Handbook of Research on Social and Organizational Dynamics in the Digital Era

Efosa C. Idemudia
Arkansas Tech University, USA

A volume in the Advances in Human Resources Management and Organizational Development (AHRMOD) Book Series

Published in the United States of America by
IGI Global
Business Science Reference (an imprint of IGI Global)
701 E. Chocolate Avenue
Hershey PA, USA 17033
Tel: 717-533-8845
Fax: 717-533-8661
E-mail: cust@igi-global.com
Web site: http://www.igi-global.com

Library of Congress Cataloging-in-Publication Data

Names: Idemudia, Efosa C. (Efosa Carroll), 1970- editor.
Title: Handbook of research on social and organizational dynamics in the digital era /
  Efosa Idemudia, editor.
Description: Hershey : Business Science Reference, [2020] | Summary:
  ""This book covers all aspects of social issues impacted by information
  technology in organizations and inter-organizational structures and
  presents the conceptualization of specific social issues and their
  associated constructs"--Provided by publisher"-- Provided by publisher.
Identifiers: LCCN 2019009418 | ISBN 9781522589334 (hardcover) | ISBN
  9781522589341 (ebook)
Subjects: LCSH: Business enterprises--Technological innovations. |
  Information technology--Social aspects. | Organizational change.
Classification: LCC HD45 .O68 2019 | DDC 303.48/33--dc23
LC record available at https://lccn.loc.gov/2019009418

This book is published in the IGI Global book series Advances in Human Resources Management and Organizational Development (AHRMOD) (ISSN: 2327-3372; eISSN: 2327-3380)

British Cataloguing in Publication Data
A Cataloguing in Publication record for this book is available from the British Library.

The views expressed in this book are those of the authors, but not necessarily of the publisher.

For electronic access to this publication, please contact: eresources@igi-global.com.

Advances in Human Resources Management and Organizational Development (AHRMOD) Book Series

Patricia Ordóñez de Pablos
Universidad de Oviedo, Spain

ISSN:2327-3372
EISSN:2327-3380

MISSION

A solid foundation is essential to the development and success of any organization and can be accomplished through the effective and careful management of an organization's human capital. Research in human resources management and organizational development is necessary in providing business leaders with the tools and methodologies which will assist in the development and maintenance of their organizational structure.

The **Advances in Human Resources Management and Organizational Development (AHRMOD) Book Series** aims to publish the latest research on all aspects of human resources as well as the latest methodologies, tools, and theories regarding organizational development and sustainability. The **AHRMOD Book Series** intends to provide business professionals, managers, researchers, and students with the necessary resources to effectively develop and implement organizational strategies.

COVERAGE

- Executive Compensation
- Employee Communications
- Disputes Resolution
- Human Relations Movement
- Succession Planning
- Workplace Culture
- Change Management
- Executive Education
- Collaborative Method
- Skills Management

IGI Global is currently accepting manuscripts for publication within this series. To submit a proposal for a volume in this series, please contact our Acquisition Editors at Acquisitions@igi-global.com or visit: http://www.igi-global.com/publish/.

Titles in this Series

For a list of additional titles in this series, please visit: www.igi-global.com/book-series

Corporate Standardization Management and Innovation
Kai Jakobs (RWTH Aachen University, Germany)
Business Science Reference • copyright 2019 • 362pp • H/C (ISBN: 9781522590088) • US $225.00 (our price)

Handbook of Research on Metaheuristics for Order Picking Optimization in Warehouses to Smart Cities
Alberto Ochoa Ortiz-Zezzatti (Autonomous University of Juarez City, Mexico) Gilberto Rivera (Autonomous University of Juarez City, Mexico) Claudia Gómez-Santillán (National Institute of Technology of Mexico, Mexico & Technological Institute of Ciudad Madero, Mexico) and Benito Sánchez–Lara (National Autonomous University of Mexico, Mexico)
Business Science Reference • copyright 2019 • 498pp • H/C (ISBN: 9781522581314) • US $345.00 (our price)

Handbook of Research on Strategic Communication, Leadership, and Conflict Management in Modern Organizations
Anthony Normore (California State University – Dominguez Hills, USA) Mitch Javidi (International Academy of Public Safety (IAPS), USA) and Larry Long (Illinois State University, USA)
Business Science Reference • copyright 2019 • 553pp • H/C (ISBN: 9781522585169) • US $245.00 (our price)

Management Techniques for Employee Engagement in Contemporary Organizations
Naman Sharma (Entrepreneurship Development Institute of India, India) Narendra Chaudhary (Symbiosis International University, India) and Vinod Kumar Singh (Gurukul Kangri Vishwavidyalaya, India)
Business Science Reference • copyright 2019 • 339pp • H/C (ISBN: 9781522577997) • US $225.00 (our price)

Emotion-Based Approaches to Personnel Management Emerging Research and Opportunities
Sara Fazzin (Niccolò Cusano Italian University in London, UK)
Business Science Reference • copyright 2019 • 235pp • H/C (ISBN: 9781522583981) • US $165.00 (our price)

Corporate Social Responsibility and Opportunities for Sustainable Financial Success
Julia Margarete Puaschunder (Columbia University, USA & The New School, USA)
Business Science Reference • copyright 2019 • 300pp • H/C (ISBN: 9781522576198) • US $200.00 (our price)

Contemporary Human Resources Management in the Tourism Industry
Demet Tüzünkan (Okan University, Turkey) and Volkan Altıntaş (Izmir Katip Celebi University, Turkey)
Business Science Reference • copyright 2019 • 405pp • H/C (ISBN: 9781522557609) • US $205.00 (our price)

Managing Diversity, Innovation, and Infrastructure in Digital Business
Nilanjan Ray (Adamas University, India)
Business Science Reference • copyright 2019 • 287pp • H/C (ISBN: 9781522559931) • US $195.00 (our price)

701 East Chocolate Avenue, Hershey, PA 17033, USA
Tel: 717-533-8845 x100 • Fax: 717-533-8661
E-Mail: cust@igi-global.com • www.igi-global.com

I dedicate this book to the following members of my family. First and foremost, I dedicate this book to my grandfather, Pa Idemudia Ogunbor, who gave me the methodology to compete and excel in the global world. Next, I wish to honor my parents, Mr. Johnson O. Idemudia and Mrs. Efe M. Idemudia, who always encouraged me with their excellent and brilliant passion for my education. In addition, I thank my two great uncles, Dr. Taiwo Idemudia and Mr. Kehinde Idemudia, and the Idemudia family for supporting my academic endeavors. I also wish to honor the memory of my late brother, Mr. Ikponmwosa K. Idemudia; who impacted/influenced my education and performance. Finally, I dedicate this work to my queen, Oluwayemisi, and my beautiful children, Osato and Ivie, all I do is dedicated to you.

List of Contributors

Alam, M. Afshar / *Jamia Hamdard, India* 344

Attaran, Mohsen / *California State University – Bakersfield, USA* 383

Attaran, Sharmin / *Bryant University, USA* 383

Bakhtiar, Toni / *IPB University, Indonesia* 461

Banodha, Umesh / *Samrat Ashok Technological Institute, India* 425

Baporikar, Neeta / *Namibia University of Science and Technology, Namibia & University of
    Pune, India* 115

Bernal, Leon Dario Parra / *Ean University, Colombia* 525

Bhusal, Roshee Lamichhane / *Kathmandu University, Nepal* 250

Bourdeau, Simon / *ESG-UQAM, Canada* 43

Calleja-Leal, Guillermo / *Royal Academy of History, Spain* 292

Cusi, Milenka Linneth Argote / *Business Intelligence and Demography SAS, Colombia* 525

Davydko, Oleksandr / *Igor Sikorsky Kyiv Polytechnic Institute, Ukraine* 305

Delgado, José Carlos Martins / *Universidade de Lisboa, Portugal* 84

Domazet, Ivana S. / *Institute of Economic Sciences, Serbia* 483

Ehrhardt, Jasmin / *University of Hamburg, Germany* 65

Elastic, Pantry / *IPB University, Indonesia* 461

Furner, Christopher P. / *East Carolina University, USA* 22

Goh, Samuel H. / *University of Alabama at Birmingham, USA* 22

Habeeb, Syed / *National Institute of Technology Warangal, India* 550

Herschel, Richard T. / *Saint Joseph's University, USA* 409

Jaharuddin / *IPB University, Indonesia* 461

Jain, Sapna / *Jamia Hamdard, India* 344

Janeš, Aleksander / *University of Primorska, Slovenia* 324

Janneck, Monique / *Luebeck University of Applied Sciences, Germany* 65

Kazmi, Niloufer Adil / *Independent Researcher, India* 344

Kirkland, Diane / *California State University – Bakersfield, USA* 383

Kumar, Ravinder / *Amity University, India* 446

Leite, Emilene / *Örebro University, Sweden & Uppsala University, Sweden* 235

Masdi, Norfarrah Binti Muhamad / *Universiti Teknologi Brunei, Brunei* 499

Mifsud, Denise / *Euro-Mediterranean Centre for Educational Research, Malta* 135

Miori, Virginia M. / *Saint Joseph's University, USA* 409

Narayana, Alamuri Surya / *Osmania University, India* 250

Nastenko, Ievgen / *Igor Sikorsky Kyiv Polytechnic Institute, Ukraine* 305

Nosovets, Olena / *Igor Sikorsky Kyiv Polytechnic Institute, Ukraine* 305

Novak, Rajko / *MRR LLC, Slovenia* 324

Pavlov, Oleksander / *Igor Sikorsky Kyiv Polytechnic Institute, Ukraine* 305
Pavlov, Volodymyr / *Igor Sikorsky Kyiv Polytechnic Institute, Ukraine* 305
Puaschunder, Julia / *The New School, USA* 157
Raimi, Lukman / *American University of Nigeria, Nigeria* 218
Saiz-Alvarez, Jose Manuel / *Tecnologico de Monterrey, Mexico* 292
Saxena, Kanak / *Samrat Ashok Technological Institute, India* 425
Seyal, Afzaal H. / *Universiti Teknologi Brunei, Brunei* 499
Siau, Nor Zainah H. / *Universiti Teknologi Brunei, Brunei* 499
Simović, Vladimir M. / *Institute of Economic Sciences, Serbia* 483
Spöhrer, Markus / *University of Konstanz, Germany* 201
Sudhakar, K. Francis / *National Institute of Technology Warangal, India* 550
Tajuddin, Sharul / *Universiti Teknologi Brunei, Brunei* 499
Vieru, Dragos / *Teluq University, Canada* 1, 43
Vincent-Hoper, Sylvie / *University of Hamburg, Germany* 65
Voronin, Albert N. / *National Aviation University, Ukraine* 276
Yoon, Tom E. / *Western Connecticut State University, USA* 22
Zinko, Robert / *Texas A&M University – Central Texas, USA* 22

Table of Contents

Preface xxii

Chapter 1
The Issue of Post-Merger Integration Boundary Management: A Sociomaterial Perspective 1
Dragos Vieru, Teluq University, Canada

Chapter 2
The Effects of Culture and Data Collection Mode on Socially Desirable Distortion and
Confidentiality Concerns in Survey Research 22
Tom E. Yoon, Western Connecticut State University, USA
Samuel H. Goh, University of Alabama at Birmingham, USA
Robert Zinko, Texas A&M University – Central Texas, USA
Christopher P. Furner, East Carolina University, USA

Chapter 3
Digital Fluency in SMEs: A Typology and a Multi-Case Study 43
Simon Bourdeau, ESG-UQAM, Canada
Dragos Vieru, TELUQ, Canada

Chapter 4
Introducing the Computer-Related Self-Concept: A New Approach to Investigate Gender
Differences in Computing Careers 65
Monique Janneck, Luebeck University of Applied Sciences, Germany
Sylvie Vincent-Höper, University of Hamburg, Germany
Jasmin Ehrhardt, University of Hamburg, Germany

Chapter 5
Improving Application Decoupling in Virtual Enterprise Integration 84
José Carlos Martins Delgado, Universidade de Lisboa, Portugal

Chapter 6
Role and Room for Knowledge Management in Small and Medium Enterprises 115
*Neeta Baporikar, Namibia University of Science and Technology, Namibia & University of
Pune, India*

Chapter 7

A Critical Review of Actor-Network Theory (ANT) and Its Use in Education Research.................. 135
Denise Mifsud, Euro-Mediterranean Centre for Educational Research, Malta

Chapter 8

Towards a Utility Theory of Privacy and Information Sharing and the Introduction of Hyper-Hyperbolic Discounting in the Digital Big Data Age.. 157
Julia Puaschunder, The New School, USA

Chapter 9

The Cochlear Implant as an Epistemic Thing: Translations of a Technical Object in Social and Scientific Contexts 201
Markus Spöhrer, University of Konstanz, Germany

Chapter 10

Breaking the Formal Financing Barriers Facing Entrepreneurs: Crowdfunding as an Alternative Financing for Enterprise Development in Nigeria in the Digital Era 218
Lukman Raimi, American University of Nigeria, Nigeria

Chapter 11

Cross-Sector Partnership in Smart City Development: The Case of Brazil 235
Emilene Leite, Örebro University, Sweden & Uppsala University, Sweden

Chapter 12

Adoption and Use of Human Information System Digital Technology for Organizational Competitiveness: An Exploratory Study in the Context of Nepal 250
Alamuri Surya Narayana, Osmania University, India
Roshee Lamichhane Bhusal, Kathmandu University, Nepal

Chapter 13

Optimization Problem: Systemic Approach.. 276
Albert N. Voronin, National Aviation University, Ukraine

Chapter 14

Fiscal Policy and Social Optimization for Developing Nations: Some Thoughts in the Digital Era . 292
Jose Manuel Saiz-Alvarez, Tecnologico de Monterrey, Mexico
Guillermo Calleja-Leal, Royal Academy of History, Spain

Chapter 15

Optimization Models for Calculation of Personalized Strategies 305
Ievgen Nastenko, Igor Sikorsky Kyiv Polytechnic Institute, Ukraine
Volodymyr Pavlov, Igor Sikorsky Kyiv Polytechnic Institute, Ukraine
Olena Nosovets, Igor Sikorsky Kyiv Polytechnic Institute, Ukraine
Oleksandr Davydko, Igor Sikorsky Kyiv Polytechnic Institute, Ukraine
Oleksander Pavlov, Igor Sikorsky Kyiv Polytechnic Institute, Ukraine

Chapter 16
Process-Oriented Organizations: Integration of Soft Factors 324
Aleksander Janeš, University of Primorska, Slovenia
Rajko Novak, MRR LLC, Slovenia

Chapter 17
Psychological Impact and Assessment of Youth for the Use of Social Network 344
Sapna Jain, Jamia Hamdard, India
M. Afshar Alam, Jamia Hamdard, India
Niloufer Adil Kazmi, Independent Researcher, India

Chapter 18
Technology and Organizational Change: Harnessing the Power of Digital Workplace 383
Mohsen Attaran, California State University – Bakersfield, USA
Sharmin Attaran, Bryant University, USA
Diane Kirkland, California State University – Bakersfield, USA

Chapter 19
Consumer Online Behavior, Data Sharing, and Ethics 409
Virginia M. Miori, Saint Joseph's University, USA
Richard T. Herschel, Saint Joseph's University, USA

Chapter 20
Collective Behavior Under the Umbrella of Blockchain 425
Kanak Saxena, Samrat Ashok Technological Institute, India
Umesh Banodha, Samrat Ashok Technological Institute, India

Chapter 21
Sustainable Supply Chain Management in the Era of Digitialization: Issues and Challenges 446
Ravinder Kumar, Amity University, India

Chapter 22
An Optimal Control Problem of Knowledge Dissemination 461
Pantry Elastic, IPB University, Indonesia
Toni Bakhtiar, IPB University, Indonesia
Jaharuddin, IPB University, Indonesia

Chapter 23
The Use of Google Analytics for Measuring Website Performance of Non-Formal Education
Institution 483
Ivana S. Domazet, Institute of Economic Sciences, Serbia
Vladimir M. Simović, Institute of Economic Sciences, Serbia

Chapter 24
Investigating the Information Perception Value (IPV) Model in Maintaining the Information
Security: Bruneian Perspective 499
Sharul Tajuddin, Universiti Teknologi Brunei, Brunei
Afzaal H. Seyal, Universiti Teknologi Brunei, Brunei
Norfarrah Binti Muhamad Masdi, Universiti Teknologi Brunei, Brunei
Nor Zainah H. Siau, Universiti Teknologi Brunei, Brunei

Chapter 25
Strengthening the Capabilities in Data Analytics: A Case Study in Bogotá, Colombia 525
Milenka Linneth Argote Cusi, Business Intelligence and Demography SAS, Colombia
Leon Dario Parra Bernal, Ean University, Colombia

Chapter 26
A Review of Antecedents of Online Repurchase Behavior in Indian E-Commerce Paradigm Shift . 550
Syed Habeeb, National Institute of Technology Warangal, India
K. Francis Sudhakar, National Institute of Technology Warangal, India

Compilation of References 569

About the Contributors 653

Index 664

Detailed Table of Contents

Preface xxii

Chapter 1

The Issue of Post-Merger Integration Boundary Management: A Sociomaterial Perspective 1
    Dragos Vieru, Teluq University, Canada

This study analyzes the interactions among individuals engaged in two information system development (ISD) projects aimed to support an organization created by the merger of previously independent entities. The literature on post-merger integration (PMI) suggests that new information systems (IS) that would span the boundaries of the previously independent firms need to be implemented to facilitate a specific level of integration. Yet, there is a lack of studies on the issue of post-merger boundary management during ISD projects. The authors draw on a sociomaterial perspective to analyze two ISD projects in a PMI context of a merger of three hospitals. In both projects, the final IS-enabled practices differed from the post-merger practices that had been planned by the new hospital management. The analysis suggests that post-merger practices were the result of dialectic processes of resistance to, and negotiation of, the two systems reconfiguration after their implementation.

Chapter 2

The Effects of Culture and Data Collection Mode on Socially Desirable Distortion and
Confidentiality Concerns in Survey Research 22
    Tom E. Yoon, Western Connecticut State University, USA
    Samuel H. Goh, University of Alabama at Birmingham, USA
    Robert Zinko, Texas A&M University – Central Texas, USA
    Christopher P. Furner, East Carolina University, USA

Internet-based surveys have emerged as a popular data collection method for researchers. Despites the popularity of Internet-based surveys, prior studies suggest that responses collected via internet-based surveys are not equivalent to those collected via paper-based survey. Thus, it is important to understand why the nonequivalence is occurred. Also, since internet-based surveys enable us to collect data from people around the globe, it would be important to understand how cultural differences influence participants' responses. In this study, the authors investigate the effects that espoused national culture and data collection mode have on confidentiality concerns and socially desirable reporting. Results indicate that data collection mode and espoused power distance influence confidentiality concerns, while data collection mode and collectivism influence socially desirable distortion.

Chapter 3
Digital Fluency in SMEs: A Typology and a Multi-Case Study 43
Simon Bourdeau, ESG-UQAM, Canada
Dragos Vieru, TELUQ, Canada

In the practitioner and the academic literatures, links between information technology (IT) adoption, IT use, and digital fluency (DF) have been emphasized by a number of authors. However, there is a lack of understanding of what exactly digital fluency is, how it can be conceptualized, and what role it plays in small and medium-sized enterprises (SMEs). Based on the DF literature and its underlying concepts such as skills, expertise, and competencies, as well as on the SME literature, a multi-case study of three Canadian SMEs is conducted to empirically evaluate a typology of DF archetypes. The typology, that is based on a change agent perspective, has three archetypes. Results suggest that SMEs' managers should focus on the complementarity nature of the cognitive, social, and technological dimensions of DF when assessing and developing their employees' DF.

Chapter 4
Introducing the Computer-Related Self-Concept: A New Approach to Investigate Gender
Differences in Computing Careers 65
Monique Janneck, Luebeck University of Applied Sciences, Germany
Sylvie Vincent-Höper, University of Hamburg, Germany
Jasmin Ehrhardt, University of Hamburg, Germany

The number of women in STEM fields, especially in computer science, is still very low. Therefore, in this chapter, the computer-related self-concept (CSC) is presented as a new approach to investigate gender differences in computing careers. The computer-related self-concept comprises computer-related attitudes, emotions, and behaviors, integrating different lines of research on computer-related self-cognitions. To establish connections with career development, an extensive online survey was conducted with more than 1100 male and female computing professionals. Results show that men have a significantly more positive computer-related self-concept than women. Furthermore, as hypothesized, the computer-related self-concept shows high correlations with career motivation. Therefore, it is concluded that the computer-related self-concept is a feasible approach to investigate and understand computer-related gender differences. Possible implications regarding measures to foster women's careers in computing are discussed along with prospects for future research.

Chapter 5
Improving Application Decoupling in Virtual Enterprise Integration... 84
José Carlos Martins Delgado, Universidade de Lisboa, Portugal

The interaction of applications belonging to several enterprise information systems (EIS), forming a collaborative network in a virtual enterprise (VE) context, raises an application integration problem that is even more stringent than within a single EIS, since a VE has a temporary nature and therefore integration requirements can change more frequently. Current integration technologies, such as web services and RESTful APIs, solve the interoperability problem but usually entail more coupling than required by the interacting applications. This is caused by sharing data schemas between applications, even if not all features of those schemas are actually exercised. The fundamental problem of application integration is therefore how to provide at most the minimum coupling possible while ensuring at least the minimum interoperability requirements. This chapter proposes compliance and conformance as the concepts to achieve this goal, by sharing only the subset of the features of the data schema that are actually used.

Chapter 6

Role and Room for Knowledge Management in Small and Medium Enterprises 115
Neeta Baporikar, Namibia University of Science and Technology, Namibia & University of Pune, India

In the present day, success and worth of businesses depend more on intellectual capital. So, knowledge is a critical resource, for any organizational growth and sustainability. For small and medium enterprises (SMEs) the latent knowledge seen as the principal component for success often tends to be over guarded. That itself is sometimes detrimental to the SMEs growth. This outlook towards knowledge by SMEs has to undergo a change as there is vast room for knowledge management (KM). Abundant studies and research exist on KM, but the focus on SMEs is limited. Current scenario of globalization, technological advances, higher returns on intellectual capital, growing significance of knowledge-intensive industries makes KM a strategic and competitive tool for SME growth, sustainability, and development. KM is indispensable for successful and sustainable business in this contemporary complex economy. Thus, the overall aim of this study done by in-depth literature review and contextual analysis is to enhance the understanding of the role and room for KM in SMEs in this globalized world.

Chapter 7

A Critical Review of Actor-Network Theory (ANT) and Its Use in Education Research.................. 135
Denise Mifsud, Euro-Mediterranean Centre for Educational Research, Malta

This chapter, which expands on a previous publication, presents a critique of actor-network theory as a sociomaterial concept. Furthermore, the author problematizes the relative under-application of this "sensibility" in education research, while simultaneously exploring its contribution as an analytical framework through its central concepts of "actor-network," "symmetry," "translation," and their constituents. This chapter zooms on the concepts of networks and power relations. The author questions the prevalent notion of the "network" metaphor promulgated by globalization discourses, setting it up against the network conception in actor-network theory, where the main principle is multiplicity. Actor-network theory is analyzed as a theory of the mechanics of power, concerning itself with the setting up of hegemony. This chapter is especially targeted for researchers of education reform who are as yet unfamiliar with the concepts of Actor-Network Theory and somewhat wary of the validity of sociomaterialism in the analysis of education issues.

Chapter 8

Towards a Utility Theory of Privacy and Information Sharing and the Introduction of Hyper-Hyperbolic Discounting in the Digital Big Data Age.. 157
Julia Puaschunder, The New School, USA

Today enormous data storage capacities and computational power in the e-big data era have created unforeseen opportunities for big data hoarding corporations to reap hidden benefits from individuals' information sharing, which occurs bit by bit in small tranches over time. Behavioral economics describes human decision-making fallibility over time but has—to this day—not covered the problem of individuals' decision to share information about themselves in tranches on social media and big data administrators being able to reap a benefit from putting data together over time and reflecting the individual's information in relation to big data of others. The decision-making fallibility inherent in individuals having problems understanding the impact of their current information sharing in the future is introduced as hyper-hyperbolic discounting decision-making predicament.

Chapter 9

The Cochlear Implant as an Epistemic Thing: Translations of a Technical Object in Social and
Scientific Contexts 201

Markus Spöhrer, University of Konstanz, Germany

This chapter examines the translations and (de)stabilizations of the cochlear implant, a subcutaneous prosthesis that is subject to ethical and judicial controversies. By looking at medical, social, and scientific contexts, the CI will be described as a technical object ascribed with certain attributes providing technical stability in those contexts that treat it and practice it as a scientific fact, a "technical thing." Scientific communities stabilize technical things by rigorously excluding attributes of the "social." However, the CI is designed to enable participation, to "gap" the supposed "disability" of not being able to hear, attributing a certain instability to it. The chapter will theoretically and methodologically approach such processes of (de)stabilization and transformation by making use of ANT and Hans-Jörg Rheinbergers concept of technical and epistemic things. This will be illustrated by analyzing certain discourses used as illustrations for the successful communication between implanted children and their parents in practical guides for parents with deaf children.

Chapter 10

Breaking the Formal Financing Barriers Facing Entrepreneurs: Crowdfunding as an Alternative
Financing for Enterprise Development in Nigeria in the Digital Era 218

Lukman Raimi, American University of Nigeria, Nigeria

Financing programs at both start-up and growth phases are confronted with a number of institutional barriers. However, the digital era with its attendant benefits of interconnectedness has provided an alternative financing option called crowdfunding for internet-savvy entrepreneurs. Crowdfunding is a digital-based tool used to raise funds for different projects contributing to socio-economic development. The chapter discusses crowdfunding as an alternative financing option for enterprise development in Nigeria. Using a desk research technique, this chapter highlights the prospects of crowdfunding and strategies for leveraging crowdfunding as a viable alternative financing alternative in Nigeria. As an internet-driven process, this chapter identifies a number of challenges, but the most fundamental is the absence of regulatory environment to protect investors, a development that is in contrast to developed countries where crowdfunding is guided by enabling legislation. The chapter concludes with a number of research implications and suggestions.

Chapter 11

Cross-Sector Partnership in Smart City Development: The Case of Brazil 235

Emilene Leite, Örebro University, Sweden & Uppsala University, Sweden

Urbanization is a persistent phenomenon. As cities have expanded, so has the demand for government ability to provide better infrastructure and public services. The "smart city" concept may form a response to these urban challenges. From a business point of view, incorporating digital technologies to address some of the city's sustainability challenges is a means to create business opportunities for firms. However, a smart city project is complex, and it requires firms interaction with government and civil society. Hence, the aim of this chapter is to understand how firms manage their relationships with socio-political actors in projects for smart city development and how socio-political actors can be a source of competitive advantage. These questions will be answered by applying business network perspective within cross-sector partnership in the context of firms operating in Brazil. The study contributes to a foundation for a better discussion among policy makers and practitioners about promoting inter-organizational cooperation in projects with a social purpose.

Chapter 12

Adoption and Use of Human Information System Digital Technology for Organizational
Competitiveness: An Exploratory Study in the Context of Nepal.. 250
Alamuri Surya Narayana, Osmania University, India
Roshee Lamichhane Bhusal, Kathmandu University, Nepal

Staying competitive in the current digitized workplace era requires, among other things, an adequate and efficient use of modern technology. Human resource information system (HRIS) is one of several tools that helps organizations remain sustainable by providing technology that can help to acquire, store, generate, analyze, and disseminate timely and accurate employee information and activities. Of late, HRIS is slowly gaining prominence in Nepal. A generic model for conditions that are necessary for successful adoption and use of HRIS in Nepali organizations is designed as the models proposed by earlier researchers in a developed context may not work well in a developing context. This sets fertile ground to carry out scholarly inquiry into the domain of HRIS in the Nepalese context. The limitations of present study are mentioned and practical/research implications of the same are discussed towards the end. Researchers are of the opinion that the findings of this preliminary study can be taken up to the next level for carrying out quantitative research in HRIS domain in Nepal.

Chapter 13

Optimization Problem: Systemic Approach.. 276
Albert N. Voronin, National Aviation University, Ukraine

A systemic approach to solving multicriteria optimization problems is proposed. The system approach allowed uniting the models of individual schemes of compromises into a single integrated structure that adapts to the situation of adopting a multi-criteria solution. The advantage of the concept of non-linear scheme of compromises is the possibility of making a multicriteria decision formally, without the direct participation of a person. The apparatus of the non-linear scheme of compromises, developed as a formalized tool for the study of control systems with conflicting criteria, makes it possible to solve practically multicriteria problems of a wide class.

Chapter 14

Fiscal Policy and Social Optimization for Developing Nations: Some Thoughts in the Digital Era . 292
Jose Manuel Saiz-Alvarez, Tecnologico de Monterrey, Mexico
Guillermo Calleja-Leal, Royal Academy of History, Spain

From the public sector's perspective, one of the healthiest ways to optimize the social and organizational dynamics of a country in the digital era is to adapt the national fiscal policy to the socioeconomic needs of the population. The objective of this work is to analyze what key factors and which strategical proposal nations can follow to improve tax efficiency and, once a fair and equitable redistribution of the collected financial resources is achieved, to offer higher levels of welfare for the entire population in the digital era.

Chapter 15

Optimization Models for Calculation of Personalized Strategies 305

Ievgen Nastenko, Igor Sikorsky Kyiv Polytechnic Institute, Ukraine
Volodymyr Pavlov, Igor Sikorsky Kyiv Polytechnic Institute, Ukraine
Olena Nosovets, Igor Sikorsky Kyiv Polytechnic Institute, Ukraine
Oleksandr Davydko, Igor Sikorsky Kyiv Polytechnic Institute, Ukraine
Oleksander Pavlov, Igor Sikorsky Kyiv Polytechnic Institute, Ukraine

The chapter considers the problem of calculating the best individual strategy based on models obtained from observations of a given sample object's reaction to the applied control actions. In order to improve the calculation efficiency, the construction of the optimization problem with line dependence on the control variables is offered. To ensure the calculation adequacy, the object state models of optimal complexity, nonlinear with respect to the initial conditions and parameters, are considered. Examples of optimal personalized treatment strategies calculation are given. The proposed approach can be extended to other practical areas to solve the decision making, provided the development of adequate the object state models in the optimization field.

Chapter 16

Process-Oriented Organizations: Integration of Soft Factors 324

Aleksander Janeš, University of Primorska, Slovenia
Rajko Novak, MRR LLC, Slovenia

The main purpose of the chapter is to represent practical approach on the empirically-evaluated business process orientation (BPO) based on the research of the Slovenian power supply business. Within the empirical investigation, the level of BPO maturity was measured in the 19 organizations. The survey was focused on the top, middle, and lower managers. As a measuring instrument, a questionnaire for the extended concept of process orientation was used. The results of the BPO measurement shows that, despite this long-standing engagement with processes, quality management system and the IT portfolio management (PoM) of operations, process orientation, and appurtenant IT PoM maturity is not very high. Results suggested the opportunities for improvement, particularly for better use and to take advantage of IT. One important reason for performing the research in the power supply business is the importance of its activities for the socio-economic and environmental impact of the whole society and therefore better understanding of the recognized "soft factors."

Chapter 17

Psychological Impact and Assessment of Youth for the Use of Social Network............................... 344

Sapna Jain, Jamia Hamdard, India
M. Afshar Alam, Jamia Hamdard, India
Niloufer Adil Kazmi, Independent Researcher, India

This chapter dissects the effect of online life on each youngster in both the negative and positive bearing of their development utilizing the social impact hypothesis. Reliance of youth via web-based networking media has both negative and beneficial outcomes. This hypothesis portrays social effect concerning social power handle that encroach upon us, pushing us to think or keep thinking about a specific goal.

These social powers have been stood out from physical powers that control the transmission of light, solid, gravity, interest, and so forth. The discoveries uncovered that the utilization of internet-based life impacts adolescent conduct when contrasted with positive aspects. This study shows a connection among contradictory and imaginative qualities of online life and displays roads for future investigations by encouraging a superior comprehension of electronic interpersonal organization use. In the chapter, the social effect felt by a person as a component of the quality, instantaneousness, and number of source people is exhibited and examined.

Chapter 18
Technology and Organizational Change: Harnessing the Power of Digital Workplace 383
Mohsen Attaran, California State University – Bakersfield, USA
Sharmin Attaran, Bryant University, USA
Diane Kirkland, California State University – Bakersfield, USA

This chapter explores the changing dimensions of the workplace and highlights the relationship between technology and organizational change. The chapter begins by briefly reviewing some key perspectives that have emerged in the information systems (IS) literature to account for the relationship between technology and organizational change. It highlights the importance of smart workplace technologies, identifies determinants of successful workplace transformation, proposes a conceptual model for implementation, identifies key factors to consider, and covers some of the potential benefits. The chapter argues that digital transformation is more than just implementing digital technologies. Successful digital transformation occurs when business strategies or major sections of an organization are altered.

Chapter 19
Consumer Online Behavior, Data Sharing, and Ethics.. 409
Virginia M. Miori, Saint Joseph's University, USA
Richard T. Herschel, Saint Joseph's University, USA

This chapter reports the results of a survey that examines how a sampling of millennials describes their online activity, their social engagement, and their priorities when they are asked to value their online activity. It also explores whether there are tenets of a specific ethical perspective that shape their thinking about what is moral behavior online. Results indicate that the online behavior of the study participants involves extensive use of social media with a variety of platforms employed. Degree of engagement is not dependent on whether the individual is introvert or extrovert. Their online priority focuses first on a concern for their privacy, followed by their appreciation for time saving technology and opportunities for money savings and promotions. No single ethical theory dominates their expressed moral values, though there is a clear pattern that is consistent with consequentialism.

Chapter 20
Collective Behavior Under the Umbrella of Blockchain 425
Kanak Saxena, Samrat Ashok Technological Institute, India
Umesh Banodha, Samrat Ashok Technological Institute, India

Any social or organization system will fetch the properties from economics, sociology, and social psychology. In the digital world everyone is trying to cope with the new technologies for the survival. The dynamics of such a system are very multifarious due to the complexity in the convergence of the digital, physical, and biological realms. The dynamics of the society and organization are rapidly changing due to the imparting of the new technologies, such as artificial intelligence, internet of things, virtual reality, etc. The resultant is revolutionizing of opportunities and expectations due to the changes in the values, norms, identities, and future potential. The collective behavior (CB) plays an important role in predicting the various dynamics which are not only coherent but also paying attention. Blockchain will not only help in detecting but also help in finding the major causes and challenges for current scenario dynamics. The chapter describes the agent-based modeling and ant colony optimization components of the CB.

Chapter 21
Sustainable Supply Chain Management in the Era of Digitialization: Issues and Challenges 446
Ravinder Kumar, Amity University, India

In the last two decades the term sustainable supply chain management (SSCM) has become quite popular. Organizations are working on sustainability of their supply chain (SC). Sustainability covers environmental, social, and economic aspects of different supply chain management activities. Organizations are continuously working in the direction of making their processes and product green. On the environmental front, use of renewable source of energy, reducing waste of energy, reducing carbon footprints is important. Simultaneously, reuse of products, re-cycling, and following environmental standards while disposing off is also recommended. In this chapter, the author has identified 13 issues and challenges of SSCM from literature review and expert opinion. Simultaneously, the author has also identified nine new technologies of modern time used in industries. Further, the author has tried to analyze the linkage between the challenges of sustainability and intelligent technologies by Jaccard's similarity coefficient methodology.

Chapter 22
An Optimal Control Problem of Knowledge Dissemination 461
Pantry Elastic, IPB University, Indonesia
Toni Bakhtiar, IPB University, Indonesia
Jaharuddin, IPB University, Indonesia

In this chapter, the authors develop an optimal control model of knowledge dissemination among people in the society. The knowledge transfer system is formulated in term of compartmental model, where the society members are categorized into four classes based on knowledge acquisition and their willingness to disseminate. The model is equipped with a set of control variables for process intervening, namely technical training for ignorant-immigrants, information dissemination through social media for solitariants and enthusiasts, and technical training for solitariants. Optimality conditions in terms of differential equations system was derived by using Pontryagin minimum principle leading to the characterization of optimal control strategies that minimizing the number of solitariants, enthusiasts, and ignorants simultaneously with the control efforts. The sweep method and the fourth order Runge-Kutta algorithm was implemented to numerically solve the equation systems. The effectiveness of the control strategies toward a set of control scenarios was evaluated through examples.

Chapter 23
The Use of Google Analytics for Measuring Website Performance of Non-Formal Education
Institution 483
Ivana S. Domazet, Institute of Economic Sciences, Serbia
Vladimir M. Simović, Institute of Economic Sciences, Serbia

The purpose of this chapter is to measure the performance of a non-formal educational institution's website using Google Analytics data and data obtained in a separate research on specific non-formal educational institution's users. The goal was to determine the best performing acquisition channel for non-formal educational institutions and the average user profile of this kind of educational programs by means of user acquisition and behavior data. Key parameters used to measure the performance of different acquisition channels were conversion rate, average session duration, and bounce rate. User gender data and age group data were used on a side of user specific data. The findings presented in this research may be applicable to other non-formal educational institutions as well.

Chapter 24

Investigating the Information Perception Value (IPV) Model in Maintaining the Information Security: Bruneian Perspective 499

Sharul Tajuddin, Universiti Teknologi Brunei, Brunei
Afzaal H. Seyal, Universiti Teknologi Brunei, Brunei
Norfarrah Binti Muhamad Masdi, Universiti Teknologi Brunei, Brunei
Nor Zainah H. Siau, Universiti Teknologi Brunei, Brunei

This pioneering study is conducted among 150 employees from various ministries of Brunei Darussalam regarding their perception in maintaining the information security and to validate the IPV model using linear regression data analysis techniques. The IPV model identifies the factors that affect the user's perception of information values and to further assess as how these perceptions of information value affect their behavior in information security environment. The results show that IPV model have significant predicting power the employees' behavior with more than half of the variance (59%) in information value is shared by these six contextual variables. However, four out of six antecedent variables monetary value, ministerial jurisdiction, spiritual, and social values are significantly predicting the information value. The study has significant impact both for the researchers and practitioners and will add value to the current repository of broad knowledge in information security behavior.

Chapter 25

Strengthening the Capabilities in Data Analytics: A Case Study in Bogotá, Colombia 525

Milenka Linneth Argote Cusi, Business Intelligence and Demography SAS, Colombia
Leon Dario Parra Bernal, Ean University, Colombia

In the framework of digital economy and the fourth industrial revolution, it is very important that companies have internal capabilities for the analysis of data and of the information they produce, as well as to generate value in the decision-making process. In 2017 the EAN University implemented the Program for Strengthening Capabilities in DA (PSCDA) with 15 companies from different economic sectors in Bogotá, Colombia. The main purpose of the program was to diagnose, qualify, and accompany the participating companies, in the process of strengthening their DA capabilities. Among the most important results we highlighted that 90% of the companies from the program have applied technological tools for the analysis of their data, while an 80% were able to design and implement a plan of improvement for their processes in data analytics and its use in decision making.

Chapter 26

A Review of Antecedents of Online Repurchase Behavior in Indian E-Commerce Paradigm Shift . 550

Syed Habeeb, National Institute of Technology Warangal, India
K. Francis Sudhakar, National Institute of Technology Warangal, India

The purpose of this chapter is to highlight research areas of customer satisfaction and repurchase intentions and their antecedents in the Indian e-commerce industry. To retain, attract, and satisfy customers, e-retailers need to understand how and why online customers evaluate a web store. The relevant areas of consumer behavior and marketing research were derived to explain the possible gaps to study with respect to e-commerce in India. To do so, a systematic review of online consumer behavior literature is conducted. Following inclusion and exclusion criteria, a total of 109 journal articles are analyzed. The major finding of the chapter was that there is very less amount of research considering the areas of customer satisfaction, trust, loyalty along with repurchase behavior of the online customer in specific to the Indian context. Therefore, it is a need of the hour to extend the study to know the repurchase behavior of the online consumer in present time.

Compilation of References 569

About the Contributors 653

Index 664

Preface

INTRODUCTION

This textbook provides important updates from research on how to implement and use social media to optimize organizational dynamics in the digital era. This textbook claims that teaching social media principles and strategies to optimize organizational dynamics is extremely important because today, directly or indirectly, companies and organizations worldwide are using social media to make better decisions and to gain competitive advantages. Directly or indirectly, all disciplines are using social media for branding, community services, to expand potential customer base, trading, competitive advantages, reputation management, agile marketing, to gain leadership/industry insights, and for recruitment. It should be noted that the concepts, techniques, methodologies, tools, and skills in this textbook can be applied to companies located in all the continents of the world. This textbook is unique because it includes case studies, concepts, techniques, skills, and methodologies from all the continents that expose students, professors, government officials, employees, and practitioners to the different types and kinds of social media to create better decision making and competitive advantage.

Worldwide companies and organizations are using social media to address and adapt to stakeholders' interests and needs. The performance of organizations and firms depends on how top management and key decision makers are using social media to address stakeholders' interests (see Figure 1). The arrows in Figure 1 are multidirectional because organizations and firms are using social media to adapt to changes in stakeholders' interests and needs for competitive advantages. In addition, most companies and organizations worldwide are using social media to improve decision makings. To date, companies and organizations are investing millions and billions of dollars to achieve social presence (IAB 2019). In the first half of 2018, digital advertisement spending hit a record-breaking $49.5 billion (IAB 2019). Both small local and global companies are using social media as a critical source and venue for business marketing strategies. Some of the important benefits of social media platforms relating to optimizing and organizational dynamics are (1) connecting with customers, (2) connecting with investors, (3) connecting with sales force, (4) connecting with employees, (5) connecting with communities, (6) connecting with government, (7) connecting with global economy, (8) connecting with political groups, (9) connecting with suppliers, (10) increasing brand awareness, (11) boosting leads in sales, and (12) making better decisions/competitive advantages. Marketing research has shown that one of the best strategies for companies and organizations to implement to make sure they have customers is to make sure that people know their business (IAB, 2019). Organizations and firms worldwide are using social media to boost their visibility to recruit customers, retain customers, reach a global audience, communicate authority, grow affordability, show authenticity, provide support, and encourage engagement.

Figure 1. Social media model within organizations and firms

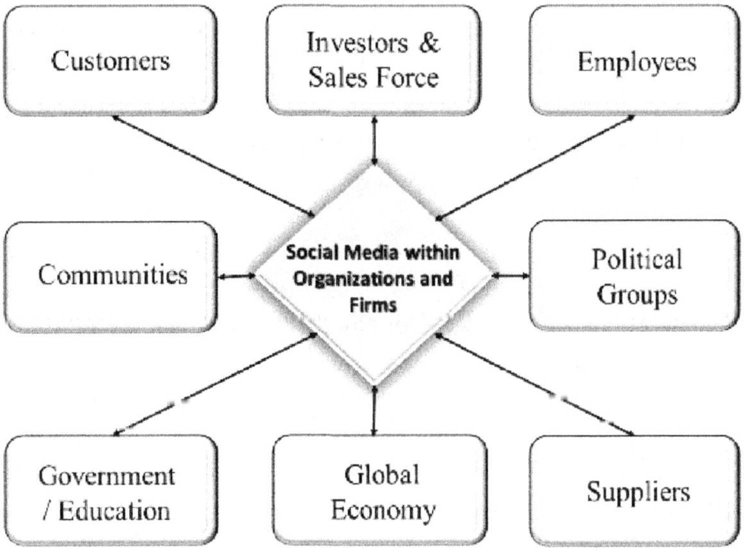

This textbook exposes students, professors, and employees, and customers to the diverse industry that exist in the world. In this textbook, readers are exposed to updated concepts, methodologies, techniques, and case studies from different continents on how to directly and indirectly use social media to make better decisions and achieve competitive advantages. One of the goals of this textbook is to expand the knowledge, skills, and abilities of individuals, firms, organizations, and governments on how to use social media to adapt to stakeholders' interests, to make better decisions, and to gain competitive advantages. To that end, each chapter in this textbook has discussion questions that empower students, professors, and employees with communication, critical thinking, analytics, and decision-making exercises to help to solve complex problems in the real world.

SOME COMPONENTS IN THE TEXTBOOK

Merger Integration

This textbook includes updated concepts, models, and methodology relating to important issues, challenges, and opportunities in merger integration. In Chapter 1, the textbooks explore the benefits, challenges, opportunities, and issues of post-merger integration boundary management to top managements, practitioners, students, and professors for strategic decision making. In addition, the textbook provides insights and instruction to students, professors, practitioners, employees, and top managements on how to support global organizations and firms that are created by a merger of previously independent entities. Chapter 1 contributes to the literature on the issues of post-merger boundary management during ISD projects by applying sociamaterial perspective and concepts. Chapter 1 presents detailed concepts relating to enterprise systems, post-merger integration, performativity, process theory, sociamaterial, and sociamaterial assemblage.

Culture and Data Collection

Technology is changing every day, and the daily advancements in software and hardware have made it possible for companies and organizations to collect data with ease from customers worldwide. In addition, advancements in technology have led to big data; this textbook discusses strategies on how to effectively and efficiently manage big data for better decision making and competitive advantages without violating data privacy, security, and governments' laws/regulations. Chapter 2 provides insights into the effects of culture and various data collection modes on socially desirable distortion and confidentiality concerns in survey research. The textbook discusses the main similarities and differences between data collected via Internet-based surveys and via paper-based survey. In addition, Chapter 2 discusses how cultural differences create challenges, issues, and benefits by influencing participants' responses on Internet-based surveys. The textbook demonstrates how important concepts such as espoused national culture, data collection mode, espoused power distance, and collectivism influence internet-based survey results. Chapter 19 explores consumer online behavior, data sharing, and ethics by examining how millennials describe their online activities/behaviors, social engagement, and priorities relating to data sharing and ethics. Chapter 20 contributes to the data collection literature by discussing in detail the collective behavior under the umbrella of blockchain.

Case Studies From Different Continents

This textbook examines cases from different parts of the world to provide insights and understanding on how various cultures and norms influence a wide variety of information technology usage and adoption. Chapter 3 presents a multi-case study of three Canadian small and medium-sized enterprises (SMEs) through links by showing the relationships between information technology adoption and IT use and digital fluency. These insights help students, professors, employees, practitioners, and top managements understand what exactly digital fluency is. In addition, Chapter 3 discusses the roles, benefits, challenges, and impact of digital fluency on small and medium-sized enterprises (SMEs) and suggests strategies that should be implemented to make better decisions. Chapter 10 presents a case study on how to break the formal financing barriers facing entrepreneurs in Nigeria and discusses how crowdfunding can serve as an alternative source of financing for enterprise development in Nigeria in the digital era. Chapter 11 presents a case study from Brazil that investigates cross-sector partnership in smart city development. Chapter 11 explores insights and understanding on how policy makers, practitioners, and top managements can make better decisions and acquire competitive advantages by promoting intra-organizational cooperation in projects with a social purpose. Chapter 12 discusses an exploratory study from Nepal that examines the adoption and use of human information systems digital technology for organizational competitiveness. Chapter 14 describes a case study from developing nations relating to fiscal policy and social optimization in the digital era. Chapter 16 presents a case study from a Slovenian power supply business relating to integrated soft factors that influence process orientation organizations. Chapter 24 discusses and presents a case study from Brunei that investigates the information perception value model in maintaining information security. Chapter 25 examines a case study from Colombia on strategies that top managements and key decision makers should implement to strengthening the capabilities in data analytics. Chapter 26 delivers a case study on Indian e-Commerce paradigm shift and a comprehensive review of antecedents of online repurchase behavior.

Gender Differences in Computing Careers

Many studies have shown that, generally, males and females perceive the adoption and usage of a wide range of technology differently (Idemudia et al., 2018; Idemudia & Raisinghani, 2017). The textbook presents strategies that top managements should implement to address the challenges and issues in gender differences in computing careers. Chapter 4 explores and provides strategies on how top managements, key decision makers, and practitioners can improve the number of minorities in STEM fields. The textbook presents computer-related self-concepts (CSC) as a new approach and method to empirically investigate gender differences in computing careers. The CSC include concepts such as computer-related attitudes, emotions, conative, motivational, cognitive, and behaviors. In addition, Chapter 4 discusses the strengths, opportunities, weaknesses, and threats relating to CSC and the effects of gender differences in the computing careers.

Decoupling in Virtual Enterprise Integration and Process Orientation Organization

Chapter 5 presents and examines the factors that positively influence decupling in virtual enterprise integration. Thus, the textbook discusses some of the main challenges, issues, strengths, weaknesses, opportunities and threats relating to decoupling in virtual enterprise integration. In addition, Chapter 5 outlines some limitations and benefits of current integration technologies such as Web Services and RESTful APIs. The textbook provides strategies to top managements, students, professors, practitioners, and employees on how to make better decisions relating to challenges and benefits of coupling, compliance, conformance, and interoperability requirements. Chapter 16 explores the integration of soft factors that influence process-oriented organization.

Knowledge Management in Small and Medium Enterprises

The textbook explores how to gain insights and knowledge from data to make better decisions and for competitive advantages. Chapter 6 presents the relationship and influence of knowledge management in small and medium enterprises; the authors argue that to date, the success, growth, and worth of companies and organizations depend on knowledge management and intellectual capital. Chapter 6 discusses how both small and medium enterprises are using and implementing knowledge management for growth and sustainability. In addition, most organizations and companies worldwide are using knowledge management as a strategic and competitive tool for growth, development, better decision making and sustainability.

Actor-Network Theory, Social Media, Sociamaterial Concepts, Digital Workplace, Systems Theory, and Optimization Models

Chapter 7 discusses a critical review of actor-network theory as a sociamaterial concept; and zooms in on the concepts relating to network and power relations for better decision making and competitive advantages. Chapter 7 presents actor-network theory as related to mechanics of power and setting up of hegemony. Chapter 13 examines in detail how top managements can use a systemic approach to solve optimization problems to make better decisions and leverage competitive advantages. Chapter 15 outlines the different types of optimization models that can be used to calculate personalized strategies for better decision makings and competitive advantages. Chapter 17 discusses the utilization of social media by today's youth. Chapter 17 provides insights and understanding on psychological impact and assessment of youth who use social networks. Chapter 18 presents a comprehensive definition of a digital workplace. In addition, Chapter 18 describe the tools with limitations and benefits that are related to the digital workplace. A successful digital transformation is driven by cultural and organizational transformation. Chapter 18 explains that digital transformation efforts succeed if top managements and key decision makers adopt an integrated approach that includes (1) training employees with new skills, (2) training employees on how to use updated tools, (3) creating a disruptive culture, and (4) exhibiting operational sustainability. Chapter 21 discusses the issues and challenges of sustainable supply chain management in the era of digitalization. In addition, Chapter 21 presents that sustainability covers environmental, social, political, and economic aspect of different supply chain management activities.

Utility Theory of Privacy, Information Sharing, Google Analytics, and Optimal Control Model

This textbook presents and discusses a lot of theories that are extremely useful in decision making and competitive advantages. Chapter 8 explains that utility theory captures people's preferences or values and demonstrates how top managements are using utility theory to make better decisions for competitive advantages. Chapter 9 explores and describes how the Cochlear implant is an epistemic thing (i.e. translation of a technical object in social and scientific contexts). Chapter 22 present an optimal control model of knowledge dissemination among people in the society; this model provides insights and understanding on how top managements and key decision makers can make better decisions relating to optimal control problems. Chapter 23 presents in detail the use of Google Analytics for measuring website performance of non-formal education institutions.

ORGANIZATION OF THE BOOK

The *Handbook of Research on Social and Organizational Dynamics in the Digital Era* is organized into 26 chapters. A brief description of each of the chapters follows:

Chapter 1 presents updated techniques and approaches that firms and organization should implement to evaluate and address the issues of post-merger integration and boundary management. Also, the authors outline the future trends, benefits, challenges, processes, and opportunities relating to sociamaterial perspective.

Chapter 2 examines the effects of culture and data collection mode on socially desirable distortion and confidentiality concerns in survey research. The authors present how culture influences online data collection. In addition, the authors provide insights on the difficulty in understanding the challenges, vital aspects, and opportunities of online data collection.

Chapter 3 delivers a typology and a multi-case study of digital fluency in small and medium-sized enterprises (SMEs). The authors present important factors top managements, practitioners, and key decision makers should consider in small and medium-sized enterprises for better decision making and competitive advantages. Also, the chapter provides insights and understanding to government officials and top managements on strategies to implement so that investment in small and medium-sized enterprises positively and significantly influences economic development of emerging, transitioning, and developing economies.

Chapter 4 explores in detail the computer-related self-concepts; it describes how top managements and key decision makers can use the concepts to make better decisions and gain competitive advantages. The authors argue that computer related self-concepts are related to attitude toward information technology. In addition, a new approach to investigate gender differences in computing is presented.

Chapter 5 provides strategies for improving application decoupling in virtual enterprise integration for better decision making and competitive advantages. The authors discuss the important relationships between application decoupling and virtual enterprise integration. In addition, the authors describe a comprehensive example of a complex enterprise technological landscape, lifecycle of an EIS, backward and forward coupling, and compliance-based interoperability.

Chapter 6 examines the role and room for knowledge management in small and medium enterprises. The authors present a scenario in India examining the relationship between knowledge management and small and medium enterprises. The authors discuss in detail the important, challenges, and rationale for knowledge management in small and medium-sized enterprises resulting in better decision making and enhanced competitive advantages.

Chapter 7 provides a holistic overview of actor-network theory (ANT) and its use in education research. The authors present a central concept of ANT and the contributions of ANT to educational research relating to better decision making and competitive advantages.

Chapter 8 presents a utility theory of privacy and information sharing and the introduction of hyperbolic discounting in the digital, big data age. The chapter examines utility theory, expected utilities, indifference curve, time preferences, behavioral economics, information sharing, and privacy concerns relating to better decision making and competitive advantages.

Chapter 9 discusses the cochlear implant as an epistemic thing. In addition, the chapter provides insights and understanding of cochlear implants by examining the translations and (de)stabilizations of the cochlear implant, a subcutaneous prosthesis that is subject to ethical and judicial controversies.

Chapter 10 addresses breaking the formal financing barriers facing entrepreneurs. The chapter provides a case study from Nigeria that presents crowdfunding as an alternative financing source for enterprise development in Nigeria in the digital era. In addition, the chapter presents insights and understanding for foreign investors planning to invest in Nigeria.

Chapter 11 presents a case study from Brazil relating to cross-sector partnership in smart city development. The authors discuss some of the challenges, problems, updated models, and proposed solutions relating to cross-sector partnership in smart city development.

Chapter 12 delivers an exploratory study in the context of Nepal relating to the adoption and use of human resources information system (HRIS) and digital technology for organizational competitiveness. The chapter presents a conceptual and generic model for successful adoption and use of HRIS. The chapter addresses the challenges and problems facing HRIS. In addition, the authors present strategies and updated models to implement to overcome the challenges and problems facing HRIS.

Chapter 13 investigates systemic approach for optimization problems. The chapter examines factors that positively and significantly influence a systems approach for optimization problems. In addition, the chapter discusses mathematical models to solve optimization problems; and the study has significant research and managerial implications.

Chapter 14 delivers some thoughts on relating to fiscal policy and social optimization for developing nations in the digital era. The authors investigate and determine factors that positively and significantly influence fiscal policy and social optimization in developing nations. This study has significant research and managerial implications relating to developing nations.

Chapter 15 reviews the optimization models for calculation of personalized strategies to make better decisions and gain competitive advantages. The chapter provides mathematical models that gives insights and understanding on calculating strategies.

Chapter 16 discusses and outlines process-oriented organizations and integration of soft factors. The authors discuss the attributes, functions, and design principles relating to process-oriented organizations for better decision making and competitive advantages.

Chapter 17 analyzes psychological impact on and assessment of youth who use social network in their daily activities and tasks. The authors present an updated predictive model that provides insights and understanding on important factors that positively and significantly influence youth using social network. In addition, the authors present the different types of social networks that exist for better decision making and competitive advantages.

Chapter 18 presents technology and organizational change and how top managements, practitioners, and key decision makers can harness the power of the digital workplace. The authors present a detailed comparison between industrial age and digital age characteristics. In addition, the authors present updated models for the digital workplace. Furthermore, the authors discuss the challenges, benefits, and opportunities of the digital workplace relating to better decision making and competitive advantages.

Chapter 19 delivers an updated discussion of consumer online behavior, data sharing, & ethics. The chapter argues that social contract theory can be used for better decision making and competitive advantages.

Chapter 20 discusses and analyses collective behavior dynamics under the umbrella of blockchain. The chapter presents an updated model for blockchain operational process and collective behavior dynamics for better decision making and competitive advantages. The authors discuss challenges, benefits, opportunities, research models, characteristics and design principles relating to blockchain.

Chapter 21 explores updated sustainable supply chain management in the era of digitalization. The chapter present updated models, issues, and challenges for sustainable supply change management in the era of digitalization for better decision making and competitive advantages.

Chapter 22 discusses the optimal control problem of knowledge dissemination. The authors present mathematical models that help to provide insights and understanding on how top managements and key decision makers can use knowledge dissemination to make better decisions and gain competitive advantages relating to optimal control problems.

Chapter 23 presents the use of Google analytics for measuring website performance of non-formal education institutions. The chapter discusses detailed reviews on how top managements and key decision makers can use Google analytics for better decision making and competitive advantages.

Chapter 24 investigates the information perception value (IPV) model in maintaining the information security. In addition, the chapter provides insights and understanding to foreign companies and investors on Brunei's technological, economical, and political environments. The chapter presents an updated information perception value (IPV) model.

Chapter 25 presents a case study from Bogotá, Colombia, on how to strengthening the capabilities in data analytics. The chapter discusses the issues, challenges, and opportunities in data analytics relating to better decision making and competitive advantages.

Chapter 26 concludes and presents a comprehensive and holistic review of *Antecedents of Online Repurchase Behavior in Indian e-Commerce Paradigm Shift*. The authors present insights and understanding on factors that positively and significant influence the adoption of online repurchase behavior. This study contributes significantly to the online repurchase behavior literature.

REFERENCES

Idemudia, E. C., Adeola, O., Achebo, N., Raisinghani, M., & Omoregbe, N. (2018). *The effects of gender on the adoption of smartphone: An empirical investigation.* 24th Americas Conference on Information Systems, TREO Talk, New Orleans, LA.

Idemudia, E. C., Raisinghani, M. S., Adeola, O., & Achebo, N. (2017). The effects of gender on the adoption of social media: An empirical investigation. *23rd Americas Conference on Information Systems*, Boston, MA.

Interactive Advertising Bureau (IAB). (2018, November 13). *Digital ad spend hits record-breaking $49.5 billion in first half of 2018, marking a significant 23% YOY increase.* Retrieved from https://www.iab.com/news/digital-ad-spend-hits-record-breaking-49-5-billion-in-first-half-of-2018/

Chapter 1

The Issue of Post–Merger Integration Boundary Management:
A Sociomaterial Perspective

Dragos Vieru
Teluq University, Canada

ABSTRACT

This study analyzes the interactions among individuals engaged in two information system development (ISD) projects aimed to support an organization created by the merger of previously independent entities. The literature on post-merger integration (PMI) suggests that new information systems (IS) that would span the boundaries of the previously independent firms need to be implemented to facilitate a specific level of integration. Yet, there is a lack of studies on the issue of post-merger boundary management during ISD projects. The authors draw on a sociomaterial perspective to analyze two ISD projects in a PMI context of a merger of three hospitals. In both projects, the final IS-enabled practices differed from the post-merger practices that had been planned by the new hospital management. The analysis suggests that post-merger practices were the result of dialectic processes of resistance to, and negotiation of, the two systems reconfiguration after their implementation.

INTRODUCTION

Merging with, or acquiring, other companies is an important component of the growth strategies of many organizations in recent decades (Hitt, Harrison, & Ireland, 2001; Vieru & Rivard, 2014). In 2017 worldwide mergers and acquisitions (M&A) activity totalled 49,447 deals valued at US$3.6 trillion and for the fourth consecutive year had surpassed $3 trillion (Thompson Reuters, 2017). However, both academic and practitioner literatures show that historically, many of these organizations have struggled to realize the business benefits that justified this strategy (Graebner, Heimeriks, Huy, & Vaara, 2017).

DOI: 10.4018/978-1-5225-8933-4.ch001

The literature identifies three phases of a merger: courtship or pre-merger, merger decision and post-merger integration (Ellis, 2004). The first two phases comprise the strategic and financial analyses that determine the potential benefits or synergies; post-merger integration (PMI) constitutes the process of actual value-creation (Haspeslagh & Jemison, 1991). Post-merger1 integration represents the process of strategic and structural combination of merging parties (Faulkner, Teerikangas, & Joseph, 2012) and during which actual value creation will hopefully occur (Haspeslagh & Jemison, 1991). The literature stresses the importance of the choice of integration approach as being one of the most important strategic decisions to make in mergers and represents a critical determinant of the post-merger outcomes (Zollo & Singh, 2004; Reus, Lamont, & Ellis, 2016). All mergers do not imply the same degree of integration among the merging parties or the same degree of autonomy retained by each (Marks & Mirvis, 2001; Zollo & Reuer, 2010).

Research on PMI reveals that when organizations try to manage differences among the merging parties, they face the conundrum of integration versus autonomy (Haspeslagh & Jemison, 1991). A number of researchers have addressed this issue by proposing four ideal-types of integration approaches based on strategic and organizational dimensions (Ellis, 2004). At one extreme, the status quo is preserved in each organization. At the other extreme, one party requires the others to adopt its practices, norms and culture. It may also happen that organizations are gradually combined by enforcing operational interdependence and a common culture, or that an organizational structure and work practices are implemented that are new to all parties. There exist four ideal-type PMI approaches (Haspeslagh & Jemison, 1991; Marks & Mirvis, 2001). Preservation refers to a situation where the demarcation lines between the merging organizations remain intact. Absorption occurs when one party imposes its work practices, norms and culture on the other parties. Symbiosis is the approach in which the merging parties gradually blend together by becoming increasingly interdependent and retaining the best aspects of each party. *Transformation* reflects the situation in which organizations are integrated by developing totally new work practices and a common organizational identity.

Depending on the PMI approach adopted, new corporate structures, rules and processes may need to be created and business functions may need to be reorganized (Wijnhoven, Stegwee, & Fa, 2006; Vieru & Rivard, 2015). It may even happen that the entire business, from product to market, will require reorganization (Vaara, 2002). Given the scale of the changes that employees from merging organizations sometimes have to experience, mergers are often beset by problems such as high levels of stress, job dissatisfaction, and resistance (Vaara & Monin, 2010). These problems have been associated with the difficult task of transforming sometimes significantly different norms, values and practices into a common set (Larsson & Finkelstein, 1999).

Among the structures and processes that need to be integrated, information technology (IT) resources - infrastructures, applications, data and management practices (Tanriverdi & Uysal, 2011; Henningsson, Yetton, & Wynne, 2018) - have been claimed to have important impacts on merger outcomes (Vieru & Rivard, 2014). For instance, a study done in 2011 by McKinsey, a global management consulting firm, found that between 40% and 60% of the expected value from a merger is dependent on post-merger IT function integration especially the software applications and data (Sarrazin & West, 2011). This often involves the implementation of new ISs to span the boundaries of the previously independent organizations (Henningsson et al., 2018). The main purpose of these systems is to facilitate the implementation of new organizational practices. At one extreme, they may be mere "bridges" across existing functionalities. At the other extreme, they may be deployed to enable completely new business processes (Wijnhoven et al., 2006). Modern large organizations usually choose to implement off-the-shelf software applications such as Enterprise Systems (ES) (Wagner, Newell, & Piccoli, 2010). However, misalignments between industry-standard practices or "best practices" embedded in these ISs and the local idiosyncratic practices have caused headaches to management and IS implementation project teams (Sia & Soh, 2007).

Organizations often realize that practice norms embedded in their ES are mismatched only after the system is implemented and users engage in resistance to adopt the system, as they can no longer perform their old practices (Delgado, 2015). This constrains some organizations to engage into a lengthy processes of negotiation and may result in substantial customizations of the system (Wagner, Moll, & Newell, 2011). The practitioner literature on PMI suggests that when significant post-merger IS-enabled changes in practices are intended, it is more difficult for users to adopt the new systems, which makes the integration task most challenging. For example, when Nokia merged with Siemens in 2007, the upper management realized that attaining post-merger synergies relies on the implementation of a common set of software applications (Accenture, 2011). The new ESs needed to sustain a new set of practices based on one common backbone and one value chain system. At the outset of the merger the two organizations were using non-standard, legacy systems. Facing significant changes in practices, organizational members built up resistance at the beginning of the PMI phase. The management was able to successfully implement the new ESs only after employees were encouraged to get involved in the PMI process and express their needs. While Nokia-Siemens merger was successful, some firms, fearing great cost and complexity, never integrate their information systems; therefore, the merger value added is minimal. Others organizations focus only on the potential synergy gains and, without much planning, implement an absorption approach by choosing one information system over another, often frustrating both customers and employees (Yetton, Henningsson, & Bjørn-Andersen, 2013).

Although these reports bring to the fore the challenges of implementing enterprise systems in a PMI context, little research, however, has been conducted on the issues related to the development of new ISs that will be necessary to bridge the demarcations between previously independent organizations (Vieru & Rivard, 2015). In view of the paucity of empirical research on post-merger IS development and of the challenges that the PMI phase entails, the present study expands knowledge on post-merger integration by focusing on the dynamics of ES development in a PMI context. More specifically, we address the following question:

How do interactions among actors engaged in post-merger ES development projects influence the resulting ES and the corresponding ES-enabled practices?

To answer this question, we adopted a sociomaterial perspective (Orlikowski & Scott, 2008; Faraj & Azad, 2012) to shed light on the outcomes of two ES implementation projects in a healthcare organization resulting from the merger of three previously independent hospitals by investigating the practices that these two systems were supposed to enable after their implementation.

THEORETICAL BACKGROUND

Post-Merger Conundrum of Integration Versus Autonomy

Researchers have addressed the issue of boundary management in PMI by proposing integration approaches based on the extent of change in the merging parties' business processes and structures (Haspeslagh &

Jemison, 1991; Graebner et al., 2017). While most of the extant empirical studies on the PMI phase provide interesting insights into post-merger success factors, they tend to offer "either/or" solutions: that is, for one given pre-merger type of combination, there is only one type of integration approach (Ellis, 2004; Vieru & Rivard, 2015). However, other researchers have observed that in some mergers, the combined organization adopts a mix of different ideal-types of integration approaches, called a *hybrid* approach (Ranft & Lord, 2002; Schweizer, 2005). For instance, in a study of a merger between a pharmaceutical firm and a biotechnology firm, (Schweizer, 2005) found that the merging organizations chose to apply different integration approaches to some of their business processes. The author identifies two different approaches (*preservation* and *absorption*), implemented at different paces (slow and fast) but simultaneously, to integrate competencies from both merging companies in order to accomplish the short- and long-term motives for the merger. On one hand, the general biotech non-R&D knowledge and business processes were rapidly absorbed by the pharmaceutical firm in order to strengthen its market position. On the other hand, decision-makers realized that in order to keep its value for the merger, specific biotech R&D knowledge needs to retain its contextuality; therefore, total organizational autonomy for the biotech R&D department was granted.

This line of research emphasizes the fact that PMI is a complex and delicate process that cannot be fully understood by considering single integration approaches in isolation. These studies promote two main ideas. The first is that the issue of boundary management should be dealt with by simultaneously providing different multi-level integration approaches that will ensure a certain degree of organizational autonomy for some business units, yet provide an environment that enables the sharing of work practices and knowledge with other business units, if required (Ranft & Lord, 2002). The second is that the boundaries to be managed should be defined not only in terms of the differences between organizational structures, but also in terms of the differences in information systems (Yoo, Lyytinen, & Heo, 2007) or work practices (Ranft & Lord, 2002; Schweizer, 2005).

A Sociomaterial Perspective on Post-Implementation IS Adoption

As mentioned earlier, PMI must be supported by ISs to enable a specific level of integration. However, implementing ISs is not a straightforward task and it tends to be even more difficult in a merger context, considering the different objectives and cultural identities of the combined organizations. While initial use is an important indicator of IS success, the desired managerial outcome is not attained unless usage continues (Kim & Malhotra, 2005). In the literature, this phenomenon has been termed post-adoption usage, IT usage, IS continuance, or post-implementation IS adoption, to name a few. To complicate things even further, not all usage are created equal and it has been said that IT, even when suited for the task at hand, can be used as to circumvent the initial objectives of the implementation (Griffith, 1999) and in non-conformity to the original spirit of the project (DeSanctis & Poole, 1994).

In recent years, post-implementation studies have mainly adopted an organizational imperative perspective, focusing on human agency, viewing technology as a social production and overseeing its material element (Orlikowski & Scott, 2008; Hultin & Mahring, 2014). This is possibly a sign of the time as many organizations are now going through system upgrade or replacement and academics and practitioners are now aware ISs are in no way silver bullets (Scott & Orlikowski, 2013). Whether they are using causal models, case studies or contingency models, most articles consider the actions and decisions of stakeholders within organizations as mainly responsible for the observed effects, a perspective also known as organizational determinism (Markus & Robey, 1988).

In the past ten years, a number of researchers have adopted a new perspective in which the material and the social intermingle to form IT-enabled practices (Wagner et al., 2010; Kautz & Jensen, 2013; Thatcher, Pu, & Pienta, 2018), described as sociomaterial. Following this line of reasoning, in this study we adopt the view that the IT (material) and the social (human) agencies can be reconciled by conceptualizing them together instead of separately (Orlikowski & Scott, 2008). Sociomateriality represents a commitment to holding meaning and matter together in the conceptualization of technology (Wagner et al., 2010). Sociomaterial approaches draw special analytic attention to the materiality of technology, allowing researchers to investigate how the social and material intertwine to give shape to complex organizational structures and practices. Thus, two different sociomaterial approaches have emerged in the literature – agential realism and critical realism (Mutch, 2013) – and each highlights important aspects. Their main difference is that critical realism views the social and the material as separate entities put into association with one another but that become inseparable only through human agency occurring over time. In contrast, agential realism argues that the social is not separated from the material, and therefore there is only the sociomaterial as something that is already ingrained in the individual's perceptions of technology (Leonardi, 2017). In this view, a technology represents a *sociomaterial assemblage* (Orlikowski and Scott, 2008) that "emerges from practice and defines how to practice" (Wagner et al., 2010, p. 279). Here, *practices* are defined as coordinated activities of individuals and groups in doing their 'real work' as they are informed by a specific organizational context (Cook & Brown, 1999). A *field of practice* may represent business units, departments or goal-driven groups, in which individuals who share practices are in pursuit of a joint interest (Levina & Vaast, 2005).

In order to make sense of their practices, the sociomaterial assemblages reflect individuals' shared understandings within the organizational context (Orlikowski and Scott, 2008). Given the research objective to understand the agency shift between the material (IT) and the social (practices performed by the organizational members), this study adopts an agential realism approach.

The introduction of an enterprise system designed to cut across pre-merger boundaries between merging entities alters the existing sociomaterial arrangements within those entities. Enterprise systems are developed based on the belief that "they represent a rationalization, encoding and abstraction of 'best practices' that, while being congruent with the logic of certain functional areas of some organizations, can be in conflict with others" (Berente, Yoo, & Lyytinen, 2007, p.14-15). However, in PMI context, the business rules underlying ESs cannot take into consideration all of the local practice idiosyncrasies. In terms of the sociomaterial perspective, the dynamic relationship between organizational actors and ISs is reflected in practices and is referred to as performativity. This is a dialectic process of resistance and accommodation that produces unpredictable reconfigurations of the sociomaterial assemblages (Wagner et al., 2010). Despite the fact that professional-based communities are usually considered global, they tend to promote practices that have a local character based on an organizational context (Knorr-Cetina, 1999). This is to emphasize the fact that there are always differences even when organizational members are supposedly engaging in the same practices. Thus, by focusing on performativity, we are able to examine how ISs are reconfigured to create agreed upon post-merger material and social arrangements.

METHODOLOGY

We adopted an explanatory theory-building-from-cases approach (Eisenhardt, 1989). An explanatory approach seeks to find relationships between an "observed state of a phenomenon and conditions that influence its development" (Avgerou, 2013, p. 428). Following Eisenhardt's (1989) methodological recommendations, we anchored our problem definition and preliminary construct specification in extant literature and we designed our data collection instruments and protocols based on this literature, following a deductive pattern. This was followed, after our entry in the field, by a "flexible and opportunistic" (Eisenhardt, 1989, p. 533) data collection approach, and a within-case and cross-case data analysis, which are inductive in nature. We used a multiple-case design and selected the cases applying a logic of replication, maximizing variation, thus predicting contrasting results but for predictable reasons (Yin, 2015), yet allowing comparison.

The two cases had two similarities: both took place in the same organization and were intended to support a new organization that would result from adopting a transformation approach to PMI. The cases varied in terms of the type of business process that was to be enabled – laboratory services and clinical information management – and the actual integration approach. The unit of analysis was the ISD project. The selected organization was the MQ Health Centre (MQHC – not its real name), that was the result of a 'merger of equals' of three large independent teaching hospitals: two adult hospitals (Community and Riverside) and Eastside, a pediatric hospital. While the term 'acquisition' refers to the purchase of a target organization for absorption into the acquiring organization, in a 'merger of equals', merging parties are considered full partners and when PMI approaches do not reflect the pre-merger promises, the result may be dissatisfaction and distrust (Marks & Mirvis, 2001). The MQHC merger was initiated with the clear goal of creating a mega-hospital that would provide outstanding health care services by implementing a business model for care management based on industry best practices. Because of the expected magnitude of the business process redesign, keeping legacy systems was considered to be an ineffective cost option. According to archival strategic documentation, the planned MQHC approach at the outset of the PMI phase was consistent with a transformation approach.

Interviews were the main method of data collection and were based on a protocol crafted from extant theory and research. In line with our theory building approach, however, we remained open to the exploration of new topics and themes during data collection (Eisenhardt, 1989). Informants were selected using a snowball sampling procedure. We interviewed key stakeholders, in particular project development and implementation committee members (i.e., department managers, IS professionals, project managers, and clinicians) who had participated in the ISD project. The interviewees were significant as agents, since they influenced the knowledge sharing process due to their roles, status, power and experience. Twenty-four interviews were conducted on site, and lasted between 45 to 90 minutes. For Case 1 we interviewed seven lab physicians, three lab technologists, three lab managers, the central lab manager, and the IS project manager. For Case 2 we interviewed three physicians, three nurses, one clinical analyst, one unit coordinator and one department manager. The interviews were recorded and transcribed. In a few instances, when clarifications were required, follow-up questions were asked via phone or email. We also conducted three follow-up interviews. One researcher was responsible for conducting all the interviews. The other researcher remained out of the field and played the role of devil's advocate (Eisenhardt, 1989) during within-case and cross-case analyses.

Although studies have shown that the participants in organizational processes do not forget key events in these processes, it is possible that a participant-informant in a retrospective study may not have judged an event as important when it occurred and therefore may not remember it later (Leonard-Barton, 1990). To avoid these shortcomings, we obtained access to a number of emails that team members exchanged during the IS development. We also followed Leonard-Barton's (1990) recommendation to engage in informal conversations (e.g., at lunch or in hallways) with individuals who were members of the project teams because useful data may emerge from this type of interaction.

Following our theory building approach (Eisenhardt, 1989), we triangulated the interview with archival sources, including project documentation, organization documents (PMI management strategy documentation, management presentations, and schemes of governance structure, communication plans, and emails). The archival documents were used in four ways. First, reports and presentations were used to assist putting together the projects chronology, including identifying the dates of important events and decision junctures. Second, emails and management presentations were used to formulate and refine interview questions. Third, reports and meeting minutes were used to corroborate and validate interview reports. Finally, meeting minutes provided an "ethnographic" sense of the project work.

The case narrative (interview data) was analyzed in an iterative process (Eisenhardt, 1989) by cycling between data, emerging themes, and relevant literature. During case analysis, themes emerged from the data. Coding was a two-phase process. In Phase 1 we built a provisional list of codes prior to the interviews. Most of the initial coding categories were based on the three theoretical constructs introduced in the previous section: practices, performativity, and reconfiguration. In Phase 2, the interview transcripts were introduced into a database, read carefully and relevant portions were marked as evidence. This allowed us to identify episodes of resistance, followed by negotiations from which the new ES were reconfigured to accommodate practices at MQHC. The final ES configurations reflected a mix of industry standards and local idiosyncrasies.

We conducted within-case and cross-case analyses. During the within-case analysis, themes emerged from the data and provided a rich understanding of each case. The outcomes of this analysis constituted the logical chains of evidence. Cross-case analysis was conducted by using methods suggested by Eisenhardt (1989), as the cases were compared to identify similarities and differences between them.

RESULTS

Case 1: Laboratory Information System (LIS)

In 2002, upper management decided to acquire an ES to provide common best practices for its unified laboratory departments. The system, developed by company LabSpec (not the real name), was based on industry standards and provided flexibility to accommodate, to a certain degree, idiosyncratic practices. The role of an LIS in a hospital is to automate laboratory clinical, financial and managerial processes and to enable lab staff to maintain accurate tracking, processing and result recording, while avoiding lost and misplaced specimens. In order to better supervise the implementation work of the project team, a Clinical Advisory Committee (CAC) was set up. Its role was to make key decisions regarding the project scope and direction. The CAC included representatives from the upper management and lab physicians. Prior to the start of the system implementation, the three lab services were asked to standardize their practices (lab request workflow). Even though the typical lab workflow (scanning barcodes that include laboratory number, patient identification and test destination – hospital department/physician) seems to be forthright, each of the three lab services was using different sequence steps and different legacy ISs.

After almost three years of development, testing and finally implementation, the new LIS was put into production at the Community hospital in 2005, followed by the Riverside and Eastside hospitals at the beginning of 2006. The management decided to have both the new and the legacy systems running in parallel for six months until lab workflows get adjusted to the new practices embedded in the new ES. While the initial design was based on best practice standards, after the six-month adjustment period, the post-implementation system configuration revealed a blend of industry standards and local contingencies. Therefore, the final LIS functionality reflected a hybrid PMI approach.

Within-Case Analysis

Theme 1: Resistance and Accommodations. At the outset of the project there were three site-based set of practices: Community, Riverside and Eastside.

"There were three different databases for each site. There were just so totally different, you know, order entry, the way they process, even in the way that they did the basic workflow." (Riverside-Lab Tech)

The need for a unique set of lab practices was clearly conveyed by the upper management to the laboratory clinicians:

"Not only do they [management] count they're going to start using the same system, but the system will work the same way for all of them. Suppliers are not going to develop a specific need for a specific site." (IS-Manager)

The evidence suggests that resistance emerged right after the new LIS was put into production due to the new ES imposing a new sociomaterial assemblage upon the lab clinicians. This set up a need for negotiations and adaptations if the new LIS were to be adopted and used by the labs user community. During the six-month period when the new and the legacy systems were running in parallel, the mindset of the clinicians reflected site-related work norms as a result of the existence of the three sets of practices for each laboratory unit. This situation is described by an interviewee:

"There was very little cooperation from the physicians that were on that committee [CAC]. So you would have physicians from the Community and Riverside coming to visit us and try to get their feet in the system and put their mark." (Community-Unit Coordinator); "I knew that there was going to be some resistance from the various departments. Just like you know the people that are in the department, and who want to be the 'top dog' and who wants to have the last say." (Eastside-Physician)

The evidence shows that while clinicians tried to preserve their pre-merger practices, the upper management started to put a constant pressure on the lab physicians to adopt and use the new ES. Thus, the Lab technicians and physicians realized they had to agree on common standard procedures. A process of negotiations followed and compromises ensued.

"There would be some shouting matches and sometimes we would have to say let's try it for six months and then see what happens [...]. So there have been times when you're trying to get a site to change and there were heated discussions, and sometimes we decided to leave it alone, depending on how important it was to change." (Riverside-Physician)

In a post-implementation meeting of the Clinical Advisory Committee, some members of the committee complained the fact that every task performed was taking more steps and time to complete than before with the old system. Workload had increased, secretaries and technicians were working a maximum amount of overtime, and doctors were not receiving reports in a timely fashion. Other members of the committee also complained that the LIS system has increased their department's daily tasks.

Our data analysis suggests that the negotiation process resulted in accommodations that enabled emergent sociomaterial assemblages. While trying to bring a closure the implementation project, the physicians from the Clinical Advisory Committee were showing commitment to the lab user community:

"We do syphilis tests, about 100 a day. So this is just one test in a typical day a microbiologist has to sign out. So at the beginning, I'm laughing because they would have to click each individual syphilis results. I was getting calls, 'this is impossible!' because you could be here until eight o'clock at night doing the results. Finally, I called one of the IS specialists who figured it out that we could verify it without doing a hundred clicks. So what normally would have taken about two hours of signing, it took ten minutes now." (Community-Physician)

Theme 2: System Reconfiguration and Resulted Practices. While neither the upper management nor the lab user community reached their goals - the former to impose new practices and the latter to keep its pre-merger workflows - the new sociomaterial arrangement (a *hybrid* approach) gained enough support from both sides to reach a stable environment. On the management side:

"What we did is that there are some different clinical practices we allowed, but we tried not to make too many because it's too difficult to keep on with quality." (Riverside-Physician)

However, on the lab user community side, the lab technologists struggled for a while and only after finding that their needs could not be entirely met through the ES design, they engaged in innovative ways to using the LIS:

"We thought that there was one way of working with the system, common to all the sites. [However], we found out that some people [lab staff] were expressing their concerns about the functionality and we found out that they resolved it. So we found out that there were some different practices ... workarounds depending on the problem." (Community-Lab Manager)

Case 2: The Clinical Results Display (CRD)

In the summer of 2004, the MQHC decided to implement a Clinical Information System (CIS) by signing a contract of collaboration with Delta (not the real name), a supplier of CIS solutions. A CIS is a software package that is the most complex IS in terms of patient data management and it offers one-stop access to patient information by centralizing all electronically available clinical data. The CIS was considered as the cross-departmental IT-lead reinvention post-merger integration approach. Seen by the upper management as the 'project that will change our lives', the MQHC and Delta decided to adopt a cautionary, multi-phased, approach to implementing the CIS.

According to CIS project documentation, this approach was structured to achieve the following three main goals: a) Show results incrementally throughout the course of the project; b) Achieve buy-in and transfer ownership of the solution developed to the clinical community; c) Introduce industry best practices for how patient information is viewed and/or captured gradually as opposed to all at once. To achieve these goals, Delta and the MQHC decided that the project would be conducted in 3 phases. Delta CIS offered in Phase 1 a Clinical Results Display (CRD) that provided a unique "smart summarization" in a series of screens that display patient demographics and clinical results. Our study focuses only on this phase of the project because the other phases were still in progress at the time of the interviews.

Phase I was completed in December 2008. In the initial design, the CRD was supposed to bring information, scattered across the THC sites, to one central access point in front of any THC caregiver. Although requirement assessment and the development of the interfaces between the ancillary systems and the CRD seemed to be a straightforward process, soon the team members realized that, due to the differences in procedures between the three sites, the task was daunting. Due to the political sensitivity of the system, upper management had involved some of the most influential MQHC clinicians in project coordination to ensure that the functionality of the new CIS would reflect the desired integration approach. Some of these clinicians were already well known to the MQHC community, while the others soon impressed the other team members. At the outset of the project it was anticipated that a first draft of the design of the CRD would be ready by the end of 2004 and a production version would start being implemented in three pilot departments each at each of the three main sites by mid-2005. However, budgetary constraints triggered important delays and the pilot test was ready in May 2006. In September 2006, the conclusions on the pilot test were presented to upper management. The team members had to strike a compromise between the needs of the respective departments and the flexibility of the CIS package.

The CRD did not lead to real changes to patient information management practices. However, on one hand, the fact that now nurses had to access patient information through a single system instead of several ancillary systems constituted a major change in their workflow. This change made their workflow more efficient but did not alter how they handled patient information. On the other hand, for the physicians, the CRD provided a single point of access to enhanced patient information, a sort of "best of all worlds." With the new system the physicians had access to comprehensive clinical information from all sites, regardless of their physical workplace.

Within-Case Analysis

Theme 1: Resistance and Accommodations. Similar to Case 1, at the outset of the post-merger integration process, three different patient information management practices were present at MQHC.

"At the Adult sites, each clinical group have drastically different workflows, so you couldn't follow patients across both sites (Community-physician); "If you looked at inter site between the Community and Riverside adult sites, they had different chart structures, different admission sheets" (Riverside-Physician); "It was clear that we were working in two different cultures [adult sites versus pediatric site] because the three major sites had different workload systems, even the information system that we were using, our legacy system, was built differently so the way things were functioning and working with it was different." (Eastside-Nurse)

According to the case narrative, overall, the team members found that the context surrounding the ISD process had a high level of novelty. First, all of the project team members were facing a completely new technology. Second, most of them were meeting people that they had never met before. Third, they were carrying with them their own field of practice's norms and values.

"There were of course a lot of new people to meet or to know because we were getting all the sites together. It was new at the beginning" (Riverside-Nurse); "I think the technical vendor's occasional reality checks were very helpful. For the rest of us since no one really had deep experience within a complete integrated system, we were just trying to, you know, blue sky and see what it is we really wanted to get out of it." (Community-Physician)

At the outset of the ISD process, upper management decided that the knowledge sharing process across the boundaries between the sites would be fostered by several agents that were influential within their fields of practice (Riverside-Physician, Community-Nurse, and Eastside-Nurse). According to Riverside-Physician, he was seen as being "pivotal" for the rest of the team members. The three agents took on the role of knowledge brokers by mediating the flow of knowledge across the boundaries between the members of the project team. They had to do the "dirty work" and try to persuade the department representatives to become CRD champions when going back to their professional communities in order to mitigate the resistance to the new system. This involved exposing the advantages of the new CRD functionalities over the limited, but comfortable functionalities of the old site-based ISs. This set up a need for negotiations and adaptations if the new CRD were to be adopted and used by the labs user community.

"We spent quite a bit of time in the work groups figuring out what people wanted to see as functionalities. We had long lists of functionalities and then we had, you know, screens made based on those functionalities, most of the time. Of course there were some trade-offs, some negotiations." (Riverside-Physician)

Theme 2: System Reconfiguration and Resulted Practices. The initial design of the CRD was to reflect upper management's objective of implementing a system that would enable new best practices: a centralized repository with one point of entry for accessing and managing patient data, hence tearing down the existing boundaries between the three fields of practice. The resulting sociomaterial arrangement reflected a unified approach to managing patient information across the MQHC sites. However, the only change in practice for the nurses was that now they were accessing patient information through a central point, whereas before they needed multiple logins on several systems to access the same information. Their workflow was not changed by the CRD; it was just streamlined. For the physicians, the new system reflected a single point of access to a blend of site-based workflows, a better way to organize the management of the patient information across all sites, yet retaining the same pre-merger practices, which were now just more efficient.

Our data analysis found a PMI *hybrid* approach (preservation and transformation - streamlined pre-merger workflows for both nurses and physicians in the resulting PMI approach) rather than a *transformation* approach, as planned by the upper management. Despite some resistance at the outset, the new sociomaterial arrangement gained enough support from both sides to reach a stable environment:

"The system was chosen to be highly configurable. The final configuration was quite different from what we thought we will have at the end" (Community-Unit coordinator physician); "You can configure it

as you prefer. For example, there was an endocrinologist who was like 'I want to see my results always this way'. Well, that's easy, we can build it or we can configure it." (Eastside-Nurse)

DISCUSSION

Cross-Case Analysis

The two cases were compared to investigate the similarities and differences between them in terms of themes and then research propositions were offered.

Planned PMI Practices, Resistance and Accommodations

Our cross-case analysis revealed that the PMI approach adopted by the MQHC (*transformation*) in both cases involved the imposition of new practices and shaped the context of the two ES implementation projects. Upper management made it very clear that unique LIS and CIS were the success factors in helping MQHC to implement new industry-based practices. The evidence shows that at the outset of the projects there were three different fields of practice, each defined by historical and patient information management-based norms. Therefore, on one hand, there were significant differences between the pre-merger site-based practices, and between these practices and the new planned practices on the other hand. In both cases, data suggest that different pre-merger sociomaterial assemblages based on common interests, organizational values and identities were at stake. This situation triggered resistance from the user communities that was followed by negotiations with the management. The resulted arrangements: (1) created the bases for new sociomaterial assemblages around IS-enabled negotiated practices; and (2) undermined the planned outcomes of the adopted PMI approach. Taking into consideration the above argumentation we propose a first research proposition:

P1: *A post-merger ES implementation triggers the creation of new sociomaterial assemblages embedded in post-merger practices that emerge through a process of dialectic of resistance and negotiation.*

System Reconfiguration and Negotiated Practices

The cross-case analysis revealed one main observation: the final configuration of the two ES was different from the initial planned/proposed system configuration. The initial design was supposed to reflect practices related to a transformation PMI approach (new practices). The members of the two project teams negotiated common interests with the stakeholders by trying to adapt industry-based best practices to 'local' requirements when possible. Both ES were reconfigured to enable workable new practices (mix of *transformation* and *preservation*) that were different than the industry standards proposed by the two manufacturers in the initial configuration (*transformation*). Our study shows that succeeding to respect industry-based practices and preserve some pre-merger (legacy) practices can help successfully pass the post-roll-out phase and avoid failure. Based on the above argumentation, we advance a second research proposition:

P2: *In a post-merger implementation of an ES, the less emphasis on an ideal PMI approach, the more likely it is that the negotiation of new practices will be successful.*

A Process Model of ES Implementation in PMI

The proposed model is based on two premises. First, ES-enabled change of existing organizational sociomaterial arrangements is met with resistance and the new ES will be accepted and used only through negotiations followed by arrangements. Second, ES do not have pre-defined structures of their own and can only be defined in relation to the practices of prospective users, or to the business processes and institutionalized values of the organization implementing the technology (Orlikowski, 2000).

We posit that major change processes in organizations, such as PMI, can be explained alternatively or complementarily in a processual manner by four different motors of change: life cycle, teleology, dialectic and evolutionary (Poole & Van De Ven, 2004). In this viewpoint, implementation of an ES can be illustrated as a process that entails a sequence of individual and collective events and activities unfolding over time. The resulting view of the process tells a rich story by explaining how the dynamics of performativity generate new sociomaterial assemblages, which collectively lead to future action.

The analysis of the two case studies led us to consider the process of a post-merger ES implementation project from a single-motor perspective: dialectical. Organizations are complex entities usually comprised of goal-driven individuals whose personal agendas might be incompatible with their organization's. As opposing individuals interact in an effort to impose their respective goals, organizations may change in response to resolutions of conflicting interests. We therefore infer that the means for driving change is dialectical as change is the outcome of the interaction between opposing forces.

Figure 1. A process model of ES implementation in PMI

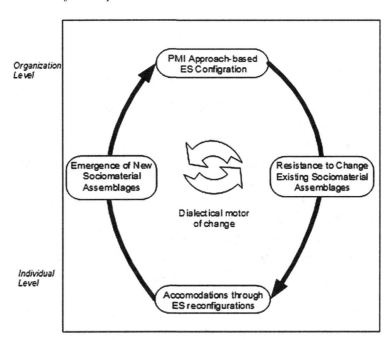

Our model, presented in Figure 1, illustrates the operation of the dialectic motor of change during the process of a post-merger ES implementation. First, we posit that the integration approach decision will reveal existing pre-merger practice-based organizational boundaries. We conjecture that users affected by the ES-enabled changes in practices, will resist system's implementation. In this context, team members will negotiate and propose accommodations through reconfigurations of the ES after the implementation. Thus, the initial functional design of the ES may be different from the final functionality once the ES is considered workable and start being used by the user community. The resulting dialectic leads to an iterative process of resistance and negotiation of common interests at the boundary, followed by a change of the existing sociomaterial assemblages which reflects a PMI approach different from the planned one.

In both cases, management decision to implement a common system caused resistance from the three site-based clinician communities (resistance was stronger in Case 1 where the lab clinicians were struggling to come up with a standardized lab workflow). The subsequent negotiations resulted in workable ESs that enabled a common set of practices and accommodated some pre-merger practice idiosyncrasies (mix of practice *transformation* and *preservation*).

CONCLUSION AND FUTURE RESEARCH DIRECTIONS

It has been argued that IT-driven organizational change is a social process (Orlikowski, 2007), and that a theory of change is best framed as a process theory rather than a variance theory (Levina & Vaast, 2005). In the case of a radical change such as a merger, process models can handle more complex causal relationships than variance models, and they can provide an explanation of how the inputs and outputs are related at different levels of analysis rather than simply identify the relationship as variance models do. From this point of view, implementation of an IS represents a process that entails a "sequence of individual and collective events, actions, and activities unfolding over time in context" (Pettigrew, 1997, p.337). The resulting view of the process tells a rich story of the events taking place within a given situation by explaining how influential factors interact, how they collectively lead to future action, and what constrains them. Thus, we adopted a sociomaterial perspective because when this theoretical lens has been used, it has allowed for the development of a temporal, process-based theory (Wagner et al., 2010). While the main constructs used by the sociomaterial perspective – such as assemblages, performativity and reconfiguration – are clearly defined in the literature, we do not have an in-depth understanding of the relationships between these constructs in the context of IS implementation and adoption in PMI settings.

The results confirm the existence of a conundrum of integration versus autonomy at the IT function level in PMI settings that can be explained by the emergence of unexpected new sociomaterial assemblages during the PMI phase. The MQHC management realized only after the implementation of the new ES that the planned PMI approach did not take into consideration the pre-merger sociomaterial arrangements in the three fields of practice. The literature on PMI suggests that while value creation results from an organization's ability to integrate practices across the previous organizational boundaries (Larsson & Finkelstein, 1999), excessive integration may render some of those practices useless due to their social and material arrangement context (Ranft & Lord, 2002). At the outset of project, the MQHC management opted for an overall ideal integration approach (*transformation*) for the new organization by planning to impose IS-enabled new practices. Yet, during the system post-implementation, it found no choice but to engage in a process of negotiation and trade-offs with the stakeholders of the ES, and in time realized that a *hybrid* integration approach (Schweizer, 2005) might be the appropriate path to take.

Our research makes a number of contributions. First, it introduces the issue of boundary management in the PMI IS literature and explains this conundrum through a dialectical motor of change. Second, by adopting a sociomaterial perspective it was found that practices are socially negotiated, rather than being permanently selected at a particular moment in time. Focusing on negotiated practices – where IT materiality exists only in relation to potential users, so that ES technology features are always subject to users' representations – explains the difference between the planned configuration and the resulted one. Consistent with the outcomes of other studies (Boudreau and Robey, 2005; Wagner et al., 2010), the MQHC's management's expectation was that clinicians use the new technology as-is, while the reality is that negotiated IT-based practices pushed the use toward a working and accepted technology.

Third, our study contributes to the IS strategy literature in presenting an ES implementation model that is neither technologically nor organizationally determined, adopting instead a sociomaterial perspective of ISs. Fourth, the theoretical explanation offered here through a field study, albeit a single organization, has the potential for exploring more in depth some of the more complex processes associated with the dynamic relationship between the social and the material in the context of organizational change.

In addressing the practitioners, our study demonstrates that negotiated practices are part of a normal course of action in enterprise systems implementation during PMI. This is an important insight for practitioners even though at odds with the popular best practice ideal associated with the packaged software such as enterprise systems (Delgado, 2015). In this context, managers who lead the development and implementation of ISs that need to bridge pre-merger practices or enable new practices need to organize another type of boundary-spanning activity: knowledge sharing about each local professional community practice. In this vein, the cross-community members of the project team need to acknowledge and understand others' old organization affiliations in terms of identity and symbolic meanings and reflect on their own past experiences in order to generate useful common knowledge required for IS development.

The main limitation of this study might be that it attempts at generalizing only from empirical statements to theoretical statements in developing a process model from a two-case study (Lee & Baskerville, 2003). However, it has been shown that statistical, sampling-based generalizability may be an unsuitable goal for qualitative studies (Denzin & Lincoln, 2000). The MQHC case is built on strong historical foundation and deal with issues of central importance to our research which makes it purposeful (Yin, 2015). Takeaways from this study should be transferred to other contexts for further refinements that eventually will offer statistical generalizability. MQHC was a unique setting in many respects and it would be fruitful to continue building the theory developed in this study based on data from other PMI settings in different industries. Looking at industry level data and data from other settings may help overcome this limitation and provide new insights.

The dynamic approach of a process model seeks a holistic explanation of an organizational process. Post-merger integration is a journey, not a discreet one-time event (Vieru & Rivard, 2015). In this vein, we consider that a cross-disciplinary, processual and multi-level perspective can help IS researchers understand the complex process of post-merger IS integration and its interdependence with the business integration process. However, in adopting this approach, they should rigorously adopt and define out-of-discipline concepts and take into account methodological issues, such as the analysis of the process data, implied by a process theory approach.

DISCUSSION QUESTIONS

This multi-case study could be used as a decision case study in a graduate course in management or in IT project management. The professor will create the following scenario for the students in order to engage the class in a dynamic discussion about the presented study.

Your task is to build a compelling recommendation to the MQHC's upper management on how to avoid the several issues related to the post-merger boundary management identified in the study. To get you started, consider the following discussion questions:

1. What were the main reasons for the differences between the planned and the resulted ES functionality in both projects?
2. What were the lessons learnt from the two ES implementation projects?
3. Analyze the pros and cons of the two PMI ES strategies: common "best practices" across the boundaries of the sites (*transformation* approach) versus context-based ES for each of the three sites (*preservation* approach).

ACKNOWLEDGMENT

This book chapter represents a substantial enhancement of the article *Unpredictable Reconfigurations: The Dilemma of the Post-Merger Information Systems Integration* published in 2013 in the *International Journal of Social and Organizational Dynamics in IT*.

Reference: Vieru, D., & Trudel, M. C. (2013). Unpredictable Reconfigurations: The Dilemma of the Post-Merger Information Systems Integration1. *International Journal of Social and Organizational Dynamics in IT (IJSODIT)*, 3(1), 47-60.

REFERENCES

Accenture. (2011). Driving Successful Change at Nokia Siemens Networks. *Accenture*.

Ahuja, M. K., & Thatcher, J. B. (2005). Moving Beyond Intentions and Toward the Theory of Trying: Effects of Work Environment and Gender on Post-Adoption Information Technology Use. *Management Information Systems Quarterly*, *29*(3), 427–459. doi:10.2307/25148691

Avgerou, C. (2013). Explaining Trust in IT-mediated Elections: A Case Study of e-Voting in Brazil. *Journal of the Association for Information Systems*, *14*(8), 420–451. doi:10.17705/1jais.00340

Berente, N., Yoo, Y., & Lyytinen, K. (2007). An Institutional Analysis of Pluralistic Responses to Enterprise System Implementations. *Proceedings of the International Conference on Information Systems*.

Boudreau, M.-C., & Robey, D. (2005). Enacting Integrated Information Technology: A Human Agency Perspective. *Organization Science*, *16*(1), 3–18. doi:10.1287/orsc.1040.0103

Cook, S. D. N., & Brown, J. S. (1999). Bridging Epistemologies: The Generative Dance between Organizational Knowledge and Organizational Knowing. *Organization Science*, *10*(4), 381–400. doi:10.1287/orsc.10.4.381

Delgado, J. C. (2015). Supporting Enterprise Integration with a Multidimensional Interoperability Framework. *International Journal of Social and Organizational Dynamics in IT*, *4*(1), 39–70. doi:10.4018/IJSODIT.2015010104

Denzin, N. K., & Lincoln, Y. S. (2000). *The Sage Handbook of Qualitative Research*. Sage.

DeSanctis, G., & Poole, M. S. (1994). Capturing the Complexity in Advanced Technology Use: Adaptive Structuration Theory. *Organization Science*, *5*(2), 121–147. doi:10.1287/orsc.5.2.121

Eisenhardt, K. M. (1989). Building Theories from Case Study Research. *Academy of Management Review*, *14*(4), 532–550. doi:10.5465/amr.1989.4308385

Ellis, K. (2004). Managing the Acquisition Process: Do Differences Actually Exist across Integration Approaches. In A. L. Pablo & M. Javidan (Eds.), *Mergers and Acquisitions: Creating Integrative Knowledge*. John Wiley & Sons.

Faraj, S., & Azad, B. (2012). The materiality of technology: An affordance perspective. In P. Leonardi, B. Nardi, & J. Kallinikos (Eds.), *Materiality and Organizing: Social interaction in a technological world*. Oxford University Press. doi:10.1093/acprof:oso/9780199664054.003.0012

Faulkner, D., Teerikangas, S., & Joseph, R. J. (2012). The handbook of mergers and acquisitions. Oxford, UK: Academic Press. doi:10.1093/acprof:oso/9780199601462.001.0001

Giacomazzi, F., Panella, C., Pernici, B., & Sansoni, M. (1997). Information systems integration in mergers and acquisitions: A normative model. *Information & Management*, *32*(6), 289–302. doi:10.1016/S0378-7206(97)00031-1

Graebner, M. E., Heimeriks, K. H., Huy, Q. N., & Vaara, E. (2017). The process of postmerger integration: A review and agenda for future research. *The Academy of Management Annals*, *11*(1), 1–32. doi:10.5465/annals.2014.0078

Griffith, T. L. (1999). Technology Features as Triggers for Sensemaking. *Academy of Management Review*, *24*(3), 472–488. doi:10.5465/amr.1999.2202132

Haspeslagh, P. C., & Jemison, D. B. (1991). *Managing Acquisitions: Creating Value through Corporate Renewal*. Free Press.

Henningsson, S., Yetton, P. W., & Wynne, P. J. (2018). A review of information system integration in mergers and acquisitions. *Journal of Information Technology*, 1–49.

Hitt, M. A., Harrison, J. S., & Ireland, R. D. (2001). *Mergers & acquisitions: A guide to creating value for stakeholders*. Oxford University Press.

Hultin, L., & Mähring, M. (2014). Visualizing institutional logics in sociomaterial practices. *Information and Organization*, *24*(3), 129–155. doi:10.1016/j.infoandorg.2014.05.002

Kautz, K., & Jensen, T. B. (2013). Sociomateriality at the royal court of IS: A jester's monologue. *Information and Organization, 23*(1), 15–27. doi:10.1016/j.infoandorg.2013.01.001

Kim, S. S., & Malhotra, N. K. (2005). A Longitudinal Model of Continued Is Use: An Integrative View of Four Mechanisms Underlying Postadoption Phenomena. *Management Science, 51*(5), 741–755. doi:10.1287/mnsc.1040.0326

Kim, S. S., & Son, J.-Y. (2009). Out of dedication or Constraint? A Dual Model of Post-Adoption Phenomena and its Empirical Test in the Context of Online Services. *Management Information Systems Quarterly, 33*(1), 49–70. doi:10.2307/20650278

Knorr-Cetina, K. (1999). *Epistemic Cultures: How the Sciences Make Knowledge*. Harvard University Press.

Larsson, R., & Finkelstein, S. (1999). Integrating Strategic, Organizational, and Human Resource Perspectives on Mergers and Acquisitions: A Case Survey of Synergy Realization. *Organization Science, 10*(1), 1–26. doi:10.1287/orsc.10.1.1

Lee, A. S., & Baskerville, R. L. (2003). Generalizing Generalizability in Information Systems Research. *Information Systems Research, 14*(3), 221–243. doi:10.1287/isre.14.3.221.16560

Leonard-Barton, D. (1990). A Dual Methodology for Case Studies: Synergistic Use of a Longitudinal Single Site with Replicated Multiple Sites. *Organization Science, 1*(3), 248–266. doi:10.1287/orsc.1.3.248

Leonardi, P. M. (2017). Methodological Guidelines for the Study of Materiality and Affordances. In M. Raza & S. Jain (Eds.), *Routledge Companion to Qualitative Research in Organization Studies*. New York: Routledge. doi:10.4324/9781315686103-18

Levina, N., & Vaast, E. (2005). The Emergence of Boundary Spanning Competence in Practice: Implications for Implementation and Use of Information Systems. *Management Information Systems Quarterly, 29*(2), 335–363. doi:10.2307/25148682

Marks, M. L., & Mirvis, P. H. (2001). Making Mergers and Acquisitions Work: Strategic and Psychological Preparation. *The Academy of Management Executive, 15*(2), 80-94.

Markus, M. L., & Robey, D. (1988). Information Technology and Organizational Change: Causal Structure in Theory and Research. *Management Science, 34*(5), 583–598. doi:10.1287/mnsc.34.5.583

Mutch, A. (2013). Sociomateriality - Taking the wrong turining? *Information and Organization, 23*(1), 28–40. doi:10.1016/j.infoandorg.2013.02.001

Orlikowski, W. (2000). Using Technology and Constituting Structures: A Practice Lens for Studying Technology in Organizations. *Organization Science, 11*(4), 404–421. doi:10.1287/orsc.11.4.404.14600

Orlikowski, W. J. (2007). Sociomaterial Practices: Exploring Technology at Work. *Organization Studies, 28*(9), 1435–1448. doi:10.1177/0170840607081138

Orlikowski, W. J., & Scott, S. V. (2008). Sociomateriality: Challenging the Separation of Technology, Work and Organization. *The Academy of Management Annals, 2*(1), 433–474. doi:10.1080/19416520802211644

Pablo, A. L. (1994). Determinants of Acquisition Integration Level: A Decision-Making Perspective. *Academy of Management Journal, 37*(4), 803–836.

Pettigrew, A. (1997). What is Processual Analysis? *Scandinavian Journal of Management, 13*(4), 337–348. doi:10.1016/S0956-5221(97)00020-1

Poole, M. S., & Van De Ven, A. H. (2004). *Handbook of Organizational Change and Innovation*. Oxford University Press.

Ranft, A. L., & Lord, M. D. (2002). Acquiring New Technologies and Capabilities: A Grounded Model of Acquisition Implementation. *Organization Science, 13*(4), 420–441. doi:10.1287/orsc.13.4.420.2952

Reus, T. H., Lamont, B. T., & Ellis, K. M. (2016). A darker side of knowledge transfer following international acquisitions. *Strategic Management Journal, 37*(5), 932–944. doi:10.1002mj.2373

Sarrazin, H., & West, A. (2011). Underestanding the Strategic Value of IT in M&A. *The McKinsey Quarterly, 1*, 1–6.

Schweizer, L. (2005). Organizational Integration of Acquired Biotechnology Companies into Pharmaceutical Companies: The Need for a Hybrid Approach. *Academy of Management Journal, 48*(6), 1051–1074. doi:10.5465/amj.2005.19573109

Scott, S. V., & Orlikowski, W. J. (2013). Sociomateriality—Taking the wrong turning? A response to Mutch. *Information and Organization, 23*(2), 77–80. doi:10.1016/j.infoandorg.2013.02.003

Sia, S. K., & Soh, C. (2007). An Assessment of Package-Organisation Misalignment: Institutional and Ontological Structures. *European Journal of Information Systems, 16*(5), 568–583. doi:10.1057/palgrave.ejis.J000700

Tanriverdi, S., & Uysal, V. (2011). Cross-Business Information Technology Integration and Acquirer Value Creation in Corporate Mergers and Acquisitions. *Information Systems Research, 22*(4), 703–720. doi:10.1287/isre.1090.0250

Thatcher, J., Pu, W., & Pienta, D. (2018). IS Information Systems a (Social) Science? *Communications of the Association for Information Systems, 43*(1), 11.

Thompson Reuters. (2017). *Mergers and Acquisitions Review, Full Year 2017*. Retrieved from http://dmi.thomsonreuters.com/Content/Files/MALegalAdvisoryReview.pdf

Vaara, E. (2002). On the Discursive Construction of Success/Failure in Narratives of Post-Merger Integration. *Organization Studies, 23*(2), 211–248. doi:10.1177/0170840602232003

Vaara, E., & Monin, P. (2010). A Recursive Perspective on Discursive Legitimation and Organizational Action in Mergers and Acquisitions. *Organization Science, 21*(1), 3–22. doi:10.1287/orsc.1080.0394

Vieru, D., & Rivard, S. (2014). Organizational Identity Challenges in a Post-Merger Context: A Case Study of an Information System Implementation Project. *International Journal of Information Management, 34*(3), 381–386. doi:10.1016/j.ijinfomgt.2014.02.001

Vieru, D., & Rivard, S. (2015). Knowledge Sharing Challenges during Post-Merger Integration: The Role of Boundary Spanners and of Organizational Identity. *International Journal of Business and Management*, *10*(11), 1–12. doi:10.5539/ijbm.v10n11p1

Wagner, E., Newell, S., & Piccoli, G. (2010). Understanding Project Survival in an ES Environment: A Sociomaterial Practice Perspective. *Journal of the Association for Information Systems*, *11*(5), 276–297. doi:10.17705/1jais.00227

Wagner, E. L., Moll, J., & Newell, S. (2011). Accounting logics, reconfiguration of ERP systems and the emergence of new accounting practices: A sociomaterial perspective. *Management Accounting Research*, *22*(3), 181–197. doi:10.1016/j.mar.2011.03.001

Wijnhoven, F. S., Stegwee, T. R., & Fa, R. T. A. (2006). Post-merger IT Integration Strategies: An IT Alignment Perspective. *The Journal of Strategic Information Systems*, *15*(1), 5–28. doi:10.1016/j.jsis.2005.07.002

Yetton, P., Henningsson, S., & Bjørn-Andersen, N. (2013). Ready to Acquire: The IT Resources Required for a Growth-by-Acquisition Business Strategy. *MIS Quarterly Executive*, *12*(1), 19–35.

Yin, R. K. (2015). *Qualitative research from start to finish*. Guilford Publications.

Yoo, Y., Lyytinen, K., & Heo, D. (2007). Closing the gap: Towards a process model of post-merger knowledge sharing. *Information Systems Journal*, *17*(4), 321–347. doi:10.1111/j.1365-2575.2007.00248.x

Zhu, Y., Li, Y., Wang, W., & Chen, J. (2010). What leads to post-implementation success of ERP? An empirical study of the chinese retail industry. *International Journal of Information Management*, *30*(3), 265–276. doi:10.1016/j.ijinfomgt.2009.09.007

Zollo, M., & Reuer, J. J. (2010). Experience spillovers across corporate development activities. *Organization Science*, *21*(6), 1195–1212. doi:10.1287/orsc.1090.0474

Zollo, M., & Singh, H. (2004). Deliberate learning in corporate acquisitions: Post-acquisition strategies and integration capability in U.S. bank mergers. *Strategic Management Journal*, *25*(13), 1233–1256. doi:10.1002mj.426

KEY TERMS AND DEFINITIONS

Enterprise Systems: Large and complex information systems, which manage large volumes of data and support organizations to integrate and coordinate their business processes.

Performativity: The dynamic relationship between organizational actors and information systems and is reflected in organizational practices. It tries to answer the question: How do things constitute reality through actors' practices?

Post-Merger Integration: The final part of a merger process, following the closing of the merger agreement itself, in which the assets, personnel, and business activities of the merging entities are combined. It constitutes the process of value-creation—actual net benefits (reduced cost per unit, increased income, etc.)—of the planned merger.

Practices: Materially bounded and situated activities engaged in by members of a community that are centrally organized around shared practical understandings.

Process Theory: It explains how a sequence of events that unfolds over time leads to some outcome. Process theory can provide explanations on how one micro-level event leads to, and affects, the ensuing one.

Sociomaterial Assemblage: Entanglements of humans and material (technology). Defined as the continuous mutual constitution of material artifacts, social actors and multiple institutional logics, continuously providing both opportunities and constraints for action.

Sociomateriality: Perspective built upon the intersection of technology, practice and organization that has as main tenet the idea that materiality acts as a constitutive element of the social world and vice versa. While materiality is the property of a technology, sociomateriality denotes the enactment of a specific set of practices that combine materiality with institutions, norms, discourses, cultures, and other phenomena that can be defined as "social."

ENDNOTE

[1]   In line with the literature, we use the term "mergers" to refer to "mergers and acquisitions" (Wijnhoven et al., 2006).

Chapter 2
The Effects of Culture and Data Collection Mode on Socially Desirable Distortion and Confidentiality Concerns in Survey Research

Tom E. Yoon
Western Connecticut State University, USA

Samuel H. Goh
University of Alabama at Birmingham, USA

Robert Zinko
Texas A&M University – Central Texas, USA

Christopher P. Furner
East Carolina University, USA

ABSTRACT

Internet-based surveys have emerged as a popular data collection method for researchers. Despites the popularity of Internet-based surveys, prior studies suggest that responses collected via internet-based surveys are not equivalent to those collected via paper-based survey. Thus, it is important to understand why the nonequivalence is occurred. Also, since internet-based surveys enable us to collect data from people around the globe, it would be important to understand how cultural differences influence participants' responses. In this study, the authors investigate the effects that espoused national culture and data collection mode have on confidentiality concerns and socially desirable reporting. Results indicate that data collection mode and espoused power distance influence confidentiality concerns, while data collection mode and collectivism influence socially desirable distortion.

DOI: 10.4018/978-1-5225-8933-4.ch002

INTRODUCTION

In the context of social science research, a great deal of data is collected from human subjects, by asking them questions (Fisher, 1993; Peterson & Kerin, 1981). Data collection for hypothesis testing is vital to the development and growth of theoretical knowledge (Dubin, 1978). Traditional methods of data collection include paper-based surveys and structured interviews. Since the emergence of Internet-based surveys in 1994 (Kehoe & Pitkow, 1996), the popularity and use of Internet-based surveys has grown considerably (Buchanan & Smith, 1999; Fan and Yan, 2010; Nulty, 2008; Sills & Song, 2002). Compared to traditional methods of data collection, Internet-based surveys have several advanatges, including lower data collection costs, shorter delivery time, more design options, and less time required for data entry (Fan and Yan, 2010; Gosling, Vazire, Srivastava & John, 2004; Fowler, 2002). Because of these advatages, researchers have increasingly adopted Internet-based surveys for data collection (Ernst, Brand, Lhachimi, & Zeeb, 2018).

Researchers often assume that their subjects will respond in the same manner regardless of the mode of data collection (Denscombe, 2006). However, prior studies suggest that responses collected via Internet are not equivalent to those collected via the traditional data collection methods (Henderson, Evans-Lacko, Flach & Thornicroft, 2012; Weigold, Weigold & Ressel, 2013). For example, participants may answer to the questions differently depending on the data collection methods (McDonald and Adam, 2003). Therefore, it is important to understand why such nonequivalence occurs, since the results of any study hinge on the validity of the responses collected. Additionally, one of the advantages of Internet based surveys is that they allow researchers to collect data from people around the globe. The findings of some previous research (i.e., Dolnicar and Grun, 2007) suggest that respondents from different cultural backgrounds demonstrate different response patterns which may lead to a response bias. This bias, in turn, may lead researchers to draw incorrect conclusions (Paulhus, 1991). It is important to understand how cultural differences may influence participants' responses.

The purpose of this study is to examine the influences of data collection modes (online versus paper surveys) and national culture on socially desirable distortion and confidentiality concerns in data collection, based on a cross-cultural sample of participants from the United States and China.

BACKGROUND

Before developing the hypotheses that will address our research question, we first review relevant literature on data collection modes, espoused national culture, confidentiality concerns and socially desirable reporting.

Data Collection Mode

Traditionally, self-administered paper-based surveys have been the mode of choice among social science researchers (Suchman & Jordan, 1990). As implied by the name, subjects are given a pen, and asked to respond to questions written on a piece of paper. A researcher must collect these answers, and if he/she intends to analyze the data from these surveys statistically, enter the responses into a computer.

Paper-based surveys have several advantages over other traditional data collection modes. For example, they are cheaper, less time consuming and more standardized across subjects than face-to-face interviews. However, paper-based surveys also suffer several disadvantages. While paper based surveys can ask open ended questions, probing questions are more difficult to ask, as incomplete responses are difficult to interpret without further elaboration. Also, if the subject is unable to understand a question, it is more difficult for them to seek clarification than face-to-face interviews. Finally, loafing can be a concern with paper-based surveys as it is easier for subjects to skip questions or provide responses without reading the questions when no human proctor is present.

Today, researchers are increasingly using the Internet as a way to collect data, particularly for survey-based research (Weigold et al.,2013; Buchanan, 2007). Generally, Internet-based survey presents questions to a subject using a web browser. Subjects are mostly limited to radio buttons, check boxes and text boxes to provide their answers. Internet-based surveys have several advantages over paper-based surveys. Internet-based surveys can draw larger, more diverse samples and access difficult-to-reach populations. (Cantrell & Lupinacci, 2007). Internet-based surveys can also lower data collection costs and eliminate the need for data entry (Gosling et al., 2004). Furthermore, Internet-based survey software can handle complex branching patterns, like automatically skipping ahead to a different question based upon a past responses as well as randomly assigning participants to experimental groups (e.g. Furner & Zinko, 2017). Also, if programmed correctly, the survey can encourage users to address data inconsistencies at the point of data entry (Fowler, 2002).

Despite of these advantages, a number of studies have found that responses collected via Internet-based surveys were not equivalent to those collected via paper-based surveys. For example, McDonald and Adam (2003) compared online and postal survey methods using the same marketing survey instruments on two groups. They found that respondents answered questions differently online that they did via postal survey. In addition, Fouladi, Mccarthy, and Moller (2002) demonstrated mean score differences between Internet and paper-based surveys in questions related to attachment to father and to mother, perceived ability to reduce negative mood, awareness of mood and mood regulation strategies. Furthermore, based on a large sample (N=763), Buchanan et al. (2005) found that responses provided online psychological tests were not equivalent to those collected using paper and pencil psychological tests.

In addition, some studies compared Internet-based surveys to other traditional data collection modes such as face-to-face interviews. For example, Pew research center (2015) compared responses between online surveys and phone surveys, and found differences in responses by those survey modes. Additionally, Duffy, Smith, Terhanian, and Bremer (2005) compared data collected via online panel surveys to data collected via face-to-face interviews, and found differences between the data, which were attributed to social desirability distortion and the interviewer effect. Furthermore, Henderson et al. (2012) found responses obtained via online surveys were differ significantly from those collected via face-to-face interviews when they administered questionnaires about intended behaviour toward people with mental health problems.

Taken together, these comparative studies suggest that even when subjects are given the same questions via different data collection modes, differences emerge, particularly when the topic of the questionnaire is sensitive in nature. Two promising theories that may help understand why subjects may not respond to questions honestly include confidentiality theory and social desirability theory.

Confidentiality Concerns

Confidentiality is the perception that the information about a subject that is collected by a researcher will not be shared with another party (Easter, Davis & Henderson, 2004). Studies using confidentiality theory suggest a variety of impacts on several data collection outcomes, including participation (Cho & LaRose, 1999; Singer, Mathiowetz, & Couper, 1993), validity (Fitzgerald & Hamilton, 1997; Kerin, Cron, & Peterson, 1977; Olson, Stander, & Merrill, 2004) and even intentional misreporting of data with the objective of frustrating the researcher (Cho & LaRose, 1999).

For example, individuals exhibited apprehension about potential secondary uses of personal information that they might have provided (Culnan, 1993). Secondary use of information refers to any use of information provided by an individual to an organization for purposes other than for the purposes identified in the initial transaction (M. Keith, Babb, Furner, & Abdullat, 2015; M. J. Keith, Babb, Furner, Abdullat, & Lowry, 2016). Cho and LaRose (1999) suggest that subjects will sometimes intentionally misreport data in retaliation for a perceived failure to protect their information, or in retaliation for a perceived invasion of privacy, if the researcher solicited participation by email or on a discussion board. Miltgen (2009) suggests that if there is no guarantee that data will remain confidential, subjects are unwilling to provide data or likely to restrict the amount of data disclosed.

Woods and McNamara (1980) proposed that subjects are more open in a confidential setting because it reduces anxiety related to potential negative outcomes of the information becoming known to others that have power over the subject. Specifically, Akers, Massey, Clark, and Lauer (1983) point out that subjects will under-report behaviors if they believe that knowledge of these behaviors by an authority will lead to disciplinary action.

Other threats to survey reliability do exist. Kerin et al. (1977) conducted an experiment in which 276 married women were given a credit card application, and assigned to one of four conditions (the factors were level of advanced notice, which was manipulated by either giving them a telephone call or sending a form letter) and the level of customization in the cover letter. They were surprised to find that even though anonymity was guaranteed in the cover letter, the subjects still misreported on several questions in the personalized conditions. The authors believe that the subjects misreported because the highly personalized cover letters indicated that the researchers already had some data on the subjects, and that they were not afraid to use this data, and presumably any further data that the subject may provide, beyond the scope of the original transaction.

In a more extreme case, Olson et al. (2004) found that only 5% of individuals who took the non-confidential Sailor's Health Inventory reported being abused as children, while 63% of individuals who took the Survey of Recruits' Behaviors and were guaranteed confidentiality reported such abuse.

Individuals tend to exhibit greater apprehension following their discovery of new threats associated with new technologies, either for better surveillance or for better transmission of personal information (M. J. Keith et al., 2016; Mason, 1986; A. Miller, 1971; Westin, 1976). Because individuals tend to perceive threats to confidentiality when faced with a new technology, subjects that have typically taken surveys on paper may experience more confidentiality concerns when switching to an internet-based format, because of their uncertainties about the capabilities of the technology and the intentions of the researcher (Andrews, Nonnecke, & Preece, 2003; Cho & LaRose, 1999). As researchers are increasing using Internet survey tools to collect data, they need to be sensitive to the confidentiality and security issues associated with the use of Internet survey tools, as participants may be unwilling to provide candid responses to a survey if their anonymity is not assured (Mitgen, 2009; Truell, 2003)

Social Desirability Distortion

Social desirability (SD) is a well-established theory, having been studied by behavioral researchers for more than 50 years (McCrae & Costa Jr, 1983). Social desirability distortion is the tendency for subjects to distort their responses to questions in order to appear to conform to the norms of some social group (Lavraka, 2008). These distortions represent a threat to the internal validity of studies, because distortions can lead to spurious correlations between variables, as well as suppression, confounding and exaggeration of relationships between constructs (Dlugosch, Klinger, Frese, & Klehe, 2018). Indeed, SD is a problem that is thought to impact all forms of self-reported data collection (Fisher, 1993; McKibben, 2017; Cerri, Thogerson & Testa, 2019) and a number of researchers cite SD as the most pervasive source of validity concerns in self-reported social science research (Krumpal, 2013; Lavraka, 2008; (Nederhof, 1985; Paulhus, 1991; Peltier & Walsh, 1990).

The theory has its roots in Medicine. Meehl and Hathaway (1946) noted that individuals taking medical surveys sometimes "fake-good" or "fake-bad," and argued that statistical corrections for this faking are necessary for medical research to be effective. Within psychology, a paradigm evolved that was aimed at understanding why individuals engage in such "faking," (Crowne & Marlowe, 1960), arguing that SD distortion affects nearly all self-reported data, and needs to be accounted for by statistical adjustments to prevent researchers from arriving at spurious conclusions.

Crowne and Marlowe (1964) postulated that individuals engage in SD distortion to satisfy their needs for social approval, social conformity and for self-protection. In addition, several researchers cite embarrassment as a stressor that people try to avoid by engaging in SD distortion (Fisher, 1993; Modigliani, 1968) as well as reputation management (Robert Zinko, Furner, Hunt, & Dalton, 2017). Researchers generally agree that needs for social approval and social conformity are triggered by social cues (e.g., Martin & Nago, 1989; Sudman & Bradburn, 1974; Robert Zinko, Tuchtan, et al., 2017), which can be as obvious as facial expressions during an interview or as subtle as the quality of the ink used in a paper-based survey (Nederhof, 1985). Martin and Nago (1989) further suggest that individuals will be particularly apt to engage in socially desirable distortion as a form of self-protection when being questioned about their ability to perform a job during an interview due to the financial implications for the interviewee of not appearing to conform.Several studies suggest that data collection modes can influence the effects of social desirability (Krumpal, 2011). For example, Henderson et al. (2012) suggests the online data collection can reduce the effect of social desirability because it can be designed to provide a greater level of anonymity than other traditional data collection methods such as in-person or telephone interviews. Also, Booth-Kewley, Larson & Miyoshi (2007) compared social desirability effects on computerized and paper-and-pencil questionnaires, and found that computer administration of surveys reduce the effects of social desirability.

Confidentiality concerns (Sills & Song, 2002) and social desirability (Joinson, 1999) play an important role in how individuals respond to surveys. We argue that confidentiality concerns are particularly strong in the case of Internet surveys, as subjects are unable to verify how their responses are connected to information that the researchers may have related to the subject, and because of recent news stories regarding information theft and misuse (Bergstein, 2006). On the other hand, it is plausible that social desirability related problems will be reduced in Internet-based surveys, because the immediacy of the embarrassment associated with making a truthful response that does not conform to socially accepted norms will be reduced.

Espoused National Culture

For some time researchers have been aware that individuals in various civilizations share common values, beliefs, norms, and customs. Researchers have labeled the socially-constructed force that embodies these factors as culture (Chang, Furner, & Zinko, 2010; Furner & George, 2012). There are several ways to conceptualize culture. Patterns of values, beliefs, norms and customs can be identified within several subgroups of people, which can be delineated by geological boundaries (Srite & Karahanna, 2006), organizational boundaries (Hofstede, Neuijen, Ohayv, & Sanders, 1990; Wilkins & Ouchi, 1983), household boundaries (Bechtel, Shepherd, & Rogers, 1995), and temporal boundaries (Oliver, 1971). There is some debate regarding which conceptualization of culture is more relevant to organizational researchers (Erez & Early, 1993), or if any study of culture is useful at all (Hickson, Hinings, McMillan, & Schwitter, 1974; G. A. Miller, 1987). What is not debatable is that due to globalization, sampling pools for data collection include more individuals from different national backgrounds (Grimm & Smith, 1997; Sivakumar & Nakata, 2001).

Numerous topologies for classifying national culture exist, the most frequently cited being the four dimensions written by Hofstede (2001). These four dimensions are Collectivism, Power Distance, Uncertainty Avoidance, and Masculinity (Thacher, Srite, Stepina, & Liu, 2003). This topology has been sharply criticized for generalizing individuals based on their nation of residence; indeed the outcome of Hofstede's original study was a table of countries and their scores on the four cultural dimensions. Nicholson and Stepina (1998) point out that these generalizations themselves may not be useful, as Hofstede's data was collected in the 1960s and 1970s, and that time is likely to have caused these values to change. Furthermore, Furner & George (2012) suggest that Hofstede's dimensions were never intended to be applied at the individual level to predict individual behavior.

As a result, researchers have developed scales that rely less on "stereotyping" by actually measuring an individual's perceptions along established cultural dimensions rather than assuming pre-held beliefs based upon national origin (Furner, Racherla, & Zhu, 2014). For example, four of the original Hofstede dimensions have been adopted by Srite and Karahanna (2006) –constituting espoused national culture. Espoused National Culture consists of four constructs: Espoused collectivism, or the extent to which an individual values relationships with their in-group, espoused power distance, or the extent to which and individual perceives a power differences between themselves and their superiors and subordinates, espoused uncertainty avoidance, or the extent to which the individuals fears risk and espoused masculinity, or the extent to which the individual views the world as competitive rather than nurturing. Espoused national culture has been effectively used in a number of studies to predict individual behavior (Furner & George, 2009, 2012; Racherla & Furner, 2009; Lu, Yu, Liu, & Wei, 2017; Hallikainen & Laukkanen, 2018).

RESEARCH MODEL

Based upon our literature review and confidentiality and social desirability theories, we posit the following hypotheses.

When an individual takes a survey on paper, there are cues that participants can watch to determine the confidentiality of their responses. For example, they can see their survey mixes anonymously into a pile of other surveys when turned in. Also, the paper media does not retain any personably identifiable information, if left unmarked other than the responses. Conversely when a person takes a survey online, there is a higher degree of uncertainty because the capabilities of the browser allow the coupling of survey responses with personably identifiable information. Also, there may be questions with regards to the security of the data if a 3rd party web host is used for administering the survey as well as the possibility of communications over the Internet being intercepted. This is expected to increase confidentiality concerns among subjects.

H1: Individuals taking Internet-based surveys will report more confidentiality concerns than individuals taking paper-based surveys

Individuals in face to face situations are more likely to perceive a pressure to adhere to norms in a face to face communication event than in a computer mediated one (Stanton, 1998). It is the pressure to adhere to these norms that creates pressure for the individual to present him/herself in socially acceptable light. In online environments, there is less pressure to adhere to norms because it is much harder to establish norms in an online environment (Richman, Kiesler, Weisband, & Drasgow, 1999). Because the social norms are not outlined, and because the subject is expected to experience less pressure to conform:

H2: Individuals taking Internet-based surveys will report less socially desirable distortion than individuals taking paper-based surveys

Individuals who score high on uncertainty avoidance are less comfortable acting in the absence of complete information (Racherla & Furner, 2009). Without knowing for sure what the effect of their actions will be, they experience stress when faced with decision. This stress is expected to be stronger when there is a risk that the individual can be identified, because unknown consequences are potentially greater the closer they hit to home. This higher degree of stress is expected to cause individuals who are high in uncertainty avoidance to experience stronger confidentiality concerns.

H3: Individuals with higher levels of espoused uncertainty avoidance will report higher confidentiality concerns

Individuals who score high on power distance typically perceive their superiors as having a great deal of control over them, and experience substantial stress when they interact with their boss (Furner & George, 2012). These individuals are likely to try to control the impression that they present to the boss. If these individuals are asked to answer questions about their work, they are likely to be mindful of what the boss would think of their answer, and be even more mindful of whether their responses are identifiable. As such:

H4: Individuals with higher levels of espoused power distance will report higher confidentiality concerns

Individuals who value collectivism prize group membership, and as such strive to adhere to and preserve group norms. Collectivists often sacrifice their own personal interests to adhere to group norms (Triandis, 1995). It is this reverence for group norms that will create pressure for collectivists to present themselves in the most positive light possible, by engaging in socially desirable distortion.

H5: Individuals with higher levels of espoused collectivism will report higher levels of social desirability distortion

As noted in above, individuals who score high on power distance typically perceive their superiors as having a great deal of control over them, and experience substantial stress when they interact with their boss (Furner & George, 2012). These individuals perceive substantial pressure to satisfy their superiors, and endeavor to avoid negative attention by not deviating from established norms. This pressure is likely to cause these individuals to engage in impression management behaviors such as socially desirable distortion.

H6: Individuals with higher levels of espoused power distance will report higher levels of social desirability distortion

When an individual is high in masculinity, s/he values a sense of achievement and superiority over her/his peers (Srite & Karahanna, 2006). These individuals seek to differentiate themselves by standing out and building a reputation. The easiest way to build a reputation is by deviating from established norms (R.; Zinko, Furner, Royal, & Hall, 2010). These deviations can be positive or negative, but to the individual who is high in masculinity, positive deviations are more likely to result in a positive reputation which can foster a sense of positive differentiation. As such, we expect individuals who are high in masculinity to engage in substantial impression management activities with the aim of impressing others.

H7: Individuals with higher levels of espoused masculinity will report higher levels of social desirability distortion

Our research model is presented in Figure 1.

Figure 1. Research model

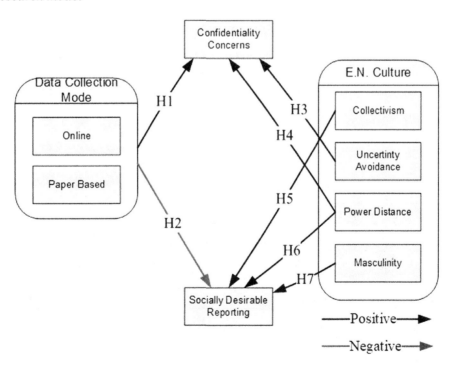

METHODOLOGY

Our research question seeks to explain the impact that data collection mode and espoused national culture have on confidentiality concerns and socially desirable distortion. A cross-sectional survey-based experiment was employed to measure the constructs of interest. This approach is consistent with a number of previous social desirability studies (Li & Reb, 2009).

Our population of interest is individuals who might become subjects in survey research and who vary in terms of espoused national culture. Since China and the United States tend to vary along the four espoused cultural dimensions, our sampling pool consists of upper level undergraduate students from the People's Republic of China and the United States. Along with using the espoused national culture measure, sampling from different countries allowed us to collect data in which there would be useful variation along cultural dimensions. Individuals from each country were randomly assigned to take an Internet-based or a paper-based survey.

Following (Furner, 2013) the instrument was developed in English and translated into Chinese by a bilingual doctoral student. The translated instrument was translated back into English by a different bilingual student. Discrepancies were resolved, and the new Chinese instrument was translated back into English by a third bilingual doctoral student. No discrepancies were identified following this translation. Table 1 indicates the number of participants assigned to each treatment.

Items were taken from existing validated scales. The 33 items used to assess socially desirable reporting were taken from Crowne and Marlowe (1960), which included reverse coded questions. The four dimensions of espoused national culture were measured using the 23 item scale by Srite and Karahanna (2006). Other items such as demographics were developed by the researchers.

RESULTS

A total of 340 subjects completed the experiment and a breakdown of the number per treatment is presented in Table 2. Before computing values for our independent variables, a reliability analysis (using SPSS 15) was conducted on the items provided in the survey. Cronbach α for each of our independent variables were strong with one exception: uncertainty avoidance had a Cronbach α of 0.684. Uncertainty

Table 1. Number of participants assigned to each treatment

	United States	P.R. China	Total
Paper	101	86	187
Online	101	86	187

Table 2. Number of subjects who completed each treatment

	United States	P.R. China	Total per Treatment
Paper	81 (39 female)	83 (48 female)	164
Online	92 (41 female)	82 (50 female)	176

Table 3. Reliabilities for independent variables

Factor	Cronbach α	Number of Items
Social Desirability	.878	33
Confidentiality Concerns	.892	4
E. Power Distance	.840	6
E. Collectivism	.906	6
E. Uncertainty Avoidance	.682	6
Masculinity	.911	5

avoidance was not analyzed as a result of the low reliability. Table 3 presents the reliabilities for each variable.

Based on the reliability analysis, we calculated our independent variables by averaging the responses to thirty-three items for Socially Desirable Distortion, four items for confidentiality concerns, six items for espoused collectivism, six items for espoused power distance and five items for espoused masculinity. However, espoused uncertainty avoidance was dropped from analysis because the Cronbach α for the variable did not exceed 0.7. We tested for common method variance using Harman's single factor method. As the variance explained using this method is 17.55%, well below the 50% threshold, this indicates that common method variance is not a cause for concern.

The Pearson's correlation matrix was examined to identify potential problems associated with multicollinearity between the independent variables. Correlations are presented in Table 4. None of the correlations exceed 0.8, indicating that multicollinearity between the independent variables is not a cause for concern (Hair, Anderson, Tatham, & Black, 1998).

To test our hypotheses, we will employ two multiple regression models: one treats confidentiality concerns as the dependent variable (Adjusted $R^2 = 0.314$), the other treats socially desirable reporting as the dependent variable (Adjusted $R^2 = 0.297$). The regression results for the model with confidentiality concerns as the dependent variable is presented in Table 5, the regression results for the model with socially desirable reporting is presented in Table 6.

Hypothesis 1 predicts that individuals who take the online survey will report more confidentiality concerns than those who take the paper-based survey. Hypothesis 1 was supported ($\beta = 1.05$, $p < 0.001$). Hypothesis 2 predicts that individuals who take the online survey will report less socially desirable

Table 4. Correlations among independent variables

	Mean	SD	1	2	3	4	5
1. Social Desirability	3.18	0.87	1				
2. Confidentiality Concerns	2.51	0.72	0.311*	1			
3. Power Distance	3.03	0.85	0.398*	0.353*	1		
4. Collectivism	3.71	0.69	0.412*	0.325*	0.260	1	
5. Masculinity	2.81	0.70	0.255	0.188	0.211	0.011	1

* p<.05

Table 5. Regression results for model with confidentiality concerns as dv

Variable	Min	Max	Mean	SD	β	p-Value
Data Collection Mode	0 (paper)	1 (online)	0.518	0.5	1.05	<0.001
E. Collectivism	1.167	6.833	3.71	0.69	0.188	0.051
E. Power Distance	1.167	7	3.03	0.85	1.01	<0.001
E. Masculinity	1.2	6.4	2.81	0.70	-0.179	0.209
Age	19	29	22.4	0.88	0.111	0.338
Gender	0 (female)	1 (male)	0.476	0.5	-0.087	0.458

Table 6. Regression results for model with socially desirable reporting as dv

Variable	Min	Max	Mean	SD	β	p-Value
Data Collection Mode	0 (paper)	1 (online)	0.518	0.5	-0.748	<0.001
E. Collectivism	1.167	6.833	3.71	0.69	0.175	0.048
E. Power Distance	1.167	7	3.03	0.85	0.099	0.056
E. Masculinity	1.2	6.4	2.81	0.70	-0.072	0.211
Age	19	29	22.4	0.88	-0.091	0.385
Gender	0 (female)	1 (male)	0.476	0.5	0.077	0.510

reporting than those who take the paper-based survey. Hypothesis 2 was supported (β = -0.748, p < 0.001). Hypothesis 3 predicted that individuals who score high on espoused uncertainty avoidance would experience stronger confidentiality concerns. Since the reliability for Espoused Uncertainty Avoidance did not meet the 0.7 threshold, hypothesis 3 cannot be analyzed. Hypothesis 4 predicted that individuals who score high on espoused power distance would experience stronger confidentiality concerns. This hypothesis was supported (β =1.01, p < 0.001).

Hypothesis 5 indicated that individuals who score highly on espoused collectivism will exhibit more socially desirable distortion. This hypothesis was supported (β = 0.175, p = 0.048). Hypothesis 6 indicated that individuals who score highly on espoused power distance will engage in more socially desirable distortion. This hypothesis is not supported (β = 0.099, p = 0.056). Hypothesis 7 indicated that individuals who score highly on espoused masculinity will engage in more socially desirable distortion. This hypothesis is not supported (β = -0.072, p = 0.211). An evaluated model is illustrated in Figure 2

DISCUSSION

The objective of this study was to understand the influence of data collection mode and espoused national cultures on social desirable reporting and confidential concerns in data collection. Based on a survey conducted in two countries: US and China. We found that both data collection mode and espoused national culture influence socially desirable reporting and confidential concerns. This section discusses the implication of our findings.

Figure 2. Evaluated model
(p < 0.05 *, p < 0.01, **, p < 0.001 ***)

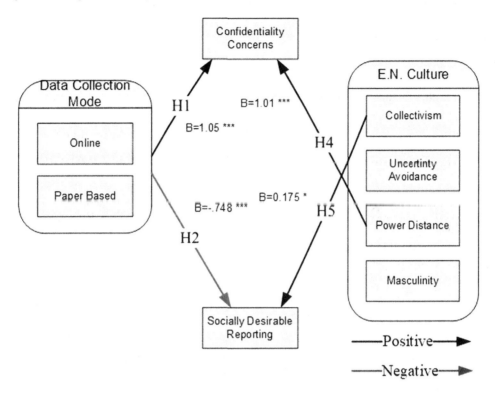

The findings of the current study offer several insights for researchers. Socially desirable distortion is a well-studied phenomena that represents a challenge to researchers in business and other social sciences (Li & Reb, 2009). With the trend toward more online research (Sills & Song, 2002) and the trend toward more cross cultural research (Furner, Mason, Mehta, Munyon, & Zinko, 2009), understanding the phenomena of socially desirable distortion becomes even more imperative. We found that online data collection results in less socially desirable distortion than paper-based data collection. This finding suggests that online data collection may be preferable in certain situation. If researchers have to ask questions that touch on potentially sensitive topics or involve behaviors that are socially desirable, they may need to consider using online data collection because respondents tend to give more honest answers online, especially when such questions are asked (Pew research center, 2015; Henderson et al., 2012).

On the other hand, we also found that confidentiality concerns were higher for subjects who took the online survey than those who took the paper-based surveys. This implication is important for researchers who collect data using online surveys. Researchers must make clear to participants that data will remain confidential. If participants perceive that there is no guarantee that data will be remain confidential, they may not participate online surveys or restrict the amount of data provided (Miltgen, 2009). Assuring confidentiality is more vital if an online survey contains sensitive or potentially embarrassing questions because participants may not provide honest responses (Dwight& Feigelson, 2000). Therefore, it is so important that researchers make abundantly clear at the beginning of online surveys that data will be remain strictly confidential and anonymous (Sue and Ritter, 2011)). For example, researchers can include additional warnings at the beginning of the online survey that notify subjects that personally identifiable data provided (e.g. IP address, browser info, cookies) will not be recorded. Alleviating these confidentiality concerns may lead to more reliable and accurate responses.

Taken together, our findings suggest that there is a tradeoff in the choice of medium and the potential biases that come along with that choice.

For the cultural dimensions, we found that power distance and collectivism had respective impacts on confidentiality concerns and social desirability reporting. As power distance increased, subjects felt that there was a higher chance that the responses they provided might be used against them. Thus, they may not provide honest answers to the survey questions (Dwight & Feigelson, 2000). Also, in highly collective culture, subjects felt the need to provide answers that they thought would better reflect group expectations than their own honest opinion. This confirms the findings of previous studies (i.e., Bernardi, 2006). These findings suggest that in addition to the data collection modes, cultural differences may affect how individuals respond to survey questions.

Taken together, researchers should be aware of these implications and carefully consider survey design to help reduce these problems. Possible remedies include an emphasis on anonymity, encouraging honesty, and clearly outlining how the data will be used. Also, researchers need to consider including a direct measure of social desirability bias in the research design.

FUTURE RESEARCH DIRECTIONS

While the findings of this study are informative, the study has noteworthy limitations. Due to the desire to create a parsimonious survey instrument, it was necessary to limit the dimensions of espoused national culture that we included in our models. The four dimensions that we identified have been used extensively in IS and social science research and have been shown to effectively influence individual level behavior (Furner & George, 2012; Srite & Karahanna, 2006). However, scholars have identified a number of cultural factors that influence human behavior, such as contextual orientation, time orientation, universalism and recently, the GLOBE Project identified nine cultural dimensions that influenced leadership behavior (House, Javidan, Hanges, & Dorfman, 2002). Certainly, these are worth of future study.

Also, our study employed student subjects. While a number of business social science studies have been conducted using students as subjects, this approach is generally considered to limit the generalizability of those findings (Furner & Goh, 2013). Future studies could be conducted using working adults to see if the relationships that we identified hold.

Our finding that subjects in the online treatment experienced stronger confidentiality concerns, but still engaged in less socially desirable reporting raises questions that should be explored in future research. The connection between confidentiality concerns and socially desirable reporting is well established, and supported by data from this study in a post-hoc analysis. What has not been as extensively explored is the "why". What is it about the online context which causes this relationship to change, or are our results simply a 'fluke?' Further investigation into this relationship in the online research context is warranted.

Changes in technology affect even Internet-based surveys. When a survey instrument is available online, we generally assume that it will be taken using either a desktop or a notebook computer. However, recent changes in infrastructure have led to the emergence of a new, more mobile form of computing facilitated by mobile devices. Future researchers should investigate the extent to which subjects using mobile devices to take surveys differ from those using desktop or laptop computers. The ability of the device to facilitate extended periods of focus, the level of effort necessary to navigate the interface and the amount of personal information contained on the mobile devices may influence the effectiveness of the survey.

Finally, while confidentiality concerns, socially desirable distortion and espoused national culture are well studied individual level factors that influence subjects' responses to surveys, a number of other factors may differ in the online environment (Kasemsap, 2016). For instance: fatigue and boredom stemming from the characteristics and constraints of the interface, the freedom to take the survey at any time and the presence of distractions may influence survey results online. Future studies should consider these factors as well as others as online data collection becomes more and more prevalent.

CONCLUSION

The trends toward online and cross-cultural data collection in business and other social science research go hand in hand, and are driven by the convergence between globalization and the adoption of web-based computing across the world. As interest in questions about cultural determinants of business behaviors began to grow, so too did the ability to survey individual across substantial geographic boundaries quickly and inexpensively. Understanding the influence of online data collection mode and cultural differences is of vital importance to researchers, and this study is a first step toward such an understanding.

DISCUSSION QUESTIONS

1. What is Socially Desirable Distortion?
2. Why do you think research subjects would distort their answers to anonymous survey questions?
3. Have you ever taken a research survey? If so, have you ever engaged in Socially Desirable Distortion? If so, Why?
4. What can researchers do to overcome the problem of Socially Desirable Distortion?
5. What does the fact that some subjects engaged in Socially Desirable Distortion mean for research findings? Are all behavioral research findings invalid?
6. What influence do Confidentiality Concerns have on how honestly you answer research questions?
7. What kind of research questions would led you to experience concerns about the confidentiality of your answers?

REFERENCES

Akers, R. L., Massey, J., Clark, W., & Lauer, R. M. (1983). Are self-reports of adolescent deviance valid? Biochemical measures, randomized response, and the bogus pipeline in smoking behavior. *Social Forces*, *62*(1), 234–251. doi:10.1093f/62.1.234

Andrews, D., Nonnecke, B., & Preece, J. (2003). Electronic survey methodology: A case study in reaching hard-to-involve Internet users. *International Journal of Human-Computer Interaction*, *16*(2), 185–210. doi:10.1207/S15327590IJHC1602_04

Bechtel, G. A., Shepherd, M. A., & Rogers, P. W. (1995). Family, culture, and health practices amond migrant farmworkers. *Journal of Community Health Nursing*, *12*(1), 15–22. doi:10.120715327655jchn1201_2 PMID:7897467

Bergstein. (2006, July 8). Questions linger over secrets on laptops. *Associated Press*.

Bernardi, R. (2006). Associations between Hofstede's cultural constructs and social desirability response bias. *Journal of Business Ethics*, *65*(1), 43–53. doi:10.100710551-005-5353-0

Booth-Kewley, S., Larson, G. E., & Miyoshi, D. K. (2007). Social desirability effects on computerized and paper-and-pencil questionnaires. *Computers in Human Behavior*, *23*(4), 463–477. doi:10.1016/j.chb.2004.10.020

Buchanan, T. (2007). Personality testing on the Internet: What we know, and what we do not. In A. Joinson, K. McKenna, T. Postmes, & U.-D. Reips (Eds.), *Oxford handbook of Internet psychology* (pp. 447–459). Oxford, UK: Oxford University Press.

Buchanan, T., Ali, T., Heffernan, T. M., Ling, J., Parrott, A. C., Rodgers, J., & Scholey, A. B. (2005). Nonequivalence of on-line and paper-and-pencil psychological tests: The case of the prospective memory questionnaire. *Behavior Research Methods*, *37*(1), 148–154. doi:10.3758/BF03206409 PMID:16097355

Buchanan, T., & Smith, J. L. (1999). Using the Internet for psychological research: Personality testing on the World-Wide Web. *British Journal of Psychology*, *90*(1), 125–144. doi:10.1348/000712699161189 PMID:10085550

Cantrell, M. A., & Lupinacci, P. (2007). Methodological issues in online data collection. *Journal of Advanced Nursing*, *60*(5), 544–549. doi:10.1111/j.1365-2648.2007.04448.x PMID:17973718

Cerri, J., Thogerson, J., & Testa, F. (2019). Social desirability and sustainable food research: A systematic literature review. *Food Quality and Preference*, *71*(1), 136–140. doi:10.1016/j.foodqual.2018.06.013

Chang, L., Furner, C. P., & Zinko, R. (2010). A study of negotiations within the ethnic Chinese community between Taiwan and Hong Kong. *Management Research and Practice*, *5*(1), 1–9.

Cho, H., & LaRose, R. (1999). Privacy issues in Internet surveys. *Social Science Computer Review*, *17*(4), 421–434. doi:10.1177/089443939901700402

Crowne, D. P., & Marlowe, D. (1960). A new scale of social desirability independent of psychopathology. *Journal of Consulting Psychology*, *24*(4), 349–354. doi:10.1037/h0047358 PMID:13813058

Crowne, D. P., & Marlowe, D. (1964). *The approval motive*. New York: Wiley.

Culnan, M. J. (1993). "How did they get my name?": An exploratory investigation of consumer attitudes toward secondary information use. *Management Information Systems Quarterly*, *17*(3), 341–363. doi:10.2307/249775

Denscombe, M. (2006). Web-based questionnaires and the mode effect: An evaluation based on completion rates and data contents of near-identical questionnaires delivered in different modes. *Social Science Computer Review*, *24*(2), 246–254. doi:10.1177/0894439305284522

Dlugosch, T. J., Klinger, B., Frese, M., & Klehe, U. C. (2018). Personality-based selection of entrepreneurial borrowers to reduce credit risk: Two studies on prediction models in low-and high-stakes settings in developing countries. *Journal of Organizational Behavior, 39*(5), 612–628. doi:10.1002/job.2236

Dolnicar, S., & Grün, B. (2007). Cross-cultural differences in survey response patterns. *International Marketing Review, 24*(2), 127–143. doi:10.1108/02651330710741785

Dubin, R. (1978). *Theory Building* (Revised ed.). New York: The Free Press.

Duffy, B., Smith, K., Terhanian, G., & Bremer, J. (2005). Comparing data from online and face-to-face surveys. *International Journal of Market Research, 47*(6), 615–639. doi:10.1177/147078530504700602

Dwight, S. A., & Feigelson, M. E. (2000). A quantitative review of the effect of computerized testing on the measurement of social desirability. *Educational and Psychological Measurement, 60*(3), 340–360. doi:10.1177/00131640021970583

Easter, M. M., Davis, A. M., & Henderson, G. E. (2004). Confidentiality: More than a linkage file and a locked drawer. *IRB, 26*(2), 13–1. doi:10.2307/3564233 PMID:15069972

Erez, M., & Early, P. (1993). *Culture, self-identify, and work.* Oxford, UK: Oxford University Press. doi:10.1093/acprof:oso/9780195075809.001.0001

Ernst, S. A., Brand, T., Lhachimi, S. K., & Zeeb, H. (2018). Combining Internet-Based and Postal Survey Methods in a Survey among Gynecologists: Results of a Randomized Trial. *Health Services Research, 53*(2), 879–895. doi:10.1111/1475-6773.12664 PMID:28217941

Fan, W., & Yan, Z. (2010). Factrors affecting response rates of the web surveys: A systematic review. *Computers in Human Behavior, 26*(2), 132–138. doi:10.1016/j.chb.2009.10.015

Fisher, R. J. (1993). Social desirability bias and the validity of indirect questioning. *The Journal of Consumer Research, 20*(2), 303–315. doi:10.1086/209351

Fitzgerald, J. L., & Hamilton, M. (1997). Confidentiality, disseminated regulation and ethico-legal liabilities in research with hidden populations of illicit drug users. *Addiction (Abingdon, England), 92*(9), 1099–1107. doi:10.1111/j.1360-0443.1997.tb03667.x PMID:9374006

Fouladi, R. T., Mccarthy, C. J., & Moller, N. P. (2002). Paper-and-pencil or online? Evaluating mode effects on measures of emotional functioning and attachment. *Assessment, 9*(2), 204–215. doi:10.1177/1079110200900201 PMID:12066835

Fowler, F. J. (2002). Survey research methods (3rd ed.). Thousand Oaks, CA: Sage.

Furner, C. P. (2013). Cultural determinants of information processing shortcuts in computer supported groups: A review, research agenda and instrument validation. *International Journal of Information Systems and Social Change, 4*(3), 17–32. doi:10.4018/jissc.2013070102

Furner, C. P., & George, J. F. (2009). Making it hard to lie: Cultural determinants of media choice for deception. *Proceedings of the 42nd Hawaii International Conference on System Sciences.*

Furner, C. P., & George, J. F. (2012). Cultural determinants of media choice for deception. *Computers in Human Behavior, 28*(4), 1427–1438. doi:10.1016/j.chb.2012.03.005

Furner, C. P., & Goh, S. H. (2013). Cultural Determinants of Socially Desirable Distortion in Computer Based Data Collection: A Multicultural Investigation. *International Journal of Social and Organizational Dynamics in IT, 3*(3), 51–67. doi:10.4018/ijsodit.2013070104

Furner, C. P., Mason, R. M., Mehta, N., Munyon, T. P., & Zinko, R. A. (2009). Cultural determinants of learning effectivness from knowledge management systems: A multinational investigation. *Journal of Global Information Technology Management, 12*(1), 30–51. doi:10.1080/1097198X.2009.10856484

Furner, C. P., Racherla, P., & Zhu, Z. (2014). A multinational study of espoused national cultural and review characteristics in the formation of trust in online product reviews. *International Journal of Services Technology and Management, 20*(1-3), 14-30.

Furner, C. P., & Zinko, R. A. (2017). The influence of information overload on the development of trust and purchase intention based on online product reviews in a mobile vs. web environment: An empirical investigation. *Electronic Markets, 27*(3), 211–224. doi:10.100712525-016-0233-2

Gosling, S. D., Vazire, S., Srivastava, S., & John, O. P. (2004). Should we trust Web-based studies? A comparative analysis of six preconceptions about Internet questionnaires. *The American Psychologist, 59*(2), 93–104. doi:10.1037/0003-066X.59.2.93 PMID:14992636

Grimm, C., & Smith, K. (1997). *Strategy as action: Industry rivalry and coordination.* Cincinnati, OH: South-Western College Publishing.

Hair, J. F., Anderson, R. E., Tatham, R. L., & Black, W. C. (1998). *Multivariate data analysis* (5th ed.). Upper Saddle River, NJ: Prentice Hall.

Hallikainen, H., & Laukkanen, T. (2018). National culture and consumer trust in e-commerce. *International Journal of Information Management, 38*(1), 97–106. doi:10.1016/j.ijinfomgt.2017.07.002

Henderson, C., Evans-Lacko, S., Flach, C., & Thornicroft, G. (2012). Responses to mental health stigma questions: The importance of social desirability and collection method. *Canadian Journal of Psychiatry, 57*(3), 152–160. doi:10.1177/070674371205700304 PMID:22398001

Hickson, D. J., Hinings, C. R., McMillan, C. J., & Schwitter, J. P. (1974). The culture free context of organization structure: A trinational comparison. *Sociology, 8*(1), 59–80. doi:10.1177/003803857400800104

Hofstede, G. (2001). *Culture's Consequences: comparing values, behaviors, institutions, and organizations across nations* (2nd ed.). Thousand Oaks, CA: Sage.

Hofstede, G., Neuijen, B., Ohayv, D., & Sanders, G. (1990). Measuring organizational cultures: A qualitative and quantitative study across twenty cases. *Administrative Science Quarterly, 35*(2), 286–316. doi:10.2307/2393392

House, R., Javidan, M., Hanges, P., & Dorfman, P. W. (2002). Understanding cultures and implicit leadership theories across the globe: An introduction to the GLOBE project. *Journal of World Business, 30*(1), 3–10. doi:10.1016/S1090-9516(01)00069-4

Joinson, A. (1999). Social desirability, anonymity, and Internet-based questionnaires. *Behavior Research Methods, Instruments, & Computers, 31*(3), 433–438. doi:10.3758/BF03200723 PMID:10502866

Kasemsap, K. (2016). Multifaceted Applications of Data Mining, Business Intelligence, and Knowledge Management. *International Journal of Social and Organizational Dynamics in IT, 5*(1), 57–69. doi:10.4018/IJSODIT.2016010104

Kehoe, C. M., & Pitkow, J. E. (1996). Surveying the territory: GVU's five www user surveys. *The World Wide Web Journal, 1*(3), 77–84.

Keith, M., Babb, J., Furner, C. P., & Abdullat, A. (2015). The role of mobile-computing self-efficacy in consumer information disclosure. *Information Systems Journal, 25*(6), 637–667. doi:10.1111/isj.12082

Keith, M. J., Babb, J., Furner, C., Abdullat, A., & Lowry, P. B. (2016). Limited Information and Quick Decisions: Consumer Privacy Calculus for Mobile Applications. *AIS Transactions on Human-Computer Interaction, 8*(3), 88–130. doi:10.17705/1thci.00081

Kerin, R. A., Cron, W. L., & Peterson, R. A. (1977). Personalization, respondent anonymity, and response distortion in mail surveys. *The Journal of Applied Psychology, 62*(1), 86–89. doi:10.1037/0021-9010.62.1.86

Krumpal, I. (2011). Determinants of Social Desirability Bias in Sensitive Surveys: A Literature Review. *Quality & Quantity, 47*(4), 2025–2047. doi:10.100711135-011-9640-9

Lavrakas, P. J. (2008). *Encyclopedia of survey research methods*. Thousand Oaks, CA: Sage Publications, Inc. doi:10.4135/9781412963947

Li, A., & Reb, J. (2009). A cross-nations, cross-cultures, and cross-conditions analysis on the equivalence of the alanced nventory of desirable responding. *Journal of Cross-Cultural Psychology, 40*(2), 214–233. doi:10.1177/0022022108328819

Lu, J., Yu, C., Liu, C., & Wei, J. (2017). Comparison of mobile shopping continuance intention between China and USA from an espoused cultural perspective. *Computers in Human Behavior, 75*(3), 130–146. doi:10.1016/j.chb.2017.05.002

Martin, C. L., & Nago, D. H. (1989). Some effects of computerized interviewing on job applicant responses. *The Journal of Applied Psychology, 74*(1), 72–80. doi:10.1037/0021-9010.74.1.72

Mason, R. O. (1986). Four ethical issues of the information age. *Management Information Systems Quarterly, 10*(1), 4–12. doi:10.2307/248873

McCrae, R. R., & Costa, P. T. Jr. (1983). Social desirability scales: More substance than style. *Journal of Consulting and Clinical Psychology, 51*(6), 882–888. doi:10.1037/0022-006X.51.6.882

McDonald, H., & Adam, S. (2003). A comparison of online and postal data collection methods in marketing research. *Marketing Intelligence & Planning, 21*(2), 85–95. doi:10.1108/02634500310465399

McKibben, W. B., & Silvia, P. J. (2017). Evaluating the distorting effects of inattentive responding and social desirability on self-report scales in creativity and the arts. *The Journal of Creative Behavior, 51*(1), 57–69. doi:10.1002/jocb.86

Meehl, P. E., & Hathaway, S. R. (1946). The K factor as a suppressor variable in the MMPI. *The Journal of Applied Psychology, 30*, 525–564. doi:10.1037/h0053634 PMID:20282179

Miller, A. (1971). *The assult on privacy: Computers, data banks and dossiers*. Ann Arbor, MI: University of Michigan Press.

Miller, G. A. (1987). Meta-analysis and the culture-free hypothesis. *Organization Studies, 8*(4), 309–326. doi:10.1177/017084068700800402

Miltgen, C. L. (2009). Online consumer privacy concern and willingness to provide personal data on the internet. *International Journal of Networking and Virtual Organizations, 6*(6), 574–603. doi:10.1504/IJNVO.2009.027790

Modigliani, A. (1968). Embarrassment and embarrassability. *Sociometry, 31*(3), 313–326. doi:10.2307/2786616 PMID:5681346

Nederhof, A. J. (1985). Methods of coping with social desirability bias: A review. *European Journal of Social Psychology, 15*(3), 263–280. doi:10.1002/ejsp.2420150303

Nicholson, J. D., & Stepina, L. P. (1998). Cultural values: A cross-national study. *Cross Cultural Management, 5*(1), 34–49.

Nulty, D. D. (2008). The adequacy of response rates to online and paper surveys: What can be done? *Assessment & Evaluation in Higher Education, 33*(3), 301–314. doi:10.1080/02602930701293231

Oliver, R. T. (1971). *Communication and culture in ancient India and China*. Syracuse, NY: Syracuse University Press.

Olson, C. B., Stander, V. A., & Merrill, L. L. (2004). The influence of survey confidentiality and construct measurement in estimating rates of childhood victimization among navy recruits. *Military Psychology, 16*(1), 53–69. doi:10.120715327876mp1601_4

Paulhus, D. L. (1991). *Measurement and control of response bias* (Vol. 1). New York: Academic Press.

Peltier, D. B., & Walsh, J. A. (1990). An investigation of response bias in the Chapman Scales. *Educational and Psychological Measurement, 50*(4), 803–815. doi:10.1177/0013164490504008

Peterson, R. A., & Kerin, R. A. (1981). *The quality of self-report data: Review and synthesis*. Chicago: American Marketing Association.

Pew Research Center. (2015). *From Telephone to the Web: The challenge of mode of interview effects in public opinion polls*. Author.

Racherla, P., & Furner, C. P. (2009). *Cultural determinants of consumers' evaluation of online product reviews: An uncertainty reduction perspective*. Paper presented at the International Conference on Information Systems - Cross Cultural Research on Information Systems SIG.

Richman, W. L., Kiesler, S., Weisband, S., & Drasgow, F. (1999). A meta-analytic study of social desirability distortion in computer-administered questionnaires, traditional questionnaires and interviews. *The Journal of Applied Psychology, 84*(5), 754–775. doi:10.1037/0021-9010.84.5.754

Sills, S. J., & Song, C. (2002). Innovations in survey research: An application of Web-based surveys. *Social Science Computer Review, 20*(1), 22–30. doi:10.1177/089443930202000103

Singer, E., Van Hoewyk, J., & Neugebauer, R. (2003). Attitudes and Behavior: The Impact of Privacy and Confidentiality Concerns on Participation in the 2000 Census. *Public Opinion Quarterly, 65*(3), 368–384. doi:10.1086/377465

Sivakumar, K., & Nakata, C. (2001). The stampede toward Hofstede's framework: Avoiding the sample design pit in cross-cultural research. *Journal of International Business Studies, 32*(3), 555–574. doi:10.1057/palgrave.jibs.8490984

Srite, M., & Karahanna, E. (2006). The role of espoused national culture values in technology acceptance. *Management Information Systems Quarterly, 30*(3), 679–704. doi:10.2307/25148745

Stanton, J. M. (1998). An empirical assessment of data collection using the Internet. *Personnel Psychology, 51.*

Suchman, L., & Jordan, B. (1990). Interactional Troubles in Face-to-Face Survey Interviews. *Journal of the American Statistical Association, 85*(409), 232–241. doi:10.1080/01621459.1990.10475331

Sudman, S., & Bradburn, N. M. (1974). *Response effects in surveys: A review and synthesis.* Chicago: Aldine Publishing Co.

Sue, V. M., & Ritter, L. A. (2011). *Conducting online surveys.* Thousand Oaks, CA: Sage.

Thacher, J. B., Srite, M., Stepina, L. P., & Liu, Y. (2003). Culture, overload and personal innovativeness with informtion technolgoy: Extending the nomological net. *Journal of Computer Information Systems, 44*(1), 74–81.

Triandis, H. (1995). *Individualism and collectivism.* Boulder, CO: Westview.

Truell, A. (2003). Use of the Internet tools for survey research. *Information Technology, Learning and Performance Journal, 21*(1), 31–37.

Weigold, A., Weigold, I. K., & Ressel, E. J. (2013). Examination of the equivalence of self-report survey-based paper-and –pencil and internet data collection methods. *Psychological Methods, 18*(1), 53–70. doi:10.1037/a0031607 PMID:23477606

Westin, A. F. (1976). *Privacy and freedom.* New York: Atheneum.

Wilkins, A. L., & Ouchi, W. G. (1983). Efficient cultures: Exploring the relationship between culture and organizational performance. *Administrative Science Quarterly, 28*(3), 468–481. doi:10.2307/2392253

Woods, K. M., & McNamara, J. R. (1980). Confidentiality: Its effects on interviewee behavior. *Professional Psychology, Research and Practice, 11*(5), 714–721. doi:10.1037/0735-7028.11.5.714 PMID:11650636

Zinko, R., Furner, C. P., Royal, M. T., & Hall, A. (2010). Self-perceptions of our personal reputations: The mediating role of image in the development of organizational citizenship behaviors. *Journal of International Management Studies, 5*(1), 1–9.

Zinko, R., Furner, Z. Z., Hunt, J., & Dalton, A. (2017). Establishing a Reputation. *Journal of Employment Counseling, 54*(2), 87–96. doi:10.1002/joec.12056

Zinko, R., Tuchtan, C., Hunt, J., Meurs, J., Furner, C., & Prati, L. M. (2017). Gossip: A channel for the development of personal reputation. *The International Journal of Organizational Analysis*, 25(3), 516–535. doi:10.1108/IJOA-07-2016-1041

KEY TERMS AND DEFINITIONS

Anonymity: A condition in which the identity of individual subjects is not known to researchers.

Confidentiality Concerns: The perception that the information about a subject that is collected by a researcher will not be shared with another party.

Espoused Collectivism: The extent to which an individual values relationships with their in-group.

Espoused Masculinity: The extent to which the individual views the world as competitive rather than nurturing.

Espoused Power Distance: The extent to which and individual perceives a power differences between themselves and their superiors and subordinates.

Espoused Uncertainty Avoidance: The extent to which the individuals fears risk.

Social Desirability Distortion: The tendency of subjects to distort their responses to questions in order to appear to conform to the norms of some social group.

Chapter 3
Digital Fluency in SMEs:
A Typology and a Multi-Case Study

Simon Bourdeau
ESG-UQAM, Canada

Dragos Vieru
TELUQ, Canada

ABSTRACT

In the practitioner and the academic literatures, links between information technology (IT) adoption, IT use, and digital fluency (DF) have been emphasized by a number of authors. However, there is a lack of understanding of what exactly digital fluency is, how it can be conceptualized, and what role it plays in small and medium-sized enterprises (SMEs). Based on the DF literature and its underlying concepts such as skills, expertise, and competencies, as well as on the SME literature, a multi-case study of three Canadian SMEs is conducted to empirically evaluate a typology of DF archetypes. The typology, that is based on a change agent perspective, has three archetypes. Results suggest that SMEs' managers should focus on the complementarity nature of the cognitive, social, and technological dimensions of DF when assessing and developing their employees' DF.

DIGITAL FLUENCY IN SMEs: A TYPOLOGY AND A MULTI-CASE STUDY

In today's world, private and public, small and large, manufacturing and service organizations have to develop and deploy strategies and processes that rely on information technologies (IT) (Catlin, LaBerge, & Varney, 2018). These organizations are overwhelmed by torrents of data and, to stay competitive or simply to survive, they have to manage those data and make sense of it (Dallemule & Davenport, 2017). This adds to the challenges related to the rapid and constant technological evolutions that organizations and their employees must face. In fact, the pressure is mainly felt by employees who must keep up the pace with the technological changes (Colbert, Yee, & George, 2016). They must make sure to maintain the appropriate knowledge, skills, abilities, and attitudes towards the various IT they have to use in their daily work. Thus, they have to stay digitally fluent (Hsi, 2007; Briggs & Makice, 2012). Maintaining the proper level of digital fluency (DF) can be challenging for any organization but even more for small and

DOI: 10.4018/978-1-5225-8933-4.ch003

medium-sized enterprises (SMEs) (Kyobe, Namirembe, & Shongwe, 2015; Lehner, 2018; Soto-Acosta, Popa, & Martinez-Conesa, 2018).

To stay competitive, SMEs need to innovate with IT and to develop new business strategies as well as processes that rely on IT (Kim, Jang, & Yang, 2016; Nguyen, Mewby, & Macaulay, 2015; Verbano & Crema, 2016). Thus, SMEs need to invest in IT infrastructures. However, the gains and benefits of such investments will materialize only if employees adopt and use IT adequately, which, in turn, depend on employees possessing the appropriate competences to maximize their use (Kotey & Folker, 2007; Palacios-Marqués, Soto-Acosta, & Merigó, 2015; Peltier, Zhao, & Schibrowsky, 2012). Moreover, SMEs have more limited means than larger organizations in terms of financial and human resources which will affect their capabilities and readiness to face the challenges imposed by constant IT evolutions strategies (P. Cragg, Mills, & Suraweera, 2013; Verbano & Crema, 2016). Therefore, it is essential that employees have a better understanding of the challenges and the opportunities related to the adoption and use of new IT in their daily works if SMEs want to benefit from their IT investments. Thus, SME employees must have the right digital competence or digital fluency to transform these IT investments in organizational value (Briggs & Makice, 2012; Caldeira & Ward, 2002; Colbert et al., 2016).

Aligning organizational strategies with existing IT expertise directly affect the extent of the adoption and use of IT in an SME (Bharadwaj & Soni, 2007; Fillis & Wagner, 2005; Marsh, 2018). Most SMEs find themselves in a difficult position because, on one hand, they must ensure that their IT strategies keep up with the constant and rapid technological evolutions and, on the other hand, they must ensure that their employees have the adequate DF to properly adopt and use these IT (Bergeron, Croteau, Uwizeyemungu, & Raymond, 2017; Dallemule & Davenport, 2017). From this discussion an important question emerges: How do SMEs' managers determine the actual level of DF of their employees and what would be the level of DF these employees need to attain?

Fluency is a concept that represents different things to different people in different contexts. The Merriam-Webster Dictionary (2018) defines it as " the quality or state of being fluent" and fluent as "having or showing mastery of a subject or skill". Such general definitions may explain why fluency has been conceptualized as an umbrella-type of notion wrapping almost every attribute that might influence performance (Bassellier, Horner, & Benbasat, 2001). In relation to information technology the concept of fluency has been labelled as digital fluency (DF). Briggs and Makice (2012) define it as "the maximum potential an individual has to achieve desired outcomes through the use of digital technology. Fluency is the results of individuals continuing to maintain and improve skills relative to the needs of your organizational context. Your fluency helps you act in a way that anticipates and support change (p.13)". For these authors, the skills and abilities related to the use of IT and the understanding of its roles in an organizational context are the central elements of DF. For Savin-Baden (2015), DF is "the ability to use digital media, of whatever sort, to manage knowledge and learning across diverse offline and online spaces. It includes the ability to understand complex issues, such as how identify can be established and faked, the ability to evaluate the trustworthiness and accuracy of information, and the ability to understand the subtext of digital media and information and place within a wider context (p.140-141)". Hsi (2007) provides a conceptualization of DF which overlaps with the knowledge, skills and attitudes to properly use IT in today's digital economy, since she defines it as "the competencies, new representational practices, design sensibilities, ownership, and strategic expertise that a learner gains or demonstrates by using digital tools to gather, design, evaluate, critique, synthesize, and develop digital media artefacts, communication messages, or other electronic expressions (p.1509)". Thus, being digitally fluent covers not only the technical skills element required for an employee to work in today's organizations but also the contextual/social and the cognitive and socio-emotional elements (Ala-Mutka, 2011; Briggs & Makice, 2012).

To be digitally fluent in today's digital economy, employees needs to have the proper skills, knowledge, attitude and awareness needed to perform, through the use of digital media and IT, various tasks such as problem-solving, communicating, collaborating, coordinating, creating, innovating and managing information, learning and socializing (Ala-Mutka, 2011; Briggs & Makice, 2012; Ferrari, 2012). Besides the technical expertise, DF emphasizes the importance of taking into consideration the social and contextual dimensions such as the cognitive and socio-emotional knowledge, skills and attitude towards IT (Ala-Mutka, 2011; Briggs & Makice, 2012; Hsi, 2007).

Various studies that have studied IT skills, competencies and/or digital fluency in SMEs suggest that the various levels of organizational DF are related to different levels of accumulated individual IT skills and knowledge in the organization. Studies have shown that the combination of the top management attitude and knowledge regarding IT, with the internal development of IT skills engendered higher levels of success with IT use in SMEs (Dibrell, Davis, & Craig, 2008). During the last two decades, most of the studies that have assessed the digital competency and/or fluency took a more "technical" perspective (Marcolin, Compeau, Munro, & Huff, 2000) and have focused on identifying: 1) IT professionals' personality characteristics (Bashein & Markus, 1997), 2) IT specialists knowledge and skill (Seppanen, 2002); or 3) business managers' technical skills (Bassellier et al., 2001). Although interesting and informative, most of these studies have adopted a limited conceptualization of the IT use and do not take into consideration other key dimensions of DF, such as the social environment sensibility and the cognitive capabilities related to the effective adoption and use of IT. Such narrow perspective is not wrong, but by putting most emphasis on the technological aspects of IT use, it might be too restrictive to be applied in the context of the today's digital economy (Burton-Jones & Grange, 2013).

The various conceptualizations and definitions of IT skills and digital fluency share one commonality, most of them have a multidimensional structure. While some conceptualizations focus on the technical and practical dimensions of IT use (Marcolin et al., 2000), others highlight the importance of conceptualizing and developing DF by encompassing the acquisition of higher order thinking skills that can be used in various contexts (Briggs & Makice, 2012; Calvani, Cartelli, Fini, & Ranieri, 2008; Ferrari, 2012). Indeed, IT are now ubiquitous and their use now spreads across various industries and organizations' levels. IT can be used to accomplish a large array of various tasks. Nevertheless, Lamb and Kling (2003) suggest the expansion of the concept of IT users, i.e. the active agents who use the IT. For these scholars, the concept of IT user should be more encompassing since IT users are, above all, social actors who are "simultaneously enabled and constrained by the socio-technical affiliations and environments of the firm, its members, and its industry" (Lamb & Kling, 2003, p.218). Thus, in the context of SMEs, this reconceptualization of the IT user means that, since each of them has to play different roles (Lamb & Kling, 2003), each of them have also a share of responsibility regarding the forecasting, the development and/or the implementation of IT in their company (Bruque & Moyano, 2007). Thus, each SME employee can be viewed as an agent of organizational change (Markus & Benjamin, 1996).

The literature on DF and all its underlying concepts such as competency, skills, expertise, knowledge, etc. reveals a myriad of various conceptualizations of DF that creates some confusions regarding what DF is. Thus, the DF conceptualization is fuzzy and falls short of providing the clarity needed by scholars and managers alike to understand the multidimensional nature of this concept. In addition, the SME's literature does not offer a clear perspective on the role played by DF in generating IT-based business value.

Taking into consideration this gap in the literature, our intention is to develop a conceptualization of DF which is more encompassing. More precisely, our goal is to address the following research questions: 1) How can digital fluency (DF) be conceptualized? 2) Do different types of DF exist in the context of SMEs? and 3) If so, how can they be characterized?

To do so, we propose a DF typology that builds on the existing body of research on SMEs, on the change agent perspective, and on the various DF definitions and conceptualization of DF and its underlying concepts. The DF conceptualization we are proposing is based on three key competence domains, i.e., technological, cognitive and social along with their learning areas, i.e. skill (know-how), knowledge (know-what) and attitude (know-why) are assembled in a theoretical framework. Our goal is to theorize on how combinations of these key competences domains and learning areas will impact IT adoption and use in SMEs. We suggest that these combinations represent DF archetypes of SMEs' employees and represent the building blocks of our proposed typology. Three different case studies of Canadian SMEs are studied to empirically test these archetypes.

Thus, this study provides "an explanation of how, why, and when things happened, relying on varying views of causality and methods for argumentation" (Gregor, 2006, p.619) and proposes a theoretical tool that enables readers to develop a broad understanding of a typology of DF in the SME context. As we pursue a theory-building approach, we put "less emphasis on the synthesis of prior literature and more emphasis on theoretical development" (Rivard, 2014, p.iv).

THEORETICAL FOUNDATIONS

Digital Fluency Conceptualization

In today' digital economy, technology is ubiquitous and plays a central role in organizations especially in SMEs (Catlin et al., 2018; Lehner, 2018; van Laar, van Deursen, van Dijk, & de Haan, 2018). To survive and navigate in this digital economy, employees have to be digitally fluent which means that they should not only know how to use digital technology but also know "how to construct ideas of significance with digital technology" (R. Wang, Wiesemes, & Gibbons, 2012, p.571). For Wang et al. (2012), digital fluency represents "the ability to reformulate knowledge to express oneself creatively and appropriately, and to produce and generate information rather than simply to comprehend it (p.2)". This definition also highlights the fact that individuals need to know not only how to use the technology but also how produce, in a specific context, things of significance with the technology. Such conceptualization goes beyond the concept of digital literacy (Ferrari, 2012). Indeed, Ala-Mutka (2011) posits that digital fluency "emphasize and encompass the need for skills, an understanding of concepts and an intellectual capability for abstract thinking about information (p.23)". For Miller and Bartlett (2012) the notion of competency and knowledge are central to the notion of digital fluency which they define "as the body of competencies and knowledge necessary to critically engage with online content [...as] a source of information that influences many consequential, even life-changing decisions (p.36)". Thus, to be digitally fluent, individuals must have the proper digital competences since " digital fluency would mean being fluent in digital competence (Ala-Mutka, 2011, p.36).

In an organizational context, different competences encompass the various skills, complementary assets, and routines used by employees to generate sustainable competitive advantage (Selznick, 1957). Thus, an organizational digital competence contains the technical skills and expertise available. Moreover, since organizational digital competence represents a combination of individuals' competences, digital competence has been mainly studied at the individual level (Pavlou & El Sawy, 2006).

In the literature, a positive correlation has been established between an organization's level of accumulated knowledge on IT innovations and its level of IT use. At the organizational level, most past studies have focused on IT management competences (e.g. Pavlou & El Sawy, 2006), while at the individual level (e.g. Bassellier & Benbasat, 2004; Bassellier et al., 2001), the focus has been on specific IT competences of managers and IS professionals. At the organizational level, Pavlou and El Sawy (2006) have proposed a general and encompassing definition of IT competence which is "…the extent to which a firm is knowledgeable about and effectively utilizes IT tools to manage information within the firm… (p 204)" However, such general and encompassing definition does not seems to find an equivalent at the individual level. Rather, scholars and practitioners have developed a wide variety of definitions and conceptualization for specific contexts. Such situation engenders some difficulties and confusion when one tries to compare and integrate research findings, to explain in a unified definition what DF exactly is and how one should integrate and compare its imbricated dimensions.

One way to conceptualize and define digital fluency is to take into consideration its underlying learning domains: i.e. knowledge, skills, and attitudes (e.g. Bassellier et al., 2001; Harisson & Boonstra, 2009; Hsi, 2007). As highlighted by several scholars, DF is sensitive to the organizational context (Briggs & Makice, 2012; Hsi, 2007; Miller & Bartlett, 2012). Thus, a conceptualization of DF should identify the main competence domains and the main learning areas associated with the specificities of a particular context. For this reason, we think that it would not be appropriate and relevant to propose a unique set of DF that could be used and applied in all the possible organizational contexts since each context is characterized by idiosyncratic practices, norms, and values. Therefore, we posit that at the conceptual level, the DF has to be constant throughout the various contexts while, at the operationalized level, the DF has to be adapted and revised to be representative of the organizations' context studied as well as aligned with the idiosyncratic social practices and technological environment (Doty & Glick, 1994). So, DF can be conceived as a multidimensional concept that encompasses the necessary set of knowledge, skills, and attitudes that an individual possesses in order to evolve in a specific technological context. In other words, IT must be appropriated by social actors that engage in the role of change agent (Burton-Jones & Grange, 2013). Based on the above argumentation, we propose the following conceptualization of individual DF:

Digital fluency is an individual capacity to use and combine one's knowledge (i.e., know-what), skill (i.e. know-how), and attitude (i.e. know-why), which represent the learning areas, associated with three related competence domains, i.e. technological, cognitive and social, to use new or existing IT to analyze, select and critically evaluate information in order to investigate and solve work-related problems and develop a collaborative knowledge base while engaging in organizational practices within a specific organizational context.

Figure 1 provides an illustration of the DF multidimensional conceptualization. The central idea of our approach is that the competence domains as well as the learning areas are simultaneously coexisting and complementary to one another.

Technological Domain

The knowledge, skills and attitudes that individuals need to possess to explore and exploit IT in a new environment as well as to apprehend the technological challenges or problems with agility are underlying

Figure 1. A multidimensional Conceptualization of Individual Digital Fluency

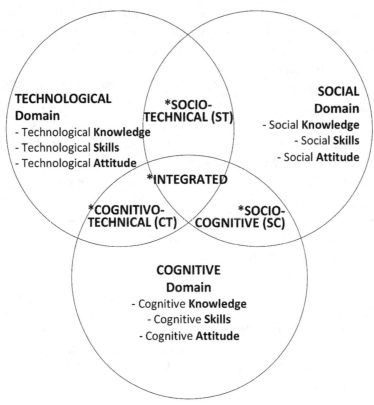

*K+S+A : Represents the Knowledge, Skill and Attitude
characterizing needed in each competence area or intersection

the technological domain (Calvani et al., 2008). Examples of challenges or problems associated with this domain could be, for instance, choosing the most appropriate IT for certain tasks, solving organizational problems using IT, recognizing and using icons and interfaces of particular IT (Ferrari, 2012). The knowledge related to IT infrastructure, such as computers, applications, networks, etc. would be examples of technological knowledge (International ICT Literacy Panel, 2007). The individuals aptitudes regarding the use of specialized tools supporting business tasks or applications for executing the technical operation aspects of digital tools would be examples of technological skills (Ala-Mutka, 2011).

Cognitive Domain

The knowledge, skills and attitudes that individuals need to possess to "read, select, interpret and evaluate data and information taking into account their pertinence and reliability" are underlying the cognitive domain (Calvani et al., 2008, p.187). Accessing, organizing and/or evaluating information are related to the cognitive domain. It includes "tasks on linguistic and numeric competences applied to the digital word" (Ferrari, 2012, p.56), reading and interpreting texts, making sense of data, assessing information, creating graphs (Calvani et al., 2008). Example of cognitive skills include "general literacy, ... as well as critical thinking and problem solving" (International ICT Literacy Panel, 2007, p.1).

Social Domain

The knowledge, skills and attitudes that individuals need to collaborate with colleagues or partners by using various IT platforms and functionalities while following the organizational work norms and values (Calvani et al., 2008). Thus, examples of social skills include "effectively express and communicate, understanding the potential and limitations of each type of media ... collaboration with possibly global reach, construct and maintain a system of personal communication links with relevant people and networks, ... participate in digital activities...", etc. (Ala-Mutka, 2011, p.51).

Integrated Domain

The integrated domain encompasses the knowledge, skills and attitudes of the three domains and focuses on their complementarities. It includes the knowledge, skills and attitudes needed for adopting and using IT for supporting and enhancing organizational practices as well as for collaborating with colleagues and partners, both internal and external, to generate value and innovate. In the integrated domain, it is essential that individuals understand "the potential offered by technologies which enable individuals to share information and collaboratively build new knowledge" (Ferrari, 2012, p.55).

An Integrative View of Digital Fluency

The literature on digital fluency several conceptualizations and definitions of the learning domains, i.e. knowledge, skills and attitude, have been proposed. This situation has engendered some confusion regarding the interpretations and the meaning each of these concepts. In order to clarify these concepts, we have decided to build our multidimensional conceptualization of DF on preexisting and relevant definitions that have been used in the context of DF (Table 1).

Table 1. Digital Fluency: Definitions of the Learning Areas

Areas	Definition	Source
Knowledge	Facts, information, principles, theories and practices acquired through experience and/or education, i.e. the theoretical or practical understanding of the nature, role and opportunities of IT in everyday contexts such as, for example, using computer applications, understanding of the opportunities and potential risks of Internet and social media, information sharing and collaborative networking, etc.	(Ala-Mutka, 2011; Genevieve Bassellier et al., 2001; Merriam-Webster, 2018; Soto-Acosta et al., 2018)
Skills	The ability to apply knowledge to complete tasks; to solve problems; to search, collect and process complex information and; to produce, present and understand it, using IT, in a critical and systematic way.	(Ala-Mutka, 2011; Marcolin et al., 2000; Merriam-Webster, 2018; van Laar, van Deursen, van Dijk, & de Haan, 2017; van Laar et al., 2018)
Attitude	The ways of thinking and the motivations for acting that shape people's action in digital environments such as intercultural, collaborative, critical, creative, responsible and autonomous aspects. For example, they include ethics, values, and priorities.	(Ala-Mutka, 2011; Ferrari, 2012; Merriam-Webster, 2018; R. Wang et al., 2012)

In a study commissioned by the European Commission Joint Research Centre Institute for Prospective Technological Studies, Ferrari (2012) suggests that the competencies underlying DF are much more encompassing than the technical skills usually associated with DF. She proposes a list of seven application domains that employees and individuals need to master to face the challenges of the digital economy. These application domains along with the domains underlying the DF conceptualization are presented in Table 2.

Digital Fluency Archetypes of SMEs' Employees

The competence domains, i.e. cognitive, social and technological and the three learning areas, i.e. knowledge, skills and attitudes are complementary to one another and could be combined in different ways in the proposed DF conceptualization. Each specific combination can describe a particular archetype (Doty & Glick, 1994). In order to combined the competencies domains and the learning areas together to identify DF archetypes, we use the change agent perspective if we consider that SMEs' employees are potential change agents (Lamb & Kling, 2003; Markus & Benjamin, 1996). This perspective is more encompassing and less limited and restrictive than user perspective adopted in previous studies (e.g. Marcolin et al., 2000). The DF conceptualization (Figure 1 and Table 1) will be used as a basis for developing the typology of SME employees DF archetypes (Doty & Glick, 1994; George & Bennett, 2005). Typologies and typological theories allow to explore a complex organizational phenomenon such as DF archetypes or profiles as well as their possible effects on IT use and IT adoption (George & Bennett, 2005). In typology, different ideal types or archetypes that are "… complex constructs that can be used to represent holistic configurations of multiple unidimensional constructs" (Doty & Glick, 1994, p.233) are developed and are posited to be maximally effective specific contexts. Typologies can be used

Table 2. An integrative view of Digital Fluency

Domains of Application	Digital Fluency Domains (Figure 1)	Description
Individual Domains		
1. Creation of content and knowledge	Cognitive domain	Construction of new knowledge through technology and media. Integrate previous knowledge; construct new knowledge.
2. Collaboration	Social domain	Link to others, participate in online networks and communities, and interact constructively and with a sense of responsibility.
3. Technical Operations	Technological domain	Use technology and media, perform tasks through digital tools.
Overlapping Domains		
4. Ethics and responsibility	Intersection of Social and Cognitive domains	Behave in an ethical and responsible way, aware of legal frame.
5. Information Management	Intersection of Technological and Cognitive domains	Identify, locate, access, retrieve, store and organize information.
6. Communication and sharing	Intersection of Technological and Social domains	Communicate through online tools, considering privacy, safety and netiquette.
Integrated Domain		
7. Evaluation and problem solving	Technological, Cognitive and Social domains	Identify digital needs, solve problems through digital means, and assess the information retrieved.

(adapted from (Ferrari, 2012; Harison & Boonstra, 2009))

to develop typological theories which adopt encompassing perspective as they take into consideration the holistic principles of inquiry and equifinality (i.e., the same outcome being attained via different pathways). In addition, such theories address complex phenomena without oversimplifying them, and identify the pathways connecting particular archetypes to specific outcomes, such as IT adoption and use (George & Bennett, 2005).

We draw on the change agentry perspective by considering SMEs' employees as change agents to identify DF archetypes. In order to change, organizations must use three different but complementary types of strategies that could be deployed by change agents: 1) political, 2) marketing, and/or 3) military campaigns (Hirschhorn, 2002). Thus, for getting support and creating a strong coalition for change, change agents should lead a political campaign. For communicating the objectives, the benefits, and the roadmap to change, as well as for getting engagement from the organization and the employees, a marketing campaign should be deployed. Finally, for identifying and securing the scarce resources needed for the change to materialize, a military campaign should be launch.

In a similar fashion, Markus and Benjamin (1996) develop three archetypes of change agents that can lead the changes efforts: traditional, facilitator, and advocate. For each archetype Markus and Benjamin (1996) identify dominant beliefs underlying a archetype's behaviors which provides "a basic orientation toward goals and means of IS work that shapes what the practitioner does and how she or he does it" (Markus & Benjamin, 1996, p.387). The three archetypes are not empirical classes or categories of a taxonomy but rather theoretical constructions of complementary characteristics that could help characterizing the DF archetypes of SMEs' employees regarding the adoption and use of IT (Harison & Boonstra, 2009; Markus & Benjamin, 1996). Hirschheim and Klein (1989) have also identified four dominant patterns or archetypes of IS specialists. The four developed archetypes, the expert, the facilitator, the social warrior, and the emancipator, describe the underlying assumptions of each archetype.

Based on the various archetypes descriptions developed by change agent scholars (Hirschheim & Klein, 1989; Hirschhorn, 2002; Markus & Benjamin, 1996) and the specificities of SMEs (Bergeron et al., 2017; Lehner, 2018; Verbano & Crema, 2016), we propose three DF archetypes of SMEs' employees: 1) Technical Expert, 2) Organizer and 3) Campaigner (see Table 3). We posit that the "technical expert" archetype would predominantly be related to the technological domain rather than the social or cognitive ones. However, this situation does not mean that the "technical expert" archetypes has no cognitive and/or social knowledge, skill and attitude. Rather, this means that, for a technical expert, his/her predominant knowledge, skills and attitude would be associated with the technical domain rather than with the cognitive and social domains. This situation also prevails for both the "organizer" and the "campaigner" archetypes. Table 3 presents the overlapping characteristics of the archetypes identified in the literature.

Table 3 provides interesting descriptions of DF archetypes, notwithstanding somewhat general and simplistic and not providing a broad conceptual perspective of the DF underlying each change agent type. These archetypes will serve as a theoretical base to build a typology of DF in an SME context. While theoretically developing DF archetypes is intuitively appealing, their inherent lack of specificity also makes them difficult to be empirically tested. So, as a first attempt to characterize the DF archetypes while considering the specificities of SMEs, the present study is an initial effort in that direction. The proposed DF conceptualization (Figure 1) will serve as a "property space" to guide the identification of empirical DF archetypes of SME employees (George & Bennett, 2005).

Table 3. Digital Fluency Archetypes of SMEs Employees

Archetypes	Technical Expert	Organizer	Campaigner
Key characteristics	1. Focuses on technical expertise; 2. Detached from stakeholders' objectives; 3. Responsible for technical aspects only; 4. Works with minimal contact from stakeholders.	1. Focuses on stakeholders' support; 2. Serves stakeholders' objectives; 3. Helps stakeholders increase their capacity for change and autonomy; 4. Provides learning advice; 5. Is responsible of changing the stakeholder's behaviors; 6. Instructs stakeholders in making informed decisions; 7. Tries to gain consensus; 8. Is organized and flexible.	1. Uses tactics (e.g. persuasion, manipulations, power) to attain his objective; 2. Responsible for attaining change objectives; 3. Makes decisions to guide the change effort in a particular direction; 4. Focuses on objectives. 5. Is well organized, and focuses on objectives.
Conceptualizations Identified in the change agent literature	• Traditional model (Markus & Benjamin, 1996) • Expert type (Hirschheim & Klein, 1989)	• Facilitator model (Markus & Benjamin, 1996) • Facilitator archetype (Hirschheim & Klein, 1989) • Political/marketing campaigns (Hirschhorn, 2002)	• Advocate model (Markus & Benjamin, 1996) • Social warrior archetype (Hirschheim & Klein, 1989) • Military campaign (Hirschhorn, 2002)

METHODOLOGY

In order to empirically evaluate the typology of DF archetypes, a qualitative research approach was adopted (Eisenhardt, 1989). More specifically a multi-case study (Yin, 2013) of three Canadian SMEs was conducted since to capture the perceptions and understandings of SMEs stakeholders' regarding the role of DF as well as to evaluate the importance of implementing new IT in the context of the digital economy. Since the literature on DF is fragmented, adopting a qualitative exploratory approach allowed us to make both empirical and theoretical contributions. Our goal was to identify and better understand the characteristics and factors that can affect the development of the DF in SMEs. Based on perceptions of experienced SME employees we were be able to identify the similarities and specificities in each of the three organizational contexts regarding how DF were developed. Relying on perceptions is an appropriate approach since we were trying to develop a theory that focuses on a "how question", i.e. how key competencies domains and learning areas can be combined and affect IT adoption and use in SMEs. Thus, a field study using case studies helped us to define the appropriate research design and data collection method but it also served as the main vehicle for generalizing the results of the case study (Yin, 2013).

The data collection was conducted in three Canadian SMEs (Castlehouse, Woolhouse & Synthouse – no real names), from the clothing industry. These companies were conducting IT implementation projects at the time of the data collection. For each project, employees of these SMEs had to adopt and use new IT in their daily tasks. To help them better use the new technologies and promote the benefits of the IT investment, each employee received a training, ranging from half a day to two days. Data were collected over a five-month period in 2015 though interviews and observations. Between five to nine employees were interviewed before and after the training and use of the new IT in each SME. Owners of the SMEs as well as managers (HR and IT), and representative employees were interviewed. Semi-structured interviews were conducted by at least two researchers each time. The interviews' objectives were to better understand/identify:

- How IT were evaluated in the SMEs,

- The role played by IT and how IT were used on a daily basis,
- Which knowledge, skills and attitude were needed for using IT in the SMEs,
- The various profiles of typical IT user in the SME,
- The characteristics of the IT infrastructure and the SME's context,
- The extent of organizational IT readiness and use,
- The employees' level of support and confidence in the IT-triggered change.

The interview questions were developed based on the competence domains and the learnings areas of the DF conceptualization (Figure 1 and Table 2) as well as on questions developed by other researchers (Cragg, Caldeira, & Ward, 2011; Harison & Boonstra, 2009).

The data collected was used to: 1) Evaluate the relevance and usefulness of the DF conceptualization, 2) Identify the characteristics, in terms of competence domains and learning areas, of the DF archetypes of SME employees, and 3) Understand the possible effects of these archetypes on IT adoption and use. Since we conducted an exploratory study of a complex phenomenon - digital fluency -, we focused our analysis on the dynamics within cases and across cases in order to build a DF typology from case studies (Eisenhardt, 1989; Yin, 2013). This theory building approach is suited for studies where a priori constructs are triangulated by multiple case studies and where within-case and cross-case analyses are combined with the literature (Eisenhardt, 1989). During the five month of data, data analyses were conducted in parallel to make adjustment during the data collection (Yin, 2013).

Cases Descriptions and Analysis

Case Study 1: Castlehouse

The first case study was conduct in Castlehouse a manufacturing and retail clothing SME of 350 employees. Castlehouse operates in a segment of the industry characterized by important pressure coming from Asian competitors as well as by and constant new demands and changes. At the time of the data collection, Castlehouse had recently deployed a new manufacturing IT platform (Lectra) to automate its sewing machines. The managers of Castlehouse were preoccupied by the implementation of this new technology and they wanted to better understand and identify the types of DF that their employees would need to develop to ensure a smooth and easy transition from the legacy technology to the new IT. In total, six employees from Castlehouse were interviewed: three managers from production, IT, and HR and three sewing workers – pattern technicians. Based on the analysis of the data collected at Castlehouse, two different DF archetypes seems to exist in this SME: the *technical expert* and the *campaigner*. In terms of competence domains and learning areas covered by those two archetypes, the technical expert at Castlehouse seems to mainly possess knowledge, skills and attitude related to the technological domain, whereas the campaigner seems to possess knowledge, skills and attitude related to both the social domain and the socio-technical intersection (see Figure 1).

At Castlehouse, it seems that the campaigner archetype is strongly embodied by the production manager. The data suggest that this person relies on both her technological and social relational skills and knowledge to promote the new manufacturing IT platform (Lectra) to both executives and floor employees. Since she has a good understanding of the technological functionalities of the new IT platform and having developed good social relations with everyone in the organization, she explained to all employees how the new IT platform would support Castlehouse's development strategy to increase its competitiveness. Thus, she played a key role in supporting and helping floor employees who would have to use, on a daily basis, this new platform:

Provide the proper working tools. Evaluate the needs. Identify who can address the needs. Send him/her to training. Some already had the training: you just have to find the right job position for them. Find the right time to move the employee to a new job position or get him/her to change his work practices. (Production manager)

The technical expert archetype was embodied by the pattern technicians. Our data analysis shows that the pattern technicians were mainly preoccupied by the technical expertise needed to master the new IT platform. In addition, they turned to colleagues to collaborate with them in order to get support, have access to new knowledge and develop their technical skills regarding Lectra. However, this collaboration is rather limited to exchanging information on how to use the system:

Once a new technology has been introduced, we get training. And then, after most of the people get trained, the ones that are more competent will be able to train some other employees [...] As soon as we discover something we will share it. We would say: 'oh look, I found a new function; it works like that, what you think about it?' Then, we will share it among us. (Pattern technician)

Based on the data collected, the Campaigner archetype at Castlehouse seems to be characterized by strong social skills and attitude as well as by technological knowledge. As for the Technical expert archetypes, it seems to be mainly characterized by the knowledge, skills and attitude related to the technological domain.

Data analysis suggests that DF archetypes at Castlehouse are mainly characterized by a mix of technological and social domains knowledge, skills and attitude. Thus, since the IT manufacturing platform is used by the patterns technicians and by the production manager to solve organizational problems and nurture organizational goals, we conjecture that the inclusion of the cognitive[1] domain of the DF (see Figure 1) is also a key factor for a successful adoption of the new IT.

Case Study 2: Woolhouse

The second case study was conducted in Woolhouse, a 40-employee family-owned company specialized in knitting. This SME operates in the field of clothing wholesale distribution and manufacturing. Their products, which are made of special fabrics coming from Egypt and Italy, are designed in Canada and have been manufactured for more than 30 years in Woolhouse's owned workshops in China. In 2014, an important strategic and operational move was made by Woolhouse by launching an online store. The underlying objective of this strategic decision was to reach new markets and grow. However, to be able to support this online store Woolhouse had to deploy a new customer relationship management (CRM) system that would affect Woolhouse's operations and value chain. Nine employees at Woolhouse were interviewed including the owner.

Data analysis suggests that three different DF archetypes exist in this SME: *the technical expert, the campaigner* and *the organizer*. In terms of competence domains and learning areas covered by those three archetypes, the technical expert at Woolhouse seems to mainly possess knowledge, skills and attitude related to the technological domain. As for the campaigner, it seems to possess, just like the campaigner at

Castlehouse, the knowledge, skills, and attitude related to both the social domain and the socio-technical intersection. Finally, the characteristics of the organizer archetype at Woolhouse are idiosyncratic and characterized by the possession of knowledge, skills, and attitude related to socio-technical, socio-cognitive, and the cognitive-technical intersections as well as to the integrated intersection (see Figure 1).

At Woolhouse the warehouse clerk played a key role in operation since he was the person with the best understanding of Woolhouse's business processes. He also had very strong technological background and was interested in technological evolutions. He had self-learned the IT infrastructures of Woolhouse and, with his understanding of the organization processes, made useful improvements in the systems. He became the de-facto IT 'expert' and our data analysis suggests that he represents the Technical Expert archetype:

I was very much accustomed with the warehouse and the POS. I became the key resource for these systems because I understood how to do reports and the inventory. I was able to master all the functionalities of those systems. (Warehouse clerk)

The Campaigner archetype was embodied by various individual at Woolhouse. Each of these individuals were in charge or responsible of various sectors of the organization, e.g. design, distribution, production, boutiques, accounting. Even if they were not technology experts, they had a good understanding of the IT platforms used in the organization as well as the possibilities offered by the upcoming platform. Thus, since they were working in different organizational sectors, they use their social skills and knowledge to promote their preoccupations and interests regarding the new technology.

Family is family, so sometimes individuals are squabbling like any family, but it gives us even more the feeling of being part of the family. However, it allows clarifying things and helps having a better understanding of the organization. Honestly, everyone means great and like I said, we're really involved. (General Manager)

Finally, the Organizer archetype was embodied by the owner's daughter who had worked in the company for the past 10 years. She knew very well the products and organizational processes and was appointed, by his father (the owner), as the responsible for all the IT projects. Even though she did not possess technical knowledge before being appointed in charge of the IT projects, she invested a lot of energy in understanding the advantages of investing in new IT by reading, attending specialized conferences, and surrounding herself with knowledgeable individuals. Thus, she became the Woolhouse's technological 'hub' once she developed a good understanding of the organization's operations as well as the functionalities of the IT platforms.

She is the one most interested with IT … she began to understand, to seek, to always push for us to be on the cutting edge of technology, … She surrounded herself with a team of young people comfortable with IT. (Staff coordinator)

Based on the data collected, the Organizer archetype at Woolhouse seems to be characterized by social knowledge, skills and attitudes, but also by technological interest and understanding of the link between IT and organizational change. As identified in the case study, the Organizer played a convergence role at Woolhouse in terms of IT. Her operational, social, and technological competencies enabled her to build connections between various employees' IT needs and requirements. In addition, data analysis suggests that the knowledge, skills and attitude of the various employees were complementary to one another. This complementarity might explain why Woolhouse did well in terms of their CRM adoption and use.

Case Study 3: Synthouse

The third case study was conduct in Synthouse, a 100-employee family-owned SME that operates in the hosiery and sock mills sector. More specifically, this SME specializes in high performance tights and competition apparel (e.g., dance and figure skating clothing). Synthouse has a large variety of diversified products which organization and is very flexible in terms of productions tasks. To develop such flexibility, the organization had to develop new competencies and to innovate in terms of production techniques. To maintain this flexibility and stay innovative, Synthouse had to develop and implement a new IT infrastructure as well as develop the DF of their employees. For this case study, five employees were interviewed.

Our data analysis suggests that at Synthouse the production/HR manager represents the main resource for knowledge and expertise regarding IT in the organization. He was also the one who understood the need for employee DF in the organization. Synthouse general manager had a more limited view and understanding of IT and approved IT investments based on their ease of use and performance, rather than on the organization's needs and strategy.

Based on our data analysis, two different DF archetypes seems to exist in this SME: The Technical Expert and the Campaigner. In this organization, the Campaigner archetype is strongly embodied by the general manager. However, compared to the campaigner archetypes identified at Castlehouse and Woolhouse, the campaigner at Synthouse seems to lack basic technical knowledge and skills. This lack of technological competencies makes it difficult for him to understand the current role played by the IT platform in the organization. Moreover, it is difficult for him to identify Synthouse's technological needs as well as adequately evaluate the strategic advantages offered by new IT solutions. This situation seemed to be problematic because Synthouse president/owner delegated most of the managerial responsibility to the general manager who used his hierarchical position and his social relational skills to promote and justify the IT solutions which he considered as being the most suitable for the organization. For instance, at the time of the data collection, the general manager was stressing the importance of the development of a web-based e-commerce solution that would communicate with the existing IT platform. However, because of his lack of IT knowledge and skills, he did not understand the technological difficulties related to the integration of the web-based in the existing legacy-based environment (a mainframe-based technology).

He knows the organization well and he is well-intentioned. However, he does not seem to understand that the technological heart of the company, the AS400, is old and not flexible. (Sales/customer service manager)

At Synthouse, the Technical Expert archetypes were embodied by the two managers, the production/HR and the sales/customer service, who were both directly reporting to the general manager. Both of these managers knew their employees very well and possessed the necessary skills to use the technology implemented in the organizational areas under their responsibility. Nevertheless, their understating was limited and they lacked the understanding of the general manager's intentions in terms of the web-based e-commerce project. They had not been informed or consulted regarding the project. In addition, the communication channels between the hierarchical levels as well as between the departments were deficient. Finally, the general manager mostly relied on the development of versatile employees, but this versatility did not take into consideration the DF its employees needed to evolve in a digital environment.

My team is open and ready. We want new technologies to be more efficient and up-to-date, but we have no idea what's coming and where we are heading. (Customer service manager).

TAKEAWAYS

An organization's ability to be resourceful and capture the value-creating opportunities presented by the growth of IT and its usage is referred as IT innovation (Kim et al., 2016; Peltier et al., 2012). For SMEs, IT innovations are essential to ensure their competitiveness and survival. Thus, an SME that has a pool of employees with the adequate DF is more likely to technologically innovate as its employees are better at identifying IT affordances and the possible benefits of IT when compared with SMEs where DF are lacking (Caldeira & Ward, 2002). Our data analysis yielded four main takeaways:

Takeaway 1#: Digital Fluency Development and Training

Except for Castlehouse, the employees at both Woolhouse and Synthouse lacked a HR formal training structure to foster the regular and constant development of their employees' DF. The training offered in those SMEs usually concerned only the employees that already had technological backgrounds. In addition, vicarious learning and knowledge sharing between employees were not stimulated. Therefore, the cognitive and social domains were largely ignored during the development of the employees' DF.

Takeaway 2#: Diffusion of Digital Fluency

The SMEs studied here lacked formalized rules or approaches to transform the existing collaborative tensions, - the tensions that exists between digitally fluent employees and less digitally fluent employees -, in an opportunity to increase their employees' general DF. With the exception of Woolhouse, both Castlehouse and Synthouse did not have any practice or mechanism to support knowledge transfer. In addition, most of the acquired knowledge during trainings was not documented and there was a lack of interest in creating an organizational memory that would support the documentation of the organizations' DF profiles.

Takeaway 3#: Management of the Cognitive and Social Domains

In all three SMEs, top managers rarely encouraged the appropriation of the information associated with the IT platform through the creations of operational manuals. We conjecture that this aspect might have been an obstacle to the reinforcement of technological, cognitive, and social innovation levels in the three SMEs. With the exception of Woolhouse, the managers of the other two SMEs did not recognize the importance of nurturing individual cognitive competences and collaboration initiatives (social competences) which usually constitute success factors in the process of creating innovative ideas.

Takeaway 4#: Socialize to be Digitally Fluent

In all of the three case studies, the collaborative dimension (social domain) of the DF was not sufficiently emphasized by the organizations. Our data analysis suggests that the collaborative level of the employees' DF was low for three reasons:

1. All three SMEs managed their departments/sectors in silos, thus preventing and limiting knowledge sharing and collaboration efforts between employees;
2. IT-driven changes in the SMEs were mainly influenced by the level of DF of the managers in charge of the IT initiatives;
3. Managers in charge of IT-driven changes lacked the communication skills, thus preventing the dissemination of the SMEs' IT vision and how the DF of employees' practices would be aligned with that vision.

CONCLUSION

Based on three case studies of IT implementation realized in three SMEs, our study suggests that the value that can be generated from IT investments is influenced by the SMEs capacities to develop their employees' digital fluency (DF) which encompasses complementary IT and non-IT knowledge, skills, and attitudes. The non-IT knowledge, skills and attitudes represents the "complementary assets" (Davern & Kauffman, 2000) that are required to transform IT investment into value and they allow organization to perform key activities exceptionally well without using IT, e.g. indigenous innovative skills, personal experiences, connections, commitment, openness of communication, and collaboration). Usually, these non-IT knowledge, skills, and attitudes will emerge in organizations that have adequate human resources (HR) capabilities and practices in terms of recruiting, developing competencies, motivating employees, and empowering them (Aral, Brynjolfsson, & Wu, 2012). Such capabilities and practices will enable organization to develop and maintain strong DF (Makadok, 2001).

Even if employees' DF represents key organizational capabilities, this concept still lacks clear conceptualization and standardization in both the IT and SME literatures. Practitioners and scholars alike need a clear conceptualization of DF to better understand and assess employees' DF. Recent studies suggest that SMEs that have employees with the appropriate DF will be better positioned to innovate from the investments made in new IT platforms and ultimately will be better at adapting their IT strategies to the constant evolving digital economy (Cragg et al., 2013; Kim et al., 2016).

The main contribution of this study represents the proposed conceptualization (Figure 1) and definition of DF. The DF conceptualization draws on a set of learning areas, i.e. knowledge, skills and attitudes (i.e. including abilities, strategies, values and awareness) and on three complementary competence domains i.e. technological, social and cognitive. The competence domains, which are possessed by employees, are employed for performing tasks, solving problems, communicating, assessing information, managing data, collaborating with colleagues, sharing knowledge, and creating and/or building knowledge with IT platforms and tools.

The second contribution of this study stems from the three case studies that were used to develop a typology of employees' DF. In this typology, three different archetypes were identified: the technical expert, the campaigner and the organizer. Our data analysis results are aligned with Harison and Boonstra's (2009) observations who argued that developing efficient employees' DF will form organizational capabilities which should help successfully manage organizational change.

Shedding light on how and why multiple combinations of cognitive, social and technological knowledge, skills and attitudes may surface in different SMEs' contexts represents the third contribution. These various combinations, which are influenced by the different contextualized HR practices, correspond to different levels of organizational competitive performance, with the possibility that some them, though different in their compositions, would have similar impacts (equifinality). By generating similar results from different combinations, it is suggested that there would be no "best way" to combine different IT and non-IT knowledge, skills, and attitudes, and the successful outcome of these combinations would stem from more "aligned" combinations with the specific organizational objectives.

In terms of practical implications, we observed that it is practically impossible for a single employee to possess all the knowledge, skills, and attitude in all the three competence domains. However, more importantly for SMEs is to be able to evaluate the DF profiles of all their employees and identify the complementarities between these profiles. Thus, we posit that, to improve IT adoption and use, SMEs need to have individuals mastering learning areas in one or two of the three DF domains and at least one employee with an organizer profiles, i.e. an employee with some knowledge, skills, and attitudes that would reflect the organization's specific needs. This combination will eventually trigger the emergence of appropriate organizational DF and processes, which would facilitate effective adoption and successful use of IT.

Our study has limitations. One limitation is that we try to generalize only from empirical statements to theoretical statements from three case studies (Lee & Baskerville, 2003). However, it has been shown that statistical, sampling-based generalizability may be an unsuitable goal for qualitative studies (Yin, 2013). We suggest that the takeaways from our case studies in the Canadian clothing industry should be assessed in other contexts for further refinements that would eventually offer statistical generalizability. Looking at different industries may also provide new understandings.

CLASS QUESTIONS

1. What does it mean for an individual to be digitally fluent in the today digital economy?
2. Why is it important for an organization to know the level of the "digital fluency" of its employees?
3. Are large organizations' and PME's challenges the same in terms of the digital fluency of their employees? Justify your answer.
4. In your own words, what are the distinctions between knowledge, skills, and attitude?
5. What are the key characteristics of the proposed multidimensional conceptualization of digital fluency (DF) in Figure 1?
6. Why the change agent perspective is used as a theoretical lens to developed the DF archetypes of SMEs' employees? What are its advantages?
7. What are the fundamental elements or characteristics of each of the three DF archetypes (the technical expert, the organizer and the campaigner) described in Table 3?
8. What are the main similarities between DF archetypes identified in each of the three case studies? What are their main differences?

REFERENCES

Ala-Mutka, K. (2011). *Mapping Digital Competence: Towards a Conceptual Understanding*. Academic Press.

Aral, S., Brynjolfsson, E., & Wu, L. (2012). Three-Way Complementarities: Performance Pay, Human Resource Analytics, and Information Technology. *Management Science*, 58(5), 913–931.

Ashurst, C., Cragg, P., & Herring, P. (2012). The role of IT competences in gaining value from e-business: An SME case study. *International Small Business Journal*, 30(6), 640–658. doi:10.1177/0266242610375703

Bashein, B. J., & Markus, M. L. (1997). A Credibility Equation for IT Specialists. *Sloan Management Review*, 35–44.

Bassellier, G., & Benbasat, I. (2004). Business Competence of IT Professionals: Conceptual Development and Influence on IT-Business Partnerships. *Management Information Systems Quarterly*, 28(4), 673–694. doi:10.2307/25148659

Bassellier, G., Blaize Horner, R., & Benbasat, I. (2001). Information technology competence of business managers: A definition and research model. *Journal of Management Information Systems*, 17(4), 159–182. doi:10.1080/07421222.2001.11045660

Bergeron, F., Croteau, A.-M., Uwizeyemungu, S., & Raymond, L. (2017). A framework for research on information technology governance in SMEs. In S. De Haes, & W. Van Grembergen (Eds.), Strategic IT Governance and alignment in business settings (pp. 53-81). IGI Global. doi:10.4018/978-1-5225-0861-8.ch003

Bharadwaj, P. N., & Soni, R. G. (2007). E-Commerce Usage and Perception of E-Commerce Issues among Small Firms: Results and Implications from an Empirical Study. *Journal of Small Business Management*, 45(4), 501–521. doi:10.1111/j.1540-627X.2007.00225.x

Briggs, C., & Makice, K. (2012). *Digital fluency: Building success in the digital age*. SociaLens.

Bruque, S., & Moyano, J. (2007). Organizational Determinants of Information Technology Adoption and Implementation in SMEs: The Case of Family and Cooperative Firms. *Technovation*, 27(5), 241–253. doi:10.1016/j.technovation.2006.12.003

Burton-Jones, A., & Grange, C. (2013). From Use to Effective Use: A Representation Theory Perspective. *Information Systems Research*, 24(3), 632–658. doi:10.1287/isre.1120.0444

Caldeira, M. M., & Ward, J. M. (2002). Understanding the Successful Adoption and Use of IS/IT in SMEs: An Explanation from Portuguese Manufacturing Industries. *Information Systems Journal*, 12(2), 121–152. doi:10.1046/j.1365-2575.2002.00119.x

Calvani, A., Cartelli, A., Fini, A., & Ranieri, M. (2008). Models and instruments for assessing digital competence at school. *Journal of e-Learning and Knowledge Society, 4*(3), 183-193.

Catlin, T., LaBerge, L., & Varney, S. (2018, October). Digital strategy: The four fights you have to win. *McKinsey Quarterly*.

Colbert, A., Yee, N., & George, G. (2016). *The digital workforce and the workplace of the future.* Academy of Management Briarcliff Manor. doi:10.5465/amj.2016.4003

Cragg, P., Caldeira, M., & Ward, J. (2011). Organizational information systems competences in small and medium-sized enterprises. *Information & Management, 48*(8), 353–363. doi:10.1016/j.im.2011.08.003

Cragg, P., Mills, A., & Suraweera, T. (2013). The Influence of IT management sophistication and IT support on IT success in small and medium-sized enterprises. *Journal of Small Business Management, 51*(4), 617–636. doi:10.1111/jsbm.12001

Dallemule, L., & Davenport, T. H. (2017). What's Your Data Strategy? *Harvard Business Review, 95*(3), 112–121.

Davern, M. J., & Kauffman, R. J. (2000). Discovering potential and realizing value from information technology investments. *Journal of Management Information Systems, 16*(4), 121–143. doi:10.1080/07421222.2000.11518268

Dibrell, C., Davis, P. S., & Craig, J. (2008). Fueling innovation through Information Technology in SMEs. *Journal of Small Business Management, 46*(2), 203–218. doi:10.1111/j.1540-627X.2008.00240.x

Doty, D. H., & Glick, W. H. (1994). Typologies as a Unique Form of Theory Building: Toward Improved Understanding and Modeling. *Academy of Management Review, 19*(2), 230–251. doi:10.5465/amr.1994.9410210748

Eisenhardt, K. M. (1989). Agency Theory: An Assessment and Review. *Academy of Management Review, 14*(1), 57–74. doi:10.5465/amr.1989.4279003

Ferrari, A. (2012). *Digital Competence in Practice: An Analysis of Frameworks.* Retrieved from Fillis, I., & Wagner, B. (2005). E-business development: An exploratory investigation of the small firm. *International Small Business Journal, 23*(6), 604–634.

George, A. L., & Bennett, A. (2005). *Case Studies and Theory Development in Social Sciences.* Cambridge, MA: MIT Press.

Gregor, S. (2006). The Nature of Theory in Information Systems. *Management Information Systems Quarterly, 30*(3), 611–642. doi:10.2307/25148742

Harison, E., & Boonstra, A. (2009). Essential competencies for technochange management: Towards an assessment model. *International Journal of Information Management, 29*(4), 283–294. doi:10.1016/j.ijinfomgt.2008.11.003

Hirschheim, R., & Klein, H. K. (1989). Four Paradigms of Information Systems Development. *Association for Computing Machinery. Communications of the ACM, 32*(10), 1199–1216. doi:10.1145/67933.67937

Hirschhorn, L. (2002). Campaigning for Change. *Harvard Business Review, 80*(7), 98–104. PMID:12140858

Hsi, S. (2007). Conceptualizing learning from the everyday activities of digital kids. *International Journal of Science Education, 29*(12), 1509–1529. doi:10.1080/09500690701494076

International ICT Literacy Panel. (2007). *Digital Transformation. A Framework for ICT Literacy.* Author.

Jones-Evans, D. (1996). Technical entrepreneurship, strategy and experience. *International Small Business Journal*, *14*(3), 15–39.

Kim, S. H., Jang, S. Y., & Yang, K. H. (2016). Analysis of the Determinants of Software-as-a-Service Adoption in Small Businesses: Risks, Benefits, and Organizational and Environmental Factors. *Journal of Small Business Management*.

Kotey, B., & Folker, C. (2007). Employee training in SMEs: Effect of size and firm type—Family and non-family. *Journal of Small Business Management*, *45*(2), 214–238. doi:10.1111/j.1540-627X.2007.00210.x

Kyobe, M., Namirembe, E., & Shongwe, M. (2015). The Alignment of Information Technology Applications with Non-Technological Competencies of SMEs in Africa. *The Electronic Journal on Information Systems in Developing Countries*, *67*(1), 1–22. doi:10.1002/j.1681-4835.2015.tb00483.x

Lamb, R., & Kling, R. (2003). Reconceptualizing users as social actors in information systems research. *Management Information Systems Quarterly*, *27*(2), 197–235. doi:10.2307/30036529

Lee, A. S., & Baskerville, R. L. (2003). Generalizing generalizability in information systems research. *Information Systems Research*, *14*(3), 221–243. doi:10.1287/isre.14.3.221.16560

Lehner, F. (2018). ICT Skills and Competencies for SMEs: Results from a Structured Literature Analysis on the Individual Level. In *The Impact of Digitalization in the Workplace* (pp. 55–69). Springer. doi:10.1007/978-3-319-63257-5_5

Leonardi, P. M. (2013). Theoretical foundations for the study of sociomateriality. *Information and Organization*, *23*(2), 59–76. doi:10.1016/j.infoandorg.2013.02.002

Makadok, R. (2001). Toward a synthesis of the resource-based and dynamic-capability views of rent creation. *Strategic Management Journal*, *22*(5), 387–401. doi:10.1002mj.158

Marcolin, B. L., Compeau, D. R., Munro, M. C., & Huff, S. L. (2000). Assessing User Competence: Conceptualization and Measurement. *Information Systems Research*, *11*(1), 37–60. doi:10.1287/isre.11.1.37.11782

Markus, M. L., & Benjamin, R. I. (1996). Change Agentry - the Next IS Frontier. *Management Information Systems Quarterly*, *20*(4), 385–407. doi:10.2307/249561

Marsh, E. (2018). Understanding the Effect of Digital Literacy on Employees' Digital Workplace Continuance Intentions and Individual Performance. *International Journal of Digital Literacy and Digital Competence*, *9*(2), 15–33. doi:10.4018/IJDLDC.2018040102

Merriam-Webster. (2018). Retrieved from http://www.merriam-webster.com/

Miller, C., & Bartlett, J. (2012). 'Digital fluency': Towards young people's critical use of the internet. *Journal of Information Literacy*, *6*(2), 35–55. doi:10.11645/6.2.1714

Nguyen, T. H., Mewby, M., & Macaulay, M. L. (2015). Information Technology Adoption in Small Business: Confirmation of a Proposed Framework. *Journal of Small Business Management*, *53*(1), 207–227. doi:10.1111/jsbm.12058

Palacios-Marqués, D., Soto-Acosta, P., & Merigó, J. M. (2015). Analyzing the effects of technological, organizational and competition factors on Web knowledge exchange in SMEs. *Telematics and Informatics, 32*(1), 23–32. doi:10.1016/j.tele.2014.08.003

Pavlou, P. A., & El Sawy, O. A. (2006). From IT Leveraging Competence to Competitive Advantage in Turbulent Environments: The Case of New Product Development. *Information Systems Research, 17*(3), 198–227. doi:10.1287/isre.1060.0094

Peltier, J. W., Zhao, Y., & Schibrowsky, J. A. (2012). Technology adoption by small businesses: An exploratory study of the interrelationships of owner and environmental factors. *International Small Business Journal, 30*(4), 406–431. doi:10.1177/0266242610365512

Rivard, S. (2014). Editor's Comments: The Ions of Construction. *Management Information Systems Quarterly, 38*(2), iii–xiii.

Savin-Baden, M. (2015). *Rethinking Learning in an Age of Digital Fluency: Is being digitally tethered a new learning nexus?* Routledge.

Selznick, P. (1957). *Leadership in Administration: A Sociological Interpretation.* Evanston, IL: Row, Peterson & Co.

Seppanen, V. (2002). Evolution of competence in software contracting projects. *International Journal of Project Management, 20*(2), 155–164. doi:10.1016/S0263-7863(00)00043-0

Soto-Acosta, P., Popa, S., & Martinez-Conesa, I. (2018). Information technology, knowledge management and environmental dynamism as drivers of innovation ambidexterity: A study in SMEs. *Journal of Knowledge Management, 22*(4), 824–849. doi:10.1108/JKM-10-2017-0448

van Laar, E., van Deursen, A. J., van Dijk, J. A., & de Haan, J. (2017). The relation between 21st-century skills and digital skills: A systematic literature review. *Computers in Human Behavior, 72*, 577–588. doi:10.1016/j.chb.2017.03.010

van Laar, E., van Deursen, A. J., van Dijk, J. A., & de Haan, J. (2018). 21st-century digital skills instrument aimed at working professionals: Conceptual development and empirical validation. *Telematics and Informatics, 35*(8), 2184–2200. doi:10.1016/j.tele.2018.08.006

Verbano, C., & Crema, M. (2016). Linking technology innovation strategy, intellectual capital and technology innovation performance in manufacturing SMEs. *Technology Analysis and Strategic Management, 28*(5), 524–540. doi:10.1080/09537325.2015.1117066

Wang, E., Myers, M. D., & Sundaram, D. (2012). *Digital Natives and Digital Immigrants: towards a Model of Digital fluency.* Paper presented at the ECIS.

Wang, R., Wiesemes, R., & Gibbons, C. (2012). Developing digital fluency through ubiquitous mobile devices: Findings from a small-scale study. *Computers & Education, 58*(1), 570–578. doi:10.1016/j.compedu.2011.04.013

Yin, R. K. (2013). *Case Study Research: Design and Methods.* Thousand Oaks, CA: SAGE Publication.

ENDNOTE

[1]   Capturing and evaluating the cognitive knowledge, skills and attitudes of each respondent via semi structured interviews have been challenging. A more appropriate approach would have been to use an evaluation questionnaire. While we have been able to collect data related to the cognitive area in each of the three case studies, we have not been able to evaluate this area and thus, we left it blank in Figures 2, 3 and 4.

Chapter 4

Introducing the Computer–Related Self–Concept:
A New Approach to Investigate Gender Differences in Computing Careers

Monique Janneck
Luebeck University of Applied Sciences, Germany

Sylvie Vincent-Höper
University of Hamburg, Germany

Jasmin Ehrhardt
University of Hamburg, Germany

ABSTRACT

The number of women in STEM fields, especially in computer science, is still very low. Therefore, in this chapter, the computer-related self-concept (CSC) is presented as a new approach to investigate gender differences in computing careers. The computer-related self-concept comprises computer-related attitudes, emotions, and behaviors, integrating different lines of research on computer-related self-cognitions. To establish connections with career development, an extensive online survey was conducted with more than 1100 male and female computing professionals. Results show that men have a significantly more positive computer-related self-concept than women. Furthermore, as hypothesized, the computer-related self-concept shows high correlations with career motivation. Therefore, it is concluded that the computer-related self-concept is a feasible approach to investigate and understand computer-related gender differences. Possible implications regarding measures to foster women's careers in computing are discussed along with prospects for future research.

DOI: 10.4018/978-1-5225-8933-4.ch004

INTRODUCTION

Even towards the end of the second decade of the 21st century, the number of women in STEM (Science, Technology, Engineering, Mathematics) fields is still very low. This holds especially true for Computer Science. Regarding western industrialized countries, the percentage of women in technical fields has stagnated at 10-20% or has even been declining (Black, Jameson, Komoss, Mehan, & Numerico, 2005; Galpin, 2002; National Science Foundation, 2011, 2014; Michelmore & Sassler, 2016; Zweben, 2011; Sax et al. 2016; Beyer, 2014). This is true despite many efforts in primary and secondary schools as well as universities to increase the number of female students.

Even worse, women who successfully graduated from a STEM-related course of study often encounter obstacles in their career development (e.g. Black et al., 2005) or even never take up a STEM-related job after graduation (Xu, 2017). In computing, women's career success is lower than men's both short-term and long-term, even though their qualification level is equal (Wolffram, Derboven, & Winker, 2009; Zweben, 2011, Fouad & Santana, 2017).

One reason for the lack of women in technical fields is that computers and information technology are still perceived as a traditionally male domain. Even though children today grow up as 'digital natives' with information technology omnipresent in their lives, girls and young women are still less confident and experienced in using computers and have lower interest in technology in general (Bamberg & Vincent-Höper, 2017; Miliszewska & Horwood, 2000; Symonds, 2000; Wetzel, 2002; Woodbury, 2002; Sassler, Glass, Levitte, & Michelmore, 2016; Sax et al., 2016; Beyer, 2014). In short, they seem to integrate computer-related activities and skills into their *self-concept* to a much lesser extent.

Therefore, in this paper we explore a new approach to analyze and understand gender differences in computing: The *computer-related self-concept (CSC),* which comprises all computer-related emotions, attitudes, and behaviors. Building on prior research on self-related cognitions and self-perceptions (Super, Starishevsky, Matlin, & Jordaan, 1963) we posit that computer-related self-perceptions will impact career choices and development in technical fields.

The chapter is structured as follows: In the Background section the related work regarding self-concept and career development is described. Building on that, we develop our model of the computer-related self-concept. Subsequently, we present the results of an extensive online survey that was conducted with over 1100 computing professionals. Using a newly developed and validated questionnaire to measure the computer-related self-concept, we investigated gender differences and the relationship with career motivation. We discuss practical implications of our findings and prospects for future research.

BACKGROUND

A person's *self-concept* is usually understood as representation of all of his / her self-referred attitudes and is seen as crucial determinant of human behavior. The self-concept is conceptualized as a multidimensional, hierarchical structure (Shavelson, Hubner, & Stanton, 1976). That means that the general self-concept is comprised of a multitude of specific self-referred cognitions which are related to different experiences and areas of life. An important aspect of the self-concept are so-called *ability concepts*, i.e. a person's notions about his/her academic performance in a variety of fields (e.g. how well one does regarding mathematical or language skills). Ability concepts have an impact on academic performance (e.g. Guay, Marsh, & Boivin, 2003) as well as a person's expectations for success in that field (see e.g. Eccles, Roeser, Wigfield, & Freedman-Doan, 2006) and might therefore also influence career development and success.

Our new approach of the *computer-related self-concept* takes up and integrates various findings regarding computer-related self-referred attitudes, thus constituting an academic ability concept comprising computer-related skills, interests, experiences, attitudes, and beliefs. Drawing on the classic Three-Components-Model of Attitudes by Rosenberg & Hovland (1960), we suggest a *multidimensional model* consisting of three components that influence each other mutually (figure 1):

- The *conative component,* representing activities, behaviors, and experiences related to computers throughout one's life.
- The *motivational component,* comprising positive as well as negative emotions, attitudes, and individual reasons and motivations for using computers.
- The *cognitive* component, involving a person's self-perceived competencies and self-efficacy regarding computer use, strategies for handling (new) information technology, and computer-related attribution processes.

The self-concept is usually conceptualized as a rather stable construct (e.g. McCrae & Costa, 1982). Nevertheless, self-referred cognitions are subject to ongoing evaluation and reappraisal. For example, positive experiences when using and mastering computers might lead to a higher feeling of self-efficacy and thus to a more positive computer-related self-concept.

In the last few decades, a large number of studies dealing with computer-related behaviors, attitudes, emotions, and cognitions have been published, most of them focusing on gender differences. In the following sections, we summarize the results with respect to conative, motivational, and cognitive aspects.

Figure 1. Model of the computer-related self-concept based on the Three-Components-Model of Attitudes (Rosenberg & Hovland, 1960)

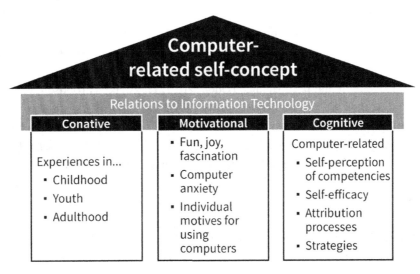

Conative Aspects

One of the most consistent findings concerning computer-related self-evaluations is that girls have significantly less experience using computers than boys do (see e.g. Nelson & Cooper, 1997; Siann, Macleod, Glissov, & Drundell, 1990; Whitley, 1997, He & Freeman, 2010; Ash, Rosenbloom, Coder, & Dupont, 2006; Varma, 2009; Schmidt, 2011). However, some authors (e.g. Beckers & Schmidt, 2001; Whitley, 1997) point out that it is not the quantity, but rather the quality and appraisal of computer-related experiences, which is crucial for future computer use.

Motivational Aspects

Boys more often report positive affects when dealing with computers, whereas girls and women tend to be more anxious (e.g. Campbell, 1990; Chua, Chen, & Wong, 1999, see also the meta-analyses by Whitley, 1997 and – most recently – Cai, Fan, & Du, 2017). According to Chua and colleagues (1999), computer anxiety is one possible reason for long-term avoidance of computers. This may also result in a disinclination to choose a career in computing, which might be especially important for girls/women.

There are also gender differences regarding individual motives for using computers: Men are often intrinsically motivated and interested in dealing with computers (Campbell, 1990; Siann et al., 1990), whereas women often pursue a more pragmatic approach, using computers as tools, without showing a deeper interest in the ways computers work (e.g. Wetzel, 2002; Beyer, 2014).

Cognitive Aspects

Although girls and women generally believe that males and females possess similar computer-related competencies (e.g. North & Noyes, 2002), they nevertheless show a strong tendency to evaluate their own, personal competencies less positively than boys and men do (e.g. Nelson & Cooper, 1997; Shashaani & Khalili, 2001; Litt, 2013; Tømte & Hatlevik, 2011). Similarly, girls and women typically rate their own computer-related self-efficacy more negatively than boys and men (e.g. Durndell, Haag, & Laithwaite, 2000; Sieverding & Koch, 2009, Fraillon et al., 2014).

Self-efficacy is defined as the personal judgment of "how well one can execute courses of action required to deal with prospective situations" (Bandura, 1986, p. 122). Whereas individuals who feel confident in their abilities are intrinsically motivated to perform, people who doubt their capabilities shy away from difficult tasks, surrender quickly in the face of obstacles, and generally tend to be less motivated and productive (Bandura, 1977). Computer self-efficacy is positively related to computer literacy, learning engagement and performance (Chen, 2017; Hatlevik, Throndsen, Loi, & Gudmundsdottir, 2018). Therefore, the lower computer-related self-efficacy seen in girls and women weakens their tendency to choose careers in computing and related fields. In contrast, boys and men benefit from their high self-efficacy, which fosters intrinsic interest and deep immersion in computer-related activities.

Closely connected to self-efficacy, patterns of *attribution* are used to subjectively explain behavior or events. Recent research has established a typology of computer-related attribution styles and shown how it influences computer use (Niels & Janneck, 2015; Niels & Janneck, 2017; Niels, Jent, Janneck, & Zagel, 2019).

Regarding computer use, girls often explain their success as being a result of external factors, such as task difficulty or general luck, whereas they attribute failures internally to a lack of ability (e.g.

Campbell, 1990; Nelson & Cooper, 1997). This attribution pattern is seen as harmful to self-efficacy and performance (Bandura, 1977).

Conversely, boys show the opposite computer-related attribution pattern. They tend to attribute successes internally to their own talents and abilities, while failure is attributed externally to task difficulty or accident, thus enhancing their motivation and performance when dealing with computers (Campbell, 1990; Nelson & Cooper, 1997).

Along with patterns of attribution, there are personal *control beliefs,* which describe the perceived control that an individual has over a particular situation (Kay, 1990). Internal control beliefs, i.e. believing that interaction with computers is determined by personal actions and not by external factors, are positively correlated with computer literacy (Kay, 1990). Sølvberg (2002) showed that boys exhibit more internal control beliefs and confidence in their computer-related activities than girls do. Gender differences vanished after participating in a computer training program.

Regarding individual strategies when dealing with computers, women are often found to be less experimental and playful (Wetzel, 2002). For example, Linn (1985) investigated strategies for playing computer games, showing that boys were more likely to experiment and to take risks, thus leading to a better understanding of the game. Girls, however, tended to follow the instructions closely, were less willing to take risks, and asked for help more often, resulting in a poorer performance.

Self-Concept, Vocational Development, and Intrinsic Career Motivation

Several well-established occupational theories have linked the self-concept to career development and career success: "The process of vocational development is essentially that of developing and implementing a self-concept." (Super, 1953, p. 190). Since the self-concept changes and is successively refined throughout people's lives as a result of experience, career success can be considered either the individual adjustment to situational requirements, or the adaptation of situational requirements to his/her needs (Super, 1953; Super et al., 1963). Similarly, in his career congruence theory, Holland (1959) emphasized the role of an accurate self-concept as people search for environments that allow them to utilize their skills and abilities, express their attitudes and values, and take on suitable problems and roles. In short, individuals are drawn to occupations that meet their personal needs and provide them with satisfaction.

One important predictor of career success is *career motivation* (Grzeda, 1999; London, 1993; London & Noe, 1997; Lopes, 2006). An especially crucial role is played by *intrinsic* career motivation (Abele, 2000), which describes one's willingness to perform well and make a determined effort based on a high interest level and enjoyment when performing a vocational task. Enjoyment of the task, deliberately taking over responsibility and making decisions, as well as the desire to explore new tasks are all prerequisites for reaching managerial positions.

Consequently, one can deduce that the computer-related self-concept can have an important impact on the career development of men and women working in information technology professions.

Research Questions

Taking into consideration the state of research on gender-specific differences in computer-related self-assessments, it can be summarized that girls and women tend to integrate computer-related attitudes *into their self-concept* in a more negative way than boys and men do. This may cause avoidance of computers and computer-related career choices. Furthermore, we assume that these differences still persist for women who indeed chose a career in computing. This is a novel approach since the bulk of existing research typically focuses on children and young adults.

Thus, as a first research question, we investigated if – and to what extent – men have a more positive computer-related self-concept than women even among information technology professionals. If so, a more negative computer-related self-concept might not only explain general underrepresentation of women in computing, but also their difficulties advancing to higher positions in this field, as the self-concept is closely related to career success and development: People strive for occupations that fit, boost, and positively influence their individual self-image.

Therefore, as a second research question we aim to investigate whether the computer-related self-concept is related to career development in information technology professions. We measured *intrinsic career motivation* as an indicator of career success, since it has been shown to be an important factor for career success and development (e. g. Abele, 2000).

METHODOLOGY

Procedure and Sample

As part of a research project on women's career advancement, especially in technical fields, we conducted an online survey among computing professionals with a total of N=1129 participants (57% male, 43% female). All participants were highly skilled, meaning they had earned a degree in Computer Science or related fields. Men and women did not differ in terms of their education and skills. Participants were recruited via professional associations and several international software companies. The mean age of the sample was 40 years (SD=7.45). 30% of participants had been employed for less than 10 years, 52% for 10-20 years, and 19% for more than 20 years (M=13 yrs). Among the respondents, 17% had managerial responsibility.

Measures

Computer-Related Self-Concept

As the computer-related self-concept constitutes a new theoretical construct, we had to develop a new psychometric instrument to assess the different aspects of computer-related cognitions described above. In the first step, we conducted a qualitative interview study with men and women working in technical professions (N=35). The results of this study served to further elaborate the CSC model and also provided the basis for the development of a CSC questionnaire. Subsequently, two quantitative studies were conducted, one with Computer Science students (N=236) and another with computing professionals (N=116), in order to test, improve, and validate the questionnaire. The number of items was reduced and in some cases items were reformulated to improve the psychometric values.

The final CSC questionnaire consists of 11 subscales with a total of 27 items, collecting conative, motivational, and cognitive computer-related self-ratings using a five-point Likert scale ("1= strongly disagree" to "5= strongly agree"). The subscales were theoretically derived from prior research and related work (see section 2), and refined by applying the results of our interview study. In particular, the three subscales measuring the motives for using computers – understanding, creating, and as a tool

Table 1. The CSC questionnaire (translation of the original German questionnaire)

	Subscales		
	Practical Experiences		
Conative	I gained practical experiences using computers at an early age.		
	(-) I did not deal with computers much in my childhood and youth.		
	In my free time, I use computers a lot (e.g. Internet, picture editing, games…).		
Motivational	**Positive Emotions**		
	I have a lot of fun using computers.		
	Computer technology fascinates me.		
	Computer Anxiety		
	When dealing with computers, I am afraid of doing something wrong.		
	When using computers, I am scared of screwing something up or accidentally deleting data.		
	I feel anxious when using computers.		
	Understanding		
	I want to understand how computers work.		
	When computer technology does not work, I want to understand the reason why.		
	Creating		
	I like to create things with computers (e.g. programming, graphics processing…).		
	I deal with computers because I can create things with them.		
	Tool Perspective		
	For me, computers are only a means to an end.		
	I simply want computers to work alright, I'm not interested in technical details.		
Cognitive	**Computer-Related Competencies**		
	I consider myself very competent at handling computer devices.		
	I'm more confident than the average person when using computers.		
	I have comprehensive computer knowledge.		
	Computer-Related Self-Efficacy		
	I keep cool when confronted with computer problems because I can always rely on my computer skills.		
	I'm up for most computer-related challenges.		
	When I'm confronted with computer problems, I find ways and means to solve them.		
	When I try hard, I generally succeed in finding solutions to computer problems.		
	Computer-Related Internal Attribution		
	When a computer device doesn't work right, generally it is because I have done something wrong.		
	When a computer problem occurs, usually I have caused it.		
	Computer-Related External Control Beliefs		
	I have no control over computer difficulties that occur.		
	Software functionality often seems random to me.		
	Computer-Related Strategies		
	I am not shy about simply trying out new software.		
	I usually try out new computer applications intuitively at first.		

– were derived from the interview study. There were clear differences in the motives reported by men and women.

The questionnaire is shown in table 1. Psychometric values are given in table 2.

Intrinsic Career Motivation

Intrinsic career motivation was measured using an adapted 6-item version of Abele's (2000) *intrinsic career motivation* scale. Items focus on openness to risk, willingness to learn, acceptance of responsibility, joy at work, individual initiative, and vocational self-efficacy, using seven-point Likert scales ("1= strongly disagree" to "7= strongly agree"). A sample item is: "I want to take responsibility in my job." The internal consistency was good (α= .80).

RESULTS

Data were analyzed using the Statistical Package for Social Sciences (version 18.0) and Amos Graphics (version 18.0). The statistical procedures included a reliability analysis and Confirmatory Factor Analysis in order to test the model quality, as well as a one-sided t-test for independent samples and bivariate Spearman's rank correlations.

Descriptive Statistics, Reliability, and Validity Estimates

Table 2 shows the mean (M), standard deviation (SD), internal consistency (Cronbach's α), and the item-total-correlation (r_{it}) for the subscales of the CSC questionnaire.

In general, as would be expected in a sample of computing professionals, respondents reported a very positive computer-related self-concept. The subscales with the highest mean responses were computer-

Table 2. CSC subscales: Mean (M), standard deviation (SD), internal consistency (Cronbach's α), of item-total-correlation (r_{it})

Subscales	M	SD	α	r_{it}
Practical experiences	3.45	1.03	.66	.37-.58
Positive emotions	3.59	1.05	.66	.66
Computer anxiety	1.32	0.52	.81	.61-.72
Understanding	3.55	1.13	.82	.71
Creating	3.66	1.10	.78	.64
Tool perspective	2.99	1.14	.74	.59
Competencies	3.88	0.84	.87	.75-.79
Self-efficacy	3.96	0.77	.90	.74-.80
Internal attribution	2.33	0.83	.82	.70
External control beliefs	1.92	0.76	.61	.44
Strategies	4.23	0.74	.72	.57

Table 3. Fit Indices of the 11-factorial CSC model

χ^2	df	p	χ^2/df	RMSEA	90% CI RMSEA	CFI
1197.033	269	.000	4.450	.055	.052-.059	.945

related *Strategies* (M=4.23), *Self-Efficacy* (M=3.96), and *Competencies* (M=3.88). The four scales indicating a negative or unfavorable self-concept – *Computer anxiety, Tool perspective, Internal attribution,* and *External control beliefs* – provided the lowest means, with the lowest values for *Computer anxiety* (M=1.32). The CSC subscales show acceptable to very good reliability coefficients (.61 $\leq \alpha \geq$ .90, see Everitt & Skrondal, 2010), particularly considering the small number of items.

The construct validity of the instrument was tested using Confirmatory Factor Analysis. The fit of the theoretical model was compared in terms of its Chi-square (χ^2) value in relation to the degrees of freedom (Normed Chi-square, NC), as well as the Comparative Fit Index (CFI) and the Root Mean Square Error of Approximation (RMSEA). General guidelines suggest an NC of χ^2/df > 5 (Marsh & Hocevar, 1985). An RMSEA < .05 indicates a close fit, .05 > RMSEA < .08 a reasonable fit, .08 > RMSEA < .10 an acceptable fit, and RMSEA > .10 an unacceptable fit (Hu & Bentler, 1999). For CFI, a value of .90 or higher indicates an acceptable fit and .94 or higher demonstrates a good fit (Hu & Bentler, 1999) (see table 3). The results indicate that the empirical data provide good fit for the theoretically postulated scales or CSC model (see table 3).

Gender Differences Regarding the Computer-Related Self-Concept

Hypothesis 1 predicts that even among computing professionals, men will have a more positive computer-related self-concept than women. In order to test this assumption, we conducted a one-sided t-test for independent samples, comparing men's and women's mean scores in computer-related self-ratings. Applying the Kolmogorov-Smirnov-test, none of the CSC variables were found to be normally distributed, a necessary precondition for the t-test. However, this procedure is resilient against violations when the sample size is large, which was the case here (Triola, 2009). Hedges "g" was used to assess the effect size of mean differences (Hedges & Olkin, 1985). Results are presented in table 4.

Results show highly significant gender differences for all CSC scales. Overall, effect sizes range from -0.54 $\leq$ g $\geq$ 0.87.

Male participants rate themselves significantly more positively on favorable aspects of the computer-related self-concept (*Practical experiences, Positive emotions, Understanding, Creating, Competencies, Self-efficacy, Strategies, External control beliefs*). The effect sizes are strong (0.66 $\leq$ g $\leq$ 0.74) or very strong (g > 0.8) for all aspects except *Strategies*, where the effect size is moderate (g = 0.32) (Cohen, 1988).

Concerning the more disadvantageous CSC facets, women score significantly higher on three out of four scales, with medium effect sizes for *Computer anxiety* (g = -0.42) and *Tool perspective* (g = -0.54), and weak effects for *External control beliefs* (g = -0.17). Men only score higher on *Internal attributions*.

In sum, men clearly show a more positive computer-related self-concept than woman.

Table 4. Gender differences in computer-related self-ratings

Subscales	Males		Females		T	df	p	g
	M	SD	M	SD				
Practical experiences	3.75	0.97	3.07	0.97	11.466	1105	.000	0.70
Positive emotions	3.90	0.96	3.18	1.02	12.114	1104	.000	0.74
Computer anxiety	1.23	0.41	1.44	0.63	-6.598	772	.000	-0.42
Understanding	3.88	1.00	3.10	1.14	11.892	941	.000	0.74
Creating	3.95	0.95	3.26	1.15	10.550	910	.000	0.66
Tool perspective	2.73	1.10	3.33	1.11	-8.900	1100	.000	-0.54
Competencies	4.15	0.74	3.51	0.84	13.000	932	.000	0.81
Self-efficacy	4.23	0.67	3.61	0.76	13.983	923	.000	0.87
Internal attributions	2.42	0.84	2.21	0.78	4.209	1035	.000	0.25
External control beliefs	1.86	0.73	1.99	0.81	-2.797	1083	.003	-0.17
Strategies	4.34	0.70	4.11	0.77	5.145	1085	.000	0.32

Note. N_{male} = 629, N_{female} = 470; M= mean, SD= standard deviation; T= test value, df= degree of freedom, p= significance level (one-sided), g= effect size.

Computer-Related Self-Concept and Intrinsic Career Motivation

Furthermore, we suggested that the computer-related self-concept is related to intrinsic career motivation in information technology professions. Since the CSC scales are not distributed normally, we used the non-parametric Spearman's rank correlation coefficient to test this assumption.

As illustrated in table 5, almost all CSC scales correlate substantially (r ≥ ±.20) and significantly (p ≤.001) with Intrinsic Career Motivation. The highest coefficients were found for *Self-efficacy* (r = .28, p ≤ .001) and *Strategies* (r = .25, p ≤ .001), whereas lowest correlations were found for *Internal attribution* (r = -.03, p ≥ .05) and *Tool perspective* (r = -.07, p ≤ .05). More importantly, results show *positive* correlations between *favorable* CSC aspects and Intrinsic Career Motivation, and *negative* correlations between *unfavorable* CSC aspects and Intrinsic Career Motivation.

Regarding career motivation in itself, slight gender differences were observed. Women score significantly lower on Intrinsic Career Motivation than men (table 6). However, the effect size is low (g=0.14).

Table 5. Spearman's Rank Correlation Coefficients between CSC scales and Intrinsic Career Motivation

		Intrinsic Career Motivation		Intrinsic Career Motivation
CSC	Experience	.22***	Competencies	.23***
	Positive emotions	.21***	Self-efficacy	.28***
	Computer anxiety	-.23***	Internal attribution	-.03
	Understanding	.17***	External control beliefs	-.20***
	Creating	.21***	Strategies	.25***
	Tool perspective	-.07*		

Table 6. Gender differences regarding Intrinsic Career Motivation

Males		Females		T	df	p	g
M	SD	M	SD				
6.02	.61	5.92	.66	2.211	977	.027*	0.14

DISCUSSION

In this chapter, the *computer-related self-concept* was presented as a new approach to analyze and understand computer-related attitudes, emotions, and behaviors, describing the three interrelated facets of *conative*, *motivational*, and *cognitive* components. We used the CSC model to investigate gender differences regarding women's underrepresentation in computing.

Our results from a large online survey with over 1100 computing professionals show that, indeed, men have a significantly more positive computer-related self-concept than women regarding conative, motivational, as well as cognitive aspects. Therefore, the assumptions of our first research question are confirmed.

Regarding the conative component, men are more *experienced* in using computers and information technology. With respect to motivational aspects, they display more *positive emotions* and less *anxiety* towards computers. Furthermore, men are more motivated to actually *understand* how information technology works and to *create* technological artifacts themselves, while women put greater emphasis on computers as useful *tools*, without having a deeper interest in them. Regarding the cognitive component, men describe themselves as more *competent* and feeling more *self-efficient* when using computers than women do. Likewise, men display more favorable *attribution patterns*, feeling more in *control* of computer-related events, and report more favorable *strategies* for dealing with computer technology.

Especially large gender differences were found for computer-related *self-efficacy* (g=.87, with substantially lower scores for women), which also showed the strongest correlation with intrinsic career motivation (r=.21***). Self-efficacy has generally been shown to be an important mediator in the relationship between ability and career intentions (e.g. Hackett & Betz; 1989). Many researchers share the view that self-efficacy is one of the most important elements of self-concepts in various areas (cf. Bong & Skaalvik, 2003).

Our results are in line with long-established previous findings on computer-related gender differences, showing girls and women generally to be more hesitant and anxious when dealing with computers and feeling less competent and in control. These findings have been persistent over many decades (e.g. Campbell, 1990; Chua et al., 1999; Durndell et al., 2000; Nelson & Cooper, 1997) and are still present in recent studies (e.g. Sieverding & Koch, 2009 Schmidt, 2011; Cai, Fan, & Du, 2017; Fraillon et al., 2014). Only one finding is marginally out of place, that is, that men score slightly higher on internal attributions of failure. This might be due to the fact that men typically also display stronger internal attributions of success, which might have influenced their answering behavior in our questionnaire. Thus, it might be advisable to include a scale measuring internal attribution of success in a revised version of the questionnaire, so that the two attribution processes can be differentiated.

Until now, studies have mostly dealt with children, teenagers, or students, whereas our study focused on highly qualified computing professionals. It is striking that even among those who have graduated in Computer Science or related fields and are actively pursuing a career in computing, there's still such a tremendous difference between men's and women's computer-related self-concepts. It seems that early experiences with information technology have a lasting effect – in an environment that is still strongly gender-stereotyped, girls are still less exposed to technology, or at least experience technology in a less playful, less experimental way (e.g. Linn, 1985; Wetzel, 2002). Furthermore, in a male-dominated environment, women lack female role models that might inspire their own career development (BarNir, Hutchins, & Watson, 2011; Beyer, 2014). This will be discussed in more detail in the next section.

It is quite reasonable to assume that having a substantially more negative self-concept is indeed detrimental to women's career development in computer-related professions. As investigated in our second research question, results show that the computer-related self-concept (CSC) is related to *intrinsic career motivation*, a concept which has previously been shown to play a crucial role in pursuing a vital and fulfilling career (Abele, 2000; Grzeda, 1999; London, 1993). Furthermore, our results show *positive* correlations between *favorable* CSC aspects and Intrinsic Career Motivation, as well as *negative* correlations between *unfavorable* CSC aspects and Intrinsic Career Motivation, thus emphasizing the plausibility of our assumptions as well as the criterion validity of the CSC questionnaire. As could be expected from our second research question, in our study women indeed showed a slightly lower level of career motivation than men.

In general, the computer-related self-concept has proven to be a feasible approach to *analyzing and understanding computer-related emotions, attitudes, and behaviors*. In our investigation, we were able to replicate findings regarding gender differences in computer use that stem from research based on a variety of theoretical approaches (cognitive, social psychological, gender studies etc.). In our view, the strength of our approach is that it *integrates different theories and findings* regarding computer-related self-referred attitudes and cognitions, thus providing a broader basis for analysis and intervention design.

Furthermore, our approach *broadens existing self-concept research* by specifically focusing on computers and information technology. While there is already a considerable amount of research on academic and ability-related self-concepts, to our knowledge there has been no theoretical work conceptualizing computer use in this manner. Since information technology plays an important part in daily life, work, and society, it is feasible that it also affects people's self-concepts in a decisive way. Therefore, better understanding of these mechanisms may provide more insight into computer-related cognitions and behaviors.

Moreover, we were able to develop and validate a *psychometric instrument* to measure conative, motivational, as well as cognitive aspects of the computer-related self-concept. Despite its broad focus, we succeeded in developing an easy-to-use and valid questionnaire that demonstrates good psychometric properties. A Confirmatory Factor Analysis affirmed the model structure of the questionnaire, thus showing its construct validity and strengthening our theoretical assumptions. Criterion validity was established by replicating findings on gender differences in computer use and the relationship with intrinsic career motivation. However, discriminant validity must still be established in further studies, e.g. by comparing the CSC questionnaire with other self-concept measures.

A limitation of our investigation is its cross-sectional design. Thus, correlations cannot be interpreted in a causal direction. Hence, for future research, longitudinal studies may help identify factors that influence career development. A second limitation is the single-source design, since only survey data – i.e. self-ratings – were collected. It would be desirable to consider further data sources – e.g. observations of computer-related behavior or diary studies – using a triangulation approach.

Regarding gender, only biological gender differences were assessed. However, for future research it might be interesting to consider gender differences in a more differentiated approach, e.g. measurement that includes gender status beliefs (Ridgeway, 2001) or sex-role stereotyping.

CONCLUSION AND FUTURE RESEARCH DIRECTIONS

Our results indicate that gender stereotypes regarding computing and technology are deeply rooted and may have a long-term impact on behavior and self-conceptions: Even highly skilled women who actively chose and pursue a career in computing show gender-stereotypical patterns regarding their computer-related self-concept.

Therefore, we posit that interventions aimed at raising girls' interest in computers and technology need to start at a much earlier age, preferably in kindergarten and elementary schools. Programs for teenagers and young adults will likely be less successful in achieving profound changes, as gender-specific behavioral patterns and self-conceptions are already rather stable and resilient to change at that age. That way, hopefully girls will develop a positive computer-related self-concept from the beginning, instead of having to overcome negative experiences and attitudes later on.

In our view, it is not necessary to provide girls with special "training" for computers. As computers and information technology are omnipresent in everyday life, girls naturally grow up surrounded by technology and learn how to use it just like boys do. However, we need to break with the stereotypes indicating that technical toys and appliances are "for boys" and "not for girls," because practical experience using computers and technology is essential for developing a sense of self-efficacy. This implies that both family members and educators must change their perspectives and behaviors.

As previously noted, the availability of *role models* has a positive effect on career development (BarNir et al., 2011, Beyer, 2014). A lack of role models has been identified as a barrier for women entering and persevering in non-traditional fields (Basow & Howe, 1980; Betz & Fitzgerald, 1987; Hackett & Betz, 1989). BarNir et al. (2011) found that the availability of role models influences the feeling of self-efficacy, especially for women. Therefore we assume that, correspondingly, the lack of female role models in computing professions might have a negative impact on women's feelings of computer related self-efficacy – with negative consequences for women's career motivation and development in computing professions. To put it positively, women might benefit from female role models in computing professions because the availability of such role models might strengthen their computer-related self-concept, and thus their career motivation as well. More research is necessary to confirm these assumptions.

While societal change is a slow and difficult process, workplace measures might help to boost the careers of women in computing professions. Supervisors should be trained to reflect on their behavior towards male and female employees: Do men and women receive similar feedback? Do they assign them similar duties and responsibilities? Do they give them equal credit for their competencies and skills? Last but not least, do they receive equal pay?

In future research, it would be interesting to take a closer look at successful women in computing as role models. What characteristics do they have, and how have they coped with gender stereotypes and the difficulties arising from them? Furthermore, research is needed on how facets of the computer-related self-concept change over time, and also what measures and interventions help people successfully overcome negative computer-related self-cognitions.

Beyond the topic of women in computing explored in this paper, the computer-related self-concept is also a feasible construct to be explored in the field of human-computer interaction. In particular, we assume that differences in the computer-related self-concept will not only influence computer-related attitudes and behaviors generally, but will also result in different usage patterns and characteristics for specific computer applications. Thus, including computer-related self-concept measurements in *user studies* might provide additional insights into user behavior. For example, our own research on attribution styles (e.g. Niels & Janneck, 2015, 2017) showed that different attribution styles (e.g. attributing computer malfunctions to technical or programming errors versus one's own lack of competencies or other external factors) leads to different evaluations of a (faulty) technical artifact (Niels & Janneck, 2016). Eventually, analyzing the computer-related self-concept might also inform *design principles* for information technology, as different types of users might respond better to different interaction styles, help documents, and types of user support, among other aspects.

DISCUSSION QUESTIONS FOR CLASSROOMS

- What are your own experiences with ICT? At what age do you remember starting to use computers / mobile devices?
- In your experience, do girls and boys still handle technology differently?
- Do you have female role models in computing or other STEM fields?
- What gender stereotypes do you experience regarding technology use?
- When do you expect current gender stereotypes regarding technology to change? 5 years? 10 years? 20 years?
- What could be done to strengthen girl's/women's computer-related self-efficacy?
- What could be done to get more girls / women interested in computing and other STEM fields?

ACKNOWLEDGMENT

This work has been funded by the German Federal Ministry of Research and Education (BMBF) and the European Social Fund (ESF) under grant no. 01FP0831/ 01FP0841.

REFERENCES

Abele, A. E. (2000). A Dual Impact Model of Gender and Career related Processes. In T. Eckes & H.-M. Trautner (Eds.), *The developmental social psychology of gender* (pp. 361–388). Mahwah, NJ: Erlbaum.

Ash, R. A., Rosenbloom, J. L., Coder, L., & Dupont, B. (2006). Personality characteristics of established IT professionals I: Big Five personality characteristics. In E. M. Trauth (Ed.), *Encyclopedia of gender and information technology* (pp. 983–989). Hershey, PA: Idea Publishing. doi:10.4018/978-1-59140-815-4.ch155

Bamberg, E., & Vincent-Höper, S. (2017). Occupation and gender. In *Reference Module Neuroscience and Biobehavioral Psychology*. Elsevier; doi:10.1016/B978-0-12-809324-5.05642-X

Bandura, A. (1977). Self-Efficacy: Towards a unifying theory of behavioral change. *Psychological Review, 84*(2), 191–215. doi:10.1037/0033-295X.84.2.191 PMID:847061

Bandura, A. (1986). *Social Foundations of Thought and Action: A Social Cognitive Theory*. Englewood Cliffs, NJ: Prentice-Hall.

BarNir, A., Watson, W. E., & Hutchins, H. M. (2011). Mediation and Moderated Mediation in the Relationship Among Role Models, Self-Efficacy, Entrepreneurial Career Intention, and Gender. *Journal of Applied Social Psychology, 41*(2), 270–297. doi:10.1111/j.1559-1816.2010.00713.x

Basow, S. A., & Howe, K. G. (1980). Role-model influence: Effects of sex and sex-role attitude in college students. *Psychology of Women Quarterly, 4*(4), 558–572. doi:10.1111/j.1471-6402.1980.tb00726.x

Beckers, J. J., & Schmidt, H. G. (2001). The structure of computer anxiety: A six factor model. *Computers in Human Behavior, 17*(1), 35–49. doi:10.1016/S0747-5632(00)00036-4

Betz, N. E., & Fitzgerald, L. F. (1987). *The career psychology of women.* San Diego, CA: Academic Press.

Beyer, S. (2014). Why are women underrepresented in Computer Science? Gender differences in stereotypes, self-efficacy, values, and interests and predictors of future CS course-taking and grades. *Computer Science Education, 24*(2-3), 153–192. doi:10.1080/08993408.2014.963363

Black, S. E., Jameson, J., Komoss, R., Mehan, A., & Numerico, T. (2005). Women in computing: A European and international perspective. *Proceedings of the 3rd European Symposium on Gender & ICT, Weston Conference Centre,* 1-13.

Bong, M., & Skaalvik, E. M. (2003). Academic self-concept and self-efficacy: How different are they really? *Educational Psychology Review, 15*(1), 1–40. doi:10.1023/A:1021302408382

Campbell, N. J. (1990). High School Student's Computer Attitudes and Attributions: Gender and Ethnic Group Differences. *Journal of Adolescent Research, 5*, 485–499. doi:10.1177/074355489054007

Chen, I.-S. (2017). Computer self-efficacy, learning performance, and the mediating role of learning engagement. *Computers in Human Behavior, 72*, 362–370. doi:10.1016/j.chb.2017.02.059

Chua, S. L., Chen, D.-T., & Wong, A. F. L. (1999). Computer anxiety and its correlates: A meta analysis. *Computers in Human Behavior, 15*(5), 609–623. doi:10.1016/S0747-5632(99)00039-4

Cohen, J. (1988). *Statistical Power Analysis for the Behavioral Sciences.* Mahwah, NJ: Erlbaum.

Corbett, C., & Hill, C. (2015). *Solving the Equation: the Variables for Women's Success in Engineering and Computing.* Washington, DC: The American Association of University Women.

Dickhäuser, O., & Meyer, W.-U. (2006). Gender differences in young children's math ability attributions. *Psychological Science, 48*(1), 3–16.

Durndell, A., Haag, Z., & Laithwaite, H. (2000). Computer self-efficacy and gender: A cross cultural study of Scotland and Romania. *Personality and Individual Differences, 28*(6), 1037–1044. doi:10.1016/S0191-8869(99)00155-5

Eccles, J. S., Roeser, R., Wigfield, A., & Freedman-Doan, C. (2006). Academic and motivational pathways through middle childhood. In L. Balter & C. S. Tamis-LeMonda (Eds.), *Child psychology: a handbook of contemporary issues* (pp. 325–356). New York, NY: Psychology Press.

Everitt, B. S., & Skrondal, A. (2010). *The Cambridge Dictionary of Statistics.* Cambridge, UK: Cambridge University Press. doi:10.1017/CBO9780511779633

Fouad, N. A., & Santana, M. C. (2017). SCCT and Underrepresented Populations in STEM Fields: Moving the Needle. *Journal of Career Assessment*, *25*(1), 24–39. doi:10.1177/1069072716658324

Fraillon, J., Ainley, J., Schulz, W., Friedman, T., & Gebhardt, E. (2014). *Preparing for Life in a Digital Age – The IEA International Computer and Information Literacy Study. International Report*. Amsterdam: IEA.

Galpin, V. C. (2002). Women in Computing Around the World. *ACM SIGCSE Bulletin*, *34*(2), 94–100. doi:10.1145/543812.543839

Grzeda, M. (1999). Career development and emerging managerial career patterns. *Journal of Career Development*, *25*(4), 233–247. doi:10.1177/089484539902500401

Guay, F., Marsh, H. W., & Boivin, M. (2003). Academic self-concept and academic achievement: Developmental perspectives on their causal ordering. *Journal of Educational Psychology*, *95*(1), 124–136. doi:10.1037/0022-0663.95.1.124

Hackett, G., & Betz, N. E. (1989). An exploration of the mathematics self-efficacy/mathematics performance correspondence. *Journal for Research in Mathematics Education*, *20*(3), 261–273. doi:10.2307/749515

Hackett, G., Esposito, D., & O'Halloran, M. S. (1989). The relationship of role model influences to the career salience and educational and career plans of college women. *Journal of Vocational Behavior*, *35*(2), 164–180. doi:10.1016/0001-8791(89)90038-9

Hatlevik, O. E., Throndsen, I., Loi, M., & Gudmundsdottir, G. B. (2018). Students' ICT self-efficacy and computer and information literacy: Determinants and relationships. *Computers & Education*, *118*, 107–119. doi:10.1016/j.compedu.2017.11.011

He, J., & Freeman, L. A. (2010). Are men more technology-oriented than women? The role of gender on the development of general computer self-efficacy of college students. *Journal of Information Systems Education*, *21*, 203–212.

Hedges, L. V., & Olkin, I. (1985). *Statistical methods for meta-analysis*. Orlando, FL: Academic Press.

Holland, J. L. (1959). A theory of vocational choice. *Journal of Counseling Psychology*, *6*(1), 35–45. doi:10.1037/h0040767

Hu, L.-T., & Bentler, P. M. (1999). Cutoff criteria for fit indexes in covariance structure analysis: Conventional criteria versus new alternatives. *Structural Equation Modeling*, *6*(1), 1–55. doi:10.1080/10705519909540118

Kay, R. H. (1990). The relation between computer literacy and locus of control. *Journal of Research on Computing in Education*, *22*(4), 464–474. doi:10.1080/08886504.1990.10781935

Linn, M. C. (1985). Gender equity in computer learning environments. *Computers and the Social Sciences*, *1*(1), 19–27. doi:10.1177/089443938500100103

Litt, E. (2013). Measuring users' internet skills: A review of past assessments and a look toward the future. *New Media & Society*, *15*(4), 612–630. doi:10.1177/1461444813475424

London, M. (1993). Relationships between career motivation, empowerment and support for career development. *Journal of Occupational and Organizational Psychology*, *66*(1), 55–69. doi:10.1111/j.2044-8325.1993.tb00516.x

London, M., & Noe, R. A. (1997). London's career motivation theory: An update on measurement and research. *Journal of Career Assessment*, *5*(1), 61–80. doi:10.1177/106907279700500105

Lopes, T. P. (2006). Career development in foreign-born workers: Where is the career motivation research? *Human Resource Development Review*, *5*(4), 478–493. doi:10.1177/1534484306293925

Marsh, H. W., & Hocevar, D. (1985). Application of confirmatory factor analysis to the study of self-concept: First and higher order factor models and their invariance across groups. *Psychological Bulletin*, *97*(3), 562–582. doi:10.1037/0033-2909.97.3.562

McCrae, R. R., & Costa, P. T. (1982). Self-concept and the stability of personality: Cross-sectional comparisons of self-reports and ratings. *Journal of Personality and Social Psychology*, *43*(6), 1282–129. doi:10.1037/0022-3514.43.6.1282

Michelmore, K., & Sassler, S. (2016). Explaining the gender earnings gap in STEM: Does field group size matter? *The Russell Sage Foundation Journal of the Social Sciences*, *2*(4), 194–215. doi:10.7758/rsf.2016.2.4.07

Miliszewska, I., & Horwood, J. (2000). Women in Computer Science. In E. Balka & R. Smith (Eds.), *Women, Work and Computerization – Charting a Course to the Future* (pp. 50–57). Boston, MA: Kluwer. doi:10.1007/978-0-387-35509-2_7

National Science Foundation. (2011). *Women, Minorities, and Persons with Disabilities in Science and Engineering*. Author.

National Science Foundation. (2014). *Integrated postsecondary education data system, 2013, completions survey*. National Center for Science and Engineering Statistics: Integrated Science and Engineering Resources Data System (WebCASPAR). Retrieved from https://webcaspar.nsf.gov

Nauta, M. M., Epperson, D. L., & Kahn, J. H. (1998). A multiple-groups analysis of predictors of higher level career aspirations among women in mathematics, science, and engineering majors. *Journal of Counseling Psychology*, *45*(4), 483–496. doi:10.1037/0022-0167.45.4.483

Nelson, L. J., & Cooper, J. (1997). Gender Differences in Children's Reactions to Success and Failure with Computers. *Computers in Human Behavior*, *13*(2), 247–267. doi:10.1016/S0747-5632(97)00008-3

Niels, A., Guczka, S., & Janneck, M. (2016). The Impact of Causal Attributions on System Evaluations in Usability Tests. In *Proceedings of the 2016 CHI Conference on Human Factors in Computing Systems* (pp. 3115-3125). ACM. 10.1145/2858036.2858471

Niels, A., & Janneck, M. (2015). Computer-Related Attribution Styles: Typology and Data Collection Methods. In *INTERACT 2015, Part II, LNCS 9297* (pp. 274–291). Springer International Publishing. doi:10.1007/978-3-319-22668-2_22

Niels, A., & Janneck, M. (2017). Understanding the Relations Between Self-concept and Causal Attributions Regarding Computer Use. In Harris, D. (Ed.), *Engineering Psychology and Cognitive Ergonomics: Performance, Emotion and Situation Awareness: 14th International Conference, EPCE 2017* (pp. 180-199). Springer International Publishing. 10.1007/978-3-319-58472-0_15

Niels, A., Jent, S., Janneck, M., & Zagel, C. (2019). Correlations Between Computer-Related Causal Attributions and User Persistence. In T. Z. Ahram (Ed.), *Advances in Artificial Intelligence, Software and Systems Engineering* (pp. 242–251). Cham: Springer. doi:10.1007/978-3-319-94229-2_23

North, A. S., & Noyes, J. M. (2002). Gender influences on children's computer attitudes and cognitions. *Computers in Human Behavior*, *18*(2), 135–150. doi:10.1016/S0747-5632(01)00043-7

Ridgeway, C. L. (2001). Gender, Status, and Leadership. *The Journal of Social Issues*, *57*(4), 637–655. doi:10.1111/0022-4537.00233

Rosenberg, M. J., & Hovland, C. I. (1960). Cognitive, Affective, and Behavioral Components of Attitudes. In Attitude organization and change: An analysis of consistency among attitude components (pp. 1-14). New Haven, CT: Yale University Press.

Sassler, S., Glass, J., Levitte, Y., & Michelmore, K. (2016). The missing women in STEM? Assessing gender differentials in the factors associated with transition to first jobs. *Social Science Research*, *63*, 192–208. doi:10.1016/j.ssresearch.2016.09.014 PMID:28202143

Sax, L. J., Lehman, K. J., Jacobs, J. A., Kanny, M. A., Lim, G., Monje-Paulson, L., & Zimmerman, H. B. (2016). Anatomy of an Enduring Gender Gap: The Evolution of Women's Participation in Computer Science. *The Journal of Higher Education*, *88*(2), 258–293. doi:10.1080/00221546.2016.1257306

Schmidt, F. (2011). A theory of sex differences in technical aptitude and some supporting evidence. *Perspectives on Psychological Science*, *6*(6), 560–573. doi:10.1177/1745691611419670 PMID:26168377

Shashaani, L., & Khalili, A. (2001). Gender and computers: Similarities and differences in Iranian college students' attitudes towards computers. *Computer Education*, *37*(3-4), 363–375. doi:10.1016/S0360-1315(01)00059-8

Shavelson, R. J., Hubner, J. J., & Stanton, G. C. (1976). Self-Concept: Validation of Construct Interpretations. *Review of Educational Research*, *46*(3), 407–441. doi:10.3102/00346543046003407

Siann, G., Macleod, H., Glissov, P., & Drundell, A. (1990). The effects of computer use on gender differences in attitudes to computers. *Computers & Education*, *14*(2), 183–191. doi:10.1016/0360-1315(90)90058-F

Sieverding, M., & Koch, S. C. (2009). (Self-) Evaluation of computer competence: How gender matters. *Computers & Education*, *52*(3), 696–701. doi:10.1016/j.compedu.2008.11.016

Sølvberg, A. M. (2002). Gender differences in computer-related control beliefs and home computer use. *Scandinavian Journal of Educational Research*, *46*(4), 409–426. doi:10.1080/0031383022000024589

Super, D. E. (1953). A theory of vocational development. *The American Psychologist*, *8*(5), 185–190. doi:10.1037/h0056046

Super, D. E., Starishevsky, R., Matlin, N., & Jordaan, J. P. (1963). *Career development: Self-concept theory*. New York, NY: College Entrance Examination Board.

Symonds, J. (2000). Why IT Doesn't Appeal to Young Women. In E. Balka & R. Smith (Eds.), *Women, Work and Computerization – Charting a Course to the Future* (pp. 70–77). Boston, MA: Kluwer. doi:10.1007/978-0-387-35509-2_9

Tømte, C., & Hatlevik, O. E. (2011). Gender-Differences In Self-Efficacy Ict Related To Various Ict-User Profiles In Finland And Norway. How Do Self-Efficacy, Gender And Ict-User Profiles Relate To Findings From Pisa 2006. *Computers & Education*, *21*, 393–402.

Triola, M. (2009). *Elementary Statistics* (11th ed.). Boston, MA: Addison Wesley.

Varma, R. (2011). Indian women and mathematics for Computer Science. *IEEE Technology and Society Magazine*, *30*(1), 39 46. doi:10.1109/MTS.2011.940294

Wetzel, I. (2002). Teaching Computer Skills: A Gendered Approach. In C. Floyd, G. Kelkar, S. Klein-Franke, C. Kramarae, & C. Limpangog (Eds.), Feminist Challenges in the Information Age (pp. 223-239). Opladen: Leske + Budrich. doi:10.1007/978-3-322-94954-7_17

Whitley, B. E. Jr. (1997). Gender Differences in Computer-Related Attitudes and Behavior: A Meta-Analysis. *Computers in Human Behavior*, *13*(1), 1–22. doi:10.1016/S0747-5632(96)00026-X

Wolffram, A., Derboven, W., & Winker, G. (2009). Women withdrawers in engineering studies: Identity formation and learning culture as gendered barriers for persistence? *Equal Opportunities International*, *28*(1), 36–49. doi:10.1108/02610150910933622

Woodbury, M. (2002). Women in Computing. In C. Floyd, G. Kelkar, S. Klein-Franke, C. Kramarae, & C. Limpangog (Eds.), Feminist Challenges in the Information Age (pp. 107-117). Opladen: Leske + Budrich. doi:10.1007/978-3-322-94954-7_9

Xu, Y. J. (2017). Attrition of Women in STEM: Examining Job/Major Congruence in the Career Choices of College Graduates. *Journal of Career Development*, *44*(1), 3–19. doi:10.1177/0894845316633787

Zweben, S. (2011). Undergraduate CS Degree Production Rises; Doctoral Production Steady. 2009-2010 Taulbee Survey. *Computing Research News*, *23*(3).

Chapter 5
Improving Application Decoupling in Virtual Enterprise Integration

José Carlos Martins Delgado
Universidade de Lisboa, Portugal

ABSTRACT

The interaction of applications belonging to several enterprise information systems (EIS), forming a collaborative network in a virtual enterprise (VE) context, raises an application integration problem that is even more stringent than within a single EIS, since a VE has a temporary nature and therefore integration requirements can change more frequently. Current integration technologies, such as web services and RESTful APIs, solve the interoperability problem but usually entail more coupling than required by the interacting applications. This is caused by sharing data schemas between applications, even if not all features of those schemas are actually exercised. The fundamental problem of application integration is therefore how to provide at most the minimum coupling possible while ensuring at least the minimum interoperability requirements. This chapter proposes compliance and conformance as the concepts to achieve this goal, by sharing only the subset of the features of the data schema that are actually used.

INTRODUCTION

Traditionally, enterprises focused on having a well-designed enterprise architecture, a web site as the customer interface, an enterprise integration solution to deal with the supply chain, and the enterprise was practically open for business, for either products or services.

However, digital-based technologies such as cloud computing, mobile devices, and the Internet of Things (IoT) (Paul, & Saraswathi, 2017) started to become ubiquitous and disruptive, and customers became more acquainted and at ease with digital services. Nowadays, customers want everything self-service, anywhere, anytime, with as little effort as possible. The world has entered a Digital Era (Liska, 2018; Chamoux, 2018), in which the simple alignment between Business and Information Technology

DOI: 10.4018/978-1-5225-8933-4.ch005

(IT) is no longer enough (Kahre, Hoffmann, & Ahlemann, 2017). Figure 1 illustrates the complexity of the current enterprise technological landscape.

Today, a classical and well-designed enterprise architecture is almost a liability, rather than an asset, due to the inertia regarding change that it entails. A small, startup enterprise can outrun an established enterprise in a short period, if its business model is innovative enough. A large organizational mass (a complex enterprise architecture), which translates to inertia and lack of agility, ability to innovate, and adaptability, is an enterprise's worst enemy. Since enterprises are usually integrated in complex supply chains, the overall business of an enterprise cluster can only be as agile and innovative as its most traditional member.

Digital technologies, and the business models they enable, are the key factor in this highly interconnected world. This means that enterprises need to become more and more digital, from top to bottom. The business itself must be inherently digital, not just enabled by digital technologies (Uhl, & Gollenia, 2016).

For an existing company, this does not mean improving the web site, moving the business to the cloud, making business processes more automated, or adding some digital features to existing products or services. This is just a digital makeup, or digital optimization. A true digital transformation (Hinings, Gegenhuber, & Greenwood, 2018; Bohnsack, Hanelt, Marz, & Marante, 2018) means reinventing the business model and providing a significant improved value as perceived by customers (Delgado, 2015), while significantly reducing the organizational inertia by taking a light approach on the supplier and resource channels.

Figure 1. An example of a complex enterprise technological landscape

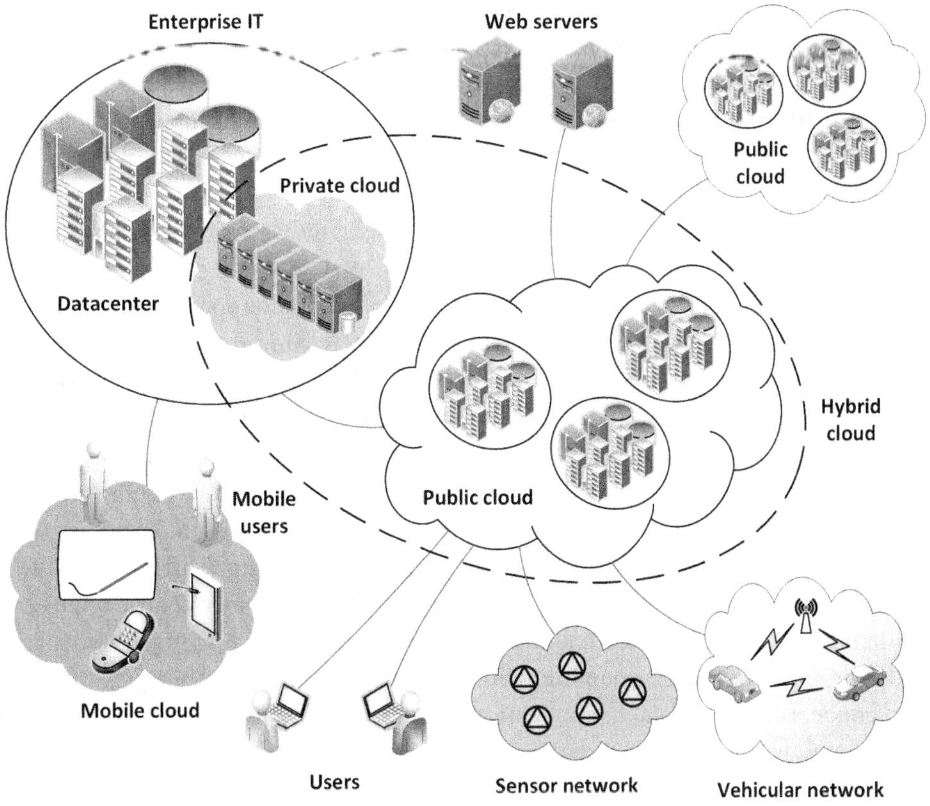

A typical strategy is to concentrate on the core business and to establish collaborative networks (Durugbo, 2016) with other enterprises that have complementary goals. Traditionally, collaborations were long-lasting partnerships. Today, the market changes very swiftly and partnerships are much more limited in their time span, usually for the duration of some project or useful lifetime of a product.

This is the idea underlying the concept of *virtual enterprise* (VE), which corresponds to a temporary partnership between several enterprises with a specific set of goals (Kovács, & Kot, 2017). A VE can encompass several enterprises and a given enterprise can participate in several VEs. This organization provides a better governance of the partnership, since it is governed as an enterprise (although virtual), than having each enterprise govern all its partnerships without clear boundaries.

The goal is also to better support the integration of the applications of the *Enterprise Information Systems* (EIS) of the various enterprises, since there should a mission, a vision, and a strategy of the VE, which are not necessarily the same as those of each of the enterprises. However, if this is already difficult within one enterprise, the challenge is far greater when several enterprises are involved, particularly when the creation and termination of VEs can occur within relatively short time spans.

One of the main challenges that need to be overcome is *integration* (He, & Da Xu, 2014; Panetto & Whitman, 2016), the ability to meaningfully and efficiently cooperate with other subsystems in order to pursue the goals of the system as a whole. Integration can be seen at all levels of abstraction and complexity, from low-level cyber-physical systems (Zanero, 2017) to high-level enterprise value chains, targeting capabilities such as those required by the fourth industrial revolution, commonly known as Industry 4.0 (Liao, Deschamps, Loures, & Ramos, 2017).

The EN/ISO 19439 standard (ISO, 2006) refers to enterprise integration as "the process of ensuring the interaction between enterprise entities necessary to achieve domain objectives". This is a very complex issue, spanning from lower levels, such as data and service interoperability, to the highest levels, including strategy and governance alignment.

Interoperability asserts the ability of two systems to understand each other's messages, whereas integration requires collaboration to achieve common goals. Interoperability is thus a necessary but not sufficient condition to achieve enterprise integration (He, & Da Xu, 2014), which usually entails cooperation and coordination at higher abstraction levels.

However, application integration entails another problem, *coupling* (Bidve, & Sarasu, 2016), which provides an indication of how much applications are intertwined. Some degree of coupling is unavoidable, since some form of mutual knowledge is necessary to make interoperability possible. However, the two most used integration approaches, SOA (Erl, Merson, & Stoffers, 2017) and REST (Fielding, Taylor, Erenkrantz, Gorlick, Whitehead, Khare, & Oreizy, 2017) achieve interoperability but do not solve the coupling problem, since they require the messages used by the interacting applications to have the same data schemas, even if only some of values of those schemas are actually used. The result is that coupling in integration is higher than actually needed. This chapter shows how to minimize the problem.

The rest of the chapter is structured as follows. It starts by describing the evolution of EIS, from traditional enterprises to virtual enterprises, describing an enterprise framework and EIS lifecycles with emphasis on changeability, agility, and digital transformation to a customer-centric approach. The fundamental problem of integration is then enunciated and models for both interoperability and coupling are presented. A proposal to reduce coupling, without impairing interoperability, is then presented by describing two concepts fundamental to application interaction: compliance and conformance. Finally, the chapter lays down the lines of future research and draws some conclusions.

BACKGROUND

Virtualization is a universal concept that spans from low-level technologies, such as compute, storage, and networking, to high-level enterprise functions, such as governance and management, enabling features such as dynamic outsourcing and reconfigurability, crucial for enterprise agility (Samdantsoodol, Cang, Yu, Eardley, & Buyantsogt, 2017). However, the automatic or semi-automatic design of an EIS implies a loss of control over the outcome of the design, unless the components comply with a general semantic framework or domain defined beforehand, to ensure their compatibility when translating goals into requirements and performing component procurement and composition.

That is why many of the examples in this area come from the manufacturing domain (Knoke, Missikoff, & Thoben, 2017), in which the goals and requirements of a component are easier to express, and reconfigurability of the production supply chain is a fundamental objective. The current trend known as Industry 4.0 (Liao, Deschamps, Loures, & Ramos, 2017; Xu, Xu, & Li, 2018) is just an example. However, the underlying principles extend to the general enterprise domain, and the Enterprise 4.0 concept (Moreira, Ferreira, & Seruca, 2018) is starting to be developed. In this digital era, the 4.0 designation is also being generalized and extended to EIS in general (Dornberger, 2018).

In any case, the notion of a VE has already been established for quite some time, as a temporary alliance of enterprises (Kovács, & Kot, 2017). More information-oriented circles (Li, & Wei, 2014) define it as a temporary consortium of partners and services, in which services are essentially Internet-based, and take a service-centric integration perspective.

In the context of the 4.0 trend (Dornberger, 2018), VE collaboration means generating and exchanging more and more data, either at business, personal, or sensor levels. This raises the application integration problem to a completely new level, in which conventional integration technologies expose their limitations and require new solutions.

Integration (Panetto & Whitman, 2016) can be broadly defined as the act of instantiating a given method to design or adapt two or more systems, so that they cooperate and accomplish one or more common goals. To interact, applications must be interoperable, i.e., able to meaningfully operate together. *Interoperability* (Agostinho, Ducq, Zacharewicz, Sarraipa, Lampathaki, Poler, & Jardim-Goncalves, 2016) is a characteristic that relates systems with this ability and is defined by the ISO/IEC/IEEE 24765 standard (ISO, 2010) as "the ability of two or more systems or components to exchange information and to use the information that has been exchanged". This means that merely exchanging information is not enough. Interacting systems must also be able to understand it and to react according to each other's expectations.

Another problem is *coupling* (Bidve, & Sarasu, 2016), which provides an indication of how much applications depend on each other. Interoperability and low coupling need to be combined to achieve an effective cooperation in the integration of distributed applications, particularly in the enterprise domain (Popplewell, 2014; Rezaei, Chiew, & Lee, 2014).

Coupling is of paramount importance but has been treated as a side issue in distributed contexts, a best-effort endeavor after achieving the primary goal, interoperability. This the case of the two most used integration approaches, Software-Oriented Architecture (SOA) (Erl, Merson, & Stoffers, 2017) and Representational State Transfer (REST) (Fielding, Taylor, Erenkrantz, Gorlick, Whitehead, Khare, & Oreizy, 2017), and of the corresponding technological solutions for distributed interoperability, Web Services (Zimmermann, Tomlinson, & Peuser, 2012) and RESTful APIs (Pautasso, 2014), respectively. These are based on data description languages such as XML (Fawcett, Ayers, & Quin, 2012) and JSON

(Bassett, 2015). Although they have achieved the basic objective of interconnecting independent and heterogeneous systems, supporting distributed application interoperability, they are not effective solutions from the point of view of coupling, since they require that the messages' data schemas used by the interacting applications are the same.

Several metrics have been proposed to assess the maintainability of service-based distributed applications, based essentially on structural features, namely for service coupling, cohesion and complexity (Babu, & Darsi, 2013). Other approaches focus on dynamic coupling, rather than static, with metrics for assessing coupling during program execution (Geetika, & Singh, 2014). There are also approaches trying to combine structural coupling and other levels of coupling, such as semantics (Alenezi, & Magel, 2014).

Compliance (Tran, Zdun, Oberortner, Mulo, & Dustdar, 2012) is a concept that can be used as the foundation mechanism to ensure partial interoperability and thus minimize coupling. It has been studied in specific contexts, such as choreography (Capel & Mendoza, 2014), modeling (Brandt & Hermann, 2013), programming (Preidel & Borrmann, 2016), and standards (Graydon, Habli, Hawkins, Kelly, & Knight, 2012).

Conformance (Khalfallah, Figay, Barhamgi, & Ghodous, 2014) is another concept underlying partial interoperability, enabling an application to replace another if it conforms to it (supports all of its features).

THE EVOLUTION OF ENTERPRISE INFORMATION SYSTEMS

The following sections establish an evolution route from a traditional EIS to the concept of what an EIS of a VE should be, in particular in what concerns the interaction between the EIS of the various enterprises in a VE and the integration of the various distributed applications involved (Delgado, 2015). This route also expresses the various degrees of an agility maturity model (Imache, Izza & Ahmed-Nacer, 2012).

The Traditional Enterprise

A traditional EIS is designed and built with classic frameworks and methods. The EIS is seen as the center of the business world, with suppliers, outsourcees and customers around it. One of the main concerns is integration with the applications and processes of other EIS (Ghobakhloo, Tang, Sabouri, & Zulkifli, 2014). Evolution can be expressed by an iterative lifecycle, such as the one depicted in Figure 2.

The *Architectural loop* is inspired by the Business Motivation Model (Vicente, Gama, & da Silva, 2014) and contemplates three main concepts, which embody three of the main questions about system development that were popularized by the Zachman framework (O'Rourke, Fishman & Selkow, 2003):

Figure 2. Lifecycle of an EIS, with emphasis on separation of conceptual and practical concerns

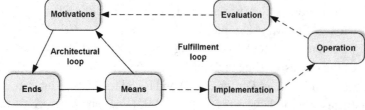

- **Motivations**: Emphasize the reasons behind the architectural decisions taken (*why* is the EIS this way), in accordance with the specification of the problem that the EIS is designed to solve.
- **Ends**: Express the desires and expectations (i.e., goals and objectives) of the stakeholders for whom the EIS is relevant (*what* is the EIS trying to achieve).
- **Means**: Describe the mechanisms (i.e., actions) used to fulfill those expectations (*how* can the EIS do it).

The *Fulfillment loop* in Figure 2 models subsequent stages in the lifecycle and is based on the organization adopted by classical development methods, such as the Rational Unified Process (Anwar, 2014). The dashed arrows are used to distinguish the two loops and to indicate that, in initial iterations, when details are scarce, the Means stage can loop directly to the Motivations stage. When enough detail and design decisions are available, the lifecycle can be enlarged to encompass both loops, with Means transitioning to Implementation, Operation and Evaluation, and back to Motivations if needed.

Designing and building an EIS is much more than a lifecycle, which can be considered just one dimension (or axis) of a larger, multidimensional architectural framework, which includes the following dimensions (or axes), depicted in Figure 3:

- **Lifecycle**: This axis is discretized into the six stages of Figure 2.
- **Concreteness**: Each stage in the lifecycle can be viewed at a very high and abstract level, or at a very detailed and concrete level. This axis has been discretized into six levels: *Conceptual*, *Strategic*, *Tactical*, *Pragmatic*, *Semantic*, and *Syntactic*. Stages of the lifecycle and their level of concreteness are orthogonal concepts. For example, the Implementation stage can be viewed at a conceptual level (just ideas on how to do it), in the same way that the Motivations stage can be detailed at a very concrete level (justification for the lowest level actions).
- **Concerns**: The focus words (*what, how, where, who, when, why*) in the Zachman framework (O'Rourke, Fishman & Selkow, 2003) are generic but do not address the entire focus range. Other questions are pertinent, such as *whence* (where from), *whither* (where to), *how much* (quantitative assessment), and *how well* (qualitative assessment). It is important to be able to express the dynamics of the EIS, its quality (how good it is, quantitatively and qualitatively), and other concerns (performance, standards, security, reliability, and so on), both functional and non-functional. This axis is discretized as needed, according to the number of concerns considered. Therefore, this is an open-ended framework. Only a few examples are shown in Figure 3, with plane details omitted for simplicity.

The Lifecycle and Concreteness axes form the front plane of Figure 3. Each cell, resulting from crossing the values of both axes, represents one lifecycle stage at a given level of concreteness. Each row is a refinement of the level above it, by including decisions that turn some abstract aspects into concrete ones. Each concern, functional or non-functional, represents a new plane, along the Concerns axis.

The levels in the Concreteness axis are organized in two categories:

- **Decisions** taken, which define, structure and refine the characteristics of the EIS, at three levels:
  - **Conceptual**: The top view of the EIS, including only global ideas.
  - **Strategic**: Details these ideas by taking usually long-lasting decisions.
  - **Tactical**: Refines these decisions into shorter-term decisions.

Figure 3. The axes of the architecture framework, with the front plane detailed

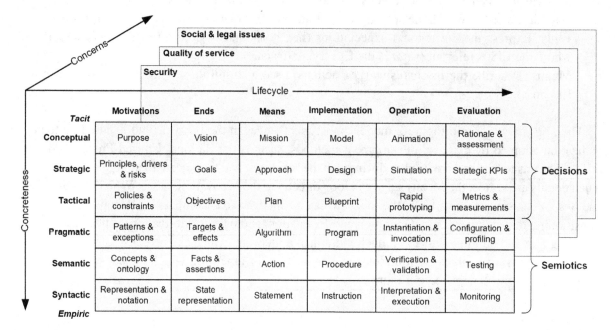

- **Semiotics** (Chandler, 2007): The study of the relationship between signs (manifestations of concepts) and their interpretation (pragmatics), meaning (semantics), and representation (syntax). In this chapter, these designations correspond to the following levels:
  - **Pragmatic**: Expresses the outcome of using the EIS, most likely producing some effects, which will depend on the context in which the EIS is used.
  - **Semantic**: Specifies the meaning of the EIS, using an ontology to describe the underlying concepts.
  - **Syntactic**. Deals with the representation of the EIS, using some appropriate notation or programming language.

All the concreteness levels express a range between two opposite thresholds, also represented in Figure 3:

- **Tacit**: This is the highest level, above which concepts are too complex or too difficult to describe. It encompasses the tacit knowledge and expertise (Oguz & Sengün, 2011) of the designers of the EIS, expressing their insight and implicit expectations and assumptions about the problem domain.
- **Empiric**: The lowest level, below which details are not relevant anymore. The EIS designers just settle for something that already exists and is known to work, such as a standard or a software library.

The Changing Enterprise

The multidimensional architecture and method described in the previous section can be powerful enough and adequate to design an EIS from a static specification, but EIS are so complex that they start being

Figure 4. The lifecycle of an EIS, emphasizing changeability

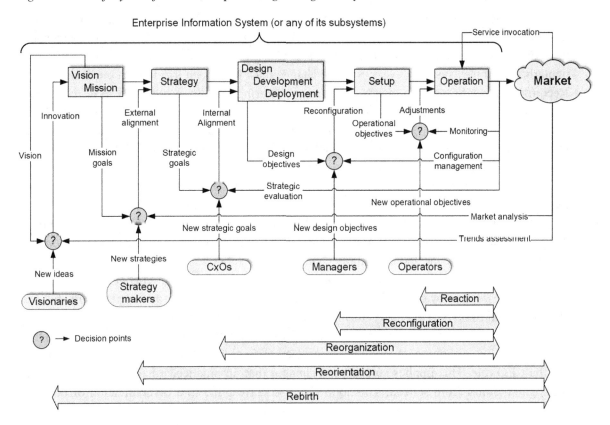

changed while they are still being conceived. Therefore, an EIS must be designed primarily for changeability, throughout its lifecycle. Figure 4 depicts an evolved system lifecycle, emphasizing changeability, which can be applied to the whole EIS, as it is usually conceived today, or to any of its subsystems. The market represents the rest of the world (namely, other EIS) or the environment in which the subsystem being modeled is immersed.

This model is maximalist, open and non-prescriptive, in the sense that any EIS (or a subsystem thereof) should go through all the stages, at least conceptually, but the level of emphasis and detail in every stage does not have to be always identical. The higher the level of the subsystem, the more important the vision and strategy will be, but it must go all the way down to operations if it is meant to work. Lower level subsystems will emphasize development and operation, but they also must have an underlying vision and mission. In the remainder of this chapter, "EIS" should be understood as the whole EIS or any of its subsystems.

Figure 4 models the lifecycle of an EIS by a pipeline of stages, each more concrete and detailed than the previous one, with several improvement loops. Each of these loops assumes that metrics (indicators) are defined, so that goals and objectives can be assessed. If the difference between the desired and measured indicators is greater than some acceptable measure, the loop should be iterated to decide and implement what needs to be changed in order to minimize that difference.

The inner loops deal with lower levels and more detail, whereas outer loops deal with higher levels and less detail. Figure 4 considers the following loops, although others are possible, with a pipeline in which the stages are more detailed:

- **Reaction**: All changes involve state only, so the cost and time to detect (monitoring) and to produce a change (of state) are usually very small. The changes can be very frequent and occur as a reaction to events or to foreseeable trends, in adaptive systems. This is the loop more amenable to automation. However, and not considering self-changing systems, which are hard to build, particularly in complex systems, every possible change must have been included in the design.
- **Reconfiguration**: Some EIS, such as in the manufacturing domain, particularly in the context of Industry 4.0 (Liao, Deschamps, Loures, & Ramos, 2017), support reconfigurability (Farid, 2017). Reconfiguration does not entail designing a new EIS but involves more than merely changing state. Some of the subsystems will be used in a different configuration or parameterization, for example to manufacture a different product in a production line. This, however, must have been included in the EIS design. Otherwise, a new version of the EIS will be needed, which is the next loop. A reconfiguration can be as frequent as its cost and benefits make it effective.
- **Reorganization**: The EIS needs to be changed in a way that has not been included in the current design. A new version needs to be produced and deployed, which may not be completely compatible with the previous one and may imply changing other subsystems as well.
- **Reorientation**: A reorientation is a profound reorganization, as result of changes in the strategy. This is usually driven by external factors, such as evolution of competitors or customers, but can also be caused by an internal restructuring to increase competitiveness.
- **Rebirth**: The vision and/or mission can also suffer significant changes, driven by factors such as stiff competition, technology evolution, merges/acquisitions, or even replacing the person fulfilling the CEO role. This implies so profound changes that, in practice, it has to be rethought and redesigned almost from scratch. This loop can also correspond to a diversification of business areas, making it necessary to build a new EIS or subsystem.

Figure 4 also indicates the typical actors involved in the change/no-change decisions taken at the decision points (the circles with a question mark). Visionaries are hard to come by and do not always exist as such (innovators are more common and frequently take on this role). The strategy makers vary from entrepreneurs, in small enterprises, to a full-fledged team driven by the CEO in large enterprises, including the various chief-level officers, or CxOs. Managers and operators take care of management and day-to-day operations, respectively.

The Agile Enterprise

Typically, a change to an EIS is decided upon when an actor realizes that the benefit of changing (BoC) is higher than the cost of implementing that change (CoC). Agile enterprises need low change costs (McLay, 2014), so that changes can be frequent, either reactively (to market changes) or proactively (anticipating market trends) (Andersen, Brunoe, & Nielsen, 2015).

Since an EIS is not synchronized with its environment (namely, customers and suppliers), it tends to progressively diverge from it, as time goes by. The misalignment of the EIS and the corresponding need for change increase. To realign the EIS, more and more changes will be needed and the CoC will be higher, as illustrated by Figure 5.

If the BoC increases faster than the CoC, as in the case of Figure 5a, then the change becomes cost effective and should be made, ideally at time T_c, when the BoC equals CoC. If the change is made too

Figure 5. Change benefits versus cost of changes: (a) Light EIS (b) Complex EIS

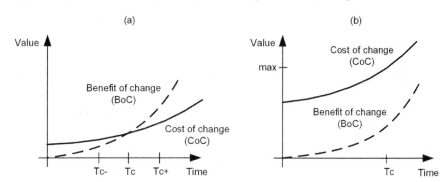

early (at T_{c-}), the cost will outweigh the benefit. If the change is made too late by waiting too much (at T_{c+}), some benefits will be lost.

If, however, the EIS is complex and resorts to diversification (spawning a new version, or introducing an adapter) instead of promoting agility to cope with changing requirements, the CoC gets higher and may never be lower than the corresponding BoC, as illustrated by Figure 5b. In this case, the time to change (T_c) is determined more by the need to limit the CoC (*max*) than by its cost-benefit effectiveness. Having a light EIS, including only what is currently needed so that it becomes reasonably easy to change, is preferable to a complex and very encompassing one, which takes a long time and effort to change.

Note that T_c is just the time at which the change is deemed necessary and ideally required to be complete and in operation. However, the change will take some time to implement and deploy. Suppose that the change starts to be implemented at T_s and is deployed at T_d. This leads to several cases, described in Table 1.

Although proactiveness is a desirable feature, the fact is that guessing the future is still an art and many things can happen between T_s and T_c. In the most unfavorable case, the change made can be completely wrong, given the latest events and market trends, and lead to losses compared to doing no change at all. Therefore, in many cases a fast reactive behavior is the best approach. In that case, the *change delay* (T_d-T_c) will determine how fast the EIS is able to realign and accommodate a change in requirements. If its average value is small compared to the MTBC (Mean Time Between Changes), the system can be classified as very agile or even real-time.

Agility, a desirable EIS property, is generally associated with quick response to a changing environment (Verbaan, & Silvius, 2014), although it has also been defined in terms of low change cost (McLay,

Table 1. Types of changes

Timings	Type of Change	Description
$T_c \leq T_s < T_d$	Reactive.	Completely reactive change, since its implementation starts only after realizing that it should be in place.
$T_s < T_c < T_d$	Mixed.	Change with a proactive and a reactive part. It starts before T_c, but some time afterwards is still needed to complete the change.
$T_s < T_d \leq T_c$	Proactive.	Completely proactive change, since its implementation starts and finishes even before it is needed. There is no much point in having T_d much before T_c.
$T_s < T_d = T_c$	Just in time.	Change is complete precisely when it is needed. The ideal case.

2014) and proactiveness (Andersen, Brunoe, & Nielsen, 2015). However, it is preferable to separate the various factors that characterize a change, with the following definitions (taken as average values) related to EIS changes:

- **Agility**: An indication of the change delay in relation to the rate at which changes are needed $((T_d-T_c)/\text{MTBC})$.
- **Dynamicity**: An indication of the implementation time of a change in relation to the rate at which changes are needed $((T_d-T_s)/\text{MTBC})$.
- **Proactiveness**: An indication of the proportion of the proactive part of the change in its implementation time, or how early the need for change is decided compared to the time required to implement the change $((T_c-T_s)/(T_d-T_s))$. Applicable only when $T_s \leq T_c$
- **Reactiveness**: An indication of the time required to implement the change in relation to the change delay $((T_d-T_s)/(T_d-T_c))$. Applicable only when $T_s > T_c$
- **Efficiency**: An indication of the average ratio between the benefit value of a change and the corresponding implementation cost (BoC/CoC).

Agility should not depend on implementation cost or proactiveness, because it is a necessity caused essentially by external factors, such as competition or technological advances. However, what the market perceives is only whether a given enterprise responds fast enough or slowly to an evolving environment. The cost of that responsiveness, or how much in advance the enterprise has to anticipate the need for change, is an internal matter of that enterprise. Sometimes, it is preferable to pay more for a faster solution and be less efficient in implementing a change, just to beat the competition and gain the competitive edge of being first on the market. If time pressure is not high, optimization can focus on the implementation cost, rather than on minimizing the change delay.

It is also important to acknowledge that these indicators can be measured in each of the loops of Figure 4 but all need to be considered, according to the theory of constraints (Şimşit, Günay, & Vayvay, 2014). If, for example, an enterprise is very agile in innovation and market perception (Reorientation loop) but sluggish in implementing and deploying changes (Reconfiguration loop), the overall agility will be hampered by this slower loop.

The Optimizing Enterprise

Ideally, resources should have 100% utilization, all the time. Unfortunately, customer demand is not constant and supplier capacity is limited. One solution is to own resources planned for an average or higher customer demand, but this translates into wasted capacity when demand is lower and will not be able to satisfy customers when demand is high. Another solution is to design an on-premises EIS for dynamic, on-demand outsourcing (minimum TCO – Total Cost of Ownership – complemented with outsourcing as needed):

- When demand for a module's functionality is higher than its capacity, the requests in excess are dynamically forwarded to one or more alternative modules (with an outsourcing contract foreseeing occasional or seasonal demand).
- When the demand is lower than the module's capacity, the business model is inverted and the module can offer its excess capacity to other enterprises needing its functionality.

This way, load balancing can be achieved both at the demand and capacity ends. The load balancing between consumption and generation should be as much as possible automatic and dynamic, although under previously agreed contractual constraints.

The Resilient Enterprise

Any enterprise should have a backup plan in case any of its EIS modules or resources fails. Resources include not only computers and other equipment, but also humans. Although replacing a sick person that holds specific knowledge is much more difficult than finding an alternative to a broken equipment, the point is that a backup plan must be built into each EIS by proper enterprise architecture design, and not dealt with only when a problem occurs. Resilience is a usual topic in IT, but sometimes enterprises tend to forget that the problem is the same in every aspect of the business (including failing employees, suppliers, outsourcees and customers).

A typical solution for a resource failure is redundancy, either in normal use (in case of failure, only capacity is reduced) or in standby, in which case the alternative resource is only put into service when the normal one fails. In hot standby, the alternative resource exists and is reserved and ready for (almost) immediate use upon failure detection. This is generally too expensive and used only for truly critical resources. The others use warm or cold standby, in which case the situation is foreseen and the actions that need to be done are known. Cold standby is the cheapest alternative solution to implement, but it takes longer to become operational. A failure usually implies a breach of the service dependent on the failed resource, and its impact and allowed recovery time should be part of the EIS design.

The Cloud-Oriented Enterprise

Cloud computing platforms (Ritter, May, & Rinderle-Ma, 2017) are now pervasive among EIS and will most likely include hybrid clouds, integrating the enterprise's owned infrastructure with one or more public clouds. Mobile cloud computing (Abolfazli, Sanaei, Sanaei, Shojafar, & Gani, 2016) is also a very relevant topic, particularly given the ever-increasing pervasiveness of smartphones and tablets that created a surge in the BYOD (Bring Your Own Device) trend (Weeger, Wang, & Gewald, 2016).

The Internet of Things (Botta, de Donato, Persico, & Pescapé, 2016), is experiencing an explosive development rate that raises the need to integrate enterprise applications with the physical world, including sensor networks (Iyengar & Brooks, 2016). Al-Fuqaha, Guizani, Mohammadi, Aledhari, and Ayyash (2015) provide estimates that indicate that the number of Internet-capable, autonomous devices greatly outnumber human-operated devices, which means that the Internet is no longer dominated by human users, but rather by small computer-based devices that require technologies adequate to them, rather than to full-fledged servers supporting web sites.

Given the huge variety and complexity of today's application scenarios, and the need to integrate many and heterogeneous applications, running on a wide range of platforms, it is only natural that enterprises resort to cloud computing as a means to provide a dynamic platform with as few constraints as possible and to simplify application integration (Mezgár & Rauschecker, 2014).

An application is a set of software modules with synchronized lifecycles, i.e., compiled and linked together. Applications are the unit of system distribution and their interaction is usually limited to message exchange. Applications are independent and each can evolve in ways that the others cannot predict or control.

The interaction between modules belonging to the same application can rely on names to designate concepts in the type system (types, inheritance, variables, methods, and so on). A name can have only one meaning in a given scope, which means that using a name is equivalent to using its definition. A working application usually assumes that all its modules are also working and use the same implementation language and formats, with any change notified to all modules. The application is a coherent and cohesive whole.

The interaction between different applications, however, is a completely different matter. Different applications may use the same name for different meanings, be programmed in different languages, be deployed in different cloud platforms, use different formats and, without notifying other applications, migrate from one server to another, change its functionality or interface, and even be down for some reason, planned or not.

This raises an interoperability problem, not only in terms of correctly interpreting and understanding exchanged data but also in keeping behaviors synchronized in some choreography. The typical solutions involve a common protocol (such as HTTP), self-describing data, at the syntactic and sometimes semantic levels, and many assumptions previously agreed. For example, XML-based interactions, including Web Services, assume a common schema. REST proponents claim that client and server are decoupled, since the client needs just the initial server´s URI – *Universal Resource Identifier*. However, RESTful applications do require previously agreed media types (schemas) and implicit assumptions by the client on the behavior of the server when executing the protocol verbs.

It is virtually impossible for one application to know how to behave in the interaction with another application if it knows nothing about the latter. Not even humans are able to achieve it. Some form of coupling (shared and agreed knowledge, prior to interaction) needs to exist. The goal is to reduce coupling as much as possible while ensuring the minimum level of interoperability required by the problem that motivated the interaction between applications.

The Virtual Enterprise

The meaning of virtual enterprise (Esposito, & Evangelista, 2014) has evolved from a classical partnership of strategic outsourcing and collaboration, in a timescale of weeks to years, to a dynamic, cost-optimizing service networks and collaborations, valid for a time span as small as a single business transaction. Cloud computing platforms and tools are the enablers that support such virtual and dynamic environments (Patrignani, & Kavathatzopoulos, 2016).

In a digital era, in which everything is seen as a service (Li, & Wei, 2014), a virtual enterprise can be conceived as a small-grain collaborative network (Durugbo, 2016), which can extend and retract, defined dynamically at the process or even at the transaction level, according to the current needs and to the functionality that needs to be implemented.

This concept, designated here VEaaS (*Virtual Enterprise as a Service*), can be characterized by the following guidelines:

- There must be a definition of a VEIS (*Virtual Enterprise Information System*), which is the EIS of the VEaaS and defines the possible variations of the configuration of the collaborative network.
- Instead of guessing what and how much the customer demand will be (introducing provisions for it in the VEIS in advance, in a static way), the VEIS should be designed so that it can assembled and/or reconfigured on the fly in reaction to concrete customer demand and requests, with a high degree of customization.

- Instead of considering the VEIS as merely a part of a value chain, see it as a value creator, or an adapter between what the customer wants and what other enterprises can provide.
- Instead of seeking static collaboration with other enterprises, build the VEIS dynamically and virtually on top of a library of services, using outsourcing as the main organizational paradigm.
- Instead of investing a lot in defining an elaborate strategy, build the entire VEIS for agility, so that strategy is easily and quickly adaptable to the fast-evolving business world.

The VEaaS builds upon a menu-based VEIS, in the sense that a new, specialized and customized VEIS can be built for each business transaction, or class of transactions, with smaller granularity and higher agility than traditional EIS. Unlike traditional scenarios, outsourcing is the main service delivery mechanism of the VEaaS model, meant to be used for all service types, including human roles.

Although VEaaS may seem similar to SaaS (Software as a Service), these are two orthogonal concepts. SaaS is essentially a service delivery mechanism, whereas VEaaS is an EIS building paradigm. SaaS offers full applications remotely, hiding management problems, but has no idea of how an EIS should be organized, and indeed current SaaS offerings (ERPs, in particular) are not that easy to configure and to integrate with other subsystems. VEaaS, on the other hand, advocates smaller granularity and promotes

Figure 6. The lifecycle of the VEIS of a VEaaS (Virtual Enterprise as a Service)

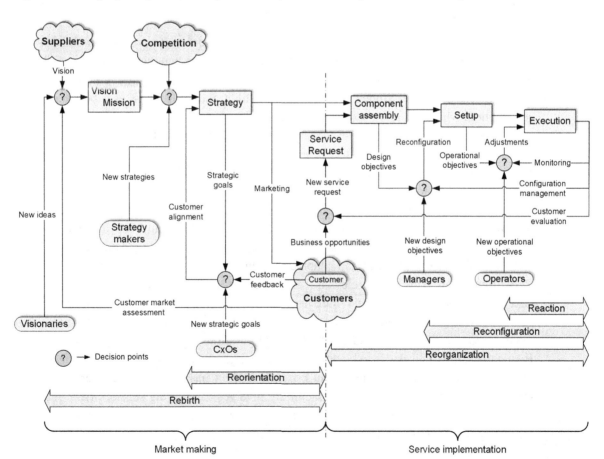

the dynamic interoperability of services, rather than their static integration into an EIS. Instead of one large application, it is better to use a library of smaller, customizable *microservices* (Dragoni, *et al.*, 2017). Agile adaptability to the customer requirements is the main tenet.

Figure 6 depicts the lifecycle of the VEIS of a VEaaS, reflecting a changeability model more dynamic than that of Figure 4, which reflects the EIS of a much more traditional enterprise. Customers are at the center of the lifecycle, by design.

The VEaaS model divides the VEIS lifecycle into two parts, with the customer precisely at the middle. The customer is the most important actor in the lifecycle, around which everything revolves. Again, this is a maximalist model, and real cases can optimize some of the aspects. This model can be briefly explained as follows:

- **The market making part**: This involves not only assessing what the customer wants but also exerting some influence by showing how a customized solution can solve that customer's problems. The VEaaS must make its own customers, not just wait for them to appear. It involves two loops:
  - **Reorientation**: This essentially recognizes business patterns and tries to contribute to the organization and structure of the service library, to capitalize on service reuse and to minimize the customization effort and implementation time. On the other hand, the customer does not always know what exactly is needed, and the service library, based on proven business patterns, can be a precious help. In other words, it contributes to the mutual alignment between the service library and the customer's needs.
  - **Rebirth**: Necessary when new technologies, innovative ideas, or competition changes appear. The VEaaS develops its market vision from the gap between the customer´s needs and the suppliers' offerings, which define the business opportunities, in particular when innovative ideas are available. Strategy, which must be light and agile, must also be attentive to competition, which has to be assumed agile as well.
- **The service implementation part**: The VEaaS should be able to provide a new VEIS design for each customer request. Naturally, most of these requests will follow common business patterns and therefore the VEIS will actually be variants of pre-established VEIS, adequate to those patterns. How easy will be to adapt these patterns to concrete cases depends on how well the library is designed. This involves the following loops:
  - **Reaction**: This is essentially the same as in a traditional EIS, but keep in mind that the VEaaS must be flexible to be adaptable, which means that monitoring and control techniques may be made more specialized and adapted to each case.
  - **Reconfiguration**: This is less relevant than in a traditional EIS because reorganization, the next loop, becomes a feasible and more flexible alternative, given the customization philosophy of a VEaaS. Nevertheless, the VEIS of a VEaaS must be able to cater for situations that require frequent choice among a fixed set of configurations.
  - **Reorganization**: This needs to be done in each change of pattern of customer requests. The Design, development, and deployment box of Figure 4 has been replaced here by an assembly box, to make clear that this essentially involves assembling services from reusable services in the library. Adapting services and in particular developing new ones should be the exception, rather than the norm.

APPLICATION INTEGRATION

The Fundamental Problem

In the context of this chapter, in which a VEIS is built as a dynamic mesh of applications provided by the collaborating enterprises, application integration is of paramount importance. Changing one of the enterprises, even if not changing anything else, will most likely mean changing objectives, processes, data formats, and so on. Therefore, reducing coupling between EIS, while ensuring the minimum business requirements for interoperability, is a fundamental factor in increasing the agility of a virtual enterprise.

The fundamental problem of application integration is how to provide *at most* the minimum coupling possible while ensuring *at least* the minimum interoperability requirements. The main goal is to ensure that each interacting application knows just enough about the others to be able to interoperate with them but no more than that. Unnecessary dependencies and constraints should be avoided.

Existing data interoperability technologies, such as XML (Fawcett, Ayers, & Quin, 2012) and JSON (Bassett, 2015), assume that interacting applications share the same message schema. This can be referred to as *symmetric interoperability* and is reminiscent of the first days of the Web and HTML documents, in which the client read the document produced by the server and both needed to use the same data specification. Today, data have been separated from their specification (schema), but both client and server still work on the same information. Coupling has not diminished.

The problem is that a server may need to serve several potentially different clients and a client may need to send requests to several potentially different servers. Sharing a schema couples both client and server for the whole set of messages that the schema can describe, even if the client only uses a subset of the admissible requests and the server only responds with a subset of the admissible responses.

The net effect of this symmetry is that, in many cases, client and server are more coupled than needed and changes in one application may very likely imply changing the other as well, even if a change does not affect the actually exchanged messages.

An Interoperability Model

Most interoperability technologies, such as Web Services (Zimmermann, Tomlinson, & Peuser, 2012) and RESTful APIs (Pautasso, 2014), usually consider only the syntactic format of messages, or at most the semantics of its terms (Verborgh, Harth, Maleshkova, Stadtmüller, Steiner, Taheriyan, & Van de Walle, 2014; Wang, Gibbins, Payne, Patelli, & Wang, 2015). However, the ability to meaningfully interact involves higher levels, naturally including behavior. Table 2 establishes a linearized systematization of interoperability at several levels of abstraction. The higher levels are particularly relevant when complex, enterprise-class applications are involved.

The abstraction levels of interoperability can be described as follows:

- **Symbiotic**: Expresses the purpose and intent of two interacting applications to engage in a mutually beneficial agreement. This can entail a tight coordination under a common governance (if the applications are controlled by the same enterprise), a joint-venture agreement (if the two applications are substantially aligned), a collaboration involving a partnership agreement (if some goals are shared), or a mere value chain cooperation (an outsourcing contract). Enterprise engineering is usually the topmost level in application interaction complexity, since it goes up to the human level,

Table 2. Abstraction levels and layers of interoperability

Abstraction Level	Layers	Description
Symbiotic (purpose and intent)	• Coordination • Alignment • Collaboration • Cooperation	• Motivations to interact, with varying levels of mutual knowledge of governance, strategy and goals.
Pragmatic (reaction and effects)	• Contract • Workflow • Interface	• Management of the effects of the interaction at the levels of choreography, process and service.
Semantic (meaning of content)	• Inference • Knowledge • Ontology	• Interpretation of a message in context, at the levels of rule, known application components and relations, and definition of concepts.
Syntactic (notation of representation)	• Structure • Predefined type • Serialization	• Representation of application components, in terms of composition, primitive components and serialization format of messages.
Connective (transfer protocol)	• Messaging • Routing • Communication • Physics	• Lower level formats and network protocols involved in transferring a message from the context of the sender to that of the receiver.

with governance and strategy heavily involved. Therefore, it maps mainly onto the symbiotic layer, although the same principles apply (in a more rudimentary fashion) to simpler applications.

- **Pragmatic**: The effect of an interaction between a client and a server is the outcome of a contract, which is implemented by a choreography that coordinates processes, which in turn implement workflow behavior by orchestrating service invocations. Languages such as Business Process Execution Language (BPEL) (Juric & Weerasiri, 2014) support the implementation of processes and Web Services Choreography Description Language (WS-CDL) (Ebrahimifard, Amiri, Arani, & Parsa, 2016) is an example of a language that allows choreographies to be specified.

- **Semantic**: Interacting applications must be able to understand the meaning of the content of the messages exchanged, both requests and responses. This implies interoperability in rules, knowledge and ontologies, so that meaning is not lost when transferring a message from the context of the sender to that of the receiver. Semantic languages and specifications, such as OWL (Matentzoglu, Parsia, & Sattler, 2017) and RDF (Tzitzikas, Manolis, & Papadakos, 2017), map onto this category.

- **Syntactic**: Deals mainly with form, rather than content. Each message has a structure, composed of data (primitive resources) according to some structural definition (its schema). Data need to be serialized to be sent over the channel as messages, using data description languages such as XML (Fawcett, Ayers, & Quin, 2012) or JSON (Bassett, 2015).

- **Connective**: The main objective is to transfer a message from the context of one application to the other's, regardless of its content. This usually involves enclosing that content in another message with control information and implementing a message protocol (such as SOAP or HTTP) over a communications network, according to its own protocol (such as the Transmission Control Protocol/Internet Protocol – TCP/IP) and possibly involving routing gateways.

All these abstraction levels are always present in all application interactions, even the simplest ones. There is always a motivation and purpose in sending a message, an effect stemming from the reaction to its reception, a meaning expressed by the message, and a format used to send it over a network under some protocol. However, what happens in practice is that some of these levels are catered for *tacitly* (implicitly assumed) or *empirically* (explicitly hidden behind some existing specification). This is consistent with the front plane of the framework depicted in Figure 3.

Also relevant is non-functional interoperability. It is not just a question of invoking the right operation with the right parameters. Adequate service levels, context awareness, security and other non-functional issues must be considered when applications interact, otherwise interoperability will be less effective or not possible at all. The abstraction levels of Table 2 must be considered for each of these concerns, which correspond to the various planes illustrated in Figure 3.

It is also important to realize that all these interoperability levels constitute an expression of application coupling:

- On the one hand, two uncoupled applications (with no interactions between them) can evolve freely and independently, which favors adaptability, changeability and even reliability (if one fails, there is no impact on the other).
- On the other hand, applications need to interact to cooperate towards common or complementary goals, which means that some degree of previously agreed mutual knowledge must exist. The more they share with the other, the easier interoperability becomes, but the greater coupling gets.

The Meaning of Application Coupling

Considering the graph of all the possible interactions between applications, any application that is not initial (does not receive requests from any other) or terminal (does not send requests to any other) will usually take the roles of both client and server.

Any interaction entails some form of dependency (coupling), stemming from the knowledge required to establish that interaction in a meaningful way. Coupling can be assessed by the fraction of the features of one application (operations, messages, data types, semantic terms, and so on) that impose constraints on another application that interacts with it, and can be expressed in two slants (Figure 7):

- **Backward Coupling**: The subset of features of an application that its clients depend on and need to use according to the application's rules. In other words, the set of constraints that an application imposes on its clients.
- **Forward Coupling**: The subset of features of an application that its clients actually use and that the application, or some other application replacing it, needs to support. In other words, the set of constraints that a client imposes on the applications that it uses.

From the point of view of a given application, these two coupling metrics can then be defined in the following way:

C_B (*backward coupling*), which expresses how much impact an application has on its clients:

$$C_B = \frac{\sum_{i \in C} \dfrac{Uc_i}{Tc \cdot M}}{|C|} \tag{1}$$

Figure 7. Backward and forward coupling

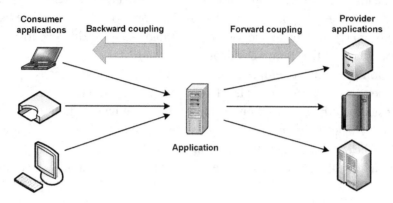

where:

C - Set of clients that use this application as a server, with $|C|$ as its cardinality

Uc_i - Number of features of this application that client i uses

Tc - Total number of features that this application has

M - Number of known applications that are compatible with this application and can replace it, as a server

C_F (*forward coupling*), which expresses how much a client is dependent on its server applications:

$$C_F = \frac{\sum_{i \in S} \dfrac{Us_i}{Ts_i \cdot N_i}}{|S|} \qquad (2)$$

where:

S - Set of server applications that this client uses, with $|S|$ as its cardinality

Us_i - Number of features that this client uses in server application i

Ts_i - Total number of features that server application i has

N_i - Number of server applications with which this client is compatible, in all uses of features of server application i by this client

These coupling metrics yield values between 0, expressing completely unrelated and independent applications, and 1, in the case of completely dependent applications, constrained by all features. These metrics can be interpreted in the following way:

- Equation (1) means that having alternatives to an application, in its role as a server, reduces the overall system dependency on it, thereby reducing the impact that application may have on its potential clients (its backward coupling C_B).

- Equation (2) indicates that the existence of alternative servers to a given application reduces its forward coupling C_F, since more applications with which this application is compatible (as a client) dilute the dependencies.
- Both equations (1) and (2) also express the fact that using a smaller fraction of features induces a lower coupling.

Alternative server applications can be found not only by designing and building them on purpose, but also by reducing the fraction of features needed for compatibility to the minimum required by the interaction between applications. The smaller the number of constraints, the greater the probability of finding applications that satisfy them.

Therefore, both factors on which coupling depends (the fraction of features used, as a client, and the number of server alternatives available) work in the same direction, with the first reinforcing the second. Reducing coupling means reducing the fraction of features used, or the knowledge of one application about another. Therefore, the integration of applications designed with these issues in mind will be easier.

Technologies such as Web Services (Zimmermann, Tomlinson, & Peuser, 2012) and RESTful APIs (Pautasso, 2014) constitute poor solutions in terms of coupling, since Web Services rely on sharing a schema (a WSDL document) and RESTful APIs are usually based on previously agreed upon media types. These technologies support the distributed interoperability problem, but do not solve the coupling problem.

In conventional systems, searching for an interoperable application is done by schema matching with similarity algorithms (Elshwimy, Algergawy, Sarhan, & Sallam, 2014) and ontology matching and mapping (Anam, Kim, Kang, & Liu, 2016). This may find similar server schemas, but does not ensure interoperability and manual adaptations are usually unavoidable.

The goal in this chapter is to be able to integrate applications with exact interoperability, rather than just approximate, even if the client and server schemas are not identical, as long as certain requirements are verified. This does not mean being able to integrate any set of existing applications, but rather being able to change an application, due to a normal evolution in specifications, while not impairing an existing interoperability. Less coupling means greater flexibility for accommodating changes.

Reducing Backward Coupling: Compliance

Figure 8 illustrates a typical client-server interaction, but with a huge difference with respect to conventional symmetric interoperability, in which both client and server share the same message schema. Here, client and server need not share the same schema. The client must only satisfy (*comply with*) the requirements established by the server to accept requests sent to it, which means that the client's schema needs only to be compliant with the server's schema in the features that it actually uses, thereby reducing the dependency of the client on the server. This is known as *compliance* (Tran, Zdun, Oberortner, Mulo, & Dustdar, 2012).

It is important to note that any client that complies with a given server can use it, independently of having been designed for interaction with it or not. Since distributed applications have independent lifecycles, they cannot freely share names, and schema compliance must be tested structurally, feature by feature, between messages sent by the client and the interface offered by the server. In the message response, the roles of client and server with respect to schema compliance are reversed.

Figure 8. Compliance-based interoperability. Only the request message validation is shown

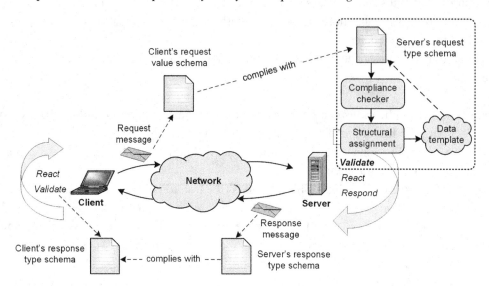

The compliance-based interoperability mechanism of Figure 8 can be detailed in the following way, for the request message (similar for the response message, with client and server roles reversed):

- The server publishes a request *type schema*, which describes the type of request message values that the server can accept.
- The actual request message, sent by the client, is described by a *value schema*. This is simply a self-description and, unlike type schemas, includes no variability (range of structured values).
- When the request message arrives at the server, the message's value schema is validated by checking it for satisfaction of, or compliance with, the type schema of the server, in the *compliance checker*. If compliance holds, the request message is one of those that satisfy the server's request type schema and is accepted.
- The request message's value is *structurally* assigned to the *data template*, which is a data structure that satisfies the server's type schema and includes default values for the components in the type schema that are *optional* (minimum number of occurrences specified as zero). The request message must include at least the minimum number of occurrences specified for each component of data template, otherwise compliance will fail.
- Structural assignment involves mapping the request message to the server's request type schema, by assigning the message to the data template, component by component, according to the following basic rules:
  - Components in the message that do not comply with any component in the data template are not assigned and simply ignored.
  - Components in the data template that are also present in the message have their values set to the corresponding message's component values.
  - Optional components in the data template missing from the message have their values set to the corresponding default values (specified in the data template).
  - Structured components are assigned by recursive application of these rules.

After this, the data template is completely populated and ready to be accessed by the server. Each request message populates a new instance of the data template. Note that this mechanism is different from the usual data binding of existing technologies, since the server deals only with its own request message schema. It does not know the actual schema of the request message and there is no need for a data binding stub to deal with it. The mapping between the request message and the data template is done in a universal manner (based on primitive data types) and does not depend on the schemas used by either the client or the server. As long as compliance holds, the structural assignment rules can be applied. This means that coupling is reduced in comparison to classical symmetric interoperability, with the following advantages:

- Coupling is limited to the actually used features of a schema and not to the full set of features of that schema.
- A client is more likely to find suitable servers based on a smaller set of features, rather than on a full schema.
- A server will be able to serve a broader base of clients, since it will impose fewer restrictions on them.

Reducing Forward Coupling: Conformance

Forward coupling limits the ability of one server application replacing another without impairing interoperability with existing clients. Replacing a server application can be useful in several cases, including the following ones:

- An application evolves (the new version replaces the old one).
- An application migrates to another cloud or environment (Figure 1), eventually with differences in its interface.
- An alternative application is used, due to a failure or lack of capacity of the original application.
- To balance the load of requests, spreading them across several (not necessarily identical) server applications.

Some management decision is taken that implies using another application.

The issue, illustrated by Figure 9, is to ascertain whether a server 1, serving a client, can be replaced by another server 2 such that the client-server relationship enjoyed by the client is not impaired.

In other words, the issue is whether server 2 is replacement compatible with server 1, a property known as *conformance* (Khalfallah, Figay, Barhamgi, & Ghodous, 2014). Server 2 must possess all the characteristics of server 1 (and probably more), therefore being able to take the form of (*to conform to*) server 1 and fulfill the expectations of the clients regarding what they expects the server to be. In particular, the schema of server 2 cannot include any additional mandatory component, regarding the schema of server 1, otherwise it would impose more requirements on the client and the interoperability could break.

By the definition of conformance, a client that complies with a server also complies with another server that conforms to the original server, as shown in Figure 9.

Figure 9. Conformance-based interoperability. A server application can be replaced by another, as long as it supports the features required by the clients of the original server application

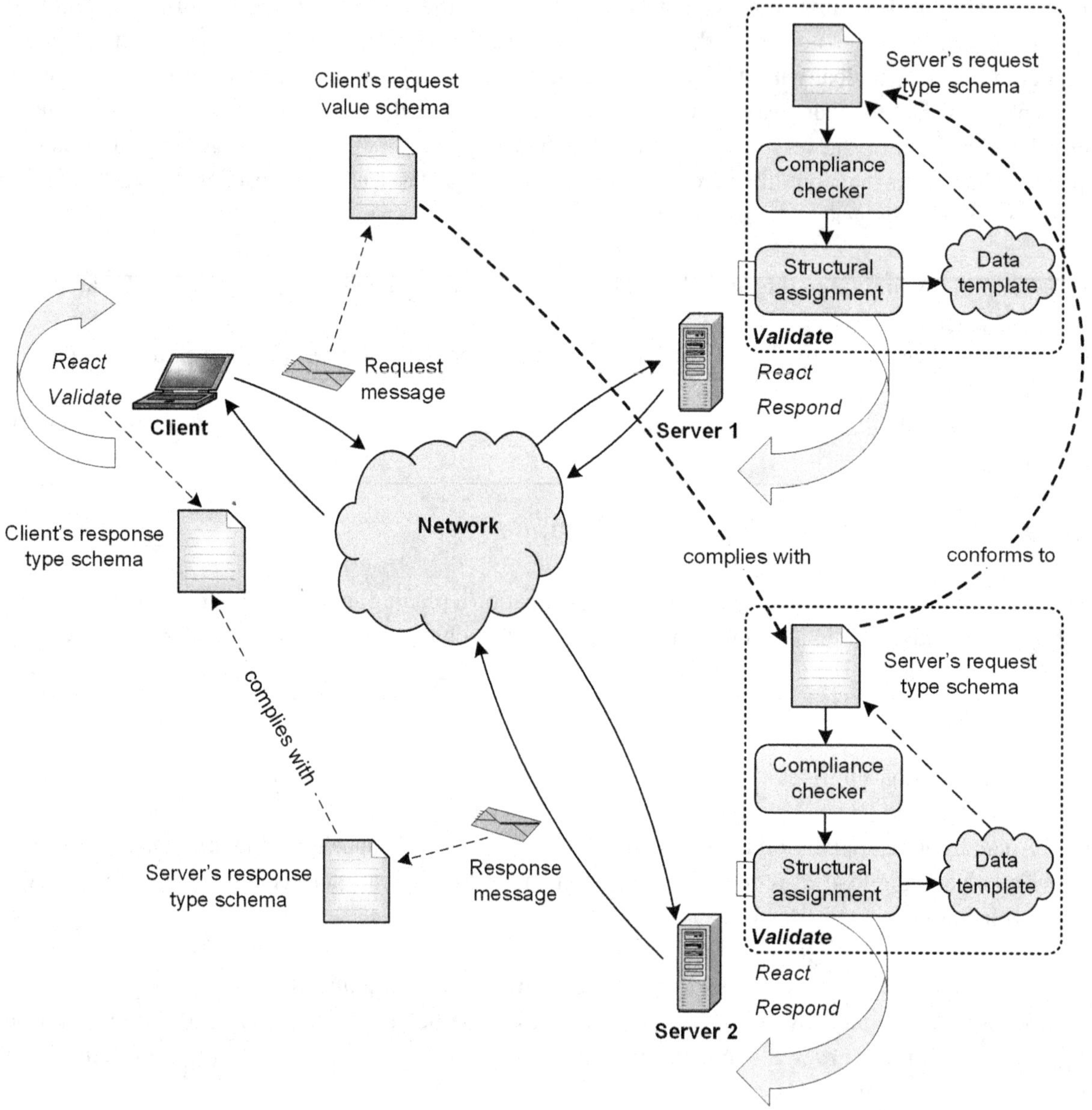

FUTURE RESEARCH DIRECTIONS

Applications in the virtual enterprise context are the focus of this chapter, but compliance and conformance are basic concepts that can be applied to all domains and levels of abstraction and complexity. Although work exists on its formal treatment in specific areas, such as choreographies (Yang, Ma, Deng, Liao, Yan, & Zhang, 2013), an encompassing and systematic study needs to be conducted to formalize the meaning of compliance and conformance at each of the interoperability layers of Table 2. Their formal definition, across all layers, needs to be made in a systematic way.

Given the current trend of increasing cloud computing adoption by enterprises, cloud interoperability (Kostoska, Gusev, & Ristov, 2016) is also a huge problem with increasing importance, in which compliance and conformance can play a role. Cloud providers favor standardization but not homogeneity, since they need differentiation as a marketing argument. A study needs to be carried out on the suitability of compliance and conformance as partial interoperability solutions for cloud-based applications.

The coupling problem is also relevant for the interoperability of non-functional aspects, namely in context-aware applications and in those involving the design and management of SLR (Service Level Requirements) with respect to virtual enterprises and supply chain interactions. Detailing how compliance and conformance can be applied in these cases requires additional research.

CONCLUSION

The application integration problem is fundamental in distributed information systems, in particular in the context of virtual enterprises, with their collaborative networks. EIS need to interact to be able to pursue common or complementary goals and their applications need to be integrated in the best possible way, which means providing the minimum interoperability requirements while minimizing application coupling.

The most common integration technologies, namely Web Services (Zimmermann, Tomlinson, & Peuser, 2012) and RESTful APIs (Pautasso, 2014), try to address this problem, but they focus more on interoperability than on coupling. Both require previous knowledge of the types of the resources involved in the interaction, which entails more coupling than actually required, since data schemas must be shared by the interacting applications. Web Services usually require a link to the schema shared by the consumer and by the provider, whereas REST-based technologies usually agree on a given schema prior to the interaction of the applications. If an application changes the schema it uses, those interacting with it must cater for these changes, to avoid breaking the interaction.

This chapter contends that both aspects, interoperability and coupling, need to be dealt with in a balanced way. The fundamental problem of application integration is how to achieve the minimum possible coupling, so that dependencies between applications that hinder changeability are kept to a minimum, while ensuring the minimum interoperability requirements, so that applications are able to effectively interact.

Structural compliance (Tran, Zdun, Oberortner, Mulo, & Dustdar, 2012) and conformance (Khalfallah, Figay, Barhamgi, & Ghodous, 2014) relax the constraint of having to share message schemas and therefore constitute an improved solution over existing integration technologies. Two applications that share at least the characteristics actually required by interoperability can interoperate, independently of knowing the rest of the characteristics, at design, compile or runtime, thereby minimizing coupling. Reducing the number of features of an application on which another depends not only reduces the perceivable width of the interface but also increases the number of providers that are compatible with a consumer, and vice-versa.

Given the huge variability in application interfaces, compliance and conformance are not universal solutions to find a server adequate for any given client, but can cater for client and/or server variants while supporting the substitution principle. An application can be replaced by another (as a server) without breaking the service or remain in service while a variant serves additional clients.

Table 3. Some questions regarding application integration

Topic	Problems	Possible Answers
Heterogeneity (types/schemas)	How can an application understand message types/schemas from another independent application?	• Self-description. • Structural compatibility.
Decoupling	Do applications need to share their entire interfaces or just the features that they actually use to interact?	Partial compatibility.
Reliability	If a service becomes unavailable, how can suitable alternatives be provided, in order to maintain the overall system working, as much as possible?	Foreseen alternatives, in either at the consumer or provider sides of an interaction, with automatic redirection.
Migration	If an application migrates from one cloud to another (due to load-balancing, maintenance, better performance or lower cost, or some other reason), how can other applications continue to interact with it transparently?	• Reverse proxy left at the original place with automatic message forwarding. • Repeat search for application (updated location returned)
Heterogeneity (portability)	How can an application be deployed to different clouds, with different APIs, platforms and processors?	• Portable platform (for interpreted languages). • Application includes several implementations.
Heterogeneity (management)	How can an application managing other applications in different clouds deal with different cloud management APIs?	Each application becomes manageable (wraps what it needs from the cloud API in its own API).

QUESTIONS

Table 3 presents some questions and hints for possible answers regarding application integration, namely in the now pervasive cloud environments.

REFERENCES

Abolfazli, S., Sanaei, Z., Sanaei, M. H., Shojafar, M., & Gani, A. (2016). Mobile Cloud Computing. In S. Murugesan & I. Bojanova (Eds.), *Encyclopedia of Cloud Computing* (pp. 29–40). Chichester, UK: John Wiley & Sons, Ltd. doi:10.1002/9781118821930.ch3

Agostinho, C., Ducq, Y., Zacharewicz, G., Sarraipa, J., Lampathaki, F., Poler, R., & Jardim-Goncalves, R. (2016). Towards a sustainable interoperability in networked enterprise information systems: Trends of knowledge and model-driven technology. *Computers in Industry*, *79*, 64–76. doi:10.1016/j.compind.2015.07.001

Al-Fuqaha, A., Guizani, M., Mohammadi, M., Aledhari, M., & Ayyash, M. (2015). Internet of things: A survey on enabling technologies, protocols, and applications. *IEEE Communications Surveys and Tutorials*, *17*(4), 2347–2376. doi:10.1109/COMST.2015.2444095

Alenezi, M., & Magel, K. (2014). Empirical evaluation of a new coupling metric: Combining structural and semantic coupling. *International Journal of Computers and Applications*, *36*(1). doi:10.2316/Journal.202.2014.1.202-3902

Anam, S., Kim, Y., Kang, B., & Liu, Q. (2016). Adapting a knowledge-based schema matching system for ontology mapping. In *Proceedings of the Australasian Computer Science Week Multiconference* (p. 27). New York, NY: ACM Press. 10.1145/2843043.2843048

Andersen, A., Brunoe, T., & Nielsen, K. (2015). Reconfigurable Manufacturing on Multiple Levels: Literature Review and Research Directions. In S. Umeda, M. Nakano, H. Mizuyama, N. Hibino, D. Kiritsis, & G. von Cieminski (Eds.), *Advances in Production Management Systems: Innovative Production Management Towards Sustainable Growth* (pp. 266–273). Cham, Switzerland: Springer International Publishing.

Anwar, A. (2014). A Review of RUP (Rational Unified Process). *International Journal of Software Engineering*, 5(2), 8–24.

Babu, D., & Darsi, M. (2013). A Survey on Service Oriented Architecture and Metrics to Measure Coupling. *International Journal on Computer Science and Engineering*, 5(8), 726–733.

Bassett, L. (2015). *Introduction to JavaScript Object Notation: A to-the-point Guide to JSON*. Sebastopol, CA: O'Reilly Media, Inc.

Bidve, V. S., & Sarasu, P. (2016). Tool for measuring coupling in object-oriented java software. *IACSIT International Journal of Engineering and Technology*, 8(2), 812–820.

Bohnsack, R., Hanelt, A., Marz, D., & Marante, C. (2018). Same, same, but different!? A systematic review of the literature on digital transformation. Academy of Management Proceedings, 2018(1), 16262.

Botta, A., de Donato, W., Persico, V., & Pescapé, A. (2016). Integration of cloud computing and internet of things: A survey. *Future Generation Computer Systems*, 56, 684–700. doi:10.1016/j.future.2015.09.021

Brandt, C., & Hermann, F. (2013). Conformance analysis of organizational models: A new enterprise modeling framework using algebraic graph transformation. *International Journal of Information System Modeling and Design*, 4(1), 42–78. doi:10.4018/jismd.2013010103

Capel, M., & Mendoza, L. (2014). Choreography Modeling Compliance for Timed Business Models. In *Proceedings of the Workshop on Enterprise and Organizational Modeling and Simulation* (pp. 202-218). Berlin, Germany: Springer. 10.1007/978-3-662-44860-1_12

Chamoux, J. (Ed.). (2018). *The Digital Era 1: Big Data Stakes*. Hoboken, NJ: John Wiley & Sons. doi:10.1002/9781119102687

Chandler, D. (2007). *Semiotics: the basics*. New York, NY: Routledge. doi:10.4324/9780203014936

Delgado, J. (2015). Supporting Enterprise Integration with a Multidimensional Interoperability Framework. *International Journal of Social and Organizational Dynamics in IT*, 4(1), 39–70. doi:10.4018/IJSODIT.2015010104

Dornberger, R. (Ed.). (2018). *Business Information Systems and Technology 4.0: New Trends in the Age of Digital Change* (Vol. 141). Cham, Switzerland: Springer. doi:10.1007/978-3-319-74322-6

Dragoni, N., Giallorenzo, S., Lafuente, A., Mazzara, M., Montesi, F., Mustafin, R., & Safina, L. (2017). Microservices: yesterday, today, and tomorrow. In M. Mazzara & B. Meyer (Eds.), *Present and Ulterior Software Engineering* (pp. 195–216). Cham, Switzerland: Springer. doi:10.1007/978-3-319-67425-4_12

Durugbo, C. (2016). Collaborative networks: A systematic review and multi-level framework. *International Journal of Production Research*, *54*(12), 3749–3776. doi:10.1080/00207543.2015.1122249

Ebrahimifard, A., Amiri, M., Arani, M., & Parsa, S. (2016). Mapping BPMN 2.0 Choreography to WS-CDL: A Systematic Method. *Journal of E-Technology*, *7*, 1–23.

Elshwimy, F., Algergawy, A., Sarhan, A., & Sallam, E. (2014). Aggregation of similarity measures in schema matching based on generalized mean. *Proceedings of the IEEE International Conference on Data Engineering Workshops* (pp. 74-79). Piscataway, NJ: IEEE Computer Society Press. 10.1109/ICDEW.2014.6818306

Erl, T., Merson, P., & Stoffers, R. (2017). *Service-oriented Architecture: Analysis and Design for Services and Microservices*. Upper Saddle River, NJ: Prentice Hall PTR.

Esposito, E., & Evangelista, P. (2014). Investigating virtual enterprise models: Literature review and empirical findings. *International Journal of Production Economics*, *148*, 145–157. doi:10.1016/j.ijpe.2013.10.003

Farid, A. (2017). Measures of reconfigurability and its key characteristics in intelligent manufacturing systems. *Journal of Intelligent Manufacturing*, *28*(2), 353–369. doi:10.100710845-014-0983-7

Fawcett, J., Ayers, D., & Quin, L. (2012). *Beginning XML*. Indianapolis, IN: John Wiley & Sons.

Fielding, R., Taylor, R., Erenkrantz, J., Gorlick, M., Whitehead, J., Khare, R., & Oreizy, P. (2017). Reflections on the REST architectural style and principled design of the modern web architecture. In *Proceedings of the 2017 11th Joint Meeting on Foundations of Software Engineering* (pp. 4-14). New York, NY: ACM Press. 10.1145/3106237.3121282

Geetika, R., & Singh, P. (2014). Dynamic coupling metrics for object oriented software systems: A survey. *Software Engineering Notes*, *39*(2), 1–8. doi:10.1145/2579281.2579296

Ghobakhloo, M., Tang, S., Sabouri, M., & Zulkifli, N. (2014). The impact of information system-enabled supply chain process integration on business performance: A resource-based analysis. *International Journal of Information Technology & Decision Making*, *13*(05), 1075–1113. doi:10.1142/S0219622014500163

Graydon, P., Habli, I., Hawkins, R., Kelly, T., & Knight, J. (2012). Arguing Conformance. *IEEE Software*, *29*(3), 50–57. doi:10.1109/MS.2012.26

He, W., & Da Xu, L. (2014). Integration of distributed enterprise applications: A survey. *IEEE Transactions on Industrial Informatics*, *10*(1), 35–42. doi:10.1109/TII.2012.2189221

Hinings, B., Gegenhuber, T., & Greenwood, R. (2018). Digital innovation and transformation: An institutional perspective. *Information and Organization*, *28*(1), 52–61. doi:10.1016/j.infoandorg.2018.02.004

Imache, R., Izza, S., & Ahmed-Nacer, M. (2012). An enterprise information system agility assessment model. *Computer Science and Information Systems*, *9*(1), 107–133. doi:10.2298/CSIS101110041I

ISO. (2006). *Enterprise integration -- Framework for enterprise modelling. ISO/CEN Standard 19439:2006*. Geneva, Switzerland: International Organization for Standardization.

ISO. (2010). *Systems and software engineering – Vocabulary. ISO/IEC/IEEE 24765:2010(E) International Standard*. Geneva, Switzerland: International Organization for Standardization.

Iyengar, S., & Brooks, R. (Eds.). (2016). *Distributed sensor networks: sensor networking and applications*. Boca Raton, FL: CRC Press.

Juric, M., & Weerasiri, D. (2014). *WS-BPEL 2.0 beginner's guide*. Birmingham, UK: Packt Publishing Ltd.

Kahre, C., Hoffmann, D., & Ahlemann, F. (2017). Beyond business-IT alignment-Digital business strategies as a paradigmatic shift: A review and research agenda. In *Proceedings of the 50th Hawaii International Conference on System Sciences* (pp. 4706–4715). Academic Press. 10.24251/HICSS.2017.574

Khalfallah, M., Figay, N., Barhamgi, M., & Ghodous, P. (2014). Model driven conformance testing for standardized services. In *IEEE International Conference on Services Computing* (pp. 400–407). Piscataway, NJ: IEEE Computer Society Press. 10.1109/SCC.2014.60

Knoke, B., Missikoff, M., & Thoben, K. D. (2017). Collaborative open innovation management in virtual manufacturing enterprises. *International Journal of Computer Integrated Manufacturing*, *30*(1), 158–166.

Kostoska, M., Gusev, M., & Ristov, S. (2016). An overview of cloud interoperability. In *Federated Conference on Computer Science and Information Systems* (pp. 873-876). Piscataway, NJ: IEEE Computer Society Press. 10.15439/2016F463

Kovács, G., & Kot, S. (2017). Economic and social effects of novel supply chain concepts and virtual enterprises. *Journal of International Studies*, *10*(1), 237–254. doi:10.14254/2071-8330.2017/10 1/17

Li, G., & Wei, M. (2014). Everything-as-a-service platform for on-demand virtual enterprises. *Information Systems Frontiers*, *16*(3), 435–452. doi:10.100710796-012-9351-3

Liao, Y., Deschamps, F., Loures, E., & Ramos, L. (2017). Past, present and future of Industry 4.0 - a systematic literature review and research agenda proposal. *International Journal of Production Research*, *55*(12), 3609–3629. doi:10.1080/00207543.2017.1308576

Liska, R. (2018). Management Challenges in the Digital Era. In R. Brunet-Thornton & F. Martinez (Eds.), *Analyzing the Impacts of Industry 4.0 in Modern Business Environments* (pp. 82–99). Hershey, PA: IGI Global. doi:10.4018/978-1-5225-3468-6.ch005

Matentzoglu, N., Parsia, B., & Sattler, U. (2017). OWL Reasoning: Subsumption Test Hardness and Modularity. *Journal of Automated Reasoning*, 1–35. PMID:30069069

McLay, A. (2014). Re-reengineering the dream: Agility as competitive adaptability. *International Journal of Agile Systems and Management*, *7*(2), 101–115. doi:10.1504/IJASM.2014.061430

Mezgár, I., & Rauschecker, U. (2014). The challenge of networked enterprises for cloud computing interoperability. *Computers in Industry*, *65*(4), 657–674. doi:10.1016/j.compind.2014.01.017

Moreira, F., Ferreira, M., & Seruca, I. (2018). Enterprise 4.0–the emerging digital transformed enterprise? *Procedia Computer Science*, *138*, 525–532. doi:10.1016/j.procs.2018.10.072

O'Rourke, C., Fishman, N., & Selkow, W. (2003). *Enterprise architecture using the Zachman framework.* Boston, MA: Course Technology.

Oguz, F., & Sengün, A. (2011). Mystery of the unknown: Revisiting tacit knowledge in the organizational literature. *Journal of Knowledge Management, 15*(3), 445–461. doi:10.1108/13673271111137420

Panetto, H., & Whitman, L. (2016). Knowledge engineering for enterprise integration, interoperability and networking: Theory and applications. *Data & Knowledge Engineering, 105*, 1–4. doi:10.1016/j.datak.2016.05.001

Patrignani, N., & Kavathatzopoulos, I. (2016). Cloud computing: The ultimate step towards the virtual enterprise? *ACM SIGCAS Computers and Society, 45*(3), 68–72. doi:10.1145/2874239.2874249

Paul, P., & Saraswathi, R. (2017). The Internet of Things – A comprehensive survey. In *Proceedings of the International Conference on Computation of Power, Energy Information and Communication* (pp. 421-426). Piscataway, NJ: IEEE Computer Society Press. 10.1109/ICCPEIC.2017.8290405

Pautasso, C. (2014). RESTful web services: principles, patterns, emerging technologies. In A. Bouguettaya, Q. Sheng, & F. Daniel (Eds.), Web Services Foundations (pp. 31-51). New York, NY: Springer. doi:10.1007/978-1-4614-7518-7_2

Popplewell, K. (2014). Enterprise interoperability science base structure. In K. Mertins, F. Bénaben, R. Poler, & J. Bourrières (Eds.), *Enterprise Interoperability VI: Interoperability for Agility, Resilience and Plasticity of Collaborations* (pp. 417–427). Cham, Switzerland: Springer International Publishing. doi:10.1007/978-3-319-04948-9_35

Preidel, C., & Borrmann, A. (2016). Towards code compliance checking on the basis of a visual programming language. *Journal of Information Technology in Construction, 21*(25), 402–421.

Rezaei, R., Chiew, T., & Lee, S. (2014). A review on E-business interoperability frameworks. *Journal of Systems and Software, 93*, 199–216. doi:10.1016/j.jss.2014.02.004

Ritter, D., May, N., & Rinderle-Ma, S. (2017). Patterns for emerging application integration scenarios: A survey. *Information Systems, 67*, 36–57. doi:10.1016/j.is.2017.03.003

Samdantsoodol, A., Cang, S., Yu, H., Eardley, A., & Buyantsogt, A. (2017). Predicting the relationships between virtual enterprises and agility in supply chains. *Expert Systems with Applications, 84*, 58–73. doi:10.1016/j.eswa.2017.04.037

Şimşit, Z., Günay, S., & Vayvay, Ö. (2014). Theory of Constraints: A Literature Review. *Procedia: Social and Behavioral Sciences, 150*, 930–936. doi:10.1016/j.sbspro.2014.09.104

Tran, H., Zdun, U., Oberortner, E., Mulo, E., & Dustdar, S. (2012). Compliance in service-oriented architectures: A model-driven and view-based approach. *Information and Software Technology, 54*(6), 531–552. doi:10.1016/j.infsof.2012.01.001

Tzitzikas, Y., Manolis, N., & Papadakos, P. (2017). Faceted exploration of RDF/S datasets: A survey. *Journal of Intelligent Information Systems, 48*(2), 329–364. doi:10.100710844-016-0413-8

Uhl, A., & Gollenia, L. (2016). *Digital enterprise transformation: A business-driven approach to leveraging innovative IT*. New York, NY: Routledge. doi:10.4324/9781315577166

Verbaan, M., & Silvius, A. (2014). The Impact of IT Management Processes on Enterprise Agility. *Communications of the IIMA, 12*(1), 7.

Verborgh, R., Harth, A., Maleshkova, M., Stadtmüller, S., Steiner, T., Taheriyan, M., & Van de Walle, R. (2014). Survey of semantic description of REST APIs. In C. Pautasso, E. Wilde, & R. Alarcon (Eds.), *REST: Advanced Research Topics and Practical Applications* (pp. 69–89). New York, NY: Springer. doi:10.1007/978-1-4614-9299-3_5

Vicente, M., Gama, N., & da Silva, M. (2014). A Business Motivation Model for IT Service Management. *International Journal of Information System Modeling and Design, 5*(1), 83–107. doi:10.4018/ijismd.2014010104

Wang, H., Gibbins, N., Payne, T., Patelli, A., & Wang, Y. (2015). A survey of semantic web services formalisms. *Concurrency and Computation, 27*(15), 4053–4072. doi:10.1002/cpe.3481

Weeger, A., Wang, X., & Gewald, H. (2016). IT consumerization: BYOD-program acceptance and its impact on employer attractiveness. *Journal of Computer Information Systems, 56*(1), 1–10. doi:10.108 0/08874417.2015.11645795

Xu, L., Xu, E., & Li, L. (2018). Industry 4.0: State of the art and future trends. *International Journal of Production Research, 56*(8), 2941–2962. doi:10.1080/00207543.2018.1444806

Yang, H., Ma, K., Deng, C., Liao, H., Yan, J., & Zhang, J. (2013). Towards conformance testing of choreography based on scenario. In *Proceedings of the International Symposium on Theoretical Aspects of Software Engineering* (pp. 59–62). Piscataway, NJ: IEEE Computer Society Press. 10.1109/TASE.2013.23

Zanero, S. (2017). Cyber-physical systems. *IEEE Computer, 50*(4), 14–16. doi:10.1109/MC.2017.105

Zimmermann, O., Tomlinson, M., & Peuser, S. (2012). *Perspectives on Web Services: Applying SOAP, WSDL and UDDI to Real-World Projects*. New York, NY: Springer Science & Business Media.

ADDITIONAL READING

Bora, A., & Bezboruah, T. (2015). A Comparative Investigation on Implementation of RESTful versus SOAP based Web Services. *International Journal of Database Theory and Application, 8*(3), 297–312. doi:10.14257/ijdta.2015.8.3.26

Chen, Y. (2015). A RDF-based approach to metadata crosswalk for semantic interoperability at the data element level. *Library Hi Tech, 33*(2), 175–194. doi:10.1108/LHT-08-2014-0078

Dahiya, N., & Parmar, N. (2014). SOA AND REST Synergistic Approach. *International Journal of Computer Science and Information Technologies, 5*(6), 7045–7049.

Hussain, T., Mehmood, R., Haq, A., Alnafjan, K., & Alghamdi, A. (2014). Designing framework for the interoperability of C4I systems. In *International Conference on Computational Science and Computational Intelligence* (102–106). Piscataway, NJ: IEEE Computer Society Press. 10.1109/CSCI.2014.102

Romero, D., & Vernadat, F. (2016). Enterprise information systems state of the art: Past, present and future trends. *Computers in Industry*, *79*, 3–13. doi:10.1016/j.compind.2016.03.001

Schumacher, A., Erol, S., & Sihn, W. (2016). A maturity model for assessing industry 4.0 readiness and maturity of manufacturing enterprises. *Procedia CIRP*, *52*, 161–166. doi:10.1016/j.procir.2016.07.040

Sharma, R., & Panigrahi, P. (2015). Developing a roadmap for planning and implementation of interoperability capability in e-government. *Transforming Government: People. Process and Policy*, *9*(4), 426–447.

Sungkur, R., & Daiboo, S. (2016). Combining the Best Features of SOAP and REST for the Implementation of Web Services. *International Journal of Digital Information and Wireless Communications*, *6*(1), 21–33. doi:10.17781/P001923

Toosi, A., Calheiros, R., & Buyya, R. (2014). Interconnected cloud computing environments: Challenges, taxonomy, and survey. *ACM Computing Surveys*, *47*(1), 7. doi:10.1145/2593512

Zhang, Z., Wu, C., & Cheung, D. (2013). A survey on cloud interoperability: Taxonomies, standards, and practice. *Performance Evaluation Review*, *40*(4), 13–22. doi:10.1145/2479942.2479945

KEY TERMS AND DEFINITIONS

Agility: The capacity of an enterprise to adapt (reactively and/or proactively) to changes in its environment in a timely and cost-efficient manner.

Compliance: Asymmetric property between a consumer C and a provider P (C is compliant with P) that indicates that C satisfies all the requirements of P in terms of accepting requests.

Conformance: Asymmetric property between a provider P and a consumer C (P conforms to C) that indicates that P fulfills all the expectations of C in terms of the effects caused by its requests.

Consumer: A role performed by a resource A in an interaction with another B, which involves making a request to B and typically waiting for a response.

Coupling: A measurement of how much an application is dependent on the interface of another application.

Interoperability: Asymmetric property between a consumer C and a provider P (C is compatible with P) that holds if C is compliant with P.

Provider: A role performed by a resource B in an interaction with another A, which involves waiting for a request from A, honoring it and typically sending a response to A.

Service: The set of operations supported by an application that together define its behavior (the set of reactions to messages that the application is able to receive and process).

Virtual Enterprise: A temporary partnership between several enterprises with a specific set of goals.

Chapter 6
Role and Room for Knowledge Management in Small and Medium Enterprises

Neeta Baporikar

iD https://orcid.org/0000-0003-0676-9913

Namibia University of Science and Technology, Namibia & University of Pune, India

ABSTRACT

In the present day, success and worth of businesses depend more on intellectual capital. So, knowledge is a critical resource, for any organizational growth and sustainability. For small and medium enterprises (SMEs) the latent knowledge seen as the principal component for success often tends to be over guarded. That itself is sometimes detrimental to the SMEs growth. This outlook towards knowledge by SMEs has to undergo a change as there is vast room for knowledge management (KM). Abundant studies and research exist on KM, but the focus on SMEs is limited. Current scenario of globalization, technological advances, higher returns on intellectual capital, growing significance of knowledge-intensive industries makes KM a strategic and competitive tool for SME growth, sustainability, and development. KM is indispensable for successful and sustainable business in this contemporary complex economy. Thus, the overall aim of this study done by in-depth literature review and contextual analysis is to enhance the understanding of the role and room for KM in SMEs in this globalized world.

INTRODUCTION

In developing countries, a vast majority of SMEs are suffering from market failures due to insufficient provision for integrated, reliable, relevant and solution-oriented business information. SMEs need support for effective linking with global markets both for their inputs and outputs. Businesses leveraging knowledge resources can make decisions faster and closer to point of action (Baporikar, 2015). It also helps in mitigating risk, exploiting business opportunities and better understanding of market signals. Economic globalization and explosive growth in flow of information have transformed the basic tenets of small and medium enterprise (SME) development strategy. Protection, developmental initiatives in

DOI: 10.4018/978-1-5225-8933-4.ch006

terms provision for infrastructure and credit and fiscal incentives are now proving to be less efficient and helpful in their sustainable growth. Structural changes and realignment in the economy, import liberalization, fierce competition and increasing quality consciousness make run-of-the-mill units less viable (Baporikar, (2014b). While various researchers and vendors have developed and implemented Knowledge Management Strategy (KMS) for large organization, many SMEs still face the challenge of selecting affordable and suitable frameworks including strategies, tools, and methods to fit their needs. A successful KMS should not only impact a critical business process, but should also build the necessary momentum for innovation and growth. Thus for SME enterprise KMS must facilitate and contribute directly to innovations, organizational strategy, productivity, and bottom line. The study accessed the status of KM in SMEs and also examined the factors that influence the adoption of KM for SMEs with focus on developing countries. Many organizations have profited from KM because they recognize the importance of the KM in business growth and development. However the study found SMEs in general and SMEs in developing countries in specific have not realized this and hence, still vulnerable. The study takes this factor into consideration and proposes a KM approach specific to SMEs. The study contributes on KM and SMEs literature and hopefully aids the researchers and practioners specially in developing economies in recognizing and understanding the role and room for KM in SMEs in this globalized world.

BACKGROUND

One of the most significant evolutions in the business environment over the past decade is the dawn of the new economy. In particular, the management of knowledge assets may provide small firms new tools for survival, growth and maintaining a sustainable competitive advantage (Omerzel & Antoncic, 2008). There is a general accord in business practices and academia on the fact that SMEs are falling behind large companies in developing KM practices and benefits of KM has not fully exploited by these firms. This is reflected in a literature gap where little research efforts have been carried out on this topic. There is abundance of literature describing how various large companies are successfully practicing KM, but the reasons why small firms show poor usage of KM tools are still unclear. In fact, little empirical studies have been conducted to identify the factors influencing KM adoption in SMEs (Finkl & Ploder, 2009). In addition, there is a growing need for qualitative analysis of the effects of knowledge management practices of networked SMEs (Valkokari & Helander, 2007). The potential which KM offers in improving efficiency and innovation has been cited as a key source of competitive advantage (MacKinnon et al., 2002).

KM is a field that consists of two important elements: either from the Information Technology (IT) and Information System (IS) research or from Strategic Knowledge Management perspectives. Alexander, Neyer. & Huizingh, (2016) elaborated the difference between 'Knowledge-based Management' and 'Strategic Knowledge Management' stating that the prior is technologically driven and dominated by 'hard' system theories. While the later, arises from softer theories such as Resource based theory (Barney 1991) and is particularly relevant for studies of dynamic capabilities (Teece, 2000). This particular research leans towards the soft theories defining strategic knowledge as resources that fits the valuable, rare, inimitable, non-substitutable, and is believed can be collectively organised for sustainable competitive advantages. These two elements of KM are illustrated by Ling (2011) as technology-centred KM strategy and people-centred KM strategy in their study testing the interaction effects of KM strategy on intellectual capital and global performance relationship. The technology centred KM strategy is IT-driven and focuses on the tangible aspects of KM, while the people-centred approach is driven by organisational learning and focuses on the tacit aspects of KM (Perez & Pablos 2003).

This chapter particularly emphasises the people-centred approach in KM strategy implementation, especially in SMEs. The people-centred KM strategy emphasised the generation of knowledge sharing through the interaction among people in the organisations and also with other stakeholders. Previous studies have found that more tacit knowledge is shared during interaction between employees (Lee, Kim, & Kim, 2014). Organisations are increasingly dependent on knowledge resources, which have particular characteristics as a strategic focus on aspects such as competencies, organisational learning, knowledge sharing, and management of tacit and explicit knowledge (Baporikar, 2013; Park, Vertinsky & Becerra, 2013). To date, many literatures in KM field agree that culture is perhaps the most influential factor in promoting or inhibiting the practice of KM (Boh, Nguyen & Xu, 2013; Haak-Saheem & K. Darwish 2014; Said, 2015). Specifically organisations that value their employees with what they know, and reward employees for sharing that knowledge create a more conducive environment. Said (2015) suggests the possible relationship between organisational culture, KM processes and organisational performance and also provides insights into the impact of organisational culture on various KM processes and their link with organisational performance. Exploring the available literature review on KM in SMEs, Durst & Edvardsson (2012: 879) define KM as "…the processes and structures provided in SMEs to support different knowledge processes, such as transfer, storage, and creation".

As knowledge is becoming more strategically important in association with organisational capabilities to achieve competitive advantage (Teece, 2000), SMEs can benefit from proper management of knowledge although 'liability of smallness' limit their capability in implementing KM strategy compared to the large organisations. Despite this pressing need, it is widely accepted that small companies – even the most knowledge-intensive ones – are characterized by a lack of uptake of KM initiatives (Nunes et al., 2006). Perhaps due to the reason that KM systems are expensive to purchase, use and maintain. Instead of usual approaches, where KM needs heavy financial and other resources, this study suggested solution centric approach (Patrick & Dotsika, 2007). Small and medium enterprises make substantial contributions to national economies and are estimated to account for 80 percent of global economic growth (Pavic et al., 2007). Today in the competitive business environment knowledge is thought to be the primary resource (Baporikar, 2016). The conventional factors of production have become secondary. It is straightforward to obtain them, provided there is knowledge (Chen et al., 2006). Davidson & Griffin (2003) pointed out small businesses have contributed many innovative ideas and technological breakthroughs in society. In order to maintain and develop further their innovative skills, SMEs need to develop their understanding of knowledge management (KM), as a key business driver rather than as a resource-intensive additional initiative (Zanjani et al., 2008). Thus, KM has become the latest strategy in increasing organizational competitiveness (DeTienne & Jackson, 2001). Today, knowledge is the primary source of competitive advantage and the key to success for organizations in the knowledge economy (MacKinnon et al., 2002; Patriotta, 2003).

KNOWLEDGE

Knowledge has been defined in multiple ways. Davenport & Prusak (1988) defined knowledge as follows a fluid mix of framed experience, values, contextual information, and expert insight that provides a framework for evaluating and incorporating new experiences and information. Delahaye (2003) concluded that knowledge is a distinctive source as it has no law of diminishing returns, grows from sharing. Wiig (1997) argued that knowledge is not a new concept, from very early times people have transferred knowledge by succession to the next generation. In ancient cultures, this has taken the form of narratives and songs, which were intended to teach the new generation new skills and survival techniques.

Samuel (1775) wrote in his early dictionary that knowledge is of two kinds: we know a subject ourselves, or we know where we can find information on it. Further, knowledge can be divided into two categories: tacit and explicit. Explicit knowledge refers to the knowledge which can be articulated in formal language such as grammatical statements, mathematical expressions, specifications, manuals, and thus can be transmitted across individuals formally and easily. On the contrary, tacit knowledge refers to the knowledge which is hard to articulate with formal language, but is personal knowledge embedded in individual experience and involves intangible factors such as personal belief, perspective, and value systems (Nonaka & Takeuchi, 1995).

The latest assessment on Resource based theory and Penrosean theory of growth by Nason & Wiklund (2015) suggests that these two theories need to be aligned in order to provide a better explanation of firm growth. However, this relationship needs managerial involvement in structuring and bundling these resources into capabilities, and leveraging the capabilities to realise competitive advantage. Sirmon et al. (2011) contribute to the Resource based theory literature by focusing on what they term resource orchestration, which explicitly addresses the role of managers' actions in effectively structuring, bundling, and leveraging organisational resources. Knowledge-based resources is defined as "valuable resources that are protected from imitation by knowledge barriers" (Miller & Shamsie 1996: 522). Lately, strategic human capital has emerged as an area of interest in both strategy and HRM literatures (Wright, Gardner & Moynihan, 2013).

Human capital theory emphasises that human capital—the composition of employee knowledge, skills, abilities, and others (KSAOs) —is a central driver of organisational performance when the return on investment in human capital exceeds labour costs (Lepak & Snell, 1999; Ployhart & Molitemo, 2011a). Researchers argue that human capital, especially high quality and/or organisation specific human capital, has the potential to serve as a source of competitive advantage ((Wright, Gardner & Moynihan, 2013; Ployhart et al. 2014). Further, strategic human capital resources is define as, "Individual or unit-level capacities based on individual KSAOs that are accessible for unit-relevant competitive advantage" (Ployhart et al. 2014: 376). The term unit is used in the definition to signify collective levels of employees like in groups, departments or organisations.

KNOWLEDGE MANAGEMENT

KM involves knowledge identification, creation, acquisition, transfer, sharing and exploitation. KM is vital for efficiency and organizational competitiveness (Egbu, 2001). Boh (2007) described that KM is a systematic process for acquiring, organizing, sustaining, applying, sharing and renewing both the tacit and explicit knowledge of employees to enhance organizational performance and create value. Menkhoff et al., (2002) defined KM as the task of developing and exploiting both tangible and intangible knowledge resources of an organization. Pillania (2006c) defined KM as "a systematic, organized, explicit and deliberate ongoing process of creating, disseminating, applying, renewing and updating the knowledge for achieving organizational objectives''. KM is a process which involves the management of explicit and tacit knowledge (Nonaka & Takeuchi, 1995). Knowledge management, like knowledge itself, is difficult to define as concepts and practices evolved quickly through the 1990s. Two main issues are evident in this evolving path: i) knowledge is a critical resource, rather than land, machines, or capital (Drucker, 1993), and ii) organizations generally poorly managed it. If more attention were paid to creating, providing, sharing, using, and protecting knowledge, the promise was that organizational performance would improve (Earl, 2001).

Current definitions of knowledge reflect a range of standpoints. The following definition contains a comparatively broad approach because it includes a range of phenomena such as values, insight, and information. According to Davenport & Prusak, (1998), knowledge is a fluid mix of framed experience, values, contextual information, and expert insight that provides a framework for evaluating and incorporating new experiences and information. It originates and is applied in the minds of knowers. In organizations also, it often becomes embedded not only in documents or repositories, but also in organizational routines, processes, practices, and norms. Thus, agreeing to Davenport & Prusak (1998), most knowledge management projects have one of the following three aims:

1. to make knowledge visible and show the role of knowledge in an organization, mainly through maps, yellow pages, and hypertext tools;
2. to develop a knowledge-intensive culture by encouraging and aggregating behaviours such as knowledge sharing (as opposed to hoarding) and proactively seeking and offering knowledge;
3. to build a knowledge infrastructure-not only a technical system, but a web of connections among people given space, time, tools, and encouragement to interact and collaborate

An understanding of the concept of knowledge and knowledge taxonomies is important because theoretical developments in the knowledge management area are influenced by the distinction among the different types of knowledge (Baporikar, 2014a). The literature offers a number of different knowledge taxonomies. Drawing on the work of Polanyi (1962, 1967), Nonaka (1994) explicated the most cited classification of knowledge distinguishing tacit and explicit knowledge dimensions. The author also views knowledge as existing in the individual or the collective. Other classifications (Alavi & Leidner, 2001) refer to knowledge as declarative (know-about or knowledge by acquaintance (Nolan Norton 1998), procedural (know-how), causal (know-why), conditional (know-when), and relational (know-with) (Zack 1998). Likewise, research in the domain of knowledge management seems fragmented. According to Sveiby (1997) the expression "managing knowledge" appears for the first time in a context of artificial intelligence at the end of 1980s. Again, in the artificial intelligence community, Wiig (1993) was one of the first scholars to recognize the limits of a primarily technological approach and he defined KM in term of creation, learning, sharing (transferring), and using or leveraging knowledge as a set of social and dynamic processes that needed to be managed (Iandoli & Zollo, 2007). Almost at the same time, Nonaka and his research group conducted a number of studies on the management of innovation processes in large Japanese companies. These studies together with the total quality management movement and the concept of continuous improvement, re-evaluate the overall role that human resources play at all levels in organizations discovering what was not yet obvious in organizational practice: the centrality of the individual in the knowledge creation process and the consequent need to recognize the person's necessary level of competence and autonomy (Nonaka & Takeuchi, 1995). Most of the contributions in the vast literature on KM can be summarized to one of these two approaches or attempts to integrate the two perspectives (Iandoli & Zollo, 2007). Bhatt, (2001) defined KM, by identifying the different phases of a KM project. These are five phases reflected in the process of knowledge creation, validation, presentation, distribution, and application and they allow an organization to learn, reflect, unlearn and relearn, usually considered essential for building, maintaining, and replenishing of core-competencies.

However, the KM definition suggested by Iandoli & Zollo (2007) has been considered as the working definition for this chapter as it simultaneously refers to objectives, knowledge involved, tools and phases of KM. According to them, KM is the process of creating, capturing, and using knowledge to enhance organizational performance. It refers to a range of practices and techniques used by organizations to identify, represent, and distribute knowledge, know-how, expertise, intellectual capital, and other forms of knowledge for leverage, reuse and transfer of knowledge and learning across the organization. As exemplified above, KM initiatives involve not only an implementation of ICT but also social and cultural facets. However, while ICT does not apply to all of the issues of knowledge management, it can support KM in different ways. In this sense, according to Alavi & Leidner, (2001), knowledge management systems (KMS) refer to a class of information systems applied to managing organizational knowledge. That is, they are IT-based systems developed to support and enhance the organizational processes of knowledge creation, storage/retrieval, transfer, and application.

Knowledge Management Approaches

The term "knowledge management" is now in widespread use, having appeared in the titles of many new books about KM as a business strategy, as well as in articles in many business publications, including The Wall Street Journal. There are, of course, many ways to slice up the multi-faceted world of KM. However, it's often useful to categorize them. There is a broad range of thought on KM with no unanimous definition and the approaches vary by author and school. KM may be viewed from each of these perspectives:

- **Techno-Centric**: A focus on technology, ideally those that enhance knowledge sharing/growth.
- **Organizational**: How does the organization need to be designed to facilitate knowledge processes? Which organizations work best with what processes?
- **Ecological**: Seeing the interaction of people, identity, knowledge and environmental factors as a complex adaptive system. In addition, as the discipline is maturing, there is an increasing presence of academic debates within epistemology emerging in both the theory and practice of KM. British and Australian standards bodies have produced documents that attempt to bound and scope the field, but these have received limited acceptance or awareness.

SMEs IN DEVELOPING COUNTRIES

According to OECD (2000) SMEs make-up the largest proportion of businesses all over the world and play tremendous roles in employment generation, provision of goods and services, creating a better standard of living, as well as immensely contributing to the gross domestic products (GDPs) of many countries. The European Commission (2005) gave rise to the term SME in 1996. The term is defined as organizations employing fewer than 250 people (Burns, 2001). In developing countries, SMEs are defined differently for various countries. The term SME covers a heterogeneous group of businesses in a developing economy, ranging from a single artisan working in a small shop making handicrafts for a village market to sophisticated engineering firms selling in overseas markets (Fischer & Reuber, 2003). Generally SMEs in developing countries have not more than 250 employees.

SMEs General Characteristics

- The company is characterized by the entrepreneur who very often the owner.
- The entrepreneur normally is the "general manager", thus he acts on his own risk.
- The entrepreneur has a network of personal contacts to customers, suppliers and the relevant public sector. So the contact is close and rather informal.
- The company usually acts very local.
- The products offered can be very individual to the customer's needs.
- The form of organization is rather informal and flat.
- The company can react quickly to changes in the environment.
- The company is not dominated or ruled by another company, e.g. part of big business concern.
- The market share is normally small.
- The products are little diversified.

SMEs Importance

SMEs are the backbone of the industrialization process of many developing countries and play a vital part in expanding a country's economy. In Thailand, SMEs account for more than 90% of the total number of establishments, 65 per cent of employment and 47 per cent of manufacturing value added while in Philippines, SMEs comprise 99 per cent of the total manufacturing establishments and contribute 45 per cent of employment and 18 per cent of value added in the manufacturing sector. Across the South Asia, the contribution of SMEs to the overall economic growth and the GDP is high. It was estimated that SMEs contribute 50% of Bangladesh's industrial GDP and provide employment to 82% of the total industrial sector employment. In Nepal, SMEs constitute more than 98% of all establishments and contribute 63% of the value-added segment. In India, SMEs' contribution to GDP is 30% (Mahmood, 2008). According to economic survey of Pakistan (2008-09) SMEs have made the most significant contribution to the economic growth in 2008-09. SMEs' sector has emerged as a lifeline of Pakistan's economy constituting nearly 99.06 percent of all economic establishments. These establishments jointly contribute 30 percent to GDP employing 80 percent of the non-agricultural labor force, 25 percent to total export and 35 percent to manufacturing value addition. SMEs' contain various advantages in income growth, entrepreneurial training, creation of technological capabilities, greater flexibility to changing market circumstances, job creation and lower wage inequality and dispersion of industry away from urban areas and regional development (Berry, 1998; Katrak & Strange, 2002). Thus, promoting SMEs would lead to: fostering an entrepreneurial culture, providing resilience in the economy, contribution to exports, employment generation, facilitate learning geographically, sectorial development, efficient resource allocation, reduction in inequalities, fair distribution of wealth and poverty reduction.

SIGNIFICANCE OF KM FOR SMEs

Both large and small firms, require continuous generation, sharing and implementation of knowledge in order to maximize their competitiveness and survival chances in the modern information society (Nunes et al., 2006; Pillania, 2008b). However SMEs relatively need more focused approach towards KM as they face severe competition. Saloja et al., (2005) described that a more conscious and systematic approach to KM enhance SMEs performance and competitive advantage. KM also promotes innovation and business entrepreneurship, help manage change, and empower employees (Nonaka & Takeuchi, 1995). Zanjani et al., (2008) stated that SMEs need to make operational, tactical and strategic decisions and without accurate information they are unable to undertake this role. The knowledge of employees of an organization is an important asset and such knowledge should be garnered for the ultimate good of the company. Wong & Aspinwall (2004) described two complementary perspectives about KM importance in SMEs. "Pull" perspective, which identified potential benefits that are crucial for small businesses, example improved competency, efficiency, innovation, etc. and "push" perspective, which deals with the external or environmental thrusts, example competitive pressure, globalization, etc. (Davenport & Prusak, 1988).

Thus the underlying reasons for which SMEs need to manage their knowledge resources are:

1. SMEs compete on the basis of their competencies and knowledge is an important resource to be competent, hence need to use knowledge more than traditional resources.
2. The owner of SMEs, usually are also managers who need to transfer knowledge to employees.
3. SMEs usually find it difficult to get or retain good minds; hence they must settle for less qualified but motivated human resources.
4. Key stake holders like lending institutions, investors, suppliers, and customers, judged SMEs on the basis of their knowledge and strategies to put knowledge in right use. (Zanjani et al., 2008)
5. Continuous 'rightsizing' trend. Starting in the 1980s, corporate downsizing measures led to the loss of valuable information and knowledge resources and subsequently to the emergence of KM as strategic countermeasure.

The driving forces like globalization have lead individuals and organizations to appreciate the important role of knowledge in an increasingly competitive world market (Davenport & Prusak, 1988). SMEs as a part of business sectors are no different from any other business sector. KM plays an important role for many SME companies in gaining competitive advantage and business survival. Knowledge in a company should be properly managed and controlled to be effective and competitive, therefore, there is no excuse or option to them to manage individual and organizational knowledge to continuously improve their process and compete in market. By and large, SMEs have a set of distinctive needs as described earlier that call for the deployment of a KM system for generating, sharing, and refining organizational knowledge. However, in practice, SMEs are still very reluctant to take KM principles into their strategic thinking and daily routines (McAdam & Reid, 2001; Nunes et al., 2006).

SMEs usually lack resources such as land, labor, and capital. Therefore, SMEs must do more with less (Desouza & Awazu, 2006). SMEs need to be creative in working in order to manage knowledge with limited resources (Zanjani et al., 2008). Though SMEs in developing countries, in comparison with large enterprises are on back step for the availability of resources to manage knowledge, SMEs do have certain advantages in KM practice. i) SMEs flat structure and short decision making process allows shorter and faster information flow which can improve communication, as well as easier to permeate new change initiatives. ii) SMEs flexible culture provides a good foundation for a change, for example the practices of quality initiatives. iii) People dominated together with organic behaviour, rather than bureaucratic and system dominated, and this helps improve the chances of success for new initiatives. iv) The high incidence of innovativeness can nurture a continuous improvement culture. Knowledge, if properly harnessed, enables SMEs to stand out in the competition and outperform their rivals, thus maintaining a competitive edge (Wong, 2005).In short, KM:

- Facilitates better, more informed decisions
- Contributes to the intellectual capital of an organization
- Encourages the free flow of ideas which leads to insight and innovation
- Eliminates redundant processes, streamlines operations, and enhances employee retention rates
- Improves customer service and efficiency
- Can lead to greater productivity

KM does not have a beginning and an end. It is ongoing, organic, and ever-evolving. Hence, the challenge of KM is to determine what information within an organization qualifies as "valuable." All information is not knowledge, and all knowledge is not valuable. The key is to find the worthwhile knowledge within a vast sea of information.

KM CHALLENGES

Organizations have a wealth of knowledge which, is embedded in people's head, work practices, and systems. The challenge for organization is to be able to capture that knowledge and to leverage it throughout the organization. Spender (2002) asserts that the intangible nature of knowledge makes it harder to identify and manage; consequently it cannot be treated in the same way as other organizational assets. SMEs in developing countries have to face many challenges regarding KM adoption. Many SME owner-managers lack even fundamental concepts about KM and are unaware about underlying benefits of KM. Cultural barriers such as distrust, lack of recognition and communication, knowledge is power mindsets, retrenchment concerns and so forth demotivate with regard to effective knowledge sharing and utilization of 'what we know'. Organizational culture plays a critical role in adoption and successful implementation of KM in SMEs. Von Krogh (1998) stated "high organizational care culture" as a key element in KM development as its helps people to share ideas, information and knowledge. Handzic & Hasan (2003a) identify two major challenges for KM: achieving an objective picture of the field, based on formal and sound research, which integrates diverse perspectives of researchers and practitioners; and bridging the gap between theory and practice, thereby providing well-established KM strategies, tools and procedures for managers. Consequently such challenges and resistance to change in KM adoption and successful implementation is natural.

ODDITIES FACED BY SME IN MANAGING KNOWLEDGE

- Lack of processes for conversion of tacit knowledge to explicit knowledge
- Defining knowledge for different audience
- Information sharing and information access
- Security issues
- Problem of capturing data
- Creation of repositories without addressing the strategy to manage content
- Failure to analyze and map knowledge management system to user's needs
- SME's inability to motivate employees by addressing their knowledge and learning needs
- Selection of right tools and technologies
- Failure to avoid re-invention of the wheel

KNOWLEDGE MANAGEMENT IN SMEs

Although introducing knowledge management systems into SME is a particular challenge because of the limited resources of these kinds of companies (Herrmann et al, 2007), the literature review on KM reveals that the most part of research in this field is focused on large companies. In fact, the understanding of the organizational theory and practice considerations of KM has mainly been derived from large company experiences. Consequently, the potential of KM seems not fully exploited by small firms and this is reflected in a literature void where little research contributions on this topic have been published. In addition, research on KM in SMEs highlights some relevant different features (Pillania, 2006 & 2008)

According to the review carried out by Thorpe et al (2005), research on KM in the SMEs context may be broken down into three distinct fields:

1. The knowledgeable SME manager or entrepreneur;
2. The knowledge systems and routines embedded within the context of the firm and their immediate networks;
3. The institutional and policy framework that is intended to support knowledge production within SMEs.

As asserted by Frey (2001), although major corporations have led the way in introducing and implementing KM, it is increasingly important for small businesses to manage their collective intellectual assets. In KM practices, issues that small businesses will face will not be simply a scaled-down replica of large-company experiences (Sparrow, 2001). Desouza & Awazu (2006) discuss five key peculiarities that differentiate knowledge management practices in SMEs and larger companies:

1. Lack of explicit knowledge repositories. Each manager/owner acts as the knowledge repository.
2. Common knowledge possessed by members of the SMEs is deep and broad. This common knowledge helps in the organization of work by easing issues of knowledge transfer, sense-making, and application.
3. SMEs by their nature and due to deliberate mechanisms are skilled at avoiding pitfalls of knowledge loss. The close social ties between members of the SME act as a deterrence against employees leaving the business. In cases where employees do leave the business, there are plenty of available knowledge resources that can be mobilized to quickly fill the void.
4. SMEs have a knack for exploiting foreign sources of knowledge. Since they are resource constrained, and cannot spend efforts to create knowledge, they look outside the organization for knowledge.
5. SMEs knowingly or unknowingly, manage knowledge the right way – the humanistic way. Technology is never made part of the knowledge management equation. The use of technology in an SME is mostly limited to acts of automation (such as the use of cash registers) and at times for informative purposes (storing of employee contact information in databases).

Similarly, McAdam & Reid (2001) firstly describe the key dimensions of KM (knowledge construction, knowledge embodiment, knowledge dissemination and knowledge use/benefit) and then, for each dimension, conduct a comparison between large firms and SMEs. Sparrow (2001) indicates four components that figure strongly in small firm knowledge projects:

1. the appreciation of personal and shared understanding;
2. knowledge bases and knowledge systems;
3. the integrated and contextualized action needed for knowledge projects in SMEs, and
4. the knowledge and organizational learning processes in SMEs

Egbu et al. (2005) highlight that knowledge generated in SMEs is tacit in nature due to various reasons. In the context of SMEs some elements of KM are practiced but in an 'ad hoc' fashion. Indeed any technological infrastructure that is put in place to support KM must be adapted to the organization's needs and not the other way round. Another stream of KM research regards factors that can influence the success of KM implementation. But in this area also, most of research efforts are heavily focused on large companies as early adopters and superior performers of KM were large and multinational corporations. As such, existing factors are mainly large companies oriented, thereby reflecting their situations and needs. Directly applying these factors into the SMEs environment may not be sufficient without an understanding of their very own and specific conditions (Wong, 2005). By integrating the common factors and introducing some new ones, Wong (2005) and Wong & Aspinwall (2005), propose a more comprehensive model for implementing KM in SMEs based on the following factors: strategy and purpose; management leadership and support; culture; organizational infrastructure; IT, processes and activities; resources; measurement; human resources management, training and education and motivational aids.

The above set of critical success factors is important because of it can act as a list of items for SMEs to address and deal with when accomplishing KM. This helps to ensure that essential issues and factors are covered when small firms are planning and developing a KM strategy. It also enables them with a basis for evaluating their KM practices (Wong, 2005).

KM STRATEGY FOR SMEs

KM strategy depicts the general approach an organization aim to take to align its knowledge resources and capabilities to the intellectual requirements of its strategy, thus reducing the knowledge gap existing between what a company must know to perform its strategy and what it does know. (Zanjani et al., 2008)

Considering the nature and requirements of SMEs in developing countries, researchers proposed personalization strategy for KM. Personalization is a strategy to manage the knowledge that is formed via human communication. Personalization strategy focuses on dialogue between individuals, not knowledge objects in a database. It is a person-to-person approach where knowledge is shared not only face-to-face, but also by electronic communications, thus building networks of people (Cendan et al., 2007). Personalization, on the other hand, provides a rich medium for communication, as it is concerned with the use of people as a mechanism for sharing knowledge (Boh, 2007). If the business strategy focuses on generating new or customer specific solutions or product innovations the personalization strategy should be chosen rather than the codification strategy (Greiner et al., 2007). Personalization strategy is more suitable for SMEs conducting tasks that are more innovative in nature (Zanjani et al., 2008).

SCENARIO IN INDIA: KM AND SMEs

India is in a period of challenge with effects of globalization and it is a time to rethink what is the purpose of SMEs, to focus on the competencies of the future, and to move towards a networked cluster based policy and organizations. The private sector has shown that KM is a key enabler in this transition to a leaner, more efficient and more focused way of working. The SME sector, with support from the government, can also use knowledge management to deliver focused, networked and learning approaches in delivery of its key services. There has never been a more pressing need for improved ways of working in the SMES as today and KM is a key tool to enable this. With this brief introduction to the emergence of KM in the globalized world and the need for it in SMES, this chapter has focused on understanding and reviewing the concept application of KM to SME Sector in India. It delves into the meaning, need, process, steps and implementation approaches of KM.

Rationale for KM in SME

In India, this is reflected in poor financials of State Financial Corporations and steep decline in number of SME accounts with public sector banks. Main reasons assigned are lacuna in creating, managing and dissemination of knowledge among SMEs in specific and SME sector in general. These can be termed as 'Gap in KM'. The gaps in KM have resulted in growth constraints and crucial among them are:

- Information available with different institutions being non-convergent, incomplete or generalised in many respects restricts its utility to the sector.
- Informational asymmetry relating to viability and return on investment in SME projects increases the risk of adverse selection for banks.
- Informational infirmities and gaps aggravate the uncertainties about cost pattern and return on investment, choice of technology, scale of production and overall business viability which discourage capital investment by small entrepreneurs.
- Lack of enabling environment hampers global connectivity for their products though some SMEs have potential
- Banks have rating modules still their lending decisions are biased on availability of tangible security. Gaps in their KM system hamper objective assessment of enterprise's worth and overall viability. Consequently, credit flows to knowledge-based SMEs remain constricted.
- KM in banks often is confined to compilation of data and traditional analysis. Contextualising and converting these data into actionable-knowledge is required for evaluation of knowledge-intensive/ innovative/ new product oriented projects.
- Majority of SMEs also do not have requisite resources and expertise to develop the infrastructure necessary to access and transform the huge information available into intelligent insight.

FUTURE RESEARCH DIRECTIONS

Apart from generic studies about KIM implementation and strategies for SMEs – sector wise studies need to be undertaken as world over the SMES are based on classified products and services. ICT enablement for better leveraging knowledge across clusters would be another interesting area to probe. Technologically, effective KM requires the efficient organization of a suitable communication and information infrastructure (e.g. intranet) based on suitable and relevant taxonomies and knowledge repositories (where applicable). In addition, methods and techniques to leverage tacit knowledge, lessons learnt, viable approaches to documentation of experiences, whether successful or unsuccessful so as to create new knowledge would go a long way. SME organizational level studies about the development of a visionary leadership and a sound organizational culture to ensure maximum sharing of innovative and creative knowledge would also benefit the future entrepreneurs. Chan & Mauborgne (2003) also suggested constructive leadership behavior and development of a healthy organizational culture as important enabler of KM.

RECOMMENDATIONS

This chapter attempts to explore KM practices in SMEs. The study revealed that there is a significant need for KM. In addition, it has been observed that SMEs adopt predominantly internal KMSs using simple ICT tools. There is greater need for wider (external) KMSs enabling inter-firm collaboration in developing collaborative projects. Hence, some of the outlined for developing KM practices are:

- *Management of market knowledge.* KMS may support relationships with customers in order to facilitate both the exchange of relevant information and improving communication with them. Furthermore, a KMS should support the retrieval of information about market opportunities.
- *Management of technology knowledge.* This is a critical area for firms operating in high technology sectors. KM tools should support the circulation of critical information about know-how and technology. In this context, this appears particularly important as firms participate in collaborative projects aimed at developing new products and services. Practical examples may be the virtual sharing of design tools (e.g. or CAD, CAE e CAM) and management and control systems (e.g. MRP and ERP) related to the same project.
- *Management of relational knowledge.* In developing and managing collaborative projects it is important to have in place tools facilitating the collaboration among participants. Nevertheless, the adoption of these tools may be inhibited by the need to protect intellectual assets and cultural barriers.

CONCLUSION

KM has evolved and today the SMEs in many countries are reaping the benefits of KM adoption as part of the strategic management. However, that is not the case in developing countries. Only few sectors like auto components in India have gone in for KM development in their organizations (Baporikar & Deshpande, 2011; 2012). Though the problems faced by SMEs depend on the sector they belong and all may not be solvable, yet there is scope for KM adoption. To some extent that will definitely help SMEs to deal effectively with demands of present competitive era by managing individual and organizational knowledge. For that there is a need to create atmosphere where interaction between individuals and teams is possible for knowledge sharing. This is by ensuring maximum participation and a high level of motivation. Moreover, the relationship between KM and organisational performance is also connected within the HRM – performance link from strategic human capital resources theory. This theory emphasises that human capital—the composition of employee knowledge, skills, abilities, and others (KSAOs) —is a central driver of organisational performance when the return on investment in human capital exceeds labour costs (Becker 1964; Lepak & Snell 1999; Ployhart & Moliterno 2011b). Hence, the management of employees' knowledge through knowledge management, elevate SMEs' capability in sustaining competitive advantage. Chadee & Raman (2012) found that proper management of external knowledge contribute positively to organisational performance from strategic human capital point of view. Furthermore, Roxas, Battisti & Deakins (2014) emphasise the importance of engagement in learning activities by owner managers or senior management as one of the mechanism through which SMEs absorb external knowledge and strengthen KM and innovation performance relationship. In addition, Dahlander, O'Mahony. & Gann (2016) suggest that the positive effects between external search and innovation outcomes is driven by employees who spend a large amount of time with external people.

In summary, the KM personalization approach is most relevant to SMEs in developing countries because this has the greatest potential for sharing of valuable tacit knowledge. The governments in developing countries also need to develop specific policy to help SMEs in their countries to build KM awareness. Government agencies, chambers of commerce and SMEs need to commit more resources and work collectively to make the KM more profitable (Baporikar, 2011). Moreover, family owned businesses, owners, entrepreneurs and managers of SMEs need to change their attitudes, adapt to the competitive globalized world by adopting first hand variations like innovative leadership, global benchmarking and professional management. Embracing KM wholeheartedly by all the stakeholders of SMEs would be first right step in this direction.

DISCUSSION QUESTIONS IN CLASSROOMS

1. Discuss major differences between the approaches to KM by large organizations and SMEs.
2. How is knowledge integrated, sourced and recombined from internal and external sources for innovation and new product development in SMEs?
3. Does and in what manner does KM improve innovation, quality, productivity, and competitive standing?
4. Is knowledge a competitive resource for SMEs in developing countries?
5. Critically evaluate what are cost –benefits of KM for SMEs

REFERENCES

Alavi, M., & Dorothy, E. L. (2001). Review: Knowledge Management and Knowledge Management Systems: Conceptual Foundations and Research Issues. *Management Information Systems Quarterly*, *25*(1), 107–136. doi:10.2307/3250961

Alexander, A. T., Neyer, A.-K., & Huizingh, K. R. E. (2016). Introduction to the special issue: Transferring knowledge for innovation. *R & D Management*, *46*(2), 305–311. doi:10.1111/radm.12195

Baporikar, N. (2011). Knowledge Management and Entrepreneurship Cases in India. In M. Al-Shammari (Ed.), *Knowledge Management in Emerging Economies: Social, Organizational and Cultural Implementation* (pp. 325–346). Hershey, PA: IGI Global. doi:10.4018/978-1-61692-886-5.ch020

Baporikar, N. (2013). Entrepreneurship in a Modern Networked Indian Economy. *International Journal of Asian Business and Information Management*, *4*(4), 48–66. doi:10.4018/ijabim.2013100104

Baporikar, N. (2014a). Organizational Barriers and Facilitators in Embedding Knowledge Strategy. In M. Chilton & J. Bloodgood (Eds.), *Knowledge Management and Competitive Advantage: Issues and Potential Solutions* (pp. 149–173). Hershey, PA: Information Science Reference. doi:10.4018/978-1-4666-4679-7.ch009

Baporikar, N. (2014b). Strategic Management Overview and SME in Globalized World. In K. Todorov & D. Smallbone (Eds.), *Handbook of Research on Strategic Management in Small and Medium Enterprises* (pp. 22–39). Hershey, PA: Business Science Reference. doi:10.4018/978-1-4666-5962-9.ch002

Baporikar, N. (2015). Knowledge Management in Small and Medium Enterprises. In J. Zhao, P. Ordóñez de Pablos, & R. Tennyson (Eds.), *Organizational Innovation and IT Governance in Emerging Economies* (pp. 1–20). Hershey, PA: Business Science Reference. doi:10.4018/978-1-4666-7332-8.ch001

Baporikar, N. (2016). Understanding Knowledge Management Spectrum for SMEs in Global Scenario. *International Journal of Social and Organizational Dynamics in IT*, *5*(1), 1–15. doi:10.4018/IJSODIT.2016010101

Baporikar, N., & Deshpande, M. (2012). Sustainable Entrepreneurship - Approach of Pune Auto Components Entrepreneurs. In A. Marcus & J. Rayappa (Eds.), Entrepreneurship, Youth and Inclusive Development for Brand India (pp. 313-320). Loyala Publications.

Barney, J. (1991). Firm resources and sustained competitive advantage. *Journal of Management*, *17*(1), 99–120. doi:10.1177/014920639101700108

Berry, A. (1998). The Potential Role of the SME Sector in Pakistan in a World of Increasing International Trade. *Pakistan Development Review*, *37*(4), 25–49. doi:10.30541/v37i4Ipp.25-49

Bhatt, G. D. (2001). Knowledge Management in Organizations: Examining the Interaction Between Technologies, Techniques, and People. *Journal of Knowledge Management*, *5*(1), 68–75. doi:10.1108/13673270110384419

Boh, W. F. (2007). Mechanisms for sharing knowledge in project-based organizations. *Information and Organization*, *17*(1), 27–58. doi:10.1016/j.infoandorg.2006.10.001

Boh, W. F., Nguyen, T. T., & Xu, Y. (2013). Knowledge transfer across dissimilar cultures. *Journal of Knowledge Management*, *17*(1), 29–46. doi:10.1108/13673271311300723

Burns, P. (2001). *Entrepreneurship and Small Business*. Academic Press.

Cerdan, A.L., Lopez-Nicolas, C., & Sabater-Sa´nchez, R. (2007). Knowledge management strategy diagnosis from KM instruments use, *Journal of Knowledge Management, 11*(2), 60-72.

Chadee, D., & Raman, R. (2012). External knowledge and performance of offshore IT service providers in India: The mediating role of talent management. *Asia Pacific Journal of Human Resources*, *50*(4), 459–482. doi:10.1111/j.1744-7941.2012.00039.x

Chen, S., Duan, Y., Edwards, S., & Lehaney, B. (2006). Toward understanding inter organizational knowledge transfer needs in SMEs: Insight from a UK investigation. *Journal of Knowledge Management*, *10*(3), 6–23. doi:10.1108/13673270610670821

Chesebrough, E. D. (2006). Knowledge Management A tool for SMEs to enhance Competitiveness. *CACCI Journal, 1*.

Dahlander, L., O'Mahony, S., & Gann, D. M. (2016). One foot in, one foot out: How does individuals' external search breadth affect innovation outcomes? *Strategic Management Journal*, *37*(2), 280–302. doi:10.1002mj.2342

Davenport, T. H., & Prusak, L. (1998). *Working Knowledge: How Organizations Manage What They Know*. Boston: Harvard Business School Press.

Davidson, P., & Griffin, R. W. (2003). *Management: An Australasian Perspective* (2nd ed.). Brisbane, Australia: John Wiley & Sons.

Dejan Nenov. (2005). *New Approaches to KM in Government: User-Centric Enterprise Information*. Accessed from, www.x1.com/download/x1_platform_whitepaper.pdf

Delahaye, B. L. (2003). Human Resource Development and the Management of Knowledge Capital. In R. Wiesner & B. Millett (Eds.), *Human Resource Management: Challenges and Future Directions*. Brisbane, Australia: John Wiley & Sons.

Deshpande, M., & Deshpande, N. (2011). Business Policy Implementation – A Case of Auto Components SMEs in Pune. In Building Competencies for Sustainability and Organizational Excellence. Macmillan.

Desouza, K. C., & Awazu, Y. (2006). Knowledge Management at SMEs: Five Peculiarities. *Journal of Knowledge Management*, *10*(1), 32–43. doi:10.1108/13673270610650085

DeTienne, K. B., & Jackson, L. A. (2001). Knowledge Management: Understanding Theory and Developing Strategy. *Competitiveness Review*, *11*(1), 1–9. doi:10.1108/eb046415

Drucker, P. F. (1993). *The Post Capitalist Society*. London: Butterworth-Heinemann.

Durst, S., & Edvardsson, I. R. (2012). Knowledge management in SMEs: A literature review. *Journal of Knowledge Management*, *16*(6), 879–903. doi:10.1108/13673271211276173

Earl, M. (2001). Knowledge Management Strategies: Toward a Taxonomy. *Journal of Management Information Systems*, *18*(1), 215–233. doi:10.1080/07421222.2001.11045670

Egbu, C. O. (2001). Knowledge management in small and medium enterprises in the construction industry: challenges and opportunities. *Managing Knowledge: conversation and Critiques. Proceedings of an international conference*.

Egbu, C. O., Hari, S., & Renukappa, S. H. (2005). Knowledge Management for Sustainable Competitiveness in Small and Medium Surveying Practices. *Structural Survey*, *23*(1), 7–21. doi:10.1108/02630800510586871

European Commission. (2005). The New SME Definition. User Guide and Model Declaration. European Commission.

Finkl, K., & Ploder, C. (2009). Knowledge Management Toolkit for SMEs. *International Journal of Knowledge Management, 5*(1), 46–60. doi:10.4018/jkm.2009010104

Fischer, E., & Reuber, R. (2003). *Competitiveness Strategy in Developing Countries: A Manuel for Policy Analysis* (G. Wignaraja, Ed.). London: Routledge.

Frey, R. S. (2001). Knowledge Management, Proposal Development, and Small Businesses. *Journal of Management Development, 20*(1), 38–54. doi:10.1108/02621710110365041

Greiner, M. E., Hmann, T. B., & Krcmar, H. (2007). A strategy for knowledge management. *Journal of Knowledge Management, 11*(6), 3–15. doi:10.1108/13673270710832127

Haak-Saheem, W., & Darwish, K. T. (2014). The role of knowledge management in creating a culture of learning. Management Decision, 52(9), 1611–1629.

Herrmann & Jahnke. (2007). Work Process Oriented Introduction of Knowledge Management: Reconsidering the Guidelines for SME. In *I-KNOW '07. 7th International Conference on Knowledge Management*. Graz, Austria: Know-Center.

Iandoli, L., & Zollo, G. (2007). *Organizational Cognition and Learning. Building Systems for the Learning Organization*. New York: Information Science Publishing. doi:10.4018/978-1-59904-313-5

Katrak, H., & Strange, R. (2002). Introduction and Overview. In H. Katrak & R. Strange (Eds.), *Small Scale Enterprises in Developing and Transition Economies*. Basingstoke, UK: Palgrave.

Lee, E. J., Kim, H. S., & Kim, H. Y. (2014). Relationships between core factors of knowledge management in hospital nursing organisations and outcomes of nursing performance. *Journal of Clinical Nursing, 23*(23–24), 3513–3524. doi:10.1111/jocn.12603

Lepak, D. P., & Snell, S. A. (1999). The Human Resource Architecture: Toward a Theory of Human Capital Allocation and Development. *Academy of Management Review, 24*(1), 31–48. doi:10.5465/amr.1999.1580439

MacKinnon, D., Cumbers, A., & Chapman, K. (2002). Learning, innovation and regional development: A critical appraisal of recent debates. *Progress in Human Geography, 26*(3), 293–311. doi:10.1191/0309132502ph371ra

Mahmood, S. (2008). *Corporate Governance and Business Ethics for SMEs in Developing Countries: Challenges and Way Forward*. Academic Press.

McAdam, R., & Reid, R. (2001). SMEs and Large Organisation Perceptions of Knowledge Management: Comparisons and Contrasts. *Journal of Knowledge Management, 5*(3), 231–241. doi:10.1108/13673270110400870

Menkhoff, T., Wah, C. Y., & Loh, B. (2002). Towards Strategic Knowledge Management in Singapore's Small Business Sector. Presented at the *International Conference on Globalization, Innovation and Human Resource Development for Competitive Advantage*, Bangkok, Thailand.

Miller, D., & Shamsie, J. (1996). The Resource-Based View of the Firm in Two Environments: The Hollywood Film Studios from 1936 to 1965. *Academy of Management Journal, 39*(3), 19–543.

Minbaeva, D. B. (2013). Strategic HRM in building micro-foundations of organizational knowledge-based performance. *Human Resource Management Review*, *23*(4), 378–390. doi:10.1016/j.hrmr.2012.10.001

Molloy, J. C., & Barney, J. B. (2015). Who Captures the Value Created with Human Capital? A Market-based View. *The Academy of Management Perspectives*, *29*(3), 309–325. doi:10.5465/amp.2014.0152

Motsenigos & Young. (2002). KM in the U.S. government sector. *KM World*, *11*.

Nason, R. S., & Wiklund, J. (2015). An Assessment of Resource-Based Theorizing on Firm Growth and Suggestions for the Future. *Journal of Management*, 1–29.

Nolan Norton Institute. (1998). *Putting the Knowing Organization to Value*. White Paper. Author.

Nonaka, I. (1994). A Dynamic Theory of Organizational Knowledge Creation. *Organization Science*, *5*(1), 14–37. doi:10.1287/orsc.5.1.14

Nonaka, I., & Takeuchi, H. (1995). *The Knowledge-creating Company*. New York: Oxford University Press.

Nunes, M. B., Annansingh, F., & Eaglestone, B. (2006). Knowledge management issues in knowledge-intensive SMEs. *The Journal of Documentation*, *62*(1), 101–119. doi:10.1108/00220410610642075

Omerzel, D. G., & Antoncic, B. (2008). Critical Entrepreneur Knowledge Dimensions for the SME Performance. *Industrial Management & Data Systems*, *108*(9), 1182–1199. doi:10.1108/02635570810914883

Organization for Economic Co-operation and Development (OECD). (2000). Small and Medium-sized Enterprises: local Strength, global reach. *OECD Policy Review*, 1-8.

Park, C., Vertinsky, I., & Becerra, M. (2013). Transfers of explicit vs. tacit knowledge and performance in international joint ventures: The impact of age. *International Business Review*, *24*(1), 89–101. doi:10.1016/j.ibusrev.2014.06.004

Patrick, K., & Dotsika, F. (2007). Knowledge sharing: Developing from within. *The Learning Organization*, *5*(14), 395–406. doi:10.1108/09696470710762628

Patriotta, G. (2003). *Organizational Knowledge in the Making - How Firms Create, Use, and Institutionalise Knowledge*. Oxford, UK: Oxford University Press.

Pavic, S., Koh, S. C. L., Simpson, M., & Padmore, J. (2007). Could e-business create a competitive advantage in UK SMEs? *Benchmarking: An International Journal*, *14*(3), 320–351. doi:10.1108/14635770710753112

Perez, J. R., & de Pablos, P. O. (2003). Knowledge management and organizational competitiveness: A framework for human capital analysis. *Journal of Knowledge Management*, *7*(3), 82–91. doi:10.1108/13673270310485640

Pillania, R. K. (2006). Leveraging Knowledge for Sustainable Competitiveness in SMEs. *International Journal of Globalisation and Small Business*, *1*(4), 393–406. doi:10.1504/IJGSB.2006.012187

Pillania, R. K. (2006c). Current status of storage and access of knowledge in Indian industry. *Journal of Information and Knowledge Management*, *5*(1), 37–46. doi:10.1142/S0219649206001347

Pillania, R. K. (2008). Strategic Issues in Knowledge Management in Small and Medium Enterprises. *Knowledge Management Research and Practice*, 6(4), 334–338. doi:10.1057/kmrp.2008.21

Pillania, R. K. (2008b). Information technology strategy for knowledge management in SMEs. *Knowledge and Process Management*, 15(3), 41–49. doi:10.1002/kpm.311

Ployhart, R. E., & Moliterno, T. P. (2011a). Emergence of the Human Capital Resource: A Mulitlevel Model. *Academy of Management Review*, 36(1), 127–150. doi:10.5465/amr.2009.0318

Ployhart, R. E., & Moliterno, T. P. (2011b). Emergence of the Human Capital Resource: A Mulitlevel Model. *Academy of Management Review*, 36(1), 127–150. doi:10.5465/amr.2009.0318

Ployhart, R. E., Nyberg, A. J., Reilly, G., & Maltarich, M. A. (2014). Human Capital Is Dead; Long Live Human Capital Resources! *Journal of Management*, 40(2), 371–398. doi:10.1177/0149206313512152

Polanyi, M. (1962). *Personal Knowledge: Toward a Post- Critical Philosophy*. New York: Harper Torchbooks.

Polanyi, M. (1967). *The Tacit Dimension*. London: Routledge and Keoan Paul.

Roxas, B., Battisti, M., & Deakins, D. (2014). Learning, innovation and firm performance: Knowledge management in small firms. *Knowledge Management Research and Practice*, 12(4), 443–453. doi:10.1057/kmrp.2012.66

Said, A. A. S. (2015). Positioning organisational culture in knowledge management research. *Journal of Knowledge Management*, 19(2), 164–189. doi:10.1108/JKM-07-2014-0287

Saloja, S., Furu, P., & Sveiby, K. (2005). Knowledge management and growth in Finnish SMEs. *Journal of Knowledge Management*, 9(2), 103–122. doi:10.1108/13673270510590254

Sirmon, D. G., Hitt, M. A., Ireland, R. D., & Gilbert, B. A. (2011). Resource Orchestration to Create Competitive Advantage: Breadth, Depth, and Life Cycle Effects. *Journal of Management*, 37(5), 1390–1412. doi:10.1177/0149206310385695

Sparrow, J. (2001). Knowledge Management in Small Firms. *Knowledge and Process Management*, 8(1), 3–16. doi:10.1002/kpm.92

Spender, J. C. (2002). Knowledge Management, Uncertainty, and an Emergent Theory of the Firm. In C. W. Choo & N. Bontis (Eds.), *The Strategic Management of Intellectual Capital and Organizational Knowledge* (pp. 149–162). Oxford, UK: Oxford University Press.

Sveiby, K. (1997). *The New Organizational Wealth: Managing and Measuring Knowledge-Based Assets*. San Francisco: Berret Koehler.

Teece, D. J. (2000). Strategies for Managing Knowledge Assets: The Role of Firm Structure and Industrial Context. *Long Range Planning*, 33(1), 35–54. doi:10.1016/S0024-6301(99)00117-X

Thorpe, R., Holt, R., Macpherson, A., & Pittaway, L. (2005). Using Knowledge within Small and Medium-Sized Firms: A systematic Review of the Evidence. *International Journal of Management Reviews*, 7(4), 257–281. doi:10.1111/j.1468-2370.2005.00116.x

Valkokari, K., & Helander, N. (2007). Knowledge Management in Different Types of Strategic SME Networks. *Management Research News*, *30*(8), 597–608. doi:10.1108/01409170710773724

Von Krogh, G. (1998). Care in Knowledge Creation. *California Management Review*, *40*(3), 133–154. doi:10.2307/41165947

Wiig, K. (1993). *Knowledge Management Foundations*. Schema Press.

Wong, K. Y. (2005). Critical Success Factors for Implementing Knowledge Management in Small and Medium Enterprises. *Industrial Management & Data Systems*, *105*(3), 261–279. doi:10.1108/02635570510590101

Wong, K. Y., & Aspinwall, E. (2005). An Empirical Study of the Important Factors for Knowledge-Management Adoption in the SME Sector. *Journal of Knowledge Management*, *9*(3), 64–82. doi:10.1108/13673270510602773

Wright, P. M., Gardner, T. M., & Moynihan, L. M. (2003). The impact of HR practices on the performance of business units. *Human Resource Management Journal*, *13*(3), 21–36. doi:10.1111/j.1748-8583.2003.tb00096.x

Zack, M. (1998). What Knowledge-Problems Can Information Technology Help to Solve. *Proceedings of the Fourth Americas Conference on Information Systems*, 644-646.

Zanjani, S., Mehdi, S. M., & Mandana, M. (2008). Organizational Dimensions as Determinant Factors of KM Approaches in SMEs. *Proceedings of World Academy of Science, Engineering and Technology, 35*.

Chapter 7
A Critical Review of Actor–Network Theory (ANT) and Its Use in Education Research

Denise Mifsud

https://orcid.org/0000-0001-6330-4528

Euro-Mediterranean Centre for Educational Research, Malta

ABSTRACT

This chapter, which expands on a previous publication, presents a critique of actor-network theory as a sociomaterial concept. Furthermore, the author problematizes the relative under-application of this "sensibility" in education research, while simultaneously exploring its contribution as an analytical framework through its central concepts of "actor-network," "symmetry," "translation," and their constituents. This chapter zooms on the concepts of networks and power relations. The author questions the prevalent notion of the "network" metaphor promulgated by globalization discourses, setting it up against the network conception in actor-network theory, where the main principle is multiplicity. Actor-network theory is analyzed as a theory of the mechanics of power, concerning itself with the setting up of hegemony. This chapter is especially targeted for researchers of education reform who are as yet unfamiliar with the concepts of Actor-Network Theory and somewhat wary of the validity of sociomaterialism in the analysis of education issues.

A CRITICAL REVIEW OF ACTOR-NETWORK THEORY (ANT) AND ITS USE IN EDUCATION RESEARCH

Actor Network Theory (ANT) is deemed to be one of the more contentious methodologies in the social sciences, mainly because of its analytical realism, which "treads on a set of ethical, epistemological and ontological toes" (Law, 1992, p. 3), through its conception of general symmetry which gives equal and undivided attention to human and non-human 'actors'. Law (2007, p. 2) describes ANT as "a disparate family of material-semiotic tools, sensibilities and methods of analysis". I analyze the diverse characterizations of ANT as expounded by different thinkers while considering the possible reasons behind

DOI: 10.4018/978-1-5225-8933-4.ch007

the relative under-application of ANT in education studies. While admitting that writing about ANT is extremely difficult due to its messy, fluid, disorderly, dynamic, chaotic and ambivalent nature, it is the very 'messiness', 'fluidity', and 'chaos' of this 'sensibility' that offers invaluable insights to researchers in the education arena (Mifsud, 2014). I sketch possible ways in which ANT can contribute to 'methodological cleansing' in the exploration of networks. Besides providing a critical literature review of the ANT concept, I explore its contribution as an analytical framework in education studies, in particular the exploration of networks and power relations, through its central concepts of 'actor-network', 'symmetry', 'translation', and their constituents.

Two concepts this paper gives prominence to are networks and power relations. In light of the way in which the 'network' metaphor has invaded social order, becoming a common conceptual horizon for contemplating about the ontological 'structure' of the construction of reality, I challenge this conception of networks propagated by globalization discourses, contrasting it in turn with the network conception in ANT, where the main premise is multiplicity, the enactment of multiple, simultaneous ontologies, as outlined by Law (2004), Mol (2002), and Moser (2008). ANT may be regarded as a theory of the mechanics of power, concerning itself with the stabilization and reproduction of some interactions over others; the construction and maintenance of network centres and peripheries; and the establishment of hegemony. I explore how Law's (1991, p. 18) suggestion that "power, whatever form it may take, is recursively woven into the intricate dance that unites the social and the technical" has been received by both ANT critics and proponents.

DEFINITIONS OF ANT

Law (2007) describes ANT as "a disparate family of material-semiotic tools, sensibilities and methods of analysis ... [it explores] the webs and the practices that carry them ... [and] the enactment of materially and discursively heterogeneous relations that produce and reshuffle all kinds of actors" (p. 2). In his exploration of the definition, Law (2007) outlines four qualifications for this concept/approach. ANT is both theoretical and empirical, as theory is embedded and extended in empirical practice. Law (2007) refuses to regard the actor-network approach as a theory, for him it is a 'toolkit' rather, a 'sensibility' for the exploration of relations and how these assemble. He even refuses to define it as a theory, preferring the term 'material semiotics' rather than 'actor-network theory', as it better captures the open, uncertain, revisable, and diverse nature of this approach, all this hinting at Law's desire to keep it implicit and volatile, he refuses to have it pinned down to something concrete. Callon (1999) denies the claim of ANT being a theory, at the same time stressing that this "gives it both its strength and its adaptability ... we never claimed to create a theory. In ANT the T is too much (*'de trop'*)" (ibid, p. 194). Law (2007) further acknowledges the relationality of texts, thereby indirectly admitting to the subjective nature of ANT, with no researcher able to make objective claims. He describes it as neither 'a creed', nor 'a dogma', with humility as a leitmotif. Latour (1999) outlines the agenda of ANT as comprising: the *attribution* of both human and nonhuman characteristics; the *distribution* of properties among them; the *connections* generated; the *circulation* of these elements; as well as their *transformation*. Thus, ANT incorporates both relational materiality and performativity (Law, 1999). It takes a semiotic world-view, embracing a negation of conventional social dualisms, where divisions are understood as 'effects' or 'outcomes' rather than being inherent in entities – "essentialist divisions are thrown on the bonfire of the dualisms" (ibid, p. 3). As a consequence of this 'semiotics of materiality', entities are *performed* in, by, and through those relations.

Cordella & Shaikh (2006) consider ANT as an *interpretative lens* for the analysis and subsequent interpretation of the complexity of dynamics present in networks. Their understanding of the word 'lens' is based on Orlikowski (2000) where certain features are focused on and emerge, with the rest falling into the background. ANT explicitly argues against the notion of constructivism, maintaining that it is the constitutive forces in the interplay among actors themselves that define, constitute and construct this interplay (Latour, 1999b; Law, 1999) – ANT views reality as an emergent phenomenon. Despite ANT's contribution to a new way of questioning reality and a new way of conceptualizing the understanding of reality, it has been misinterpreted. As Law (1999) states, ANT has "been reduced to a few aphorisms that can be quickly passed on", which has tended to "defuse the power and the tension originally and oxymoronically built into the expression [actor-network]" (pp. 8-9). He attacks the assumption of heterogeneity and incompatibility being mistaken for homogeneity – this defies its theoretical richness and hybrid methodology. ANT offers the challenging opportunity of exploring the concept of becoming and change in a network, by studying reality as transitional in its unfolding and as a trajectory of creation, constantly being made and remade, never constant/static. Parker (2017) describes ANT as a 'relational epistemology', therefore promoting itself as a valuable instrument for 'slowing things down', in order to make visible the complex processes of change and transformation. Furthermore, ANT may lead to the problematization of the traditional concepts of "what we know" and "how we know what we know" in what the analysis chooses to render visible. Notably, ANT is "its own ontology – we are only able to *know* what is made visible by traceable associations" (p. 155, original emphasis). As Nespor (2002) describes, ANT ideas are "ontological acids undermining reductive explanations and pushing us towards engagements with evidence" (p. 368). Lee & Stenner (1999) give an alternative interpretation of ANT – as "a moral commitment to the inclusion of the disenfranchised" (ibid, p. 96), thus extending the possibility of infinite inclusion. The disturbing 'unsecuring' of belonging that ANT involves, 'belonging-by-banishment' and 'belonging-by-assemblage' raise ethical questions about the nature of belonging, questions which remain unanswered, contributing further to the abiding controversy of ANT.

Baiocchi et al. (2013) problematize the purchase of ANT for educational research, questioning its purpose as a theory or method depending on how it is approached and conceptualized. They regard it as a set of sensibilities, placing an emphasis on four particular ethnographic engagements and entanglements. ANT sensibilities call for particular kinds of descriptions – the assembling, disassembling, and reassembling of associations – with ANT giving the possibility of expansion to what is worthy of description. ANT sensibilities comprise a different relationship to theory, rejecting the top-down mobilization of theory to explain, rather than to facilitate further examination. ANT theorists regard the reliance on theory to 'frame' reality as constituting the failure of research to sufficiently trace associations and connections. ANT sensibilities empower all actors with a voice to speak their sociologies, being especially concerned with the discursively and materially heterogeneous 'world-making' activity of actors. ANT flags up "what actors achieve by *scaling*, *spacing*, and *contextualizing* each other" (Latour 2005, p. 184, original emphasis). ANT sensibilities raise the question of politics in research, with knowledge itself being an actor-network. Consequently, "Though sometimes decried as apolitical, ANT has the potential to open the door for more subtle kinds of political engagements … It encourages questions about the kinds of worlds we are helping to make and legitimate in our accounts, and the ways in which we are helping to compose and reconfigure the very communities, processes, and actors under our ethnographic gaze … [with] ethnographic research act[ing] *in* and *on* the world" (Baiocchi et al. 2013, p. 337, original emphasis).

A constellation of ideas have developed around ANT and associated themselves with it. In my writings, I choose to employ the all-encompassing definition given by Fenwick & Edwards (2010), to employ "ANT as a marker – understood to be a contingent and conflicted signifier – for approaches that share notions of symmetry, network broadly conceived, and translation in multiple and shifting formulations" (p. 3). In this sense, "the infralanguage of ANT is seen as a tool to help explicate, amplify, and link – not as a detailed series of rigorous, cohesive, general, and substantive claims concerning the world" (Sayes 2014, p. 142). Fenwick & Edwards (2011) are concerned that "the risk in explaining ANT is *distorting* and *domesticating* it" (p. 2, added emphasis), with its ideas being "practices for understanding, not a totalizing theory of the world and its problems". ANT helps researchers reflect on the different kinds of connections and associations created among things; the networks produced through these connections; in addition to the different ends served through these networks. ANT can demonstrate how assemblages in educational practices can be simultaneously made and unmade, with unconventional forms and spaces taking shape and developing strength.

CENTRAL CONCEPTS OF ANT

Symmetry

ANT treats human entities in an equal way to nonhumans, they are regarded as relational effects, taking away the strength/force of human agency and intentionality. Humans are not assumed to be privileged with an 'a priori' status in the world, on the other hand/conversely, "without the nonhuman, the humans would not last for a minute" (Latour, 2004a: 91). ANT subsequently traces *how* these entities assemble and *hold* together, being both capable of 'translating' each other. Fenwick & Edwards (2010) remark that this concept of generalized symmetry is difficult to keep hold of and operationalize, arguing that the very notion of actor-network itself inscribes this symmetrical approach.

Murdoch (1998) claims that through the principle of general symmetry, ANT "questions the very status of the term 'human'" (p. 367), by 'flattening' all distinctions between the network entities, in so doing, questioning if the dichotomy between humans and nonhumans is negligible. According to Rose (1996b), when humans are aggregated and 'black-boxed' in networks, they are conferred stable identities *as* 'humans' – relating to oneself as a "subject of unique capacities" or as the "target of discipline and docility" (p. 141). Following the same argument, Murdoch (1998) describes how humans can either "be networks" or be "situated in networks" (p. 368) – in this way, ANT analysts may end up "struggling for symmetrical perspective on heterogeneous relations while at the same time relying on intentionally motivated humans as key actors" (p. 369). The principle of symmetry may turn out to be a hindrance when addressing the question of network negotiation processes by those that are "partial and ambivalent" members (Murdoch, 1998).

Latour (2005) confirms that this concept of 'symmetry' is not an attempt at a 'reconciliation' of the *(in)famous* object/subject dichotomy, or at the privileging of 'objective' matter over 'subjective' language, reasoning instead that any social ties will zigzag between human and object connections. "... objects are suddenly highlighted not only as being full-blown actors, but also as what explains ... the over-arching powers of society, the huge asymmetries, the crushing exercise of power" (Latour, 2005,

p. 72). The designation of agency to material artefacts leads to taking advantage of their 'functional blankness (Brown & Capdevila, 1999), their 'lack of meaning', to forge alliances based on possibilities. With respect to actor-network symmetry, this 'functional blankness' can also be exhibited by human actors, who form relations on the basis of absence, what is not uttered, where 'agency' shines through, triggering an intense provocation of the *will-to-connect*.

Sayes (2014) argues that ANT portrays a coherent methodology for incorporating non-humans into social scientific accounts, amid claims of it bordering on chaos even by those who are ANT supporters. For example, Mol (2010) proposes that the position merely possesses a "repertoire" and a "set of contrary methodological reflexes" without a "consistent method" (p. 261). Sayes (2014) presents an outline of the four main contributions that non-humans make to social life as illustrated by the Actor-Network position. The actions and capacities of non-humans are regarded as a condition for the possibility of the formation of human society. A non-human is also conceived as a mediator, providing an added value to an association, with non-humans understood as continually modifying relations between actors, rather than just treating them as ingenuous ancillaries for human actors. Non-humans may also be regarded as members of moral and political associations, which brings forward the question of responsibility. Finally, non-humans are regarded as gatherings, where action is always "*inter*action", shared with variable actors, of variable ontologies, of variable times, of variable spaces, and of variable durability (Latour 1996, p. 239). In ANT terms, agency is decoupled from criteria of intentionality, subjectivity, and free will, mirroring a "complicated but nonetheless minimal conception" (Sayes 2014, p. 141) of the term [agency]. Notwithstanding, "whether this action is locatable in humans or non-humans is meaningless – or at least sociologically irrelevant. An a priori distinction between the agential capacities of humans and non-humans ceases to be helpful if it acts to occlude, to stack our accounting enterprises before we have even commenced counting" (Latour 1987, p. 232).

Translation

ANT has also been described as a "sociology of translation", that according to Latour (1987) occurs when human and nonhuman entities assemble and connect, changing each other to form links/nodes. At each connection, one entity works upon another to change it to become part of a network. The working entity is an '*actor*', while the worked-upon entity is an '*actant*'- with the 'action' aspect being emphasized. The more heterogeneous elements an actor is implicitly or explicitly able to align, the more it becomes. Nothing lies outside the network of relations. Actors can then be considered as a sum of other, smaller actors, an effect known as '*punctualization*'. These '*ordering struggles*' by actors to translate one another may appear to become stabilized, in ANT terms '*black-boxed*', the stability of which is influenced by the costs of re-opening it. Through translation, network elements are converted to '*immutable mobiles*', by being defined and ascribed roles. These 'immutable mobiles', acting at a distance, are only visible within a particular network of relations, functioning as the delegates of these other networks, extending their power by crawling into novel geographical spaces and working on the translation of other entities to widen the web. Actors are connected into a network through '*intermediaries*' – which can be understood as the "language of the network" (Stalder, 1997, p. 6) through which actors communicate with one another, thus translating their intentions into other actors. On the other hand, '*mediators*' are entities which multiply difference and which should be taken up as the object of study – their outputs cannot be predicted by their inputs.

When it comes to the understanding of network growth, Callon (1986) proposes a four-stage typology by which networks assemble and extend themselves through *'moments'* of translation. Through *'problematization'*, an entity attempts to establish itself as an *'obligatory point of passage'*, in the meantime attracting other entities to join the network in the moment of *'interressement'*. Those entities to be included experience *'enrolment'*, while the moment of 'mobilization' reveals network durability as its translations have been extended to other locations. This fixed model has been criticized for being too mechanical, trying to fit moments in a pre-given framework, tending to distort the complexity it was intended to liberate.

According to Cooper & Law's (1995) definition of retrospection, networks emerge out of pure action, preceding any thought, ordering or organization – they simply happen. The ANT approach, disregarding any adherence to chronology, circulates around the fold, "where 'after' comes 'before' the 'beginning' ... moving simultaneously away from and toward the end of things" (Brown & Capdevila, 1999, p. 35). This eventually leads to ambivalence in the conception of the 'outside' of the network, a withdrawing space in constant pursuit by the network.

POSSIBLE EXPLANATIONS BEHIND THE UNPOPULARITY OF ANT IN EDUCATION STUDIES

Literature reveals that ANT is still relatively under-utilized in education research – in fact, one may safely state/conclude that it has barely gone beyond its youth stage/reached its stage of maturity since its inception/conception in the 1980s. In the words of Fenwick & Edwards (2010, p. 1), it is "not terribly familiar" in education studies, being taken up "sporadic[ally] rather than [in a] sustained [manner]". Writing about ANT is extremely difficult due to its messy, fluid, disorderly, dynamic, chaotic and ambivalent nature. However, Law (1999, p. 10) warns that "only dead theories and dead practices celebrate their identity" – any attempt at a re-establishment and imposition of a purity of ANT-ness is unthought of. It is perhaps the "slippery and diffuse" (Fenwick & Edwards, 2010, p. 2) nature of ANT that puts off scholars from applying it as a frame of analysis. Proof of this is Latour's (1999) own reasoning of the difficulty of grasping this theory – attributing to "the fusion of three hitherto unrelated strands of preoccupations" (p. 6) – the intertwining of semiotics, methodology, and ontology. Meaning production becomes the only important thing to study due to its contribution to entity building, becoming opaque while relishing the "thick, rich, layered and complex matter" (ibid, p. 6). Meaning turned from a means to an end in itself, becoming a 'mediator' rather than an 'intermediary'. Consequently, every entity can be comprehended as a choice, thus leading to "an extraordinary liberty of analysis" (ibid, p. 6). ANT took up adaptations from semiotics to suit its own purposes of exploring actor flow in network assemblages. Semiotics attributes and distributes action, competences, performances and relations. Actors are considered as flowing, circulating objects rather than fixed entities while context definition is relegated to texts and discourses, shifting the responsibility of author, reader, and metalanguage demarcation. Semiotics was further extended to define a completely empty frame enabling the path recording of any assemblage of heterogeneous entities, becoming a method to describe the deployment of associations. ANT removes the burden from the 'observed' actor to the 'observation' act, from the specific 'shape' that is recorded to the recording. Latour (1999) defines ANT as an 'infralanguage', with an "infinite pliability and absolute freedom" (p. 7) due to its irreductionist, unassumptive and uncommitted nature, making any heterogeneous association possible through translation. This theory distribution provides another source of misunderstanding, with the twin accusations of mere description *versus* dogma levelled at ANT. It is only when the third ontological strand is added to methodology and semiotics that the criticism is mitigated, as bracketing out reference and social context does not lead to the solution of meaning, while deploying shapes of associations is not in itself explanatory. The 'networky' character of the entities leads to a blurring of distinction between representation and things, providing connections among unrelated elements. The explanation is found within the network itself, surrounding itself with "its own frame of reference, its own definition of growth, of referring, of framing, of explaining". It seems that the best features of ANT are their very deterrent, especially for researchers who do not embrace the postmodern or poststructuralist turn.

Another issue stems from the production of ANT accounts – one dealing with analytical symmetry. McLean & Hassard (2004) argue that "the primary challenge facing ANT researchers is to produce accounts that are robust enough to negate the twin charges of symmetrical absence and symmetrical absurdity" (p. 493). A major dilemma presents itself with the inclusion/exclusion issue, involving a continual process of deciding which actors to follow and how to represent them, described by Strathern (1996) as a question of where and when to 'cut the network'. Law (1991) indicates the problematic nature of 'following the actors' as analytical distance by the researcher is difficult to maintain as the world is viewed and experienced through *their* constructs and practices, but then reiterates by the reassurance that "we can never, really, reduce our categories to those of our subjects" (ibid, p. 11). Furthermore, ANT accounts have also been accused of giving prominence to 'high profile' actors, while ignoring/disregarding significant 'others' who make a somewhat 'silent' contribution to the network. Another problem arises from ANT's insistence on the agency of non-humans, due to its notion of 'general symmetry' that Collins & Yearley (1992) criticize as 'radical' in its attempts to 'suspend all dichotomies'. However, in ANT, the social and the technical are analytically composite as "there is no thinkable social life without the participation ... ... of non-humans ..." (Callon & Latour, 1992, p. 359). For Callon (1986), the process of representing others relies on the observer's agnosticism to ensure that "no point of view is privileged and no interpretation is censored" (p. 200). ANT scholars maintain that while their conception of agency does not presuppose intentionality which is not attributed to nonhumans, agency is located in the heterogeneous associations of humans and nonhumans - neither in human "subjects" nor in non-human "objects" (Wikipedia Online Resource). Despite these clarifications, McLean & Hassard (2004) maintain that the problem of actor 'relevance' remains due to the "... question of how we represent those who are viewed as unrepresentable? Do we exclude them as 'monsters' (Law, 1991), as not providing an acceptable attribution of agency, or do we include them through our role as the political representative of these entities, and reintroduce them through semiotic processes?" (p. 504).

Some writers have also questioned the way by which nonhumans are regaled with a higher status in terms of their relation to humans under the lens of ANT, with Collins & Yearley (1992) suggesting that material actors are "over-granted" 'reality' and 'potency'. Proponents of ANT (Callon & Latour, 1992; Pels, 1995), rather than denying such differences, question their 'a priori' status and make them understood as 'effects' or 'outcomes'.

ANT has also been attacked for attending to the local, contingent and processual, while failing to attend to broader social structures, for focusing on the 'micro' at the expense of the 'macro'. Latour (1991) describes how the 'macro-structure' is constituted by the same basic connections as the 'micro-structure', so when exploring the 'social', one gets closer to the local, thus transforming the 'social' into a 'circulation' (Latour, 1999a), highlighting the need to examine the 'empty space' between networks. ANT can provide concepts to study 'spaces' – at Gomart & Hennion's (1999) suggestion, "The network is not a black pool in which to drop, dilute, criticise, and lose the subject. It is ... an opening – pried loose with a partly rhetorical liberation of things and an attentiveness to spaces, dispositions, and events ..." (p. 226).

Whittle & Spicer (2008) accuse ANT of failing to live up to its promise, that of "developing critical theories of organization after the so-called 'postmodern turn' (Calas & Smirchich, 1999)" (p. 611), arguing that while providing a valuable framework for empirical analysis, it fails to provide a critical account of organization. Whittle & Spicer (2008) subject ANT to critique on the premise of its reliance on a naturalizing ontology; an un-reflexive epistemology; and a conservative politics. Despite frequent claims of ANT being anti-essentialist, anti-dualist, and anti-determinist, Whittle & Spicer (2008) prove otherwise, claiming that it "is unable to develop an account of how the capacities of actors are emergent and interpretively flexible; how the split between humans and nonhumans is created in social practice and how actors escape the process of translation" (p. 617). ANT fails to uncover the limits too causality and recognize power relations as failing operations, while not giving resistance its due importance.

Sayes (2017) suggests that ANT has been subject to "a cascade of criticism" (p. 295), identifying four strands of broadly Marxist critiques that conclude that ANT is of insignificant value to contemporary social science. The conception of non-humans and non-human agency presented by ANT has been harshly criticized (Hartwick 2000). A second strand chastises ANT for its reductionism, in other words, for ignoring potentiality in favour of the positive (Noys 2010), and for disregarding materialist abstractions in favour of the empirical (Rudy 2005). A third strand of critique emphasizes the manner in which ANT neglects social structure (Soderberg & Netzen 2010), context (Gareau 2005), deep causes (Holifeld 2009), and the systemic (Fine 2005). A fourth strand can be outlined as a political criticism, accusing ANT of retaining political indeterminacy (Winner 1993) and of embracing dangerous political implications (Wacjcman 2000).

On the epistemological level, it has been suggested that despite its claim to objectivity, ANT tends to impose its own theoretical lexicon, being ethnocentric in gaining power over member interpretations; providing a lack of resonance between the network of human and nonhuman actors and the linear four-stage model of translation; as well as its failure to provide a thoroughly reflexive theory of knowledge. Whittle & Spicer (2008) further question the assertion that ANT provides a 'radical' political framework, rejecting its claim that existing power relations are natural, in turn accusing it of missing the 'meaningful' character of human action and tending to legitimize hegemonic power relations – being limited to the description of surface-level of power relations (Winner, 1993). According to Fountain (1999), ANT has been criticized for being too post-modernist and post-structuralist, yet Latour (2005) strenuously attacks postmodern or post-structuralist positions as intellectual and moral dead-ends. However, Crawford (2004) states that ANT does not have affinities with post-modernism or post-structuralism, due to its sharing some similarities with Foucauldian material-semiotics and borrowing from his conception of power/knowledge.

Latour (1999) himself subjects ANT to critique, finding fault with four things: the "actor", "network" "theory", and they hyphen, later changing his position by accepting the wide use of the term, "including the hyphen" (Latour, 2005, p. 9) – qualitative hallmarks/characteristics of actor/network epistemology. Latour (1999) deplores the use of the word 'network' due to the change in meaning with the new popularization of the word – from a series of transformations, translations and transductions, similar to Deleuze & Guattari's term 'rhizome' – it came to signify "transport without deformation" (ibid, p. 15). The term 'actor-network', which brings the agency/structure cliché to the fore, should instead be regarded as "two faces of the same phenomenon" (ibid, p. 19), as ANT concentrates on a movement, a circulation that can travel without any close encounter with either the micro-level or the macro-level, raising awareness of the empty space 'in between' networks, the 'terra incognita' that offers potential for change. Latour (1993) criticizes Callon's coining of the notion 'actor-network', reasoning that it is a way of getting rid of system and structure, while nonchalantly claiming that it is "just one of the many words we have to invent and use and drop after a while in order to trace and define a social relation that is not social and a natural relation that is not naturalized", further criticizing the whole notion of ANT as "not [being] a very well packaged argument", moreover with a vocabulary that is "voluntarily poor" (Latour in Latour & Crawford, 1993, pp. 262-3). Latour, later tries to correct himself and retract from his initial comment/impression by saying that "ANT has been sliding in a sort of race to overcome its limits and to drop from the list of its methodological terms any which would make it impossible for new actors to define the world in their own terms, using their own dimensions and touchstones" (Latour, 1999, p. 20). Consequently, ANT proposes to "follow the actors".

While celebrating the 'diffusion' and 'translation' of ANT, which he regards as signs of respectability and reputation-building, Law (1999) is against labelling, which although indicating the transportability of ANT, unfortunately reveals its adaptation into "a specific strategy with an obligatory point of passage, a definite intellectual place within an equally definite intellectual space" (ibid, pp. 3). Law (1999) purports not to defend it against criticism, voicing his desire of escaping "the multinational monster, 'ANT'" (p. 2) which was never meant to be regarded as a fixed, rigid, localized point. He then seemingly contradicts himself by paradoxically stating that it is "the performance of an irony", confessing to having made "a fixed point" (by establishing ANT) "... in order to argue *against* fixity and singularity" (p. 3). The term 'ANT', originating from '*acteur reseau*', is '*intentionally oxymoronic*' (Law, 1999, p. 5), embodying a tension between the centred 'actor' and the decentred 'network', 'agency' versus 'structure', a difference/dichotomy which lends identity, hinting at strategic discourses of network assemblage attempting to struggle to centre and order from a centre, leading in turn to problems of heterogeneity and 'actor ... network' orderings.

Strathern (1996) draws attention to the metaphorical baggage carried by the term 'network' due to notions of relatedness, topology, and regionalism, which according to Law (1999), can be circumvented by topological non-conformity, by embracing Deleuze & Guattari's concept of 'the fold'. However, this theory, this 'sociology of association' (Latour, 2005) "has been broken on the altar of transparency and simplicity ... of rapid transformability" (Law, 1999, p. 12) due to the naturalization and homogenization of spatial and relational possibilities. Law (1999) argues for the 'complexity' of ANT, lost in the labelling process and in its 'diaspora', arguing instead for the metaphor of the fractal, which defies singularity, multiplicity, and plurality.

Latour (2005) outlines five sources of uncertainty researchers come up against when working with ANT. The main and constant uncertainty, giving rise to all the others is wondering over the intimate nature of entities in their behaviour as 'intermediaries' or 'mediators'. Closely following are the origin of the actor's 'action'; assigning agency to nonhuman actors; matters of fact versus matters of concern; as well as writing down these 'risky accounts', ANT interpretations.

THE POSSIBLE CONTRIBUTIONS OF ANT TO EDUCATION RESEARCH

Fenwick & Edwards (2010) firmly believe that ANT offers invaluable insights when taken up by researchers in the education arena, mainly due to its mutations into a "highly diffuse, diverse and contested set of framings and practices" (p. 1). They regard ANT as "a virtual 'cloud', continually moving, shrinking and stretching, dissolving in any attempt to grasp it firmly ... [it] is more like a sensibility, a way to sense and draw nearer to a phenomenon" (p. 1). ANT approaches generate unique analysis of educational reform by tracing the rich material trajectories of the actors being followed by the researcher. Moreover, ANT's language can open up new questions, following an approach that enables the researcher to "discern the difficult ambivalences, messes, multiplicities and contradictions" (Fenwick & Edwards 2010, p. 1) entrenched in numerous educational matters.

ANT claims "no final word, no line to draw under an analysis to bring it to a close, no necessary completion of accounts ... no necessary end to the elements that may contribute to a network" (Lee & Stenner, 1999, p. 93), a feature also noted by Strathern (1996). It is this infinity of ANT that makes it ideal for educational research, coupled with its de-centring which is better understood as a method of analysis. The centredness of agentic responsibility is dispersed among interdependencies and co-responsibilities, while the unpredictable nature of responsibility, dependency and ownership are set in motion.

ANT has often been reprimanded for failing to offer a satisfactory theory of the actor endowed with limitless power or deprived of any possibility for adaptation, the absence of which, in combination with the role/agency attributed to nonhumans, proves to be one of its strengths, according to Callon (1999). This combination makes it possible to explain the existence and intricacies of networks due to their disentanglement, framing, internalization, and externalizations.

Sorensen (2009) argues that there is a "blindness toward the question of how educational practice is affected by materials" (p. 2), suggesting that materials are treated as mechanisms to advance educational performance. According to Fenwick et al. (2011), sociomaterial approaches offer 'resources' that simultaneously consider both "the patterns as well as the unpredictability" that makes educational activity possible. Consequently, these promote methods that enable the recognition and tracing of the "multifarious struggles, negotiations and accommodations whose effects constitute the 'things' in education", thus exploring these concepts as "effects of heterogeneous relations" (p. 3-4). Education is viewed as an assemblage, "only becoming possible through its own enactment as a separate domain" (Fenwick & Landri 2012, p. 2). As a result of this, "Socio-material studies shift the conversation from issues defined by the personal and the social to questions about these assemblages, how they move, and how they produce what may appear to be distinct objects, subjects, and events. How and why do certain combinations of things come together to exert particular effects? ... How do some assemblages become stable, and what force do they wield? How can more oppressive assemblages be interrupted and weakened?" (ibid, p. 3).

ANT helps us deal with research that is 'messy', 'unknowable', and 'heterogeneous' (Law, 2007, p. 596), just as 'the largest part of the world is'. According to Sorensen (2009), "The logical meaning and coherence of the concepts we use is less important: what is crucial is how they help us do empirical studies and analyses and the kinds of studies and analyses in which they result" (p. 12). Law & Urry (2003) confess that the time has arrived for a review of methodological inheritance, we no longer need research that seeks to purify through its enactments. Globalization has altered social reality, with due prominence being given to "... connection and flow ... the fleeting, the ephemeral, the geographically distributed and the suddenly proximate ..." (ibid, 2003, p. 10). Methods are never innocent as they enact what they describe into reality, leading into the issue of 'ontological politics', as lack of innocence has political implications. Therefore, Law & Urry (2003) advise that sensibilities appropriate to a methodological decentering need to be developed – method "... needs to find ways of knowing the slipperiness of 'units that are not' as they move in and beyond old categories" (p. 11).

How will ANT help to generate this *'ontological cleansing'*? Law (2004b) suggests the exploration of research approaches that are "broader, looser, more generous, and in certain respects quite different to that of many of the conventional understandings" (p. 4). ANT research allows us to "follow the actors" (Latour, 2005), by gathering information about the 'how' and 'why' of actors' actions (Latour, 1999, p. 20), tracing complexity and heterogeneity, without enacting any boundaries between "the individual and the environment" (Law, 2004a, p. 23). The focus is on the particular and the local, tracing micro-movements and relations, with the entity being studied regarded as an *effect* of multiple, material connections. ANT helps us to explore the ambivalence and ambiguity, marginality and multiple identities of educational phenomena, where the researcher not only notices the ambivalence, but following the suggestion of Fenwick & Edwards (2010), dwells within it throughout the analysis process, by paying attention to "the strains, the uncanny, the difficult and the ill-fitting ..." (p. 156). ANT also allows for the confrontation and acceptance of multiplicity, what Mol (2002) labels as "the problem of difference" – for the co-existence of multiple worlds. ANT offers three ontological possibilities, outlined by Law (1999) in his case studies of *'traduction'* and *'trahison'*. *'Ontological choreography'* draws attention to the "dance-like nature of ontological performance" (p. 10), to retrospective and prospective dance where momentary connections are made. In the world of *'ontological ambivalences'*, ontology becomes inconsistent, with reality built on a pattern of incoherences. The third version of *'ontological patchwork'* involves "... multiple realities, many ontological interactions and intersections ... ceaseless making and linking and clashing" (p. 10). This resonates with Mol's (1999) claim that ANT and its semiotic relatives have reshaped ontology by underlining that the reality we live in is performed in a variety of practices, therefore revealing its multiplicity, opening up the notion of choice, which problematizes the presupposition of an actor who actively chooses, with potential actors being inextricably linked up with their *'enactment'*. To describe this, Mol (1999) coins the term "ontological politics", suggesting a link between the 'real' (the present potential) and the 'political'.

Due to its emphasis on the sociomaterial, ANT gives importance to 'things' through the principle of 'symmetry', which treats human and nonhuman actors alike. In the words of Latour (1996), "Our collective is woven together out of speaking subjects, perhaps, but subjects to which poor objects, our inferior brothers, are attached at all points" (p. viii). ANT brings 'things' to the fore, whereas before the focus was mainly on human "subjects" – we are now made aware of the interdependency of things in education reform. Things respond to human intentions, relationships, meanings, force, perceptions of self, changing and shaping them in the process. Waltz (2006) argues for the importance of material nonhuman things in education research as while things circulate amid connections, they also bring about change. Fenwick & Edwards (2010) state that this materiality in the associative work of networking is often overlooked, strengthening Sorensen's (2009) complaint about "the blindness toward the question of how educational practice is affected by materials" (p. 2).

Sociomaterialists are spurring researchers to retrace the practices of critique by experimenting with the social and the natural, the human and non-human as political entities (Edwards & Fenwick 2015). This is in line with the reasoning of Latour (2005) regarding critical practices of attachment and experimentation, with the critic being defined as "not the one who debunks, but the one who assembles ... not the one who lifts the rugs from under the feet of the naïve believers, but the one who offers the participants arenas in which to gather" (Latour 2004, p. 246). Fenwick & Edwards (2015) propose that educational researchers should reflect on the gathered practices of critique, considering the process as "a politics of attachment and experimentation, of materialities and intensities, of the human and non-human" (p. 1394), turning into an attempt to develop an enactment of politics through sociomateriality.

Fenwick (2010) draws our attention to the various ways in which ANT sensibilities can help us explore networks – in helping to trace the emergent forms of powerful networks; the connections assembling objects and people into these extended networks; what and who becomes included and excluded; the translation of individual entities and behaviours; elements of negotiation, resistance or competition. The whole focus seems to circulate around the dynamics of interaction, concurring with Cordella & Shaikh's (2006) proposition of ANT as "an analytical tool that provides the theoretical and methodological underpinning for the study of these dynamic relationships" (p. 8). This analysis of relationships involves having a close look at the actor-network; the various actor characteristics and levels of flexibility; the diverse forces at play; the actor as 'network'; the actantiality (potential) for action generated in negotiation; the multiple trajectories resulting in stabilization or instability; the different levels of rigidity of actor inscription and alignment; as well as the concept of circularity.

Kamp (2018) concludes that the engagement with distinct actors at play in the network society's 'space of flows' (Castells & Ince 2003) leads to a portrayal of the fluid spaces (Fenwick 2011) of localized net-work, in addition to the structural, technological and intrapersonal actants involved in the commencement or foreclosing of the 'flow'. Accordingly, "ANT's commitment to symmetry for humans and non-humans and the suspension of assumptions about the ways they make us act offers greater scope for understanding the 'how' in our attempts to net-work" (Kamp 2018, p. 788). Networking as a practice reconceives leadership as a practice, with ANT providing alternative conceptualizations of leadership dynamics. Leadership involves "active hybrids composed of networks of associations", that people should gain an understanding of via a 'flat' analytical basis, without giving priority to a nominated human 'leader' (Grint 2004, p. 5).

An ANT reading of educational reform offers tangible understandings about the unfolding of the dynamics of change. Typical lines of inquiry an ANT-ish research may follow are: "How does a new state initiative seeking to generate 'school improvement' produce itself into a 'thing'? How does 'it' become enacted over time and across different regions? What diverse negotiations and responses are generated through material practices, and how do these affect its durability and force? What exactly becomes engaged and connected, what becomes excluded, and how do these involvements shift over time? Where and how does power accumulate through these negotiations?" (Fenwick 2011, p. 117-118). Nespor (2002) argues that a network reading presents reforms and contexts as mutually creating one another, constituting materially heterogeneous networks that have unfolded geographically and historically, thus overlapping and relating with one another. Attention to the sociomaterial connections and their patterns can distinguish "not only closures but also openings in mass reform efforts, spaces for flux and instability", as well as the possibility "to realize alternative educational change" where appropriate (Fenwick 2011, p. 131-132).

ANT may turn out to be an invaluable resource in the field of education studies, in the words of Fenwick & Edwards (2010), these ANT-ish researchers are showing the "multiple heterogeneous layers and fragile connections that make up the 'actants' of education", as well as "signalling new ways to frame educational problems, and new entry points for interventions" (p. 164). ANT can be combined with other methodological approaches, drawing on concepts which are most likely to suit the research rather than applying it as a rigid framework to the entity under scrutiny. The trend in education research seems to be to use ANT "not as a stable body of work, but one that provides some tools and perspectives with which to think and analyze" (Leander & Lovvorn, 2006, p. 295) education reform practices as sociomaterial processes.

ANT AND THE 'NETWORK' METAPHOR: TRACING 'ASSEMBLAGES'

Society can no longer be conceptualized as independent of networks as the metaphor of hierarchy has been transformed and abandoned by discourses, images, theories, and institutions that now embrace an idea of "whole", of "totality". Eriksson (2005) reveals how the metaphor of network has become a common conceptual horizon for thinking about society and for contemplating about the conditions of co-being, that is, the ontological "structure" of the construction of truth/reality. Riles (2000) makes claims to the 'institutionalized utopianism' of 'the network' and how networks are presented as an unproblematized solution to knowledge development and dissemination. This is further elaborated on by Frankham (2006) who subjects the notions of conventional network thinking to harsh critique by illustrating how due to its malleability and flexibility, the discourse of networks has been applied to learning, equating 'learning networks' with the discourse of the commodification of knowledge, of its easy transfer across domains and of claimed future benefits. Frankham (2006) questions the amenability of the abstraction/decontextualization and recontextualization (Strathern, 2002) of network theories into the field of education – can the deployment of the "network" metaphor be accused of only having a superficial fit? Should we not be looking at *dis*connections instead, in terms of 'network talk'?

Globalization discourses lead 'networks' towards the *cradling* of the global and the local and their connection, with Riles (2000) suggesting that in such a context, the network acknowledges these problems while positing itself as the local solution. Angus (2004) voices his concern over the 'learning network' thus becoming a "totalizing structure which imposes its will without much, if any, consideration of agency, local politics or resistance" (p. 24). In a paper exploring the changing forms of education governance in England, Ozga (2009) argues how recent attempts to 'rebalance' steering through 'intelligent accountability' invoke network principles, thus giving the appearance of deregulation, while the 'centre' retains control through decision-making. Frankham (2006) concludes that the most vital criterion for judging network success are the network 'workings' rather than the connections or structures. People's behaviour in a network is what matters most – especially "... their capacity to tolerate loose ends, to deal with upredictability, and to revel in the disconnections that means that they live in multiple worlds and traverse different domains" (Strathern, 2002, p. 309). This sort of detailed work is required to counter the rhetoric of the network that is repeated as if it were "some kind of educational magic bullet" (McLaren & Giarelli, 1995, p. 301), as if merely using the term will transform the potential for mutual gain.

In direct opposition to the use of the 'network' metaphor problematically suggesting flat linear chains, enclosed pipelines and ossified tracks, ANT-associated writings (Mol & Law, 1994) have explored alternate metaphors of regions and fluid spaces. In ANT terms, a network is "an assemblage or gathering of materials brought together and linked through processes of translation, that together perform a particular enactment" (Fenwick & Edwards, 2012, p. 5). The main premise in ANT is *multiplicity*, the enactment of multiple simultaneous ontologies, as outlined by Law (2004b); Mol (2002); Moser (2008). According to Fenwick (2010), a network in ANT "does not connect things that already exist, but actually configures ontologies" (p. 3). Fenwick & Edwards (2012) delineate the utility of ANT's network ontology in education, discussing how it renders a detailed contextual analysis that is very much dependent on network relations, as well as tracing how certain relations of power may be strengthened through assemblages. Latour (2005) defines the term network as "a concept ... a tool to help describe something, not what is being described ... a network is not what is represented in the text, but what readies the text to take the relay of actors as mediators" (p. 131). This conceptual understanding enables researchers to generate actor-network accounts of topics that do not constitute the shape of a network or are not even remotely related to it. The most important feature of the network metaphor is the flow of translations, "the trace left behind by some moving agent" (ibid, p. 132).

Latour (1999) points out misunderstandings that are generated due to common mistakes in the usage of the word 'network' – this happens when it is ascribed with a common technical meaning denoting finality and stability, and also when it is equated with the study of social networks. ANT is not concerned with the social relations of individual human actors, in fact, the word 'actor' or 'actant' is extended to include nonhuman, non-individual entities. This may lead to question the wisdom of Latour in his persistence of the use of the word 'network', being open to such misinterpretation. He answers that ANT is "a change of metaphors to describe *essences*: instead of surfaces one gets filaments (or rhizomes in Deleuze's parlance)" Latour, 1999, p. 2). ANT represents a change in topology from surfaces to multi-dimensional nodes; a process where strength comes from the netting of ties weak by themselves (somewhat equivalent to Foucault's analysis of micro-powers); as well as background/foreground reversal as the theory starts from irreducible, incommensurable realities, accounting for the exceptions. ANT really is a reductionist/relativist theory paradoxically leading to an irreductionist/relationist ontology. Latour (1999) discusses the three properties he considers to be common to all networks: far/close, small scale/ large scale; inside/outside. The 'network'notion lifts the tyranny of space definition, offering a notion of 'associational' space. The whole metaphor of scales becomes a metaphor of connections, while it is all boundary without inside and outside.

Networks generate effects – agency, power, identity, knowledge – ANT regards all entities as relational effects. 'Immutable mobiles' (Latour, 1987), things that act at a distance are only visible within a particular network of relations as they move into different spaces to translate additional entities. ANT's ontology of folding and unfolding networks does not rely on the agency/structure dichotomy, instead focusing on the circulating forces and the myriad translations. Some 'immutable mobiles' become 'obligatory points of passage' (Latour, 1987), central assemblages through which all network relations must flow – both signalling important dynamics in the power relations circulating in education.

Murdoch (1998) regards ANT as a way of thought about how spatial relations get wrapped up in complex networks through a navigation of dualisms and a re-definition of geography by overthrowing the "'tyranny of distance' (Latour, 1997), a beast which tends to impose a single conception of undifferentiated space upon variable landscapes of relations and connections" (Murdoch, 1998, p. 358). ANT regards space as constructed within networks, thus holding relations/associations as building and stratification blocks of the world. Spaces emerge from within networks through a consideration of heterogeneity, via the translation of materials into networks with their own space-time trajectories, which are "reshaped (and variably stabilized, temporarily) in the ... heterogeneous processes of co-construction and mutual reinforcement" (Wynne, 1996, p. 362). Law (1997, p. 3) himself refers to translated spaces as "oxymoronic" as the 'actor-network' refers to both a network and a point, a decentred network and a centred actor, both "individual and collective" (Callon & Law, 1997, p. 174) – this "centred subjectivity" consolidating the associations between all elements.

Work on translation identifies two network types: stabilized networks that move towards convergence, what Latour (1992) labels "spaces of prescription", and provisional and divergent networks that are known as "spaces of negotiation" (Callon & Law, 1989). Stalder (1997) remarks that convergence does not necessarily imply homogeneity, but only that "any one actor's activity fits easily with those of the other actors, *despite* their heterogeneity" (Callon, 1992, p. 87), thus "non-linearity and path dependence can be seen to be integral to the dynamics of [a network]" (ibid, 1992, p. 92). On the other hand, in networks of variation and flux, spaces will be fluid, interactional and unstable. Murdoch (1998) argues how such differing spaces may emerge from within the *same* networks, perhaps shading, dissolving or flowing into one another.

Hetherington & Law (2000) voice their concern regarding the all-too-encompassing nature of the network metaphor which can take a firm hold on all the layers, folds, and constituents of a phenomenon, assuming that everything that exists is drawn into the network web. This problem also raises issues about space and action division according to questions of relation and difference – spaces and discontinuities may be enacted through conventional network readings.

Law (2007) lists all the ingredients needed to brew the actor network theory: semiotic relationality; heterogeneity; materiality; process and its precariousness; power, space, and scale as effects. The 'network', in ANT, enjoys durability in the material and strategic areas, as well as discursive stability. It is the web configuration that produces stability, not the materials themselves, while patterns of relations are indifferent to human intentions. Law (2007) borrows from Foucault in regarding modes of ordering as mini-discourses – discourses define conditions of possibility and the fact that they are different contributes to their stability – it is this 'multi-discursive' ordering that secures relative stability. Fenwick (2010) reveals the possibility of different assemblages due to their constant shifting, emerging, and dissolving, for as Law (2003) states "there are no orders, only orderings – that are always precarious". Fenwick's (2010) advice to researchers applying the ANT approach in education is to "... focus on this mess and particularly on the materializing processes it accomplishes ... follow the interplays that occur at the most local levels of practice, in ways that resist the urge to clarify, order and distinguish" (p. 14).

ANT AND POWER RELATIONS

ANT may be regarded as a theory of the mechanics of power, concerning itself with the stabilization and reproduction of some interactions over others, the construction and maintenance of network centers and peripheries, and the establishment of hegemony. Crawford (2004) regards this kind of power as "persuasion" rather than "possession", obtained through the number of entities networked and generated in a relational and distributed manner through "ordering struggles".

Brown & Capdevila (1999) regard networks as "assemblages of forces", emerging from and dissolving into the "play of power" (pp. 38), attributing both their existence and their eventual collapse to power, without which they would come to resemble "perpetuum mobile, curious structures which function endlessly without apparent reference to the world around them" (p. 38). However, in order for this to materialize, the network has to appear as the model of power itself – the same objection made by both Star (1991) and Pels (1996), problematizing the notion of all power being 'networked-power'.

Law (1992) studies how power is generated as an 'effect' through an exploration of the metaphor of heterogeneous network, network consolidation, as well as network ordering and the materials and strategies involved. Order is an effect generated by heterogeneous means through "heterogeneous engineering". Law (1992) confesses that ANT exhibits analytical radicalism since it "treads on a set of ethical, epistemological and ontological toes" (p. 2), mainly through its concept of general symmetry. Ordering is a precarious process due to the constant struggle and resistance, recursive generation and reproduction – it can never be considered complete, autonomous or final. Law (1992) explains how ANT is all about power as a concealed effect, with a close affinity to Foucault (1979), but not solely

Foucauldian, with a Machiavellian touch in the method. ANT is really concerned with "demystify[ing] the power of the powerful ... [by saying that] there is no difference in kind, no great divide, between the powerful and the wretched ..." (Law, 1992, p. 8). This claim, of ANT's rejection of the notion of power relations being natural and just is rejected by Whittle & Spicer (2008) who argue that in its *apparently* neutral descriptions of actor-networks, it reinforces the state of affairs described. Law (2003) acknowledges the fact of ANT simply reproducing hegemony rather than challenging it. Furthermore, the focus on translation celebrates the "victors" (Leigh-Star, 1991; Lee & Brown, 1994); a flat ontology leads to a total disregard of the hierarchical/unequal distribution of opportunity (Reed, 1997; Star, 1991), while through a reduction of 'right' to 'might', ANT refuses to explore *how* power is established (Amsterdamska, 1990). As Law (1991) similarly suggests, "No one, no thing, no class, no gender, can have power unless a set of relations is constituted and held in place ... power, whatever form it may take, is recursively woven into the intricate dance that unites the social and the technical" (p. 18). For Law (1997), politics is about hierarchical distributions, "where the Other becomes the mirror image of order, that which is told and performed into being as an exemplification of the evils of dis/order" (p. 9). Latour (1997) argues that despite its criticisms of putting humans and nonhumans on the same level, ANT seeks to banish reified boundaries that may otherwise blind us from seeing how humans and nonhumans are intermeshed. McLean & Hassard (2004) draw attention to the fact that this intermeshing needs to be examined in order to account for issues of exclusion and distribution.

ANT attempts to map the "hidden geography" (Latour, 2005) of the political, of the spaces in which we are situated and the persuasive, influential, and powerful actors working to translate us. Murdoch (1998) reveals how tracing network topology is simultaneous to tracing power typology due to the spatial dimensions of actor-networks, especially the distribution of positions and the untangling of geographical relations. According to Murdoch (1998), this becomes a geography that "is inscribed from within the networks but which also seeks to balance the perspectives of multiple network positions. It is ... a geography of folds and striations ... seeking to hold the central and the peripheral" (p. 370), alluding to a continual negotiation of the ordering of time and space. Leigh-Star (1995) views space as an "arrangement of priorities", where certain priorities compete with others to inscribe themselves in socio-material arrangements, ultimately shaping actors and agency (Munro, 1997b).

CONCLUSION

Researchers in education are encouraged to enact aspects of Actor-Network Theory as a 'sensibility', keeping in mind that, "Travelling with ANT ... will turn out to be agonizingly slow. Movements will be constantly interrupted, interfered with, disrupted, ... no displacement seems possible without costly and painful translations ..." (Latour, 2005, p. 25). Rather than gliding like an angel, "the ANT scholar has to trudge like an ant, carrying the heavy gear in order to generate even the tiniest connection" (Latour, 2005, p. 25). This chapter depicts a portrayal of Actor-Network Theory, providing a critical literature review of both its criticisms and accomplishments. Furthermore, the author problematizes the relative under-application of this 'sensibility' in education research, while simultaneously exploring its contribution as an analytical framework through its central concepts of 'actor-network', 'symmetry', 'translation', and their constituents. The relation of Actor-Network theory to the 'network' metaphor and to power relations is given prominence.

DISCUSSION QUESTIONS

1. Give a definition of ANT.
2. How may ANT lead to the problematization of the traditional concepts of "what we know" and "how we know what we know"?
3. Describe ways in which ANT empowers all actors with a voice to speak.
4. According to Fenwick and Edwards (2011), "the risk in explaining ANT is distorting and domesticating it", with its ideas being "practices for understanding, not a totalizing theory of the world and its problems" (p. 2). How far do you agree with this concern? Discuss.
5. Discuss the concept of symmetry and how this can be a help and/or hindrance in carrying out educational research.
6. ANT has been described as a "sociology of translation". Discuss this, drawing on examples of specific research projects being carried out by you as researcher.
7. Literature reveals that ANT is still relatively under-utilized in education research. How far do you agree or disagree with this? What reasons lie behind this so-called "under-utilization"?
8. What are the challenges facing ANT researchers?
9. ANT as a sociomaterial approach has often been critiqued. Discuss.
10. What are the possible contributions of ANT to education research?
11. How can ANT sensibilities aid in the exploration of networks and assemblages?
12. ANT may be regarded as a theory of the mechanics of power. Discuss.

REFERENCES

Amsterdamska, O. (1990). 'Surely you are joking, Monsiour Latoru! *Science, Technology & Human Values*, *15*(4), 495–504. doi:10.1177/016224399001500407

Baiocchi, G., Graizbord, D., & Rodriguez-Muniz, M. (2013). Actor-network theory and the ethnographic imagination: An exercise in translation. *Qualitative Sociology*, *36*(4), 323–341. doi:10.100711133-013-9261-9

Brown, S. D., & Capdevila, R. (1999). Perpetuum mobile: Substance, force and the sociology of translation. In J. Law & J. Hassard (Eds.), *Actor network theory and after* (pp. 26–50). Oxford, UK: Blackwell. doi:10.1111/j.1467-954X.1999.tb03481.x

Calas, M., & Smirchich, L. (1999). 'Past postmodernism? reflections and tenative directions. *Academy of Management Review*, *24*(4), 649–671. doi:10.5465/amr.1999.2553246

Callon, M. (1986). Some elements of a sociology of translation: Domestication of the scallops and the fishermen of St.Brieuc bay. In J. Law (Ed.), *Power, action, and belief: A new sociology of knowledge?* London: Routledge & Kegan Paul.

Callon, M. (1992). The dynamics of techno-economic networks. In R. Coombs, P. Saviotti, & V. Walsh (Eds.), *Technological change and company strategies: Economic and sociological perspectives* (pp. 77–102). London: Harcout Brace Jovanovich.

Callon, M. (1999). Actor-network theory - the market test. In J. Law & J. Hassard (Eds.), *Actor network theory and after* (pp. 181–195). Oxford, UK: Blackwell.

Callon, M., & Latour, M. (1992). Don't throw the baby out with the bath school. In A. Pickering (Ed.), *Science as practice and culture*. Chicago, IL: University of Chicago Press.

Callon, M., & Law, J. (1997). After the individual in society: Lesson on collectivity from science, technology and society. *Canadian Journal of Sociology, 22*(2), 165–182. doi:10.2307/3341747

Castells, M., & Ince, M. (2003). *Conversations with Manuel Castells*. London: Polity Press.

Collins, H., & Yearley, S. (1992). Epistemological chicken. In A. Pickering (Ed.), *Science, practice and culture*. Chicago, IL: University of Chicago Press.

Cordella, A., & Shaikh, M. (2006). *From epistemology to ontology: Challenging the constructed "truth" of ANT. Working Paper Series, No. 143*. London: Department of Information Systems, London School of Economics and Political Science. Retrieved from http://is2.lse.ac.uk/WP/PDF/wp143.pdf

Crawford, C. (2004). Actor network theory. In *Ritzer encyclopaedia* (pp. 1-3). Retrieved from: http/www.sagepub.com/upm-data/5222_Ritzer_Entries_beginning_with_A_%5B1%5D.pdf

Edwards, R., & Fenwick, T. (2015). Critique and politics: A sociomaterialist intervention. *Educational Philosophy and Theory, 47*(13-14), 1385–1404. doi:10.1080/00131857.2014.930681

Fenwick, T. (2010). (Un)doing standards in education with actor-network theory. *Journal of Education Policy, 25*(2), 117–133. doi:10.1080/02680930903314277

Fenwick, T. (2011). Reading educational reform with actor network theory: Fluid spaces, otherings, and ambivalences. *Educational Philosophy and Theory, 43*(S1), 114–134. doi:10.1111/j.1469-5812.2009.00609.x

Fenwick, T., & Edwards, R. (2010). *Actor-network theory and education*. London: Routledge. doi:10.4324/9780203849088

Fenwick, T., & Edwards, R. (2011). Introduction: Reclaiming and renewing actor network theory for educational research. *Educational Philosophy and Theory, 43*(S1), 1–14. doi:10.1111/j.1469-5812.2010.00667.x

Fenwick, T., Edwards, R., & Sawchuk, P. (2011). *Emerging approaches to educational research: Tracing the sociomaterial*. London: Routledge.

Fenwick, T., & Landri, P. (2012). Materialities, textures and pedagogies: Socio-material assemblages in education. *Pedagogy, Culture & Society, 20*(1), 1–7. doi:10.1080/14681366.2012.649421

Fine, B. (2005). From actor-network theory to political economy. *Capitalism, Nature, Socialism, 16*(4), 91–108. doi:10.1080/10455750500376057

Foucault, M. (1979). *Discipline and punish: The birth of the prison*. Harmondsworth, UK: Penguin.

Fountain, R. M. (1999). Socio-scientific issues via actor network theory. *Journal of Curriculum Studies, 31*(3), 339–358. doi:10.1080/002202799183160

Frankham, J. (2006). Network utopias and alternative entanglements for educational research and practice. *Journal of Education Policy, 21*(6), 661–677. doi:10.1080/02680930600969191

Gareau, B. J. (2005). We have never been human: Agential nature, ANT, and marxist political economy. *Capitalism, Nature, Socialism, 16*(4), 127–140. doi:10.1080/10455750500376081

Gomart, E., & Hennion, A. (1999). A sociology of attachment: Music amateurs, drug users. In J. Law & J. Hassard (Eds.), *Actor network theory and after* (pp. 220–247). Oxford: Blackwell. doi:10.1111/j.1467-954X.1999.tb03490.x

Grint, K. (2004). Actor network theory. In G. Goethals, G. Sorensen, & J. MacGregor (Eds.), Encyclopaedia of leadership (pp. 5-8). Burns: Sage. doi:10.4135/9781412952392.n3

Hartwick, E. R. (2000). Towards a geographical politics of consumption. *Environment & Planning A, 32*(7), 1177–1192. doi:10.1068/a3256

Hetherington, K., & Law, J. (2000). After networks. *Environment and Planning D. Space and Society, 18*, 127–132.

Holifeld, R. (2009). Actor-network theory as a critical approach in environmental justice: A case against synthesis with urban political ecology. *Antipode, 41*(4), 637–658. doi:10.1111/j.1467-8330.2009.00692.x

Kamp, A. (2018). Assembling the actors: Exploring the challenges of 'system leadership' in education through actor-network theory. *Journal of Education Policy, 33*(6), 778–792.

Latour, B. (1987). *Science in action: How to follow scientists and engineers through society*. Cambridge, MA: Harvard University Press.

Latour, B. (1992). Where are the missing masses the sociology of a few mundane artifacts. In W. Bijker & J. Law (Eds.), *Shaping technology/building society: Studies in socio-technical change* (pp. 225–264). London: MIT Press.

Latour, B. (1996). On interobjectivity. *Mind, Culture, and Activity, 3*(4), 228–245. doi:10.120715327884mca0304_2

Latour, B. (1997). The trouble with actor-network theory. *Soziale Welt, 47*, 369–381.

Latour, B. (1999a). On recalling ANT. In J. Law & J. Hassard (Eds.), *Actor network theory and after* (pp. 15–25). Oxford, UK: Blackwell.

Latour, B. (1999b). *Pandora's hope*. Cambridge, MA: Harvard University Press.

Latour, B. (2004). Why has critique run out of steam? From matters of fact to matters of concern. *Critical Inquiry, 30*(2), 225–248. doi:10.1086/421123

Latour, B. (2005). *Reassembling the social: An introduction to actor-network theory*. Oxford, UK: Oxford University Press.

Latour, J., & Crawford, T. (1993). An interview with Latour. *Configurations, 2*(2), 247–269. doi:10.1353/con.1993.0012

Law, J. (1991). Introduction. In J. Law (Ed.), *A sociology of monsters: Essays on power, technology and domination*. London: Routledge.

Law, J. (1992). *Notes on the theory of the actor network: Ordering, strategy and heterogeneity.* Lancaster, UK: Centre for Science Studies, Lancaster University. Retrieved from http://www.comp.lancs.ac.uk/sociology/papers/Law-Notes-on-Ant.pdf

Law, J. (1996). Ontology and the mode of accounting. In J. Mouritsen & R. Munro (Eds.), *Accountability, power and ethos.* London: Chapman Hall.

Law, J. (1997). *Heterogeneities.* Paper presented at the 'Uncertainty, Knowledge and Skill Conference', Limburg University.

Law, J. (1999). After ANT: Complexity, naming and topology. In J. Law & J. Hassard (Eds.), *Actor network theory and after* (pp. 1–14). Oxford, UK: Blackwell.

Law, J. (2003). *Traduction/Trahison: Notes on ANT.* Lancaster, UK: Centre for Science Studies, Lancaster University. Retrieved from http://www.comp.lancs.ac.uk/sociology/papers/Law-Notes-on-Ant.pdf

Law, J. (2004a). And if the global were small and noncoherent? Method, complexity, and the baroque. *Environment and Planning D. Space and Society, 22*(1), 13–26.

Law, J. (2004b). *After method: Mess in social science research.* London: Routledge.

Law, J. (2007a). *Actor network theory and material semiotics, version of 25th April 2007.* Retrieved from: http://www.heterogeneities.net/publications/Law2007AntandMaterialSemiotics.pdf

Law, J. (2007b). Making a mess with method. In W. Outhwaite & S. P. Turner (Eds.), *The Sage handbook of social science methodology* (pp. 595–606). London: Sage. doi:10.4135/9781848607958.n33

Law, J., & Hassard, J. (Eds.). (1999). *Actor network theory and after.* Oxford, UK: Blackwell Publishing/The Sociological Review.

Law, J., & Urry, J. (2003). *Enacting the social.* Lancaster, UK: Centre for Science Studies, Lancaster University. Retrieved from http://www.comp.lancs.ac.uk/sociology/papers/Law-Notes-on-Ant.pdf

Leander, K. M., & Lovvorn, J. F. (2006). Literacy networks: Following the circulation of texts, bodies, and objects in the schooling and online gaming of one youth. *Cognition and Instruction, 24*(3), 291–340. doi:10.12071532690xci2403_1

Lee, N., & Brown, S. (1994). Otherness and the actor-network: The undiscovered continent. *The American Behavioral Scientist, 37*(6), 772–790. doi:10.1177/0002764294037006005

Lee, N., & Hassard, J. (1999). Organization unbound: Actor-network theory, research strategy and institutional flexibility. *Organization, 6*(3), 391–404. doi:10.1177/135050849963002

Lee, N., & Stenner, P. (1999). Who pays? Can we pay them back? In J. Law & J. Hassard (Eds.), *Actor network theory and after* (pp. 90–112). Oxford, UK: Blackwell. doi:10.1111/j.1467-954X.1999.tb03484.x

McLaren, P. L., & Giarelli, J. M. (Eds.). (1995). *Critical theory and educational research.* Albany, NY: State University of New York Press.

McLean, C., & Hassard, J. (2004). Symmetrical absence/Symmetrical absurdity: Critical notes on the production of actor-network accounts. *Journal of Management Studies, 41*(3), 493–519. doi:10.1111/j.1467-6486.2004.00442.x

Mifsud, D. (2014). Actor-Network Theory: An assemblage of perceptions, understandings, and critiques of this 'sensibility' and how its relatively under-utilized conceptual framework in education studies can aid researchers in the exploration of networks and power relations. *International Journal of Actor-Network Theory and Technological Innovation, 6*(1), 1–16. doi:10.4018/ijantti.2014010101

Mol, A. (1999). Ontological politics. A word and some questions. In J. Law & J. Hassard (Eds.), *Actor network theory and after* (pp. 74–89). Oxford, UK: Blackwell. doi:10.1111/j.1467-954X.1999.tb03483.x

Mol, A. (2002). *The body multiple: Ontology in medical practice*. Durham, NC: Duke University Press. doi:10.1215/9780822384151

Mol, A. (2010). Actor-network theory: Sensitive terms and enduring tensions. *Kölner Zeitschrift für Soziologie und Sozialpsychologie, 50*(1), 253–269.

Mol, A., & Law, J. (1994). Regions, networks and fluids: Anaemia and social topology. *Social Studies of Science, 24*(4), 641–671. doi:10.1177/030631279402400402 PMID:11639423

Moser, I. (2008). Making Alzheimer's disease matter: Enacting, interfering and doing politics of nature. *Geoforum, 39*(1), 98–110. doi:10.1016/j.geoforum.2006.12.007

Munro, R. (1997). Proceedings of the 5th interdisciplinary Perspectives on Accounting Conference. *Power, Conduct and Accountability: Re-Distributing Discretion and the Technologies of Managing.*

Murdoch, J. (1998). The spaces of actor-network theory. *Geoforum, 29*(4), 357–374. doi:10.1016/S0016-7185(98)00011-6

Nespor, J. (2002). Networks and contexts of reform. *Journal of Educational Change, 3*(3/4), 365–382. doi:10.1023/A:1021281913741

Noys, B. (2010). *The persistence of the negative: A critique of contemporary continental thought*. Edinburgh, UK: Edinburgh University Press. doi:10.3366/edinburgh/9780748638635.001.0001

Orlikowski, W. J. (2000). Using technology and constituting structures: A practical lens for studying technology in organizations. *Organization Science, 11*(4), 404–428. doi:10.1287/orsc.11.4.404.14600

Ozga, J. (2009). Governing education through data in England: From regulation to self-evaluation. *Journal of Education Policy, 24*(2), 149–162. doi:10.1080/02680930902733121

Parker, E. (2017). An actor-network theory reading of change for children in public care. *British Educational Research Journal, 43*(1), 151–167. doi:10.1002/berj.3257

Pels, D. (1996). The politics of symmetry. *Social Studies of Science, 26*(2), 277–304. doi:10.1177/030631296026002004

Reed, M. I. (1997). In praise of duality and dualism: Rethinking agency and structure in organizational analysis. *Organization Studies, 18*(1), 21–42. doi:10.1177/017084069701800103

Riles, A. (2000). *The network inside out*. Ann Arbor, MI: University of Michigan Press. doi:10.3998/mpub.15517

Rose, N. (1996). *Inventing ourselves: Psychology, power and personhood*. Cambridge, UK: Cambridge University Press. doi:10.1017/CBO9780511752179

Rudy, A. P. (2005). On ANT and relational materialism. *Capitalism, Nature, Socialism, 16*(4), 109–125. doi:10.1080/10455750500376065

Sayes, E. (2014). Actor-network theory and methodology: Just what does it mean to say that nonhumans have agency? *Social Studies of Science, 44*(1), 134–149. doi:10.1177/0306312713511867 PMID:28078973

Sayes, E. (2017). Marx and the critique of actor-network theory: Mediation, translation, and explanation. *Distinktion: Journal of Social Theory, 18*(3), 294–313. doi:10.1080/1600910X.2017.1390481

Soderberg, J., & Netzen, A. (2010). When all that is theory melts into (hot) air: Contrasts and parallels between actor network theory, autonomist Marxism, and open Marxism. *Ephemera, 10*(2), 95–118.

Sorensen, E. (2009). *The materiality of learning: Technology and knowledge in educational practice*. Cambridge, UK: Cambridge University Press. doi:10.1017/CBO9780511576362

Stalder, F. (1997). *Actor-network theory and communication networks: Toward convergence*. Toronto: Faculty of Information Studies, University of Toronto. Retrieved from http://felix.openflows.com/html/Network_Theory.html

Star, S. L. (1991). Power, technologies and the phenomenology of conventions: On being allergic to onions. In J. Law (Ed.), *A sociology of monsters: Essays on power, technology and domination*. London: Routledge.

Star, S. L. (1995). The politics of formal representations: Wizards, gurus, and organisational complexity. In S. L. Star (Ed.), *Ecologies of knowledge: Work, and politics in science and technology* (pp. 89–118). New York: State University of New York Press.

Strathern, M. (1996). Cutting the network. *Journal of the Royal Anthropological Institute, 2*(3), 517–535. doi:10.2307/3034901

Wacjcman, J. (2000). Reflections on gender and technology studies: In what state is the art? *Social Studies of Science, 30*(3), 447–464. doi:10.1177/030631200030003005

Waltz, S. B. (2006). Nonhumans unbound: Actor-network theory and the reconsideration of "things" in educational foundations. *Journal of Educational Foundations, 20*(3/4), 51–68.

Whittle, A., & Spicer, A. (2008). Is actor network theory critique? *Organization Studies, 29*(4), 611–625. doi:10.1177/0170840607082223

Winner, L. (1993). Upon opening the black box and finding it empty: Social constructivism and the philosophy of technology. *Science, Technology & Human Values, 18*(3), 362–378. doi:10.1177/016224399301800306

Wynne, B. (1996). SSK's identity parade: Signing-up, off-and-on. *Social Studies of Science, 26*(2), 357–391. doi:10.1177/030631296026002007

Chapter 8
Towards a Utility Theory of Privacy and Information Sharing and the Introduction of Hyper-Hyperbolic Discounting in the Digital Big Data Age

Julia Puaschunder
The New School, USA

ABSTRACT

Today enormous data storage capacities and computational power in the e-big data era have created unforeseen opportunities for big data hoarding corporations to reap hidden benefits from individuals' information sharing, which occurs bit by bit in small tranches over time. Behavioral economics describes human decision-making fallibility over time but has—to this day—not covered the problem of individuals' decision to share information about themselves in tranches on social media and big data administrators being able to reap a benefit from putting data together over time and reflecting the individual's information in relation to big data of others. The decision-making fallibility inherent in individuals having problems understanding the impact of their current information sharing in the future is introduced as hyper-hyperbolic discounting decision-making predicament.

CHAPTER CONTENT

In the age of instant communication and social media big data storage and computational power; the need for understanding people's trade-off between communication and privacy has leveraged to unprecedented momentum. Today enormous data storage capacities and computational power in the e-big data era have created unforeseen opportunities for big data hoarding corporations to reap hidden benefits from individual's information sharing, which occurs bit by bit in small tranches over time. The utility theory of contradicting information sharing and privacy predicaments is presented in this paper for the first time

DOI: 10.4018/978-1-5225-8933-4.ch008

and a nomenclature of different personality types regarding information sharing and privacy preferences is theoretically introduced. Unravelling the utility of information sharing versus privacy conflict but also shedding light at the current commodification of big data holds economic theory advancement and governance improvement potentials in the digital age. The article is a first step towards advocating for reclaiming the common good of knowledge via taxation of big data harvesting and self-determination of information sharing based on education about information sharing to curb harmful information sharing discounting fallibility. From legal and governance perspectives, the outlined ideas may stimulate the e-privacy infringement regulations discourse in the pursuit of the greater goals of democratisation of information, equality of communication surplus and upheld humane dignity in the realm of e-ethics in the big data era.

1. INTRODUCTION

Economics is concerned about utility. Utility theory captures people's preferences or values. As one of the foundations of economic theory, the wealth of information and theories on utility lacks information about decision-making conflicts between preferences and values. The preference for communication is inherent in human beings as a distinct feature of humanity. Leaving a written legacy that can inform many generations to come is a humane-unique advancement of society. At the same time, however, privacy is a core human value. People choose what information to share with whom and like to protect some parts of their selves. Protecting people's privacy is a codified virtue around the globe grounded in the wish to uphold individual dignity. Yet to this day, no utility theory exists to describe the internal conflict arising from the individual preference to communicate and the value of privacy. In the age of instant communication and social media big data storage and computational power; the need for understanding people's trade-off between communication and privacy has leveraged to unprecedented momentum. Today enormous data storage capacities and computational power in the e-big data era have created unforeseen opportunities for big data hoarding corporations to reap hidden benefits from individual's information sharing, which occurs bit by bit in small tranches over time. Behavioral economics describes human decision making fallibility over time but has – to this day – not covered the problem of individuals' decision to share information about themselves in tranches on social media and big data administrators being able to reap a benefit from putting data together over time and reflecting the individual's information in relation to big data of others. The decision-making fallibility inherent in individuals having problems understanding the impact of their current information sharing in the future is introduced as hyper-hyperbolic discounting decision-making predicament. Individuals lose control over their data without knowing what surplus value big data moguls can reap from the social media consumer-workers' information sharing, what information can be complied over time and what information this data can provide in relation to the general public's data in drawing inferences about the innocent individual information sharer. Big data derived personality cues have recently been used for governance control purposes, such as border protection and tax compliance surveillance. The utility theory of contradicting information sharing and privacy predicaments is presented in this paper for the first time and a nomenclature of different personality types regarding information sharing and privacy preferences is theoretically introduced. Unravelling the utility of information sharing versus privacy conflict but also shedding light at the current commodification of big data holds economic theory advancement and governance improvement potentials in the digital age. The article is a first step towards advocating for reclaiming the common good of knowledge via taxation of big data harvesting and self-determination of information sharing based on education about information sharing to curb harmful information sharing discounting fallibility. From legal and governance perspectives, the outlined ideas may stimulate the e-privacy infringement regulations discourse in the pursuit of the greater goals of democratisation of information, equality of communication surplus and upheld humane dignity in the realm of e-ethics in the big data era.

Utility theory is concerned with people's choices and decisions based on preferences and values (Fishburn, 1968). Representing satisfaction experienced, utility is derived from the self-attributed worth and goodness of an option compared to other options. Standard neo-classical economic theory describes utility as a set of internally-consistent assumptions about options in the wish to maximize utility (Fishburn, 1968). Utility theory has leveraged as one of the most dominant theories in economics as an underpinning of rational choice and game theory. Utility is usually revealed in people's willingness to pay different money amounts for different options, leading to the concept of revealed preferences (Samuelson, 1937)

Whereas economic utility studies primarily focus on prescriptive approaches to guide how people should behave to maximize their well-being (Arrow, 1951, 1958; Majumdar, 1958; Simon, 1959); decision sciences started capturing how people actually decide regarding choices in an uncertain world and over time (Becker & McClintock, 1967; Edwards, 1954, 1961; Luce & Suppes, 1965). Expected utility theory introduces a first temporal discussion of expectations of utility rather than the actual utility derived from a choice (Alchian, 1953; Marschak, 1950; Strotz, 1953). Von Neumann and Morgenstern (1953) introduced that outcomes of choices are not known with certainty but have probabilities of occurrence, which weighted linear combination allows inferences about the overall utility derived over time.

Since the end of the 1970ies, a wide range of psychological, economic and sociological laboratory and field experiments proved human beings deviating from rational choices as standard neo-classical profit maximization axioms to fail to explain how human actually behave (Kahneman & Thaler, 1991). Human beings were shown to use heuristics in the day-to-day decision making as mental short cuts that enable to cope with information overload in a complex world (Bazerman & Tenbrunsel, 2011; Kahneman & Tversky, 1979; Thaler & Sunstein, 2008).

As one of the most recent developments in utility theory studies, behavioral economics find human utility choices biased (Bowles, 2004; Camerer, Loewenstein & Rabin, 2004; Ebert & Prelec, 2007; Kahneman, 2011; Okada & Hoch, 2004; Putnam, 2002; Sen, 1971, 1993, 1995, 1997, 2002a; Zauberman, Kim, Malkoc & Bettman, 2009) by heuristics (Kahneman, Slovic & Tversky, 1982; Simon, 1979), analogical thinking (Colinsky, 1996; Gentner, 2002), and minimized effort (Allport, 1979; Shah & Oppenheimer, 2008).

In particular, people's cognitive capacities to consider future outcomes in today's decisions are limited (Doyle, 2013; Laibson, 1997; Loewenstein, 1992; Milkman, Rogers & Bazerman, 2009; Read, Loewenstein & Kalyanaraman, 1999; Read & van Leeuwen, 1998). Laibson's (1997) hyperbolically decreasing discounting functions more accurately describe choice behaviors of individuals, who tend to be impatient for smaller rewards now rather than waiting for larger ones later (e.g., Ainslie, 1992; Becker & Murphy, 1988; Doyle, 2013; Estle, Green, Myerson & Holt, 2007; Frederick, Loewenstein & O'Donoghue, 2002; Green, Fry & Myerson, 1994; Green & Myerson, 2004; Hansen, 2006; Henderson & Bateman, 1995; Kirby, 1997; Kirby & Marakovic, 1995; Laibson, 1997; Loewenstein & Prelec, 1993; Mazur, 1987; Meyer, 2013; Murphy, Vuchinich & Simpson, 2001; Myerson & Green, 1995; Rachlin, Raineri & Cross, 1991; Sterner, 1994). Dynamically inconsistent preferences reverse as people are patient when deciding for the future and impatient when choosing for now (Hornsby, 2007; Laibson, 1997; McClure, Ericson, Laibson, Loewenstein & Cohen, 2007; Meyer, 2013; Reed & Martens, 2011; Thaler, 1981).

Field and laboratory experiments provide widespread empirical evidence for hyperbolic discounting and self-control failures (Frederick et al., 2002; Hoch & Loewenstein, 1991; Sen, 1971, 2002b) on money management (Alberini & Chiabai, 2007; Chabris, Laibson & Schuldt, 2008; Coller & Williams, 1999; Harrison, Lau & Williams, 2002; Keller & Strazzera, 2002; Kirby & Marakovic, 1995; Laibson, 1997; Laibson, Repetto & Tobacman, 2003; Salanié & Treich, 2005; Slonim, Carlson & Bettinger, 2007; Thaler & Shefrin, 1981; Warner & Pleeter, 2007), financial benefits (Cairns & van der Pol, 2008), credit card debt (Meier & Sprenger, 2010; Shui & Ausubel, 2004), medical adherence (Trope & Fishbach, 2000), public health (Bosworth, Cameron & DeShazo, 2006; Cameron & Gerdes, 2003; Chapman, 1996; Duflo, Banerjee, Glennerster & Kothari, 2010; Horowitz & Carson, 1990; van der Pol & Cairns, 2001), addiction (Badger, Bickel, Giordano, Jacobs, Loewenstein & Marsch, 2007; Becker & Murphy, 1988; Heyman, 1996; Laux & Peck, 2007; Madden, Bickel & Jacobs, 1999; Petry & Casarella, 1999), social security (Mastrobuoni & Weinberg, 2009), fiscal policies (Keeler & Cretin, 1983), commitment (Duflo, Kremer & Robinson, 2008; Sen, 1977, 2002b), health exercise (DellaVigna & Malmendier, 2004, 2006), employment (DellaVigna & Paserman, 2005), procrastination (Reuben, Sapienza & Zingales, 2010), diet (Read & van Leeuwen, 1998), subscription discipline (Oster & Scott-Morton, 2005), animal care (Green et al., 1994; Mazur, 1987), and consumption (Milkman, Rogers & Bazerman, 2008; Read et al., 1999; Wertenbroch, 1998). Failures to disciplinedly stick to plans for giving in to immediate desires (Ainslie & Haslam, 1992; Read, Frederick & Airoldi, 2012; Strotz, 1956) are explained by people caring less about future outcomes in the eye of future uncertainty (Luce & Raiffa, 1957; Shackle, 1955), perceived risk (Mas-Colell, Whinston & Green, 1995), and transaction costs (Chung & Herrnstein, 1967; Epper, Fehr-Duda & Bruhin, 2011; Frederick et al., 2002; Kirby & Herrnstein, 1995; Mazur, 1987; Read, 2001). Presenting temporal snapshots for now and later concurrently helps overcome myopia and decision-making fallibility (Puaschunder & Schwarz, 2012). In all these studies missing is an investigation of human decision making on preferences for information sharing and privacy.

Although communication and non-communication are day-to-day decisions of individuals; to this day, there is no stringently tested utility theory of information sharing and privacy. We lack a coherent decision science framework about when people choose to share information and when they rather want to stay silent for the sake of privacy. From the economic perspective, information sharing may impose temporal irreversible lock-ins or tipping points. The point of information sharing may be a reference point, in which one bit of more communication gives less utility than one bit of less information shared, hence one bit of more privacy, grants more utility in the sense of Kahneman & Tversky's (1979) behavioral decision science finding 'losses loom larger than gains.' There may also be a marginal decreasing utility derived from one bit more information shared but an exponential marginal utility gain from one more unit of information received given the fact that information can be put into context and an exponentially increasing marginal utility of information. Education, for instance, is the only good with an exponential marginal utility increase, as the more information one holds, the more complex connections one can make and use.

In the past, communication was depicted to decentralize organizations (Crémer, Garicano & Prat, 2007). Media was initially promoted to offer means of information transfer, political participation and protection against political abuse (Delli Carpini & Keeter, 1989; Neuman, Just & Crigler, 1992; Norris & Sanders, 2003; Prat & Strömberg, 2005; Snyder & Strömberg, 2010). Evidence suggests that media coverage increases voter information, which increases the responsiveness of votes to policy, which increases the effort and selection of politicians, thus producing better policies (Prat & Strömberg, 2013). Media thus traditionally was portrayed as helping to keep politicians accountable (Prat & Strömberg, 2013). Media coverage was found to improve selection and incentives of politicians alongside voting responsiveness (Iyengar & Kinder, 1987; Snyder & Strömberg, 2010).

Critical studies in this regard show that there are negative downsides of transparency (Prat, 2005). Mass media can also erode social capital, as they potentially isolate people from real-world experiences (Olken, 2009; Putnam, 2000). A positive relation between federal funds per capita allocation to areas where the media covered political parties in power was found (Snyder & Strömberg, 2010). Research has been done on the effect of conventional media on politics including a nomenclature of biases that impose problems – especially against minority opinions (Prat & Strömberg, 2013). Ideological biases are found in conventional media and media effects captured on vote choice (Prat & Strömberg, 2013). While the negative facets of information on elections and the role of social media on voting outcomes has been widely discussed recently; yet to this day no stringent theoretical or empirical framework for the utility of privacy and information sharing on social media exits.

In the digital age, to study the trade-off between information sharing and privacy has leveraged into unprecedented importance. Social media revolutionized human communication around the globe. As never before in the history of humankind, information about individuals can be stored and put in context over time and logically placed within society thanks to unprecedented data conservation and computational powers. The big data era, however, also opened gates to unprecedentedly reap benefits from information sharing and big data generation (Puaschunder, 2017). The so-called nudgital society was recently introduced, shedding light onto the undescribed hidden social class division between social media users and social media providers, who can benefit from the information shared by social media users. Social media users share private information in their wish to interact with friends and communicate to public. The social media big data holder can then reap surplus value from the information shared by selling it to marketers, who can draw inferences about consumer choices. The big data can also be used for governance control purposes, for instance border protection and tax compliance control.

Drawing from the economic foundations of utility theory, this paper seeks the introduce the first application of utility theory to a preference-values predicament between communication and privacy in the new media era. Behavioral economics insights are advanced in shedding novel light on the conflict between the humane wish to communicate now versus combined information held by unknown big data compilers in the future. An exponential loss of privacy and hyper-hyperbolic risks in the future for the information sharer are introduced as behavioral economic decision-making fallibilities. For the overconfident information sharer, it remains largely unforeseeable what the sum of the individual information sharing tranches can lead to over time and what information its Gestalt holds for those who have big data insights over time, which can also be analyzed in relation to the general population. Governance gains a critical stance on new media use for guiding on public concerns regarding privacy and information sharing in the digital age (Puaschunder, 2017). While there is some literature on the history of media on politics (Prat & Strömberg, 2013), the wide societal implications of fake news and discounting misinformation has widely been overlooked in contemporary behavioral economics research and the externalities literature. Social sciences literature on privacy and information sharing has to be reconsidered in the age of social media.

The article is structured as follows: An introduction of the theory of utility and communication and information sharing is followed by an outline of the impetus of the digital big data age on privacy. The first utility theory of information sharing and privacy will be theoretically introduced. Hyperbolic decision making fallibility will become the basis of argumentations around hyper-hyperbolic discounting – the novel argument that information sharing in tranches may lead to an underestimation of the privacy infringements when these bits of information can be put together over time and are compared to big data in order to infer about the individual in relation to the general population.

The subjective additive utility of information-shared tranche by tranche may underestimate the big data holder's advantage to reap benefits from information shared. The discussion introduces problems of the contemporary nudgital society (Puaschunder, 2017), in which big data compilers can reap a surplus value from selling compiled information (Madsbjerg, 2017) or manipulate vulnerable population segments based on their previously shared information (The Economist, 2017). Implications lead to open questions about ethics in the information age and recommendations for a reclaiming of the common good of shared knowledge in education about information sharing in the digital age as well as the democratization of information. Challenging contemporary behavioral insights theory aims at fostering a more informed, self-determined and protected digital society in the wish to uphold e-ethics in the 21st century big data social media era.

2. THEORY

2.1 Utility Theory

Economic theory is built upon the idea of utility, which captures people's preferences or values (Fishburn, 1968). Human are believed to strive to maximize utility on a constant basis by weighting their preferences and values on the pleasure they would receive from different options. In neoclassic economics, utility theory primarily focuses on prescriptive utility maximization giving recommendations how individuals should behave to maximize their utility. Prescriptive utility maximization theory serves as normative guide in helping the decision maker codify preferences. If preferences would violate rational preference choices, the theory suggests strategies so the informed decision maker can revise their rational reference choices and judgments to eliminate preference inconsistency. Using utility theory, preferences are constantly transformed into corresponding numerical utility data that is portrayed to maximize the individual's pursuit of happiness. Utility theory provides a powerful set to determine how to compare actual alternatives. It enables the decision maker's optimal preferences to be transformed into a numerical utility structure guided by an optimization algorithm.

In doing so, standard microeconomic utility theory has been of aid to explain how to maximize individual outcomes in very many different domains ranging from marketing research (Greenberg & Collins, 1966; Marquardt, Makens & Larzelere, 1965; Stafford, 1966), food industry quality control of products and corporate strategies (Read, 1964; Stillson, 1954) and production (Aumann & Kruskal, 1958, 1959; Suzuki, 1957).

2.1.1 Expected Utilities

Utility maximization lies at the heart of common sense rational decision making. It provides a powerful tool to resolve multidimensional value maximization by weighting the pros and cons of alternatives in additive utility theory. Uncertainty can be coped with by comparing expectations as to what might result from alternative choices in expected utility theory. The so-called stochastic utility theory makes assumptions in terms of probabilities of choice rather than capturing actual preferences (Debreu, 1958, 1960; Fishburn, 1968; Suppes, 1961). Expected utility theory therefore introduces a first temporal discussion of expectations of utility rather than the actual utility derived from a choice later (Alchian, 1953; Marschak, 1950; Strotz, 1953). Given future uncertainty, the utility of any *P* can be computed as the weighted sum of the utilities of the x in X, the weights being the probabilities assigned by *P*. The expected utility equation reads (Bernoulli, 1954):

$$u\left(P\right) = P\left(x^1\right)u\left(x^1\right) + P\left(x^2\right)u\left(x^2\right) + \dots + P\left(x^m\right)u\left(x^m\right), \tag{1}$$

whereby u stands for utility, P denotes probability of the u of the separate alternatives x^1, $x^2 \dots x^m$. The weighting of different alternatives in relation to each other is exhibited in indifference curves (Edgeworth, 1881; Pareto, 1906/2014).

2.1.2 Indifference Curves

According to utility theory, individuals are constantly evaluating competing choice options. Given a consumer's budget constraints and prices of goods, commodity bundle arise, in which consumers weight alternative options based on their expected utility derived. Indifference curves connect points on a graph representing different quantities of two goods, between which a consumer is indifferent. For instance, if a consumer weights whether or not to buy good *x* or good *y*, the indifference curves would outline how much of good *x* and good *y* can be consumed to end with the same utility given the budget of the consumer. This is how much the utility of one good must be increased to offset a decrease in the utility of another good.

Figure 1 represents standard indifference curves for two competing goods, good *x* and good *y*. The indifference curve outlines that the consumer has no preference for one combination or bundle of goods over a different combination of the same curve. All points on the curve hold the same utility for the consumer. The indifference curve is therefore the locus of various points of different combinations of two goods providing equal utility to the consumer. Indifference curves represent observable demand patterns for individual consumers over commodity bundles (Edgeworth, 1881; Pareto, 1906/2014).

In classical economics, an individual is believed to always being able to rank any consumption bundles by order of preference (Jevons, 1871). The curves are negatively sloped curves – as the quantity consumed of one good *x* increases, total satisfaction increases if not offset by a decrease in the quantity of good *y*. Indifference curves fulfill the axioms of completeness, transitivity and strictly convex preferences. Preferences are complete, meaning the consumer ranks all available alternative combinations of commodities in terms of satisfaction provided. Preference rankings are reflexive, transitive, continuous and strongly monotonous. There is a strongly holding substitution assumption, meaning that consumers are believed to willingly give up or trade-off some of one good to get more of another. The fundamental assertion is that there is a maximum amount that a consumer is willing to give up of one commodity to get another commodity, which will leave the consumer indifferent between the new and the old situation (Silberberg, 2000). Indifference curves are determined by the prices of goods and budget constraints of consumers.

Indifference curves for substitute goods are straight lines – see the straight line in green in Figure 2 representing a budget constraint for substitute goods.

Figure 1. Indifference curve (blue curve) for two goods, good x and good y given their budget constraint (red line)

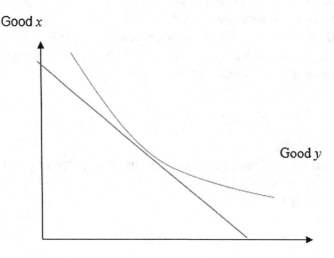

Figure 2. Indifference curve (green line) for substitute goods, good x and good y

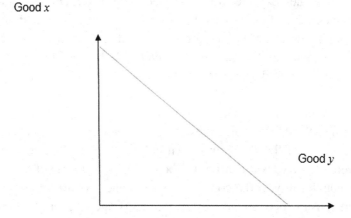

The slope of an indifference curve in absolute value is the marginal rate of substitution, which explains the rate at which consumers are willing to give up one good in exchange for more of the other good. For most goods the marginal rate of substitution is not constant so their indifference curves are curved.

2.1.3 Time Preferences

When making decisions, people may contemplate a sequence of choices – some with outcomes now and some with outcomes later. The so-called hyperbolic conundrum lies in the present utility often turning into future disutility. Building on standard neoclassical utility theory offering a first nomenclature of time preferences among the population, standard utility theory (Fishburn, 1968) therefore categorized types of decision makers over time into:

1. **Extreme Impatience**: Only immediate pleasures are valued, people are overwhelmingly concerned with immediate pleasures.

2. **Impatience**: Discounting the future, e.g. featured in work of Diamond, Koopmans and Williamson (1962), Feldstein (1965), Koopmans (1960), Koopmans, Diamonds and Williamson (1964), Marglin (1963), and Strotz (1957).

3. **Eventual Impatience**: Discounting may not occur in the present and the near future, but all periods sufficiently far away will be discounted at some point in the future, for instance discussed in Diamond (1965).

4. **Time Perspective:** Related to hyperbolic-discounting as in Koopmans et al. (1964) and Laibson (1997).

5. **No Time Preference:** At the present time, the individual neither discounts nor overcounts the future with respect to the present – find this idea in the work of Diamond (1965), Fishburn (1966), Ramsey (1928), Wold (1952).

6. **Persistence**: Stationarity of a consistent preference structure in Diamond (1965), Koopmans (1960), Koopmans et al. (1964).

7. **Variety**: Or nonpersistence as consistently varying preference structure as described in Wold (1952).

Overall, all these notions apply to preferences concerning the future, viewed from the present given general uncertainty about what our preferences for future events will be in the future. This nomenclature addresses the problem of capturing valid preference structures over time that allow stringent predictions of choice behavior and strategies for future planning (Fishburn, 1968).

While standard neoclassical economic theory defines utility to be about preferences and values maximization, no theory framework for the predicament between preferences and values exists to date, which may be theoretically grounded in the critical extension of neoclassical economics.

On a large scale, utility theory provides inferences about behavioral tendencies of individuals to predict the reaction of a social group to changes in commodity prices and incomes. Economists are enabled to evaluate changes of income and prices for consumers following the greater goal of improving the social good on the basis of utility predictions. Governance can derive recommendations for prescribing economic policies that will be overall most beneficial to a society. Welfare economics is a powerful example of the prescriptive use of utility theory in practice (Debreu, 1964; Rothenberg, 1961).

2.2 Behavioral Economics

Behavioral economics found individuals having difficulties to make preference comparisons on a constant basis in a multidimensional world of uncertainty. Behavioral economists therefore set out to aid decision makers to discover how to determine the optimal preference structure in a complex world.

Starting with psychological studies in the wish to derive a predictive ability of utility preference choices and choice behavior, behavioral economics (Simon, 1957) revolutionized economic theory by finding human decision making persistently deviating from rational choice axioms (Sen, 1971, 1993, 1997, 2002a). Whereas economic utility studies primarily focus on prescriptive approaches to guide how people should behave to maximize their well-being (Arrow, 1974, 1978; Majumdar, 1958; Simon, 1959); behavioral economists and decision sciences specialists have rather captured how people actually decide on choices (Becker & McClintock, 1967; Edwards, 1954, 1961; Luce & Suppes, 1965). Behavioral economics offers an alternative description how individual actually choose to pursuit their utility maximization in more intuitive decision approaches. Predictive utility and behavioral economics thereby follow the wish to aid decision maker cope with a complex world and discover his or her preference architecture in a set of alternatives under uncertainty.

Behavioral economists finds human time perception biased (Bowles, 2004; Camerer et al., 2004; Ebert & Prelec, 2007; Kahneman, 2011; Okada & Hoch, 2004; Putnam, 2002; Zauberman et al., 2009) by heuristics (Kahneman et al., 1982; Simon, 1979), analogical thinking (Colinsky, 1996; Gentner, 2002), and minimized effort (Allport, 1979; Shah & Oppenheimer, 2008). An impressive line of research has shown that heuristics lead to predictable and systematic errors (Tversky & Kahneman, 1974). Individuals are therefore believed to satisficing regarding their options, meaning to break them down in less complex choice sets than the actual alternatives (Simon, 1957).

By studying human decision-making fallibility and its consequences, behavioral economics argues that people make decisions based on rules of thumb heuristics that dominate human choices (Gigerenzer, 2014, 2016; Kahneman & Tversky, 2000). Laboratory experiments have captured heuristics as mental short cuts easing mentally constrained human in a complex world (Cartwright, 2011; Sen, 1977; Simon & Bartel, 1986). Mental short cuts were outlined to simplify decision-making and substitute difficult questions with easy applicable automatic behavioral reactions (Kahneman, 2011).

Heuristics cause people to make choices much faster, but ultimately less logically than more careful, long-form, decision making. From these insights gained, decision-making failures became studied in order to improve human decision-making outcomes over time and in groups (Camerer et al., 2004). These cognitive mental shortcuts are most crucial if they set humans on a path to erroneous choices over time. Multi-period decision-making addresses that for each time period, another set of preferences for the same options can be expected. Decision preference vary over time in the eye of uncertainty.

One of the major problems detected by behavioral economics lies in preferences being dependent on past experiences and present expectations, which are time inconsistent as people's cognitive capacities (Doyle, 2013) to consider future outcomes in today's decisions are limited (Laibson, 1997; Loewenstein, 1992; Milkman et al., 2009; Read et al., 1999; Read & van Leeuwen, 1998). In carefully designed repetitive-choice situations, individuals exhibited to have shifting preferences and malleable choices. In laboratory and field experiments, individuals were found to consider alternatives on a constant basis based on many factors and attributes that can span a number of time periods. They have difficulty in arriving at an overall preference between alternatives, especially when weighting some importance factors on one dimension and other importance determinates on another (Fishburn, 1968).

While standard microeconomic theory captures exponential temporal discounting to explain rational decision-making; Laibson's (1997) hyperbolically decreasing discounting functions describe choice behavior of individuals more accurately. Decision makers were found to be impatient for smaller rewards now rather than waiting for larger ones later (e.g., Ainslie, 1992; Becker & Murphy, 1988; Doyle, 2013; Estle et al., 2007; Frederick et al., 2002; Green et al., 1994; Green & Myerson, 2004; Hansen, 2006; Henderson & Bateman, 1995; Kirby, 1997; Kirby & Marakovic, 1995; Laibson, 1997; Loewenstein & Prelec, 1993; Mazur, 1987; Meyer, 2013; Murphy et al., 2001; Myerson & Green, 1995; Rachlin et al., 1991; Sterner, 1994). Dynamically inconsistent preferences reverse as people are patient when deciding for the future and impatient when choosing for now (Hornsby, 2007; Laibson, 1997; McClure et al., 2007; Meyer, 2013; Reed & Martens, 2011; Thaler, 1981). Field and laboratory experiments provide widespread empirical evidence for hyperbolic discounting and self-control failures (Frederick et al., 2002; Hoch & Loewenstein, 1991; Sen, 1971, 2002b) on money management (Alberini & Chiabai, 2007; Chabris et al., 2008; Coller & Williams, 1999; Harrison et al., 2002; Keller & Strazzera, 2002;

Kirby & Marakovic, 1995; Laibson, 1997; Laibson et al., 2003; Salanié & Treich, 2005; Slonim et al., 2007; Thaler & Shefrin, 1981; Warner & Pleeter, 2007), financial benefits (Cairns & van der Pol, 2008), credit card debt (Meier & Sprenger, 2010; Shui & Ausubel, 2004), medical adherence (Trope & Fishbach, 2000), public health (Bosworth et al., 2006; Cameron & Gerdes, 2003; Chapman, 1996; Duflo et al., 2010; Horowitz & Carson, 1990; van der Pol & Cairns, 2001), addiction (Badger et al., 2007; Becker & Murphy, 1988; Heyman, 1996; Laux & Peck, 2007; Madden et al., 1999; Petry & Casarella, 1999), social security (Mastrobuoni & Weinberg, 2009), fiscal policies (Keeler & Cretin, 1983), commitment (Duflo et al., 2008; Sen, 1977, 2002b), health exercise (DellaVigna & Malmendier, 2004, 2006), employment (DellaVigna & Paserman, 2005), procrastination (Reuben et al., 2010), diet (Read & van Leeuwen, 1998), subscription discipline (Oster & Scott-Morton, 2005), animal care (Green & Myerson, 1994; Mazur, 1987), and consumption (Milkman et al., 2008; Read et al., 1999; Wertenbroch, 1998). Failures to disciplinedly stick to plans for giving in to immediate desires (Ainslie & Haslam, 1992; Read et al., 2012; Strotz, 1956) are explained by people caring less about future outcomes in the eye of future uncertainty (Luce & Raiffa, 1957; Shackle, 1955), perceived risk (Mas-Colell, Whinston & Green, 1995), and transaction costs (Chung & Herrnstein, 1967; Epper et al., 2011; Frederick et al., 2002; Kirby & Herrnstein, 1995; Mazur, 1987; Read, 2001). Presenting temporal snapshots for now and later concurrently helps overcome myopia (Puaschunder & Schwarz, 2012). The wealth of behavioral economics theories on utility maximization deviations is – to this day – silent about decision-making conflicts between preferences and values in regard to information sharing and privacy.

3. INFORMATION SHARING AND PRIVACY

The wish for communication is inherent in human beings as a distinct feature of humanity. Leaving a written legacy that can inform many generations to come is a humane-unique advancement of society. At the same time, however, privacy is a core human value. People choose what information to share with whom and like to protect some parts of their selves in secrecy. Protecting people's privacy is a codified virtue around the world to uphold the individual's dignity. Yet to this day, no utility theory exists to describe the conflict arising from the individual preference to communicate and the value of privacy.

3.1 The Humane Preference For Communication

The act of conveying intended meanings from one entity or group to another through the use of mutually understood signs and semiotic rules is the act of communication. Communication is a key feature of humans, animals and even plants (Witzany, 2012). Steps inherent to all human communication are the formation of communicative motivation and reason, message composition as further internal or technical elaboration on what exactly to express, message encoding, transmission of the encoded message as a sequence of signals using a specific channel or medium, noise sources influencing the quality of signals propagating from the sender to one or more receivers, reception of signals and reassembling of the encoded message from a sequence of received signals, decoding of the reassembled encoded message and interpretation or sense making of the presumed original message (Shannon, 1948). Information sharing implying giving up privacy is at the core of communication. Communication can be verbal and non-verbal. Comprising very many different domains ranging from business, politics, interpersonal, social to mass media; communication is a humane-imbued wish and center core of every functioning society.

In society, language is used to exchange ideas and embody theories of reality. Language is the driver of social progress (Orwell, 1949). Linguists find discourse and information sharing inseparable from socio-economic societal advancement (Fowler, Hodge, Kress & Trew, 1979). Language and communication modes are implicit determinations of social strata (Orwell, 1949). Different institutions and media sources have different varieties of language and information sharing styles. Access to information is related to social status and market power. Social visibility is a powerful and cheap incentive to make people contribute more to public goods and charities and be less likely to lie, cheat, pollute or be insensitive and antisocial (Ali & Benabou, 2016). Information receipt is an implicit determinant to classify and rank people to assert institutional or personal status in society (Fowler et al., 1979). Mass communication echoes in economic cycles in the creation of booms and busts (Puaschunder, work in progress). Media is also a hallmark of propaganda and political control (Besley & Prat, 2006; Prat & Strömberg, 2013). At the same time, privacy is a human virtue around the world.

3.2 Privacy as a Human Virtue

Privacy is the ability of an individual or group to seclude themselves, or information about themselves, and thereby share information about themselves selectively. The right to privacy grants the ability to choose which information about parts of the self can be accessed by others and to control the extent, manner and timing of the use of those parts we choose to disclose. Privacy comprises of the right to be let alone, the option to limit the access others have to one's personal information and secrecy as the option to conceal any information about oneself (Solove, 2008).

The degree of privacy varies in autonomy levels throughout individualistic and collectivism cultures. While the boundaries and contents protected and what is considered as private differ widely among cultures and individuals, the common sense in the world is that some parts of the self should be protected as private.

Privacy has a valued feature of being something inherently special or sensitive to a person, which can create value and specialty if shared with only a selected person or group. The domain of privacy partially overlaps with security, confidentiality and secrecy, which are codified and legally protected throughout the world, mainly in privacy laws but also in natural laws of virtues of integrity and dignity. Privacy is seen as a collective core human value and fundamental human right, which is upheld in constitutions around the world[1] (Johnson, 2009; Warren & Brandeis, 1890).

In personal relations, privacy can be voluntarily sacrificed, normally in exchange for reciprocity and perceived benefits. Sharing private information can breed trust and bestow meaningfulness to social relations. Giving up privacy holds risks of uncertainty and losses, which are undescribed in economics and in particular the behavioral economics literature on intertemporal decision-making (Gaudeul & Giannetti, 2017). People tend to be more willing to voluntarily sacrifice privacy if the data gatherer is seen to be transparent as to what information is gathered and how the information will be used (Oulasvirta, Suomalainen, Hamari, Lampinen & Karvonen, 2014). Privacy as a prerequisite for the development of a sense of self-identity is a core of humanness (Altman, 1975). Privacy is often protected to avoid discrimination, manipulation, exploitation, embarrassment and risks of reputational losses, for instance, in the domains of body parts, home and property, general information of private financial situations, medical records, political affiliation, religious denomination, thoughts, feelings and identity.

Technological shocks have a history of challenging privacy standards (Warren & Brandeis, 1890). The age of instant messaging and big data, however, has leveraged the idea of privacy to another dimension. The concept of information privacy has become more significant as more systems controlling big data appear in the digital age. With advances in big data, face recognition, automated licence-plate readers and other tracking technologies, the upholding privacy and anonymity has become increasingly expensive and the cost is more opaque than ever before (Ali & Benabou, 2016).

3.3 Privacy in the Digital Big Data Era

The amount of big data stored each second has reached an all time high in the digital era. Internet privacy is the ability to determine what information one reveals or withholds about oneself over the internet, who has access to personal information and for what purpose one's information may be used. Privacy laws in many countries have started to adapt to changes in technology in order to cope with unprecedented constant information surveillance possibilities, big data storage opportunities and computational power peaks. For instance, Microsoft reports that 75 percent of U.S. recruiters and human-resource professionals use online data about candidates, often using information provided by search engines, social-network sites, photo and video sharing tools, personal web appearances like websites and blogs, as well as Twitter.

Social media tools have become large-scale factories with unpaid labor (Puaschunder, 2017). For instance, Facebook accounts for the largest social-network site with nearly 1,490 million members, who upload over 4.75 billion pieces of content about their lives and that of others daily. The accuracy of this information also appears questionable, with about 83.09 million accounts assumed to be fake. Aside from directly observable information, social media sites can also easily track browsing logs and patterns, search queries or secondary information giving inferences about sexual orientation, political and religious views, race, substance use, intelligence and overall personality, mental status, individual views and preferences (Kosinski, Bachrach, Stillwell, Kohli & Graepel, in press; Kosinski, Stillwell & Graepel, 2013).

As for the unprecedented possibilities to collect data, store big data and aggregate information that can be compared to big data Gestalt over time and society, privacy has leveraged into one of the most fragile areas of concern in the electronic age, demanding for legal protection, regulatory control and e-ethics (Flaherty, 1989). Today, the existing global privacy rights framework in the digital age has been criticized to be incoherent, inefficient and in need for revision. Global privacy protection shields are demanded to be established. Yet to this day there is no economic framework on information sharing and privacy control. While – for instance – Posner (1981) criticizes privacy for concealing information, which reduces market efficiency; Lessig (2006) advocates for regulated online privacy. As of now we lack a behavioral decision making frame to explain the privacy paradox of the individual predicament between the humane-imbued preference to communicate and information share versus value of privacy. We have no behavioral economics description of inconsistencies and moderator variables in the decision between online information sharing behavior and retroactive preference reversal preferences in the eye of privacy concerns in the digital big data era.

4. A UTILITY THEORY OF INFORMATION SHARING AND PRIVACY

Building on classical utility theory, individuals are constantly evaluating competing choice options. Individuals weight alternative options based on their expected utility derived. Indifference curves would

*Figure 3. Indifference curve (blue line) for information sharing s and privacy p given the total informa-
tion and communication constraint*

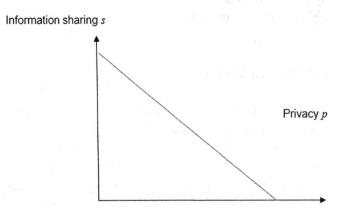

then connect points on a graph representing different quantities of two goods, between which an individual is indifferent.

In the case of the privacy paradox of information sharing preferences and privacy values, a person
would weights whether or not to share information s or choose the information to remain private p. The
respective indifference curves would outline how much of information sharing s and privacy p can be
enabled to end with the same utility given the budget of overall information held by the decision maker.

Figure 3 represents the respective indifference curves for information sharing s and privacy p. That
is, the individual has no preference for one combination or bundle of information sharing or privacy
over a different combination of the same curve. All points on the curve hold the same utility for the
individual. The indifference curve is therefore the locus of various points of different combinations
of privacy and information sharing providing equal utility to her or him. Indifference curves are
thereby seen to represent potentially observable behavioral patterns for individuals over information
bundles. The indifference curve for information sharing s and privacy p is subject to communication
and information constraints, hence all information budgets and communication opportunities. There is
only a finite amount of information and there may be environmental conditions determining if people
can exchange and share information. As exhibited in graph 3, the indifference curve for information
sharing s and privacy p is a straight line given the assumption that information sharing or privacy are
substitutes.

While in classical economics, an individual was believed to always being able to rank any consumption bundles by order of preference (Jevons, 1871); the indifference curve for information sharing s
and privacy p subject to communication and information constraints may feature a hyper-hyperbolic
element or temporal dimension. The information share moment may thereby be a reference point. At
the moment of the information sharing decision, it may not be foreseeable what the future implication
of the information sharing is.

In general, the costs and benefits of communication are assumed as linear subtraction of positive
benefits of communication b_c minus the negative consequences of communication c_c. The nature of the
problem is intertemporal as information sharers cannot foresee the future implications of their information sharing divided by variance σ (Prat, 2017).

$$\frac{b_c - c_c}{\sigma} \qquad\qquad (2)$$

However, the digital social media era has heralded a hyper-hyperbolic discounting fallibility. Individuals have lost oversight of the consequences of their individual information sharing given big data hoarding capabilities, which also allow drawing inferences about the individual in relation to others.

In the digital big data era, information share online may hold unforeseen risks of privacy merchants or social media capitalists that commercialize information reaping hidden benefits from the information provided (Etzioni, 2012; Puaschunder, 2017; The Economist, November 4, 2017). The subjective additive utility of information shared tranche by tranche may underestimate the big data holder's advantage to reap benefits from information shared given unprecedented data storage and big data computation power advantages of the big data era. Unprecedented computational power and storage opportunities have created the possibility to hoard information over time and put it in context with the rest of the population in order to draw inferences about the information sharer (Madsbjerg, 2017). The digital age and era of instant information sharing have therefore heralded problems of individuals who give in their basic humane need for information communication to become vulnerable over time. The big data information holder may thereby benefit from the history of information and the relation of the individual's information in comparison to the general population to an unknown degree given missing e-literacy and transparency. Comparison to the general public may lead to an implicit underrepresentation and hence discrimination of vulnerable groups. For instance, certain groups that may not be represented online will therefore likely face an under-advocacy of their rights and needs.

While regular hyperbolic discounting captures a game theoretical predicament of the self now versus the self later, the information offering more of a Gestalt in the eyes of the big data holder, leverages hyperbolic discounting to a game theory against uncertainty on the end of the big data holder. The hyper-hyperbolic discounting fallibility therefore may describe that at the moment of information sharing, the individual has hardly any grasp what is implied in the giving up of privacy. The individual only focuses on the current moment trade-off between information sharing and privacy upholding, but hardly has any insights what the compiled information over time holds for big data moguls. As for holding computational and storage advantages, the social media big data moguls can form a *Gestalt* which is more than the sheer sum of the individual information shared, also in comparison to the general populace's data. The shared information can also be resold to companies (Etzioni, 2012; Madsbjerg, 2017). In relation to other people's information, the big data moguls can make predictions about their choices and behaviors (Madsbjerg, 2017). Information can also be used for governance purposes, for instance tax compliance and border control mechanisms (Puaschunder, 2017). Some governments have recently used big data to check the accuracy of tax reports but also to detect people's political views when crossing borders (Puaschunder, 2017). Lastly, the use of big data inferences also implies hidden persuasion means – nudging can be turned against innocent information sharers who have no long-term and computational advantage to foresee the impact of the information share (The Economist, 2017; Puaschunder, 2017).

While behavioral economics hyperbolic discounting theory introduces the idea of time-inconsistency of preferences between an individual now and the same individual in the future; hyper-hyperbolic discounting underlines that in the case of information sharing preferences this fallibility is exacerbated since individuals lose control over their data and big data moguls can reap surplus value from the social media consumer-workers' information sharing and derive information complied over time and in relation to the general norm to draw inferences about the innocent information sharer. With the modern digital era, all these features open an information sharer versus information reaper divide in the big data age (Puaschunder, 2017).

From the social media big data capitalist view, the information gain of one more person sharing information is exponentially rising. Hence, the marginal utility derived from one more person providing information is increasing exponentially and disproportionally to the marginally declining costs arising from one more person being added to the already existing social media platform. Communication costs and benefits are assumed to not be additive and separable.

4.1 Expected Utility and Subjective Probability in the Digital Big Data Era

In accordance with neo-classical utility theory, decision makers weight alternatives based on the resulting consequences dependent on uncertain aspects of the environment. But in the digital big data era, individuals simply lack an oversight of the consequences of information sharing. Assumptions on preferences of information sharing are skewed leading to an underestimation of the consequences of amalgamated information and private information evaluated in relation to other's data. Assignment of utilities to the consequences are underinflated. The utility of information sharing is thus the underweighted sum of the utilities of the consequences.

4.2 Time Preferences

Following the standard neo-classical nomenclature of time preferences among the population, an information sharing preference over time is introduced. Multi-period decision-making addresses that for each time period, another set of preferences for the same options can be expected. The populace may therefore be theoretically categorizes into

1. **Extreme Impatience:** Extreme information sharing as the individual values immediate pleasure of information sharing, information is shared without hesitation, impression management may play a role in this.
2. **Impatience:** Discounting the future impact of information, uninformed information sharing nature. This is the case if an individual shares information although having a hunch that this information sharing may create problems in the future, called the privacy paradox.
3. **Eventual Impatience:** Discounting the future impact of information at some point in the future leads to controlled information sharing, very likely choosing what categories to expose to public.
4. **Time Perspective:** Related to hyper-hyperbolic discounting awareness, individuals may control information sharing, for instance, these individuals may participate in social media only to reap information from others but not contribute additional information beyond what is required. This type has a controlled privacy and is engaged in social media solely to reap benefits of other's information from social media networks.
5. **No Time Preference:** At the present time the individual neither discounts nor overcounts the future with respect to the present, which may be true for individuals who do not at all participate in social media communication and are blasé about information sharing and gaining information on social media,

6. **Persistence:** Consistent preference structure regarding information sharing may result in informed information sharing with no regrets.

7. **Variety:** Consistently varying preference structure regarding information sharing, likely dependent on the content of information shared, may result in information sharing with regrets afterwards. These individuals have no stringent position towards information sharing or privacy preference, likely have categories for what to share and what not. This type varies in information preferences over time and by subject category.

This nomenclature addresses the problem of capturing valid preference structures over time that allow stringent predictions of choice behavior and strategies for future planning (Fishburn, 1968). The nomenclature also highlights that the selection of information sharing or privacy has an impact on our later choices. Addressing this predicament, Klein and Meckling (1958) suggest the best strategy given future uncertainties is to concentrate attention on immediate decisions that lead toward the main objective while preserving a reasonable degree of freedom in future choices. While Strotz (1957) considers the maximization of utility in an additive, discounted form over a continuous-time future and powerful research on hyperbolic discounting has unraveled pre-commitment and consistent planning as means to curb harmful decision-making fallibility. Yet the age of social media generated big data may impose novel hyperbolic discounting fallibility onto the information-sharing individual (Behears, Choi, Laibson, Madrian & Sakong, 2011; Chabris et al., 2008; Koopmans, 1964). Future research may test the reliability and validity of the nomenclature and unravel moderator variables and variances between different populations, e.g., such as age, cultural heritage, gender, etc.

4.3 Expected Utility and Subjective Probability

In accordance with neo-classical utility theory, alternatives are weighted based on the resulting consequences dependent on uncertain aspects of the environment. Assumptions on preferences between such alternatives lead to an assignment of utilities to the consequences and to the alternatives plus an assignment of subjective probabilities to the possible states of the environment. The utility of an alternative can therefore be written as a weighted sum of the utilities of the consequences. The weight for any alternative-consequence pair is the subjective probability associated with the states of the environment that yield the given consequence when the given alternative is used (Fishburn, 1968).

Regarding expected utility, the overall expected utility equation for information sharing and privacy reads

$$u = \sum w * u_s + w * u_p, \tag{3}$$

whereby w stands for weight, u_s is the utility of information sharing and u_p the utility of privacy.

The weighted expected utility equation reads

$$u(P) = P(x^1) u_s(x^1) + P(x^2) u_p(x^2), \tag{4}$$

whereby $P(x^1) u_s(x^1)$ is the probability of information sharing utility and $P(x^2) u_p(x^2)$ the probability of privacy.

In the digital age, the utility of privacy is expected to have a marginal exponential value given the exponential rise of utility for the big data holder to reap benefits from data. The more data is held, the more complex relations can be unraveled by the big data holder. Information can be put into context of time and population correlates. While there is a marginally declining cost of an additional social media user using an established social network, there is an disproportionally large social network gain with another person joining for the social network provider, who can reap an excessive exponentially increasing marginal utility of another person joining and sharing another piece of information. Given the absence of any taxation of this gain (Madsbjerg, 2017), social media has leveraged into an IT monopoly (Soros, 2018).

5. DISCUSSION: RECLAIMING THE COMMONS OF KNOWLEDGE: A THEORY OF SELF-DETERMINATION IN THE DIGITAL BIG DATA AGE

In the age of instant communication and social media big data; the need for understanding people's tradeoff between communication and privacy has leveraged to unprecedented momentum. For one, enormous data storage capacities and computational power in the e-big data era have created unforeseen opportunities for big data hoarding corporations to reap hidden benefits from individual's information sharing.

In the 21st century, the turnover of information and the aggregation of social informational capital has revolutionized the world. In the wake of the emergence of new social media communication and interaction methods, a facilitation of the extraction of surplus value in shared information has begun. Computational procedures for data collection, storage and access in the large-scale data processing have been refined for real-time and historical data analysis, spatial and temporal results as well as forecasting and now casting throughout recent decades. All these advancements have offered a multitude of in-depth information on human biases and imperfections as well as social representations and collective economic trends (Minsky, 1977; Moscovici, 1988; Puaschunder, 2015; Wagner & Hayes, 2005; Wagner, Lorenzi-Cioldi, Mankova & Rose, 1999).

The digital age has brought about unprecedented opportunities to amalgamate big data information that can directly be used to derive inferences about people's preferences in order to nudge and wink them in the nudgitalist's favor. In today's nudgital society, information has become a source of competitive advantage. Technological advancement and the social media revolution have increased the production of surplus value through access to combined information. Human decisions to voluntarily share information with others in the search for the humane pleasure derived from communication is objectified in human economic relations. Unprecedented data storage possibilities and computational power in the digital age, have leveraged information sharing and personal data into an exclusive asset that divides society in those who have behavioral insights derived from a large amount of data (the nudgers) and those whose will is manipulated (the nudged).

The implicit institutional configuration of a hidden hierarchy of the nudgital society is structured as follows: Different actors engage in concerted action in the social media marketplace. The nudgital-brokers are owners and buyers of social media space, which becomes the implicit means of the production. In the age of instant global information transfer, the so-called social media industrialist-capitalist provides the social media platform, on which the social media consumer-workers get to share information about their life and express their opinion online for free. In their zest for a creation of a digital identity on social media platforms, a 'commodification of the self' occurs. Social media consumer-producer-worker are sharing information and expressing themselves, which contributes to the creation of social media experience (Puaschunder, 2017).

The hidden power in the nudgitalist society is distributed unevenly, whereby the social media consumer-workers are slaves, who receive no wages in return for their labor, falling for their own human nature to express themselves and communicate with one-another. Social media consumer-workers also engage in social media expression as for their social status striving in the social media platforms, where they can promote themselves. By posing to others in search for social status enhancement and likes, they engage in voluntary obedience to the social media capitalist-industrialist who sells their labor power product of aggregated information to either capitalists or technocrats. The social media consumer-worker's use value is inherent in their intrinsic motivation to satisfy a human need or want to communicate and gain respect from their community. The use value of the commodity is a social use value, which has a generally accepted use-value derived from others' attention and respect in the wake of information sharing in society. The social media provider gives the use value an outlet or frame, which allows the social media consumer-worker to express information, compare oneself to others and gain information about the social relation to others. The consumer-laborer thereby becomes the producer of information, releasing it to the wider audience and the social media industrialist. This use value only becomes a reality by the use or consumption of the social media and constitute the substance of consumption. The tool becomes an encyclopedic knowledge and joy source derived from the commodity.

But the use of social media is not an end in itself but a means for gathering more information that can then be amalgamated by the social media capitalist-industrialist, who harvests its use value to aid nudgers (Marx, 1867/1995). It is a social form of wealth, in form of social status and access to knowledge about others that the use value materializes on the side of the industrialist in the exchange value. For the social media industrialist, who is engaged in economic and governmental relations, the exchange value of the information provided by his or her social media consumer-laborers is the information released and consumption patterns studied. In exchange this allows to derive knowledge about purchasing and consumption patterns of the populace and therefore creates opportunities to better nudge consumers and control the populace. With the amalgamated information, the social media industrialist-capitalist can gain information about common trends that can aid governmental officials and technocrats in ensuring security and governance purposes. Further, the social media platform can be used for marketing and governmental information disclaimers as media influences politics (Calvo-Armengol, de Marti & Prat, 2015; Prat, 2017; Prat & Strömberg, 2013).

Exchange value is a social process of self-interested economic actors taking advantage of information sharing based on utility derived from consuming the social media. The social media industrialist-capitalist can negotiate a price based on the access to the social media consumer-worker's attention and sell promotion space to marketers. The exchange value of the commodity of information share also derives from the subjective perception of the value of amalgamated data. Exchanged information can be amalgamated by the social media industrialist-capitalist and traded to other market actors. Exchange value is derived from integrating everything the worker is and does, so both in his creative potential and how he or she relates to others. Exchange value also stems from the exchange of the commodity of amalgamated information that enables an elite to nudge the general populace. The amalgam of information as a premium signals the average opinion and how the majority reacts to changing environments, which allows inferences about current trends and predictions how to react to market changes.

Underlying motives may be the humane desire for prestige and distinction on both sides – the industrialist-capitalist's and the consumer-worker's. From the industrialist-capitalist's perspective, monetary motives may play a role in the materialization of information; on the consumer-worker's side it is the prestige gained from likes, hence respect for an online identity created (Ali & Benabou, 2016). Individuals may experience a warm glow from contributing to the public good of common knowledge (Ali & Benabou, 2016). The benefits of the superior class are the power to nudge, grounded on the people's striving for prestige and image boosts. Impression management and emotions may play a vital role in seducing people to share information about themselves and derive pleasure for sharing (Evans & Krueger, 2009; Horberg, Oveis & Keltner, 2011; Lerner, Small & Loewenstein, 2004). Social norms and herding behavior may be additional information sharing drivers (Paluck, 2009). The realization of prestige stems from creating a favorable image of oneself online, which signs up the workers in a psychological quasi-contract to provide more and more information online and in a self-expanding value. Prestige is also gained in the materialization of information as asset by the capitalist-industrialist, who reaps the surplus value of the commodification of the self of the consumer-worker based on socio-psychological addiction to social media (Marx, 1867/1995; Soros, 2018). In the wake of an addiction to social media, users get distracted from profitability for their own terms and experience a loss of autonomy bit by bit. The social media capitalist-industrialist therefore increases their capital based on the social media consumer-worker's innocent private information share. The social media capitalist-industrialist also accumulated nudgital, the power to nudge.

This information sharing opens a gate for the social media provider to reap surplus value from the information gathered on social platforms and to nudge the social media consumer-producers or resell their amalgamated information to nudgers. Crucial to the idea of exploitation is the wealth or power of information in the digital age. While classical economic literature finds value in organizational hierarchy to economize transaction costs, the age of big data has opened a gate to reap disproportional benefits from individual data and information sharing. Surplus of information can be used to nudge in markets and by the force of governments. To acknowledge social media consumers as producers leads to the conclusion of them being underpaid workers in a direct wage labor exploitation. Surplus gravitates towards the social media owning class. Information becomes a commodity and commodification a social product by the nature of communication. Commodification of information occurs through the trade of information about the consumer-worker and by gaining access to nudge consumer-workers on social platforms. The transformation of a labor-product into a commodity occurs if information is used for marketing or governance purposes to nudge people. In the contemporary big data society, the nudged social media user therefore end up in a situation where they are unwaged laborers, providing the content of entertainment within social media, whereas the social media industrialist-capitalist, who only offers the information brokerage platform and is not subject to tax per information share, reaps extraordinary benefits from the amalgamated information shared. Not just labor power but the whole person becomes the exchange value, so one could even define the consumer-worker as utility-slave.

The technological complexity of digital media indicates how interrelated social, use and exchange value creation are. All commodities are social products of labor, created and exchanged by a community, with each commodity producer contributing his or her time to the societal division of labor. Use value is derived by the consumer-worker being socially related insofar as private consumption becomes collective. The use value thereby becomes the object of satisfaction of the human need for social care and want for social interaction. The use value becomes modified by the modern relations of production in the social media space as the consumer-worker intervenes to modify information. What the consumer-worker says on social media, for the sake of communication and expression but also in search for social feedback, is confined by the social media industrialist-capitalist, who transforms the use value into exchange value by materializing the voluntary information share by summing it up and presenting it to nudgers, who then derive from the information marketability and nudgitability of the consumer-workers. All information sharing has value, or labor value, the abstract labor time needed to produce it. The commodification of a good and service often involves a considerable practical accomplishment in trade. Exchange value manifests itself totally independent of use value. Exchange means the quantification of data, hence putting it into monetary units. In absolute terms, exchange value can be measured in the monetary prices social media industrialist-capitalists gain from selling advertisement space to nudging marketers but also to public and private actors who want to learn about consumer behavior in the digital market arena and influence consumers and the populace (Shaikh, 2016). The exchange value can also be quantified in the average consumption-labor hours of the consumers-workers. While in the practical sense, prices are usually referred to in labor hours, as units of account, there are hidden costs and risks that have to factored into the equation, such as, for instance, missing governmental oversight and taxing of exchange value.

Overall, there is a decisive social role difference between the new media capitalist-industrialist and the social media consumer-worker. The social media provider is an industrialist and social connection owner, who lends out a tool for people to connect and engage with. As the innovative entrepreneur who offers a new media tool, the industrialist also becomes the wholesale merchant in selling market space to advertisement and trading information of his customers or workers, who are actively and voluntarily engaging in media tools (Schumpeter, 1949). The social media consumers turn into workers, or even slaves if considering the missing direct monetary remuneration for their information share and since being engaged in the new media tool rather than selling their labor power for money in the market place holds opportunity costs of foregone labor. While selling their commodity labor power, the social media consumer-workers are also consumers of the new media tool laden information, which can be infiltrated with advertisement. The social media capitalist-industrialist not only reaps exchange value benefits through access to people's attention through selling advertisement space, but also grants means to nudge the consumers into purchasing acts or wink the populace for governance authorities (Marx, 1867/1995). The social media capitalist-industrialist thereby engages in conversion of surplus value through information sharing into profit as well as selling attention space access and private data of the consumer-workers.

When the new media consumer-workers' amalgam of provided information gets added up to big data sets, it can be used by capitalists and governance specialists. Over time the nudgital society emerges, as the nudging social media industrialist-capitalists form a Gestalt of several bits and pieces put together about the nudged social media consumer-producer-worker-slaves. Information gets systematically added up providing invaluable behavioral insights. Information in its raw form and in amalgamated consistency then gets channeled from the broad working body on social media into the hands of a restricted group or societal class. This circulation of information and the distribution into those who provide a medium of information exchange and those who exchange information that then forms a society in those who nudge and those who are nudged implying an inherent social class divide.

In the nature of exchange, nudgital becomes an abstract social power, a property claim to surplus value through information. Value can be expropriated through the exchange of information between the industrialist-capitalist and the nudgitalist. Exchange value has an inherent nature of implicit class division. Exchange value represents the nudgitalists' purchasing power expressed in his ability to gain labor time that is required for information sharing as a result of the labor done to produce it and the ability to engage in privacy infringements. The social media industrialist-capitalists implicitly commands labor to produce more of data through social nudging and tapping into humane needs to communicate and express themselves, whereby he or her use a reacting army of labor encouraging information share through social gratification in the form of likes and emoticons (Posner, 2000). The reacting army of labor is comprised of social media users, who degrade into hidden laborers that are not directly compensated for their information share and cheerleading others to do the same. The nudgital society's paradox is that information sharing in the social compound gets pitted against privacy protecting alienation.

In all these features apparent becomes the rise of the monopolistic power of giant IT platform companies (Soros, 2018). For instance, Facebook and Google are believed to control over half of all internet advertising revenue (Soros, 2018). While these companies initially played an important innovative and liberating role, by now it has become apparent that they also exploit the social environment (Soros, 2018). Social media companies know how people think and influence them to behave in a certain way without their users having insights or being aware of the hidden influence (Soros, 2018). As George Soros points out at the World Economic Forum 2018, this has far-reaching adverse consequences on the functioning of democracy, particularly on the integrity of elections. It is believed that social media can prime how people evaluate politicians consciously and unconsciously based on the available content (Iyengar & Kinder, 1987). The profitability of these corporations is based on the absence of direct payments for the information shared to the social media users or taxation being imposed on the IT giants (Soros, 2018; Madsbjerg, 2017). While these platforms were initially set up to make the world more flat, by now they have turned to monopoly distributors of the public good knowledge. Acknowledging these monopolistic IT giants as public utilities will help making them more accountable and subject to stringent regulations, aimed at preserving competition, innovation and fair and open universal access to information (Soros, 2018).

The nudgitalist exploitation also holds when technocrats use heuristics and nudges to create selfish outcomes or undermine democracy. Ethical abysses of the nudgital society open when the social media is used for public opinion building and public discourse restructuring. Social media not only allows to estimate target audience's preferences and societal trends but also imposes direct and indirect influence onto society by shaping the public opinion with real and alternative facts. Government officials' gaining information about the populace that can be used to interfere in the democratic voting process, for instance in regards to curbing voting behavior or misinformation leading people astray from their own will and wishes. The social intertwining of the media platform and the democratic act of voting has been outlined in recent votes that were accused to have been compromised by availability heuristic biases and fake news. Data can also be turned against the social media consumer-worker by governance technocrats for the sake of security and protection purposes, for instance, social media information can be linked together tax verification purposes.

Governments have been transformed under the impact of the digital revolution. Instant information flow, computational power and visualization techniques, sophisticated computer technologies and unprecedented analytical tools allow policy makers to interact with citizens more efficiently and make well-informed decisions based on personal data. New media technologies equip individuals with constant information flows about informal networks and personal data. Novel outreach channels have created innovative ways to participate in public decision making processes with a partially unknown societal impact at a larger scale, scope and faster pace than ever before. Big data analytics and the internet of things automate many public outreach activities and services in the 21st century. Not only do we benefit from the greatly increasing efficiency of information transfer, but there may also be potential costs and risks of ubiquitous surveillance and implicit persuasion means that may threaten democracy. The digital era governance and democracy features data-driven security in central and local governments through algorithmic surveillance that can be used for corporate and governmental purposes. Open source data movements can become a governance regulation tool. In the sharing economy public opinion and participation in the democratic process has become dependent on data literacy. Research on the nudgital society holds key necessary information about capacity-building and knowledge sharing within government with respect for certain inalienable rights of privacy protection. The nudgital society's paradox that information sharing in the social compound gets pitted against privacy protecting alienation requires an ideological superstructure to sustain and tolerate hidden exploitation.

All these features are modern times phenomena as the technology and big data creating computational power is currently emerging. The transferability of the commodity of information itself, hence the big data amalgamation over time and space to store, package, preserve and transport information from one owner to another appears critical. The legal leeway to allow private information sharing implicitly leads to individuals losing their private ownership rights to the commodity of information upon release on social media and the right to trade information. The transferability of these private rights from one owner to another may infringe on privacy protection, human rights and humane dignity upholding mandates.

Not only pointing at the ethical downfalls of the nudgital society, also defining social media users as workers is of monumental significance to understand the construction of the nudgital society and bestow upon us social media consumer-workers labor rights. The technical relationship between the different economic actors are completely voluntary and based on trust (Puaschunder, 2016). The creation of use value is outsourced to the community (e.g., in likes) and the share of information about the workers from the social media capitalist to the market or nudgitalists remains without a clear work contract and without protection of a labor union. The worker-employer relationship needs to be protected and a minimum wage should settle for the market value of the worker producing during the working day. Wages would be needed to maintain their labor power of the workers minus the costs of the production. Unpaid laborers should not only be compensated for their opportunity costs of time but should enjoy the workers' privilege of right to privacy, prevention of misuse of the information they share and have the right to access to accurate information but also protection from nudging in the establishment of the right to voluntary fail.

The nature of making profit from information in exchange value is questionable. Information exchange of the industrialist-capitalist is different than neoclassical goods and services trade insofar since for the capitalist-industrialist making money off privacy and the consumer-workers share of information without knowledge and/or control over the recipient of the amalgamated mass of privacy released. Workers are never indifferent to their use value and their inputs may also produce unfavorable outcomes for them. The exchange value will sell for an adequate profit and is legally permitted, yet it can destroy the reputation and standing as well as potentially the access of the individual to country entrance if considering the proposed social media information release mandate at border controls. Care must be taken for privacy infringement and the product of amalgamated big data and how useful it is for society.

By shedding light on these risks of the social media age and the implicit dynamism of capitalism forming around information, a social formation of social media workers' right can be heralded. Social media user-workers should be defined to hold inalienable rights to privacy and be forgotten (part 4.1), to be protected from data misuse of information they share (part 4.2), they should be granted the right to access of accurate information (part 4.3) and – in light of the nudgitalist audacity – the right to fail (part 4.4).

5.1 People's Right to Privacy and to Be Forgotten

The transformation of a use value into a social use value and into a commodity has technical, social and political preconditions. Information gets traded and ownership of privacy transferred in information sharing. Upon sharing information on social media, the consumer-worker bestows the social media capitalist-industrialist with access to previously private information. The social media capitalists then transforms the information into use value by offering and selling the bundled information to nudgitalists, who then can draw inferences about certain consumer group's preferences and guide their choices.

Overall, the nudgital society leads to a dangerous infringement upon the independence of individuals in their freedom of choice and a social stratification into those who have access to the amalgamated information of social media consumer-workers. There is a trade-off between communication and privacy in an implicit contract of the use of personal data. Power is exercised through the accumulation of information, including the quality of insatiability of social media consumer-workers to constantly upload information and the social media capitalist-industrialist reaping profits from selling it.

Social media thereby reveals to hold a sticky memory that allows storage of information in the international arena eternally. Privacy and information share regulations depend on national governments. For instance, in the commodification of privacy, the EU is much more beneficial to consumers than that of the US. Data protection and commercial privacy are considered as fundamental human rights to be safeguarded in Europe. Europe appears in a better position, since it does not have any IT platform monopolistic giants of its own (Soros, 2018). Not only does Europe have much stronger privacy and data protection laws than America. EU law also prohibits the abuse of monopoly power irrespective of how it is achieved (Soros, 2018). US law measures monopoly by the inflated price paid by customers for a service received, which is impossible to prove when the services are free and there is no utility theory of privacy and information sharing that captures the value and price of information (Soros, 2018). In contrast, the US approach towards commercial privacy focuses on only protection the economic interests of consumers. Current privacy regulations are considered as not sufficient in targeting actions that cause non-economic and other kinds of harm to consumers.

Privacy and information sharing guidelines appear to be culturally-dependent phenomena. Information about privacy boundary conditions can be obtained from the transatlantic dialog between the US and Europe on privacy protection. While in Europe health care data is public, in Canada, there is a public interest to make the data more public. The EU's privacy approach is based on Article 7 and 8 of the Charter of the Fundamental Rights of the EU, which grants individuals rights to protection, access and request of data concerning him or herself. European privacy is oriented around consumer consent. The 2016 EU General Data Protection Regulation (GDPR) ruled the right to be forgotten under certain circumstances. Consumer consent and dealing with incomplete, outdated and irrelevant information is legally regulated. GDPR establishes regulatory fines for non-complying companies applicable to foreign companies whose data processing actions are related to 'good and services' that they provide to data subjects in the EU, so also including US companies operating in the virtual space accessible by European citizens. The EU privacy approach offers member states flexibility in data management for national security and other exceptional circumstances but also protects civilians from common potential circumstances for data abuse; while there are standardized data management policy procedures regardless of a companies' country-of-origin or operational locations. The EU's privacy approach has higher regulatory costs, is not specified by sectors and the right to be forgotten still needs enforcement validity.

The US approach to privacy is sector specific. Commercial privacy is pitted against economic interests and neither seen as civil liberty nor as constitutional right. US privacy is regulated by the Federal Communications Commission (FCC) and the Federal Trade Commission (FTC). Overall in the US, the general definitions of unfair and deceptive give the FTC a wider scope for monitoring and restricting corporate privacy infringements. The FTC has a wide variety of tools for data protection, yet the responsibility is split between the FTC and the FCC, which increases bureaucratic and regulatory costs and limits industry oversight.

So while the EU framework treats commercial privacy as a basic human right leading to a more extensive protection of individual's privacy including data collection, use and share; the EU framework is also non-sectoral and allows sovereign nation states to overrule common data management policies for the sake of national security and protection. The US framework lacks a centralized privacy regulation approach, yet is sector but split regarding oversight in the domains of the FCC and FTC.

5.2 People's Right to Prevent Misuse of Information They Share

By US standards, social media is required by the FTC to ask users for permission if it wants to alter its privacy practices. Under Section 5 of the FTC Act that states that (1) unfair practices are causes or is likely to cause substantial injury to consumers or cannot reasonably be avoided by consumers; and (2) deceptive practices are practices that likely are misleading or actually misleading the consumer.

In August 2016, the decision of WhatsApp to share more user data – especially user phone numbers – with Facebook in order to track customer-workers' use metrics and refine targeted user advertising also opened a gate to discriminatory pricing. This decision faced a huge backlash in the EU, where data sharing was ordered to be halted and Germany deemed these practices as illegal. In the US the Federal Trade Commission (FTC) began reviewing joint complaints from consumer privacy groups. The recent WhatsApp data sharing is a possible violation of this requirement since it only allowed consumers to opt out of most of the data sharing while lacking clarity and specificity. WhatsApp's restrictive opt out option and incomplete data sharing restrictions were argued to be perceived as unfair and deceptive (Tse, in speech, March 25).

5.3 People's Right to Access to Accurate Information

Traditional media studies advocate for independence of the media. Commercial motives have ever since raised doubts about reputation and credibility of outlets (Prat & Strömberg, 2013). Technological shocks have always created new opportunities but also opened gates to novel downfalls in the communication realm. Novel technologies for information sharing but also monitoring of communication are prone to significant change in the nature of communication. In such technological leaps, attention to privacy is recommended (Ali & Benabou, 2016).

In the nudgital society, profits appear in the circuit of information and take on different forms in the new media age. The possibility of trading information and reaping benefits from information sharing of others determines the unequal position of people in society. The possession of knowledge stems from the surplus derived from the activity of production, hence the information share of social media consumer-producers. This confrontation of labor and consumption is not apparent in the modern marketplace. The class division remains quite invisible in the implicit workings of the system.

The nudgitalist act becomes problematic when being coupled with infiltration with fake news and alternative facts that curb democratic acts, e.g. manipulating voting behavior. Ethical questions arise if it there is a transparency about the capitalist's share of information and a fair social value benefits distribution among the capitalist and the worker. In addition, under the cloak of security and protection, privacy infringements by sharing information with the nudgitalist is questionable. In the political domain, knowledge has been acknowledged as a public good. Voters who spend resources on obtaining information to keep their government accountable produce a positive externality for their fellow citizens (Prat & Strömberg, 2013).

By outlining the nudgital market procedures and acknowledging knowledge as a public good, fairness in the distribution of gains should be accomplished and privacy infringing information sharing limited, curbed by taxation or guided by the legal oversight. Access to information about the storage, preservation, packaging and transportation of data is non-existent, demanding for more information about behind-the-scenes' social media conduct. Transforming private information from use value to exchange value is an undisclosed and therefore potentially problem-fraught process that holds implicit inequality within itself. From a societal standpoint, also the missing wealth production in the social media economy appears striking. Thereby the dangers of information release and transfer and the hidden exchange value accrued on the side of the media innovator are left unspoken. The importance of shedding light on such, though, is blatant as for stripping the populace from inalienable rights of privacy while reaping benefits at the expense of their susceptibility. Nudges in combination with misinformation and power abuse in the shadow of subliminal manipulation can strip the populace from democratic rights to choose and voluntary fail (Benabou & Laroque, 1992).

As a policy response to the negative implications of the nudgital society, taxing IT giants may enable to raise revenue for reducing cost and noise in collecting political information. For instance, by making news freely available without commercial interruptions. A mixture strategy could be introduced, in which consumers are given the choice to either choose a free account that releases information or pay for a private account, which restricts third party use of their data.

Facebook has recently acknowledged the rise of fake news having an impact on voting behavior and therefore roles out a bottom-up accuracy check mechanism (Crilly, 2018). Truthfulness appears hard to quantify on social media since truth is not easily verifiable and integrity of information embodied in prices is missing through the free information exchange on social media. Reputation and social self-determination mechanism appear as alternate sources of information accuracy checks in the absence of classical price mechanisms (Benabou & Laroque, 1992).

5.4 People's Right to Choose and Fail

In the personal information sharing age and nudgital society, attention must be given to privacy and human dignity. The nudgital society opens a gate to gain information about consumer choices and voting preferences. The uneven distribution of key information about people's choices opens a gate to tricking people into choices. The so-called nudging attempt though raises ethical questions about human dignity and the audacity of some to know better what is better for society as a whole. Because governance is a historical process, no one person can control or direct it, thereby creating a global complex of governance connections that precedes the individual administration. Structural contradictions describe the class struggle between the nudged in opposition to the nudgers in the nudgital society. Since societal actors who involuntarily are nudged are separated from an active reflection process when being nudged, the moral weight is placed on the nudger. Though democratically elected and put into charge, the nudgers checks-and-balances of power seem concentrated and under disguise through the middle man of social media capitalist-industrialists who collect information. Rather focusing on how to trick people into involuntary choices, the revelations should guide us to demand to educate people on a broad scale about their fallibility in choice behavior.

In a self-enlightened society, people have a right to voluntary fail. Nudging implies a loss of degrees of freedom and disrespect of human dignity, hence the nudgital society will lead to structural contradictions. Their rational thinking and voluntary engagement in governmentally-enforced action becomes divorced from rational reflection. No one entity should decide to control or direct other's choices, thereby creating a global complex of social connections among the governed for the sake of efficiency for the common good. The economic formation of human decision making in society should never precede the human voluntary decision.

There is an inherent inequality of social positions, manifested primarily in the respective capacities of reaping benefit from amalgamated information, which leads to a disparity of social position. The distribution of power leads to a natural order of human activity, in which the nudgers are in charge of nudging the populace. Moral value is separated from economic value and hence placing the fate of the populace into the arms of the behavioral economists raises problems of lack of oversight and concentration of objective economic value rule in the nudgital society.

Overall, with the communication on the nudgital society just having started, it remains on us to redesign the apparatus of production in ways that make the infringement on private information through the natural tendency to share information, care about others and express oneself. Governance crises are rooted in the contradictory character of the value creation through big data. The formation of value is a complex determination and we still need more research to understand the deep structures of market behavior in the digital age.

6. CONCLUSION AND FUTURE PROSPECTS

The article presented a first theoretical introduction of a utility theory of information sharing and privacy. Potential limitations are that some communication may not be integrated in the framework, such as non-verbal communication or emotional responses. In general information exchange is very heterogeneous and vast international differences are assumed to exist. In addition, in what time online communication and under what circumstances decisions regarding communication and privacy are made, remains a completely undiscussed topic.

As a next research step, a stringent hypotheses testing of the presented problem is recommended. For instance, future research projects featuring a multi-methodological approach will help gain invaluable information about the actual performance and behavior regarding information sharing and privacy upholding. Interaction of individuals on social media should be scrutinized in order to derive real-world relevant economic insights for legal and policy making purposes alongside advancing an upcoming scientific field.

Following empirical investigations should employ a critical survey of the intersection of analytic and behavioral perspectives to decision making in information sharing. Literature discussion featuring a critical analysis how to improve e-literacy should be coupled with e-education and enhancement of e-ethicality. Research should be directed towards a critical analysis of the application of behavioral economics on hyper-hyperbolic discounting in the digital age. In the behavioral economics domain, both approaches, studying the negative implications of information sharing and decision making to uphold privacy but also finding ways how to train new media users wiser decisions should be explored. Interdisciplinary viewpoints and multi-method research approaches should be covered in the heterodox economics readings but also in a variety of independent individual research projects. Research support and guidance should be targeted at nurturing interdisciplinary research interests on privacy and information sharing in the fields of behavioral economics and public affairs.

More concretely, future studies should define the value that data has to individuals and data sovereignty in the international context. When people share information, they should be informed to consider what the benefit and value from information sharing is for them and what the benefit for social media industrialists-capitalists is. The sovereignty of data and the human dignity of privacy should become debated as civic virtual virtue in the 21st century. Individuals should be informed that sharing data is a personal security risk, if considered to be asked for social media information upon entry of a country.

Future studies should describe what companies and institutions constitute the complex system that helps establishing the nudgital society and the influence that social media has. The implicit underlying social structure of the nudgital society based on a complicated information gathering machinery should become subject to scrutiny and how, in particular, the nudgital class division is supported by a comprehensive social network data processing method. How social media advertising space can be used to specialize on targeted propaganda and misleading information to nudge the populace in an unfavorable way should be unraveled. The role of politicians' use of various channels and instruments to manipulate the populace with targeted communication should be scrutinized.

In the recent US election the profit and value of detailed market information has been found to have gained unprecedented impetus. Future research should also draw a line between the results of the 2016 US presidential election, and the study of heuristics to elucidate that heuristics played a key role in Trump's election as they made people less likely to vote logically. This would be key as it would help explain how people chose to vote, and why they do not always make the most logical choice when voting. This line of research could help to more accurately promote future elections' candidates, how to better predict election outcomes and how to improve democracy.

In addition, nudging through means of visual merchandising, marketing and advertising should be captured in order to uphold ethical standards in social media. Nudging's role in selling products, maximizing profits but also creating political trends should be uncovered. While there is knowledge on the visual merchandising in stores and window displays, little appears to be known how online appearances can nudge people into making certain choices. In particular, the familiarity heuristic, anchoring and the availability heuristic may play a role in implicitly guide people's choices and discreetly persuade consumers and the populace. Not to mention advancements of online shopping integrity and e-commerce ethics, the prospective insights gained will aid uphold moral standards in economic market places and hopefully improve democratic outcomes of voting choices.

Contemporary studies could also address if the age of instant messaging has led to a loss of knowledge in information sharing. Future research should also investigate how search engines can be manipulated to make favorable sources more relevant and how artificial intelligence and social networks can become dangerous data manipulation means. The role of data processing companies may be studied in relation to the idea of data monopoly advantages – hence situations in which data processing companies may utilize data flows for their own purposes to support sponsored causes or their own ideals. Due to the specific time period of the digital age not extrapolations to past time periods is possible but the results appear useful in determining future behaviors.

The current research in this area lacks empirical evidence, demanding for further investigations on how nudges can directly impact individual's choices and new media can become a governance manipulation tool. What social instruments are employed on social media and what prospects data processing has in the light of privacy infringement lawsuits should be uncovered. How social media is utilized to create more favorable social personas for political candidates should be explored. How internet online presences allow to gain as much attraction as possible for the presence of political candidates is another question of concern. Another area of concern is how selective representations influence the voting population and what institutions and online providers are enabling repetitiveness and selectivity. How gathered individual information is used to parse data to manipulate social internet behavior and subsequent action is another topic to be investigated. Future research goals will include determining what this means for the future political landscape and how internet users should react to political appearances online. Information should be gathered how we choose what media to watch and if political views play a role in media selection and retention. Does distrust in the media further political polarization and partisanship, needs to be clarified. Future studies should also look into the relationship between individual's political ideologies and how they use and interact on social media, especially with a focus on the concept of fake news and alternative facts. Where do these trends come from and who is more susceptible to these negative impacts of the digital society? Has social media become a tool to further polarize political camps, is needed to be asked. All these endeavors will help outlining the existence of social media's influence in governance and data processing to aid political campaigning in order to derive inferences about democracy and political ethicality in the digital age.

How social media tools nudge people to not give everything at once but put it together in a novel way that it creates surplus, should be analyzed. In small bits and pieces individuals give up their privacy tranche be tranche. Small amounts of time are spent time for time. People, especially young people, may have a miscalibration about the value of information released about them. Based on hyperbolic discounting myopia, they may underestimate the total future consequences of their share of privacy.

The time spent on social media should become closer subject to scrutiny and the impact on opportunity costs onto the labor market. For instance, countries that ban social media, such as China, or restrict internet, like slowing it down or censoring certain media, could become valuable sources of variance to compare to. Network theories for e-blasting information should become another area of interest to be studied in relation to hyper-hyperbolic discounting fallibilities. Emotional reactions and emotional externalities of communication could be another area of behavioral economics research in the privacy and information sharing predicament domain. The role of attention should be addressed as another moderator variable that is quite unstudied in the digital media era (Prat, in speech, November 2017). Thereby interesting new questions arise, such as how to measure attention – is it the time allocation or the emotional arousal information bestows individuals with (Wouter & Prat, forthcoming)?

The preliminary results may be generalized for other user-generated web contents such as blogs, wikis, discussion forums, posts, chats, tweets, podcastings, pins, digital images, videos, audio files, advertisements but also search engine data gathered or electronic devices (e.g., wearable technologies, mobile devices, Internet of Things). Certain features of the nudgital society may also hold for tracking data, including GPS, geolocation data, traffic and other transport sensor data and CCTV images or even satellite and aerial imagery. All preliminary results should be taken into consideration for future studies in different countries to examine other cultural influences and their effects on social class and heuristics.

Innovative means should be found to restore trust in media information and overcome obstacles such as the availability heuristic leading to disproportionate competitive advantages of media controlling parties. As remedies, consumer education should target at educating social media users about their rights and responsibilities on how to guard their own and other's privacy. E-ethicality trainings could target at strengthening the moral impetus of big data and artificial ethicality in the digital age. Moral trade-offs between privacy infringements and security should also become subject to scrutiny.

Promoting governance through algorism offers novel contributions to the broader data science and policy discussion (Roberts, 2010). Future studies should also be concerned with data governance and collection as well as data storage and curation in the access and distribution of online databases and data streams of instant communication. The human decision-making and behavior of data sharing in regards to ownership should become subject to scrutiny in psychology. Ownership in the wake of voluntary personal information sharing and data provenance and expiration in the private and public sectors has to be legally justified (Donahue & Zeckhauser, 2011). In the future, institutional forms and regulatory tools for data governance should be legally clarified. Open, commercial, personal and proprietary sources of information that gets amalgamated for administrative purposes should be studied and their role in shaping the democracy. In the future we also need a clearer understanding of the human interaction with data and their social networks and clustering for communication results. The guarantee of safety of the information and the guarantee of the replacement or service, should a social media fail its function to uphold privacy law as intended, is another area of blatant future research demand. Novel qualitative and quantitative mixed methods featuring secondary data analysis, web mining and predictive models should be tested for holding for the outlined features of the new economy alongside advancing randomized controlled trials, sentiment analysis and smart contract technologies. Ethical considerations of machine learning and biologically inspired models should be considered in theory and practice. Mobile applications of user communities should be scrutinized.

As for consumer-worker conditions, unionization of the social media workers could help uphold legal rights and ethical imperatives of privacy, security and personal data protection. Data and algorithms should be studied by legal experts on licensing and ownership in the use of personal and proprietary data. Transparency, accountability and participation in data processing should also become freed from social discrimination. Fairness-awareness programs in data mining and machine learning coupled with privacy-enhancing technologies should be introduced in security studies of the public sector. Public rights of free speech online in the dialogue based on trust should be emphasized in future educational programs. Policy implications of the presented ideas range from security to human rights and law to civic empowerment. Citizen empowerment should feature community efforts to protect data and information sharing to be free of ethical downfalls. Social media use education should be ingrained in standard curricula and children should be raised with an honest awareness of their act of engagement on social media in the nudgital society of the digital century.

Future research may also delve into moderator variables of the utility derived from information sharing and privacy. For instance, extraversion and introversion could be moderating the overall pleasure derived from communication or silence. Future research may also address prescriptive recommendations how to educate individuals about the risks and dangers of information sharing in the digital age. Attention must also be paid to how to uphold accuracy in times of fake news and self-created social information. Certain societal segments that are not represented strongly online should somehow be integrated into big data in order to democratize the information, which is considered as big data 'norm,' or standard by which the social media user is measured on. At the same time, psychologically guide studies could unravel a predictive approach and validate the outlined ideas' validity by testing the proposed theoretical assumptions in laboratory and field study settings. In particular, the proposed nomenclature's validity could be studied and the percentage of information sharing types captured in the population. The moderator variable age could be phased in as it appears to be conundrum why younger people, who have more to lose given a longer time ahead to live are in particular prone to use new social media and lavishly share their lives in e-blasts to public. Regarding direct implications, a tax may be used to offset problems of the costs and risks of social media privacy infringements in the big data era (Madsbjerg, 2017). Drawing from utility usually measured by the willingness to pay different amounts of money for different options, laboratory experiments may operationalize the value of privacy by measuring how much money people would be willing to pay for repurchasing their data or having a social media account that can only be viewed but no personal data can be resold or put in context to others. These attempts could also serve as a guideline for policy regulations and free market solutions. Social media could offer services of having accounts that are private in that sense that no surplus value can be reaped by reselling information or big data storage and computation can occur. This may serve as an indicator of revealed preferences of social media privacy. The privacy paradox may be scrutinized in behavioral economics laboratory and field experiments. Potential individual influencing factors such as gender, age, trust and personality differences may be tested for in order to retrieve information on how to educate the social media user and regulate the social media provider. Regarding regulation, splitting social media power cartels may be one solution to decrease the big data social media user disadvantage. Taxation for information sharing may create another incentive to slow down unreflected information share. The tax revenues could be used to offset some of the societal costs of privacy infringement. In addition, fines for privacy infringement could help to uphold e-ethics in the digital age. From the economics perspective, interesting moderator variables for future studies is the distinction between active and passive communication. Further, model robustness checks could follow and learning effects depicted. Access to information what happens with data and how big data is used appears crucial for learning people a well-calibration of their relation to their information. Communication costs and benefits are assumed to not be additive and separable, leaving an interesting field for future studies in this domain. The communication patterns could be classified in different types of communication in the future, e.g., certain node specificities detected, such as communication within a family, with friends and in hierarchical situations like at work. The absolute and relative influence of information sharers could become part of a network description approach as well. Impact factor measurements could be based on status, search engine rank and connections to capture global influence. Complexity of information would need to be controlled based on information processing times and time allocation preferences to information, hence attention. Communication costs should in the future to be separated in economic models in fixed and variable communication costs and a potential separation between fixed communication costs for social media providers and a variable communication costs for social media users be depicted (Prat, 2017).

Overall, the presented piece can also serve as a first step towards advocating for education about information sharing in order to curb harmful information sharing discounting fallibility. From legal and governance perspectives, the outlined ideas may stimulate the e-privacy infringement regulations discourse in the pursuit of the greater goals of democratization of information, equality of communication surplus and upheld humane dignity and e-ethics in the big data era.

DISCUSSION QUESTIONS

- What is economics of information?
- What is the utility of privacy and information sharing?
- Why has attention to utility of privacy and information sharing become essential in our current times?
- What are the advantages but also the challenges and risks of the digital age?
- Who are the stakeholders regulating information and capitalization of information?
- Should we tax wealth accumulation based on information usage? If so, how? If so, who should be the beneficiary of the tax?
- What are future developments prospected regarding information flow and usage of big data

REFERENCES

Ainslie, G. (1992). *Picoeconomics: The interaction of successive motivational states within the person.* Cambridge, UK: Cambridge University Press.

Ainslie, G., & Haslam, N. (1992). Hyperbolic discounting. In G. Loewenstein & I. Elster (Eds.), *Choice over time.* New York: Russel Sage.

Alberini, A., & Chiabai, A. (2007). Discount rates in risk versus money and money versus money tradeoffs. *Risk Analysis, 27*(2), 483–498. doi:10.1111/j.1539-6924.2007.00899.x PMID:17511713

Alchian, A. A. (1953). The meaning of utility measurement. *The American Economic Review, 32,* 26–50.

Ali, N. S., & Benabou, R. (2017). *Image versus information: Changing societal norms and optimal privacy.* Cambridge, MA: National Bureau of Economic Research working paper 22203. Retrieved from https://scholar.princeton.edu/sites/default/files/rbenabou/files/imagevsinfo-21_002.pdf

Allport, G. W. (1979). *The nature of prejudice.* Reading, UK: Addison-Wesley.

Altman, I. (1975). *The environment and social behavior: Privacy, personal space, territory, and crowding.* Monterey, CA: Brooks.

Arrow, K. J. (1951). Alternative approaches to the theory of choice in risk-taking situations. *Econometrica, 19*(4), 404–437. doi:10.2307/1907465

Arrow, K. J. (1958). Utilities, attitudes, and choices: A review note. *Econometrica, 26*(1), 1–23. doi:10.2307/1907381

Arrow, K. J. (1974). *The limits of organization.* New York: Norton.

Arrow, K. J. (1978). Extended sympathy and the possibility of social choice. *Philosophia, 7*(2), 223–237. doi:10.1007/BF02378811

Aumann, R. J., & Kruskal, J. B. (1958). The coefficients in an allocation problem. *Naval Research Logistics Quarterly, 5*(2), 111–123. doi:10.1002/nav.3800050204

Aumann, R. J., & Kruskal, J. B. (1959). Assigning quantitative values to qualitative factors in the naval electronics problem. *Naval Research Logistics Quarterly, 6*(1), 1–16. doi:10.1002/nav.3800060102

Badger, G. J., Bickel, W. K., Giordano, L. A., Jacobs, E. A., Loewenstein, G., & Marsch, L. (2007). Altered states: The impact of immediate craving on the valuation of current and future opioids. *Journal of Health Economics, 26*(5), 865–876. doi:10.1016/j.jhealeco.2007.01.002 PMID:17287036

Bazerman, M. H., & Tenbrunsel, A. E. (2011). *Blind spots: Why we fail to do what's right and what to do about it*. Princeton, NJ: Princeton University Press. doi:10.1515/9781400837991

Becker, G. M., & McClintock, C. G. (1967). Values: Behavioral decision theory. *Annual Review of Psychology, 18*(1), 239–286. doi:10.1146/annurev.ps.18.020167.001323 PMID:5333424

Becker, G. S., & Murphy, K. M. (1988). A theory of rational addiction. *Journal of Political Economy, 96*(4), 675–700. doi:10.1086/261558

Benabou, R., & Laroque, G. (1992). Using privileged information to manipulate markets: Insiders, gurus, and credibility. *The Quarterly Journal of Economics, 107*(3), 921–958. doi:10.2307/2118369

Bernoulli, D. (1954). Specimen theories novae de mensura sortis. *Commentarii Academiae Scientiarum Imperialis Petropolitanae, 5*, 175–192.

Beshears, J. L., Choi, J. J., Laibson, D. I., Madrian, B. C., & Sakong, J. (2011). *Self-control and liquidity: How to design a commitment contract*. RAND Working Paper Series, WR- 895-SSA.

Besley, T., & Prat, A. (2006). Handcuffs for the grabbing hand? Media capture and government accountability. *The American Economic Review, 96*(3), 720–736. doi:10.1257/aer.96.3.720

Bosworth, R., Cameron, T. A., & DeShazo, J. R. (2006). *Preferences for preventative public health policies with jointly estimated rates of time preference*. School of Public Health and International Affairs: North Carolina State University.

Bowles, S. (2004). *Microeconomics: Behavior, institutions & evolution*. Princeton, NJ: Princeton University Press.

Cairns, J., & van der Pol, M. (2008). Valuing future private and social benefits: The discounted utility model versus hyperbolic discounting models. *Journal of Economic Psychology, 21*(2), 191–205. doi:10.1016/S0167-4870(99)00042-2

Calvo-Armengol, A., de Marti, J., & Prat, A. (2015). Communication and influence. *Theoretical Economics, 10*(2), 649–690. doi:10.3982/TE1468

Camerer, C. F., Loewenstein, G., & Rabin, M. (2004). *Advances in behavioral economics*. Princeton, NJ: Princeton University Press.

Cameron, T. A., & Gerdes, G. R. (2003). *Eliciting individual-specific discount rates*. Department of Economics, University of Oregon. doi:10.2139srn.436524

Cartwright, E. (2011). *Behavioral economics*. London, UK: Routledge.

Chabris, Ch., Laibson, D., & Schuldt, J. (2008). *Intertemporal choice*. New York: Palgrave Dictionary of Economics.

Chapman, G. B. (1996). Expectations and preferences for sequences of health and money. *Organizational Behavior and Human Decision Processes*, *67*(1), 59–75. doi:10.1006/obhd.1996.0065

Chung, S. H., & Herrnstein, R. J. (1967). Choice and delay of reinforcement. *Journal of the Experimental Analysis of Behavior*, *10*(1), 67–74. doi:10.1901/jeab.1967.10-67 PMID:16811307

Colinsky, J. (1996). Why bounded rationality? *Journal of Economic Literature*, *34*, 669–700.

Coller, M., & Williams, M. B. (1999). Eliciting individual discount rates. *Experimental Economics*, *2*(2), 107–127. doi:10.1023/A:1009986005690

Crémer, J., Garicano, L., & Prat, A. (2007). Language and the theory of the firm. *The Quarterly Journal of Economics*, *122*(1), 373–407. doi:10.1162/qjec.122.1.373

Crilly, R. (2018). *Facebook to Start 'Trust Ratings' for Media Outlets as it Fights Back Against Fake News*. Retrieved from http://www.telegraph.co.uk/news/2018/01/19/facebook-start-trust-ratings-media-outlets-fights-back-against/

Debreu, G. (1958). Stochastic choice and cardinal utility. *Econometrica*, *26*(3), 440–444. doi:10.2307/1907622

Debreu, G. (1960). Topological methods in cardinal utility theory. In K. J. Arrow, S. Karlin, & S. Suppes (Eds.), *Mathematical models in the social sciences* (pp. 16–26). Stanford, CA: Stanford University press.

Debreu, G. (1964). Continuity properties of Paretian utility. *International Economic Review*, *5*(3), 285–293. doi:10.2307/2525513

DellaVigna, St., & Malmendier, U. (2004). Contract design and self-control: Theory and evidence. *The Quarterly Journal of Economics*, *119*(2), 353–402. doi:10.1162/0033553041382111

DellaVigna, St., & Malmendier, U. (2006). Paying not to go to the gym. *The American Economic Review*, *96*(3), 694–719. doi:10.1257/aer.96.3.694

DellaVigna, St., & Paserman, M. D. (2005). Job search and impatience. *Journal of Labor Economics*, *23*(3), 527–588. doi:10.1086/430286

Delli Carpini, M. X., & Keeter, S. (1989). *What Americans know about politics and why it matters*. New Haven, CT: Yale University Press.

Diamond, P. A. (1965). The evaluation of infinite utility streams. *Econometrica*, *33*(1), 170–177. doi:10.2307/1911893

Diamond, P. A., Koopmans, T. C., & Williamson, R. (1962). Axioms for persistent preference. In R. E. Machol & P. Gray (Eds.), *Recent developments in information and decision processes*. New York: Macmillan.

Donahue, J. D., & Zeckhauser, R. J. (2011). *Collaborative governance: Private sector roles for public goals in turbulent times*. Princeton, NJ: Princeton University Press. doi:10.1515/9781400838103

Doyle, J. R. (2013). Survey of time preference, delay discounting models. *Judgment and Decision Making, 8*(2), 116–135.

Duflo, E., Banerjee, A., Glennerster, R., & Kothari, D. (2010). Improving immunization coverage in rural India: A clustered randomized controlled evaluation of immunization campaigns with and without incentives. *British Medical Journal, 340*(1), 2220. doi:10.1136/bmj.c2220

Duflo, E., Kremer, M., & Robinson, J. (2008). How high are rates of return to fertilizer? Evidence from field experiments in Kenya. *The American Economic Review, 98*(2), 482–488. doi:10.1257/aer.98.2.482

Ebert, J. E., & Prelec, D. (2007). The fragility of time: Time-insensitivity and valuation of the near and far future. *Management Science, 53*(9), 1423–1438. doi:10.1287/mnsc.1060.0671

Edgeworth, F. Y. (1881). *Mathematical physics: An essay on the application of mathematics to the moral sciences.* London: Kegan. Retrieved from https://archive.org/details/mathematicalpsy01goog

Edgeworth, F. Y. (1881). *Mathematical Physics: An Essay on the Application of Mathematics to the Moral Sciences.* Retrieved from https://archive.org/details/mathematicalpsy01goog/page/n6

Edwards, W. (1954). The theory of decision making. *Psychological Bulletin, 51*(4), 380–417. doi:10.1037/h0053870 PMID:13177802

Edwards, W. (1961). Behavioral decision theory. *Annual Review of Psychology, 12*(1), 473–498. doi:10.1146/annurev.ps.12.020161.002353 PMID:13725822

Epper, T., Fehr-Duda, H., & Bruhin, A. (2011). Viewing the future through a warped lens: Why uncertainty generates hyperbolic discounting. *Journal of Risk and Uncertainty, 43*(3), 169–203. doi:10.100711166-011-9129-x

Estle, S. J., Green, L., Myerson, J., & Holt, D. D. (2007). Discounting of money and directly consumable rewards. *Psychological Science, 18*(1), 58–63. doi:10.1111/j.1467-9280.2007.01849.x PMID:17362379

Etzioni, A. (2012). The privacy merchants: What is to be done? *The Journal of Constitutional Law, 14*(4), 929–951.

Evans, A. M., & Krueger, J. I. (2009). The psychology and economics of trust. *Social and Personality Psychology Compass, 3*(6), 1003–1017. doi:10.1111/j.1751-9004.2009.00232.x

Feldstein, M. S. (1965). The derivation of social time preference rates. *Kyklos, 18*(2), 277–287. doi:10.1111/j.1467-6435.1965.tb02482.x

Fishburn, P. C. (1966). Stationary value mechanisms and expected utility theory. *Journal of Mathematical Psychology, 3*(2), 434–457. doi:10.1016/0022-2496(66)90023-X

Fishburn, P. C. (1968). Utility theory. *Management Science, 14*(5), 335–378. doi:10.1287/mnsc.14.5.335

Flaherty, D. (1989). *Protecting privacy in surveillance societies: The federal republic of Germany, Sweden, France, Canada, and the United States.* Chapel Hill, NC: The University of North Carolina Press.

Fowler, R., Hodge, B., Kress, G., & Trew, T. (1979). *Language and control.* London: Routledge.

Frederick, S., Loewenstein, G., & O'Donoghue, T. (2002). Time discounting and time preference: A critical review. *Journal of Economic Literature, 40*(2), 351–401. doi:10.1257/jel.40.2.351

Gaudeul, A., & Giannetti, C. (2017). The effect of privacy concerns and social network formation. *Journal of Economic Behavior & Organization, 141*, 233–253. doi:10.1016/j.jebo.2017.07.007

Gentner, D. (2002). The psychology of mental models. In N. J. Smelser & P. B. Bates (Eds.), *International encyclopedia of the social and behavioral sciences* (pp. 9683–9687). Amsterdam: Elsevier.

Gigerenzer, G. (2014). *Risk savvy: How to make good decisions.* New York, NY: Viking.

Gigerenzer, G. (2016). Towards a rational theory of heuristics. In R. Frantz & L. Marsh (Eds.), *Minds, models and milieux: Commemorating the centennial of the birth of Herbert Simon.* Basingstoke, UK: Palgrave Macmillan. doi:10.1057/9781137442505_3

Green, L., Fry, A. F., & Myerson, J. (1994). Discounting of delayed rewards: A life-span comparison. *Psychological Science, 5*(1), 33–36. doi:10.1111/j.1467-9280.1994.tb00610.x

Green, L., & Myerson, J. (2004). A discounting framework for choice with delayed and probabilistic rewards. *Psychological Bulletin, 130*(5), 769–792. doi:10.1037/0033-2909.130.5.769 PMID:15367080

Greenberg, A., & Collins, S. (1966). Paired comparison taste tests: Some food for thought. *JMR, Journal of Marketing Research, 3*(1), 76–80. doi:10.1177/002224376600300109

Hansen, A. (2006). Do declining discount rates lead to time inconsistent economic advice? *Ecological Economics, 60*(1), 138–144. doi:10.1016/j.ecolecon.2006.03.007

Harrison, G. W., Lau, M. I., & Williams, M. B. (2002). Estimating individual discount rates in Denmark: A field experiment. *The American Economic Review, 92*(5), 1606–1617. doi:10.1257/000282802762024674

Henderson, N., & Bateman, I. (1995). Empirical and public choice evidence for hyperbolic social discounting rates and the implications for intergenerational discounting. *Environmental and Resource Economics, 5*(4), 413–423. doi:10.1007/BF00691577

Heyman, G. M. (1996). Resolving the contradictions of addiction. *Behavioral and Brain Sciences, 19*(4), 591–610. doi:10.1017/S0140525X00042990

Hoch, St., & Loewenstein, G. (1991). Time-inconsistent preferences and consumer self-control. *The Journal of Consumer Research, 17*(4), 492–507. doi:10.1086/208573

Horberg, E. J., Oveis, C., & Keltner, D. (2011). Emotions as moral amplifiers: An appraisal tendency approach to the influences of distinct emotions upon moral judgments. *Emotion Review, 3*(3), 237–244. doi:10.1177/1754073911402384

Hornsby, J. (2007). *An empirical investigation of the effects of discounting on privacy related decisions* (Dissertation). Nova Southeastern University.

Horowitz, J. K., & Carson, R. T. (1990). Discounting statistical lives. *Journal of Risk and Uncertainty, 3*(4), 403–413. doi:10.1007/BF00353349

Iyengar, S., & Kinder, D. R. (1987). *News that matter.* London: University of Chicago Press.

Johnson, D. (2009). *Ethical theory and business*. Upper Saddle River, NJ: Pearson Prentice Hall.

Kahneman, D. (2011). *Thinking, fast and slow*. New York: Farrar, Straus and Giroux.

Kahneman, D., Slovic, P., & Tversky, A. (1982). *Judgment under uncertainty: Heuristic and biases*. New York: Cambridge University Press. doi:10.1017/CBO9780511809477

Kahneman, D., & Thaler, R. (1991). Economic analysis and the psychology of utility: Applications to compensation policy. *The American Economic Review, 81*, 341–346.

Kahneman, D., & Tversky, A. (1979). Prospect theory: An analysis of decision under risk. *Econometrica, 47*(2), 263–291. doi:10.2307/1914185

Kahneman, D., & Tversky, A. (2000). *Choices, values, and frames*. Cambridge, MA: Cambridge University Press. doi:10.1017/CBO9780511803475

Keeler, E. G., & Cretin, S. (1983). Discounting of life-saving and other non-monetary effects. *Management Science, 29*(3), 300–306. doi:10.1287/mnsc.29.3.300

Keller, L.R. & Strazzera, E. (2002). Examining predictive accuracy among discounting models. *Journal of Risk and Uncertainty, 24*(2), 143-160.

Kirby, K. N. (1997). Bidding on the future: Evidence against normative discounting of delayed rewards. *Journal of Experimental Psychology. General, 126*(1), 54–70. doi:10.1037/0096-3445.126.1.54

Kirby, K. N., & Herrnstein, R. J. (1995). Preference reversals due to myopic discounting of delayed reward. *Psychological Science, 6*(2), 83–89. doi:10.1111/j.1467-9280.1995.tb00311.x

Kirby, K. N., & Marakovic, N. N. (1995). Modeling myopic decisions: Evidence for hyperbolic delay-discounting within subjects and amounts. *Organizational Behavior and Human Decision Processes, 64*(1), 22–30. doi:10.1006/obhd.1995.1086

Klein, B., & Meckling, W. (1958). Application of operations research to development decisions. *Operations Research, 6*(3), 352–363. doi:10.1287/opre.6.3.352

Koopmans, T. C. (1960). Stationary ordinary utility and impatience. *Econometrica, 28*(2), 287–309. doi:10.2307/1907722

Koopmans, T. C. (1964). On flexibility of future preferences. In M. W. Shelly & G. L. Bryan (Eds.), *Human Judgments and Optimality*. New York: Wiley.

Koopmans, T. C., Diamonds, P. A., & Williamson, R. E. (1964). Stationary utility and time perspective. *Econometrica, 32*(1/2), 82–100. doi:10.2307/1913736

Kosinski, M., Bachrach, Y., Stillwell, D. J., Kohli, P., & Graepel, T. (in press). Manifestations of user personality in website choice and behavior on online social networks. *Machine Learning*.

Kosinski, M., Stillwell, D., & Graepel, T. (2013). Private traits and attributes are predicable from digital records of human behavior. *Proceedings of the National Academy of Sciences of the United States of America, 110*(15), 5802–5805. doi:10.1073/pnas.1218772110 PMID:23479631

Laibson, D. (1997). Golden eggs and hyperbolic discounting. *The Quarterly Journal of Economics*, *11*(2), 443–477. doi:10.1162/003355397555253

Laibson, D., Repetto, A., & Tobacman, J. (2003). A debt puzzle. In P. Aghion, R. Frydman, J. Stiglitz, & M. Woodford (Eds.), *Knowledge, information, and expectations in modern economics: In honor of Edmund S. Phelps* (pp. 228–266). Princeton, NJ: Princeton University Press.

Laux, F. L., & Peck, R. M. (2007). *Economic perspectives on addiction: Hyperbolic discounting and internalities*. Social Science Research Network working paper. Retrieved November 3, 2015 at http://papers.ssrn.com/sol3/papers.cfm?abstract_id=1077613

Lerner, J. S., Small, D. A., & Loewenstein, G. (2004). Heart strings and purse strings: Carryover effects of emotions on economic transactions. *Psychological Science*, *15*(5), 337–341. doi:10.1111/j.0956-7976.2004.00679.x PMID:15102144

Lessig, L. (2006). *Code: Version 2.0*. New York, NY: Basic.

Loewenstein, G. (1992). The fall and rise of psychological explanations in the economics of intertemporal choice. In G. Loewenstein & J. Elster (Eds.), *Choice over time* (pp. 3–34). New York: Sage.

Loewenstein, G., & Prelec, D. (1993). Preferences for sequences of outcomes. *Psychological Review*, *100*(1), 91–108. doi:10.1037/0033-295X.100.1.91

Luce, R. D., & Raiffa, H. (1957). *Games and decisions: Introduction and critical survey*. New York: Dover.

Luce, R. D., & Suppes, P. (1965). Preference, utility, and subjective probability. In R.D. Luce, R.R., Bush, & E. Galanter (Eds.), Handbook of mathematical psychology, (pp. 103-189). New York: Wiley.

Madden, G. L., Bickel, W. K., & Jacobs, E. A. (1999). Discounting of delayed rewards in opioid-dependent outpatients: Exponential or hyperbolic discounting functions? *Experimental and Clinical Psychopharmacology*, *7*(3), 284–293. doi:10.1037/1064-1297.7.3.284 PMID:10472517

Madsbjerg, S. (2017). *It's Time to Tax Companies for Using Our Personal Data*. Retrieved from https://www.nytimes.com/2017/11/14/business/dealbook/taxing-companies-for-using-our-personal-data.html?rref=collection%2Fsectioncollection%2Fbusiness&action=click&contentCollection=business&region=stream&module=stream_unit&version=latest&contentPlacement=8&pgtype=sectionfront

Majumdar, T. (1958). *The measurement of utility*. London: Macmillan.

Marglin, S. A. (1963). The social rate of discount and the optimal rate of investment. *The Quarterly Journal of Economics*, *77*(1), 95–111. doi:10.2307/1879374

Marquardt, R., Makens, J., & Larzelere, H. (1965). Measuring the utility added by branding and grading. *JMR, Journal of Marketing Research*, *2*(1), 45–50. doi:10.1177/002224376500200106

Marschak, J. (1950). Rational behavior, uncertain prospects, and measurable utility. *Econometrica*, *18*(2), 111–141. doi:10.2307/1907264

Marx, K. (1995). *Capital: A critique of political economy*. Moscow: Progress. (Original work published 1867)

Mas-Colell, A., Whinston, M. D., & Green, J. R. (1995). *Microeconomic theory*. New York: Oxford University Press.

Mastrobuoni, G., & Weinberg, M. (2009). Heterogeneity in intra-monthly consumption patterns, self-control, and savings at retirement. *American Economic Journal. Economic Policy*, *1*(2), 163–189. doi:10.1257/pol.1.2.163

Mazur, J. E. (1987). An adjusting procedure for studying delayed reinforcement. In M. M. Commons, J. A. Nevvin, & H. Rachlin (Eds.), *Quantitative analyses of behavior*. Hillsdale, NJ: Lawrence Erlbaum.

McClure, S., Ericson, K., Laibson, D., Loewenstein, G., & Cohen, J. (2007). Time discounting for primary rewards. *The Journal of Neuroscience*, *27*(21), 5796 5804. doi:10.1523/JNEUROSCI 4246-06.2007 PMID:17522323

Meier, S., & Sprenger, C. (2010). *Stability of time preferences*. IZA Discussion Paper 4756, Institute for the Study of Labor.

Meyer, A. G. (2009). *Estimating individual level discount factors and testing competing discounting hypotheses* (Dissertation). University of Colorado.

Meyer, A. G. (2013). Estimating discount factors for public and private goods and testing competing discounting hypotheses. *Journal of Risk and Uncertainty*, *46*(2), 133–173. doi:10.100711166-013-9163-y

Milkman, K. L., Rogers, T., & Bazerman, M. H. (2008). Harnessing our inner angels and demons: What we have learned about want/should conflicts and how that knowledge can help us reduce short-sighted decision making. *Perspectives on Psychological Science*, *3*(4), 324–338. doi:10.1111/j.1745-6924.2008.00083.x PMID:26158952

Milkman, K. L., Rogers, T., & Bazerman, M. H. (2009). Highbrow films gather dust: Time- inconsistent preferences and online DVD rentals. *Management Science*, *55*(6), 1047–1059. doi:10.1287/mnsc.1080.0994

Minsky, H. P. (1977). Banking and a fragile financial environment. *Journal of Portfolio Management*, *3*(4), 16–22. doi:10.3905/jpm.1977.408609

Moscovici, S. (1988). Notes towards a description of social representations. *Journal of European Social Psychology*, *18*(3), 211–250. doi:10.1002/ejsp.2420180303

Murphy, J. G., Vuchinich, R. E., & Simpson, C. A. (2001). Delayed reward and cost discounting. *The Psychological Record*, *51*, 571–588.

Myerson, J., & Green, L. (1995). Discounting of delayed rewards: Models of individual choice. *Journal of the Experimental Analysis of Behavior*, *64*(3), 263–276. doi:10.1901/jeab.1995.64-263 PMID:16812772

Neuman, W., Russel, M. R. J., & Crigler, A. N. (1992). *Common knowledge*. Chicago: Chicago University Press. doi:10.7208/chicago/9780226161174.001.0001

Norris, P., & Sanders, D. (2003). Message or medium? Campaign learning during the 2001 British General Election. *Political Communication*, *20*(3), 233–262. doi:10.1080/10584600390218878

Okada, E. M., & Hoch, S. J. (2004). Spending time versus spending money. *The Journal of Consumer Research*, *31*(2), 313–323. doi:10.1086/422110

Olken, B. A. (2009). Do television and radio destroy social capital? Evidence from Indonesian villages. *American Economic Journal. Applied Economics, 1*(4), 1–33. doi:10.1257/app.1.4.1

Orwell, G. (1949). 1984. New York: Harcourt Brace.

Oster, S.M. & Scott-Morton, F.M.S. (2005). Behavioral biases meet the market: The case of magazine subscription prices. *Advances in Economic Analysis & Policy, 5*(1), 1-32.

Oulasvirta, A., Suomalainen, T., Hamari, J., Lampinen, A., & Karvonen, K. (2014). Transparency of intentions decreases privacy concerns in ubiquitous surveillance. *Cyberpsychology, Behavior, and Social Networking, 17*(10), 633–638. doi:10.1089/cyber.2013.0585 PMID:25226054

Paluck, E. L. (2009). What's in a norm? Sources and processes of norm change. *Journal of Personality and Social Psychology, 96*(3), 594–600. doi:10.1037/a0014688 PMID:19254106

Pareto, V. (2014). *Manual of political economy*. Oxford, UK: Oxford University Press. (Original work published 1906)

Petry, N. M., & Casarella, T. (1999). Excessive discounting of delayed rewards in substance abusers with gambling problems. *Drug and Alcohol Dependence, 56*(1), 25–32. doi:10.1016/S0376-8716(99)00010-1 PMID:10462089

Posner, R. A. (1981). The economic of privacy. *The American Economic Review, 71*(2), 405–409.

Posner, R. A. (2000). *Law and social norms*. Cambridge, MA: Harvard University Press.

Prat, A. (2005). The wrong kind of transparency. *The American Economic Review, 95*(3), 862–877. doi:10.1257/0002828054201297

Prat, A. (2017). *Lecture notes 'Industrial Organization*. New York: Columbia University.

Prat, A., & Strömberg, D. (2005). *Commercial television and voter information*. CEPR Discussion Paper 4989.

Prat, A., & Strömberg, D. (2013). *The political economy of mass media*. New York: Columbia University Working Paper. Retrievable at http://www.columbia.edu/~ap3116/papers/mediasurvey11.pdf

Puaschunder, J. M. (2015). On the social representations of intergenerational equity. *Oxford Journal of Finance and Risk Perspectives, 4*(4), 78–99.

Puaschunder, J. M. (2016). Trust and reciprocity drive common goods allocation norms. In *Proceedings of the Cambridge Business & Economics Conference*. Cambridge, UK: Cambridge University. 10.5465/ambpp.2016.17526abstract

Puaschunder, J. M. (2017). Nudgital: Critique of Behavioral Political Economy. *Archives of Business Research, 5*(9), 54–76. doi:10.14738/abr.59.3623

Puaschunder, J. M. (in progress). *On the collective soul of booms and busts*. Retrievable at https://papers.ssrn.com/sol3/papers.cfm?abstract_id=2799646

Puaschunder, J. M., & Schwarz, G. (2012). *The future is now: How joint decision making curbs hyperbolic discounting but blurs social responsibility in the intergenerational equity public policy domain.* Harvard University Situationist Law and Mind Sciences Working Paper.

Putnam, H. (2002). On the rationality of preferences. In H. Putnam (Ed.), *The Collapse of the Fact-Value Dichotomy and Other Essays.* Cambridge, MA: Harvard University Press.

Putnam, R. D. (2000). *Bowling alone: The collapse and revival of American community.* New York: Simon & Schuster.

Rachlin, H., Raineri, A., & Cross, D. (1991). Subjective probability and delay. *Journal of the Experimental Analysis of Behavior, 55*(2), 233–244. doi:10.1901/jeab.1991.55-233 PMID:2037827

Ramsey, F. P. (1928). A mathematical theory of savings. *Economic Journal (London), 38*(152), 543–559. doi:10.2307/2224098

Read, D. (2001). Is time-discounting hyperbolic or subadditive? *Journal of Risk and Uncertainty, 23*(1), 1, 5–32. doi:10.1023/A:1011198414683

Read, D., Frederick, S., & Airoldi, M. (2012). Four days later in Cincinnati: Longitudinal tests of intertemporal preference reversals due to hyperbolic discounting. *Acta Psychologica, 140*(2), 177–185. doi:10.1016/j.actpsy.2012.02.010 PMID:22634266

Read, D., Loewenstein, G., & Kalyanaraman, S. (1999). Mixing virtue and vice: The combined effects of hyperbolic discounting and diversification. *Journal of Behavioral Decision Making, 12*, 257–273. doi:10.1002/(SICI)1099-0771(199912)12:4<257::AID-BDM327>3.0.CO;2-6

Read, D. R. (1964). A quantitative approach to the comparative assessment of taste quality in the confectionery industry. *Biometrics, 20*(1), 143–155. doi:10.2307/2527623

Read, D. R., & van Leeuwen, B. (1998). Predicting hunger: The effects of appetite and delay on choice. *Organizational Behavior and Human Decision Processes, 76*(2), 189–205. doi:10.1006/obhd.1998.2803 PMID:9831521

Reed, D. D., & Martens, B. K. (2011). Temporal discounting predicts student responsiveness to exchange delays in a classroom token system. *Journal of Applied Behavior Analysis, 44*(1), 1–18. doi:10.1901/jaba.2011.44-1 PMID:21541113

Reuben, E., Sapienza, P., & Zingales, L. (2010). Time-discounting for primary and monetary rewards. *Economics Letters, 106*(2), 125–127. doi:10.1016/j.econlet.2009.10.020

Roberts, A. S. (2010). *The logic of discipline: Global capitalism and the architecture of government.* New York: Oxford University Press. doi:10.1093/acprof:oso/9780195374988.001.0001

Rothenberg, J. (1961). *The measurement of social welfare.* Englewood Cliffs, NJ: Prentice Hall.

Salanié, F., & Treich, N. (2005). Over-savings and hyperbolic discounting. *European Economic Review, 50*(6), 1557–1570. doi:10.1016/j.euroecorev.2005.05.003

Samuelson, P. A. (1937). A note on measurement of utility. *The Review of Economic Studies, 4*(2), 155–161. doi:10.2307/2967612

Schumpeter, J. A. (1949). *Economic theory and entrepreneurial history.* Cambridge, MA: Harvard University Press.

Sen, A. K. (1971). Choice functions and revealed preference. *The Review of Economic Studies, 38*(3), 307–317. doi:10.2307/2296384

Sen, A. K. (1977). Rational fools: A critique of the behavioral foundations of economic theory. *Philosophy & Public Affairs, 6*(4), 317–344.

Sen, A. K. (1993). Internal consistency of choice. *Econometrica, 61*(3), 495–521. doi:10.2307/2951715

Sen, A. K. (1995). Rationality and social choice. *The American Economic Review, 85*(1), 1–24.

Sen, A. K. (1997). Maximization and the act of choice. *Econometrica, 65*(4), 745–780. doi:10.2307/2171939

Sen, A. K. (2002a). Consistency of choice. In A. Sen (Ed.), *Rationality and freedom.* Cambridge, MA: Harvard University Press.

Sen, A. K. (2002b). Goals, commitment, and identity. In A. Sen (Ed.), *Rationality and freedom.* Cambridge, MA: Harvard University Press.

Shackle, G. L. S. (1955). *Uncertainty in economics and other reflections.* Cambridge, UK: Cambridge University Press.

Shah, A. K., & Oppenheimer, D. (2008). Heuristics made easy: An effort-reduction framework. *Psychological Bulletin, 134*(2), 207–222. doi:10.1037/0033-2909.134.2.207 PMID:18298269

Shaikh, A. (2016). *Capitalism: Competition, conflict, crises.* Oxford, UK: Oxford University Press. doi:10.1093/acprof:oso/9780199390632.001.0001

Shannon, C. E. (1948). A mathematical theory of communication. *The Bell System Technical Journal, 27*(3), 379–423. doi:10.1002/j.1538-7305.1948.tb01338.x

Shui, H., & Ausubel, L. M. (2004). *Time inconsistency in the credit card market.* Social Science Research Network working paper. Retrieved October 25, 2015 at http://ssrn.com/abstract=586622

Silberberg, S. (2000). *The structure of economics: A mathematical analysis.* Boston: McGraw-Hill.

Simon, H. A. (1957). *Models of man: Social and rational.* New York: Wiley.

Simon, H. A. (1959). Theories of decision making in economics and behavioral science. *The American Economic Review, 49*, 253–283.

Simon, H. A. (1979). Rational decision making in business organizations. *The American Economic Review, 69*(4), 493–513.

Simon, H. A., & Bartel, R. D. (1986). The failure of armchair economics. *The Challenge (Karachi), 29*(5), 18–25. doi:10.1080/05775132.1986.11471113

Slonim, R., Carlson, J., & Bettinger, E. (2007). Possession and discounting behavior. *Economics Letters*, *97*(3), 215–221. doi:10.1016/j.econlet.2007.03.018

Snyder, J. M. Jr, & Strömberg, D. (2010). Press coverage and political accountability. *Journal of Political Economy*, *118*(2), 355–408. doi:10.1086/652903

Solove, D. J. (2008). *Understanding privacy*. Cambridge, MA: Harvard University Press.

Soros, G. (2018). *Remarks delivered at the World Economic Forum in Davos*. Retrieved at https://www.georgesoros.com/2018/01/25/remarks-delivered-at-the-world-economic-forum/

St. Jevons, W. (1871). *The theory of political economy*. London: Macmillan. Retrieved from http://www.econlib.org/library/YPDBooks/Jevons/jvnPECover.html

Stafford, J. E. (1966). Effects of group influences on consumer brand preferences. *JMR, Journal of Marketing Research*, *3*(1), 68–75. doi:10.1177/002224376600300108

Sterner, T. (1994). Discounting in a world of limited growth. *Environmental and Resource Economics*, *4*(5), 527–534. doi:10.1007/BF00691927

Stillson, P. (1954). A method for defect evaluation. *Industrial Quality Control*, *11*, 9–12.

Strotz, R. H. (1957). Myopia and inconsistency in dynamic utility maximization. *The Review of Economic Studies*, *23*(3), 165–180. doi:10.2307/2295722

Suppes, P. (1961). Behavioristic foundations of utility. *Econometrica*, *29*(2), 186–202. doi:10.2307/1909288

Suzuki, G. (1957). Procurement and allocation of naval electronic equipments. *Naval Research Logistics Quarterly*, *4*(1), 1–7. doi:10.1002/nav.3800040103

Thaler, R. H. (1981). Some empirical evidence on dynamic inconsistency. *Economics Letters*, *8*(3), 201–207. doi:10.1016/0165-1765(81)90067-7

Thaler, R. H., & Shefrin, H. M. (1981). An economic theory of self-control. *Journal of Political Economy*, *89*(2), 392–406. doi:10.1086/260971

Thaler, R. H., & Sunstein, C. R. (2008). *Nudge. Improving decisions about health, wealth, and happiness*. New Haven, CT: Yale University Press.

The Economist. (2017). *Do Social Media Threaten Democracy?* Retrieved from https://www.economist.com/news/leaders/21730871-facebook-google-and-twitter-were-supposed-save-politics-good-information-drove-out

Trope, Y., & Fishbach, A. (2000). Counteractive self-control in overcoming temptation. *Journal of Personality and Social Psychology*, *79*(4), 493–506. doi:10.1037/0022-3514.79.4.493 PMID:11045735

van der Pol, M., & Cairns, J. (2001). Estimating time preferences for health using discrete choice experiments. *Social Science & Medicine*, *52*(9), 1459–1470. doi:10.1016/S0277-9536(00)00256-2 PMID:11286369

von Neumann, J., & Morgenstern, O. (1953). *Theory of games and economic behavior*. Princeton, NJ: Princeton University Press.

Wagner, W., Lorenzi-Cioldi, F., Mankova, I., & Rose, D. (1999). Theory and method of social representations. *Asian Journal of Social Psychology*, *2*(1), 95–125. doi:10.1111/1467-839X.00028

Warner, J. T., & Pleeter, S. (2007). The personal discount rate: Evidence from military downsizing programs. *The American Economic Review*, *91*(1), 33–53. doi:10.1257/aer.91.1.33

Warren, S., & Brandeis, L. (1890). The right to privacy. *Harvard Law Review*, *4*(5), 193–220. doi:10.2307/1321160

Wertenbroch, K. (1998). Consumption self-control by rationing purchase quantities of virtue and vice. *Marketing Science*, *17*(4), 317–337. doi:10.1287/mksc.17.4.317

Witzany, G. (2012). *Biocommunication of fungi*. Dordrecht: Springer. doi:10.1007/978-94-007-4264-2

Wold, H., Shackle, G. L. S., & Savage, L. J. (1952). Ordinal preferences or cardinal utility? *Econometrica*, *20*(4), 661–664. doi:10.2307/1907647

Wouter, D., & Prat, A. (forthcoming). Attention in organizations. In Y. Bramoulle, A. Galeotti, & B. Rogers (Eds.), *The Oxford handbook of network economics*. Oxford, UK: Oxford University Press.

Zauberman, G., Kim, B. K., Malkoc, S. A., & Bettman, J. R. (2009). Discounting time and time discounting: Subjective time perception and intertemporal preferences. *JMR, Journal of Marketing Research*, *46*(8), 543–556. doi:10.1509/jmkr.46.4.543

ENDNOTE

[1]   e.g., Asian-Pacific Economic Cooperation, Australia, Brazil, Canada, China, European Union, Italy, Japan, Korea, Organisation for Economic Co-operation and Development, South Africa, United Kingdom, United Nations, United States, Universal Declaration of Human Rights – to name a few.

Chapter 9

The Cochlear Implant as an Epistemic Thing:
Translations of a Technical Object in Social and Scientific Contexts

Markus Spöhrer
University of Konstanz, Germany

ABSTRACT

This chapter examines the translations and (de)stabilizations of the cochlear implant, a subcutaneous prosthesis that is subject to ethical and judicial controversies. By looking at medical, social, and scientific contexts, the CI will be described as a technical object ascribed with certain attributes providing technical stability in those contexts that treat it and practice it as a scientific fact, a "technical thing." Scientific communities stabilize technical things by rigorously excluding attributes of the "social." However, the CI is designed to enable participation, to "gap" the supposed "disability" of not being able to hear, attributing a certain instability to it. The chapter will theoretically and methodologically approach such processes of (de)stabilization and transformation by making use of ANT and Hans-Jörg Rheinbergers concept of technical and epistemic things. This will be illustrated by analyzing certain discourses used as illustrations for the successful communication between implanted children and their parents in practical guides for parents with deaf children.

INTRODUCTION[1]

Disability and disabling practices (cf. Schillmeier, 2007) are tightly related to specific forms of knowledge and the way this knowledge is conditioned by the context it is produced in. Different discourses, though relating to the same topic, concern or situation, can be diverse and not seldom contradictory or incommensurable. As I showed and argued in an article on a disputation about the cochlear implants (cf. Spöhrer, 2013) – led by deaf communities on the one hand and medical experts on the other hand-, the incongruity of such discourses can generate a range of both socially, medically and politically charged debates and controversies. In this case, I argued, the controversy was generated by the fact that stabi-

DOI: 10.4018/978-1-5225-8933-4.ch009

lized forms of knowledge (medical/scientific 'facts' and deaf-cultural concerns), were supposed to be transferred (or even: applied) 'seamlessly' to other contexts.

The following refers to this question from a techno-philosophical or Actor-Network Theory-inspired approach by (re)considering one of the central questions of techno-social and philosophical studies of science related to knowledge transfer: How does knowledge act "if it leaves its laboratory context and is adapted into science and society" (Hoof et al., 2011, p.7, trans. MS). Already when objects of knowledge (epistemic things) – the central objects of the research process (Rheinberger, 1997, p.28) - are assembled, they are fabricated, marked and stabilized as either scientific or social things in relation to specific media environments (Hörl, 2017) and discursive practices (cf. Lösch et al., 2001, p.7). However, this does not mean that technical objects are necessarily permanent or unchangeable as far as their use or attributes are concerned once they leave their laboratory context – they are rather metastable, which means that they are stable in relation to the specific networks, events or situations they are linked with and enrolled in. Just as any other non-human and human entity, technical objects are *processual* and *relational* (cf. for example Spöhrer, 2017a), they change and (de)stabilize in relation to the elements they are interwoven with and in relation to their discursive arrangement and framing as well as the usage and their users' sensory conditions (cf. Gibson, 1986, pp.127-146). Following this theoretical framing of "technical objects" allows for describing "technical things" as defined by Rheinberger (1997) or as Latourian "Black Boxes" (1999). Rheinberger, referring to Latour, describes technical things (also in the sense of 'facts') as 'entities' in the research process, whose stability or "identity" (cf. Callon, 1986) significantly depends on their technical, discursive and medial conditions. Rheinberger's perspective allows for on the one hand to inquire about the processes of stabilization of such technical objects and fields of knowledge and on the other hand about the "[…] interfaces between different kinds of fields of knowledge and the processes of transformation, which knowledge experiences while passing through these different fields of knowledge" (Hoof et al., 2011, p.7, trans. MS). Such processes of transformation are the object of investigation of this paper. However, in this case an effort is made to describe transformations of fields of knowledge / discourses on the basis of a specific case study: The (re-)socialization of the otolaryngologic-technical object called

'Cochlear Implant (CI)'. As an acoustic prosthesis for hearing impaired, the CI was developed to function as a means of eliminating social hardships – mainly the supposed disabling consequences of the 'lack' of hearing. The need for the development of an implant for the improvement (or restoration) of physiological hearing is based on the discourses on psychosocial, emotional or pedagogical disadvantage that arise for hearing impaired (cf. Hermann-Röttgen, 2010; Arndt, 2010, p.3). Such medical discourses construct the situation of deaf or hearing-impaired persons as a divide between social activities (or the entirety of the 'sounding world') and the respective individual. Thus, in a sense, the CI is supposed to act as a socio-technical "mediator" or "medium" between the 'disabled' individual and the social world they are excluded from (cf. Ochsner & Stock, 2014, p. 423; Ochsner, 2013). During the process of its technical stabilization in an experimental system[2] the implant is translated from an uncertain, vaguely defined and partially contradictory epistemic thing into a well-defined, technical thing, a technical component or device (cf. Rheinberger, 1997, pp. 28-29) that is supposed to fulfil the distinct function of bridging the gap between the 'social world' and the deaf individual. However, 'the social' as well as the broad spectrum of individual subjective, communicational and everyday situations can impossibly be summarized or generalized and additionally, the need for an enabling technology such as the CI is subject to a multitude of (political) controversies (cf. Spöhrer, 2013), the CI appears to be an indistinct, paradox and oftentimes vague network of discourses. It is inscribed with contradictory and incommensurable attributes. In this respect, it might be considered as an "epistemic thing" (Rheinberger XXXX), that, in order to function in medical and bio-scientific terms ('bridging the gap'), requires distinct definition and concretization. As I will show, during the process of stabilization, the CI in the form of an epistemic thing is isolated from the aforementioned inscriptions of the social, which is conditioned by the stabilized environment of the corresponding experimental system (particular disciplinary traditions, discourses, viscourses[3] and other stabilized technical objects). Not until the translation, the enrolement, the re-habilitation or re-socialization in patient networks (cf. Cal-lon, 1986), the technical object CI is inscribed with attributes of the social again. In the case of the CI, such a "transfer of knowledge" (from scientific context to a social context) caused "otolaryngological controversies" (cf. Hodges et al., 2001, pp.417-433), which is a result of the destabilization of the technical object during its retranslation into the state of an epistemic thing.

The premise of this paper is thus, that the technical object is subject to production or inscription at any given time. It is subject to constant processes of translation, which, in relation to the experimental environment, become manifest in specific processes of mediation producing and reproducing certain discourses or viscourses. The same applies for attributions to and demarcations of disabled / normal and deaf / hearing. In order to exemplify such processes, scientific-medicinal and popularized representations of the ear as well as representations of successful communication in guidebooks for parents with deaf children will be analyzed.

LABORATORIES OF THE SOCIAL: SOCIAL ORIGINS OF THE COCHLEAR IMPLANT

According to social discourses and discourses of medical history, the development of technical objects and techniques of the body (cf. Mauss, 2005) to rehabilitate deafness result from the intention of eliminating social hardships and inequality (cf. Arndt, 2010). For the principle of mechanical amplification of sound - e.g. by placing the hand behind the ear or by using a technical device such as an ear-trumpet – evidence is provided by literary representations since antiquity (cf. Hüls, 1999, p.13). Paleoanthropological research even supports the hypothesis that humans as "homo audiens" have developed hearing aids ever since as a means of eliminating social and existential hardships (e.g. for communication during hunting) (cf. Hüls 1999, p.13). However, otolaryngologic techniques and technologies are not and have not always been "blessed" social equalizers (cf. Hüls 1999, p.15). In the antiquities and the middle age socially discriminating hardness of hearing could be relativized with certain prostheses (e.g. an ear-trumpet). However, with the enrollment of such technical objects into established social collectives, new agencies were formed which presented themselves as "socially conditioned" and "socially conditioning:"

If hearing aids existed, why are there no historical visual representations? The reason for that may be the same reason as today: People tried to hide and deny their hearing deficiency. An if hearing aids existed, we do not recognize them as such but interpret the objects in question as jewelry or decoration. (cf. Hüls, 1999, p.15, trans. MS)

The hearing aid as an actor which was translated into a social collective in turn de-mands a certain translational effort of its users: The regained social ability of hearing enables the desired normalization and the social inclusion of its users in this case. However, in order to stabilize these processes for their users, the disguising of the technical object becomes necessary, because undisguised it functions as a marker for social disadvantage and disability (cf. Spöhrer, 2013): In contemporary society, a visible technical object that is attached to certain sensory body parts, such as the as the ear or the head, in a manner that does not resemble an ordinary headphone or any other music device, is interpreted as an 'aid' – an instrument used by 'disabled' people in order to regain 'missing' sensory capacities. Conditioned by the technological development of technical hearing aids, this stabilization of socializing and normalizing processes is inscribed in modern hearing aids and subcutaneous inner ear implants like the CI (cf. Hüls, 1999, p.459), since "the miniaturization of electronic components" (cf. Hüls, 1999, p.459) made possible the reduction of certain social issues related to the size and visibility of hearing aid devices (cf. Hüls, 1999, p. 459, also cf. Mills, 2011a). One of the new possibilities of the technological development and the miniaturization of hearing aids is thus the assumed elimination of the technical object as a social marker of disability. The inner ear prosthesis is considerably smaller and less noticeable as aforementioned earlier hearing prostheses (and other modern hearing aids). Nevertheless "speech processor and microphone as well as a transmitter coil are visibly attached to the head" (Schlenker-Schulte & Weber, 2009, p. 93, trans. MS). However according to social discourses of 'normal' and 'disabled' by which social collectives are formed, these visible markers are not excluding attributes but instead the technical object enables participation in 'social activities' (cf. Spöhrer, 2013). The argument is made that the peculiar visibility of the CI is negligible, as long as it enables "barrier-free communication" (Schlenker-Schulte & Weber, 2009, p. 93). Hearing and talking are considered reciprocally conditioning requirements for partaking in social life and the inability ('disability') or refusal of these communicative abilities supposedly result in psychosocial, emotional and pedagogical disadvantages which may cause depression and/or social exclusion (cf. Hermann-Röttgen, 2010, p.18).

However, disability is not an essentialist category, but instead is produced by the network which is called 'normality' and consequently, as Ingun Moser states, [t]his implies that disability is not something a person is, but something a person becomes" (Moser,2005 p.668). Just as communication, 'normality' can be considered a black box: "A black box contains that which no longer needs to be considered, those things whose contents have become a matter of indifference. The more elements one can place in black boxes – modes of thought, habits, forces and objects – the broader the constructions one can raise" (Callon & Latour, 1981, pp. 284-285). Successful communication as well as 'normal' acting and operating in social collectives require a merely incomprehensible ensemble of translational efforts and processes of stabilization. However, in the moment in which communication is successful and functioning these elements become invisible. Only when this stable network of practices, statements and techniques breaks down at some point – when communication is unsuccessful or simply disturbed – abnormality respectably disability becomes visible (cf. Spöhrer, 2013). While normality remains the stabilized, invisible black box, disability becomes visible in its instability and at the same time becomes a stabilizing factor for normality. In the same manner in which social collectives produce disability in this way, techniques and technologies of (re-)normalization respectively invisibilization of disability are produced in such collectives: "Technology and medical progress are supposed to help removing [communicational] barriers, on the side of the individuals with hearing disorders and on the side of their communication partners" (Schlenker-Schulte & Weber, 1999, p. 93, trans. MS). Even if a merely endless spectrum of technical objects precedes the CI, which is de-socialized by labels such as "history of technological developments" (cf. e.g. Hüls, 1999), the history of technical objects is nevertheless always a history of the social collectives of whose hardships they originate. According to approaches of Science and Technology Studies like Actor-Network-Theory, which commits to theoretical premises such as "free association" and "generalized symmetry" (cf. Callon, 1986, pp. 200-201), the dichotomy of technology versus social can be described as discoursivation that results from certain collectives of knowledge (and their specific constellations). In this respect discourses on the "rehabilitation" or even the "infiltration of society by technical artifacts and procedures" (Lösch et al., 2001, p.7, trans. MS) imply that there is a basic isolation of technology from social and cultural processes (Lösch et al., 2001). The thesis of this paper is that the isolation of technology from the social or the invisibilization of the social attributes attached to the technical object respectively, is put into effect during the transfer of knowledge from collectives which are marked as 'social', to collectives which are marked as 'scientific'. Since the title of this paragraph suggests that social collectives can be described as laboratories, this analogy will be discussed in the following. In order to describe processes of emergence, stabilization, transformation and transfer of the CI, I will refer to Hans-Jörg Rheinberger's model of experimental systems in *Toward a History of Epistemic Things* (1997) and use approaches of Actor-Network-Theory (Callon, 1986; Latour 2005). At first it should be mentioned that Rheinberger actually refers to the production of knowledge in scientific contexts (or collectives). However, I would like to show that his approach of the reciprocal constitution of epistemic things and technical objects and the translation and stabilization of knowledge can be transferred to the production and transformation of knowledge in non-scientific collectives.

According to Rheinberger, experimental systems are the „smallest integral working units of research" (1997, p.28). In these operational units the objects of knowledge (the epistemic things) are indissolvably connected with the stabilized technical conditions of their production (Rheinberger, 1997, pp. 28-29). At this point it should be mentioned (as will be described in detail later), that objects of knowledge are also produced in social collectives – for example in the form of discourses on disability or the social hardships of (re-)normalization mentioned before (which also are indissolvably connected to the environments they are produced in). According to Rheinberger, two distinct but inseparable structures interact with each other in experimental systems. Firstly, the epistemic things and secondly the technical things Epistemic things are the objects of research – the objects of knowledge: "They are material entities or processes – physical structures, chemical reactions, biological functions – that constitute the objects of inquiry" (Rheinberger, 1997, p. 28). Epistemic things are characterized by inevitable vagueness which results from the fact that within the experimental system they are produced in, they are not yet well defined (unstable). Epistemic things paradoxically embody that which one does not yet know, which renders them absent in their experimental presence. Experimental systems produce an indissolvable connection between their material units, which also includes a list of attributes, concepts or ideas which accumulate around these units. Thus, during the process of stabilization, the epistemic thing is subject to the process of operational redefinition, attribution and inscription (Rheinberger, 1997). The possibility of stabilization and redefinition is only given if a stable environment, the experimental conditions, is provided. In social collectives such stable environments can also be given and epistemic things (knowledge formations) can be produced in such collectives in the same manner as in scientific laboratories: In this paper 'normality' is considered an element of social collectives, which is produced via a well-defined set of practices, statements and techniques that mark and generate 'normal' or 'normality' (invisibility). Just as certain ideas, attributes or concepts condense into stabilized discourses and become actors in scientific contexts, this is also possible in social collectives. The stabilization of epistemic things in social collectives – here using the example of the social need for a normalizing technical object – provides them to translate into other collectives and to suggest and execute agencies. In this example the agency inscribed in social discourse is the development of a technical object that enables "barrier-free communication" (cf. Schlenker-Schulte & Weber, 2009) and eliminates psychosocial hardships. In this moment, the CI has accepted the identity of a partly contradictory composite being consisting of technical and social attributes (cf. Callon, 1986).

Thereby it is insignificant which point of the history of deafness as a social factor or of the history of the CI as a normalizing technical object is set as an initial point of research. And it is insignificant whether these developments are observed from the technological or social perspective:[4] Technical objects and social needs reciprocally condition each other and are indissolvable allies of a single broad network, in which further networks (collectives) coexist, which, due to their specific conditions, appear as separated: They are discoursified as dichotomies and stabilized as singularities although they coexist solely in relation to that which they are not. Rheinberger defines the stable elements, the stable environment of an experimental system as "technical things" – the second structures in experimental systems that are nevertheless inseparable from the epistemic things. Epistemic things are framed by technical things and thus „become entrenched and articulate themselves in a wider field of epistemic practices and material cultures" (Rheinberger, 1997, p.29). Depending on whether the conditions of an experimental system are produced and stabilized by technical and scientific attributes or by attributes of the social, it is subject to isolation from the particular other. In order to be stabilized as a normalizing otolaryngologic technical object, the epistemic thing as an idea or discourse of social collectives needs to be transferred to a stabilized scientific experimental system. The phantasm of the social equalizer – the normalizing technical object – becomes an actor which, by translating into the collective of science, commits to a superordinate agenda (cf. Callon 1986): its stabilization as a medicinal technical object and thus its de-socialization, its isolation from social attributes.

DE-SOCIALIZATION OF THE COCHLEAR IMPLANT IN THOUGHT COLLECTIVES OF SCIENCE

Experimental systems are nothing else but specific collectives, networks of heterogeneous actors which are connected to each other and condition each other reciprocally (cf. Spöhrer, 2017b, pp. 128-132). They are "connections between human and non-human entities and are the results of interactions, intermediations and negotiations whereby the participants are attributed with certain qualities, competences, agencies, roles and functions" (Kneer, 2009, p.24, trans. MS). The dynamic relationship existing between technical things and epistemic things can be considered reciprocal negotiations and testing of identities and at the same time as either acceptance of or resistance to translations, in the senses of Michel Callon's actor-network approach (cf. Callon, 1986). It is a matter of a mutual constitution of identities in dependence of the collective in which the particular epistemic and technical things circulate. A stabilized technical thing is thus an entity which is exceedingly resistant to translations and the epistemic thing is an entity which is exceedingly translatable, flexible and redefinable. According to Rheinberger, examples for technical things are instruments and tools, recording devices or standardized model organisms – those things in which certain stocks of knowledge are stabilized and "entrenched" (cf. Rheinberger, 1997, p.29).[5] Then, former epistemic things can be implemented as stabilized technical things (as technical components) into existing experimental arrangements and thus themselves may become the technical conditions for new epistemic things (Rheinberger, 1997, p. 30). Stabilized technical things are usable, practical, implementable, transportable, transferrable and reliable. In Bruno Latour's (1987) terminology such intensively stabilized entities are comparable to what he calls "immutable mobiles":

The concept of 'immutable mobiles has been adopted by sociologists of scientific knowledge to describe objects, representations, or processes that remain unchallenged when moved between different cultural settings, usage, or locations. The concept of immutable mobiles assumes that objects are hybrids: neither 'natural' nor 'social', but a combination of social experiences and framings of biophysical objects that evolve over time as the result of different political and social factors. 'Immutable mobiles,' by their very definition, however, have not changed in this manner when faced with different social and political factors, and are therefore apparently fixed. (Forsyth, 2004, p. 178)

This is true for the CI as a technological entity, as a piece of scientific, medical and technological endeavor. The technical units of the CI do, as a matter of fact, not easily change when faced with "social and political factors" (Forsyth, 2004, p. 178). However, its social function as a 'normalizer' Is a thoroughly different part of its discourse and one, that is veiled in the process of its technical stabilization. In the case of the CI, microphones, electric cables, speech processors, wire coils as well as processes of transmission, processing of data and the interconnectivity which links these units can also be considered as intensively stabilized technical units (cf. Zeng, 2004, pp. 186-187). In this respect stabilized knowledge of human biology and its connectivity to other technical units such as the processes of conversion of sound waves into electrical impulses being transmitted to the auditory nerve can be considered technical things too (Zeng, 2004, p.186). On the one hand, Rheinberger defines technical objects by their stability and on the other hand by their function, by "the place or 'node' it occupies in the experimental context" (1997, p.30). This functional aspect of the technical thing, which is inscribed into it in collectives that are marked as scientific, will be discussed later.

For the time being it is more important to emphasize the fact that technical things in contrast to epistemic things need to be characteristically determined, since they define the horizon and the limits of the experimental system: "The experimental conditions 'contain' the scientific objects in the double sense of this expression: they embed them, and through that very embracement, they restrict and constrain them" (Rheinberger, 1997, p. 29). Also, technical things define the realm of possible representations of an epistemic thing. At this point I would like to get back at the inseparable connection between technical and epistemic things in experimental systems: "Within a particular experimental system both types of elements are engaged in a nontrivial interplay, intercalation, and interconversion, both in time and space" (Rheinberger, 1997). Both elements may switch roles when the epistemic thing is stabilized enough to be relatively resistant to translational efforts by other actors enrolled in such an experimental collective – in this case the epistemic thing has become a technical thing. This kind of technical stabilization depends significantly on the coherence of the attributes which are attributed to the epistemic thing in the process of research. Rheinberger quotes Bruno Latour in order to clarify this aspect of experimental systems:

The new object, at the time of its inception, is still undefined. [At] the time of its emergence, you cannot do better than explain what the new object is by repeating the list of its constitutive actions. [The] proof is that if you add an item to the list you redefine the object, that is, you give it a new shape. (Latour in Rheinberger, 1997, p. 29)

In the process of translation of the CI from the collective marked as social into the collective marked as scientific, its stability as an actor in this network is put to the test (cf. Callon, 1986, 207). In social collectives in which the CI (as an epistemic thing) emerges as an actor inscribed with the agenda of social equalization (or annihilate social inequality or disabling conditions) its list is also produced by a list of attributes of the social or the human register respectively and thus, again, is subject to destabilization. As Lösch et al. show, the 'social' versus the 'technical' is discoursified and structured as a dualism of incongruency, vagueness and unpredictability on the social side and as distinctive, functioning and predictable on the technical side:[6]

If technologies and technical processes are contrasted to human actions and statements in this manner, 'socio-cultural' and 'technical' processes show contrary characteristics: Human actions and statements appear as spontaneous and versatile and are attributed ambiguous meanings. Technologies on the contrary seem to be characterized by their regularity, materiality and unambiguous functioning. (Lösch et al., 2001, p.7)

As soon as the technical object is subject to technical and scientific stabilization in a specific (well-defined) experimental system, it is necessary to eliminate these incoherences, unreliabilities and tensions, which result from the inscription of contradictory and incommensurable attributes of the social and the technical register.[7] To put it differently: Stabilization as a technical thing in the sense of a scientific technical object (or otolaryngologic object), which is characterized by unambiguousness, requires crossing off the social attributes of the list of its features and activities.

At this point I would like to come back to the functional aspects of technical things: As stated before, technical things, as technical conditions, define the realm of possible representations of an epistemic thing. This is not necessarily restricted to a certain apparatus which visualizes the epistemic thing[8], but can be extended to modes of representations which are conditioned by discursive sedimentations of local or disciplinary research traditions – in the words of Ludwig Fleck, as "a result of the development of and confluence of several lines of collective thought" (Fleck, 1981, p.23). According to medical and scientific thought collectives, scientific facts as well as medicinal technical objects need to be stabilized in a specific way. As described before, because of its incoherent attributes, the CI emerges as vague, irritating and contradictory as soon as it is enrolled into a technical scientific collective. The functioning of the technical thing, which the CI is supposed to become, depends on whether these identitary tensions can be made invisible and the corresponding coherence can be made visible: The implant needs to translate its indistinct dysfunctional elements to a distinct functionality. Thereby the practice of scientific thought collectives is the following: "The object of research needs to be defined and isolated artificially by decontextualization, reflection and systematic research" (Spychinger, 2010, p.40).[9] In scientific viscourses (cf. Knorr-Cetina 1999) such practices and thought styles (cf. Fleck 1981) manifest in the form of de-socialized, highly schematized and denaturalized representations of the CI as in Figure 1.

Such illustrations show the schematized section of the human ear respectively the translation of a specific viscourse of a specific scientific thought collective: On the one hand a certain area was isolated and thus defined and on the other hand 'extracted' from its social contexts. While the assumed isolated area is 'unfolded' in the foreground, the social attributes are 'folded in' into the background. This kind of schematizing can be considered a form of translation, which decontextualizes and de-socializes the representation of the human ear. In these illustrations a viscourse is made visible which is blackboxed as the 'process of hearing' in human medicine – this process and aspect of the CI can for example be considered as a relatively fixed "immutable mobile" (Latour, 1987). As can be seen in these illustrations, the process of hearing is assembled by various further stabilized technical components (technical things), which in turn can emerge as separate isolated and decontextualized elements: ear-drum, auditory canal, auditory nerve, cochlea, malleus, incus, stapes etc. Each of these elements can thus be considered

Figure 1.

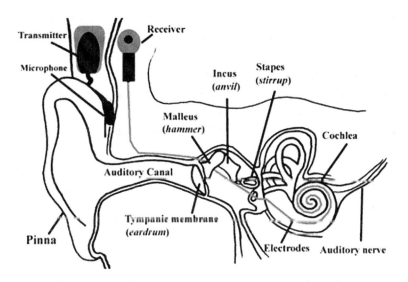

a blackbox and immutable mobile themselves. Oftentimes the isolation of the separate elements in such illustrations is highlighted by the use of different coloring. The verbal semantization of such visual representations also draws on the conventionalized register of medicinal technical collectives which seems to be 'cleaned' from the attributes of the social: "They are the inescapably historical product of a 'purification' procedure" (Rheinberger, 1997, 28). The description for a similar illustration, in Zeng (2004), presents itself as follows:

A typical cochlear implant system showing how it directly converts sound to electric impulses delivered to the auditory nerve. A microphone picks up the sound (1) and sends it via a wire (2) to a behind the ear speech processor (3). The processor converts the sound into a digital signal and sends the processed signal to a head piece (4). The headpiece is held in place by a magnet attracted to the implant on the other side of the skin [...]. (Zeng, 2004, p. 184, MS)[10]

Here the different elements, which are stabilized within the thought collectives of medicinal science and science of technology, are named and numbered and thus emerge as isolated and well-defined (and thoroughly incontestable, immutable) fields of knowledge. The CI as well as the human body are dealt with as technical things, which are assembled by a variety of definable single components. As it seems "each of them is made of several parts, each with its own role and function and its relatively independent goals" (Latour, 1999, p.183). Now each of the parts has" individual existence, each its own 'black box'" (Latour, 1999). Black boxes fold in into themselves relatively stable relationships, associations or networks. As shown by the example of the experimental systems, stabilization of such elements is possible through the reference to other stabilized elements (black boxes, immutable mobiles). Theoretically the tracks of translations, or "strings of translations" (cf. Latour, 1995), black boxes consist of, could be traced back infinitely – traced back far enough, the social unfolds itself at some point (cf. Latour, 1999). The scientific practice of stabilization and the simultaneous folding in of the attributes of the social, functions by the corresponding conventionalized practice of decontextualization, as the visual and textual representation in the example above show: The different stabilized elements are related to each other. Each new actor, which is enrolled and translated from another specifically conditioned collective, is consequently subject to being related to the already stabilized elements. Those elements (or attributes) which cannot be related to each other in this manner get folded in and made invisible, but at the same time enable the impression of a well-defined identity of the object in question. Well-defined and sharply separated from each other, each of the components visualized in such schemes appear as thoroughly unsocial. Each of them was carefully cleaned through the processes of the thought collectives of medicinal science. During an endless track of translations, isolation, abstraction, decontexualization, simplification and systematization they were condensed into "the darkest black box[es]" (Latour, 1987, p. 137, MS).

Only in this manner is it possible to connect and associate the technical components which belong to the discourses and viscourses of human biology (e.g. ear-drum, cochlea, auditory nerve etc.) with the technical components of the technical object CI (e.g. speech processor, wire coils, microphone etc.), which belong to the discourses and viscourses of science of technology.

THE (RE-)SOCIALIZATION OF THE COCHLEAR IMPLANT AND ITS REDEFINITION THROUGH PARTICIPATION IN SOCIAL COLLECTIVES

Born as an idea in social collectives, as an eliminator of social hardship, the CI is inscribed and assigned with an inevitable social agenda right from the beginning. As a stabilizer of communication and as an enablement of inclusion of assumed socially excluded individuals, it

is bound to enhance disabled individuals with the "most important social sense": hearing (Silverthorn, 2007, p.511, trans. MS). Thus, it is attached to the agenda of being reintroduced to and re-socialized into 'society' after its scientific and technical isolation and stabilization. In this respect, the CI was assembled as a participatory object (cf. Ochsner, 2013). During its assemblage, in the process of reciprocal translations between stabilized things, the epistemic thing CI was inscribed with a participatory claim. Thus, after its technical stabilization, the CI is subject to rehabilitation or reintegration into social collectives. Following its inscribed social agenda, it is bound to act as an actor in patient networks and other networks marked as social. The process of reintegration is termed 'translation' in Actor-Network-Theory: "Translations are [...] all forms of (re-)definitions of identity, abilities and attributes of any given entity, which are aimed at establishing connections that is establishing networks" (Schulz-Schäffer, 2000, p. 189, trans. MS).

When translated into social collectives, the de-socialized technical objects collide with the social (or socialized) identities of actors enrolled and acting in such networks. As a participatory object assembled as an object with social claims – to recapitulate: in order to normalize and eliminate social hardships – the CI unfolds its social attributes again and thereby establishes new social links, affinities and attachments (cf. Hennion & Gomart, 1999): An example for that is the discussion on the question of the „right of deaf children to get a CI", an ethical and judicial controversy on the forced implantation of infants by law. Müller and Zaracko (2010) plead for the legal incapacitation of parents if they refuse to let their infants be implanted, basing their arguments on medicinal facts (again: blackboxes, immutable mobiles): "If a child gets implanted a cochlear implant before the age of two, there is a good chance that they will develop normal faculties of speech and be able to attend normal educational facilities" (Müller & Zaracko, 2010, p.244, trans. MS). Here the scientific fact, a stabilized component and technical thing in the Rheinbergian sense, is translated into an actor to enforce normality. However, 'forced commitment' cannot become an actor with a thoroughly stabilized identity which is resistant to translations of the opposing network: The diverging and partly contradictory answers, that are the contra arguments of this discussion, are thus resistant to translations that it is impossible for the 'forced commitment' to become stable. The alliance of another (social) collective is knotted much more stable: In her polemic *Zur Frage des Umgangs mit der Frage nach dem Cochlea-Implantat* (translates: *How to handle the question on the cochlear implant*) (2010) Katrin Bentele argues that Müller and Zaracko refer to a medicinal model of disability, which is highly problematic and old-fashioned (cf. Bentele, 2010, p.411) and which consequently is surrounded by diverging ethical, social and political discourses. While the technological components, which provide the stability of the technical thing CI (microphones, electric cables, speech processors etc.), remain resistant to translations for the most part, diverging, conflicting and contradictory social attributes are added to the list of the CI as a whole. To put it differently: The technical components of the CI remain stable and coherent whereas the social elements are subject to incoherence. However, as networks try to stabilize their actors, in order to prevent the network from collapsing, they have to translate and transform themselves into states of identity in which conflicting attributes are folded in. Such identity transformations and the strategies which allow stabilization of the CI can also be observed in specific social collectives, in which specific discourses are generated. To exemplify this statement, I will consider two cover illustrations of guidebooks for parents with deaf children: Marion Hermann-Röttgen's *Cochlea-Implantat: Ein Ratgeber für Betroffene und Therapeuten* (2010)[11] and Dorothea Senf's *Cochlea-Implantat: Mit dem CI leben, hören und sprechen: Ein Ratgeber für Eltern* (2004).[12] In both illustrations a parent and an assumed deaf child are visualized, represented by 'real' photographed humans in an assumed social context:[13] The successful communication between the parent and their formerly deaf child. Already with the choice of a specific frame for the illustrations, certain elements are included into the image section while others are excluded and rendered invisible. As in the schematized scientific representations of communication, certain images are thus isolated. However, in the photographic visualizations the elements can be described as pars pro toto: Although the faces and torsi of the people in the illustrations are cut and could be perceived as isolated separate and mutilated body fragments, this is usually not the case (with average observers). Rather, average observers cognitively complete the missing body parts as an effect of culturally and socially acquisitioned knowledge on 'reading of images'. Thereby, the effect of this specific kind of framing is a different one, as in the image sections of such cover illustrations the social phantasms of the CI have become reality: The bringing together of groups of persons (disabled/abled) which are discoursified as mutually excluding each other. Both illustrations represent functioning communication, enabled by the technical object CI. In the scientific representations discussed above, communication is a thoroughly technical, biological, dehumanized and de-socialized process. In the cover illustrations of guidebooks for parents with deaf children, the technical and biological aspects and elements of communication play a minor role. They become barely visible or even invisible elements which are folded in into the background. In the foreground however unfolds the social: Humans, close to each other, united again and successfully and happily communicating with each other.[14]

CONCLUSION

In this paper, an effort was made to show that technical objects can be subject to a range of translations and negotiations, that knowledge, materialities and practices are interconnected and reciprocally influence each other – not only on the technological, but also on the discoursive level. From the perspective of Actor-Network Theory, objects cannot be considered 'singular' or self-containing, but instead appear as actor-networks themselves – they are made up, maintained, transformed, and "made to act by a large star-shaped web of mediators flowing in and out of it" (Latour, 2005, p. 217). However, one aspect, that seems to be neglected by Latour frequently, is the fact, that the researcher studying an object and its relations to specific networks (such like me, writing this paper on the cochlear implant), are part of these very networks, too. Researchers not only 'un- or discover' facts, they generate, relate and translate objects such as the cochlear implant, by giving them a specific form and function as well as a specific meaning. In this respect, scientific facts, technologies or objects, such as the cochlear implant in my example, can and do have 'political agendas' (cf. Winner, 1980; Mills, 2011b) related to the actor-networks they are enrolled in and these agendas can change during the course of time and in relation to their use and discoursivation. Researchers play a major role in this, because the way in which they generate scientific facts and inscribe them with certain meanings, determines how these facts can be functionalized. Thus, researchers and the forms of representation they use act as 'mediators' instead of 'intermediators': they are not merely "static and passive channels" (Spöhrer, 2018, p. 15) through which 'reality flows' without transformation. Rather, "traditional scientific methods tend to create a particular version of reality through what amounts to performative acts" (Felluga, 2015, p. 7). The particular version of reality is not only conditioned by the specific method the researcher uses, but also by the medium of choice (representational medium). There is a difference between a fact da is conditioned by an optical or visual medium such as and image or a drawing and facts, that are generated by written or oral language. In this case, academic writing itself emerges as an experimental system, with the author of the paper as the experimenter, bringing together a set of stabilized fields of knowledge in order to produce new discourses (cf. Spöhrer, 2016b). The goal of this experiment was to rise on a 'meta-level' and to relate and connect fields of knowledge which were discoursified as separate and isolated, led by the question of how certain stabilized fields of knowledge act and react if they are transferred from one stabilized ('experimental') context to another. Thereby a certain set of stabilizing factors and methods were used, which are traditionalized elements of sociology, science and media studies, and most notably Actor-Network-Theory's 'inderministic heuristic' (cf. Schüttpelz, 2008, p. 239): In order to stabilize and bring together the presumably incommensurable discourses of the CI as a technical object on the one hand and as a social actor on the other hand, the CI had to be historically trivialized, decontextualized, isolated and purified from irritating attributes just to be reassembled with attributes which produce the desired effect: To show that the CI is both social and scientific, both human and technical, but depending on the system and arrangement of the corresponding experimental and medial environment it can be produced to appear as thoroughly and exclusively social or scientific or human or technical. With a rearrangement of the technical things, the technical components and the specific experimental and medial environments, the CI was destabilized, de-socialized, technically stabilized and finally re-socialized into patient networks, presenting itself as an epistemic thing containing a wide spectrum of potentialities.

DISCUSSION QUESTIONS IN CLASSROOM

Question 1: What other forms of stabilized scientific, religious, cultural or social knowledge can you name? How is this knowledge used by certain though collectives as usable, functioning, transferrable or transportable knowledge?

Question 2: Can 'everyday' knowledge (e.g. stereotypes, clichés also be considered stabilized knowledge, that is used as a means of 'functioning' operations and procedures?

Question 3: Are there any other disabling techniques, technologies or knowledges you can name and describe?

Question 4: How does stabilized knowledge relate to power? How can scientific, religious or other fields of knowledge be used for political agendas?

REFERENCES

Arndt, S. (2010). *Sonderfälle der Kochleaimplantation: Aktuelle Aspekte zur Indikationserweiterung.* Freiburg, UV.

Bentele, K. (2010). Zur Frage des Umgangs mit der Frage nach dem Cochlea-Implantat (CI): Ein Kommentar. *Das Zeichen, 86,* 408–415.

Callon, M. (1986). Some elements of a sociology of translation: Domestication of the scallops and the fishermen of St. Brieuc Bay. In J. Law (Ed.), *Power, action and belief: A new sociology of knowledge?* (pp. 196–233). London, UK: Routledge & Kegan Paul.

Callon, M., & Latour, B. (1981). Unscrewing the big Leviathan; or how actors macrostructure reality and how sociologist help them to do so. In K. Knorr-Cetina (Ed.), *Advances in social theory and methodology: Toward an integration of micro- and macro-sociologies* (pp. 277–303). London, UK: Routledge & Kegan Paul.

Felluga, D. F. (2015). *Critical theory. The key concepts.* New York: Routledge. doi:10.4324/9781315718873

Fleck, L. (1981). Genesis and development of a scientific fact. Chicago, IL: UP. doi:10.7208/chicago/9780226190341.001.0001

Forsyth, T. (2004). *Critical political ecology. The politics environmental science.* London, New York: Routledge. doi:10.4324/9780203017562

Gibson, J. (1986). *The ecological approach to visual perception.* Hillsdale, NJ: Lawrence Erlbaum.

Grebe, A., Spöhrer, M., & Stock, R. (2018). Popular narratives of the cochlear implant. In A. Görgen, G. Alfonso Nunez, & H. Fangerau (Eds.), *Handbook of popular culture and biomedicine. Knowledge in the life sciences as cultural artefact* (pp. 229–243). Cham: Springer.

Hennion, A., & Gomart, É. (1999). A sociology of attachment: Music lovers, drug addicts. In J. Law & J. Hassard (Eds.), *Actor-network-theory and after* (pp. 220–247). Oxford, UK: Blackwell.

Hermann-Röttgen, M. (2010). *Cochlea-Implantat: Ein Ratgeber für Betroffene und Therapeuten.* Trias.

Hodges, A., Balkany, T. J., & Butts, S. L. (2001). Cochlear implants in congenitally deaf children. In M. L. Pensak (Ed.), *Controversies in otolaryngology* (pp. 417–433). New York, NY: Thieme.

Hoof, F., Jung, E.-M., & Salascheck, U. (2011). *Jenseits des Labors: Transformationen von Wissen zwischen Entstehungs- und Anwendungskontext.* Bielefeld: Transcript. doi:10.14361/transcript.9783839416037

Hörl, E. (2017). *General ecology: The new ecological paradigm*. London: Bloomsbury.

Hüls, R. (1999). *Geschichte der Hörakustik: 2000 Jahre Hören und Hörhilfe*. Heidelberg, Germany: Median.

Kneer, G. (2009). Akteur-netzwerk-theorie. In G. Kneer & M. Schroer (Eds.), *Handbuch Soziologische Theorien* (pp. 19–38). Wiesbaden, Germany: VS. doi:10.1007/978-3-531-91600-2_2

Knorr-Cetina, K. (1999). 'Viskurse' der Phyisk: Wie visuelle Darstellungen ein Wissenschaftsgebiet ordnen. In J. Huber & M. Heller (Eds.), *Konstruktionen Sichtbarkeiten* (pp. 245–263). Wien, Germany: Springer.

Latour, B. (1987). *Science in action: How to follow scientists and engineers through society*. Cambridge, MA: Harvard UP.

Latour, B. (1995). The "pedofil" of Boa Vista: A photo-philosophical montage. *Common Knowledge*, *4*, 144–187.

Latour, B. (1999). *Pandora's hope: Essays on the real-ity of science studies*. Cambridge, MA: Harvard UP.

Latour, B. (2005). Reassembling the social: An in-troduction to actor-network-theory. Oxford, UK: UP.

Lösch, A., Spreen, D., Schrage, D., & Stauff, M. (2001). Technologien als Diskurse – Einleitung. In *Technologien als Diskurse: Konstruktionen von Wissen, Medien und Körpern* (pp. 7–20). Heidelberg, Germany: Synchron.

Mauss, M. (2005). Techniques of the body. In M. Fraser (Ed.), The body: A reader (pp. 73–77). London, UK: Routledge.

Mills, M. (2011a). Hearing aids and the history of electronics miniaturization. *IEEE Annals of the History of Computing*, *33*(2), 24–45. doi:10.1109/MAHC.2011.43

Mills, M. (2011b). Do signals have politics? Inscribing abilities in cochlear implants. In The Oxford handbook of sound studies (pp. 320-346). Oxford UP. doi:10.1093/oxfordhb/9780195388947.013.0077

Moser, I. (2005). On becoming disabled and articulating alternatives. The multiple ordering of disability and their interferences. *Cultural Studies*, *19*(6), 667–700. doi:10.1080/09502380500365648

Müller, S., & Zaracko, A. (2010). Haben gehörlose Kleinkinder ein Recht auf ein Cochleaimplantat? *Nervenheilkunde: Zeitschrift für Interdisziplinaere Fortbildung*, *29*(04), 244–248. doi:10.1055-0038-1628755

Ochsner, B. (2013). Teilhabeprozesse oder: Das Versprechen des Cochlea-Implantats. Augenblick. *Konstanzer Hefte zur Medienwissenschaft*, *58*, 112–123.

Ochsner, B., & Stock, R. (2014). Das Hören des Cochlea Implantats. *Historische Anthropologie*, *22*(3), 408–425. doi:10.7788/ha-2014-0308

Racevskis, K. (1983). *Michel Foucault and the subversion of the intellect*. Ithaca, N.Y.: Cornell UP.

Rheinberger, H.-J. (1997). *Toward a history of epistemic things: Synthesizing proteins in the test tube*. Stanford, CA: Stanford UP.

Schillmeier, M. (2007). Dis/abling practices: Rethinking disability. *Human Affairs, 17*(2), 195–208. doi:10.2478/v10023-007-0017-6

Schlenker-Schulte, C., & Weber, A. (2009). Teilhabe durch barrierefreie Kommunikation für Menschen mit Hörbehinderung. In Rhetorik: Ein internationales Jahrbuch. Band 28. Rhetorik und Verständlichkeit (pp.92-102). Tübingen: Max Niemeyer Verlag. doi:10.1515/9783484605817.92

Schulz-Schäffer, I. (2000). *Sozialtheorie der Technik*. Frankfurt, Germany: Campus.

Schüttpelz, E. (2008). Der Punkt des Archimedes. Einige Schwierigkeiten des Denkens in Operationsketten. In G. Kneer, M. Schroer, Markus, & E. Schüttpelz (Eds.), Bruno Latours Kollektive. Kontroversen zur Entgrenzung des Sozialen (pp. 234-258). Frankfurt a. M., Germany: Suhrkamp.

Senf, D. (2004). *Cochlea-Implantat: Mit dem CI leben, hören und sprechen: Ein Ratgeber für Eltern*. Idstein: Schulz-Kirchner.

Serres, M. (1982). *The parasite*. Baltimore, MD: Johns Hopkins UP.

Silverthorn, D. U. (2007). *Physiologie*. München, Germany: Pearsons.

Spöhrer, M. (2013). Bilder der gelungenen Kommunikation. Das Cochlea Implantat in sozialen und medizinischen Denkkollektiven. *Das Zeichen*, 382-389.

Spöhrer, M. (2016a). *Film als epistemisches Ding*. Marburg: Schüren.

Spöhrer, M. (2016b). Vom Eigen- und Stellenwert der geisteswissenschaftlichen Wissensproduktion: Schreiben als Experimentalsystem. In A. Bartl & M. Famula (Eds.), *Vom Eigenwert der Literatur* (pp. 195 212). Würzburg: Königshausen & Neumann.

Spöhrer, M. (2017a). A cyborg perspective: The cochlear implant and actor-networking perception. In M. Spöhrer & B. Ochsner (Eds.), *Applying the Actor-Network Theory in Media Studies* (pp. 80–95). Hershey, PA: IGI Global. doi:10.4018/978-1-5225-0616-4.ch006

Spöhrer, M. (2017b). Applying actor-network theory in Production Studies: The formation of the film production network of Paul Lazarus' Barbarosa (1982). In M. Spöhrer & B. Ochsner (Eds.), *Applying the actor-network theory in media studies* (pp. 114–141). Hershey, PA: IGI Global. doi:10.4018/978-1-5225-0616-4.ch008

Spöhrer, M. (2018). Applying Actor-Network theory in media Studies: Theoretical (im)possibilities. In M. Spöhrer (Ed.), *Analytical frameworks, applications, and impacts of Actor-Network theory* (pp. 1–27). Hershey, PA: IGI Global.

Spychinger, M. B. (2010). Fehler als Erfahrung: Zur Rolle von Koordination und Diskoordination in bewussten Prozessen. In Was aus Fehlern zu lernen ist in Alltag, Wissenschaft und Kunst (pp. 31-54). Berlin, Germany: Lit.

Stäheli, U. (2011). Das Soziale als Liste. Zur Epistemologie der ANT. In F. Balke, M. Muhle, & A. von Schöning (Eds.), *Die Wiederkehr der Dinge* (pp. 83–102). Berlin: Kadmos.

Winner, L. (1980). Do artifacts have politics? In The social shaping of technology (pp. 26-38). Buckingham, YJ: Open UP.

Zeng, F.-G. (2004). Compression and Cochlear Im-plants. In Compression: From cochlea to cochlear implants (pp. 184-220). New York, NY: Springer.

ENDNOTES

1   This is an updated and revised version of my 2013 paper published in IJANTTI (International Journal of Actor-Network Theory).

2   By the term "experimental system" I do not necessarily mean a concrete laboratory situation (or a specific space of scientific research and experimentation). Although Rheinberger (1997) mostly uses the term like that, in my paper, an experimental system represents a broad 'field of knowledge', a thought style (Fleck, 1981). Experimental systems here are meant as specific thought collectives or "discourse communities", people and sociotechnical and discursive relations that share a body of "truth statements" (Racevskis 1983), which influence, structure and determine all kinds of social actions and articulations.

3   The term "viscourse" refers to Knorr-Cetina's concept of stabilized visual discourses used in science (cf. Knorr-Cetina, 1999).

4   According to Michel Serres (1982), each history of science is constructed by an arbitrary point of origin, which however is a necessity of research and (scientific) historiography: "Someone comes alone in these parts, no gloves, no hat. He opens the black box, Pandora's box with all its gifts. Attracted by such a source, some join the first, organize the work site, bringing light, equipment, documentation, increasing sophistication of means and the ever more complex organization of their group" (Serres, 1982, p.17).

5   However, as I have shown in a number of case studies, technical things are neither not reduced to inanimate objects nor to the scientific context. Dependent on the collective they both form and are formed in, a technical thing can be anything from a film animal, a discourse, a specific perspective, a medium, habits, actions etc. Technical things are not defined by the quality but instead by their stability (cf. Spöhrer, 2017a, 2017b, 2016a, 2016b).

6   The concept of the "list" with all its epistemic implications and theortical and methodological consequences is described in detail in Stäheli (2011).

7   On conradictions and incommensurabilites of heterogenuous fields of knowledge see Spöhrer, 2016a.

8   Written, oral, haptic or bodily verbalization of scientific knowledge can also be considered as visualization (cf. Spöhrer, 2016b), which besides photography is not necessarily restricted to technical scientific collectives.

9   Interestingly even scientific descriptions of scientific practice are described as 'artificial', which is usually attributed to the realm of technology and science in contrast to "natural" (which is rather attributed to human beings as such) (cf. Spychinger, 2010, p.40).

10   For further similar examples see the illustra-tions in Zeng, 2004, p. 186; or in Arndt, 2005, p.5.

11   The cover illustration of this guidebook can be found on the official website of the publishing company Thieme-Verlag: https://www.thieme.de/medias/sys_mas-ter/8806088769566/9783830435303_

12   The cover illustration of this guidebook can be found on the official website of the publishing company Schulz-Kirchner-Verlag: http://www.schulz-kirchner.de/cgi-bin/sk/medium.pl?F=1&E=333572

13 Similar illustrations are produced for similar social contexts. See for example the web presence of Implant Centrum Freiburg (University Hospital of Freiburg): http://www.uniklinik-freiburg.de/icf/live/implantate/cochlearimplant.html. The trivialized, but nonetheless similarly operating representations of this discourse can also be found in a number of children's comic books and other popular narratives of the cochlear implant (cf. Grebe, Spöhrer, & Stock, 2018).

14 For a detailed analysis of the communicational and disabling situations represented in such images and their respective relation to Ludwik Flecks "thought collectives" see Spöhrer, 2013.

Chapter 10

Breaking the Formal Financing Barriers Facing Entrepreneurs:
Crowdfunding as an Alternative Financing for Enterprise Development in Nigeria in the Digital Era

Lukman Raimi
American University of Nigeria, Nigeria

ABSTRACT

Financing programs at both start-up and growth phases are confronted with a number of institutional barriers. However, the digital era with its attendant benefits of interconnectedness has provided an alternative financing option called crowdfunding for internet-savvy entrepreneurs. Crowdfunding is a digital-based tool used to raise funds for different projects contributing to socio-economic development. The chapter discusses crowdfunding as an alternative financing option for enterprise development in Nigeria. Using a desk research technique, this chapter highlights the prospects of crowdfunding and strategies for leveraging crowdfunding as a viable alternative financing alternative in Nigeria. As an internet-driven process, this chapter identifies a number of challenges, but the most fundamental is the absence of regulatory environment to protect investors, a development that is in contrast to developed countries where crowdfunding is guided by enabling legislation. The chapter concludes with a number of research implications and suggestions.

INTRODUCTION

Financing programs at both start-up and growth phases are confronted with a number of institutional barriers. These barriers prevent entrepreneurs from accessing the required external financing support for survival at the early phases of their development. There are many entrepreneurs, whose dreams of establishing innovative businesses and creative projects have long been forgotten due to lack of start-up funds. Apart from the stringent conditions attached to conventional financing programs, there are dif-

DOI: 10.4018/978-1-5225-8933-4.ch010

ferent conditions tied to loan disbursement by the commercial banks, venture capitalists, angel investors and development banks. Personal savings as of most entrepreneurs are often grossly inadequate to grow their businesses beyond start-up and early growth stages. For formal loans from commercial banks, microfinance banks and other financial institutions, Bazza, Maiwada & Daneji (2014) noted that these banks provide short-term loans at higher interest rates, as well as impose very stringent conditions on fund-seeking entrepreneurs that approach them for funding support. Apart from very high interest rates, there are other associated transaction costs – a situation that makes commercial loans too expensive and unfriendly to both new businesses and existing businesses (Onakoya et al., 2013). Unfriendly interest rates charged by the commercial banks discourage start-ups and early growth businesses from patronizing them for loans. Loans from commercial banks are also inhibited by the inability of most borrowers to provide the needed collateral securities when requested by financial institutions (Ehimagunmwende 2016). Provision of collateral securities – a precondition required by the commercial banks and development banks is a major barrier in accessing financing in Nigeria. Without collateral securities, banks do not provide financial support regardless of the viability of the business models. This negative attitude of banks is borne out of the past experiences they had with defaulting entrepreneurs. However, the digital era with its attendant benefits of interconnectedness has provided an alternative financing option called crowdfunding for internet-savvy entrepreneurs. Crowdfunding is a digital-based tool used to raise funds for different businesses and social projects impacting on socio-economic development in different parts of the world. While crowdfunding is popular in developed economies such as the US, UK, France, Canada and Italy, it is an emerging financing option in Nigeria. The purpose of this chapter is to discuss crowdfunding as an alternative financing option for enterprise development in Nigeria. The less popularity of crowdfunding in Nigeria in spite of the growing number of internet users justifies the need for this exploratory chapter. Another important justification is the unique advantages it offers entrepreneurs and project owners as an alternative financing program. By unveiling the prospects of crowdfunding to fund-seeking entrepreneurs, investing publics and the academic, this chapter will enrich the understanding of the stakeholders as well as open the door for richer and indepth research on the subject matter.

In view of the foregoing, this chapter discusses crowdfunding as an alternative financing for enterprise development in Nigeria in the digital era. Specifically, the two research questions that this chapter intends to answer are: (a) What are the prospects of crowdfunding for enterprise development in Nigeria in the Digital Era? (b) What are the typologies of crowdfunding and the key challenges facing this alternative financing option in the developing context of Nigeria?

There are eight (8) sections in this chapter. Section 1 discusses the background to the chapter including the methodology and approach. Section 2 discusses financing options in Nigeria and imperative of crowdfunding. Section 3 defines crowdfunding, best practices and typologies. Section 4 provides a theoretical underpinning for crowdfunding in Financing leveraging social exchange theory (SET). Section 5 highlights the prospects of crowdfunding in a developing context. Section 6 explains systematically the strategies for crowdfunding venture financing. Section 7 highlights the challenges of crowdfunding in a developing economy. Section 8 concludes with summary of discussion and implications of research including suggestions for further research.

Methodology and Approach

A qualitative research method is adopted, while relying on desk research as the preferred technique for conducting the study. The approach is effective for exploring poorly researched issue or new phenomenon in social research before undertaking an empirical investigation. A desk research technique entails a review of relevant literature on crowdfunding to gain a broader understanding about the phenomenon. In line with the desk research tradition, the extracted pieces of information from scholarly articles and relevant internet resources on crowdfunding were systematically reviewed and synthesized to provide answers to the research questions. Scholars in the fields of social and management sciences have used desk research for a number of exploratory studies and field investigations (see Mbow, et al., 2012; Gulaid & Kiragu, 2012; Hedger et al., 2008). The essence of desk research is to systematically identify, assess and record the extent to which the phenomenon being investigated impacted and contributed to intended outcomes; it also allows researchers record lessons learned, report field challenges and highlight best practices. By-and-large, desk research assists researchers formulate insights that can be applied when conducting an empirical investigation after the exploration.

FINANCING OPTIONS IN NIGERIA AND IMPERATIVE OF CROWDFUNDING

The literature on entrepreneurial financing discussed different financing programs, which are mostly influenced by the predilections of different entrepreneurs as well as the alternatives that are available to entrepreneurs (Eniola & Entebang, 2015). The various financing options for start-up businesses and those at the growth phase of business development could be broadly categorized as formal financing and informal financing (Gbandi & Amissah, 2014). From the formal and the informal categorizations, the sources of financing can be further sub-grouped into debt financing and equity financing. Nigeria's formal financing landscape comprises licensed financing organizations such as development finance institutions (DFIs), microfinance institutions (MFIs), commercial banks and international development agencies (Gbandi & Amissah 2014, Central Bank of Nigeria 2018). The formal financing organizations (commercial banks and thrift & credit societies) have well-organized structure with highly regulated financial activities (Olawumi, Lateef & Oladeji, 2017). Nigeria's informal financial sector, on the other hand, comprises savings and loans associations, credit unions, family members and friends, informal money lenders and co-operative societies (Gbandi & Amissah 2014). Broadly, there are equity and debt sources of financing. It is important to mention that the formal financing sources are well regulated by the government and other agencies, while the informal financing sources are not well regulated by the government (Terungwa 2012).

It is imperative to state that the different sources of financing mentioned-above fit different business growth stages. For start-ups and early growth businesses, the appropriate financing programs are personal savings, support of business angels, equity funding of venture capitalists and well-designed internet-driven crowdfunding campaigns. For most start-ups and early growth businesses in Nigeria, access to the capital markets for sales of shares is institutionally restricted. Also, access to equity capital for start-ups is further restricted because bankers and business angels may not be willing to take on new businesses deemed to be too risky to be supported. Even venture capitalists that may be interested in providing financing support would do so after carrying out thorough due diligence on the business plan and supporting documents (Yung, 2009). Considering the rigidities in the Nigerian financial industry, the most flexible alternative financing for internet-savvy entrepreneurs is the crowdfunding. The next section discusses with clarity the definitions of crowdfunding, the best practices and typologies.

DEFINITION OF CROWDFUNDING AND BEST PRACTICES AND TYPOLOGIES

Crowdfunding is a novel source of financing made popular in Nigeria by the advent of social media platforms and growing internet usage by the technology-savvy entrepreneurs. Crowdfunding is an internet-driven and digital-based tool for fundraising to support different projects contributing to socio-economic development (Abdullahi, 2018). But, Schwienbacher & Larralde (2010) defined crowdfunding as an open call on the internet, initiated by the entrepreneurs and/or project owners requesting for financial resources from a large pool of small-scale investors/funders in the forms of donation, lending and equity participation in exchange for tangible and intangible rewards for their support. Crowdfunding can also be defined as a system of raising capital from diverse individuals through an online platform without the stress of due diligence and direct scrutiny of business proposals that characterized the formal financing program. Crowdfunding platforms are operationally flexible, as they enable prospective entrepreneurs and/or project owners raise funds for their business ideas or social projects through donations in return for rewards or equities (Agrawal, Catalini & Goldfarb, 2014). Another definition by Jegelevičiūtė & Valančienė (2015) view crowdfunding as a novel method of financing through an intermediary internet platform that connects backers/investors that are interested in investing into impactful projects of entrepreneurs seeking start-up capitals.

From practitioners' viewpoint, crowdfunding is a funding method designed to allow all types of entrepreneurs raise start-up funds from the crowd to fund their personal or business projects because of financing barriers (Falcon, 2017). Kuti and Madarász (2014) explained that globally, the sum of USD 2.7 billion was raised through the crowdfunding platforms in 2012. Another study on crowdfunding in Europe's alternative finance market indicated that this financing option increased by 101% from € 1019m to € 2063m in 2016. The study further states that there is an average annual growth of 85% in crowdfunding between 2013 and 2016 (Ziegler et al, 2018). Unlike the formal financing programs, crowdfunding does not have continent-wide acceptability and popularity in the developing countries because there no far-famed laws that guide crowdfunding activity, a development that is in contrast to developed climes such as the US, Canada, Turkey, the United Kingdom and Europe where it is properly guided by enabling rules and regulations (Eniola & Entebang 2015). Crowdfunding has been described as an effective entrepreneurial financing alternative for commercial and social enterprises for sourcing investible funds from a large number of people that believe in their ideas (Eniola & Entebang 2015; Belleflamme et al, 2014, Nehme 2018). From the foregoing definitions, crowdfunding can be defined as an internet-driven fundraising that enables entrepreneurs and project owners raise the need funds at initial stage of their businesses from small investors/donors/funders across the globe to fund their projects with less hassles because of the difficulties in accessing formal financing programs through bank loans or equity capital from corporate investors. It is a funding option made easy as a result of globalisation and digital interconnectedness.

With regards to redemption of funds raised by the crowdfunding sites, the project owners should make up their mind on selecting between fixed and flexible crowdfunding. Fixed crowdfunding means that the project owners are allowed to access the funds, only when the campaign hit its original funding target, but if the target is not met, no transaction takes place and the entire funded raised will returned back to the backers/funders for transparency and accountability. Flexible crowdfunding on the other hand, allow for flexibility, as the project owners gets to keep the funds raised even if the funding target is not reached. The flexible funding campaign is ideal and suitable for charitable causes (CrowdFund Buzz, 2018).

In view of the fact that crowdfunding is beneficial to large spectrum of stakeholders including the governments, some countries have proactively developed financial regulations and best practices to guide crowdfunding activities thereby bolstering entrepreneurial activity in these countries (Allison et al., 2015). According to Crowdfunding Centre (2014), the foremost countries where crowdfunding projects have been most successful are the USA, UK, Canada, Germany, France, Australia and Italy. These countries have different, but well-established regulations guiding crowdfunding as a digital-driven financing alternative.

Let us do a comparative analysis of the best practices and regulations in US, UK and Germany to serve as reference point for the development of best practices and enabling legislation for crowdfunding in Nigeria. In the US, best practices on crowdfunding are set and promoted by four different associations established in 2012 with mutually reinforcing objectives. The National Crowdfunding Association (NLCFA) supports, educates and protects American crowdfunding market; the American Crowdfunding Investment Association (ACFIA) encourages and promotes responsible financing of small businesses in US through crowdfunding; the Crowdfund Intermediary Regulatory Advocates (CFIRA) interfaces with the Securities & Exchange Commission (SEC), the Financial Industry Regulatory Authority (FINRA), and relevant governmental and quasi-governmental agencies to help establish industry standards and best practices on crowdfunding; and the Crowdfunding Professional Association (CfPA) boosts the capacities of fundraisers and their supporters, by providing education, resources and assistance to all stakeholders in the Crowdfunding community. The Jump Start Our Business Act (Jobs) Act of 2012, provides regulatory backing for equity crowdfunding in US for non-accredited investors (title III), while the US Securities and Exchange Commission promulgates rules for such offerings and the Financial Industry Regulatory Authority (FINRA) establishes specific rule regulating funding on crowdfunding portals (Jegelevičiūtė & Valančienė, 2015).

In the UK, the UK Crowdfunding Association (UKCFA) was established as the voice of all crowdfunding businesses. UKCFA promotes crowdfunding as a valuable fundraising platform for supporting businesses, projects and other ventures. It also publishes a code of practice guiding UK crowd funding businesses. With regards to legislation, the Financial Conduct Authority (FCA) is responsible for regulating loan and investment-based crowdfunding platforms guided by enabling crowdfunding rules promulgated in April 1, 2014 (FCA, 2015; Hulme, 2014).

In Germany, the German Crowd-funding Network (GCN) that was established in 2011 represents the interests of all crowdfunding stakeholders in the country. It also offers advisory services to fundraisers and funders for mutually beneficial relationship. Whereas, Australia established the Crowdfunding Institute of Australia (CFIA) in 2014 as an association vested with the responsibility of lobbying for crowdfunding reforms, increases public awareness, and create a more cohesive industry structure in the country (Jegelevičiūtė & Valančienė, 2015).

In Nigeria, crowdfunding is less popular, but there are a growing number of crowdfunding platforms such as Naijafund, Fundanenterprise, CircleUp, MicroVentures (Invoice, 2019), but no standard best practices nor laws exist to guide crowdfunding activity – a situation that makes crowdfunding vulnerable to financial risks (Eniola & Entebang 2015). Based on the financial risk associated with online lending, online marketing and crowdfunding activities, Ojo and Nwaokike (2018) call for a collaborative and inclusive process of stakeholders' engagement to discuss the need to enact relevant guidelines and regulations that would guide online financial transactions as well as protect the interests of customers, investors and other stakeholders in the Fintech industry.

The crowdfunding best practices and regulations in US, UK and Germany as discussed above, provide a rich learning curve and reference point for policymakers in Nigeria. The operational best practices and enabling regulations in these developed countries have largely assisted to safeguard and balance the interests of the fundraisers, funders and crowdfunding platforms for the sustainable growth and development of businesses in the developed countries in the digital era charcterised by financial innovation and technology.

With regards to crowdfunding typologies, Bone and Baeck (2016) stated that there are five (5) types of crowdfunding in practice, namely: donation-based crowdfunding, rewards-based crowdfunding, equity-based crowdfunding, community share crowdfunding and lending-based crowdfunding. But, Forbes & Schaefer (2017) identified four (4) crowdfunding models, namely: reward-based model (investment in exchange for products or gifts), equity-based model (investment for a percentage stake), lending-based model (peer-to-peer lending) and donation-based model (charitable giving). Reward-based model of crowdfunding is widely practised on Kickstarter and Indiegogo platforms, equity-based model is available on Seedrs and Crowdcube; Donation-based model is provided on crowdfunding platforms such as Just Giving, Global giving and other charity platforms; and lending-based model is provided on The Funding Circle (Cholakova & Clarysse, 2015; Bock, et al, 2014; Forbes & Schaefer, 2017). Each crowdfunding typology has its inherent costs and benefits for both fundraisers and donors/investors.

Definite explanations of the five typologies of crowdfunding are provided hereunder.

1. **Donation-Based Crowdfunding:** In this type of crowdfunding, interested individuals and corporate donors within the crowdfunding community donate small amounts for specific projects, which are pooled together to meet the purpose of the crowdfunding while the donors receive no tangible benefits. However, they are appreciated, thanked, praised and provided feedbacks on the projects periodically.
2. **Rewards-Based Crowdfunding:** This type of crowdfunding allows individual donors and groups contribute towards specific projects with the anticipation of receiving a tangible (but non–financial) reward in the form of a product when the project kicks off – a concept otherwise called pre-purchasing in the crowdfunding literature.
3. **Equity-Based Crowdfunding:** This crowdfunding typology gives individual investors and donors the opportunity to invest in equity ownership of start-up businesses with a view to earning financial return from the businesses at maturity.
4. **Community Shares Crowdfunding:** This is a unique crowdfunding project carefully designed as a sub-type of investment model, which offers investors specifically co-operative societies, community benefit societies (CBS) and charities a unique form of community share capital as co-owners. The community shares make these societies critical stakeholders with a democratic say in the ownership and running of the funded businesses. The community shares could be liquidated, swapped for cash and they may be paid interest on their shares based on performance of the business. However, the community shares cannot appreciate in value, but can depreciate in value.
5. **Lending-Based Crowdfunding:** This type of crowdfunding allows prospective fundraisers seeking debt facilities for starting their projects/businesses apply through the crowdfunding site, with donors and investors taking small chunks of the overall loan facilities as debt–based securities. This type of crowdfunding is usually allowed for commercial-oriented projects and projects with a combined commercial and social mission. The UK-based Abundance is a classic example of crowdfunding site that issues debt–based securities for raising shares for innovative projects and pays return to investors.

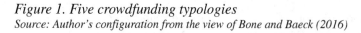

Figure 1. Five crowdfunding typologies
Source: Author's configuration from the view of Bone and Baeck (2016)

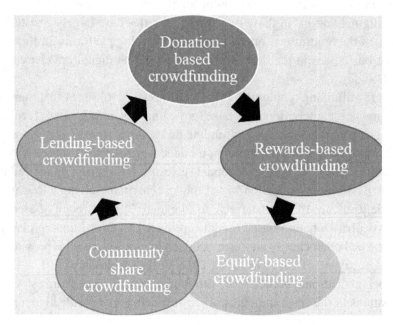

The nature of projects, target investors and fundraising platforms largely determines which of the five crowdfunding typologies to be chosen by the entrepreneurs and project owners.

THEORIZING CROWDFUNDING IN FINANCING

Crowdfunding is a disruptive approach to financing, which is driven partly by economics and by a set of shared values that unite communities of funders and the fundraisers for mutually-beneficial purpose of actualizing business projects and social causes (Gleasure & Feller, 2016). Therefore, the most appropriate theory that explains the functionality of crowdfunding (as an alternative financing program) is the social exchange theory (SET). According to Cook, Cheshire, Rice & Nakagawa (2013), social exchange is defined as the exchange of activity/opportunity that is tangible or intangible, between two or more people – the activity traded in the social exchange process are more or less rewarding or costly to the actors. The hallmark of the theory is emphasis on a series of interactions that are based on obligations or interdependent transactions, which all the actors are expected to fulfill (Cropanzano & Mitchell, 2005). In other words, social exchange relationship is a series of sequential transactions between two or more parties that is premised on reciprocity, trust and flexibility (Mitchell, Cropanzano, & Quisenberry, 2012, Cropanzano et al, 2017).

Furthermore, Social exchange theory as a relational theory measures the interplay of actors using the framework of cost-benefit analysis (otherwise called measurement of the pluses and minuses) (Crossman, 2019). The formula for predicting the behavior of actors within the social exchange process is: ***Behavior (profits) = Rewards of interaction – Costs of interaction***. SET is hinged on four key assumptions associated with rewards and punishments. The first proposition (success assumption) states that behavior that creates positive result is likely to be repeated. The second proposition (stimulus assumption) presumes that rewarded behavior in particular circumstances in the past will be performed in similar circumstances. The third proposition (value assumption) stipulates that the more valuable the result of an action is to an actor, the more likely that action is to be performed. The fourth proposition (deprivation-satiation assumption), states that the more frequently a person is rewarded for an action, the less valuable is an additional unit of that reward because humans react emotionally to different reward situations (Cook et al, 2013).

The import of social exchange theory when applied to the phenomenon of crowdfunding is that, prospective crowdfunding is an exchange relationship between communities of funders and the fundraisers for mutually-beneficial purpose of actualizing business projects and social causes. The exchange relationship is premised on cost-benefit analysis. The fundraisers sign up for crowdfunding financing, if the anticipated benefits are higher than the costs. For the investors and donors, they provide the needed financing resources in support of social causes or innovative start-up businesses when the anticipated benefits are higher than the costs.

PROSPECTS OF CROWDFUNDING IN A DEVELOPING CONTEXT

Crowdfunding has great prospects especially for developing economies where internet usage has increased and the process of financing start-ups is constrained by institutional barriers imposed by financial intermediaries and capital markets. In view of the liberty and sustained growth associated with raising funds on the internet by businesses, entrepreneurs as alternative fundraising mechanism to support creative projects and social causes, the phenomenon of crowdfunding has been described as the democratization of fundraising (Noyes 2014). In developed countries, crowdfunding as a novel tool provides a new opportunity for aspiring entrepreneurs to launch their start-ups seamlessly without going through the lengthy due diligence process of banks, venture capitalists and angel investors as pre-condition for funding ((Hui, Greenberg & Gerber, 2014). Crowdfunding therefore represents a paradigm shift from the traditional rigid financing schemes to a flexible social exchange platform where individuals and organizations interact online for mutually-beneficial benefits. The crowdfunding communities (investors, backers and donors) are bonded by shared values provide capital investment for specific projects and campaigns that meet their expectations (Gleasure & Feller, 2016). Unlike the conventional financing programs, the operational flexibility of crowdfunding allows fundraisers bypass conventional banks, angel investors, fund managers, and venture capitalists and other financial intermediaries (Pope & Sydnor, 2011; Wang & Greiner, 2011). After signing up to a reliable crowdfunding platform, what is required is for fund-seekers to pitch their social projects and innovative business proposals. This should be followed up with social network campaign and intense publicity because the success of crowdfunding activities rest largely on publicity support mechanisms that range from web applications tracking that boost page views to social online forums (Facebook, Instagram, Twitter and others) that connect fundraisers with investors and donors (Hui, Gerber, & Gergle, 2014). Some of the useful crowdfunding sites include Kickstarter, IndieGoGo, ProFounder, Buzzbnk, 33needs, CauseVox and FirstGiving and AppBackr (The Punch, 2018). Unlike conventional financing programs whose reward is premised on return on investment (ROI), the reward for backers of crowdfunding or crowdfunding communities is expressed in the forms of equity ownership, reward for donating, perks, products, sense of entitlement, credit points, reputation building, psychological satisfaction (Burtch, Ghose, & Wattal, 2013; Kuppuswamy & Bayus, 2013; Mollick, 2014). Apart from being an incredibly powerful platform for raising funds from ideological investors to fund laudable projects, crowdfunding also simultaneously creates the needed awareness among crowd of people as early prospective customers backing the products and services hosted on crowdfunding sites (Miller, 2018).

In the face of institutional barriers slowing down industrial development in emerging economies, crowdfunding could be an effective mechanism for launching new products, new services and creative ideas with fewer hassles. In other words, it provides a pragmatic and easy approach for internet-savvy entrepreneurs to raise for early start-up funding for their creative ideas (Kuppuswamy & Bayus 2014). One classic example of the flexibility of crowdfunding is the Oculus Rift virtual reality headset developer kits (DK1) supported by Kickstarter fundraising platform. The funding was successful to the delight of funders such that, the company was subsequently bought and taken over by Facebook for US$2 billion, a deal than angered the backers/investors because the deal contradicted the principles of crowdfunding (Gleasure, & Feller, 2016). Furthermore, crowdfunding has been used effectively to support successful social campaigns such as Pebble smart watch and the Veronica Mars movie project hosted on Kickstarter crowdfunding site. It is reported that Kickstarter overtime had raised over US$2 billion from 12 million backers for over 112,000 crowdfunding campaigns (Kickstarter, 2016). It has also been reported that TikTok+LunaTik successfully raised $941,718 from 13,512 crowd funders through pre-ordering of the product called multi-touch watch kit. Active crowd funders also pre-ordered watches from "Pebble" on Kickstarter platform raising more than $10 million in few weeks of the campaign (Belleflamme et al, 2014). Similarly, the Crowdsourcing Organization (2012) reported that for 2011 and 2012 financial years, one million successful campaigns have been launched leading to raising of almost $1.5 billion in 2011 and at least $3 billion in 2012. For 2019, the transaction value of crowdfunding amounts to US$6,923.6m, which is expected to increase of US$11,985.6m by 2023. Curiously, the highest transaction value of US$5,572m was recorded in China in 2019 – an indication that China is indeed a growing economy that would overtake the known bigger economies soon (Statista, 2019).

In spite of the growing popularity of crowdfunding, the success rate of this funding mechanism is not as impressive as often portrayed. Attention should therefore be given to the design of the crowdfunding campaign because well-designed campaigns attract funders, while poorly-designed campaigns often end up in failure. Evidence-based statistics indicated that large number of crowdfunding campaigns do not meet the funding goal. Specifically, 81% of failed crowdfunding campaigns attained less than 20% of their funding goal (Forbes & Schaefer, 2017).

In Nigeria with growing number of internet-savvy entrepreneurs and large population of crowd funders and empathetic investors/donors, the idea of crowdfunding would definitely be an attractive funding alternative, if the growing demographic of funders is well coordinated and sensitised at individual, organisational and national levels about the prospects of crowdfunding for enterprise development. This is instructive because crowdfunding as a viable funding mechanism thrives where there is a well-developed community of small funders/backers poised to support entrepreneurs in actualising their dream projects (Belleflamme, Lambert & Schwienbacher, 2014).

STRATEGIES FOR CROWDFUNDING VENTURE FINANCING

Before launching a crowdfunding campaign in any context, the project owners must understand the interconnectedness of three pillars of crowdfunding, namely: (a) the fundraiser, (b) the funders, and (c) the crowdfunding platform. The funder as the entrepreneur must be a project manager with commitment, business acumen and communication skills, as the are required to attract the community of funders. The funders are the backers/donors that provide the financial resources. The crowdfunding platform act as intermediary that brings the fundraiser and funders together for mutually-beneficial relationships (Fondevila Gascón et al, 2015). Literature also explains that the operational success/outcome of crowdfunding campaigns is largely dependent on a number of factors. These are: (a) goal size (amount targeted to be raised), contribution frequency, fundraising duration (timeline/deadline set for the campaign), creator's network size (social networks of the fundraisers/degree of endorsement), and signals of quality (Mollick 2014; Kuppuswamy & Bayus 2014; Zheng et al. 2014). Therefore, prospective fundraisers need to understand the dynamics of crowdfunding before using for venture financing. A crowdfunding approach, unlike conventional financing programs, is internet-driven and relies heavily on ideology, shared-values and social networks. Therefore, fundraising on online platforms requires well-thought-out strategies, as different crowdfunding sites have their core interests, distinct features and operational rules. The key strategies for leveraging crowdfunding for venture financing include:

- Developing a proposal for pitch on crowdfunding sites stating clearly the project idea, funding goal, amount targeted, funding deadline and rewards to donors;
- Identifying relevant crowdfunding platforms with communities of funders that share fundraisers' social values, ideals and worldviews;
- Signing up after agreeing to the rules and operational procedures of the crowdfunding platform including service charge;
- Getting third–party/expert endorsements to validate and bridge information gaps about the start–up projects;
- Launching intensive publicity to attract traffic to the crowdfunding sites because crowdfunding practically leverages social network to reach campaign goals (Hui, Greenberg & Gerber, 2014).

For an effective crowdfunding project or social cause, Forbes & Schaefer (2017) suggested that the project owner should provide clear answers to the following questions:

1. What crowdfunding platform should I use after reflecting on the expertise of the various platforms?
2. What should my funding goal be – flexible or fixed funding goals?
3. What should my reward options be after weighing the pros and cons of the variable reward models?
4. How should I construct my video to elicit interest and empathetic support of backers/funders?

CHALLENGES OF CROWDFUNDING IN A DEVELOPING ECONOMY

Globally, crowdfunding faces a number of surmountable challenges. First and foremost, crowdfunding financing is very popular in the developed countries with highly enlightened investing publics and backers that have social media visibility. This implies that crowdfunding would be appealing to the internet-compliant donors that are very active on the social media; hence, it is not an appropriate financing alternative for the internet-shy fundraisers. However, in Nigeria, crowdfunding is fairly popular and is just emerging. Secondly, globally-recognised and impactful crowdfunding sites with records of successful projects are located in the developed countries specially US, UK, Germany and Italy where

Table 1. Crowdfunding sites, features and terms

SN	Name of Crowdfunding Site	Terms and Conditions
1	Kickstarter is one of the most effective crowdfunding sites on the internet. It is reported that, it has so far assisted in raising $220 million for 61,000 creative projects launched on its site. It does not allow social causes, charity and scholarships. Donors/backers are promised rewards when they pay up the price point.	Fundraiser is charged 5% fee for successful project. The donations are redeemed on Amazon.
2.	Indiegogo is a crowdfunding site that provides swift financing for personal businesses and projects. It allows all projects such as business, social causes, and donation for charity. The backers' rewards are called perks.	Indiegogo charges 4% from the fund raised, 3% is charged for credit card processing and $25 wire fee for non-U.S. campaigns.
3	RocketHub is a crowdfunding platform for projects or campaigns targeted at top-notch brands, donors, investment companies and marketers. It accepts projects from artists, photographers and musicians. The backers' rewards are photography exhibition venues, 4-week media outreach campaigns with top marketers and rare publicity.	RocketHub charges 4% from the successful projects, 8% for project that ended without attaining the financial goal, and 4% of credit card processing.
4	GoFundMe is a good crowdfunding platform for personal campaigns, charities and business projects. This platform rewards backers with words of empathy 'Sharing is caring'.	5% fee is charged from each donation. The payment modes are WePay or PayPal that attract charge fees ranging from 2.9% to 3.5%.
5	Crowdrise focuses on helping to solve real world problems such as social wellness of people, endangered culture, arts, diseases, educational intervention projects, charities and religion. The backers are rewarded with CrowdRise Points (impact rating points) which boost the popularity and reputation of the donors.	A dual fee system applies. There is a flat 4.95% charge for the fundraising event and an extra monthly transaction fee.
6	Razoo is a renowned hi-tech fundraising website. It has raised over $97,000,000 for thousands of social causes, campaigns and problem-solving projects. Razoo allows the fundraisers to interact with the donors.	2.9% of the total fund is charged as service fee, thereby making it the most considerate crowdfunding site.
7	PledgeMusic is a crowdfunding site created to support new musicians and talented artists in the music industry. Backers are rewarded and appreciated for supporting a digital download of the artist music album.	PledgeMusic charges 15% out of the fund donated. Users have to weigh the cost and benefits before signing up.
8	Sellaband is a crowdfunding site that focused music development. It has raised over $4,000,000 donations for music bands, and handled recording sessions for over 80 music artists. Backers/donors are rewarded with opportunity to make a deal with the musicians on label, CD production & printing, sales & marketing and other third party management solution.	Sellaband charges 15% of the amount raised in order to cover professional expenses.
9	Appbackr is a high-tech crowdfunding site that offers support for apps developers having financial challenges at the developmental stages. Backers of the apps are given return on investment (ROI), which is redeemed through a payback system, after the sale of the app.	Appbackr has a service fee that depends on the price of the apps supported, but there is no fixed percentage.
10	Crowdfunder is a funding platform for providing financing support for new start-up and small companies by selling equities, debt and revenue-based securities to angel investors, venture capitalists and people with idle funds. Crowdfunder select companies to be supported through a startup contest. Best adjudged startups pitch their ideas at the live event of the Vegas Tech Fund. The winner is given $500,000 in funding.	Crowdfunder has a service fee, but there is no fixed percentage.

Source: Author's compilation from Falcon (2017)

the culture of crowdfunding is well entrenched. Unfortunately, impactful crowdfunding platforms with records of success are very few in developing economy like Nigeria. Online search revealed Naijafund, Fundanenterprise, CircleUp, MicroVentures (Invoice, 2019).

Besides, fraudulent crowdfunding is a serious challenge, whereas by default, crowdfunding is a financing technique built on shared values such as credibility, trust and openness. Upsurge in the number of fraudulent internet users and proliferations of crowdfunding platforms have compromised these shared values; as such investors, backers and donors have become weary of crowdfunding and have therefore tightened their pockets. Even where investors and donors show some interests in online campaigns, they carry out background checks to ascertain the authenticity of such crowd fundraising. It is therefore very challenging for people with creative ideas to win the trust, faith and conviction of the investing public through crowdfunding these days. In the past, several fraudulent business projects and social causes had been funded, and the fundraisers disappeared without redeeming their promises nor providing progress reports (Carbajo, 2017). This challenge fundamentally inhibits the success of many crowdfunding campaigns.

Another major challenge facing crowdfunding is inability of project owners/promoters of creative ideas to raise the required amount through crowdfunding platforms. The media and crowdfunding platforms have over-celebrated crowdfunding, but several projects and social causes have actually fallen short of their funding goals (financing targets). Research indicated that 56% of projects launched on crowdfunding platforms fail to meet their financial targets (Hui, Gerber & Gergle, 2014). Although, a study linked the impeding factor for inability of promoters to meet their targets to weak publicity efforts because crowdfunding as a tool practically leverages social network to reach campaign goals (Hui, Greenberg & Gerber, 2014).

Finally, the absence of regulatory environment to protect investors, a development that is in contrast to developed countries where crowdfunding is guided by enabling legislation. In developed countries, there are enabling laws guiding and best practices for crowdfunding, in all its forms. The relationship between crowdfunding sites and fund-seekers are well articulated within the ambit of the laws. Furthermore, the capital and money market in the developed countries especially US, UK, Canada and Germany are well developed to accommodate crowdfunding financing option. For instance, Europe has in place an alternative finance market for coordination of crowdfunding, a move that led to 85% average annual growth in crowdfunding between 2013 and 2016 (Ziegler et al, 2018). This is not the case in Nigeria where there exists no alternative finance market for crowdfunding because of weak development of the financial market in the country.

CONCLUSION

This chapter sets out to discuss crowdfunding as an alternative financing option for enterprise development in Nigeria. Leveraging a desk research technique to gain a broader understanding about the phenomenon of crowdfunding, the chapter reviewed the various definitions of crowdfunding and came up with an operational definition for this slippery concept – it is defined as an internet-driven fundraising campaign that enables aspiring entrepreneurs, project owners and charities raise the need funds from backers/donors/funders across the globe to support their projects because of the difficulties in accessing external finance at initial stage through bank loans or equity capital from corporate investors. It is a funding option made easy as a result of globalisation and digital interconnectedness. The chapter identified two crowdfunding redemptions - fixed and flexible crowdfunding campaigns. The fixed crowdfunding campaign does not allow the project owners access the funds, if the funding goal is not reached, but flexible crowdfunding allows for flexibility, as the project owners gets to keep the funds raised even if the funding target is not reached. Furthermore, the chapter identified five typologies of crowdfunding namely: donation-based crowdfunding, rewards-based crowdfunding, equity-based crowdfunding, community share crowdfunding and lending-based crowdfunding. It was established that crowdfunding is a paradigm shift from the traditional and rigid financing schemes because it provides a new opportunity for aspiring entrepreneurs to launch their innovative projects seamlessly without going through the stringent terms and conditions imposed by commercial banks, venture capitalists and angel investors as pre-condition for funding. Key challenges to crowdfunding in Nigeria as a financing alternative include poor awareness about crowdfunding, rising incident of fraudulent fundraisers, inability of promoters to meet funding targets and absence of strong legislation and regulatory environment.

Practical and Theoretical Implications

The implications of this chapter are diverse. First, the chapter makes a modest contribution to understanding crowdfunding in a developing context of Nigeria, by conceptualizing, contextualizing and theorizing crowdfunding as an emerging model of business investment. This exploit has helped to translate academic research on the subject matter into a practitioner-friendly chapter for practical application in a developing context such as Nigeria. Theoretically this chapter builds and enriches social exchange theory (SET) by embedding it as the most appropriate theory for explaining how crowdfunding communities leverage shared values for providing investible funds for fundraisers on dedicated websites and online platforms. The issues raised in this chapter contribute to scholarly understanding of crowdfunding and its various typologies as well as the challenges facing crowdfunding as an alternative financing option in a developing context. This conceptual research has laid a theoretically sound foundation for empirical research in the field of crowdfunding in Nigeria.

Discussion Questions in Classrooms

1. What is the uniqueness of crowdfunding option compared to other conventional financing programs?
2. For developing economy, what are the key challenges that may inhibit the functionality of crowdfunding as an alternative financing?
3. Can early career scientists, graduate students, and researchers in developing countries leverage crowdfunding as a means for raising fund for research?
4. What role does legislation play in the embedment of crowdfunding as a financing program in both developed and developing economy?
5. What are the major typologies of crowdfunding in the literature? Discuss the unique differences of the five typologies of crowdfunding.
6. Considering the fact that crowdfunding leverages internet technology and high level publicity, can it be a viable option for entrepreneurs living in remote part of the world with limited internet access and low media visibility?
7. In view of rising incidence of fraudulent fundraisers on the internet platforms, how can prospective fundraisers elicit trust and confidence of funders/donors for their crowdfunding projects and campaigns?

8. Crowdfunding community comprising investors, donors, ideological backers and operators of crowdfunding sites are very active in the developed countries; do you think projects from developing countries will meet their expectations and funding support?

REFERENCES

Abereijo, I. O., & Fayomi, A. O. (2005). Innovative approach to SME financing in Nigeria: A review of small and medium industries equity investment scheme (SMIEIS). *Journal of Social Sciences, 11*(3), 219–227. doi:10.1080/09718923.2005.11893635

Agrawal, A., Catalini, C., & Goldfarb, A. (2014). Some simple economics of crowdfunding. *Innovation Policy and the Economy, 14*(1), 63–97. doi:10.1086/674021

Allison, Th. H., Davis, B. C., Short, J. C., & Webb, J. W. (2015). Internal Social Capital and the Attraction of Early Contributions in Crowdfunding. *Entrepreneurship Theory and Practice, 39*, 53–73. doi:10.1111/etap.12108

Bazza, M. I., Maiwada, B. Y., & Daneji, B. A. (2014). Islamic Financing: A Panacea To Small and Medium Scale Enterprises Financing Problems In Nigeria. *European Scientific Journal, 10*(10), 432–444.

Belleflamme, P., Lambert, T., & Schwienbacher, A. (2014). Crowdfunding: Tapping the right crowd. *Journal of Business Venturing, 29*(5), 585–609. doi:10.1016/j.jbusvent.2013.07.003

Bock, J. A., Frydrych, D., Kinger, T., & Koeck, B. (2014). Exploring Entrepreneurial Legitimacy in Reward-Based Crowdfunding. *Venture Capital,* (16): 247–269.

Bone, J., & Baeck, P. (2016). *Crowdfunding Good Causes - Opportunities and challenges for charities, community groups and social entrepreneurs.* Working Paper of Nesta United Kingdom. Available: https://media.nesta.org.uk/documents/crowdfunding_good_causes-2016.pdf

Carbajo, M. (2017). Key Challenges and Drawbacks with Crowdfunding - How to Avoid the Crowdfunding Mindfield. *The Balance Small Business.* Available: https://www.thebalancesmb.com/key-challenges-and-drawbacks-with-crowdfunding-4116031

Central Bank of Nigeria. (2018). *Economic report for the first half of 2017.* Retrieved from http://www.cbn.gov.ng/Out/2018/RSD/half%20year%202017%20innerx.pdf

Cholakova, M., & Clarysse, B. (2015). Does the Possibility to Make Equity Investments in Crowdfunding Projects Crowd Out Reward–Based Investments? *Entrepreneurship Theory and Practice, 39*(1), 145–172. doi:10.1111/etap.12139

Cook, K. S., Cheshire, C., Rice, E. R., & Nakagawa, S. (2013). Social exchange theory. In *Handbook of social psychology* (pp. 61–88). Dordrecht: Springer. doi:10.1007/978-94-007-6772-0_3

Cropanzano, R., Anthony, E. L., Daniels, S. R., & Hall, A. V. (2017). Social exchange theory: A critical review with theoretical remedies. *The Academy of Management Annals, 11*(1), 479–516. doi:10.5465/annals.2015.0099

Crossman, A. (2019). *Understanding Social Exchange Theory*. Available: https://www.thoughtco.com/social-exchange-theory-3026634

CrowdFund Buzz. (2018). *Your Crowdfunding Campaign: Flexible Funding or Fixed Funding?* Available: https://www.crowdfundbuzz.com/your-crowdfunding-campaign-flexible-funding-or-fixed-funding/

Crowdfunding Centre. (2014). *Mapping: the state of the crowdfunding nation*. Available: thecrowdfundingcentre.com/downloads/eFunding__The_State_of_The_Crowdfunding_Nation_-_Q2_2014_HEADLINE_EDITION.pdf.

Crowdsourcing Organization. (2012). *Crowdfunding industry report*. Available: https://www.slideshare.net/samgold007/crowdfunding-industry

Ehimagunmwende, C. (2016). *Challenges Facing SMEs Financing in Nigeria*. Available: https://www.linkedin.com/pulse/challenges-facing-smes-financing-nigeria clifford-nosa/

Eniola, A. A., & Entebang, H. (2015). SME firm performance-financial innovation and challenges. *Procedia: Social and Behavioral Sciences*, *195*, 334–342. doi:10.1016/j.sbspro.2015.06.361

Falcon, A. (2017). *10 Crowdfunding Sites To Fuel Your Dream Project*. HongKiat. Available: https://www.hongkiat.com/blog/crowdfunding-sites/

Financial Conduct Authority. (2015). *A review of the regulatory regime for crowdfunding and the promotion of non-readily realisable securities by other media*. Available at: www.fca.org.uk/static/documents/crowdfunding-review.pdf

Fondevila Gascón, J. F., Rom Rodríguez, J., Mata Monforte, J., Santana López, E., & Masip Masip, P. (2015). Crowdfunding as a formula for the financing of projects: an empirical analysis. *Hermes Scientific Journal*. Available at: http://www.redalyc.org/articulo.oa?id=477647161003

Forbes, H., & Schaefer, D. (2017). Guidelines for successful crowdfunding. *Procedia CIRP*, *60*, 398–403. doi:10.1016/j.procir.2017.02.021

Gbandi, E. C., & Amissah, G. (2014). Financing options for small and medium enterprises (SMEs) in Nigeria. *European Scientific Journal*, *10*(1), 327–340.

Gleasure, R., & Feller, J. (2016). A rift in the ground: Theorizing the evolution of anchor values in crowdfunding communities through the oculus rift case study. *Journal of the Association for Information Systems*, *17*(10), 708–736. doi:10.17705/1jais.00439

Gulaid, L. A., & Kiragu, K. (2012). Lessons learnt from promising practices in community engagement for the elimination of new HIV infections in children by 2015 and keeping their mothers alive: summary of a desk review. *Journal of the International AIDS Society, 15*.

Hedger, M. M., Mitchell, T., Leavy, J., Greeley, M., & Downie, A. (2008). *Desk review: evaluation of adaptation to climate change from a development perspective*. Available: http://citeseerx.ist.psu.edu/viewdoc/download?doi=10.1.1.575.1027&rep=rep1&type=pdf

Higgins, R. C. (2012). *Analysis for financial management* (10th ed.). Irwin, NY: McGraw-Hill.

Hui, J. S., Gerber, E. M., & Gergle, D. (2014). Understanding and leveraging social networks for crowdfunding: opportunities and challenges. In *Proceedings of the 2014 conference on Designing interactive systems* (pp. 677-680). Academic Press. Available: https://collablab.northwestern.edu/pubs/DIS2014_HuiGerberGergle.pdf

Hui, J. S., Greenberg, M. D., & Gerber, E. M. (2014). Understanding the Role of Community in Crowdfunding Work. In *Proceedings of the 17th ACM conference on Computer supported cooperative work & social computing* (pp. 62-74). Available: https://dl.acm.org/citation.cfm?id=2531715

Hulme, A. (2014, June). Consumer credit roundup. *Credit Management*, 32–33.

Invoice. (2019) *Best Crowdfunding Sites To Fund Your Business Ideas In Nigeria*. Available: https://invoice.ng/blog/best-crowdfunding-sites-in-nigeria/

Jegelevičiūtė, S., & Valančienė, L. (2015). Comparative analysis of the ways crowdfunding is promoted. *Procedia: Social and Behavioral Sciences, 213*, 268–274. doi:10.1016/j.sbspro.2015.11.536

Kickstarter. (2016). *Seven things to know about Kickstarter*. Retrieved from https://www.kickstarter.com/about

Kuppuswamy, V., & Bayus, B. L. (2014). *Crowdfunding Creative Ideas: The Dynamics of Project Backers in Kickstarter*. UNC Kenan-Flagler Research Paper:2013-15.

Mbow, C., Skole, D., Dieng, M., Justice, C., Kwesha, D., Mane, L., & Virji, H. (2012). *Challenges and prospects for REDD+ in Africa: desk review of REDD+ implementation in Africa. Global Land Project Reports, 5. World Agroforestry Centre*. Nairobi, Kenya: ICRAF.

Miller, Z. (2018). *The Entrepreneur's Guide to the Fees on Crowdfunding Platforms*. Available: https://www.thebalancesmb.com/entrepreneurs-guide-to-fees-on-crowdfunding-platforms-985187

Mitchell, M. S., Cropanzano, R. S., & Quisenberry, D. M. (2012). Social exchange theory, exchange resources, and interpersonal relationships: A modest resolution of theoretical difficulties. In *Handbook of social resource theory* (pp. 99–118). New York, NY: Springer. doi:10.1007/978-1-4614-4175-5_6

Mollick, E. (2014). The Dynamics of Crowdfunding: An Exploratory Study. *Journal of Business Venturing, 29*(1), 1-16.

Nehme, M. (2018). Regulating crowd equity funding–the why and the how. *Journal of Law and Society, 45*(1), 116–135. doi:10.1111/jols.12082

Noyes, K. (2014). Why Investors Are Pouring Millions into Crowdfunding. *Fortune Magazine*. Available: http://fortune.com/2014/04/17/why-investors-arepouring-millions-into-crowdfunding/

Ojo, O., & Nwaokike. (2018). Disruptive Technology and the Fintech Industry in Nigeria: Imperatives for Legal and Policy Responses. *Gravitas Review of Business and Property Law, 9*(3). Available: SSRN: https://ssrn.com/abstract=3306164

Olawumi, S. O., Lateef, L. A., & Oladeji, E. O. (2017). Financial Deepening and Bank Performance: A Case Study of Selected Commercial Banks in Nigeria. *Journal of Mathematical Finance, 7*(03), 519–535. doi:10.4236/jmf.2017.73028

Olowe, F. T., Moradeyo, O. A., & Babalola, O. A. (2013). Empirical study of the impact of microfinance bank on small and medium growth in Nigeria. *International Journal of Academic Research in Economics and Management Sciences*, 2(6), 116–124.

Onakoya, A., Fasanya, I., & Abdulrahman, H. (2013). Small and Medium Scale Enterprises Financing and Economic Growth in Nigeria-. *European Journal of Business and Management*, 5(4), 2222–2839.

Pope, D. G., & Sydnor, J. R. (2011). What's in a picture? Evidence of discrimination from Prosper.com. *The Journal of Human Resources*, 46(1), 53–92. doi:10.3368/jhr.46.1.53

Schwienbacher, A., & Larralde, B. (2010). Crowdfunding of small entrepreneurial ventures. In D. J. Cumming (Ed.), *The Oxford Handbook of Entrepreneurial Finance*. Oxford, UK: Oxford University Press.

Statista. (2019). *Crowdfunding Worldwide*. Available: https://www.statista.com/outlook/335/100/crowd-funding/worldwide

Terungwa, A. (2011). An empirical evaluation of small and medium enterprises equity investment scheme in Nigeria. *Journal of Accounting and Taxation, 3*(3), 79-90.

The Punch Newspaper. (2018). *Crowdfunding: How to raise money from strangers*. Available: https://punchng.com/crowdfunding-how-to-raise-money-from-strangers/

Wang, H., & Greiner, M. E. (2011). Prosper—The eBay for money in lending 2.0. *Communications of the Association for Information Systems*, 29, 243–258. doi:10.17705/1CAIS.02913

Yung, C. (2009). Entrepreneurial financing and costly due diligence. *Financial Review*, 44(1), 137–149. doi:10.1111/j.1540-6288.2008.00213.x

Zheng, H., Li, D., Wu, J., & Xu, Y. (2014). The Role of Multidimensional Social Capital in Crowdfunding: A Comparative Study in China and Us. *Information & Management, 51*(4), 488-496.

Chapter 11

Cross–Sector Partnership in Smart City Development:
The Case of Brazil

Emilene Leite
Örebro University, Sweden & Uppsala University, Sweden

ABSTRACT

Urbanization is a persistent phenomenon. As cities have expanded, so has the demand for government ability to provide better infrastructure and public services. The "smart city" concept may form a response to these urban challenges. From a business point of view, incorporating digital technologies to address some of the city's sustainability challenges is a means to create business opportunities for firms. However, a smart city project is complex, and it requires firms interaction with government and civil society. Hence, the aim of this chapter is to understand how firms manage their relationships with socio-political actors in projects for smart city development and how socio-political actors can be a source of competitive advantage. These questions will be answered by applying business network perspective within cross-sector partnership in the context of firms operating in Brazil. The study contributes to a foundation for a better discussion among policy makers and practitioners about promoting inter-organizational cooperation in projects with a social purpose.

INTRODUCTION

Urbanization is a persistent phenomenon and its impact is evident in today's society and in the environment. With more people living in urban areas, streets become congested, environmental degradation levels have increased and public health may decline (UN, 2014). As cities have expanded, so has the demand for government capacity to provide better cities' infrastructure and public services. The increasing trajectory of urban population is not only an interesting fact but it urges the need to make cities sustainable. With regards to sustainability - a main UN goal - cities and urban population merit attention. The 'smart city' concept may form a response to these urban challenges.

DOI: 10.4018/978-1-5225-8933-4.ch011

A city is defined as 'smart' when the government participates in the efficient distribution of resources aligned with economic development (Caragliu, Del Bo & Nijkamp, 2011). The term has also been used to refer to the integration of public and private services using technological innovation, which typically involves ICT (information and communications technology). Although there is no prevalent or universally acknowledged definition of 'smart city, its goal 'is to better allocate public resources, increase the quality of services offered to citizens while reducing the operational costs of the public administration' (Zanella Bui, Castellani & Vangelista, 2014) and therefore public authorities are the potential buyers of such technologies. This objective for making cities smart can be pursued by the development of IoT (Internet of Things) based services, which integrate several technologies and communication infrastructures via the internet. Such technologies facilitate remote monitoring, the management and optimization of traditional public services such as – but not limited to - transport and parking, public street lighting, education, etc. (Atzori, Iera, & Morabito, 2010). Furthermore, these technological solutions can also combine data from several connected devices and, therefore, help public authorities to improve their decision-making through data analysis.

From a business point of view, incorporating digital technologies to address some of the city's sustainability challenges is a way of creating business opportunities. However, the development and implementation of technologies applied to cities require companies to interact with a range of actors outside their traditional business network. In this study the central concern is on companies that are considered to be embedded in relationships containing both business and nonbusiness actors. Firms' relationship with nonbusiness actors refers to other stakeholders beyond the traditional business network of customers, suppliers, and competitors. In this study, 'social' refers to nongovernmental organizations (NGOs) while 'political' refers to public officials and politicians. In such relationships, companies and socio-political actors may benefit from each other if they perceive possibilities for achieving common goals.

When examining development of products and services, literature within business research commonly focuses on companies and their performance in relation to short-term and incremental aspects of innovation, while little attention has been paid to public-private benefits (Bhanji & Oxley, 2013; Mahoney, McGahan, & Pitelis, 2009). Such relationship development becomes even more relevant in a market for smart city technologies, in which nonbusiness actors are the potential buyers and system users. I argue that there is a need to learn more about how firms cope with the inherent complexity in such relationships where actors with different values and limited resources attempt to find novel smart city solutions. Based on that, the aim of this chapter is twofold: 1) to understand how firms manage their relationships with socio-political actors in projects for smart city development and 2) how socio-political actors can be a source of competitive advantage. These questions will be answered by applying business network perspective in the context of firms operating in Brazil.

An interesting aspect is that the dominant literature studying smart cities focuses specifically on technology and its infrastructure (Andersson & Mattsson, 2015), and there is a lack of academic inquiries analyzing these suppliers' business relationships and network formation. As mentioned above, particular focus is made in this chapter is on the role of the socio-political actors on the firms' business activities linked with the smart city projects. Therefore, the investigation of the influence of these actors on the firms' cooperative behavior as well as what kind of solution can be achieved, needs to be further studied. Investigating cross-sector cooperation within smart city development and implementation may help broaden business-to-business research and industrial business network.

Following this introduction of the chapter, next section provides theoretical background regarding cross-sector cooperation. In addition to that, challenges and opportunities faced by companies in such a partnership as well as companies' resource allocation is also discussed. Subsequently the data and methods applied to address the research questions are outlined. Afterwards, the findings of the empirical analysis are presented. Finally, the chapter ends with a summary of the main contributions and suggests avenues for further research.

CROSS-SECTOR COOPERATION: CHALLENGES AND OPPORTUNITIES

In this study business and socio-political actors are co-developers of a smart city solution. To develop the solution, different pieces of knowledge are expected to be combined and integrated. Thus, the development is seen as an interaction process. The potential users of the technology will be politicians, public officials, and citizens. The producers are those contributing resources such as technological expertise that comes from the business sphere and also those, such as socio-political actors, contributing local knowledge expertise about the needs of the society and the needs of the city specifically.

From the business point of view, socio-political actors become an important resource not only because they may contribute to the adjustment of the technology but also because companies need social acceptance for their specific products/services. However, this type of partnership requires a lot of coordination from companies. When examining MNEs (multinational enterprise) and local cross-sector cooperation in the Baltic Sea, Ritvala et al., (2014) observed that in order to reduce tensions and conflicts, such interactions required greater social, resource, and organizational coordination mechanisms. Their study also highlights a type of partnership that is characterized by absence of necessary resources, and collaborative experience. In the same line of thinking, Le Ber and Branzei (2010; p.145) affirm that cross-sector cooperation is complex and the relationship is commonly marked by constant adjustments and interrupted by temporary successes and failures. In projects for smart city development which involves business, government and civil society coordination becomes relevant not only in terms of organizational mechanisms but also to understand the different actors' expectations and goals.

Figure 1 illustrates a business network view that includes three different main actors: business, social, and political. The triangle indicates that each actor belongs to a different sphere, sustains a different legitimacy, and therefore has different objectives. Challenges and opportunities are located at the center of the triangle. The arrows represent the heterogeneity in terms of actors and their respective resources. Thus, challenges in this context concerns the type of relationship among different actors where the resource exchange is aimed at developing a new technological solution. Challenges can be related to difficulties in managing, coordinating different goals and interests. However, challenges can be turned into opportunities. Actors with different background and heterogeneous resources can be a source of competitive advantage to firms aiming to develop solution with a social purpose such as smart city.

It is worth mentioning that complexity in the relationship between companies, government and NGOs is observed in several ways. In the triangle, business represents the firms which develop and sell the technology. They differ in size (small, medium, and/or multinationals). Social actors are the NGOs whose representatives are the individuals of civil society. Political actors include public officials and politicians at different levels of public administration. They differ in terms of power and interests. For instance, public officials tend to have a more permanent position as opposed to temporary politicians. The temporary position of politicians implies that priorities, objectives, and values change over time, or are at least expected to change from election to election when new politicians are placed in office. As Hadjikhani et al., (2008) affirm, politicians can be directly or indirectly connected to different ac-

Figure 1. Business, social, and political actors: a business network view

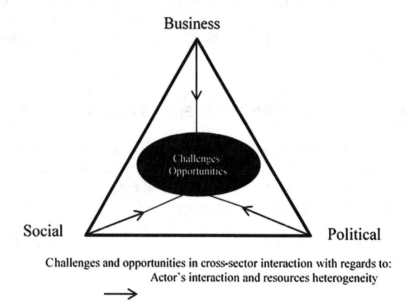

Challenges and opportunities in cross-sector interaction with regards to:
Actor's interaction and resources heterogeneity

tors such as citizens, voters, media, unions, consumers, etc. all of whom influence their behavior and decisions. Political actions towards business can be coercive or supportive, where coercive means that companies need to adapt their business activities to political norms and social rules, while supportive means that companies are able to influence political decisions to benefit their own business interests (Hadjikhani et al., 2008).

From one side, political actors attempt to incorporate values from different groups as a way to enhance their political legitimacy in the society. On the other side, companies make investments that affect groups like media, citizens, and others on which politicians are dependent. Such heterogeneity in the structure of the network also can be related to the NGOs, once that they are also connected to actors outside the political and business network. They form a heterogeneous group with different working scope and of course interests. Their actions may influence both political and corporate behavior. Similarly to political actions, NGOs' actions towards firms can also be supportive and/or coercive. NGOs can be indirectly coercive by creating pressure on government to influence more socially responsible corporate behavior. Direct coercive action includes regulation of hazardous wastes to a global ban of certain companies' products/services for instance. Such a pressure exerted by NGOs as a way to force companies to exercise sustainability. Hence, developing close cooperation with NGOs can help companies to transform a coercive action into a supportive one (Ghauri, et al., 2012). The same may occur with regards to political actors. I.e., companies may change a coercive into a supportive action depending on the context. In a cross sector partnership companies and socio-political actors are interdependent, not only on one another but also on the actors surrounding them as their activities influence each other's network connections. However it is important to highlight that not all NGOs will be interested to collaborate with companies. Some may prefer to remain at a certain distance, by monitoring, publicizing, and criticizing in cases where companies fail to take seriously their impacts on society.

In a traditional companies' business network, a broad array of resources is often exchanged within a frame of relationships between two companies. But in a network with nonbusiness actors, exchange takes another form. In the examination of the influence of socio-political actors on firms' business networks, Hadjikhani and Thilenius, (2005) stress that in such relationships the aspects of trust and commitment as well as the understanding how knowledge can be combined are dissimilar to business-to-business relationships. The authors emphasize that knowledge, for instance, is not related to technological development or adaptation but is instead related to a specific community or context. For companies, acquiring knowledge about political and societal objectives is necessary because these actors are expected to satisfy different groups with specific demands (Boddewyn & Doh, 2011; Choi, Jia & Lu, 2014). Given such differences in the type of exchange, such cooperation is more susceptible to conflicts. But despite all of the aforementioned challenges, Mahoney et al., (2009) argue that private and public action may also activate the degree of alignment in interests. For that reason, it is possible to innovate through cooperation activities, but motivation depends on the constant adaptation of each actor role since heterogeneity is inherent in such cooperation (Le Ber & Branzei, 2010). Turn challenges into opportunities by managing relationships with nonbusiness actors can enhance firms' competitive advantage mainly with respect to resource allocation in projects for smart city development.

RESOURCE ALLOCATION

Managing Relationships as a Means to Turn Challenges Into Opportunities

In a city setting, business resources are directly linked to capabilities and technological competences, while socio-political resources refer to the understanding of the social context, challenges and opportunities faced by the city, etc. Political actors also exercise control over the city's resources in terms of urban planning and therefore they have the power and legitimacy to decide if a share of the city's budget will be allocated for buying technologies that the companies develop. The understanding of the political agenda helps companies to know where they will be allocating their resources, i.e., investment decisions in areas that the government has an interest.

Another important aspect it to know how firms may succeed in a new market for IoT based-services applied to cities whose users and co-developers are not traditional business partners. In a city setting users differ, i.e., the client is not a company and challenges become the process in which integrating resources means incorporating business resources into the needs of socio-political actors. As can be observed, the resource dimension is expected to be intrinsically interwoven with the actor dimension and at the intersection between actors and resources, the concept of smart city solution emerges. Thus, resources from actors become interdependent and relationship development facilitates the knowledge and learning process. In addition to this, it is interesting to understand the influence of nonbusiness actors in contributing to technological development with non-financial assets that may indirectly influence both the development and implementation of innovation. Examples include ideas, relationship knowledge, tacit knowledge, contextual knowledge, advice, emotional support, positive word of mouth, etc., which will indirectly impact on companies' focal networks and their business opportunities. There is, for instance, a large body of research showing consumer interaction through internet technology and cooperation with companies as producers of new ideas (Kazadi, Lievens & Mahr, 2016).

By studying service multinationals in Brazil, Hadjikhani, Leite and Pahlberg, (2019) emphasize that, as a mean to strengthen competitive market position, companies have to manage socio-political relationships that are essential and supplement their business activities. In the case of the smart city, socio-political actors may contribute to and/or hinder firms from managing resource allocation as well as help them to create market opportunity for a novel solution. In addition to that, UN Global Compact Program (2016) asserts that government may play a significant role in helping business to be more innovative, socially and environmentally responsible mainly in respect to areas related to urban development. Hence, urban development represents one of the UN development goals (UN, 2014) and it is also in many government agenda in both developed and developing nations.

From the technological point of view, companies will take strategic actions with regard to learning how to combine different resources and finding ways to use the knowledge in a different situation. For example, part of the solution developed in a city setting might be used in another setting; examples may include solutions for consumers in smart homes, private schools, private security, smart parking solution in malls, etc., therefore expanding the company's knowledge and its strategy to explore novelty in different settings. In the network way of reasoning, knowledge is not given and there is always a way of learning something new about a particular way of combining resources (Håkansson & Snehota, 1995; 2006). This has implications for learning, adaptation, development and implementation. Within the network, actors are expected to share both resources and knowledge (Håkansson & Snehota, 1995; 2006).

METHOD

An analysis of a single case is used to understand how firms manage their relationships with socio-political actors in projects for smart city development and how socio-political actors as co-developers may be a source of competitive advantage. The contextual richness provided by case studies in a more complex cooperative structure, for instance involving private and public spheres, is helpful when capturing actors' differences in values, beliefs and intentions (Yin, 2017). Moreover a case study is recommended when 'how' questions are asked (Ghauri & Grønhaug 2005). A network perspective, therefore, is applied in order to consider the views of diverse actors with the purpose of producing a holistic explanation of the context but also with a deliberate focus on business actor engagement with the public domain (e.g., public authorities and NGOs).

Data Selection and Data Gathering

With regard to case selection, factors such as product/service innovation, an emerging market economic context and community impact have been considered. Although the case involves a smart city project within one country, an international dimension is given since the firms involved are from several countries. Two strategies were used for data gathering: 30 in-depth interviews collected within three years (2015-2018) and the analysis of secondary sources such as company reports, local and international media coverage about the project. Managers, engineers and heads of marketing, strategy and R&D departments within the companies have been interviewed. Questions were divided into the following themes: 1) general questions about the project, activities developed and actors' motivations for the development of a smart city solution and; 2) specific, detailed questions about the relationship development as well as challenges and opportunities faced by companies within the interaction with social and political actors.

Case Description

The city in which the smart city project has been developed and implemented is located in Brazil. The country deserves a brief overall description from a social and economic perspective. In 2012, the Brazilian economy was steadily growing. An emerging middle class was expanding its domestic consumption, and this attracted new foreign direct investment (FDI). With a population of over 200 million inhabitants, the Brazilian market provides great business opportunities. Brazil's economic and social progress between 2003 and 2014 raised 29 million people out of poverty. The income level of the poorest 40 percent of the population rose on average by 7.1 percent (in real terms) between 2003 and 2014, compared to a 4.4 percent income growth for the population as a whole (World Bank, 2017). Despite the positive Brazilian context, unexpected economic, social, and political changes have impacted the Brazilian economy in recent years (2014-2017). Recent political election (2018) seems to have a potential to put the country back to economic progress, mainly because the new president has promised political reforms and investment in urban development. His aim is to improve cities infrastructure and make cities more inclusive. Brazil has 5500 municipalities and technologies helping the local government to better allocate resources can be a source of business opportunities for companies from the ICT industry. Hence, in a business environment which combines both opportunities and challenges, Brazil has become an interesting market to study, primarily when observation leads to an understanding of the strategies used by firms to succeed in such an unstable market.

Aguas City Smart City Project

The main objective of the pilot project was to transform Aguas city into a digital hub with technology improving public services. The project included a range of applications such as smart parking, smart street lightning, and e-government platforms. The major actors from the business side were Telefonica/Vivo, Ericsson, Huawei, and ISPM, as well as several local startup companies. Ericsson and Telefonica/Vivo have worked together in several projects in Brazil such as "the Amazon project" in which connectivity was implemented in rural areas and "the Buses of Curitiba" in which 3G connectivity was applied in the city's public transportation.

Huawei is a Chinese company specializing in telecommunication equipment and services, while ISPM is a Brazilian company specializing in the development of IoT platforms within 4G technologies. Other actors included the city mayor, public officials, and two NGOs, Vanzolini Foundation and Telefonica Foundation. Telefonica/Vivo initially invested over 560,000 US dollars in the project in 2015, after making a proposal to the city mayor to expand technological solutions aligned with the city's social needs. There was no financial investment by the city, but the companies received permission to use the city as a lab for their technology as well as to demonstrate the technology being used in a real city context. With approximately 3300 inhabitants (IBGE, 2016) and a high level on the human development index, the city was chosen due to its small size and low level of required investment by companies. For the Telefonica/ Vivo's partners, investment was also made in equipment, labor force, and training. The estimated total investment in this project was around 4 to 5 million US dollars. Telefonica/Vivo's team was formed by 15-20 people consisting of technicians, developers, managers, etc. to give support to both the city and the business partners. Although the technology had previously been developed by the firms, it required adjustment for the city context. The tourism secretary was interested in the smart parking solution, because the city doubles in population during weekends since it is famous for its waters used for hydrotherapic purpose.

In the project, Ericsson was responsible for the smart parking and smart street lighting solutions while Huawei was responsible for smart security with surveillance cameras installed in the city. Additionally, ISPM was in charge of integrating all services into its IoT platform. The company developed digital application solutions in the health service, such as a service to schedule appointments and remote monitoring of clinical symptoms of patients via the web. Moreover, two apps were developed which enable more direct engagement between citizens and the local government. In the education area, Telefonica/Vivo donated 410 netbooks and tablets to students in the city's public schools and developed an education digital platform. The service allows access to digital content (e.g., books, videos, and news). As part of the project, the Telefonica Foundation and Vanzolini Foundation together have trained school teachers to use the new interactive platform.

Project Outcome: The project was successfully implemented in 2015, benefiting the citizens of Aguas and improving public services as well as citizen satisfaction. The project received substantial local media coverage and also received international visibility among the entrepreneurial community with recognition as being an innovative project by TM Catalyst Forum.

CASE ANALYSIS

In this project the cross-sector partnership emerged with a clear objective of creating new business opportunities. By showing integrated solutions for a smart city the idea was to create a smart city concept. The main point was to show the technology functioning in a real city setting while helping firms to sell the solution to several mayors in Brazil and then also to expand in the Latin America region. The project was an initiative that came from Telefonica/Vivo and as a project leader it coordinated activities between business and nonbusiness actors.

In the process of developing and implementing the technology companies faced opportunities and challenges. Interviews indicate that business opportunities were created not only in the city that the project was developed but also in other cities in Brazil. In addition to that, knowledge was developed about the local context and companies also learnt the needs of the city and worked to adjust the technology, companies also learnt how to develop relationships with the local government, etc. This observation is in line with Håkansson and Snehota (2006) who claim that in a network reasoning there are always a way of learning something new and a particular way of combining resources differently.

Furthermore, companies had the opportunity to show their technology while creating brand awareness. Smart city project has become an important reference case for companies like Ericsson, Huawei and Telefonica/Vivo. They have used it in their corporate sustainability report. Furthermore, firms can also gain legitimacy by showing how technology can solve society's problems. One of the Ericsson's main corporate message is "Technology for Good" and the firm's Vice President of Latin America emphasized that *"The smart parking solution is an example of what we can do in the future, especially at Aguas de São Pedro, the first smart city in Brazil."*

In the same line, Huawei's senior manager's stressed that *"showing the technology functioning in practice in a city would create business opportunities and demonstrate that we could deliver such a solution to any city in the world"*. For him, it is much easier to convince a client when it is possible to show how things function in practice, i.e., shows how to solve a city problem. He claimed that the pilot project has generated several new business opportunities - around 20 different municipalities, i.e., mayors have shown interest and the deals are in the process of negotiation. The head of marketing and strategic department at Ericsson has a similar view and he also explained the importance of such projects. He claimed that a smart city case initiatives like the one developed in Brazil is good to increase their visibility in the local market and get public attention. He mentioned that *"A pilot project is very important to show up. If it is a successful story it generates confidence to the market and to the government eyes"*. This statement exemplifies what Hadijikhani and Thilenius (2005) highlight about the differences between business-to-business relationships in comparison to business with nonbusiness actors. In accordance with them, it is clear that knowledge created in this project is not only about technological development or adaptation but also it is related to knowing what the government would be interested in. Hence, success in this type of partnership is intrinsically linked to adjust the technology to meet the political and social objectives.

For the President of Telefonica/Vivo *'the pilot project serves as a laboratory for the creation of public-private partnerships (PPPs) mainly for the implementation of technology in more populated municipalities'*. The project included a range of applications called by companies as – but not limited to – smart parking, smart street lightning, digitized education and e-government platforms. But an interesting aspect is that, despite the innovative idea, Telefonica/Vivo had a hard time to be understood (see Table 1). When presenting the project, Telefonica/Vivo' managers asked how they could help the city with technology. The tourism secretary was one of the few who understood and liked the idea. He mentioned that the lack of understanding about such type of new technology, especially in small municipalities in Brazil is an issue since the body of the city hall is not formed by technicians but by people who only care about politics. He said that: *"Some of them are illiterate in respect to technology. In this first contact with the companies it was really funny. The companies asked all secretaries, including me, how they could help us with the city's problems through technologies. Some of the secretaries asked for more ambulances for example. They did not understand the project as such; they did not know how the technology could help them"*.

For Huawei managers, the main challenge was to make the public officials to use the technology. They have installed 15 surveillance cameras that could improve the city security. But, Huawei's managers faced a certain disappointment after installing the control room in the city hall. The solution manager said to the mayor: *"We gave you the technology but you need to have a team to operate it but the mayor said we do not know who can do that. After that we at Huawei realized that it was necessary to educate people how to monitor the city trough the cameras"*. It seems a common sense but gradually both the city as well as the managers began to learn together this whole dynamic highlighted the Huawei's managers. It was clear that interactions among actors were challenging and the implementation was a learning process according to the solution manager at Huawei. Another difficulty Huawei faced was the city context. He affirmed that: *"We didn't have the practical experience in cities. For example, it is easy to define places where the cameras could be installed but we did not think about a camera above the city bus terminal which required electricity and connectivity."*

In the project, the tourist secretary was an important partner for the companies. He became the co-ordinator from the city side and was interested in the potential visibility that the project would bring to the city. Committed to the project idea, he started facilitating the project development by removing some practical obstacles, such as license requirements. But he also put demands on the firms. For instance, when the companies wanted to charge for some of their services he stressed: *"You –guys – came to us proposing to use the city as a showroom for your technologies, but you forgot to measure the value of the city. We have much more to lose than you. You are "multinationals", we are a small town. If it works*

- great! both can win, but if not, you will leave while the city stays". After presenting the arguments, companies understood our rules, our values, affirmed the secretary. Once the project has been better understood from both sides the next phase was the process of implementing the technology.

It is clear that lack of understanding of the usage of the technology (see in table 1) and its applicability from the political actors was detected but misunderstandings were not only observed from the political side with respect to the technology, companies also did not understand the city hall objectives. These findings are in accordance with the Ritvala et al., (2014) research findings that stress cross sector partnership as a type of relationship that is characterized by the lack of required resources, common understanding and collaborative experience. In the project successful collaboration is related to know how to coordinate different actors and also to accommodate different goals. Thus the type of partnership observed in this smart city project requires the need for actors to find a balance between economic and social goals. This implies that company's success in projects involving socio-political actors demand knowledge and understanding about what are the interests of society as a whole and politicians as claimed by Boddewyn and Doh (2011) as well as Choi, Jia and Lu, (2014). An interesting aspect to highlight is the role of the project leader, i.e., Telefonica/Vivo. The company learned along the way how to accommodate various interests and solve clashes and misunderstands among actors during the cooperation. However, the task of coordinating different actors was complex due to the different pool of resources and actors. Put differently, coordination in projects for smart city development as the one observed in this study requires ability to make a link between the project leaders' business partners and their specific resources from one side, and socio-political actors and their local knowledge expertise from another side.

The above statement clears show what Hadjikhani et al., i (2008) highlight about the behavior of political actors. I.e., they can be supportive and/ or coercive towards companies. The tourism secretary behaved in a very supportive way by reducing the bureaucracy and facilitating the implementation of the technology. However, he was also coercive with regards to the charge of services. In such a situation, companies need to comply and accept as a means to reduce tension and to assure the success of the project.

When asked about the importance of the project for the city as well as the relationship between the private and public sector, the secretary highlighted that the cooperation has been very good. For example, "*Ericsson has helped us to reduce our electricity bill 35 percent. Bulbs send message to us when they are close to expiring*". However, there has been a negative link between Telefonica/Vivo's image in respect to the city hall image. He highlights that: "*Citizens complain that they live in a smart city but with poor connectivity at home. The bad service was perceived as a city hall's failure although it was out of our control and the scope of the project*". For the companies, they have benefited from feedback provided by both the municipality and the citizens with regards to the apps developed (see table 1). These findings are in line with the results from Coviello and Joseph (2012), as well as Kazadi et al., (2016), that show how close interaction with consumers can provide companies with new ideas. The difference in this study is that here the users of the system are the socio-political actors, who are seen as producers of new ideas and can provide companies with feedback about the technology in use and, thus, can be considered a source of competitive advantage.

DISCUSSION AND CONCLUSION

The findings show that the networks investigated in this study emerged because firms' limitation in the pursuit of complex knowledge, thus collective behavior, i.e., cooperation becomes a corner-

Table 1. Opportunities and Challenges in Cross-Sector Partnership

Actors	Opportunities	Challenges
Ericsson	*"A pilot project is very important to show up. If it is a successful story it generates confidence to the market and to the government eyes".* [The head of marketing and strategic department at Ericsson]	*"In business-to-business the relationship is for the developing of new business opportunities. The objective is more on the short run while for the business-to-government, the aim is to develop markets and therefore the target is more on the medium and long run"[Ericsson's Government Relationship Manager]*
Huawei	*"Showing the technology functioning in practice in a city would increase our market legitimacy that we could deliver such a solution to any city in the world"* [Huawei's senior manager] *"The pilot project serves as a laboratory for the creation of public-private partnerships (PPPs) mainly for the implementation of technology in more populated municipalities".* [Telefonica President]	*"We gave you the technology but you need to have a team to operate it but the mayor said we do not know who can do that. After that we at Huawei realized that it was necessary to educate people how to monitor the city trough the cameras"* [Huawei's Solution Manager]
Telefonica/ Vivo	*"At Telefonica/Vivo, we decided to work in mobility, smart lighting, education and health, in many areas where the mayor and public managers have informed they have a need"* [Telefonica/Vivo relationship manager]	Telefonica/ Vivo had a hard time to be understood. Telefonica/Vivo needed to coordinate activities among different groups and accommodate different demands and expectations.
ISPM	To gain legitimacy and be recognized by a solution provider for smart city technology [ISPM's director of innovation]	The development of two apps which enabled more direct engagement between citizens and the local government.
City Hall	*"Citizens prefer to complain directly to the city hall because they start to rely more on our response and problem solving"* [Tourism Secretary] *"Before the project not many people have heard about a small municipality such as Aguas de Sao Pedro, our city is now known by this interesting project"*	*"You –guys – came to us proposing to use the city as a showroom for your technologies, but you forgot to measure the value of the city. We have much more to lose than you. You are "multinationals", we are a small town. If it works - great! both can win, but if not, you will leave while the city stays".* *"Some of them are illiterate in respect to technology. In this first contact with the companies it was really funny. The companies asked all secretaries, including me, how they could help us with the city's problems trough technologies. Some of the secretaries asked for more ambulances for example. They did not understand the project as such; they did not know how the technology could help them"* [Tourism secretary]
Non-Profit	Training school teacher has helped Telefonica Foundation to create a communication channel between teachers and the municipality [Telefonica Foundation's Relationship Manager]	Telefonica Foundation has also reduced conflicts and even punishment from regulators to the Telefonica Group

stone for sustaining competitiveness. The novelty, however, is that the locus of innovation is not limited to traditional business to business relationships – where marketing and business researchers center their analysis – but it can also emerge from non-business actors such as government and NGOs, mainly if public administrations become early adopters of emerging technologies such as IoT-based services. Having government as early users can help companies to speed up adoption of the technology on a broad scale (c.f. Zanella, Castellani & Vangelista, 2014). A further interesting aspect is that within IoT-based services applied to cities, local government is knowledgeable in terms of the need of the society and they can exchange ideas about the reality of the cities while helping companies to design and/or adjust their technology to meet such societal needs. However developing relationships with such important partners is not an easy task and it requires coordination to balance economic and social goals.

By studying such complex interactions, the study addresses recent calls that highlight the need to include other actors in the firm's business network as a means to explore new theoretical and empirical territories (see, for example, Ritvala et al., 2014; Thilenius et al., 2016). In addition to this, a recent criticism in the literature is that studies examining interaction between business and the public sphere are lagging behind practice (Salmi & Heikkilä, 2015; Welch & Wilkinson, 2004, Leite & Bengtson, 2018). The cooperation between actors observed in this study provides a practical perspective, by explaining how socio-political actors can be a source of competitive advantage. Examples include socio-political actors' contributions to ideas and advocating in favor of the benefits of the technology developed. An interesting observation has also been made by Hadjikhani, Lee and Park (2016) on companies' CSR activities as a strategy to address corporate citizenship. However, unlike his study where CSR is commonly linked to charity projects, this study shows firms using their core business activities to demonstrate corporate social issues. Such a perspective certainly needs further examination and requires more understanding of how companies align their core business while addressing societal complex problems such as urban development.

Limitations and Directions for Future Research

This chapter has some limitations that also offer opportunities for future research. First, it is based on one single case within the same industry and limited to the same country, Brazil. Hence, the phenomenon should be investigated through large scale empirical studies. By incorporating multiple context and case studies, it will be possible to carry out further analysis and then improve our understanding of such complex networks of partners.

An interesting aspect is that, ICT and its related IoT developments open new opportunities to connect activities, resources, and actors in business networks. ICT players, for instance, are becoming newcomers in several industries due to the digital transformation of products and services, and this will allow cross industry partnerships. For example, traditional city services such as transit and transport, security or public street lighting which are recognized as low-tech are now moving towards the integration of high-tech solutions. So a natural question arises about which actors will play a central role in bridging different industries and sectors? Will the overall competitive behavior of companies increase or decrease as cooperation across sectors or industries increases? I hope that future studies will address these interesting questions.

Managerial Implications

It was clear that the cooperation was not easily achieved. Actors faced several challenges, misunderstanding, conflicts and frictions in the relationship, but coordination helped companies to turn challenges into opportunities. Observations show that successful cooperation in this network type relies on the need to accommodate both economic and social goals. Therefore, managers need to identify the differences in values, expectations and economic logic as a means to facilitate cooperation. Understanding such differences will help managers to achieve both the firms' respective goals and expectations and the overall goals of the cooperation involving social and political actors. Thus, managers are required to cope with the challenges inherent in such type of relationships, primarily due the fact that interactions with nonbusiness actors represent a valuable intangible resource. Support from socio-political actors is essential to legitimize companies' technological know-how, increase their business legitimacy, provide them with users' knowledge related to a specific setting, and enhance companies' market positioning. As a result, the accomplishment of the cooperation goes above and beyond the benefits from simply generating immediate revenues. Consequently, knowing how to manage such relationships constitute a source of competitive advantages for firms.

DISCUSSION QUESTIONS

1. In projects for smart city development, social and political actors seem to be important partners for companies. What are the main motivations for companies to develop and nurture such a type of relationship?
2. Le Ber and Branzei (2010; p.145) affirm that cross-sector cooperation is complex and the relationship is commonly marked by constant adjustments and interrupted by temporary successes and failures. Explain what are the opportunities and benefits for companies to get involved in a cross-sector partnership? How managers should develop relationships with nonbusiness actors? Do you think that the way managers approach to companies should be similar to the way managers approach to nonbusiness actors? What would be the similarities and differences and why?
3. In order to achieve mutual goals and succeed in the implementation of smart city technologies development, actors may have their own and common goals. From a business network perspective which personal and common goals can be observed from the project developed in Aguas City?
4. Despite the overall challenges faced by all actors in the smart city project, what are the main contributors for success? How actors have benefited each other? What companies have learned in this specific partnership that can be used in other projects for smart technological application?

REFERENCES

Andersson, P., & Mattsson, L. G. (2015). Service innovations enabled by the 'internet of things'. *IMP Journal, 9*(1), 85–106. doi:10.1108/IMP-01-2015-0002

Atzori, L., Iera, A., & Morabito, G. (2010). The internet of things: A survey. *Computer Networks, 54*(15), 2787–2805. doi:10.1016/j.comnet.2010.05.010

Bhanji, Z., & Oxley, J. E. (2013). Overcoming the dual liability of foreignness and privateness in international corporate citizenship partnerships. *Journal of International Business Studies, 44*(4), 290–311. doi:10.1057/jibs.2013.8

Boddewyn, J., & Doh, J. (2011). Global strategy and the collaboration of MNEs, NGOs, and governments for the provisioning of collective goods in emerging markets. *Global Strategy Journal, 1*(3-4), 345–361. doi:10.1002/gsj.26

Caragliu, A., Del Bo, C., & Nijkamp, P. (2011). Smart cities in Europe. *Journal of Urban Technology, 18*(2), 65–82. doi:10.1080/10630732.2011.601117

Choi, S. J., Jia, N., & Lu, J. (2014). The structure of political institutions and effectiveness of corporate political lobbying. *Organization Science, 26*(1), 158–179.

Ghauri, P., Hadjikhani, A., & Elg, U. (2012). The three pillars: Business, state and society: MNCs in emerging markets. In Business, Society and Politics (pp. 3-16). Emerald Group Publishing Limited.

Ghauri, P. N., & Grønhaug, K. (2005). *Research methods in business studies: A practical guide*. Pearson Education.

Hadjikhani, A., Lee, J. W., & Ghauri, P. N. (2008). Network view of MNCs' sociopolitical behavior. *Journal of Business Research*, *61*(9), 912–924. doi:10.1016/j.jbusres.2007.10.001

Hadjikhani, A., & Thilenius, P. (2005). 'The impact of horizontal and vertical connections on relationships' commitment and trust'. *Journal of Business and Industrial Marketing*, *20*(3), 136–147. doi:10.1108/08858620510592759

Hadjikhani, A., Leite, E., & Pahlberg, C. (2019). Business and Socio-Political Interaction in International Service Projects: The Case of Brazil. *Management International Review*, *59*(1), 171–200. doi:10.100711575-018-0368-9

Hadjikhani, A., Lee, J. W., & Park, S. (2016). Corporate social responsibility as a marketing strategy in foreign markets: The case of Korean MNCs in the Chinese electronics market. *International Marketing Review*, *33*(4), 530–554. doi:10.1108/IMR-03-2014-0104

Håkansson, H., & Snehota, I. (1995). *Developing relationships in business networks*. Academic Press.

Håkansson, H., & Snehota, I. (2006). "No business is an island" 17 years later. *Scandinavian Journal of Management*, *22*(3), 271–274. doi:10.1016/j.scaman.2006.08.001

IBGE. (2016). *Aguas de Sao Pedro*. Retrieved May 8, 2019, from https://cidades.ibge.gov.br/brasil/sp/aguas-de-sao-pedro/panorama

Kazadi, K., Lievens, A., & Mahr, D. (2016). Stakeholder co-creation during the innovation process: Identifying capabilities for knowledge creation among multiple stakeholders. *Journal of Business Research*, *69*(2), 525–540. doi:10.1016/j.jbusres.2015.05.009

Le Ber, M. J., & Branzei, O. (2010). Value frame fusion in cross sector interactions. *Journal of Business Ethics*, *94*(S1), 163–195. doi:10.100710551-011-0785-1

Leite, E., & Bengtson, A. (2018). A business network view on value creation and capture in public-private cooperation. *Industrial Marketing Management*, *73*, 181–192. doi:10.1016/j.indmarman.2018.02.010

Mahoney, J. T., McGahan, A. M., & Pitelis, C. (2009). Perspective-the interdependence of private and public interests. *Organization Science*, *20*(6), 1034–1052. doi:10.1287/orsc.1090.0472

Ritvala, T., Salmi, A., & Andersson, P. (2014). MNCs and local cross-sector partnerships: The case of a smarter Baltic Sea. *International Business Review*, *23*(5), 942–951. doi:10.1016/j.ibusrev.2014.02.006

Salmi, A., & Heikkilä, K. (2015). Managing relationships with public officials—A case of foreign MNCs in Russia. *Industrial Marketing Management*, *49*, 22–31. doi:10.1016/j.indmarman.2015.05.026

Welch, C., & Wilkinson, I. (2004). The political embeddedness of international business networks. *International Marketing Review*, *21*(2), 216–231. doi:10.1108/02651330410531411

World Bank. (2017). *Global Outlook – A fragile recovery*. Retrieved March 8, 2019, from http://pubdocs. worldbank.org/en/216941493655495719/Global-Economic-Prospects-June-2017-Global-Outlook.pdf

Yin, R. K. (2017). *Case study research and applications: Design and methods*. Sage Publications.

UNCTAD. (2014). *Findings on Services, Development and Trade*. Retrieved March, 29, from http://unctad.org/en/pages /PublicationWebflyer.aspx?publicationid=549

Zanella, A., Bui, N., Castellani, A., Vangelista, L., & Zorzi, M. (2014). Internet of things for smart cities. *Internet of Things Journal, IEEE, 1*(1), 22–32. doi:10.1109/JIOT.2014.2306328

Chapter 12

Adoption and Use of Human Information System Digital Technology for Organizational Competitiveness:
An Exploratory Study in the Context of Nepal

Alamuri Surya Narayana
Osmania University, India

Roshee Lamichhane Bhusal
Kathmandu University, Nepal

ABSTRACT

Staying competitive in the current digitized workplace era requires, among other things, an adequate and efficient use of modern technology. Human resource information system (HRIS) is one of several tools that helps organizations remain sustainable by providing technology that can help to acquire, store, generate, analyze, and disseminate timely and accurate employee information and activities. Of late, HRIS is slowly gaining prominence in Nepal. A generic model for conditions that are necessary for successful adoption and use of HRIS in Nepali organizations is designed as the models proposed by earlier researchers in a developed context may not work well in a developing context. This sets fertile ground to carry out scholarly inquiry into the domain of HRIS in the Nepalese context. The limitations of present study are mentioned and practical/research implications of the same are discussed towards the end. Researchers are of the opinion that the findings of this preliminary study can be taken up to the next level for carrying out quantitative research in HRIS domain in Nepal.

DOI: 10.4018/978-1-5225-8933-4.ch012

INTRODUCTION

An adequate and efficient use of technology, *inter alia*, is a *sine qua non* to stay competitive in the current workplace of digitized era. Human Resource Information System (HRIS) is one of the several tools that helps modern organizations remain competitive by providing technology that can help to acquire, store, generate, analyze, and disseminate timely and accurate employee information. HRIS is an intersection of human processes and technology through a HR software solution that allows electronic processing of HR processes and activities (Gupta, 2013). In similar lines, Anitha and Aruna (2013) state that HRIS provides a pool of information systems that integrate different HR processes for business excellence. In organizations that have adopted Information Technology, HRIS has invariably become an essential part of it as it helps organizations in carrying out their HRM functions efficiently. HRIS has now become an integral part of organization information management along with the development of computer and database network techniques (Jie, 2014). Research report published by Sage People (2017) found that though 83% of global HR leaders agree that all people decisions should be based on data and analytics, only 37% are actually using them. For instance, HRIS has *not* been implemented in Pakistani health sector owing to multitude of factors ranging from infrastructure, lack of expertise, low budget, and lack of maintenance (Kumar et. al. 2013).

Earlier research studies suggest that adoption of HRIS and its use has not been fully functional in majority of organizations globally and we can surmise a similar situation in Nepal as well. However, of late, **HRIS** is slowly gaining prominence in Nepal. It was implemented in some nascent form since early 90s by mid to large-sized firms largely due to individual, organizational, environmental, and technological factors. Last decade has witnessed virtually a HRIS wave in a majority of Nepali organizations. However, adoption of an Integrated HRIS in Nepal is an exception rather than a reality. Further, there is wide gap between the intended and actual use of HRIS demanding an inquiry into factors that affect successful adoption of HRIS. There is no precise data on the number of organizations using HRIS or IT enabled HR systems in Nepal despite the fact that the use of HRIS is increasing even more rapidly in the last five years compared to the earlier decades. Use of HRIS is found to be more in banking sector followed by other sectors such as Private, MNCs, Development, and Public. Among total number of businesses, only 250-300 organizations have HRIS in place. This information can be supported by the fact that there are already 12-15 major developers of HR software in Nepal. Each of them has some 15-20 clients as listed in their websites on an average and the cumulative number totals to 250-300.

In the global context also, literature on HRIS has remained limited. Though researchers have focused mostly on the barriers and conditions for successful adoption, the findings cannot be generalized for all sectors and contexts. Additionally, the models proposed by previous researchers in a developed context may not work well in a developing context. This aptly sets a fertile ground to carry out scholarly inquiry into the domain of HRIS in the context of Nepal. For the present research, information was elicited through interviews with 18 key informants working for MNCs, Government, and Private sector representing education and development domains. After the coding process, different HRIS themes emerged and they were further grouped to form sub-themes. The overarching goal of this study is to develop an initial understanding of HRIS in Nepal and its current usage status. After exploring the dynamics and various dimensions of HRIS domain, a Generic Model for conditions that are necessary for successful adoption and use of HRIS in Nepali organizations is designed. It is believed that the models proposed by previous researchers in a developed context may not work well in a developing context.

This sets fertile ground to carry out scholarly inquiry into the domain of HRIS in the context of Nepal. This exploratory study could uncover not only the conditions necessary for successful adoption and implementation of HRIS but also the factors that pose as stumbling blocks in the process. The limitations of the present study are mentioned and practical/research implications of the same are discussed towards the end. The researchers are of the opinion that the findings of this preliminary study can be taken up to the next level for carrying out quantitative research in HRIS domain in the context of Nepal.

LITERATURE REVIEW

Modern HRIS includes a comprehensive set of Human Resource functions in organizations including transaction processing, communication systems, decision support systems, and some elements of Artificial Intelligence (AI). A number of researchers have traced the evolution of HRIS. An attempt is made now to present an elaborate literature currently available in the area of HRIS. It provides a multitude of definitions on HRIS and offers explanations of different concepts and constructs that are related to the domain of HRIS. It also explores several research studies carried out on the barriers and factors aiding successful adoption and use of HRIS.

The definition of Human Resource Information System (HRIS) seems to have evolved with the advancement of technology. HRIS has increasingly transformed since its introduction in General Electric in the 1950s (Shiri, 2012). DeSanctis (1986) contends that HRIS is a system that is designed to support the planning, administration, decision making, and control of Human Resource Management. In similar lines, Kovach and Cathcart, Jr (1999) defined HRIS as a systematic procedure for collecting, storing, maintaining, retrieving, and validating data needed by an organization about its human resources, personnel activities, and organization unit characteristics. They believed that HRIS need not be complex or be computerized. Likewise, Hendrickson (2002) defined HRIS as "an integrated system used to gather, store and analyze information regarding an organizations' human resource." This definition also includes people, policies, processes, and procedures, along with the technical part of the system.

However, with the advancement in IT, the early conceptualization of HRIS has undergone some changes. While the earlier definition focused on the operational side of HR, latest definition of HRIS has focused on the strategic role of HRIS. Bedell (2003) put forward that modern HRIS has been designed to assist HR professionals in all areas of his/her job ranging from performing administrative tasks to making high level decisions governing the future direction of an organization. He defined HRIS system as a software application that stores employee, applicant, and other "people-related data" so that HR professionals can make accurate and timely decisions. In similar lines, Shani and Tesone (2010) noted that by saving time on the operational issues of the employees, HRIS allows employees to focus on strategic planning and implementation. Iwu and Benedict (2013) stated that HRIS is part of organizations' strategic philosophy. Modern HRIS includes comprehensive set of Human Resource functions in organizations which includes transaction processing, communication systems, decision support systems, and some elements of artificial intelligence (Weeks, 2013). A number of researchers have traced the evolution of HRIS. For example, Johnson, Lukaszewski, and Stone (2016) reviewed the professional and academic development of HRIS to assess its progress. They examined the interplay between HR and IT though four areas of technology, namely, mainframe, client server, ERP, and web-based systems.

It can be observed that with the transformation of HR function from administrative to function with strategic value, role of HRIS has widened (Bedell, 2003). Current organizations are using web based system or corporate intranet as top cost cutting strategy to utilize HRIS (Weeks, 2013). Thite, Kavanagh, and Johnson (2009) contend that HRIS has come due to focus of HR from transactional to transformational activities. They argue that HRIS now includes applications in large scale integrated ERP architecture or web based applications.

e-HRM and HRIS

Electronic HRM or e-HRM reflects a philosophy for the delivery of HR; it uses information technology, particularly the web, as the central component of delivering efficient and effective HR services (Kavanagh, Thite, & Johnson, 2015). In similar lines, Strohmeier (2006) defined e-HRM as the planning, implementation and application of information technology for both networking and supporting at least two individuals and collective actors in their shared performing of HR functions. Thus, e-HRM improves service delivery by speeding up transaction processing, reducing information errors, and tracking and control of HR actions (Hall, & Moritz, as cited in Bondarouk, Ruel, & Heijden, 2009). "Though they may look similar but they are different as organizations embracing e-HRM approach don't simply utilize technology in the support of human resources but instead see technology as enabling the HR function to be done differently by modifying "information flows, social interaction patterns, and communication processes" (Stone, & Lukaszewski, as cited in Kavanagh, Thite, & Johnson, 2015). One the other hand, Kavanagh, Thite, and Johnson (2015) point out that HRIS comprises the technology and processes underlying this new way of conducting Human Resource Management.

Studies About Barriers for Adoption and Implementation

A number of researches on HRIS have focused on the barriers for adoption and implementation suggesting that these barriers or constraints are context specific. Rahman, Islam, and Qi (2017) found that high investment, costly maintenance, long term benefits, organizational culture, structure, top management support, lack of experts and users as some of the financial, management and organizational related barriers for adoption of HRIS in Bangladeshi garment industry. Rahman, Qi and Jinnah (2016) found that social influence lead to behavioral intention that eventually influenced the adoption of HRIS in Bangladeshi bank and finance sector. In a similar manner, management reluctance, employee privacy issues, organizational internal resistance, and conversion cost were some of the factors that influenced the implementation (Ferdous, Chowdhury, & Bhuiyan, 2015).

In contrast, Al-Mobaideen, Allahawiah, and Basioni (2012) found that IT infrastructures significantly determined HRIS adoption in Jordon. Similarly, Altarawneh, and Al-Shqairat (2010) found that insufficient financial support, difficulty in changing organizational culture, and lack of commitment from top managers were the major HRIS implementation barriers. Likewise, in a study of Kenyen Universities, lack of skilled staff, high set up and maintenance cost, and resistance to change were cited as some of the challenges to HRIS implementation (Kananu, & Nyakego, 2016). In similar light, Ferdous, Chowdhury, and Bhuiyan (2015) found management reluctance, employee privacy issues, organizational internal resistance, and conversion cost are some of the potential barriers that impedes implementation of HRIS in Bangladesh. David, Shukla and Gupta (2015) found inadequate knowledge, lack of expertise, lack of cooperation, network problem, and technical issues are barriers to HRIS implementation.

In another educational context, it was found that lack of commitment of top management, inadequate knowledge and lack of expertise in IT, unavailability of suitable HRIS software, fear of changing the way people do things, difficulty in changing the organizational culture, insufficient financial support, and lack of commitment and involvement by employees were the barriers to HRIS usage (Bamel, Bamel, Sahay, & Thite, 2014). Now, most of the barriers as found in different researches can be classified as individual, organizational, environmental, and technological barriers.

Research Studied on Factors for Successful Adoption and Use of HRIS

Despite the fact that adoption of HRIS is important for smooth functioning of organization, it has remained an under- researched phenomenon (Troshani, Jerram, & Gerrard, 2010). A number of factors in the individual, organizational, environmental, and technological aspects affect the successful adoption of HRIS.

For example, Troshani, Jerram, and Hill (2011) found environmental context (regulations, successful adoptions), organizational context (technology competency, management commitment, organization size, and degree of centralization), and technology context (perceived benefit cost and organization fit) as some of the factors influencing the public-sector adoption of HRIS in Australia.

Likewise, relative advantage, compatibility, complexity, visibility and trialability are some of the factors that determine the extent of use of HRIS (Kassim, Ramayah, & Kurnia, 2012). Anitha and Aruna (2013) revealed that technological factors (making technology operational, potential benefits of technology, organization adoption capacity), organizational factors (degree of centralization, information technology infrastructure, financial resources, competitiveness), environmental factors (competitive capability, cost saving limited resources, external resources), and psychological resources (user perception and intention, user satisfaction) as some of the conditions for adoption of HRIS. In similar light, Chakraborty and Mansor (2013) found that organizational factors (top management support, HRIS expertise, degree of centralization), technological factors (organization technology infrastructure, IT, Human Resources, organization fit, adoption cost, complexity or user friendliness, efficiency), environmental factors (industry characteristics, governmental regulation, and supporting infrastructure) determine adoption of HRIS. Haines and Petit (1997) found that individual characteristics (understanding of hardware, software and programming), organizational characteristics (size of organization and HR department), and nature of system are conditions for successful adoption of HRIS. All these researches point out the fact that whatever is the context of HRIS adoption and use, the facilitating conditions relate to factors relating to the individual, organization, technology and environment.

STATEMENT OF THE PROBLEM

Given the backdrop provided in the Introduction section, the basic research questions this study intends to explore in the context of Nepali Organizations are:

1. What is the current status of *adoption and use* of HRIS and the key HR functions for which it is used? What is the general understanding of HRIS among Nepali HR professionals?
2. What are the barriers/constraints in and facilitating conditions for the *adoption and use* of HRIS?

OBJECTIVES OF THE STUDY

While the overarching goal of this study is to develop an initial understanding of HRIS in Nepal and its current usage status, it also aims to delve into issues related to constraints and factors for successful adoption and use of HRIS. *More specifically this research aims:*

1. To gain insights about HRIS use and its adoption status in Nepal and generate understanding of the same through practicing HR professionals.
2. To understand the factors that pose as barriers in the adoption and use of HRIS.
3. To understand the facilitating conditions for successful adoption and use of HRIS.
4. To explore the dynamics and dimensions of HRIS domain and design a Generic Model for conditions that are necessary for successful adoption and use of HRIS in Nepali organizations

SIGNIFICANCE OF THE STUDY

The findings of the study have both theoretical and practical implications. On the theoretical side, it has the potential to add to the domain knowledge of HRIS besides filling in the research gap by identifying factors that lead to successful adoption and use of HRIS in the Nepali organizations. Organizations intending to adopt HRIS come to know about the required measures to be kept in mind before using it effectively. For the academicians, benefits lie in home grown knowledge about factors leading to successful adoption.

It becomes the initial reference point for researchers and scholars for pursuing further quantitative researches by setting the tone on the existing condition of HRIS and its current usage status. Information about the barriers and conditions for its adoption can be used for subsequent empirical research and also by HR practitioners.

RESEARCH METHODOLOGY

There is no single published or unpublished qualitative or quantitative research in the domain of HRIS conducted in Nepal. This has called for an exploratory research for inquiry into its nature, current adoption status, usage, barriers and conditions for successful adoption. Researcher aims to explore the dynamics and dimensions of HRIS in the context of Nepal through qualitative research.

Research Approach

Whenever the nature of inquiry into a given subject matter is exploratory, qualitative research is generally suggested and the proposed research gets rooted into subjective Ontology, interpretive Epistemology, and Grounded Theory for the purpose of data collection. Given the nature of the study which requires exploration of the existing conditions and usage of HRIS, Grounded Theory approach of research was deemed fit. This approach is suitable for this study as Grounded Theory helps in developing inductive theories that are grounded in systematically gathered and analyzed data (Bitsch, 2005). Furthermore, as stated by Myers (2013), Grounded Theory method also helps in systematically gathering and analyzing real world data that is close to the phenomenon under study. Under the Grounded Theory technique, multiple rounds of interviews were taken to ensure adequate data is generated to a point where no evidence is generated and reaches a state of "category saturation". This is a primary means of verification in Grounded Theory (Strauss & Corbin, 1998 as cited in Suddaby, 2006). Since Grounded Theory allows systematic and detailed analysis of data and allows researchers to analyze data from the early stage (Myers, 2013), this was considered the best way for getting immersed into the domain of inquiry.

Research Design

Under the Grounded Theory approach, semi-structured in-depth interviews with key informants are collected. Semi-structured interview is chosen as it provides the required flexibility (Myers, & Newmann, 2007). In-depth interviews are taken with the HR Managers and Professionals to unearth issues related to the conditions of HRIS usage and successful conditions for adoption and usage. Given the nature of HRIS, this method is appropriate as their adoption and use can be better understood from the perspectives of the users of such systems, consisting of HR managers and professionals. Using grounded theory approach, this study has explored themes that posed as barriers and conditions for successful adoption and use of HRIS. This can be developed into a model to depict conditions for successful adoption of HRIS. Based on interactions and discussions and with key representatives of HR and four key representatives of HR, including a software developer, organizations having a minimum 200 employees within Kathmandu valley that adopted HRIS or are in the process of adoption are considered. It is ensured that all informants are knowledgeable about HRIS and its adoption status or at least are influential in arranging the interview with the key informants useful for the study.

Population and Sample Selection

Based on the preliminary discussions with the personnel concerned in the HR industry, the prospective informants are identified. Additional respondents are decided based on *snow ball technique* where one respondent also refers other prospective respondents.

Data Collection

Once the interviews are taken, data is transcribed and open coding is done. Open coding is the first stage of qualitative data analysis (Myers, 2013). Data collection and data generation for production of qualitative information primarily relies on the method adopted for data analysis. Semi-structured interviews are utilized as technique to gather information about the current usage status of HRIS, barriers for adoption, and conditions for successful adoption and use.

Interviews

For the purpose of data transcribing, the number of respondents is 18. However, two respondents each from two organizations are considered as one respondent apiece as the responses obtained from them for that particular organization are similar.

Transcribing

Interview data collected are transcribed through the help of audio and researchers note. Attempt is made to produce a verbatim account with sincerity to the original language and also maintain the flow of information while transcribing.

Data Analysis

Once all the interviews are compiled, themes and sub- themes are generated. Since grounded theory follows iterative process, data collection and analysis is done till the point where any additional data stopped generating any new themes or categories.

RESULTS

Results derived from the Grounded Theory approach are presented here. As per the grounded theory methodology, the demographic profiles of the participants and background of the organizations have been presented. Then with the help of coding process and method of constant comparison, themes and sub-themes and categories generated during the data analysis have been presented. Themes for each case have been mentioned separately.

Contextual Analysis

Characteristics of each of the participants and their organizations are analyzed to find out the contextual and situational relevance of the research. This information mainly has come through the predesigned fact sheet.

Participant Characteristics

All the 18 participants chosen for the study, of which six are female, belong to different age groups, educational backgrounds, and know-how on the subject matter. Their ages varied from 29 to 57 years. Two have Bachelor's and all others have Masters Degrees with a minimum of 3 and a maximum of 25 years experience. All have been working in their current organizations for more than a year and are aware of HRIS, its requirements, necessary conditions, and have been involved in its implementation. General Profiles of all the 18 Participants are provided at **APPENDIX-I** at the end. An overview of the participant's characteristics is captured in the form of a Summary of Demographic Profile of Participants at **APPENDIX-II.**

Organization Characteristics

The selected organizations for this study ranged from private, government, development, educational, and MNC sectors having their HRIS at different stages of its adoption—nascent stage to full scale. They also differ in terms of their investment appetite for procuring HRIS related software. All the organizations have a minimum of 150 and a maximum of 2500 staff members. Majority of the organizations procured software from local vendors while one or two used software from Indian vendors.

Important characteristics of the participants' organizations are captured in the form of in a summary form under the heading 'Profiles of Participants' Organizations' at APPENDIX-III.

Initial Coding of Interviews and Grouping

The initial coding of interviews and grouping them according to different cases helped in identifying the major sub-themes related to current adoption status, barriers for adoption and use, and conditions for successful adoption and use. It can be fairly surmised that when barriers for adoption and use are removed, it leads to facilitating conditions for successful adoption and use. The same are grouped under three categories viz., individual, organizational, environmental, and technological factors as identified through discussions with the people concerned. Interviews with all the participants (Case I to XVIII) are analyzed by dividing them into three basic themes, namely, (i) current adoption status, (ii) barriers for adoption and usage, and (iii) conditions for successful adoption and usage. The samples of groupings, coding, and sub-themes generated from interviews with the participants (Case I to XVIII) have been included in **APPENDIX-IV**. Finally, the summary of Findings is captured in the form of a Generic Model for Successful Adoption and Use of HRIS in Nepali organizations and is shown in **Figure-I** at the end of the Chapter.

Through this exploratory study in the domain of HRIS in Nepal involving in-depth interviews with the HR professionals, researchers intend to discuss about the findings obtained in the light of existing literature and presents the practical/research implications, limitations of the study, and a critique there of. An increase in organization's size and capabilities as well as advancements made in IT are making it imperative for organizations to migrate to automated HR systems and processes for better organizational productivity and efficacy. Even Governmental regulatory mechanisms and legal provisions under the Labor Act have mandated that the employees be duly compensated and provided with benefits. Tracking of employee's personal records, their compensation, and benefits is bound to become cumbersome in the absence of an automated system making the use of HRIS limited only to operational purposes than for strategic uses.

HRIS in Nepali Organizations

First, the answers derived from interviews were coded and sub-themes were generated for each interview. After analyzing the findings of each interview, major themes were derived. These major themes have been categorized as individual, organizational, environmental and technological factors. These are discussed in detail below.

Individual Factors Influencing Adoption of HRIS

Majority of the participants believed that '*attitude*' holds the key in the adoption of HRIS.

Attitude is needed along with the technical expertise and experience of the HR professionals for effective implementation and use. Fortunately current well-educated and informed employees are more open for experimentation and risk taking with new systems and are aware of the benefits of software.

Organizational Factors Influencing Adoption of HRIS

Top management's non-ambivalent support in terms of the needed investment for enabling infrastructure such as cell phones and other hand-held devices for employees in the field and commitment for implementation is crucial. As long as the acquired software gives returns, cost ceases to be an issue for management. While Training and Development opportunities facilitate better adoption, the technical role of IT department in adoption of software and liaising with software vendors on a continuous basis can't be overemphasized.

Environmental Factors Influencing Adoption of HRIS

One of the compelling factors for adoption of HRIS is the imperative of complying with a plethora of recent governmental regulatory and legal provisions. The current fierce competition among the software vendors is undoubtedly beneficial to organizations as it helps in acquiring most economical and quality software along with more knowledgeable HR Software developers. As against cumbersome and costly manual systems, any HRIS adopted in large-sized firms is always hassle-free and cost effective in the long-run. However, organizations need to provide enabling IT infrastructure that is handy for employees travelling to remotest places. There is always a risk in adopting free or cheap pirated software and firms have to go for customized solutions offering the most critical *after sales support* especially when HR professional do not have the requisite knowledge of the software.

Technological Factors Influencing Adoption of HRIS

It is no denying the fact that IT infrastructure has to be simple to understand, user-friendly, and robust to support the software and to facilitate easier and better HRIS adoption. Systems should be safe, secure, and free from privacy concerns maintaining end-to-end data about the employees

Findings of the study are similar to those from earlier studies. Under the organizational factors, top management from pre-entry to post-exit stages. Implementation of the software on online platforms or even in handheld devices requires reliable technology as some HRIS software is available as mobile applications.

SUMMARY, DISCUSSION, AND IMPLICATIONS

Discussion

Top management support and commitment have been identified as key factors in influencing adoption of HRIS which was similar to the findings by (Ahmer, 2013; Chakraborty, & Mansor, 2013; Troshani, Jerram, & Gerrard, 2010) and contradictory to the findings by Al-Mobaideen, Allahawiah, & Basioni, 2013. Similarly, under the environmental factors, competition and governmental regulation were identified as factors influencing the adoption of HRIS. These findings were similar to the findings by (Anitha, & Aruna, 2013; Chakraborty, & Mansor, 2013). Likewise, under the technological factors, technology infrastructure or state of technology use were found to be affecting the adoption of HRIS which was similar to the finding by (Chakraborty, & Mansor, 2013). It was also found that HRIS currently has been used for operational purpose than strategic one. Hence, the better use of HRIS needs to incorporate strategic aspects in the days to come such as succession planning, competency mapping, linking their appraisal with training need assessment. This requires knowledgeable HR professionals, provision of technology and skilled HR software vendors who can understand the needs of clients better and serve them accordingly.

Practical Implications

First, the findings of the research can be used by practitioners to suggest their management in adoption of software. Second, they can understand and realize the importance of creating necessary infrastructure for adoption and prepare beforehand. Third, this research will help HR practitioner to understand the relevance of HRIS in our Nepali organization by following the home-grown models and identify factors for successful adoption. Findings from the research have practical implications for those in education to share the home-grown model on adoption of HRIS.

Research Implications

This research adds value to the existing domain of knowledge on HRIS by providing a home-grown model for adoption of HRIS. Digging into issues related to adoption requires exploratory studies especially in the developing nations' context (Zikmund, Babin, Carr, & Griffin, as cited in Rahman, Qi, & Jinnah, 2013) for which the method adopted for this study is justifiable. Additionally, this research now allows for further quantitative study in the area of HRIS in the Nepali organizations.

Critiquing of the Study

Researcher, through this exploratory study, aimed to investigate the factors that influence successful adoption and use of HRIS in Nepal. The individual perceptions and judgments of the informant-HR professionals are bound to influence the answers. The environment, context, and timing of the study might also have impacted on the participants interviewed. The fact that the setting for interviews is their offices also might have restricted them to be very open about the systems, processes, and barriers in adoption. Samples for the study represent people with diverse backgrounds and hence the viewpoints are expected to be distinctly different. Approachability is the yardstick for targeting and selecting respondents initially on a convenience basis while the remaining ones are referred ones by the participants themselves causing selection bias on the part of researcher.

DISCUSSION QUESTIONS

1. Several new and emerging technologies can help improve the effectiveness of the HRM function. In this context, discuss the role and importance of Human Resources Information System.
2. How might HRIS be useful for recruitment? Training and Development? For payroll? For Benefits Administration? For Performance Management?
3. Do you think it is easier to tie HRIS to the Strategic HRM Process in a large or small organization? Why?

Figure 1. Conceptual and generic model for successful adoption and use of HRIS

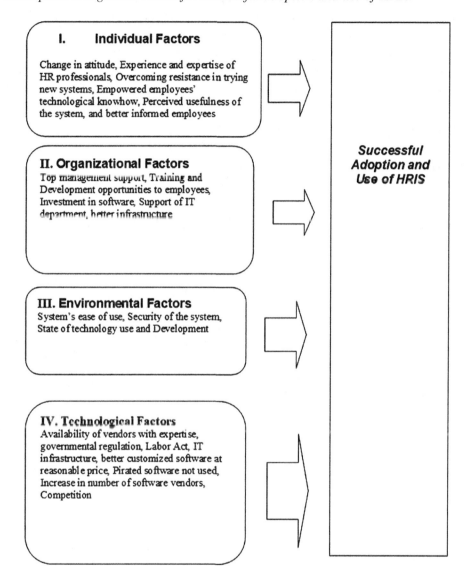

4. Restructuring the internal HRM function and redesigning the processes represent internal approaches to improving HRM effectiveness. In this backdrop, why and how do HR executives seek to improve the effectiveness of the systems, processes, and services HR function delivers through "Outsourcing"?

5. Employees in your company currently choose and enroll in benefits programs after reading communications brochures, completing enrollment forms, and sending them their HR representative. A temporary staff has to be hired to process the large amount of paperwork that is generated. Enrollment forms need to be checked, sorted, batched, sent to data entry, keypunched, returned, and filed. The process is slow and prone to errors. How could you use HRIS to make benefit enrollment more efficient and effective?

6. Some argue that outsourcing an activity is not good as the activity is no longer a means of distinguishing the firm from competitors. All competitors can buy the same service from the same provider, so it cannot be a source of competitive advantage. Is this true with regard to the procurement and adoption of HRIS Software? If so, why would a firm go for outsourced HRIS software rather than a home-grown one? Discuss the pros and cons.

EXPERIENTIAL EXERCISE

Building an HRIS

- **Purpose:** The purpose of this exercise is to give the students in creating a HRIS.
- **Required Understanding**: Students should be fully acquainted with the material in the Book Chapter.

How to set up the Exercise/Instructions: Divide the class into teams of five or six students. Each team will need access to the Internet.

Assume that the owners of a small business come to you with the following problem. They have a company with less than 40 employees and have been taking care of all types of HR paperwork informally, mostly on little slips of paper and with memos. They want you to build them a HRIS—how computerized it is will be up to you, but they can only afford a budget of $5,000 upfront (not counting your consulting), and then about $500 per year for maintenance. You know from your HR training that there are various sources of paper-based and online systems.

Required: Write a two-page proposal telling them exactly what your team would suggest, based on its accumulated existing knowledge, and from online research.

REFERENCES

Ahmer, Z. (2013). Adoption of Human Resource Information Systems Innovation in Pakistani Organizations. *Journal of Quality and Technology Management*, 9(2), 25–50.

Al-Mobaideen, H., Allahawiah, S., & Basioni, E. (2013). Factors Influencing the Successful Adoption of Human Resource Information System: The Content of Aquaba Special Economic Zone Authority. *Intelligent Information Management*, 5(01), 1–9. doi:10.4236/iim.2013.51001

Alharthey, B. K., & Rasli, A. (2012). The Use of Human Resource Management Systems in the Saudi Market. *Asian Journal of Business Ethics*, 1(2), 163–176. doi:10.100713520-012-0015-7

Altarawneh, I., & Al-Shqairat, Z. (2010). Human Resource Information Systems in Jordanian Universities. *International Journal of Business and Management*, 5(10), 113–127. doi:10.5539/ijbm.v5n10p113

Anitha, J., & Aruna, M. (2013). Adoption of Human Resource Information System in Organizations. *SDMIDD Journal of Management*, 4(2), 5–16.

Ankrah, E., & Sokro, E. (2016). Intention and Usage of Human Resource Information Systems among Ghanaians Human Resource Managers. *International Journal of Business and Management, 11*(2), 241–248. doi:10.5539/ijbm.v11n2p241

Arora, K. (2013). Importance of HRIS: A Critical Study on Service Sector. *Global Journal of Management and Business Studies, 3*(9), 971–976.

Bailey, J. (2008). First Steps in qualitative data analysis: transcribing. *Family Practice Advance Access,* 127-131.

Bamel, N., Bamel, U. K., Sahay, V., & Thite, M. (2010). Usage, Benefits, and Barriers of Human Resource Information System in Universities. *Vine, 44*(4).

Bedell, M. (2003). Human Resource Information Systems. Encyclopedia of Information Systems, 2, 537-550.

Bitsch, V. (2005). Qualitative Research: A Grounded Theory Example and Evaluation Criteria. *Journal of Agribusiness, 23*(1), 75–91.

Bondarouk, T., Ruel, H., & Heijden, B. (2009). e-HRM effectiveness in a public-sector organization. A multi-stakeholder perspective. *International Journal of Human Resource Management, 20*(3), 578–593. doi:10.1080/09585190802707359

Chakraborty, A. R., & Mansor, N. N. A. (2013). Adoption of Human Resource Information System: A Theoretical Analysis. *Procedia: Social and Behavioral Sciences, 75,* 473–478. doi:10.1016/j.sbspro.2013.04.051

Corbin, J., & Strauss, A. (1990). Grounded Theory Research. Procedures, Canons, and Evaluative Criteria. *Zeitschrift für Soziologie, 19*(6), 418–427. doi:10.1515/zfsoz-1990-0602

David, S., Shukla, S., & Gupta, S. (2015). Barriers in Implementing Human Resource Information System in Organization. *International Journal of Engineering Research and Management, 2*(5), 116–120.

DeSanctis, G. (1986). Human Resource Information Systems: A Current Assessment. *Management Information Systems Quarterly, 10*(1), 15–27. doi:10.2307/248875

Di-Cicco-Bloom, C., & Crabtee, B. F. (2006). The Qualitative Research Interview. *Medical Education, 40*(4), 314–321. doi:10.1111/j.1365-2929.2006.02418.x PMID:16573666

Ferdous, F., Chowdhury, M. M., & Bhuiyan, F. (2015). Barriers to the Implementation of Human Resource Information Systems. *Asian Journal of Management Sciences and Education, 4*(1), 33–43.

Francis, J. J., Johnston, M., Robertson, C., Glidewall, L., Entwistle, V., Eccles, M. P., & Grimshaw, J. M. (2010). What is an adequate sample size? Operationalizing Data Saturation for Theory-based Interview Studies. *Psychology & Health, 25*(10), 1229–1245. doi:10.1080/08870440903194015 PMID:20204937

Gupta, B. (2013). Human Resource Information System (HRIS): Important Element of Current Scenario. *IOSR Journal of Business and Management, 13*(6), 41–46. doi:10.9790/487X-1364146

Haines, V. Y., & Petit, A. (1997). Conditions for Successful Human Resource Information System. *Human Resource Management*, *36*(2), 261–275. doi:10.1002/(SICI)1099-050X(199722)36:2<261::AID-HRM7>3.0.CO;2-V

Harris, S., & Spencer, E. (2015). *2015-2016 HR Systems Survey* (18th ed.). Academic Press.

Hosnavi, R., & Ramezan, M. (2010). Measuring the effectiveness of Human Resource Information System in National Iranian Oil Company. *Education, Business and Society*, *3*(1), 28–39. doi:10.1108/17537981011022797

HRIS Technology Trends and Next-Generation Needs. (2015). Retrieved from https://www.comparehris.com/hris-technology-trends-and-next-generation-needs/

HRIS Trends for 2017. (2017). Retrieved from https://www.peoplematters.in/article/hcm-hrms-hris/hris-trends-for-2017-15025

Iwe, C., & Bendict, H. (2013). Economic recession and investment on Human Resource Information Systems (HRIS). Perspectives on some South African firms. *Journal of Management Development*, *32*(4), 404–418. doi:10.1108/02621711311326383

Jahan, S. (2014). Human Resources Information System (HRIS): A Theoretical Perspective. *Journal of Human Resource and Sustainability Studies*, *2*(02), 33–39. doi:10.4236/jhrss.2014.22004

Jie, X. (2014). Research on the Realization of Human Resource Management System. *Advanced Materials Research*, *926-930*, 3930–3933. doi:10.4028/www.scientific.net/AMR.926-930.3930

Johnson, R. D., Lukaszewski, K. M., & Stone, D. L. (2016). The Evolution of the Field of Human Resource Information Systems: Co-Evolution of Technology and HR Processes. *Communications of the Association for Information Systems*, *38*(28), 533–553. doi:10.17705/1CAIS.03828

Kananu, K. M., & Nyakego, M. O. (2016). Challenges and Strategies in the Implementation of Human Resource Information Systems in Kenyan Universities. *Research on Humanities and Social Sciences*, *6*(18), 148–161.

Kariuki, M. M. (2015). Human Resource Information System and Competitive Advantage of Companies Listed in Nairobi Security Exchange in Kenya. *European Journal of Business and Management*, *7*(21), 198–206.

Kassim, N. M., Ramayah, T., & Kurnia, S. (2012). Antecedents and Outcomes of HRIS use. *International Journal of Productivity and Performance Management*, *61*(6), 603–623. doi:10.1108/17410401211249184

Kavanagh, M.J., Thite, M., & Johnson, R.D. (2009). The Future of HRIS. *Emerging Trends in HRM and IT*. Retrieved from file:///C:/Users/Matilda/Desktop/HRIS/Chapter17The%20future%20of%20HRIS.pdf

Kavanagh, M. J., Thite, M., & Johnson, R. D. (2015). *Human Resource Information Systems*. Sage Publications.

Kaygusuz, I., Akgemci, T., & Yilmaz, A. (2016). The impact of HRIS usage on Organizational Efficiency and Employee Performance: A Research in Industrial and Banking Sector in Ankara and Istanbul cities. *International Journal of Business and Management*, *4*(4), 14–52.

Khashman, I. M. A., & Khashman, A. M. (2016). The Impact of Human Resource Information System (HRIS) Applications on Organizational Performance (Efficiency and Effectiveness) in Jordanian Private Hospitals. *Journal of Management Research*, 8(3), 31–44. doi:10.5296/jmr.v8i3.9419

Kothari, C. R. (2004). *Research Methodology: Methods and Techniques*. New Age International.

Kovach, K. A., & Cathcart, C. E. Jr. (1999). Human Resource Information System (HRIS): Providing Business with Rapid Data Access, Information Exchange and Strategic Advantage. *Public Personnel Management*, 28(2), 275–283. doi:10.1177/009102609902800208

Kumar, R., Shaikh, B. T., Ahmed, J., Khan, Z., Mursalin, S., Memon, M. I., & Zareen, S. (2013). The Human Resource Information System. A rapid appraisal of Pakistan's capacity to employ the tool. *BMC Medical Informatics and Decision Making*, 13(1), 104. doi:10.1186/1472-6947-13-104 PMID:24016066

Mujeeb, L. M. (2013). Importance of best human resource management practices and the need for human resource information system (HRIS) for the public health sector in Sri Lanka. *Sri Lanka Journal of Bio-Medical Informatics*, 3(2), 55–62. doi:10.4038ljbmi.v3i2.2449

Myers, M. D. (2013). *Qualitative Research in Business and Management*. Sage Publications Inc.

Myers, M. D., & Newman, M. (2007). The qualitative interview in IS research: Examining the craft. *Information and Organization*, 17(1), 2–26. doi:10.1016/j.infoandorg.2006.11.001

Nagendra, A., & Deshpande, M. (2014). Human Resource Information Systems (HRIS) in HR planning and development in mid to large sized organizations. *Procedia: Social and Behavioral Sciences*, 133, 61–67. doi:10.1016/j.sbspro.2014.04.169

Noutsa, F. A., Kamdjoug, J. R. K., & Wamba, S. F. (2017). *Acceptance and Use of HRIS and Influence on Organizational Performance of SMEs in a Developing Economy: The Case of Cameroon*. Presented at World Conference on Information System and Technologies.

Oliver, D. G., Serovich, J. M., & Mason, T. L. (1995). Constraints and Opportunities with Interview Transcription: Towards Reflection in Qualitative Research. *Social Forces*, 84(2), 1273–1289. doi:10.1353of.2006.0023 PMID:16534533

Poland, B. D. (1995). Transcription Quality as an Aspect of Rigor in Qualitative Research. *Qualitative Inquiry*, 1(3), 290–310. doi:10.1177/107780049500100302

Qureshi, M. O., Kaur, M. K., & Sajjad, S. R. (2013). An empirical analysis of organizations using Human Resource Information System (HRIS) in India: An employee perspective. *International Journal of Economics and Management Sciences*, 2(9), 54–63.

Rahman, M. A., Islam, M. D., & Qi, X. (2017). Barriers in Adopting Human Resource Information System (HRIS): An Empirical Study on Selected Bangladeshi Garments Factories. *International Business Research*, 10(6), 98–105. doi:10.5539/ibr.v10n6p98

Rahman, M.A., Qi, X., Jinnah, M.S. (2016). Factors affecting the adoption of HRIS by the Bangladeshi banking and financial sector. *Cogent Business and Management, 3*, 1-10.

Rangriz, H., Mehrabi, J., & Azadegan, A. (2011). The Impact of Human Resource Information System in Strategic Decisions in Iran. *Computer and Information Science, 4*(2), 81–88. doi:10.5539/cis.v4n2p81

Sadiq, U., Khan, A. F., & Ikhlaq, K. (2012). The Impact of Information Systems on the Performance of Human Resource Department. *Journal of Business Studies Quarterly, 3*(4), 77–91.

SagePeople. (2017). *Becoming a People Company-the Way to unlock fast track growth.* Retrieved from file:///C:/Users/Matilda/Downloads/Sage_People_Research_Report.pdf

Seven Reasons HR Technology Is So Hot Today. (2013, May). Retrieved from https://www.forbes.com/sites/joshbersin/2013/05/31/7-reasons-hr-technology-is-so-hot-today/#7dc154176fdc

Shani, A., & Tesone, D. V. (2010). Have human resource information system evolved into internal e-commerce? *Worldwide Hospitality and Tourism Themes, 2*(1), 30–48. doi:10.1108/17554211011012586

Shibly, H. A. (2011). Human Resource Information Systems Success Assessment: An Integrative Model. *Australian Journal of Basic and Applied Sciences, 5*(5), 157–169.

Shiri, S. (2012). Effectiveness of Human Resource Information System on HR Functions of the Organization- A Cross Sectional Study. *US-China Education Review, 9,* 830–839.

Soloman, A., Breunlin, D., Panattoni, K., Gustafson, M., Ransburg, D., Ryan, C., ... Terrian, J. (2011). "Don't Lock Me Out": Life-Story Interviews of Family Business Owners Facing Succession. *Family Process, 50*(2), 149–166. doi:10.1111/j.1545-5300.2011.01352.x PMID:21564058

Strohmeier, S. (2006). Research in e-HRM: Review and Implications. *Human Resource Management Review, 17*(1), 19–37. doi:10.1016/j.hrmr.2006.11.002

Thite, M., Kavanagh, M. J., & Johnson, R. D. (2009). *Evolution of Human Resource Management and Human Resource Information Systems.* Retrieved from https://s3.amazonaws.com/academia.edu.documents/38322126/EVOLUTION.pdf?AWSAccess KeyId=AKIAIWOWYYGZ2Y53UL3A&Expires=1509386148&Signature=Ru%2BRbIY6CJD8 p%2FK2PXUN57lA5x8%3D&response-content-disposition=inline%3B%20filename%3DEvolution_of_Human_REsouRcE_managEmEnt_a.pdf

Troshani, I., Jerram, C., & Gerrard, M. (2010). Exploring the Organizational Adoption of Human Resource Information Systems (HRIS) in the Australian public sector. *21st Australian Conference on Information Systems.*

Turner, J. R. (2014). Grounded Theory Building for the Workplace. *Performance Improvement, 53*(3), 31–39. doi:10.1002/pfi.21401

Weeks, K. O. (2013). An Analysis of Human Resource Information Systems impact on Employees. *Journal of Management Policy and Practice, 14*(3), 35–49.

Wimpenny, P., & Gass, J. (2000). Interviewing in Phenomenology and Grounded Theory: Is there a difference? *Journal of Advanced Nursing, 31*(6), 1485–1492. doi:10.1046/j.1365-2648.2000.01431.x PMID:10849162

APPENDIX I

Participants' Profiles

Case I: Respondent is General Manager (HR) in a private Trade and Services organization with 185 regular and 180 outsourced employees. He is 40 years old and has been working for a year having worked earlier in the capacity of HR managers in hospitality industry and other private organizations in Nepal and India with total 15 years of HR experience and a master's degree in HR. HRIS adoption is in progress with ongoing talks with local vendor though basic processes such as employee payroll, employee record, and attendance have been automated though not fully functional and integrated.

Case II: Respondent is a 29-year old female Deputy Manager (HR) working for four years in private organization dealing in trade and services with 1500 employees. She has total five years of experience in the HR with a master's degree in HR. HRIS adoption is complete to a large extent and we find some HR processes like appraisal both in manual and automated formats due to the difficulty in migrating to online system with ease. Despite going in for automation from the beginning 20 years ago, it takes some more time before HRIS as a part of ERP gets functional.

Case III: Respondent is 57-year old Corporate Human Resource Manager with one year stint at private organization dealing in trade and service having 900 employees. He has worked earlier in the capacity of HR consultant for many different service organizations for 25 years as Head-HR in banks, service, hospitality, and MNC sectors. He holds an international degree in the area of HR and works as visiting faculty. He is a certified trainer in the area of Performance Management. HRIS adoption is not complete despite automating major HR processes such as employee records, leave, attendance, payroll, training and development, and appraisal though not yet integrated into one system using Software provided by a local vendor.

Case IV: Respondent is 38-year old VP (HR) at private organization dealing in trade and services having, both on rolls/outsourced, 2500 employees. In his 2-year stint, he was instrumental in introducing HRIS using his earlier 10-year experience as HR manager in MNCs and service/IT sectors. With a Master's in Business Studies, also works as trainer/coach. Adoption of HRIS has been completed to a large extent with automated basic processes like employee records, payroll, leave, attendance, appraisal, and T&D while rest need to be integrated using the local software.

Case V: Respondent is 35-year old Senior Manager (HR & Admin.) for one year with this 700 employee strong private organization dealing in trading and services with an overall five years HR experience. He holds a HR Masters Degree. Adoption of HRIS is substantial maintaining employee records, leave, attendance, and appraisal using local software.

Case VI: Respondent is 34-years old HR Officer in a Commercial Bank with 870 employees. He has 8 years experience and holds an MBA (HR) Degree. Though not fully integrated yet, adoption of HRIS is complete to a large extent having automated employee records, payroll, leave, attendance, appraisal, and T&D using local vendor provided software.

Case VII: Respondent is 34-year old working as Acting Assistant Director (HR) in a Government Bank with 1200 employees. He holds a Masters degree and has 4 years of HR experience. Using local software, HRIS was adopted two years and automated only basic HR processes like attendance and leave and continuing the rest largely on manual basis.

Case VIII: Respondent is 56-years old female with a Masters in English and working for 13 years as Chief Human Resource Manager at this service organization with 200 employees. Using no software, adoption of HRIS is not yet complete though major HR processes such as employee records, leave, attendance, payroll, training and development, and appraisal are automated.

Case IX: Respondent is 38-year old Business Manager and Head of HR in a private hospital with 100 plus employees. With a Bachelor's degree in Commerce, she has been working in the organization for 5 years. HRIS is 5 years old and except for payroll, most of the other processes are manual and are looking for local software vendor to get a customized solution.

Case X: Respondent is 29-year old HR Manager at a construction company with 800 regular and 200 outsourced employees and he is working for over one an year. With a Masters in HR, he has 7 years HR experience. HRIS is 3-years old using IT-Department developed in-house Software.

Case XI: Respondent is a 39-year old HR and OD Coordinator at 270-employee strong development organization for four years. She has 10 years experience and has a Post Graduate Diploma in HRM and Services. Two-year old HRIS is adopted for basic processes like employee records, time sheets, attendance, and payroll using Software provided by local vendor.

Case XII: Respondent is a HR manager in a development organization. Respondent is 33 years old female and has been working in the organization for last one year. She has 9 years of experience in the area of HR. Organization has around 250 staffs. She has an MBA in the area of HR. HRIS is partially implemented in the sense that HR processes are automated and maintained in excel. There is no software being used at the moment.

Case XIII: Respondent is Corporate HR and admin officer at MNC. Respondent is 29 years old female and has 3.5 years of experience in the area of HR. She has an MBA in area of HR. Organization has around 230 employees. HRIS is implemented to a large extent since most HR processes are automated. International software for HRIS is being used.

Case XI: Respondent is Senior-HR manager at a private organization dealing in trade and services. Respondent is 32 years old male and has worked in the organization for more than 5 years. He has 8 years of experience in the area of HR. He has masters' degree. The organization employs some 850 people. HRIS has been adopted for almost 6 years and used more for operational purpose than strategic one. Software by local vendor is being used.

Case XV: Respondent is 39-year old with a Masters Degree and working as HR Manager at an Educational Institution with 100 employees for 13 years. HRIS Software is being used for only 500 employees and is also not fully integrated.

Case XVI: Respondent, 45 years old is Vice President (Operations) in an internet service provider company with 1400 employees for past 11 years and also looks after HR and has an international Bachelor's degree in Information Systems. Adoption of HRIS is partial with HR processes yet to be integrated and procurement of software from a local vendor is awaited.

Case XVII: Respondent is 30-year old female Associate HR manager in an IT company with 200 employees for past two years. She holds an MBA having 4.5 years overall HR experience. Adoption of HRIS using local software is complete to a large extent with most automated HR processes while others still needing to be integrated.

Case XVIII: Respondent is 50-year old Head of (HR & Admin.) and is working for Development Sector organization employing 230 people for past 2.5 years with over 25 years HR experience and having an international Masters' Degree in HR. Adoption of HRIS is partial and is 2.5 years old with automated basic HR processes. Local vendor based software being used.

APPENDIX II

Table 1. Summary of demographic profile of participants

Case	Age	Gender	Education	Experience	Job Title
I	40	M	MBA	15	General Manager-HR
II	29	F	MBA	5	Deputy Manager-HR
III	57	M	MSM	25	Corporate HR Manager
IV	38	M	MBS	10	Vice President-HR
V	35	M	MBA	5	Senior Manager-HR and Admin
VI	34	M	MBA	8	HR Officer
VII	34	M	MBA	4	Acting-Asst Director-HR
VIII	56	M	Masters	13	Chief HR Manager
IX	38	F	Bachelors	5	Business Manager and Head of HR
X	29	M	Masters	7	HR Manager
XI	39	F	PGD	10	HR and OD Coordinator
XII	33	F	MBA	9	HR Manager
XIII	29	F	MBA	3.5	Corporate HR and admin officer
XIV	32	M	MBA	8	Senior-HR manager
XV	39	F	MBA	13	HR Manager
XVI	45	M	Bachelors	11	Vice President-Operations
XVII	30	M	MBA	4.5	Associate HR Manager
XVIII	50	M	Masters	25	Head-HR and Administration

APPENDIX III

Table 2. Profile of the participants' organizations

Case	Type	Number of Employees	Adoption of HRIS
I	Private-Trading and Service	350 plus	Yes, in process
II	Private-Trading and Service	1500	Adopted almost fully
III	Private-Trading and Service	900	Adopted almost fully
IV	Private-Trading and Service	2500	Adopted to a large extent
V	Private-Trading and Service	700	Adopted to a large extent
VI	Public	870	Adopted to a large extent
VII	Government	1200	Adopted to a large extent
VIII	Private- Service	200 plus	Not fully adopted
IX	Private-Service	100 plus	Not fully adopted
X	Private- Construction	2800 plus	Adopted to a large extent
XI	Development	270	Not fully adopted
XII	Development	250	Not fully adopted
XIII	MNC	230	Adopted to a large extent
XIV	Private-Trading and Service	850	Adopted to a large extent
XV	Educational institute	1000	Not fully adopted
XVI	Private- Internet Service Provider	1400	Not fully adopted
XVII	Private- IT based company	200	Adopted to a large extent
XVIII	Development	230	Not fully adopted

APPENDIX IV

Grouping of Interview Scripts Into Sub-Themes (For Case-I to Case Xviii)

Table 3. Grouping of interview scripts into sub-themes of Case I

Issues	Sub-Themes
Current Adoption Status	HR Status, Importance of HR increasing, Need to work internationally, Employees more aware and informed, Shift in role of HR from operational to strategic, Realization by Businesses that HRIS is important, Most HR processes are automated but not yet integrated.
Barriers for Adoption and Use	International Software too costly, lack of good Software Developer in Nepal, inadequate knowledge of the part of HR professionals, people are not tech savvy, fear, Complexities in the system, Inadequate support from Management, lack of support systems, Systems need to be configured as per need, lack of trainings, HRIS is also not error free.
Conditions for Successful Adoption	Support from Top Management and Organization, Knowledgeable HR professionals, Quality Vendors to choose from, Training opportunity

Table 4. Grouping of interview scripts into subthemes of Case II

Issues	Sub-Themes
Current Adoption Status	Most HR processes such as payroll, attendance, appraisal, compensation and benefits are automated, not all HR processes are interlinked, Migration from manual to automated form, Both maintained for appraisal, Old and established company, HR processes have been automated, HR systems tied up with the ERP, HRIS is now no longer a choice.
Barriers for Adoption and Use	Technological hassles, High cost of international software, lack of training and development, there is limitation in the number of users, cost of adopting HRIS difficult to justify, employee resisting to use, HR issues highly sensitive, privacy concerns, interlink with other departments, individual resistance
Conditions for Successful Adoption	Dedicated after-sales support team from vendors, Reasonable price of software, Training& Development

Table 5. Grouping of interview scripts into subthemes of Case III

Issues	Sub-Themes
Current Adoption Status	Major HR processes in Employees' Life Cycle embedded in HRIS, Attendance, Payroll, Movement of staff recorded, Appraisal, TNA is carried out and has been integrated.
Barriers for Adoption and Use	Employee attitude not open to trying new things, even HR professionals don't have required technical knowledge, Turnover of staff, those with technical knowhow are gone, extra work to HR department, need to help those employees not familiar with technology
Conditions for Successful Adoption and Use	Changing the Mindset of people, Better post-sale service, better coordination with IT department and software vendor, provision of authentic software over pirated ones, Ownership by the employees, Supportive conditions for technology adoption, providing Training and Developmental opportunities

Table 6. Grouping of interview scripts into subthemes of Case IV

Issues	Sub-Themes
Current Adoption Status	HRIS makes things easily accessible, reporting easy and as per need, allows logical analysis, a must for employee management in large organization, HRIS adopted after his joining, his role instrumental in establishing HRIS in previous organizations, HRIS almost fully integrated, most organizations using local software, employees are more aware
Barriers for Adoption and Use	International software costly to afford, local vendors not able to develop customized solutions, insecurity in part of employees, Old employees reluctant, lack of training and development, errors in software, not authentic, privacy concerns, security issues, lack of competent vendors
Conditions for Successful Adoption and Use	Vendor after-sales support, Authentic Software, Competent Software developers

Table 7. Grouping of interview scripts into subthemes of Case V

Issues	Sub-Themes
Current Adoption Status	HR is graduating, Personnel/ labor department to HR department, HRIS is well maintained, employee records, appraisal, insurance, benefits of employees, compensation, HRIS now being prioritized, last 5 years HRIS is growing in value
Barriers for Adoption and Use	Incompetent HR professionals, can't understand the complete functionalities, lack of quality vendors, incompetent staffs, after sales support not available
Conditions for Successful Adoption	employee attitude, willing to adapt to new systems, HR Ministry to start, Labor Act to be strictly followed, Guidelines on making HR stronger, HR professionals need to be experienced to understand practical challenges. Training and Development, Top Management Support, IT Department and software vendors to work cordially,

Table 8. Grouping of interview scripts into subthemes of Case VI

Issues	Sub-Themes
Current Adoption Status	HRIS is almost fully integrated in the organizations, employee records, attendance, T&D, payroll, appraisal, etc all automated, data retrieval made easy, NRB guidelines has made it compulsory to address competency mapping,
Barriers for Adoption and Use	Investment commitment from top management, technical hassles, turnover in IT professionals on the vendors side, International software too costly,
Conditions for Successful Adoption	Cost benefit analysis by organizations willing to adopt, proper coordination between IT and Software Developer, After-sales support by vendors

Table 9. Grouping of interview scripts into subthemes of Case VII

Issues	Sub-Themes
Current Adoption Status	HR function not yet systematized, HR is merely Personnel Administration, HRIS is in place in the organization, employee records all maintained in system, however other processes such as appraisal are not automated
Barriers for Adoption and Use	Lack of skills on the part of employees, internal auditing, software does not support, lack of training, budget issues, lack of customized software, return on software not estimated, pirated software available so genuine software are found to be costly, employee resistance, challenges in government procurement system
Conditions for Successful Adoption	Top level Management Commitment, organization ready to adopt, training and development, awareness

Table 10. Grouping of interview scripts into subthemes of Case VIII

Issues	Sub-Themes
Current Adoption Status	HRIS is in use, Central Repository or data system being maintained, HRIS use increasing in Nepal, next 5 years huge scope, use most for operational tasks than strategic
Barriers for Adoption and Use	IT department and vendor incompatibility, lack of capacity of local vendors, some technical issues with software, not compatible as per audit requirement, security issues, confidentiality of data
Conditions for Adoption and Use	Proper coordination between IT department and vendor, Customized software,

Table 11. Grouping of interview scripts into subthemes of Case IX

Issues	Sub-Themes
Current Adoption Status	Medical professional is a different field altogether, they are not used to software, difficult to get implemented, different in and out time, doctors are not willing to punch their attendance, sooner or later all computerized, so can be positive about HRIS, as organization and employees grow, HRIS important, in this organization HRIS not fully automated, except for attendance, other processes manual, now employee data maintained in excel
Barriers for Adoption and Use	Attitudinal change, has to start from school level, medical professionals need to change their attitude, lack of quality software, lack of customized solutions, lack of infrastructure for HRIS adoption,
Conditions for Adoption and Use	Acceptance of tech-friendly environment, Top management support, Availability of Software and Vendor support,

Table 12. Grouping of interview scripts into subthemes of Case X

Issues	Sub-Themes
Current Adoption Status	HRIS is almost fully implemented in the organization, employee records, payroll, attendance, KPIS, KRAs, manpower planning, need of HRIS slowing increasing, employees are empowered, organization has adopted HRIS for 25 years, use of HRIS from operational to strategic
Barriers for Adoption and Use	Resistance from employees, infrastructure is a challenge especially in rural location, local vendors not able to provide customized solutions, confidentiality issues, leakage of data,
Conditions for Adoption and Use	availability of technology, and confidentiality agreement with vendors before set up, dedicated team of vendor for support, provision of quality software

Table 13. Grouping of interview scripts into subthemes of Case XI

Issues	Sub-Themes
Current Adoption Status	HR is largely administrative in many organizations of Nepal, HRIS in this organization is slowly progressing, most HR processes are still manual, since 2015 few processes automated, Personnel Activity Report, Time Sheets, Leave, Employee Records are automated, HRIS slowly progressing, making it paperless, Local software being used, not a customized system used, some basic changes to suit the existing software, HR manager came from an organization that had HRIS, insisted on adopting HRIS, took 3-4 years to adopt the system
Barriers for Adoption and Use	Employees in all places do not have access to automation, field based activity mostly common, payroll handled by accounts, may have to adopt HQ based software, privacy
Conditions for Adoption and Use	Better infrastructure, internet facilities, Training and development opportunities, Data Security

Table 14. Grouping of interview scripts into subthemes of Case XII

Issues	Sub-Themes
Current Adoption Status	HRIS not fully adopted, employee related data maintained in excel, appraisal, training and other information maintained in excel, data sent to head office, no software procured, present system allows data retrieval
Barriers for Adoption and Use	Small size of employees, no separate budget for HRIS, since organizational expenses are project based, turnover of people having requisite skills to function
Conditions for Adoption and Use	Management Support, good vendor support, reasonable cost for software

Table 15. Grouping of interview scripts into subthemes of Case XIII

Issues	Sub-Themes
Current Adoption Status	All major HRIS processes automated, payroll, attendance, employee records, HR processes are not integrated, process of integration on
Barriers for Adoption and Use	Lack of Technological capabilities, Employee resistance in the initial days, lack of infrastructure
Conditions for Adoption and Use	Provision of required infrastructure, Support by the management, Better training and development opportunities

Table 16. Grouping of interview scripts into subthemes of Case XIV

Issues	Sub-Themes
Current Adoption Status	HRIS has been adopted for over 6 years, Basic HR processes, Attendance, Leave, Employee records, other processes not integrated
Barriers for Adoption and Use	Individual resistance, at initial stages, Privacy issues, no after-sales support from vendors, Vendor and IT incompatibility, HR Software vendor doesn't receive feedback positively,
Conditions for Adoption and Use	Support from top management, availability of software at reasonable price, return on software to be computed, proper research before software development,

Table 17. Grouping of interview scripts into subthemes of Case XV

Issues	Sub-Themes
Current Adoption Status	Local software used for last 4-5 years, attendance, payroll, employee records automated, other processes largely manual
Barriers for Adoption and Use	Individual resistance, lack of technical support, locational disadvantage for software vendors
Conditions for Adoption and Use	Good quality software, customized solutions, after sales support from vendors

Table 18. Grouping of interview scripts into subthemes of Case XVI

Issues	Sub-Themes
Current Adoption Status	Some form of automation exists, no software, in the process of procurement, data on employee records, attendance, leave automated, appraisal, TNA is manual
Barriers for Adoption and Use	resistance from old employees, lack of customized software, HRIS used more of operational purpose, need to support strategic use
Conditions for Adoption and Use	Knowledgeable HR software developers

Table 19. Grouping of interview scripts into subthemes of Case XVII

Issues	Sub-Themes
Current Adoption Status	Most of HR processes automated but not integrated, employee records, attendance, leave, appraisal, TNA automated
Barriers for Adoption and Use	Lack of customized software, software meets only certain requirement, organizations of small size cannot afford, employee resistance, issues of piracy
Conditions for Adoption and Use	Availability of authentic software at reasonable price

Table 20. Grouping of interview scripts into subthemes of Case XVIII

Issues	Sub-Themes
Current Adoption Status	HRIS adopted to some extent; Attendance and Payroll automated
Barriers for Adoption and Use	Nature of organization, Employee movement to work sites, difficulty in implementing certain systems, lack of adequate infrastructure, network issues, lack of training
Conditions for Adoption and Use	Better infrastructure facilities

Chapter 13
Optimization Problem:
Systemic Approach

Albert N. Voronin
National Aviation University, Ukraine

ABSTRACT

A systemic approach to solving multicriteria optimization problems is proposed. The system approach allowed uniting the models of individual schemes of compromises into a single integrated structure that adapts to the situation of adopting a multi-criteria solution. The advantage of the concept of non-linear scheme of compromises is the possibility of making a multicriteria decision formally, without the direct participation of a person. The apparatus of the non-linear scheme of compromises, developed as a formalized tool for the study of control systems with conflicting criteria, makes it possible to solve practically multicriteria problems of a wide class.

INTRODUCTION

The essence of many practical problems in different subject areas is the choice of conditions that allow the object of research in a given situation to show its best properties (optimization problems). The conditions on which the properties of the object depend are expressed quantitatively by some variables $x_1, x_2, ..., x_n$, given in the domain of definition X and called optimization arguments. External actions r do not depend on us, but it is known that they can take their values from a compact set R. Usually it is assumed that the calculations are carried out for a given and known external action vector $r^0 \in R$, which ultimately determines the decision-making situation.

In turn, each of the properties of the object in the domain M is quantitatively described by the variable y_k, $k \in [1,s]$, the value of which characterizes the quality of the object in relation to this property.

In the general case, the parameters $y_1, y_2, ..., y_s$, called the quality criteria, form the vector $y = \{y_k\}_{k=1}^s \in M$. Its components quantify the properties of the object for a given set of optimization arguments $x = \{x_i\}_{i=1}^n \in X$.

DOI: 10.4018/978-1-5225-8933-4.ch013

As an example of technology can result in the design of the aircraft. Here, the discrete components of the vector of independent variables x can be schematic solutions (monoplane, biplane), characteristics of materials, etc. The components of the vector of quality criteria y are altitude, speed, maneuverability, cost.

In agrotechnology, x - crop rotation schemes (legumes for sunflower, black pairs, etc.). The components of the - gross yield, indicators of soil erosion.

In pharmacology, the x components of the composite drug. Criteria for the effectiveness of y - the duration of the cure of the disease, the presence of contraindications.

In the economy of x - tax rates, tariffs, excise taxes. Criteria y - gross product, standard of living, unemployment, income differentiation of citizens.

We draw attention to the fact that quality criteria are usually contradictory. The art of the researcher is in the system linking conflicting indicators. So, Jean Colbert (Minister of Louis XIV) in 1665 said "The art of taxation is to pluck a goose, to get the maximum amount of feathers with the minimum hiss".

More fully examples of applied multi-criteria tasks are given in Albert Voronin (2017).

SYSTEMIC APPROACH

The term "systemic approach" means that a real object represented as a system is described as a set of interacting components that implements a specific goal. At the same time, a finite, but ordered set of elements and relations between them is "cut out" from the variety of components of a real object. We can say that the system is a model of a real object only in the aspect of the goal that it implements. The goal, requiring for its achievement certain functions, determines through them the composition and structure of the system.

The goal isolates, outlines the contours of the system in the object. In this system (object model) only what is necessary and sufficient to achieve the goal will come from the real object. If the same object can realize several goals, then with respect to each it acts as an independent system. The systemic approach assumes that not only the object, but also the research process itself acts as a complex system, the task of which, in particular, consists in combining in a single whole various models of the object.

Thus, with the systemic approach, the researcher receives only that information about a real object, which is necessary and sufficient to solve the task.

OPTIMIZATION

If the object realizes only one goal, then the effectiveness of achieving the goal is quantitatively expressed by the single criterion of optimality y. The solution of the optimization problem involves reaching the extreme value of the criterion by choosing the set of optimization arguments.

The extremalization of the optimality criterion is often identified with the concept of goal realization, while in reality these are different concepts. We can say that the criterion and goal are correlated with each other as a model and an original with all the consequences that follow from this. This is understandable, if only because the original is usually put in line not one, but several models reflecting this or that aspect of the original. Some goals are difficult, and sometimes impossible to describe with the help of quantitative criteria. In any case, the criterion is just a surrogate of the goal. Criteria characterize the goal only indirectly, sometimes better, sometimes worse, but always approximately (Antonov(2004), Peregudov (1989)).

The decision of optimization problems assumes presence of some estimation of quality of work of a system from which it is possible to tell that one system works better, and another – is worse and how much. The fundamental problem of the quantitative assessment of objects and processes is that the notions of "better" and "worse" be put in line with the concepts "more" and "less." For certainty, it is believed that, for example, "better" means "less".

According to S. Stevens, if the description opens the way for measurement, then the discussions are completely replaced by calculations. In application to our problems, this means that if there are reasonable quantitative criteria for the quality of a complex system, then its study can be carried out through a formalized mathematical apparatus. Otherwise, subjective assessments, multivalued interpretations and arbitrary decisions are inevitable.

The function $y = f(x)$ relates the quality criterion to the optimization arguments. In estimation problems, the function $f(x)$ is called the *evaluation* function, and in optimization problems it is called the *objective* function. With some reservations, the optimization problem is formulated as finding such a combination of arguments from their domain, in which the objective function acquires an extreme value:

$$x^* = \arg \operatorname*{extr}_{\substack{x \in X \\ y \in M}} f(x)_{r^O \in R}$$

If "better" means "less", then in practice, for fixed $r^O \in R$ and guaranteed $y \in M$, expression

$$x^* = \arg \min_{x \in X} f(x)$$

is applied.

MULTICRITERIA PROBLEMS

A complex object of research can not be characterized by any one (for example, the most "important" or "typical") attribute. When describing it, many inseparable properties must be taken into account simultaneously. In other words, to study complex objects, a modern systemic approach requires the involvement of the entire spectrum of their properties. A complex object and any fragment of it must be viewed not in isolation, but in numerous contradictory interactions and, importantly, in various possible situations.

Complex systems, being in different conditions (situations, modes), reveal different system properties, including those that are incompatible with none of the other situations separately. In their study, an approach is used that consists in the creation and simultaneous coexistence of not one but a set of theoretical models of the same phenomenon, some of which conceptually contradict each other. However, not one can be neglected, since each characterizes some property of the phenomenon under study and neither can be accepted as a single one, since it does not express the complete complex of its properties. It is interesting to compare what was said with the principle of complementarity introduced into science by Niels Bohr: "... To reproduce the integrity of the phenomenon it is necessary to apply mutually exclusive "additional" classes of concepts, each of which can be used in its own special condition, but only taken together, exhaust all the determinable information".

Multiple properties of a complex system in a given situation of its functioning are quantitatively estimated by corresponding partial criteria. In different situations, the rank of "the most important" acquire different properties and, accordingly, different partial criteria. Thus, mutually exclusive "additional" classes of concepts, in which the role individual theoretical models are presented, are characterized by conflicting partial criteria, each of which is applicable in its own special condition. And only a complete set of partial criteria (vector criterion) makes it possible to adequately assess the functioning of a complex system as a manifestation of the contradictory unity of all its properties. Therefore, it can be assumed that multicriteriality is the embodiment of the principle of complementarity in the methodology of research of the complex systems.

However, this possibility is only a necessary, but not sufficient, condition for vector estimation of the entire system as a whole. Indeed, let it be known the numerical values of all the partial criteria of the system. Does this mean that we, knowing these values, can evaluate the effectiveness of the system as a whole? No we can not.

It is appropriate to recall the old Indian parable about the blind men that got to know the elephant. One touched the trunk and decided that the elephant was like a snake. The second picked up an ear and said that the elephant reminds him of a sheet. The third felt a foot and said that the elephant is a pillar.

For a holistic assessment, it is necessary to rise to the next level, i.e. carry out the act of composing the criteria. Let us compare this with Kurt Gödel's incompleteness theorem: "... In any sufficiently complex first-order theory there is an assertion that can not be proved or disproved by the means of the theory itself. But the consistency of one particular theory can be established by means of another, more powerful, second-order formal theory. But then the question arises of the consistency of this second theory, and so on." Gödel's theorem seems to be the methodological basis for composing criteria, which is a sufficient condition for vector estimation of the system as a whole.

A scalar convolution of the criteria can serve as an instrument of the composition act. Scalar convolution is a mathematical method of compressing information and quantifying its integral properties by one number.

In general, the simultaneous description of the phenomenon (object) from several sides always gives a qualitatively new, more perfect idea of the described phenomenon (object) in comparison with any "one-sided" description. So, even two flat images that form a stereo pair make up a three-dimensional image of the object, not to mention the possibilities of holography. A multi-criteria approach that gives a "stereoscopic" look at the evaluation of the functioning of the system opens up new ways for improving complex management systems and decision making. So, for a holistic perception of a complex system in different conditions of its work, it is necessary to apply a multi-criteria approach.

In practical problems, a real object usually implements not one, but several goals and, accordingly, is characterized by several partial criteria of efficiency (quality). Let's pay attention to the fact that quality criteria, as a rule, are contradictory. The art of the researcher consists in the systemic linking models characterized by contradictory indicators. Thus, Jean Colbert (Minister of Louis XIV) in 1665 said: "The art of taxation is to get a maximum number of feathers while digging a goose, with a minimal hiss." At the systemic approach there is a task which consists in connection in a single whole of various models of object. The problem is solved by applying the act of criteria composition.

For the systemic linking in multicriteria problems, the scalar convolution of the particular criteria $Y=f[y(x)]$, where y is no longer a scalar, but an s-dimensional vector of the criteria $y = \{y_k\}_{k=1}^{s}$, is used as the objective (or evaluation) function instead of $y=f(x)$. Scalar convolution acts as an instrument of the act of composing criteria.

In the notion of optimality, in addition to the criteria, limitations $x \in X$ on the optimization arguments as well as $y \in M$ on the efficiency of the solution play an equally important role. Even small changes can significantly affect the solution. And very serious consequences can be obtained by removing certain restrictions and adding others with the same system of criteria. There is a great danger in the optimization of complex systems, as N. Wiener pointed out in his first publications on cybernetics. The fact is that, without setting all the necessary restrictions, we can, simultaneously with the extremization of the objective function, obtain unforeseen and undesirable accompanying effects.

To illustrate this N. Wiener liked to bring an English fairy tale about a monkey's foot. The owner of this talisman could fulfill any desire with its help. When he once wished to receive a large sum of money, it turned out that for this he paid the life of his beloved son. We will agree that it is often very difficult, and sometimes it is simply impossible to foresee in advance all the consequences of adopting multi-criteria decisions.

The idea of N. Wiener that in complex systems, we are fundamentally unable to determine in advance all the conditions and limitations that guarantee the absence of undesirable optimization effects, allowed him to make a gloomy assumption about the catastrophic consequences of cybernation of society.

Nevertheless, from the standpoint of system analysis, the attitude to optimization can be formulated as follows: it is a powerful means of increasing efficiency, but it should be used more cautiously as the complexity of the problem increases.

We formulate the formulation of the multicriteria optimization problem in a fairly general form.

FORMULATION OF THE PROBLEM

A set of possible solutions $X \subset E^n$ consisting of vectors $x=\{x_i\}_{i=1}^n$ of n-dimensional Euclidean space is given. By the physical nature of the problem the vector holonomic (in static) or nonholonomic (in dynamics) connection $B(x) \leq 0$ is given. The decision is made at external influences, described by the vector r, given on the set of possible factors R.

The quality of the solution is estimated from the set of contradictory partial criteria that form the s-dimensional vector $y(x)=\{y_k(x)\}_{k=1}^s \subset F$, which is defined on the set X. The expression $y \subset F$ denotes the vector y belonging to the class F of admissible efficiency vectors. The partial criteria vector is bounded by the admissible domain: $y \in M$.

The situation that results from the adoption of a multi-criteria solution x under given external conditions r, is characterized by the Cartesian product $S = X \times R$.

The problem is to determine a solution $x^* \in X$, which, under given conditions, connections, and constraints, optimizes the efficiency vector $y(x)$.

This formulation is so general that, according to a famous comic expression, it can not be applied in any particular case. For the constructive solution of the task in various particular statements, it is necessary to carry out the structuring of certain concepts. To do this, we need to make additional special assumptions that help solve the following problems of vector optimization:

- Determination of the range of Pareto optimal solutions;
- Choice of the scheme of compromises;

- Normalization of partial criteria;
- Consideration of priority.

Difficulties in solving vector optimization problems are not computational, but conceptual in nature (this is not *how* to find the optimal solution, but *what* should be understood by it). Therefore, the development of a formal apparatus for solving multicriteria problems is one of the most difficult problems in the modern theory of decision-making and management. Its solution is important both in theoretical and applied terms.

SELECTION OF THE SCHEME OF COMPROMISES

From the problems of vector optimization, we will pay special attention to the problem of choosing a scheme of compromises. One of the most important theses of the theory of decision-making under many criteria is that there is no best solution in some absolute sense. The decision made can be considered the best only for the person making the decision (decision maker, DM) in accordance with the goal set by him and taking into account the specific situation. The normative models for solving multicriteria problems are based on the hypothesis of the existence in the consciousness of the DM some utility function (Fishburn (1978)), measured both in nominal and in ordinal scales. The reflection of this utility function is the scheme of compromises and its model in a given situation – the scalar convolution of partial criteria $Y[y(x)]$, which allows constructively solving the problem of multicriteria optimization.

The determination of a multi-criteria solution is by its nature compromise and fundamentally based on the use of subjective information. Having received this information from the decision maker and choosing a scheme of compromises, one can move from a general vector expression to a scalar convolution of partial criteria, which is the basis for formation a constructive apparatus for solving multicriteria problems. If the scalar convolution method is used, the mathematical model of solving the vector optimization problem is represented in the form of the extremization of the function $Y[y(x)]$. This is a scalar function that has the meaning of a scalar convolution of the vector of partial criteria, the form of which depends on the chosen scheme of compromises.

The most commonly an additive (linear) scalar convolution is used

$$Y\Big[y(x)\Big] = \sum_{k=1}^{S} a_k y_k(x)$$

where a_k are the weight coefficients determined by the decision maker, starting from his utility function in the given situation. The Laplace principle in the theory of decision-making consists in the extremization of a linear scalar convolution. The drawback (specificity) of the application of linear scalar convolution is the possibility of "compensating" one criterion at the expense of others.

Multiplicative convolution

$$Y\Big[y(x)\Big] = \prod_{k=1}^{S} y_k(x)$$

is free of this shortcoming. The Pascal principle is the extremization of the multiplicative scalar convolution.

Historically, Blaise Pascal's principle was first described in the work of Pensees, published in 1670. It is believed that this work laid the foundation for the whole theory of decision-making. Here are introduced two key concepts of the theory: 1) partial criteria, each of which evaluates any one side of the effectiveness of the solution and 2) the principle of optimality, i.e. rule, allowing by the values of the criteria to calculate a single numerical measure of the effectiveness of the solution (act of criteria composition).

The Pascal principle is adequate in tasks with a cumulative effect, when the effect of certain efficiency factors is, as it were, increasing or decreasing the influence of other factors. When maximizing partial criteria, the zero value of any of them completely suppresses the contribution of all others to the overall effectiveness of the solution. In the aerospace industry, this approach can be partly justified when each criterion (for example, reliability and safety) is critical and no improvement in other criteria can compensate for its low value. If at least one of the partial criteria is zero, then the global criterion is also zero.

Shortcoming of application of multiplicative scalar convolution: a very expensive and very effective system can have the same estimation as a cheap and low effective. We will compare such "weapon systems" as an atomic bomb and a slingshot, which at a low cost has some damaging effect. Guided by the multiplicative convolution, it is possible to select a slingshot for the armament of the army.

Similar to the Laplace principle, one can generalize the Pascal principle by introducing weighting coefficients:

$$Y\left[y(x)\right] = \prod_{i=1}^{S}\left[y_i(x)\right]^{a_i}$$

Convolution according to the Charnes-Cooper concept. The concept of Charnes-Cooper is based on the principle of "closer to the ideal (utopian) point." In the space of criteria under given conditions and constraints, an unknown a priori vector y^{id} is determined, for which the optimization problem is solved s times (by the number of partial criteria), each time with one (the next) criterion, as if the rest were not exist at all. The sequence of "single-criterion" solutions of the initial multicriteria problem gives the coordinates of an unattainable ideal vector $y^{id} = \left\{y_k^{id}\right\}_{k=1}^{S}$.

After that, the criterion function $Y(y)$ is introduced as a measure of approximation to the ideal vector in the space of optimized criteria in the form of some non-negative function of the vector y^{id}-y, for example, in the form of a square of the Euclidean norm of this vector:

$$Y(y) = \left\|\frac{y^{id} - y}{y^{id}}\right\| = \sum_{k=1}^{S}\left[\frac{y_k^{id} - y_k}{y_k^{id}}\right]^2 .$$

The disadvantage of this method is the cumbersome procedure for determining the coordinates of an ideal vector. In addition, the possibility of violation of restrictions is not ruled out.

The choice of the scheme of compromises is carried out by the person making the decision (DM) and has a conceptual character.

FORMALIZATION

Depending on the availability and type of information on the preferences of DM, the approaches to solving multicriteria tasks can be different. If there is no such information at all, then sometimes we are limited to finding any solution vector x^* that ensures only the fulfillment of the constraints $A = \left\{ A_k \right\}_{k=1}^{S}$ condition:

$$y^* \in M = \left\{ y \mid 0 \leq y_k(x^*) \leq A_k, k \in [1,s] \right\}, x^* \in X .$$

(Here we have the structuring of the concept of the domain of constraints M).

The disadvantages are obvious – the solution obtained is often rough and, as a rule, not Pareto-optimal. Consequently, the capabilities of the system in this case are not fully used.

The method is recommended to be used to optimize very complex systems, when it is far from easy to carry out even such a simple reconciliation of conflicting criteria ("just to get into limitations"). A variation of this approach is the widely accepted technique, when for optimization of the set y_k, $k \in [1,s]$, the decision maker chooses only one criterion (for example, the first one), and the remaining criteria are reclassified into the category of constraints. Thus, the original multicriteria problem is artificially replaced by a one-criterion problem with constraints:

$$x^* = \arg \min_{x \in X} y_1(x), 0 \leq y_k(x) \leq A_k, k \in [1,s] .$$

A consequence of this approach is the solution in the form of a polar point of the Pareto region, i.e. frankly rude and subjective decision.

The scalar convolution approach with minimized criteria involves the use of the formula

$$x^* = \arg \min_{x \in X} Y[y(x)] .$$

It is more reasonable in terms of formalization.

ANALYSIS OF THE SCALAR CONVOLUTION

The problem is that the form of the function $Y[y(x)]$ depends on the situation of the adoption of the multicriteria solution and is usually not known. Since the function $Y[y(x)]$ is difficult to obtain throughout the entire domain, we are often limited to an analysis of its behavior in the vicinity of that point in the arguments space that corresponds to the most typical situation. Since we are talking about *small* neighborhoods of the operating point, then, using the hypothesis of the smoothness of the criterion function, we replace it by a hyperplane tangent to the surface of equal values of $Y[y(x)]$ at the operating point. Then the approximating dependence $Y[\alpha, y(x)]$ takes the form of a linear scalar convolution

$$Y^{O}[a, y(x)] = \sum_{k=1}^{S} a_{k}^{O} y_{k}(x),$$

where α^{o}_{k} is the regression coefficient having the meaning of the partial derivative of the criterion function with respect to the k-th criterion, calculated at the base operating point. To calculate the coefficients α with the use of information from the DM, it is possible to solve the problem using the least squares method, but it is better to use the heuristic modeling technique described in Voronin (2010).

Using the expression obtained, it must always be remembered that this is only a linear approximation of the scalar convolution of criterial functions, and in situations that differ from the base one, it can lead to significant distortions.

To obtain a criterion function over the entire domain, it is necessary to specify the form of the approximation dependence. As usual in the practice of approximation, success depends on how adequately the form of the given function reflects the physics of the phenomenon being studied. If you use information about the mechanisms of phenomena, then the model you specify is meaningful. In the absence of such information, the "black box" approach is used, and formal regression models of a general type (polynomial, power, etc.) are given for approximation. The quality of meaningful models is usually much better than formal ones.

CONTENT ANALYSIS OF UTILITY FUNCTION

To improve the quality of the research, one should always involve a priori information about the physics of the phenomenon under investigation and, at every opportunity, move from formal models to meaningful ones. In our case, the subject of investigation is such a subtle substance as an imaginary utility function that arises in the mind of the decision-maker when solving a particular multicriteria problem. In addition, even if it does exist, then each DM has its own utility function. Nevertheless, it is possible to obtain information for specifying the type of the meaningful model of a criterial function if one reveals and analyzes some general laws observed in the process of making multicriteria decisions by various decision-makers in different situations.

Comparison of partial criteria of a different physical nature is possible only in a normalized (dimensionless) space. We normalize the efficiency vector y by the constraint vector A and obtain a vector of relative partial criteria (the normalized efficiency vector)

$$y_{0}(x) = \left\{ y_{k}(x) / A_{k} \right\}_{k=1}^{S} = \left\{ y_{0k}(x) \right\}_{k=1}^{S}.$$

This operation is monotonic, and, in accordance with the well-known theorem of Hermeyer, any monotonic transformation does not change the results of the comparison. Therefore, we replace the model of the solution of the vector optimization problem with the original criterion functions by the model

$$x^{*} = \arg \min_{x \in X} Y\left[y_{0}(x) \right], y_{0k}(x) \in [0;1], k \in [1, s],$$

in which the practically used schemes of compromises have a physical meaning. The form of the function $Y[y_0(x)]$ depends on the chosen scheme of compromises.

The scheme of compromises determines in what sense the multicriteria solution obtained is better than other Pareto-optimal solutions. At present, the choice of the scheme of compromises is not determined by theory, but is carried out heuristically, on the basis of individual preferences and professional experience of the developer, as well as information about the situation in which a multi-criteria decision is taken.

The main difficulty of the transition from the vector quality criterion to the scalar convolution is that the convolution should be a conglomeration of partial criteria, the significance (importance) of each of which in the overall assessment changes depending on the situation. In various situations, the rank of "the most important" can acquire different partial criteria. In other words, the scalar convolution of partial criteria must be an expression of a scheme of compromises that *depends on the situation*. When analyzing the possibilities of formalizing the choice of the scheme of compromises, let's put this thesis in the basis.

It is assumed that there are some invariants, rules that are usually common to all decision-makers, regardless of their individual inclinations, and which they equally adhere to in any given situation. The inevitable subjectivity of a decision maker has its limits (Larichev (1979)). In business decisions, a person must be rational in order to be able to convince others, explain the motives of his choice, the logic of his subjective model. Therefore, any preferences of decision-makers should be within the framework of a certain rational system. This makes possible formalization.

The concept of the situation, expressed by the deuce $S=<r,x>$ from the Cartesian product $R{\times}X$, is fundamental to the theory of vector optimization, since it, being objective, is the only support for attempts to formalize the choice of the compromise scheme. We introduce the concept of tension of the situation as a measure of the closeness of relative partial criteria to their limiting value (unit):

$$\rho_k(r,x) = 1 - y_{0k}(r,x), \rho_k \in [0;1], k \in [1,s]$$

This system is a structured characteristic of the concept of the situation $S=<r,x>$, $r{\in}R$, $x{\in}X$.

If a multicriteria solution is taken in a stressful situation, then it means that under given external conditions r, one or more partial criteria $y_{0k}(r,x), k \in [1,s]$, as a result of the solution x, may be in dangerous proximity to the limiting value $(\rho_k = 0)$. And if one of them reaches the limit (or exceed it), then this event is not compensated by a possible low level of the remaining criteria – it is usually not allowed to violate any of the restrictions.

In this situation, it is necessary to prevent in every possible way the dangerous growth of the most unfavorable (i.e., closest to its limit) partial criterion, not taking very much into account the behavior of the others at this time. Therefore, in sufficiently stressful situations (for small values of ρ_k), the DM, if it admits the deterioration of the maximal (most important in the given conditions) partial criterion per a unit, then only compensating by a large number of units for improving the remaining criteria. And in a very tense situation (the first polar case: $\rho_k{\approx}0$), the DM generally leaves only this one, the most unfavorable partial criterion, in view, without paying attention to the others.

Consequently, an adequate expression of the scheme of compromises in the case of a stressful situation is the minimax (Chebyshev) model

$$x^* = \arg \min_{x \in X} \max_{k \in [1,s]} y_{0k}(x).$$ (1)

In less stressful situations, it is necessary to return to the simultaneous satisfaction of other criteria, taking into account the contradictory unity of all interests and goals of the system. In this case, the DM varies his estimate of the winnings according to one criteria and the losses on the other, depending on the situation. In intermediate cases, schemes of compromises are chosen, giving different degrees of partial equalization of partial criteria. With a decrease in the tension of the situation, preferences for individual criteria are aligned.

And, finally, in the second polar case ($\rho_k \approx 1$) the situation is so calm that the partial criteria are small and there is no threat of violation of the restrictions. DM here considers that the unit of deterioration of any of partial criteria is completely compensated by an equivalent unit of improvement of any of the others. This case corresponds to an economical scheme of compromises, which provides the minimum for the given conditions, the total losses by partial criteria. Such a scheme is expressed by the model of integral optimality

$$x^* = \arg \min_{x \in X} \sum_{k=1}^{S} y_{0k}(x).$$ (2)

Analysis shows that schemes of compromises are grouped at two poles, reflecting different principles of optimality: 1) egalitarian – the principle of uniformity and 2) utilitarian – the principle of economy.

The application of the principle of uniformity expresses the aspiration uniformly, i.e. equally reduce the level of all relative criteria in the functioning of the management system. A very important realization of the principle of uniformity is the Chebyshev model (1) – the polar scheme of this group. This scheme makes it necessary to minimize the worst (greatest) of the relative criteria, reducing it to the level of the others, i.e. leveling all the partial criteria. The disadvantages of egalitarian schemes of uniformity include their "economic inefficiency". Providing the closest to each other level of relative criteria is often achieved by significantly increasing their total level. In addition, sometimes even a small digression from the principle of uniformity can significantly improve one or more important criteria.

The principle of economy, which is based on the possibility of compensating for some deterioration in quality according to one criteria with a certain improvement for others, is devoid of these shortcomings. The polar scheme of this group is realized by the model of integral optimality (2). The utilitarian scheme provides the minimum total level of relative criteria. A common drawback of schemes of the principle of economy is the possibility of a sharp differentiation of the level of individual criteria.

The analysis reveals a pattern by which the decision maker varies from a model of integral optimality (2) in calm situations to a minimax model (1) in stressful situations. In intermediate cases, the decision maker chooses compromise schemes that give different degrees of satisfaction of individual criteria in accordance with his individual preferences, but in accordance with the given situation. If we take the conclusions from the analysis as a logical basis for formalizing the choice of the compromise scheme, then we can suggest various constructive concepts, one of which is the concept of a nonlinear scheme of compromises.

NONLINEAR SCHEME OF COMPROMISES

From the standpoint of the systemic approach, it is advisable to replace the problem of *choosing* the scheme of compromises with the equivalent problem of synthesizing a certain *single* scalar convolution of partial criteria, which in different situations would express different principles of optimality. Separate models of compromise schemes are combined into a single holistic model, the structure of which adapts to the situation of a multi-criteria decision making. The requirements for the synthesized function $Y[y_0(x)]$:

- it should be smooth and differentiable;
- in tense situations, it should express the principle of minimax;
- in calm conditions – the principle of integral optimality;
- in intermediate cases it should lead to Pareto-optimal solutions, giving various measures of partial satisfaction of the criteria.

In other words, such a universal convolution should be an expression of a scheme of compromises that *adapts* to the situation. We can say that adaptation and the ability to adapt are the main substantive essence of the study of multi-criteria systems. For this it is necessary that the expression for the scalar convolution explicitly include the characteristics of the tension of the situation. We can consider several functions that satisfy the above requirements. The simplest of these is a scalar convolution

$$Y(\alpha, y_0) = \sum_{k=1}^{S} \alpha_k \left[1 - y_{0k}(x)\right]^{-1}; \alpha_k \geq 0, \sum_{k=1}^{S} \alpha_k = 1,$$

where α_k=const are the formal parameters defined on the simplex and having a double physical meaning. On the one hand, these are the coefficients that express the preferences of the decision-maker for certain criteria. On the other hand, these are the coefficients of regression of a meaningful regression model based on the concept of a nonlinear scheme of compromises.

Thus, the nonlinear scheme of compromises is considered as the basic one, to which corresponds the model of vector optimization, which explicitly depends on the characteristics of the tension of the situation:

$$x^* = \arg \min_{x \in X} \sum_{k=1}^{S} \alpha_k \left[1 - y_{0k}(x)\right]^{-1}. \tag{3}$$

From this expression it is clear that if any of the relative partial criteria, for example, $y_{0i}(x)$, approaches closely to its limit (unit), i.e. the situation becomes strained, then the corresponding term $Y_i = \alpha_i / [1 - y_{0i}(x)]$ in the minimized sum increases so much that the problem of minimizing the entire sum is reduced to minimizing only the given worst term, i.e., ultimately, the criterion $y_{0i}(x)$. This is equivalent to the action of the minimax model (1). If the relative partial criteria are far from unit, i.e. the situation is calm, then the model (3) acts equivalent to the model of integral optimality (2). In intermediate situations, different degrees of partial alignment of the criteria are obtained.

This means that the nonlinear compromise scheme has the property of continuous adaptation to a multi-criteria decision making situation. From this point of view, traditional schemes of compromises can be considered as a result of the "linearization" of a nonlinear scheme at various "work points" - situations.

This, by the way, explains the name of the proposed *nonlinear* scheme of compromises, since in other respects it is no more "nonlinear" than other schemes considered in decision theory. We emphasize that the adaptation of the nonlinear scheme to the situation is carried out *continuously*, while the traditional choice of the compromise scheme is done discretely, which adds to the subjective errors also the errors associated with the quantization of the compromise schemes.

We have repeatedly stressed above that the choice of a compromise scheme is a person's prerogative, a reflection of his subjective utility function when solving a particular multicriteria task. Nevertheless, we managed to identify some regularities and, on this objective basis, construct a scalar convolution of criteria, the form of which follows from meaningful ideas about the essence of the phenomenon under study. The phenomenon of individual preferences of the DM is formally represented by the presence of the vector α in the structure of the meaningful model (3).

The Pareto optimality questions of the nonlinear scheme of compromises and its axiomatics were investigated in Voronin (2010), Albert Voronin (2017).

UNIFICATION

Various assessments of the role of subjective factors in the solution of multicriteria problems are possible. Subjectivity is permissible and even desirable if such a task is solved in the interests of a particular person. Therefore, the mechanism of individual preferences is rather intensively applied in the practice of solving multicriteria problems.

However, subjectivity in their decision is permissible and desirable only as long as the result is intended for specific decision-makers or narrow collectives of people with similar preferences. If it is intended for general use, then it must be completely objective, unified.

When the result of solving a multicriteria problem is intended for wide use, it is unified and individual preferences are leveled by statistics. If there is no a priori information about the differentness of the criteria, then the principle of the insufficient foundation of Bernoulli-Laplace says that in this case we must accept all the weight coefficients in expression (3) *equal to each other*. It follows from the normalization on the simplex that $\alpha_k \equiv 1/s, \forall k \in [1,s]$. Then

$$Y(\alpha, y_0) = \frac{1}{s} \sum_{k=1}^{S} \left[1 - y_{0k}(x)\right]^{-1}$$

Taking into account that multiplication by $1/s$ is a monotonic transformation, which, by the theorem of Hermeyer, does not change the results of the comparison, we pass to the unified (without weight coefficients) expression for the scalar convolution of the criteria

$$Y(y_0) = \sum_{k=1}^{S} \left[1 - y_{0k}(x)\right]^{-1}. \tag{4}$$

This formula is recommended to be applied in all cases when a multicriteria problem is solved not in the interests of one particular DM, but for wide use.

The unified scalar convolution by the nonlinear scheme has the form (4) or, in an equivalent form,

$$Y(y) = \sum_{k=1}^{S} A_k \left[A_k - y_k(x) \right]^{-1},$$

i.e., without preliminary normalization of partial criteria. The concept of a non-linear scheme of compromises corresponds to the principle "away from restrictions".

For the criteria being maximized, the unified scalar convolution has the form

$$Y(y) = \sum_{k=1}^{g} B_k \left[y_k(x) - B_k \right]^{-1}$$

where $B_k, k \in [1, s]$ is the minimum permissible values of the criteria to be maximized.

THE DUAL METHOD

If a multicriteria problem is solved in the interests of a particular decision maker, it is recommended first to obtain a unified (basic) solution and present it to the person. And only if this solution does not satisfy him and correction is required, it is necessary to proceed to the determination of weight coefficients reflecting his individual preferences. It is important that the search process does not start from an arbitrary point in the criteria space, but from a unified, basic solution.

The practice of solving multicriteria problems shows that the assumption that there is a ready and stable (at least implicitly) utility function of the decision maker is not always fair. Solving a multi-criteria task, the decision maker compares sets of specific criteria values with different alternatives, makes trial steps, makes mistakes and interprets the relationship between his needs and the possibilities of meeting them with a given object in a given situation.

With contradictory criteria, this ratio is by its nature a compromise, however, a decision maker does not have a consciously a priori scheme of compromises, or so far it is only in its infancy. Usually, the idea of a compromise scheme that is necessary to solve a problem arises and is gradually improved only as a result of attempts by the decision maker to improve a multi-criteria solution in a series of test steps. It is clear that the presence of interactive computer technology is implied. "In kind" such a procedure is usually impossible.

Thus, simultaneously and interdependent, on the one hand, a person adapts to the multicriteria problem being solved, carrying out the structuring of preferences and improving his understanding of the utility function, and on the other, consistently finds a series of solutions optimal in the sense of the current utility function. The mutually conditioned processes of adaptation of the decision maker to the task and finding the best result are of a dual nature and are, in principle, part of the methodology of the human-machine solution of multicriteria problems.

As noted, in the initial stage of the decision process, the DM practically lacks not only an analytic description of the utility function, but also a ready a priori idea of it. Therefore, the interactive procedure should be organized as dual, and the search optimization method should allow dialog programming in ordinal scales and use minimal information about the utility function. This method, based on the comparison of preferences with specially calculated alternatives, is an ordinal analogue of the simplex-planning method (Voronin (2010), Albert Voronin (2017)).

An important factor contributing to the effectiveness of the method is that the starting point of the search is chosen not as an arbitrary point in the Pareto set, but as an axiomatically grounded basic solution that should only be adjusted in accordance with the informal preferences of a particular decision maker. The process of adjustment provides mutual adaptation: a person adapts to this particular multicriteria task, and the model of a non-linear scheme of compromises becomes a reflection of the individual preferences of the person.

The fundamental difference between convolution in a nonlinear scheme and other known scalar convolutions is the organic connection with the situation of a multi-criteria decision. In fact, the proposed convolution is a non-linear regression function (linear in parameters), chosen for physical reasons and therefore effective. The coefficients α in the expression for the nonlinear scalar convolution have the meaning of the parameters of the nonlinear meaningful regression function, therefore, when found, they do not change from situation to situation, as in the case of linear and other known convolutions that do not adapt to the situation.

The problem of determining the coefficients α in a dual procedure can be considered as the problem of synthesizing a decision rule, which, when applied formally, adequately reflects the logic of a particular decision maker in any possible situation. Such a problem arises, for example, when a multi-criteria system operates in the mode of the operator's advisor in the conditions of time deficit. Here, it is desirable that the system in any situation quickly made the same decision as this operator, if he had the opportunity to calmly think. Similar problems have to be solved in the development of a decisive system for an intelligent robot that functions in changing and uncertain dynamic environments, if you want it to act in the same way a person who trained it would act in its place, etc.

CONCLUSION

As a result of a systemic approach, a multi-criteria optimization model is obtained, which allows an object to achieve all of its goals in the whole range of possible situations. A systemic approach to the problem of multi-criteria optimization allowed us to combine the models of individual compromise schemes into a single holistic structure, adapting to the situation of multi-criteria decision making. The advantage of the concept of a non-linear compromise scheme is the possibility of making a multi-criteria decision formally, without direct human participation. At the same time, on a single ideological basis, both tasks that are important for general use and those whose main content essence is the satisfaction of individual preferences of decision makers are solved. The apparatus of the non-linear compromise scheme, developed as a formalized tool for the study of control systems with conflicting criteria, allows us to practically solve multi-criteria tasks of a wide class.

We hope that in our chapter will find something new and useful for themselves and our colleagues - specialists in the field of research of complex technical and ergatic systems, and students of relevant specialties.

DISCUSSION QUESTIONS

- What is the essence of multi-objective optimization tasks?
- Why N. Wiener warned about the dangers in the optimization of complex systems?
- Why should a systematic approach be used to solve multicriteria problems?
- What are the advantages and disadvantages of such scalar convolutions of partial criteria as additive, multiplicative, and convolutions according to the Charns-Cooper concept?
- What is the main advantage of a non-linear compromise scheme?

REFERENCES

Antonov, A. V. (2004). *System analysis: a textbook for universities*. Moscow. Higher School.

Fishburn, P. (1978). *Theory of utility for decision-making*. Moscow: Science.

Larichev, O. I. (1979). *Science and the art of decision making*. Moscow: Science.

Peregudov, F.I., & Tarasenko, F.P. (1989). *Introduction to system analysis*. Moscow: Radio and Communication.

Voronin. (2017). *Multi-Criteria Decision Making for the Management of Complex Systems*. IGI Global; doi:10.4018/978-1-5225-2509-7

Voronin, A. N., Ziatdinov, Yu. K., & Kuklinsky, M. V. (2010). *Multi-criteria solutions: Models and methods*. Kiev: NAU.

Chapter 14
Fiscal Policy and Social Optimization for Developing Nations:
Some Thoughts in the Digital Era

Jose Manuel Saiz-Alvarez
https://orcid.org/0000-0001-6435-9600
Tecnologico de Monterrey, Mexico

Guillermo Calleja-Leal
Royal Academy of History, Spain

ABSTRACT

From the public sector's perspective, one of the healthiest ways to optimize the social and organizational dynamics of a country in the digital era is to adapt the national fiscal policy to the socioeconomic needs of the population. The objective of this work is to analyze what key factors and which strategical proposal nations can follow to improve tax efficiency and, once a fair and equitable redistribution of the collected financial resources is achieved, to offer higher levels of welfare for the entire population in the digital era.

INTRODUCTION

From the public sector's perspective, one of the healthiest ways to optimize the social and organizational dynamics of a country in the digital era is to adjust national fiscal policy to the socioeconomic needs of the population. The European Union (from now on EU) is laying the foundations for a single fiscal policy throughout the Eurozone. This budgetary centralization aims to be more efficient in controlling public debt with the final goal of reducing public deficit and corruption. All these good managerial practices carried out in the public sector are possible to achieve, only when Governments do not carry out two-hand policies, defined by the combination of anti-inflationary monetary policy and expansive fiscal policy with the increase in public spending. Although such economic policy is forbidden after

DOI: 10.4018/978-1-5225-8933-4.ch014

the signature of the Maastricht Treaty in 1992, some non-Eurozone European governments tend to use fiscal policy for electoral purposes, leading to corrupt practices and the deterioration of their economic fundamentals. The government will avoid these problems by applying a single budgetary system in Europe, which leads to a public deficit's decrease, and a lower need for issuance of public debt. As a result, both economic and social welfare increase to benefit all the countries belonging to the Eurozone.

The European tax model is characterized, unlike the Latin American one, by the existence of higher control carried out by public tax officials by using metadata with the help of Information and Communication Technologies (ICTs), combined with the exchange of Interpol's tax information, tax inspectors and national public security agencies. As a result, Governments can jointly fight against currency evasion and tax fraud. Struggle against fraud increasingly carried out in the European Union with the help of the Financial Action Task Force on Money Laundering (FATF) currently composed of 26 countries, the European Commission and the Gulf Cooperation Council.

The objective of this work is to analyze what key factors and which strategical proposal nations can follow to improve tax efficiency and, once a fair and equitable redistribution of the collected financial resources is achieved to offer higher levels of welfare for the entire population in the digital era. Tax efficiency is framed within an institutionalist vision (North, 1990) that presents a perspective contrary to the populist theory of endogenous development, where economic growth must be autonomous, self-dependent, and centered on the use of national resources. This institutionalist system, primarily supported in the private sector, does not achieve steady economic development. So, in this work, the authors advocate for the use of a neo-institutionalist vision where public-private initiatives are fundamental, because "the strategy to achieve economic development must be based on adequate coordination in the areas of public and private action, because the lack of communication, many of the goals are opposed and contrary to the goals sought" (González, 2009: 94).

These public-private initiatives develop in territories defined by their high degree of economic and social inequality, where institutions only favor the most influential lobbies (World Bank, 2005). As a result, it is necessary for States to be involved in the economy because "the persistence of internal inequalities limits the institutional change that is necessary for the inclusion of the middle classes and the poor use in the processes of change, for economic development and the reduction of poverty. Under these conditions, public and private can cooperate to benefit social groups at risk of social exclusion" (Vázquez-Barquero, 2007: 197).

To achieve the proposed objective, the authors will analyze below how entrepreneurial values are useful and inserted into a Decalogue to implement fiscal-based measures to benefit society. Within these traits, it is worth highlighting the implementation of public-private initiatives for the study of which, in this case, the application of the European fiscal model in other regions, a SWOT analysis is developed. Finally, the authors introduce some conclusions.

A DECALOGUE OF MEASURES TO IMPLEMENT THE EUROPEAN FISCAL MODEL

From a budgetary point of view, the application of the European model in the developing countries' social and economic reality is given, among others, by the following measures:

1. The need to develop an efficient and fair tax system in the redistribution of income;

2.   Fight against corruption and tax evasion;
3.   The design of a system to achieve universal and free coverage in its most fundamental sections of the basic needs of the population: health, justice, and education;
4.   The design of an intelligent eGovernment with the use of ICTs;
5.   The implementation of a transparency policy to know what the destination of taxes is;
6.   Greater control in commercial operations, including in small transactions, avoiding fraud, especially in the use of electronic means of payment;
7.   The approval of a penal code that introduces jail sentences for corrupt officials;
8.   The signing of agreements with other countries to avoid double taxation and to control tax evasion and money laundering;
9.   The design of policies to achieve greater control of public spending always seeking efficiency and the common good, without there being the need to increase the tax burden and, finally,
10. The implementation of policies aimed at a higher degree of public-private collaboration. The need to develop an efficient and fair tax system in the redistribution of income is given by tax equity, according to which the distribution of tax burden among taxpayers is weighted according to their financial capacity due to the nature and purposes of the tax in question.

Fiscal equity will be better as tax fraud decreases because public spending has to be distributed among all the population with a legal obligation to declare the payment of taxes. Today, a minority only,

Table 1. Corruption Perceptions Index (CPI) in the Americas (Low CPI, high corruption rate)

North America		The Caribbean	
Canada	81	Bahamas	65
Mexico	28	Barbados	68
United States	71	Cuba	47
Central America		Dominica	57
Costa Rica	56	Dominican Republic	30
El Salvador	35	Grenada	52
Panama	37	Haiti	20
Honduras	29	St Lucia	55
Guatemala	27	St Vincent and the Grenadines	58
Nicaragua	25	Suriname	43
		Trinidad and Tobago	41
South America			
Uruguay	70	Peru	35
Chile	67	Ecuador	34
Argentina	40	Bolivia	29
Guyana	37	Paraguay	29
Colombia	36	Venezuela	18
Brazil	35		

Source: Adapted from Transparency International (2019)

generally middle class, pay taxes while a good part of the population is excluded from payment, either for economic reasons or due to lack of control by the tax authorities.

Higher payment of taxes is directly related to low corruption levels. The least corrupt countries in the world, and where the middle class is extensive, is where tax fraud is least. The reasons for this fact are (a) high educational levels; (b) adequate compensation (excellent health services, sufficient means of public transport, excellent road infrastructures, ...) by the public authorities after the payment of taxes, and (c) an effect of imitation by politicians who live in austerity and at the service of society. At this respect, Nawawi and Salin (2019) affirm that the capital statement analysis can be a useful tool in detecting under-reported income and tax evasion, only if taxpayers cooperate.

Therefore, as shown in Table 1, the corruption level expressed through fraud and tax evasion is one of the most important structural problems in the Americas, especially in Venezuela, Haiti, Nicaragua, Guatemala, and Mexico, whose solution has to come from the public sector by reducing tax fraud. In this regard, Giachi (2014) shows that the fight against tax fraud is given by tax morality, confidence in the tax system, and the trust in the known taxpayers. So, tax fraudsters justify their actions in the absence of faith in the system and inequity in the exchange, given by the differences between the amount paid and the goods and services received in exchange.

Thus, tax compliance is given by the conjunction of four complementary factors

1. Political trust, by which the rulers have to set an example to the population avoiding corrupt practices;
2. Perception of fiscal justice on the part of the taxpayers who must observe that vertical equity, that is, strict compliance with the progressivity in the tax;
3. Perception of fairness in the exchange, so that taxpayers see a return to the payment of fees under the form of free public essential services (mainly education, justice, and health); and
4. The existence of fiscal morality that legitimizes the rule without there being an abuse of power by the Government. Increased tax revenue because of success in the fight against evasion and tax fraud causes positive externalities in the countries. Thus, and for the Spanish case, Gómez-Plana and Arzoz (2011) show that an increase of 1.4% in the collection of the Value Added Tax (VAT) increases the Gross National Product (GNP) by 1.33%, employment by 1.57%, real wages by 0.76%, and income by 0.06%.

On the other hand, when the population finds that essential public services are offered in exchange for taxes, it is willing to pay even more for the services already enjoyed or expected to be received. Thus, for example, in work carried out by Vásquez and Espaillat (2016) to assess the availability of the population in the small Guatemalan municipality of San Lorenzo to pay for quality drinking water supply. Results show that future beneficiaries would be willing to pay more than 200% on their water bill to receive drinking water for their daily consumption. This fact explains why countries with lower levels of financial corruption in the world are defined by enjoying quality public services, as well as a high perception of equity in the exchange.

The structural transformation of the public administration as a whole would be given by the creation of an intelligent e-Government with the intensive use of ICTs. One of the challenges that e-Government has is the quality of the public service offered to users, which is achieved thanks to the high degree of adaptability of the different computer programs according to local, regional or national needs (Sa, Rocha & Cora, 2016). In other words, instead of having a single data receiving center, which creates the so-called "inefficiencies X" due to the bottlenecks generated, the idea is to digitize the entire territory so that there are information flows in different operational levels transmitted in real time. This land digitalization would make the fight against corruption more efficient and would contribute to a higher degree of economic equity.

Also, the implementation of an adequate transparency policy to know the final destination of taxes paid is one of the challenges that, from a perspective of optimizing public spending, countries have. This high degree of information and transparency of the Government to taxpayers legally exists in the European Union (Law 11/2007, of June 22, of Electronic Access of Citizens to Public Services (BOE 150, June 23, 2007, also known as the e-Government Law), but it is not enough. This Law allows the use of metadata, which in turn leads to higher control in commercial operations, even in small economic exchanges. Transactions whose amounts have been decreasing to be detected by the Tax Agency (up to EUR 2,500) (Law 7/2012, October 29) to prevent and fight fraud, being expressly forbidden to pay workers in cash. All payments must be made through the bank for the electronic record to inform tax authorities and Social Security. In this regard, if a cash transaction exceeds 2,500 euros (or an equivalent amount in foreign currency), and one of the parties denounces the other, this part will have to pay a fine of 25% of the amount traded, but the complainant is exempt from the fine (article 7.2 section 5 of Law 7/2012).

In general, it is a common practice in many micro and SMEs to pay cash to their stakeholders, and more particularly to suppliers. Even to their employees for fortnights, weeks, and even days, which is beyond the control of the authorities. This fact, from a vision of the European tax authorities, encourages corruption, and money laundering. The implementation of such a drastic measure requires a minimum degree of social acceptance by the population. That is why, in my opinion, it is so challenging to implement e-Government in this region.

This type of fiscal measures is complemented by the signing of agreements with other countries to avoid double taxation and control tax evasion and money laundering, as well as the so-called "friendly procedure" that allows the interaction of administrations of different nations directly, without having to resort to diplomatic channels. This procedure is found in the Article 25 of the Model Agreement of the Organization for Economic Cooperation and Development and the Article 25 of the Model Convention between the United States and the United Nations (Abeniacar, 2008: 79). That is why a fluid exchange of tax information between the tax administrations that signed the agreement to achieve distributive and fiscal justice is necessary.

Lastly, in the fight against fraud, the use of the Penal Code that introduces jail sentences for tax fraudsters stands out. In this regard, the authors would like to highlight the legal treatment of the German Criminal Code concerning tax fraud (Kindhäuser, 2007), by distinguishing between corruption offenses arising from commercial and financial transactions and corruption offenses born in the public administration. This difference is significant because the "acceptance of an advantage" (in German, Akzeptanz von Vorteil) by the public official (Article 331 of the German Criminal Code) is considered a particular crime, which has an aggravating penalty. These anti-corruption mechanisms in Germany lead to a tendency toward optimization in the control of public spending, always-seeking efficiency, and the common good, without there being any need to increase the tax burden. As a result, the primary requirements, in terms of health, justice and education, are covered, to which is added an increasing degree of public-private collaboration that we will see, due to its importance, in the following section.

THE PUBLIC-PRIVATE COLLABORATION IN THE EU

In the EU, active public-private cooperation can be observed in practically all of the economic sectors defined as being a mixed system of private capitalization and public provision, which explains in part the substantial degree of State interventionism in Europe, mainly derived from German Ordoliberalism. Following Eucken (1983[1956]) and quoted by Noejovich (2011), Ordoliberalism is based on the following constituent principles:

1. The objective of monetary policy is the stabilization of the currency to control both the monetary base and interest rates (Lombard type);
2. The market must be open, but monopolies must be regulated;
3. Absolute respect must be given to private property;
4. There must be free to contract in the labor market;
5. Economic policy must be guided by corporate social responsibility (CSR); and
6. The Government must have the ultimate objective of stability in the financial system so countries can achieve sound economic fundamentals in the economy, both internal (low unemployment and low-interest rates) and external (equilibrium in the balance of payments).

Contrary to the Anglo-Saxon vision fostering individualism, Europe favors solidarity interests without losing individuality, which makes economic and social progress go along a common evolutionary path (Jellinek, 1954, cited by Noejovich, 2011). A reality that is closer to the situation in Latin America and the Caribbean, given the high importance of the family in the continent, as well as the existence of a tendency to act in a group, especially in rural communities. Thus, in the developing countries of the Americas, the fundamental role of local leaders in small peasant communities surpasses even the leadership carried out by the State in terms of efficiency and struggle against poverty in the post-conflict era (Klick, 2016). Therefore, the population must agree with the measures to be taken by the Government, primarily if they affect the environment (Wayland & Kuniholm, 2015) and want to avoid tensions with the local and regional populations. However, this public intervention, if carried out, must be as small as possible to avoid that the harmful effects of the intervention (crowding-out effect or displacement effect) exceed the positive results generated after this intervention (crowding-in effect). Correct public planning will lead to a harmonious development of the territory to avoid migratory flows to the cities and emigration to foreign countries. To this end, it is essential to increase the levels of public security in these countries, with the reduction of the very high levels of crime in some developing countries.

This public intervention must insert the developing into the new technologies emerged in globalization. According to Greenfield (2106), the global sociodemographic tendencies in the world are given by the passage from a rural to an urban society; the change from agriculture to trade; a growing degree of loneliness due to the interconnectivity of ICT, mainly the Internet, and an increasing tendency to have less extensive families in the number of children. All this leads to the existence of cultural losses (social and family interdependence, respect and tradition) that more than compensate, in many countries, the advantages derived from the adoption of new technologies and global interconnectivity.

These cultural losses can, at least, be partially compensated by business policies based on CSR, ethics, and support for micro-entrepreneurs and collaboration with SMEs through their participation in clusters in business incubators and accelerators. Incubators and accelerators of companies directly connected with universities and research centers, as well as in the European case mainly, with municipalities and local, regional and regional development entities.

Although Panama presents the lowest levels of citizen insecurity, as well as the least desire to emigrate given its better relative economic situation due to sound economic fundamentals, however, scandals with the so-called "Panama Papers" endanger in the short and medium term the attraction of capital and foreign investors who benefit from the existence of a looser tax regulation, which will tend to harm the Panamanian economy in the medium and long-term.

Gately and Cunningham (2014) show that the technology applied to entrepreneurship generates four types of relational capital, namely,

1. Development of networks of contacts;
2. Construction of personal and professional relationships;
3. Access to experts and the membership of associations, and
4. Leveraging of knowledge internalized in the firm's production and commercial processes.

The creation of relation capital is the result of a process of transfer and transformation of individual relationships (Paoloni, Cesaroni, & Demartini, 2019). This transformation process accelerates with the use of ICTs and social networks. The larger the relational capital, the higher the value of the individual in the labor market, and the best relationships with banks (Cucculelli, Peruzzi, & Zazzaro, 2019). Therefore, one of the selection criteria used by headhunter companies is the selection of candidates by observing the number of contacts on LinkedIn pages.

Hence, in terms of job creation and wealth, greater collaboration between universities (public, private, and pontifical) and public administrations (local, regional, national, and international) should be desirable to create positive externalities that benefit society as a whole. Externalities generate employment and wealth for the whole community, and its impact becomes more significant when the principles of justice and equity guide public intervention. X-inefficiencies should be reduced to a minimum with the optimization in making decisions and the use of ICTs to give rise to e-Government for solving administrative procedures quickly.

Bridging innovation, Terstriep and Lüthje (2018) argue that structural and relational embeddedness, relational capital, and absorptive capacity influence clustered firms' innovativeness. The acquisition of high levels of innovation makes the company more competitive in global environments and accelerates its growth by reaching new market niches and building loyalty to existing niches, and throughout this process, the fiscal policy carried out by the government has crucial importance. In this sense, the European example can be a guide to implement it in developing countries, where the leading role of aid by the state is usually less active.

A SWOT ANALYSIS OF THE EUROPEAN FISCAL MODEL FOR DEVELOPING COUNTRIES

As a result, to implement the European budgetary model in the developing countries, it has to adapt to the economic, business, political, and social reality of these countries. A SWOT analysis will be shown to have a unified vision of the positive and negative aspects of its possible implementation.

Weaknesses

The first significant gap in the developing countries' fiscal systems is the absence of strict control between the amounts received, and those declared. This fact makes both a lack of budgetary culture at the time of paying taxes and a fear of fines and penalties so that in these cases only the ethical part of the tax (moral tax) remains when the individual is aware that he is committing illegality (Williams & Franic, 2016). This problem is born due to the low relative levels of computerization about the most developed countries of the planet. Therefore, the implementation of e-Government would solve this problem.

However, to achieve its correct implementation, it is necessary to organize specific training courses for the population to obtain a minimum degree of digital literacy and thus execute structural changes in the tax system. Changes more evident when arising different levels of literacy rates between cities and the developing countries' most isolated areas. A large part of the community is indigenous and does not have access to ICTs, which constitutes a disadvantage because the "bandwidth today is not only a technological trigger but also an economic driver" (Vargas, 2014). Given the current technology, it is possible to achieve high levels of economic growth in rural areas without damaging the environment thanks to the use of clean technologies. However, sometimes the rejection of the population to adopt the paradigms of modernity preserves its culture, language, customs and local customs, which is a special incentive for the maintenance of the cultural and linguistic diversity of the territory for the next generations.

Another weakness for the adoption of the European tax system in the developing countries is given by the existence of a fragile and not very extensive middle class. Expanding the middle class will enrich the lower social levels, and it is essential to achieve the sustainability of the system while reducing public debt and structural fiscal deficit. The significant inequalities between social classes give one of the most severe social problems. This fact leads to a very high level of insecurity and crime in some countries of the region, and the impossibility, because of low tax collection and tax evasion, to achieve a fair redistribution of income and wealth that would reduce these differences.

Threats

The existence of a widespread corruption negatively affects the attraction of capital (foreign and domestic) to be invested into productive investment, which directly influences on the undercapitalization of a future fiscal system, like increase the political and economic instability that augments the country-risk. Regardless of the country considered, corruption negatively affects the growth and welfare of a nation because of the decrease in job creation (Beltrán, 2016). A generation of stable and quality employment that must be sustainable over time if the state wants to avoid migratory flows to third countries.

As a result of corruption and inefficiency in the reallocation of productive resources, and in contrast with most of the developed countries, government policies on taxes and spending have little influence on the increase in the size of the middle class in Latin American nations (Pressman, 2011), which aggravates the existing social imbalance in the region.

The proximity of tax gives a second threat to the implementation of an efficient tax system in the collection havens since there is a risk of a good tax evasion towards them if there is no control of the flow of capital generated by work and productive investment. This threat is unusually intense in those countries where there is no traditional culture on the need to pay taxes, although it considers there is no fair return on the benefit of services offered by Public Administrations towards taxpayers.

Strengths

The application of ICT to increase fiscal transparency and make it easier to file taxes is one of the bases for improving tax collection, and financing public spending for social redistribution of resources. This application primarily favors digital natives whose adaptation to new tax systems based on ICTs leads to better adoption and internalization of e-Government with consequent increases in efficiency. Having a higher degree of fiscal transparency increases the degree of certainty about the destination of the collection obtained, as well as reduces the sovereign risk (Arbatti & Escolano, 2015) by positively influencing the efficiency of its application. Education is of fundamental importance to achieving these higher levels of productivity. A culture based on values, including the value of intergenerational solidarity, provides the basis for the young population to more efficiently support future retirees, including through a system of non-contributory pensions, whose adoption will be obligatory due to the lack of previously quoted (Galiani, Gertler, & Bando, 2016). This type of pensions thus becomes an instrument in the fight against poverty and social inequality, and contribute to reducing the high rates of insecurity in the region. The process of redistribution of income and wealth generated from the implementation of fairer and more efficient tax systems will lead to the creation of a broad-based middle class, which will guarantee the future of the system by reducing social differences. However, the expansion of the middle class will have to emerge with a public intervention, as salaries are meager in relative terms. As shown by Pressman (2011), and except Brazil and Mexico where employment increases the size of the middle class, labor markets in the rest of Latin America do not have a substantial effect on increasing the size of the middle class. In this sense, I agree with this author when he states that

"what is important for a large middle class to exist is government policy: a progressive tax system and a series of generous government spending programs that benefit families of low and medium income. The lack of these policies explains largely the fact that Latin American nations do not have a large middle class compared to that of developed nations. To increase the Latin American middle class, it will be necessary for the State to develop and expand policies that support the existence of a large middle class: child allowances and family allowances, unemployment, and disability insurance and a more inclusive and generous retirement system" (Pressman, 2011: p. 149).

When starting from shallow levels of wealth, the public administration must promote development alone, or preferably, in the process of public-private collaboration. The inhibition of the State in this sense will contribute to the maintenance of a status quo that favors only the oligarchies located near the Government and large corporations. Nevertheless, it is essential to emphasize that once they have been able to lay the foundations for economic growth, the State has to give way to private initiative and prevent very predatory tax systems. In terms of economic policy, Europe has always followed this strategy by fulfilling the precepts of the social market economy. As a result, seven out of the top ten countries in the world in terms of HDI (Human Development Index) are Europeans, which indicates the high standards achieved in terms of economic and social well-being in the continent.

Opportunities

The introduction of an efficient tax system in the region is an excellent opportunity to digitalize the territory, as well as to create pension funds to guarantee the future of the population. The small relative size of the community makes it easier to change, but only if obstacles (corruption and endogenous resistance) are controlled, and ideally eliminated. Economic efficiency, also, allows reducing the tax burden on taxpayers, as well as achieving a fairer redistribution of the tax collection. Without an efficient tax system, it is not possible to create a large middle class and to make higher rates of economic growth. One of the most severe social problems in the developing countries, the small size of the middle class, which prevents economic growth from benefiting society, and as a result, to reduce the high levels of poverty existing in the continent.

Along with this, the adoption of higher levels of tax control tends to break with the inertia effect of not paying taxes by the taxpayers obliged to do so. When this inertia effect ends, it is necessary to continue the process of tax supervision with data crossing to analyze the origin of taxpayers' revenues if a country wants to be successful in collecting taxes. Unless such collection is insufficient due to the impact of the Tanzi-Oliveira effect (high inflation rates cause a fiscal deficit because of inadequate tax collection in real terms), it is advisable to keep the tax pressure as low as possible to avoid reducing consumption or private investment.

Finally, the introduction of higher levels of efficiency in the developing countries' tax systems by using e-Government will achieve more significant levels of economic equity due to the redistributive process of income and wealth generated to benefit the entire population. In other words, the economy has moved from a Pareto suboptimal to a Pareto Optimum, which reduces fiscal pressure in the medium term because of less tax fraud.

CONCLUSION

The adoption of fiscal policy measures and strategies stemming from the European experience to be applied in developing countries would contribute to achieving more significant levels of equity and efficiency in the region, which in turn would result in a reduction of the current high levels of poverty. For this, it is necessary to promote education in values to reduce tax fraud, as well as to lay the foundations for inserting an e-Government with the help of ICTs. E-Government will improve the results achieved on fighting against tax fraud, as well as will contribute to a better reallocation of resources among the population, to favor especially the most disadvantaged and those at risk of social exclusion.

The fight against poverty in the developing countries should go through the improvement of high-quality education and the fight against corruption, mainly to achieve political and economic transparency. Therefore, combating crime is the priority objective that should be at the core of any administrative or fiscal reform of any kind approved in these countries. Without economic and financial transparency, it is not possible to have good results, especially in the Public Administration, generally defined by the existence of bottlenecks in the transmission of information, which creates X-inefficiencies that can be solved by using ICT-based technologies in the digital era.

The process of changing values is a process of systemic change to integrate gradually, as a result of education and culture, new values (independence, self-sufficiency, and gender equality) (Manago, 2012) with traditional values (respect for elders and family obligations). Therefore, educational programs must respect human rights (Schimmel, 2007) and inculcate public benefits, such as equity and justice (Schimmel, 2007). However, it is very different from integrating, respecting local customs and practices, that to impose a "superior" culture on another. Hence, models that have triumphed in other latitudes may fail if they are not adapted to the economic and social reality where they want to be implemented.

The increasing speed in the transmission of information has turned the planet into a global village. As a result of this process, more significant divergence between the richest and poorest of the earth is taking place in the world, which generates injustice and widespread famine. The planet does not have a problem of food production, but the key is in the distribution. Therefore, to improve this distributive process and thus achieve social optimization, it is essential to implement a fiscal policy that raises and disseminate welfare levels throughout the population. But for the correct implementation of fiscal policy to be successful in developing countries, the first issue is to fight corruption. Because when the levels of corruption are widespread, they lead to failure in all economic policies applied to increase the standard of living of the population and, unfortunately, widespread corruption is one of the main problems of developing countries.

DISCUSSION QUESTIONS

1. Do you approve that widespread corruption is one of the significant problems that exist in developing countries? And in developed nations?
2. Do you agree that higher tax rates decrease tax revenues? Why?
3. Is a State intervention good for the economy, or is it better to let the market be free?
4. Do taxpayers in your country perceive fairness in the exchange? In other words, do they see a real return after their tax payment by receiving free public and essential services?
5. Do you like the existence of tax havens? Would you take them away or leave them? Why?

REFERENCES

Abeniacar, P. (2008, October 1). Sobre el Reglamento de Procedimientos Amistosos y la Nueva Cláusula de Arbitraje Internacional en los Convenios para Evitar la Doble Imposición. *Actualidad Jurídica*.

Arbatti, E., & Escolano, J. (2015). Fiscal Transparency, Fiscal Performance and Credit Ratings. *Fiscal Studies*, *36*(2), 237–270. doi:10.1111/1475-5890.12051

Beltrán, A. (2016). Does Corruption Increase or Decrease Employment in Firms? *Applied Economics Letters*, *23*(5), 361–364. doi:10.1080/13504851.2015.1076137

Cucculelli, M., Peruzzi, V., & Zazzaro, A. (2019). Relational capital in lending relationships: Evidence from European family firms. *Small Business Economics*, *52*(1), 277–301. doi:10.100711187-018-0019-3

Eucken, W. (1983). El orden de la competencia y su realización. In *La economía social de mercado: un proyecto económico alternativo* (pp. 21–40). Buenos Aires, Argentina: Centro Interdisciplinario de Estudios para el Desarrollo Latinoamericano. (Original work published 1956)

Galiani, S., Gertler, P., & Bando, R. (2016). Non-Contributory Pensions. *Labour Economics*, *38*, 47–58. doi:10.1016/j.labeco.2015.11.003

Gately, C. G., & Cunningham, J. A. (2014). Building Intellectual Capital in Incubated Technology Firms. *Journal of Intellectual Capital*, *15*(4), 516–536. doi:10.1108/JIC-07-2014-0087

Giachi, S. (2014). Dimensiones sociales del fraude fiscal: Confianza y moral fiscal en la España contemporánea. *Revista Espanola de Investigaciones Sociologicas, 145*, 73–98.

Gómez-Plana, A. G., & Arzoz, P. P. (2011). Fraude Fiscal e IVA en España: Incidencia en un modelo de equilibrio general. *Hacienda Pública Española, 199*(4), 9–52.

González, J. (2009). *Teoría del desarrollo económico neoinstitucional. Una alternativa a la pobreza en el siglo XXI*. Porrua.

Greenfield, P. M. (2016). Social Change, Cultural Evolution, and Human Development. *Current Opinion in Psychological, 8*, 84–92. doi:10.1016/j.copsyc.2015.10.012 PMID:29506809

Kindhäuser, U. (2007). Presupuestos de la corrupción punible en el Estado, la economía y la sociedad. Los delitos de corrupción en el Código penal alemán. *Política Criminal, 3*(A1), 1–19.

Klick, M. T. (2016). The Effect of State-Local Complementarity and Local Governance on Development: A Comparative Analysis from Post-War Guatemala. *World Development, 82*, 1–13. doi:10.1016/j.worlddev.2016.01.005

Manago, A. M. (2012). The New Emerging Adult in Chiapas, Mexico: Perceptions of Traditional Values and Value Change among First-Generation Maya University Students. *Journal of Adolescent Research, 27*(6), 663–713. doi:10.1177/0743558411417863

Nawawi, A., & Salin, A. S. A. P. (2019). Capital statement analysis as a tool to detect tax evasion. *International Journal of Law and Management, 60*(5), 1097–1110. doi:10.1108/IJLMA-03-2017-0024

Noejovich, H. (2011). Ordoliberalismo ¿alternativa al "neoliberalismo"? *Economía, 67*, 203–211.

North, D. C. (1990). *Institutions, Institutional Change, and Economic Performance*. Cambridge University Press. doi:10.1017/CBO9780511808678

Paoloni, P., Cesaroni, F. M., & Demartini, P. (2019). Relational capital and knowledge transfer in universities. *Business Process Management Journal, 25*(1), 185–201. doi:10.1108/BPMJ-06-2017-0155

Pressman, S. (2011). La clase media en países latinoamericanos. *Revista Problemas del Desarrollo, 164*(42), 127–152.

Sa, F., Rocha, A., & Cora, M. P. (2016). Potential Dimensions for a Local e-Government Services Quality Model. *Telematics and Informatics, 33*(2), 370–376. doi:10.1016/j.tele.2015.08.005

Schimmel, N. (2007). Indigenous Education and Human Rights. *International Journal on Minority and Group Rights, 14*(4), 425–453. doi:10.1163/138548707X247419

Terstriep, J., & Lüthje, C. (2018). Innovation, knowledge, and relations–on the role of clusters for firms' innovativeness. *European Planning Studies, 26*(11), 2167–2199. doi:10.1080/09654313.2018.1530152

Transparency International. (2019). *Corruption Perceptions Index 2018*. Berlin: Author.

UNESCO. (2008). *Teacher Training Curricula for Media and Information Literacy*. Report of the International Expert Group Meeting. Paris: International UNESCO.

Vargas, J. E. G. (2014). Universal Broadband Access in Developing Countries-The Case of Bolivia. *Proceedings of the 4th IEEE Global Humanitarian Technology Conference*, 597-602. 10.1109/GHTC.2014.6970344

Vásquez, W. F., & Espaillat, R. (2016). Willingness to Pay for Reliable Supplies of Safe Drinking Water in Guatemala: A Referendum Contingent Valuation Study. *Urban Water Journal*, *13*(3), 284–292. doi:10.1080/1573062X.2014.991741

Vázquez-Barquero, A. (2007). Desarrollo endógeno. Teorías y políticas de desarrollo territorial. *Investigaciones Regionales*, *11*, 183–210.

Wayland, J., & Kuniholm, M. (2015). Legacies of Conflict and Natural Resource Resistance in Guatemala. *The Extractive Industries and Society*, *3*(2), 395–403. doi:10.1016/j.exis.2016.03.001

Williams, C. C., & Franic, J. (2016). Beyond a Deterrence Approach Towards the Undeclared Economy: Some Lessons from Bulgaria. *Journal of Balkan & Near Eastern Studies*, *18*(1), 90–106. doi:10.1080/19448953.2015.1094269

KEY TERMS AND DEFINITIONS

ALPF2: Acronym of "assets liquid in the hands of the public plus the investment funds and insurance instruments," it embraces all these financial instruments that can be made liquid for their tenants.

Digital Literacy: The ability to locate, organize, understand, evaluate, and analyze information using digital technology.

E-Government: The use of ICTs in the internal processes of government and the delivery of products and services following private sector-related (e-business) or public-related strategies.

Fiscal Policy: Type of economic policy related to public spending and taxes to maintain financial stability, cushion economic cycles, and generate economic growth and employment.

Inefficiencies X: Generated by the bottlenecks caused when solving problems in bureaucratic organizations. A correct vertical-horizontal and horizontal-horizontal communication process can eliminate these inefficiencies with the help of ICTs and the digitalization of the entire territory, so information flows in different operational levels transmitted in real time.

Moral Tax: The ethical part of the charge that remains when the individual is aware that he or she is committing something illegal.

Ordoliberalism: Born at the University of Freiburg (Germany), this School of Thought advocates that the State must act to avoid monopolies born in free market economies derived from fair competition. Therefore, for Ordoliberalism, the State must ensure the general welfare by creating an adequate legal environment to maintain a healthy level of competitiveness while following free market principles.

Tanzi-Oliveira Effect: Caused by fiscal deficits fueled by high inflation rates, which creates an inadequate tax collection in real terms.

Chapter 15
Optimization Models for Calculation of Personalized Strategies

Ievgen Nastenko
Igor Sikorsky Kyiv Polytechnic Institute, Ukraine

Volodymyr Pavlov
Igor Sikorsky Kyiv Polytechnic Institute, Ukraine

Olena Nosovets
Igor Sikorsky Kyiv Polytechnic Institute, Ukraine

Oleksandr Davydko
Igor Sikorsky Kyiv Polytechnic Institute, Ukraine

Oleksander Pavlov
Igor Sikorsky Kyiv Polytechnic Institute, Ukraine

ABSTRACT

The chapter considers the problem of calculating the best individual strategy based on models obtained from observations of a given sample object's reaction to the applied control actions. In order to improve the calculation efficiency, the construction of the optimization problem with line dependence on the control variables is offered. To ensure the calculation adequacy, the object state models of optimal complexity, nonlinear with respect to the initial conditions and parameters, are considered. Examples of optimal personalized treatment strategies calculation are given. The proposed approach can be extended to other practical areas to solve the decision making, provided the development of adequate the object state models in the optimization field.

DOI: 10.4018/978-1-5225-8933-4.ch015

INTRODUCTION

Optimizing the dynamics of social and organizational processes is quite a challenge and is a multi-step procedure. There are a stage of process identification (Kiparissides, Koutinas, Kontoravdi, Mantalaris & Pistikopoulos, 2011), a stage of constructing an area in which control actions take place (Cevikalp, Larlus, Neamtu, Triggs & Jurie, 2010), and finally, the most important stage is the formation of a goal and optimization criteria (Jakob & Blume, 2014). Then you should construct an optimization problem and find effective means of solving it (Crown et al., 2017). However, the solving the original problem process also requires optimization since the problems successful solution of individual stages (except the last) does not guarantee the problem effective solution as a whole. For a successfully formalized dynamic optimization problem with adequate process and optimization domain models, there may simply not exist an effective solution tool. Therefore, it is desirable to simplify the problem representation at each stage of the solution search in order to obtain a sufficiently effective tool in terms of the calculation procedure. Following the above in the task below, the dynamic essence of the optimization problem is simplified to the maximum extent. This led the problem formulation to a single management stage: the input state of the object with the applied control action - the output state of an object. Simplified, this is a one-step optimization task "in" - "out". Since the above representation assumes the Markov property possession during the object transition from state to state, the problem has a good prospect for generalization to n control stages. Then, to solve a multi- stage optimization problem, it is possible to apply dynamic programming. The controlled object structural identification of state equations should also strive to obtain the most simple structures (or structures of optimal complexity). If simple with respect to control variables (for example, linear) equations of the object state can be obtained, then effective computational procedures can be applied to solve the optimization problem. The authors tried to follow the above principles in solving the delivered problem - the calculation of the optimal individual impact strategies according to the monitoring data or the active experiment on objects from a given sample. The considered approach to the formalization of the calculation is illustrated by examples of obtaining optimal personalized treatment strategies for patients undergoing coronary artery bypass grafting.

BACKGROUND

Almost any formalized problem can be assigned to one of the three problem classes: design, control, and modeling. And each of these tasks is always dominated by the requirement to solve it in the best way within a definition given area. It would seem that any practical task would have to be formulated and solved as a kind of optimization problem. However, now the optimization statements in the problems of decision making or control actions calculation are usually used only in case when the constraints and the object state models can be obtained analytically. Researchers often avoid statistical estimates of parameters or statistical models due to the introduction of uncertainty related to the modeling error. Nevertheless, the use of stochastic programming methods, the creation of statistical models with an appropriate level of adequacy in the problem variables study area allows us to count on obtaining solutions suitable, at least for expert evaluation of specialists and application in practice. However, the first report of the ISPOR dedicated to best practices in the optimization techniques implementation in medicine marked an extremely rare their application in optimization of therapeutic intervention for individual patients (Crown et al., 2017). One of the few examples of personalized strategies calculation for a particular dynamic programming model is given by Denton, Kurt, Shah, Bryant & Smith (2009). The calculation involves determining the optimal start time for statin treatment of patients with type 2 diabetes. The strategy is personalized depending on the presence in the history of coronary artery disease and cholesterol levels. However, the work does not offer a broader view of the problem as a whole, which leaves the need for common approaches to the task of personalizing strategies. Thus, it can be considered expedient the development and study of this optimization problems class, the development of tools for studying the solutions obtained.

The task of calculating personalized strategies presented below arose from the need to develop a mechanism for determining treatment strategies for specific patients in accordance with their parameters and initial conditions. Note that accounting some important parameters, such as weight, age of the patient, the presence of factors that complicate the excreting function of the body and is now an integral part of the recommendations for the use of therapeutic drugs. However, it is possible to calculate the strategy taking into account and other essential parameters in the presence of which the treatment process is implemented.

The calculation of personalized strategies can be formulated as a solution to the problem of determining the optimal control actions, decision-making, optimal control, which are equivalent representable in the mathematical programming problems form of complexity different levels (Van Slyke, 1968, Tabak & Kuo, 1971 and Betts, 2010). In the general case the calculation of the optimal control will introduce a non-linear programming problems (Tabak & Kuo, 1971).

The task presented in this Chapter also falls into the specified task class. We show the idea of such formalization. Let the available data allow us to construct adequate models for the object(s) output states $E_i^{\text{out}} = F_i(\mathbf{p}, q^{\text{in}}, \mathbf{E}^{\text{in}}, \mathbf{u})$, $i = 1, ..., d$, for the criterion variable $q^{\text{out}} = F_q(\mathbf{p}, q^{\text{in}}, \mathbf{E}^{\text{in}}, \mathbf{u})$ and for the domain of solution existence $\mathbf{F}(\mathbf{p}, q^{\text{in}}, \mathbf{E}^{\text{in}}, \mathbf{E}^{\text{out}}, \mathbf{u}) \leq 0$, where $\mathbf{p}$ is a vector of the object parameters, $\mathbf{E}^{\text{in}}, \mathbf{E}^{\text{out}}$ are the input and output vectors of the object's state, q^{in}, q^{out} are the criterion variable values on the input and output of the controlled period, $\mathbf{u}$ is vector of applied control actions. Then we can formally write the following optimization problem:

$$\begin{cases} \underset{\mathbf{u}}{\text{extr}} \, q^{\text{out}} = \underset{\mathbf{u}}{\underset{U}{\text{extr}}} \, F_q(\mathbf{p}, q^{\text{in}}, \mathbf{x}^{\text{in}}, \mathbf{u}) \\ x_{1\,\min}^{\text{out}} \leq F_1(\mathbf{p}, q^{\text{in}}, \mathbf{x}^{\text{in}}, \mathbf{u}) \leq x_{1\,\max}^{\text{out}} \\ \ldots\ldots \\ x_{d\,\min}^{\text{out}} \leq F_d(\mathbf{p}, q^{\text{in}}, \mathbf{x}^{\text{in}}, \mathbf{u}) \leq x_{d\,\max}^{\text{out}} \\ \mathbf{F}(\mathbf{p}, q^{\text{in}}, \mathbf{x}^{\text{in}}, \mathbf{x}^{\text{out}}, \mathbf{u}) \leq 0 \\ \mathbf{u}_{\min} \leq \mathbf{u} \leq \mathbf{u}_{\max} \end{cases} \tag{1}$$

Substituting in (1) the patient object data $\mathbf{p}, q^{\text{in}}, \mathbf{E}^{\text{in}}$ we obtain an optimization problem (2) and it is focused on the optimal effect calculation for the selected object and its input state:

$$\begin{cases} \min_{\mathbf{u}} q^{\text{out}} = \min_{\mathbf{u}} \ \mathbf{f}_u(\mathbf{u}) + c' \\ E_{1\min}^{\text{out}} \leq f_1(\mathbf{u}) + a_{01}' \leq E_{1\max}^{\text{out}} \\ \ldots\ldots \\ E_{d\min}^{\text{out}} \leq f_d(\mathbf{u}) + a_{0d}' \leq E_{d\max}^{\text{out}} \\ \mathbf{f}(\mathbf{x}^{\text{out}}, \mathbf{u}) \leq 0 \\ \mathbf{u}_{\min} \leq \mathbf{u} \leq \mathbf{u}_{\max} \end{cases} \tag{2}$$

This non-linear programming problem should be solved to calculate the individual control strategy of this object. In some cases, the calculating problem the influence strategies providing the transfer the system from some initial state to some attractor can be described by the linear evolution operator, as shown in works Draško & Božica (2014) and Tomic, Muftic & Baksa, (2019), and solved as a semi-definite optimization problem:

$$\min_{\mathbf{X}} tr(\mathbf{CX}) \mid tr(\mathbf{A}_i \mathbf{X}) = b_i, \ i = 1,\ldots, m, \ \mathbf{X} \geq 0, \ \mathbf{C}, \mathbf{A}_i \in \mathbf{S}_n, \ i = 1,\ldots, m, \ tr\mathbf{A} = \sum_{i=1}^{n} a_{ii}, \tag{3}$$

where S_n is the symmetric matrices set of dimension (n × n). An effective representation example and solution of such a problem is shown in the work of Tomic (2002). In the particular case when $\mathbf{X} = \text{diag}(x_1,\ldots,x_n)$, $\mathbf{C} = \text{diag}(c_1,\ldots,c_n)$, $\mathbf{A}_i = \text{diag}(a_{i1},\ldots,a_{in})$ there is a special effective from the point of view of computing technology option - linear optimization problem:

$$\min_{\mathbf{x}} \mathbf{c}^{\mathrm{T}} \mathbf{x} \mid \mathbf{A}\mathbf{x} = \mathbf{b}, \ \mathbf{x} \geq 0, \tag{4}$$

where matrix A consists of elements a_{ij}, $i = 1,\ldots, m$, $j = 1,\ldots, n$, and x, c, b are vectors $(x_1,\ldots,x_n)^T$ $(c_1,\ldots,c_n)^T$, $(b_1,\ldots,b_m)^T$.

We point out that the problem formalization in this form requires obtaining qualitatively and quantitatively adequate, linear, relative to the control influence of statistical or analytical models for evolution operator. Then, in the future, it is possible using an effective computational tool to solve such problems - linear programming methods (Rosen, Lane, Morrill & Belli, 1991, Hacisalihzade & Mansour, 1985, Crown et al., 2018).

However, if the objects under consideration are patients, then obtaining adequate models is faced as a rule with the lack of experimental data with a sufficient level of control variables variability. The problems arise due to the specifics of clinical trials methods oriented, as a rule, to the proof of the therapeutic effect importance in the sample (Brody, 2016), and not to obtain experimental data, providing the best adequacy of the models. As a result, when solving the optimization problem for a particular patient, researchers are forced to rely either on the specified data of clinical trials or on the monitoring data of the treatment process (Kuzmich & Todurov, 2015).

One of the possible mechanisms for increasing the models adequacy in these conditions is the use of the optimization models tuning to the specific conditions of drugs using: parameters and initial conditions of the patient. Note that the parameters and the object initial states after substitution in the model are converted to the model parameters fixed values. So to improve the models adequacy, it is possible to search for their structures as optimal complexity structures, non-linear in the indicated variables, while not going beyond the linear class of optimization problems in control variables. To build the models of optimal structure it is natural to apply algorithms of Group Method of Data Handling - GMDH (Ivakhnenko & Stepashko, 1985, Madala & Ivakhnenko, 1994). For ensuring the quantitative adequacy of the object state models, the Learning sample data will be divided into Training and Testing data, on the basis of which an external criterion for the selection of generalized variables to the model structure will be formed.

The purpose of the study under consideration is:

- to formalize the calculation of personalized strategies as the object state forecast optimizing task;
- to construct the specified class of optimization problems as linear in control actions and nonlinear in parameters and initial conditions of the object state;
- to carry out examples of calculating the optimal personalized treatment strategy on real monitoring data of the treatment process.

The formulated approach is implemented below.

CALCULATION OF PERSONALIZED STRATEGIES AS A FORECAST OPTIMIZATION PROBLEM

The problem of transferring an object from some initial state to the final one by means of applying a vector of control actions is considered. The effect of interference is present, but not fixed. No information is available on the noise nature. Mark the state variables initial values of the object with the marker "in", the final with the marker "out". Then, in the block matrix object-properties X the block $\mathbf{X}^{in}$ is a matrix of variables values that describe the object initial state, the block $\mathbf{Q}^{in}$ is a vector of the criterion variable initial values, the block $\mathbf{X}^{out}$ is a matrix of variable values that describe the object final state, the block $\mathbf{Q}^{out}$ is a vector of the criterion variable final values, the block $\mathbf{U}$ is a matrix of known control actions:

$$\text{\%} = | \mathbf{X}^{in} | \mathbf{Q}^{in} | \mathbf{X}^{out} | \mathbf{Q}^{out} | \mathbf{U} |, \tag{5}$$

where $\mathbf{X}^{in} = \begin{vmatrix} x_{11}^{in} & \cdots & x_{1d}^{in} \\ \cdots & \cdots & \cdots \\ x_{n1}^{in} & \cdots & x_{nd}^{in} \end{vmatrix}$, $\mathbf{X}^{out} = \begin{vmatrix} x_{11}^{out} & \cdots & x_{1d}^{out} \\ \cdots & \cdots & \cdots \\ x_{n1}^{out} & \cdots & x_{1d}^{out} \end{vmatrix}$, d is the number of object state variables,

$\mathbf{Q}^{in} = (q_1^{in}, q_2^{in}, ..., q_n^{in})^T$, $\mathbf{Q}^{out} = (q_1^{out}, q_2^{out}, ..., q_n^{out})^T$ is the criterion values vector before and after applying the control action, $\mathbf{U} = \begin{vmatrix} u_{11} & \cdots & u_{1h} \\ \cdots & \cdots & \cdots \\ u_{n1} & \cdots & u_{nh} \end{vmatrix}$, h is the number of control variables.

This means that the matrix X represents the data of the object transition, which is in the state x_{ij}^{in}, q_V^{in} $j = 1,...,d$, to the state x_{ij}^{out}, q_V^{out} $j = 1,...,d$, using the values of the control action u_{ij}, $j = 1,...,h$, for each of the known states $i = 1,..., n$.

Next, we will form an optimization problem that is linear in controls, but we will allow to form relations for x_j^{out} $j = 1,...,d$ and q^{out} nonlinear in q^{in} and $\mathbf{x}^{in}$:

$$x_j^{out} = \mathbf{f}_j(q^{in}, \mathbf{x}^{in}) \cdot \mathbf{u} + f_{0j}(q^{in}, \mathbf{x}^{in}) + a_{0j}, \ i=1,...,d, \ q^{out} = \mathbf{f}'(q^{in}, \mathbf{x}^{in}) \cdot \mathbf{u} + f_0'(q^{in}, \mathbf{x}^{in}) + A_0. \tag{6}$$

Also, if necessary, it is possible to construct the area of finite state constraints of the problem as

$$\mathbf{F}_x(q^{in}, \mathbf{x}^{in}) \cdot \mathbf{x}^{out} + \mathbf{F}_u(q^{in}, \mathbf{x}^{in}) \cdot \mathbf{u} + \mathbf{f}_0(q^{in}, \mathbf{x}^{in}) + \mathbf{b}_0 \leq 0. \tag{7}$$

Then it is possible to write a task for criterion optimization q^{out} with constraints on x_j^{out}, $j = 1,..., d$, u_{ij}, $j = 1,...,h$ and the optimization region (7) in the form

$$\begin{cases} \min_{\mathbf{u}} \mathbf{f}'(q^{in}, \mathbf{x}^{in}) \cdot \mathbf{u} + f_0'(q^{in}, \mathbf{x}^{in}) + A_0 \\ x_{1\,min}^{out} \leq \mathbf{f}_1(q^{in}, \mathbf{x}^{in}) \cdot \mathbf{u} + f_{01}(q^{in}, \mathbf{x}^{in}) + a_{01} \leq x_{1\,max}^{out} \\ ...... \\ x_{d\,min}^{out} \leq \mathbf{f}_d(q^{in}, \mathbf{x}^{in}) \cdot \mathbf{u} + f_{0d}(q^{in}, \mathbf{x}^{in}) + a_{0m} \leq x_{d\,max}^{out} \\ \mathbf{F}_x(q^{in}, \mathbf{x}^{in}) \cdot \mathbf{x}^{out} + \mathbf{F}_u(q^{in}, \mathbf{x}^{in}) \cdot \mathbf{u} + \mathbf{f}_0(q^{in}, \mathbf{x}^{in}) + \mathbf{b}_0 \leq 0 \\ \mathbf{u}_{min} \leq \mathbf{u} \leq \mathbf{u}_{max} \end{cases} \tag{8}$$

where the capital F denotes the corresponding matrices, the small f - the vectors, and the f- the scalar functions, $x_{i\,min}^{out}$, $x_{i\,max}^{out}$, $i = 1,...,d$, $u_{i\,min}$, $u_{i\,max}$, $i = 1,...,h$ are the limit values of state variables and controls, limiting the permissible area of the optimization problem.

Since the strings of matrix $\mathbf{X}^{in}$ and vector $\mathbf{Q}^{in}$ are known as the state of the object before optimization, substituting their specific values in the model, we form the corresponding constants instead of nonlinear terms that adjust the models to the state history. The problem (8) after such substitution takes a linear form:

$$\begin{cases} \min_{\mathbf{u}} q^{out} = \min_{\mathbf{u}} \mathbf{c}_u \cdot \mathbf{u} + c' \\ x_{1\,min}^{out} \leq \mathbf{a}_1 \cdot \mathbf{u} + a_{01}' \leq x_{1\,max}^{out} \\ ...... \\ x_{d\,min}^{out} \leq \mathbf{a}_d \cdot \mathbf{u} + a_{0d}' \leq x_{d\,max}^{out} \\ \mathbf{B}_x \cdot \mathbf{x}^{out} + \mathbf{B}_u \cdot \mathbf{u} + \mathbf{b}_0' \leq 0 \\ \mathbf{u}_{min} \leq \mathbf{u} \leq \mathbf{u}_{max} \end{cases} \tag{9}$$

Problems (8), (9) can be used to make optimal decisions in the case of a sufficient adequacy level representation of the object reactions the statistical models of the form (6).

The calculating problem the optimal control action can be reduced to the form (9) not only in the presence of an observation matrix of the same object (5), but also in the presence of statistics for a set of sufficiently homogeneous objects. Statistics at the same time can be represented by the object-property matrix, similar to (5):

$$\% = \mid \mathbf{X}^{\text{in}} \mid \mathbf{Q}^{\text{in}} \mid \mathbf{X}^{\text{out}} \mid \mathbf{Q}^{\text{out}} \mid \mathbf{U} \mid, \tag{10}$$

where each row of the matrix (10) corresponds to a separate object.

Homogeneity is understood in the sense of the representation possibility by adequate statistical models of relations (8), (9) according to the object-properties matrix (10), where the corresponding rows of the matrix X are no longer related to different variants of the same object transition from different initial states to the corresponding finals, but describe the transition from some initial state to the final one for different objects. In this case, the object features are taken into account due to the expedient expansion of the object-property matrix by their characteristic parameter block. The block matrix of the source data takes the form:

$$\% = \mid \mathbf{P} \mid \mathbf{X}^{\text{in}} \mid \mathbf{Q}^{\text{in}} \mid \mathbf{X}^{\text{out}} \mid \mathbf{Q}^{\text{out}} \mid \mathbf{U} \mid, \tag{11}$$

where $\mathbf{P} = \begin{vmatrix} p_{11} & \cdots & p_{1g} \\ \cdots & \cdots & \cdots \\ p_{n1} & \cdots & p_{ng} \end{vmatrix}$ is the object parameter matrix, and where each of its rows contains g the

corresponding object parameter values. The optimization problem type does not change, and the model terms, which are associated with the object characteristics parameters are added to relations (6) and (7):

$$x_i^{\text{out}} = \mathbf{f}_i(\mathbf{p}, q^{\text{in}}, \mathbf{x}^{\text{in}}) \cdot \mathbf{u} + f_{0i}(\mathbf{p}, q^{\text{in}}, \mathbf{x}^{\text{in}}) + a_{0i}, \text{ i=1,...,d,} \tag{12}$$

$$q^{\text{out}} = \mathbf{f}'(\mathbf{p}, q^{\text{in}}, \mathbf{x}^{\text{in}}) \cdot \mathbf{u} + f_0'(\mathbf{p}, q^{\text{in}}, \mathbf{x}^{\text{in}}) + A_0. \tag{13}$$

$$\mathbf{F}_{\text{x}}(q^{\text{in}}, \mathbf{x}^{\text{in}}) \cdot \mathbf{x}^{\text{out}} + \mathbf{F}_u(q^{\text{in}}, \mathbf{x}^{\text{in}}) \cdot \mathbf{u} + \mathbf{f}_0(q^{\text{in}}, \mathbf{x}^{\text{in}}) + \mathbf{b}_0 \leq 0 \tag{14}$$

The criterion optimizing task q^{out} with constraints on $x_j^{\text{out}}, j = 1,..., d$, u_{ij}, $j = 1,...,h$ and the optimization region (14) become the form:

$$\begin{cases} \min_{u} f'(\mathbf{p}, q^{\text{in}}, \mathbf{x}^{\text{in}}) \cdot \mathbf{u} + f'_{0}(\mathbf{p}, q^{\text{in}}, \mathbf{x}^{\text{in}}) + A_{0} \\ x_{1\min}^{\text{out}} \leq \mathbf{f}_{1}(\mathbf{p}, q^{\text{in}}, \mathbf{x}^{\text{in}}) \cdot \mathbf{u} + f_{01}(\mathbf{p}, q^{\text{in}}, \mathbf{x}^{\text{in}b}) + a_{01} \leq x_{1\max}^{\text{out}} \\ \ldots\ldots \\ x_{d\min}^{\text{out}} \leq \mathbf{f}_{d}(\mathbf{p}, q^{\text{in}}, \mathbf{x}^{\text{in}}) \cdot \mathbf{u} + f_{0d}(\mathbf{p}, q^{\text{in}}, \mathbf{x}^{\text{in}}) + a_{0m} \leq x_{m\max}^{\text{out}} \\ \mathbf{F}_{x}(\mathbf{p}, q^{\text{in}}, \mathbf{x}^{\text{in}}) \cdot \mathbf{x}^{\text{out}} + \mathbf{F}_{u}(\mathbf{p}, q^{\text{in}}, \mathbf{x}^{\text{in}}) \cdot \mathbf{u} + \mathbf{f}_{0}(\mathbf{p}, q^{\text{in}}, \mathbf{x}^{\text{in}}) + \mathbf{b}_{0} \leq 0, \\ \mathbf{u}_{\min} \leq \mathbf{u} \leq \mathbf{u}_{\max} \end{cases} \quad (15)$$

To calculate the specific controls of object "a" we substitute the values of its parameters and background $p_{aj}, x_{aj}^{\text{in}}, q_{a}^{\text{in}}, j = 1, \ldots, d$, in the obtained models of form (12), (13), (14) thereby adjusting the system of restrictions and criteria for the specified object. The problem (15) takes a linear form with respect to the control variables, similar to (9). Thus, the objects partially nonlinear models description are formed, thereby increasing the forecast accuracy and at the same time, the problem does not go out of the linear optimization stage class.

In order to ensure the calculation adequacy, the values $E_{i\min}^{\text{out}}, E_{i\max}^{\text{out}}, j = 1, \ldots, d, u_{i\min}, u_{i\max}, i = 1, \ldots, h$ should limit the search area of the problem solution to the area of variable values, where the adequacy the objects state models are confirmed. Quantitative and partially qualitative adequacy of object state models can be provided if the models are calculated by the Grup Method of Data Handling (Ivakhnenko & Stepashko, 1985, Madala & Ivakhnenko, 1994, Vanin & Pavlov, 2004, Pavlov, 2010), with the appropriate choice of the algorithm external criterion. On more advanced approaches that can provide the model qualitative adequacy, we will indicate in FUTURE RESEARCH DIRECTIONS section.

EXAMPLES OF A PERSONALIZED CALCULATION STRATEGY

As examples, consider the calculation of optimal strategies for the specific patients' treatment based on their conditions models, built on the monitoring results the treatment process. In the first example, one of the surgical intervention parameters and the parameters of postoperative treatment therapy are considered as control actions. In the second example, assume the optimization only the post-operative treatment.

Example 1

As a first example, consider the calculation of the surgical intervention parameter (u_0 is the implantable shunts number) and drug therapy (u_1 is the medication duration and u_1, u_2, u_3 are the drugs doses) in the postoperative period of coronary artery bypass grafting. The task criterion q^{out} is the patient's life duration after the operation and the treatment process. The observations sample contains 129 patients. The initial database contains 271 patient characteristics. As parameters and variables of the patient's states, 17 variables were selected, which have a significant correlation with the task criterion q^{out} and three variables of the state $E_1^{\text{out}}, x_2^{\text{out}}, x_3^{\text{out}}$ the final values of which are fundamental to characterize the treatment effectiveness.

Here is a list of variables studied in the notation convenient for recording the optimization problem: p_1 is the time that patient spent in hospital and outpatient under the doctor's supervision (days), p_2 is the patient age, p_3 is the functional class of the patient's heart failure, p_4 is the final systolic volume upon the patient admission to the hospital, p_5 is the final systolic cavity size upon the patient admission, p_6 is the stenotic arteries number, p_7 is the percentage of viable myocardial tissue, p_8 is a part of the lactic acid salts in the patient's blood upon admission to hospital, p_9 is the pulmonary vascular resistance index upon admission, E_1^{in} is the systolic pressure during hospitalization, E_2^{in} is the saturation of hemoglobin mixed venous blood with oxygen upon the patient admission, E_3^{in} is the oxygen utilization factor during hospitalization, u_0 is the number of coronary artery shunts implanted during surgery, u_1 is the medication duration after surgery (days), u_2 is the dose of the drug A, u_3 is the dose of the drug B, u_4 is the dose of the drug C, q^{out} is the duration of life after surgery and subsequent treatment (months), x_1^{out} is the systolic pressure after surgery and treatment, x_2^{out} is the saturation of hemoglobin mixed venous blood with oxygen after surgery and treatment, x_3^{out} is the oxygen utilization rate after surgery and treatment.

In our case, the composition of the block matrix X has the form: $\mathbf{P} = (\mathbf{p}_1,...,\mathbf{p}_9,\mathbf{p}_{10})$, $\mathbf{X}^{in} = (\mathbf{x}_1^{in},\mathbf{x}_2^{in},\mathbf{x}_3^{in})$ are sub-matrices of the parameters and the condition of patients before surgery, respectively, $\mathbf{X}^{out} = (\mathbf{x}_1^{out},\mathbf{x}_2^{out},\mathbf{x}_3^{out})$ is the sub-matrix condition after treatment, $\mathbf{Q}^{out} = (q^{out})$ is a vector of criterion values after treatment, $\mathbf{U} = (u_0,u_1,u_2,u_3,u_4)$ is the sub-matrix of values of medical treatment, and where u0 is an integer variable.

The calculation task is formulated as follows: to determine the number of shunts, duration and optimal combination of the therapeutic drugs doses for a particular patient based on the achievement of maximum life expectancy after treatment in the permissible area of the patient's condition. As a result of the calculation, the following models were obtained:

$$q^{out} = 14.586 + 0.122 \cdot p_3^2 - 0.018 \cdot p_7^2 + 0.003 \cdot u_0 \cdot p_1 p_6 + 0.0007 \cdot u_1 p_3 p_6 - 0.00126 \cdot u_2 x_2^{in} p_4 - \\ -0.0003 \cdot u_3 p_3 p_9 + \cdot u_4 (0.00104 \cdot p_3 p_3 + 0.0001 \cdot p_8 p_9) \tag{16}$$

Normalized relative mean square error (NRMSE) $\Delta_w = \sqrt{\dfrac{\sum_{i=1}^{w}(q_i - \hat{q}_i)^2}{\sum_{i=1}^{w}(q_i - \overline{q})^2}}$ on the Learning sample

of w objects has reached the value $\Delta_w = 0.158$.

$$x_1^{out} = 66.654 - 2.566 \cdot p_2 + 14.42 \cdot \frac{p_3}{x_1^{in}} + 9.015 \cdot \frac{x_3^{in}}{x_1^{in}} - 4.231 \cdot \frac{x_3^{in}}{p_4} - 0.246 \cdot p_3 x_2^{in} \\ +1.982 \cdot u_0 + 12.615 \cdot u_1 \frac{x_2^{in}}{p_1} - 0.056 \cdot u_2 \frac{p_4}{p_1} - 0.002 \cdot u_3 p_1 x_2^{in} - 0.0007 \cdot u_4 \frac{p_3}{p_1} \tag{17}$$

NRMSE on the Learning sample reached the value $\Delta_w = 0.341$.

$$x_2^{\text{out}} = 0.805 - 0.033 \cdot p_2 + 0.065 \cdot \frac{p_3}{x_1^{\text{in}}} - 0.001 \cdot x_1^{\text{in}} + 0.006 \cdot u_0 + 0.0005 \cdot u_1 \frac{x_3^{\text{in}}}{p_1} - 0.0001 \cdot u_2 \frac{p_4}{x_3^{\text{in}}} -$$

$$-0.0004 \cdot u_3 \frac{x_2^{\text{in}}}{p_4} - 0.0001 \cdot u_4 \frac{p_3}{p_1} \tag{18}$$

NRMSE on the Learning sample reached the value $\Delta_w = 0.379$.

$$x_3^{\text{out}} = 12.987 - 12.3 \cdot \frac{p_3}{x_1^{\text{in}}} + 3.179 \cdot p_2 + 0.148 \cdot x_1^{\text{in}} + 5.668 \cdot \frac{p_1}{x_1^{\text{in}}} + 0.118 \cdot p_3 x_2^{\text{in}}$$

$$-0.782 \cdot u_0 - 0.035 \cdot u_1 \frac{p_1}{x_1^{\text{in}}} + 0.01 \cdot u_2 \frac{p_4}{x_3^{\text{in}}} + 0.034 \cdot u_3 \frac{p_1}{p_4} - 0.002 \cdot u_4 \tag{19}$$

NRMSE on the Learning sample reached the value $\Delta_w = 0.355$.

We form the task constraints by setting them for the state and control variables based on the variable area where the adequate modeling results were obtained.

Set constraints on the following output state variables $60 \leq x_1^{\text{out}} \leq 120$, $0.2 \leq x_2^{\text{out}} \leq 1$, $21 \leq x_3^{\text{out}} \leq 50$ and controls $0 \leq u_0 \leq 5$, $0 \leq u_1 \leq 200$, $0 \leq u_2 \leq 300$, $0 \leq u_3 \leq 200$, $0 \leq u_4 \leq 250$

Taking into account the found models, we write down the optimization problem

$$\begin{cases} \max_{\mathbf{u}} \quad q^{\text{out}} = \max_{\mathbf{u}} \ [14.586 + 0.122 \cdot p_3^2 - 0.018 \cdot p_7^2 + 0.003 \cdot u_0 \cdot p_1 p_6 + 0.0007 \cdot u_1 p_3 p_6 - \\ -0.00126 \cdot u_2 x_2^{\text{in}} p_4 + -0.0003 \cdot u_3 p_3 p_9 + u_4 (0.00104 \cdot p_3 p_3 + 0.0001 \cdot p_8 p_9)] \\ 60 \leq 66.654 - 2.566 \cdot p_2 + 14.42 \cdot \frac{p_3}{x_1^{\text{in}}} + 9.015 \cdot \frac{x_3^{\text{in}}}{x_1^{\text{in}}} - 4.231 \cdot \frac{x_3^{\text{in}}}{p_4} - 0.246 \cdot p_3 x_2^{\text{in}} + 1.982 \cdot u_0 + \\ +12.615 \cdot u_1 \frac{x_2^{\text{in}}}{p_1} - 0.056 \cdot u_2 \frac{p_4}{p_1} - 0.002 \cdot u_3 p_1 x_2^{\text{in}} - 0.0007 \cdot u_4 \frac{p_3}{p_1} \leq 120 \\ 0,5 \leq 0.805 - 0,033 \cdot p_2 + 0.065 \cdot \frac{p_3}{x_1^{\text{in}}} - 0,001 \cdot x_1^{\text{in}} + 0.006 \cdot u_0 + 0.0005 \cdot u_1 \frac{x_3^{\text{in}}}{p_1} - \\ -0.0001 \cdot u_2 \frac{p_4}{x_3^{\text{in}}} - 0.0004 \cdot u_3 \frac{x_2^{\text{in}}}{p_4} - 0,0001 \cdot u_4 \frac{p_3}{p_1} \leq 1 \\ 21 \leq 12.987 - 12.3 \cdot \frac{p_3}{x_1^{\text{in}}} + 3.179 \cdot p_2 + 0.148 \cdot x_1^{\text{in}} + 5.668 \cdot \frac{p_1}{x_1^{\text{in}}} + 0.118 \cdot p_3 x_2^{\text{in}} - \\ -0.782 \cdot u_0 - 0.035 \cdot u_1 \frac{p_1}{x_1^{\text{in}}} + 0.01 \cdot u_2 \frac{p_4}{x_3^{\text{in}}} + 0.034 \cdot u_3 \frac{p_1}{p_4} - 0.002 \cdot u_4 \leq 50 \\ 0 \leq u_0 \leq 5, \quad 0 \leq u_1 \leq 200, \quad 0 \leq u_2 \leq 300, \quad 0 \leq u_3 \leq 200, \quad 0 \leq u_4 \leq 250 \end{cases} \tag{20}$$

where u_0 is an integer variable.

Now the task is written in the form (20) corresponding to the task (15). The next step is to convert it to a particular form, configured for a specific object. Choose a patient with parameters and initial conditions: $p_1 = 32$, $p_2 = 36$, $p_3 = 4$, $p_4 = 183.3$, $p_6 = 4$, $p_7 = 86$, $p_8 = 2.4$, $p_9 = 750.61$, $x_1^{out} = 72$, $x_2^{out} = 0.64$, $x_3^{out} = 36$. After substitution of patient data, the optimization problem (20) acquires a special form (21) related to the Mixed Integer Linear Programming problem (MILP problem):

$$\begin{cases} \max_{\mathbf{u}} \left[39,56 + 1,67 \cdot u_0 + 0,0756 \cdot u_1 + 0.147 \cdot u_2 - 8,106 \cdot u_3 + 0,204 \cdot u_4 \right] \\ 60 \leq x_{15} = 61,608 + 1,982 \cdot u_0 + 0,13 \cdot u_1 - 0,16 \cdot u_2 - 0.079 \cdot u_3 - 0,00406 \cdot u_4 \leq 120 \\ 0,2 \leq 0,83 + 0,06 \cdot u_0 + 0,00029 \cdot u_1 - 0.0094 \cdot u_2 - 0.00015 \cdot u_3 - 0,000058 \cdot u_4 \leq 1 \\ 21 \leq 14,43 - 0,782 \cdot u_0 - 0.0301 \cdot u_1 + 0.0509 \cdot u_2 + 0.0115 \cdot u_3 - 0,002 \cdot u_4 \leq 50 \\ 0 \leq u_0 \leq 5, \quad 0 \leq u_1 \leq 200, \quad 0 \leq u_2 \leq 300, \quad 0 \leq u_3 \leq 200, \quad 0 \leq u_4 \leq 250 \end{cases} \qquad (21)$$

where u_0 is an integer variable.

The Calculation Result

Solving (21), we obtain the drug dose A of 2.36 units, the drug dose C of 240 units and medication duration of 200 days. At the drugs discontinuation time, the systolic pressure must be 96, the saturation - 1, the oxygen utilization rate - 27.51. The life duration is 72 months.

Example 2

Consider a task, similar to the example 1 where the number of implanted shunts is no longer the task controlling effect but is a preliminary decision made by doctors based on the patient preoperative analysis. Thus, the task control variable u_0 in example 1 assumes the role of one of the patient's input parameters p_{10}, which will change the criterion model parameters and (formally) the structure of the object state models. Next, we consider the optimization of the postoperative therapy calculation.

The patient parameters matrix includes an additional parameter p_{10} that is the number of implanted shunts, and the control vector contains only four components - $\mathbf{U} = (u_1, u_2, u_3, u_4)$. The rest of the notation in example 2 coincide with the example 1 notation. The obtained models have the following form:

$$q^{out} = -27.379 - 153.064 \frac{p_3}{p_1} + 1.045 \cdot x_2^{in} + 5.808 \cdot p_3 \cdot p_3 - 12.132 \cdot p_2 + 24.445 \cdot u_1 \frac{x_2^{in}}{x_3^{in}} +$$
$$+ 0.489 \cdot u_2 \cdot x_2^{in} \cdot x_2^{in} - 0.796 \cdot u_3 \frac{x_3^{in}}{p_1} - 12.295 \cdot u_3 \frac{1}{p_4 \cdot x_2^{in}} + 0.529 \cdot u_4 \frac{p_3}{x_3^{in}} \qquad (22)$$

Normalized relative mean square error (NRMSE) on the Learning sample of W objects has reached the value $\Delta_w = 0.155$.

$$x_1^{out} = 68.654 - 2.066 \cdot p_2 + 14.42 \cdot \frac{p_3}{x_1^{in}} + 9.015 \cdot \frac{x_3^{in}}{x_1^{in}} + 1.982 \cdot x_2^{in} - 4.231 \cdot \frac{x_3^{in}}{p_4} - 0.246 \cdot p_3 \cdot x_2^{in}$$
$$+ 12.615 \cdot u_1 \frac{x_2^{in}}{p_1} - 0.056 \cdot u_2 \frac{p_4}{p_1} - 0.002 \cdot u_3 \cdot p_1 \cdot x_2^{in} - 0.0007 \cdot u_4 \frac{p_3}{p_1} \tag{23}$$

NRMSE on the Learning sample reached the value - $\Delta_w = 0.341$.

$$x_2^{out} = 0.805 - 0.033 \cdot p_2 + 0.065 \cdot \frac{p_3}{x_1^{in}} - 0,001 \cdot x_1^{in} + 0.006 \cdot p_{10} + +0.0005 \cdot u_1 \frac{x_3^{in}}{p_1}$$
$$- 0.0001 \cdot u_2 \frac{p_4}{x_3^{in}} - 0.0004 \cdot u_3 \frac{x_2^{in}}{p_4} - 0.0001 \cdot u_4 \frac{p_3}{p_1} \tag{24}$$

NRMSE on the Learning sample reached the value - $\Delta_w = 0.379$.

$$x_3^{out} = 12.987 - 12.3 \cdot \frac{p_3}{x_1^{in}} + 3.179 \cdot x_2 + 0.148 \cdot x_1^{in} - 0.782 \cdot p_{10} + 5.668 \cdot \frac{p_1}{x_1^{in}} + 0.118 \cdot p_3 \cdot x_2^{in}$$
$$- 0.035 \cdot u_1 \frac{p_1}{x_1^{in}} + 0.01 \cdot u_2 \frac{p_4}{x_3^{in}} + 0.034 \cdot u_3 \frac{p_1}{p_4} - 0.002 \cdot u_4 \tag{25}$$

NRMSE on the Learning sample reached the value - $\Delta_w = 0.355$.

Taking into account the found models, we write down the optimization problem (26) corresponding to (15):

$$
\begin{cases}
\max_{u} \ q^{out} = \max_{u} - 27.379 - 153.064 \frac{p_3}{p_1} + 1.045 \cdot x_2^{in} + 5.808 \cdot p_3 \cdot p_3 - 12.132 \cdot p_2 \\[2mm]
+ 24.445 \cdot u_1 \frac{x_2^{in}}{x_3^{in}} + 0.489 \cdot u_2 \cdot x_2^{in} \cdot x_2^{in} - 0.796 \cdot u_3 \frac{x_3^{in}}{p_1} - 12.295 \cdot u_3 \frac{1}{p_4 \cdot s_2^{in}} + 0.529 \cdot u_4 \frac{p_3}{x_3^{in}} \\[2mm]
s_{1\,min}^{out} \leq 68.654 - 2.066 \cdot p_2 + 14.42 \cdot \frac{p_3}{x_1^{in}} + 9.015 \cdot \frac{x_3^{in}}{x_1^{in}} + 1.982 \cdot x_2^{in} - 4.231 \cdot \frac{x_3^{in}}{p_4} - 0.246 \cdot p_3 \cdot x_2^{in} \\[2mm]
+ 12.615 \cdot u_1 \frac{s_2^{in}}{p_1} - 0.056 \cdot u_2 \frac{p_4}{p_1} - 0.002 \cdot u_3 \cdot p_1 \cdot s_2^{in} - 0.0007 \cdot u_4 \frac{p_3}{p_1} \leq s_{1\,max}^{out} \\[2mm]
s_{2\,min}^{out} \leq 68.654 - 2.066 \cdot p_2 + 14.42 \cdot \frac{p_3}{s_1^{in}} + 9.015 \cdot \frac{s_3^{in}}{s_1^{in}} + 1.982 \cdot s_2^{in} - 4.231 \cdot \frac{s_3^{in}}{p_4} - 0.246 \cdot p_3 \cdot s_2^{in} \\[2mm]
+ 12.615 \cdot u_1 \frac{s_2^{in}}{p_1} - 0.056 \cdot u_2 \frac{p_4}{p_1} - 0.002 \cdot u_3 \cdot p_1 \cdot s_2^{in} - 0.0007 \cdot u_4 \frac{p_3}{p_1} \leq s_{2\,max}^{out} \\[2mm]
s_{3\,min}^{out} \leq 12.987 - 12.3 \cdot \frac{p_3}{s_1^{in}} + 3.179 \cdot x_2 + 0.148 \cdot s_1^{in} - 0.782 \cdot p_{10} + 5.668 \cdot \frac{p_1}{s_1^{in}} + 0.118 \cdot p_3 \cdot s_2^{in} \\[2mm]
- 0.035 \cdot u_1 \frac{p_1}{s_1^{in}} + 0.01 \cdot u_2 \frac{p_4}{s_3^{in}} + 0.034 \cdot u_3 \frac{p_1}{p_4} - 0.002 \cdot u_4 \leq s_{3\,max}^{out} \\[2mm]
\quad u_{1\,min} \leq u_1 \leq u_{1\,max}, \quad u_{2\,min} \leq u_2 \leq u_{2\,max}, \quad u_{3\,min} \leq u_3 \leq u_{3\,max}, \quad u_{4\,min} \leq u_4 \leq u_{4\,max}
\end{cases} \tag{26}
$$

Next, we form the constraints of the problem by setting the boundaries for the state variables and controls based on the variables area where adequate simulation results were obtained:

$$64 \leq x_1^{\text{out}} \leq 120, \, 0.2 \leq x_2^{\text{out}} \leq 1, \, 21 \leq x_3^{\text{out}} \leq 50, \, 21 \leq x_3^{\text{out}} \leq 50, \, 0 \leq u_1 \leq 100,$$

$$0 \leq u_2 \leq 300, \, 0 \leq u_3 \leq 200, \, 0 \leq u_4 \leq 250.$$

Then let convert (26) to its particular form (27), tuned to the patient. Substitute the parameters and initial conditions of the selected patient $p_1 = 32$, $p_2 = 36$, $p_3 = 4$, $p_4 = 183.3$, $p_{10} = 3$, $x_1^{in} = 72$, $x_2^{in} = 0.64$, $x_3^{in} = 36$ in (26). The patient-oriented task takes the form of a linear programming problem:

$$\begin{cases} \max_u \quad -75,23 + 0,434 \cdot u_1 + 0,2002 \cdot u_2 - 0.462 \cdot u_3 + 0.0424 \cdot u_4 \\ 60 \leq 61,608 + 0,13 \cdot u_1 - 0,16 \cdot u_2 - 0.079 \cdot u_3 - 0,00406 \cdot u_4 \leq 120 \\ 0,5 \leq 0,83 + 0,00029 \cdot u_1 - 0.0094 \cdot u_2 - 0.00015 \cdot u_3 - 0,000058 \cdot u_4 \leq 1 \\ 21 \leq 14,43 - 0.0301 \cdot u_1 + 0.0509 \cdot u_2 + 0.0115 \cdot u_3 - 0,002 \cdot u_4 \leq 50 \\ 0 \leq u_1 \leq 100, \quad 0 \leq u_2 \leq 300, \quad 0 \leq u_3 \leq 200, \quad 0 \leq u_4 \leq 250 \end{cases} \quad (27)$$

The Calculation Result

Solving (27), we obtain the drug dose A of 32 units, the drug dose C of 240 units and medication duration of 100 days. At the drugs discontinuation time, the systolic pressure must be 84, the saturation 1, the oxygen utilization rate - 30.1. The life duration is 52.3 months.

THE RESULT DISCUSSION AND RECOMMENDATIONS

As can be seen, the calculations results satisfy the established restrictions. At the same time, it is obvious that any "computer" solution should receive a compliance expert assessment the treatment Protocol and its possible implementations. And only after that, is possible to implement it in practice. Recall that the task of finding the optimal strategy is preceded by checking the behavior adequacy of the object state models under study in the optimization region and, if necessary, this area is narrowed (expanded) to the required limits.

The most natural solution to the problem of using linear statistical models in optimization tasks is to achieve the highest possible accuracy of the models. If the desired accuracy cannot be achieved then the further approach development may be in the way of linear approximation in its individual subdomains. In particular, using different formations from the admissible area of some sets of convex subdomains, the sum of which forms the initial admissible area, and the pairwise intersection forms some paths from the initial to the best state. Next, in each set, we will look for a chain (pairwise intersecting by areas) of the generated optimization tasks leading to the best solution. Let us take as the solution to the initial problem the best of the obtained solutions. This approach may be effective if the quality and sample size allow obtaining the adequate and linear by controls the models in each of the generated subdomains.

If the modeling results will be unsatisfactory or there are problems in the chain construction of linear programming tasks will have to move to the nonlinear optimization problem.

In the case that the experiment or observations data of the process contain controlling variables with insufficient variation, the authors recommend using the algorithm versions with the patronage for certain variables providing of entering them in the model. Thus, the qualitative adequacy problem of object state models can be partially solved. More radical mechanisms for solving this problem will be discussed in the next section.

In conclusion, we note the obvious fact that in accordance with (5) - (9) can be calculated the optimal strategy of transfer from the initial state to the final for the same object.

FUTURE RESEARCH DIRECTIONS

The solution of MILP problems is usually based on multiple solutions to linear programming problems. Therefore, we will further consider the results from the point of view of the simplex method mechanisms application. We note the proposed approach significant feature from the point of view of evaluating the solution optimality: the iterate mechanism over the simplex vertices has an algebraic nature, so is correct applying it to analytical relations, and not to statistical ones. And only the initial relations will correspond to the most probable values of the modeled quantities. Any transformation of the original system forms a ratio different from the most likely. The analytical transformations replacement in the transition to the neighboring simplex vertex with statistical ones will require modeling of independent variables, which formally contradicts the statistical modeling logic. The theoretical obstacle here, to a certain extent, is the need to interpret the control variables as dependent variables. However, in the essence of the problem, it is not a contradiction, since the value choice of medical treatment by a doctor in the treatment process are interrelated and depend on the patient state. And as we noted above, the problem can be solved radically by obtaining a model of the objects state the qualitative and quantitative adequacies of which are close to analytical analogs. If the models' error is significant, then the problem can be solved by developing mechanisms for obtaining the best statistical relations with equal standard deviations for each variable, when they are used as a model output. Such relations can be considered as coarsened analogs of the corresponding analytical ones, and for them the analytical procedures of the simplex method for moving along the vertices of the simplex may be considered as correct. Improving the models' quantitative adequacy, it is desirable to have a number of object subgroups in the sample with sufficiently close parameter values (rows of submatrix P, ideally belonging to almost identical objects). The impact results in such subgroups can be interpreted as the control results for one object in the definition field the optimization problem. Then, using the GMDH algorithms (Ivakhnenko & Stepashko, 1985, Madala & Ivakhnenko, 1994), we can form external criteria on test samples from a part of objects with similar parameter values. This approach will allow calculating the optimal complexity models and will be reasonable expectations to obtain quantitatively adequate forecasts in the field of input states, represented by the object-properties matrix.

A separate problem for the optimization problem successful solution is to obtain qualitatively and quantitatively adequate the objects state models. The problem with the data for modeling, that indicated above in the work, contained in the fact that the treatment process observations contain insufficient variations for control variables, has repeatedly led to qualitatively inadequate model structures. To ensure the control variables entered into the model without significantly impairing the quantitative adequacy, the authors used the modeling algorithms with the patronage for the control variables. In the future, it is planned to develop modeling algorithms that ensure both the forecast accuracy and the object state models structure consistency to the essence of the extreme problem. The fulfillment of these conditions will allow us to reasonably assume the possibility of the personalized strategies adequate calculation. Note that decision the key issue qualitative adequacy of models can be provided by the means of mathematical programming algorithms. This problem is extremely extensive and deserves a separate in-depth study and development. Here we note that many useful ideas in this direction can be found in (Zgurovsky & Pavlov, 2019). The list of authors ' works, each of which is constructive research, is given in the sections ADDITIONAL READING and DISCUSSION QUESTIONS to those interested in the ideas of solving combinatorial problems used to build effective algorithms for selecting structures.

As we said above, most often a "computer" solution should receive expert evaluation and only after that it should be applied in practice. This requires the development of a decision support system so that the validity of the individual strategy calculation system is evident to the decision maker. Therefore, as an analytical tool to support the optimal strategy calculation system, it is advisable developing an analysis subsystem for visual assessment of the models' qualitative adequacy and a subsystem for analyzing the optimization problem solution. The analysis the multidimensional models' visual representation by the slices for the specific values of separate variables will allow to estimate the qualitative adequacy of the objects state models in areas where there is not enough training data to assess the quantitative adequacy. The subsystem of the optimization problem solution analysis should provide a study of the optimal solution stability degree found when compared with the variance of the task functional and constraints parameters.

And in conclusion, we note the organizational problem, the solution of which will dramatically increase the efficiency of the objects state models and, as a consequence, the validity of the optimization problem solution. Currently used the clinical trial methodology is aimed solely at providing the therapeutic effect significance in the study group in comparison with the placebo. Variants of methodology allow comparison of the new drug effect with the effects in the groups in which the therapy is carried out by known methods. Note that the circumstances that allow detailing the individual treatment strategy are limited by the parameters of the patient, such as weight, partially age (discretely - children, adults, elderly contingent) and factors that complicate the excreting function of the body. The current clinical trial methodology does not provide data with a sufficient degree of therapeutic impacts variability so that it would be possible to build adequate changes models in the patients' condition under the therapy influence. This is what causes for the need of application is quite artificial patronage methods for control variables when building models. And in these conditions, it is not always possible to obtain qualitatively adequate models. This is due to the fact that the patient parameters variability and the treatment initial conditions are significantly higher than the therapeutic impacts variability in the main group. And the statistical models' accuracy is achieved to a greater extent by increasing the complexity of the model structures for these parameters, while the use of algorithms with variables protection may lead to an inadequate form of inclusion in the model of therapeutic effects. A natural problem solution is the creation of subgroups in the main object group, one of which is aimed at proving the therapy effect significance, and the other to allow the use of therapeutic impacts variability, sufficient to obtain the best in these conditions, the statistical models' accuracy. For the first subgroup, there are results that allow for a given significance level to obtain estimates for the minimum required objects number in order to prove the difference effect. The estimates are based on the application of Hill's hypothesis to symmetric absolutely continuous distributions [18]. In the thesis of author D. Klyushin, the hypothesis proof in these conditions is given. There are also the proposed nonparametric tests of equivalence of General populations based on measures of proximity between the hypothetical and empirical samples, which are composed of symmetrically dependent random variables. Their advantage over Kolmogorov-Smirnov and Wilks statistics is proved. For the second subgroup, it is expedient to apply the experiment multilevel planning, with the give of necessary level for impacts variability. In sufficiently homogeneous objects subgroups in the linear case, it is possible to apply the principles of a multi-factorial experiment. Express the opinion that the main problem here is the need to convince the doctors' community in the feasibility of changing the clinical trials' methodology so that trials results can be effectively used to build personalized strategies.

CONCLUSION

The Chapter formalizes the problem of calculating personalized strategies that optimize the object predicted state. A class of optimization problems, linear in control actions and nonlinear in parameters and initial conditions of the object state, is constructed. The application correctness conditions of the offered optimization models are specified. The examples of optimal treatment strategy calculation in the period after coronary artery bypass grafting are considered. The results obtained imply the doctor expert evaluation use but demonstrate the fundamental possibility of calculating the optimal personalized strategies. The proposed approach can be extended to other decision-making practical tasks areas, provided that the object state adequate models in specified optimization area are developed.

DISCUSSION QUESTIONS

1. What statistical estimates allow us to assess the models' quantitative adequacy?
2. What features will you suggest to assess the models' qualitative adequacy?
3. What tools can be offered to study the models' qualitative adequacy?
4. What class of problems solves the proposed approach in the Chapter, what is the main idea of the approach?
5. What ways can be considered to summarize the approach proposed in the Chapter?
6. What are the main limitations of the method?
7. How can the approach be modified if the accuracy of the obtained models that are linear in controls and nonlinear in parameters and initial States of the object is obtained unsatisfactory?
8. Under what conditions it is necessary to pass to the formation of a nonlinear optimization problem?
9. Express your opinion on the ways of the system development proposed in the DIRECTIONS OF FUTURE RESEARCH section.
10. Why is the direct application of statistical models with a significant modeling error to form the constraints of the LP problem is not correct? What are the possible ways to solve the problem?
11. What are the possible reasons for the use of modeling the objects state equations of algorithms with the patronage for some variables? What variables do you need to specify patronage?
12. Justify the need to develop an analytical tool to support the system of calculation the optimal individual strategy. What functionality would you offer for such an analytical system?

13. What are the methodology provisions of clinical trials limit the obtaining possibility on the basis of their statistics adequate models of patient states?
14. In what areas other than medicine the proposed tool for calculating individual strategies can be applied?

REFERENCES

Betts, J. (2010). *Practical methods for optimal control and estimation using nonlinear programming* (2nd ed.). Philadelphia, PA: Society for Industrial and Applied Mathematics. doi:10.1137/1.9780898718577

Brody, T. (2016). Study Design, Endpoints and Biomarkers, Drug Safety, and FDA and ICH Guidelines. In T. Brody (Ed.), Clinical Trial (2nd ed.; pp. 31-68). Academic Press.

Cevikalp, H., Larlus, D., Neamtu, M., Triggs, B., & Jurie, F. (2010). Manifold Based Local Classifiers: Linear and Nonlinear Approaches. *Journal of Signal Processing Systems for Signal, Image, and Video Technology*, *61*(1), 61–73. doi:10.100711265-008-0313-4

Crown, W., Buyukkaramikli, N., Sir, M., Thokala, P., Morton, A., Marshall, D., ... Pasupathy, K. S. (2018). Application of Constrained Optimization Methods in Health Services Research: Report 2 of the ISPOR Optimization Methods Emerging Good Practices Task Force. *Value in Health*, *21*(9), 1019–1028. doi:10.1016/j.jval.2018.05.003 PMID:30224103

Crown, W., Buyukkaramikli, N., Thokala, P., Morton, A., Sir, M., Marshall, D., ... Pasupathy, K. S. (2017). Constrained Optimization Methods in Health Services Research—An Introduction: Report 1 of the ISPOR Optimization Methods Emerging Good Practices Task Force. *Value in Health*, *20*(3), 310–319. doi:10.1016/j.jval.2017.01.013 PMID:28292475

Denton, B., Kurt, M., Shah, N., Bryant, S., & Smith, S. (2009). Optimizing the Start Time of Statin Therapy for Patients with Diabetes. *Medical Decision Making*, *29*(3), 351–367. doi:10.1177/0272989X08329462 PMID:19429836

Draško, T., & Božica, P. (2014). Control and optimization of complex biological systems. In *37th International Convention on Information and Communication Technology, Electronics and Microelectronics* (pp. 222-227). Opatija: IEEE.

Hacisalihzade, S., & Mansour, M. (1985). Solution of the multiple dosing problem using linear programming. *International Journal of Bio-Medical Computing*, *17*(1), 57–67. doi:10.1016/0020-7101(85)90073-X PMID:3840459

Ivakhnenko, A., & Stepashko, V. (1985). *Noise-immunity modeling*. Kiev: Naukova dumka.

Jakob, W., & Blume, C. (2014). Pareto Optimization or Cascaded Weighted Sum: A Comparison of Concepts. *Algorithms*, *7*(1), 166–185. doi:10.3390/a7010166

Kiparissides, A., Koutinas, M., Kontoravdi, C., Mantalaris, A., & Pistikopoulos, E. (2011). 'Closing the loop' in biological systems modeling— From the in silico to the in vitro. *Automatica*, *47*(6), 1147–1155. doi:10.1016/j.automatica.2011.01.013

Klyushin, D., & Petunin, Y. U. (2019). *Evidence-based medicine. The use of statistical methods.* Dialektika-Vil'yams. (in Russian)

Kuzmich, I., & Todurov, B. (2015). Dynamics of Secondary Pulmonary Hypertension after Cardiac Surgical Procedures in Patients with Low Left Ventricular. *Clinical Anesthesiology & Intensive Care,* *2*(6), 82–90.

Madala, H., & Ivakhnenko, A. (1994). *Inductive learning algorithms for complex systems modeling.* Boca Raton, FL: CRC Press.

Pavlov, A. (2010). Modified algorithm with combinatorial selection and variables orthogonalization and its analysis. In Inductive modeling of complex systems (pp. 130-139). Academic Press.

Rosen, I., Lane, R., Morrill, S., & Belli, J. (1991). Treatment plan optimization using linear programming. *Medical Physics,* *18*(2), 141–152. doi:10.1118/1.596700 PMID:2046598

Tabak, D., & Kuo, B. (1971). *Optimal control by mathematical programming.* Englewood Cliffs, NJ: Prentice-Hall.

Tomic, D. (2002). Spectral performance evaluation of parallel processing systems. *Chaos, Solitons, and Fractals,* *13*(1), 25–38. doi:10.1016/S0960-0779(00)00223-X

Tomic, D., Muftic, O., & Baksa, S. (2005). *Computer 3D Spectral Analysis of Human Movements.* In Conference on Computer-Aided Ergonomics, Kosice, Slovakia. Retrieved from https://bib.irb.hr/prikazi-rad?rad=212840

Van Slyke, R. (1968). *Mathematical programming and optimal control theory.* Berkeley, CA: University of California.

Vanin, V., & Pavlov, A. (2004). Development and application of self-organization algorithms for modeling of complex processes and objects which are represented by the point former. In *Proceedings of Tavria State agrotechnical academy* (pp. 51–56). Melitopol.

Zgurovsky, M., & Pavlov, A. (2019). The Four-Level Model of Planning and Decision Making. In *Combinatorial Optimization Problems in Planning and Decision Making: Theory and Applications* (pp. 347–406). Cham: Springer. doi:10.1007/978-3-319-98977-8_8

KEY TERMS AND DEFINITIONS

External Criterion: A suitably chosen criterion for model structure evaluating.

Generalized Variable: Member of a complete polynomial of a given degree.

GMDH: Group method of data handling; the structural-parametric synthesis method with an implicit fine for the model complexity.

Learning Sample: The whole sample of objects for which is known the class accordance.

Model of the Optimal Structure: Is understood in a sense of achieving an extremum of the algorithm external criterion.

Testing Sample: A sample of objects that using in GMDH algorithms mainly for selection of model structure.

Training Sample: A sample of objects that using in GMDH algorithms mainly to calculate the model parameters.

Chapter 16
Process–Oriented Organizations:
Integration of Soft Factors

Aleksander Janeš
University of Primorska, Slovenia

Rajko Novak
MRR LLC, Slovenia

ABSTRACT

The main purpose of the chapter is to represent practical approach on the empirically-evaluated business process orientation (BPO) based on the research of the Slovenian power supply business. Within the empirical investigation, the level of BPO maturity was measured in the 19 organizations. The survey was focused on the top, middle, and lower managers. As a measuring instrument, a questionnaire for the extended concept of process orientation was used. The results of the BPO measurement shows that, despite this long-standing engagement with processes, quality management system and the IT portfolio management (PoM) of operations, process orientation, and appurtenant IT PoM maturity is not very high. Results suggested the opportunities for improvement, particularly for better use and to take advantage of IT. One important reason for performing the research in the power supply business is the importance of its activities for the socio-economic and environmental impact of the whole society and therefore better understanding of the recognized "soft factors."

INTRODUCTION

Owing to constantly changing business requirements and challenges, such as decreasing product life cycles, international competition and increasing cost pressure (e.g. due to the demand to apply latest state-of-the-art technology), companies are forced to improve their processes in order to keep pace with fast-changing market requirements. As a consequence, business process management (BPM) is among the most important managerial topics because it allows companies an agile adaptation to changing business requirements (Neubauer, 2009). Choong's (2013) literature review indicate that BPM is a holistic

DOI: 10.4018/978-1-5225-8933-4.ch016

management philosophy that uses a systematic approach and information technology (IT) to improve processes that focus on aligning all aspects of an organization with the wants and needs of customers. Ravesteyn and Batenburg (2010) claim, that BPM-systems are the typical result of developments in both the business and IT-domain.

The definition of the business process orientation (BPO) construct has a somewhat intangible nature, which represents a barrier to its conceptualization. Many studies into process management use proxy variables (e.g. ISO 9001 certification) as an indicator for BPO (Kohlbacher & Gruenwald, 2011; Peršič, Markič, & Peršič, 2016; Xiaofen, 2013). BPO is extremely important for the success of business process management (BPM) efforts within organizations. McCormack and Johnson (2001) research results indicate a surprisingly strong relationship between BPO and overall performance (Hammer & Champy 1993 as cited in Reijers, 2006; Sikdar & Payyazhi 2014; Škrinjar, Bosilj-Vukšić, & Indihar-Štemberger, 2008). Since both concepts are closely intertwined, surveys focusing on BPM and BPO are considered in the literature review (Roeser & Kern, 2015; Škrinjar & Trkman, 2013; Nadarajah & Kadır, 2016).

The Neubauer's (2009) survey showed that only a small number of the participating organizations can be determined as process focused organizations (PFOs) according to the criteria taken from the literature. The vast majority of organizations are still on their way towards a PFO that includes the design of end-to-end business processes and measuring and managing of process level results (Işik, Mertens, & Van den Bergh, 2013). Business processes are the core building blocks of an organization's operations and provide a plethora of information that can be tapped into. However, today business process analytics is often only the second step of consideration in BPM. Likewise, near real-time insight into processes is rare or almost non-existent in practice (Janiesch, Matzner, & Müller, 2012).

Among the reasons for struggling to evolve and expand BPM practices across the organization are the lack of positive organizational culture (Wilson, 2015), lack of support among senior management, the absence of clear roles and responsibilities (Sikdar & Payyazhi, 2014; Young, Young, & Zapata, 2014) in implementing the BPM methodology, and insufficient budget and available resources.

The majority of academic work on BPM, but also its practical implementation across several industries, is focused on tools, systems and techniques, and less on the managerial, organizational, strategic or cultural challenges of BPM (Adamides, 2015; Gębczyńska, 2016). Because the BPM community is doing this extremely well, to the extent that the ability to eliminate problems within an operational process has become a commodity, as a consequence, massively streamlined processes, rather than highly innovative processes have been encountered (Kohlborn, Mueller, Poeppelbuss, & Roeglinger, 2014).

From the process maturity research perspective the Slovenian power supply business organizations are interesting because of their engagement with processes and process approach over many years. Most involved organizations have a certified Quality Management System according to ISO 9001. One feature of their activity is that it demands that a lot of resources and efforts are directed to the automation and digitalization of operations in the technical field, as clearly defined and documented processes are required in this business. The power supply business consists of all the installations and equipment for the generation, transmission and distribution of electricity, ensuring the maintenance of a balance between production and consumption, with appropriate regulation. The Slovenian electricity market is an integral part of the common energy market of the European Union (EU). Production of electricity to the public network in Slovenia amounted to 16.281 gigawatt hours (GWh) in 2014 and 14.984 GWh in 2017. Therefore the consumption coverage with domestic production resources amounted to 98% in 2014 and 82% in 2017 (Ministry of Infrastructure, 2015, 2017).

The research purpose and goal is being achieved through represented practical approach on the empirically evaluated BPO, analysis of results and opportunities for improvement in the power supply business. The research's basic thesis is linked to the introduction of BPM and BPO, in which organizations management devote too little attention to so-called 'soft factors' i.e. values, organizational culture (Wilson, 2015), organizational structure, human resource (HR) management and behavior that promotes process functioning. The remainder of the chapter proceeds as follows. In the next section, the research background is represented. The process orientation of the power supply business section presents methodology, hypothesis, data collection procedures and discussion. This is followed by the solutions and recommendations and future research directions. The paper then concludes with the overall coverage of the chapter and concluding remarks.

BACKGROUND

In the European Union (EU), the information and communication technology (ICT) industry is regarded as the main source of productivity growth in the present time. At the same time, the ICT sector is a key driver of innovation, growth and employment in other industries or economy sectors (Schröder, 2011). The adoption of ICT differs between economy sectors but is important in all industries at macro and micro economic level. According to Tisdell (2017) estimates are not available for all countries but the largest proportionate contribution to GDP of internet-related value added appears to be for the United States of America (USA) and the United Kingdom (UK) followed by Australia and Germany but with somehow lower contribution for several European countries and for Hong Kong (China). Overall, the greatest value added by ICT is in the tertiary or service sector (Tisdell, 2017).

The factors impacting the decision to adopt Information Technology (IT) or ICT may differ in importance depending on the context, e.g. organizational strategy, technology, organization, environment, industry, market segment, socio-economic, tasks and employees. Namely, ICT can dramatically improve the accuracy, reliability, speed and productivity of organization's processes (Carayon et al., 2006 as cited in Huang & Gramopadhye, 2016; Cordes Feibert & Jacobsen, 2019).

ICT reduces market transaction costs and the amount of resources required to deliver many commodities. As a result effective prices of many commodities are reduced, consumer surplus rises in most cases, and producer surplus may also rise. The advent of ICT has resulted in significant restructuring of labor markets. Although the internet has had some positive social consequences, it has also had negative social impacts which were identified and which call for public intervention. ICT employee's jobs are characterized by a high workload, competitive, innovative and deadline-driven work, including the permanent pressure of keeping the professional knowledge up-to-date in a globalized world. Hence, the working conditions in ICT jobs are also associated with the development of mental disorders (Boes et al., 2011; Gerlmaier, 2011; Jung et al., 2012; Lehner et al., 2013).

In addition, the environmental consequences of ICT technology appear to be mixed. Considerable benefits from the use of ICT in the education, research (Roblek, Meško, Dimovski, & Peterlin, 2019) and health sectors were identified. Nevertheless, the increased use of ICT in education and research can have also negative consequences. Furthermore, as pointed out, increased use of ICT and the internet have both positive and negative consequences for the welfare of rural commodities. There is a problem of accurately measuring the socioeconomic impact of ICT; given the multidimensional nature of these impacts, no simple solution is being proposed. While most economic studies of the value of ICT concentrate on the use of the internet, it should also be realized that there are many modern information technologies that do not depend on the internet, or do so only to a limited extent e.g. robots, drones, satellite communications and CT scans. Some of these techniques are of considerable value in agriculture, health care and other industries but their economics has not received much attention yet (Tisdell, 2017).

Information technology and adequate information system (IS) support organizations in three vital ways: in improving business processes and operations, in rational decision making by managers and employees, and in strengthening strategies for competitive advantage. Internet, the World Wide Web (WWW), and electronic data interchange (EDI), have already changed, and are changing continuously, the ways organizations do business with the use of contemporarily IT (Mandal & Gunasekaran, 2003 as cited in Mandal & Bagchi, 2016).

Benitez-Amado, Llorens-Montes, & Perez-Arostegui (2010) argue that IT resources and capabilities per se do not enhance firm performance, although they can act as key enablers of valuable higher-order organizational capabilities, or interact with business processes and resources to increase business performance. The integration and synergy between IT resources and capabilities, and organizational processes and non-IT resources can develop higher-order capabilities that might be unique, rare and imperfectly mobile across other businesses. López and Alegre's (2012) research showed that IT capability and competency, on its own, is insufficient to generate and maintain a competitive advantage and managers should not only focus on allocating sufficient resources for IT investments. Indeed, the IT enabled capability perspective has been consistently successful in justifying the importance of IT among organizations in many industries (Ghobakhloo, Azar, & Fathi, 2018; Wade & Hulland, 2004).

According to many authors, the maturity and capability of business processes and IT resources is acknowledged as a key determinant of an organization's ability to adapt and respond to emerging threats and opportunities, and thus its sustainability (Janeš, 2014; Novak & Janeš, 2018). Based on the literature, it is clear that business processes have an important role to play in defining how organizations perform. It is commonly accepted that operational processes together with support processes determine an organization's current performance. Nowadays, many managers are looking for ways to make their organization more process-oriented. Findings of several authors indicate that BPM involves many different aspects, ranging from process agility and performance measurement (Benmoussa, Abdelkabir, Abd, & Hassou, 2015) to process-oriented organizational structure combined with industry-specific and IT expertise (Antonucci & Goeke, 2011). Along with the development of internet technology and applications, the associated network standardization, and a web services orientation, BPM started as the automation of an organization's internal processes and then became more externally oriented towards the digitization of supply chains (Ravesteyn & Batenburg, 2010).

The concept of process maturity stems from the understanding that the processes have their life cycle or development stages, which can be clearly defined, measured and managed over time. The higher the degree of maturity of any process resulting in improved forecasting objectives, costs and operating efficiency, the greater are the presumed performance and achievement of goals in an improved performance and in proposing new, higher target levels of business performance (Jin, Chai, & Tan, 2014; McCormack et al., 2009; Pöppelbuß & Röglinger, 2011).

Several authors linked use of IT portfolio management (PoM) to benefits and found that the latter could be at one of four stages of the organization's business process orientation (BPO) maturity: ad hoc, defined, linked (or managed), and integrated (or synchronized). At the first, ad hoc stage organizations make IT investment decisions in uncoordinated ways resulting in missed opportunities. At the defined stage all the key components of IT are documented along with estimates of benefits and costs. At the linked (managed) stage IT assets are aligned with the business strategy (Carmo et al., 2017) and an objective process to select projects is used. At the integrated (synchronized) stage, all portfolio investments are aligned with business strategy and their risk, value, and option value are constantly assessed at different stages of the IT asset life cycle. These differences in maturity leading to different levels of benefits highlight the importance of finding out what IT PoM processes are necessary to yield higher levels of returns for the organization. Therefore the IT PoM is a contemporary real-life phenomenon which embraces a gap between benefits expectations from IT PoM and the actual results that organizations are experiencing. The implementation of an IT PoM solution constitutes not only a large and complex effort for an organization but requires major changes in business processes and organizational structure. Quantitative approaches at this researches, projects and practices typically refer to decision or optimization models, whereas qualitative approaches propose reference processes and classifications, as well as enable the integration of 'soft factors' (Ajjan, Kumar, & Subramaniam, 2016; Jeffery & Leliveld, 2004; Lehnert, Linhart, & Roeglinger, 2017; McCormack, 2001, 2007; McCormack et al., 2009; Novak & Janeš, 2018).

IT PoM implementation can be conceptualized as a social process that focuses on the interplay between forces supporting IT PoM and forces opposing IT PoM. The identified organizational structure, appropriation process, and outcomes can serve as the basis for a deeper understanding of the organizational wide implementation of IT PoM, spirit interpretations, and resistance issues that arise when implementing IT PoM. In addition, it uncovers important features that make up IT PoM, and relationship between structures and actual appropriation of processes within the organization. The study results of Ajjan et al. (2016) indicate that IT PoM features are made up of three processes: creating the portfolio; assessing and analyzing the portfolio characteristics based on risk, benefits, alignment, criticality, and cost; and balancing decisions to start projects or terminate under-performing IT assets.

According to the literature review, BPM is a holistic management philosophy that uses a systematic approach and IT or ICT to improve processes that focus on aligning all aspects of an organization with the wants, expectations and needs of customers which is resulting in developments in both the business and IT-domain (Choong 2013; Ravesteyn & Batenburg 2010). Contemporary literature acknowledges the importance of business process (BP), BPM and BPO maturity of the organization. Therefore scope of used terminology comprises; BP is included by BPM, which is further embraced by BPO (Nadarajah & Kadir, 2016; Tarhan, Turetken, & Reijers, Hajo, 2016; Van Looy, De Backer, & Poels, 2011; Van Looy, De Backer, Poels, & Snoeck, 2013). However, thus far, the phenomenon has been so under-researched and under-theorized that it merits a systematic research (Estruch & Álvaro, 2012; Carmo et al., 2017).

PROCESS ORIENTATION OF THE POWER SUPPLY ORGANIZATIONS

Methodology

Within the framework of an empirical study, the level of BPO maturity was measured with the selected survey instrument in the 19 organizations from the production, transmission and distribution of electricity of the Slovenian power supply business. Presented research is the first one which considers the business process orientation maturity in the Slovenian power supply (McCormack & Johnson, 2001; Hair, Babin, Anderson, & Tatham, 2006).

The purpose of BPO maturity measurement is being concisely described as: 'to help organizations where they are today, where they should go in the future and the value of doing so, and how to get there' (Masalskyte, Andelin, Sarasoja, & Ventovuori, 2014). In order to achieve the research purpose, BPO measurements of the power supply business were performed between February and March, 2016. One definitely important reason for performing the maturity measurement in the power supply business is the importance of its activities for the operation and development of the whole of Slovenian society.

Selected survey instrument was a questionnaire for the extended concept of process orientation with nine elements (i.e. Strategic perspective, Determination and documenting of processes, Measurement and management of processes, Process oriented organizational structure, HR management, Process oriented organizational culture, Market orientation, Suppliers' perspective (business partners) and Process oriented information technology) which were developed through studies of several researchers e.g. McCormack and Johnson (2001), McCormack et al., (2009), Škrinjar, Bosilj-Vukšić, and Indihar-Štemberger (2008), and Škrinjar (2010). Concept of elements stems from three main dimensions (i.e. management and organization, architecture which means the development of process and information architectures and IT integration) of BPM implementation projects (Ravesteyn & Batenburg, 2010; Roeser & Kern, 2015). Elements were evaluated with 7 Likert-scale levels, allowing ample opportunity to express a level of agreement, ranging from a rating of 1 (the statement is not true) through to a rating of 7 (the statement is absolutely true) and additional choice 'I do not know'. Intermediate ranging reflects the level of agreement, with higher agreement rates meaning more established process orientation. Each element is consisted of several issues that altogether represent 51 statements. Beside that questionnaire included multiple choices items about some demographic and organizational data. To determine the level of maturity, McCormack's (2007) four development stages maturity model was used (Ajjan et al., 2016; Jeffery & Leliveld, 2004; Lehnert et al., 2017; McCormack, 2001, 2007; Novak & Janeš 2018; Škrinjar, 2010). In doing this, the degree of Ad Hoc (maturity level boundary including 4), Defined (4.01 to 5.5), Linked (5.51 to 6.5) and Integrated (6.51 to 7) was taken into account. The survey comprised the top, middle and lower managers, and project managers, thus representing the whole population of 450 managers.

The research's basic thesis is linked to the introduction of BPM and BPO, in which organizations management devote too little attention to so-called 'soft factors' i.e. values, organizational culture (Wilson, 2015), organizational structure, human resource (HR) management and behavior that promotes process functioning. BPM is supporting business processes using methods, techniques, and software to design, enact, control, and analyze operational processes involving employees, organizations, applications, documents and other sources of information (van der Aalst, Dumas, & ter Hofstede, 2003 as cited in Neubauer, 2009). Successful implementation of BPM is significantly influenced by the strategic commitment of leadership and the established role of process holders (Gębczyńska, 2016; Hernaus, Vukšić, & Štemberger, 2016; Ravesteyn & Batenburg, 2010) with clearly defined and understood processes ownership, proper processes performance indicators e.g. Key performance indicators (KPI) (Estruch & Álvaro 2012; Carmo et al., 2017; Janeš, 2014; Janiesch et al., 2012), process organizational culture and process oriented IT (Adamides, 2015; Ajjan et al., 2016; Jeffery & Leliveld, 2004; Lehnert et al., 2017).

In practice, the BPM is often carried out only in certain parts of the organization, with no real connection to the organization's strategy (Cordes Feibert & Jacobsen, 2019) and sometimes the BPM-system is regarded as 'just another' software application, while others consider it as the basis for a new paradigm (Gębczyńska, 2016; Jeston & Nelis, 2007; Ravesteyn & Batenburg, 2010; Sikdar & Payyazhi, 2014). In many organizations functional boundaries between organizational units are explicit and remain significant barriers to the effective implementation of cross-functional and inter-organizational processes (i.e. end-to-end processes) and the performance of BPM (McCormack, 2007; Wendland, Lerch Lunardi, & Bittencourt Dolci, 2019). Estruch and Álvaro (2012) and Carmo et al. (2017) argue that the BPM system can be the main component of the proposed IT solution. Traditionally, BPM system means a software platform, which provides organizations the ability to model, manage, and optimize processes. The usage of standards to model how each operations scenario must be handled, describing it in a formally way (i.e. at the same time the main operation process activities, the logic to detect and handle complex events and the related KPIs evaluation) (Janiesch et al., 2012), helps to communicate across all involved employees how organization's operations are done and their implications. This way, common understanding is achieved and future improvement proposals could be obtained from more employees, not only particular operation specialists.

Based on recognized problems from literature review and practice, and chosen methodology, originates the first hypothesis, which was subjected to statistical evaluation:

Hypothesis One: Poor development of 'soft factors' associated with leadership, such as process oriented organizational culture, process oriented organizational structure and human resource (HR) management, reduces the level of an organization's process maturity.

The second hypothesis relates to the perception of the BPO by the top, middle and lower management (Peslak, 2012; Ajjan et al., 2016). Practice often points out that top management assesses the BPO maturity and performance of BPM more positively because of theirs influence on the performance of an organization (Peršič et al., 2016; Novak & Janeš, 2018). From that originates the hypothesis two.

Hypothesis Two: Middle and lower management assesses the performance of realized business process orientation and business process management more critically than the top management.

Findings and Discussion

Questionnaires were submitted to respondents in agreement and with the support of the top managers of organizations through established channels of internal communication. Namely, 240 fully completed questionnaires were received, which represented a 53.33% response rate. The survey was conducted via an online portal 'EnKlikAnketa' using the open source application named 1KA (1KA is the name of the application for a free service online survey developed by the Centre for Social Informatics, Faculty of Social Sciences at University of Ljubljana). The questionnaire was pre-tested on a test sample of 34 respondents in one organization of the power supply business. The research was supported by the Section for Quality and Excellence in the power supply business with an invitation to organizations to complete the questionnaire.

Based on the replies to the questionnaires, descriptive statistics and testing of assumptions for normality and reliability for every element of the BPO's questionnaire were calculated (e.g. frequencies calculation, mean values, standard deviation, Cronbach's Alpha, correlation analysis, factor analysis, and t-test for independent samples; (Hair et al., 2006) using the Statistical Package for Social Sciences (SPSS). The questionnaire included a control question: Do you agree with the statement 'Our organization is very process-oriented'?

Hypothesis Testing

Hypothesis One: Was tested in two steps. Firstly, the correlation analysis was performed, which established the dependence between 'soft' elements related to leadership and the level of the BPO maturity, and where, as a level of business process orientation, the responses of managers to the control question were taken into account.

Correlation analysis revealed that between process oriented organizational culture, process oriented organizational structure, HR management and the organization's business process orientation, there is a positive medium strong correlation (correlation range from 0.599, to 0.639 and to 0.649; all three correlations were significant at 0.01). From the results it was evident that underdeveloped 'soft' BPO elements, which are associated with leadership, such as process oriented organizational culture, process oriented organizational structure and HR management; reduce the level of the organization's BPO.

Secondly, the influence of 'soft' elements of BPO associated with leadership (independent variables), on the level of the organization's business process orientation (dependent variable) was analyzed using multiple regression analysis. As previously, the impact of individual 'soft' BPO elements on the level of the organization's business process orientation was of central interest. To this end, multiple regression analysis, using method Enter, was conducted. A histogram and graph of standardized regression residues demonstrated that the residues were normally distributed.

Multiple regression analysis results showed that dependent variable BPO (Business process orientation was a dependent variable) is positively affected by all three 'soft' elements associated with leadership, namely: process oriented organizational structure ($\beta 1 = 0.252$; sig $= 0.039$), process oriented organizational culture ($\beta 2 = 0.493$; sig $- 0.000$) and HR management ($\beta 3 = 0.298$; sig $= 0.010$). The regression model explained 52.5% of the variability of BPO of 19 surveyed organizations of the power supply business.

In the regression model, partial regression coefficient βi explains how much the dependent variable BPO has changed, if there is a change of the independent variable e.g. process oriented organizational culture for one unit, with constant values of all other independent variables (lat. ceteris paribus). In other words all three 'soft' elements associated with leadership: process oriented organizational structure, process oriented organizational culture and HR management pointed out their relevance towards the BPO maturity. Consequently the hypothesis one was accepted.

Hypothesis Two: For the verification of the second hypothesis and analysis validation the three (top, middle and lower) surveyed groups of managers were divided into two:
- ◦ **First group:** Top management;
- ◦ **Second group:** Middle and lower-level management.

Hypothesis H2 was tested with t-test for independent samples. Results represented in Table 1 indicate that evaluation of BPO elements' averages cannot be seen as statistically significant (for all nine elements sig. > 0.05) between the two groups of respondents' i.e. top management and middle and lower-level management. On average, both groups' relatively equally assessed individual elements of business process orientation maturity (differences of averages were between 0.02 to 0.32, see Table 1). According to this finding the hypothesis two was rejected.

Hypothesis testing confirmed that managers should put much more emphasis on developing the 'soft factors' of the BPO (Ajjan et al., 2016; Hernaus et al., 2016; Nadarajah & Kadir, 2016; Novak & Janeš, 2018; Tisdell, 2017) and that there is still much room for improvements despite of fact that most power supply organizations have a certificate for a quality management system in accordance with the requirements of the ISO 9001 standard.

Discussion

Regarding the questionnaire's control question: Do you agree with the statement 'Our organization is very process-oriented'?, managers on average agreed, with a score of only 4.73 out of 7 levels on the Likert scale. An almost identical assessment was obtained by statistical evaluation of measured values of the nine individual BPO elements (nine elements average = 4.68, see Table 1).

Study of Peršič et al. (2016) investigates organizations that have generally introduced at least one ISO 9001 quality management standard. Though the study incorporated exclusively a population of medium and large enterprises, authors argue that top management, who, as a rule, have a better understanding of management standards and models at the same time have possession of a greater influence on the performance of an organization. As presented through their study, upgrading and optimization of socially responsible management standards integration may, in the future, focus on even greater investments into employee education and training.

Regarding represented research the top-rated BPO elements were the Determination and documenting of processes (5.21), Strategic perspective (4.92) and Measurement and management of processes (4.92). Determination and documenting of processes was, as expected, the highest rated element, with 70.8% of respondents recognizing the special organizational unit or part of an organizational unit, which provides professional support to the processes' owners. Process oriented organizational structure (4.76), Process oriented organizational culture (4.61) and Market orientation (4.61), were relatively medium assessed. The lowest evaluated elements were Process oriented information technology (4.22), HR management (4.41) and Suppliers' perspective (4.46) (see Table 1). The lowest score for information technology represents a surprise, which, within individual power supply organizations deserves a more detailed analysis and appropriate action.

Researchers suggest that IT is value, but depends on many other issues and factors in an organization. According to survey among managers potential key issues facing IT of contemporary organizations are; level of IT PoM investment, IT priority investments and upgrading or replacing legacy systems, establishing and maintaining effective dialogue between IT and users, identifying the appropriate level of security for information and software applications, business processes, using technology to drive business change (Neubauer, 2009; Wendland et al., 2019), disaster recovery capabilities, and aligning business and IT strategy. Therefore it is important to understand what problems still exist in IT and also measure progress with regard to these issues. Understanding what the most important IT issues are will allow for improvements in IT implementation and appropriation success due to focused efforts to address these problems (Melville, Kraemer, & Gurbaxani, 2004; Peslak, 2012). Average values of BPO elements are represented in Table 1.

Based on the calculated average value of BPO, the power supply business is located on the second level as defined in McCormack's Business Process Orientation Maturity Model (BPOMM). This level is characterized by the defined and documented processes e.g. all the key components of IT are documented along with estimates of benefits and costs (Ajjan et al., 2016). Changes to processes are taking

Table 1. Statistically evaluated estimates and t-test results of the nine BPO elements

Statistically Evaluated Estimates of the Nine BPO Elements		t-Test			
	Stat. Eval. Estimates	Group	N	Av.	Sig.
Strategic perspective	4.92	TM	33	4.91	0.931
		MLM	158	4.93	
Determination and documenting of processes	5.21	TM	32	5.23	0.943
		MLM	165	5.20	
Measurement and management of processes	4.92	TM	32	4.76	0.543
		MLM	183	4.95	
Process oriented organizational structure	4.76	TM	31	4.93	0.351
		MLM	171	4.73	
HR management	4.41	TM	33	4.53	0.139
		MLM	192	4.39	
Process oriented organizational culture	4.61	TM	31	4.75	0.165
		MLM	184	4.58	
Market orientation	4.61	TM	32	4.54	0.085
		MLM	140	4.63	
Suppliers' perspective (business partners)	4.46	TM	31	4.53	0.080
		MLM	141	4.45	
Process oriented information technology	4.22	TM	31	3.97	0.312
		MLM	115	4.29	

Note: Two groups of managers are: Top Management (TM); Middle and lower management (MLM)
Source: Adapted from Novak and Janeš, 2018

place on the basis of formal procedures. Jobs and organizational structures already include a process perspective, but actually remain functional (Peršič, et al., 2016). Representatives from functional areas meet regularly to coordinate with each other, but only as representatives of their traditional functions (McCormack, 2007; Neubauer, 2009).

Research results in the Slovenian power supply business showed that, despite this long-standing process orientation engagement, the implementation of the process approach, quality management systems (ISO 9001 certified), business ICT, and IT PoMm, business process orientation maturity is not high. This may be due to the fact that BPM is often understood very narrowly only by completing the ISO 9001 requests (Kohlbacher & Gruenwald, 2011; Peršič, et al., 2016; Xiaofen, 2013), sometimes also in a very technically perspective. Including that sometimes the BPM system is regarded as a software application. That consideration is probably the perspective of the power supply business which is a highly technical activity and should be further investigated and subjected to appropriate action. According to Peslak (2012) and Tisdell (2017) identifying how IT can improve business processes has dramatically increased suggesting that businesses should fully appreciate the importance of BPM and the necessity of optimizing processes for effective operations performance. However the BPM system should be rather considered as the basis for a new paradigm in the BPO context. In practice, BPM confirms itself as an appropriate way to innovate and transform organizations and develop their agility.

SOLUTIONS AND RECOMMENDATIONS

Results analysis pointed to the need for better communication with employees. Lowest estimates of the individual elements are for statements concerning the acquaintance of employees with strategic goals, indicator results and achievement of processes and the expected changes. The power supply business is a highly technical activity, which is dominated by managers from technical sciences. Therefore it is not a surprising that the second lowest evaluated element is HR management (4.41). Employees are unfamiliar with methods for processes improvement and are not stimulated for process improvement proposals, which may represent a serious obstacle to the further improvement of the processes' effectiveness and efficiency, and consequently the performance of organizations. Namely, 29.2% of respondents think that they do not have special organizational units for process management. Here is an opportunity for managers to devote more attention to 'soft factors' i.e. values, organizational culture (Wilson, 2015) and behavior that promotes process orientation deployment and functioning (Hernaus et al., 2016; Nadarajah & Kadir, 2016; Tisdell, 2017; Novak & Janeš, 2018). Results therefore point out the need for further process orientation development and deployment and transition to the next, third, stage of BPO maturity level (McCormack 2001, 2007).

Therefore it is essential for IT PoM team members, to recognize the need to adapt the IT PoM methodology to fit the organization it is being implemented in and to understand factors that may result in resistance such as lack of communication of IT PoM plans as it relates to progress and value. The research results highlight specific practices that adaptation of some practices may be interpreted differently among the stakeholders involved; e.g. the challenges to implementation and appropriation such as resistance, lack of information availability, neglected 'soft factors', and poor communication are also important (Ajjan et al., 2016).

Further statistical analysis (i.e. correlation and regression analysis) confirmed that underdeveloped 'soft factors' of BPO, associated with leadership, such as process oriented organizational culture, process oriented organizational structure and HR management, reduce the level of an organization's BPO. Findings partially coincide with the findings put forward by Antonucci and Goeke (2011) regarding the need to clearly define the roles and responsibilities for BPM process to be successful in the long run. Research findings represent valuable feedback on the necessity of investing in employees, about the importance of the development of process oriented organizational culture and process oriented organizational structure for the top management of the involved organizations and also other industries.

At last but not least the t-test (see Table 1) for independent samples indicated that between the estimates of individual BPO elements by the top management on the one hand and the middle and lower management on the other, there were no statistically significant differences. This fact that is definitely encouraging, as managers at different management levels gave similar estimates of the situation in the field of BPO.

According to the findings of the research the basic thesis, that the management of organizations devoted too little attention to the so-called 'soft factors', was confirmed. The chosen BPO maturity model focuses on the organization as a whole; therefore it gives an average overall picture and does not allow for more detailed insights into the maturity of individual processes. However, organizational factors have a significant impact on each process in the organization, which is especially true for lower levels of maturity. Ramdani, Kawalek and Lorenzo (2009) showed that small and medium enterprises (SMEs) are more influenced by technological and organizational factors than environmental factors. It's being argued that the likelihood to adopt these systems is greater for larger organizations, greater perceived relative advantage and ability to experiment with the system previous to implementation and adoption, top management support and organizational maturity which includes 'soft factors' (Molinillo & Japutra, 2017). BPO also leads to better non-financial outcomes and indirectly to better financial performance which was ascertained by researchers from several EU countries (Škrinjar et al., 2008; McCormack et al., 2009; Saragiotis, 2019). According to Roeser and Kern (2015), several studies examine data from industrial countries like EU (Germany, England, Holland, Croatia, Norway, Austria, Portugal, Switzerland and Slovenia), America (Brazil, Canada and USA) and Asia (China, India, Japan and South Korea). USA, Canada, Germany, Austria and Japan. One study uses a sample of organizations from emerging countries, i.e. Croatia and Slovenia while the remaining study investigates organizations all over the world. Studies examine different industries e.g. manufacturing companies, public administration, service companies, automobile industry and computer industry (Roeser & Kern, 2015).

According to several authors, if the task environment is stable, IT reinforces centralization in decision making. On the other hand, if the task environment is quite dynamic, IT reinforces decentralization in decision making. Organizations adopt strategies which enable them to cope with uncertainty in the environment; they process information in ways which help to reduce as much uncertainty as possible. They attempt to shield themselves through the formation of new organizational designs and models. In fact, advanced IT contributes to the formulation of organizational structures, business models (Janeš, Biloslavo, & Faganel, 2017), processes and systems based on rules, and appropriate maintenance of these designs (Robey 1980 as cited in McCleary, Asubonteng, & Munchus, 1995).

Research results are aligned with findings and recommendations of several authors: e.g. strategic commitment of leadership and the established role of process holders by Gębczyńska (2016); behavior that promotes process orientation deployment and functioning by Hernaus et al. (2016) and Tisdell, (2017); BPO as the basic function of developing and managing processes by Nadarajah and Kadir (2016), alignment of IT and business strategy by Carmo et al. (2017); and scarcity of empirical works confirming the validity and usefulness of the models or empirically validated BPOMM cases by McCormack and Johnson, (2001), Škrinjar et al. (2008), Škrinjar and Trkman (2013), Tarhan et al. (2016), and Novak and Janeš (2018).

The adoption of ICT differs between industries or sectors of the economy but is important in all industries. Ghobakhloo et al. (2018) presented examples of IT-enabled higher-order organizational capabilities that significantly improved business performance, which are; mass-customization (Jitpaiboon Dobrzykowski, Ragu-Nathan, & Vonderembse, 2013; Xiaosong Peng, Liu, & Heim, 2011), production capability (Ayabakan, Bardhan, & Zheng, 2017), lean-agile manufacturing (Ghobakhloo and Azar, 2018), operational agility (Tan, Tan, Wang, & Sedera, 2017), proactive corporate environmental strategy (Benitez-Amado & Walczuch, 2012), management of knowledge resources (Wagner, Vollmar, & Wagner, 2014) and primary health care (Wendland et al., 2019). Identifying how IT can improve business processes has dramatically increased suggesting that organizations of nowadays fully appreciate the importance of BPM and the necessity of optimizing processes for excellent performance of operations (Peslak, 2012; Tisdell, 2017).

FUTURE RESEARCH DIRECTIONS

Further impetus and research direction may also represent the insight into the relationship between the development level of BPO and the business performance of power supply chain organizations. Given the observed deficiencies in the HR management perspective, especially with communication, checking the differences between the estimates of managers and employees could provide an opportunity for future research. The lowest evaluated elements i.e. Process oriented information technology, HR management and Suppliers' perspective are among future research initiatives. Particularly the lowest score for information technology represents a surprise, which, within individual power supply organizations deserves a more detailed analysis, planning and executing appropriate action. The chosen BPOM model focuses on the organization as a whole; therefore research for more detailed insights into the maturity of individual processes is another research direction. Future research should involve conducting investigations in different industries in order to gain further insight on the factors supporting or preventing the use of BPOMM in practice.

CONCLUSION

One important reason for performing the maturity measurement in the power supply business is the importance of its activities for the operations and development, socio-economic and environmental impact of the whole of Slovenian society. Especially the hydroelectric power plants are important part of Slovenian renewable energy sources which provides electricity for industry and citizens and represents necessary power supply foundation for smart technologies and digitalization.

Based on the lowest estimated statements and BPO elements (Novak & Janeš, 2018; Škrinjar, 2010) a definite improvement program can be planned for the implementation of BPO and transition to the third stage of maturity. For faster implementation of BPO, leaders will have to pay more attention to the implementation of relevant values, communication, empowerment, training and organizational culture.

This chapter makes significant contributions to the literature and above all to managers, project managers, professionals, practitioners and scholars who are engaged in this field and will find useful guidance for a better understanding of applying BPO and suitable maturity models (i.e. McCormack and Johnson's BPOMM) in different industries.

DISCUSSION QUESTIONS

1. How could you define Business Process (BP)? Can you recognize and describe BP that is most familiar to you? Are processes generally defined as sequences of activities performed within or across organizations or something else? Are activities considered to be the basic entity used to build a process? Can activities be further divided?
2. What kind of discipline is the Business process management (BPM)? Is a discipline which is dealing with the management of portfolio of Business processes (BP)? It has anything to do with the continuous improvement in organizations? How would you characterize the added value of BPM approach for profit and nonprofit organizations?
3. Business process orientation (BPO) is a construct which has a somehow intangible nature. How can be explained the categorization of following: BP is included by BPM, which is further embraced by BPO? Which soft factors are included in the BPO? How they can be explained?
4. McCormack and Johnson's Business process orientation maturity model (BPOMM) is the most disseminated model based on the number of studies that report on its testing in a business environment.

Could you recognize and explain the life cycle of the process in general? Which process maturity stages are included in this model? Please explain the statement that maturity model provides a 'big picture' overview, composed of small elements, and thus comprehensively explains how to implement the development of a product or a process?

5. What would entirely describe the information technology (IT) knowledge? It is the degree to which the organization understands the capabilities of existing and emerging IT or an awareness of IT 'possibilities' which exposes the universe of digital options available to the organization? Could the IT knowledge be the provider of the flexibility to quickly adapt to emerging market(s) opportunities? If not, please share your reasons.

6. Based on the last 10 years of Business process orientation deployment, what do you envision in the next decade? Will process orientation prevail over functional organizational structure? Will managers be able to accept that kind of organization?

ACKNOWLEDGMENT

This research was supported by the Slovenian power supply organizations which are listed according to the descending order of the number of respondents in survey:

- ELES, d.o.o. (Limited liability company),
- Electricity distribution companies (Elektro Maribor, d.d.; Elektro Celje, d.d.; Elektro Ljubljana, d.d.; Elektro Primorska, d.d., and Elektro Gorenjska, d.d.) all are Joint stock companies,
- Holding Slovenske elektrarne (HSE Company), and
- GEN Group.

REFERENCES

Adamides, E. D. (2015). Linking operations strategy to the corporate strategy process: A practice perspective. *Business Process Management Journal*, *21*(2), 267–287. doi:10.1108/BPMJ-07-2013-0107

Ajjan, H., Kumar, R. L., & Subramaniam, C. (2016). Information technology portfolio management implementation: A case study. *Journal of Enterprise Information Management*, *29*(6), 841–859. doi:10.1108/JEIM-07-2015-0065

Antonucci, Y. L., & Goeke, R. J. (2011). Identification of appropriate responsibilities and positions for business process management success: Seeking a valid and reliable framework. *Business Process Management Journal*, *17*(1), 127–146. doi:10.1108/14637151111105616

Ayabakan, S., Bardhan, I. R., & Zheng, Z. E. (2017). A data envelopment analysis approach to estimate it-enabled production capability. *Management Information Systems Quarterly*, *41*(1), 189–205. doi:10.25300/MISQ/2017/41.1.09

Benitez-Amado, J., Llorens-Montes, F. J., & Perez-Arostegui, M. N. (2010). Information technology enabled intrapreneurship culture and firm performance. *Industrial Management & Data Systems*, *110*(4), 550–566. doi:10.1108/02635571011039025

Benitez-Amado, J., & Walczuch, R. M. (2012). Information technology, the organizational capability of proactive corporate environmental strategy and firm performance: A resource-based analysis. *European Journal of Information Systems*, *21*(1), 664–679. doi:10.1057/ejis.2012.14

Benmoussa, R., Abdelkabir, C., Abd, A., & Hassou, M. (2015). Capability/maturity based model for logistics processes assessment. *International Journal of Productivity and Performance Management*, *64*(1), 28–51. doi:10.1108/IJPPM-08-2012-0084

Boes, A., Baukrowitz, A., Kämpf, T., & Marrs, K. (2011). Globalisation 2.0 - professional qualification and skilled worker development in the IT branch. In R. Reichwald, M. Frenz, S. Hermann, & A. Schipanski (Eds.), *Zukunftsfeld Dienstleistungsarbeit* (pp. 319–346). Wiesbaden: Springer Gabler.

Carayon, P., Schoofs Hundt, A., Karsh, B. T., Gurses, A. P., Alvarado, C. J., Smith, M., & Flatley Brennan, P. (2006). Work system design for patient safety: The SEIPS model. *Quality & Safety in Health Care*, *15*(1), i50–i58. doi:10.1136/qshc.2005.015842 PMID:17142610

Carmo, A., Fantinato, M., Thom, L., Prado, E., Spinola, M., & Hung, P. (2017) A method for eliciting goals for business process models based on nonfunctional requirements catalogues. In *Proceedings of the 19th International Conference on Enterprise Information Systems* (pp. 262-273). Porto: Portugal: Academic Press. 10.5220/0006314702620273

Choong, K. K. (2013). Are PMS meeting the measurement needs of BPM? A literature review. *Business Process Management Journal*, *19*(3), 535–574. doi:10.1108/14637151311319941

Cordes Feibert, D., & Jacobsen, P. (2019). Factors impacting technology adoption in hospital bed logistics. *International Journal of Logistics Management*, *30*(1), 195–230. doi:10.1108/IJLM-02-2017-0043

Estruch, A., & Álvaro, J. A. H. (2012). Event-driven manufacturing process management approach. In *10th Int. Conf. on Business Process Managament*, (pp. 120–133). Berlin: Springer.

Gębczyńska, A. (2016). Strategy implementation efficiency on the process level. *Business Process Management Journal*, *22*(6), 1079–1098. doi:10.1108/BPMJ-01-2016-0004

Gerlmaier, A. (2011). Stress and burnout among IT professionals – searching for causes. In Burnout in der IT-Branche (pp. 53-89). Kröning: Asanger.

Ghobakhloo, M., & Azar, A. (2018). Business excellence via advanced manufacturing technology and lean-agile manufacturing. *Journal of Manufacturing Technology Management*, *29*(1), 2–24. doi:10.1108/JMTM-03-2017-0049

Ghobakhloo, M., Azar, A., & Fathi, M. (2018). Lean-green manufacturing: The enabling role of information technology resource. *Kybernetes*, *47*(9), 1752–1777. doi:10.1108/K-09-2017-0343

Hair, J. H., Babin, B. J., Anderson, R. E., & Tatham, R. L. (2006). *Multivariate Data Analysis*. Pearson Prentice Hall.

Hammer, M., & Champy, J. (1993). *Reengineering the Corporation: A Manifesto for Business Revolution*. New York: HarperCollins.

Hernaus, T., Vukšić, V. B., & Štemberger, M. I. (2016). How to go from strategy to results? Institutionalising BPM governance within organisations. *Business Process Management Journal, 22*(1), 173–195. doi:10.1108/BPMJ-03-2015-0031

Huang, Y.-H., & Gramopadhye, A. K. (2016). Recommendations for health information technology implementation in rural hospitals. *International Journal of Health Care Quality Assurance, 29*(4), 454–474. doi:10.1108/IJHCQA-09-2015-0115 PMID:27142953

Işik, Ö., Mertens, W., & Van den Bergh, J. (2013). Practices of knowledge intensive process management: Quantitative insights. *Business Process Management Journal, 19*(3), 515–534. doi:10.1108/14637151311319932

Janeš, A. (2014). Empirical verification of the balanced scorecard. *Industrial Management & Data Systems, 114*(2), 203–219. doi:10.1108/IMDS-04-2013-0195

Janeš, A., Biloslavo, R., & Faganel, A. (2017). Sustainable business model: A case study of Fonda.si. *Annales Series Historia et Sociologia, 27*(1), 175–190.

Janiesch, C., Matzner, M., & Müller, O. (2012). Beyond process monitoring: A proof-of-concept of event-driven business activity management. *Business Process Management Journal, 18*(4), 625–643. doi:10.1108/14637151211253765

Jeffery, M., & Leliveld, I. (2004). Best practices in IT portfolio management. *MIT Sloan Management Review, 45*(3), 41–49.

Jeston, J., & Nelis, J. (2007). *Business Process Management. Practical Guidelines to Successful Implementations*. Amsterdam: Butterworth–Heinemann.

Jin, D., Chai, K.-H., & Tan, K.-C. (2014). New service development maturity model, *Managing Service Quality. International Journal (Toronto, Ont.), 24*(1), 86–116.

Jitpaiboon, T., Dobrzykowski, D. D., Ragu-Nathan, T., & Vonderembse, M. A. (2013). Unpacking IT use and integration for mass customisation: A service-dominant logic view. *International Journal of Production Research, 51*(8), 2527–2547. doi:10.1080/00207543.2012.720727

Jung, J., Ernstmann, N., Nitzsche, A., Driller, E., Kowalski, C., Lehner, B., ... Pfaff, H. (2012). Exploring the association between social capital and depressive symptoms: Results of a survey in German information and communication technology companies. *Journal of Occupational and Environmental Medicine, 54*(1), 23–30. doi:10.1097/JOM.0b013e318237a1b6 PMID:22157802

Kohlbacher, M., & Gruenwald, S. (2011). Process orientation: Conceptualization and measurement. *Business Process Management Journal, 17*(2), 267–283. doi:10.1108/14637151111122347

Kohlborn, T., Mueller, O., Poeppelbuss, J., & Roeglinger, M. (2014). Interview with Michael Rosemann on ambidextrous business process management. *Business Process Management Journal, 20*(4), 634–638. doi:10.1108/BPMJ-02-2014-0012

Lehner, B. S., Jung, J., Stieler-Lorenz, B., Nitzsche, A., Driller, E., Wasem, J., & Pfaff, H. (2013). Psychosocial factors in the information and communication technology sector. *Management Decision, 51*(9), 1878–1892. doi:10.1108/MD-12-2012-0876

Lehnert, M., Linhart, A., & Roeglinger, M. (2017). Exploring the intersection of business process improvement and BPM capability development: A research agenda. *Business Process Management Journal*, *23*(2), 275–292. doi:10.1108/BPMJ-05-2016-0095

Mandal, P., & Bagchi, K. (2016). Strategic role of information, knowledge and technology in manufacturing industry performance. *Industrial Management & Data Systems*, *116*(6), 1259–1278. doi:10.1108/IMDS-07-2015-0297

Mandal, P., & Gunasekaran, A. (2003). Issues in implementing ERP: A case study. *European Journal of Operational Research*, *146*(2), 274–283. doi:10.1016/S0377-2217(02)00549-0

Masalskyte, R., Andelin, M., Sarasoja, A.-L., & Ventovuori, T. (2014). Modelling sustainability maturity in corporate real estate management. *Journal of Corporate Real Estate*, *16*(2), 126–139. doi:10.1108/JCRE-09-2013-0023

McCleary, K., Asubonteng, P., & Munchus, G. (1995). The effects of advanced information technology on organizational design. *Health Manpower Management*, *21*(2), 20–23. doi:10.1108/09552069510085870 PMID:10143260

McCormack, K. (2001). Business process orientation: Do you have it? *Quality Progress*, *34*(1), 51–58.

McCormack, K. (2007). *Business Process Maturity. Theory and Application*. BookSurge Publishing.

McCormack, K., & Johnson, W. C. (2001). *Business process orientation: gaining the e-business competitive advantage*. Boca Raton, FL: St. Lucie Press. doi:10.1201/9781420025569

McCormack, K., Willems, J., van den Bergh, J., Deschoolmeester, D., Willaert, P., Indihar Štemberger, M., ... Vlahović, N. (2009). A global investigation of key turning points in business process maturity. *Business Process Management Journal*, *15*(5), 792–815. doi:10.1108/14637150910987946

Melville, N., Kraemer, J., & Gurbaxani, V. (2004). Information technology and organizational performance: An integrative model of IT business value. *Management Information Systems Quarterly*, *28*(2), 283–322. doi:10.2307/25148636

Ministry of Infrastructure. (2015). *Report on the Energy Sector in Slovenia in 2014*. Retrieved February 7, 2019, from http://www.energetika-portal.si/dokumenti/poslovna-porocila/porocilo-o-stanju-na-podrocju-energetike/

Ministry of Infrastructure. (2017). *Report on the Energy Sector in Slovenia in 2017*. Retrieved March 5, 2019, from http://www.energetika-portal.si/fileadmin/dokumenti/publikacije/agen_e/porae_2017.pdf

Molinillo, S., & Japutra, A. (2017). Organizational adoption of digital information and technology: A theoretical review. *The Bottom Line (New York, N.Y.)*, *30*(01), 33–46. doi:10.1108/BL-01-2017-0002

Nadarajah, D., & Kadir, S. L. S. A. (2016). Measuring Business Process Management using business process orientation and process improvement initiatives. *Business Process Management Journal*, *22*(6), 1069–1078. doi:10.1108/BPMJ-01-2014-0001

Neubauer, T. (2009). An empirical study about the status of business process management. *Business Process Management Journal*, *15*(2), 166–183. doi:10.1108/14637150910949434

Novak, R., & Janeš, A. (2018). Business process orientation in the Slovenian power supply. *Business Process Management Journal*. doi:10.1108/BPMJ-05-2017-0130

Pérez-López, S., & Alegre, J. (2012). Information technology competency, knowledge processes and firm performance. *Industrial Management & Data Systems*, *112*(4), 644–662. doi:10.1108/02635571211225521

Peršič, A., Markič, M., & Peršič, M. (2016). The impact of socially responsible management standards on the business success of an organisation. *Total Quality Management & Business Excellence*. doi:10. 1080/14783363.2016.1174059

Peslak, A. R. (2012). An analysis of critical information technology issues facing organizations. *Industrial Management & Data Systems*, *112*(5), 808–827. doi:10.1108/02635571211232389

Pöppelbuß, J., & Röglinger, M. (2011). What makes a useful maturity model? A framework of general design principles for maturity models and its demonstration in business process management. In *Proceedings of the 19th European Conference on Information Systems*. Helsinki, Finland: ECIS.

Ramdani, B., Kawalek, P., & Lorenzo, O. (2009). Predicting SMEs' adoption of enterprise systems. *Journal of Enterprise Information Management*, *22*(1/2), 10–24. doi:10.1108/17410390910922796

Ravesteyn, P., & Batenburg, R. (2010). Surveying the critical success factors of BPM-systems implementation. *Business Process Management Journal*, *16*(3), 492–507. doi:10.1108/14637151011049467

Reijers, H. A. (2006). Implementing BPM systems: The role of process orientation. *Business Process Management Journal*, *12*(4), 389–409. doi:10.1108/14637150610678041

Robey, D. (1980). Computers and management structure: some empirical findings re-examined. In D. Katz, R. L. Kahn, & J. S. Adams (Eds.), *The Study of Organizations* (pp. 33–42). San Francisco, CA: Jossey-Bass.

Roblek, V., Meško, M., Dimovski, V., & Peterlin, J. (2019). Smart technologies as social innovation and complex social issues of the Z generation. *Kybernetes*, *48*(1), 91–107. doi:10.1108/K-09-2017-0356

Roeser, T., & Kern, E. M. (2015). Surveys in business process management–a literature review. *Business Process Management Journal*, *21*(3), 692–718. doi:10.1108/BPMJ-07-2014-0065

Saragiotis, P. (2019). Business process management in the port sector: A literature review. *Maritime Business Review*, *4*(1), 49–70. doi:10.1108/MABR-10-2018-0042

Schröder, C. (2011). Regional and enterprise-specific factors of growths dynamics in German ICT companies. In P. J. J. Welfens (Ed.), *Cluster- und Innovationsdynamik in Europa: Neue Perspektiven der Automobil- und ITK-Wirtschaft* (pp. 237–308). Stuttgart: Lucius & Lucius.

Sikdar, A., & Payyazhi, J. (2014). A process model of managing organizational change during business process redesign. *Business Process Management Journal*, *20*(6), 971–998. doi:10.1108/BPMJ-02-2013-0020

Škrinjar, R. (2010). *Increasing the process orientation maturity with the renovation and computerization of operations* (Unpublished doctoral dissertation). University of Ljubljana, Ljubljana, Slovenia.

Škrinjar, R., Bosilj-Vukšić, V., & Indihar-Štemberger, M. (2008). The impact of business process orientation on financial and non-financial performance. *Business Process Management Journal, 14*(5), 738–754. doi:10.1108/14637150810903084

Škrinjar, R., & Trkman, P. (2013). Increasing process orientation with business process management: Critical practices. *International Journal of Information Management, 33*(1), 48–60. doi:10.1016/j.ijinfomgt.2012.05.011

Tan, F. T. C., Tan, B., Wang, W., & Sedera, D. (2017). IT-enabled operational agility: An interdependencies perspective. *Information & Management, 54*(3), 292–303. doi:10.1016/j.im.2016.08.001

Tarhan, A., Turetken, O., & Reijers, H. A. (2016). Business process maturity models: A systematic literature review. *Information and Software Technology, 75*, 122–134. doi:10.1016/j.infsof.2016.01.010

Tisdell, C. (2017). Information technology's impacts on productivity and welfare: A review. *International Journal of Social Economics, 44*(3), 400–413. doi:10.1108/IJSE-06-2015-0151

van der Aalst, W. M., Dumas, M., & ter Hofstede, A. H. (2003). Web service composition languages: old wine in new bottles? In *Proceedings of the 29th Conference on EUROMICRO*. Washington, DC: IEEE. 10.1109/EURMIC.2003.1231605

Van Looy, A., De Backer, M., & Poels, G. (2011). Defining business process maturity: A journey towards excellence. *Total Quality Management & Business Excellence, 22*(11), 1119–1137. doi:10.1080/14783363.2011.624779

Van Looy, A., De Backer, M., Poels, G., & Snoeck, M. (2013). Choosing the right business process maturity model. *Information & Management, 50*, 466-488. doi: .06.002 doi:10.1016/j.im.2013

Wade, M., & Hulland, J. (2004). Review: the resource-based view and information systems research: review, extension, and suggestions for future research. *Management Information Systems Quarterly, 28*(1), 107–142. doi:10.2307/25148626

Wagner, D., Vollmar, G., & Wagner, H.-T. (2014). The impact of information technology on knowledge creation: An affordance approach to social media. *Journal of Enterprise Information Management, 27*(1), 31–44. doi:10.1108/JEIM-09-2012-0063

Wendland, J., Lerch Lunardi, G. & Bittencourt Dolci, D. (2019). Adoption of health information technology in the mobile emergency care service. *RAUSP Management Journal*. Retrieved January 9, 2019, from . doi:10.1108/RAUSP-07-2018-0058

Wilson, F. (2015). The Quality Maturity Model: Your roadmap to a culture of quality. *Library Management, 36*(3), 258–267. doi:10.1108/LM-09-2014-0102

Xiaofen, T. (2013). Investigation on quality management maturity of Shanghai enterprises. *The TQM Journal, 25*(4), 417–430. doi:10.1108/17542731311314890

Xiaosong Peng, D., Liu, G. J., & Heim, G. R. (2011). Impacts of information technology on mass customization capability of manufacturing plants. *International Journal of Operations & Production Management, 31*(10), 1022–1047. doi:10.1108/01443571111182173

Young, M., Young, R., & Zapata, J. R. (2014). Project, programme and portfolio maturity: A case study of Australian Federal Government. *International Journal of Managing Projects in Business*, 7(2), 215–230. doi:10.1108/IJMPB-08-2013-0034

KEY TERMS AND DEFINITIONS

Business Process Management (BPM): Is a discipline dealing with the management of business processes (BPs) for the achievement of continuous improvement in organizations. BPM refers to a collection of tools and methods for achieving an understanding of and then for managing and improving an organization's process portfolio.

Business Process Orientation (BPO): BPO construct has a somehow intangible nature because the BP is included by BPM, which is further embraced by BPO.

Business Process Orientation Maturity Model (BPOMM): The McCormack and Johnson's BPOMM is the most disseminated model based on the number of studies that report on its testing in a business environment and provides a 'big picture' overview, composed of small elements, and thus comprehensively explains how to implement the development of a product or a process.

Information Technology (IT) or Information Communication Technology (ICT): Is a generic term fundamentally used to refer to programs, computers and telecommunications.

ISO 9001: Is the title of an ISO standard that outlines the requirements an organization must maintain in its quality system for certification to ISO 9001. The current version is ISO 9001:2015. The standard can help companies meet their customers' requirements for their product/service while fulfilling any regulatory requirements.

IT Infrastructure: IT infrastructure refers to artifacts, tools and resources that contribute to the acquisition, processing, storage, dissemination and use of information. According to this definition, the IT infrastructure includes elements such as hardware, software and employees.

IT Knowledge: Describes the degree to which the organization understands the capabilities of existing and emerging IT. An awareness of IT 'possibilities' exposes the universe of digital options available to the organization, providing the flexibility to quickly adapt to emerging market(s) opportunities.

IT Operations: This concept refers to the IT-related methods, processes and techniques that may be needed if these technologies are to create value. IT operations can be defined as the extent to which the firm uses IT to improve its effectiveness, agility and decision-making.

Maturity Model: A maturity model is a conceptual model that consists of a sequence of discrete maturity levels for a class of processes in one or more business domains, and represents an anticipated, desired, or typical evolutionary path for these processes.

Chapter 17
Psychological Impact and Assessment of Youth for the Use of Social Network

Sapna Jain
Jamia Hamdard, India

M. Afshar Alam
Jamia Hamdard, India

Niloufer Adil Kazmi
Independent Researcher, India

ABSTRACT

This chapter dissects the effect of online life on each youngster in both the negative and positive bearing of their development utilizing the social impact hypothesis. Reliance of youth via web-based networking media has both negative and beneficial outcomes. This hypothesis portrays social effect concerning social power handle that encroach upon us, pushing us to think or keep thinking about a specific goal. These social powers have been stood out from physical powers that control the transmission of light, solid, gravity, interest, and so forth. The discoveries uncovered that the utilization of internet-based life impacts adolescent conduct when contrasted with positive aspects. This study shows a connection among contradictory and imaginative qualities of online life and displays roads for future investigations by encouraging a superior comprehension of electronic interpersonal organization use. In the chapter, the social effect felt by a person as a component of the quality, instantaneousness, and number of source people is exhibited and examined.

INTRODUCTION

This section gives an understanding how web based life has turned out to be interlinking into the material of most recent youth. Youth trust vigorously via web-based networking media for correspondence, cooperation, and subsequently the dispersal of information. Web based life could be a territory that is

DOI: 10.4018/978-1-5225-8933-4.ch017

supercharged by people, and can, in this way, reverberation individuals' best aims, yet as their awfully most exceedingly terrible; those that search for to hurt others region unit strong by the web, by indistinguishable will be aforementioned for those that search for exclusively to help others. Online life makes our social relationship inside the feeling that, being on field we'd not be prepared to manufacture a great deal of companions. The reliance of young people on the online life has come to at such dimension that, while not web based life, every adolescent can't depend on the course of their development. Reliance of youth via web-based networking media has each negative and positive effect .

Researchers have discovered that abuse of innovation ordinarily, and web based life most importantly, makes an incitement design equivalent to the example made by various propensity shaping practices. a fresh out of the plastic new investigation demonstrates that getting "likes" via web-based networking media actuates indistinguishable circuits inside the youthful mind that territory unit enacted by nourishing chocolate or winning money. The pros and cons of social network affects the psychological behaviour of youth when interacting on a social network. It is basic for teenagers to check sources and truth, rather than taking all that youth should see as truth. They tend to wish to be "pulled over the coals" as a result of a wrong move that they tend to work by posting one thing that is inadequately investigated and eventually exposed. The technique by which the youth convey their contemplations when online defines the impact of the features and facilities on the social network.

BACKGROUND

Online Social Networks (OSNs) area unit seen because the pay attention of framework resource for affiliations that association key regard and business execution (Zhou, Wu, and Luo, 2007). On bigger casual network areas, people area unit commonly not eager to meet new individuals however rather area unit logically enthused regarding supervision associations by maintaining contacts with recent mates WHO area unit beginning at currently a part of their wide comprehensive relative association (Boyd and Ralph Waldo Ellison, 2007). To total up, casual association goals will be seen as elective specific mechanical assemblies that support existing associations and activities during a fun and hanging method that may build up the customers' experiences several relative association destinations have risen; actuation specifically get-togethers of consumers subject to their economic science and a few be careful for systems with unequivocal shared interests (Palmer and Koenig-Lewis, 2009). there's nowadays a good deal of affirmation that easy going affiliation zones have pushed toward obtaining the prospect to be normal and it's been spoken to it all around, these objectives address one in at traditional intervals spent on the net (Jones, 2009). fifty four % of internet shoppers some spot within the extent of sixteen and twenty four have created their terribly own exceptional page or profile on someone to singular correspondence website page (Palmer and Koenig-Lewis, 2009). Social affiliation locales have party of individuals quite another on-line life these days. Facebook accomplishes 710 million customers (H. Hanafizadeh and Behboudi, 2012). Meanwhile, if Facebook were a rustic, it'd be the third greatest nation on earth, waiting behind simply China and Asian country. half those "locals" check in faithfully and victimization the positioning once per day (Zarrella and Zarrella, 2011). the standard client has one hundred thirty partners and is expounded with eighty system pages, social affairs, and events each pay a normal of forty six minutes out of systematically on Facebook (Facebook.com, 2011). Moreover, one hundred million individuals build a social proceed onward YouTube faithfully and 800 million distinctive customers visit this website every month (Youtube.com). Casual association districts provide opportunities to attach with these arduous to-contact social affairs of people sailplaning faraway from normal media. it would be deduced that utilization of relative association is extending at Associate in Nursing large speed, and it's influencing however individuals share information over the world. SNS may be a crisp out of the plastic new purpose for authorities thanks to its relative peculiarity, and one or two of researchers in numerous settings tried to contemplate this new phonemena. The impact of casual associations is logically bound, with activities running from the financial e.g., shopping and advancing e.g. complete building, advertising) to the social (e.g., social and physiological impacts) and enlightening (e.g., separate preparing) (for instance mangold-wurzel and Smith, 2011; golf player and Koenig-Lewis, 2009; S. Pookulangara and K. Koesler, 2011; Teo, Chan, Weib, and Zhang, 2003). In any case, paying very little mind to its noteworthiness within the new info time, no total composition review has been driven within the field of casual networks beside a review paper coordinated by Hanafizadeh, et al. (2012) on casual correspondence business effects composing. Everything thought of, there's a necessity for driving this type of analysis works, since it'll fill in as a guide for the 2 scholastics and specialists. it'll in like manner show the lilting movement state and course of analysis subjects, and will be of interest. a web relative association (OSN) may be a growth of the quality casual association on the web, that is very internet based mostly programming that individuals use to develop social affiliations. OSN fuses numerous on-line headways, for example, blog, Twitter, Facebook, Mashup, content, video gathering, virtual world, linguistics destinations, . (S. M. Lee and subgenus Chen, 2011). OSNs use computer support because the reason of correspondence among its individuals (Andrews, Preece, and Turoff, 2001). Drawing on Boyd and Ralph Waldo Ellison (2007), OSNs area unit represented as on-line associations that (1) have interaction individuals to create Associate in Nursing open or semi-open profile for themselves within Associate in Nursing obligated framework, (2) show a fast summary of various shoppers with whom they're connected, and (3) see and investigate their summation of affiliations and people created out by totally different shoppers within the structure. In express settings, as an example, the propellant structure, the terms 'online social affiliation' and 'virtual framework' area unit frequently utilised synonymously. Virtual society area unit seen as consumer parties of adjusting sizes that expire habitually and for a few zero in a managed manner over the web through a typical zone or fragment to accomplish individual additionally as shared focuses of their kin (Dholakia, Bagozzi, and Pearo, 2004; Ridings, Gefen, and Arinze, 2002). the $64000 nice position of OSN is its capability to grant a lot of important long vary easygoing correspondence openings than the quality social affiliation transversally over numerous geographical, social, social, or institutional settings. OSN doesn't uproot the quality easygoing affiliation, rather supplements it and starts new social affiliations. The affront of OSN is that people have low trust and faithfully feel nervous or unsure within the virtual condition (S. M. Lee and subgenus Chen, 2011).

WHAT IS A SOCIAL NETWORK?

Social network is online unit organizations that helps people to build up an and open profile, to develop an online posting platform of different users with whom they share an affiliation and read their once-over of affiliations and people made by others users on the network.

CHARACTERISTICS OF SOCIAL NETWORKS

Interpersonal interaction Sites like Facebook and Linkedin are the most prevalent web goals today . They give a stage to individuals to interface with companions, relatives and colleagues over the world. They have basic characteristics that make them well known and utilized by today's youth.

Core Characteristics of Social Networks.

Those characteristics are as follows.

1. User-based: Before online social network like Facebook or twitter turned into the standard, sites depended on substance that was refreshed by all youth age group users. The progression of data was in a solitary bearing, and the course of future updates was dictated by the website admin, or author. Online social organizations, then again, are manufactured and coordinated by users themselves. Without the users, the system would be an unfilled space loaded up with void discussions, applications, and talk rooms. Clients populate the system with discussions and substance .

2. Interactive: In the present day informal communities is the way that they are so intuitive that an informal community isn't only a gathering of chatrooms and discussions any longer for youth. Sites like Facebook are loaded up with system based gaming applications, where you can play poker together or challenge a companion to a chess competition.

3. Community-driven: Social systems are fabricated and flourish from network ideas. This implies simply like networks or social gatherings around the globe are established on the way that individuals hold basic convictions or leisure activities, interpersonal organizations depend on a similar standard.

4. Relationships: The ability to viably utilize web search tools and see has been contemplated by United Nations office or what associations made or support the information; wherever the data originates from and its believability . Join that have some expertise in morals, style and cooperation make a significant commitment to discussions round the job of internet based life in scholarly settings, giving numerous chances to inventive reasoning and articulation, while maintaining a strategic distance from the over-disentangled investigation that might be identified with sane evaluate of online networking writings. In any case, while concurring that such open doors should be important elements of online networking in scholastic settings, we will in general contend that there's as yet a need for reflexive scrutinize.

5. Emotion over content: Another one of a kind normal for social network is the passionate factor. While sites of the past were focused essentially around giving data to a guest, the online community really furnishes young users with enthusiastic security and a feeling that regardless of what occurs, their companions are inside simple reach.

6. Persistence: Unlike the fleeting nature of discourse in unmediated publics, arranged interchanges are recorded for descendants. This empowers offbeat correspondence however it likewise expands the time of presence of any discourse demonstration. Accessibility can be improved in light of the fact that articulations are recorded and character is set up through content, hunt and disclosure devices help individuals discover like personalities. While individuals can't at present procure the geological directions of any individual in unmediated spaces, discovering one's computerized body online is simply an issue of keystrokes. While we can outwardly identify a great many people who

can catch our discourse in unmediated spaces, it is for all intents and purposes difficult to discover each one of the individuals who may keep running over our appearances in arranged publics.

Emprical Characteristics of Social Network

Unlike the fleeting nature of discourse in unmediated publics, arranged interchanges are recorded for descendants. This empowers offbeat correspondence however it likewise expands the time of presence of any discourse demonstration. Accessibility can be improved in light of the fact that articulations are recorded and character is set up through content, hunt and disclosure devices help individuals discover like personalities. While individuals can't at present procure the geological directions of any individual in unmediated spaces, discovering one's computerized body online is simply an issue of keystrokes. While we can outwardly identify a great many people who can catch our discourse in unmediated spaces, it is for all intents and purposes difficult to discover each one of the individuals who may keep running over our appearances in arranged public.

Facebook

Facebook is an Internet-based administration going for interfacing individuals, sharing substance and transferring photographs among companions and relationship. Facebook cases to have in excess of 55 million clients and a normal of 250,000 new enrolled clients every day (by April 2008), consequently being one of the world most prevalent administrations. Usefulness and configuration show an emphasis on private use and contacts are alluded to as "companions". The framework is created and kept up by the proprietors yet the substance, similar to pictures, diversions and connections, are transferred and kept up by the clients. Each client creates and keeps up their very own online profile, which should concur with their disconnected character, yet no genuine control is made (or is conceivable). Users are urged to create applications inside the structure of the site, bringing about in excess of 20,000 one of a kind applications. Facebook has progressively grown new highlights, as Facebook Notes and news channels showing the ongoing exercises of part's companions. The organic reach for pages has nearly flatlined, it is popularly utilised by seventy two of all adult net users in America as shown in Figure 1 . More women users: seventy seven of on-line female users area unit on Facebook. The Younger audience: eighty 2 of all on-line users between 18-29 area unit on Facebook. The Facebook Demographics analysis results show as USA (14%), Republic of India (9%) and Brazil (7%) kind the three largest markets.

Twitter

Twitter, propelled in 2006, is an on-line application planned around the idea of smaller scale blogging. The on-line stage enables clients to send open updates ("tweets") about themselves as short content based presents available on different clients who have joined to get them. Presents are constrained on 140 characters, which make them reasonable for conveyance through texting administrations, (e.g.: MSN Messenger), or short message benefits on cell phones. Twitter is likewise intended to coordinate inside outsider informal communication programming, for example, Facebook. Facebook clients can buy in to Twitter and control it's administrations through Facebook. Clients who become companions, can peruse each other's posts on either the Twitter site, a cell phone, another SNS stage, or a texting administration. Clients can control which companions get their updates, and confine the updates got from others: for

Figure 1. Facebook demographics usage

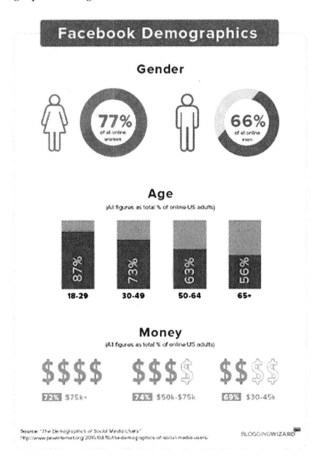

example, short message administration on cell phones can be turned off around evening time, or undesired clients' updates can be won't. The product permits the expansion of client made applications, for example, realistic representation of the systems made by client memberships to individual miniaturized scale postings. Twitter's snappy streaming 'data stream' pulls in A crowd of people that swings more youthful and is normally urban and semi-urban. The Youngers utilized it by thirty seventh of all on-line clients somewhere in the range of eighteen and twenty-nine. The Educated community has fifty-four of users have either graduated faculty or have some faculty experience. The Richer square measure fifty-four of on-line adults World Health Organization produce over $50,000 and have area unit on Twitter (Figure 2). Overall, twenty third of on-line adult's area unit on Twitter.

Instagram

Instagram recently overtook Twitter to become the second largest social network. bench estimates that twenty sixth of all on-line adults unit on Instagram inside the USA as shown in figure 5.There are a lot of women victimisation than, twenty ninth of all on-line women unit on Instagram, vs. alone twenty second of all men. fifty 3 of all 18 to 29 year olds unit on Instagram in figure 3. The Less educated on Instagram users unit college graduates, whereas thirty initial have some college experience that is fitting as primarily younger audience.

Figure 2. Twitter demographics usage

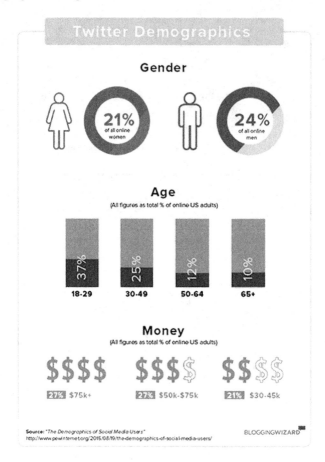

LinkedIn

Linkedin is an Internet-based virtual world propelled in 2003, created by Linden Research, Inc. A down-loadable customer program called the Second Life Viewer empowers its clients (occupants) to cooperate with one another's symbols, giving a propelled long range informal communication administration. Linden Labs guarantees more than 6,000,000 occupants from 106 nations. Occupants can investigate, meet different inhabitants, mingle, take an interest in individual and gathering exercises, and make and exchange things (virtual property) and administrations. Second Life has its own in-world monetary market and money (Linden dollar - replaceable for genuine monetary forms). Though the geo-spatial foundation is overseen by the proprietors, the destinations (islands) are principally worked by inhabitants in-world, utilizing three-dimensional graphical control and scripting. Organizations, intrigue gatherings and NGOs are generally spoken to, as are government offices and ideological groups. Second Life's computerized world has numerous associations with the outside world. The more seasoned network has only twenty third of clients unit between 18-29 years later. Twenty first percent were more than sixty five years, and thirty one percent somewhere in the range of thirty and forty nine years versed people as appeared in figure 4.The Urban individuals truly limited differ of provincial clients – solely 14 July. sixty one unit either urban or regional territory. The Wealthier people square measure seventy fifth of

Figure 3. Instagram demographics usage

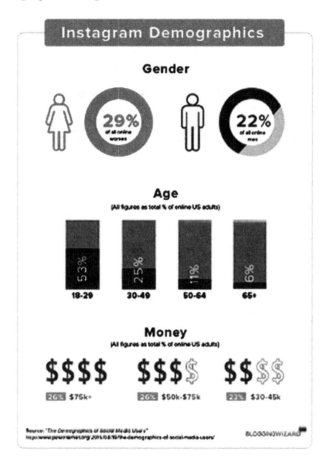

clients acquire over $50,000.The incredibly instructed contribute 5 hundredth of LinkedIn clients unit personnel graduates. An additional twenty second have some workforce understudies.

SOCIAL NETWORK PSCHYCOLOGY

An social network is comprised of people or associations who impart and connect with one another. Long range informal communication destinations for example, Facebook, Twitter, and LinkedIn – are characterized as innovation empowered instruments that help clients with making and keeping up their connections. The users identified with long range interpersonal communication is affected by real individual contrasts. The individuals contrast methodically in the amount and nature of their social connections. Two of the principle character attributes that are in charge of this fluctuation are the characteristics of extraversion and introspection. Extraversion alludes to the inclination to be socially prevailing, apply authority, and impact on others. Contrastingly, introspection alludes to the propensity of an individual to have an air of modesty, social fear, or even maintain a strategic distance from social circumstances through and through, which could prompt a decrease in the quantity of potential contacts that individual may have. These individual contrasts may result in various long range interpersonal communication

Figure 4. LinkedIn demographics usage

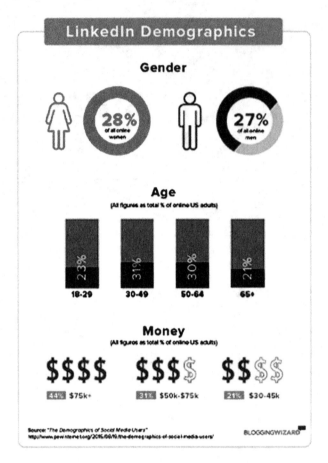

results. Other mental variables identified with internet based life are: melancholy, uneasiness, connection, self-character, and the need to have a place. Internet based life and mind capacity go connected at the hip. Our cerebrum is the 'social organ' of our bodies and the maker of online networking itself. The mind needs to associate with other individuals, to submerge and comprehend other individuals' encounters through correspondence, regardless of whether that be up close and personal or through broad communications. Internet based life requires a lot of self-referential idea. Individuals utilize internet based life as a stage to express their suppositions and hotshot their over a wide span of time selves. Self-referential idea includes movement in the average prefrontal cortex and the back cingulate cortex. The cerebrum utilizes these specific frameworks when considering oneself. The information encased in a profile shifts by interpersonal organization, anyway some of the time incorporates a picture of the client and a client name, also as information in regards to socioeconomics and demeanour, similar to sexual orientation, dates of birth, training, business, and interests. Facebook is by and by the premier wide utilized on-line interpersonal organization, with 1.5 billion ordinary clients on various informal communities spend significant time in explicit employments. LinkedIn, Twitter with a microblogging centre, and Instagram with a photograph partaking in various significant classes of informal organization . System sharing stages, as twitter and Instagram, give people a field to share system like recordings or photographs. This class normally covers with informal communities, because of system sharing stages commonly give profiles, remarks, or input on indicate content. for example, Instagram has been classified as each an informal organization focused on sharing, also as a system sharing stage. Social news stages, as Reddit and Digg, give people with a field to share and talk about news. The users will create, alter, and erase content, anyway ordinarily don't move as socially as in various platforms.

The online users give a stage for people to fulfil these rudimentary social drives. In particular, interpersonal organization license youth to join with others and husband to be our name through at least 5 key practices (Figure 5)- *Social network users can:*

1.   Broadcast information;
2.   Receive feedback on this information;
3.   Observe the broadcasts of others;
4.   Provide feedback on the broadcasts of others;
5.   Compare themselves with others.

For instance, an online user may require photographs of an excursion that she might truly want to impart to other people. The online user photographs to informal community so various users give criticism by remarking on the pictures and additionally giving an image of endorsement (e.g., a 'like' or 'top choice', looking on the interpersonal organization stage). This correspondence works inside the other route also: (iii)users watch information communicated by others; and (iv) users give criticism on others' posts. for example, a user would conceivably observe a picture of a companion's get-away, 'similar to' the picture on Facebook, so address what amount fun the occasion looked. Input is here and there noticeable to the client's system or, at times, people in general. In either case, (v) user communicate in social correlation, by various their very own communicates and input to other people, similar to the amount of preferences got.

Web-based social networking has turned out to be interlaced into the texture of most recent youthfulness. Youth trust vigorously web-based networking media for correspondence, association, and consequently the scattering of data. Web based life may be a space that is supercharged by individuals, and can, accordingly, reverberation individuals' best goals, in any case as their most noticeably terrible;

Figure 5. Five key social network behaviours

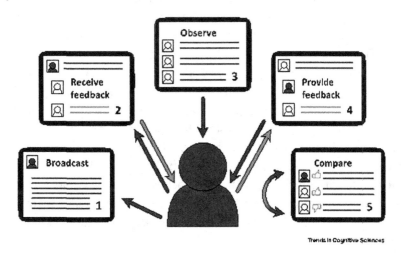

Trends In Cognitive Sciences

individuals who scrounge around for to hurt others square measure brave by the net, still indistinguishable are previously mentioned for individuals who scavenge around for just to help other people. Web based life shapes social relationship inside the feeling that, being on field online who are capable not have the option to construct huge amounts of companions.

Web based life may be a stage in making new companions. It causes the young to frame relationship by knowing ourselves higher and apparently inside the more drawn out term, we'd end up serving to ourselves. Our reality isn't planning to alteration, and innovation will at present infiltrate society much more profound exertion next to zero opportunity to respond to the clearly day by day augmentations to our lives. Utilization of online long range interpersonal communication is accomplice principal a region of Indian youth today. Over utilization of web based life, has gotten the thought of youth completely. The dependence of youngsters on the online life has come to at such measurement that, while not web based life, each juvenile can't recognize the course of their advancement. Dependence of youth by means of online systems administration media has each negative and constructive outcome. Specialists have found that maltreatment of advancement unremarkably, and electronic long range informal communication exceptionally, makes a prompting structure unclear in light of the way that the model made by absolutely novel addictive lead. The points of interest and drawbacks of electronic life through and through depend on yet we tend to use it. regardless, it's as one essential to expect the opposite side thusly on keep up a key separation from any sort of complexities. it's central for U.S. to check sources and truth, instead of taking all that we should constantly see as truth. we tend to should be "pulled over the coals" inferable from a wrong move that we tend to make by posting one factor that is deficiently researched and finally uncovered! the framework by that we will when all is said in done pass on our thoughts to our gathering of spectators might be raised to quality on condition that those contemplations zone unit a unit particularly contained with checked convictions and sources.

It has right now turned into a clear and normal sight to face individuals being unfeeling toward talk in revering places, homes once relatives and visitors square measure around, expressways, schools, schools and parties whereby youth is so distracted and charmed into their telephones that they are doing not bother to appear up on wherever they're which finishes in their failure to put on what's fundamental and what isn't. The essential target of this section is to toss light on anyway viably has the use of person to person communication destinations influenced the young by assessing every one of its positive and negative angles.

With connection to the discoveries it completely was obviously confounded out anyway reasonable, insightful, humorous and mindful the young is inside the present time. Through the help of the data that was gathered and examined very couple of ends have been drawn down which might be explained and intricate as pursues .The young now a days isn't exclusively mindful to what fits in best for them in any case, are sharp and ardent to draw their own needs and fix on to which of them square measure most critical and the way. similarly these destinations fill to their need of associating them with people the whole way across the globe by not hampering their work hours and timetables. Be that as it may, interpersonal interaction destinations supply them a stage to append with new individuals, share encounters and increase presentation. With connection to the normal result the investigation has delighted to an unmistakable edge whereby not exclusively negative effects have well-endeavoured to exist through the utilization of long range informal communication locales be that as it may likewise the presence of positive effects have involved a zone in one's life. The teenagers have decided their own limits and have set their possess restrains on be that as it may and once to utilize online networking paying little respect to the positive and negative impacts .

SOCIAL NETWORK ACTIONS

Why We've Got an Inclination to Post on Social Network

People dedicate concerning thirty to four-hundredth ever talking concerning themselves. be that as it may, on-line that determination bounces to concerning eightieth of interpersonal organization posts. Talking eye to eye is chaotic and genuinely is concerned. We don't have sufficient energy to acknowledge what to state, we must peruse facial prompts and correspondence on-line. We have time to develop and refine clinicians call of self-introduction, situating yourself the way you'd like to be seen. The inclination we have a tendency to prompt from self-introduction is seeing your own Facebook profile has been appeared to expand your vainness. What's together captivating for advertisers is that the preeminent extraordinary proposes that we have a tendency to will in general work on self-introduction is through things, purchasing things and stress things that mean UN office we have a tendency to demonstrate.

Why We've a Bent to Share on Social Network

On the off chance that we have a bowed to love talking concerning ourselves such loads, what might create our picture to share one issue of somebody else's. It encourages for Self-introduction and reinforcing connections that help to make our own self-esteem. As indicated by review directed sixty eight of individuals state they offer to oversee others the following feeling of United Nations organization they are and what they care concerning. But the chief fundamental reason we've a twisted to share is concerning different people: seventy eight folks} state they share as a consequences of it causes them to remain associated with individuals. various investigations have demonstrated that the preeminent powerful indicators of infectious ideas among the cerebrum square measure related with the components that attention on contemplations concerning people. this suggests substance intended for informal community doesn't need to be constrained to appeal to A curiously large bunch or a mean group. it only should appeal to a chose individual. Informal community Currency is by having one issue captivating to state.

Why We've Got a Bent to Like on Social Network

Facebook, with over an attempt of billion month to month dynamic clients could likewise be a wonderful case of a stage where individuals wish to like. Truth be told, since Facebook implemented the "Like" catch, it has been utilized over one.13 multiple times, therewith choice developing by the day. We do this as a consequences of we will in general need to require care of connections. when we watch out for most loved and like each other's posts. Teenagers got a bowed to highlight an incentive to the connection, and strengthen that closeness. we will in general set up together turn out a correspondence result. We have a bowed to feel committed to oversee back to the individuals who have given to North American nation to redesign the scales. A man of science sent Christmas cards to 600 arbitrary outsiders and got two hundred equally. That is the intensity of correspondence. Youth can correspondence on Instagram in like manner, where getting a tag or direct message makes you feel constrained to send one back. What's more, whenever anyone get a like on your profile, they potentially feel scarcely dismantle to respond in be that as it may, regardless of whether or not by sharing one factor proportionally, language up upgrades out social connections.

Why We've Got a Bent to Comment

The selling organizations will in general guess discussions with clients region unit massively significant. The commitment, cooperation with the most clients the greatest sum as potential forms long help. An overview of over seven thousand clients found that only twenty third percent people did that what they did, solely 13 referred to visit associations with the whole as an explanation behind having a relationship. The customers same shared qualities were a so a lot bigger driver for a relationship than unnumbered cooperation with a whole clients. this can be to not say that remarks aren't amazing. Indeed, they will be unrealistically so there's an advancement alluded to as shared reality that claims our entire experience of 1 issue is stricken by if and in this manner the way we have a twisted to impart it to others.85% various individuals' reactions on an issue helps U.S.A. comprehend and approach data and occasions. This implies remarks even have the ability to change our psyches, and science backs this up. An investigation on news destinations demonstrated that remarks that simply assault the creator, without any realities the littlest sum bit, are sufficient to shift our impression of an issue. On the elective hand, well-mannered audits – even once they're negative – cause a whole to be viewed as a lot of legitimate and healthy. Clients were truly ready to pay concerning $41 a lot of for a watch once they saw courteous negative audits than once the surveys were evacuated. Essentially, any remark concerning you, anyplace on-line, is to a customer an impression of what very organization you are. It's not explicitly coherent, yet that is nevertheless our cerebrums work. This implies being effectively connected inside the remarks area of your diary and with the customer audits of your item is critical, not such a lot to the individual you're reacting to beside everybody taking an interest inside the mutual truth of remarks and surveys.

Selfie Craze

Historically, portraits are relating to standing, and dominant the means that our image is perceived.

Today, they're the thanks to estimate for the tendency WHO we tend to are . The "looking-glass self" could also be a psychological thought that claims that we can, we will, we are able to ne'er be really see ourselves. We would really like our reflection from others therefore on grasp who we have an inclination to are. Selfies put together work as a results of we have an inclination to pay loads of attention to faces than we've an inclination to try and do to the remainder. The profile image is that the first place the eye is drawn to on Facebook and different social network sites. On Instagram, footage with human faces are thirty eight percent loads of in all probability to receive likes and thirty 2% that is loads of in all probability to attract comments. Eye-tracking studies show that on-line, we've an inclination to follow the eyes of the oldsters we've an inclination to check on screen.

Emoji Power on Social Network

Most people have a bent to mimic each other's expressions in face-to-face spoken communication. In on-line arena, we have a bent to recreate that crucial a part of sympathy using emoticons and emoji. Today, ninety 2 of people out hundreds of times use stickers, emoticons or emojis in their on-line communication, and 10 billion emoji are sent around the world every day. Emoji may be a powerful link between emoji use and social network power. it's Associate in Nursing analysis of over 5 years in social network found that emoji were a customary issue among important and customary social network sharers. A study that had participants chat on-line with various forms of specialists found that participants rated the specialists friendlier and tons of competent once they used emoticons in their communication. There are several fun ways that during which to incorporate emoji into your merchandising campaigns. Brands like Ikea, Coca-Cola, Burger King and Comedy Central have even created their own branded emoji for their popularity.

Network Nostalgia

Sometimes the network and life moves thus fast that we have a tendency to would like things to dam. This is where craving comes in, and this longing for the past is an unbelievable strategy for modern social network selling. yearning is universal across all cultures and it provides U.S. the way of social connectedness, feelings of being favourite and protected.

CONCEPTUAL FRAMEWORK

See Figure 6.

Figure 6. Conceptual framework

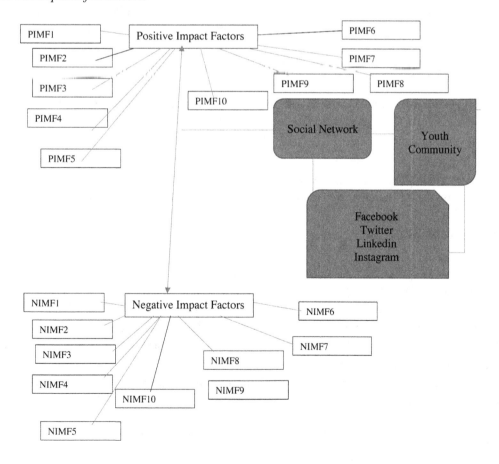

POSITIVE SOCIAL NETWORK PSYCHOLOGY

Web-based social networking is progressively turning into a basic component of human culture by changing our social standards, qualities, and culture. Data sharing and the conveyance of substance are getting to be significant social wants . Web based life has changed how individuals, including college understudies impart, cooperate, and associate through the span of their learning forms at instructive establishments. This new type of media is assuming an imperative job in substance sharing among colleges understudies and the remainder of society. Understudies currently have the chance to partake in social talk by sharing pictures and pictures, posting their remarks, scattering thoughts, . . Advanced media and person to person communication are altering strategies for ordinary correspondence, coordinated effort, data sharing, and data utilization .

Media Skill

The ability to viably utilize web search tools and see has been contemplated by United Nations office or what associations made or support the information; wherever the data originates from and its believability . Join that have some expertise in morals, style and cooperation make a significant commitment to discussions round the job of internet based life in scholarly settings, giving numerous chances to inventive reasoning and articulation, while maintaining a strategic distance from the over-disentangled investigation that might be identified with sane evaluate of online networking writings. In any case, while concurring that such open doors should be important elements of online networking in scholastic settings, we will in general contend that there's as yet a need for reflexive scrutinize.

Technical Acquirement

The information and skills needed to use a laptop, application or specific package program or application. company learners World Health Organization have a high degree of technical acquirement acumen to use technology to their advantage. they will realize all the knowledge they have by looking out the net and exploitation the tech-based resources that square measure out there. These people even have the ability to beat everyday challenges and reach their goals with the assistance of their mobile devices. Technical acquirement is important in our tech-centric society.

Critical Content Skill

The ability to viably utilize web search tools and see has been contemplated by United Nations office or what associations made or support the information; wherever the data originates from and its believability . Join that have some expertise in morals, style and cooperation make a significant commitment to discussions round the job of internet based life in scholarly settings, giving numerous chances to inventive reasoning and articulation, while maintaining a strategic distance from the over-disentangled investigation that might be identified with sane evaluate of online networking writings. In any case, while concurring that such open doors should be important elements of online networking in scholastic settings, we will in general contend that there's as yet a need for reflexive scrutinize.

Communicative and Social Networking Literacy

Open partner studied informal communication process in different totally various zones of correspondence on the online web. The formal standards that administer guide the material conduct, dimension of protection to influence undesirable or unseemly correspondence through them; creative substance and visual securing furthermore to the capacities to shape and exchange picture and video content this incorporates seeing how on-line visual substance is adjusted and developed, what sensibly substance is satisfactory and the manner in which copyright applies to their exercises. Research shows that the work of long range interpersonal communication administrations will bolster the occasion of media procurement. The creation and sharing of substance on administrations like Myspace has been believed to expand every youthful people groups specialized education, as they figure out how to utilize code to frame their profiles, and inventive substance and visual literacy.

Formal Education Outcome

The potential of public SNS and social media like blogs to helps to conduct formal tutorial activities and enhance learning outcomes. whereas e-learning frameworks square measure presently integrated into most tutorial settings, the use of SNS could be a smaller quantity comprehensively used. The SNS varies in keeping with state and there's inadequacy of proof on the impact of SNS on young people's formal education . SNS is in addition obtaining accustomed increase opportunities for formal learning across geographical contexts. Using SNS, youngsters from the two schools act with learners from over forty various SNS use between lecturers and students can improve rapport and motivation and engagement with education .Studies conducted inside the point on the role of ICT in learning and development .

On-line forums and SNS can support the continuation and extension of learning and discussion outside formal as Peer based learning can be a key characteristic of the strategy throughout that teenagers direct their own learning outside school & formal organisations .Evaluations of e-learning ways that have found SNS platforms enable the extension of learning discussion outside the formal area setting, therefore promoting deeper learning as teenagers not exclusively interact with the material for extended but square measure further apparently to relate thereto and incorporate it into their everyday lives. Finally, studies conducted on the use of hand-held devices to deliver point learning demonstrable that regular accessibility suggests that children can access resources in a very technique that is every convenient and relevant to them. The elearning tutorials have positive impact on learners and help socio-economic backgrounds and folks living in remote areas, face persistent challenges of internet access and skill . Increasing the benefits of SNS for these groups specifically wants addressing access and digital skill.

Creativity

Rapid uptake of digital technologies have displayed unexampled prospects for amateur users to make and distribute content specified media users became producers. User-generated content describes each the generation of „original" inventive content and „remixed" content that creatively reworks or repurposes existing content. The interrelatedness between SNS and social media has provided a key impetus (via platforms like youtube.com and flickr.com) for the sharing of this self-generated content with broader networks. teens particularly area unit additional immersed during this democratic media surroundings than the other age-group. They currently produce and share their own 'small media' in their everyday communicative, inventive and social activities.

Creative content sharing practices such as blogs, animations, videos, photos associate degreed digital collages . It plays a big role in young people developing sense of identity and community. inventive content production and sharing empowers individual teens through the subsequent incontestable benefits. Developing a way of aspiration, personal action and self-worth, and fostering additional creative thinking and self-Notley of all of that area unit key predictors of wellbeing.

Individual Identity and Self-Expression

Individual Identity SNS area necessary for the expression of identity. This articulation is not simply egotistic, but supports essential peer-based nature. As a results of SNS area unit essentially versatile and designed to push individual customisation youngsters use SNS to experiment nonetheless as notice legitimacy for his or her political, ethnic, cultural or sexual identity .

SNS can offer youngsters with a part to work out identity and standing, add from cultural cues and discuss public life. Free from adult regulation young people's articulation and expression of assorted components of their identity to their friends et al. supports essential peer-based nature . Such processes of socialisation area unit essential for psychosocial development at a time once many youngsters are consolidating their identities, propulsion up roots from their family, pains for independence and developing new sorts of relationships, yet as intimate ones .

Strengthening Existing Relationships

Having positive social relationships in web use, generally, has been found to strengthen young people's existing social relationships Most analysis has centered on the role SNS play within the maintaining and strengthening of existing offline relationships. However, for a few teenagers, notably those that area unit marginalised or otherwise socially isolated, on line relationships provided a major, and generally the sole, chance for such socialisation. As a study of SNS for teenagers that suffer chronic sickness and/or incapacity demonstrates, not solely did it offer the chance to develop such friendships however participants represented these friendships as "true friends" that were amongst their most dependable and enduring . Another study incontestable however Facebook helped teenagers with lower levels of social skills develop friendships on-line that then translated offline .Indeed, teenagers area unit more and more partaking at the same time in on-line and offline social networking. As an example, multi-player gambling includes a long tradition of mixing on-line and offline interactions of players with web cafes and computer network parties providing such areas .whereas there has been very little analysis it seems that teenagers typically work collaboratively within the on-line area through SNS, making and commenting on YouTube videos or different such activities, whereas physically co-located. teenagers not solely can take into account their on-line and offline worlds together however truly mix the two during a physical and temporal sense. This insight is additional emphatic by analysis demonstrating that the potential of SNS for promoting social inclusion depends upon finding ways that of bridging online communication .

Belonging and Collective Identity

SNS facilitates people, children, kids, youngsters, teenagers, teens, adolescents, youth. The sexually and gender varied to meet folks and learn from each other, creating the sense of happiness to a broader community. This sense of happiness and acceptance can mean that youth United Nations agency might even be tons of in danger of isolation like those with chronic malady or a incapacity usually keep members of an online community long once their initial impetus is content sharing plays a major role in cultivating happiness and some way of collective identity. Sharing written, visual or audio content on SNS that represents or portrays a private or community experience invites others to act and relate. This phenomenon is associated with current visual access to a small-scale communication cluster or community via spontaneous and everyday photos uploaded to a cooperative media space. Such a mode of sharing and connection does not want of time communication and will to boot mitigate feelings of social isolation.

Civic and Political Participation

SNS speak to new territories for municipal commitment and political cooperation just as information sharing and transferral along new systems for activity using email, client produced substance and distinctive systems administration rehearses. Concentrates inside the U.S. understand that thirty seventh of eighteen – twenty multi year olds use online journals and SNS for political or community commitment. Political competitors zone unit increasingly using SNS and online life, as territory unit backing and issue-situated groups. SNS zone unit getting utilized for dialog, association and assembly as a piece of rising political talk in youthful people groups presence. despite the fact that focused on balloting, efforts like Rock the Vote, The Hip Hop Summit Action Network, subject adjustment and Voces del Pueblo zone unit tests of the technique that long range informal communication is inserted in new assortments of network and political sorting out and electioneering. For youth United Nations organization don't consider their investment in community or issue-based exercises as inside the old or institutional sense, SNS region unit thought of a great deal of fundamental than ,,civic locales. Person to person communication administrations, as <u>web.</u> <u>myspace.com</u> region unit acclimated choose what individuals do by associating with individuals with comparable interests, existing efforts or distributive data in regards to their own comes.

NEGATIVE SOCIAL NETWORK PSYCHOLOGY

The threatening effects of these individual to individual correspondence goals surpass the helpful ones. The study suggests that electronic life is an engaging way for understudies to keep up a vital separation from weariness while they are thinking about or glancing through their course material web, diverting their thought from their work. The online network filling has a net-negative effect on one life. For instance, the going with electronic life stages have been situated from the most to the least negative reliant on customer evaluations: Twitter, Facebook, linkedin, and Instagram.

Sedentary Behaviour

Inactive practices square measure exercises that include sitting or resting and square measure described by an espresso Metabolic Equivalent Total (MET) vitality use. Inert practices square measure performed at or somewhat over the resting rate go 1 to 1.5 METS and grasp an assortment of exercises like television seeing, PC use, appreciating computer games, and latent diversion These dormant practices square measure unavoidable in our general public, grown-ups pay a middle of twenty eight hours out of each week recognition . Internet based life more supports these sorts of dormant practices. Commonly, an individual uses web based life on their workstation or cell phone while hanging loose all through a dormant movement: sitting on the train or transport, holding up in line, and so on. In any case, very that, internet based life commonly works as Associate in Nursing movement amid and of itself – as in an individual will plunk down all through relaxation time explicitly to imagine their web-based social networking destinations, making idle conduct rather than only exploiting it. Inactive practices, similar to those propelled by web based life use, are joined to physical wellbeing dangers. The raised danger of kind polygenic infection lard, issue, high weight level, and metabolic disorder square measure all identified with idle conduct. Be that as it may, less is thought in regards to the consequences of idle conduct on the peril of mental state issues.

Displaced Behaviour

As per uprooting hypothesis, it isn't simply the web based life use all by itself that effects affects emotional wellness, but instead the nonattendance of different exercises. One idea may put forth a defense for anyway the dormant practices motivated by web based life influence mental state is that of uprooting. people that compensation longer in inert practices like web based life use possess less energy for up close and personal social association and physical movement, both of that are attempted to ensure against mental issue. In accordance with removal hypothesis, it's not simply the online networking use all by itself that affects mental state, anyway rather the nonattendance of various exercises. As per Open Thinking Exchange (2013), Americans matured 18-64 United Nations office utilize informal communities report that they pay a mean of three.2 hours every day doing in this manner. This range is significantly higher for youthful grown-ups: 18-34-year-olds report abuse internet based life a mean of three.8 hours out of every day, with one out of five clients matured 18-34 reportage that they're on interpersonal interaction destinations six or a great deal of hours out of each day. NBC News reports that in July 2012 alone, Americans went through a joined 230,060 years via web-based networking media destinations. concerning hundredth of the time Americans utilize their PCs, they are via web-based networking media; half-hour of the time region on their cell phones they're completing a proportional. Whatever the reason, work up is all around archived to support mental state. The dangers of supplanting physical exercises with an inert conduct, together with web based life use, must be thought of as an achievable issue once talking about the outcomes of web based life use on mental health. Face-to-confront social cooperation conjointly plays an occupation in uprooted conduct hypothesis. Like work out, it diminishes the opportunity of creating mental state issues and eases mental state issues that exist as of now. The uprooted conduct hypothesis contends that dormant practices like web-based social networking use could be dislodging this vis-à-vis cooperation and along these lines the edges it offers. The social withdrawal theory is one system of clarifying the relationship between expanding latent practices and expanding danger of despondency. This speculation recommends that the a ton of generally people stare at the TV or utilize the PC/web, the any they expel themselves from social collaboration, that progressively will build their danger of despondency. Krout (2002) expanded this hypothesis alongside his social confinement speculation, recommending that drawn out commitment in latent practices, similar to TV survey or pc use, not just expels the client from social connection, anyway conjointly results in the breakdown of social help or correspondence systems which can result in expanded danger of mental sick wellbeing.

Sleep Interruption Due to Blue Light-Weight

Wright. (2013) found that individuals United Nations association went through consistently spot to remain inside the Rocky Mountains, displayed to solely ordinary light-weight and no electronic contraptions, had their unit of time tickers synchronized with the development and fall of the sun. Regardless, these normal unit of time rhythms are not by any means the standard in the present snappy and involved world. Our typical rest cycles are being meddled with .An Associate in Nursing said our workstations, cell phones what's more, cell phones and pc screens wont to peruse internet based life destinations all share one issue practically speaking. The concealed interims their which sparkle, they emanate abnormal amounts of blue light weight. This fake light-weight upsets sound rest cycles demonstrated that evening time introduction to fake light-weight disturbs the body's organic time, or the 24-hour system that controls our rest cycle. In what capacity will this counterfeit light-weight disturb rest per Holzman (2010), the blue light-weight encased in fake light-weight is that the most destructive to people. Blue light-weight smothers inner discharge, or the mind's "sluggish compound," creation extra keenly than various wavelengths. Blue light-weight stifles inner discharge through one in every one of the sensors in our eye: the essentially light-delicate retinal neural structure cells, or RGCs. The RGCs are most delicate to blue light; in this way, it exclusively takes alittle amount of blue light-weight for the mind to flag the ductless organ to forestall causation out interior discharge, making it problematic to desire to rest. This inside discharge smothering blue light-weight is blessing in our TVs, pc screens and cell phones. Perusing internet based life before bed isn't just diverting from rest, it will for all intents and purposes prevent you from being drowsy peered toward in any regard.

Rapid Task Switch

Fast errand change (additionally alluded to as performing various tasks), propelled by online life, could likewise be one root clarification for wretchedness. Rosen et al. (2013) states that "while performing various tasks is innately a character's property, innovation has possibly excessively roused and advanced it by our multi-window workstation situations, multi-application cell phone screens and furthermore the wide-going tangible incitement (and diversion) offered by top notch, adjustable visual and methodology flag also material incitement through vibration.

Cybersickness

Cybersickness is tantamount to kinetosis and for the most part occurs all through or once drenching in an exceedingly virtual climate. Cybersickness is accepted to happen essentially as an aftereffects of contentions between 3 tangible frameworks: visual, proprioception and interoception. therefore, the eyes comprehend a development that is out of alter by a few milliseconds with what's apparent by the vestibular device, while the remainder of the body remains for all intents and purposes unmoving . Cybersickness might be brought about by elements related with the work of video game instrumentation (for example largeness of the head protector, closeness of screen to the eyes. As per Kennedy, Lane, Berbaum and Lilienthal (1993), the transitory feature impacts related to cybersickness will be isolated into 3 classes of indications related with the tactile clashes and to the work of computer game gear: (1) visual side effects (eyestrains, obscured vision, cerebral pains), (2) confusion (vertigo, unevenness) and (3) sickness (regurgitating, tipsiness). Visual side effects normally happen as an aftereffects of closeness of the screen and square measure limited fundamentally to the work of a virtual protective cap. The sickness and bewilderment extreme square measure brief, like perusing in an exceedingly moving vehicle and square measure caused essentially as an after-effects of tactile clash.

In any event hour of computer game climate clients report having felt side effects of cybersickness all through an essential session. The extent of individual who feel extra serious and long-run auxiliary impacts is like the extent of individuals who are experiencing an affectability to kinetosis. around five-hitter of clients really feel no feature impacts of any sort as an after-effects of being drenched inside the computer game air.

Cyberbullying

Cyberbullying is harassing that happens over computerized gadgets like phones, PCs, and tablets. Cyberbullying will happen through SMS, Text, and applications, or on-line in online life, gatherings, or redirection wherever people will peruse, take an interest in, or offer substance. Cyberbullying incorporates causation, posting, or sharing negative, unsafe, false, or mean substance with respect to another person. It will grasp sharing individual or non-open data in regards to another person perpetrating shame or embarrassment. Some cyberbullying crosses the street into unlawful or criminal conduct. The most widely recognized places wherever cyberbullying happens are: Online life, as Facebook, Instagram, Snapchat, and Twitter, SMS (Short Message Service) moreover alluded to as Text Message sent through gadgets Text (by means of gadgets, email provider administrations, applications, and online networking electronic informing highlights) email. With the predominance of internet based life and computerized gatherings, remarks, photographs, posts, and substance shared by individuals will ordinarily be seen by outsiders besides as associates. The substance an individual offers on-line – each their own substance moreover as any negative, mean, or pernicious substance – makes a type of lasting open record of their perspectives, exercises, and conduct. This open record will be thought of as a web name, which can be available to universities, businesses, schools. UN organization is likewise exploring an individual right now or inside what's to come. Cyberbullying will hurt the net notorieties of everyone concerned isn't just the individual being scared, anyway those doing the harassing or partaking in it .

Cyberaddiction

Internet addiction is represented as an impulse management disorder, that doesn't involve use of an intoxicating drug and is extremely the same as pathological gambling. Some web users could develop AN emotional attachment to on-line friends and activities they produce on their laptop screens. web users could get pleasure from aspects of the web that enable them to satisfy, socialize, and exchange concepts through the utilization of chat rooms, social networking websites, or "virtual communities." different web users pay endless hours researching topics of interest on-line or "blogging". Blogging may be a contraction of the term "Web log", within which a private can post commentaries and keep regular chronicle of events. It may be viewed as journaling and also the entries area unit primarily matter. Similar to different addictions, those full of web addiction use the virtual phantasy to attach with real individuals through the web, as a substitution for real-life human association, that they're unable to realize ordinarily.Internet addiction leads to personal, family, academic, financial, and activity issues that area unit characteristic of different addictions. Impairments of real world relationships area unit non continuous as a results of excessive use of the web. people full of web addiction pay longer in solitary seclusion, pay less time with real individuals in their lives, and area unit usually viewed as socially awkward. Arguments could result thanks to the degree of your time spent on-line. Those full of web addiction could conceive to conceal the quantity of your time spent on-line, which ends in distrust and also the disturbance of quality in once stable relationships. Some full of web addiction could produce on-line personas or profiles wherever they're ready to alter their identities and fake to be somebody apart from himself or herself. Those at highest risk for creation of a secret life area unit those that suffer from low-self esteem feelings of inadequacy, and concern of disapproval. Such negative self-concepts result in clinical issues of depression and anxiety.

Many persons United Nations agency conceive to quit their web use expertise withdrawal including: anger, depression, relief, mood swings, anxiety, fear, irritability, sadness, loneliness, boredom, restlessness, procrastination, and dyspepsia. Being captivated with the web may also cause physical discomfort or medical issues such as: Carpal Tunnel Syndrome, dry eyes, backaches, severe headaches, consumption irregularities such as skipping meals, failure to attend to non-public hygiene, and sleep disturbance.

Cyber Depression

Another research presumes that there's if in all honesty a causative connection between the use of online networking and negative impacts on prosperity, basically despondency and dejection. The investigation was uncovered inside the Journal of Social and psychotherapeutics. "What we tend to establish by and large is that in the event that you utilize less web based life, you're extremely less discouraged and less forlorn, which implies that the decreased internet based life use is the thing that causes that subjective move in your prosperity," previously mentioned Jordyn Young, a creator of the paper and a senior at the University of Pennsylvania. The scientists state this is frequently the essential time a causative connection has ever been built up in research venture. The examination encased 143 understudies from the University of Pennsylvania. They were helter and skelter named 2groups: one that may proceed with their online networking propensities as was normal or one that may significantly restrain access to internet based life. For three weeks, the exploratory group had their web based life utilize decreased to half-hour of the day for ten minutes on 3 entirely using Facebook, Instagram, and Twitter.In request to remain these trial conditions, the specialists looked at telephone use data, that reported what amount time was spent exploitation each application every day. The majority of the examination members needed to utilize iPhones. The outcomes were clear: The bunch that utilized less web-based social networking, despite the fact that it wasn't completely disposed of, had higher mental state results. Gauge readings for members were taken toward the beginning of the preliminary in numerous zones of prosperity: social help, stress of passing up a great opportunity, forlornness, tension, dejection, vanity, independence, and self-acknowledgment. At the tip of the preliminary, those inside the test group saw every forlornness and burdensome side effects decay, with the most significant changes occurring in those that revealed greater dimensions of melancholy.

Eating Disorders

"Selfies, self-image, vanity and therefore the "self" is incredibly abundant at the guts of socialmedia these days. It pay loads of your time urging folks with ingestion disorders to be additional crucial of the bloggers they give the impression of being at, as a result they're promoting their lifestyles on social media . Whether clean ingestion, fitspiration or the virtues of veganism, several celebrities and "vloggers" use social media sites to push their food decisions, exercise regimes and toned bodies. For folks fighting low vanity and body confidence, the constant timeline of body and food-related posts could cause heightened levels of stress and anxiety around what they understand because the perfect lifestyle.

Attention Deficit Upset Disorder

Teens diagnosed having Attention Deficit Disorder Disorder (ADD) expertise identical core symptoms as younger youngsters with the disorder, including: basic cognitive process, impulsivity, and, in some cases, disorder. Teens conjointly face exaggerated expectations socially and academically throughout this point, which may work to accentuate some symptoms of attention deficit disorder. Developmentally, teenagers may be characterised by higher educational and social expectations. Teens have additional autonomy and fewer structure each in school and reception, and fewer teacher oversight once it involves finishing assignments and maintaining with work. For teens with minimal brain dysfunction which is new independence will backfire.

Many youngsters with minimal brain dysfunction exhibit difficulties in peer relationships thanks to impulsivity, hyperactivity, and aggression. Frequent interruptions, issue dealing with frustration, and poor social skills will negatively impact early friendships, which pattern will continue into adolescence. The importance of peer relationships will increase throughout adolescence, as teens pay additional of their time engaged with peers. Lack of follow with social skills within the early years will build it troublesome to ascertain new friendships throughout the teenager years. Many teens with minimal brain dysfunction expertise alternative difficulties. analysis shows high levels of comorbidity between minimal brain dysfunction and mood disorders, anxiety disorders, and conduct disorder.4 One study found that adolescent females with minimal brain dysfunction have a a pair of 0.5 times higher risk of major depression than feminine adolescents while not minimal brain dysfunction.

Teens with minimal brain dysfunction want further emotional support from their folks and lecturers. The behaviours that folks and lecturers take for frustrating or annoying are the terribly behaviours that trigger anxiety and low vanity in teens with minimal brain dysfunction. Left uncurbed, these behaviours will intensify and end in symptoms of tension depressive disorders. Due to impulsivity, emotional regulation may be a struggle for teens with minimal brain dysfunction. mix exaggerated pressure, high educational demands, low social interaction skills with low emotional regulation skills and it all adds up to teens with minimal brain dysfunction combating varied social-emotional struggles day after day.

SOCIAL IMPACT THEORY

Social Impact Theory become created turned into by Bibb Latane in 1981 as a shape for comprehension the general regulations that guide the association of networks and connections. Social effect alludes to, as Latane noticed, "the pleasant form of adjustments in physiological states and abstract sentiments, thought tactics and feelings, perceptions and convictions, qualities and conduct, that manifest in an individual as an aftereffects of the large, inferred, or whimsical nearness or activities of non-compulsory people. Latane stated that take a seat wasn't produced for its explicitness or its ability to explain the exact methodologies by using that social effect is exchanged from person to an change. sit down just shows that social effect is a part into 'social powers' along with high-quality, instantaneousness, and quantity, which the impact of every social strength are regularly spoken to numerically. Latane(1981) displays each social power and its essential examination, regardless of the fact that he concedes that most of his related statistics alludes to his third social electricity. run as an detail of social effect alludes, most sensibly, to the amount of humans that shape up an impacting supply. Latane contends that enthusiastic or intellectual element sway on an man or woman will increment in light of the reality that the affecting institution develops in length. however, the impact of each affecting individual is a littler sum than that of the individual that preceded. Latane clarifies the idea through a similarity: while price of a person's first dollar is as much as the unique estimation in their one centesimal dollar, the impact of the one hundredth greenback is a littler sum than the effect of the important. eventually, the social impact of quite a few 100 humans is not a couple of times as massive in mild of the truth that the effect of 1 character. Latane communicates the instance part of team spirit thru a situation, wherever "I" is social impact, "s" could be a scaling regular, "N" is that the scope of resources, and "t" will be a value but one: $I = sNt$. research that, Latane closes, is confirmative of sit down and typically confirmative of his clinical articulation of bunch size consists of an expansion of each human and non-human practices, collectively with ingesting spot tip estimate in regard to bolstering gathering size, situation in guinea pigs, and similarity amongst understudies. The social powers, great and quickness, are not any reduced, Latane (1981) states, however he exhibits this kind of terrific deal much less confirmative examination. every quality (i.e. the standing or depth of an affecting source) and quickness, or "the closeness in house or time and nonappearance of interceding hindrances or channels," are represented as Latane reviews the outcomes of news events. Latane alludes to his own exam with Bassett, gave in 1976, that researched every of the 3 social powers with the aid of displaying numerous fake functions and test information memories to technology understudies. Understudies have been entrusted with deciding on what quantity article inches each story ought to be relegated. The status (or strength) of the issues concerned in each story perceived to haven't any have an impact on at the users choices, but the quantity of subjects concerned and also the space of the occasion (Columbus, close to; Phoenix, some distance) did. Fewer column inches had been committed to occasions in Phoenix, and even though the amount of topics worried collected column inches for each near and far off occasions, the gap among the 2 sets widened as cluster size collected. Latane concludes that distance would not boom impact logarithmically, and later is going on to specify that impact, "might be an mathematical feature of the sq. of the space among people. The result would possibly, perhaps, be extra associated with strength than Latané supposes. Latane in 1996 redeveloped sit as dynamic Social impact idea. Dynamic Social Impact Theory conceives of social effect as an repetitious approach inside which probably haphazardly distributed attributes cluster over the years supported, in part, physical distance through immediacy. Latane shows that much less well favored attributes persist thru minority subgroups. therefore, dynamic take a seat proposes that these social forces are responsible for a backside-up formation of culture thru communication. As a consequences of Latane development, this principle will become in general concerning styles and social groupings, cultural shifts and social commonalities.

Legal Guidelines of Conduct

Latané contends that every individual is conceivably a "source" or an "objective" of social impact now and then each on the double. He supposes there are three recommendations or legal guidelines at paintings.

Social Pressure

Social force is made by impact, danger, amusingness, disgrace and diverse consequences that is contained power, Immediacy and Numbers:

1. Power: that is how a whole lot strength you believe the man or woman influencing you has. for example, if the man or woman has rank in an association, their solicitations could have extra fine.
2. Immediacy: that is the methods via which later the effect is and the way close you, from a solicitation a minute again out of your leader standing suitable with the aid of you (fast) to an electronic mail you obtain out of your director seven days prior (now not fast)
3. Numbers: The extra people placing weight on you to attain something, the extra social power they'll have

The Psychosocial Law

The Psychosocial law in social impact will occur within the advancement from 0 to one source .the amount of assets are manufactures. The condition Latané uses for this regulation is impact = s.Nt. The electricity (t) of the quantity of people (N) copied with the aid of the scaling unfaltering (s) chooses social impact. Asch's stated of congruity in understudies denies the psychosocial law, displaying up or three wellsprings of social impact have little impact. Regardless, Gerard, Wilhelmy, and Conolley drove a practically equal document on closeness testing from auxiliary school understudies. The Auxiliary school understudies were regarded as greater against be impenetrable to likeness than college students. Latane explained his law to pantomime likewise, the use of Milgram's sizeable check. in this exam diverse amounts of confederates stayed on a road nook in new york expanding and expanding on the sky. The outcomes showed that greater confederates inferred greater spectators, and the trade ended up being logically beside the point as more confederates were available. In an exam Latane and Harkins proved before a set of human beings warning and shame, the effects in like manner renowned the psychosocial law seeming moreover assembling of individuals human beings inferred steadily great uneasiness and that the pleasant distinction existed some location within the scope of 0 and 1 swarm human beings.

Divisions of Effect

The regulation of division impact communicates that the exceptional, immediacy, and wide variety of targets take delivery of an occupation . The more pleasant and immediacy and the more essential quantity of centers in a social scenario reasons the social effect to be apportioned amongst maximum of the destinations. The condition that addresses this division is affect = f(SIN) .The social effect hypothesis is each a generalizable and a particular hypothesis. It uses one parcel of conditions, that are cloth to diverse social situations. for instance, the psychosocial regulation may be used to ascertain times of comparability, pantomime and shame. in any case, it's miles in like way unequivocal in light of the truth that the gauges that it makes are express and can be associated with and noticed on earth. The concept is falsifiable furthermore. It makes dreams making use of conditions; in any case, the conditions could be undeserving to correctly predict the consequence of social situations. Social impact principle is in like way accommodating. It might be used to fathom which social situations result in the exceptional impact and which conditions gift exceptions to the gauges. Even as Social effect hypothesis explores social conditions and can assist count on the consequences of social situations, it moreover has multiple inadequacies and questions which might be left uncertain. The regulations coordinating the idea depict human beings as recipients that latently understand social effect and do not take into account the social impact that human beings may accurately hunt out. The model is in like manner static, and does no longer completely compensate for the additives drew in with social participations. The principle is tolerably new and fails to address some pertinent problems. those issues consolidate finding dynamically genuine approaches to address degree social results, know-how the "t" type in psychosocial law, considering, perceiving how flashing results can shape into steady outcomes, utility to accumulate affiliations, know-how the version's inclination .

APPLYING SOCIAL IMPACT THEORY

Survey Approach

Social impact theory facilities around the non-separate social powers, which might be the span of the affecting accumulating and the influencer's high-quality popularity or intensity of the influencer. This exploration turned into meant to restrict or dispense with impedance from those social powers. right off the bat, it turned into clarified to participants that their mission companion turned into someone. This element was communicated whilst booking project aid and amid project hobby in some exceptional ways. to begin with, the challenge companion changed into continuously alluded to as a specific detail. second, a particular separation become given to each member to their errand partner. ultimately, amid challenge funding, the elements included had been recorded within the "Babbles online" place of the speak application, and the main names recorded had been the member, the expert, and the gazing scientist. exceptional as a social strength became an increasing number of muddled to represent. Conversationalists are in all likelihood going to border conclusions approximately the status in their cooperating accomplices dependent on subsequent to no facts. because of the want of giving the equivalent printed contributions to every member, it turned into considered as full-size that the pre-composed reactions suggest subsequent to no approximately the mission partner/specialist. Reactions have been composed with insignificant slang and internet-specific expressing or truncations, general spelling, popular accentuation and capitalization, and negligible but responsive utilization of emoticons. This changed into finished to restriction the opportunity that members would create suppositions about the age, instructive status, or sexual orientation of their undertaking accomplice (Marwick, 2013). In light of time limitations, reactions sent amid undertaking interest should have been brisk. Hence, the pre-composed reactions were sent, reliably crosswise over errand cooperation, as fast as it was esteemed conceivable to have kept in touch with them at a sensible speed in order to keep away from suggestions that may have identified with age or capacity. At last, on the grounds that an enormous concern in regards to much past SIT research is that members may have predispositions about specific places, this investigation tried member conduct and observation utilizing a separation and not a spot.

Data was collected from University Students of Jamia Hamdard through survey. A self administered questionnaire was used for data collection. In the survey the data was collected from students (n = 560) to examine the validity and reliability of the adapted scales. The questionnaire pattern for the study was

Figure 7. SIT survey analysis

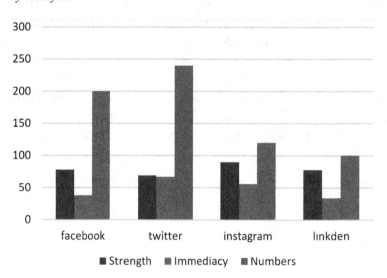

prepared in two portions to examine the opinions of the respondents. This investigation additionally incorporated an open-finished inquiry to assemble data about the view of understudies' learning conduct through web based life. The study asked college understudies to answer inquiries dependent on positive and negative elements, demonstrating how such components influenced their every day lives, particularly regarding maintainable instructive learning. The study depended on a five-point Likert scale to survey the level of understanding. The information of study one was incorporated into the complete information to keep up the consistency in the information gathered from arbitrary example of understudies. Total 560 questionnaires were distributed online using google forms among the randomly chosen students and the response rate was 83%. The age ranges of the sample students were as follows. The sample students were enrolled in undergraduate degree programs, graduate degree programs, and postgraduate degree programs respectively. The result analysis shown in figure 7 analysed that facebook has strength 60%, immediacy as 48% with approx. 200 users,twitter has strength 51%, immediacy as 50% with 240 users, Instagram has strength 93%, immediacy 50% with 120 users, linkden has strength 51%, immediacy 20% with 100 users.

The Psychosocial Law Impact for the survey is calculated as Impact which is 224 people per transcation can be used to understand which social situations and behaviour. The division of impact for all the users has impact of diffusion of responsibility refers to the decreased responsibility of action each member of a group feels when she or he is part of a group. As per the diffusion of responsibility, people feel that their need to intervene in a situation decreases as the number of other (perceived) witnesses increases which has both negative and positive effect on the behaviour of the user. Group size significantly influenced the likelihood of helping behaviour in a staged emergency: 85% of participants responded with intervention when alone, 62% of participants took action when with one other person, and only 31% did when there were four other bystanders. Figure 8 shows the behaviour impact analysis on the user according to the age groups. The analysis resulted that >21 age group have most changing behaviour on online networks,age group between 21-29 shows steady change in behaviour analysis as compared to age group > 31.

Figure 8. Behaviour impact analysis

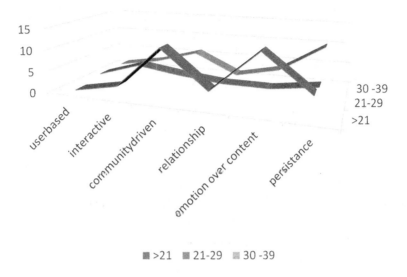

Figure 9. Positive and negative psychological impact factors

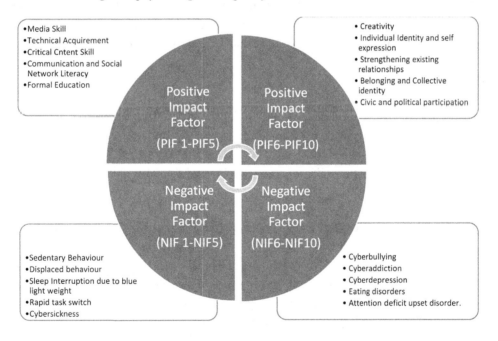

Psychological Impact Factors List

The data we gathered from the surveys from the users through google forms, the information was checked, sent into the SPSS programming variant 25. Next, expressive measurements, recurrence investigation, dependability, graphic insights examination, ANOVA, and a t-test were performed on the legitimate information of the 560 respondents. The reaction rate resulted to be 87.033%, which is an incredible reaction rate. Our discoveries demonstrate that 53.08% of the respondents hold a graduate degree; 36.02% of

Table 1. Cronbach's alpha values for psychological impact positive and negative factors

Reliability Test -Positive factors	
Scale Items No of Items -10 Positive Psychological Impact Factors of Social Network	Data Reliability 0.862 Crobach's alpha values
Scale Items No of Items -10 Negative Psychological Impact Factors of Social Network	Data Reliability 0.715 Crobach's alpha values

the respondents hold a four year certification, and 10.90% of the understudy respondents hold an expert degree. Table 1 presents 10 chose web-based social networking factors. The estimation of Cronbach's alpha for the positive web based life elements estimated was agreeable ($\alpha = 0.7$), and the negative web based life factors likewise introduced a palatable Cronbach's alpha esteem ($\alpha = 0.9$). Information consistency mirrors the information source, and it requires data about the respondents' comprehension of the chose survey. This investigation connected Cronbach's alpha (α) to evaluate the dependability of the got information, and the ascertaining instrument was SPSS rendition 25. Accordingly, the unwavering quality of the overview poll uncovered a satisfactory estimation of Cronbach's alpha ($\alpha = 0.762$, $\alpha = 0.815$) for both the positive and negative internet based life factors, and these outcomes demonstrate that the respondents had a full hold and comprehension of the data incorporated into the study and great nature with the effect of the positive and negative components of web based life use on the online network.

Data Processing

In the data processing the primary challenge of this specific study was to explore and determine the most influential social media factors and their ultimate impact on the students' communities. These factors were identified from the previous literature after an in-depth investigation, and each element was analysed independently. Table 2 displays the mean score (M) and standard deviation (SD) of the selected positive social media factors.

Positive Psychological Impact Positive Factor Social Network Analysis

Table 3 describes the mean scores (M) and standard deviations (SD) of selected positive social media factors. The results of all the positively related factors are close to each other. The most significant impacts

Table 2. Participants using various applications of social media

Social Network Types	Frequency	Percent	Valid Percent	Cumulative Percent (%)
Facebook	*280*	*41*	*41*	*41*
Twitter	*160*	*11.6*	*11.6*	*52.6*
Instagram	*100*	*7.8*	*7.8*	*60.4*
Linkedin	*120*	*31.6*	*31.6*	*92.1*
All	*66*	*7.9*	*7.9*	*100*

Table 3. Mean scores and standard deviations of positive psychological impact positive factors

PIF	Positive Psychological Impact Positive Factor	M	SD
PIF1	Media Skill	4.0241	1.355
PIF2	Technical Acquirement	4.0144	1.3101
PIF3	Critical Content Skill	4.0903	1.3566
PIF4	Communication and Social network literacy	4.0542	1.3101
PIF5	Formal education outcome	4.0830	1.3431
PIF6	Creativity	3.042	0.342
PIF7	Individual Identity and self-expression	3.219	0.231
PIF8	Strengthening existing relationship	4.0557	1.3282
PIF9	Belonging and collective identity	4.001	1.562
PIF10	Civic and Political Participation	3.780	1.674

of social media include the following: Media Skill (M = 4.0241, SD = 1.3566), Technical Acquirement (M = 4.0144, SD = 1.3298), Critical Content Skill (M = 4.0903, SD = 1.1955), Communication and Social network literacy (M = 4.0542, SD = 1.3101), Formal education outcome (M = 4.0830, SD = 1.3431), and Strengthening existing relationship (M = 4.0457, SD = 1.3282).

Negative Psychological Impact positive Factor Social Network Analysis

Table 4 shows the antagonistic effects of the unreasonable utilization of web based life and nine basic variables chose from the writing. Figure 12 demonstrates the most significant negative factors, the particular mean score (M) and standard deviation (SD), and the situating of the components of this gathering dependent on the respondents' perspectives: Sedentary Behaviour (M = 4.0975, SD = 1.3076), Cyberbullying (M = 3.2058, SD = 1.0664), Cyberdepression (M = 4.0241, SD = 1.3566), Cybersickness

Table 4. Mean scores and standard deviations of negative psychological impact positive factors

NIF	Negative Psychological Impact Positive Factor	M	SD
NIF1	Sedentary Behaviour	4.0975	1.3076
NIF2	Displaced Behaviour	4.0144	1.3101
NIF3	Sleep Interruption due to blue light	4.0903	1.3566
NIF4	Rapid Task switch	4.0542	1.3101
NIF5	Cybersickness	4.0878	1.3374
NIF6	Cyberbullying	3.2058	1.0664
NIF7	Cyberaddiction	4.0866	1.3566
NIF8	Cyberdepression	4.0241	1.3566
NIF9	Eating Disorders	4.001	1.562
NIF10	Attention deficit upset disorder	4.0710	1.3285

(M = 4.0878, SD = 1.3374), Cyberaddiction (M = 4.0866, SD = 1.3207), and Attention deficit upset disorder (M = 4.0710, SD = 1.3285). The mean scores of the selected factors are shown respectively.

CONCLUSION AND RECOMMENDATIONS

Web-based social networking has a few advantages, it is a spot to make associations, for private and gifted work. Anyway there are standard issues with web-based social networking, especially on the long range informal communication destinations, there are some elective online life issues which establish that the Update Syndrome issue delineates the extra you keep and take a gander at what others have shared, or see the welcome to make diversions, or visit unnecessary pages, the more you squander subsequently ignoring family and duties. Today's youth assemble associations with on-line companions, check their profiles before making companions with them and depend on-line companions rather than physical companions. This survey shows new exact discoveries with respect to internet based life utilization, and it expected to look at the impacts of online networking on college understudies learning conduct and social change . The point of this investigation is bolstered by the earlier writing, as online life has turned into a fundamental component of training, and it has turned out to be progressively significant in both course conveyance and course appraisals. Crafted by Stathopoulou et al. (2019) uncovered that consolidating internet based life in training positively affects understudies' profound learning knowledge. Internet based life is a supporting device for understudies amid the learning procedure, and it is useful for teachers also. Be that as it may, instructors and guardians have been encouraged to keep up a sound equalization when permitting the utilization of web-based social networking, as inordinate use may result in unfavourable consequences for understudies . These examination discoveries uncovered that internet based life has both positive and negative effects on understudies' learning forms, and a fair methodology is suggested while utilizing online networking applications .The social effect hypothesis indicates the impacts of social factors quality, quickness, and number of sources . In this way, in the use of the social impact theory to instigate somebody with a restricting position to change, and strength, the capacity to enable the individuals who to concur with somebody's perspective to oppose the impact of others, is presented. Eventually, a person's probability of progress and being affected is an immediate capacity influence, promptness and the quantity of promoters and is an immediate opposite capacity of solidarity steadiness, instantaneousness and number of target people.

DISCUSSION QUESTIONS

1. Define the Social Networking.
2. What are the advantages and disadvantages of social networking?
3. Do you think that excessive social networking affects lifestyle and food habits? Do teenagers get influenced with the popular trends going online?
4. What is Social Impact theory.
5. Today's youth has knowledge of the contrasts between who you appear to be and who you think you are. Does spending pretending to be someone you are in deepest darkest fear for teenagers? What do you think Attention Syndrome is responsible for Cyber Crimes ?

6. How can Strength factor of social impact theory help to improve the psychological analysis of behaviour on social network websites?

7. What are characteristics of social network?

8. Communication may be evolving but being a quality communicator will remain a critical success factor. What are the implications for building effective lines of communication with different generation?

9. Teasing, lying, gossiping, threatening, spreading rumours, and harassing are all forms of bullying. If these things occur online, are they perceived as harming? How these actions can be prevented?

10. The usage of social media on youth affects the physical, social emotional, and psychological feature development. Does the problems concerning body image, educational action, and behaviour interrelated? Does it affect social relationships?

11. Social networks have failed to tackle cyber-bullying which results in affecting the mental health of young people. The teenagers just delete your account to stop the bullying, but that's taking something away from that young person's life for something that's not their fault. Do you think it is best way to avoid it?

12. What is Cyberaddiction?

13. What is Social Network literacy?

14. What is cyberdepression?

15. What is division of impact?

REFERENCES

Abbas, J., Aman, J., Nurunnabi, M., & Bano, S. (2019). The Impact of Social Media on Learning Behavior for Sustainable Education: *Evidence of Students from Selected Universities in Pakistan. Sustainability, 11*(6), 1683. doi:10.3390u11061683

Aravindh & Baratwaj. (2016). Examining the Regularity and consistency level of profile updation in social media applications by active users in Tamil Nadu. *International Journal for Innovative Research in Multidisciplinary Field, 2*(11).

Pink, B. (n.d.). *Australian Social Trends*. Australian Bureau of Statistics Catalogue no. 4102.

Baumeister, R.F., & Leary, M.R. (1995). The need to belong, desire for interpersonal attachments as a fundamental human motivation. *Psychological Bull., 117*, 497–529.

Bazarova, N. N. (2015). Online disclosure. In C. R. Berger & M. E. Roloff (Eds.), *The International Encyclopedia of Interpersonal Communication*. Hoboken, NJ: Wiley-Blackwell. doi:10.1002/9781118540190.wbeic251

Berson. (2003). Grooming cybervictims: The psychosocial effects of online exploitation for youth. *Journal of School Violence, 2*(1), 5-18.

Besley. (2008). Cyberbullying: An Emerging Threat to the always on Generation. *Canadian Teacher Magazine*, 18-20.

Blanchard, M., Metcalf, A., & Burns, J. M. (2007). *Bridging the digital divide: creating opportunities for marginalised young people to get connected. Report for the Inspire Foundation & Orygen Youth Health Research Centre*. Melbourne: University of Melbourne.

Blanchard, M., Metcalf, A., Degney, J., Hermann, H. & Burns, J.M. (2008). Rethinking the digital divide: findings from a study of marginalised young people's information communication technology (ICT) use. *Youth Studies Australia*.

Boase, J., Horrigan, J. B., Wellman, B., & Raine, L. (2006). *The Strength of Internet Ties: The Internet and email aid users in maintaining their social networks and provide pathways to help when people face big decisions*. Washington, DC: Pew Internet & American Life Project.

Dahl, S. (2018). Social Media Marketing: Theories and Applications. Thousand Oaks, CA: SAGE Publications.

Ding, C., Cheng, H. K., Duan, Y., & Jin, Y. (2017). The power of the "like" button*: The impact of social media on box office. Decision Support Systems, 94*, 77–84. doi:10.1016/j.dss.2016.11.002

Dunbar, R. I. M. (2012). Social cognition on the Internet: Testing constraints on social network size. *Philosophical Transactions of the Royal Society of London. Series B, Biological Sciences, 367*(1599), 2192–2201. doi:10.1098/rstb.2012.0121 PMID:22734062

Haferkamp, N., & Krämer, N. C. (2011). Social comparison 2.0: Examining the effects of online profiles on social-networking sites. *Cyberpsychology, Behavior, and Social Networking, 14*(5), 309–314. doi:10.1089/cyber.2010.0120 PMID:21117976

Harton, H., Green, L., Jackson, C., & Latane, B. (1998). Demonstrating Dynamic Social Impact: Consolidation, Clustering, Correlation, and (Sometimes) the Correct Answer. *Teaching of Psychology, 25*(1), 31–35. doi:10.120715328023top2501_9

Hawk, S. T., van den Eijnden, R. J., van Lissa, C. J., & ter Bogt, T. F. M. (2019). Narcissistic adolescents' attention-seeking following social rejection: Links with social media disclosure, problematic social media use, and smartphone stress. *Computers in Human Behavior, 92*, 65–75. doi:10.1016/j.chb.2018.10.032

Helliwell, J. F., & Putnam, R. D. (2004). *The social context of well-being*. Philos. doi:10.1098/rstb.2004.1522

Hogg & Tindale. (n.d.). *Blackwell Handbook of Social Psychology: Group Processes*. John Wiley.

Holt-Lunstad, J., Smith, T. B., & Layton, J. B. (2010). Social relationships and mortality risk: A meta-analytic review. *PLoS Medicine, 7*(7), e1000316. doi:10.1371/journal.pmed.1000316 PMID:20668659

Issa, T., Isaias, P., & Kommers, P. (2016). *Social Networking and Education: Global Perspectives*. Cham, Switzerland: Springer International Publishing. doi:10.1007/978-3-319-17716-8

Jošanov, Pucihar, & Vrgović. (2016). Opinions and behavior of students about abuse of internet in social involvements: Gender analysis. *Business School*.

Karau, S., & Williams, K. (1995). Social Loafing: Research Findings, Implications, and Future Directions. *Current Directions in Psychological Science, 4*(5), 135. doi:10.1111/1467-8721.ep10772570

Kwahk, G. (2012). Social impact theory: An examination of how immediacy operates as an influence upon social media interaction in Facebook fan pages. *The Marketing Review*.

Luck, B. (2007). *Cyberbullying: an emerging issue bernadette luck, record of the communications policy & research forum*. Retrieved from https://apo.org.au/sites/default/files/resource-files/2007/10/apo-nid69033-1106296.pdf

Meshi, Tamir, & Heekeren. (2015). The Emerging Neuroscience, Trends in Cognitive Science. *Trends in Cognitive Sciences*, *19*(12), 771–782.

Osatuyi, B., & Passerini, K. (n.d.). Twittermania: Understanding how social media technologies impact engagement and academic performance of a new generation of learners, *Communications of the AIS*.

Radovic, A., Gmelin, T., Stein, B.D., & Miller, E. J. (2017). *Depressed adolescents' positive and negative use of social media*. Academic Press.

Ravasan, A. Z., Rouhani, S., & Asgary, S. (2013). A Review for the Online Social Networks Literature (2005-2011). *European Journal of Business and Management*, *6*(4).

Shabir, Hameed, Safdar, & Gilani. (2014). The impact of social media on Youth: A case study of Bahawalpur City. *Asian Journal of Social Sciences & Humanities*, *3*(4).

Siddiqui, S., & Singh, T. (2016). Social Media its Impact with Positive and Negative Aspects. *International Journal of Computer Applications Technology and Research*, *5*(2), 71 - 75. Retrieved from http://www.ijcat.com/archives/volume5/issue2/ijcatr05021006.pdf

Tamir, D. I., & Ward, A. F. (2015). Old desires, new media. In The Psychology of Desire (pp. 432–455). Guilford Press.

Van Schaik, C. P. (1983). Why are diurnal primates living in groups? *Behaviour*, *87*(1-2), 120–144. doi:10.1163/156853983X00147

Ward, M. L. (2003). *Understanding the role of entertainment media in the sexual socialization of American youth: A review of empirical research*. Academic Press.

KEY TERMS AND DEFINITIONS

Brain Science: It is the logical investigation of the human personality and its capacities, particularly those influencing conduct in a given setting.

Cyberbullying: Cyberbullying is tormenting that happens over computerized gadgets like mobile phones, PCs, and tablets.

Cybersickness: Cybersickness for the most part occurs all through or once submersion in an exceedingly virtual air.

Digital Laws: Cyber law is the piece of the generally lawful framework that manages the Internet, the internet, and their particular lawful issues.

Dispersion of Responsibility: Being a piece of a huge gathering makes individuals feel mysterious and this lessens their sentiments of obligation. It may make them less inclined to obey orders.

Informal Organization: The stage online unit that administers the license individuals to develop an open or open profile and construct a posting of various clients with whom they share an association and read their rundown of associations and individuals made by others among the framework.

Media Skill: It is the capacity to. get to, dissect, assess, make, and act utilizing all types of correspondence.

APPENDIX

Research Into Social Impact Theory

Latané (1981) discusses various instances of Social Impact with an intriguing findings with US Christian TV minister Billy Graham (see left). The theory was that Billy Graham would make more believers before little gatherings of people. Latané looked into the quantities of individuals who reacted to Graham's intrigue for proselytes and found that when the groups of onlookers were little, individuals were all the more ready to sign cards enabling nearby vicars to reach them later. This exhibits divisions of effect (otherwise called dispersion of duty). Sedikides and Jackson (1990) did a field try in the perch room at a zoo. A confederate advised gatherings of guests not to incline toward the railings close to the winged creature confines.

Applying Social Impact Theory (Ao2)

With regards to submission, a ton relies upon whether you see the individual giving the requests to be an expert figure or not. Various types of Power helps to provide details of applying the theory-
   French and Raven (1959) distinguished various sorts of power:

1.   Genuine power which expert figures with high status
2.   Remunerate influence with the individuals who have cash or who can perform favors
3.   Coercive power with individuals who can rebuff others
4.   Master control individuals which are proficient), and
5.   Referent power with individuals users have a place with gatherings you regard.

This fits in well with Social Impact Theory since it clarifies the various reasons why an individual's requests may have Social Force. "Referent Power" likewise applies to Tajfel's Social Identity Theory since it demonstrates that requests originating from an individual from our ingroup convey more Social Force than requests originating from an outgroup part. This is the reason a group part may have more specialist over a young man than an instructor: the educator has authentic expert however the posse part may have reward control, coercive power and referent power since he can give the teenager favors, they will hurt you in the event that him cross him and the teenager sees him as his ingroup.

Dispersion of Responsibility

Being a piece of a huge gathering makes individuals feel unknown and this diminishes their sentiments of duty. It may make them less inclined to obey orders. Latané and Darley (1968) completed a celebrated analysis into this. Members sat in corners examining medical problems over a radio. One of the speakers was a confederate who might profess to show at least a bit of kindness assault. In the event that there was just a single other member, they went for assistance 85% of the time; this dropped to 62% if there were two different members and 31% if there were 4+. Nobody was giving requests in this investigation, however the standard "proceed to get help when somebody breakdown" is a kind of request that is available all the time in the public eye. Following these kind of social guidelines is called prosocial conduct and defying the norms is standoffish conduct. Social Impact Theory clarifies prosocial conduct just as dutifulness.

There's a developing assemblage of research supporting Social Impact Theory. What's more, the hypothesis likewise comprehends a ton of Classic investigations from the '60s and '70s that used to appear irrelevant – like Latané and Darley (1968) into dispersion of duty, Tajfel (1970) into intergroup separation also, Milgram (1963) into compliance. Looking back, these investigations can be viewed as taking a gander at various viewpoints of Social Impact. There have been later augmentations to Social Impact Theory. Lateen et al. (1996)developed Dynamic Social Impact Theory to focus on how minorities and larger parts impact one another, for example, how individuals will in general change their perspectives to coordinate the gathering they are in yet why they now and then "adhere to their weapons".

Protests

Social Impact gives a ton of consideration to the attributes of the individual giving the requests however very little to the individual accepting them. For instance, there might be character types that are especially consistent (oblige anything) or defiant. An individual might be glad to oblige a few sorts of requests yet adhere to a meaningful boundary at others –, for example, arranges that annoy them ethically or humiliate them socially. A comparative issue is that Social Impact Theory treats individuals as latent. It suggests that anyone will do anything if the appropriate measure of Social Force is applied as a powerful influence for them. In any case, individuals here and there obey orders while in the meantime subverting them. A model may be Oskar Schindler who given Jewish representatives over to the Nazis amid WWII while covertly helping numerous others to get away.

Contrasts

Milgram's Agency Theory is oversimplified contrasted with Social Impact Theory. Milgram recommends we have advanced to go into a respectful mental state around anybody we perceive as an expert. There's very little proof for this by and large. Social Impact Theory recommends numerous highlights of Agency Theory are valid – that the quality (S) of the expert figure is a significant indicator of how devoted somebody will be – yet there are other situational factors too, similar to the quantities of individuals included (N) and the instantaneousness (I) of the requests. In any case, Agency Theory clarifies a few things superior to Social Impact Theory. For instance, in Variation #10, compliance was let in a summary office contrasted with Yale University. Milgram clarifies this through the eminence of the setting adding to the expert figure's status, yet this is hard for Latane to give a scientific incentive to. Also, Milgram has a clarification for the shaking and sobbing his members occupied with – moral strain. There's no discourse of good strain in Social Impact Theory, which perspectives individuals as either obeying or ignoring and nothing in the middle.

Applications

The possibility of a numerical equation to compute Social Impact is valuable. Lateen trusts that, in the event that you know the number (N) of individuals included and the instantaneousness (I) of the request and the quality (S) of the expert figure, you can ascertain precisely that somebody is so liable to comply

(I) utilizing the recipe I = f (SIN). This implies you can anticipate whether laws will be pursued, regardless of whether mobs will break out and whether 9B will get their work done.

The hypothesis proposes in the event that you need to get individuals to comply, you have to coordinate Social Force at them when they are in little gatherings and in a perfect world stop them getting together into enormous gatherings. This is the reason some oppressive governments endeavour to stop individuals utilizing internet based life and social occasion for open gatherings. Since requests should be prompt it is essential to rehash them frequently and put them on signs, TV adverts and customary declarations.

Dynamic Social Impact Theory

The Dynamic Social Impact Theory by Bibb Latane and his associates has great impact of individuals among dominant part and minority gatherings. Dynamic social effect hypothesis recommends that culture is made and moulded by neighbourhood social impact as characterized by four wonders:

1. Clustering, or provincial contrasts in social components;
2. Relationship, or rising relationship between components;
3. Combination, or a decrease in fluctuation; and (iv) proceeding with assorted variety.

The hypothesis fills in as expansion of the beginning Social Impact Theory (i.e., impact is controlled by the quality, quickness, and number of sources present) as it clarifies how gatherings, as intricate frameworks, change and create after some time. Gatherings are always sorting out and re-arranging into four essential examples: combination, grouping, relationship, and proceeding with decent variety. These examples are predictable with gatherings that are spatially appropriated and interfacing more than once after some time.

1. **Union**: As people communicate with one another normally, their activities, demeanours, and suppositions become increasingly uniform. The assessments done have good effect all through the gathering and the minority diminishes in size.
   a. E.g., Individuals who live in a similar school residence will, after some time, create comparable demeanors on an assortment of subjects.
2. **Bunching**: Happens when gathering individuals convey all the more as often as possible as an outcome of closeness. As the law of social effect recommends, people are defenseless to impact by their nearest individuals, thus bunches of gathering individuals with comparative suppositions rise in gatherings. Minority bunch individuals are regularly protected from larger part impact because of grouping. In this manner, subgroups can develop which may have comparative plans to each other, however hold unexpected convictions in comparison to the greater part populace. E.g., Neighbors on a sub-urban road persuade different neighbors to shape a network watch gathering.
3. **Connection**: After some time, singular gathering individuals' conclusions on an assortment of issues of join, with the goal of suppositions to become associated. E.g., Individuals on an official society, discover they concede to subjects they have talked about all through a gathering -, for example, the best money related arrangement, however that they likewise concur on points which they have not examined.

4.   **Proceeding With Diversity**: As referenced beforehand, minority individuals are frequently protected from larger part impact because of bunching. Assorted variety exists if Sedikides and Jackson (1990) did a field try in the perch room at a zoo. The confederate suggested gatherings of guests not to rail close to the winged creature confines. The guests were then seen to check whether they complied.

In the event that the confederate was wearing the uniform of a zookeeper, submission was high, yet on the off chance that he was dressed coolly, it was lower. This shows differing Social Force, specifically S (Strength) due to the apparent expert of the confederate. As time passed, more guests began overlooking the guidance not to incline toward the railing. This likewise indicates Social Force, particularly I (Immediacy), on the grounds that as the guidance gets less prompt it has less effect. Divisions of effect were additionally considered.

Chapter 18
Technology and Organizational Change:
Harnessing the Power of Digital Workplace

Mohsen Attaran
California State University – Bakersfield, USA

Sharmin Attaran
Bryant University, USA

Diane Kirkland
California State University – Bakersfield, USA

ABSTRACT

This chapter explores the changing dimensions of the workplace and highlights the relationship between technology and organizational change. The chapter begins by briefly reviewing some key perspectives that have emerged in the information systems (IS) literature to account for the relationship between technology and organizational change. It highlights the importance of smart workplace technologies, identifies determinants of successful workplace transformation, proposes a conceptual model for implementation, identifies key factors to consider, and covers some of the potential benefits. The chapter argues that digital transformation is more than just implementing digital technologies. Successful digital transformation occurs when business strategies or major sections of an organization are altered.

INTRODUCTION

In the past ten years, office work has been shifting from repetitive tasks to knowledge based, flexible, and adaptive tasks. It has been proven that employees waste significantly less time and company resources when they have access to the right information at the right time, and by working in accordance with productive work practices (Igloo, 201, 2019). Therefore, increases in information related productivity need to be the focus of modern organizations, as much as industry automation used to be in past decades. "Information Mastery" was considered the Industry Automation of the 21st Century.

DOI: 10.4018/978-1-5225-8933-4.ch018

Companies are realizing the importance of workplace transformation which reflects modern work styles, user preferences, and maturing technologies. A large portion of work today is "Information Work"—work that requires information to be executed, and in which information often determines the outcome of the work (Dority, 2016). Many enterprises do not consider information as an organizational resource and therefore do not manage it as such. It is erroneously assumed that information is managed automatically through technology. This mis-treatment of information oftentimes has immense effects on employee productivity, efficiency, effectiveness, and profitability (Avanade, Inc. 2017).

On the other hand, the proper treatment of information as an important organizational resource is key in gaining a competitive advantage-in a globalized economy. According to widespread research, quality and productivity are affected by employees not having access to the right information, such as where, when, and which information is required for the respective tasks (Igloo, 2917, 2019). A meta-analysis of nine studies on wasted employee time found that an average of 1.1 hours per day was lost on unproductive information searches. This is a tremendous waste of time and productivity, considering that 1.1 hours per day is more than 12 percent of total work time summing up to more than 30 work days per year per person (Schillerwein, 2011). In a study conducted by IDC and commissioned by the Information Overload Research Group, significant numbers of employees indicated that less than half of the information they need is searchable and that searching is time consuming and frustrating (Gantz, Boyd, and Dowling, 2009).

This study also found that employees waste 25 percent of their time dealing with information overload related interruptions and distractions. Reducing the time wasted by 15% could save a company with 500 employees more than $2 million a year. According to this study, a large percentage of managers and business leaders are also affected by information overload. They do not have sufficient information across their organization to do their jobs. Over 40 percent of surveyed managers said they use incorrect information at least weekly and had the information they needed less than 75% of the time (Gantz, Boyd, and Dowling, 2009). A mature digital workplace has the potential to revolutionize both the way information is treated in the organization and the way work gets done.

The Evolution of Digital Age

The world of business is rapidly evolving. Several studies highlight the differences which characterize organizations and work within the industrial and information age (Schillerwein, 2011). According to these studies, industrial age or traditional organizations are efficient but both rigid and hierarchical—they are frequent users of chains of commands.

The digital workplace allows employees to work flexible hours and connect to people and information anytime, anywhere, and on any device. This means that an employee can work from a home office, a satellite office, a co-working building, or a coffee shop. Employees can share their ideas, thoughts, and content, and have the unique opportunity to become leaders by sharing what they know and what they care about. Employees have a voice within their organizations, can be recognized for their contributions, and ultimately shape their own career paths.

Traditional organizations are formed like silos and are fragmented. It is challenging to find the right people and information to get work done as employees in different departments or geographies often-times do not communicate and collaborate with one another, nor do they share information. Digital-age organizations are internetworked, flexible, and have high level of uncertainty. Employees are organized around flexible cross-functional teams where they are dynamically linked to each other, in ways that both empower them and allow them to share information and knowledge. The economic environment of digital age organizations is uncertain, highly dynamic, and based on mass customization and value-added products and processes. The nature of jobs is complex and requires e-skills. Figure 1 highlights the nature of organizations for both traditional and digital age workplaces.

One of the big advantages of the digital workplace is that new technologies enable worker mobility, flexibility, and improved efficiency and productivity. Organizations are implementing ongoing deliberate approaches to create a more flexible environment that is better able to facilitate innovative and flexible working practices. A recent study conducted by several companies and published by MarketsandMarkets™, estimated the Digital Workplace Market will grow from $13.4 billion in 2018 to $ 35.7 billion by 2023. This is a compound annual growth rate of nearly 22 percent during this period (Amador, 2019).

Changing Workplace Demographics

Today's workplaces characteristics are also changing. A recent study conducted 3801 online interviews of adults who work more than 35 hours a week across nine different markets. The report analyzed adults who work in one of seven target industries: Education, Government, Financial Services, Healthcare, Manufacturing, Media & Entertainment, and Retail (Berland, 2016). The report found that the global workforce is at a tipping point. 44 percent of employees worldwide feel that their workspace is not smart enough, while more than half expect to be working in a smart office within the next five years. This study

Figure 1. Industrial vs. digital age characteristics

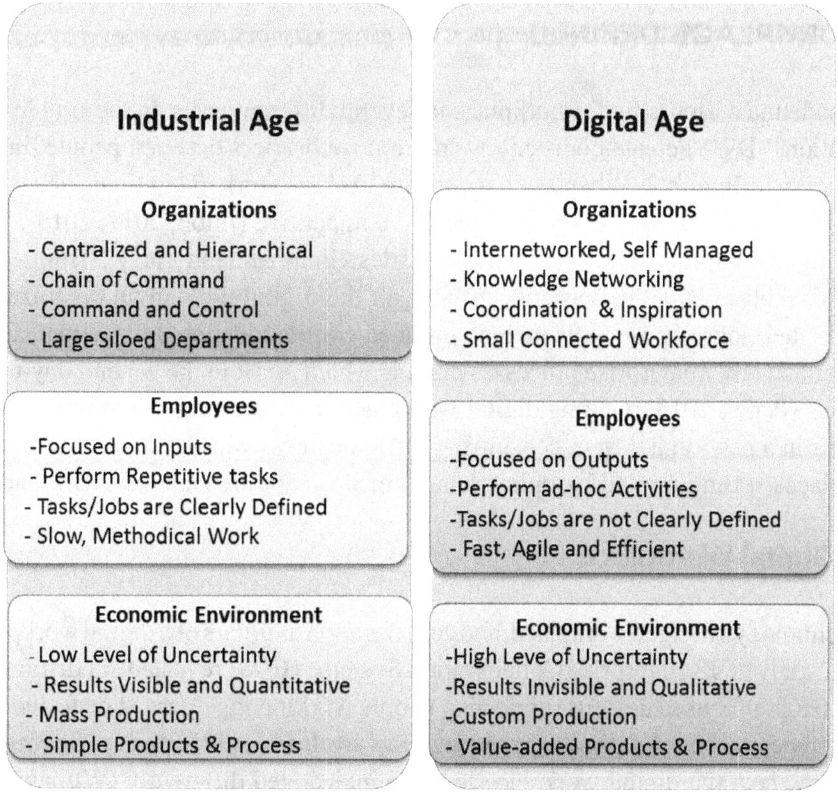

Industrial Age

Organizations
- Centralized and Hierarchical
- Chain of Command
- Command and Control
- Large Siloed Departments

Employees
-Focused on Inputs
- Perform Repetitive tasks
- Tasks/Jobs are Clearly Defined
- Slow, Methodical Work

Economic Environment
- Low Level of Uncertainty
- Results Visible and Quantitative
- Mass Production
- Simple Products & Process

Digital Age

Organizations
- Internetworked, Self Managed
- Knowledge Networking
- Coordination & Inspiration
- Small Connected Workforce

Employees
-Focused on Outputs
-Perform ad-hoc Activities
-Tasks/Jobs are not Clearly Defined
- Fast, Agile and Efficient

Economic Environment
-High Leve of Uncertainty
-Results Invisible and Qualitative
-Custom Production
- Value-added Products & Process

also revealed that half of global employees currently work remotely one or more times a week. 50 to 60 percent of the time, employees of Fortune 1000 companies around the globe are not at their desks. More than 30 percent said that the biggest time-wasters at their jobs were tech-related (slow, glitch software or devices) and that the technology they had available in their homes was more cutting-edge than what was available at their place of work (Berland, 2016). Additionally, a study by Wainhouse Research revealed that the vast majority of meeting rooms have little or no teleconferencing and collaboration technologies in place and that 34 percent of office meetings start late because of technical difficulty (Haskins and Nilssen, 2015). A 2011 study by Price Waterhouse Coopers identified that by 2020, Millennials (22-37 years old) and Generation X (38-53 years old) will be 50 percent of the global workforce by 2020 and are reshaping the workplace (Price Waterhouse Coopers, 2011). Compared to their predecessors, Millennials are more willing to embrace workplace technology and are more likely to quit a job with substandard workplace technology (Berland, 2016). These changes in technology and workforce require a workplace that boosts competitiveness, collaboration, and agility, and that also reduces the cost of both IT and business operations.

Today's workplace should provide employees with consistent, consumer-like user experience—one that is wholly aligned with the way people work today. Business leaders expect their digital workplace solutions (DWS) to raise employee engagement, enable employees to achieve business outcomes faster, and empower employees to reduce cost and increase efficiency. These leaders desire a robust IT service that is aligned with the way people work today, regardless of platform and location. Employees now expect a digitally-driven work experience that is personal, real-time, mobile-enabled, collaborative, and able to exploit consumer oriented styles and technologies.

DIGITAL WORKPLACE DEFINED

Industry and academia define a digital workplace in several different ways. In the simplest terms, digital workplace solutions (DWS) create connections and remove barriers between people, information, and processes as shown in Figure 2. When the barriers are broken, workers do their jobs more effectively and efficiently, and make the business more agile and competitive (Igloo, 2017, 2019).

The term "Digital Workplace" was coined by Charles Grantham and Larry Nichols in 1993 (Perks, 2015). Digital workplace is defined as collection of all the digital tools in an organization that allow employees to do their jobs. Those tools include intranet, communication tools, email, CRM, ERP, HR system, calendar and other enterprise processes or tools which assist in the general day-to-day functioning of a business (Perks, 2015). Getting digital workplace transformation right is vital for sustainable business success in a new digital first, consumer-centric business world. The digital workplace affects physical workplaces, technology, and people. Changes made in one area may result in changes in another.

Pillars of a Digital Workplace

Intel defines technology, the agile workplace, and collaboration as pillars of a digital workplace (Constant, 2017). A recent study of 13 Enterprise Collaboration Systems (ECS) revealed six distinctive workplace designs. Three people-focused designs supporting people working together to create and share information and three process-focused designs supporting joint work towards business improvement projects. The findings show how the digital workplace is being interpreted differently (Williams and Schubert,

Figure 2. Breaking down barriers and creating connections

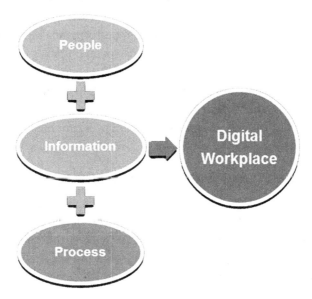

2018). Another study by Infocentric Research identified a framework for the digital workplace that includes three building blocks: personal performance, team performance, and organizational performance as described in Figure 3 (Schillerwein, 2011). These building blocks provide all of the information and function relevant to a person, team, or organization. They serve as a depository of all project tasks, thereby

Figure 3. A framework for the digital workplace

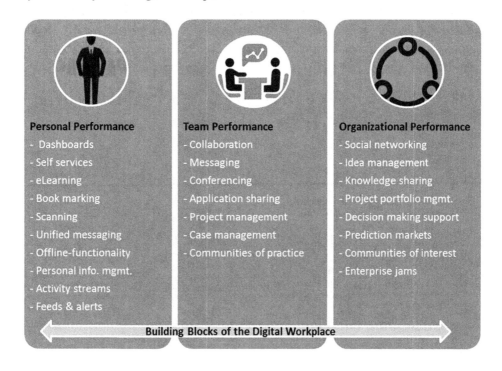

enabling team members' access to the projects and activities. The personal block provides all the necessary digital tools for employees including but not limited to self-services, eLearning, and book marking in order to facilitate efficient task performance. The team performance block provides digital tools for effective team building and communication. It integrates social collaboration, including voice, video, and messaging. The organizational performance block facilitates idea generation, promotes knowledge sharing, provides decision making support, and creates communities of interest. These building blocks do not exist in isolation from each other within the digital workplace. They blend into each other based on respective tasks and situations. They serve as a logical framework for creating the strategy and concept design of the digital workplace.

The Evolution of Enterprise Workplace

Over years, the workplace has evolved from referring to a physical space including offices, meeting rooms, and desk phones, to being focused on always connected environment with instantaneous access to what employees need to work. Many office documents and projects have gone online. Instant messaging has become a popular communication choice within office communities and email is a heavily used mode of correspondence.

Gartner divides the evolution of digital workplace into 4 generations (Microsoft Ignite, 2017). They are shown in Figure 4 and further discussed here. The first generation of the digital workplace was about improving productivity and communication. Tools such as audio and video conferencing, group scheduling, and discussion forums improved communications between employees and between employees and customers. In the second generation of the digital workplace we used the power of the Internet for instant messaging, web conferencing, and virtual teams to promote team building and to integrate and empower social collaboration. Many organizations are still in the third generation of the digital workplace where mobile devices, the cloud, and smart phones are used to provide platforms for knowledge sharing, decision making, and the creation of communities of interest. Multiple employees can easily communicate and collaborate with each other on projects, and work synergistically. Technologies in the third generation increase-productivity, engage employee collaboration, simplify communication, and boost cohesiveness. Employees can store files on a secure cloud and can access, share, edit, and

Figure 4. The evolution of the digital workplace

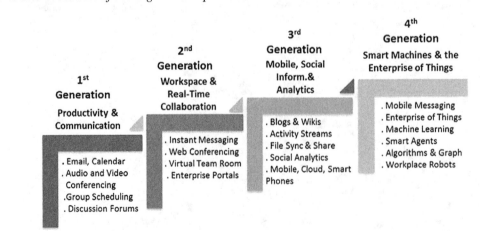

work on them from anywhere and at any time. Newsfeed tools enable organizations to disseminate the latest information, broadcast corporate messages, and get real-time feedback to create a cooperative organizational culture. The fourth generation is the innovative new digital workplace that will rely on technologies such as Artificial Intelligence (AI), Machine Learning (ML), and the Enterprise of Things (EoT) to provide pertinent, robust, and accurate information for timely decision making in the organization. Technologies in this new generation of the digital workplace will give organizations the tools and systems they need to become efficient, productive, and lean. AI implemented through Chatbot and workplace robots will help teams automate routine office activities so employees can spend their time on more productive enterprises. It provides streamlined customer support, improved response times, and heightened customer experiences. Business analytics tools compile data from variety of sources and create actionable plans for forecasting, activity tracking, and resource management. Finally, 5G networking technology will provide fast Internet connections and enable employees to access anytime, anywhere service on mobile devises.

Factors Influencing Accelerated Change

The popularity of digital workplaces has soared in recent years. This accelerated change can be attributed to the emergence of some fundamental trends (Hamburg, 2019; Morgan, 2013; Deloitte, 2014). Organizations need to understand these trends to better prepare and adapt to the changes which are impacting the working environment. These trends require a digital transformation and a reshaping of work environment.

1. **Workforce Demographics:** Businesses struggle to meet the varying needs of a multi-generational workforce. Knowledge is leaving the company as the baby boomers retire. The baby boomers (population age 55 to 73) are the largest generation in U.S. with 72 million in 2018. Boomers peaked in size at nearly 79 million in 1999. The aging of boomers will continue to put pressure on the U.S. economy. According to the Census Bureau, by 2030, one in five U.S. residents will be of retirement age. The number of millennials is projected to reach 73 million and they will overtake baby boomers as the largest U.S. population group in 2019 (National Post, 2019). According to a study by Hartford, millennial workers are dominating the workforce. By the end of this decade nearly half of employees will come from this group of tech-savvy, mobile-centric, socially networked workers (Hartford Business, 2014). The same study estimated millennials will make up 75 percent of workforce by 2025. Millennial workers are IT savvy and expect to have flexible working hours and easy to use tools. Cross-generational understanding and collaboration will be important for organizations as Millennials takeover a much larger percentage of the workforce in the next 10 years.

2. **Information Overload:** The amount of data is continuously growing at exponential rates. These extreme large data sets need to be analyzed computationally to reveal patterns, trends, and associations relating to consumers. Businesses are struggling to find filter and forward information to the right workers at the right time. For example, declining customer satisfaction resulting from an inability of customer service agents to access the requisite information to solve their challenge is very high. In a survey conducted by IDC and sponsored by Xerox, 40 percent of those surveyed said they had the information they needed less than 75 percent of the time (Gantz, Boyd and Dowling, 2019). A survey conducted by Omega Management Group Corp. and Coveo found out that 70 percent of customer service agents are facing significant challenges as a result of not being able to find necessary customer information. 73 percent of respondents identified improving informa-

tion access and quality along with knowledge management as areas they are investing to improve customer care (Omega Management Group Corp. and Coveo, 2011).

3. **Social Media:** Technologies such as Facebook, Twitter, Linkedin, and many others in the consumer web help encourage and support new behaviors such as creating communities, being open and transparent, sharing information and ideas, and being able to find people and information easily. These social media technologies are now making their way into our organizations and are helping shape the future of work.

4. **The Need for Speed and Collaboration:** Today's work environment moves at a much quicker pace than it used to. Employees are required to work faster, collaborate more effectively, and work more efficiently to meet deadlines and to successfully do their jobs. Collaborative technologies give employees the freedom and flexibility to work from anywhere, anytime, and on any device. Organizational structure is flattened as employees now have a voice within their organizations and virtually any employee can connect or communicate with anyone else and information is being opened up instead of being locked down.

5. **Mobility:** Organizations are starting to allow for more flexible work environments. Most organizations employ mobile worker which means employees can work from anywhere, anytime, and on any device. The Internet and communication technologies enable employees to access everything they need to get their jobs done.

ADVANTAGES OF DIGITAL WORKPLACE

Scholars have conducted intensive research on digital workplace advantages, which include collaboration, compliance, mobility, reduced stress and overload, reduced waste, and productivity improvement. (Hamburg, 2019; Dery, Sebastion, and Meulen, 2016; Koeffer, 2015; Haas, Criscuolo, and George, 2015; Perlow, 2012; Przybylski, Weinstein, 2013; Reyt and Wiesenfeld, 2015; Sykes, 2011; Turkle, 2015; Mazmanian, Orlikowski, & Yates, 2013; Aaltonen et al, 2012).

The following sections summarize advantages of DWS in major areas of productivity, employee morale, and waste reduction:

Improving Productivity

Effectively planned, communicated, and implemented, digital workplaces reduce costs and delivers compelling benefits. Integrating workplace technologies like mobile, cloud, analytics, and social tools into the workplace will empower employees to work faster and communicate more easily – at anytime, anywhere. In 2015, Wakefield Research surveyed 500 global C-level executives and IT decision-makers across seven countries regarding the advantages of a truly digital workplace. The results were clear and compelling: reduced costs, improved productivity, increased innovation, revenue growth, and employee engagement (Avanade, 2017). The digital workplace addresses existing challenges and provides measurable business value. For example, one company saved 43 minutes each month per manager with improved DWS. The company estimated an annual saving of $12 million (Deloitte, 2014). A 2011 New Ways of Working survey, which included more than 100 Fortune 500 respondents, found that between 2008 and 2011, alternative workplace programs resulted in improved employee productivity, increased business agility, increased employee attraction/retention, improved collaboration, faster access to customers/

co-workers, and business continuity (Miller, 2012). Based on the transformational journeys of three established companies, a 2017 study showed how digital workplaces drive success and how the digital transformation is a key to digital innovation (Dery, Sebastion, and Meulen, 2016).

As discussed above, improved productivity of employees is perceived as the main benefit of the digital workplace. According to several recent studies, a digital workplace in a modern enterprise provides many advantages for employees and businesses including increased staff satisfaction, improved employee experience, closer collaboration, reduced operational costs, enhanced innovation, improved customer experience, and increased revenue. Figure 5 summarizes benefits gained by employees and organizations (Gantz, Boyd, and Dowling, 2009; Schillerwein, 2011; Miller, 2012; Ruostela and Lönnqvis, 2013; Deloitte, 2014; Miller and March, 2016).

Improving Employee's Moral

Flexible working hours, shared information, and engaging, empowering, and inspiring leadership have created a more relaxing organization's environment for employees. In 2018, a survey of a large global manufacturing company was conducted to validate the factors that drive an employee's satisfaction within the current work environment. The survey concluded that the highest impact on the user's satisfaction level is driven by the knowledge exchange amongst peers, followed by the perceived productivity and creativity (Kissmer, et al. 2018).

A survey of HR professionals by the Society for Human Resource Management showed that the majority of respondents thought that flexible work arrangements and digital workplaces had a positive impact on absenteeism including fewer minor health problems, fewer signs of depression, fewer sleep problems, and reduced stress levels (Miller, 2012).

Figure 5. Benefits of digital workplace solutions

Employees

- Empowers employees with a richer IT experience
- Provides a consistent user experience across all devices
- Raises employee engagement
- Helps employees experience greater flexibility and choice
- Improves employee and customer experiences
- Enables access to expert knowledge and discovery of project-critical information
- Improves communications interfaces and collaboration
- Enables agility
- Prevents time wasted in recreating information that already exists
- Reduces employee absenteeism
- Decreases staff turnover
- Enables secure access for users, from anywhere at any time
- Supports closer collaboration with customers, partners & coworkers

Business

- Accelerates decision-making & innovation
- Provides more effective ways of working - Increases productivity
- Speeds up the release of new products and services
- Provides efficient information distribution channels
- Strengthens talent attraction & retention
- Prevents information overload
- Reduces sales cycles
- Exploits consumer oriented styles and technologies
- Increases the chances of a project successfully meeting its outcomes by using cross-functional teams
- Facilitates technical improvements including better performance, platform support, improved security, etc.
- Enables environmental gains due to a reduction in travel (thereby improving the carbon footprint)

Reducing Waste

One of the major advantages of DWS is the reduction of waste. There are plenty of distractions and time-wasters that take workers away from the task at hand. DWS breaks down barriers between people, information, and processes, thereby enabling workers to do their jobs more efficiently and effectively. IDC identified annual costs of the most costly time-wasters at work (Schubmehl, 2014). They are summarized in Figure 6 and are described below:

1. **Ineffective Meetings**: Meetings are costly. On average, a single employee attends 62 meetings per month and spends over 30 hours a week in meetings. According to a research study by Infocom, 30-50 percent of time in meetings is considered wasted. Also the majority of meeting attendees admit to daydreaming during meetings, while over one-third have dozed. This cost companies on average $9000.00 per employee per year (Infocom, 2018).
2. **Managing eMail:** A typical office worker spends almost 7 hours per week reading, replying, and sorting through emails. 33 percent of this time is spent on time-wasting tasks such as reading "Reply all" and trying to locate the email. IDC estimates that on average, the cost per employee is $8,000.00 per year (Schubmehl, 2014).
3. **Searching for People and Information:** People and information search are costly for companies. Workers spend 2.5 hours per week searching for people and information that are scattered throughout the organization. The annual cost is on average $7,000 per employee per year (Schubmehl, 2014).
4. **Re-Creating Work**: A typical office worker spends almost 2.5 hours a day duplicating work that has already been done. This costs companies on average $5,000 per employee per year (Schubmehl, 2014).

MAKING THE DIGITAL WORKPLACE A EALITY

Intel defines workplace transformation, technology transformation, and enterprise collaboration as three pillars of making the digital workplace a reality (Constant, 2017). These pillars are shown in Figure 7. The following section describes theses pillars in detail.

Figure 6. Average annual costs per employee for top time wasters

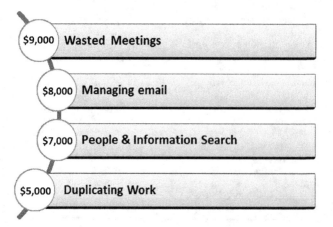

Physical Workplace Transformation: Agile Workspace

The Digital Workplace is about changing the physical workplace and empowering the workforce through a well-thought-out workplace strategy that leverages a common platform that is integrated with front and back office tools. Traditional offices are expensive, inefficient, inflexible, and difficult to scale and modify. The digital workplaces should stand up to certain criteria as discussed in detail below:

1. **Distributed Workspaces**: Because of mobile technologies, knowledge workers are often absent from the office and spend their working time on the road or at customer locations (Bosch-Sijtsema et al. 2010). The workplace is seen as a place of interaction, collaboration, knowledge transfer, and communication (Harrison et al. 2004). A workplace is no longer only the physical office space, but rather a combination of physical, virtual, social, and mental spaces, which are interlinked with each other to form a collaborative working environment (Vartiainen 2009). The physical space is the environment where work is conducted, such as the main workplace, home, or the premises of customers and partners. The virtual space is an electronic working environment such as the Internet which provides a platform that can be used for collaboration in a distributed workplace. Examples are e-mail, and more complex collaboration tools such as video conferencing (Vartiainen et al. 2007). The social space is the whole social network of team members, managers and customers.

   The mental space refers to thoughts, beliefs, ideas, and mental states that employees share through communication and collaboration. The work environment should be understood as an entity comprising all the previously described spaces (see Figure 8). The challenge of digital organizations is how to make these four spaces support the knowledge workers' tasks in a distributed work setting. There is no one rule to follow. Organizations should start the process by analyzing the work of knowledge workers (Ruostela, and Lönnqvis, 2013).

2. **Digital Environments**: Work is shifting from the physical to the digital workplace resulting in reduced office size. Office configuration is also changing, and its role in the workplace is being adapted. The nature of work has changed and primary office space is unoccupied nearly one-third of the time (Miller, 2012). The Telework Research Network estimates the average business could save $2,500 to $5,000 a year in real estate and related costs for each half-time teleworker (Miller,

Figure 7. Pillars of a digital workplace transformation

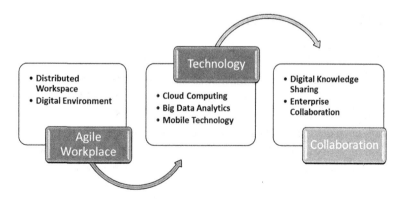

Figure 8. Distributed workspaces

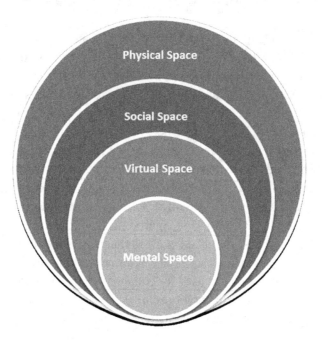

2012). According to Miller, digital environments, whether they are repurposed offices, home of-fices, or co-working or "third places", should stand up to certain criteria. Among the criteria are the quality of digital environments, the ease of intuitive accessibility, the ease of portability, the ability to operate consistently across the organization – in one region or globally, the security, and the ability to enable working beyond corporate borders (Miller, 2012). Physical workplaces and buildings play important roles in providing more flexible work capabilities and facilities, more open and shared spaces, more collaborative interactions. Workspaces should be designed around activities. Each agile workplace should have special "zones" connecting individuals and offering easier collaboration. At the same time, the agile workplace should also provide a more relaxing and informal environment. An effective workspace design should provide more mobility and office dispersion, less paper, less storage, more attractive facilities, and increased utilization of available space (Constant, 2017).

Digital Technology Transformation

Having the right technology in place is critical. To support uninterrupted collaboration, the agile work-place requires a carefully designed IT infrastructure. The cross-functional delivery team should fix system constraints and upgrade the organization's network infrastructure to include the entire backbone and every switch, router, and firewall. The objective should be to shift to open workspaces, accessible meeting rooms, and modern devices. This shift should include the installation of operating systems that allow for increased productivity and for the attraction of new talent. Each employee should be provided with upgraded tools, including a universal laptop, collaboration tools including video-conferencing, and voice-over-internet phones (VOIP) that ride on the network without constraint. The installation of a low cost, open, easy to use hardware, software and collaboration solution that can be easily upgraded and expanded over time is highly recommended. The tools needed to support the digital workplace needs will vary, depending on business and job functions. These tools need to be implemented not in silos but in an environment that benefits a holistic digital workplace strategy. A summary of suggested tools divided into different categories is-shown in Table 1.

It is suggested that four technologies of cloud computing, big data, enterprise collaboration, and mobile and search-based applications should be integrated to achieve a digital workplace (White, 2012). The following sections describe these technologies in more detail:

1. **Cloud Computing**: Cloud Computing Technology (CCT) has drastically changed the landscape for workplace collaboration and enabled virtual, visual, and anywhere meetings. In a highly competitive business landscape, CCT enables dynamic collaboration between workers. Using web-based software, organizations can facilitate communication between suppliers, customers, and distributors and use this communication platform to make judgments about a firm's external environment. CCT has emerged as an exciting new means for empowering this type of communication (Gartner Report, 2017).

Table 1. Digital workplace solutions for managing various business activities

Software Tools	Service Provided	Digital Workplace Solutions
Business Applications	Provides employees access to online applications	• HR • CRM • ERP • Help desk • Accounting & Payroll • Contract Management
Messaging & Communication	Provides effective information sharing and communication	• Instant messaging, Helpdesk • Mobile messaging • E-mail and blogs • E-mail Marketing and Chat-based communication • Video conferencing • Voice over IP (VOIP)
Productivity	Reduces time and increase efficiency of employees	• Word processing • Presentation software • Spreadsheet • Document management • Backup storage • Employee time tracking • Survey and campaign monitoring
Collaboration	Provides effective collaboration between employees and customers	• Teamwork • Online meeting • Team rooms • Web conferencing • File sharing
Workplace Mobility	Provides employees access to tools away from the office	• Mobile and smart phone • Laptop and tablet • Home office

Usually, CCT is delivered as a paid service in exchange for third-party management of IT infrastructure. Companies rely on cloud-based workplace collaboration tools to increase employees' productivity. Mobile and remote end-users can use cloud-based messaging services or team collaboration platforms to interact and exchange information with multiple contributors. Collaboration platforms like Fuze, Slack, Workplace, and Microsoft Teams focus on broadly defined productivity improvements for employees by offering voice and video conferencing, and messaging. Cloud messaging services are an integral part of an enterprise digital workplace strategy. Cloud messaging services can assist geographically dispersed organizations to improve their productivity and project workflows. Team collaboration tools offer group messaging, file sharing, and voice and video conferencing support. These same tools also allow in-house and remote employees to easily interact and exchange information among themselves, and their customers and partners.

Software services in this category make teamwork easy, fun, and inexpensive. They are easy to set up and provide collaboration tools such as shared desktops, white boarding, and in-app private chat. One can easily run and manage robust and easily-automated email campaigns by creating chat rooms for employees and by creating email templates that help send emails expeditiously. E-mail Marketing tools can be used for sending promotions, announcements of new features or services, and discounted coupons to customers.

2. **Big Data Analytics**: A big challenge for many companies is proper management of big data. Data is growing faster than ever before and it is everywhere: documents, the Internet, social networks, appliances, devices, sensors, etc. It is no surprise that the past few years have seen an explosion in business use of analytics. According to Gartner Research, data volume will grow 800 percent over the next 5 years (Gartner Report, 2017). Corporations around the world are using analytical tools, including business intelligence (BI), dashboards and data mining, to gain a better understanding of their present customers and to predict who will potentially become customers. Organizations are evolving from generating static and passive reports to proactive analytics with real-time dashboards. The factors that have contributed to underlying shifts include large volumes of data, the Internet, the evolution to the Cloud, and the changing demands of customers. The Internet revolution has created an environment where consumers desire ever increasing amounts of information and have greater expectations. Management and analysts expect immediate information without latency. Consequently, a new genre in BI tools has emerged offering data exploration and rapid prototyping. These new tools empower users to choose when, where, and how they interact with an organization.

Although most organizations already empower their employees with analytics tools to access data and improve decision making, many are now embedding analytics into their core business applications. The objective is twofold: first, to broaden their reach and second, to improve the timeliness of insights. While embedded analytics is not a new concept, the technology for the integration of reports, charts, dashboards, and self-service tools has evolved rapidly over the past 30 years. While current users of embedded analytics are primarily large corporations, there are numerous additional industries and organizations where embedded analytics tools could advantageously assist decision makers.

3. **Mobile Technology:** Mobile technology is used for cellular communication. There has already been a huge explosion in the use of *mobile technology*. The technology has evolved from being used for

phone call and messaging into a multi-tasking device used for internet browsing, instant messaging tool, GPS navigation, etc. Tablet and portable computers are becoming more and more popular and employees' use of wireless networking and mobile computing is increasing. Marketers are able to sell their products with ease through mobiles technology. Employees have the ability to gain information, download files, and transfer files through Bluetooth and wifi. Inexpensive collaboration tools such as shared desktops, white boarding, in-app private chat, video call conferencing, and online meeting are making it easy for employees to connect with customers and peers. Skype allows professionals to collaborate through screen sharing, instant messages, video conferencing, and audio conferencing and file sharing (Adobe, 2016).

4.   **Network Connectivity:** Most network providers are offering 4G networks connectivity. The 5G network, which will be offered by end of 2019, enables a high speed data transmission with low latency in the channels, making surfing the internet easier and faster. 5G networks will provide a fantastic mobile experience for consumers and enable them to access free-roaming immersive services on mobile devices anytime, anywhere. Additionally, digital transformation is starting to shift user experience away from text, image, and video into immersive virtual reality (VR) and augmented reality (AR). Fifth generation cellular technology offers high speed, superior reliability, extreme bandwidth capacity, and low latency. It is a perfect fit for this new shift.

Workplace/Enterprise Collaboration

Digital knowledge-sharing platforms have become central to problem solving in geographically dispersed offices (Hass, Criscuoolo, and George, 2015). Information and its flow through an organization are important enablers for the successful execution of business strategy. Information is an integral part of each and every task that gets executed in an organization and the outputs of these tasks are directly dependent upon information. The amount of digitized data continues to grow at an exponential rate and workplace collaboration tools for information sharing and meeting organizational needs are becoming increasingly important.

"Enterprise Collaboration" is defined as a system of communication among enterprise employees. It may include the use of some or all of the following: a collaboration platform, social networking tools, a corporate intranet, and the public Internet. Enterprise collaborations enable employees to share information and work together on projects remotely through a combination of software technologies, networking capabilities, and collaborative processes.

The way today's knowledge worker collaborates is changing and involves a mix of both in-person and virtual attendees. Collaboration technologies include video conferencing, document-sharing, and groupware. Modern collaboration Wainhouse Research surveyed 200 commercial enterprises with 250 or more employees, and inquired into the various collaboration tools the respondents used to get their work done. They found that on average, over half of meetings included remote participants attending via audio, video and/or web conferencing (Haskins, and Nilssen, 2015).

IMPLEMENTATION CHALLENGES AND OBSTACLES

Most existing information management systems deliver only limited value to their organizations. These systems are products of many years of organic growth and change. They often create as many new problems as they solve existing ones. These systems largely exist in isolation from each other. They are mostly static and passive, dated and primitive, and they set an expectation with employees that the organization need not be efficient. An effective digital workplace cannot be merely a combination of existing tools. The workplace must be enhanced by context, structured and unstructured information, and consistent coverage of information flows. The lack of a clear distinction between tools and business needs can also make an information management system ineffective. Without a proper business case, business need, and goal, technology delivers only limited value. An on-going employee education on the proper usage of workplace technology is a necessary foundation for productivity and quality improvements.

There are numerous challenges in applying DWS for businesses in ways that allow for significant and rapid growth. For example, the 2017 State of Digital Transformation Survey conducted by Altimeter identified the following as the most important digital transformation challenges facing organizations (Solis, and Littleton, 2017; Hamburg, 2019):

- Lack of digital literacy and expertise among employees and leadership
- Mistaken view of digital transformation as a short term cost center instead of long-term investment
- Lack of empowered culture focused on agility and growth
- Lack of leadership and purpose
- Lack of budget
- Lack of staff resources
- Lack of sense of urgency to compete differently
- Human barriers— Politics, egos, fear, and skepticism

A recent study by Forester Research identified several reasons for lack of effective employee use of DWS (Forrester Research, 2017). Among them:

- Struggling to log onto multiple apps
- Inability to access data and apps inside and outside of the office
- Requiring help to access data

IMPLEMENTING A LEADING–EDGE WORKPLACE TRANSFORMATION

A leading-edge workplace transformation initiative should take a holistic and cross-functional approach, spanning people, places, and technology. However, not all organizations experience success in implementing digital workplace transformation projects. Increasingly, digital projects are not strategically focused. All too often, organizations overly concentrate on technology rather than on the people using the systems. Technology, in and of itself, will never be the solution to all problems. As with any new investment, the key is to ensure that selected technology reflects the overall business strategy, and that it will significantly add value to the business (Perks, 2015). Therefore, a cross-functional delivery team that includes senior leaders as well as IT, HR, and Marketing should be formed. This cross-functional delivery team should assist future projects by providing access to expert knowledge, helping with the discovery of project-critical information, and enabling more efficient ways of working. The team should create a digital workplace strategy that clearly articulates the business focus and guides the development of digital solutions.

A Conceptual Model for Implementation

Gartner recently conducted a 12-month survey of enterprises with cloud management strategies and identified the three phases of cloud adoption strategy. We adopted this model and modified it to fit a leading-edge workplace transformation initiative described below and summarized in Figure 9 (Smith, 2016):

In **Phase 1**, relevant employees should:

1. Learn about digital technology solutions and perform a detailed analysis of the applications and services the company requires.
2. Identify the business goals the company is trying to achieve with the digital solutions and translate them into guiding principles to drive development, and
3. Implement a digital strategy, which incorporates technological implications and alignments with corporate objectives.

The workplace strategy should set clear priorities and serve as a blueprint for the roles and relationships of each department. Define a clear business case and timings for the enterprise digital strategy. Identify which digital services, workplace tools, and solutions are needed. The most impactful deployments start with users fully understanding their desired business outcomes and then identifying the services that will be offered. This requires asking questions such as what services users need, how much of each service will be consumed, when each service will be consumed, which users will consume each service, and what is a reasonable price for each service.

In Phase 2, relevant employees should work with the CIO and business stakeholders to document and analyze the internal processes that will be affected by the selected digital solutions. During this analysis, they should study the internal processes involved with offering relevant digital solutions. This might bring to light the need to flatten, reconfigure, realign, refine, or eliminate inefficient processes and target repetitive manual processes for automation. The types of security that will be applied to the deployment must also be addressed. Companies should enable and bring together user-friendly systems, data integration, social, mobile, analytics and cloud computing technologies to create a digital workplace that responds to the informational needs of employees. Companies should also integrate social collabo-

Figure 9. Implementation phases

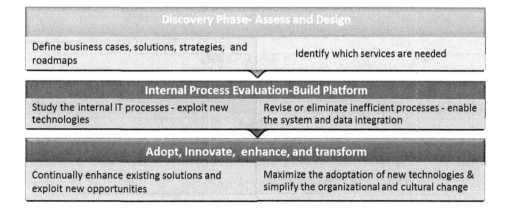

ration technologies such as voice, video, messaging, and workspace tools in order to make knowledge sharing more effective. Finally, companies should provide the requisite platform to access and secure information across multiple devices and channels.

In Phase 3, companies should continually enhance existing solutions, maximize the adoption of digital solutions, and ensure user adoption. As the needs of workers evolve, these companies should continually exploit new opportunities and deliver a consumer-like experience and a consistent user experience across multiple platforms for internal employees. Corporations should simplify the organizational and cultural changes that hinder the adoption of DWS. They should engage with users, to understand their needs and articulate how the digital workplace enables them to work productively. Firms must ensure that employees have access to training that enables them to use the digital solutions to their advantage, and that technical personnel and trainers are properly trained to support the digital solutions technology. Lastly, firms must provide policy training for employees on the types of information they should or should not share, on the handling of personnel data, and on the avoidance of potentially damaging their organizational data.

GUARANTEEING DIGITALTRANSFORMATION SUCCESS

According to a 2017 survey, executives are paying attention to digital workplace. With the initial rise of digital transformation, Chief Information Officers (CIOs) were charged with coordinating digital transformation. As customer experience and digital marketing rose in importance, Chief Marketing Officers (CMOs) and Chief Technology Officers (CTOs) took over the digital transformation initiatives (Solis and Littleton, 2017).

In order to fully reap the benefits in the digital workplace, organizations need to take a holistic view of the scope of digital work projects, exploit different technologies, identify needed services, and maximize the adoption of new technologies. The following section reviews some of the factors that will guarantee a successful digital workplace transformation.

Figure 10. Key drivers of digital transformation

Critical Factors to Consider

To improve the chances of successful implementation, it is important to consider the following critical issues (Hamburg, 2019):

- Take a cross-functional and holistic view of the organization's digital work place and involve representatives from key stakeholders on the delivery team
- Ensure that the project is enterprise-wide and encompasses a significant proportion of the workforce
- Enable employees to have a choice of workplace locations – involve employees
- Help to improve employee and customer experiences
- Aim to change the way employees actually work-Invest in training
- Choose collaborative tools that are easy to use and accessible – support collaboration
- Foster a culture where experimentation is allowed and encourage

Key Drivers for Digital Transformation

In 2017, Altimeter released the third annual State of Digital Transformation Survey. This report, based on a survey of 528 digital transformation leaders and strategists, revealed how, why, and to what extent organizations were investing in digital workplace technologies (Solis and Littleton, 2017). The surveyed companies were experiencing both increased competition and growth opportunities in new markets. These findings revealed the urgency within organizations to optimize operations, satisfy evolving customer demands, and compete in new markets. According to this report, surveyed organizations cited multiple reasons for pursuing digital transformation, including customer preferences, competitive pressures, opportunities in new markets, lack of understanding of digital trends, and decline in business performance as highlighted in Figure 10.

IT Transformation vs. Cultural Transformation

According to Forbs, 84 percent of digital transformation efforts fail. According to a 2017 survey, many organizations consider digital transformation as an integration of digital technologies and merely as IT transformation (Solis and Littleton, 2017). Their objective is to optimize IT services for organizational needs. They fail to recognize that a successful digital workplace transformation is first and foremost, a cultural and organizational transformation rather than a technology-driven endeavor. The first step in the digital transformation is a cultural change in organizations (Hamburg, 2019).

Change Management

Implementing a leading-edge workplace transformation requires managing change effectively. Effective digital transformation requires businesses to develop and realign priorities and operate with a sense of purpose and urgency (Solis and Littleton, 2017). Many organizations fail at change because often, leaders have not given change management the proper attention. Effective management of change increases the effectiveness of the implementation and acceptance of changes. Ineffective management of change oftentimes affects employees in a negatively and makes the next change objective more difficult to imple-

Figure 11. Steps for implementing change management

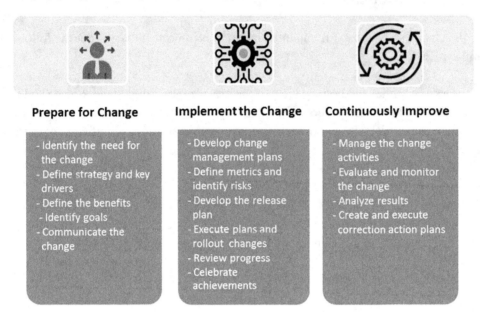

ment. Additionally, the fear of managing the change is a leading cause of anxiety in managers. There are several models for successful management of change (Markovic, 2008; Marek, 2017; Drucker, 2017). Figure 11 highlights a sample model.

Continuous Monitoring

The rate of organizational change is increasing and rapid and continual innovation in digital technologies is driving changes to organizational systems and processes. Digital transformation is a continuous innovation and requires rapid response to change, challenges and, opportunities in the business world. We should expect change to occur across all the pillars of digital transformation including strategy, people, process, and technology. Innovative and successful organizations must respond rapidly as new technologies and opportunities for improving the digital workplace emerge.

SUMMARY AND CONCLUSION

In recent years, work has shifted from the physical to the digital and the popularity of digital workplaces has soared. Today, global employees still prefer to exchange face to face conversation with their colleagues. However, the nature of work will change substantially and will likely be very different in the next 5 to 10 years. Remote teams and better communications technology will make face-to-face communications obsolete. Employees' changing lifestyles and their desire to work outside of the office are driving this evolution. Additionally, the millennial generation, now entering employment in vast numbers, is reshaping the workplace. They will dominate the global workforce and are more willing to embrace workplace technology. They prefer to communicate electronically at work, rather than face to face. They care strongly about having access to advanced technologies, believe that access to technology makes them more effective at work, and are more likely to quit a job with substandard technology.

The workplace is experiencing an unprecedented transformation driven by technology. Technologies like AI help organizations to automate simple tasks and create better experiences for customers. 5G networking technologies is expected to greatly increase the capacity of networks and data speeds, thereby enabling network providers to meet the growing demand for data-intensive services, such as digital and media streaming services. This enhanced streaming would greatly enhance remote teams' communications and make employees more effective at work. Technologies like cloud computing and business intelligence has also evolved rapidly–companies are using them to fully reap the benefits of the information age. Properly planned and implemented, (CCT) has the potential to drastically improve the operational efficiency in three types of performances: personal, team, and organizational. The Software as a Service (SaaS) model of CCT offers applications over a network (Internet), and is accessible via browser or program interface. Since applications are delivered via on-demand software, they can be deployed quickly and from anywhere.

This chapter concludes that a digital workplace is the foundation for a successful business strategy- it enhances collaboration and leads to increased productivity. Digital workplace solutions introduce both challenges and new possibilities to many aspects of the physical workplace, internet architecture, protocols, services, and applications. Managing a digital workplace program for a large organization can be a challenging task and is growing more complex every year. Many companies are still struggling with technological and human challenges of digital transformation. Many company leaders are risk-averse and do not feel a sense of urgency to create a digital workplace. Politics, egos, and fear are the main obstacles to achieving the collaboration and solidarity needed within companies to make the digital changes.

Successful change initiatives require effective persuasion and a clear understanding of organizational change as a long-term, multi-step process rather than a singular event. To realize the business benefits of a truly digital workplace, organizations need to prepare for a massive workplace change, use digital workplace technologies, and head in the direction of creating intelligence context around people. The agile workplace transformation initiative, discussed in this chapter, should provide a balanced work-life program for its employees while simultaneously advancing organizational goals in productivity, efficiency, and space planning. Progressive companies provide their employees with easy-to-use hardware and software collaboration tools that can be upgraded and expanded over time, with minimal training and effort. The success of the digital workplace will be constituted by a well-orchestrated approach that addresses all of steps highlighted in this chapter.

DISCUSSION QUESTION

1. Define the Digital Workplace
2. Briefly define advantages of digital workplace solutions
3. What are some barriers that digital workplace solutions (DWS) remove?
4. What are the differences between traditional (industrial) organizations and digital age organizations?
5. Briefly define pillars of a digital workplace
6. Name 5 advantages of digital workplace solutions for employees
7. What are the most costly time-wasters at work?
8. Describe the changing dimensions of the workplace

9. Define the relationship between technology and organizational change
10. Identifies determinants of successful workplace transformation
11. The chapter argues that digital transformation is more than just implementing digital technologies. Explain.
12. Successful digital transformation is first and foremost a cultural and organizational transformation. Discuss
13. In the past ten years, office work has been shifting from repetitive tasks to knowledge based, flexible, and adaptive tasks. Explain the reasons for the shift.
14. Millennials are more willing to embrace workplace technology. Discuss their expectations of digital workplace solutions
15. The evolution of digital workplace can be dived into 4 generations. Briefly describe each generation
16. Explain how cloud computing has changed the landscape for workplace collaboration
17. Explain the role of mobile technologies in improving digital workplace
18. The popularity of digital workplaces has soared in recent years. Briefly define 5 factors that have attributed to this trend.
19. A workplace is no longer only the physical office space, but rather a combination of physical, virtual, social, and mental spaces. Discuss
20. Briefly discuss three phases of workplace digital solutions adoption strategy

REFERENCES

Aaltonen, L., Ala-Kotila, P., Laarni, J., Määttä, H., Nykänen, E., Schembri, I., . . . Nagy, G. (2012). State-of-the-art report on knowledge work-new ways of working. VTT Technical Research Centre of Finland.

Adobe. (2016). *Driving Competitive Advantage with enterprise mobile app*. Retrieved March 2, 2019, from https://offers.adobe.com/content/dam/offer-manager/en/na/marketing/Experience%20Manager%20 PDF's/2016/Adobe-Report_Driving_competitive_advantage_enterprise_apps.pdf

Amador, C. (2018). *The future of work: The rise of the digital workplace*. Retrieved March 2, 2019, from https://allwork.space/2019/02/the-future-of-work-the-rise-of-the-digital-workplace

Avanade, Inc. (2017). *Global survey: companies are unprepared for the arrival of a true digital workplace*. Retrieved March 2, 2019, from https://www.avanade.com/~/media/asset/research/digital-workplace-global-study.pdf

Bailey, D. (2017). *30 Online small businesst to use in 2017*. Retrieved March 2, 2019, from https://blumint.co/30-online-small-business-tools-use-2017

Berland, P. S. (2016). *Dell & Intel future works global report*. Retrieved March 2, 2019, from http://www.workforcetransformation.com/workforcestudy/assets/report/Dell-future-workfoce-study_GLOBAL.pdf

Bosch-Sijtsema, P., Ruohomäki, V. & Vartiainen, M. (2010). Multi-locational knowledge workers in the office: navigation, disturbances and effective-ness. *New Technology, Employment and Work Journal, 25*(3), 183–195.

Constant, C. (2017). Three steps to making the digital workplace ar. *Gartner Symposium 2016*. Retrieved March 2, 2019, from https://www.slideshare.net/IntelITCenter/three-steps-to-making-a-digital-workplace-a-reality-chad-constant-at-gartner-symposium-2016

Deloitte. (2014). *The digital workplace: think, share, do transform your employee experience*. Retrieved March 6, 2019, from https://www2.deloitte.com/content/dam/Deloitte/be/Documents/technology/The_digital_workplace_Deloitte.pdf

Dery, K., Sebastian, I. M., & Van Der Meulen, N. (2016). The digital workplace is key to digital innovation. MIS Quarterly Executive, 16(2), 135-152.

Dority, G. K. (2016). *Rethinking Information Work: a Career Guide for Liberian and other Information Professionals* (2nd ed.). Santa Barbara, CA: ABC-CLIO, LLC.

Forrester Research. (2017). *The digital transformation race has begun*. Retrieved March 5, 2019, from http://www.virtusadigital.com/wp-content/themes/the-box/images/digital-transformation/The%20Digital%20Transformation%20Race%20Has%20Begun.pdf

Gantz, J., Boyd, A., & Dowling, S. (2009). *Cutting the clutter: tackling information overload at the source*. IDC. Retrieved March 2, 2019, from https://www.xerox.com/assets/motion/corporate/pages/programs/information-overload/pdf/Xerox-white-paper-3-25.pdf

Gartner Report. (2017). *Gartner says worldwide public cloud services market to grow 18 percent in 2017*. Retrieved March 2, 2019, from https://www.gartner.com/newsroom/id/3616417

Haas, M. R., Criscuolo, P., & George, G. (2015). Which problems to solve? Online knowledge sharing and attention allocation in organizations. Academy of Management Journal, 58, 680–711. doi:10.5465/amj.2013.0263

Hamburg, I. (2019). Implementation of a digital workplace strategy to drive behavior change and improve competencies. In *Strategy and Behaviors in the Digital Economy*. IntechOpen. Retrieved May 16, 2019 from https://www.researchgate.net/publication/332494626_Implementation_of_a_Digital_orkplace_Strategy_to_Drive_Behavior_Change_and_Improve_Competencies

Harrison, A., Wheeler, P., & Whitehead, C. (2004). *The Distributed Workplace: Sustainable Work Environments*. London: Spon Press.

Hartford Business. (2014). *Millennials to take over by 2025*. Retrieved March 4, 2019. From http://www.hartfordbusiness.com/article/20140818/PRINTEDITION/140819969/millennials-to-take-over-by-2025

Haskins, B., & Nilssen, A. (2015). The collaborative enterprise: how enterprises are adapting to support the modern meeting. *Wainhouse Research*. Retrieved March 2, 2019, from https://www.logitech.com/assets/65076/wainhouse-wp-the-collaborative-enterprise.pdf

Igloo. (2017). Ro-Why: The business value of a digital workplace. Retrieved March 6, 2019, from https://www-cmswire.simplermedia.com/rs/706-YIA-261/images/RO_Why.pdf

Igloo. (2019). 2019 State of the digital workplace report. Retrieved June 18, 2019, from http://igloosoftware.lookbookhq.com/c/report-igloo-digital?x=QOKHau&_ga=2.218919897.1310781544.1560897722-686124159.1560897722

Ignite, M. (2017). *Spark the Future.* Retrieved March 6, 2019, from https://slideplayer.com/slide/4875602/

Infocom. (2018). *Meetings in America: A study of trends, costs, and attitudes toward business travel and teleconferencing, and their impact on productivity.* A Verizon Conferencing White paper. Retrieved March 6, 2019, from https://e-meetings.verizonbusiness.com/global/en/meetingsinamerica/uswhitepaper.php#INTRODUCTION

Kissmer, T., Stieglitz, S., Knoll, J., & Gross, R. (2018). *Knowledge workers' expectations towards a digital workplace. Americas Conference on Information Systems.* Retrieved May 16, 2019. From https://www.researchgate.net/publication/325809547_Knowledge_Workers%27_Expectations Towards_a_Digital_Workplace

Koeffer, S. (2015). Designing the digital workplace of the future -what scholars recommend to PR actioners. *International Conference on Information Systems*, Fort Worth, TX.

Marek, E. (2017). *Redefining change management in the digital age.* Retrieved March 6, 2019, from https://www.itchronicles.com/itsm/redefining-change-management/

Markovic, M. R. (2008). Managing the organizational change and culture in the age of globalization. January 8. *Journal of Business Economics and Management*, 9(1), 3–11. doi:10.3846/1611-1699.2008.9.3-11

Mazmanian, M., Orlikowski, W. J., & Yates, J. (2013). The autonomy paradox: the implications of mobile email devices for knowledge professionals.' Organization Science, 24, 1337–1357.

Microsoft Ignite. (2017). Spark the Future. Retrieved March 6, 2019, from https://slideplayer.com/slide/4875602/

Miller, P. (2012). Digital workplace business case: What is the financial value of investing in digital working? *Digital Workplace Group.* Retrieved March 6, 2019, from http://www.digitalworkplace-group.com/wp-content/downloads/dwg-free/DWG-Digital-Workplace-Business-Case-Free-Report.pdf#page=1&zoom=auto,-274,848

Miller, P. (2012). *The Digital Workplace: How Technology is Liberating Work.* TECL Publishing.

Miller, P., & March, A. (2016). *The Digital Renaissance of Work: Delivering digital workplaces fit for the future.* Routledge.

Morgan, J. (2013). *Five trends shaping the future of work.* Retrieved March 6, 2019, from https://www.forbes.com/sites/jacobmorgan/2013/06/20/five-trends-shaping-the-future-of-work/#777c696aece0

National Post. (2019). *Millennials will overtake baby boomers as the largest U.S. population group in 2019.* Retrieved March 6, 2019, from https://nationalpost.com/news/world/millennials-will-overtake-baby-boomers-as-the-largest-u-s-population-group-in-2019

Omega Management Group Corp. and Coveo. (2011). *The knowledge-driven support organization and its impact on the customer experience.* Retrieved March 6, 2019, from http://www.omegascoreboard.com/pdf/finalresults.pdf

Perks, M. (2015). *Everything you need to know but were afraid to ask: the Digital Workplace*. Retrieved October 6, 2018, from https://www.unily.com/media/23747/the-digital-workplace-guide-whitepaper.pdf

Perlow, L. A. (2012). *Sleeping with your Smartphone: How to Break the 24/7 Habit and Change the Way You Work*. Boston, MA: Harvard Business School Press.

PricewaterhouseCoopers. (2011). *Millennials at work: reshaping the workplace*. Retrieved March 6, 2019, from https://www.pwc.com/co/es/publicaciones/assets/millennials-at-work.pdf

Przybylski, A. K., & Weinstein, N. (2013). Can you connect with me now? How the presence of mobile communication technology influences face-to-face communication quality. *Journal of Social and Personal Relationships, 30*, 237 –246.

Reyt, J., & Wiesenfeld, B. M. (2015). Seeing the forest for the trees: exploratory learning, mobile technology, and knowledge workers' role integration behaviors. Academy of Management Journal, 58, 739–762.

RightScale. (2017). *State of the Cloud Report*. Retrieved March 6, 2019, from https://www.rightscale.com/blog/cloud-industry-insights/cloud-computing-trends-2017-state-cloud-survey#cloud-workloads

Ruostela, J., & Lönnqvis, A. (2013). Exploring more productive way of working. World Academy of Science, Engineering and Technology, 73, 711-719.

Schillerwein, S. (n.d.). *The Digital Workplace: Redefining productivity in the Information Age*. Infocentric Research AG. Retrieved March 6, 2019, from file:///C:/Users/Admin/Downloads/The_Digital_Workplace_-_Whitepaper_-_Infocentric_Research.pdf

Schubmehl, D. (2014). Unlocking the hidden value of information. *IDC*. Retrieved March 6, 2019, from https://idc-community.com/groups/it_agenda/bigdataanalytics/unlocking_the_hidden_value_of_information

Smith, D. (2016). *Cloud computing deployments should begin with service definition*. Gartner Report. Retrieved March 6, 2019, from https://www.gartner.com/doc/reprints?id=1-G2H8FE&ct=160826&st=sb

Solis, B., & Littleton, A. (2017). *The 2017 state of digital transformation. altimeter*. Retrieved March 6, 2019, from file:///C:/Users/Mohsen/AppData/Local/Temp/Altimeter%20_%202017%20State%20of%20DT.pdf

Sykes, E. R. (2011). Interruptions in the workplace: A case study to reduce their effects. *International Journal of Information Management, 31*, 38–394.

Turkle, S. (2015). *Reclaiming Conversation: The Power of Talk in a Digital Age*. New York, NY: Penguin Press.

Vartiainen, M. (2009). Working in multi-locational office – how do collaborative working environments support human centered design? *HCI, 10*, 1090–1098.

Vartiainen, M., Hakonen, M., Koivisto, S., Mannonen, P., Nieminen, M. P., Ruohomäki, V., & Vartola, A. (2007). *Distributed and Mobile Work – Places, People and Technology*. Helsinki: University Press Finland.

White, M. (2012). Digital workplaces: vision and reality. *Business Information Review*, *29*(4), 205-214.

Williams, S., & Schubert, P. (2018). Designs for the digital workplace. *Procedia Computer Science*, *13*, 478-485. Retrieved May 16, 2019 from https://www.researchgate.net/ publication/328472149_Designs_for_the_Digital_Workplace

Chapter 19
Consumer Online Behavior, Data Sharing, and Ethics

Virginia M. Miori
Saint Joseph's University, USA

Richard T. Herschel
Saint Joseph's University, USA

ABSTRACT

This chapter reports the results of a survey that examines how a sampling of millennials describes their online activity, their social engagement, and their priorities when they are asked to value their online activity. It also explores whether there are tenets of a specific ethical perspective that shape their thinking about what is moral behavior online. Results indicate that the online behavior of the study participants involves extensive use of social media with a variety of platforms employed. Degree of engagement is not dependent on whether the individual is introvert or extrovert. Their online priority focuses first on a concern for their privacy, followed by their appreciation for time saving technology and opportunities for money savings and promotions. No single ethical theory dominates their expressed moral values, though there is a clear pattern that is consistent with consequentialism.

INTRODUCTION

This chapter examines consumer online behavior and the ethical perspectives that may underlie their values and inform their actions. This information is especially relevant for organizations today since issues with data sharing, data usage, and data privacy have recently received so much attention in the press. In some instances, new legislative actions now define how organizations must manage information captured and stored from their interactions with consumers online. However, here it is argued that there is a larger social issue involved: organizations need to not only respect customer data, but also to appreciate how consumers engage online (their data footprint) and the values that inform their behavior. This would seem fundamental in helping organizations to manage risk by maintaining an effective relationship with their stakeholders.

DOI: 10.4018/978-1-5225-8933-4.ch019

BACKGROUND

Consumer data is a major component of Big Data. Big Data is a term that describes the structured and unstructured data that inundates business on a day-to-day basis. Big Data has been described as encompassing a number of dimensions, including volume, variety, velocity, veracity, variability, and complexity (SAS, 2019). Improvements to the telecommunications infrastructure combined with the rapid deployment of high-speed wireless technologies worldwide have enabled greater bandwidth for transferring an assortment of data types data that can quickly be shared globally. For instance, every minute Facebook users send roughly 31.25 messages and watch 2.77 million videos (New Generation Applications, 2018).

The Big Data that is generated online has become essential to organizations. It provides the critical raw material that is scrutinized via analytics to generate the business intelligence that will inform decision-making activities. IBM (2019) notes that this Big Data comes from organizational internal data sources and their external data sources. Internal data sources include transactions, log data, and emails. External data sources include social media, audio, and photos and video. IBM states that 43% of external data comes from social media alone and this information can be used to gain information about and insights into consumer behavior.

When examining the contribution of social media on Big Data, Statistica (2019) reports that in 2017, 81 percent of the population in the United States had a social networking profile, representing a three percent growth compared to the previous year. They also comment that, according to estimates, the number of worldwide social media users is expected to grow to almost 3 billion by 2021.

Globalwebindex (2018) reports that 98% of digital consumers are social media users and that they spend an average of 2 hours and 22 minutes per day on social media and messaging. Their research indicates that 22 percent of online consumers like or follow a brand on a social network and that more than 4 in 10 use social networks to research new brands or products. They also find that people have an average of 8.5 social media accounts, using each platform for different purposes.

A Pew Research Center (February 5, 2018) survey of social media usage by U.S. adults found that Facebook dominates the social media landscape with 68% using it. However, when Pew Research examined the behavior of younger adults 18-24-years of age, they found that they differ from the overall trend in social media consumption. They report that 78% of this younger population are substantially more likely to use platforms such as Snapchat, Instagram, and Twitter than the other age groups. These findings may help explain why Edison Research (2018), who has been tracking Facebook usage since 2008, found that in 2018, the portion of Americans reporting that they currently ever use Facebook declined for the first time. Their data revealed that among 12- to 34-year-olds, Facebook usage declined 15 percent in one year.

The widespread use of social media is not without consequence for consumers. Social media companies have demonstrated a long-term pattern of sharing user data with or without consumers being aware of it. When they are aware of it, Maheshwari (2018) reports that they give up personal information due to a sense of futility, since they do not know what to do about it. Moreover, he says, most consumers will also give up their data for relevant ads on their social media sites hosts, not because of convenience, but due to a resignation that they are powerless.

Data is the currency that makes free or near-free services possible. As Johnson (2018) notes, the only reason Skype, Facebook, or any online service is free is due to data. Most consumers understand this conceptually, though not always specifically. Furthermore, consumers may be willing to accept the tradeoff between a value-added service and disclosure of information about them in a classic quid-pro-quo arrangement. However, the challenge is that all this information is buried in a 60-page privacy policy of which, Johnson says, most consumers will never read, nor understand if they did read it.

While social media companies argue that their goal is to make the world more open and connected, the process of actually doing this while respecting and protecting an individual's data privacy has been shown to be problematic. There is serious doubt that social media hosts can or will protect user information. Moreover, Harris (2018) notes that social networking sites have come under scrutiny by both the press and governments due to (deliberate or inadvertent) actions that foster deception, social grooming, and/or the creation of defamatory content that adversely impacts consumers.

In 2018, a survey by the Pew Research Center (March 27, 2018) found that only 9% of American social media users were 'very confident' that social media companies could guard their privacy. The survey findings also reported that two-thirds of the participants felt that current laws were sufficient to protect their privacy. The paradox, the Pew Research Center concludes, is that people are using social media platforms even as they express great concern about the privacy implications of doing so – and the social woes they encounter.

This concern is justified. Recently, British and US lawyers launched a joint class action against Facebook, Cambridge Analytica and two other companies for allegedly misusing the personal data of more than 71 million people. The lawsuit claims that these firms obtained their users' private information from the social media network to develop "political propaganda campaigns" in the UK and the US. It is asserts that Facebook failed to act responsibly to protect the data of 1 million British users and 70.6 million people in America (Bowcott & Hern, 2018).

The misuse of personal information by social media companies and other organizations has had real consequences for all organizations who interact with consumers online. There is now new legislation intended to protect the privacy of personal information. For example, the General Data Protection Regulation (GDPR), introduced by the European Union in 2018, represents an attempt to protect EU citizens from privacy and data breaches in an increasingly data-driven world (EU GDPR, 2018). This legislation mandates that organizations must take consumer online behavior and preferences seriously. It also implies that it is in an organizations best interest to be proactive in monitoring social norms on an ongoing basis. Vartabedian, Wells, and O'Reilly (2018) report that in June of 2018, California also passed new consumer-privacy legislation – the California Consumer Privacy Act. The regulation provides consumers with the right to know all data collected by a business about them and the right to say "no" to the sale of their information.

DATA SHARING AND ETHICS

Culnan and Williams (2009) have documented the potential for abuses of informational reuse and unauthorized data that could result in privacy problems. They state that information reuse involves organizations making decisions about new uses of personal information they have collected, while unauthorized access involves employees viewing personal information they are not authorized to view. Both activities threaten the organization's legitimacy in its interactions with consumers, shareholders, and regulators. These unethical activities can lead to a breach of consumer confidentiality and trust, or the financial harm to individuals from identity theft or identity fraud.

In 2014, King and Richards noted that large datasets were being mined for predictions that could influence all kinds of human activities and decisions, including dating, shopping, medicine, education, voting, law enforcement, terrorism prevention, and cybersecurity. In this process, individuals were ignorant of the fact that their data was being collected, let alone shared with third parties.

In trying to reign the abuse of people's privacy, the GDPR widened the definition personal data. It describes it as any information that can be used to identify an individual. This can include genetic, mental, cultural, economic, or social information (Ashford, 2016). Then, to ensure that organizations are protecting this data, GDPR compliance requires that organizations create a "map" of all personal data being processed in a given network and then be able to justify exactly why they are processing this data (Gambardella, 2018).

Accenture Labs (2016) argues that a best-practice approach in addressing data sharing issues is to ensure that ethics are properly considered throughout the data management process so that risks are appropriately identified and mitigated. They note that risk management has become part of compliance law and, they argue, it must necessarily be applied to questions of data privacy, protection, and sharing.

A risk management strategy embeds ethics as a driving force in the enterprise. Pain (1994) states that in such a strategy, ethical values shape the search for opportunities, the design of organizational systems, and the decision-making processes used by individuals and groups. Shared moral values provide a common frame of reference and serve as a unifying force across different functions, lines of business, and employee groups. In essence, Pain argues that an organizational ethic helps define what a company is and what it stands for. She believes that creating an organization that encourages exemplary conduct may be the best way to prevent damaging misconduct.

Monitoring of social norms can also have important implications for organizations. For example, Verschoor (2013), reported the findings of an Ethics Resource Center study that detailed millennials' posting of questionable workplace-related information on their social networking sites. Abril, Levin, and Del Riego (2012) believe that these millennial's actions can be explained by their preference for open communications, which includes offering traditionally private information online. The problem with these actions is that millennials' apparent desire for network privacy is not supported by technology, law, or prevailing business practices.

Many managers think of ethics as a question of personal scruples, a confidential matter between individuals and their consciences. However, Paine notes that ethics has *everything* to do with management. Business practices involve the tacit, if not explicit, cooperation of others and reflect the values, attitudes, beliefs, language, and behavioral patterns that define an organization's operating culture. Ethics, she concludes, is an organizational issue. Paine believes that managers must acknowledge their role in shaping organizational ethics and seize opportunities to create a climate that can strengthen the relationships and reputations on which their companies' success depends. This should extend to how they deal with their business partners and their customers.

Understanding ethics is pertinent and valuable when assessing risk, since ethical perspectives shape perceptions about what is right or wrong. It helps us to understand how people perceive certain situations and what they judge to be appropriate behavior. Our moral perceptions shape our actions, our responses, and our feelings about what happens in our face-to-face encounters and our online activity.

Ethics perspectives are articulated by theories that provide specific philosophical principles that allow the individual to construct persuasive, logical, and reasoned arguments that reflect their moral values. Below are four well-known ethical theories that illustrate how this is accomplished. These theories are Virtue Ethics, Social Contract Theory Utilitarianism, and Kantianism.

Virtue Ethics

Virtue ethics emphasizes virtues, or moral character, rather than duties, rules, or the consequences of actions. Rooted in the arguments of Aristotle (384 BC-322 BC) and Plato (428 BC-347 BC), this theory defines a virtue as a character trait or disposition that is well entrenched in its possessor which makes that person good. There are two types of virtues, intellectual and moral virtues. Intellectual virtues are those derived from reasoning and truth. Moral virtues are deep-seated habits or dispositions formed through the repetition of virtuous actions over time. Morally good people realize happiness by consistently acting out their virtues, doing what any virtuous person would know to be right. For example, honesty, justice, generosity, and loyalty may be seen to be core virtues (Stanford University, 2019). A person who adhered to a Virtue Ethics perspective would evaluate social media behavior and respect for data as a reflection of one's moral character.

Social Contract Theory

Social Contract Theory [based on the arguments made by philosophers Thomas Hobbs (1588-1679), John Locke (1632-1704), Jean-Jacques Rousseau (1712-1778), and John Rawls (1921-2002)] is an ethical perspective that states that a person's moral and/or political obligations are dependent upon a contract or agreement that people have made to form the society in which they live. In this theory, people are seen as rationale beings who understand that in order to create and maintain a society, people must cooperate and agree to follow certain guidelines in order to gain the benefits of social living. To do this, that people must choose rationality over their natural selfish instincts. That is, they must be willing to submit to a government and its laws in order to live in a civil society, rather than live in a "natural" state of anarchy and chaos. The social contract provides the justification for the establishment of moral rules to govern relationships among citizens as well as the mechanism capable of enforcing these rules – government (Friend, 2019). The EU's creation and imposition of the GDPR could be seen as a reflection of a society's intent to mandate respect for peoples' privacy by reigning in the free will of social media platforms.

Utilitarianism

Unlike Kantianism, Utilitarianism [originating from Jeremy Bentham (1748-1832) and John Stuart Mill (1806-1873)] examines right or wrong based on the consequences of an act or a rule. The act utilitarian perspective applies the principle of utility to individual moral actions and the rule utilitarian applies the principle of utility to moral rules. The right act is one that produces the greatest happiness for a community or society. A wrong act decreases the total happiness of the affected parties. The right moral rule of conduct is one where if it is adopted by everyone, will lead to the greatest net increase in happiness for all involved. Hence, in the Utilitarianism ethical perspective, one must calculate what action or rule achieves the best results. That is, one must literally account for and the weigh the good and the bad elements affecting a situation to determine the net consequences of the action or rule. In Utilitarianism, it is the "happiness" or the maximum well-being outcome that is most critical (Cavalier, 2019). Hence, to evaluate ethical behavior online, one would need to get an impression that someone seriously weighs both the pros and cons of their participation in social media to determine what actions is acceptable.

Kantianism

Kantian ethics, originating with the German philosopher Immanuel Kant (1724-1804), is an ethical theory concerned about not about what we do, but what we ought to do. What we ought to do reflects our dutifulness. Dutifulness reflects good will – the desire to do things right based upon rules that everyone ought to follow. That is, a dutiful person acts the way they do because of a morale rule. These rules are imperatives that are either hypothetical or categorical and they are the means by which reason commands our will and our actions. Hypothetical imperatives equate basically to conditional if, then statements relative to what you are trying to accomplish. Categorical imperatives command unconditionally as they are unequivocal. For example, one categorical imperative states that you should only follow moral rules that you would expect everyone else to follow. Another states that you should never treat people as means to an end, but as an end unto themselves since all persons have moral worth and should be treated with dignity. For Kant, rules are paramount. Everyone is held to the same standard and there are clear guidelines for appropriate behavior. Hence, in Kantianism it is not the outcome of a behavior that matters, rather it is the rule behind the action that is most critical (California State University Sacramento, 2019). With regards to social media and privacy, for example, one might condemn social media for providing a service whose real intent is capture and manipulate people's personal information – using it as a means to their own ends.

Three of the ethical theories described above have been employed to make moral assessments about the value of outcomes. This is referred to as ethical consequentialism, which describes a class of normative ethical theories holding that the consequences of one's conduct are the ultimate basis for any judgment about the rightness or wrongness of that conduct. Ethical consequentialism evaluates acts, rules, motives, or institutions to evaluate our choices (Mulligan, 2016). Utilitarianism and Social Contract Theory are typically classified as consequentialist theories while Kantianism oftentimes is not. Instead, Kantianism can be classified as representing deontology ethics, which states that the morality of an action should be based on whether that action itself is right or wrong under a series of rules, rather than based on the consequences of the action. However, Cummiskey (2003) argues that Kant's basic rationalist, internalist approach to the justification of normative principles, his conception of morality as a system of categorical imperatives, his account of the nature of the goodwill and the motive of duty, and his principle of universalizability are all compatible with normative consequentialism. Virtue Ethics, however, is definitely not compatible with consequentialism since it is solely focused on one's moral character and not the consequences of their actions.

EXPLORATORY RESEARCH

Our research employed these ethical perspectives to conduct an exploratory research study to examine how a group of active social media users describe their digital behavior and the moral perspectives that shape their online attitudes and actions. A 25-question survey was administered to 110 graduate business students to gather information about their use of social media, loyalty card ownership, streaming services subscriptions, data sharing, online shopping, and other forms of digital interaction. This data essentially provides a social profile of their online activity. The subjects were primarily millennials.

The survey also employed a series of questions that asked participants to identify their moral values. When choosing an answer to these questions, respondents had to choose among four different viewpoints,

Figure 1. Age distribution of respondents

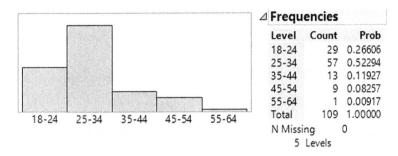

◢ Frequencies		
Level	Count	Prob
18-24	29	0.26606
25-34	57	0.52294
35-44	13	0.11927
45-54	9	0.08257
55-64	1	0.00917
Total	109	1.00000
N Missing	0	
5 Levels		

Figure 2. Educational level of respondents

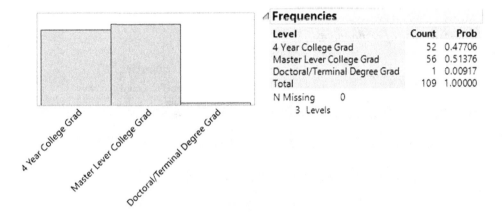

◢ Frequencies		
Level	Count	Prob
4 Year College Grad	52	0.47706
Master Lever College Grad	56	0.51376
Doctoral/Terminal Degree Grad	1	0.00917
Total	109	1.00000
N Missing	0	
3 Levels		

each of which represented the tenets of one of the ethical theories discussed above. These questions examined issues pertaining loyalty cards, social media, data management, data leaks, and the use of their personal data by organizations for business intelligence activities.

While participant views on ethics were confined to the values ascribed to Virtue Ethics, Social Contract Theory, Utilitarianism, and Kantianism, the larger intent was to see if a single ethical perspective was dominant in shaping their views or if there was inconsistency in how the respondents expressed their moral views. Either outcome would have relevance for organizational risk management activities. Being able to identify a dominant ethical theory employed by a social group would make it easier to anticipate their reaction to organizational behavior and actions. However, if there is variability in their ethical choices, this suggests that situational changes can give rise to consequential behavioral inconsistencies, which makes risk management activities much more complicated (Hartwig & Gigerenzer, 2011).

Findings

Survey Respondent Summary

The respondents were asked to identify themselves demographically. Figures 1 – 4 provide summaries of these demographics.

Figure 3. Respondent area of study

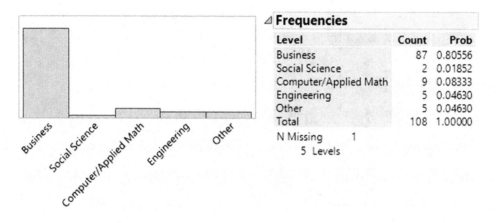

Figure 4. Gender identity of respondents

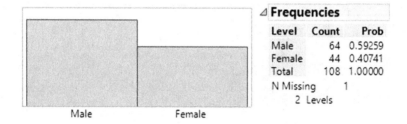

Social Media Tolerance

Respondents were asked about their use of social media platforms. These included:

- Instagram
- Twitter
- Snapchat
- Facebook/Messenger
- LinkedIn
- Tumblr
- Pinteret
- WeChat
- WhattsApp
- Pokemon Go
- YouTube

Participants were then asked how often they used them:

1. never (1 point)
2. yearly (2 points)
3. monthly (3 points)

Figure 5. Total social media score distribution

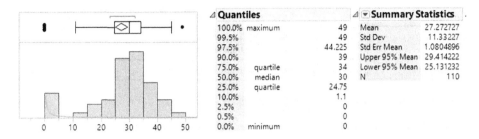

4.   weekly (4 points)
5.   daily (5 points)
6.   multiple times per day (6 points)

The social media tolerance was calculated as a sum. For each social media platform, the response was translated to the number of points (as stated in the list). The sum of these point yields a maximum score of 66 and a minimum score of 11. The distribution shown in Figure 5 indicates that the top 50% of the respondents fell above a score of 30. Of the 11 social media platforms listed above, Tumblr, WeChat and Pokemon Go, which were almost never used. This tells us that 8 social media platforms are chiefly responsible for the total social media tolerance score.

The top four social media platforms (by use in this group of respondents) were Instagram, Facebook/Messenger, LinkedIn and YouTube. Figure 6 summarized the accumulated score for these four platforms. This analysis indicated that the top 50% of respondents recorded a score above 17 (indicating that all four of these platforms were used at least weekly).

We also note that:

- 57.1% of respondents used Instagram daily or multiple times per day
- 42.8% of respondents used Facebook/Messenger daily or multiple times per day
- 34.7% of respondents used Linked daily or multiple times per day
- 60.0% of respondents used YouTube daily or multiple times per day

Analysis of Variance (ANOVA) models completed for the Top Four Sum found significant differences for two variables as seen in Table 1. In other words, social media usage for the top four platforms differs based on age group and educational status.

Figure 6. Top four social media platform usage

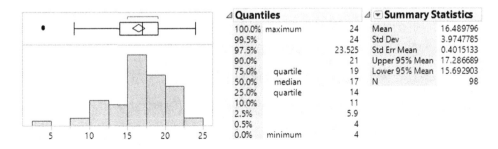

Table 1. ANOVA results for top four sum

Variable	Difference Between	Significance Level
Age Group	Ages: 25-34 and 45-54 Ages: 18-24 and 45-54	0.0477
Educational Status	Masters Level and Doctoral Level/Terminal	0.0493

Introversion or Extroversion

Eight questions were employed to identify behavioral preferences that were consistent with expressions of either introversion or extroversion. These questions inquired about such things as their attitudes about and preferences for engaging with others or being alone and whether they were inwardly focused or active in interacting with their environment.

In Figure 7, higher scores indicate a greater degree introversion, while lower score suggest a greater leaning towards extroversion. The mean score of the data was 29.28, suggesting that the vast majority of respondents self-identify as being a blend of both introvert and extrovert. An ANOVA did however indicate a difference in level of introversion based on gender identity. Among our respondents, females tested as tending toward introversion more than males.

An initial hypoesis was that the degree of introversion and extroversion would impact social media tolerance. After testing this hypotheses using ANOVA, it was detemined that the degree of introversion did not yield differences in social media tolerance.

Priority Preferences in Valuing Online Activity

A series of questions were presented in which respondents were asked to compare two factors (of social media usage) at a time. These factors included privacy, social connection, time saving technology, money saving and promotions, and loyalty reward. Participants were ask to split 11 points between each pair of factors. Table 2 provides a summary analysis of these questions. In interpreting the table, we read as the

Figure 7. Introversion score distribution

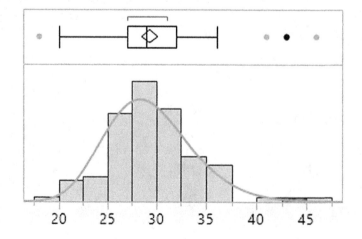

Table 2. Online priority preferences

	Privacy	Social Connection	Time Saving Technology	Money Savings and Promotions	Loyalty Rewards
Privacy	-	1.676	1.006	1.210	1.655
Social Connection	0.596	-	0.781	0.723	1.134
Time Saving Technology	0.994	1.280	-	1.132	1.600
Money Savings and Promotions	0.827	1.383	0.883	-	1.614
Loyalty Rewards	0.604	0.882	0.625	0.620	-

row header being preferred over the column header by the factor contained in the intersecting cell. For example, privacy is preferred 1.676 times over social connection. Note that a factor of less than 1.000 indicates that the row header is less preferred than the column header.

Table 2 reveals is that Privacy is valued more than Social Connection (by a factor of 1.676), Time Saving Technology (by a factor of 1.006), Money Savings and Promotions (by a factor of 1.210), and Loyalty Rewards (by a factor of 1.655). Social Connection is preferred over Loyalty Rewards (by a factor of 1.134), while Time Saving Technology is valued over Social Connection (by a factor of 1.280), Money Savings and Promotion (by a factor of 1.132), and Loyalty Rewards (by a factor of 1.614). Finally, Money Savings and Promotions are preferred over Social Connection (by a factor of 1.383) and Loyalty Rewards (by a factor of 1.614).

The factors are then ranked, with participants valuing privacy most, followed by time saving technology, money and promotions, social connection, and least of all loyalty rewards.

Social Media Followers and Following

Respondents were asked how many followers they have on social media. Figure 8 shows the frequency distribution of these responses. This distribution indicates that the likelihood of large numbers of fol-

Figure 8. Followers on social media

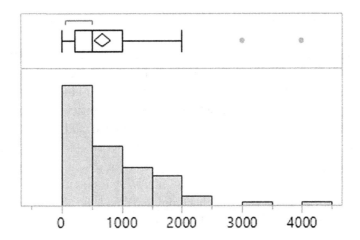

Figure 9. People followed on social media

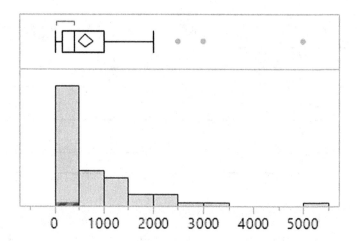

lowers is very low among our population. Note also that the number of followers was not impacted by degree of introversion.

Further, respondents were asked how many people they follow; Figure 9 shows this frequency distribution. The distribution indicates that the likelihood of following larger numbers of people is very low among our population.

Expressed Ethical Values

Participants were asked a series of questions to probe their ethical values concerning risks associated with data sharing, Big Data, loyalty cards, social media activity, data management, data leaks, and analytics. Analysis indicated that there was no one ethical theory that consistently shaped how participant values were expressed. That said, the choice of responses that are consistent with the values expressed by Virtue Ethics were significantly less chosen than those consistent with social Contract Theory, Utilitarianism, or Kantianism. This means that ethical the ethical values of participants can be characterized as being grounded in varying expressions of consequentialism.

CONCLUSION AND RECOMMENDATIONS

These millennials clearly engaged in social media. Our results indicate that participant use of social media platforms were consistent with this reported by Smith and Anderson (2018). They found YouTube, Facebook, Snapchat, Instagram, and Twitter to be especially popular among those ages 18-24.

We found and engagement in social media activities was not exclusive to or dominated by extroverts, which is not consistent with research conducted by Azucar, Marengo, and Settanni (2018) and Harbaugh (2010). Our results also contradict the assertion made by Burke, Kraut, and Marlow, (2011) that introverts spend more time in online social engagement than extroverts do.

That study participants expressed a primary focus on privacy issues may be influenced by the dominance of this issue in the media. Reports of data hackings and data leaks are unfortunately commonplace events that are routinely covered in the media. This has led to recent well-publicized privacy legislation is imposing how social media may interact with its clientele. Hence, there is every reason to believe that participant in this study have been especially sensitized to this issue.

We conjecture that valuing of time and money savings/promotions over social connections may simply reflect a preference for valuing their own self-interest before their need for social interaction.

The fact that survey participants explain their moral perspectives using multiple ethical theories is not problematic. Donaldson (1996) addresses this when he refutes the concept of ethical imperialism. The fundamental argument underlying ethical imperialism, he says, is absolutism, which insists that there is a single list of moral truths. Donaldson states that the problem with absolutism is the presumption that people must express moral truth using only one set of concepts; that there is a single global standard of ethical behavior. Instead, he contends that context must be allowed to shape ethical practice. Donaldson asserts that what is more important than variations in the use of different ethical theories to justify one's values is the ability to express consistent respect for core human values, which he defines as respect for human dignity, respect for basic rights, and good citizenship.

Indeed, Rosenthal (2019) makes the case that situation ethics may explain the variations in the expression of moral views. Situation ethics takes the position that moral decision making is contextual or dependent on a set of circumstances. That is, situation ethics holds that moral judgments must be made within the context of the entirety of a situation and that all normative features of a situation must be viewed as a whole. Hence insisting that one ethical viewpoint consistently define one's ethical views is unreasonable, because an absolute position pays no attention to the complexity and uniqueness of each situation being examined.

Hence to think that survey participants should be consistent in their use of a specific ethical theories to explain their views should not be expected. Norms of rightness or correctness in practical thinking should not require us to think along a single prescribed pathway. Indeed, when examining people moral choices, Richardson (2018) states that we should not expect people to necessarily attend to the moral facts nor apply a single moral theory that exhausts or sufficiently describes their moral reasoning. What is important is that moral considerations enter into their thinking and that they are able to recognize and choose a moral action. In this study, theories characterized by the tenets of ethical consequentialism dominate. There is scant expression of moral virtue as the preferred means for judging online behavior.

The findings suggest there is risk in managing their relationships with these stakeholders. It is clear that these millennials are sensitive to the fact that organizations need to respect their privacy. They also value time saving technology and money savings and promotions are valued and to a lesser extent so are loyalty rewards. Whether their online consumers are introverts or extroverts may not be important for organizations to ponder. Both personality types are engaged with organizations online and both types employ principles of consequential ethics in their judgement of organizational behavior.

All analyses available upon request.

DISCUSSION QUESTIONS

1. The ability to communicate via social media implies a willingness to sacrifice personal privacy. How would you characterize the value placed on privacy by individuals in society today? Is social connectedness worth the sacrifice of privacy?
2. Do you feel that existing ethical foundations are sufficient (if expanded to include data collection and usage) to represent progressing societal norms and expanding social media platforms?

3. Have you searched for yourself on the internet? If not, do so now. Do you find your universally available information (internet footprint) acceptable? Do you feel that you have the ability to sufficiently control the information available? Should users have a greater ability to control their internet footprint?

4. Do corporations have the right to gather and use private data (without consent)? Are you willing to share your own private data in the name of marketing advancements? Is it worth sharing data to receive individually targeted ads?

5. Should corporations and organizations be subject to legislation on their collection and use of personal data? If so, what should be included in this legislation? If not, please share your reasons.

6. Based on the last 5-10 years of expansion in the collection and use of personal data, what do you envision in the next decade? Will privacy be completely forfeited or will it be enhanced? Will legislators effective address data collection and usage?

REFERENCES

Abril, P. A., Levin, A., & Del Riego, A. (2012, Spring). Blurred Boundaries: Social Media Privacy and the Twenty-First-Century Employee. *American Business Law Journal, 49*(1), 63–124. doi:10.1111/j.1744-1714.2011.01127.x

Accenture Labs. (2016). The ethics of data sharing: A guide to best practices and governance. *Accenture Technology.* Retrieved March 7, 2019, from https://www.accenture.com/t20161110T001618Z__w__/ca-en/_acnmedia/PDF-35/Accenture-The-Ethics-of-Data-Sharing.pdf

Ashford, W. (2016). 10 facts businesses need to note about the GDPR. *Computer Weekly.* Retrieved January 7, 2019, from https://www.computerweekly.com/news/450296306/10-key-facts-businesses-need-to-note-about-the-GDPR

Azucar, D., Marengo, D., & Settanni, M. (2018). Predicting the Big 5 personality traits from digital footprints on social media: A meta-analysis. *Personality and Individual Differences, 124,* 150–159. doi:10.1016/j.paid.2017.12.018

Baer, J. (2018). 6 Unexpected Trends in 2018 Social Media Research. *Convince & Convert.* Retrieved June 9, 2018, from http://www.convinceandconvert.com/social-media-measurement/6-unexpected-trends-in-2018-social-media-research/

Bowcott, O., & Hern, A. (2018). Facebook and Cambridge Analytica face class action lawsuit. *The Guardian.* Retrieved April 3, 2018, from https://www.theguardian.com/news/2018/apr/10/cambridge-analytica-and-facebook-face-class-action-lawsuit

Burke, M., Kraut, R., & Marlow, C. (2011). Social capital in Facebook: Differentiating uses and users. *CHI'11 Proceedings of the SIGCHI Conference on Human Factors in Computing Systems,* 571-580.

California State University Sacramento. (2019). *Kantian Ethics.* Retrieved February 5, 2019, from https://www.csus.edu/indiv/g/gaskilld/ethics/kantian%20ethics.htm

Cavalier, R. (2019). Utilitarian theories. *Online Guide to ethics and moral philosophy.* Retrieved February 4, 2019, from http://caae.phil.cmu.edu/Cavalier/80130/part2/sect9.html

Culnan, M. J., & Williams, C. C. (2009). How ethics can enhance organizational privacy: Lessons from the Choicepoint and TJX data breaches. *Management Information Systems Quarterly*, *33*(4), 673–687. doi:10.2307/20650322

Cummiskey, D. (2003). Kantian Consequentialism. *Oxford Scholarship Online*. Retrieved March 23, 2019, from http://www.oxfordscholarship.com/view/10.1093/0195094530.001.0001/acprof-9780195094534

Donaldson, T. (1996). Values in tension: Ethics away from home. *Harvard Business Review*. Retrieved March 12, 2019, from https://hbr.org/1996/09/values-in-tension-ethics-away-from-home

Edison Research. (2018). Facebook declines for the first time in infinite dial history. *Blog – Latest news*. Retrieved February 15, 2019, from https://www.edisonresearch.com/facebook-declines-first time-infinite-dial-history/

EU GDPR. (2018). The EU General Data Protection Regulation (GDPR) is the most important change in data privacy regulation in 20 years. *EU GDPR.ORG*. Retrieved June 1, 2018, from https://www.eugdpr.org/

Friend, C. (2019). Social contract theory. *Internet Encyclopedia of Philosophy*. Retrieved February 4, 2019, from https://www.iep.utm.edu/soc-cont/

Gambardella, T. (2018). Gearing up to meet GDPR compliance requirements. *TechTarget*. Retrieved February 15, 2019, from https://searchcompliance.techtarget.com/video/Gearing-up-to-meet-GDPR-compliance-requirements

Globalwebindex. (2018). Social: Flagship Report 2018. *Globalwebindex*. Retrieved March 4, 2019, from https://www.globalwebindex.com/hubfs/Downloads/Social-H2-2018-report.pdf

Harbaugh, E. R. (2010). The effect of personality styles (level of introversion-extroversion) on social media use. *The Elon Journal of Undergraduate Research in Communications*, *1*(2), 70–86.

Harris, J. (2018). Ethical issues in social networking. *Cariblogger*. Retrieved April 7, 2018, from https://cariblogger.com/ethical-issues-in-social-networking/

Hertwig, R., & Gigerenzer, G. (2011). Behavioral inconsistencies do not imply inconsistent strategies. *Frontiers in Psychology*, *2*(292), 1–3. PMID:22110447

IBM. (2019). Where does big data come from. *Big Data & Analytics Hub*. Retrieved January 21, 2019, from https://www.ibmbigdatahub.com/infographic/where-does-big-data-come

Johnson, K. (July 9, 2018). What is consumer privacy and where is it headed? *Forbes*. Retrieved March 4, 2019, from https://www.forbes.com/sites/forbestechcouncil/2018/07/09/what-is-consumer-data-privacy-and-where-is-it-headed/#4f7fab731bc1

King, J. H., & Richards, N. M. (March 28, 2014). What's up with Big Data ethics? *Forbes*. Retrieved February 27, 2018, from https://www.forbes.com/sites/oreillymedia/2014/03/28/whats-up-with-big-data-ethics/#a344d0035913

Maheshwari, S. (December 24, 2018). Sharing Data for Deals? More Like Watching It Go With A Sigh. *The New York Times*. Retrieved March 5, 2019, from https://www.nytimes.com/2018/12/24/business/media/data-sharing-deals-privacy.html

Mulligan, T. (2016). Ethical Consequentialism. *Oxford Bibliographies*. Retrieved March 23, 2019, from http://www.oxfordbibliographies.com/view/document/obo-9780195396577/obo-9780195396577-0026.xml

New Generation Applications. (2018). 21 Big Data Statistics & Predictions on the Future of Big Data. *Blog*. Retrieved March 5, 2019, from https://www.newgenapps.com/blog/big-data-statistics-predictions-on-the-future-of-big-data

Paine, L. S. (1994). Managing for organizational integrity. *Harvard Business Review*. Retrieved October 10, 2018, from https://hbr.org/1994/03/managing-for-organizational-integrity

Pew Research Center. (2018a). Social Media Use in 2018. *Pew Research Center: Internet & Technology*. Retrieved March 4, 2019, from http://www.pewinternet.org/2018/03/01/social-media-use-in-2018/

Pew Research Center. (2018b). American's complicated feelings about social media in an era of privacy concerns. *Pew Research Center: FACTTANK*. Retrieved March 4, 2019, from http://www.pewresearch.org/fact-tank/2018/03/27/americans-complicated-feelings-about-social-media-in-an-era-of-privacy-concerns/

Quinn, M. J. (2017). *Ethics for the Information Age*. Hoboken, NJ: Pearson.

Richardson, H. S. (2018). Moral Reasoning. *Stanford Encyclopedia of Moral Reasoning*. Retrieved March 1, 2019, from https://plato.stanford.edu/entries/reasoning-moral/

Rosenthal, S. B. (2019). Situation Ethics. *Encyclopedia Britannica*. Retrieved March 12, 2019, from https://www.britannica.com/topic/situation-ethics

SAS. (2019). Big Data: What it is and why it matters. *Big Data Insights*. Retrieved February 2, 2019, from https://www.sas.com/en_us/insights/big-data/what-is-big-data.html

Smith, A., & Anderson, M. (2018). Social Media Use in 2018. *Pew Research Center: Internet & Technology*. Retrieved March 25, 2019, from https://www.pewinternet.org/2018/03/01/social-media-use-in-2018/

Stanford University. (2019). Virtue ethics. *Stanford Encyclopedia of Philosophy*. Retrieved February 3, 2019, from https://plato.stanford.edu/entries/ethics-virtue/

Statistica. (2019). Number of social media users worldwide from 2010 to 2021 (in billions). *Statistica: The Statistics Portal*. Retrieved March 8, 2019, from https://www.statista.com/statistics/278414/number-of-worldwide-social-network-users/

Vartabedian, M., Wells, G., & O'Reilly, L. (2018), Businesses Blast California's New Data-Privacy Law. *The Wall Street Journal*. Retrieved August 2, 2018, from https://www.wsj.com/articles/businesses-blast-californias-new-data-privacy-law-1530442800

Verschoor, C. V. (2013). Ethical Behavior Differs Among Generations. *Strategic Finance*. Retrieved January 5, 2019, from https://sfmagazine.com/wp-content/uploads/sfarchive/2013/08/ETHICS-Ethical-Behavior-Differs-Among-Generations.pdf

Chapter 20
Collective Behavior Under the Umbrella of Blockchain

Kanak Saxena
Samrat Ashok Technological Institute, India

Umesh Banodha
Samrat Ashok Technological Institute, India

ABSTRACT

Any social or organization system will fetch the properties from economics, sociology, and social psychology. In the digital world everyone is trying to cope with the new technologies for the survival. The dynamics of such a system are very multifarious due to the complexity in the convergence of the digital, physical, and biological realms. The dynamics of the society and organization are rapidly changing due to the imparting of the new technologies, such as artificial intelligence, internet of things, virtual reality, etc. The resultant is revolutionizing of opportunities and expectations due to the changes in the values, norms, identities, and future potential. The collective behavior (CB) plays an important role in predicting the various dynamics which are not only coherent but also paying attention. Blockchain will not only help in detecting but also help in finding the major causes and challenges for current scenario dynamics. The chapter describes the agent-based modeling and ant colony optimization components of the CB.

INTRODUCTION

The concept of social & organizational dynamics belongs to the social physics that dealt with the current rules and regulations by the global policies. This will not only change the society but also help out the organization to work out in an efficient and effective manner. The purpose of any study depends on the following factors especially when the era is sound enough to tackle the problems as and when occurred. Of course, the nature of the problem changes as the environment of the society/organization changes and more over the technology gets change. This is also very true that the technology changes very drastically as compared to the old era and to make society accustomed with the technology are bit easier in comparison to have trust on the technology. Thus, to keep in mind, one has to focus on the following factors:

DOI: 10.4018/978-1-5225-8933-4.ch020

1. *Provisional Functions*: The collective behavior must have the provision of contribution with control in the group/organization. This may include (i) Services, (ii) Documentation, (iii) Verified and validated information, (iv) Stored Data security and (v) Authentication verification at each step.
2. *Work Approach*: The approach and task defined in any group/organization depends on its nature and objective. However, the fundamental approaches are based on the following concepts: (i) Calibration, (ii) Monitoring, (iii) Job sharing, (iv) Communication and (v) Training.
3. *Required Resources*: For accomplishing the work with a particular approach, certain resources are required and it's well known that the resources may be shared in various approaches or may be recursively used in used one approaches. This may be due to the following reasons: (i) External queries, (ii) Internal queries, (iii) Problem solving, (iv) System monitoring and (v) System calibration.
4. *Work Technologies*: This is the most important and difficult task to choose among the existing one. There are many techniques which resembles one or other with minute differences. Conceptually, but had a huge impact if wrongly chosen. Thus, one has to very clear in their objectives and outcomes. In general, to name a few the techniques may be used for (i) shared information, (ii) applying hardware and software, (iii) Monitoring the information, (iv) storage optimization and (v) computational priorities. The idea brings togetherness from the complex system. The complex system modeling is very difficult due to its global environment components which directly or indirectly interconnected. These have the impact on climate, ecosystem, health, human brain, education and infrastructure. The following are the seven major sub-systems of the complex system.
    a. Game theory
    b. Non linear Dynamics
    c. Networks
    d. System Theory
    e. Pattern Formation,
    f. Evolution & Adaptation.
    g. Collective Behavior.

The components which demonstrate the environment of collective behavior are (i) Social dynamics, (ii) Collective Intelligence, (iii) Self – organized critically, (iv) Phase – transition, (v) Synchronization, (vi) Herd Mentality, (vii) Agent – based modeling (viii) Ant – colony optimization, (ix) Particle swarm optimization and (x) Swarm behavior. The collective behavior is the response to the unexpected events emerged which do not follows any rules and regulations. There are many theories which explain the collective behavior.

1. Contagion Theory – The theory is based on the emotional driving of the activities which either rational or irrational.
2. Convergence Theory – The similar attitude people comes together to intensify the sentiments. One can also say that it is based on the "learning theory".
3. Emergent Norm Theory – Based on the facts of mixed people mentality and motions.
4. Value Added Theory – Based on the above three theories with the added factors of location, weather and current situation environment wise.
5. Complex Adaptive System Theory – The above theories are just the affect of the instances of the synergy. This theory dealt with the patterns, path discovery and dependence, new entities and many more.

The technology plays an important role to demonstrate and address a wide range of social impact. The chapter focuses to demonstrate their capacity of the block chain to create scalable impact on collective behavior and to indentify the subfield that needs to be addressed to mitigate challenges in its applications. Though, the blockchain popularity is in the financial market, but in current scenario, the society is enhanced with the new technology with new solutions and models. It helps in transforming the inefficient operations to humanize the society. The general architecture leads to steps forward for covenant promises with the preservation of the traditional factors and theories. Consider case in point, the loans can be sanctioned to the individuals without the proper identification of documents. The problems of distributing aids for various governments polices and scheme for the different section of the citizens are handled with more transparency and in efficient manner. There are many social and organization impact applications where the blockchain plays a vital role as emergent technologies which is powerful and long term, to name a few era, health tracking, voter records, and education data. The chapter delineates a framework to guide policy makers and social impact organizations which have long term implications. The framework use the approach of blockchain to relates with the collective behavior key questions, design and analysis by examine the key attributes with its applicability.

The chapter will sum up with the discussion of Blockchain tools which will enhance the transforming process. The discussion will also highlight on the challenges and complexity that will arise while implementing to smooth the progress of the transition to a rational collective behavior dynamics. It describes the Agent Based Modeling and Ant Colony Optimization components of the CB.

BACKGROUND

Joseph Lubin et. al., (2018) put their efforts to express the early Blockchain applications, i.e., financial, and the future of the Blockchain applications that will change over the organization, societies, institutions and many more not merely at local stage but also at the global stage. The point they quoted, it's the fact that the tools of Blockchain are in their infant stage and will mature slowly but surely day by day. This will be through the iterative use of the technology for the transformation of the social structure that consists of the technology used for individual as well as the collectives and examine the projected and uncontrolled consequences followed by the development of the new technologies. The article enhanced with the possibility of self-governing identity, consumer service tokens and work in economics. The smart contracts will help in the participation of the individuals which will prove true in the longer run. This concept will avoid the problem of "authoritarian paternalism" presented by the author William Easterly (2006).

Philip Boucher (2017-2018) elaborated the change occurred in one's life by the Blockchain technology. In spite of its use in currency transactions it may apply on other tasks which are not related with finance like e-voting, document accessible at appropriate instance, supply chains, digital media and various types of communal services like health care, economic benefits, self-executing contracts, road map for companies to operate themselves with human intervention devoid. Further, the tasks that can be performed for the services such as land records maintenance, boost productivity, support compliance, land registries, patient records to name a few. The development of the Blockchain technology would be in manner where the impact must be significant at the common social stages of individual or collective.

Marcella Atzori (2015) focused on the existence of the Blockchain technology in connection to business, politics and society at broader level. With the help of the artificial intelligence, the Blockchain technology will derive the agents which are self-sufficient in order to perform the tasks at their own. The author also extended the description by enhancing the requirements of well established & multi-disciplinary efforts through each and every area where human knowledge plays an important role in respect to theory of politics, humanities and social sciences to best access pitfalls, rewards and results.

Walid Al-Saqaf, et. al., (2017) emphasizes on the opportunities and challenges for the technology on the social impact. The article objective is to understand the factors on society that are responsible in relation to the probable impact of Blockchain technology with its pros and cons like self-sufficiency, risk in recentralization, government resistance, trust, equality facts and factors, unequal access, transparency, accountability and limits of anonymity and many more. Though, the Blockchain technology is in infant stage but will facilitate the progress in online identity, fraud, human trafficking, hoax, autonomous membership and liberty to expression.

In 2018, the pwc (UK) believed that there are following five global shifts with reference to the smart city which are reshaping the world, (i) rapid urbanization, (ii) demographic and social changes, (iii) technological breakthroughs, (iv) shift in global economic power and (v) climate change and resource scarcity. To name a few, the major areas where the Blockchain technology can have high impact are healthcare, education, intelligent government services, economy and employment, safety, waste management, citizen participation.

Young H.P. (2005) quoted that the social dynamics can be very complex due to their high complexity. The author designed the framework for analyzing the asymptotic behavior of a wide variety of agent based models. The Markova chain theory makes the quantitative predictions about the long-run probability of various outcomes and thus avoids the hazards of drawing conclusions solely from simulation.

In 2017 the Cognizant reported the glimpse of the financial institutions that how are they making themselves ready to adopt the new technology especially in the Asia-Pacific region. The reason behind is to empower the institutions with trusted and flexible transactional applications with an eye on security, privacy, scalability and interoperability challenges.

Fidanova S. et. al.,(2018) proposed the hybrid Ant Colony Optimization (ACO) algorithm to solve the workforce problem, which is a combination between ACO and an appropriate local search procedure. The main idea is to remove part of the workers in the solution in a random way and to include new workers in their place. The focus is on the reduction of the assignment cost.

BLOCKCHAIN

According to Don & Alex, the blockchain is a digital ledger that meant for not only the financial transaction but virtually everything of value. There were many definitions which describes the blockchain in terms of the distributed ledgers and economics. In order to describe the blockchain in simplest form that covers the entire applications is bit intricate. Thus, at bests of the effort, the simplest definition is "the distributed invariant records that were time-stamped sequenced in the respective domain". In the blockchain, the term block is the collection of the records that are grouped to form the blocks and are actually the data blocks which in short term as block and chain is the cryptographic principle used to bind the blocks with each other in secure manner. The information in the blockchain dependable for the actions involved in the event is transparent and open to all. The blocks can transfer the information automatically in secure form by the verification process which can be done by number of distributed computers on the internet. The verified inimitable information is further the part of chain.

Table 1. Key attributes of blockchain

Distributed	The participants of social and organization have the full transparency
Immutable	Untouched and non modifiable records
Secure	Cryptographic Records
Programmable	Ability to be programmed
Time-Stamped	Records added is time sequenced
Anonymous	Identity of the participant
Trust	Belief in direct communication without the intervention of any centralized authority
Unanimous	Globally validity of records.

It deals with inefficiencies and maneuver with respect to social dynamics for the improvement of the one's living. Due to its property of immutability and decentralization, it approaches to engender transparency, make available verification, and build up trust from corner to corner among various organizations. The prospective of Blockchain technology in this chapter is in relation to view of collective behavior. Though, till date the major focus is on the financial applications, but still many researchers are working on the possibilities of the Blockchain such as healthcare domain, education domain, etc. which will transform the society, institute and the organization. Thus, it refers to an iterative collective behavior process that will observe its anticipated or not projected consequences. The affect is based on the aspect of the adoption of the new technology by the society and the organization. At what extent it gets utilized. Hence, for the proper implementation one has to keep an eye on the working style where it can be incorporated and acceptable by the world easily.

There are many applications other than the bitcoin, such us purchase of online tickets, where the operators move the complete ticket purchasing process through the credit card to the blockchain. In this the ticket is the new block in the blockchain that is also a record of the entire transaction which contain the complete validity of the ticket for the said duration. There are many more examples and can be illustrated with the music, eBooks, reservations, stock exchange etc. can eliminate the involvement of the third party and connect the retailer and consumer directly. In short, the blockchain formulate the world-shattering transformation.

The following are the advantages of the blockchain which describes the reason of its popularity and trust area.

- It is distributed with the decentralized property.
- The data is secured in the block with the cryptography process.
- The data cannot be corrupt in the block as it is immutable.
- The data in the block is transparent and available as and when require.

The above can be summarized in three main properties (i) Transparency, (ii) Immutability and (iii) Decentralization with the additional properties as Programmable, Anonymous, Time-stamped and Unanimous. The table 1 illustrates the key attributes of the blockchain.

The figure 1 depicts the operation process of blockchain. To build the unchanged blocks of information, the process commence with the validation of the transaction all the way through distributed network. The process initiated with the participant's request in the form of the transaction which is broadcasted

Figure 1. Blockchain operational process

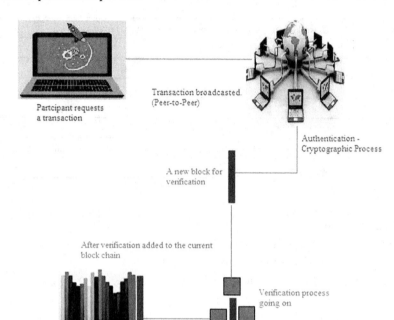

(peer-to-peer) to a set of computers generally termed as nodes. The node authenticates the cryptographic process (by means of existing algorithm) with the verification process. The verified block may contain the records, contracts, crypto currency and many more information. After the verification of the transaction over, the transaction is collectively with other transactions form the block and the new block added to the current blockchain and hence the process gets completed.

The major negative aspects of the Blockchain technology in concerned with collective behavior in organizations are

- **Performance:** In spite of various advantages the Blockchain technology suffers with the drawbacks but with the hope that as the technology become more mature the performance may increase. In this, the every transaction must be secure through digitally signed using the cryptography may be public or private. Thus, the computation increases at both level (source for creation and destination for verification).
- **Work Consensus:** In any organization or group, the efforts are to put in ensuring the work consensus among the individuals. Thus, the focus is on to adopt the appropriate mechanism which might involve significant communication and involvement of the individuals with the concept of rollback that will leads towards the computational complexity and operational redundancy.
- **Flexible Governance:** the group or the organizations are dependent on the government policies and if any changes in the dynamics occurred the resultant is in situation of uncertain authoritarian. This will have the direct impact on the complexity in implementation of the Blockchain and also reflects in the large energy consumption.

- **Work Culture Approval:** Though the Blockchain applications offer a variety of quick solutions, but require the major changes or the complete changeover of the existing system. Hence, these transformations reflect on the work culture of any group or organization. Always the question remains open that how can it be welcome by the members and the organization/society/group.
- **Preliminary Cost:** The advantage is in the diminution of the cost, but at preliminary level the cost could be restraint.

COLLECTIVE BEHAVIOR PROSPECTIVE OF BLOCKCHAIN

Collective behavior is actually framed as the "power of many". The fact is that the smartest organizations are not the ones with the intelligent individuals, but to a certain extent those with the ability to swiftly summative can influence with their collective intelligence. It somehow the top management of an organization fails at certain point, the resultant is neither in collapsing state of the organization nor have the adverse effect on the society with the distribution of the power. Not only they help to overcome the problem but also save the organization or group from eradication. This is the importance on one side but the other side of the coin also has a different story. The performance of collective behavior gets affected by the Diversity of opinion. Due to different perception, one's opinion gets affect the behavior.

The block chain gives the social and organizational collective behavior to built and create the ability to secure the information with its verification in the form of digitization. The collective behavior is also not remaining unaffected with the latest technologies. The following are the areas where blockchain affects the collective behavior.

1. **Social Connections:** The common characteristics are grouped and executed with the positive impact after the verification and validation process. A derivative could be applied to the society when meet certain benchmark with the use of the blockchain technology and enabling the applicability automatic.
2. **Sharing Outlook:** In today's world the sharing of the views through the social media is proven and in practice too. The blockchain opens a gateway where there is no interaction of the third parties and a direct peer-to-peer transaction took place. In general, there will be no norms and the individual reputation plays an important role on the collective behavior.
3. **Funding Agencies:** Blockchain took the opportunity to ease the work of funding to agencies by creating the validation of the group/individual according to the need and requirement for the beneficial of the society or organization. Thus, is keeping one step ahead using the technology.
4. **Governance:** Blockchain helps the organization in decision-making by making it transparent and verifiable with the digital information. The impact of the governance through the blockchain on the collective behavior will result in changes in the parameter's characteristics.
5. **Intellectual Property Protection:** The usage of the internet resulted in the production of the digital information which may be new or reproduced infinitely and thus, the changes occurs for the theft of the intellectual property. The blockchain technology will help in creating the peer-to-peer distribution system where the individual know that who all are using their intellectual property. This property will reduce the chanced of mishandling of the information on one hand and on other will help to create the environment which will be beneficial to the society and organization for growing up.

Figure 2. Collective behavior dynamics

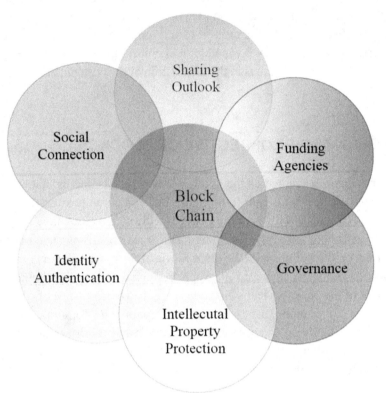

6. **Identity Authentication:** As with the increase of the internet usage, some mechanism is require to authenticate the identity of the group/individual/organization. A good reputation is the most significant condition for conducting transaction online based on the information provided on the net. This is very complex problem due to the variations in the norms from state to state and country to country. Hence, the blockchain will maintain the track of the previous transactions and could be abridged through the cross institution client verification, and at the same point in time will augment monitoring and analysis effectiveness.

The figure 2 represents the responsibility of the blockchain in the collective behavior dynamics. The amalgamation of the dynamics is essential and the resultant is that it's not the professional or code developers show. Now, for the best results of the blockchain completion, the interdisciplinary endeavor from all the era of collective development where knowledge/wisdom works with the benefits and permissible risk factors.

From the above discussion, it is very clear that the blockchain is the mechanism that involved every unit to its highest accountability. This emphasize on the fact that it keeps the record with its validity not only at one master file but a distributed linked master file with a secure validation mechanism.

While applying the changes, the organization's management or the government must perform the planning implementation in intelligent manner by keeping in view of the participants' culture, emotions and behavior patterns. They must also analyze the effects on the resultant design, its structure and

Figure 3. State of technology

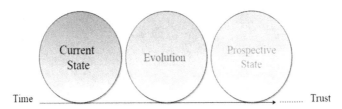

technology systems. The stakeholder psychological contracts must be well understood by the system engineers as the technology handles the new innovations but still the focus is on TRUST. Trust is crucial for any civilization and thus it should be for technology too. The Blockchain gain the TRUST as no one know about the bitcoin miner, but still the world rely on the mining algorithms that the system will successively work. One even not bother to have the TRUST as one of the measuring attribute while considering various key attributes. As the scenario changes, the meaning and the value of the TRUST also gets effected. The figure 3 illustrates the state of the technology impact on the group/organization. It presents the state technology from the current state to the future after the transition state and it tend towards the TRUST.

The collective behavior is having its own importance due to the factors that it has the collective intelligence. The collective intelligence works on the theme that the task must be efficiently taken by everyone in the group with the collective performance for a shared ambition. The technology helps to do by keeping the information processed to be knowledge ready with supportive hardware and software. The collective intelligence is the compilation of the (i) information which congregates from the experts (group/organization) and the associated data/knowledge/information or wisdom, (ii) Provisional function with work approach which is based on the hardware and software required for processing the provisional functions by the expert from the group or organization and (iii) Resource requirement and Work Technology is on the combination of the data/information/knowledge/wisdom and the required hardware & software for the technology in use. The above concept is represented in figure 4. Collective intelligence helps out in decision process from various perceptions of the individuals, having different level of harmony among individuals and the intellectual level. Thus, the focus is on the 3Cs, (i) cognition, (ii) coordination and (iii) cooperation. The collective intelligence plays a vital role in upgrading the success rate of any organization and the group.

In order to maintain the blockchain process intact, the group/organization must be familiar with the symbolic manipulation in the collective behavior. These symbols will help in understanding the group/organization and thus ease in understand the behavior of the society with respect to that group/organization. The symbolic manipulations are:

1. **Algorithmic (Automatic Transfer of the Symbols):** Digital information authentication and its relevance.
2. **Typographic (Automatic Reproduction and Transmission of Symbols):** The basis of any society/organization with objectives and outcomes.
3. **Literate (Optimization of the Symbols Manipulation):** Efficient prediction of the information on the basis of the knowledge and wisdom data hierarchy.
4. **Scribal (Self Conversation of Symbols):** Systematic knowledge.

Figure 4. Collective intelligence

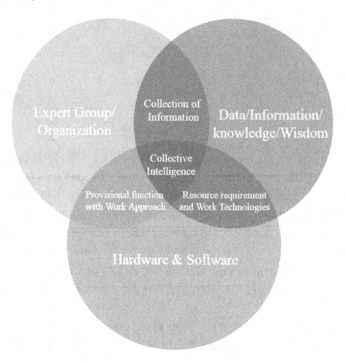

In order to have an elucidation of the problem, the organization / group make sure the involvement of each member. There are many techniques for integrating the context of member's opinion and observation. The aggregation mechanism has the influence to transform the situation into favorable or adverse, but to know well in advance is still an open challenge as the prediction of one's perception is not well defined. The blockchain helps in envisage the situation which is dependent on the aggregation. It will keep track of the group past behavior with keeping an eye on the characteristics of the individual with the level of the intelligence. This will be based on the knowledge and previous experience in the said situation well in advance. As it is well known that the phenomenon of collective behavior is not visible in plain sight because it illustrates about the psychology of individual which reflect in the said situation. In short, blockchain can assist the group/organization to visualize the situation at point in time so that the timely decision can improve the authentication of the authority. It follows the business impact and insight intelligence of neighbor's behavior by maintaining the chain of individual's cognition, i.e., collective cognition.

The two components were discussed to shape the collective behavior components for any group/organization in optimize and efficient behavior.

AGENT BASED MODELING (ABM)

The system operates with the help of agents and the agent may be the instrument, mediator, manager and many more whose function is to changeover or communicate within the system circumstances. The efficiency is in the selection of the mechanism and the procedure used to incorporate in the system. The vital important feature of any agent is used to model the system of homogenous agents or heterogeneous agents with significant interaction. It is used for simulating the action and interactions of individual or group/organization to have a look on the outcomes of the efforts proposed on the system as a complete process. The ABM can visualize as a network of the agents and process commence from lower level to higher level which cumulate the level behavior. Hence, the resultant is the collective behavior intelligence of agents on the path which may or may not interact with the neighbor's path (it's not necessary that the agents are independent for all the process of the system). The complete path is the outward appearance of chain and to implement the ABM under the umbrella of blockchain, the blockchain is composed of

1. **Block Degree Based on the Agent's Extent:** To which group/organization of smaller imperceptible entities attached jointly to turn out to be larger perceptible entities.
2. **Block Strategic Heuristic Function:** To determine the exact position in the blockchain.
3. **Supportive Knowledge Base System by Means of Appropriate Procedure:** To adapt when to update the blockchain on responsive changes in the group/organization.
4. **Operational Strategies and Environment:** Refers to reach the objective of the group/organization by optimum and efficient utilization of the individuals' strength and the environment which reflect the impact on achieving it.

The blockchain varies as per the nature of the system for which the ABM is to perform. The system may be (i) Complex, (ii) Exploratory, (iii) Descriptive and (iv) Validate. Thus, for the Complex ABM the blockchain will assist to identify the knowledge mechanism blocks of one or more analogous systems. For the Exploratory ABM, the blockchain give a hand to analyzing the previous track of individuals' and is feasible for proof-of-concept. For the Descriptive ABM, the blockchain illustrates the possibilities of the new perspective from the old with its description by comparing with the analogous systems, and for the Validate ABM, blockchain will facilitate in validation and verification of the information a block consists of.

The figure 5 illustrates the role of the blockchain in ABM and working with the blockchain, the system avails its important property of decentralization. Thus the smart contract is between the various types of the ABM system. The smart contract facilitates the transaction with the automatic trust; agree-

Figure 5. Impact of blockchain on ABM

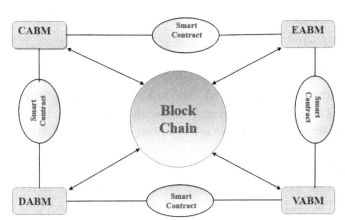

Figure 6. Hybrid blockchain architecture

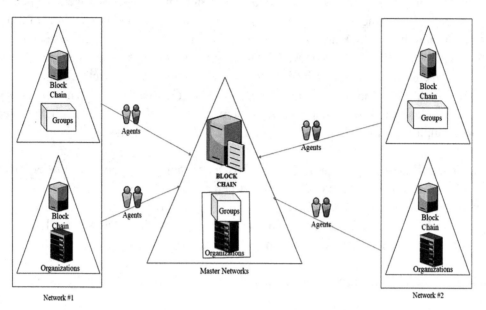

ments and related software objects for contribute into the group/organization. This can be processed by the self executable actions on the basis of the predefined rules and regulations and thus, the agreement without any intervention will sustain.

The blockchain for group and the organization has its strengths and weaknesses. The group blockchains are more apparent and flexible in sharing the information but are expensive and slow in nature. On the other hand the organization blockchains are focused on the rules and having a touch of centralized but bring out high throughput and fast. To improve the blockchain formation of the group and organization, one can form the hybrid blockchain by combining the advantages of the both the blockchains. The figure 6 portrays the hybrid blockchain ABM architecture. The hybrid blockchain ABM is the multi-realization of the knowledge base mechanisms of multilevel organization or of analogous groups. This will useful for approximate the structure of the group/organization from the activities and events role played by the individuals in the world and on the other hand will assist the top management or authorities that which set of the individuals with the knowledge mechanism an environment are more likely to have the convenient collective behavior intelligent. For this reason, the hybrid blockchain will maintain the master network that will regularly judge for its parent network by means of the agents and can straighten out the transaction by the agents were some disagreement arrives. The resultant will be in the terms of the selection of the individuals with the cognitive intelligence level.

The input of the blockchain are well defined at originate of the system (at any level) and then authorities can calibrate the components of the blockchain to know the cognitive intelligence evolution level among the individuals. On the basis of the analysis the changes can be made at the components level in order to achieve stability by analyzing the fellow felling as well as ill felling between and within the group/organization. The blocks can be trained at certain well defined norms for realistic environment with the relation ascertain based on the current rational level of the group/organization. The blockchain is now get classified on the selected level of the group/organization in relation with the individuals' thinker level to upgrade the societal level. The agents' eventual can changes the level of thicker and can maintain the long-term relationships in comparison to short-term relationship.

Figure 7. Updating the block

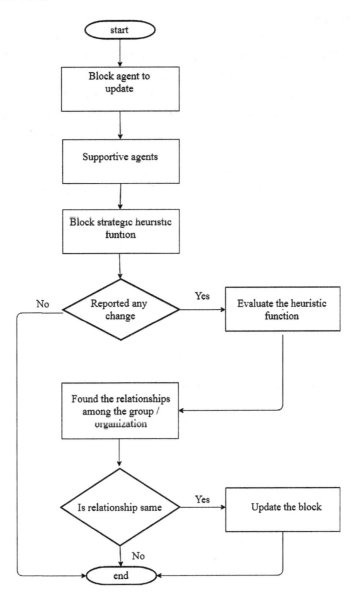

The blockchain agent defines the following agent roles for the group/organization.

Individual role: The sense of the social behavior in an individual which is the starting point of collective behavior. This may include the patience level, friendship level, fellow feeling, dedication and work style towards the society and the very important is moral. These can be acquired by analyzing the master blockchain. This agent can include the following category of the individuals as quite agents, participated agents, constructive agents, destructive agents and obedient agents.

Chief Officer (Authority) role: On one hand they have to update the information of the individual and on the other hand they themselves are individual. So the role is very sophisticating and has to handle with care.

The following flowcharts will depict the dataflow for updating the blocks in blockchain and updating the relationships among the blocks. The figure 7 mainly accepts the input from the blockchain agent and other supportive agents. It uses the block strategic heuristic function to report any changes from the previous update. If the function value reported no change then the blockchain will not encompass any change otherwise the new block will get updated on the evaluation of the block strategic heuristic function.

Once the decision for updating the block is over the next step is to identify the relation between two blocks agent on the group/organization. If the relation is positive correlation then groups has larger perceptible entities otherwise the groups are imperceptible. If there relation had no change then the groups are impartial.

The behavior of the individual agents imitates the group/organization which relies on certain mechanism. The validity of the blocks must be incorporated in the complete process as to legality the group/organization.

Advantages

1.   Blockchain provides the operational platform for agents to deal with the hypothesis.
2.   The blockchain agents are more capable to control the experimental theories generated well in time and can support it when such instances can occur.

Figure 8. Updating the groups according to relationships

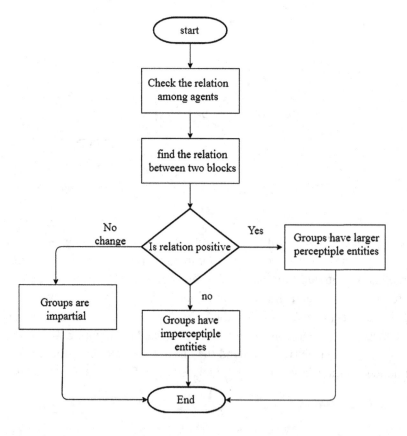

3. The organization is having the various managerial levels and the blockchain treats as multilevel organization and at every level the agents were clearly distinguish the various level. The blockchain facilitate the agent properties and the interaction among the agents at various levels can be observed.
4. Blockchain have the better control and one way or another optimize the systematic planning process for social dynamics.

ANT COLONY OPTIMIZATION

In order to analyze the collective behavior of the organization, one has to learn the group and individual behavioral performance and activities. The major aim is to enhance the skills of individuals/resources in the course of the workforce planning in terms of size, type, knowledge, wisdom, experience and information. The workforce planning is the group effort of the human resource management and the finance, to observe and discover the talent and contribute as per the future prospects with the appropriate gaps and solution workforce map. In continuance, to formulate the intellectual judgment on the subject of the future prediction of any organization/groups the challenging job is to distribute and coordinate the task in a group/organization in order to get the optimum utilization of the person and resources to avoid the overloading. The Ant Colony Optimization (ACO) will help in assigning the task in optimum and efficient manner. The purpose to do so with the help of ACO across the defined group or organization to carry out the well defined task efficiently. In this section, the blockchain concept is proposed which will consider the features to estimate the collective behavior with respect to the group/organization environment. Today, the social dynamics are governing with the government policies and it becomes the responsibilities of the officers to provide the services timely with the high success rate. The success rate depends on (i) speedy delivery without any hazard, (ii) collective satisfaction and (iii) duration it last long. Thus, there is a need to have a flexible and dynamic model that facilitates the group/organization with improvement in the cognitive behavior. The model should be optimizing to satisfy and incorporate the changes as early as possible. Hence the Meta heuristics application can show the way towards the solution which is not only reasonable but also reach within permissible time limit. For solving such cases, the ACO gained the popularity and have the results up to the mark. The hybrid ACO algorithm under the umbrella of blockchain approach is proposed in this section. The proposed approach is characterized by the heuristic information utilization, adequate parameters and local-optima methods. The ACO is based on the blockchain; each block has a direction which expresses its utility and cost. The block contains the demands and services required by the group/organization with the required/current weights. The number of blocks and the number of times it has been accessed can be reflecting the decision. The goal is to extract the speedy information with minimum cost, deliver the information and to know the stream of the collective decision.

Hybrid ACO Blockchain

A block consists of the following components: (i) multiple blockchain networks indicator, (ii) types of the group/organization, (iii) cost of the service, (iv) time of the service and (v) the meta heuristic function. The blockchain presents a motivated meta heuristic function which will be used successfully in order to obtain the high quality solution to the optimization problems in efficient time complexity. It basically works on the heuristic search and knowledge base module. The knowledge base module dealt with the

Figure 9. Hybrid blockchain ACO

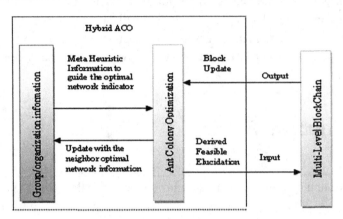

information that used for the optimizing the process to speed up the search process. The heuristic search dealt with the local as well global search throughout the solution space and combining it termed as the meta heuristic. The local heuristic with reduce the number of the searches in the respective blockchain. The figure 9 illustrates the architecture. The following are the blockchain components that help in the above said processes

1. **Network Indicator Optimization:** It will found the proper chain of blocks related to the network of groups with the help of the heuristic information. This dealt mainly to discover the minimum number of the blocks which fulfills the time constraint imposed. The heuristic information used to upgrade the knowledge of the network optimization which enhances the eminence selection. In order to initiate the process, the selection is done randomly for the blocks in a chain. Thereafter, update the heuristic information. The process is to continue till the termination condition rose or reached the threshold value. The architecture of hybrid ACO is illustrated in the following figure 9. The meta heuristic information of group/organization is transferred to the Ant colony optimization and the updated information is again transferred to the group/organization, if required. The multi-level blockchain will have the input derived from the ACO and on the foundation of the optimization the block is updated and if it is essential it will be the productivity which may be the input of the ACO.

2. **Parameters Initialization:** The parametric values must be initializing at this point and also have the insight vigilance on the parameters. If found some parameters are of the flexible than based on their previous optimization performance, the new value must be assigned. The block clustering with the priority information is also required for the appropriate initialization.

3. **Derived Feasible Elucidation:** With the help of the ACO the feasible elucidation of the group from the network indicator optimization is derived from the possible rationalization the group. This is the necessity as only 20 to 25 percent blocks were initialized and the reality is the knowledge is in multilevel blockchain.

4. **Blocks Update:** The blocks were getting updated according the information received from the neighbor optimal network blockchain. The selected blocks are also govern with defined rules and are also optimize by the local as well as the global meta heuristic information.

The following is the operational flow of the algorithm in which the process of derived feasible elucidation and blocks update will iteratively continue till reaches to the termination condition

Network indicator optimization → Parameters initialization → Derived feasible elucidation → Blocks update. The utilization of the heuristic information, weighted sum approach which is generated on the basis of the multiple objective functions and local optimization techniques exemplifies the hybrid ACO principally.

Advantages

The advantages of the ACO is well known as speedy detection of the best solution, distributed computation keep away from untimely convergence, heuristic will lend a hand for early solution and agents collective interactions with the inherent parallelism. The disadvantages of the ACO also become the advantages with the collaboration of blockchain. For example, the blocks are updated by meta heuristic information and hence maintain the appropriate selection process for the best derived elucidation. The dependent sequence becomes the independent and significant as per the scenario.

CONCLUSION

The blockchain technology gains the significant attention to individuals, groups/organization and legislators across the world. In general, the governments of the nation allocate the budgets and launch the schemes for the poorer, handicaps, health, insurance and many more to serve the society. The same is provided to the groups and the organization governed by the government. Unfortunately, the benefits of the budgets and scheme are out of the reach the real needy individuals which reflect the social dynamics. The same concept is adopted in the groups' as well as organization. The chapter describes the impact of collective behavior as one of the dynamics on the group/organization. The group or the organization is considered as multilevel complex setup where the interdisciplinary interaction of the individuals accomplished. For this, the blockchain technology is discussed seeing the importance of it. The technology is appropriate only at the time when several parties (individuals' from group/organization) contribute the data (component's services) and required common information. The general introduction is followed by the role of the blockchain on the collective behavior, i.e., how the key attributes of the blockchain influence the various areas of the collective behavior. This provides the improvement in customizing the local social collective behavior contexts supported by the blockchain. Blockchain supports the spectators and the members to hold the accountability of each other in the group/organization. It enhances the complete coordination (production, planning, operational) and the sense of the responsibility. Further, the chapter introduces the two components of the collective behavior which demonstrate the environment (i) Agent-Based Modeling and (ii) Ant Colony Optimization. These components illustrate the role of the agents and optimization in the blockchain effective working with respect to the group/organization. The novel approach is characterized by the utilization of the heuristic information, flexible parameters to get adjusted on the basis of the information, local optimization techniques and the action on the relationship survival.

The blockchain took the edge of the challenges with respect to the social dynamics. Earlier the major challenges that alleviated were

1. Adaptability
    a. It amplifies the involvement at every step of process in the group/organization.
    b. Increase the empowerment
    c. Enhancement of the system with the integration of additional services with ease.
2. Accountability
    a. More reliable on availing the services.
    b. Build the strong bond between the government, management and the employees.
    c. Immediate incorporation of the changes occurred at any permissible level through interconnection of the systems.
3. Efficiency
    a. Efficient in delivering the services to the target cluster of individuals.
    b. Well-timed execution guaranteed the efficiency of the system.
4. Transparency
    a. Direct peer to peer communication.
    b. Clear transparency in all the settlements.
    c. No leakage in service providing to individuals.

Though, the blockchain gain the significant importance and made the understandable clarification to many challenges, but still the lots of challenges are still unturned. Still it's not accepted nor has faith by the general public. It has to acquire acceptance in sensitive and insightful problems. The ground reality is that still many of the citizens are uncomfortable to access the internet and are not rely on the digital applications. For the final fruition of the blockchain technology all the sectors (government, non-government, private and public) must put the efforts together.

DISCUSSION QUESTIONS

Q1. What is the role of the collective behavior in the world of digitization?

Q2. How important is the collective behavior in decision making with respect to diverse group/organization.

Q3. What are the various components of the collective behavior for the knowledge and its consequences?

Q4. How can the efficiency of any group/organization are improved through blockchain.

Q5. "The induction of blockchain technology will have change in the working style of organization". Comment.

Q6. What are various measures of success rate with the impact of blockchain on the organization?

Q7. What is the mechanism of the blockchain to work as a tool for optimization task?

Q8. How the blockchain does helps in fighting against the world of antisocial activities.

Q9. What is the necessity of the knowledge of contracts and heuristic information for the successful functioning of the blockchain?

REFERENCES

Almeida, V., Getschko, D., & Afonso, C. (2015). The Origin and Evolution of Multi Stakeholder Models. *IEEE Internet Computing*, *19*(1), 74–79. doi:10.1109/MIC.2015.15

Arentz, T. A. (2013). An Agent-Based Random-Utility-Maximization Model to Generate Social Networks with Transitivity in Geographic Space. *Social Networking, 35*(3), 451–459. doi:10.1016/j.socnet.2013.05.002

Blockchain. (2018). *The next innovation to make our cities smarter*. Retrieved from www.pwc.in

Blum, C. (2005). Beam-ACO – Hybridizing Ant Colony Optimization with Beam Search: An Application to Open Shop Scheduling. *Computers & Operations Research, 32*(6), 1565–1591. doi:10.1016/j.cor.2003.11.018

Burke, W. (2008). *Organizational Change: Theory and Practice* (2nd ed.). Sage Publications.

Burke, W., & Litwin, G. (1992). A Causal Model of Organizational Performance and Change. *Journal of Management, 18*(3), 523–545. doi:10.1177/014920639201800306

Chanyapurn, C. (2016). *Here's what Asian Leaders are Doing with Blockchain Technology*. Blommber Technology.

Chen, S. (2017). A Blockchain Based Supply Chain Quality Management Framework. *e-Business Engineering (ICEBE), IEEE 14th International Conference*, 172–176. 10.1109/ICEBE.2017.34

Close, K. (2016). Almost Nobody Trusts Financial Institutions. *Money*.

Cognizant Report. (2017). *The Future of Blockchain in Asia-Pacific Digital System & Technology*. Author.

Cummings, D. (2016). *Use Cases of Ethereum in Different Sectors 2016*. Academic Press.

Desai, V. (2017). *Counting the Uncounted: 1.1 Billion People without IDs*. Academic Press.

Dirk, A. (2017). *The ICO Gold Rush: It's a Scam, it's a bubble, it's a super Challenge for Regulators*. University Luxembourg Law Working Paper 11.

Doerr, B. (2012). Why Rumors Spread so Quickly in Social Networks. *Communications of the ACM, 55*(6), 70–75. doi:10.1145/2184319.2184338

Doug, J. G. (2018). Blockchain for Social Impact: Moving Beyond the Hype. *Technical Report*. Stanford Graduate School of Business.

Drahota, A., & Dewey, A. (2008). The Sociogram: A Useful Tool in the Analysis of Focus Groups. *Nurs. Re., 57*(4), 293–297. doi:10.1097/01.NNR.0000313489.49165.97 PMID:18641498

Eric, P. (2016). *Blockchain: Democratizes Trust Distributed Ledgers and the Future of Value*. Technical Report. Deloitte.

Fehler, M. (2005). Techniques for Analysis and Calibration of Multi-Agent Simulations. Lecture Notes Computer Science, 3451, 305-321. doi:10.1007/11423355_22

Flint & David. (2005). *The User's View of Why IT Projects Fail*. Gartner Report.

Garcia, M. (2015). A process for developing efficient agent-based simulators. *Engineering Applications of Artificial Intelligence, 46*, 104–112. doi:10.1016/j.engappai.2015.09.003

Garcia, M. (2016a). A hybrid approach with agent-based simulation and clustering for sociograms. *Inf. Sci.*, *345*, 81–95. doi:10.1016/j.ins.2016.01.063

Garcia, M. (2016b). A technique for automatically training agent-based simulators. *Simulation Modelling Practice and Theory*, *66*, 174–192. doi:10.1016/j.simpat.2016.04.003

Garcia, M. (2017). A technique for developing agent-based simulation apps and online tools with nondeterministic decisions. *Simulation Modelling Practice and Theory*, *77*, 84–107. doi:10.1016/j.simpat.2017.05.006

Hassan, S. (2011). Friendship dynamics: Modeling social relationships through a fuzzy agent-based simulation. *Discrete Dynamics in Nature and Society*, *2*, 118–124.

Jin, F. (2013). Epidemiological Modeling of News and Rumors on twitter. In *Proc. 7th workshop on Social Network Mining and Analysis*. ACM. 10.1145/2501025.2501027

Joseph, L. (2018). Blockchain for Global Development. *Innovations, 12*(1/2), 10-17.

Kelman, S. (2005). *Unleashing Change: A Study of Organizational Renewal in Government*. The Brookings Institute.

Kotter John, P. (1998). Winning at Change. *Leader to Leader*, *10*(10), 27–33. doi:10.1002/ltl.40619981009

Lapointe, C., & Fishbane, L. (2015). *The Blockchain Ethical Design Framework*. Georgetown.

Lawson, E., & Price, C. (2003). The Psychology of Change Management. *The McKinsey Quarterly*.

Lim, K. K., Ong, Y.-S., Lim, M. H., Chen, X., & Agarwal, A. (2008). Hybrid ant colony algorithm for path planning in sparse graphs. *Soft Computing*, *12*(10), 981–994. doi:10.100700500-007-0264-x

Lin, J. W., & Lai, Y. C. (2013). Online formative assessments with social network awareness. *Comput. Educ.*, *66*, 40–53. doi:10.1016/j.compedu.2013.02.008

Lin, S., & Kemighan, B. W. (1973). An Effective Heuristic Algorithm for the Traveling Salesman Problem. *Operations Research*, *21*(2), 498–516. doi:10.1287/opre.21.2.498

Marcella, A. (2015). *Blockchain Technology and Decentralized Governance: Is the State Still Necessary?* Academic Press.

Marsden, P. (2010). *Social Commerce: Monetizing Social media*. London: GRIN Verlag.

Mclean. (2017). Melbourne's RMIT to Explore the Social Sciences of Blockchain. *ZDNet*. Retrieved from http://www.zdnet.com/article/melbournes-rmit-to-explore-the-social-science-of-blockchain/

Microsoft. (n.d.). *What is Blockchain?* Author.

Miller, R. (2017). *The Promise of Managing Identity on the Blockchain*. Academic Press.

Ostroff, F. (2006, May). Change Management in Government. *Harvard Business Review*. PMID:16649704

Peyton Young, H. (2005). Social Dynamics: Theory and Applications. *Computational Economics*, 1–45.

Philip, B. (2017). How Blockchain Technology Could Change Our Lives. *European Union*, 1–24.

Pisa & Juden. (2017). *Blockchain and Economic Development: Hype vs. Reality. Technical Report.* Center for Global Development.

Santos, S. J. D. (2015). Association Between Physical Activity, Participation in Physical Education Classes, and Social Isolation in Adolescents. *The Journal of Pediatrics*, *91*(6), 543–550. doi:10.1016/j.jped.2015.01.008 PMID:26113429

Sweet, T. M., & Zheng, Q. (2017). A mixed membership model-based measure for subgroup integration in social networks. *Social Networking*, *48*, 169–180. doi:10.1016/j.socnet.2016.08.001

Thiele, J. C., & Grimm, V. (2010). NetLogo meets R: Linking agent-based models with a toolbox for their analysis. *Environmental Modelling & Software*, *25*(8), 972–974. doi:10.1016/j.envsoft.2010.02.008

Tommy, K., & Erik, P. (2018). What Blockchain Alternative Do You Need? In *Workshop on Cryptocurrencies and Blockchain Technology (LNCS)*, *11025*. Springer.

Vitalik, B. (2016). *Privacy on the Blockchain*. Ethereum Blog.

Walid, A., & Nicolas, S. (2017). Blockchain technology for social impact: opportunities and challenges ahead. *Journal of Cyber Policy*, 1-17.

Walter, F. E., Battiston, S., & Schweitzer, F. (2008). A Model of Trust Based Recommendation System on Social Network. *Autonomous Agents and Multi-Agent Systems*, *16*(1), 57–74. doi:10.100710458-007-9021-x

Williamson, D. (2010). Social Network Demographics and Usage. *eMarketer*.

Wüst, K., & Gervais, A. (2018). Do you need a Blockchain? *Conference on Blockchain Technology*.

Chapter 21
Sustainable Supply Chain Management in the Era of Digitialization:
Issues and Challenges

Ravinder Kumar
Amity University, India

ABSTRACT

In the last two decades the term sustainable supply chain management (SSCM) has become quite popular. Organizations are working on sustainability of their supply chain (SC). Sustainability covers environmental, social, and economic aspects of different supply chain management activities. Organizations are continuously working in the direction of making their processes and product green. On the environmental front, use of renewable source of energy, reducing waste of energy, reducing carbon footprints is important. Simultaneously, reuse of products, re-cycling, and following environmental standards while disposing off is also recommended. In this chapter, the author has identified 13 issues and challenges of SSCM from literature review and expert opinion. Simultaneously, the author has also identified nine new technologies of modern time used in industries. Further, the author has tried to analyze the linkage between the challenges of sustainability and intelligent technologies by Jaccard's similarity coefficient methodology.

INTRODUCTION

In last two decades the term sustainable supply chain management (SSCM) has become quite popular. Organizations are working on sustainability of their supply chain (SC). Sustainability covers environmental, social and economic aspect of different supply chain management activities. Organizations are continuously working in the direction of making their processes and product green. On environmental front, use of renewable source of energy, reducing waste of energy, reducing carbon footprints is important. Simultaneously reuse of products, re-cycling and following environmental standards while disposing

DOI: 10.4018/978-1-5225-8933-4.ch021

off is also recommended. On similar front while implementing sustainable practices in business, social aspect of processes and polices keeping in mind the SC members i.e. suppliers, vendors and customers should also be framed and implemented.

In current scenario, digitalization of organizations has raised the global competition to new heights of quality and service standards. Digitalization of organizations has influenced the management of supply chain management too. So organizations can take advantage of intelligent technologies while dealing with issues and challenges of SSCM.

In this chapter author has identified thirteen issues and challenges of SSCM from literature review and expert opinion. Simultaneously author has also identified nine new technologies of modern time used in Industries such as: Internet of things (IOT), Additive manufacturing, System integration, Big data, Augmented reality, Simulation, Cyber security, Cloud computing and Autonomous robots (elements of Industry 4.0). Further author have tried to analysis the linkage between the challenges of sustainability and intelligent technologies by Jaccard's similarity coefficient methodology. By this analysis author tried to observe possibility of reducing/managing these challenges with the help of new technologies. The sustainability issues and modern technologies are identified keeping in mind the Indian scenario and recent trends.

From analysis author observed that intelligent manufacturing techniques such as simulation, augmented reality and big data have similarity of 88% with challenges of sustainability. This mean that these techniques can help in managing sustainability challenges. Similarly intelligent techniques such as IOT, additive manufacturing and autonomous robots working with techniques like simulation, augmented reality and big data have similarity of 86% with challenges of sustainability. This implies that these intelligent manufacturing techniques help in managing challenges of sustainability in developing countries at both micro and macro-level when applied together in coordination.

SUSTAINABILITY AND SUSTAINABLE MANUFACTURING

U.S. Department of Commerce (2010) defined sustainable manufacturing (SM) as "creation of manufactured products that use processes that are nonpolluting, conserve energy and natural resources, and are economically sound and safe for employees, communities and consumers". The basic concepts of lean, green and sustainable manufacturing are explained graphically in Figure 1. India as a growing economy is using its natural resources like land, hydrocarbons, water and minerals at a very faster rate. Demand of basic amenities of industrial development like energy and raw materials are very high. Excessive and unsystematic use of hydrocarbons and other natural resources leads to pollution of land, air and water and overall growth seems unsustainable (Mittal et al., 2013). Sustainable manufacturing means ability to sustain, producing less-waste or carbonless manufacturing (Bhanot et al., 2015). Practices of reprocess, recreate and recycling make both products and processes sustainable in long run. Intelligent and interconnecting production processes can help in reducing pollution and waste of natural resources (Kulatunga et al., 2013). Three aspects of sustainability are shown in Figure 2.

In today's globalised trend, the collaboration of academia and industry professionals is imperative when it comes to identifying the solutions for the sustainability issues (Bhanot et al., 2015).

On the way to sustainability there are number of challenges. Current manufacturing trends have become extremely competitive in the global market. Sustainability has three basic fronts in manufacturing i.e. economic, environmental and social (Mutingi et al., 2017). To be globally competitive, organizations

Figure 1. Lean vs Green vs Sustainable Manufacturing

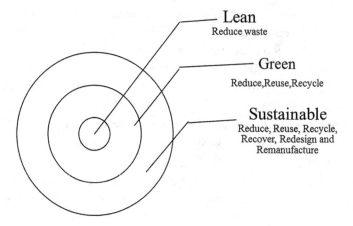

should focus on drivers and barriers of green manufacturing and strategically plan to reduce the barriers (Mittal et al., 2013). Sustainability assessment framework for manufacturing sector consists of elements/performance measures to improve organizational policies, people, products, processes, and performance from triple bottom line perspective (Bhakar et al., 2018). These days' sustainability approaches, reducing barriers to implement sustainability and integration sustainability into business are gaining popularity (Stewart et al., 2016). Identifying, prioritizing green manufacturing barriers is gaining popularity these days (Mittal et al., 2014). Organizations need to strategically plan for value creation through sustainable manufacturing and should have a future vision for sustainable products, processes and systems (Badurdeen & Jawahir, 2017). From literature review author have identified different issues and Challenges on the path of sustainability both at micro and macro level (Table1).

SUPPLY CHAIN MANAGEMENT

SCM integrate all business functions and members of chain for timely flow of products, information and revenue (Mentzer et al., 2001). The basic idea behind the SCM is that companies and corporations involve themselves in a supply chain by exchanging information regarding market fluctuations and production capabilities. Supply chain members are dependent on each other and these dependencies can be managed by improving coordination between members of supply chain (Disney & Towill, 2003). To

Figure 2. Sustainability and its different issues

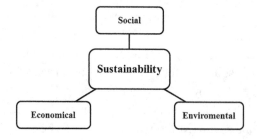

sustain in global competition, individual competencies of enterprises are not enough. It's the time of chain to chain competition and chain to chain development (Koh et al., 2006).

SUSTAINABILITY AND SCM ON MICRO-LEVEL

Supply chain can be said sustainable if it manages the products from suppliers to customers and their associated returns, accounting for social, environmental and economic impacts (Barbosa-Povoa, 2014). These days awareness toward the environmental and social problems is increasing, which motivates the companies to focus and pay more attention toward sustainable issues. The United Nations Global Corporate Sustainability report has observed considerable shift in the attitude of corporates towards sustainability (Compact, 2013).

Economic slowdown has even strength the belief in principle of sustainable supply chain in last one decade. But companies are facing problems due to different challenges of supply chain sustainability (as discussed in Table 1) and failing in implementing its measures. Sometimes the companies are not able to understand the meaning and fails in implementing the best practices of sustainability. Companies need to take strategic decisions to reduce uncertainty and risks toward implementing sustainability in SCM.

Sustainability of SC is "flow of material, money, and information among SC members by considering its social, economic and environmental aspects" (Seuring & Miller, 2008). However, a widely accepted definition for sustainability was proposed by (Brundtland, 1987), which describes meeting today's needs of the people without compromising the future needs of the generations to come. Different supply chains have faced different issues in recent times such as flaws in automobile design, harmful chemicals in baby's toys, and dangerous chemicals in food (Roth et al., 2008). By developing vendors, improving services at suppliers ends can help in improving performance of organizations and can help in reducing lot of accidents (Yuan & Woodman, 2010). Motivating working atmosphere for staff can help in producing better quality products, reduce health and safety costs, so adoption of social sustainability issues in supply chain add economic benefits (Carter & Rogers, 2008). Social sustainability deals with social assets of organization such as skills, ability of employees (Sarkis et al., 2010). Discussion on social issues in the supply chain is primarily focused on inter and intra level issues and customer issues (Klassen & Vereecke, 2012). Hug et al. (2016) discussed different social sustainability issues in Bangladesh's apparel industry. Authors explored different issues concerned about employee's health, working conditions, quality of life and rights. Sodhi & Tang (2011) observed different aspects of social sustainability such as safe drinking water, healthy food, services of health and educations in developing countries. Competitive sustainable manufacturing is a fundamental enabler of globalization and also proposing global & local approaches for manufacturing (Jovane et al., 2017).

In current emerging & developing economies, the governments and stakeholders are under immense pressure to sustain manufacturing growth for improving quality of life of their citizens. The manufacturing sector consumes lot of natural resources & energy and in results emits lot of green-house gases. Green manufacturing & Sustainable manufacturing currently faces many challenges but government, stakeholder & industries should need to provide motivation to make this change possible. Motivating factors concerning environmental, social & economic perspectives are prioritized in this paper (Mittal & Sangwan, 2014). Awareness about all perspectives of sustainability is growing in companies. Authors examined the social perspective of sustainability & its influence on successful business models (Schonborn et al., 2019). Manufacturing is concerned by all the three perspectives of sustainability (economic, environmental & social). In manufacturing industry decision makers only focuses on technological & economical perspectives but social perspective in sustainable manufacturing is also important which helps in evolving business models (Sutherland et al., 2016).

Table 1. Issues and challenges of sustainable supply chain management

S.No.	Issues & Challenges	Descriptions	References
1	Lack of end-to-end engineering in value chain	Need of Sustainable Supply Chain Management (SSCM) practices & Improved SCM	Carvalho et al.(2018), Bhakar et al.(2018), Badurdeen & Jawahir (2017)
2	Poor knowledge of customers/ Original equipment manufacturers (OEMs) about sustainable products	Less orientation & awareness toward sustainability	Kulatunga et al. (2013), Bhanot et al. (2015), Mittal et al.(2013), Bhakar et al.(2018), Mittal & Sangwan (2014), Luthra et al.(2011), Koho et al.(2011)
3	Lack of dedicated funds for sustainable technologies/ practices	Poor Government support, Neglected approach for judicious funds distribution	Kulatunga et al. (2013), Bhanot et al. (2015), Mutingi et al.(2017), Stewart et al.(2016), Luthra et al.(2011)
4	Lack of standardized metrics or performance benchmarks	Absence of practicable guidelines and parameters	Bhanot et al. (2015), Mutingi et al.(2017), Bhakar et al.(2018), Moldavska & Welo(2017), Stewart et al.(2016), Badurdeen & Jawahir (2017)
5	Lack of support from top management	Lack of awareness/ knowledge about long term benefits of Sustainability	Stewart et al.(2016), Bhakar et al.(2018), Mittal & Sangwan(2014), Luthra et al.(2011), Bhanot et al. (2015)
6	High cost of sustainable techniques/practices	Initial high costs for sustainable technology implementation	Bhanot et al.(2015), Mutingi et al.(2017), Stewart et al.(2016), Luthra et al.(2011)
7	Shortage of Green energy	Need of improving green power production and distribution	Bhanot et al.(2015), Stewart et al.(2016)
8	Lack of skills in employee about sustainable technologies	Lack of training & skills up-gradation programs towards new concepts of sustainability	Mutingi et al.(2017), Bhakar et al.(2018), Stewart et al.(2016), Sutherland et al. (2016).
9	Implementation and operational challenges	Difficulties in implementing and operating sustainability technologies	Mutingi et al.(2017), Luthra et al.(2011), Ariffin & Ghazilla (2015), Sutherland et al. (2016).
10	Weak Legislation on sustainable practices	Absence of environmental laws.	Mittal et al.(2013), Mittal & Sangwan (2014)
11	Poor implementation of laws	Complexity of law	Mittal et al.(2013), Steward et al.(2016), Mittal & Sangwan (2014)
12	Technological Risk	Risk of implementing new technology, Outsourcing of environmental problems	Mittal et al.(2013), Steward et al.(2016), Mittal & Sangwan (2014)
13	Lack of foreign direct investment (FDI) and import-export policies focused on sustainable practices	Technological and financial motivation from Global partners	Geng et al.(2017), Zhang et al.(2018), Khan et al.(2018)

SUSTAINABILITY AND SCM ON MACRO-LEVEL

In developing countries of Asia continent, organization type, size, ISO certification and planning for export affects its green supply chain management practices and performance (Geng et al., 2017). In developed countries renewable energy is a driver for green logistics and supply chain practices and finally contributes to sustainability on environmental and economic front. Zhang et al. (2018) observed that green practices of logistics affects directly the foreign direct investments, green energy generators and import-export policies.

Use of hydrocarbons as energy source produce greenhouse gases and has negative effect on environmental and economic sustainability. Use of renewable energy and green practices can reduce harmful effect of logistics operations on sustainability (environmental and economic front) (Khan et al., 2018). Khan et al. (2017) observed that emission of pollutants like carbon di-oxide and other greenhouse gases influence organization profit, and different shares of gross domestic product like industry, manufacturing and service. Green practices and global practices of transportation help in improve exports and sustainability (Khan & Qianli, 2017). Combined focus on both environmental and operational issues with the help of environmental management practices improves competitiveness of Indian firms (Das, 2018).

DIGITALIZATION AND DIGITAL TECHNOLOGIES

Modern competition on quality and service standards has raised the need of digitalization of manufacturing facilities all over the globe. Digitalization of organizations has influenced the management of supply chain management too. So organizations can take advantage of intelligent technologies while dealing with issues and challenges of SSCM. In this chapter author has identified nine new technologies of modern time used in Industries from literature review and experts opinion such as:

- **IOT**: IOT is the ever-growing infrastructure of internet-connected devices which can transfer data and commands between points (Mourtzis et al., 2016; Wollschlaeger et al., 2017).
- **Additive Manufacturing:** Advances in 3D printing and other enabling technologies mean that product components can be made lighter and for less cost (Iyer, 2018; Zhang et al., 2018).
- **System Integration:** A business can have many different pieces of hardware of software which need to be utilized in unison so that maximum value can be derived (Santos et al., 2017; Mengoni et al., 2017).
- **Big Data:** Businesses can create huge volumes of data without realizing it and this data can be a source of untapped value for business improvement and growth (Vallhagen et al., 2017; Jain et al., 2017).
- **Augmented Reality:** Virtually augmenting what we can see with our own eyes with data and hidden systems can be immensely powerful when it comes to process and product improvement (Miller and Weising, 2018; Bauer et al., 2015).
- **Cyber Security:** Connected systems require optimized and current security so that your assets and information are safe from intrusion (Tvengea and Martinsena, 2018); Mueller et al., 2017).
- **Simulation:** It can often be more cost-effective to trial something in the virtual world than to make a physical prototype for each variable being tested (Taborga et al., 2018; Khan et al., 2016).

- **Autonomous Robot:** Robotics and artificial intelligence have evolved to a point where systems can operate to high standards on various tasks without constant human intervention (Pederson et al., 2016; Bahrin et al., 2016).
- **Cloud Computing:** IT services are increasingly being provided by the 'cloud' to generate cost and space savings as well as to offer innovative use models (Ramachandra et al., 2017; Alsmadi and Prybutok, 2018).

METHODOLOGY TO CHECK LINKAGE

Author has tried to analysis the linkage between the challenges of sustainability and intelligent technologies by Jaccard's similarity coefficient methodology. By this analysis author tried to observe possibility of reducing/managing these challenges with the help of new technologies. This technique was developed by Paul Jaccard. In this technique one coefficient (Jaccard's coefficient) is used for comparing the similarity and diversity of sample variables. Bag et al. (2019) observed that Jaccard's similarity methodology is more accurate and effective in all traditional similarity models.

Jaccard's Similarity Coefficient or Jaccard's Similarity Index compares two sets of data and finds out whether the data entries are same or identical. In other words, it is a measurement to check the similarity of two sets of data, where similarities range from 0% to 100%. If this similarity factor is high, then we can say that the data or population of each set are same. In order to calculate Jaccard's Similarity, from the Table 2, we take two columns, say IT 1 and IT 2, then we find out all the similar entries that include rating 1 from both the columns of IT1 and IT 2 and then we find total number of rating 1 from both the columns IT1 and IT 2.

Then we use following formula:

$$S_{ij} = \frac{Total\,number\,of\,1\,that\,are\,similar\,in\,both\,columns\,of\,i\,and\,j}{Total\,number\,of\,1\,in\,both\,columns\,of\,i\,and\,j}$$

Where i and j are for the number of columns which are being compared.

For example, if we are comparing entries of IT 1 and IT 2, then

Total number of 1 that are similar in columns of IT 1 and IT 2 = 3

Total number of 1 in both the columns of IT 1 and IT 2 = 8

So, according to the given formula:

$$S_{12} = \frac{Total\,number\,of\,1\,that\,are\,similar\,in\,both\,columns\,of\,IT\,1\,and\,IT\,2}{Total\,number\,of\,1\,in\,both\,of\,columns\,of\,IT\,1\,and\,IT\,2}$$

Similarity Coefficient for IT 1 and IT 2 is, $S_{12} = \frac{4}{7} = 0.57$

Similarly, all similarity coefficients are calculated for their respective filled in their respective cells to generate a matrix (Table 3(a) and Table 3(b)). Relationships are shown graphically by diagram known as dendogram (Figure 3).

Table 2. Intelligent technologies of digital era and sustainability issues incidence matrix

Challenges on the Path of Sustainability		Intelligent Technologies of Digital Era								
		IT1	IT2	IT3	IT4	IT5	IT6	IT7	IT8	IT9
C1	Lack of end-to-end engineering in value chain	1	1	1	0	1	1	1	1	1
C2	Lack of awareness on sustainability	1	1	0	1	1	1	1	1	0
C3	Lack of dedicated funds for sustainable technologies	0	0	0	0	0	0	0	0	0
C4	Lack of performance Standards on sustainability	1	1	0	1	1	1	1	1	0
C5	Lack of support from top management	0	0	0	0	0	1	0	0	0
C6	High cost of sustainable techniques/ practices	0	0	0	0	0	0	0	0	0
C7	Shortage of Green energy	0	0	0	0	0	0	0	0	0
C8	Lack of skills in employee about sustainable practices	0	0	1	0	1	0	1	0	0
C9	Implementation and operational challenges	1	0	1	1	1	1	1	1	1
C10	Weak Legislation on sustainable practices	0	0	0	0	0	0	0	0	0
C11	Poor implementation of laws	0	1	1	1	1	1	0	1	0
C12	Technological Risk	1	1	1	1	1	1	1	1	1
C13	Lack of FDI and import-export policies focused on sustainable practices	1	0	1	1	1	1	1	1	1

Note: IT1-Internet of things (IOT); IT2-Additive Manufacturing; IT3-Cloud Computing; IT4-Autonomous Robot;
IT5-Simulation; IT6-System Integration; IT7-Augmented Reality; IT8-Big Data; IT9-Cyber Physical System;
1 – Particular Intelligent technology can reduce corresponding challenge to Sustainability
0 = No significant impact of Intelligent technology on corresponding challenge to Sustainability

Table 3a. Similarity coefficient matrix

	IT1	IT2	IT3	IT4	IT5	IT6	IT7	IT8	IT9
IT1	0	5/7=0.714	4/8=0.5	5/7=0.71	6/8=0.75	5/8=0.625	6/8=0.75	6/7=0.86	4/6=0.67
IT2		0	4/8=0.5	5/7=0.71	6/8=0.75	5/8=0.625	5/8=0.625	6/7=0.86	3/7=0.43
IT3			0	4/8=0.5	6/8=0.75	4/9=0.44	5/8=0.625	5/8=0.625	4/6=0.67
IT4				0	5/8=0.625	5/8=0.625	5/8=0.625	6/7=0.86	3/7=0.43
IT5					0	6/9=0.67	7/8=0.875	7/8=0.875	4/8=0.5
IT6						0	5/9=0.56	6/8=0.75	3/8=0.375
IT7							0	6/8=0.75	4/7=0.571
IT8								0	4/7=0.571
IT9									0

Table 3b. Similarity coefficient matrix

	IT1	IT2	IT3	IT4	IT5	IT6	IT7	IT8	IT9
IT1	0	0.57	0.5	0.71	0.75	0.63	0.75	**0.86**	0.67
IT2		0	0.5	0.71	0.75	0.63	0.63	**0.86**	0.43
IT3			0	0.5	**0.75**	0.44	0.63	0.63	0.67
IT4				0	0.63	0.63	0.63	**0.86**	0.43
IT5					0	0.67	**0.88**	**0.88**	0.5
IT6						0	0.56	**0.75**	0.38
IT7							0	**0.75**	0.57
IT8								0	**0.57**
IT9									0

Figure 3. Dendogram showing relation between different factors

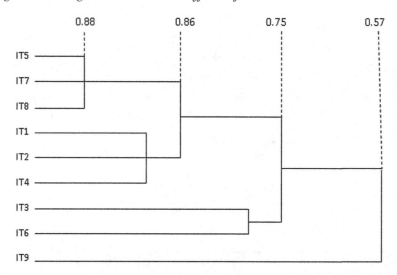

OBSERVATION FROM RESULTS OF METHODOLOGY AND DENDOGRAM

Few of key observations from results obtained from analysis and graphical representation shows that:

- Technologies IT5, IT7 and IT8 (i.e. intelligent technologies i.e. Simulation, Augmented Reality and Big Data analysis) if implemented together, then possess a similarity of 88% on the sustainability challenges. This implies that these technologies (IT5, IT7 and IT8) can help in managing challenges of SSCM.
- Technologies IT1, IT2 and IT4 (i.e., IOT, Additive Manufacturing and Autonomous Robot respectively)} and IT5, IT7 and IT8 if implemented together, then these modern technologies, possess a similarity of 86% with the sustainability challenges. This implies that these technologies can help in managing challenges of SSCM.

- Technologies IT3 and IT6 (i.e., Cloud Computing and System Integration respectively)}, IT1,IT2 and IT4 and IT5,IT7 and IT8 if implemented together, then these modern technologies, possess a similarity of 75% on the sustainability challenges (as shown in Figure 3). This implies that these technologies can help in managing challenges of SSCM.
- The overall similarity of these intelligent technologies with challenges to implement sustainability, if implemented together is 57%.

From above discussed points author observed that any industry need not to invest on all nine type of digital technologies but by choosing any pair of technologies from (IT5, IT7 and IT8), (IT1, IT2 and IT4) and (IT5, IT7 and IT8) etc. can solve different issues of sustainability.

CONCLUSION

Sustainable manufacturing, sustainable supply chain management and sustainable development are very commonly used terms these days all over the globe. But policy makers, government agencies and organizations working on ground level have to work altogether to make sustainability a success on both theoretical and practical front.

In this chapter, author has identified different challenge on the path of sustainable supply chain from literature review. In all, thirteen factors which are creating challenges for sustainability of supply chain and nine modern technologies have been identified from literature review and expert opinion. Analysis of the combination of technologies and sustainability challenges shows clear affinity in resolving challenges of sustainability by adoption of modern technologies.

A pair of simulation, augmented reality and big data analysis technologies (IT5, IT7 and IT8) shows an affinity to resolve sustainability challenges by 88% if implemented strategically with planning. Similarly pair of technologies such IOT, Additive Manufacturing and Autonomous Robot if implemented with simulation, augmented reality and big data analysis (IT5, IT7 and IT8), then these modern technologies, possess an affinity 86% in resolving the sustainability challenges. This implies that issues and challenges of sustainability can be resolved by modern technologies but need strategic planning and action accordingly. These finding can be helpful for both organizations of developed and developing economies.

DISCUSSION QUESTIONS IN CLASSROOM

- What is need of sustainable SCM?
- What are different elements of sustainability?
- What are modern digital technologies used in manufacturing organizations?
- What are different issues and challenges in the path of sustainability?
- What are different issues in adopting digital technologies in manufacturing organizations?

REFERENCES

Alsmadi, D., & Prybutok, V. (2018). Sharing and storage behavior via cloud computing: Security and privacy in research and practice. *Computers in Human Behavior*, 85, 218–226. doi:10.1016/j.chb.2018.04.003

Ariffin, R., & Ghazilla, R. (2015). Drivers analysis and barriers in green manufacturing practices in Malaysian SMEs: A preliminary findings. *Procedia CIRP*, *26*, 658–663. doi:10.1016/j.procir.2015.02.085

Badurdeen, F., & Jawahir, I. S. (2017). Strategies for Value Creation through Sustainable Manufacturing. *Procedia Manufacturing*, *8*, 20–27. doi:10.1016/j.promfg.2017.02.002

Bag, S., Kumar, K. S., & Tiwari, M. K. (2019). An efficient recommendation generation using relevant Jaccard similarity. *Information Sciences*, *483*, 53–64. doi:10.1016/j.ins.2019.01.023

Bahrin, M.A.K., Othman, M.F., Azli, N.N., & Talib, M.F. (2016). Industry 4.0: A review on industrial automation and robotic. *JurnalTeknologi, 78*(6-13), 137-143.

Barbosa-Póvoa, A. P. (2014). Process supply chains management–where are we? Where to go next? *Frontiers in Energy Research*, *2*, 23.

Baucr, W., Hämmcrlc, M., Schlund, S., & Vocke, C. (2015). Transforming to a hyper-connected society and economy–towards an "Industry 4.0". *Procedia Manufacturing*, *3*, 417–424. doi:10.1016/j.promfg.2015.07.200

Bhakar, V., Digalwar, A. K., & Sangwan, K. S. (2018). Sustainability assessment framework for manufacturing sector- a conceptual model. *Procedia CIRP*, *69*, 248–253. doi:10.1016/j.procir.2017.11.101

Bhanot, N., Rao, V. P., & Deshmukh, S. G. (2015). Enablers and Barriers of Sustainable Manufacturing: Results from a Survey of Researchers and Industry Professionals. *Procedia CIRP*, *29*, 562–567. doi:10.1016/j.procir.2015.01.036

Brundtland, G.H. (1987). *World Commission on Environmental and Development: Our common Future*. World Commission for Environment and Development.

Carter, C. R., & Rogers, D. S. (2008). A framework of sustainable supply chain management: Moving toward new theory. *International Journal of Physical Distribution & Logistics Management*, *38*(5), 360–387. doi:10.1108/09600030810882816

Carvalho, N., Chaim, O., Cazarini, E., & Gerolamo, M. (2018). Manufacturing in the fourth industrial revolution: A positive prospect in Sustainable Manufacturing. *Procedia Manufacturing, 21*, 671-678.

Compact, U. G. (2013). Global corporate sustainability report 2013. *UN Global Compact Reports*, *5*(1), 1–28. doi:10.5848/UNGC.5720.2014.0009

Das, D. (2018). The impact of Sustainable Supply Chain Management practices on firm performance: Lessons from Indian organizations. *Journal of Cleaner Production*, *203*, 179–196. doi:10.1016/j.jclepro.2018.08.250

Disney, S. M., & Towill, D. R. (2003). The effect of vendor managed inventory (VMI) dynamics on the Bullwhip Effect in supply chains. *International Journal of Production Economics*, *85*(2), 199–215. doi:10.1016/S0925-5273(03)00110-5

Feng, L., Zhang, X., & Zhou, K. (2018). Current problems in China's manufacturing and countermeasures for industry 4.0. *EURASIP Journal on Wireless Communications and Networking*, *2018*(1), 90. doi:10.118613638-018-1113-6

Geng, R., Afshin Mansouri, S., & Aktas, E. (2017). The relationship between green supply chain management and performance: A meta-analysis of empirical evidences in Asian emerging economies. *International Journal of Production Economics*, *183*, 245–258. doi:10.1016/j.ijpe.2016.10.008

Hug, F. A., Choudhary, I. N., & Klassen, R. D. (2016). Social management capabilities of multinational buying firms and their emerging market suppliers: An exploratory study of the clothing Industry. *Journal of Operations Management*, *46*(1), 19–37. doi:10.1016/j.jom.2016.07.005

Iyer, A. (2018). Moving from Industry 2.0 to Industry 4.0: A case study from India on leapfrogging in smart manufacturing. *Procedia Manufacturing*, *21*, 663–670. doi:10.1016/j.promfg.2018.02.169

Jain, S., Shao, G., & Shin, S. J. (2017). Manufacturing data analytics using a virtual factory representation. *International Journal of Production Research*, *55*(18), 5450–5464. doi:10.1080/00207543.2017. 1321799 PMID:28924330

Jovane, F., Seliger, G., & Stock, T. (2017). Competitive Sustainable Globalization General Considerations and Perspectives. *Procedia Manufacturing*, *8*, 1–19. doi:10.1016/j.promfg.2017.02.001

Khan, M., Wu, X., Xu, X., & Dou, W. 2017. Big data challenges and opportunities in thehype of Industry 4.0. *2017 IEEE International Conference on Communications(ICC)*, 1–6.

Khan, S. A. R., & Qianli, D. (2017). Does national scale economic and environmental indicators spur logistics performance? Evidence from UK. *Environmental Science and Pollution Research International*, *24*(34), 26692–26705. doi:10.100711356-017-0222-9 PMID:28956233

Khan, S. A. R., Qianli, D., SongBo, W., Zaman, K., & Zhang, Y. (2017). Environmental logistics performance indicators affecting per capita income and Sectoral growth: Evidence from a panel of selected global ranked logistics countries. *Environmental Science and Pollution Research International*, *24*(2), 1518–1531. doi:10.100711356-016-7916-2 PMID:27785719

Khan, S. A. R., Zhang, Yu., Anees, M., Golpîra, H., Lahmar, A., & Qianli, D. (2018). Green supply chain management, economic growth and environment: A GMM based evidence. *Journal of Cleaner Production*, *185*, 588–599. doi:10.1016/j.jclepro.2018.02.226

Klassen, R. D., & Vereecke, A. (2012). Social issues in supply chains: Capabilities link responsibility, risk (opportunity) and performance. *International Journal of Production Economics*, *140*(1), 103–115. doi:10.1016/j.ijpe.2012.01.021

Koh, S. C. L., & Tan, K. H. (2006). Operational intelligence discovery and knowledge mapping approach in a supply network with uncertainty. *Journal of Manufacturing Technology Management*, *17*(6), 687–699. doi:10.1108/17410380610678747

Koho, M., Torvinen, S., & Romiguer, A. T. (2011). Objectives, enablers and challenges of sustainable development and sustainable manufacturing: Views and opinions of Spanish companies. In *International Symposium on Assembly and Manufacturing (ISAM)*. IEEE. 10.1109/ISAM.2011.5942343

Kulatunga, A., Jayawickrama, M., & Jayatilaka, P. R. (2013). Drivers and barriers to implement sustainable manufacturing concepts in sri lankan manufacturing sector. *Proceedings of the 11th Global Conference on Sustainable Manufacturing - Innovative Solution*, 172-177.

Luthra, S., Kumar, V., Kumar, S., & Haleem, A. (2011). Barriers to implement green supply chain management in auto industries using Interpretes structural modeling technique-an Indian perspective. *JIEM*, *4*(2), 231–257. doi:10.3926/jiem.2011.v4n2.p231-257

Mengoni, M., Perna, A., Bevilacqua, M., & Giraldi, L. (2017). The role of business relationships in new product development. The case of Antrox-Nel Design. *Procedia Manufacturing*, *11*, 1351–1357. doi:10.1016/j.promfg.2017.07.264

Mentzer, J. T., DeWitt, W., Keebler, J. S., Min, S., Nix, N. W., Smith, C. D., & Zacharia, Z. G. (2001). Defining supply chain management. *Journal of Business Logistics*, *22*(2), 1–25. doi:10.1002/j.2158-1592.2001.tb00001.x

Mitta, V.K., Egede, P., Herrmann, C., & Sangwan, K.S. (2013). Comparison of Drivers and Barriers to Green Manufacturing: A Case of India and Germany. *Procedia CIRP*, 723-728.

Mittal, V. K., & Sangwan, K. S. (2014a). Prioritizing Barriers to Green Manufacturing: Environmental, Social and Economic Perspective. *Procedia CIRP*, *17*, 559–564. doi:10.1016/j.procir.2014.01.075

Mittal, V. K., & Sangwan, K. S. (2014b). Prioritizing Drivers for Green Manufacturing: Environmental, Social and Economic Perspectives. *Procedia CIRP*, *15*, 135–140. doi:10.1016/j.procir.2014.06.038

Moldavska, A., & Welo, T. (2017). The concept of sustainable manufacturing and its definitions: A content-analysis based literature review. *Journal of Cleaner Production*, *166*, 744–755. doi:10.1016/j.jclepro.2017.08.006

Mourtzis, D., Vlachou, E., & Milas, N. (2016). Industrial Big Data as a result of IoT adoption in manufacturing. *Procedia CIRP*, *55*, 290–295. doi:10.1016/j.procir.2016.07.038

Müller, J. M., Buliga, O., & Voigt, K. I. (2018). Fortune favors the prepared: How SMEs approach business model innovations in Industry 4.0. *Technological Forecasting and Social Change*, *132*, 2–17. doi:10.1016/j.techfore.2017.12.019

Müller, J. M., Kiel, D., & Voigt, K. I. (2018). What Drives the Implementation of Industry 4.0? The Role of Opportunities and Challenges in the Context of Sustainability. *Sustainability*, *10*(1), 247. doi:10.3390u10010247

Mutingi, M., Musiyarira, H., Mbohwa, C., & Kommula, V. P. (2017). *An Analysis of Enablers and Barriers of Sustainable Manufacturing in Southern Africa* (Vol. 2). WCECS.

National Manufacturing Competitiveness Council. (2006). *The National Strategy for Manufacturing*. Available from: http://nmcc.nic.in/pdf/strategy_paper_0306.pdf

Pedersen, M. R., Nalpantidis, L., Andersen, R. S., Schou, C., Bøgh, S., Krüger, V., & Madsen, O. (2016). Robot skills for manufacturing: From concept to industrial deployment. *Robotics and Computer-integrated Manufacturing*, *37*, 282–291. doi:10.1016/j.rcim.2015.04.002

Ramachandra, G., Iftikhar, M., & Khan, F. A. (2017). A Comprehensive Survey on Security in Cloud Computing. *Procedia Computer Science*, *110*, 465–472. doi:10.1016/j.procs.2017.06.124

Roth, A. V., Tsay, A. A., Pullman, M. E., & Gray, J. V. (2008). Unraveling the food supply chain: Strategic insights from China and the 2007 recalls. Journal Supply chain Management. *Global Rev. Purch. Supply, 44*(1), 22–39.

Santos, K., Loures, E., Piechnicki, F., & Canciglieri, O. (2017). Opportunities assessment of product development process in industry 4.0. *Procedia Manufacturing, 11*, 1358–1365. doi:10.1016/j.promfg.2017.07.265

Sarkis, J., Helms, M. M., & Hervani, A. A. (2010). Reverse logistics and social sustainability. *Corporate Social Responsibility and Environmental Management, 17*(6), 337–354. doi:10.1002/csr.220

Schönborn, G., Cecilia Berlin, C., Pinzone, M., Hanisch, C., Georgoulias, K., & Lanz, M. (2019). Why social sustainability counts: The impact of corporate social sustainability culture on financial success. *Sustainable Production and Consumption, 17*, 1–10. doi:10.1016/j.spc.2018.08.008

Seuring, S., & Miller, M. (2008). From literature review to a conceptual framework for sustainable Supply Chain Management. *Journal of Cleaner Production, 16*(15), 1699–1710. doi:10.1016/j.jclepro.2008.04.020

Sodhi, M. S., & Tang, C. S. (2011). Social enterprises as supply chain enablers for the poor. *Social-Economical Planning Science., 45*(4), 146–153. doi:10.1016/j.seps.2011.04.001

Stewart, R., Bey, N., & Boks, C. (2016). Exploration of the barriers to implementing different types of sustainability approaches. *Procedia CIRP, 48*, 22–27. doi:10.1016/j.procir.2016.04.063

Sutherland, J.W., Richter, J.S., Hutchins, M.J., Dornfeld, D., Dzombak, R., Mangold, J., … Friemann, F. (2016). The role of manufacturing in affecting the social dimension of sustainability. *CIRP Annals - Manufacturing Technology, 65*, 689–712.

Taborga, C. P., Lusa, A., & Coves, A. M. (2018). A proposal for a green supply chain strategy. *Journal of Industrial Engineering and Management, 11*(3), 445–465. doi:10.3926/jiem.2518

Tvenge, N., & Martinsen, K. (2018). Integration of digital learning in industry 4.0. *Procedia Manufacturing, 23*, 261–266. doi:10.1016/j.promfg.2018.04.027

U.S. Department of Commerce. (2010). *How does commerce define sustainable manufacturing?* Retrieved from .http://www.trade.gov/competitiveness/sustainablemanufacturing/how_doc_defines_SM.asp

Vallhagen, J., Almgren, T., & Thörnblad, K. (2017). Advanced use of Data as an Enabler for Adaptive Production Control using Mathematical Optimization–An Application of Industry 4.0 Principles. *Procedia Manufacturing, 11*, 663–670. doi:10.1016/j.promfg.2017.07.165

Wollschlaeger, M., Sauter, T., & Jasperneite, J. (2017). The future of industrial communication: Automation networks in the era of the internet of things and industry 4.0. *IEEE Industrial Electronics Magazine, 11*(1), 17–27. doi:10.1109/MIE.2017.2649104

Yuan, F., & Woodman, R. W. (2010). Innovative behavior in the workplace: The role of performance and image outcome expectations. *Academy of Management Journal, 53*(2), 323–342. doi:10.5465/amj.2010.49388995

Zhang, Yu, Hêriş, G., & Khan, S. A. R. (2018). The relationship between green supply chain performance, energy demand, economic growth and environmental sustainability: An Empirical evidence from developed countries. *The Central European Journal of Social Science and Humanities, 14*(4), 479-494.

Chapter 22
An Optimal Control Problem of Knowledge Dissemination

Pantry Elastic
IPB University, Indonesia

Toni Bakhtiar
ⓘ https://orcid.org/0000-0002-7426-1620
IPB University, Indonesia

Jaharuddin
IPB University, Indonesia

ABSTRACT

In this chapter, the authors develop an optimal control model of knowledge dissemination among people in the society. The knowledge transfer system is formulated in term of compartmental model, where the society members are categorized into four classes based on knowledge acquisition and their willingness to disseminate. The model is equipped with a set of control variables for process intervening, namely technical training for ignorant-immigrants, information dissemination through social media for solitariants and enthusiants, and technical training for solitariants. Optimality conditions in terms of differential equations system was derived by using Pontryagin minimum principle leading to the characterization of optimal control strategies that minimizing the number of solitariants, enthusiants, and ignorants simultaneously with the control efforts. The sweep method and the fourth order Runge-Kutta algorithm was implemented to numerically solve the equation systems. The effectiveness of the control strategies toward a set of control scenarios was evaluated through examples.

INTRODUCTION

Knowledge management is a framework to maximize the value and application of knowledge. It refers to a multidisciplinary approach to achieve the objective of organization by making the best use of knowledge in distributing and sharing. As a part of knowledge management system, knowledge dissemination (also known as knowledge transfer or knowledge exchange) plays crucial roles in ensuring the availability of

DOI: 10.4018/978-1-5225-8933-4.ch022

knowledge to those who may need it. Knowledge dissemination can be as simple as posting a news into social media, or it can be a time-consuming activity such as seminar and training. The right pathway for knowledge dissemination can be decided according to the format of knowledge, the user, the speed of change, and the speed of sharing. Milton's approach in classification of systems for capturing and disseminating knowledge includes formal-informal dimension on how supply of knowledge to users is conducted in either structured format or conversational text, as well as connect-collect dimension on how knowledge is recorded or communicated (Milton, 2010). The pros and cons of knowledge dissemination systems within each of Milton's four quadrants of learning approaches was highlighted by Kingston (2012). Four knowledge dissemination techniques were also examined in this report: informal-connect, formal-connect, informal-collect, and formal-collect. Communities of practice can be seen as an informal-connect approach in term of conversation among those who need knowledge and those who have knowledge. Formal-connect approach includes knowledge portals in information technology systems. Knowledge codification as a formal-collect strategy can be conducted by revealing additional indexing features of knowledge. While mentoring and training can be treated as either informal-connect or formal-connect.

A number of qualitative and quantitative models have been developed to describe various aspects of knowledge dissemination in knowledge-based organizations, with or without intervention (see for instance, Kelliher et al. (2010), Chen et al. (2014), Su et al. (2018), Li et al. (2017), and Liu et al. (2017)). In the field of operation and supply chain management, it has been identified opportunities and challenges of knowledge creation and dissemination for the future development. A review of the major developments during the past 25 years has been conducted and ways to accelerate some of them have been proposed (Roth et al, 2016).

Knowledge dissemination intervention can be defined as an active intervention to communicate information, data, or knowledge to a target audience through certain channels, using designed strategies such that it creates a positive impact on the acquisition of knowledge, attitudes, and practice (Lafrenière et al. 2013). A number of researchers in community empowerment have proposed different knowledge dissemination techniques. Some of these studies have demonstrated the success of intervention strategies using various media including audio-visual aids. Bell et al. (2005) introduced a knowledge dissemination model in education of Tanzanian smallholder farmers about mastitis in their dairy cattle. The effectiveness of interventions in the forms of diagrammatic handout, video, and village meeting (and their combinations) were evaluated against a control group of no intervention. Analysis using generalized linear mixed models suggested that all five interventions are more effective than no intervention.

Motivated by the same urges, this chapter aims at developing a dynamical intervention model of knowledge dissemination in a society. The authors adopt an approach generally used in epidemiological model by classifying society members into four different compartments based on knowledge acquisition and the willingness to share. To assess the effectiveness of the intervention strategies, the model is formulated in an optimal control problem. Therefore, it enables us to characterize the optimal intervention strategies in term of model variables and parameters.

The rest of this chapter is organized as follows. In Section 2 the authors overview some previous works carried out by other researchers, especially those relate to knowledge dissemination model and mathematical models of information transfer. Compartmental model of knowledge dissemination as well as its optimal control version proposed by the authors are respectively presented in Section 3 and Section 4. In Section 5, an example is pointed out to illustrate the effectiveness of control strategy. The authors conclude in Section 6.

RELATED WORKS

The conventional models of scientific knowledge dissemination face some consequences and limitations regarding the information overload, outdated notion of scientific contributions, ineffective organization, slower processes and outdated research activity rewarding (Baez, 2012). The internet has drastically changed the way we create, consume and disseminate data and information. Vast amounts of data are generated massively and continuously every second by machines, networks and human interaction on systems like social media in a number of new types of data such as messages, blog, conversations, photos, sensor data, video and audio. From the viewpoint of scientific knowledge dissemination, internet has offered new opportunities and challenges. The advent of internet emerges the new paradigm of scientific knowledge dissemination and collaboration. Kondratova and Goldfarb (2004) proposes generic architecture and design principles for a knowledge portal that fulfil the basic community of practice portal requirements. The requirements include a conversation space for online discussions on a variety of topics, a discussion forum for posing questions to the community, a shared workspace for synchronous electronic collaboration, a virtual laboratory for discussion or meeting, and a repository for documents storing.

The excellent work of Baez (2012) has identified models and developed tools and services for knowledge dissemination by embracing the benefits of the internet while addressing the problems caused by volume, variety, velocity and veracity of data. A web-based model of scientific contribution was proposed in this work, separating the nature of the contribution, the level of certification and degree of maturity, which enables us to have new perspective on knowledge creation and evaluation. In addition, the so-called liquid journal as a prototype of scientific journal for the web era and knowledge spaces for capturing, sharing and discovering scientific knowledge in all of its forms, and tools for knowledge sharing in seminars, conferences and courses, are prominent contributions of this work. These platforms are supported by space management systems for resources dissemination across multiple services on the web and universal resource lifecycle management system for scientific artifacts.

Since knowledge dissemination is a multifaceted complex process, the study on the fundamental nature of knowledge dissemination within an organization is emerged to effectively support the organization in managing knowledge. Lombari (2019) provides a note to advance existing theories in the field of knowledge transfer directed to propose advances on which are organizational performance and business process's main issues in the past, present and future perspectives. From mathematical modeling point of view, the dissemination of knowledge as an important part of knowledge management has been the topic of research for years. Yu & Zhang (2008) set up a system dynamic model of short-term and long-term knowledge dissemination within an organization in term of SIR and SI models. Rumor spreading in social networks, as a kind of knowledge dissemination, was studied by Zhao et al. (2012) in term of Susceptible-Infected-Hibernator-Removed (SIHR) model and was reviewed by Ndii et al. (2018). Further, Qichao et al. (2014) presented the information dissemination model in mobile social networks using graph theory. Kowalska-Styczen et al. (2018) performed more recent and advanced research on knowledge transfer within organization, where the factors influence the efficiency and effectiveness of knowledge dissemination was evaluated using cellular automata technique. Wang et al. (2015) presented an improved knowledge diffusion hypernetwork (IKDH) model where the knowledge will spread from the target node to all its neighbors. Study by Wilke et al. (2017) deals with the dissemination and implementation of research on the prevention of occupational skin diseases using quantitative impact analysis.

Study by Li et al. (2017) investigated the dynamic dissemination process of the knowledge in the cooperative learning network. The knowledge dissemination model of a cooperative learning network was constructed in the framework of complex network transmission dynamics theory. Two epidemic based models was proposed, namely the susceptible-infected-susceptible-leader (SISL) model and the susceptible-infected-removed-leader (SIRL) model. The former considers both students' forgetting and leaders' inspiration and the later allows students' interest in spreading and leaders' inspiration. It has been shown that both model can effectively describe the dynamic behavior of knowledge dissemination on cooperative learning network.

Literature study by Lafrenière et al. (2013) examined the knowledge dissemination interventions implemented in health research. It was deduced that most of interventions were evaluated in term of knowledge acquisition, changes in agents' attitudes, and changes in practice, provided a positive impact on the first two outcomes, but a limited one on the last.

It is worth mentioning that at the present time there are only a few researches using the optimal control framework to model the effect of intervention on knowledge dissemination process. From the perspective of epidemiology, Chen et al. (2014) developed a dynamical model for epidemic information dissemination over networks. Each node in the network is categorized into three states, namely susceptible, infected, and recovered states. In the infected state, a node receives the information and disseminates it. A node that refuses to receive the information, i.e., immune, is classified in recovered state. Otherwise, the node is still vulnerable to the information and is in susceptible state. The control capability, i.e., the ability to recover from infection, was expressed as a function of its distribution time and the optimal control problem is to determine the optimal signal distribution time in mobile and social networks. The best control was derived by utilizing Pontryagin minimum principle to minimize the accumulated cost caused by infected nodes jointly with the control effort. Liu et al. (2017) proposed a periodic impulsive knowledge dissemination model to improve the knowledge dissemination process. The model considers the quantity of knowledge already hold in the brain before guidance as state variable and the teaching effort as control variable. The teaching effort is defined as the portion of the remaining knowledge that needs to be taught correspond to the current learning performance, which is constrained by knowledge absorptive capacity of a learner. In particular, the optimal teaching strategy that maximizes the effectiveness of knowledge dissemination was investigated in the framework of discrete time optimal control theory.

KNOWLEDGE DISSEMINATION MODEL

In this chapter, the authors develop an optimal control model of knowledge dissemination among members of society, namely the DSEI model. It adopts the environment advanced by Cahyono et al. (2017) by which the society is categorized into four compartments, namely Disseminant (D), Solitariant (S), Enthusiant (E), and Ignorant (I). Variables $D(t)$ and $S(t)$ represent the number of people in society at time t who have knowledge and are willing to disseminate their knowledge, and those who have knowledge, but are not willing to disseminate their knowledge, respectively. While, variables $E(t)$ and $I(t)$ denote the number of individuals at time t in the society who have no knowledge, but they are willing to learn and are not willing to learn, respectively. The classification of DSEI model shares some similarities with that of SHIR model in Zhao et al. (2012), where Disseminant is similar to Spreader (or Infected in well-known SIR model), Solitariant comes close to Stifler (or Removed in SIR model), and an Enthusiant seems like a Hibernator. Both DSEI and SHIR models possess Ignorant class, which

Figure 1. The DSEI compartmental model

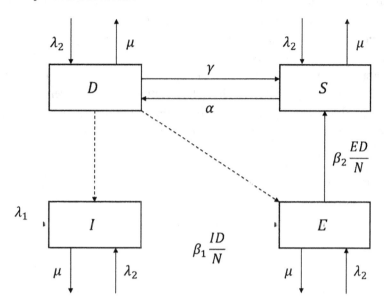

consists of individuals with no knowledge/rumor to spread. The DSEI compartmental model is depicted in Figure 1.

As shown in Figure 1, the DSEI knowledge dissemination model assumptions can be summarized as follows.

- Model consists of four compartments (disseminant, solitariant, enthusiant, and ignorant) and it is possible to categorize the member of society into a compartment based on his/her knowledge acquisition and willingness to transfer. The number of populations in compartments at time t given by $D(t)$, $S(t)$, $E(t)$, and $I(t)$, respectively. The total members of society at time t is denoted by $N(t) = D(t) + S(t) + E(t) + I(t)$.

- Individuals from outside, i.e., immigrants, with different knowledge acquisition and willingness to share may enter the society as new members with rate λ_2. In addition, there is a possibility with rate λ_1 that individuals from inside are promoted to be ignorant newcomers. These individuals can be seen as susceptible newborn babies in epidemiology model.

- The natural death rate is μ.

- The interaction between ignorants and disseminants may encourage an ignorant to become an enthusiant. The interaction between enthusiant and disseminants may motivate an enthusiant to become a solitariant. Both interactions are indicated by dashed lines in Figure 1. Terms $\beta_1 I / N$ and $\beta_2 E / N$ can be seen as the force of promotion or per capita contact rates, where β_1 and β_2 are the transmission rates.

- A solitariant may change his/her attitude in willingness to transfer knowledge with rate α. However, there is a possibility a disseminant decides to become a solitariant with rate γ, due to knowledge withholding.

Two significant improvements toward the work of Cahyono et al. (2017) are proposed in this model. Firstly, the authors relax the restrictions by considering an open society, i.e., society with inflow and outflow of members due to demographic changes: fertility, mortality, and immigration flows. The authors also assume that there is a possibility with certain rate that a disseminant can be transformed into solitariant compartment, for instance, due to knowledge withholding (Das & Chakraborty, 2018; Webster et al., 2008). Secondly, the authors introduce a number of intervening instruments in term of dynamical control variables. The dynamic of DSEI model in Figure 1 is mathematically represented by the following system of nonlinear ordinary differential equations:

$$\frac{dD}{dt} = \alpha S + \left(\lambda_2 - \mu - \gamma\right) D, \tag{1}$$

$$\frac{dS}{dt} = \frac{\beta_2 ED}{N} + \left(\lambda_2 - \mu - \alpha\right) S + \gamma D, \tag{2}$$

$$\frac{dE}{dt} = \frac{\beta_1 ID}{N} - \frac{\beta_2 ED}{N} + \left(\lambda_2 - \mu\right) E, \tag{3}$$

$$\frac{dI}{dt} = \left(\lambda_1 + \lambda_2 - \mu\right) I - \frac{\beta_1 ID}{N}. \tag{4}$$

OPTIMAL CONTROL MODEL

The theory of optimal control deals with the problem of determining a control law for a given process, normally expressed in a nonlinear ordinary differential equations system, such that a certain performance criterion is attained. Control theory as an extension of the calculus of variations has progressed rapidly since the work of Lev Pontryagin and Richard Bellman in the 1950s, and is now established as a leading research area of applied mathematics. The application of optimal control covers many areas of modeling and control in engineering, and nowadays are commonly applied in many other fields of sciences, such as population dynamics, disease transmission, and production-inventory management.

In a control model, the process that causes state variable $x(t)$ to change can be controlled, at least partially, by control variable $u(t)$. It is assumed that the rate of change of $x(t)$ depends on time t, $x(t)$ itself, and control $u(t)$, i.e., the process is given by $\dot{x} = f(x, u, t)$. In this section the optimal control model, i.e., model (1)-(4) equipped with a number of the so-called control variables, is presented. Optimality conditions as the main result is also provided in this section.

The Maximum Principle

Consider a system evolving in time. At any time t, the system is in some state, which can be described by state variables $x(t) = (x_1(t), x_2(t), \ldots, x_n(t))$. It is assumed that the process going on in the system can be controlled to a certain extent in the sense that there are a number of control variables $u(t) = (u_1(t), u_2(t), \ldots, u_m(t))$ that influence the process. The dynamic of the system is given by ordinary differential equations system $\dot{x} = f(x, u, t)$. Suppose that the state of the system is known at time $t = 0$, so that $x(0) = x_0$, where x_0 is a given vector in $\mathbb{R}^n$. It is associated with each control variable $u(t)$ and its response $x(t)$ the number $J = S(x(T), T) + \int_0^T f_0(x, u, t)dt$, where S is a scrap or salvage function which describes system in the final time. Here T is not necessarily fixed, and $x(T)$ might have some terminal condition on it at the end point T. The optimal control problem is a problem of finding a control law $u(t)$. among all admissible controls which brings the system from the initial state x_0 to a final state satisfying the terminal conditions such that J is either as large as or as small as possible. Such a control function $u^*(t)$ is called an optimal control and the associated path $x^*(t)$ is called an optimal path. J is often called the objective functional.

The necessary optimality condition for the existence of optimal control $u^*(t)$ is provided by the Pontryagin maximum principle (Pontryagin et al., 1962). Let $u^*(t)$ be a piecewise continuous control defined on $[0, T]$ which solves the control problem and let $x^*(t)$ be the associated optimal path. Then there exists a continuous and piecewise continuously differentiable function $p(t)$ such that for all $t \in [0, T]$:

1. 1. Optimal control $u^*(t)$ maximizes $H(x^*(t), u(t), p(t), t)$ for all admissible controls $u(t)$, that is

$$H(x^*(t), u^*(t), p(t), t) \geq H(x^*(t), u(t), p(t), t).$$

This condition can be achieved by solving $H_u = 0$.

2. State variable $x(t)$ and adjoin variable $p(t)$ satisfy the differential equations system $\dot{x} = H_p$ and $\dot{p} = -H_x$. We call the former dynamical system and the later adjoin system.
3. 3. The following transversality condition is satisfied:

$$(S_x - p)\delta x \mid_T + (H + S_t)\delta t \mid_T = 0.$$

In the case of $x(T)$ is free and $S \equiv 0$, then the transversaility condition is reduced to $p(T) = 0$.

Here H denotes the hamiltonian defined by

$$H\left(x,u,p,t\right) := f_0\left(x,u,t\right) + p\left(t\right)\cdot f\left(x,u,t\right).$$

In the case of linear H with respect to u, i.e.,

$$H = \psi\left(x,p,t\right) + \sigma\left(x,p,t\right)u,$$

the optimal control law governed by the first condition is lead to bang-bang control: $u^*\left(t\right) = u_{min}$ for $\sigma < 0$ and $u^*\left(t\right) = u_{max}$ for $\sigma > 0$, where u_{min} and u_{max} are respectively the lower and upper bounds of u. When the switching function σ is zero, then it refers to a singular control.

Model

In this work, the model by Cahyono et al. (2017) is reformulated in the framework of optimal control, by which it enables us to intervene the system by means a set of dynamical variables. As stated in Lafrenière et al. (2013), there are three forms of communication that can be regarded as intervention mechanisms in knowledge dissemination: written material, electronic material, and interpersonal communication activities or events. These forms of communication include newsletter, policy briefs, website, online registry of research evidence, seminar, and training. Obviously, other types of control strategies in term of dynamical control variables as per demographic changes, fertility, mortality, and immigration flows can also be introduced. However, in knowledge dissemination environment, it should be noted that fertility cannot be seen as newborn babies in epidemiology, instead newcomers that promoted into society of knowledge dissemination. In this case, early childhood education may be considered as an intervening instrument.

In this present work, the authors incorporate into the model three control variables as intervention instruments, namely training for ignorant-immigrants $u_1\left(t\right)$, information dissemination through social media for enthusiants and ignorants $u_2\left(t\right)$, and training for solitariants $u_3\left(t\right)$. Thus, model (1)-(4) is modified as follows:

$$\frac{dD}{dt} = \alpha u_3 S + \left(\lambda_2 - \mu - \gamma\right)D \tag{5}$$

$$\frac{dS}{dt} = \beta_2\left(1 + u_2\right)\frac{ED}{N} + \left(\lambda_2 - \mu - \alpha u_3\right)S + \gamma D \tag{6}$$

$$\frac{dE}{dt} = \beta_1\left(1 + u_2\right)\frac{ID}{N} - \beta_2\left(1 + u_2\right)\frac{ED}{N} + \left(\lambda_2 - \mu\right)E \tag{7}$$

$$\frac{dI}{dt} = \left(1 - u_1\right)\lambda_2 I - \beta_1 \left(1 + u_2\right)\frac{ID}{N} + \left(\lambda_1 - \mu\right)I, \tag{8}$$

where the following initial conditions are imposed

$$D(0) = D_0 > 0, S(0) = S_0 > 0, E(0) = E_0 > 0, I(0) = I_0 > 0, \tag{9}$$

and all terminal conditions $D(T), S(T), E(T)$, and $I(T)$ are assumed to be undetermined (free), with T is the control period. Thus, it is assumed in the model that training and information sharing among members can control the dynamics of the number of disseminants, solitariants, enthusiants, and ignorants in the society.

From equations (5) and (6) it is known that if the training for solitariants (u_3) is encouraged then the number of solitariants will be reduced by $-u_3 \alpha S$ to become disseminants. The control variable of information dissemination through social media for enthusiants and ignorants (u_2) will promote some enthusiants to become solitariants and those of ignorants to become enthusiants through their interaction with disseminants by $u_2 \beta_2 ED / N$ and $u_2 \beta_1 ID / N$ terms in (7) and (8), respectively. Both parameters β_1 and β_2 indicate how intense the interaction among ignorants, enthusiant, and solitariants. In this setting, it is assumed that it is not possible yet for an enthusiant as well as an ignorant to directly become a disseminant. Special training for ignorant-immigrants (u_1), if effectively delivered, will reduce the number of ignorant-immigrants by $-u_1 \lambda_2 I$.

From model (5)-(8), it is denoted by $x(t) = \left(D(t), S(t), E(t), I(t)\right)$ the vector of state variables and by $u(t) = \left(u_1(t), u_2(t), u_3(t)\right)$ the vector of control variables. The set of all admissible controls is given by

$$U = \{u(t) | 0 \le u_i(t) \le \overline{u}_i, t \in [0, T]\} \tag{10}$$

for $i \in \{1, 2, 3\}$. Thus, a bounded control strategy in a bounded period of control $[0, T]$ is considered with upper bound $\overline{u}_i$ reflects the practical limits on the maximum rate of control. If, for instance, $\overline{u}_i = 1$ is set, then a result of $u_i(t) = 0.5$ can be interpreted as control implementation with half effort. Further, if $\overline{u}_i = 0$ is assigned, then all control variables will be inactive and it refers to the model without control. It is preferred to implement controls with lowest possible effort. This objective along with the aim to have a society with more disseminating members is then formulated in the following performance index:

$$J = \int_0^T \left[A_1 S(t) + A_2 E(t) + A_3 I(t) + \frac{1}{2}C_1 u_1^2(t) + \frac{1}{2}C_2 u_2^2(t) + \frac{1}{2}C_3 u_3^2(t)\right]dt, \tag{11}$$

where A_i and C_i are balancing cost weights incurred by the size and the relative importance among compartments and controls. Term with larger weight gets more importance in optimization process.

The optimal control problem is then stated as follows: among all pairs of state and control variables $\left(x(t), u(t) \right)$ that obey the system of differential equation (5)-(8) with initial conditions (9) and free terminal conditions, find one that minimizes performance index (11). In other words, the primary objective of the control model is to determine the best possible control strategies in minimizing the number of solitariants, enthusiants, and ignorants simultaneously with the control efforts.

Optimality Conditions

Pontryagin's maximum principle (Pontryagin et al. 1962) constitutes as the first order necessary optimality condition of a control problem and holds a prominent role in theory of optimal processes. In this work, the authors utilize Pontryagin maximum principle by introducing a number of adjoin functions, representing the underlying optimal control in terms of the state and adjoin functions. Firstly, the problem of minimization functional (11) is converted into one of minimization the hamiltonian. To facilitate the analysis, let denote the integrand of (11) by $f_0\left(x, u, t\right)$ and the right-hand sides of (5)-(8) by $f_1\left(x, u, t\right)$, $f_2\left(x, u, t\right)$, $f_3\left(x, u, t\right)$, and $f_4\left(x, u, t\right)$, respectively. The hamiltonian H is defined as follows:

$$H\left(x, u, p, t\right) = f_0\left(x, u, t\right) + \sum_{i=1}^{4} p_i\left(t\right) f_i\left(x, u, t\right) \tag{12}$$

where $p_i\left(i = 1, 2, 3, 4\right)$ are adjoin functions corresponding to D, S, E and I, respectively. In accordance to Pontryagin minimum principle, the necessary optimality conditions for the optimal control problem are governed by the following set of requirements:

$$\frac{\partial H}{\partial u_i} = 0, \quad i = 1, 2, 3, \tag{13}$$

$$\frac{dx_i}{dt} = \frac{\partial H}{\partial p_i}, \quad i = 1, 2, 3, 4, \quad x_i \in \left\{D, S, E, I\right\}, \tag{14}$$

$$\frac{dp_i}{dt} = -\frac{\partial H}{\partial x_i}, \quad i = 1, 2, 3, 4, \quad x_i \in \left\{D, S, E, I\right\}. \tag{15}$$

By applying condition (13), the optimal control variables u_1^*, u_2^*, and u_3^* are obtained and provided as follows:

$$u_1^* = \frac{\lambda_2 p_4 I}{C_1},$$
(16)

$$u_2^* = \frac{\beta_1 \left(p_4 - p_3\right) ID + \beta_2 \left(p_3 - p_2\right) ED}{C_2 N},$$
(17)

$$u_3^* = \frac{\alpha \left(p_2 - p_1\right) S}{C_3}.$$
(18)

It is obvious that the application of condition (14) provides the dynamical system (5)-(8). Condition (15) is rather complicated as the right-hand side of (6)-(8) involve $N = D + S + E + I$ in the denominator making partial derivation longer than expected. However, one may arrive at the following adjoin system:

$$\frac{dp_1}{dt} = \gamma \left(p_1 - p_2\right) + \frac{\left(1 + u_2^*\right)\left(N - D\right)\left(\beta_2 \left(p_3 - p_2\right) E + \beta_1 \left(p_4 - p_3\right) I\right)}{N^2},$$
(19)

$$\frac{dp_2}{dt} = -A_1 + \alpha u_3^* \left(p_2 - p_1\right),$$
(20)

$$\frac{dp_3}{dt} = -A_2 + \left(\mu - \lambda_2\right) p_3 + \frac{\beta_2 \left(1 + u_2^*\right)\left(p_3 - p_2\right)\left(N - E\right) D}{N^2},$$
(21)

$$\frac{dp_4}{dt} = -A_3 - \left(\lambda_1 - \mu + \left(1 - u_1^*\right)\lambda_2\right) p_4 + \frac{\beta_1 \left(1 + u_2^*\right)\left(p_4 - p_3\right)\left(N - I\right) D}{N^2}.$$
(22)

Therefore, the optimal control variables (16)-(18) can be obtained by numerically solving the dynamical system (5)-(8) simultaneously with adjoin system (19)-(22) under initial conditions (9) and transversality conditions

$$p_1\left(T\right) = p_2\left(T\right) = p_3\left(T\right) = p_4\left(T\right) = 0$$
(23)

as it is assumed that terminal conditions $D(T), S(T), E(T)$, and $I(T)$ are all undetermined (free). The complete derivation of the optimality conditions are provided in Appendix.

In this control model, Pontryagin minimum principle poses both necessary and sufficient conditions for optimality as it is guaranteed by fact that the admissible control set U in (10) is closed and convex, and the integrand of functional objective (11) is also convex in S, E, I and u_i. Thus, the optimal controls (16)-(18) minimize (11).

ILLUSTRATIVE EXAMPLE

Now the authors provide an example for illustrating the effectiveness of the control strategy. A small open society initially with 100 members dominated by enthusiasts and ignorants is considered. It is assumed that there are 5 disseminants, 20 solitariants, 25 enthusiasts, and 50 ignorants, i.e., $D_0 = 5$, $S_0 = 20$, $E_0 = 25$, and $I_0 = 50$. New members can enter the society either as newcomers with promotion rate of $\lambda_1 = 0.0015$, or as immigrants with entrance rate of $\lambda_2 = 0.0010$. The natural death rate is $\mu = 0.0006$. The level of interaction among populations from different classes is reflected by $\alpha = 0.05$, $\beta_1 = 0.15$ and $\beta_2 = 0.15$. The transfer rate between disseminant and solitariant is $\gamma = 0.01$. The level of importance among terms in the functional objective (11) is given by $A_1 = 20$, $A_2 = 30$, $A_3 = 50$, $C_1 = 10$, $C_2 = 40$, and $C_3 = 40$. It means that reducing the number of ignorants is considered more important than decreasing the number of solitariants and enthusiasts. However, providing training for ignorant-immigrants is considered less important than that for enthusiasts and solitariants. Bounded optimal controls with $\overline{u}_1 = \overline{u}_2 = \overline{u}_3 = 1$ should be determined within control period of $T = 60$ days.

An indirect approach, namely the forward-backward sweep method, was implemented to numerically solve the differential equations system characterized by Pontryagin minimum principle. The dynamical system (5)-(8) was initially solved in forward by fourth order Runge-Kutta algorithm, then the adjoin system (19)-(22) was solved backwards in time with the same algorithm, following by controls updating. This step generates a new approximation of the state, adjoin, and control variables (x, p, u). The process loops by exploiting these new updates and generating new Runge-Kutta approximations and control updates with the goal of reaching fixed variables (x, p, u). The sweep method is terminates when a sufficiently small level of tolerance reached. McAsey et al. (2012) discusses the convergence issue of this method.

Figure 2 portrays the dynamics among society members in each compartments, where those without intervention are depicted in solid lines and ones with control are indicated by dashed lines. Case without intervention was obtained by setting $\overline{u}_1 = \overline{u}_2 = \overline{u}_3 = 0$, forcing all control variables to zero all the time. It can be seen in this case that the number of disseminants is almost constant, while that of ignorants is slightly decreased. Normal interaction among society members significantly increases the number of solitariants and slightly that of enthusiasts. Application of control by means of training for ignorant-immigrants (u_1), information sharing through social media for enthusiasts and ignorants (u_2), and specific training for solitariants (u_3) changes the dynamics. These efforts are proven in eliminating the number of ignorants and enthusiasts in sixty days. Hence, in the end of control period, the society is dominated by disseminants and solitariants. The social group comparison and analysis can be represented according to the each compartment as follows:

Figure 2. The dynamics of society with and without control

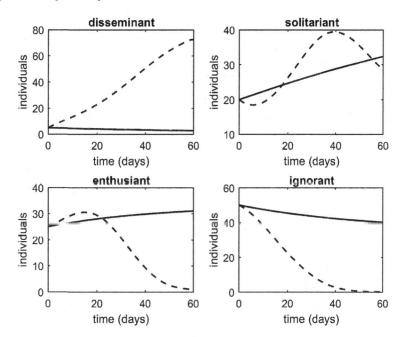

1. The number of disseminants will increase from 5 to more than 70 individuals in the end of period. Based on compartmental model in Figure 1, the rise in the number of disseminants is caused by solitariants which change their attitude in willingness to transfer knowledge to become disseminants with rate α. Even though there is a possibility that a disseminant becomes a solitariant with rate γ, due to knowledge withholding, the rate is smaller than that of opposite direction, i.e., $\alpha = 0.05$ and $\gamma = 0.01$. The flow from solitariant to disseminant is speeded up by the application of control u_3 (special training for solitariants).

2. The number of solitariants fluctuates during the period: decreasing in the beginning of control period and then increasing up to 40 individuals in day forty and achieving 30 in the end. In-flows to this class come from disseminants which decide to be solitariants with rate $\gamma = 0.01$ and from enthusiasts which, due to their interaction with disseminants, transform to become solitariants with transmission rate $\beta_2 = 0.15$. This interaction is boosted up by the application of control u_2 (information sharing through social media between enthusiasts and disseminants). It seems that the in-flows are greater than out-flow, i.e., solitariant-to-disseminant flow, results in the increase in trend of the number of solitariants.

3. The number of enthusiasts slightly increases in the early period of time due to interaction of some ignorant with disseminants through social media to become enthusiast with transmission rate $\beta_1 = 0.15$. However, the number of enthusiasts is decreasing tends to zero as more and more enthusiasts are promoted to be solitariants.

4. The in-flows to ignorant compartment are coming from newcomer promotion with rate of $\lambda_1 = 0.0015$ and from immigrant with entry rate of $\lambda_2 = 0.0015$. However, this compartment is a target of control application through training for ignorant-immigrants (u_1) and information sharing via social media between ignorants and disseminant (u_2). Thus, a significant number of ignorants is transferred to enthusiast class, declining straightforwardly the number of ignorants to zero.

Figure 3. The intensity of optimal control application

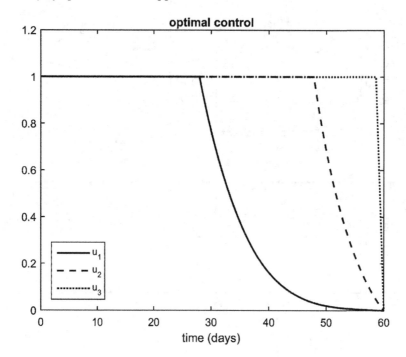

This simple simulation, however, reveals that the characteristic of people in learning and disseminating knowledge might be influenced by training and information sharing.

Figure 4. The number of enthusiasts and ignorants under single and multiple controls

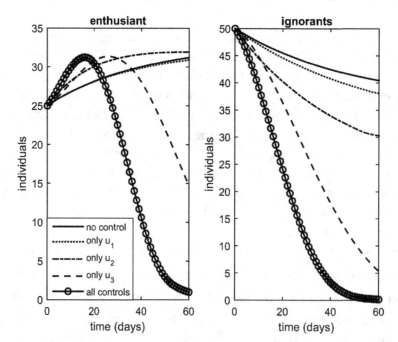

Figure 3 depicts the intensity of optimal control application within the period in order to attain the above result. It is suggested that the training for ignorant-immigrant should be fully given only in the first half of the period. The intensity is gradually diminished afterward. The second intervention strategy, i.e., information dissemination through social media for enthusiants and ignorants (u_2), should be fully delivered a bit longer but no more than day fifty. While, the specific training for solitariants (u_3) should be fully conveyed almost all the time. With three control strategies in the hand, a set of scenarios might be proposed regarding the single or multiple use of controls. Figure 4 describes the effectiveness of the control strategies when each control variable is applied independently and all control variables are introduced concurrently. It can be seen that in the case of single control application, the intervention through training for solitariants (u_3) exhibits the most effective method in reducing the number of enthusiants and ignorants. Under this strategy, the number of enthusiants is 15 and that of ignorants is 5 in the end of period. In addition to this result, Figure 5 in Appendix shows the fulfillment of transversality conditions $p_1(T) = p_2(T) = p_3(T) = p_4(T) = 0$ by adjoin functions.

CONCLUSION

The authors have proposed a mathematical model for quantitatively evaluating the process of knowledge dissemination among population. A small open society with four classes of member, namely disseminant, solitariant, enthusiant and ignorant, has been considered and the interaction among member of different classes has been analyzed. The knowledge dissemination problem in the society was formulated in the framework of optimal control model. Three intervention strategies, namely the training for ignorant-immigrants, dissemination of information by means of social media for enthusiants and ignorants, and specific training for solitariants were introduced to the system. The effect of intervention on the flow of people among compartment were then examined. In particular, the characterization of optimal control strategies has been derived by using Pontryagin minimum principle in the form of first order differential equation systems. The numerical solutions have been obtained by utilizing the forward-backward sweep method and the fourth order Runge-Kutta algorithms. The solutions minimize the number of solitariant, enthusiant and ignorant as well as the control efforts.

It has been revealed that the proposed control strategies can effectively decrease the number of enthusiants and ignorants but increase the number of solitariants as the later was assigned with the smallest weight of balancing cost. It seems that the class of solitariant plays key role in control strategies as the introduction of specific training for solitariants into the society provides the most impact in reducing the number of enthusiants and ignorants.

DISCUSSION QUESTIONS

In the end of chapter, the authors raise a few questions, which are intended to stimulate readers and students to discuss about its contents and to encourage new angles of research with similar topic.

1. In functional objective (11), the authors consider an L_2-type criterion, which consists of six terms. The first three terms reflect the number of individuals in S, E, and I to be minimized (remember,

realizing a society with more number of disseminants is preferable). The quadratic terms denote the amount of control effort, which should also be jointly minimized. Obviously, mathematically there are several nonequivalent ways to measure the effectiveness of control. For instance, it is possible to consider the following L_1-type criterion (linear in the control):

$$J = \int_0^T \left(A_1 S(t) + A_2 E(t) + A_3 I(t) + C_1 u_1(t) + C_2 u_2(t) + C_3 u_3(t) \right) dt.$$

What is the main advantage of the L_1-type and L_2-type criteria? What are the optimal controls in the L_1 case?

2. In the study of epidemiological phenomena, the SIR model is one of the simplest representation of the population dynamic. Since published in 1927, this model has been developed into numerous refinements and improvements to cope up with emerging new infections and invention of new approach and basis of existing infections. This effort includes the introduction of a new compartment or state, such as E for exposed, V for vaccinated, and Q for quarantined. Toward the model of knowledge dissemination depicted in Figure 1, what kind of improvement can be made? Is the addition of a new compartment making the model more realistic? Can we consider different control strategies, e.g., by making few parameters dynamic?

3. The presentation of optimal control model is usually preceded by the analysis of model without control, which may include the finding of the equilibria, the calculation of the basic reproductive number, and the stability analysis of linearized system in the vicinity of equilibrium. This preliminary step can be conducted towards the knowledge dissemination model (1)-(4). Beyond an equilibrium at origin, one may found other equilibria by solving

$$\frac{dD}{dt} = \frac{dS}{dt} = \frac{dE}{dt} = \frac{dI}{dt} = 0.$$

In epidemiology, the basic reproductive number R_0 is used to measure the potential of transmission of a disease within a population. It is defined as the average number of secondary cases that would be generated by a primary case in an entirely susceptible population. By arguing that disseminant is similar to infected in SIR model, is it relevant to derive the corresponding basic reproductive number for model (1)-(4)? Do we still have the same interpretation for $R_0 > 1$ and $R_0 < 1$?

ACKNOWLEDGMENT

This research received no specific grant from any funding agency in the public, commercial, or not-for-profit sectors.

REFERENCES

Baez, M. (2012). *Knowledge dissemination in the web era* (PhD Dissertation). University of Trento.

Bell, C. E., French, N. P., Karimuribo, E., Ogden, N. H., Bryant, M. J., Swai, E. M., & Fitzpatrick, J. L. (2005). The effects of different knowledge-dissemination interventions on the mastitis knowledge of Tanzanian smallholder dairy farmers. *Preventive Veterinary Medicine*, *72*(3-4), 237–251. doi:10.1016/j.prevetmed.2005.05.004 PMID:16154215

Cahyono, E., Mukhsar, & Elastic, P. (2017). Dynamics of knowledge dissemination in a four-type population society. *Far East Journal of Mathematical Sciences*, *102*(6), 1065–1076. doi:10.17654/MS102061065

Chen, P. Y., Cheng, S. M., & Chen, K. C. (2014). Optimal control of epidemic information dissemination over networks. *IEEE Transactions on Cybernetics*, *44*(12), 2316–2328. doi:10.1109/TCYB.2014.2306781 PMID:25415940

Das, A. K. & Chakraborty, S. (2018). Knowledge withholding within an organization: the psychological resistance to knowledge sharing linking with territoriality. *RISUS - Journal on Innovation and Sustainability, 9*(3), 94–108. doi: . doi:10.24212/2179-3565.2018v9i3p94-108

Kelliher, F., Harrington, D., & Galavan, R. (2010). Spreading leader knowledge: Investigating a participatory mode of knowledge dissemination among management undergraduates. *Irish Journal of Management*, *29*(2), 170–125.

Kingston, J. (2012). Choosing a knowledge dissemination approach. *Knowledge and Process Management, 19*(3), 160–170. doi:10.1002/kpm.1391

Kondratova, I., & Goldfarb, I. (2004). Knowledge portal as a new paradigm for scientific publishing and collaboration. *Journal of Information Technology in Construction*, *9*, 161–174.

Kowalska-Styczen, A., Malarz, K., & Paradowski, K. (2018). Model of knowledge transfer within an organisation. *Journal of Artificial Societies and Social Simulation*, *21*(2), 3. doi:10.18564/jasss.3659

Lafrenière, D., Menuz, V., Hurlimann, T., & Godard, B. (2013). Knowledge dissemination interventions: A literature review. *SAGE Open*, 1–14. doi:10.1177/2158244013498242

Li, J., Zhang, Y., Man, J., Zhou, Y., & Wu, X. (2017). SISL and SIRL: Two knowledge dissemination models with leader nodes on cooperative learning networks. *Physica A*, *468*, 740–749. doi:10.1016/j.physa.2016.11.126

Liu, D. Q., Wu, Z. Q., Wang, Y. X., Guo, Q., & Liu, J. G. (2017). Optimal teaching strategy in periodic impulsive knowledge dissemination system. *PLoS One*, *12*(6), e0178024. doi:10.1371/journal.pone.0178024 PMID:28665961

Lombardi, R. (2019). Knowledge transfer and organizational performance and business process: Past, present and future researches. *Business Process Management Journal*, *25*(1), 2–9. doi:10.1108/BPMJ-02-2019-368

McAsey, M., Mou, L., & Han, W. (2012). Convergence of the forward-backward sweep method in optimal control. *Computational Optimization and Applications*, *53*(1), 207–226. doi:10.100710589-011-9454-7

Milton, N. (2010). *The Lessons Learned Handbook: Practical Approaches to Learning from Experience*. Witney, UK: Chandos Publishing. doi:10.1533/9781780631929

Ndii, M. Z., Carnia, E., & Supriatna, A. K. (2018). Mathematical models for the spread of rumors: a review. In F. L. Gaol, F. Hutagalung, & C. F. Peng (Eds.), *Issues and Trends in Interdisciplinary Behavior and Social Science, 8*. London: CRC Press; doi:10.1201/9781315148700-8

Pontryagin, L. S., Boltyanskii, V. G., Gamkrelidze, R. V., & Mishchenko, E. F. (1962). *The Mathematical Theory of Optimal Processes (English translation)*. Geneva: Interscience.

Roth, A., Singhal, J., Singhal, K., & Tang, C. S. (2016). Knowledge creation and dissemination in operations and supply chain management. *Production and Operations Management*, *25*(9), 1473–1488. doi:10.1111/poms.12590

Su, J., Yang, Y., & Duan, R. (2018). A CA-based heterogeneous model for knowledge dissemination inside knowledge-based organizations. *Journal of Intelligent & Fuzzy Systems*, *34*(4), 2087–2097. doi:10.3233/JIFS-162116

Wang, J.-P., Guo, Q., Yang, G.-Y., & Liu, J.-G. (2015). Improved knowledge diffusion model based on the collaboration hypernetwork. *Physica A*, *428*, 250–256. doi:10.1016/j.physa.2015.01.062

Webster, J., Brown, G., Zweig, D., Connelly, C. E., Brodt, S., & Sitkin, S. (2008). Beyond knowledge sharing: knowledge withholding at work. In Research in Personnel and Human Resources Management. Bradford: Emerald Group Publishing. doi:10.1016/S0742-7301(08)27001-5

Wilke, A., Bollmann, U., Cazzaniga, S., Hübner, A., John, S. M., Karadzinska-Bislimovska, J., & Wulfhorst, B. (2017). The implementation of knowledge dissemination in the prevention of occupational skin diseases. *Journal of the European Academy of Dermatology and Venereology*, *32*(3), 449–458. doi:10.1111/jdv.14653 PMID:29055149

Xu, Q., Su, Z., Zhang, K., Ren, P., & Shen, X. S. (2015). Epidemic information dissemination in mobile social networks with opportunistic links. *IEEE Transactions on Emerging Topics in Computing*, *3*(3), 399–409. doi:10.1109/TETC.2015.2414792

Yu, J., & Zhang, R. (2008). A dynamic analysis upon the knowledge dissemination within an organization. *2008 4th International Conference on Wireless Communications, Networking and Mobile Computing*. doi: 10.1109/WiCom.2008.2613

Zhao, L. J., Wang, J. J., Chen, Y. C., Wang, Q., Cheng, J. J., & Cui, H. (2012). SIHR rumor spreading model in social networks. *Physica A*, *39*(7), 2444–2453. doi:10.1016/j.physa.2011.12.008

KEY TERMS AND DEFINITIONS

Compartmental Models: Model that classifies individuals into different population groups or compartments based on certain characteristics, which are connected by the flow (migration or transformation) of individuals. This model is usually governed by nonlinear ordinary differential equations system that tracks the population as a function of time.

Optimal Control Model: A dynamical model for evaluating the time varying values of a certain process variable. The model aims at determining the control policy and state law that maximize or minimize a specific performance criterion over a period of time, subject to the constraints imposed by the physical nature of the problem.

APPENDIX

In this appendix, the authors provide the detailed derivation of the necessary optimality conditions. By considering dynamical system (5)-(8) and the functional objective (11), the hamiltonian H is defined as follows

$$H = A_1 S + A_2 E + A_3 I + \frac{1}{2} C_1 u_1^2 + \frac{1}{2} C_2 u_2^2 + \frac{1}{2} C_3 u_3^2 + p_1 \left(\alpha u_3 S + \left(\lambda_2 - \mu - \gamma \right) D \right)$$

$$+ p_2 \left[\beta_2 \left(1 + u_2 \right) \frac{ED}{N} + \left(\lambda_2 - \mu - \alpha u_3 \right) S + \gamma D \right] + p_3 \left[\beta_1 \left(1 + u_2 \right) \frac{ID}{N} - \beta_2 \left(1 + u_2 \right) \frac{ED}{N} + \left(\lambda_2 - \mu \right) E \right]$$

$$+ p_4 \left[\left(1 - u_1 \right) \lambda_2 I - \beta_1 \left(1 + u_2 \right) \frac{ID}{N} + \left(\lambda_1 - \mu \right) I \right].$$

As the control model involves three control variables, Pontryagin minimum principle (13) consists of three conditions: $H_{u_1} = 0$, $H_{u_2} = 0$, and $H_{u_3} = 0$, where H_{u_i} is an alternate notation for partial derivative $\partial H / \partial u_i$. Each of these conditions can further be described as follows:

$$H_{u_1} = 0 \Leftrightarrow C_1 u_1 - \lambda_2 p_4 I = 0 \Leftrightarrow u_1^* = \frac{\lambda_2 p_4 I}{C_1},$$

$$H_{u_2} = 0 \Leftrightarrow C_2 u_2 + \frac{\beta_2 ED p_2}{N} + \frac{\beta_1 ID p_3}{N} - \frac{\beta_2 ED p_3}{N} - \frac{\beta_1 ID p_4}{N}$$

$$= 0 \Leftrightarrow u_2^* = \frac{\beta_1 \left(p_4 - p_3 \right) ID + \beta_2 \left(p_3 - p_2 \right) ED}{C_2 N},$$

$$H_{u_3} = 0 \Leftrightarrow C_3 u_3 + \alpha S p_1 - \alpha S p_2 = 0 \Leftrightarrow u_3^* = \frac{\alpha S \left(p_2 - p_1 \right)}{C_3}.$$

Since all control variables are bounded, i.e., $0 \leq u_i \leq \overline{u}_i$, then for numerical programming purposes, the expression of optimal controls can also be given by

$$u_1^* = \min \left\{ \overline{u}_1, \max \left\{ 0, \frac{\lambda_2 p_4 I}{C_1} \right\} \right\},$$

$$u_2^* = \min \left\{ \overline{u}_2, \max \left\{ 0, \frac{\beta_1 \left(p_4 - p_3 \right) ID + \beta_2 \left(p_3 - p_2 \right) ED}{C_2 N} \right\} \right\},$$

$$u_3^* = \min\left\{\bar{u}_3, \max\left\{0, \frac{\alpha S\left(p_2 - p_1\right)}{C_3}\right\}\right\}.$$

The second principle (14) consists of

$$\frac{dD}{dt} = \frac{\partial H}{\partial p_1}, \frac{dS}{dt} = \frac{\partial H}{\partial p_2}, \frac{dE}{dt} = \frac{\partial H}{\partial p_3}, \frac{dI}{dt} = \frac{\partial H}{\partial p_4}.$$

It is easy to verify that the above conditions lead to dynamical system (5)-(8). The number of conditions insisted by the last principle (15) is as many as the number of state variables, that is four, and those are expressed below:

$$\frac{dp_1}{dt} = -\frac{\partial H}{\partial D} \Leftrightarrow \frac{dp_1}{dt} = -\left[\begin{matrix} -\gamma p_1 + \beta_2\left(1+u_2\right)p_2 E \dfrac{N-D}{N^2} + \gamma p_2 + \beta_1\left(1+u_2\right)p_3 I \dfrac{N-D}{N^2} \\ -\beta_2\left(1+u_2\right)p_3 E \dfrac{N-D}{N^2} - \beta_1\left(1+u_2\right)p_4 I \dfrac{N-D}{N^2} \end{matrix}\right] \Leftrightarrow \frac{dp_1}{dt}$$

$$= \gamma\left(p_1 - p_2\right) + \frac{\left(1+u_2^*\right)\left(N-D\right)\left(\beta_2\left(p_3 - p_2\right)E + \beta_1\left(p_4 - p_3\right)I\right)}{N^2},$$

$$\frac{dp_2}{dt} = -\frac{\partial H}{\partial S} \Leftrightarrow \frac{dp_2}{dt} = -\left(A_1 + \alpha u_3 p_1 - \alpha u_3 p_2\right) \Leftrightarrow \frac{dp_2}{dt} = -A_1 + \alpha u_3^*\left(p_2 - p_1\right),$$

$$\frac{dp_3}{dt} = -\frac{\partial H}{\partial E} \Leftrightarrow \frac{dp_3}{dt} = -\left[\begin{matrix} A_2 + \beta_2\left(1+u_2\right)p_2 D \dfrac{N-E}{N^2} \\ -\beta_2\left(1+u_2\right)p_3 D \dfrac{N-E}{N^2} + \left(\lambda_2 - \mu\right)p_3 \end{matrix}\right] \Leftrightarrow \frac{dp_3}{dt}$$

$$= -A_2 + \left(\mu - \lambda_2\right)p_3 + \frac{\beta_2\left(1+u_2^*\right)\left(p_3 - p_2\right)\left(N-E\right)D}{N^2},$$

$$\frac{dp_4}{dt} = -\frac{\partial H}{\partial I} \Leftrightarrow \frac{dp_4}{dt} = -\left[\begin{matrix} A_3 + \beta_1\left(1+u_2\right)p_3 D \dfrac{N-I}{N^2} + \lambda_2\left(1-u_1\right)p_4 \\ +\left(\lambda_1 - \mu\right)p_4 - \beta_1\left(1+u_2\right)p_4 D \dfrac{N-I}{N^2} \end{matrix}\right] \Leftrightarrow \frac{dp_4}{dt}$$

$$= -A_3 - \left(\lambda_1 - \mu + \left(1-u_1^*\right)\lambda_2\right)p_4 + \frac{\beta_1\left(1+u_2^*\right)\left(p_4 - p_3\right)\left(N-I\right)D}{N^2}.$$

The above adjoin system must be simultaneously solved with the dynamic system under transversality conditions $p_1\left(T\right) = p_2\left(T\right) = p_3\left(T\right) = p_4\left(T\right) = 0$. Figure 5 confirms that these terminal conditions are satisfied with $T = 60$.

Figure 5. The adjoin functions

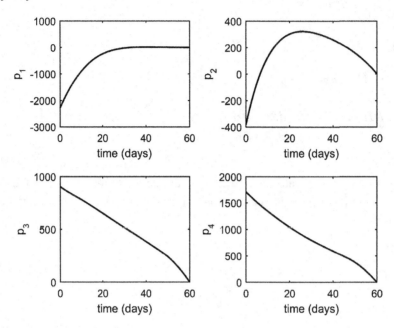

Chapter 23

The Use of Google Analytics for Measuring Website Performance of Non-Formal Education Institution

Ivana S. Domazet

ⓘ https://orcid.org/0000-0002-3493-4616

Institute of Economic Sciences, Serbia

Vladimir M. Simović

Institute of Economic Sciences, Serbia

ABSTRACT

The purpose of this chapter is to measure the performance of a non-formal educational institution's website using Google Analytics data and data obtained in a separate research on specific non-formal educational institution's users. The goal was to determine the best performing acquisition channel for non-formal educational institutions and the average user profile of this kind of educational programs by means of user acquisition and behavior data. Key parameters used to measure the performance of different acquisition channels were conversion rate, average session duration, and bounce rate. User gender data and age group data were used on a side of user specific data. The findings presented in this research may be applicable to other non-formal educational institutions as well.

INTRODUCTION

Non-formal educational programs are experiencing tremendous growth worldwide. Numerous reasons can be identified as being important in this regards. The fact that non-formal educational programs are more flexible and adaptive in terms of modern business environment, needs can be observed as one of the leading reasons. As a direct consequence of a growing popularity of non-formal education in global terms, non-formal education institutions, which organize and conduct different non-formal educational

DOI: 10.4018/978-1-5225-8933-4.ch023

programs, are also witnessing the intensive growth. Non-formal educational programs are facing many challenges and changed learning environment, which should enhance students' satisfaction and strong motivation (Simović, Radović-Marković, 2018).

Some of those educational institutions are focused exclusively on domestic markets whilst others are targeting international markets as well. Some of those institutions are performing their educational programs exclusively in traditional settings, others are exclusively using e-learning, as a tool for their educational content delivery, whilst some are combining those two approaches.

Regardless of their strategic approach in terms of educational content delivery channel and their targeted markets, all of those educational institutions are investing lots of efforts and resources to reach to their targeted audience. Nowadays all of them are focusing on using their websites for promoting their activities and educational programs. The websites have become their leading mechanism in attracting new customers and retaining the existing ones. In other words, their websites have become a hub for all of their digital traffic. Therefore, it has become essential for them to measure the performance of their websites in terms of aforementioned goals.

There are many different methods and tools the organizations can use in order to measure the performance of their websites. One of them is especially efficient and well known, and widespread. It is the Google Analytics. Google Analytics represents one of the leading industry solutions specialized in analyzing the website traffic, the effects of different marketing campaigns and the overall performance. The tool launched in 2005 represents a response of a company Google to a growing need for a website performance measurement. It enables the website administrators to simply copy the line of tracking code into the XML code of their website, and thereby track the website's performance on several levels:

- **User Level:** Which refers to an actions of an individual user.
- **Session Level:** Which relates to each individual visit.
- **Page View Level:** Which refers to visited pages.
- **Event Level:** Which relates to actions undertaken by individual visitor.

In its core essence, the Google Analytics helps the companies to collect two categories of data relevant for measurement and evaluation purposes:

1. User acquisition data, which refers to user demographic characteristics such as age, gender, interests etc, on one side, and user acquisition channel data (referrals, organic, paid etc.), on the other side.
2. The user behavior data, which refers to the behavior of the users who reached the targeted website (the landing page data, average session duration data, bounce rate data, user pathway etc).

BACKGROUND RESEARCH

Non-formal education was the subject of interest and research by many authors, including Eshach, 2007, who focused on cognitive and affective aspects of non-formal learning, as well as on defining the different types of out-of-school learning such as formal, informal and non-formal learning. The author focuses on different models of learning and identifies the clear distinction between them, since the terms informal and non-formal learning are often misused and misunderstood. For exactly the same reason, Malcolm et al. (2003) focus on identifying the clear distinction between the aforementioned types of education.

Romi and Schmida, 2009, focused on the role of non-formal education, as a major educational force in a postmodern world. The authors argue that non-formal education challenges the traditional concept of education and brings significant changes to a society as a whole.

Many authors analyzed the use of Google Analytics, as a tool for measuring website performance. Plaza (2011) uses the time series to determine the effectiveness of entries, measured by visitors' behavior and length of sessions, in regards to traffic sources represented by direct visits, in-link visits and search engine visits.

Google Analytics can be successfully used for measuring website usability and determining the usability problems. As suggested by Hasan et al (2009) Google Analytics can be used to target the e-commerce website usability issues. The authors suggest that Google Analytics cannot be used to provide in depth analysis about the nature of the issue, but instead it could be used to point to a usability issues present on a website.

In a current academic literature, there is no evidence on a research targeted towards using the Google Analytics as a tool for measuring the performance of a non-formal education institution's website. Similar attempts were made in a case of different industries but never in the case of non-formal education. For example, Plaza (2011) uses Google Analytics to measure the performance of a tourist industry website. Similarly, Fang (2007) has used Google Analytics to evaluate and propose measures for improvement of the library website content. Based on Google Analytics data, the author redesigned the library's website and the results showed that the redesigned website fitted better the information needs of library users. Besides this author, others also examined the use of Google Analytics in regards to digital library website. Barba et al (2013) argue that Google Analytics cannot be used to predict users' needs but can be very useful in describing users' behavior. Furthermore, web analytics can reveal blind spots in predictive website usage and can allow the modification based on real user behavior.

Pakkala et al (2012) were using Google Analytics to measure visitors' statistics in a case of three food composition websites. Their findings suggest that Google Analytics can be easily and effectively used to compare data on a different websites, and to improve the website design.

Besides being a tool for analyzing past users data, Google Analytics can effectively be used as a prediction tool. Gunter and Onder (2016) conducted a study aimed at forecasting the actual tourist arrivals into the city of Vienna using Google Analytics website traffic indicators. Their findings suggest that for a longer horizon forecast combination methods based on Google Analytics data work the best thus confirming the predictive nature of Google Analytics data.

There were some theoretical works trying to investigate the role of Google Analytics in regards to learning process. Filva et al (2014) suggest that Google Analytics provides a temporal dimension as a possible behavior measurement for learning process that takes place in virtual environment. This research, along with others, represents a broader concept, which some authors even define as the entirely new discipline called learning analytics. As suggested by Siemens (2013) the learning analytics is focused on better understanding of teaching, learning, intelligent content and personalization and adaptation in learning as well as the use of data analytics in education.

MEASURING THE PERFORMANCE OF NON-FORMAL EDUCATION INSTITUTION'S WEBSITE USING GOOGLE ANALYTICS

The aim of this paper is to identify all relevant aspects of website performance in a case of a specific non-formal education institution's website. The institution in question is the Institute of Economic Sci-

Table 1. Number of users visiting center's website in a period between January 2017 and January 2019, by acquisition channels

Acquisition Channel	Number of Users	% of the Sample
Organic Search	8.630	68.45
Social	2.160	17.13
Direct	1.439	11.41
Referral	378	3.01
Total	12.607	100

Source: (Google Analytics, 2019)

ences in Belgrade, Serbia and the website of its operating unit, called Center for Professional Education. The Center was established within Institute in January 2017 with the purpose of providing high quality non-formal educational programs in accounting and financial reports analysis. The educational content is delivered to a targeted audience in traditional settings, and so far, no e-learning approach has been adopted. The fact that the learning content is presented traditionally, in the classroom, means that the targeted audience is identified as being situated in Belgrade and the surrounding area. Consequently, the marketing campaigns and activities are directed towards this targeted group of customers. As stated by Domazet and Neogradi (2018) all marketing activities use the Internet as a channel of communication. That is exactly the case in the situation of Center for Professional Education.

The Center's website performance was tracked and analyzed in a period since its establishment, from January 2017 until January 2019. Two categories of data provided by Google Analytics were used to measure the Center's website performance:

1. User acquisition data
2. User behavior data

The first set of data is the data regarding user acquisition. By analyzing those data and comparing them with data on users who converted, and became the users of Center's educational content and learning programs, the goal was to identify the best acquisition channels, and the reasons behind the success of paid marketing campaigns. The overall goal of this part of the research was to identify the profile of the average non-formal accounting and financial reports analysis course user. In order to achieve this goal a data regarding Center's acquisition channels in a period between January 2017 and January 2019 were collected with the use of Google Analytics (Table 1).

As shown in Table 1, organic search represents the main acquisition channel in terms of frequency for the Center's website. This fact is understandable considering that extensive search engine optimization was conducted for some keywords relevant for Center's educational programs. For some keywords, the Center is ranked high within organic results in Google, which results in large number of visitors originating from the search engine. As argued by Evans (2007) successful search engine optimization ensures a high page rank in Google and is affected by number of factors including links, directories and social bookmarking sites. Shin et al. (2012) emphasize the role of search engine as an important tool for reaching a destination websites. These authors conclude that well designed search engine optimization in combination with social networking can significantly improve website's visibility and overall traffic.

Table 2. Number of converted users of center's educational programs in a period between January 2017 and January 2019, by acquisition channels

Acquisition Channel	Number of Users	% of the Sample
Organic Search	43	27.92
Social	22	14.29
Direct	87	56.49
Referral	2	1.30
Total	154	100

Source: (Authors, 2019)

In order to compare data regarding acquisition channels and their effectiveness in terms of converting users from visitors to Center's educational programs buyers, a research among users of Center's educational programs revealed very useful data in terms of their demographic and behavior characteristics. The data on total number of Center's educational programs users in a period between January 2017 and January 2019, and the acquisition channel they used to interact with Center's website are shown below.

The data in Table 2 show the distribution of acquisition channels among the actual users who converted and became the buyers of the Center's non-formal educational programs. As provided, the majority of users came directly to a Center's website. It is important to emphasize that these users have not actually typed in a Center's website URL into their browser. Instead, the majority of users originated from a Serbian website specialized in non-formal educational programs in various areas and topics. This website serves as a hub for users in Serbia who are in search for non-formal educational programs. Various institutions are representing their educational programs on this website and Google counts these visits as direct visits. This is a reason why this channel proved to be the most frequent one from customers' perspective.

Besides direct visits, users emphasized organic search as being one of the important acquisition channels from their perspective. In this regards, their view is somehow similar with data earlier presented on acquisition channels, obtained from Google Analytics. The explanation for organic search, being observed as important acquisition channel by the users, is the same as in the case of data presented in Table 2. Search engine was considerably optimized for some keywords relevant to Center's educational programs.

After identifying the most frequent acquisition channels in users' opinion, it would be very useful to identify the actual effectiveness of every acquisition channel, by analyzing the data on acquisition channels originating from Google Analytics on one side, and data originating from Center's educational programs users, on the other. This analysis should provide the most relevant data regarding various acquisition channels effectiveness. The data are shown in the Table below.

The data in Table 3 show that 154 out of 12.607 users who visited the Center's website in a period between January 2017 and January 2019 converted and became the users od Center's educational programs. This means that the overall conversion rate for the Center's website in aforementioned period was 1.22. The results became quite different when observed by alternative acquisition channels. The data show that direct visits provided the best conversion rate to a Center's website. In case of direct visits, 87 users became customers out of 1.439 visitors of the Center's website, thus making the conversion rate for this acquisition channel the highest in the sample of available data – 6.05. The fact that the conversion rate for this acquisition channel is so high compared to other acquisition channels is because, as explained

Table 3. Number of website visitors and converted users of Center's educational programs in a period between January 2017 and January 2019, by acquisition channels

Acquisition Channel	Number of Users GA	Number of Converted Users	Conversion Rate
Organic Search	8.630	43	0.49
Social	2.160	22	1.02
Direct	1.439	87	6.05
Referral	378	2	0.53
Total	12.607	154	1.22

Source: (Authors Research and Google Analytics, 2019)

earlier, the direct visitors came from a web location on which they had the opportunity to gather almost all necessary data regarding Center's educational programs. Consequently, they were visiting the Center's website in order to gather the additional information, and to make contact with the sales representatives.

Although it appeared that organic search represents very efficient channel in terms of acquiring new customers, the data from Table 3 show that this acquisition channel had the lowest conversion rate in the sample. The conversion rate for organic search was 0.49 for Center's website in the aforementioned period. This acquisition channel definitely plays a significant role in terms of providing a traffic volume on a Center's website. When observed in absolute numbers, this channel ranks second, right after direct visits. Low conversion rate for this acquisition channel can be explained by the fact that the content on a Center's website is in some aspect irrelevant, faulty etc. Website visitors' conversion rate is affected by many different factors. Various authors were analyzing the factors which affect conversion rates, ranging from website features (McDowell et al, 2016), content repetitions (Jankowski, 2013), placement of call to action buttons on a website (Hernandez, Respnick, 2013) etc.

Besides direct visits, social proved to be a fair acquisition channel with a conversion rate greater than 1 (1.02). The fact that 1 out of 100 visitors to a Center's website originating from social media became the Centers user, represents a fair result, but brings attention to the efficiency issue of the social media marketing campaigns.

We can conclude that the most efficient acquisition channel, in the case of a Center's website, was a direct channel, for the reasons explained earlier in this chapter. In terms of acquisition channels efficiency, we must emphasize that some channels proved to be inefficient in a case of non-formal education institution's website. The reasons behind this lie in multiple internal and external factors.

In addition, the purpose of this part of the research was to identify the profile of the Center's educational programs average users. The possibility to more closely identify the average users represents a great opportunity for the Center to improve its marketing efforts and to make them more focused and targeted to a specific user group.

The first personal characteristic of the Center's educational programs users is their gender. The following table represents the gender structure of the sample of Center's users.

The data in Table 4 show female are dominant in terms of converting and becoming a user of Center's educational programs. As shown, 83.11% of users are female. This is expected having in mind the fact that the Center's educational programs are directed towards accounting and financial reports analyses, which are believed to be dominantly female occupation nowadays (CPAExamGHub, 2017).

Table 4. Number of converted users of Center's educational programs in a period between January 2017 and January 2019, by gender

Gender	Number of Converted Users	% of the Sample
Male	26	16.88
Female	128	83.11
Total	154	100

Source: (Authors, 2019)

Table 5. Number of Center's website visitors in a period between January 2017 and January 2019, by gender

Gender	Number of Website Visitors	% of the Sample
Male	6.827	54.15
Female	5.780	45.85
Total	12.607	100

Source: (Google Analytics, 2019)

Google Analytics data regarding gender structure of the users who visited Center's website in afore-mentioned period reveal a different situation. This data is presented in Table 5.

As shown in Table 5, males are dominant in terms of visiting a Center's website with 54.15% of all visits in a period between January 2017 and January 2019. This data is opposite to a data previously presented in Table 4. In order to gain a clear understanding of the conversion rate of the users depending on their gender, the following table integrates the data regarding users' gender from both sources – actual users of Center's educational programs and Google Analytics.

The data in Table 6 suggest that the conversion rate in a case of female website visitors is much higher than in a case of male visitors. Males are visiting the Center's website more often than females, but females are preferably converting into Center's users. The conversion rate in a case of female visitors is 6 times higher than in a case of male visitors. This key question, which arises here, is why is this happening? It is obvious that in a case of male visitors the Center's website does not provide enough evidence to make them convert and become the users of Center's educational programs. Unfortunately, the available data does not provide enough evidence to determine the reasons behind this behavior.

Table 6. Number of website visitors and converted users of Center's educational programs in a period between January 2017 and January 2019, by gender

Gender	Number of Users GA	Number of Converted Users	Conversion Rate
Male	6.827	26	0.38
Female	5.780	128	2.21
Total	12.607	154	1.22

Source: (Google Analytics, 2019)

Table 7. Number of converted users of Center's educational programs in a period between January 2017 and January 2019, by age groups

Age Groups	Number of Converted Users	% of the Sample
18-24	4	2.59
25-34	27	17.53
35-44	79	51.30
45-54	35	22.74
55-64	9	5.84
65+	0	0
Total	154	100

Source: (Authors, 2019)

The second personal characteristic of Center's educational programs users is their age. Table 7 presents the data regarding the age groups of users of the Center.

The data in Table 7 show that most of the Center's educational programs users are in age group between 35 and 44 years (51.30% of the sample). This is important information in terms of targeting this group in future marketing campaigns and in terms of optimizing marketing budget. Second most engaged group of users in Center's educational programs are those between 45 and 54 years of age (22.74% of the sample).

Besides data originating from converted users, this research encompasses the data regarding users' age groups originating from Google Analytics. The following table presents those data.

According to Google, the most engaged group of users on a Center's website in terms of visits are users between 25 and 34 years of age (33.50% of the sample). The second most engaged group in terms of website visits are users between 18 and 24 years of age (27.50% of the sample). It is interesting that these data are not in line with results presented in previous Table. According to those data, the most engaged group of users are those between 35 and 44 years of age.

As in case of gender, the best way to gain the clear understanding of age group as a personal characteristic in terms of conversion rate for Center's educational programs is to put the data originating

Table 8. Number of Center's website visitors in a period between January 2017 and January 2019, by age groups

Age Groups	Number of Website Visitors	% of the Sample
18-24	3.467	27.50%
25-34	4.223	33.50%
35-44	1.954	15.50%
45-54	1.577	12.50%
55-64	693	5.50%
65+	693	5.50%
Total	12.607	100

Source: (Google Analytics, 2019)

Table 9. Number of website visitors and converted users of Center's educational programs in a period between January 2017 and January 2019, by age groups

Age Groups	Number of Users GA	Number of Converted Users	Conversion Rate
18-24	3.467	4	0.12
25-34	4.223	27	0.64
35-44	1.954	79	4.04
45-54	1.577	35	2.22
55-64	693	9	1.30
65+	693	0	0
Total	12.607	154	1.22

Source: (Google Analytics and Authors, 2019)

from converted users and Google Analytics data side by side. The data in this regards are presented in the following Table.

The data in Table 9 prove that definitely the most engaged category of users are those in age range between 35 and 44 years, whose conversion rate is 4.04. Besides this user group, the second most engaging user groups are users between 45 and 54 years of age. As shown in Table 9, the conversion rate for this category of users is 2.22. Data in Table shows that the conversion rate for the category of users who are the most frequent visitors of Center's website (users between 25 and 34 years of age) is 0.64, and that it is even significantly lower than for group of users between 55 and 64 years of age. This fact, as in a case of user's gender, points to a conclusion that website content and something in Center's offering is inadequately optimized for this category of users. The data show that these users are frequently visiting the Center's website but their conversion rate is very low.

The overall conclusion of this part of the research, which was directed towards identifying the profile of the average user of the Center's educational programs in accounting and financial reports analysis, is that according to available data, presented in previous part of this chapter, the average user is a female between 35 and 44 years of age. The presented data suggested that this category of users has the highest conversion rate when compared with other user groups. This fact represents significant information in terms of planning marketing campaigns in the future, and reaching the right potential customers. As stated in the introductory section of this paragraph, the research was based on the use of user acquisition data, provided by Google Analytics, and the research conducted among the users of the Center's educational programs.

The second category of data used in this research were the data regarding user behavior on the Center's website, such as average session duration, bounce rate, user flow etc. The overall goal of this part of the research was to establish a correlation between user behavior data on the Center's website and the financial parameters of non-formal courses organized by the Center. The financial parameters were observed using the number of users who attended various courses organized by the Center. Those data were used to calculate the conversion rates for different acquisition channels, which served as a base for the analysis conducted in this part of the research.

The table which represents the data regarding average session duration for a Center's website, depending on acquisition channels, is provided below.

Table 10. Average session duration on a Center's website in a period between January 2017 and January 2019, by acquisition channels

Acquisition Channel	Average Session Duration
Organic Search	00:01:38
Social	00:00:47
Direct	00:02:19
Referral	00:01:03
Average session duration	00:01:32

Source: (Authors, 2019)

The data from Table 10 show that the average session duration for all acquisition channels is 00:01:32. The users who visited the Center's website directly spent more time then users originating from other acquisition channels on average. This can be explained by the fact that was emphasized earlier in this chapter that direct visitors are actually originating from a website, which serves as a hub for all non-formal educational programs in Serbia. Users visiting the Center's website have already gathered the basic information regarding Center's educational programs, and are visiting the Center's website in search for additional and more detailed information. Their decision to visit the Center's website represents a significant step towards their final decision of becoming a Center's educational programs users, and therefore they are expected to spend some additional time in gathering necessary information on the Center's website. These are the reasons which affect the length of session duration in case of direct visits. In order to have even more clear understanding on the efficiency of different acquisition channels, as explained in the first part of this chapter, it would be useful to compare those data with data regarding average session duration by different channels.

The data in Table 11 confirm that the channel which has the highest conversion rate also has the longest average session duration time. The reasons in this regards were explained in details in previous parts of this paper.

In addition, we have tried to confirm the existence of correlation between Conversion Rate (CR) for different acquisition channels and Average Session Duration (ASD). Pearson's correlation coefficient was used for the purpose of this correlation analysis. The results of correlation analysis are presented in the following Table 12.

Table 11. Comparative data on conversion rate and average session duration on a Center's website in a period between January 2017 and January 2019, by acquisition channels

Acquisition Channel	Conversion Rate	Average Session Duration
Organic Search	0.49	00:01:38
Social	1.02	00:00:47
Direct	6.05	00:02:19
Referral	0.53	00:01:03
Total	1.22	00:01:32

Source: (Google Analytics and Authors, 2019)

Table 12. Pearson's Correlation coefficient between conversion rate and average session duration for a Center's website in a period between January 2017 and January 2019

	CR	ASD
CR	1	
ASD	0.79187	1

Source: (Authors, 2019)

The value of Pearson's correlation coefficient in the case of Conversion Rate and Average Session Duration data is 0.79187, and it confirms the existence of strong positive correlation between the two set of parameters. This fact leads to a conclusion that higher conversion rate is associated with longer average session duration time. In other words, the visitors who spend more time on an institution's website are more likely to convert and to become the users of the Center's educational programs.

In order to gain the better understanding of the user's behavior depending on different acquisition channels a data regarding bounce rate can be introduced into analysis. The relevant data are presented in the following Table.

The data in Table 13 show that the bounce rate for all sessions, which occurred on a Center's website between January 2017 and January 2019, is the highest in the case of social acquisition channel and the lowest in the case of organic search. The direct channel, which had the best conversion rate, as proved earlier, ranks second in regards to lowest bounce rate. A possible explanation of the low organic search bounce rate is the fact that organic search helps acquiring the customers who are already interested in the subject matter. Those customers are visiting a website to gather additional information regarding specific educational program and therefore are bouncing fewer that the customers originating from other acquisition channel.

As in the case of average session duration, an additional analysis was conducted aimed in determining the existence of correlation between acquisition channel efficiency measured by Conversion Rate (CR) and Bounce Rate for different acquisition channels (BR). Again, Pearson's correlation coefficient was used in order to quantify the possible correlation. The results in this regards are presented in Table 14.

The correlation coefficient in Table 14 prove the existence of the moderate negative correlation between Conversion Rate of different acquisition channels and Bounce Rates associated with them. The value of Pearson's correlation coefficient for those two sets of variables is -0.41458. This actually means that the better conversion rates of some acquisition channels are associated with lower bounce rates and vice versa.

Table 13. Bounce rate on a Center's website in a period between January 2017 and January 2019, by acquisition channels

Acquisition Channel	Bounce Rate %
Organic Search	18.74
Social	80.70
Direct	29.11
Referral	77.14

Source: (Google Analytics, 2019)

Table 14. Pearson's Correlation coefficient between conversion rate and bounce rate for a Center's website in a period between January 2017 and January 2019

	CR	BR
CR	1	
BR	-0.41458	1

Source: (Authors, 2019)

The overall conclusion of this part of the research is that there is a positive correlation between conversion rate and average session duration for different acquisition channels, meaning that users are converting better if they spend more time on a non-formal educational institution's website. Some acquisition channels are performing better in this regards than the others (direct visits and social). On the other side, there is a moderate negative correlation between conversion rates and bounce rates for different acquisition channels. It was proved in this regards that some acquisition channels are performing better than the others (organic search and direct visits). Based on all available data, it may be conclude that in a case of Center for professional education of the Institute of Economic Sciences, the best performing acquisition channel were direct visits.

RECOMMENDATIONS AND FUTURE RESEARCH DIRECTIONS

The method used in this paper can serve as a tool for successful performance evaluation of any other non-formal educational institution's website. The findings presented in this paper can also serve marketers employed in those institutions, to more successfully identify and target the prospective customers, and to apply marketing activities more effectively. As stated in introductory part, the tremendous growth of non-formal education worldwide led to a significant increase in numbers of non-formal education providers. Due to enormous competition and a tough fight for every customer, those institutions must optimize their websites and their overall efforts in successfully attracting new and retaining the existing customers.

In terms of recommendation for future research, it would be very useful if the data and conclusions of this research could be evaluated against a larger number of non-formal educational institutions. Therefore, it would be possible to check the relevance of the conclusions of this research, and to draw more specific conclusions and implications, which would be useful for the complete non-formal education industry.

In addition, one of the conclusions of the research, presented in this chapter, was that female visitors are converting into non-formal educational institution users six times more than male visitors. Therefore, it would be very useful to plan and execute a research, which would try to identify the exact reasons of such disproportion in conversion rates between the two categories of users.

As in a case of gender as one of personal characteristics of a user group, the research regarding age groups visiting the Center's website and using the Center's educational programs revealed that some age groups are converting better than the others are. The research also revealed that one specific user group (users between 25 and 34 years of age) are frequently visiting the Center's website, but are converting rarely with a conversion rate of 0.64, almost the smallest in a sample. A future research should be directed towards identifying the reasons for such a low conversion rate for this user group. If the true reasons were identified, the overall performance of a Center's website would be improved, since this users group represents the majority of Center's website visits.

CONCLUSION

The main purpose of this chapter was to measure a non-formal education institution's website performance using data originating from Google Analytics and a data originating from visitors who converted and became the users of Center's educational programs. A several specific objectives were set and analyzed in this chapter.

The first specific objective was to determine the most efficient acquisition channel in a case of a non-formal educational institution's website. The presented data and comparative analysis of different acquisition channels showed that the direct visits were the most efficient acquisition channel in a case of non-formal educational institution, with the highest conversion rate among all other acquisition channels. The reasons behind the high efficiency of direct visits in terms of high conversion rate were thoroughly explained and the implications could be important for other non-formal educational institutions as well.

The second specific objective of this chapter was to determine the average user profile in a case of non-formal educational institution focused on traditional learning context in classroom. The user characteristics were analyzed from different perspectives. The first one was the user gender. The results showed that females are converting six times more frequent than males and becoming the users of the non-formal institution's educational programs. It must be emphasized that this conclusion stands for the educational programs focused on accounting g and financial reports analysis. Besides gender, the users were analyzed in terms of their age as well. The results showed that the users in user group between 35 and 44 years of age are converting much more often than those from other age groups. The results also revealed that some user groups are frequently visiting the non-formal education institution's website but are rarely converting. This fact rises a question why is that so but the data available in this research could not provide enough evidence to investigate and understand the causes of such a situation.

The overall conclusion in terms of average profile of non-formal educational program focused on accounting and financial report analysis user is that it is a female between 35 and 44 years of age. This conclusion is very important for every non-formal educational institution, which is focused on similar educational programs and it could significantly improve the efficiency of their marketing endeavors and campaigns.

The second part of the research and performance evaluation which results were also presented in this chapter was directed towards user behavior data obtained from Goggle Analytics. The goal of this part of the research was to establish the existence of the correlation between conversion rates for different acquisition channels and average session duration and bounce rates, on the other side. This research can be observed as complementary to the first part of the research, directed towards best performing acquisition channel. The research revealed the existence of positive correlation between conversion rates and average session duration for different acquisition channels, and proved that the best performing acquisition channels in the case of Center's website were direct visits and social media. The research revealed the existence of negative correlation between conversion rates and bounce rates for different acquisition channels and proved that the best performing acquisition channels in this regards were organic search and direct visits.

Based on a data presented in this chapter, it can also be concluded that in terms of performance, which was measured for non-formal educational institution's website using Google Analytics data and combined with data collected in a separate research of institution's users, the best performing acquisition channel were direct visits for reasons explained earlier in this chapter.

DISCUSSION QUESTIONS

1. Do you find some other metrics in Google Analytics useful in terms of evaluating a website performance?
2. Are the results presented in this chapter applicable in the case of formal learning environment?
3. Which factors in your opinion drive the learners' readiness to participate in non-formal educational programs?
4. What are the reasons behind the fact that women are more interested in accounting and financial analysis educational programs?
5. Based on evidence in this chapter and other sources, how would you explain the relation between acquisition channels and average session duration?
6. Besides Google Analytics, what other solutions can be useful in terms of website performance evaluation?
7. Propose a set of measures for reduction of high bounce rate of a website's homepage.

ACKNOWLEDGMENT

This chapter is written as a part of research projects numbers III47009 (European integrations and social and economic changes in Serbian economy on the way to the EU) and OI179015 (Challenges and prospects of structural changes in Serbia: Strategic directions for economic development and harmonization with EU requirements), financed by the Ministry of Education, Science and Technological Development of the Republic of Serbia.

REFERENCES

Amo Filvà, D., Casany Guerrero, M. J., & Alier Forment, M. (2014). Google Analytics for Time Behavior Measurement in moodle. *Proceedings of the 9th Iberian Conference on Information Systems and Technologies*, 1-6. DOI: 10.1109/CISTI.2014.6877095

Barba, I., Cassidy, R., De Leon, E., & Williams, B. (2013). Web Analytics Reveal User Behavior: TTU Libraries' Experience with Google Analytics. *Journal of Web Librarianship*, 7(4), 389–400. doi:10.1080/19322909.2013.828991

Domazet, I. (2018). Digital Transformation of Business Portfolio through DCRM. In M. Radović (Ed.), *Digital Transformation - New Challenges and Business Opportunities* (pp. 214–235). London, UK: Silver and Smith Publishers.

Domazet, I., Lazić, M., & Zubović, J. (2018). Driving Factors of Serbian Competitiveness: Digital Economy and ICT. *Strategic Management: International Journal of Strategic Management and Decision Support Systems in Strategic Management*, 23(1), 20–28. doi:10.5937/StraMan1801020D

Domazet, I., & Neogradi, S. (2018). Digital Marketing and Service Industry: Digital Marketing in Banking Industry. In N. Ray (Ed.), *Managing Diversity, Innovation, and Infrastructure in Digital Business* (pp. 20–41). Hershey, PA: Information Science Publishing.

Eshach, H. (2006). Bridging In-school and Out-of-school Learning: Formal, Non-Formal, and Informal Education. *Journal of Science Education and Technology*, *16*(2), 171–190. doi:10.100710956-006-9027-1

Evans, M. (2007). Analysing Google rankings through search engine optimization data. *Internet Research*, *17*(1), 21–37. doi:10.1108/10662240710730470

Fang, W. (2007). Using Google Analytics for improving library website content and design: a case study. *Library Philosophy and Practice*, 1-17.

Gunter, U., & Önder, I. (2016). Forecasting city arrivals with Google Analytics. *Annals of Tourism Research*, *61*, 199–212. doi:10.1016/j.annals.2016.10.007

Hernandez, A., & Resnick, M. (2013). Placement of Call to Action Buttons for Higher Website Conversion and Acquisition. *Proceedings of the Human Factors and Ergonomics Society Annual Meeting*, *57*(1), 1042–1046. doi:10.1177/1541931213571232

Jankowski, J. (2013). Increasing Website Conversions Using Content Repetitions with Different Levels of Persuasion. *Intelligent Information and Database Systems*, 439-448. doi:10.1007/978-3-642-36543-0_45

Malcolm, J., Hodkinson, P., & Colley, H. (2003). The interrelationships between informal and formal learning. *Journal of Workplace Learning*, *15*(7/8), 313–318. doi:10.1108/13665620310504783

McDowell, W., Wilson, R., & Kile, C. Jr. (2016). An examination of retail website design and conversion rate. *Journal of Business Research*, *69*(11), 4837–4842. doi:10.1016/j.jbusres.2016.04.040

Plaza, B. (2011). Google Analytics for measuring website performance. *Tourism Management*, *32*(3), 477–481. doi:10.1016/j.tourman.2010.03.015

Romi, S., & Schmida, M. (2009). Non-formal education: A major educational force in the postmodern era. *Cambridge Journal of Education*, *39*(2), 257–273. doi:10.1080/03057640902904472

Shih, B., Chen, C., & Chen, Z. (2012). Retracted: An Empirical Study of an Internet Marketing Strategy for Search Engine Optimization. *Human Factors and Ergonomics in Manufacturing & Service Industries*, *23*(6), 528–540. doi:10.1002/hfm.20348

Siemens, G. (2013). Learning Analytics. *The American Behavioral Scientist*, *57*(10), 1380–1400. doi:10.1177/0002764213498851

Simovic, V., & Radovic-Markovic, M. (2018). Modern business environment and entrepreneurship education. In M. Radović (Ed.), *Digital Transformation - New Challenges and Business Opportunities* (pp. 148–169). London, UK: Silver and Smith Publishers.

The Future of Accounting is Female: Women in Accounting are on the Rise - CPA Exam Hub. (2019). Retrieved from https://cpaexamhub.com/blog/future-accounting-female-women-accounting-rise/

ADDITIONAL READING

Beckerman, Z., & Silberman-Keller, D. (2003). Professing nonformal education. *Educational Research for Policy and Practice*, *2*(3), 237–256. doi:10.1023/B:ERPP.0000034518.97695.88

Domazet, I., Đokić, O., & Milovanov, O. (2018). The Influence of Advertising Media on Brand Awareness. *Management: Journal of Sustainable Business and Management Solutions in Emerging Economies,* *23*(1), 13–22.

Domazet, I., Stošić, I., & Hanić, A. (2016). New technologies aimed at improving the competitiveness of companies in the services sector. In X. Richet (Ed.), *Europe and Asia: Economic Integration Prospects* (pp. 363–377). Nice, France: CEMAFI International.

Falk, J. H., & Storksdieck, M. (2005). Using the contextual model of learning to understand visitor learning from a science center exhibition. *Science Education, 89*(5), 1–35. doi:10.1002ce.20078

Farney, T. A. (2011). Click Analytics: Visualizing Website Use Date. *Information Technology and Libraries, 30*(3), 141–148. doi:10.6017/ital.v30i3.1771

Grable, J. E., & Britt, S. L. (2011). An Investigation of Response Bias Associated with Electronically Delivered Risk-Tolerance Assessment. *Journal of Financial Therapy Association, 2*(1), 43–52.

Little, G. (2012). Managing Technology: Where Are You Going, Where Have You Been? The Evolution of the Academic Library Website. *Journal of Academic Librarianship, 38*(2), 123–125. doi:10.1016/j.acalib.2012.02.005

Tamir, P. (1990). Factors associated with the relationship between formal, informal, and nonformal science learning. *The Journal of Environmental Education, 2*(2), 34–42. doi:10.1080/00958964.1991.9943052

KEY TERMS AND DEFINITIONS

Acquisition Channels: A type of route user takes to reach to the desired website. It can be organic search, referral, direct, social, paid search, etc.

Bounce Rate: The percentage of website visitors who left the website immediately after viewing one page only.

Conversion Rate: Number of website visitors who became the customers and buyers of the certain product/service.

Informal Learning: This type of learning takes place outside schools and colleges and usually is not initiated with a learning purpose in mind.

Non-Formal Leaning: A type of learning which takes place outside the traditional learning environment and within some kind of organizational framework

Search Engine Optimization: A set of different techniques used to improve a page rank of the certain web page on a search engine. Many factors affect search engine optimization and search engines are constantly changing the algorithms used for page ranking.

URL: Uniform resource locators or a complete address of a website.

Web Analytics: The process of website users' behavior analysis, performed in order to attract more visitors to a specific web location.

Chapter 24
Investigating the Information Perception Value (IPV) Model in Maintaining the Information Security:
Bruneian Perspective

Sharul Tajuddin
Universiti Teknologi Brunei, Brunei

Afzaal H. Seyal
https://orcid.org/0000-0002-2571-5366
Universiti Teknologi Brunei, Brunei

Norfarrah Binti Muhamad Masdi
Universiti Teknologi Brunei, Brunei

Nor Zainah H. Siau
Universiti Teknologi Brunei, Brunei

ABSTRACT

This pioneering study is conducted among 150 employees from various ministries of Brunei Darussalam regarding their perception in maintaining the information security and to validate the IPV model using linear regression data analysis techniques. The IPV model identifies the factors that affect the user's perception of information values and to further assess as how these perceptions of information value affect their behavior in information security environment. The results show that IPV model have significant predicting power the employees' behavior with more than half of the variance (59%) in information value is shared by these six contextual variables. However, four out of six antecedent variables monetary value, ministerial jurisdiction, spiritual, and social values are significantly predicting the information value. The study has significant impact both for the researchers and practitioners and will add value to the current repository of broad knowledge in information security behavior.

DOI: 10.4018/978-1-5225-8933-4.ch024

INTRODUCTION

The first decade of 21ˢᵗ century has brought a radical shift in ICT paradigm with emergence of new technologies such as IoT, Big Data, Cloud Computing, Artificial Intelligence and Virtual Reality. These technologies have changed the corporate world by empowering the end user with better operative command and communication to have a competitive advantage among businesses. At the same time when end users are getting the benefits of the pervasive and ubiquitous computing, the CEOs and CIOs, especially of Fortune 500 companies have been given a more difficult task to protect their valuable assets-data not only from the outside intruders- but to continuously developing a policy to protect it from the inside loss.

Information is still one of the major assets in an organization or business. A loss in information can greatly produce negative impacts on an organization. In the case of Target's data breach in 2013 there was a loss of 70 million customers financial data which caused customers to lose trust towards the company that resulted in reduced sales during that month of the event (Plachkinova & Maurer, 2018). It was identified that the point of entry of the attack was from the use of stolen credentials of third-party service providers. Therefore, it is important to protect information to prevent negative impacts on businesses.

It is widely known in information security that the human aspect is the weakest link in security defence (Bashorun, Worwui, & Parker, 2013) and every organization must address this issue within their domain and framework. Before managing the people factor in information security, security experts must know how the people behave towards the information. The IPV (Information Perception Value) model was developed to understand the human factor in the information security environment.

The IPV model is a model which identifies the factors that affect the user's perception of information values and how these perceptions of information value affect their behaviour in the information security environment (Doherty & Tajuddin, 2018). This research project extends the research on the current IPV model because the model itself is newly developed and has not been tested in a larger population. The IPV model had been proven valid and true using qualitative research conducted in the public sector in Brunei Darussalam (Doherty & Tajuddin, 2018).

Problem Statement

The IPV model is built and verified using qualitative methods. Although the model is proven to be valid, there are two problems that are associated with the IPV model. There is a need to prove it using statistical measures to ensure that the model will work if the model is used in maintaining information security.

The first problem is whether the model can be used in managing different individuals with different backgrounds in a different environment. It is unknown whether the model can be used by different types of organizations that employ a lot of people with a different background or the model can only be used in a certain organization. The importance of the IPV model is that it helps gain insight into the factors that dominate people's behaviour towards protecting information. These insights help the organization to manage the people aspects in an information security environment by developing countermeasures to handle the factors affecting the people. Therefore, it is important to ensure that the model can be generalized to the population as suggested by a group of researchers who question whether the model can be generalized to a large population or as individuals or groups (Alohali, Clarke, Furnell, & Albakri, 2018). If the model can be used with the general population, different management can implement the model in their organization to manage the human aspect of information security.

The second problem is the importance of each of the influencing factors that affect an individual's perception and behaviour. The impact of each factor towards the assignment of information value is not known in the model. There are a lot of influential factors that contribute to the IPV model. Thus, prioritizing the factors becomes crucial in this study. Tajuddin (2016) and Albrechtsen, (2007) proposed different models but both suggest the use of statistical measure to determine the importance of each factor that affects the user's perceived value of information. In a study, it was discovered by the researchers that age, working industry, and education level are the factors that affect compliance behaviour (Chua, Wong, Low, & Chang, 2018). Other studies suggest that to encourage compliance behaviour, the management should focus on the personal norm (established PIV) which is usually influenced by an external factor which is the social norm (Yazdanmehr & Wang, 2016). Studies also found that social factors affect the compliance behaviour because individuals want to act based on the group norms due to the social power that the group has (Sowden, Lymberopoulos, Militaru, & Catmur, 2018). A different researcher believes that different characteristics of important factors affect people's behaviour towards information. Therefore, it is crucial to discover what factors have a high impact on a person's perception of information.

The importance of each factor can help management to prioritize which factor that needs to be managed well within an organization. Some factors might not have a big impact on an individual's behaviour. Depending on the importance of the factors, an organization can put a different level of effort in managing the different factors that affect the people in the organization. If a factor has a high impact level on an individual's perception of information, then the organization might want to put extra effort into managing that specific factor. It might take a lot of the organization's resources to manage all the influencing factors. Management would want to manage their resources properly without wasting resources on factors that might not have an impact on the individual.

Objectives of the Study

This study is conducted to test the validity of the IPV model in maintaining the security of information in a different geographical setting with different sets of the users. However, the specific objectives are mentioned below:

1. To determine the validity and suitability of the IPV model to test and augment with the quantitative methodology approach and to compare the results with previous studies.
2. To identify the significant factors in IPV model that dominates an individual's behaviours towards information?

LITERATURE REVIEW

At the outset, the review of literature section is composed of four sections. The first section will be focusing on information value and information security followed by section that will address the human aspects of information security, information security in the government sector. The fourth and final section will discuss the IPV model that will be used in this quantitative research.

Information Value and Information Security

Information is considered an asset by many organizations in the world. A lot of organizations rely on information to conduct their businesses. Information value refers to how important the information is to the individual or an organization. It means that whether the information can cause harm to others or whether information can benefit an individual or organization. Information is considered a fundamental asset for the organization and information security is a process of protecting the information assets (Thomson & Von Solms, 2005).

Information security can be defined as countermeasures implemented to protect information in order to maintain information confidentiality, integrity, and availability. They further group in physical and virtual security. Information security's main objectives are to protect and safeguard the information assets. Currently, the objectives of information security include accountability, authenticity, non-repudiation, and the reliability of the information resources. Without achieving all of these objectives, information is not secure (Von Solms & Van Niekerk, 2013).

Information Security Challenges

Information security challenges focus on the challenges arises from different elements of security. To identify the challenges, the BMIS (Business Model for Information Security) model will be used to classify challenges based on the elements of the BMIS. Based on the BMIS model, the information security takes into account of organization, technology, process and the people and all the four elements affect each other which means that changes in one of the elements, the management should manage the change not only on the changed element but on the other elements too (ISACA, 2009). For example, when adding in new technology to information security, it will affect the people who will be using the technology. It also will affect the process since the technology is used to enhance the process and organization might need to revise their organization strategy to adapt to the change in technology.

The biggest threats to information security are the people elements due to the unpredictable behaviour of people. People are the biggest threats within an organization because of their personal knowledge and access to the organization's information (Colwill, 2009). Some information security attacks can only be done by people working in the organization (the insider) and not people from outside the organization, the outsiders (Colwill, 2009), This suggests that people can commit attacks from inside or from the outside.

There are three different categories of users (insiders) based on their errors made towards information security in an organization. The three categories are the neutral user who has no intention to do harm but has bad security behaviour, such as, choosing the date of birth as passwords; benevolent users whose intention is to protect information and thus adopt a good security behaviour, such as, reporting any security incident; and finally the malicious users where the user has the intention to cause harm to the information or by using the information (Stanton, Stam, Mastrangelo, & Jolton, 2005). The problematic behaviours are from malicious and neutral users.

An example of a neutral user's behaviours is posting information on social media. The most common task affecting information security was the posting of information and the sharing of information through email (Evans, and He, 2018). It was also identified that most security incidents occur where the task that is routine and required a low-level of skill to complete (ibid). Sarkar (2010) provided an example in his study that most of the time where the end users' rely heavily on technologies to protect their organization's information they tend to practice insecure behaviour.

People also tend to circumvent information security measures or policy because they perceived that the measures complicate or delay their tasks (Sarkar, 2010). In a study conducted for final-year medical students at the University of Toronto, the students were asked about the use of smartphone in sharing information with their colleagues during their residency and it was found that they perceived that the use of smartphones increased their efficiency but most of the student's smartphones are not properly equipped with security features to protect information which increases the risk of privacy breaches (Tran et al., 2014).

Sarkar (2010) described more trends from insider threats, such as, framing people to take the blame for causing information security incidents, planting malicious code to be triggered when needed, social engineering which involves in manipulating other people to disclose sensitive information. People called moles are inadvertently hired to enter an organization to commit espionage, fraud or embezzlement. Finally, social networking is where employees might unintentionally release the organization's information (Sarkar, 2010)

Another challenge from the people elements is the ability of the user to determine the sensitivity or confidentiality of the information. Some users found it difficult to determine which information is sensitive and which information can be legally be disclosed. This is the case if users are dealing with a large amount of information (Cross, 2002).

The review of the literature on information security challenges focused on challenges posed by the insiders. The challenges discovered were that people may not fully understand the sensitivity of a piece of information and even when they understand it, they might still trade the protection of information to increase their efficiency.

Information Security in Government

Government agencies like any other organization face information security challenges. The difference is that the government has a hierarchical structure which can impact decision-making especially in regards to information security (Fyfe & Crookall, 2010). It was stated in a study that the government serves the people of a country, therefore it is required of them to have an information security that follows the laws of the country and at the same time the government needs to maintain a trusting relationship between the government and the citizens (AlKalbani, Deng, & Kam, 2015). Information handled by the government is considered as highly security sensitive since misusing the population's data invites tough penalty (Pandya & Patel, 2017). Governments are also concerned with the security of a system but they are less concerned about the privacy of the data which means they tend to underestimate the human factor of information security (Pandya & Patel, 2017).

The disclosing of information and the misuse of information exists in the public sector even before the social media introduction (Fyfe & Crookall, 2010). Based on a study conducted in Greece, it was discovered that the Greek public sector values the confidentiality of information due to the information containing personal and sensitive data but that the populace lacks extensive awareness of information system security (Loukis, 2001). An analysis using the UK Information Commissioner's Office (ICO) and the UK National Health Service (NHS)'s reports on the public sector incidents and data breach identified that 64% of incidents are caused by human error while another 27% of the incidents have the possibility of being caused by human error which suggested that a total of 91% of incidents reported are caused by human error (Evans & He, 2018).

According to Global Cybersecurity Index 2017, Brunei Darussalam global rank is 53rd and Brunei is categorized as at a maturing stage and is defined as having developed complex commitments to cybersecurity, taking initiatives towards cybersecurity and engaging in cybersecurity programmes (ITU, 2017). It was also mentioned that about 38% of governments globally have published a cybersecurity strategy. Brunei also has developed strategic plans which are called the Digital Government Strategic Plans for the year 2015 to 2020 and one of the focus areas in the plan is for the government to be aware of its digital assets and environment, and to respond to cyber-incidents effectively ("Digital Government Strategy 2015 - 2020 Brunei Darussalam," 2015).

Based on the review of the literature, employees under the employment of the public sector are concerned with information privacy and confidentiality although they only have a basic awareness of information security which means they know and take countermeasures such as creating a backup and using a firewall.

IPV Model

The Information Perception Value (IPV) model acts as a guideline for the organization to manage the people's security behaviour through managing the views of the people on information within the organization. The IPV model is based on the perception of people towards information rather than focusing on people information security compliance's behaviour done by the other researchers.

There are many studies that were conducted in the information security area, more specifically on information security compliance behaviour. One research concentrates on the relationship between cognitive processing, social influence and social bonding with information security compliance behaviour (Ifinedo, 2014). Another researcher concentrates on using the health belief model to study user's compliance behaviour (Ng, Kankanhalli, & Xu, 2009). Another study focuses on managing behaviour of the organizations in levels where the levels are divided into three, which are the individual level, workgroup level and the formal organization (Vroom & Von Solms, 2004). The IPV model is also one of the models that not only focus on improving information security behaviour but also focuses on the information valuation.

The IPV model suggested that the higher the perceived information value, the higher the value assignment which would increase the compliance behaviour of the individual. The model believes that if the information is important to an individual, the individual would take actions willingly such as adopting protective behaviour on the information. Figure 1 shows the general IPV model. IPV model is a model that shows different criteria that can affect an individual's value assignment, the perception of information value and the compliance behaviour.

In the models, the main factors that affect the value assignment are the espoused information value, established perceived information value (PIV) and the work-group PIV. Espoused information value is how the organizations value their information. Established PIV is an individual's own principle without the influence of the organization, workgroup and the contextual factors and this is further influenced by rewards and penalty, their work contexts, instructions, awareness education and training, peer actions and environment elements. Contextual factors that influenced workgroup PIV are the information's monetary value and ministerial jurisdiction. The other four contextual factors influenced all of the main factors. Under the contextual factors, the other four factors are the cultural demand, spiritual, social value and information sensitivity. Cultural demand is influenced by spiritual and social value. Therefore, the construct used in the model contributes and affect the value assignment. (Tajuddin, 2016)

Figure 1. IPV model
(Tajuddin, 2016)

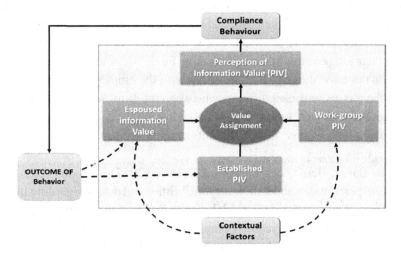

How the individuals value the information will change the individual's PIV and how they perceive the information will drive their compliance behaviour. The outcome of their compliance behaviour can then affect the individual's established PIV. It is a cyclic model that implies that any changes in any of the factors in the model can affect other factors in the model especially the three major factors of the model. Based on the above assertion, it is evident that there is a strong need to conduct a study with data collected quantitatively in order to augment and to further test the parsimony and robustness of the model within the context of Brunei Darussalam.

Research Model

From the IPV model, it is seen that the focus is on three main perspectives of information value. There are individual priorities, organizational priorities, and cultural demand. Not all factors that affect the three main factors will be included in this research due to research constraints. Only six out of 11 of the contextual factors are selected for the proposed research model. For the proposed research model, the three main perspectives will be the major parts of the model. Under each of these perspectives, there are only two factors selected to develop the model.

Individual Priorities

Individual priorities refer to how an individual prioritizes the information they handle. In other words, individual priorities can be defined as the individual perception of the importance of information. Personal norms (individual's belief and value) finds a relationship between information security compliance and behaviour (Sohrabi, Von Solms, & Furnell, 2016; Yazdanmehr & Wang, 2016). From these studies, personal norms have a positive influence on information security compliance and behaviour. The two factors under individual priorities are the work context and peer actions and environment.

Work Context

Work context for an individual means how an individual perceives their task or responsibilities associated with their job, the importance of their job, and the condition under which they perform their work. The work context itself describes the job itself. The work context can include the job level, the types of responsibilities and their job position. In a research done by da Veiga and Martins (2017), it was discovered that job levels do not have significant relationship with the employee's perception when protecting the information but there is a significant difference between the employees who work in IT (Information Technology) and those that do not work in IT which is due to the nature of their work. The study also indicates that employees who worked in IT value information security more and they do adhere closer to the information security policy.

In a study done by Bauer, Bernroider, and Chudzikowski (2017) in a bank setting, it was identified that users have different perceptions about their responsibilities and duties regarding information security policy (ISP) compliance. The user from the bank branch perceived that they are burdened with a heavy workload daily which led to the employees to complete their main task at the cost of noncompliance to ISP (Bauer, Bernroider, & Chudzikowski, 2017). They also determine that both users from the bank's branch and headquarters perceived that information security is handled by the IT personnel and not by themselves (Bauer et al., 2017). Lee, Lee, and Kim (2016) also suggested that information ISP compliance cause work overload which led to being one of the major ISS stressors which led to noncompliance. Work context is important in determining the value of information (Engelsman, 2007). Thus, it is hypothesized that:

H1: Work context is positively related to an information value assignment.

Peer Actions and Environment

Peer actions and environment refers to an individual's co-workers and superior's behaviours within the organization. In this factor, it is assumed that the superior's and co-worker's affect individual behaviour. In simple terms, an individual will mimic the perceived behaviour of the people within the environment of the organization.

Johnston and Warkentin use the term 'social influence' to define the perception of individual of acceptable or unacceptable behaviour by their peers and supervisor (Johnston & Warkentin, 2017). The research determined that 'social influence' is positively related to behaviour intention in using information security. In a research conducted by da Veiga and Martins it was shown that the perception of the employee towards their superior's adherence to information security policy helps in developing a strong information security culture (da Veiga & Martins, 2017).

Herath and Rao (2009$_b$) also supported the social influence factor. Jaafar and Ajis (2013) found that the co-worker socialization factor is significantly related to information security compliance behaviour but the upper management practice and direct supervisory practice are found to be insignificant. Upper management practice refers to top management behaviours that the employee's perceived while direct supervisory practice refers to the repeated actions taken by their immediate supervisor.

Ifinedo conducted two kinds of research where it is found that the subjective norm (supervisor's and co-worker's perception of the individual's actions) have a positive and significant correlation with the information system security policy compliance behavioural intention (Ifinedo, 2012, 2014). Ifinedo suggested that an individual may follow another co-worker or their superior as a role model in determining whether specific beliefs or actions are acceptable or suitable within the organization (Ifinedo, 2014).

According to another study in a hospital setting, Cross, (2002) found that therapist would seek advice from their superior or their senior when deciding to disclose their patient's confidential information shared by the patient themselves.

Based on these reviews of literature, a hypothesis is created for the research model which is:

H2: Peer actions and the environment are positively related to an information value assignment.

Organizational Priorities

Organizational priorities refer to the perceptions of information as a group instead of as an individual. A group can be formed within the organization by a department, by similar interest/goals, by their responsibilities or by the whole organization itself. The two factors under organizational priorities are the monetary value and ministerial jurisdiction.

Monetary Value

Su, (2006, p-4) quotes: *"Today information security is shifting from what is technically possible to what is economically effective"*. Several financial metrics such as return on investment (ROI), net present value (NPV) and internal rate of return (IRR) that have been developed previously, are now being used by the majority of the organizations to measure the organizational performance in keeping information security (Sue, 2006). Whereas, Chai et al. (2011) pointed out that besides these parameters other methods, such as, firm's reputation, customer's trust and competitive advantages could be measured to estimate the information security investment. Researchers focused on the cost and benefit of sharing data on security breaches, threats and potential solution with so called Information Sharing Alliances (ISAs) (Anderson and Choobinch, 2008; Goodman and Ramer, 2007). Monetary value is one of the factors of the IPV model which refers to information that is associated with money. The higher the information value in terms of money, the higher is the perception of the importance of that information. Information that has high monetary value may include the organization's budget and salaries. Therefore, departments that deal with money might have better security and stricter security policy than other departments. The financial sector is always sensitive to security issues since they deal with money (Locher, 2005).

H3: Monetary value is positively related to information value assignment.

Ministerial Jurisdiction

A ministry is a government functional entity that is established to handle specific functions for the country. There are thirteen (13) ministries in Brunei and each ministry performs a specific function. Thus, they also deal with the different information they need in order to manage the affairs. Ministerial jurisdiction refers to the way a different ministry manages the same information. In other words, sensitivity of the information and its perceived value is dependent on specific functions of each ministry so it is plausible to say that each ministry might value the same information differently. Unfortunately, study could not get much support for the inclusion of this variable from the literature. Up to our knowledge and exhaustive search the variable in the present context was not used explicitly especially among ASEAN and in Asia-Pacific countries. So we self-developed the construct by borrowing items from the various sources and rephrasing them to capture better meaning and image. That may be added as one of the limitations of this study.

Researchers further narrated that the development of an information security culture is affected by the strategy and vision of the management (da Veiga & Martins, 2017). The research also recommended a study conducted on different industries and sectors to identify whether industries or sectors affect the information culture over different jurisdictions.

In another study conducted in Taiwan, it was found that organization types can be a good predictor for building information security policy (Hong, Chi, Chao, & Tang, 2006). They also emphasized on understanding the organization because organizations have different core operations. Therefore, in some organizations, information security is considered as a big asset compared to other organizations and needs to be seriously protected (Hong et al. 2006).

Chang and Ho, (2006) highlighted the importance of organization's type on information security management. The researchers state that some organizations, such as, financial institutions, internal and external security agencies would weight information security heavily and in return they passionately dedicate themselves to the management of information security on top priority basis.

H4: Ministerial jurisdiction is positively related to information value assignment.

Cultural Demand

The studies on cultural demand explicitly discuss culture from two aspects, namely, national and organizational culture. Some countries that are high in collectivism, masculine and power distance have a dominating national culture (Hofstede et al. 1990). Whereas, organizational culture is defined as "the way things are done in an organization" (Lundy and Cowling, 1996). Yeats and Cadel, (1996) defined as unwritten rules of life and the assumption about the way in which work is done. Thus, the organizational culture is also different for every organization each having its own set of characteristics that it values, such as working in teams rather than as individuals (Robbins, 2001). Martins and Eloff (2002, p-25) in their study of information security culture stated that every organization has certain information security practices that are followed and incorporated into the working environment that will become part of the organizational culture in the organization. This notion continues with the emergence of information security culture that leads to the collection of set of information security characteristics. In other words, information security culture is an assumption of what is and what is not acceptable (ibid). In the presence of information security culture, the information security compliance behaviour among employees could be easily adopted. Cultural demand in the context of IPV model refers to the behaviour of the environment surrounding an individual. Cultural demand does not only refer to the immediate surrounding's behaviours and perception but also include a bigger surrounding, such as a country's population behaviours and perception. In Brunei Darussalam, it employs MIB (Melayu Islam Beraja or Malay Islamic Monarchy) ideology which affects the country's perceptions and behaviours.

Researchers continuously reported that information security behaviour is affected by factors and national and organizational culture plays a significant role (Tajuddin, 2016; Doherty & Tajuddin, 2017). Parsons et al. (2011) conducted a study for the Department of Defence, Australian Government regarding human factors and information security from individual, cultural and security environments. They (ibid) concluded that culture and climate not only have significant impact on values, attitudes and behaviours but culture plays an important aspect in information security. In another study, the researcher developed a framework for developing an information security culture where one of the building blocks of the framework was the national culture (Alhogail, 2015). Colwill, (2009) also emphasized the regional culture, national culture and religion factors in order to identify and manage insider threats. Greene and D'Arcy (2011) conducted a study in the USA to assess the impact of security culture and the employee-organizational relationship on information systems security compliance and found that security culture and job satisfaction lead to increased compliant security behaviour.

The two factors proposed under the cultural demands are the spiritual which relates to the religion and social values which focused on how an individual's relationship affects their own behaviours.

Spiritual

Spiritual in this model relates to one's ethics and religion. The main religion in Brunei is Islam where 78% of the people have Islam as their religion in 2011 (Perangkaan & Menteri, 2015). Therefore, the spiritual context in this research will mainly involve the Islamic concept which is 'Amanah' which means trust or trustworthiness.

There are previous researches that focused on different religion and how a person's religion or religiosity relates to different behaviours in different contexts. In their study Grullon, Kanatas and Weston, (2009) found that organizations that are located in an area where communities have high religiosity have a lower likelihood of unethical corporate behaviour (Grullon, Kanatas, & Weston, 2009).

In another research conducted by Keller, Smith, and Smith, focused on studying the students in a university in the U.S. which shows that the most influential factor on ethical decision making is religiosity regardless of gender (Keller, Smith, & Smith, 2007). Rettinger and Jordan (2005) in their study on student's cheating behaviour in an examination found that the higher the religiosity the lesser is the cheating behaviour among students. Abar, Carter, and Winsler, (2009) conducted another study on student's religiosity and found that the higher the religiosity of the students, the lower their risk-taking behaviour.

Several studies have focused on Islam as religion and to its moral and ethical teaching. Yousef (2000) in his study indicated that the Islamic Work Ethics relationship is significant with organizational commitment. In another study, Rokhman, (2010) and Yousef, (1999) concluded that Islamic work ethics have positive and significant relationship with organizational commitment which means that higher the Islamic work ethics, the greater individuals are committed to the organization. Within the context of this study, commitment would mean an individual who will dedicate themselves to protect the organization's information.

Whereas, Zulhuda, (2010) in her study described the principles and practices of information security within Islamic perspective including the "Amanah" concept. Abdulmunir, (2018) suggested the four Islamic values which are trustworthiness, truthfulness, intelligence, and advocacy that the top management must have in order to have a better information security governance. Based on these findings, a hypothesis is proposed:

H5: Spirituality is positively related to information value assignment.

Social Values

The term social value in this IPV model context refers to the perception of people who have a close relationship with the individual outside the organization's environment. This relationship can be in the form of family ties, marriage relationship (an individual's spouse) or just simply an individual's close

Figure 2. Proposed research model

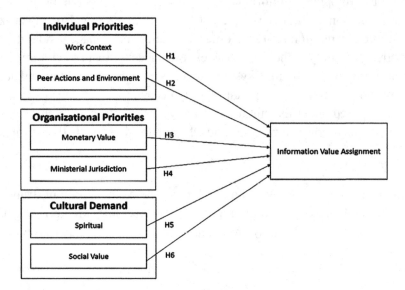

friends. Social values in the IPV model suggest that an individual's behaviours are affected by the perception of those closely related to them.

There is research that found that there is a negative relationship between family and friend discovery and software piracy's behaviour disapproval which means that the greater the family and friend disapproval of such action, the lesser the software's piracy behaviour demonstrated by the students (Higgins, Wilson, & Fell, 2005).

In another research that was conducted on Saudi Arabia focused on giving high value to the family and personal relationship leading to decisions that are affected by the individual's desires to please their family or friends (Alkahtani, Lock, & Dawson, 2013). Similarly, a study in China states that the Chinese people value relationship higher than others ethical guidelines, thus they prefer to deal with any situation or decision by confiding with their family or friends which can be good and bad depending on the situations (Luo, Warkentin, Johnston, & Luo, 2009). In the same study, it was stated that Westerners value law, rules, and guidelines compared to their personal relationship with others (Luo et al., 2009).

H6: Social value is positively related to information value assignment.

Based on the contextual variables a normative model was developed to highlight the relationship and to test its suitability to the context of Brunei Darussalam.

METHODOLOGY

Design of Instrument

The standard instrument used to collect the survey responses of the employees consist of seven parts. The part A or section 1 is to collect information about demographics. Section 2 to 7 was included to collect responses on six specific constructs that were grouped in individual, organizational and cultural factors. Each item measured on five-point Likert scale from 1 to 5 whether the respondents strongly disagree to strongly agree with the statement. This study used existing questions from the various studies referenced in review of literature with the exception of one construct "ministerial jurisdiction" which is self-developed for this study. Dependent variable for this study is information value assignment that measured the items on the users 'behaviour towards information whether they have safe behaviours towards information because the higher the perceived value of the information, the higher the security behaviour. The construct measured three items from safeguarding, recommending and assisting others in protecting organizational information assets. All these three items were adapted after Siponen et al. (2010). The question of validity is undertaken in a similar way of all independent variables.

Pilot Study

After designing the questionnaire it was then sent to senior staff members of an academic institution to improve the content and face validity. Some items were rephrased and reworded for clarity. In order to test the reliability, validity of the questionnaire and sensitivity of the study, it was very important to undergo pilot testing. Therefore a pilot study was conducted with 31 reusable samples of the randomly selected employees of some ministries that are located close to the researchers' work place The purpose of the pilot study is to discover errors or faulty in the questionnaires and to check whether the items measuring various constructs were logical. If questions were cleared and easily understood it further allows the researchers to check on the selected variables that could easily be processed and analysed. Every item in each constructs was passed through SPSS procedure on reliability and any item that was found to have value less than 0.40 on corrected-item total was dropped out from the construct. Based on this procedure, the original questionnaire that measured 38 items were reduced to 30 items with Cronbach's alpha values ranging .76 to .89. Table 2 shows the quality control statistics of the pilot study.

Population and Sample

Before distributing the questionnaires, it is best to determine enough sample size that can be used to obtain the correct result from the data analysis. To determine the sample size, use a sample size calculator that is based on the confidence level, population size, and margin of error. For the population size, the total numbers of employees working with 13 ministries were considered.*(Brunei Darussalam Key Indicators (BDKI)*, 2016).

Before the dissemination of the questionnaires, the questionnaires were developed on an online questionnaires tool which is the Google Form. The distribution of the questionnaires will be through the link provided by the online questionnaire's tools. To focus on the target population, the link will be sent through the target population's email. For the distribution to the target's email, there is a plan to liaise with the EGNC (E-Government National Centre). Several methods were used to distribute the questionnaires through the use of social media and distributing those using paper-based questionnaires that are delivered to different ministries.

The Survey

At the outset, 200 questionnaires were distributed randomly to all the ministries, out of them; we received 160 questionnaires and out of these ten questionnaires were discarded because of incomplete information. A total number of 150 responses were retained with the response rate of 75% which is adequate for survey research.

Reliability and Validity

The reliability and the validity of the questionnaires are measured using the SPSS software. SPSS software also was used to generate a demographic summary of the respondents. Table 3 shows the demographics of the respondents. It shows that most of the respondents are female (53%) and it also shows that the highest number of respondents comes from the age of 40 to 49 (45%). The highest number of respondents are from the Ministry of Education (47%) compared to the other three ministries selected for the pilot study.

The first method used to test reliability was the Cronbach's Alpha which was used to purify the data. The result of the measure is shown in Table 1 which is the reliability and validity statistics table. The table shows that some construct's original number of items in the first column is larger compared to the second column which is the number of items retained after the purification. Items were dropped when the Cronbach's Alpha value is less than 0.70 or the Corrected Item-Total Correlation is less than 0.40 (Gliem & Gliem, 2003). The mean and standard deviation is also shown in Table 2. The mean can show the answers that respondents prefer. All constructs have a low standard deviation that indicates that responses do not deviate much which is good for the constructs.

The reliability coefficient was taken for each construct which is in the range 0.76 to 0.89 and it is considered a very good indicator of the reliability and validity. From the retained items, the composite reliability (CR) was calculated and composite reliability is an indicator of validity which further shows that all the constructs account for greater than 50% variance except the monetary value construct where it is slightly below 50%. There were two options available to handle the monetary value construct. The options are either to drop the construct or to use the construct with caution. The monetary value construct was not dropped. All the constructs are then used for the final analysis which is the regression analysis.

Table 1. Reliability statistics of pilot study

	No. of Original Items	**No. of Items Retained**	**Mean**	**Std. Dev**	**Cronbach's Alpha**	**CR**	**Source**
Work Context	9	5	4.03	.71	.76	.63	Wright 2004; Chen 2008
Peer Actions & Environment	4	4	4.08	.77	.83	.75	Herath & Rao 2009[b]
Monetary Value	5	3	4.10	.72	.83	.48	Tang 2003; Lim 2003
Ministerial Jurisdiction	5	5	3.96	.73	.83	.56	Self-developed
Spiritual	8	7	4.10	.58	.84	.54	Keller 2007; Rokhman, 2010
Social Value	4	3	4.38	.62	.89	.69	Herath &Rao 2009[b]
Information Value Assignment	3	3	4.33	.63	.86	.71	Siponen et al. 2010
TOTAL ITEMS	38	30					

Table 2. Reliability statistics for full study

	No. of Items After Pilot Study	No. of Items Retained Full study	Mean	Std. Dev	Cronbach's Alpha	CR	AVE
Work Context	5	3	4.12	.68	.71	.58	.50
Peer Actions & Environment	4	4	3.96	.70	.81	.72	.52
Monetary Value	3	3	4.10	.83	.86	.58	.50
Ministerial Jurisdiction	5	5	3.76	.73	.88	.84	.54
Spiritual	7	6	4.21	.58	.82	.76	.50
Social Value	3	3	3.95	.78	.88	.81	.60
Information Value Assignment	3	3	4.23	.70	.87	.80	.58
TOTAL ITEMS	30	**27**					

After purifying the data, the correlation analysis was done and the results are shown in Table 4. The correlation analysis indicates that most constructs correlate with each other and the entire constructs correlate with the dependent variable which is the information value assignment.

In order to assess the validity and reliability, tests were performed in this study. To get the reliability of the questionnaire, the coefficient of Cronbach's alpha (Cronbach, 1951) was taken into account. Minimum Cronbach's alpha values were greater than 0.70 to indicate reliability of the instrument (Nunnally, 1978). Convergence validity measured by average variance extracted (AVE) should be at least 0.5 (Indrawati and Mas-Marhaeni, 2015). Table 2 shows AVE in the last column and one half of all the values are above .50 and one half is at marginal value cut off value of .50 that does not represent an ideal value, however for the study it shows that the validity is acceptable.

RESULT

The data obtained from the survey were analysed using descriptive statistic features of SPSS-21. The model was tested by correlation and linear regression method.

Background Profile

Table 3 summarizes the background data and characteristics of participants. Most were females in the age group of 40-49 (45%) who represented mature respondents. Majority of the surveyed participants were from Ministry of Education.

Prior to the analyzing the data by regression analysis, we conducted zero-order correlational analysis. Results are shown in Table 4 that further confirms the presence of moderate to slightly higher but significant correlation between all seven constructs.

While Pearson correlation is useful for testing individual hypotheses, it does not provide the means for studying the combined efforts of all independent variables and their relative importance. A regres-

Table 3. Demographic profile

Variable	Description	Percentage
Gender	Male	47%
	Female	53%
Age	20 – 29	11%
	30 – 39	24%
	40 – 49	45%
	50 – 59	20%
Ministries	Ministry of Defence	4%
	Ministry of Home Affairs	3%
	Ministry of Education	47%
	Ministry of Health	8%
	Ministry of Religious Affairs	13%
	Ministry of Development	2%
	Ministry of Culture & Youth Affairs	1%
	Ministry of Energy & Manpower	3%
	Prime Minister's Office	11%
	Ministry of Industry & Primary Resources	6%
	Ministry of Transport & Info Communications	2%

Table 4. Correlation analysis

	WC	PAE	MV	MJ	SP	SV	IV
WC	1						
PAE	.378**	1					
MV	.442*	.457**	1				
MJ	.425**	.566**	.330**	1			
SP	.478**	.400**	.431**	.350**	1		
SV	.384**	.664**	.361**	.566**	.453**	1	
IV	.481**	.536**	.511**	.577**	.599**	.614**	1

**. *Correlation is significant at the 0.01 level (2-tailed)*

WC – Work Context PAE – Peer Actions & Environment MV – Monetary Value MJ – Ministerial Jurisdiction SP – Spiritual SV – Social Value IV – Information Value Assignment

sion analysis was carried out to provide meaningful interpretations of the relative importance of the six constructs. When the six independent variables were regressed on predicting the information value assignment as the dependent variable using the regression function in SPSS, the following results shown in Table 5 were obtained.

In order to predict the significant variables and predictors to test the hypotheses we conducted regression analysis. The results are shown in Table 5 below further indicated that three out of four hypotheses were supported. Regression analysis was done after the correlation analysis. It was found that the R^2 is

Table 5. Regression analysis

Items	Beta	t	Sig.	Ranking	Remarks	Hypotheses Tested
Work Context	.058	.704	.483		Not Significant	H1 not supported
Peer Actions and Environ	.011	.109	.914		Not Significant	H2 not supported
Monetary Value	.185	2.30	.023	4	**Significant**	**H3 supported**
Ministerial Jurisdiction	.244	2.82	.006	3	**Significant**	**H4 supported**
Spiritual	.290	3.54	.001	1	**Significant**	**H5 supported**
Social Value	.248	2.59	.011	2	**Significant**	**H6 supported**

R=.77, R^2 = 59%, Adjusted R^2 = 57%, F= 22.763 (p<0.01), Durbin Watson= 1.96

Dependent variable. IVA (information value assignment)

59% which indicates that the model has sufficient predicting power. Based on the regression analysis shown in Table 5, it was found that four factors are found to be significant which are the monetary value, the ministerial jurisdiction, spiritual and social value factors. Based on these findings, the revised model obtained is shown in Figure 3.

Table 5 shows that the multiple correlation coefficient (R), using all the predictors simultaneously, is 0.77. The coefficient of determination R^2 for our multiple regression model is 0.59, indicating that more than one half percent of the total variation is explained by this equation. The adjusted R^2 (0.57) is used to incorporate the effect of including additional independent variables in a multiple regression equation. The adjustment is necessary because of the several number of variables used. Results further suggested on the basis of high F-Statistic value of 22.76 that the regression model is statistically significant (P<0.01).

DISCUSSION

In this section the results and findings of the research will be discussed with respect to the literature. The study examined the IPV model with the standardized linear regression techniques and has fulfilled its objectives. The results of this study provide an insight into the employees of thirteen ministries in Brunei Darussalam, in terms of how they perceived the factors that led to the information value assignment. At the outset, the revised model was tested to augment its validity. Based on the significant F-value and subsequent R^2 (59%) parsimony of the model would be ascertained. Examining the beta coefficients provide further insight about the relationship in regression equation. The coefficients of the independent variables are expressed in standardized form. They are used to compare the relative importance of each independent variable directly in relation to the dependent variable. Out of four significant independent variables; spiritual value has the largest beta coefficient (.290) and ranked as 1st, followed by social value (.248) which ranked as 2nd. Whereas, ministerial jurisdiction and monetary value have subsequent beta values of .224 and .185 and thus ranked as 3rd and 4th place. If we group the variables then the cultural factors become a significant predictor of information value assignment.

The results explicitly indicated that four variables from organizational and cultural demand factors significantly contributed to information value assignment. These help us to understand how these factors affect the employees' preferences prevalence to information security value and perception. Accordingly, the main results indicated that cultural factors followed by the organizational factors were significant

Figure 3. Final model

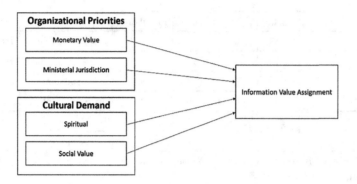

contributors to the IPV model. This is a unique finding and in the following paragraphs we discuss the findings.

Under the organizational factor, the two variables; monetary value and ministerial jurisdiction were studied in the revised IPV model. Monetary value measures the impact of the value of information in terms of dollar value. The study found that if the information is sensitive and is of a vital nature, organizations will do their upmost attempt to protect it from natural, technical and man-made hazards and threats. Our result therefore supports the previous studies of Locher, (2005); Sue (2006) and Anderson and Choobinch, (2008). Therefore, hypotheses H3 stating monetary value is positively related to the information value is supported.

Similarly, our second variable within organizational context measured 'ministerial jurisdiction': this is new variable and as far as we know has not been studied in the Bruneian context or in the perspective of ASEAN (Association of Southeast Asian nations). In previous Brunei-based studies, this variable was studied in the context of business type and organizational type to study the various public sector SMEs on the basis of different business type and remained as one of the significant predictors of technology adoption (Seyal, 2019; Seyal et al. 2003). The variable of ministerial jurisdiction measured various items to capture how the information is perceived as valuable, assigned, ranked, used and protected it according to its sensitivity with an emphasis on how each ministry defines and treats the information as vital. The significance of this variable in our study further indicates how much various ministries in Brunei Darussalam perceive and value the information, its sensitivity and develops safety and security measures to protect it. Our results therefore support the previous studies of Hong et al. (2006); Chang and Ho, (2006) and daVeiga and Martins, (2017).

The second factor that was found significant in our study of predicting information value assignment (IVA) is the cultural demand factor. In this study, the cultural factor measured items from spiritual and social value constructs and were found to be a significant determinant of IVA.

Spiritual values were measured by eight items focusing on specific questions on morality, spirituality and religiously. The result found that majority of the respondents (mean=4.21) weighted high on the spiritual and moral aspects of the information especially in sharing it with anyone else. Our results support the work of Rettinger and Jordan, (2005); Keller, Smith and Smith, (2007); Grullon, Kanatas and Weston, (2009); and Rokhman, (2010). Thus, hypotheses five (H5) was supported.

Next the social value variable in the context of social norms has been used as one of the significant variables to study various technological features and their adoption to augment the TRA and TPB.

However, in the present context it measures "seeking the advice from family and friends exclusively" and was found to be significant. Thus, our findings support the previous studies by Alkahtani, Lock and Dawson, (2013); Luo et al. (2009); and Seyal et al. (2017). Our hypothesis (H6) was also supported.

Lastly the non-significance of two variables; work context and peer action that were grouped in the individual priorities factor, mainly asked respondents about the individual work in a general format and not specifically on task variety, e.g., job level, type of responsibility and job position. This might be of this reason that both variables were non-significant. The results are in contrast with previous studies (Johnston and Warkentin, 2017; daVeiga and Martin, 2017; Lee et al. 2016; and Herath and Row, 2009). Therefore our hypotheses 1 and 2 could not be supported.

CONCLUSION

The study examines the information value assignment by developing a normative model. The model was tested by capturing the data from 150 randomly selected employees of 13 ministries in Brunei Darussalam. The model has good predicting power and parsimony as indicated from a high R^2 value. Two out of three factors measuring four variables were found significant thus supporting our hypotheses H3-H6. Results are consistent with the several of the previous studies mentioned in section 2 of the review of literature. A majority of the respondents in our study are spiritual, morally-oriented and having strong religious and internal belief of protecting organizational information security and due to this they are unlikely to indulge in non-compliance behavior. In addition, the respondents are given to listening to their friends and family and that provides a social platform which helps the employee to take extra care towards security issues. Results further elaborated the importance of organizational factors along the cultural factors. Under the organizational factor the study captured responses on ministerial jurisdiction and monetary value. That ministerial jurisdiction is positively related with information value assignment. This is an interesting finding that emerged from this study and provided support for the inclusion of ministerial level variable. In other words, there is a significant difference in perception as how each ministry value information differently. In addition, the relevant importance of monetary value variable further highlights the users 'behavior as they agree to allocate financial resources to protect the highly sensitive information from the outside intruders and threats. By combining these two factors, the policy makers at the organizational/ministerial level could enhance the information security culture with the minimum retaliation from the employees. The policy makers can also look in depth as how to improve the individual factors to make the working more rewarding and challenging at the workplace in relation to information security culture.

- *Limitations*: There are limitations in the study as our samples of all thirteen ministries are skewed especially on assigning the value to information in terms of dollar value and did not address the sensitivity of the information which might in turn be able to provide a better picture. Secondly, the items used in the individual constructs might need to be revised and demographics should add type of duties and task performed which could make the study more interesting.
- *Practical Implications:* - Besides its limitation, the study can be viewed as being a pioneering one among thirteen ministries in Brunei Darussalam. It brings new insights by providing empirical evidence of the factors that have contributed to the parsimony of the IPV model. This might provide more justification of preparing and enacting information security policies at workplace.

- *Future Studies:* In the future cross culture studies, especially within ASEAN region, in addition to conducting longitudinal studies might not only increase the generalizability but bring new dimensions to the existing body of knowledge.

DISCUSSION QUESTIONS

1. Why the information systems security has become pivotal for the organizations relying much on Big Data, and Cloud Computing?
2. Why the information system security culture has become an important part of the corporate culture?
3. Suggest how organization should design a policy to deal with neutral and problematic employees while addressing the information security issues.
4. How does the IPV model help the organizations to address the issues of information systems security?

REFERENCES

Abar, B., Carter, K. L., & Winsler, A. (2009). The effects of maternal parenting style and religious commitment on self-regulation, academic achievement, and risk behavior among African-American parochial college students. *Journal of Adolescence, 32*(2), 259–273. doi:10.1016/j.adolescence.2008.03.008 PMID:18692235

Ajzen, I. (1991). The Theory of Planned Behavior. *Organizational Behavior and Human Decision Processes, 50*(2), 179–210. doi:10.1016/0749-5978(91)90020-T

Ajzen, I., & Fishbein, M. (1980). *Understanding attitudes and predicting social behaviour.* Prentice-Hall.

Albrechtsen, E. (2007). A qualitative study of users' view on information security. *Computers & Security, 26*(4), 276–289. doi:10.1016/j.cose.2006.11.004

Alhogail, A. (2015). Design and validation of information security culture framework. *Computers in Human Behavior, 49*, 567–575. doi:10.1016/j.chb.2015.03.054

Alkahtani, H., Lock, R., & Dawson, R. (2013). The impact of culture on Saudi Arabian information systems security. *21st International Conference on Software Quality Management (SQM)*, 201–210.

AlKalbani, A., Deng, H., & Kam, B. (2015). Organisational Security Culture and Information Security Compliance for E-Government Development: The Moderating Effect of Social Pressure. *Pacific Asia Conference on Information Systems (PACIS)*, 1–12.

Alohali, M., Clarke, N., Furnell, S., & Albakri, S. (2018). Information security behavior: Recognizing the influencers. *Proceedings of Computing Conference 2017, 2018*, 844–853. 10.1109/SAI.2017.8252194

Anderson, R., & Moore, T. (2006). The Economics of Information Security. *Science, 13*(314), 610.

Barsky, A. (2011). Investigating the Effects of Moral Disengagement and Participation on Unethical Work Behavior. *Journal of Business Ethics, 104*(1), 59–75. doi:10.100710551-011-0889-7

Bashorun, A., Worwui, A., & Parker, D. (2013). Information security: To determine its level of awareness in an organization. *AICT 2013 - 7th International Conference on Application of Information and Communication Technologies, Conference Proceedings*. 10.1109/ICAICT.2013.6722704

Bauer, S., Bernroider, E. W. N., & Chudzikowski, K. (2017). Prevention is better than cure! Designing information security awareness programs to overcome users' non-compliance with information security policies in banks. *Computers & Security*, *68*, 145–159. doi:10.1016/j.cose.2017.04.009

Brunei Darussalam Key Indicators (BDKI). (2016). Retrieved from http://www.depd.gov.bn/DEPD Documents Library/DOS/BDKI/BDKI 2016.pdf

Chai, S., Kim, M., & Rao, H. R. (2011). Firms' Information Security Investment Decisions. Stock Market Evidence of Investors' Behavior. *Decision Support Systems*, *50*(4), 651–661. doi:10.1016/j.dss.2010.08.017

Chang, S. E., & Ho, C. B. (2006). Organizational factors to the effectiveness of implementing information security management. *Industrial Management & Data Systems*, *106*(3), 345–361. doi:10.1108/02635570610653498

Chen, L. H. (2008). Job satisfaction among information system (IS) personnel. *Computers in Human Behavior*, *24*(1), 105–118. doi:10.1016/j.chb.2007.01.012

Chia, P. A., Maynard, S. B., & Ruighaver, A. B. (2002). Understanding Organizational Security Culture. *Proceedings of PACIS2002*.

Chia, P. A., Maynard, S. B., & Ruighaver, A. B. (2003). Understanding Organizational Security Culture. In Mg. Hunter & Kk. Dhanda (Eds.), *Information Systems: The Challenges of Theory and Practice*. Las Vegas, NV: Information Institute.

Chua, H. N., Wong, S. F., Low, Y. C., & Chang, Y. (2018). Impact of Employees’ Demographic Characteristics on the Awareness and Compliance of Information Security Policy in Organizations. *Telematics and Informatics*, *35*(6), 1770–1780. doi:10.1016/j.tele.2018.05.005

Clark, M., Greenberg, A., Hill, E., Lemay, E., Clark, P.-E., & Roosth, D. (2011). Heightened Interpersonal Security Diminishes the Monetary Value of Possessions. *Journal of Experimental Social Psychology*, *47*(2), 359–364. doi:10.1016/j.jesp.2010.08.001

Colwill, C. (2009). Human factors in information security: The insider threat - Who can you trust these days? *Information Security Technical Report*, *14*(4), 186–196. doi:10.1016/j.istr.2010.04.004

Cronbach, L. J. (1951). Coefficient alpha and the internal structure of tests. *Psychometrika*, *16*(3), 297–336. doi:10.1007/BF02310555

Cross, S. (2002). Confidentiality within physiotherapy: Perceptions and attitudes of clinical practitioners. *Journal of Medical Ethics*, *26*(6), 447–453. doi:10.1136/jme.26.6.447 PMID:11129846

da Veiga, A., & Martins, N. (2017). Defining and identifying dominant information security cultures and subcultures. *Computers & Security*, *70*, 72–94. doi:10.1016/j.cose.2017.05.002

Digital Government Strategy 2015 - 2020 Brunei Darussalam. (2015). Retrieved from http://www.digitalstrategy.gov.bn/Themed/index.aspx

Doherty, N. F., & Tajuddin, S. T. (2018). Towards a user-centric theory of value-driven information security compliance. *Information Technology & People, 31*(2), 348–367. doi:10.1108/ITP-08-2016-0194

Dor, D., & Elovici, Y. (2016). A Model of the Information Security Investment DecisionMaking Process. *Computers & Security, 63*, 1–13. doi:10.1016/j.cose.2016.09.006

Engelsman, W. (2007). *Information Assets and their Value*. Academic Press.

Evans, Y., He, I. Y., & H. J. (2018). Analysis of published public sector information security incidents and breaches to establish the proportions of human error. *Proceedings of the Twelfth International Symposium on Human Aspects of Information Security Assurance (HAISA) 2018, 12*, 191–202.

Finne, T. (1998). Special Feature: A Conceptual Framework for Information Security Management. *Computers & Security, 17*(4), 303–307. doi:10.1016/S0167-4048(98)80010-2

Fitzgerald, T. (2007). Building Management Commitment through Security Councils, or Security Council Critical Success Factors. In H. F. Tipton (Ed.), *Information Security Management Handbook* (pp. 105–121). Hoboken, NJ: Auerbach Publications.

Fyfe, T., & Crookall, P. (2010). *Social Media and Public Sector Policy Dilemmas*. Academic Press.

Gliem, J. A., & Gliem, R. R. (2003). Calculating, Interpreting, and Reporting Cronbach's Alpha Reliability Coefficient for Likert-Type Scales. Academic Press.

Goodman, S. E., & Ramer, R. (2007). Global Sourcing of IT Services and Information Security: Prudence before Playing. *Communications of the Association for Information Systems, 20*(1), 812–823.

Grullon, G., Kanatas, G., & Weston, J. (2009). *Religion and Corporate (Mis)Behavior*. doi:10.2139srn.1472118

Helokunnas, T., & Kuusisto, R. (2003). Information Security Culture in a Value Net. *Engineering Management Conference, 2003. IEMC'03. Managing Technologically Driven Organizations: The Human Side of Innovation and Change*. 10.1109/IEMC.2003.1252258

Herath, T., & Rao, H. R. (2009a). Encouraging information security behaviors in organizations: Role of penalties, pressures and perceived effectiveness. *Decision Support Systems, 47*(2), 154–165. doi:10.1016/j.dss.2009.02.005

Herath, T., & Rao, H. R. (2009b). Protection motivation and deterrence: A framework for security policy compliance in organisations. *European Journal of Information Systems, 18*(2), 106–125. doi:10.1057/ejis.2009.6

Higgins, G. E., Wilson, A. L., & Fell, B. D. (2005). An application of deterrence theory to software piracy. *The Journal of Criminal Justice and Popular Culture, 12*(3), 166–184.

Hofstede, G., Neuijen, B., Ohayv, D. D., & Sanders, G. (1990). Measuring Organizational Cultures: A Qualitative and Quantitative Study across Twenty Cases. *Administrative Science Quarterly, 35*(2), 286–316. doi:10.2307/2393392

Hong, K. S., Chi, Y. P., Chao, L. R., & Tang, J. H. (2006). An empirical study of information security policy on information security elevation in Taiwan. *Information Management & Computer Security*, *14*(2), 104–115. doi:10.1108/09685220610655861

Ifinedo, P. (2012). Understanding information systems security policy compliance: An integration of the theory of planned behavior and the protection motivation theory. *Computers & Security*, *31*(1), 83–95. doi:10.1016/j.cose.2011.10.007

Ifinedo, P. (2014). Information systems security policy compliance: An empirical study of the effects of socialisation, influence, and cognition. *Information & Management*, *51*(1), 69–79. doi:10.1016/j.im.2013.10.001

Indrawati & Mas-Marhaeni. (2015). Predicting Instant Message Application Adoption using a Unified Theory of Acceptance & Use of Technology. *Proceedings of 5*[th] *International Conference on Computing and Informatics*.

ISACA. (2009). An Introduction to the Business Model for Information Security. *ISACA Journal*, 1–28.

ITU. (2017). *Global Cybersecurity Index (GCI) 2017*. ITU Report. doi:10.1111/j.1745-4514.2008.00161.x

Jaafar, N. I., & Ajis, A. (2013). Organizational Climate and Individual Factors Effects on Information Security Faculty of Business and Accountancy. *International Journal of Business and Social Science*, *4*(10), 118–131.

Johnston & Warkentin. (2017). Fear Appeals and Information Security Behaviors: An Empirical Study. *MIS Quarterly, 34*(3), 549. doi:10.2307/25750691

Keller, A. C., Smith, K. T., & Smith, L. M. (2007). Do gender, educational level, religiosity, and work experience affect the ethical decision-making of U.S. accountants? *Critical Perspectives on Accounting*, *18*(3), 299–314. doi:10.1016/j.cpa.2006.01.006

Lee, C., Lee, C. C., & Kim, S. (2016). Understanding information security stress: Focusing on the type of information security compliance activity. *Computers & Security*, *59*, 60–70. doi:10.1016/j.cose.2016.02.004

Lim, J. S., Chang, S., Maynard, S., & Ahmad, A. (2009). Exploring the Relationship between Organizational Cultural and Information Security Culture. *7th Australian Information Management Conference*.

Locher, C. (2005). Methodologies for Evaluating Information Security Investments - What Basel II Can Change in the Financial Industry. *Proceedings of the 13th European Conference on Information Systems*, 1–12.

Luo, X., Warkentin, M., Johnston, A. C., & Luo, X. (2009). The Impact of National Culture on Workplace Privacy Expectations in the Context of Information Security Assurance. *Proceedings of the Fifteenth Americas Conference on Information Systems*, 1–6.

Martin, A., & Eloff, J. (2003). Information Security Culture. *Proc. of IFIP TC11 17th International Conference on Information Security*.

Ng, B. Y., Kankanhalli, A., & Xu, Y. (2009). Studying users' computer security behavior: A health belief perspective. *Decision Support Systems*, *46*(4), 815–825. doi:10.1016/j.dss.2008.11.010

Nunnally, J. C. (1978). *Psychometric Theory*. New York, NY: McGraw-Hill.

Oost, D., & Chew, E. (2007). *Investigating the Concept of Information Security Culture: UTS*. Hoboken, NJ: Auerbach Publications School of Management Working Paper: No. 2007/6.

Pandya, D. C., & Patel, D. N. J. (2017). Study and analysis of E-Governance Information Security (InfoSec) in Indian Context. *IOSR Journal of Computer Engineering, 19*(1), 4–7. doi:10.9790/0661-1901040407

Perangkaan, J., & Menteri, J. P. (2015). *Brunei Darussalam Statistical Yearbook 2015*. Academic Press.

Plachkinova, M., & Maurer, C. (2018). Teaching case security breach at target. *Journal of Information Systems Education, 29*(1), 11–20. Retrieved from http://jise.org/Volume29/n1/JISEv29n1p11.html

Rahman, Z. A., & Shah, I. M. (2015). Measuring Islamic Spiritual Intelligence. *Procedia Economics and Finance, 31*(15), 134–139. doi:10.1016/S2212-5671(15)01140-5

Rettinger, D. A., & Jordan, A. E. (2005). The relations among religion, motivation, and college cheating: A natural experiment. *Ethics & Behavior, 15*(2), 107–129. doi:10.120715327019eb1502_2

Rokhman, W. (2010). The Effect of Islamic Work Ethics on Work Outcomes. *Electronic Journal of Business Ethics and Organization Studies, 15*(1), 21–27. doi:10.4103/1817-7417.104699

Ross, S. (2011). ROSI Scanarios. *Information Systems Control Journal, 3*. Available: https://www.isaca.org/Journal/archives/2011/Volume-2/Pages/What-is-the-value-of-security.aspx

Sarkar, K. R. (2010). Assessing insider threats to information security using technical, behavioural and organisational measures. *Information Security Technical Report, 15*(3), 112–133. doi:10.1016/j.istr.2010.11.002

Seyal, A. H. (2003). *An Investigation of E-Commerce Adoption in Micro Business Enterprise: Bruneian Evidence*. In 4th We-B conference, Perth, Australia.

Seyal, A. H. (2019). Evaluating Strategic Information Technology Planning Process: Lesson Learnt from Bruneian Small Businesses. In Strategy and Behavior in the Digital Economy. IntechOpen.UK.

Seyal, A. H., & Rahman, M. N. (2003). A Preliminary Investigation of E-Commerce Adoption in Small and Medium Enterprises in Brunei. *Journal of Global Information Technology Management, 6*(2), 6–26. doi:10.1080/1097198X.2003.10856347

Seyal, A. H., Rahman, M. N., Sy, M. Y., & Siau, N. Z. (2017). Examining m-Learning in Higher Education: An Application of Theory of Planned Behavior. In A. H. Seyal & M. N. Rahman (Eds.), *Theory of Planned Behaviour: New Research*. Nova Publisher.

Siponen, M. (2005). Analysis of Modern Is Security Development Approaches: Towards the Next Generation of Social and Adaptable ISS Methods. *Information and Organization, 15*(4), 339-375.

Siponen, M., Pahnila, S., & Mahmood, M. A. (2010). Compliance with information security policies: An empirical investigation. *Computer, 43*(2), 64–71. doi:10.1109/MC.2010.35

Sohrabi, S. N., Maple, C., Watson, T., & Solms, R. (2017). *Motivation and opportunity based model to reduce information security insider threats in organisations*. doi:10.1016/j.jisa.2017.11.001

Sohrabi, S. N., Von Solms, R., & Furnell, S. (2016). Information security policy compliance model in organizations. *Computers & Security*, *56*, 1–13. doi:10.1016/j.cose.2015.10.006

Sowden, S., Lymberopoulos, E., Militaru, E., & Catmur, C. (2018). *Quantifying compliance and acceptance through public and private social conformity*. doi:10.1016/j.concog.2018.08.009

Stan, S. (2007). Beyond Information Security Awareness Training: It Is Time to Change the Culture. In H. F. Tipton (Ed.), Information Security Management Handbook (pp. 555–565). Academic Press.

Stanton, J. M., Stam, K. R., Mastrangelo, P., & Jolton, J. (2005). Analysis of end user security behaviors. *Computers & Security*, *24*(2), 124–133. doi:10.1016/j.cose.2004.07.001

Su, X. (2006). *An Overview of Economic Approaches to Information Security Management*. Centre for Telematics and Information Technology, University of Twente.

Tajuddin, S. T. (2016). *The Role of "perceptions of information value" in information security compliance behaviour: a study in Brunei Darussalam's public organisations*. Loughborough University. Retrieved from https://dspace.lboro.ac.uk/2134/23261

Thomson, K. L., & Von Solms, R. (2005). Information security obedience: A definition. *Computers & Security*, *24*(1), 69–75. doi:10.1016/j.cose.2004.10.005

Tran, K., Morra, D., Lo, V., Quan, S. D., Abrams, H., & Wu, R. C. (2014). Medical students and personal smartphones in the clinical environment: The impact on confidentiality of personal health information and professionalism. *Journal of Medical Internet Research*, *16*(5), 1–8. doi:10.2196/jmir.3138 PMID:24855046

Von Solms, B. (2000). Information Security -- the Third Wave? *Computers & Security*, *19*(7), 615–620. doi:10.1016/S0167-4048(00)07021-8

Von Solms, R., & Van Niekerk, J. (2013). From information security to cyber security. *Computers & Security*, *38*, 97–102. doi:10.1016/j.cose.2013.04.004

Vroom, C., & von Solms, R. (2004). Towards information security behavioural compliance. *Computers & Security*, *23*(3), 191–198. doi:10.1016/j.cose.2004.01.012

Wahab, M. A., Quazi, A., & Blackman, D. (2016). Measuring and validating Islamic work value constructs: An empirical exploration using Malaysian samples. *Journal of Business Research*, *69*(10), 4194–4204. doi:10.1016/j.jbusres.2016.03.005

Wright, B. E. (2004). The Role of Work Context in Work Motivation: A Public Sector Application of Goal and Social Cognitive Theories. *Journal of Public Administration: Research and Theory*, *14*(1), 59–78. doi:10.1093/jopart/muh004

Yazdanmehr, A., & Wang, J. (2016). Employees' information security policy compliance : A norm activation perspective. *Decision Support Systems*, *92*, 36–46. doi:10.1016/j.dss.2016.09.009

Yousef, D. A. (1999). Commitment and Job Satisfaction in a. *Personnel*, (1958).

Yousef, D. A. (2000). *Organizational commitment as a mediator of the relationship between Islamic work ethic and attitudes toward organizational change*. doi:10.1177/0018726700534003

Zaib, T. (2017). Evaluating Narcissisim, Intention and Selfie Posting Behaviour among Housewives in Australia: An Extended TPB. In A. H. Seyal & M. N. Rahman (Eds.), *Theory of Planned Behaviour: New Research*. Nova Publisher.

Zulhuda, S. (2010). *Proceeding 3rd International Coriference on ICT4M 2010 Information Security in the Islamic Perspective: The Principles and Practices*. Academic Press.

Chapter 25
Strengthening the Capabilities in Data Analytics:
A Case Study in Bogotá, Colombia

Milenka Linneth Argote Cusi
Business Intelligence and Demography SAS, Colombia

Leon Dario Parra Bernal
Ean University, Colombia

ABSTRACT

In the framework of digital economy and the fourth industrial revolution, it is very important that companies have internal capabilities for the analysis of data and of the information they produce, as well as to generate value in the decision-making process. In 2017 the EAN University implemented the Program for Strengthening Capabilities in DA (PSCDA) with 15 companies from different economic sectors in Bogotá, Colombia. The main purpose of the program was to diagnose, qualify, and accompany the participating companies, in the process of strengthening their DA capabilities. Among the most important results we highlighted that 90% of the companies from the program have applied technological tools for the analysis of their data, while an 80% were able to design and implement a plan of improvement for their processes in data analytics and its use in decision making.

INTRODUCTION

The strengthening of data management capabilities in economically emerging companies is fundamental for economical development. The need becomes stronger in a context in which information technologies allow access to a huge amount of structured and unstructured data, that companies should benefit from as a competitive advantage (Parra y Argote, 2017; Bell & Pavitt, 1992).

Information is power. Data and information have been gaining prominence in the field of business over the past 30 years. The computer systems have responded to the needs of companies and institutions for the management of data in relation to management of inventory, of individuals, products, financial accounts and many other variables that could be systematized, however, this area

DOI: 10.4018/978-1-5225-8933-4.ch025

was relegated to a technical staff of the organizations for many years. In a knowledge society we can not treat data, tmanagement and generation of information as an isolated area of the strategic part of organizations, as the previous situation weakens the potentials of the technological capabilities that strengthen companies. Actually a global and integral vision is necessary and Data Analytics (DA) is a set of tangible and intangible technologies that allow the transformation of information into power (Castellanos, Funeque, Ramires, 2011; Parra y Argote, 2017:188; Argote y Parra, 2016a:9; Argote, 2016b:230; Bell & Pavitt, 1993).

Eventhough there is a perspective or, as defined by other authors (Park and Lee 2011; Castellanos et al 2011; Argote, 2016b) a theory of resources and capabilities that define a set of capabilities that organizations have or don't have, but no references were found about the capabilities in Data Analytics. First of all, it is not feasable to translate the English term since it defines a multidisciplinary topic in relation to the tools it uses and the term of "data analysis" or "Analysis is different because it refers only to a process of disintegration for the understanding of the parts as the whole of a particular theme. Which is why, throughout the chapter the concept of DA is defined, in order to understand the case of the Program for Strengthening Capabilities in DA (PSCDA) in Colombian companies.

Once the importance of DA is recovered in the field of business the reason for being in the program was born, with the question: Which Colombian companies have capabilities in DA? According to various researches, which were reviewed and carried out by the authors of the present chapter and by other (Parra & Argote, 2015, 2016), important exponents of economical development in Latin America and of the structural change, such as Katz (2000, 2007, 2013), Kantis, Angelelli, Moori (2004); Kantis, Postigo, Federico and Tamborini (2002ª); Kantis, Ishida, and Komori (2002b) it was expected to find a low percentage of companies in Latin America that have such capabilities, according to several researches who allowed us to show that approximately 80% of the companies are micro and small (SMEs) with a low capacity in data management (Audrestch, Kuratko & Link, 2016; Acs, Astebro, Audrestch & Robinson, 2016; Acs, Audrestch & Strom, 2009; Parra y Argote, 2016ª). Although the percentage of companies with growth potential in the Colombian economy could be growing as a result of support policies, to research, development and innovation (R+D+I) at country level, and the strengthening of the National Research System (NRS) with investment and politicies to support entrepreneurship, even if the probability of finding companies with DA capacity is very low, as we are going to show in the following sections (Bell y Pavitt, 1993).

In this order, the present chapter begins with the development of the theoretical framework, which is fundamental when you bear in mind that no referents have been found for the term "capabilities in DA", it goes on with the description of the socio-eonomical context of emerging economies, within which is Colombia, and the details of the Colombian context, from the support poplicies to the economical development which has been implemented in the last 10 years. With this frame of reference, we proceed to present the data and methods used to design and implement the program beginning with a survey collected in the companies (main input for diagnostic in DA). After that we describe the characteristics of the PSCDA, developed during the first semester of 2017. Finally, we present the results of the program and the conclusions. As it is one of the few DA programs that has been completed in itself from the diagnosis up to the implementation of specific solutions, we considered it was necessary to include the section of learned lessons with the objective of generating knowledge for future versions of the program, either with a larger sample of companies or its replication in different socio-economical contexts.

THE PERSPECTIVE OF RESOURCES AND CAPABILITIES

The concept of capabilities comes from the perspective or resources theory, topic that is developed by Park and Lee (2011), within the framework of technological transfer. In that research the authors assume the point of view of resources, and capabilities, to contribute to the definition of technological transfer strategies of 361 Korean companies. This perspective suggests that the resources and capabilities available to the firm influence its development and performance. In this framework of analysis, the question that guides research in this area is related to identifying what type of resources and capabilities generate competitive advantages to the firm.

The issue of resources and capabilities of organizations is extensive, so much so, that it has led to the development of a theory of capabilities. The capabilities can be framed in the proper capabilities of human resource management, own capabilities of the organization and enterprise culture (Barney, 1997). The literature that reviews and systematizes the capabilities identified in an organization is extensive, among the main works we have: Aguirre J.J. (2010), Domínguez y Brown (2004), Castellanos et al (2011), y Argote (2016b), which allows the visualization of the background of capabilities that give rise to different types of classifications (see table 1). In table 1 it can be seen that the "Analitical capacity"

Table 1. Type of capabilities found by researches

References	Type of Capabilities
Aguirre, 2010	Research and Development capacity
	Strategic Direction capacity
	Marketing capacity
	Manufacturing capacity
	Resource management capacity
Wang, Lu and Chen, 2008	Transference capacity
	Decision making capacity
	Commercialization capacity
	Manufacturing capacity
	Financing capacity
Domínguez and Brown, 2004	Production capacity
	Networking capacity
	Investment capacity
Ranga et al, 2018	Technological capacity
	Legal capacity
Turriago, 2014	Production capacity
	Investment capacity
	Innovation capacity
Others	Management capacity
	Learning capacity
	Innovation capacity

Source: Taken from Argote C. Milenka Linneth (2016a)

is considered one of the most valuable attributes of business management, which can be found in the seventh position among 25 attributes of the company that the article analyzes (in ascending order). So, before defining, what is considered in the present chapter as "DA capabilities", it is important to clarify the difference between Data Analysis and Data Analytics.

THE DIFFERENCE BETWEEN DATA ANALYSIS AND DATA ANALYTICS (DA)

It is normal to translate "Data Analytics" into "Data Analysis" but they have quite different meanings. In fact, there is no translation for the concept of Data Analytics since more than a concept it is a set of concepts that are relared to the discovery, interpretation and communication of patterns in the data, through the use and simultaneous application of: statistics, computer programming and operation research to performance measurement.

Nowadays, organizations collect analyze and communicate large amounts of data in the framework of what is the BIG DATA (BD), due to volume, processing speed and variety that comes from the internet and social networks. According to Watson (2013), the BD is generating a new data management system to support decision making in which the key question is, how to analyze that data? Now, Data Analytics offers a set of technologies that require the intensive use of computing through algorithms and software that make use of techniques provided by computer science, statistics and mathematics. The business sector is one of which recognizes the importance of data and is the area in which the latest applications of analysis have been made in processes of prediction, decision making, optimization, risks, fraud, among other areas, which currently form part of the so-called "Data Science" (Rodriguez, 2017).

The analysis of data refers to a process of reflection and is interpreted more as a personal task, while the DA is a concept that includes a set of technologies that allow the analysis of large amounts of data as a key support, in the process of decision making. In this sense, since Data Analytics is a new set of tools and technologies for the management of information, in its incipient stage of development, there are few or no researches that refer to "DA capabilities". This situation highlights the relevance and contribution of this chapter.

What Are the Capabilities in Data Analytics (DA)?

Beyond the information management, the concept of capabilities of DA in the context of this chapter refers to: the technological, human talent, strategies and management capabilities oriented towards achieving a sophisticated[1] data analysis, with the objective of generating strategic data for companies which will allow them to be innovative and competitive in a determined sector (Argote, 2016a; Castellanos, Fúguene, Ramirez, 2013; Rodriguez, 2017; Wang et. al., 2008).

DA is a set of tools that derive from information and communication technologies (ICTs) to carry out data analysis by using the latest technologies that facilitate their processing, at a time when an enormous amount of information is available, and also sophisticated methodologies for analyzing information, that a while back were unattainable for the real sector, and were limited to being published in scientific journals. (Ramachandran R., 2013).

In this context of new advances in data management technologies, companies cannot be left out. Product of the dynamics of the companies and their daily transactions, these generate large amounts of information. Likewise, the environment in which companies are currently immersed, it is feasible to access and obtain other types of information such as videos, sound, text messages, from which valuable data can be obtained for the company; data that had not been available before. The technologies of today allow us to integrate both worlds of data (structured and unstructured) through the DA supporting strategic business decision making and transforming the social and organizational dynamic.

Which Are the Companies That Have These Technologies and These Capabilities to Face This New Technological Dynamic?

According to statistical data from the Global Entrepreneurship Monitor (GEM), approximately 80% of companies worldwide are micro and small (SMEs) with less tan 10 employees (Goméz et al, 2018). These undertakings or companies, in their majority, lack many capabilities since they were conceived, not by opportunity but by necessity, as an escape from unemployment. According to Kantis (2000), those companies that were created from an academic and work experience, with a certain network capacity, which have considerably increased, within a few years, their level of sales as well as the number of employees, are known as dynamic companies (Kantis, 2000). According to the statistics mentioned at the beginning of the paragraph, it is clear that the number of these companies is very scarce, considering that only 20% of the companies worldwide are large companies that could become part of the category of "dynamic companies". The later are more likely to have capabilities in technology, financial management and human resources, from the most basic capabilities, since the size of their companiy demands it. However, they also have a high probability of not having capabilities of analysis, which is a higher level of business management, as mentioned by Kopsco & Pachamanova (2017), in their maturity levels of companies. By contrast, in developed economies the scenario is different (Audrestch et al, 2016; Acs et al, 2016; Acs et. al., 2009).

In developing countries, the situation is more precarious. The level of technological development, at country and regional level, does not allow a high percentage of internet access, which is the basic technology to access data for technological surveillance processes, market intelligence, etc. Countries such as Bolivia and Ecuador have an approximated 20% of telephony and internet penetration, while in Colombia, Chile, México and Argentina the percentage is close to 60% (Katz, 2000, Kantis, 2007).

However, beyond the tangible capabilities there are huge gaps in the intangible capabilities. The problem of education, health, economy, structural change, make that independently from the policies of entrepreneurship and strengthening of small and medium enterprises, there are structural problems that do not allow the migration from economies of narrow base to economies based on knowledge and technology (Parra, Argote y Farro, 2018). Even so, in countries such as Colombia, Peru, Chile, México and Argentina, the implementation of policies aimed to strengthening research, development and innovation is bearing fruit in establishing the bases for the formation of the National Innovation Systems and the link between University-Company-State as is the case of Colombia through several institutions such as Colciencias, CONNECT and INNPULSA (Dill, JC, Kask, D.J. & Darvill, 2011).

Latin America is in an embryonic stage, not in the theoretical and academic field in R+D+I, but in the application of these developments in the real sector of the economy. There is still a long way to go in the Business-University relationship, although initiatives such as the calls from COLCIENCIAS for the financing of projects between both entities and the university-business technology transfer, and the development of spin-off to promote their interaction. The organizational culture is a barrier that has not allowed the achievement of the desired results (GEM Bogotá, 2018).

In this context, the question of: which companies have capabilities in DA? The answer is that there is a very low percentage and a high probability that even medium and large companies do not have these capabilities. Kim, Trini and Chung (2014), in their analysis of applications of BIG DATA in the government, affirm that the business sector is the world leader in the development of applications in BD, while the public sector is considering if they apply these technologies to support their decision making. A review of the word wide initiatives shows that most of the initiatives in BD and DA projects in countries like Korea, US and Japan are starting at government level and only a low percentage are being implemented or are currently operating. The biggest challenge is the integration of structured and non structured information in the real sector (Kim et al, 2014).

In Colombia, according to the mapping of technological capabilities in medium-sized companies that allowed the PSCDA, before the implementation, in 15 companies from different sectors, the result of this is that capabilities in DA are very low. Most companies do not have strategies in DA, data is handled rudimentally and although some rely on technology for the management of information with SAP and Oracle, this becomes a passive of the company or is underused only for information management activities and not for DA. Beyond tangibles, in relation with intangibles, it is necessary to give importance to data for the construction of valuable information for decision making, that is, training is needed to raise awareness among entrepreneurs, businessmen, managers and middle staff, of the importance of the collection, processing and analysis of data for decision making, since it is mostly based on their intuition. BD and DA are still unknown technologies for company managers.

Therefore, the present pilot Program for Strengthening Capabilities in DA is pertinent and necessary for companies in Bogota and throughout the country, the context of the program, the methodology; mapping results and the main conclusions and learned lessons are detailed below.

CONTEXT OF THE PROGRAM

Colombia is at a very interesting moment, in terms of financing support programs and strengthening of the productive system. Several government institutions, in alliance with universities, have developed programs that seek to strengthen the different faces of entrepreneurship and innovation in companies, such as financing R + D + I, qualification of human resources, incubation, sustainability, among other important issues.

Thus, the Ministry of Telecommunications, the Mayor's Office of Bogota, and Colciencias together with universities instituted the VIVELAB point program in 2016, with the objective of strengthening the capabilities of the Information and Communication Technologies (ICTs) of companies in Bogota. The EAN University, who mainstreams the subject of entrepreneurship through the Institute of Sustainable Entrepreneurship sees as an opportunity to be part of the VIVELAB program to carry out several projects within which the "Program for the Strengthening of Capabilities of DA of companies located in Bogota, Colombia (PSCDA), is proposed.

The PSCDA, unlike other business oriented programs for companies, is integral since it starts form a mapping of the capacities in DA, qualification of the managerial personnel of the company, to the implementation of a solution in management of the data of the company that forms part of the program. That is to say, the objective of the PSCDA was to establish the base line of the company in regard to the capabilities in DA in an initial stage and to transform this situation towards a posterior stage in which the company applies DA, in support of market decision-making, sales or other variables of a firm's interest.

Figure 1. Phases of the program of strengthening data analytics capabilities
Source: Own elaboration

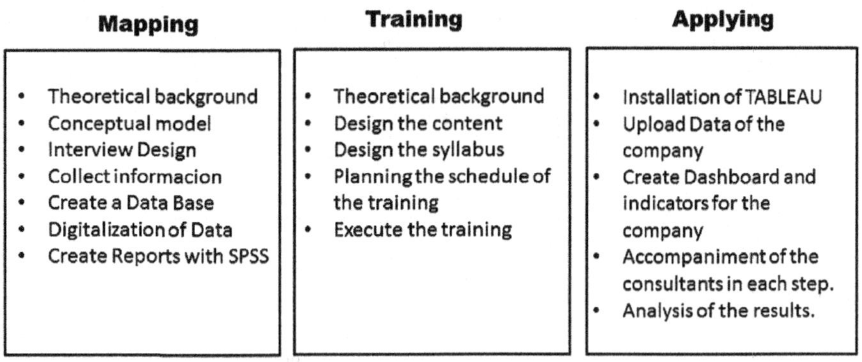

Mapping	Training	Applying
• Theoretical background • Conceptual model • Interview Design • Collect informacion • Create a Data Base • Digitalization of Data • Create Reports with SPSS	• Theoretical background • Design the content • Design the syllabus • Planning the schedule of the training • Execute the training	• Installation of TABLEAU • Upload Data of the company • Create Dashboard and indicators for the company • Accompaniment of the consultants in each step. • Analysis of the results.

METHODOLOGY

The program is designed in three phases, a mapping phase of technological capabilities, another phase of training in capabilities of DA for decision making and the last phase in the implementation of a platform (TABLEAU) to carry out DA with the Company data. In spite of the program being designed to be developed in six months, he program has been developed in three months. Due to administrative terms, the impact of the program must be evaluated as a pilot test tof the achievement lifecycle of Data Analytics from the identification of the problem to the implementation of a pilot solution using the TABLEAU tool. These results constitute a base line for the future Data Analytics Strategy in each company.

MAPPING OF CAPABILITIES IN DA

Before beginning an intervention to transform the initial situation, it is important to map the technological cababilities in general and the capabilities in DA of companies in the program to identify the state of the companies in DA. The development of this phase implied in turn several scientific activities, related to the conceptual framework from which the thematic is approached, the design of an instrument to collect information about the base line (see table 2), knowledge of the company's history for which field trips are carried out, and an analysis of the data collected. This set of activities made it possible to objectively and sustainably demostrate in a map the DA capabilities of each company.

Table 2 shows the dimensions considered for the mapping of DA capabilities. The first section allows us to create a record of demographic and economical characteristics of the company. In second instance, it was important to know the strategic direction of the company, its mission and vision, to identify whether of not there is a strategy in DA. What data does the company generate? How is the data managed? With, among others, the questions that allowed us to delve into the complex topic of data management in the sample of companies. The fourth section is innovative in the sense that it seeks, with a few questions, to visualize, in a general way how decisions are being made in the company from the availability of the information, its processing, analysis and support for the DM. Because the first natural application of the DA is to study the market, it is important to know what the company is doing in this regard. To finish, and as a product of the trayectory through the dimensions, it closes with a triggering question that guides all the process of application of the DA. What is the need or the main problem of the company

Table 2. Dimensions and Variables

Dimensions	Variables
Characterization of companies	Data register of the companies
	Age of the companies
	Main product or service
	Main and second economic activity
	Number of employees
	Total amount of anual sales
	Export activities
Strategic Directioning	Scenario planning
	Availability of human resources for planning
	Indicators to evaluate planning
	Processes of evaluation of strategies according to the market
	Strategic design based on information about the evironment
Information management of the company	Type of information
	Register of organizational and operational data of the company
	Technology in information management
	State of the information of the company
	Activities related to the management of technology
	Which users would make use of BD and DA?
	What type of information would you like to integrate?
	Which is the main utility of this technology?
Information for Decision Making	Process and analysis of the information for Decision Making (DM)
	Type of information required for DM
	Area of the company that carries out this type of reports
	Assertive frequency of the DM
	Impact of the company's decision in the last 5 years
	Behavior of the profit curve in the last 5 years
	How are decisions made iin the companies
	Components of strategic planning
	Distribution of budget
Use of Information for marketing	Information the company uses for market knowledge
	Planning and control of marketing
	Market research, Business Intelligence
	Planning and distribution of publicity
Triggering question	Which is the main problem of your company that you want to solve?

Source: Own elaboration

Table 3. Sample of road map

Variables	Indicator or KPI	Indicators o KPI (Expected in a year)	Activities oriented to improve the indicators	Deriverables	Responsible	Means of verifying the deliverables	Time line			
							t	t+1	t+2	t+3
Dimension 1: Strategic addressing										
Dimension 2: Information Management										
Dimension 3: Information for Decision Making										
Dimension 4: Marketing management										

KPI. Key Productive Indicator
Source: Own elaboration

that it wants to solve? This question seeks to generate reflection and analysis from decision makers to face the next phases.

Based on the mapping of the analitical capabilities of the company, a roadmap and a schedule are established. The roadmap is a planning matrix in the analysis of capabilities of analysis, with their respective indicators and means of verification, in order to operationalize the strengthening of capabilities, based on established goals over time (see Table 3). Later, these matrixes are the input for the improvement plan that each company develops.

TRAINING IN DATA ANALYTICS

One of the main assets is the trained human capital and since the area of DA is a new area for companies, a training process is necessary. The PSCDA developed training for company managers through eight sessions (eight hours by session) on the main topics of the DA, from the exploration of the state of the art, the thematic and knowledge of the sector, passing through the basic tools necessary to carry out DA, up to learning to answer the questions about the needs of the company through the TABLEAU (Chen, Chiang & Storey, 2012; Davenport, 2006; McAfee, Brynjolfsson, Davenport, Patil & Barton, 2012). To conclude, we studied in depth, the concepts and the importance of data for decision making through a case study with data from the "*UC Machine Learning Repository*" in particular the "Bank Marketing" database that contains information about a telephone marketing strategy that a Portugal bank made (http://archive.ics.uci.edu/ml/). It is important to remark that the objective of each session is to develop a specific product with the knowledge acquired during the training, as you can observe in table 4.

DATA ANALYTICS APPLICATION

The program from the beginning was conceived to implement a DA technological tool to practical cases of the company. Thus the post-training application phase involved the on-site visit of TABLEAU partner

Table 4. Content of data analytics training program

Thematic	Products That Each Company Have to Develop
Theme 1 Corporate planning and business intelligence	Exploratory analysis of the Company sector, introspective analysis of the Company in relation to its capabilities in analysis and identification of specific needs
Theme 2 .Information management: identification and application of structures and non-structured information sources	Identification of structured and non-structured information which is of interest to the company
Theme 3. Practical concepts of descriptive and inferential statistics applied to decision making	Search, processing and selection of the information of interest to the Company and application of basic statistical techniques
Theme 4. Construction of indicators applied to the managerial decision making	Constructed and established indicators for the company in the dimension of the capabilities of analysis (roadmap).
Theme 5 Data visualization and Analytical Prospective	Dashboard constructed by the Company managers in matters of interest
Theme 6 The generation of value from the Data Science	Analytics strategy defined from the analysis of Company data. Awareness of the importance of data in the decision making of the Company.
Theme 7. Organizational improvement plan	Improvement plan of the capabilities of DA
Theme 8. Presentation of the Final Projects / close	Presentation of proposals and exchange of learning in networks.

Source: Own elaboration

to companies for the installation of the tool and the generation of specific "Dashboards" for the needs of the company. It is important to remark that each company, before the implementation of tTABLEAU, which has the products detailed in table 4 that integrate a value change of data science: identify needs, identify specific problems, collect data, analysis of data, create a mode give, results and apply the new information to DM.

This process also counted on the support of the consulting team, who with the knowledge of the DA capabilities of each firm and their expertise in the different processes allowed guide strategically and productively the implementation of these solutions. Keeping in mind the specific problem that each company wants to resolve, the consultants guide participants in tdeveloping a dashboard and other information with TABLEAU (from three to four visits had been made for each company, in the implementation stage), in order to support the decision making.[2]

The accompaniment of the consultants from the beginning of the program also allowed the development of a road map and an improvement plan for the company integrated with the products developed by the businessmen and managers in the different phases of the program (see table 3).

DATA

A database has been generated with companies enrolled to the program, product of the mapping of the DA capabilities that was carried out to each company through a survey of 35 closed questions in the following areas: characterization of the company, strategic direction management, information for decision making and use of information for marketing (see table 2 and 3). The database collected the information of the 17 companies that started the program with the mapping, of which 88% finalized the program. See detailed information of the data base in the annex A (matrix of 102 rows x 98 columns).

Table 5. Sample of companies of PSCDA

Companies	Antiquity Years	Number of Employees	Sector
AUROS COPIAS S.A	22	More than 200	Wholesale and retail commerce and personal service
LITO PRINT SA	57	between 50 and 199	Manufacturing industry
INCOLNOX SA	29	between 10 and 49	Manufacturing industry
PRODICAUCHOS SA	35	between 10 and 49	Manufacturing industry
ABACOL SAS	20	between 50 and 199	Construction
ANILLO DOBLE O SAS	12	between 10 and 49	Manufacturing industry
DAMATIC LTDA	12	between 50 and 199	Manufacturing industry
ORGANIZACIÓN SANPRO	23	between 50 and 199	Wholesale and retail commerce and personal service
CREATING IDEAS SAS	16	between 50 and 199	Manufacturig industry
ADRIALPETRO SAS	20	between 10 and 49	Exploitation of mines and quarries
CMESPORT SAS	10	less than 10	Manufactruing industry
DESKTOP SYSTEM	24	less than 10	Information and Telecomunications
NNERCIA	18	between 50 and 199	Arts and Design
INDUCARTON	40	between 10 and 49	Manufacturing industry
TWOTOTANGO	2	between 10 and 49	Wholesale and retail commerce and personal service
MODULASER	28	between 50 and 199	Manufacturing industry
COLEGIO REFOUS	58	more than 200	Education

Source: Own elaboration

SAMPLE OF COMPANIES

The program counted with the participation of small, medium and large companies of Bogotá D.C. from different productive sectors such as the energertic and oil industry, metal-mechanic industry, rubber industry and design and arts industry, which manifested the need to innovate in their organizations with DA processes for knowledge of the market and the customers (see table 5).

A first analysis of the answers allows us to show that 82% are medium and large companies with more tan 10 years of antiquity, consequently they are established companies, 52% are in the manufacturing industry, 14% in wholesale and retail trade and personal services, and the rest in other sectors such as construction, education arts and design.

FINDINGS

A 90% rate was achieved in the successful competition of the companies in the program strengthen capabilities in DA. From the total of those who completed the program, approximately 80% implemented TABLEAU and an improvement plan that became evident when the program was completed.

Table 6. Companies by economic sector and export

Main Activities	Do they Export?				Total	%
	Yes	%	No	%		
Explotation of mines and quarries	1	0	1	7	1	7,1
Manufacturing industires	0	0	2	14	8	57,1
Construction	0	0	1	7	1	7,1
Wholesale and retail commerce and personal service	0	0	2	14	2	14,3
Other	1	7	1	7	2	14,3
Total	7	50	7	50	14	100,0

Source: Own elaboration based on the survey

Among the main problems to be solved in the companies, there were those related to disorganized data, fragmented data, non-systematic records, no up-to-date data on sales or historical data, so as to be able to know the trends, there is no adequate inventory control system (for manufacturing companies), they need to collect data from the market (for service companies), etc.

Approximately 10% of the companies in the program were in the process of implementing the ERP (Enterprise Resource Planning) system. Companies such as ABACOL (medium Company) and AUROS COPIAS (large Company) with more than 50 employees, due to their needs, take the decision to implement an integral solution for storage, processing and reporting. Even if the project was oriented towards strengthening the capabilities of small and medium companies of less than 50 employees, the sample has large companies that were also benefited at an opportune moment.

CHARACTERIZATION OF COMPANIES

The majority of the participating PSCDA companies (57%) operate in the manufacturing industry, followed by the commercial sector, personal services and to a less extent the companies of construction and exploitation of mining and quarries. According to the number of employees 50% of companies have between 50 and 199 employees, and 7% more than 200, consequently, most of the companies in the program are medium-large companies (see table 6 and 7) in relation to sales, all of them claimed they have sales that are superior to 300 million COP per year (approximately more than 100.000 dollars per year).

Table 7. Companies by number of employees

Number of Employess	Cases	Percentage
Less than 10 employees	2	14,3
Between 10 and 49 employees	4	28,6
Between 50 and 199 employees	7	50,0
More than 200 employees	1	7,1
Total	14	100,0

Source: Own elaboration based on the survey

STRATEGIC DIRECTION

A 50% affirm that they have trained personnel, for planning, while the rest do not. In relation to indicators to evaluate planning, you can observe that a 57% of the companies do not execute them or they do it in a basic way, while 48% do it in a more sophisticated way.

The evaluation processes apparently are not systematized in the group, given that 50% do not have processes for evaluating strategies according to the market and 48% have a basic process. Only 7% do it systematically.

A very important aspect of Analyses is the integration of internal data with external data. In this respect, 57% of the companies in the program do not carry out this integration, 14% only take into account macroeconomical indicators and 28% also take other sources.

Table 8. Is there planning of scenarios for decision making in the company?

Answers	Cases	Percentage
No	2	14,3
Sometimes	4	28,6
It is planned for one year	8	57,1
Total	14	100,0

Source: Own elaboration based on the survey

Table 9. Use of indicators to evaluate planning

Answers	Cases	Percentage
No	4	28,6
Yes. Basic indicators and less than 5	4	28,6
Yes. More sophisticated indicators and more than 10	6	42,9
Total	14	100,0

Source: Own elaboration based on the survey

Table 10. Does it integrate internal information with the environment?

Answers	Cases	Percentage
No	8	57,1
Yes. Indicators are taken into account Macroeconomics (M)	2	14,3
Yes (N) is taken into account as well as information from other sources	4	28,6
Total	14	100,0

Source: Own elaboration based on the survey

INFORMATION MANAGEMENT IN THE COMPANY

The management of information in the company is very important for monitoring the company and making decisions. When asking the group of companies of the program, if they considered that their information was organized or not, 40% answered no and 57% answered yes.

When inquiring about a specialized analytical department whose main function is the monitoring and evaluation of information management, more than 90% responded that it does have such an area.

Regarding the type of information that companies have, 100% manage standard information, only 43% incorporate social networks and 4% information from censors.

As can be seen in table 12, the organizational and operational information of the company is registred in a traditional analytical media. Additionally, the 4% of companies have acquired, in the last year, integrated information systems and are on the process of adaptation..

Currently, companies handle different technologies for information management, ones more sophisticated than others.100% handle standard technologies, 50% more specialized technologies and 6% a specific technology related to networks.

Regarding the findings on the use of new technologies, approximately 25% carry out certain activities related to the management of technology, as the application of prospective analysis techniques, technological surveillance or technological evaluation and selection and 28% say that there is no activity.

Table 11. Does it have a specialized area in DA?

Answers	Cases	Percentage
No	13	92,9
NR	1	7,1
T	144	100,0

Source: Own elaboration based on the survey

Table 12. The type of information that the company handles

Answers	Cases	Percentage
Standard information, salaries, sales, financial transferences, register, supplies, accounting info.	14	100.0
Marketing through social network	6	42,9
Censor data	2	14.3

Source: Own elaboration based on the survey

Table 13. Where is the information of the company registered?

Answers	Cases	Percentage
Physical files, Excel sheets, information systems, (isolated software)	14	100,0
Integrated information system / ERP SAP), technologies in the cloud or data warehouse (OLAP)	3	21,4

Source: Own elaboration based on the survey

Table 14. Companies according to the technology they use

Answers	Cases	Percentage
Standard internet (Web page) management system (organizational,, accounting, inventories, (sales)	14	100.0
Logistic systems, BD management monitoring and, software of ID	7	50,0
Call centers, electronic commerce, social media	8	57.1

Source: Own elaboration based on the survey

If they had implemented a technology in Data Analytics, approximately 64% indicated that the users would be from the senior and middle management, a 14% everyone. Regarding the type of information that would be integrated, we found that 50% of the companies say that all types, 78% data from the network and 42% from international institutions. The main usefulness of this technology, according to the companies would be information compilation, 48%, processing 57%, data analysis 68% and visualization 64%.

DATA FOR DECISION MAKING

The objective of this section is to diagnose how decisions are made in companies and what is the management of data for support. When we inquired if the company processes and analyzes their information for the TD, 57% answered yes and the rest said no.

When we inquired about the types of reports on information generated in the company, we found that 92% generate standard information, 64% generate basic statistics, 14% more sophisticated statistics and 29% prospective exercises. In 50% of the companies, this type of activity is carried out by the manager, 7% by a specialized professional and 43% by a specific area. The highest frequency with which these reports are elaborated is 57% every month, 21% every week and 14% every day.

We found that in 21,4% of the companies the decisions of cases are taken intuitively and in the majority of cases, 86%, basic data is analyzed.

To asses the percentage of assertiveness in decision making and the impact on the company, two questons were asked. As it can be observed in figure 1, 98% affirm that out of 10 decisions made, approximately 50% were correct and only 7% indicate that 8 out of 10. It is striking that 24% affirm that no decisión is correct.

Table 15. Type of information that the company generates

Answers	Cases	Percentages
Basic accounting data of production	13	92,0
Descriptive indicators	9	64,3
Complex markers	2	14,3
Analytical perspective	4	28,6

Source: Own elaboration based on the survey

Figure 2. Percentage of assertiveness in decisions
Source: Own elaboration based on the survey

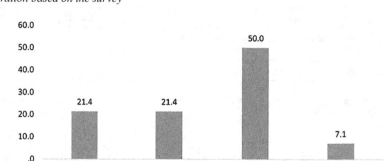

Once decisions are made they have an effect on the company, which we will call a positive or negative impact. According to the following chart 50% of the companies said that the impact has been positive and that productivity has been increased by 50%, 21% of the companies perceive that there has been no impact and that the company is stable and 14% indicate that the impact of the last 10 decisions has been negative and this has reduced sales.

You can observe below the distribution of the percentage of profit from the companies in the program, during rthe last five years. The behavior of the net profit, in the last five years, of the companies that provided the information

As it can be seen in Figure 4 and Table 16, the percentage of profit from the companies in the last five years has been variable, presenting negative data in certain cases. The highest growth percentage is 40%, as CME sport and the loss of profit are around al least 10%, as in the case of LITOPRINT in 2015. Companies such as INERCIA, INCOLNOX, REFOUS, ANILLO DOBLE O have had a stable behavior in their profits, around 10% over the last five years. On the other hand, there are cases such as TWO TO TANGO, LITOPRINT and SINGPRO that have been abrupt in growth or decline. Also, AUROS and INDUCARTON stand out for their constant growth.

Figure 3. Impact of making decisions
Source: Own elaboration based on the survey

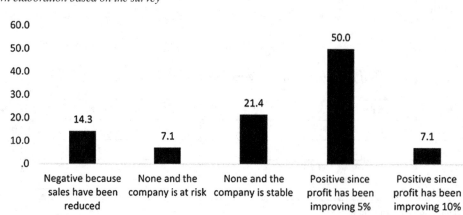

Table 16. Behavior of the profit in the companies in the last 5 years

Company	2012	2013	2014	2015	2016
AUROS COPIAS SA	10	16	20	28	30
LITO PRINT SA.	1	0	-8	-12	7
INCOLNOX SA	1	5	8	9	12
ABACOL SAS	18	-5	-3,7	-3,7	24
ANILLO DOBLE O SAS	10	20	13	8	16
DIMATIC LTDA	14	14	20	20	10
SINGPRO	5	15	11	3	-10
CREATING IDEAS SAS	8	9	12	9	8
CME SPORT SAS	21	25	12	40	30
DESKTOP SYSTEM	20	2,7	25	22	15
INNERCIA	2,5	1.5	2	2	14
INDUCARTON	1,1	10	18	25	30
TWOTOTANGO	0	0	0	30	40
MODULASER	10	15	10	14	12
REFOUS SCHOOL	10	10	10	10	10

Source: Own elaboration based on the survey

Note: The ABACOL data is not taken into account for the profit analysis because the data which was declared was considered unrealistic.

Figure 4. Percentage of the profit from the companies in the last five years
Source: Own elaboration based on the survey

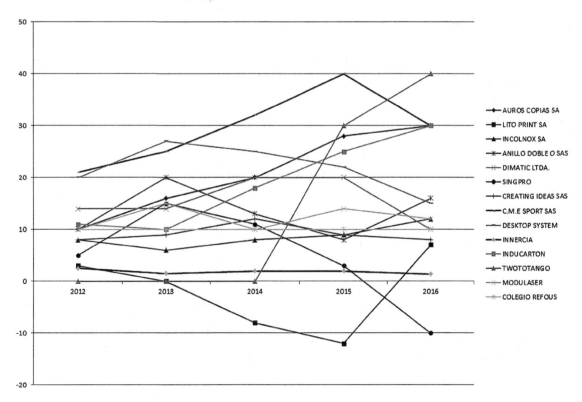

USE OF THE INFORMATION FOR MARKETING

The use of the information for knowledge of the market is one of the activities that accounts for the interest of the company in its costumers, because of the competition with the aim of improving and innovating to maintain growth. When we asked Colombian companies about the strategies they used to access market information, 64,3% declared they read the news and ask members, friends, relatives, etc. Another percentage of companies (42.9%), although tney conduct trend studies, these processes are carried out in a very basic way, this leaves only about 30% of the companies who accomplish more sophisticated studies (see Table 17).

A marketing strategy combined with the planning and control of this process reflects a high level of development in companies. Of the group of the PSCDA, only 28,6% get to carry out marketing planning and control and this percentage is reduced to 21,4% for those who carry out market research. That is, about 80% of the companies in the program do not carry out market research that is related to the DA.

LEARNED LESSONS

The design, planning and execution of this type of project, further than the availability of financial, technological and human resources, requires the trust of entrepreneurs to participate actively in the program. It is a complete program that includes the mapping, training and implementation of a strategic solution based on data analytics, the collaboration and willingness of the participants is required to achieve an impact on the real situation of each company.

On the other hand, the belief that the answer is in the technological tool of DA, rather than, in the identification of what needs to be solved by the technology, is a commom problem in the entrepreneur's mind. This belief is due to the overevaluation of technologies in tautomatic problem solving. This illusion can be frustrating for the users of technology and for the companies, which in some cases, end up acquiring new technologies that end up forming part of the archives. Accordingly, the training of entrepreneurs was key to clarifying those technologies and most importantly the identification of the problem and the data that will allow its solution. Consequently, the program was oriented to the search of the question that needs an answer, for which there is not always an answer with data or for which data is not available.

To finish, another of the challenges of the program was building basic DA capabilities in entrepreneurs and their companies diagnose analytical capabilities and implement the solution in a short time, due to the administrative processes tied for this type of financing. Initially, the program was designed

Table 17. Sources of information and marketing techniques

Answers	Cases	Percentage
Reads the news/ asks their associates	3	64.3
Carry out specific studies of market trends and needs	6	42,5
Apply techniques for market analysis	4	28.6
Hires on external for it	1	7.1

Source: Own elaboration based on the survey

to be executed in six months, however it was executed in half of the time expected after the funds were released. In this sense, it is important to consider contingency plans for the following problems that may be frequent in the scenarios, possible desertion of the program, entry barriers, exit barriers, disruption in providing information of the organization, etc.

CONCLUSION

This pogram was innovative in the framework of the reviewed literature by incorporating and giving importance to the term "capabilities in Data Analytics", as part of the strategic capabilities of companies, in the context of the fourth industrial revolution. What is understood as capabilities in DA is defined to decant the need to strengthen these capabilities of Colombian companies, in a context of availability of a huge amount of information (BIG DATA), revolutionized support systems that integrate mathematics, statistics, engineering, computing and business in what is called today DATA ANALYTICS.

We took advantage of the opportunity the technological laboratories offered, which was an initiative of the Technological and Communication Ministry of Colombia, to implement a Program for Strengthening Capabilities in DATA ANALYTICS in Colombian companies, in three phases: mapping of capabilities, training in DA and application of TABLEAU software, to practical cases generated by each Company.

According to the results found in the mapping of capabilities, preview to the implementation of the Program, in general terms, 90% of the companies don't have Data Analytics capabilities, according to the definition used in this chapter. Consequently, the objective of the program was relevant, necessary and allowed the strengthening of these capabilities through the training stage and the application of tools such as TABLEAU, to carry out analytics in each case. Finally, the companies were left with the following products that show their learning and the contribution of the program. diagnostic of DA capabilities, roadmap for strengthening their DA capabilities, improvement plan based on a DA strategy, scorecards for each company and license for one year of the TABLEAU tool. These products are the company's base line to introduce them in the change of the 4th industrial revolution related to management and analysis of the information using the latest technology to support the strategic decision making in the future.

It is important to highlight that the development of capacity in DA is not solved by buying software. According to the theory of resources and capabilities, these capabilities go much further because it is not possible to develop them without a DA strategy, human resources, fuancing in DA and technological capabilities in DA, among others. Even so, according to Park and Lee (2011), developing skills in DA is a complex and multidisciplinary task which is difficult for small and medium companies, so it could be more feasible for them to hire specialized services with organizations that specialize in these matters. (Schiller S, Goul M., Iyer L., Sharda R. & Schrader D., 2015:815, Parra and Argote, 2017).

DISCUSSION QUESTIONS

According to previous secctions some questions emerge that a teacher could analyce with students about the case of SPCDA:

1. In the context of Revolution 4.0, what percentaje of the companies have DA capabilities al local, regional or global level? Why?

2. Which are the key factors related to developing DA capabilities in the companies?

3. Do you know the difference between Tangible versus Intangible capabilities? DA capabilities are intangible; do you believe that they are important for the companies? Why?

4. We found that a hight percentaje of "bogotanas" companies believe that buingy a software was a solution of their problems. Which is the importance of the identification of needs and of a clear objective in a DA project? Which is the importance of identification of needs and of a clear objective in the value chain of a company?

5. Kopsco and Pachamanova (2017:2) mention stages of analytics maturity of the companies: Data quality, Data visualization and descriptive analysis, Diagnostics, Predictive analytics and Prescriptive analytics. The business value of DA depends of the maturity level of the company, at which level is your company?

6. As directive of your company, if you have the most brilliant DA tool, but you don't have clear objectives, which is the result? If you don't have a good data quality, which is the result?

REFERENCES

Acs, Z. J., Audretsch, D. B., & Strom, R. J. (Eds.). (2009). *Entrepreneurship, Growth, and Public Policy*. Cambridge University Press. doi:10.1017/CBO9780511805950

Aguirre Ramírez, J. (2010). *Metodología para medir y evaluar las capacidades tecnológicas de innovación aplicando sistemas de lógica difusa caso fábricas de software* (Doctoral dissertation). Universidad Nacional de Colombia.

Argote, M. (2016a). *Identification of the technological capabilities of the "Fundación Universitaria de Ciencias de la Salud"*. Paper presented at the Congress of Science and Technology 2016, Quito, Ecuador.

Argote, M. (2016b). Identification of the technological capabilities of the "Fundación Universitaria de Ciencias de la Salud". *Yura relaciones internacionales, 9*, 230. Retrieved from http://world_business.espe.edu.ec/revista-yura/

Audretsch David, B., Kuratko, D., & Link, A. (2016). *Dynamic Entrepreneurship and Technology-Based Innovation*. Department of Economics Working Paper Series, April 2016, Working Paper 16-02. Retrieved from http://bae.uncg.edu/econ/

Bell, M., & Pavitt, K. (1992). Accumulating technological capability in developing countries. *The World Bank Economic Review, 6*(suppl 1), 257–281. doi:10.1093/wber/6.suppl_1.257

Bell, M., & Pavitt, K. (1993). Technological accumulation and industrial growth: Contrasts between developed and developing countries. *Industrial and Corporate Change, 2*(2), 157–210. doi:10.1093/icc/2.2.157

GEM Bogota. (2018). *GEM report Bogotá*. Secretaria Distrital de Desarrollo Economico de Bogota in alliance with EAN University.

Bray, M. J., & Lee, J. N. (2000). University revenues from technology transfer: Licensingfees versus equity positions. *Journal of Business Venturing, 15*(5–6), 385–392. doi:10.1016/S0883-9026(98)00034-2

Castellanos Domínguez, Ó. F., Fúquene Montañez, A. M., & Ramírez Martínez, D. C. (2011). *Análisis de tendencias: de la información hacia la innovación*. Universidad Nacional de Colombia.

CEPAL. (2007). *Progreso técnico y cambio estructural en América Latina. Project document of the United Nations*. Author.

Chapple, W., Lockett, A., Siegel, D. S., & Wright, M. (2005). Assessing the relative performance of U.K. University technology transfer offices: Parametric and nonparametricevidence. *Research Policy*, *34*(3), 369–384. doi:10.1016/j.respol.2005.01.007

Chen, H., Chiang, R. H., & Storey, V. C. (2012). Business intelligence and analytics: From big data to big impact. *Management Information Systems Quarterly*, *36*(4), 1165. doi:10.2307/41703503

Cimoli, M. (2000). Creación de redes y sistema de innovación: México en un contexto global. *El Mercado de Valores*, *60*(1), 3–17.

Davenport, T. H. (2006). Competing on analytics. *Harvard Business Review, 84*(1), 98.

Dill, J. C., Kasik, D. J., & Darvill, D. J. (2013). Case study: successful deployment of industry-university collaborative visual analytics research. In *System Sciences (HICSS), 2013 46th Hawaii International Conference on* (pp. 1505-1511). IEEE. 10.1109/HICSS.2013.126

Domínguez, L., & Brown, F. (2004). Measuring technological capabilities in Mexican. *CEPAL Review*, *83*(83), 129–144. doi:10.18356/872c3189-en

García del Junco, J., & García, R. (1995). Análisis de las principales capacidades de la gestión empresarial. *Dirección y Organización*, (13), 32-44.

Hoyos, T. A. (2014). Innovación y cambio tecnológico en la sociedad del conocimiento (2nd ed.). Ediciones ECOE, Universidad de la Sabana.

Kantis, H., Angelelli, P., & Moori, V. (2004). *Desarrollo emprendedor: América Latina y la experiencia internacional*. BID-FUNDES Internacional.

Kantis, H., Ishida, M., & Komori, M. (2002b). *Empresarialidad en economías emergentes: Creación y desarrollo de nuevas empresas en América Latina y el Este de Asia (No. 56558)*. Washington, DC: Inter-American Development Bank.

Kantis, H., Postigo, S., Federico, J., & Tamborini, F. (2002a). El surgimiento de emprendedores de base universitaria: en qué se diferencian? Evidencias empíricas para el caso de Argentina. Presentado en: RENT XVI Conference, Barcelona, Spain.

Katz, J. (1986). Desarrollo y crisis de la capacidad tecnológica Latinoamericana, el caso de la industria metalmecánica. Estudios sobre desarrollo tecnológico por BID/CEPAL/CIID/PNUD.

Katz, J. (2000). Cambios estructurales y productividad en la Industria Latinoamericana, 1970-1996. *Revista de la CEPAL, 71*, 65–84.

Katz, J. (2007). Cambios estructurales y desarrollo económico. Ciclos e creación y destrucción de capacidad productiva y tecnológica en América Latina. Revista de Economía Política de Buenos Aires, 1, 71-92.

Kopcso, D., & Pachamanova, D. (2017). *Case Article—Business Value in Integrating Predictive and Prescriptive Analytics Models.* INFORMS Transactions on Education.

McAfee, A., Brynjolfsson, E., Davenport, T. H., Patil, D. J., & Barton, D. (2012). Big data: The management revolution. *Harvard Business Review, 90*(10), 60–68. PMID:23074865

Parra, L., & Argote, M. (2013). La gestión en el proceso de creación empresarial: el caso de IN3 de la Universidad EAN de Colombia. In *Emprendimiento: diferentes aproximaciones.* Cuaderno de investigación. Editorial Universidad EAN.

Parra, L., & Argote, M. (2016a). Marco Conceptual para el Análisis de Brechas tecnológicas en el Sector Metalmecánico. Análisis de brechas tecnológicas en el sector.

Parra, L., & Argote, M. (2017). Data Analytics to Characterize UniversityBased Companies for Decision Making in Business Development Programs. In E. Rodriguez (Ed.), *Data Analytics Applications in Latin America and Emerging Economies.* CRC Press, Taylor and Francis.

Porter, M. E., & Stern, S. (2002). National Innovative capacity. Academic Press.

Ranga, M., Temel, S., Ar, I. M., Yesilay, R. B., & Sukan, F. V. (2016). Building Technology Transfer Capacity in Turkish Universities: A critical analysis. *European Journal of Education, 51*(1), 90–106. doi:10.1111/ejed.12164

Rodriguez, E. (Ed.). (2017). *Data Analytics applications in Latin America and emerging economies* (1st ed.). New York: Taylor and Francis. doi:10.4324/9781315164113

Rothaermel, F. T., Agung, S. D., & Jiang, L. (2007). University entrepreneurship: A taxonomy of the literature. *Industrial and Corporate Change, 16*(4), 691–791. doi:10.1093/icc/dtm023

Parra, Argote, & Farro. (2018). Emprendimiento universitario: análisis de contraste entre la Universidad EAN Colombia y la Universidad Continental Perú. *Universidad EAN, 2018,* 7–38.

Wang, C. H., Lu, I. Y., & Chen, C. B. (2008). Evaluating firm technological innovation capability under uncertainty. *Technovation, 28*(6), 349–363. doi:10.1016/j.technovation.2007.10.007

Zoltan, A. (2016). Public policy to promote entrepreneurship: A call to arms. *Small Business Economics, 47*(1), 35–51. doi:10.100711187-016-9712-2

ENDNOTES

[1] We understand sophisticated techniques as they use statistics, mathematics and computational algorithms for predictive and prescriptive analysis (Kopcso & Pachamanova, 2017).

[2] Each Company saves the results of the implementation of TABLEAU (dashboard and indicators). The analysis of this informacion is in the improvement plan of each company.

APPENDIX

Table 18. Descriptives of the data base of Bogotanas companies of the PSCDA

Name	Type	Long	Label	Values	Missings	Colums
sec	Numérico	12	id	Ninguna	Ninguna	12
preg0_1	Cadena	16	consultor	Ninguna	Ninguna	16
preg0_2	Cadena	30	c_name	Ninguna	Ninguna	30
preg0_3	Numérico	12	c_cedula	Ninguna	Ninguna	12
preg0_4	Fecha	11	fecha_e	Ninguna	Ninguna	11
preg1	Cadena	35	e_name	Ninguna	Ninguna	35
preg1_1	Cadena	24	e_dir	Ninguna	Ninguna	24
preg1_2	Cadena	12	e_nit	Ninguna	Ninguna	12
preg1_3	Numérico	12	e_telf	Ninguna	Ninguna	12
preg1_4	Cadena	23	e_web	Ninguna	Ninguna	23
preg1_5	Cadena	54	e_mail	Ninguna	Ninguna	50
preg2	Cadena	2	antigu	{1, entre 10 y 20 años}...	Ninguna	10
preg3	Cadena	84	prod_serv	Ninguna	Ninguna	50
preg4	Numérico	12	e_act	lotación de minas y cant(	Ninguna	12
preg4_1	Numérico	12	e_act_1	olo una actividad princip	Ninguna	12
preg5	Numérico	12	e_emple	Menos de 10 empleados	Ninguna	12
preg6	Numérico	12	e_ventas	e 51 y 100 millones de p(	Ninguna	12
preg7	Numérico	12	e_exp	{1, Si}...	Ninguna	12
preg8	Numérico	12	plan_esc	{1, No}...	Ninguna	12
preg9	Numérico	12	per_cal	{1, Si}...	Ninguna	12
preg10	Numérico	12	ind_eval	{1, No}...	Ninguna	12
preg11	Numérico	12	est_mercado	{1, No}...	Ninguna	12
preg12	Numérico	12	int_ext	{1, No}...	Ninguna	12
preg13_1	Numérico	12	tipo_inf_1	{0, No}...	Ninguna	12
preg13_2	Numérico	12	tipo_inf_2	{0, No}...	Ninguna	12
preg13_3	Numérico	12	tipo_inf_3	{0, No}...	Ninguna	12
preg13_4	Cadena	44	tipo_otra	Ninguna	Ninguna	44
preg14_1	Numérico	12	reg_inf_1	{0, No}...	Ninguna	12
preg14_2	Numérico	12	reg_inf_2	{0, No}...	Ninguna	12
preg15_1	Numérico	12	tec_inf_1	{0, No}...	Ninguna	12
preg15_2	Numérico	12	tec_inf_2	{0, No}...	Ninguna	12
preg15_3	Numérico	12	tec_inf_3	{0, No}...	Ninguna	12
preg16	Numérico	12	inf_org	{1, Si}...	Ninguna	12
preg17	Cadena	2	dep_anali	{1, Si}...	Ninguna	2
preg18_1	Numérico	12	act_ges_1	{0, No}...	Ninguna	12
preg18_2	Numérico	12	act_ges_2	{0, No}...	Ninguna	12

continued on following page

Table 18. Continued

preg18_3	Numérico	12	act_ges_3	{0, No}...	Ninguna	12
preg18_4	Numérico	12	act_ges_4	{0, No}...	Ninguna	12
preg18_5	Cadena	46	act_ges_otra	Ninguna	Ninguna	46
preg19_1	Numérico	12	us_tec_1	{0, No}...	Ninguna	12
preg19_2	Numérico	12	us_tec_2	{0, No}...	Ninguna	12
preg19_3	Numérico	12	us_tec_3	{0, No}...	Ninguna	12
preg19_4	Numérico	12	us_tec_4	{0, No}...	Ninguna	12
preg19_5	Numérico	12	us_tec_5	{0, No}...	Ninguna	12
preg19_6	Cadena	3	us_tec_6	Ninguna	Ninguna	7
preg20_1	Numérico	12	int_inf_1	{0, No}...	Ninguna	12
preg20_2	Numérico	12	int_inf_2	{0, No}...	Ninguna	12
preg20_3	Numérico	12	int_inf_3	{0, No}...	Ninguna	12
preg20_4	Numérico	12	int_inf_4	{0, No}...	Ninguna	12
preg20_5	Numérico	12	int_inf_5	{0, No}...	Ninguna	12
preg21_1	Numérico	12	uso_tecno_1	{0, No}...	Ninguna	12
preg21_2	Numérico	12	uso_tecno_2	{0, No}...	Ninguna	12
preg21_3	Numérico	12	uso_tecno_3	{0, No}...	Ninguna	12
preg21_4	Numérico	12	uso_tecno_4	{0, No}...	Ninguna	12
preg22	Numérico	12	inf_td	{1, Si}...	Ninguna	12
preg23_1	Numérico	12	tipoinf_td_1	{0, No}...	Ninguna	12
preg23_2	Numérico	12	tipoinf_td_2	{0, No}...	Ninguna	12
preg23_3	Numérico	12	tipoinf_td_3	{0, No}...	Ninguna	12
preg23_4	Numérico	12	tipoinf_td_4	{0, No}...	Ninguna	12
preg24_1	Numérico	12	area_td_1	{0, No}...	Ninguna	12
preg24_2	Numérico	12	area_td_2	{0, No}...	Ninguna	12
preg24_3	Numérico	12	area_td_3	{0, No}...	Ninguna	12
preg24_4	Numérico	12	area_td_4	{0, No}...	Ninguna	12
preg24_5	Numérico	12	area_td_5	{0, No}...	Ninguna	12
preg24_6	Numérico	12	area_td_6	{0, No}...	Ninguna	12
preg24_otro	Cadena	7	area_td_otro	Ninguna	Ninguna	10
preg25_1	Numérico	12	frec_repo_1	{0, No}...	Ninguna	12
preg25_2	Numérico	12	frec_repo_2	{0, No}...	Ninguna	12
preg25_3	Numérico	12	frec_repo_3	{0, No}...	Ninguna	12
preg25_4	Numérico	12	frec_repo_4	{0, No}...	Ninguna	12

continued on following page

Table 18. Continued

preg25_6	Numérico	12	frec_repo_6	{0, No}...	Ninguna	12
preg26_1	Numérico	12	como_td_1	{0, No}...	Ninguna	12
preg26_2	Numérico	12	como_td_2	{0, No}...	Ninguna	12
preg26_3	Numérico	12	como_td_3	{0, No}...	Ninguna	12
preg26_4	Numérico	12	como_td_4	{0, No}...	Ninguna	12
preg27	Numérico	12	veces_td	n 0 de 10 ocasiones en q	Ninguna	12
preg28	Numérico	12	impacto_td	o ya que se ha reducido la	Ninguna	12
preg29_1	Cadena	3	uti_1	Ninguna	Ninguna	3
preg29_2	Cadena	3	uti_2	Ninguna	Ninguna	3
preg29_3	Cadena	3	uti_3	Ninguna	Ninguna	3
preg29_4	Cadena	3	utl_4	Ninguna	Ninguna	3
preg29_5	Cadena	3	uti_5	Ninguna	Ninguna	3
preg30_1	Numérico	12	com_estra_1	{0, No}...	Ninguna	12
preg30_2	Numérico	12	com_estra_2	{0, No}...	Ninguna	9
preg30_3	Cadena	3	com_estra_3	{0, No}...	Ninguna	7
preg31_1	Numérico	12	presupuesto_1	{0, No}...	Ninguna	12
preg31_2	Numérico	12	presupuesto_2	{0, No}...	Ninguna	12
preg31_3	Numérico	12	presupuesto_3	{0, No}...	Ninguna	12
preg31_4	Cadena	3	presupuesto_4	{0, No}...	Ninguna	11
preg32_1	Numérico	12	cono_mer_1	{0, No}...	Ninguna	12
preg32_2	Numérico	12	cono_mer_2	{0, No}...	Ninguna	12
preg32_3	Numérico	12	cono_mer_3	{0, No}...	Ninguna	12
preg32_4	Cadena	3	cono_mer_4	{0, No}...	Ninguna	8
preg33	Numérico	12	plan_mer	{1, Si}...	Ninguna	12
preg34	Numérico	12	inv_mer	{1, Si}...	Ninguna	12
preg35	Numérico	12	publicity	{1, Si}...	Ninguna	12
Preguntadetonante	Cadena	116	preg_deton	Ninguna	Ninguna	50
preg5m	Cadena	2	recodificada	Ninguna	Ninguna	8
filter_$	Numérico	1	SSING(preg5) (FIL	{0, Not Selected}...	Ninguna	10
antiguedad	Numérico	8	ntigu recodificad	{,00, No responde}...	Ninguna	12

Chapter 26
A Review of Antecedents of Online Repurchase Behavior in Indian E–Commerce Paradigm Shift

Syed Habeeb
National Institute of Technology Warangal, India

K. Francis Sudhakar
National Institute of Technology Warangal, India

ABSTRACT

The purpose of this chapter is to highlight research areas of customer satisfaction and repurchase intentions and their antecedents in the Indian e-commerce industry. To retain, attract, and satisfy customers, e-retailers need to understand how and why online customers evaluate a web store. The relevant areas of consumer behavior and marketing research were derived to explain the possible gaps to study with respect to e-commerce in India. To do so, a systematic review of online consumer behavior literature is conducted. Following inclusion and exclusion criteria, a total of 109 journal articles are analyzed. The major finding of the chapter was that there is very less amount of research considering the areas of customer satisfaction, trust, loyalty along with repurchase behavior of the online customer in specific to the Indian context. Therefore, it is a need of the hour to extend the study to know the repurchase behavior of the online consumer in present time.

INTRODUCTION

India is one among the fast-moving and drastically growing countries with respect to e-commerce when compared with developed and developing countries. Now a day's internet is playing a vital role in person's life as well as for corporate houses. Because of expanding noticeable quality of e-retailing, enthusiasm among researchers and professionals have expanded towards customer perception and reception.

DOI: 10.4018/978-1-5225-8933-4.ch026

Researchers have attempted to speculate e-shopping regarding social brain science and data framework perspective of view to investigate its different determinants (Celik, 2016).

Nowadays, people are so involved in their way of life and they claim that it is difficult to go outside and shop. For such factors, the online stores give them countless options to peruse, including refunds that a standard store can never stand while they sit in their home. It should also be noted that if individualists unsatisfied with psychological needs in a face-to-face relationship then they would seek to satisfaction in other contexts such as the online buying (Li, Zhang et al, 2016; Li and Zhou, 2016; Ibrahim Arpaci et al, 2018). Electronic business has become immeasurably worldwide and its aggressiveness is expanding over the previous decades. The most important aspect of the business is to not only attract customers but also retain them to survive and withstand the competition. Hence repurchase from a customer is ending up increasingly noticeable for web-based shopping sites and sellers than at any other time (Jansen et al, 2008).

The number of users when compared around the world, Asia ranks the first with 50.2% internet users, Europe 17.1%, Latin America 10.3%, Africa 9.3%, the remaining percentage is shared by North America, Middle East and Australia (Internet World stats, Mar 31, 2017). Headway in the computer supported innovation and the quick development of web based apps has helped internet business drastic growth (Oh *et al.*, 2012). Web based business has turned into a vital piece of the virtual space and has brought about quick development of e shopping space and online shopping websites (Alden *et al.*, 2006; Kamarulzaman, 2007).

E-commerce business makes open doors for business endeavors to acquire purchasers globally (Al-Maghrabi *et al.*, 2011). It engages buyers with a broad determination, colossal item data and minimal fleeting and spatial restrictions, which urge them to buy items and services through online rather than physical stores (Wen *et al.*, 2011).

The KPMG Report (2017) on E commerce Retail Logistics India stated that the infiltration of online retail in India's aggregate retail advertise is relied upon to go up from 2.5% in 2016 to 5% by 2020. Aranca Research (March 2018), the report quantified that the online business advertising is expected to reach US$ 64 billion in 2020 from US$ 38.5 of 2017 and US$ 200 billion by the ending of 2026. With developing web infiltration, web clients in India are expected to reach 829 million by 2021 against 481 million as of December 2017 (Ibef, March 2018).

Morgan Stanley (2017) stated that India's e-commerce market will rise to 30 percent to $200 billion by 2026. This milestone will also raise market penetration to increase from 2% to 12% in coming decade and there will be an increment in new internet users from 14% in 2016 to 50% by 2026 and it will help e-commerce industry to grow (India's Digital Leap report 2018). Thus there is a vast market for new entry and as well as the existing e-retailers to grow in future. This marks that research should be done to know the mindset or new consumer's behavior.

In order to predict consumer behavior of online shopping, many models highlighting socio psychological items and informational system items have been developed which includes technology acceptance model, motivation theory, theory of planned behavior and unified theory of acceptance. These studies contributed in support to online consumer behavior, they failed to accomplish keeping online buyers retaining and repurchasing. In the Indian scenario, online shopping portals are increasing drastically. Many retailers that were only into brick and mortar business are forcing themselves to be in electronic commerce due to change in the market environment. Several multinational online shopping players also have made their existence in the Indian market as the usage of online shopping is growing among the Indian consumer

As the e-commerce market becomes increasingly dynamic and competitive, the marketers have to acknowledge that the best core marketing strategy is to retain existing customers by satisfying them through service in terms of delivery and service quality (Bai et al, 2008; Udo et al, 2010; Kim, 2010; Ankit keshawani et al, 2017). Indian market conditions have become more competitive than before, there is a need for a business to deliver consumer value by enchanting customers in long term relationships in order to increase greater chances of re-purchase.

Number of e-commerce players though are trying to reach out to the customers, are not successful since they could not grab the customer base. Only very few online sellers have converted themselves into giant sellers. Even though these giants provide high discounts but still fail to create loyalty to its customers and could not create repurchase intention.

Hence, in order to grab customers and take advantage of the smart Indian market, firstly the online sellers need to understand different determinants and dimensions that drive for repurchase intention from the last purchased website. Sullivan et al. (2018) repurchase intentions are influenced by website reputation and online trust. This work makes an attempt to finding out the different determinants that can cause repurchase intention.

Why Study E-Commerce in India?

The e-commerce players have come up with mobile apps or user-friendly browsers and these forces drive the consumers to taste the online experience at their convenience. Research seems to be interesting may be because of various comparisons made by the consumers like mobile versus desktop and online shop versus in-store. The state of mind or perception of consumers comparing the prices of online and in-store gives the interest to make a study of their behavior.

Indian customers are heterogeneous in nature; they like to pay online since they are found shopping online since a decade and want to have greater shopping experience in terms of fast delivery, steep discounts, replacement facility etc. The other kinds of customers are those who bargain and never mind about fast delivery, but the price of the product does matter. No loyalty is found in them when big discounts are given by the sellers.

Nowadays there are multiple competitors in online shopping such as Amazon, Flipkart, Myntra, Snapdeal, Jabong etc. So, it is a challenging job for the online shopping inc. to differentiate their products/service than others to attract as much as online shopping customers. The differentiation can be based on multiple factors (Athira A Nair, Feb 2017).

Table 1. Reasons for online shopping popularity

Researchers	Reasons
Poulter et al, 2013; Duarte, P et al, 2018	convenience
Palmer, 2013; Bodur, H. O et al, 2015; Gorodnichenko, Y et al, 2017	price comparisons online, product comparision
Poulter, 2013; Delacroix, E 2016	avoiding long queues
Eckler, 2013; Anil Bilgihan 2016; Lee, C. R et al, 2017	consumers can shop online anywhere, anytime
Poulter, 2013	one third of consumers shop in bed, 24/7
Lauden & Traver, 2013; Shehu, E et al, 2016; Ma, S 2017	Free offers, No crowds or no queues, Easier to find items, Direct shipping to home

Table 2. Reasons why online shopping seems to be dissatisfying and annoying

Researchers	Reasons
Rackspace (2013)	complicated check out procedures
Adeshara, 2013, Palmer, 2013; Chen, H. M et al, 2016; Wang, Y et al, 2016	High shipping costs, product information lack, security issues and few online payment options

BACKGROUND

Measuring consumer behavior and perception is an ongoing process for every industry since no business can survive without consumers/Customers. Measuring consumer behavior is also important because it helps the organization in understanding the target audience. Considering past decade it is found that there is internet usage growing and also found that businesses expanding by adopting e-commerce to mark their presence globally. Considering Asia Pacific region internet penetration for the year 2017, the top position is taken by China with 731 million internet users and India takes second place with 462 million internet users (Statista, 2017).

The Internet and Mobile Association of India and market research firm IMRB International mentioned that Indian internet penetration present is around 31% and digital transformation will take India's internet users to 829 million (59 percent of the Indian population) in 2021 from 373 million (28 percent of the population) in 2016. This indicates there is much positive to happen in e-business and online shopping in India.

Internet users increasing day by day and prefer shopping online because of social networking sites are seen increasing. But a question arises irrespective of time, how to attract the customer and make him/her as a loyal customer to the online shopping seller. To answer this question, many academicians, researcher and consulting firms have tried to answer this question but failed to give a proper solution. This may be due to the changes in the consumer behavior and market advancements. For effective marketing strategy development studying consumer behavior is used as a key phenomenon.

Online shopping is the topic that has been researched and provided proven outcomes from past to nowadays, but still, as the time passes there is a need to study to know consumer behavior. The post-purchase behavior of consumer should be studied regularly since making consumers stick to the same e-commerce is difficult these days because of steep discounts and cheap products. To measure post-purchase behavior, the consumers need to test whether they are satisfied or dissatisfied.

The satisfaction and dissatisfaction of consumers falls between product performance and consumer's expectations. The larger the gap between product performance and consumer's expectations, there will be greater consumer's dissatisfaction. Also retaining customers these days is not that easy, so a gap is open to study why these customers do shopping with different e-stores and need to find out which factors lead them to shop with other online sellers. Thus there is still a need to study post purchase behavior of the online customer in present days.

Several factors are found that govern the growth of e-commerce in India. Online players need to understand the need that holds the customer stick to their earlier purchased company or seller. This can only happen with a thorough understanding of the Indian online consumer behavior. Online shopping behavior is governed by quality, price offered and seller's reputation (Genrt et al, 2012). In the quality at any price offered, reputation will be the most dominant segment in the online shopping behavior. May be this is the reason why customers tent to buy from prominent online seller's. Once the customers found to be satisfied with online shopping, they will tend to repeat purchase (Jiang and Rosenbloom, 2005).

The needs and wants of the consumers keep on changing as time goes and this needs to be remembered by the company. It's seen too often that brands focus on product catalog and forget about its customers. Always consider who your business is being built for. Remembering the wants and needs of the consumer's should be important for a company. As time goes on the tastes of the consumer's change and studies should regularly be done in knowing how to retain the consumer make him repurchase again and again. Thus, this study is focused on the factors that develop trust and repurchase intention of Indian consumers in the present competitive market.

Overview of Reviewed Articles

A systematic approach was followed to literature search. The academic publications from 2005 to 2018 were focused. In the journal papers considered more focus was made with respect to repurchase behavior and its antecedents were high lightened. Major journal papers in the areas of consumer behavior, services marketing and e-commerce were also included.

India is competing with global retailers because India is having a very good potential market. Since the internet users number is growing day by day and thus it is very necessary to identify the various factors that affect Indian consumers online shopping behavior in order to research hoe these factors stimulate the online shopping behavior (Jayendra Sinha, 2012).

Hong-Youl Ha et al. (2008) carried out a study that employs a cross-cultural perspective which explores alternative explanations in the development of the online repurchase intentions model. Structural equation modeling was applied to test the model which deals with key consumer behavior factors such as customized information, web use applications, online service and perceived interactivity which lead to formation of purchase intentions. The results explain the power of customized information that lies in its ability to influence consumer satisfaction and perceived interactivity that are proximate to repurchase intentions.

Fang, Y et al. (2009) have focused on the relationship between customer satisfaction and repurchase intention and showed that the customer satisfaction is not predominantly result in the frequent repurchase. There are many possible factors connecting to the relationship in repurchase behavior. Vinerean, S et al, (2013), worked with the psychological and social factors and cheeked their influence on online shopping behavior. The results conclude that social media or social networks influence online perception and trust with respect to a specific website through word of mouth. Hsu, C. L (2009) studied external & internal factors that influence customer satisfaction and loyalty relationship using structural equation modeling as an analytical tool. Their findings show customer satisfaction and website service quality has a positive effect on loyalty and also states that technology acceptance model factors positively influence customer satisfaction and loyalty.

Grewal *et al.* (2009) establish that online satisfactory shopping knowledge can increase in repeat purchase plan. According to self-perception theory (Johnson *et al.*, 2001), people may frequently modify their perceptions as they procure new information about the pivotal behavior. Hand et al. (2009) explored situational factors that influence adoption of online grocery shopping and posited that due to service issues some customers discontinued grocery shopping. Doherthy & Ellis (2010) in their comprehensive literature review stated that consumer has become more powerful and also stated that competitive pricing wins competition in e-retailing environment.

Mummalaneni V et al (2009) reported that service quality induce online customers to repurchase from the previous seller. Zhang et al (2011) mentioned in their research that repurchase intentions exert influences with service quality. Bhupinder ps chandar et al (2016) mentioned that with the increasing players in online market, the marketers need to have an edge in terms of service quality to gain a large market share in competitive market. This study explained the service quality concept along with most significant factor in e-service quality which attracts consumer online buying. The results say that the most important factor in measuring service quality is the privacy of website and delivery of goods on time. The growth of internet and online shopping will increase in larger number in coming years; so online sellers should think about how to make customers repeat purchase.

Richard M. O. et al. (2010) the influences of web atmosphere and internet experience on consumer e-shopping behavior is examined in this paper, which developed to the model of web navigation behavior. They assessed the role of men and women for online shopping behavior. Results revealed that, women engaged more exploratory behavior and website involvement than men. The key attitudes of website are effectiveness of information content, entertainment and challenge.

Boudhayan Ganguly et al. (2010) to provide empirical evidence that trust in online stores is positively influencing the purchase intention and reduces the perceived risk; the mediating role of trust is tested in this paper. Confirmatory Factor Analysis is performed to analyze the questionnaire. The factors such as website design, information design, visual effects and navigation influence trust through which purchase intensions increase

Su & Huang (2011) analyzed online shopping intention of China's undergraduate consumer based on theory of planned behavior. Their results posited that price of products and student' computer knowledge influences the online shopping intentions.

Mustafa I. Eid (2011) a conceptual framework which hypothesizes the relationship between the constructs of e-commerce and their antecedents to identify the factors that influence consumers trusts, satisfaction and loyalty towards B2C e-commerce. Results proved that customer's loyalty is more influenced by customer satisfaction and less influenced by customer trust. Kim Hee-Woong et al. (2011) the relative influence of price and trust on online purchase decisions of potential and repeat customers are examined in this paper. For developing customized sales strategies to target different groups of customers the relative impacts and the relative roles over customer transaction experience is useful. From the results it is observed that perceived trust has more effect than the price on purchase intensions. The repeat customers purchase intensions are much influenced by perceived price.

Ha & Stoel (2012) tested the influence of e-shopping quality on e-shopping satisfaction and e-shopping intention and also testing consumer experiential e-shopping motives as a moderator on USA apparel retail store. The results posit that website content have a significant influence on e-shopping satisfaction which indeed contributes to e-shopping intention, also found that security and consumer service have a significant impact on e-shopping intention but not on e-shopping satisfaction. Dwivedi et al. (2012) studied review of existing literature with respect to online retailing in India and identified some factors that motivate consumers to shop online. These factors include convenience, payment mode, delivery and cost saving. The challenges found out were security and transaction fraud issues, competitors are click away and consumers waiting for best offers.

Gong W et al. (2013) studied the factors those influence Chinese consumers to shop online considering the effect of demographic characteristics on e-shopping intentions. The results depict that age, income, education and marital status show significant impact on online shopping intention. Nachiappan Subramanian et al (2013) studied the impact of customer satisfaction and Chinese electronic retailer's competitiveness considering quality factors. This Study proposed two conceptual models based on asset-process-performance (APP) competitive theoretical framework. By using SEM, the researchers could identify reliability in service quality along with purchasing experience in e-service quality as dominant customer satisfaction elements. They made a conclusion that to be competitive e-retailers, they have to focus more on delivery of products (logistics) compared to other intangible service quality factors.

Ariff M S M et al. (2013) the study showed the relationship and the impacts of e- SQ and e- satisfaction on e- loyalty in internet banking are examined in this research. The modified version of E-SERVQUAL instrument was used to determine e- SQ. Survey was conducted and data is collected from 265 internet banking users. The factors that affected e-satisfaction are assurance, efficient system availability, privacy, contact-responsiveness and guide constitute e- service quality for the internet banking service, and these are shown in results. The results highlighted the important features of internet banking that attractiveness and appearance of bank's website and the information and guidance provided by the websites.

Waseso Segoro (2013) this study was done seeing in the decline of customer satisfaction and loyalty in service firms. The factors such as customer perception on service quality, mooring factors and relationship quality are identified as influences of customer satisfaction and loyalty. To measure these factors questionnaire was distributed to students who subscribed to cellular operated services. The Structural Equation Model (SEM) was used for data analysis. Results showed that customer perception and relationship quality had positive correlation with mooring factors, these also have positive direct influence on customer loyalty.

Hana Uzun (2014) in a study about factors affecting online shopping behavior which measures consumer's previous experience and mentioned that if consumers are satisfied with the online seller with minimal risk level then they will buy more in future. Thus the consumers become loyal to the online seller. Brady & Cronin Jr. (2014) the effects of being customer oriented and outcome behaviors on service performance perceptions are studied in this paper. Using the two step approach the model was tested. The results showed the link between physical goods quality, services cape quality and performance service quality.

Chinho Lin, Watcharee Lekhawipat (2014) examined the effects of online shopping experience and pattern in relation to adjusted expectations for increasing online repurchase intention. Study used partial least square (PLS) as a method to analyze the measurement and structural models. The results showed that online shopping pattern acts as a moderator of both customer satisfaction and adjusted expectations, whereas online shopping experience can be perceived as a key driver of customer satisfaction. If the product or service meets the customer satisfaction will develop an intention to repurchase. Since customer satisfaction is known as bunch of many factors such as good feeling when comparing product with others, expectations match with the product and service etc.

Giovanis & Athanasopoulou (2014) in their study they tested the customer loyalty in e-tailing. They investigation was done to determine e-SQ and their dimensions to e-satisfaction and e-trust, the relevant impact of e- satisfaction and e-trust on e-loyalty. Data was collected from 451 customers of consumer electronics e-tailers. The results showed that the e-loyalty is positively affected by e-satisfaction and e- trust, the antecedents of e-satisfaction and e-trust are the e-SQ dimensions such as reliability, privacy and usability. The relationship between the information quality/benefits, responsiveness and web design & e-trust are mediated by e- satisfaction.

Srivastava M & Alok Kumar Rai (2014) this paper discussed the service quality -customer loyalty relationship in life insurance sector. By assessing the moderating influences of trust it offers further insights. Results proved that relationships are statistically significant. Customer loyalty has a strong and positive relationship with service quality and trust. Zeki Atıl Bulut (2015) investigated Turkish consumers intentions considering e-satisfaction, e-trust and e-loyalty and revealed that there exists a positive relationship between repurchase intentions and these construct. Also found that e-trust is a very important determinant for online repurchase intentions. Michelle Carter et al. (2014) in this research paper the authors did an empirical study of the relative influence of trust versus switching costs on e-loyalty for online service providers. They also examined whether the relationship between switching costs and e-loyalty are moderated by trust. Results showed that trust is the important factor of e-loyalty than the switching costs. It also revealed that switching costs depends on the trust that customers have.

Mubbsher Munawar Khan, Mariam Fasih (2014) made a study to determine the satisfaction level of banking customers regarding quality of different services provided by their bank and their loyalty with the respective bank. This study was made to find out which service quality dimensions may enhance customer satisfaction and customer loyalty in a better way. Descriptive statistics, one sample t-test, correlation and regression are used to analyze the data. The results indicate that service quality and all its dimensions have significant and positive association with customer satisfaction and customer loyalty. Today's online businesses lack loyal customers. Making customers stick to the company and purchase again and again is a question raising issue. Thus it is very important for a business to manage satisfaction, belief, and customer loyalty in the adoption of E-commerce services for business development.

Gerson Tontini et al. (2015) considered the nonlinear impact of online retail stores quality dimensions on general customer satisfaction and loyalty. Using factorial analysis with verimax rotation, five service-quality dimensions are studied: service accessibility/speed, fault recovery, buying reliability, service and site flexibility and site interaction/ feedback. Penalty and reward difference analysis identifies the Kano model classification of the service-quality dimensions, and the nonlinear impact of these dimensions, and customer satisfaction, on customer loyalty. The findings show that there is a nonlinear impact of these dimensions, and customer satisfaction, on customer loyalty.

Muita Sobihah et al. (2015) has made a study which deals with E-commerce service quality on customer satisfaction, belief and loyalty. The collected data was tested by confirmatory factor analysis. This paper has sought to examine the perception of foreign tourists towards e-commerce service quality in Malaysian hotel websites that influence their satisfaction, belief and loyalty. On basis of discussions throughout this paper, it was found that customer satisfaction and consumer belief will be influenced by E-commerce service quality and also the mediator that will influence customer loyalty in using the website as a substitute for traditional purchases. The researchers conclude as, In order to have a loyal customer, the hotel industry should fulfill the service quality expected by the customer that will satisfied and have belief with the service provider.

Siqi Ma (2016) investigated delivery time interacting with shipping charges on customer satisfaction and purchase intentions and found that increase in delivery time increases customer ambiguity and perceived riskiness which negatively impact purchase intentions. Further Edlira Shehu et al (2016) worked on free shipping promotions and their impact on online retailers, his findings state that free shipping promotions will increase return shares to the sellers. Jorge Matute (2016) explored the characteristics of consumer reviews taking e-word of mouth in to consideration and its impact on repurchase intentions. The results indicate that e-word of mouth quality has a positive effect on repurchase intentions.

Lin and Jing Luo et al (2016) explored the quality factors influencing customer satisfaction in the e-commerce context using a triadic view of customer, e-retailer, third-party logistics provider, and to investigate the impacts of service quality on customer satisfaction and loyalty provider in the e-retailing supply chain. Structural equation modeling is used to analyze collected data and test the hypothesis.

The findings indicate that e-service quality and logistics service quality are strongly linked to customer satisfaction. Also found that e-Service quality positively impacts customer satisfaction with logistics services, but logistics service quality negatively impacts customer satisfaction with e-services. The results show that e-retailers should not only focus on e-service quality, but also logistics service quality, which is critical to the success of e-commerce.

Ibrahim Elbeltagi Gomaa Agag (2016) studied online shoppers in Egypt to develop a new framework that explains impact of e-retailing ethics customer satisfaction and repurchasing intention and mentioned that the factors like Security, Privacy, non-deception, fulfilment/reliability, and service recovery are strongly predict the customer satisfaction and repurchase intention.

Hong-Youl Ha et al. (2016) in their paper using trust as a mediator in online shopping they examined the effects of perceptions of information obtained from social networks. For this, they have conducted an email survey. They adopted a two dimensional view of trust i.e.., cognitive and affective trust. Using longitudinal approach direct and indirect effects of information perceptions on behavioral intentions are empirically explored. Results show that there is a significant carryover effects from time T to time $T+1$ in perceptions of information obtained. The study revealed that over time, the influence of affective trust is greater than that of cognitive trust, both in its effect on behavioral intentions as well as in its mediating role between information perceptions and behavioral intentions.

Thi Song Hanh Pham et al. (2017) studied the determinants of online customer satisfaction taking online shopping experience based on UK consumers. The items include order fulfillment, ease of return and customer service and found these items showed significant influence to online customer satisfaction. The most important interpretation was that website appearance on customer satisfaction found insignificant. Their findings also state that customer satisfaction leads to repurchase behavior and also spreading positive recommendations. Xiabing Zheng et al. (2017) this paper highlighted about that e-loyalty is the driver of online shopping. The theoretical analysis of coupon proneness and value consciousness in e-loyalty are examined. Results said that value consciousness and coupon proneness plays a important role in e-loyalty.

Yeolib Kim & Robert A. Peterson (2017) this study examined the role of online trust in B2B e-commerce. A meta-analysis on antecedents and consequences of online trust was conducted where related relationships were influenced by moderated variables. 16 pairwise relationships derived from 150 empirical studies were analyzed. This analysis revealed that online trust exhibits significant relationships with selected antecedents (perceived security, disposition to trust, perceived reputation, perceived risk etc.,) and consequences (purchase intention, attitude, satisfaction, loyalty etc.,). The Hedges and Olkin (1985) procedure for analyzing correlated coefficients was suggested for analysis of each pairwise relationship.

Oliveira, T et al. (2017) this paper tested the path model that can have solutions to increase trust for internet vendors. The three main dimensions of trust in this path model are competence, integrity, and benevolence. And assessed the influence of overall trust of consumers. The analyzed various sources of trust i.e. consumer & firm characteristics, website design and interactions with consumers. The model is tested through collecting data from email survey. Results suggest that consumers with high overall trust demonstrate a higher intention in online purchasing.

Al-dweeri et al. (2017) e-satisfaction and e-trust as mediators the present study analyzes the relationship between e-SQ and e-loyalty (both behavioral and attitudinal elements) in online shopping. Confirmatory factor analysis and structural equation model were performed to a sample of 302 website users of amazon.com. Results showed that factors such as efficiency, privacy and customer services are considered as important factors of e-SQ. the relationship between e-SQ and behavioral and attitudinal loyalty are mediated by satisfaction.

Xiaolin Lin et al. (2018) this paper investigated on gender differences in the effects of perceived risk, vividness, interactivity and diagnosticity of consumers in making web-based purchase decisions. Attitude formation influences the perceived risk & interactivity more in males, in females it was vividness & diagnosticity. The results highlighted that importance must be given to gender while developing a website.

Dung H. Nguyen (2018) performed a systematic review of consumer behavior and order fulfillment in online retailing. The findings state that future research on developing consumer service strategies responses which found significant impact of order-fulfillment elements on consumer behavior.

Habeeb S & Francis K F (2019) examined the effects of service quality and satisfaction on consumer behavioral intentions. The results posit that e-service quality has a positive effect on e-satisfaction and influences behavioral Intentions like word of mouth, website revisit and repurchase intentions.

Based on internet growth, online shopping is growing fast and could see great number of opportunities for e-vendors to rise and preserve interaction with customers. There is a difference between customers with respect to spending more money or spend less and buy often. Thus customer retention states to be very important concern for firms wishing to obtain a competitive advantage. Prior studies show that increase in customer retention leads to higher profits for the companies. In customer retention process, satisfaction of customer plays a vital role. Lee *et al.*, (2009), stated that a satisfied customer is more likely to return. Further it develops loyalty towards the product or service.

Till today, most of the researchers have focused on how to acquire the customer, especially focusing on the service quality and satisfaction. As the technology advancements in the online shopping and competition among the major players in India, companies such as Amazon, Flipkart, Snapdeal, Myntra, Homeshop18, pepperfry, Infibeam etc trying to satisfy the customer and making them to repurchase the product or service. It is the need of the hour to study how repurchase intention will develop in the Indian consumers and what factors influence it.

In Asia, India shares half billion of internet users. Rababah et al (2011) mentioned that the success of e-commerce is not just because of web site, low price but also because of the delivery and quality of the web site; if these factors are good, customers are willing to pay more for the product or service. This represents that quality plays a crucial role in attracting and retaining customers to the success of the company on online shopping.

Variety of firms and organizations are creating business opportunities on the internet and these corporations are spending more and more money on websites, advertising with a hope of creating customers to buy product and services through online. (Bahram Ranjbarian, Saeed Fathi, 2012) stated in a study that the success or failure for e-commerce businesses is not because of web existence or low price but delivering right quality of e-service. The researchers have conducted an empirical investigation which proposes and tested an e-satisfaction model. The adopted model categorizes five dimensions representing satisfaction with internet purchase experience and analyzes online-customers attitude towards internet shopping based on their perceptions based convenience, the kind of merchandising, website design, security in doing transaction and serviceability in e-satisfaction. Factor analysis was used and the findings shown that four factors such as convenience, merchandising, security and serviceability have influence on customer e-satisfaction but the influence of website design on e-satisfaction was not sustained despite its indirect impact on security and serviceability.

RESEARCH GAP

Considering the development in e-commerce, growth in number of internet users, competition the market, the websites or online sellers are not able to meet the demands and needs of their customers like before, the reason could be continuous rise in customers' expectations and demand for better and cheap products or services. Seyed & Jamalabad (2011), stated in a study that there is a danger of attracting our unsatisfied customers by the competitors and this ends up in losing profits to the company. So, the business specialists should understand that losing customers is very costly to the company and developing customers trust, making repurchase happening is what needed. One of the main goals of a marketer is that look for satisfying the customers, develop trust in them which in return makes the customer to become loyal to the company and repurchase.

As the e-commerce market becomes increasingly dynamic and competitive, the marketers have acknowledge that the best core marketing strategy is to retain existing customers by satisfying them through service in terms of delivery and service quality (Bai et al, 2008; Udo et al, 2010; Kim, 2010; Ankit keshawani et al, 2017). Indian market conditions has become more competitive than before, there is need for a business to deliver consumer value by enchanting customers in long term relationships in order to increase greater chances of re-purchase.

The review of literature on online shopping has revealed that majority of research in this area has conducted outside India. There is dearth of literature available in India which explores the acceptance of online shopping by identifying the motivating factors and various challenges of online shopping. Earlier studies have focused on the influence of e- Word of mouth on consumer behavior along with antecedents and consequences (Hennig T et al, 2014; Khammash & Griffiths, 2011). Few studies have focused considering online shopping habits and experience (Khalifa et al, 2007; Meng-Hsiang Hsu et al, 2015). Most of the studies have explored the effect of isolated dimensions of information (quality & credibility) separately (Park et al, 2007; Cheung et al, 2008). Other studies have focused on the trust and website usefulness as the important determinants in explaining consumer behavior in the context of online shopping (Gefen et al, 2003; Chiu et al. 2012). However, very few studies have explained the influence of diverse online shopping determinants and consumer characteristics on e-trust and repurchase from a holistic perspective. Indian market conditions has become more competitive than before, there is need for a business to deliver consumer value by enchanting customers in long term relationships in order to increase greater chances of re-purchase.

To address the above gap, the present study develops a model to explain how quality attributes influence customer satisfaction and then the impact on customer trust and customer loyalty and their influence on customer repurchase intentions.

Conceptual Framework of the Study

Boston Consulting Group (BCG) and Internet and Mobile Marketing Association of India (IAMAI) stated in a report that Indian internet users could cross 550 million in 2018 making India online population to stand in second position in the world. The report also states that Indian e-commerce is being used by only 11 percent of internet population when compared China internet population uses 50 percent of e-commerce. With the upcoming on 4G network and cheap internet providers Indian online shopping is emerging fastly. There exist a great number of opportunities for the Indian online players to rise. The Indian e-players or e-vendors have to rise up and grab the customer base in India. There are several factors contributing to the growth of e-commerce in India, firms need to understand and build on competencies that will hold the customer. Thus to with stand in a fierce competition the Indian ecommerce players had to think about customer retention.

Among the most important researched concepts in practice and in academia customer loyalty, satisfaction, service quality and repurchase had to be given more important in order to study about a consumer behavior. In order to have an upper hand in competitive markets and to stand tall in grabbing the competitive advantage; customer satisfaction, loyalty, service quality and repurchase intentions shows powerful impact on e-commerce vendors (Tamilla Curtis 2013, Zineldin 2006). Despite of ample research on the relationships between customer satisfaction, service quality, loyalty and repurchase, these relationships look to be complex and are therefore not well understood. Thus this study would be performed to know which among the above relationships would grab and retain the online customers to repurchase again and again.

For setting efficient and effective business objectives and implement them, the e-commerce players should know it's customers needs, characteristics and behaviors. Allessandro Russieri, Cecilia Silvestri, (2014); Srivastava Rai, (2013); Cussignani Mular, (2009); mentioned in their studies that e-commerce players need to adopt new strategies in order to target new customers. E-commerce players should also care about retaining the old customers by making them do repeat purchases.

Yingsheng Du & Youchun Tang (2014), mentioned that in any industry customer satisfaction is to know their needs and fulfilling their needs by offering something extra. Once the customer is satisfied with the products and services provided by the e-commerce sellers, the customers become loyal to the e-commerce company. On the other hand, service quality is known to be the antecedent of customer satisfaction and service quality cannot exist without customer satisfaction. Allessandro Russieri &Cecilia Silvestri (2014), pointed that customer loyalty cannot be taken for granted since customers are attracted to cheap products and discounts from other competitors. If customer satisfaction can be pursued with service quality, there are greater choices of having satisfied customers.

(Caruana, 2000; Hou Xinggi, 2008; Deng Yingsu, 2013; Peng yan, 2006) carried out studies on relationships containing service quality, customer satisfaction, customer loyalty and proved that service quality affects customer loyalty indirectly through customer satisfaction. The model is represented in figure 1. These relationships were examined in various industries like training, catering and hotel industries and online securities trading. So the scope of future research can be done on online shopping or e-commerce industry.

Chang Yaping et al (2009) and Zou Jianping (2010) worked on the concepts including service quality, customer satisfaction, customer trust and customer loyalty in the network and express industries. From

Figure 1. Caruana (2000), Hou Xingqi (2008) Model stating relationship between service quality, customer satisfaction and customer loyalty

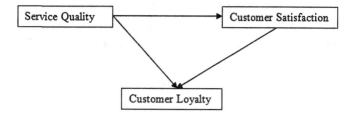

Figure 2. Chang Yaping et al (2009); Zou Jianping (2010) Model stating relationship between service quality, customer satisfaction, customer loyalty and customer trust

Figure 3. Proposed model 1

Figure 4. Proposed model 2

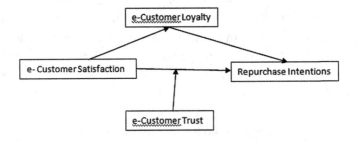

the figure 2 it is seen, researchers stated that service quality affects customer loyalty through intervening variables like customer satisfaction and customer loyalty separately.

In above both models the researchers discussed stipulated variables such as service quality, customer satisfaction, customer loyalty and customer trust. To make the present study more interesting and result oriented, the researcher would like to add another variable i.e. repeat purchase. Because researcher have found the variable repeat purchase is yet to be tapped with respect to online shopping in India.

There are no fixed research models containing above relationships like service quality, customer satisfaction and customer loyalty. Based on existing literatures researchers or scholars should build their own research models for future study. Thus the literature reviewed in this paper gives a scope to add one more variable called repurchase intentions. Thus Zou Jianping (2010) model can be extended with adding repurchase intention or repurchase behavior to the existing model. The proposed models 1, 2, 3 are respectively shown in figure 3, figure 4, and figure 5.

Our study tries to attempt considering previous reported findings to explain the various relationships of above mentioned proposed model. The questions with respect to the model will be asked like;

1. Does e-customer satisfaction antecedents impact directly or indirectly on customer repurchase behavior.

Figure 5. Proposed model 3

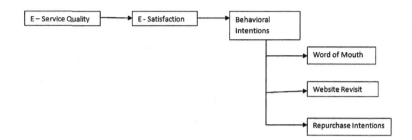

2. Does e-customer satisfaction and e-trust influence positively the e-customer loyalty and leads to customer repurchase behavior.
3. Does e-customer trust moderately influence the relationship between e-customer satisfaction and repurchase intentions?

DISCUSSION

Cameran et al (2010); Deng et al (2010); Ojo et al (2010); Pantouvakis, (2010); in their studies found that customer satisfaction is an effective post purchase evaluation with respect to service management literature. Bayraktar et al (2010), stated that customer may switch to other online sellers if they are not satisfied with the service provided by the seller. Cameran et al (2010); Grigoroudis et al (2007); Sanchez-Hernandez et al (2010); mentioned in their studies that service quality was found to be the main determinant of customer satisfaction and also influences purchase intentions.

Caceres & Paparoidamis (2007), mentioned in his study that customer trust has more influence on customer loyalty. The online customers will continually purchase and even recommend the service if there is a prompt service is provided, this is when the customer trust the sellers (Deng et al., 2010). Grewal (2004), mentioned that positive customer trust gives high-level repurchase intentions to the online seller. Trust is a critical factor influencing repurchase behavior (Gounaris, 2005), because it makes a strong bond between the supplier and the customer.

In order to remain loyal to the sellers the consumers wants satisfaction (young & Peterson, 2004). Since the nature of the business in present days is aggressive and competitive, thus the need exists for a retailer to give some advantage and Importance to their customers to retain them (McElheran, 2013). (Ali & Sankaran, 2010: Mattson, 2009) stated that customer satisfaction is one of the main antecedent to the variables like customer loyalty, customer trust and repurchase behavior. Bagram & Khan (2012), customers becoming loyal to a company is that easy, because they do not get satisfy that easily. Thompsom (2005), in achieving competitive advantage over other online sellers, the customer loyalty plays an important role with respect to making repurchasing decisions. Thus there is a link between customer loyalty and repurchase intentions (Van Vuuren, Roberts-Lombard & Tonder 2012; Singh & Khan, 2012; Vesel & Zabkar, 2009; Ang & Buttle, 2006; Thompson, 2005).

Owusuah, (2012); Rust & Chung, (2006); Thompson, (2005); mentioned in their studies that repurchase behavior or repurchase intention is the main variable considered for sales and business growth. Observing various relationships mentioned in the above literature and this leaves a gap to be filled in future studies measuring customer satisfaction influence on both trust and loyalty as mediator variables and results in causing a repurchase behavior. Thus from the above literature there exists a gap to fill, that there is very little research done on repurchase intentions along with service quality, customer satisfaction, trust and loyalty with respect to online shopping in India.

Thus there is a need to research with the combination of customer satisfaction, service quality, trust, loyalty and repurchase behavior of an online customer in India. From the above literature it is proven that customer satisfaction, service quality, loyalty, trust and repurchase intentions together are not studied. Thus studies in Indian e-commerce can be done in specific to this relationship.

CONCLUSION

Repurchase intention refers to the consumer's willingness to buy for a long time from the same company (Gounaris, Dimitriadis & Stathakopoulos, 2010). It can also refer to the individual's judgment about buying again a designated service from the same company (Lacey & Morgan, 2009).). Consumer buying behavior can be understood in two stages, thus encouraging people to purchase and enhancing them to repurchase (Zhang et al 2011). Customer repurchase expectation is of principal significance to business specialists since it means that business progression, future revenue prospects and henceforth business productivity (Chang, 2012). The intention to re-purchase is a post purchase behavioral intention that influences customer loyalty, complaint and switch intentions (Meng et al, 2011). The goal of shoppers to repurchase is subject to customer's assessment of the past purchase transactions (Maziriri et al, 2015).

Thus, both business experts and academicians alike have been keen on recognizing the precursors of customer repurchase goal. Strikingly to note, customer satisfaction, customer trust and customer loyalty are reliably among a portion of those elements that have progressively being perceived in the surviving writing as indicators of customer goal to repurchase (Flavian et al, 2006; Kandampully & Juwaheer, 2009; Sirdeshmurk et al, 2012; Chinomona, R., & Sandada, M. 2013). Many other researchers also mentioned that it very necessary to provide products and services which satisfy customer since satisfied customers develop trust in the company and become loyal and ends up in repurchase (Boshoff & du Plessis, 2009; Hong & Cho, 2011; Dabholkar & Sheng, 2012; Kun D, 2013, Zeki et al, 2015).

FUTURE RESEARCH

The future of E-Commerce is not that easy to predict. There are various factors responsible for the growth of e-commerce. E-commerce industry is also faced with serious challenges; these challenges have to be overcome for an online player to succeed in this tense competition.

Future research could collect a broader, more controlled sample and use a greater variety of products. Prospective research could also investigate elements influencing consumers' subsequent purchase behaviors, such as product quality, delivery methods, and after-sales service. In future research, Researcher may study other possible factors affecting online initial trust, such as marketing tactics, product varieties, price ranges, online service, web site quality and levels of convenience.

Today's consumers continue to desire more and for a business to withstand in such a fierce competition, the businesses should target the consumers with providing services in a better manner, faster and cheaper. Businesses should target new consumer needs and trends since internet is available cheaply, internet audience have various choices to prefer. Considering the advancement in technology, the e-commerce players' need's to grab the advantage. E-commerce has to look forward to consumers repurchase and also look forward to grab loyal customer. So an e-commerce player should target in retaining the old customer and use its positive features in attracting new customers. However, e-commerce has its disadvantages including consumer uncertainties, thus these uncertainties have to be resolved with better business practices. This literature will guide the e-commerce players or sellers to prosper with much success and profitability.

DISCUSSION QUESTIONS

1. What are the steps to be taken to grab the customer's attention in the present competitive Indian online market?
2. Compare and contrast online shopping with that of offline shopping.
3. What are the main factors that affect the online consumer when considering a repurchase over the internet?
4. Explain the connection between customer satisfaction and repurchase intentions. Do customers repurchase if satisfied. Why and Why not?
5. Do you agree that studying antecedents of repurchase intentions give some scope for solutions to the organizations over the competition in present fierce online Indian market? Give your suggestions.

REFERENCES

Al-dweeri, R. M., Obeidat, Z. M., Al-dwiry, M. A., Alshurideh, M. T., & Alhorani, A. M. (2017). The impact of e-service quality and e-loyalty on online shopping: Moderating effect of e-satisfaction and e-trust. *International Journal of Marketing Studies*, *9*(2), 92–103. doi:10.5539/ijms.v9n2p92

Ariff, M. S. M., Yun, L. O., Zakuan, N., & Ismail, K. (2013). The impacts of service quality and customer satisfaction on customer loyalty in internet banking. *Procedia: Social and Behavioral Sciences*, *81*, 469–473. doi:10.1016/j.sbspro.2013.06.462

Brady, M. K., & Cronin, J. J. Jr. (2001). Some new thoughts on conceptualizing perceived service quality: A hierarchical approach. *Journal of Marketing*, *65*(3), 34–49. doi:10.1509/jmkg.65.3.34.18334

Bulut, Z. A. (2015). Determinants of repurchase intention in online shopping: A Turkish consumer's perspective. *International Journal of Business and Social Science*, *6*(10), 55–63.

Carter, M., Wright, R., Thatcher, J. B., & Klein, R. (2014). Understanding online customers' ties to merchants: The moderating influence of trust on the relationship between switching costs and e-loyalty. *European Journal of Information Systems*, *23*(2), 185–204. doi:10.1057/ejis.2012.55

Chandar & Sarangal. (2016). A study of significance of E-servqual in determining service quality of online websites. *International Journal of Business Management and Scientific Research, 15*.

Doherty, N. F., & Ellis-Chadwick, F. (2010). Internet retailing: The past, the present and the future. *International Journal of Retail & Distribution Management*, *38*(11/12), 943–965. doi:10.1108/09590551011086000

Dwivedi, A. (2012). A higher-order model of consumer brand engagement and its impact on loyalty intentions. *Journal of Retailing and Consumer Services, 24*, 100–109. doi:10.1016/j.jretconser.2015.02.007

Eid, M. I. (2011). Determinants of e-commerce customer satisfaction, trust, and loyalty in Saudi Arabia. *Journal of Electronic Commerce Research, 12*(1), 78.

Elbeltagi, I., & Agag, G. (2016). E-retailing ethics and its impact on customer satisfaction and repurchase intention: A cultural and commitment-trust theory perspective. *Internet Research, 26*(1), 288–310. doi:10.1108/IntR-10-2014-0244

Fang, Y., Qureshi, I., Sun, H., McCole, P., Ramsey, E., & Lim, K. H. (2014). Trust, satisfaction, and online repurchase intention: The moderating role of perceived effectiveness of e-commerce institutional mechanisms. *Management Information Systems Quarterly, 38*(2), 407–427. doi:10.25300/MISQ/2014/38.2.04

Ganguly, B., Dash, S. B., Cyr, D., & Head, M. (2010). The effects of website design on purchase intention in online shopping: The mediating role of trust and the moderating role of culture. *International Journal of Electronic Business, 8*(4-5), 302–330. doi:10.1504/IJEB.2010.035289

Giovanis, A. N., & Athanasopoulou, P. (2014). Gaining customer loyalty in the e-tailing marketplace: the role of e-service quality, e-satisfaction and e-trust. *International Journal of Technology Marketing, 9*(3), 288-304.

Gong, W., Stump, R. L., & Maddox, L. M. (2013). Factors influencing consumers' online shopping in China. *Journal of Asia Business Studies, 7*(3), 214–230. doi:10.1108/JABS-02-2013-0006

Grewal, D., Levy, M., & Kumar, V. (2009). Customer experience management in retailing: An organizing framework. *Journal of Retailing, 85*(1), 1–14. doi:10.1016/j.jretai.2009.01.001

Ha, H. Y., Janda, S., & Muthaly, S. K. (2010). A new understanding of satisfaction model in e-re-purchase situation. *European Journal of Marketing, 44*(7/8), 997–1016. doi:10.1108/03090561011047490

Ha, H. Y., Muthaly, S. K., & Akamavi, R. K. (2010). Alternative explanations of online repurchasing behavioral intentions: A comparison study of Korean and UK young customers. *European Journal of Marketing, 44*(6), 874–904. doi:10.1108/03090561011032757

Ha, H. Y., Muthaly, S. K., & Akamavi, R. K. (2010). Alternative explanations of online repurchasing behavioral intentions: A comparison study of Korean and UK young customers. *European Journal of Marketing, 44*(6), 874–904. doi:10.1108/03090561011032757

Ha, S., & Stoel, L. (2012). Online apparel retailing: Roles of e-shopping quality and experiential e-shopping motives. *Journal of Service Management, 23*(2), 197–215. doi:10.1108/09564231211226114

Habeeb, S., & Sudhakar, K. F. (2019). Analyzing Causality Among the Service Quality, Customer Satisfaction and Behavioral Intention Variables with Respect to E-Shopping: An Empirical Take. *International Journal of Online Marketing, 9*(1), 38–59. doi:10.4018/IJOM.2019010103

Hsu, C. L., Wu, C. C., & Chen, M. C. (2013). An empirical analysis of the antecedents of e-satisfaction and e-loyalty: Focusing on the role of flow and its antecedents. *Information Systems and e-Business Management, 11*(2), 287–311. doi:10.100710257-012-0194-8

Khan, M. M., & Fasih, M. (2014). Impact of service quality on customer satisfaction and customer loyalty: Evidence from banking sector. *Pakistan Journal of Commerce and Social Sciences*, 8(2), 331–354.

Kim, H. W., Xu, Y., & Gupta, S. (2012). Which is more important in Internet shopping, perceived price or trust? *Electronic Commerce Research and Applications*, 11(3), 241–252. doi:10.1016/j.elerap.2011.06.003

Kim, Y., & Peterson, R. A. (2017). A Meta-analysis of Online Trust Relationships in E-commerce. *Journal of Interactive Marketing*, 38, 44–54. doi:10.1016/j.intmar.2017.01.001

Lin, C., & Lekhawipat, W. (2014). Factors affecting online repurchase intention. *Industrial Management & Data Systems*, 114(4), 597–611. doi:10.1108/IMDS-10-2013-0432

Lin, X., Featherman, M., Brooks, S. L., & Hajli, N. (2018). Exploring gender differences in online consumer purchase decision making: An online product presentation perspective. *Information Systems Frontiers*, 1–15.

Lin, Y., Luo, J., Cai, S., Ma, S., & Rong, K. (2016). Exploring the service quality in the e-commerce context: A triadic view. *Industrial Management & Data Systems*, 116(3), 388–415. doi:10.1108/IMDS-04-2015-0116

Matute, J., Polo-Redondo, Y., & Utrillas, A. (2016). The influence of EWOM characteristics on online repurchase intention: Mediating roles of trust and perceived usefulness. *Online Information Review*, 40(7), 1090–1110. doi:10.1108/OIR-11-2015-0373

Mummalaneni, V., & Meng, J. (2009). An exploratory study of young Chinese customers' online shopping behaviors and service quality perceptions. *Young Consumers*, 10(2), 157–169. doi:10.1108/17473610910964732

Nguyen, D. H., de Leeuw, S., & Dullaert, W. E. (2018). Consumer behaviour and order fulfilment in online retailing: A systematic review. *International Journal of Management Reviews*, 20(2), 255–276. doi:10.1111/ijmr.12129

Oliveira, T., Alhinho, M., Rita, P., & Dhillon, G. (2017). Modelling and testing consumer trust dimensions in e-commerce. *Computers in Human Behavior*, 71, 153–164. doi:10.1016/j.chb.2017.01.050

Pham, T. S. H., & Ahammad, M. F. (2017). Antecedents and consequences of online customer satisfaction: A holistic process perspective. *Technological Forecasting and Social Change*, 124, 332–342. doi:10.1016/j.techfore.2017.04.003

Rahim Mosahab, P. C. (2010). *Service Quality, Customer Satisfaction and Loyalty: A Test of Mediation*. Academic Press.

Ranjbarian, B., Fathi, S., & Jooneghani, R. B. N. (2012). The Effect of Brand Extension Strategies upon Brand Image in the Sport Apparel Market. *International Journal of Academic Research in Business and Social Sciences*, 2(10), 48.

Richard, M. O., Chebat, J. C., Yang, Z., & Putrevu, S. (2010). A proposed model of online consumer behavior: Assessing the role of gender. *Journal of Business Research*, 63(9-10), 926–934. doi:10.1016/j.jbusres.2009.02.027

Segoro, W. (2013). The influence of perceived service quality, mooring factor, and relationship quality on customer satisfaction and loyalty. *Procedia: Social and Behavioral Sciences*, *81*, 306–310. doi:10.1016/j.sbspro.2013.06.433

Shehu, E., Papies, D., & Neslin, S. (2016). *Free Shipping and Product Returns*. Tuck School of Business Working Paper, (2864019).

Sinha, J., & Kim, J. (2012). Factors affecting Indian consumers' online buying behavior. *Innovative Marketing*, *8*(2), 46–57.

Sobihah, M., Mohamad, M., Ali, N. A. M., & Ismail, W. Z. W. (2015). E-commerce service quality on customer satisfaction, belief and loyalty: A proposal. *Mediterranean Journal of Social Sciences*, *6*(2), 260.

Srivastava, M., & Rai, A. K. (2013). Investigating the Mediating Effect of Customer Satisfaction in the Service Quality-Customer Loyalty Relationship. *Journal of Consumer Satisfaction, Dissatisfaction & Complaining Behavior*, 26.

Su, D., & Huang, X. (2011). Research on online shopping intention of undergraduate consumer in China-based on the theory of planned behavior. *International Business Research*, *4*(1), 86.

Subramanian, N., Gunasekaran, A., Yu, J., Cheng, J., & Ning, K. (2014). Customer satisfaction and competitiveness in the Chinese E-retailing: Structural equation modeling (SEM) approach to identify the role of quality factors. *Expert Systems with Applications*, *41*(1), 69–80. doi:10.1016/j.eswa.2013.07.012

Sullivan, Y. W., & Kim, D. J. (2018). Assessing the effects of consumers' product evaluations and trust on repurchase intention in e-commerce environments. *International Journal of Information Management*, *39*, 199–219. doi:10.1016/j.ijinfomgt.2017.12.008

Tontini, G., da Silva, J. C., Beduschi, E. F. S., Zanin, E. R. M., & Marcon, M. D. F. (2015). Nonlinear impact of online retail characteristics on customer satisfaction and loyalty. *International Journal of Quality and Service Sciences*, *7*(2/3), 152–169. doi:10.1108/IJQSS-02-2015-0021

Uzun, H., & Poturak, M. (2014). Factors Affecting Online Shopping Behavior of Consumers. *European Journal of Social and Human Sciences*, (3), 163-170.

Vinerean, S., Cetina, I., Dumitrescu, L., & Opreana, A. (2013). Modeling Trust To Study Consumers Acceptance Of Online Shopping. *Revista Economica*, *65*(2), 72–90.

Zhang, Y., Fang, Y., Wei, K. K., Ramsey, E., McCole, P., & Chen, H. (2011). Repurchase Intention in B2C e-commerce - A relationship quality Perspective. *Information & Management*, *48*(6), 192–200. doi:10.1016/j.im.2011.05.003

Zheng, X., Lee, M., & Cheung, C. M. (2017). Examining e-loyalty towards online shopping platforms: The role of coupon proneness and value consciousness. *Internet Research*, *27*(3), 709–726. doi:10.1108/IntR-01-2016-0002

Compilation of References

Aaltonen, L., Ala-Kotila, P., Laarni, J., Määttä, H., Nykänen, E., Schembri, I., . . . Nagy, G. (2012). State-of-the-art report on knowledge work-new ways of working. VTT Technical Research Centre of Finland.

Abar, B., Carter, K. L., & Winsler, A. (2009). The effects of maternal parenting style and religious commitment on self-regulation, academic achievement, and risk behavior among African-American parochial college students. *Journal of Adolescence*, *32*(2), 259–273. doi:10.1016/j.adolescence.2008.03.008 PMID:18692235

Abbas, J., Aman, J., Nurunnabi, M., & Bano, S. (2019). The Impact of Social Media on Learning Behavior for Sustainable Education: *Evidence of Students from Selected Universities in Pakistan. Sustainability*, *11*(6), 1683. doi:10.3390u11061683

Abele, A. E. (2000). A Dual Impact Model of Gender and Career related Processes. In T. Eckes & H.-M. Trautner (Eds.), *The developmental social psychology of gender* (pp. 361–388). Mahwah, NJ: Erlbaum.

Abeniacar, P. (2008, October 1). Sobre el Reglamento de Procedimientos Amistosos y la Nueva Cláusula de Arbitraje Internacional en los Convenios para Evitar la Doble Imposición. *Actualidad Jurídica*.

Abereijo, I. O., & Fayomi, A. O. (2005). Innovative approach to SME financing in Nigeria: A review of small and medium industries equity investment scheme (SMIEIS). *Journal of Social Sciences*, *11*(3), 219–227. doi:10.1080/097189 23.2005.11893635

Abolfazli, S., Sanaei, Z., Sanaei, M. H., Shojafar, M., & Gani, A. (2016). Mobile Cloud Computing. In S. Murugesan & I. Bojanova (Eds.), *Encyclopedia of Cloud Computing* (pp. 29–40). Chichester, UK: John Wiley & Sons, Ltd. doi:10.1002/9781118821930.ch3

Abril, P. A., Levin, A., & Del Riego, A. (2012, Spring). Blurred Boundaries: Social Media Privacy and the Twenty-First-Century Employee. *American Business Law Journal*, *49*(1), 63–124. doi:10.1111/j.1744-1714.2011.01127.x

Accenture Labs. (2016). The ethics of data sharing: A guide to best practices and governance. *Accenture Technology*. Retrieved March 7, 2019, from https://www.accenture.com/t20161110T001618Z__w__/ca-en/_acnmedia/PDF-35/Accenture-The-Ethics-of-Data-Sharing.pdf

Accenture. (2011). Driving Successful Change at Nokia Siemens Networks. *Accenture*.

Acs, Z. J., Audretsch, D. B., & Strom, R. J. (Eds.). (2009). *Entrepreneurship, Growth, and Public Policy*. Cambridge University Press. doi:10.1017/CBO9780511805950

Adamides, E. D. (2015). Linking operations strategy to the corporate strategy process: A practice perspective. *Business Process Management Journal*, *21*(2), 267–287. doi:10.1108/BPMJ-07-2013-0107

Adobe. (2016). *Driving Competitive Advantage with enterprise mobile app*. Retrieved March 2, 2019, from https://offers.adobe.com/content/dam/offer-manager/en/na/marketing/Experience%20Manager%20PDF's/2016/Adobe-Report_Driving_competitive_advantage_enterprise_apps.pdf

Agostinho, C., Ducq, Y., Zacharewicz, G., Sarraipa, J., Lampathaki, F., Poler, R., & Jardim-Goncalves, R. (2016). Towards a sustainable interoperability in networked enterprise information systems: Trends of knowledge and model-driven technology. *Computers in Industry*, *79*, 64–76. doi:10.1016/j.compind.2015.07.001

Agrawal, A., Catalini, C., & Goldfarb, A. (2014). Some simple economics of crowdfunding. *Innovation Policy and the Economy*, *14*(1), 63–97. doi:10.1086/674021

Aguirre Ramírez, J. (2010). *Metodología para medir y evaluar las capacidades tecnológicas de innovación aplicando sistemas de lógica difusa caso fábricas de software* (Doctoral dissertation). Universidad Nacional de Colombia.

Ahmer, Z. (2013). Adoption of Human Resource Information Systems Innovation in Pakistani Organizations. *Journal of Quality and Technology Management*, *9*(2), 25–50.

Ahuja, M. K., & Thatcher, J. B. (2005). Moving Beyond Intentions and Toward the Theory of Trying: Effects of Work Environment and Gender on Post-Adoption Information Technology Use. *Management Information Systems Quarterly*, *29*(3), 427–459. doi:10.2307/25148691

Ainslie, G. (1992). *Picoeconomics: The interaction of successive motivational states within the person*. Cambridge, UK: Cambridge University Press.

Ainslie, G., & Haslam, N. (1992). Hyperbolic discounting. In G. Loewenstein & I. Elster (Eds.), *Choice over time*. New York: Russel Sage.

Ajjan, H., Kumar, R. L., & Subramaniam, C. (2016). Information technology portfolio management implementation: A case study. *Journal of Enterprise Information Management*, *29*(6), 841–859. doi:10.1108/JEIM-07-2015-0065

Ajzen, I. (1991). The Theory of Planned Behavior. *Organizational Behavior and Human Decision Processes*, *50*(2), 179–210. doi:10.1016/0749-5978(91)90020-T

Ajzen, I., & Fishbein, M. (1980). *Understanding attitudes and predicting social behaviour*. Prentice-Hall.

Akers, R. L., Massey, J., Clark, W., & Lauer, R. M. (1983). Are self-reports of adolescent deviance valid? Biochemical measures, randomized response, and the bogus pipeline in smoking behavior. *Social Forces*, *62*(1), 234–251. doi:10.1093f/62.1.234

Ala-Mutka, K. (2011). *Mapping Digital Competence: Towards a Conceptual Understanding*. Academic Press.

Alavi, M., & Dorothy, E. L. (2001). Review: Knowledge Management and Knowledge Management Systems: Conceptual Foundations and Research Issues. *Management Information Systems Quarterly*, *25*(1), 107–136. doi:10.2307/3250961

Alberini, A., & Chiabai, A. (2007). Discount rates in risk versus money and money versus money tradeoffs. *Risk Analysis*, *27*(2), 483–498. doi:10.1111/j.1539-6924.2007.00899.x PMID:17511713

Albrechtsen, E. (2007). A qualitative study of users' view on information security. *Computers & Security*, *26*(4), 276–289. doi:10.1016/j.cose.2006.11.004

Alchian, A. A. (1953). The meaning of utility measurement. *The American Economic Review*, *32*, 26–50.

Al-dweeri, R. M., Obeidat, Z. M., Al-dwiry, M. A., Alshurideh, M. T., & Alhorani, A. M. (2017). The impact of e-service quality and e-loyalty on online shopping: Moderating effect of e-satisfaction and e-trust. *International Journal of Marketing Studies*, *9*(2), 92–103. doi:10.5539/ijms.v9n2p92

Alenezi, M., & Magel, K. (2014). Empirical evaluation of a new coupling metric: Combining structural and semantic coupling. *International Journal of Computers and Applications*, *36*(1). doi:10.2316/Journal.202.2014.1.202-3902

Alexander, A. T., Neyer, A.-K., & Huizingh, K. R. E. (2016). Introduction to the special issue: Transferring knowledge for innovation. *R & D Management*, *46*(2), 305–311. doi:10.1111/radm.12195

Al-Fuqaha, A., Guizani, M., Mohammadi, M., Aledhari, M., & Ayyash, M. (2015). Internet of things: A survey on enabling technologies, protocols, and applications. *IEEE Communications Surveys and Tutorials*, *17*(4), 2347–2376. doi:10.1109/COMST.2015.2444095

Alharthey, B. K., & Rasli, A. (2012). The Use of Human Resource Management Systems in the Saudi Market. *Asian Journal of Business Ethics*, *1*(2), 163–176. doi:10.100713520-012-0015-7

Alhogail, A. (2015). Design and validation of information security culture framework. *Computers in Human Behavior*, *49*, 567–575. doi:10.1016/j.chb.2015.03.054

Ali, N. S., & Benabou, R. (2017). *Image versus information: Changing societal norms and optimal privacy*. Cambridge, MA: National Bureau of Economic Research working paper 22203. Retrieved from https://scholar.princeton.edu/sites/default/files/rbenabou/files/imagevsinfo-21_002.pdf

Alkahtani, H., Lock, R., & Dawson, R. (2013). The impact of culture on Saudi Arabian information systems security. *21st International Conference on Software Quality Management (SQM)*, 201–210.

AlKalbani, A., Deng, H., & Kam, B. (2015). Organisational Security Culture and Information Security Compliance for E-Government Development: The Moderating Effect of Social Pressure. *Pacific Asia Conference on Information Systems (PACIS)*, 1–12.

Allison, Th. H., Davis, B. C., Short, J. C., & Webb, J. W. (2015). Internal Social Capital and the Attraction of Early Contributions in Crowdfunding. *Entrepreneurship Theory and Practice*, *39*, 53–73. doi:10.1111/etap.12108

Allport, G. W. (1979). *The nature of prejudice*. Reading, UK: Addison-Wesley.

Almeida, V., Getschko, D., & Afonso, C. (2015). The Origin and Evolution of Multi Stakeholder Models. *IEEE Internet Computing*, *19*(1), 74–79. doi:10.1109/MIC.2015.15

Al-Mobaideen, H., Allahawiah, S., & Basioni, E. (2013). Factors Influencing the Successful Adoption of Human Resource Information System: The Content of Aquaba Special Economic Zone Authority. *Intelligent Information Management*, *5*(01), 1–9. doi:10.4236/iim.2013.51001

Alohali, M., Clarke, N., Furnell, S., & Albakri, S. (2018). Information security behavior: Recognizing the influencers. *Proceedings of Computing Conference 2017, 2018*, 844–853. 10.1109/SAI.2017.8252194

Alsmadi, D., & Prybutok, V. (2018). Sharing and storage behavior via cloud computing: Security and privacy in research and practice. *Computers in Human Behavior*, *85*, 218–226. doi:10.1016/j.chb.2018.04.003

Altarawneh, I., & Al-Shqairat, Z. (2010). Human Resource Information Systems in Jordanian Universities. *International Journal of Business and Management*, *5*(10), 113–127. doi:10.5539/ijbm.v5n10p113

Altman, I. (1975). *The environment and social behavior: Privacy, personal space, territory, and crowding*. Monterey, CA: Brooks.

Amador, C. (2018). *The future of work: The rise of the digital workplace*. Retrieved March 2, 2019, from https://allwork.space/2019/02/the-future-of-work-the-rise-of-the-digital-workplace

Amo Filvà, D., Casany Guerrero, M. J., & Alier Forment, M. (2014). Google Analytics for Time Behavior Measurement in moodle. *Proceedings of the 9th Iberian Conference on Information Systems and Technologies*, 1-6. DOI: 10.1109/CISTI.2014.6877095

Amsterdamska, O. (1990). 'Surely you are joking, Monsiour Latoru! *Science, Technology & Human Values*, *15*(4), 495–504. doi:10.1177/016224399001500407

Anam, S., Kim, Y., Kang, B., & Liu, Q. (2016). Adapting a knowledge-based schema matching system for ontology mapping. In *Proceedings of the Australasian Computer Science Week Multiconference* (p. 27). New York, NY: ACM Press. 10.1145/2843043.2843048

Andersen, A., Brunoe, T., & Nielsen, K. (2015). Reconfigurable Manufacturing on Multiple Levels: Literature Review and Research Directions. In S. Umeda, M. Nakano, H. Mizuyama, N. Hibino, D. Kiritsis, & G. von Cieminski (Eds.), *Advances in Production Management Systems: Innovative Production Management Towards Sustainable Growth* (pp. 266–273). Cham, Switzerland: Springer International Publishing.

Anderson, R., & Moore, T. (2006). The Economics of Information Security. *Science, 13*(314), 610.

Andersson, P., & Mattsson, L. G. (2015). Service innovations enabled by the 'internet of things'. *IMP Journal*, *9*(1), 85–106. doi:10.1108/IMP-01-2015-0002

Andrews, D., Nonnecke, B., & Preece, J. (2003). Electronic survey methodology: A case study in reaching hard-to-involve Internet users. *International Journal of Human-Computer Interaction*, *16*(2), 185–210. doi:10.1207/S15327590IJHC1602_04

Anitha, J., & Aruna, M. (2013). Adoption of Human Resource Information System in Organizations. *SDMIDD Journal of Management*, *4*(2), 5–16.

Ankrah, E., & Sokro, E. (2016). Intention and Usage of Human Resource Information Systems among Ghanaians Human Resource Managers. *International Journal of Business and Management*, *11*(2), 241–248. doi:10.5539/ijbm.v11n2p241

Antonov, A. V. (2004). *System analysis: a textbook for universities*. Moscow: Higher School.

Antonucci, Y. L., & Goeke, R. J. (2011). Identification of appropriate responsibilities and positions for business process management success: Seeking a valid and reliable framework. *Business Process Management Journal*, *17*(1), 127–146. doi:10.1108/14637151111105616

Anwar, A. (2014). A Review of RUP (Rational Unified Process). *International Journal of Software Engineering*, *5*(2), 8–24.

Aral, S., Brynjolfsson, E., & Wu, L. (2012). Three-Way Complementarities: Performance Pay, Human Resource Analytics, and Information Technology. *Management Science*, *58*(5), 913–931.

Aravindh & Baratwaj. (2016). Examining the Regularity and consistency level of profile updation in social media applications by active users in Tamil Nadu. *International Journal for Innovative Research in Multidisciplinary Field*, *2*(11).

Arbatti, E., & Escolano, J. (2015). Fiscal Transparency, Fiscal Performance and Credit Ratings. *Fiscal Studies*, *36*(2), 237–270. doi:10.1111/1475-5890.12051

Arentz, T. A. (2013). An Agent-Based Random-Utility-Maximization Model to Generate Social Networks with Transitivity in Geographic Space. *Social Networking*, *35*(3), 451–459. doi:10.1016/j.socnet.2013.05.002

Argote, M. (2016a). *Identification of the technological capabilities of the "Fundación Universitaria de Ciencias de la Salud"*. Paper presented at the Congress of Science and Technology 2016, Quito, Ecuador.

Argote, M. (2016b). Identification of the technological capabilities of the "Fundación Universitaria de Ciencias de la Salud". *Yura relaciones internacionales, 9*, 230. Retrieved from http://world_business.espe.edu.ec/revista-yura/

Ariffin, R., & Ghazilla, R. (2015). Drivers analysis and barriers in green manufacturing practices in Malaysian SMEs:A preliminary findings. *Procedia CIRP, 26*, 658–663. doi:10.1016/j.procir.2015.02.085

Ariff, M. S. M., Yun, L. O., Zakuan, N., & Ismail, K. (2013). The impacts of service quality and customer satisfaction on customer loyalty in internet banking. *Procedia: Social and Behavioral Sciences, 81*, 469–473. doi:10.1016/j.sbspro.2013.06.462

Arndt, S. (2010). *Sonderfälle der Kochleaimplantation: Aktuelle Aspekte zur Indikationserweiterung*. Freiburg, UV.

Arora, K. (2013). Importance of HRIS: A Critical Study on Service Sector. *Global Journal of Management and Business Studies, 3*(9), 971–976.

Arrow, K. J. (1951). Alternative approaches to the theory of choice in risk-taking situations *Econometrica, 19*(4), 404–437. doi:10.2307/1907465

Arrow, K. J. (1958). Utilities, attitudes, and choices: A review note. *Econometrica, 26*(1), 1–23. doi:10.2307/1907381

Arrow, K. J. (1974). *The limits of organization*. New York: Norton.

Arrow, K. J. (1978). Extended sympathy and the possibility of social choice. *Philosophia, 7*(2), 223–237. doi:10.1007/BF02378811

Ashford, W. (2016). 10 facts businesses need to note about the GDPR. *Computer Weekly*. Retrieved January 7, 2019, from https://www.computerweekly.com/news/450296306/10-key-facts-businesses-need-to-note-about-the-GDPR

Ash, R. A., Rosenbloom, J. L., Coder, L., & Dupont, B. (2006). Personality characteristics of established IT professionals I: Big Five personality characteristics. In E. M. Trauth (Ed.), *Encyclopedia of gender and information technology* (pp. 983–989). Hershey, PA: Idea Publishing. doi:10.4018/978-1-59140-815-4.ch155

Ashurst, C., Cragg, P., & Herring, P. (2012). The role of IT competences in gaining value from e-business: An SME case study. *International Small Business Journal, 30*(6), 640–658. doi:10.1177/0266242610375703

Atzori, L., Iera, A., & Morabito, G. (2010). The internet of things: A survey. *Computer Networks, 54*(15), 2787–2805. doi:10.1016/j.comnet.2010.05.010

Audretsch David, B., Kuratko, D., & Link, A. (2016). *Dynamic Entrepreneurship and Technology-Based Innovation*. Department of Economics Working Paper Series, April 2016, Working Paper 16-02. Retrieved from http://bae.uncg.edu/econ/

Aumann, R. J., & Kruskal, J. B. (1958). The coefficients in an allocation problem. *Naval Research Logistics Quarterly, 5*(2), 111–123. doi:10.1002/nav.3800050204

Aumann, R. J., & Kruskal, J. B. (1959). Assigning quantitative values to qualitative factors in the naval electronics problem. *Naval Research Logistics Quarterly, 6*(1), 1–16. doi:10.1002/nav.3800060102

Avanade, Inc. (2017). *Global survey: companies are unprepared for the arrival of a true digital workplace*. Retrieved March 2, 2019, from https://www.avanade.com/~/media/asset/research/digital-workplace-global-study.pdf

Avgerou, C. (2013). Explaining Trust in IT-mediated Elections: A Case Study of e-Voting in Brazil. *Journal of the Association for Information Systems, 14*(8), 420–451. doi:10.17705/1jais.00340

Ayabakan, S., Bardhan, I. R., & Zheng, Z. E. (2017). A data envelopment analysis approach to estimate it-enabled production capability. *Management Information Systems Quarterly, 41*(1), 189–205. doi:10.25300/MISQ/2017/41.1.09

Azucar, D., Marengo, D., & Settanni, M. (2018). Predicting the Big 5 personality traits from digital footprints on social media: A meta-analysis. *Personality and Individual Differences, 124*, 150–159. doi:10.1016/j.paid.2017.12.018

Babu, D., & Darsi, M. (2013). A Survey on Service Oriented Architecture and Metrics to Measure Coupling. *International Journal on Computer Science and Engineering, 5*(8), 726–733.

Badger, G. J., Bickel, W. K., Giordano, L. A., Jacobs, E. A., Loewenstein, G., & Marsch, L. (2007). Altered states: The impact of immediate craving on the valuation of current and future opioids. *Journal of Health Economics, 26*(5), 865–876. doi:10.1016/j.jhealeco.2007.01.002 PMID:17287036

Badurdeen, F., & Jawahir, I. S. (2017). Strategies for Value Creation through Sustainable Manufacturing. *Procedia Manufacturing, 8*, 20–27. doi:10.1016/j.promfg.2017.02.002

Baer, J. (2018). 6 Unexpected Trends in 2018 Social Media Research. *Convince & Convert*. Retrieved June 9, 2018, from http://www.convinceandconvert.com/social-media-measurement/6-unexpected-trends-in-2018-social-media-research/

Baez, M. (2012). *Knowledge dissemination in the web era* (PhD Dissertation). University of Trento.

Bag, S., Kumar, K. S., & Tiwari, M. K. (2019). An efficient recommendation generation using relevant Jaccard similarity. *Information Sciences, 483*, 53–64. doi:10.1016/j.ins.2019.01.023

Bahrin, M.A.K., Othman, M.F., Azli, N.N., & Talib, M.F. (2016). Industry 4.0: A review on industrial automation and robotic. *JurnalTeknologi, 78*(6-13), 137-143.

Bailey, D. (2017). *30 Online small businesst to use in 2017*. Retrieved March 2, 2019, from https://blumint.co/30-online-small-business-tools-use-2017

Bailey, J. (2008). First Steps in qualitative data analysis: transcribing. *Family Practice Advance Access,* 127-131.

Baiocchi, G., Graizbord, D., & Rodriguez-Muniz, M. (2013). Actor-network theory and the ethnographic imagination: An exercise in translation. *Qualitative Sociology, 36*(4), 323–341. doi:10.100711133-013-9261-9

Bamberg, E., & Vincent-Höper, S. (2017). Occupation and gender. In *Reference Module Neuroscience and Biobehavioral Psychology*. Elsevier; doi:10.1016/B978-0-12-809324-5.05642-X

Bamel, N., Bamel, U. K., Sahay, V., & Thite, M. (2010). Usage, Benefits, and Barriers of Human Resource Information System in Universities. *Vine, 44*(4).

Bandura, A. (1977). Self-Efficacy: Towards a unifying theory of behavioral change. *Psychological Review, 84*(2), 191–215. doi:10.1037/0033-295X.84.2.191 PMID:847061

Bandura, A. (1986). *Social Foundations of Thought and Action: A Social Cognitive Theory*. Englewood Cliffs, NJ: Prentice-Hall.

Baporikar, N., & Deshpande, M. (2012). Sustainable Entrepreneurship - Approach of Pune Auto Components Entrepreneurs. In A. Marcus & J. Rayappa (Eds.), Entrepreneurship, Youth and Inclusive Development for Brand India (pp. 313-320). Loyala Publications.

Baporikar, N. (2011). Knowledge Management and Entrepreneurship Cases in India. In M. Al-Shammari (Ed.), *Knowledge Management in Emerging Economies: Social, Organizational and Cultural Implementation* (pp. 325–346). Hershey, PA: IGI Global. doi:10.4018/978-1-61692-886-5.ch020

Baporikar, N. (2013). Entrepreneurship in a Modern Networked Indian Economy. *International Journal of Asian Business and Information Management*, 4(4), 48–66. doi:10.4018/ijabim.2013100104

Baporikar, N. (2014a). Organizational Barriers and Facilitators in Embedding Knowledge Strategy. In M. Chilton & J. Bloodgood (Eds.), *Knowledge Management and Competitive Advantage: Issues and Potential Solutions* (pp. 149–173). Hershey, PA: Information Science Reference. doi:10.4018/978-1-4666-4679-7.ch009

Baporikar, N. (2014b). Strategic Management Overview and SME in Globalized World. In K. Todorov & D. Smallbone (Eds.), *Handbook of Research on Strategic Management in Small and Medium Enterprises* (pp. 22–39). Hershey, PA: Business Science Reference. doi:10.4018/978-1-4666-5962-9.ch002

Baporikar, N. (2015). Knowledge Management in Small and Medium Enterprises. In J. Zhao, P. Ordóñez de Pablos, & R. Tennyson (Eds.), *Organizational Innovation and IT Governance in Emerging Economies* (pp. 1–20). Hershey, PA: Business Science Reference. doi:10.4018/978-1-4666-7332-8.ch001

Baporikar, N. (2016). Understanding Knowledge Management Spectrum for SMEs in Global Scenario. *International Journal of Social and Organizational Dynamics in IT*, 5(1), 1–15. doi:10.4018/IJSODIT.2016010101

Barba, I., Cassidy, R., De Leon, E., & Williams, B. (2013). Web Analytics Reveal User Behavior: TTU Libraries' Experience with Google Analytics. *Journal of Web Librarianship*, 7(4), 389–400. doi:10.1080/19322909.2013.828991

Barbosa-Póvoa, A. P. (2014). Process supply chains management–where are we? Where to go next? *Frontiers in Energy Research*, 2, 23.

Barney, J. (1991). Firm resources and sustained competitive advantage. *Journal of Management*, 17(1), 99–120. doi:10.1177/014920639101700108

BarNir, A., Watson, W. E., & Hutchins, H. M. (2011). Mediation and Moderated Mediation in the Relationship Among Role Models, Self-Efficacy, Entrepreneurial Career Intention, and Gender. *Journal of Applied Social Psychology*, 41(2), 270–297. doi:10.1111/j.1559-1816.2010.00713.x

Barsky, A. (2011). Investigating the Effects of Moral Disengagement and Participation on Unethical Work Behavior. *Journal of Business Ethics*, 104(1), 59–75. doi:10.100710551-011-0889-7

Bashein, B. J., & Markus, M. L. (1997). A Credibility Equation for IT Specialists. *Sloan Management Review*, 35–44.

Bashorun, A., Worwui, A., & Parker, D. (2013). Information security: To determine its level of awareness in an organization. *AICT 2013 - 7th International Conference on Application of Information and Communication Technologies, Conference Proceedings*. 10.1109/ICAICT.2013.6722704

Basow, S. A., & Howe, K. G. (1980). Role-model influence: Effects of sex and sex-role attitude in college students. *Psychology of Women Quarterly*, 4(4), 558–572. doi:10.1111/j.1471-6402.1980.tb00726.x

Bassellier, G., & Benbasat, I. (2004). Business Competence of IT Professionals: Conceptual Development and Influence on IT-Business Partnerships. *Management Information Systems Quarterly*, 28(4), 673–694. doi:10.2307/25148659

Bassellier, G., Blaize Horner, R., & Benbasat, I. (2001). Information technology competence of business managers: A definition and research model. *Journal of Management Information Systems*, 17(4), 159–182. doi:10.1080/07421222.2001.11045660

Bassett, L. (2015). *Introduction to JavaScript Object Notation: A to-the-point Guide to JSON*. Sebastopol, CA: O'Reilly Media, Inc.

Bauer, S., Bernroider, E. W. N., & Chudzikowski, K. (2017). Prevention is better than cure! Designing information security awareness programs to overcome users' non-compliance with information security policies in banks. *Computers & Security, 68*, 145–159. doi:10.1016/j.cose.2017.04.009

Bauer, W., Hämmerle, M., Schlund, S., & Vocke, C. (2015). Transforming to a hyper-connected society and economy–towards an "Industry 4.0". *Procedia Manufacturing, 3*, 417–424. doi:10.1016/j.promfg.2015.07.200

Baumeister, R.F., & Leary, M.R. (1995). The need to belong, desire for interpersonal attachments as a fundamental human motivation. *Psychological Bull., 117*, 497–529.

Bazarova, N. N. (2015). Online disclosure. In C. R. Berger & M. E. Roloff (Eds.), *The International Encyclopedia of Interpersonal Communication*. Hoboken, NJ: Wiley-Blackwell. doi:10.1002/9781118540190.wbeic251

Bazerman, M. H., & Tenbrunsel, A. E. (2011). *Blind spots: Why we fail to do what's right and what to do about it.* Princeton, NJ: Princeton University Press. doi:10.1515/9781400837991

Bazza, M. I., Maiwada, B. Y., & Daneji, B. A. (2014). Islamic Financing: A Panacea To Small and Medium Scale Enterprises Financing Problems In Nigeria. *European Scientific Journal, 10*(10), 432–444.

Bechtel, G. A., Shepherd, M. A., & Rogers, P. W. (1995). Family, culture, and health practices amond migrant farmworkers. *Journal of Community Health Nursing, 12*(1), 15–22. doi:10.120715327655jchn1201_2 PMID:7897467

Becker, G. M., & McClintock, C. G. (1967). Values: Behavioral decision theory. *Annual Review of Psychology, 18*(1), 239–286. doi:10.1146/annurev.ps.18.020167.001323 PMID:5333424

Becker, G. S., & Murphy, K. M. (1988). A theory of rational addiction. *Journal of Political Economy, 96*(4), 675–700. doi:10.1086/261558

Beckers, J. J., & Schmidt, H. G. (2001). The structure of computer anxiety: A six factor model. *Computers in Human Behavior, 17*(1), 35–49. doi:10.1016/S0747-5632(00)00036-4

Bedell, M. (2003). Human Resource Information Systems. Encyclopedia of Information Systems, 2, 537-550.

Bell, C. E., French, N. P., Karimuribo, E., Ogden, N. H., Bryant, M. J., Swai, E. M., & Fitzpatrick, J. L. (2005). The effects of different knowledge-dissemination interventions on the mastitis knowledge of Tanzanian smallholder dairy farmers. *Preventive Veterinary Medicine, 72*(3-4), 237–251. doi:10.1016/j.prevetmed.2005.05.004 PMID:16154215

Belleflamme, P., Lambert, T., & Schwienbacher, A. (2014). Crowdfunding: Tapping the right crowd. *Journal of Business Venturing, 29*(5), 585–609. doi:10.1016/j.jbusvent.2013.07.003

Bell, M., & Pavitt, K. (1992). Accumulating technological capability in developing countries. *The World Bank Economic Review, 6*(suppl 1), 257–281. doi:10.1093/wber/6.suppl_1.257

Bell, M., & Pavitt, K. (1993). Technological accumulation and industrial growth: Contrasts between developed and developing countries. *Industrial and Corporate Change, 2*(2), 157–210. doi:10.1093/icc/2.2.157

Beltrán, A. (2016). Does Corruption Increase or Decrease Employment in Firms? *Applied Economics Letters, 23*(5), 361–364. doi:10.1080/13504851.2015.1076137

Benabou, R., & Laroque, G. (1992). Using privileged information to manipulate markets: Insiders, gurus, and credibility. *The Quarterly Journal of Economics, 107*(3), 921–958. doi:10.2307/2118369

Benitez-Amado, J., Llorens-Montes, F. J., & Perez-Arostegui, M. N. (2010). Information technology enabled intrapreneurship culture and firm performance. *Industrial Management & Data Systems, 110*(4), 550–566. doi:10.1108/02635571011039025

Benitez-Amado, J., & Walczuch, R. M. (2012). Information technology, the organizational capability of proactive corporate environmental strategy and firm performance: A resource-based analysis. *European Journal of Information Systems*, *21*(1), 664–679. doi:10.1057/ejis.2012.14

Benmoussa, R., Abdelkabir, C., Abd, A., & Hassou, M. (2015). Capability/maturity based model for logistics processes assessment. *International Journal of Productivity and Performance Management*, *64*(1), 28–51. doi:10.1108/IJPPM-08-2012-0084

Bentele, K. (2010). Zur Frage des Umgangs mit der Frage nach dem Cochlea-Implantat (CI): Ein Kom-mentar. *Das Zeichen*, *86*, 408–415.

Berente, N., Yoo, Y., & Lyytinen, K. (2007). An Institutional Analysis of Pluralistic Responses to Enterprise System Implementations. *Proceedings of the International Conference on Information Systems*.

Bergeron, F., Croteau, A.-M., Uwizeyemungu, S., & Raymond, L. (2017). A framework for research on information technology governance in SMEs. In S. De Haes, & W. Van Grembergen (Eds.), Strategic IT Governance and alignment in business settings (pp. 53-81). IGI Global. doi:10.4018/978-1-5225-0861-8.ch003

Bergstein. (2006, July 8). Questions linger over secrets on laptops. *Associated Press*.

Berland, P. S. (2016). *Dell & Intel future works global report*. Retrieved March 2, 2019, from http://www.workforce-transformation.com/workforcestudy/assets/report/Dell-future-workfoce-study_GLOBAL.pdf

Bernardi, R. (2006). Associations between Hofstede's cultural constructs and social desirability response bias. *Journal of Business Ethics*, *65*(1), 43–53. doi:10.100710551-005-5353-0

Bernoulli, D. (1954). Specimen theories novae de mensura sortis. *Commentarii Academiae Scientiarum Imperialis Petropolitanae*, *5*, 175–192.

Berry, A. (1998). The Potential Role of the SME Sector in Pakistan in a World of Increasing International Trade. *Pakistan Development Review*, *37*(4), 25–49. doi:10.30541/v37i4Ipp.25-49

Berson. (2003). Grooming cybervictims: The psychosocial effects of online exploitation for youth. *Journal of School Violence*, *2*(1), 5-18.

Beshears, J. L., Choi, J. J., Laibson, D. I., Madrian, B. C., & Sakong, J. (2011). *Self-control and liquidity: How to design a commitment contract*. RAND Working Paper Series, WR- 895-SSA.

Besley. (2008). Cyberbullying: An Emerging Threat to the always on Generation. *Canadian Teacher Magazine*, 18-20.

Besley, T., & Prat, A. (2006). Handcuffs for the grabbing hand? Media capture and government accountability. *The American Economic Review*, *96*(3), 720–736. doi:10.1257/aer.96.3.720

Betts, J. (2010). *Practical methods for optimal control and estimation using nonlinear programming* (2nd ed.). Philadelphia, PA: Society for Industrial and Applied Mathematics. doi:10.1137/1.9780898718577

Betz, N. E., & Fitzgerald, L. F. (1987). *The career psychology of women*. San Diego, CA: Academic Press.

Beyer, S. (2014). Why are women underrepresented in Computer Science? Gender differences in stereotypes, self-efficacy, values, and interests and predictors of future CS course-taking and grades. *Computer Science Education*, *24*(2-3), 153–192. doi:10.1080/08993408.2014.963363

Bhakar, V., Digalwar, A. K., & Sangwan, K. S. (2018). Sustainability assessment framework for manufacturing sector- a conceptual model. *Procedia CIRP*, *69*, 248–253. doi:10.1016/j.procir.2017.11.101

Bhanji, Z., & Oxley, J. E. (2013). Overcoming the dual liability of foreignness and privateness in international corporate citizenship partnerships. *Journal of International Business Studies*, *44*(4), 290–311. doi:10.1057/jibs.2013.8

Bhanot, N., Rao, V. P., & Deshmukh, S. G. (2015). Enablers and Barriers of Sustainable Manufacturing: Results from a Survey of Researchers and Industry Professionals. *Procedia CIRP*, *29*, 562–567. doi:10.1016/j.procir.2015.01.036

Bharadwaj, P. N., & Soni, R. G. (2007). E-Commerce Usage and Perception of E-Commerce Issues among Small Firms: Results and Implications from an Empirical Study. *Journal of Small Business Management*, *45*(4), 501–521. doi:10.1111/j.1540-627X.2007.00225.x

Bhatt, G. D. (2001). Knowledge Management in Organizations: Examining the Interaction Between Technologies, Techniques, and People. *Journal of Knowledge Management*, *5*(1), 68–75. doi:10.1108/13673270110384419

Bidve, V. S., & Sarasu, P. (2016). Tool for measuring coupling in object-oriented java software. *IACSIT International Journal of Engineering and Technology*, *8*(2), 812–820.

Bitsch, V. (2005). Qualitative Research: A Grounded Theory Example and Evaluation Criteria. *Journal of Agribusiness*, *23*(1), 75–91.

Black, S. E., Jameson, J., Komoss, R., Mehan, A., & Numerico, T. (2005). Women in computing: A European and international perspective. *Proceedings of the 3rd European Symposium on Gender & ICT, Weston Conference Centre*, 1-13.

Blanchard, M., Metcalf, A., Degney, J., Hermann, H. & Burns, J.M. (2008). Rethinking the digital divide: findings from a study of marginalised young people's information communication technology (ICT) use. *Youth Studies Australia*.

Blanchard, M., Metcalf, A., & Burns, J. M. (2007). *Bridging the digital divide: creating opportunities for marginalised young people to get connected. Report for the Inspire Foundation & Orygen Youth Health Research Centre*. Melbourne: University of Melbourne.

Blockchain. (2018). *The next innovation to make our cities smarter*. Retrieved from www.pwc.in

Blum, C. (2005). Beam-ACO – Hybridizing Ant Colony Optimization with Beam Search: An Application to Open Shop Scheduling. *Computers & Operations Research*, *32*(6), 1565–1591. doi:10.1016/j.cor.2003.11.018

Boase, J., Horrigan, J. B., Wellman, B., & Raine, L. (2006). *The Strength of Internet Ties: The Internet and email aid users in maintaining their social networks and provide pathways to help when people face big decisions*. Washington, DC: Pew Internet & American Life Project.

Bock, J. A., Frydrych, D., Kinger, T., & Koeck, B. (2014). Exploring Entrepreneurial Legitimacy in Reward-Based Crowdfunding. *Venture Capital*, (16): 247–269.

Boddewyn, J., & Doh, J. (2011). Global strategy and the collaboration of MNEs, NGOs, and governments for the provisioning of collective goods in emerging markets. *Global Strategy Journal*, *1*(3-4), 345–361. doi:10.1002/gsj.26

Boes, A., Baukrowitz, A., Kämpf, T., & Marrs, K. (2011). Globalisation 2.0 - professional qualification and skilled worker development in the IT branch. In R. Reichwald, M. Frenz, S. Hermann, & A. Schipanski (Eds.), *Zukunftsfeld Dienstleistungsarbeit* (pp. 319–346). Wiesbaden: Springer Gabler.

Bohnsack, R., Hanelt, A., Marz, D., & Marante, C. (2018). Same, same, but different!? A systematic review of the literature on digital transformation. Academy of Management Proceedings, 2018(1), 16262.

Boh, W. F. (2007). Mechanisms for sharing knowledge in project-based organizations. *Information and Organization*, *17*(1), 27–58. doi:10.1016/j.infoandorg.2006.10.001

Boh, W. F., Nguyen, T. T., & Xu, Y. (2013). Knowledge transfer across dissimilar cultures. *Journal of Knowledge Management, 17*(1), 29–46. doi:10.1108/13673271311300723

Bondarouk, T., Ruel, H., & Heijden, B. (2009). e-HRM effectiveness in a public-sector organization. A multi-stakeholder perspective. *International Journal of Human Resource Management, 20*(3), 578–593. doi:10.1080/09585190802707359

Bone, J., & Baeck, P. (2016). *Crowdfunding Good Causes - Opportunities and challenges for charities, community groups and social entrepreneurs*. Working Paper of Nesta United Kingdom. Available: https://media.nesta.org.uk/documents/crowdfunding_good_causes-2016.pdf

Bong, M., & Skaalvik, E. M. (2003). Academic self-concept and self-efficacy: How different are they really? *Educational Psychology Review, 15*(1), 1–40. doi:10.1023/A:1021302408382

Booth-Kewley, S., Larson, G. E., & Miyoshi, D. K. (2007). Social desirability effects on computerized and paper-and-pencil questionnaires. *Computers in Human Behavior, 23*(4), 463–477. doi:10.1016/j.chb.2004.10.020

Bosch-Sijtsema, P., Ruohomäki, V. & Vartiainen, M. (2010). Multi-locational knowledge workers in the office: navigation, disturbances and effective-ness. *New Technology, Employment and Work Journal, 25*(3), 183–195.

Bosworth, R., Cameron, T. A., & DeShazo, J. R. (2006). *Preferences for preventative public health policies with jointly estimated rates of time preference*. School of Public Health and International Affairs: North Carolina State University.

Botta, A., de Donato, W., Persico, V., & Pescapé, A. (2016). Integration of cloud computing and internet of things: A survey. *Future Generation Computer Systems, 56*, 684–700. doi:10.1016/j.future.2015.09.021

Boudreau, M.-C., & Robey, D. (2005). Enacting Integrated Information Technology: A Human Agency Perspective. *Organization Science, 16*(1), 3–18. doi:10.1287/orsc.1040.0103

Bowcott, O., & Hern, A. (2018). Facebook and Cambridge Analytica face class action lawsuit. *The Guardian*. Retrieved April 3, 2018, from https://www.theguardian.com/news/2018/apr/10/cumbridge-analytica-and-facebook-face-class-action-lawsuit

Bowles, S. (2004). *Microeconomics: Behavior, institutions & evolution*. Princeton, NJ: Princeton University Press.

Brady, M. K., & Cronin, J. J. Jr. (2001). Some new thoughts on conceptualizing perceived service quality: A hierarchical approach. *Journal of Marketing, 65*(3), 34–49. doi:10.1509/jmkg.65.3.34.18334

Brandt, C., & Hermann, F. (2013). Conformance analysis of organizational models: A new enterprise modeling framework using algebraic graph transformation. *International Journal of Information System Modeling and Design, 4*(1), 42–78. doi:10.4018/jismd.2013010103

Bray, M. J., & Lee, J. N. (2000). University revenues from technology transfer: Licensingfees versus equity positions. *Journal of Business Venturing, 15*(5–6), 385–392. doi:10.1016/S0883-9026(98)00034-2

Briggs, C., & Makice, K. (2012). *Digital fluency: Building success in the digital age*. SociaLens.

Brody, T. (2016). Study Design, Endpoints and Biomarkers, Drug Safety, and FDA and ICH Guidelines. In T. Brody (Ed.), Clinical Trial (2nd ed.; pp. 31-68). Academic Press.

Brown, S. D., & Capdevila, R. (1999). Perpetuum mobile: Substance, force and the sociology of translation. In J. Law & J. Hassard (Eds.), *Actor network theory and after* (pp. 26–50). Oxford, UK: Blackwell. doi:10.1111/j.1467-954X.1999.tb03481.x

Brundtland, G.H. (1987). *World Commission on Environmental and Development: Our common Future*. World Commission for Environment and Development.

Brunei Darussalam Key Indicators (BDKI). (2016). Retrieved from http://www.depd.gov.bn/DEPD Documents Library/ DOS/BDKI/BDKI 2016.pdf

Bruque, S., & Moyano, J. (2007). Organizational Determinants of Information Technology Adoption and Implementation in SMEs: The Case of Family and Cooperative Firms. *Technovation, 27*(5), 241–253. doi:10.1016/j.technovation.2006.12.003

Buchanan, T. (2007). Personality testing on the Internet: What we know, and what we do not. In A. Joinson, K. McKenna, T. Postmes, & U.-D. Reips (Eds.), *Oxford handbook of Internet psychology* (pp. 447–459). Oxford, UK: Oxford University Press.

Buchanan, T., Ali, T., Heffernan, T. M., Ling, J., Parrott, A. C., Rodgers, J., & Scholey, A. B. (2005). Nonequivalence of on-line and paper-and-pencil psychological tests: The case of the prospective memory questionnaire. *Behavior Research Methods, 37*(1), 148–154. doi:10.3758/BF03206409 PMID:16097355

Buchanan, T., & Smith, J. L. (1999). Using the Internet for psychological research: Personality testing on the World-Wide Web. *British Journal of Psychology, 90*(1), 125–144. doi:10.1348/000712699161189 PMID:10085550

Bulut, Z. A. (2015). Determinants of repurchase intention in online shopping: A Turkish consumer's perspective. *International Journal of Business and Social Science, 6*(10), 55–63.

Burke, M., Kraut, R., & Marlow, C. (2011). Social capital in Facebook: Differentiating uses and users. *CHI'11 Proceedings of the SIGCHI Conference on Human Factors in Computing Systems*, 571-580.

Burke, W. (2008). *Organizational Change: Theory and Practice* (2nd ed.). Sage Publications.

Burke, W., & Litwin, G. (1992). A Causal Model of Organizational Performance and Change. *Journal of Management, 18*(3), 523–545. doi:10.1177/014920639201800306

Burns, P. (2001). *Entrepreneurship and Small Business*. Academic Press.

Burton-Jones, A., & Grange, C. (2013). From Use to Effective Use: A Representation Theory Perspective. *Information Systems Research, 24*(3), 632–658. doi:10.1287/isre.1120.0444

Cahyono, E., Mukhsar, & Elastic, P. (2017). Dynamics of knowledge dissemination in a four-type population society. *Far East Journal of Mathematical Sciences, 102*(6), 1065–1076. doi:10.17654/MS102061065

Cairns, J., & van der Pol, M. (2008). Valuing future private and social benefits: The discounted utility model versus hyperbolic discounting models. *Journal of Economic Psychology, 21*(2), 191–205. doi:10.1016/S0167-4870(99)00042-2

Calas, M., & Smirchich, L. (1999). 'Past postmodernism? reflections and tenative directions. *Academy of Management Review, 24*(4), 649–671. doi:10.5465/amr.1999.2553246

Caldeira, M. M., & Ward, J. M. (2002). Understanding the Successful Adoption and Use of IS/IT in SMEs: An Explanation from Portuguese Manufacturing Industries. *Information Systems Journal, 12*(2), 121–152. doi:10.1046/j.1365-2575.2002.00119.x

California State University Sacramento. (2019). *Kantian Ethics*. Retrieved February 5, 2019, from https://www.csus.edu/indiv/g/gaskilld/ethics/kantian%20ethics.htm

Callon, M. (1986). Some elements of a sociology of translation: Domestication of the scallops and the fishermen of St. Brieuc Bay. In J. Law (Ed.), *Power, action and belief: A new sociology of knowledge?* (pp. 196–233). London, UK: Routledge & Kegan Paul.

Callon, M. (1986). Some elements of a sociology of translation: Domestication of the scallops and the fishermen of St.Brieuc bay. In J. Law (Ed.), *Power, action, and belief: A new sociology of knowledge?* London: Routledge & Kegan Paul.

Callon, M. (1992). The dynamics of techno-economic networks. In R. Coombs, P. Saviotti, & V. Walsh (Eds.), *Technological change and company strategies: Economic and sociological perspectives* (pp. 77–102). London: Harcout Brace Jovanovich.

Callon, M. (1999). Actor-network theory - the market test. In J. Law & J. Hassard (Eds.), *Actor network theory and after* (pp. 181–195). Oxford, UK: Blackwell.

Callon, M., & Latour, B. (1981). Unscrewing the big Leviathan; or how actors macrostructure reality and how sociologist help them to do so. In K. Knorr-Cetina (Ed.), *Advances in social theory and methodology: Toward an integration of micro- and macro-sociologies* (pp. 277–303). London, UK: Routledge & Kegan Paul.

Callon, M., & Latour, M. (1992). Don't throw the baby out with the bath school. In A. Pickering (Ed.), *Science as practice and culture*. Chicago, IL: University of Chicago Press.

Callon, M., & Law, J. (1997). After the individual in society: Lesson on collectivity from science, technology and society. *Canadian Journal of Sociology*, *22*(2), 165–182. doi:10.2307/3341747

Calvani, A., Cartelli, A., Fini, A., & Ranieri, M. (2008). Models and instruments for assessing digital competence at school. *Journal of e-Learning and Knowledge Society, 4*(3), 183-193.

Calvo-Armengol, A., de Marti, J., & Prat, A. (2015). Communication and influence. *Theoretical Economics*, *10*(2), 649–690. doi:10.3982/TE1468

Camerer, C. F., Loewenstein, G., & Rabin, M. (2004). *Advances in behavioral economics*. Princeton, NJ: Princeton University Press.

Cameron, T. A., & Gerdes, G. R. (2003). *Eliciting individual-specific discount rates*. Department of Economics, University of Oregon. doi:10.2139srn.436524

Campbell, N. J. (1990). High School Student's Computer Attitudes and Attributions: Gender and Ethnic Group Differences. *Journal of Adolescent Research*, *5*, 485–499. doi:10.1177/074355489054007

Cantrell, M. A., & Lupinacci, P. (2007). Methodological issues in online data collection. *Journal of Advanced Nursing*, *60*(5), 544–549. doi:10.1111/j.1365-2648.2007.04448.x PMID:17973718

Capel, M., & Mendoza, L. (2014). Choreography Modeling Compliance for Timed Business Models. In *Proceedings of the Workshop on Enterprise and Organizational Modeling and Simulation* (pp. 202-218). Berlin, Germany: Springer. 10.1007/978-3-662-44860-1_12

Caragliu, A., Del Bo, C., & Nijkamp, P. (2011). Smart cities in Europe. *Journal of Urban Technology*, *18*(2), 65–82. doi:10.1080/10630732.2011.601117

Carayon, P., Schoofs Hundt, A., Karsh, B. T., Gurses, A. P., Alvarado, C. J., Smith, M., & Flatley Brennan, P. (2006). Work system design for patient safety: The SEIPS model. *Quality & Safety in Health Care*, *15*(1), i50–i58. doi:10.1136/qshc.2005.015842 PMID:17142610

Carbajo, M. (2017). Key Challenges and Drawbacks with Crowdfunding - How to Avoid the Crowdfunding Mindfield. *The Balance Small Business*. Available: https://www.thebalancesmb.com/key-challenges-and-drawbacks-with-crowdfunding-4116031

Carmo, A., Fantinato, M., Thom, L., Prado, E., Spinola, M., & Hung, P. (2017) A method for eliciting goals for business process models based on nonfunctional requirements catalogues. In *Proceedings of the 19th International Conference on Enterprise Information Systems* (pp. 262-273). Porto: Portugal: Academic Press. 10.5220/0006314702620273

Carter, C. R., & Rogers, D. S. (2008). A framework of sustainable supply chain management: Moving toward new theory. *International Journal of Physical Distribution & Logistics Management, 38*(5), 360–387. doi:10.1108/09600030810882816

Carter, M., Wright, R., Thatcher, J. B., & Klein, R. (2014). Understanding online customers' ties to merchants: The moderating influence of trust on the relationship between switching costs and e-loyalty. *European Journal of Information Systems, 23*(2), 185–204. doi:10.1057/ejis.2012.55

Cartwright, E. (2011). *Behavioral economics.* London, UK: Routledge.

Carvalho, N., Chaim, O., Cazarini, E., & Gerolamo, M. (2018). Manufacturing in the fourth industrial revolution: A positive prospect in Sustainable Manufacturing. *Procedia Manufacturing, 21,* 671-678.

Castellanos Domínguez, Ó. F., Fúquene Montañez, A. M., & Ramírez Martínez, D. C. (2011). *Análisis de tendencias: de la información hacia la innovación.* Universidad Nacional de Colombia.

Castells, M., & Ince, M. (2003). *Conversations with Manuel Castells.* London: Polity Press.

Catlin, T., LaBerge, L., & Varney, S. (2018, October). Digital strategy: The four fights you have to win. *McKinsey Quarterly.*

Cavalier, R. (2019). Utilitarian theories. *Online Guide to ethics and moral philosophy.* Retrieved February 4, 2019, from http://caae.phil.cmu.edu/Cavalier/80130/part2/sect9.html

Central Bank of Nigeria. (2018). *Economic report for the first half of 2017.* Retrieved from http://www.cbn.gov.ng/Out/2018/RSD/half%20year%202017%20innerx.pdf

CEPAL. (2007). *Progreso técnico y cambio estructural en América Latina. Project document of the United Nations.* Author.

Cerdan, A.L., Lopez-Nicolas, C., & Sabater-Sa´nchez, R. (2007). Knowledge management strategy diagnosis from KM instruments use, *Journal of Knowledge Management, 11*(2), 60-72.

Cerri, J., Thogerson, J., & Testa, F. (2019). Social desirability and sustainable food research:A systematic literature review. *Food Quality and Preference, 71*(1), 136–140. doi:10.1016/j.foodqual.2018.06.013

Cevikalp, H., Larlus, D., Neamtu, M., Triggs, B., & Jurie, F. (2010). Manifold Based Local Classifiers: Linear and Nonlinear Approaches. *Journal of Signal Processing Systems for Signal, Image, and Video Technology, 61*(1), 61–73. doi:10.100711265-008-0313-4

Chabris, Ch., Laibson, D., & Schuldt, J. (2008). *Intertemporal choice.* New York: Palgrave Dictionary of Economics.

Chadee, D., & Raman, R. (2012). External knowledge and performance of offshore IT service providers in India: The mediating role of talent management. *Asia Pacific Journal of Human Resources, 50*(4), 459–482. doi:10.1111/j.1744-7941.2012.00039.x

Chai, S., Kim, M., & Rao, H. R. (2011). Firms' Information Security Investment Decisions: Stock Market Evidence of Investors' Behavior. *Decision Support Systems, 50*(4), 651–661. doi:10.1016/j.dss.2010.08.017

Chakraborty, A. R., & Mansor, N. N. A. (2013). Adoption of Human Resource Information System: A Theoretical Analysis. *Procedia: Social and Behavioral Sciences, 75,* 473–478. doi:10.1016/j.sbspro.2013.04.051

Chamoux, J. (Ed.). (2018). *The Digital Era 1: Big Data Stakes.* Hoboken, NJ: John Wiley & Sons. doi:10.1002/9781119102687

Chandar & Sarangal. (2016). A study of significance of E-servqual in determining service quality of online websites. *International Journal of Business Management and Scientific Research, 15.*

Chandler, D. (2007). *Semiotics: the basics.* New York, NY: Routledge. doi:10.4324/9780203014936

Chang, L., Furner, C. P., & Zinko, R. (2010). A study of negotiations within the ethnic Chinese community between Taiwan and Hong Kong. *Management Research and Practice, 5*(1), 1–9.

Chang, S. E., & Ho, C. B. (2006). Organizational factors to the effectiveness of implementing information security management. *Industrial Management & Data Systems, 106*(3), 345–361. doi:10.1108/02635570610653498

Chanyapurn, C. (2016). *Here's what Asian Leaders are Doing with Blockchain Technology.* Blommber Technology.

Chapman, G. B. (1996). Expectations and preferences for sequences of health and money. *Organizational Behavior and Human Decision Processes, 67*(1), 59–75. doi:10.1006/obhd.1996.0065

Chapple, W., Lockett, A., Siegel, D. S., & Wright, M. (2005). Assessing the relative performance of U.K. University technology transfer offices: Parametric and nonparametricevidence. *Research Policy, 34*(3), 369–384. doi:10.1016/j. respol.2005.01.007

Chen, S. (2017). A Blockchain Based Supply Chain Quality Management Framework. *e Business Engineering (ICEBE), IEEE 14th International Conference*, 172–176. 10.1109/ICEBE.2017.34

Chen, H., Chiang, R. H., & Storey, V. C. (2012). Business intelligence and analytics: From big data to big impact. *Management Information Systems Quarterly, 36*(4), 1165. doi:10.2307/41703503

Chen, I.-S. (2017). Computer self-efficacy, learning performance, and the mediating role of learning engagement. *Computers in Human Behavior, 72*, 362–370. doi:10.1016/j.chb.2017.02.059

Chen, L. H. (2008). Job satisfaction among information system (IS) personnel. *Computers in Human Behavior, 24*(1), 105–118. doi:10.1016/j.chb.2007.01.012

Chen, P. Y., Cheng, S. M., & Chen, K. C. (2014). Optimal control of epidemic information dissemination over networks. *IEEE Transactions on Cybernetics, 44*(12), 2316–2328. doi:10.1109/TCYB.2014.2306781 PMID:25415940

Chen, S., Duan, Y., Edwards, S., & Lehaney, B. (2006). Toward understanding inter organizational knowledge transfer needs in SMEs: Insight from a UK investigation. *Journal of Knowledge Management, 10*(3), 6–23. doi:10.1108/13673270610670821

Chesebrough, E. D. (2006). Knowledge Management A tool for SMEs to enhance Competitiveness. *CACCI Journal, 1*.

Chia, P. A., Maynard, S. B., & Ruighaver, A. B. (2002). Understanding Organizational Security Culture. *Proceedings of PACIS2002*.

Chia, P. A., Maynard, S. B., & Ruighaver, A. B. (2003). Understanding Organizational Security Culture. In Mg. Hunter & Kk. Dhanda (Eds.), *Information Systems: The Challenges of Theory and Practice*. Las Vegas, NV: Information Institute.

Cho, H., & LaRose, R. (1999). Privacy issues in Internet surveys. *Social Science Computer Review, 17*(4), 421–434. doi:10.1177/089443939901700402

Choi, S. J., Jia, N., & Lu, J. (2014). The structure of political institutions and effectiveness of corporate political lobbying. *Organization Science, 26*(1), 158–179.

Cholakova, M., & Clarysse, B. (2015). Does the Possibility to Make Equity Investments in Crowdfunding Projects Crowd Out Reward–Based Investments? *Entrepreneurship Theory and Practice, 39*(1), 145–172. doi:10.1111/etap.12139

Choong, K. K. (2013). Are PMS meeting the measurement needs of BPM? A literature review. *Business Process Management Journal, 19*(3), 535–574. doi:10.1108/14637151311319941

Chua, H. N., Wong, S. F., Low, Y. C., & Chang, Y. (2018). Impact of Employees’Demographic Characteristics on the Awareness and Compliance of Information Security Policy in Organizations. *Telematics and Informatics*, *35*(6), 1770–1780. doi:10.1016/j.tele.2018.05.005

Chua, S. L., Chen, D.-T., & Wong, A. F. L. (1999). Computer anxiety and its correlates: A meta analysis. *Computers in Human Behavior*, *15*(5), 609–623. doi:10.1016/S0747-5632(99)00039-4

Chung, S. H., & Herrnstein, R. J. (1967). Choice and delay of reinforcement. *Journal of the Experimental Analysis of Behavior*, *10*(1), 67–74. doi:10.1901/jeab.1967.10-67 PMID:16811307

Cimoli, M. (2000). Creación de redes y sistema de innovación: México en un contexto global. *El Mercado de Valores*, *60*(1), 3–17.

Clark, M., Greenberg, A., Hill, E., Lemay, E., Clark, P.-E., & Roosth, D. (2011). Heightened Interpersonal Security Diminishes the Monetary Value of Possessions. *Journal of Experimental Social Psychology*, *47*(2), 359–364. doi:10.1016/j.jesp.2010.08.001

Close, K. (2016). Almost Nobody Trusts Financial Institutions. *Money*.

Cognizant Report. (2017). *The Future of Blockchain in Asia-Pacific Digital System & Technology*. Author.

Cohen, J. (1988). *Statistical Power Analysis for the Behavioral Sciences*. Mahwah, NJ: Erlbaum.

Colbert, A., Yee, N., & George, G. (2016). *The digital workforce and the workplace of the future*. Academy of Management Briarcliff Manor. doi:10.5465/amj.2016.4003

Colinsky, J. (1996). Why bounded rationality? *Journal of Economic Literature*, *34*, 669–700.

Coller, M., & Williams, M. B. (1999). Eliciting individual discount rates. *Experimental Economics*, *2*(2), 107–127. doi:10.1023/A:1009986005690

Collins, H., & Yearley, S. (1992). Epistemological chicken. In A. Pickering (Ed.), *Science, practice and culture*. Chicago, IL: University of Chicago Press.

Colwill, C. (2009). Human factors in information security: The insider threat - Who can you trust these days? *Information Security Technical Report*, *14*(4), 186–196. doi:10.1016/j.istr.2010.04.004

Compact, U. G. (2013). Global corporate sustainability report 2013. *UN Global Compact Reports*, *5*(1), 1–28. doi:10.5848/UNGC.5720.2014.0009

Constant, C. (2017). Three steps to making the digital workplace ar. *Gartner Symposium 2016*. Retrieved March 2, 2019, from https://www.slideshare.net/IntelITCenter/three-steps-to-making-a-digital-workplace-a-reality-chad-constant-at-gartner-symposium-2016

Cook, K. S., Cheshire, C., Rice, E. R., & Nakagawa, S. (2013). Social exchange theory. In *Handbook of social psychology* (pp. 61–88). Dordrecht: Springer. doi:10.1007/978-94-007-6772-0_3

Cook, S. D. N., & Brown, J. S. (1999). Bridging Epistemologies: The Generative Dance between Organizational Knowledge and Organizational Knowing. *Organization Science*, *10*(4), 381–400. doi:10.1287/orsc.10.4.381

Corbett, C., & Hill, C. (2015). *Solving the Equation: the Variables for Women's Success in Engineering and Computing*. Washington, DC: The American Association of University Women.

Corbin, J., & Strauss, A. (1990). Grounded Theory Research: Procedures, Canons, and Evaluative Criteria. *Zeitschrift für Soziologie*, *19*(6), 418–427. doi:10.1515/zfsoz-1990-0602

Cordella, A., & Shaikh, M. (2006). *From epistemology to ontology: Challenging the constructed "truth" of ANT. Working Paper Series, No. 143.* London: Department of Information Systems, London School of Economics and Political Science. Retrieved from http://is2.lse.ac.uk/WP/PDF/wp143.pdf

Cordes Feibert, D., & Jacobsen, P. (2019). Factors impacting technology adoption in hospital bed logistics. *International Journal of Logistics Management, 30*(1), 195–230. doi:10.1108/IJLM-02-2017-0043

Cragg, P., Caldeira, M., & Ward, J. (2011). Organizational information systems competences in small and medium-sized enterprises. *Information & Management, 48*(8), 353–363. doi:10.1016/j.im.2011.08.003

Cragg, P., Mills, A., & Suraweera, T. (2013). The Influence of IT management sophistication and IT support on IT success in small and medium-sized enterprises. *Journal of Small Business Management, 51*(4), 617–636. doi:10.1111/jsbm.12001

Crawford, C. (2004). Actor network theory. In *Ritzer encyclopaedia* (pp. 1-3). Retrieved from: http/www.sagepub.com/upm-data/5222_Ritzer_Entries_beginning_with_A_%5B1%5D.pdf

Crémer, J., Garicano, L., & Prat, A. (2007). Language and the theory of the firm. *The Quarterly Journal of Economics, 122*(1), 373–407. doi:10.1162/qjec.122.1.373

Crilly, R. (2018). *Facebook to Start 'Trust Ratings' for Media Outlets as it Fights Back Against Fake News.* Retrieved from http://www.telegraph.co.uk/news/2018/01/19/facebook-start-trust-ratings-media-outlets-fights-back-against/

Cronbach, L. J. (1951). Coefficient alpha and the internal structure of tests. *Psychometrika, 16*(3), 297–336. doi:10.1007/BF02310555

Cropanzano, R., Anthony, E. L., Daniels, S. R., & Hall, A. V. (2017). Social exchange theory: A critical review with theoretical remedies. *The Academy of Management Annals, 11*(1), 479–516. doi:10.5465/annals.2015.0099

Crossman, A. (2019). *Understanding Social Exchange Theory.* Available: https://www.thoughtco.com/social-exchange-theory-3026634

Cross, S. (2002). Confidentiality within physiotherapy: Perceptions and attitudes of clinical practitioners. *Journal of Medical Ethics, 26*(6), 447–453. doi:10.1136/jme.26.6.447 PMID:11129846

CrowdFund Buzz. (2018). *Your Crowdfunding Campaign: Flexible Funding or Fixed Funding?* Available: https://www.crowdfundbuzz.com/your-crowdfunding-campaign-flexible-funding-or-fixed-funding/

Crowdfunding Centre. (2014). *Mapping: the state of the crowdfunding nation.* Available: thecrowdfundingcentre.com/downloads/eFunding__The_State_of_The_Crowdfunding _Nation_-_Q2_2014_HEADLINE_EDITION.pdf.

Crowdsourcing Organization. (2012). *Crowdfunding industry report.* Available: https://www.slideshare.net/samgold007/crowdfunding-industry

Crowne, D. P., & Marlowe, D. (1960). A new scale of social desirability independent of psychopathology. *Journal of Consulting Psychology, 24*(4), 349–354. doi:10.1037/h0047358 PMID:13813058

Crowne, D. P., & Marlowe, D. (1964). *The approval motive.* New York: Wiley.

Crown, W., Buyukkaramikli, N., Sir, M., Thokala, P., Morton, A., Marshall, D., ... Pasupathy, K. S. (2018). Application of Constrained Optimization Methods in Health Services Research: Report 2 of the ISPOR Optimization Methods Emerging Good Practices Task Force. *Value in Health, 21*(9), 1019–1028. doi:10.1016/j.jval.2018.05.003 PMID:30224103

Crown, W., Buyukkaramikli, N., Thokala, P., Morton, A., Sir, M., Marshall, D., ... Pasupathy, K. S. (2017). Constrained Optimization Methods in Health Services Research—An Introduction: Report 1 of the ISPOR Optimization Methods Emerging Good Practices Task Force. *Value in Health, 20*(3), 310–319. doi:10.1016/j.jval.2017.01.013 PMID:28292475

Cucculelli, M., Peruzzi, V., & Zazzaro, A. (2019). Relational capital in lending relationships: Evidence from European family firms. *Small Business Economics*, *52*(1), 277–301. doi:10.100711187-018-0019-3

Culnan, M. J. (1993). "How did they get my name?": An exploratory investigation of consumer attitudes toward secondary information use. *Management Information Systems Quarterly*, *17*(3), 341–363. doi:10.2307/249775

Culnan, M. J., & Williams, C. C. (2009). How ethics can enhance organizational privacy: Lessons from the Choicepoint and TJX data breaches. *Management Information Systems Quarterly*, *33*(4), 673–687. doi:10.2307/20650322

Cummings, D. (2016). *Use Cases of Ethereum in Different Sectors 2016*. Academic Press.

Cummiskey, D. (2003). Kantian Consequentialism. *Oxford Scholarship Online*. Retrieved March 23, 2019, from http://www.oxfordscholarship.com/view/10.1093/0195094530.001.0001/acprof-9780195094534

da Veiga, A., & Martins, N. (2017). Defining and identifying dominant information security cultures and subcultures. *Computers & Security*, *70*, 72–94. doi:10.1016/j.cose.2017.05.002

Dahl, S. (2018). Social Media Marketing: Theories and Applications. Thousand Oaks, CA: SAGE Publications.

Dahlander, L., O'Mahony, S., & Gann, D. M. (2016). One foot in, one foot out: How does individuals' external search breadth affect innovation outcomes? *Strategic Management Journal*, *37*(2), 280–302. doi:10.1002mj.2342

Dallemule, L., & Davenport, T. H. (2017). What's Your Data Strategy? *Harvard Business Review*, *95*(3), 112–121.

Das, A. K. & Chakraborty, S. (2018). Knowledge withholding within an organization: the psychological resistance to knowledge sharing linking with territoriality. *RISUS - Journal on Innovation and Sustainability*, *9*(3), 94–108. doi: . doi:10.24212/2179-3565.2018v9i3p94-108

Das, D. (2018). The impact of Sustainable Supply Chain Management practices on firm performance: Lessons from Indian organizations. *Journal of Cleaner Production*, *203*, 179–196. doi:10.1016/j.jclepro.2018.08.250

Davenport, T. H. (2006). Competing on analytics. *Harvard Business Review*, *84*(1), 98.

Davenport, T. H., & Prusak, L. (1998). *Working Knowledge: How Organizations Manage What They Know*. Boston: Harvard Business School Press.

Davern, M. J., & Kauffman, R. J. (2000). Discovering potential and realizing value from information technology investments. *Journal of Management Information Systems*, *16*(4), 121–143. doi:10.1080/07421222.2000.11518268

David, S., Shukla, S., & Gupta, S. (2015). Barriers in Implementing Human Resource Information System in Organization. *International Journal of Engineering Research and Management*, *2*(5), 116–120.

Davidson, P., & Griffin, R. W. (2003). *Management: An Australasian Perspective* (2nd ed.). Brisbane, Australia: John Wiley & Sons.

Debreu, G. (1958). Stochastic choice and cardinal utility. *Econometrica*, *26*(3), 440–444. doi:10.2307/1907622

Debreu, G. (1960). Topological methods in cardinal utility theory. In K. J. Arrow, S. Karlin, & S. Suppes (Eds.), *Mathematical models in the social sciences* (pp. 16–26). Stanford, CA: Stanford University press.

Debreu, G. (1964). Continuity properties of Paretian utility. *International Economic Review*, *5*(3), 285–293. doi:10.2307/2525513

Dejan Nenov. (2005). *New Approaches to KM in Government: User-Centric Enterprise Information*. Accessed from, www.x1.com/download/x1_platform_whitepaper.pdf

Delahaye, B. L. (2003). Human Resource Development and the Management of Knowledge Capital. In R. Wiesner & B. Millett (Eds.), *Human Resource Management: Challenges and Future Directions*. Brisbane, Australia: John Wiley & Sons.

Delgado, J. C. (2015). Supporting Enterprise Integration with a Multidimensional Interoperability Framework. *International Journal of Social and Organizational Dynamics in IT*, *4*(1), 39–70. doi:10.4018/IJSODIT.2015010104

DellaVigna, St., & Malmendier, U. (2004). Contract design and self-control: Theory and evidence. *The Quarterly Journal of Economics*, *119*(2), 353–402. doi:10.1162/0033553041382111

DellaVigna, St., & Malmendier, U. (2006). Paying not to go to the gym. *The American Economic Review*, *96*(3), 694–719. doi:10.1257/aer.96.3.694

DellaVigna, St., & Paserman, M. D. (2005). Job search and impatience. *Journal of Labor Economics*, *23*(3), 527–588. doi:10.1086/430286

Delli Carpini, M. X., & Keeter, S. (1989). *What Americans know about politics and why it matters*. New Haven, CT. Yale University Press.

Deloitte. (2014). *The digital workplace: think, share, do transform your employee experience*. Retrieved March 6, 2019, from https://www2.deloitte.com/content/dam/Deloitte/be/Documents/technology/The_digital_workplace_Deloitte.pdf

Denscombe, M. (2006). Web-based questionnaires and the mode effect: An evaluation based on completion rates and data contents of near-identical questionnaires delivered in different modes. *Social Science Computer Review*, *24*(2), 246–254. doi:10.1177/0894439305284522

Denton, B., Kurt, M., Shah, N., Bryant, S., & Smith, S. (2009). Optimizing the Start Time of Statin Therapy for Patients with Diabetes. *Medical Decision Making*, *29*(3), 351–367. doi:10.1177/0272989X08329462 PMID:19429836

Denzin, N. K., & Lincoln, Y. S. (2000). *The Sage Handbook of Qualitative Research*. Sage.

Dery, K., Sebastian, I. M., & Van Der Meulen, N. (2016). The digital workplace is key to digital innovation. MIS Quarterly Executive, 16(2), 135-152.

Desai, V. (2017). *Counting the Uncounted: 1.1 Billion People without IDs*. Academic Press.

DeSanctis, G. (1986). Human Resource Information Systems: A Current Assessment. *Management Information Systems Quarterly*, *10*(1), 15–27. doi:10.2307/248875

DeSanctis, G., & Poole, M. S. (1994). Capturing the Complexity in Advanced Technology Use: Adaptive Structuration Theory. *Organization Science*, *5*(2), 121–147. doi:10.1287/orsc.5.2.121

Deshpande, M., & Deshpande, N. (2011). Business Policy Implementation – A Case of Auto Components SMEs in Pune. In Building Competencies for Sustainability and Organizational Excellence. Macmillan.

Desouza, K. C., & Awazu, Y. (2006). Knowledge Management at SMEs: Five Peculiarities. *Journal of Knowledge Management*, *10*(1), 32–43. doi:10.1108/13673270610650085

DeTienne, K. B., & Jackson, L. A. (2001). Knowledge Management: Understanding Theory and Developing Strategy. *Competitiveness Review*, *11*(1), 1–9. doi:10.1108/eb046415

Diamond, P. A. (1965). The evaluation of infinite utility streams. *Econometrica*, *33*(1), 170–177. doi:10.2307/1911893

Diamond, P. A., Koopmans, T. C., & Williamson, R. (1962). Axioms for persistent preference. In R. E. Machol & P. Gray (Eds.), *Recent developments in information and decision processes*. New York: Macmillan.

Dibrell, C., Davis, P. S., & Craig, J. (2008). Fueling innovation through Information Technology in SMEs. *Journal of Small Business Management*, *46*(2), 203–218. doi:10.1111/j.1540-627X.2008.00240.x

Di-Cicco-Bloom, C., & Crabtee, B. F. (2006). The Qualitative Research Interview. *Medical Education*, *40*(4), 314–321. doi:10.1111/j.1365-2929.2006.02418.x PMID:16573666

Dickhäuser, O., & Meyer, W.-U. (2006). Gender differences in young children's math ability attributions. *Psychological Science*, *48*(1), 3–16.

Digital Government Strategy 2015 - 2020 Brunei Darussalam. (2015). Retrieved from http://www.digitalstrategy.gov.bn/Themed/index.aspx

Dill, J. C., Kasik, D. J., & Darvill, D. J. (2013). Case study: successful deployment of industry-university collaborative visual analytics research. In *System Sciences (HICSS), 2013 46th Hawaii International Conference on* (pp. 1505-1511). IEEE. 10.1109/HICSS.2013.126

Ding, C., Cheng, H. K., Duan, Y., & Jin, Y. (2017). The power of the "like" button: *The impact of social media on box office. Decision Support Systems*, *94*, 77–84. doi:10.1016/j.dss.2016.11.002

Dirk, A. (2017). *The ICO Gold Rush: It's a Scam, it's a bubble, it's a super Challenge for Regulators*. University Luxembourg Law Working Paper 11.

Disney, S. M., & Towill, D. R. (2003). The effect of vendor managed inventory (VMI) dynamics on the Bullwhip Effect in supply chains. *International Journal of Production Economics*, *85*(2), 199–215. doi:10.1016/S0925-5273(03)00110-5

Dlugosch, T. J., Klinger, B., Frese, M., & Klehe, U. C. (2018). Personality-based selection of entrepreneurial borrowers to reduce credit risk: Two studies on prediction models in low-and high-stakes settings in developing countries. *Journal of Organizational Behavior*, *39*(5), 612–628. doi:10.1002/job.2236

Doerr, B. (2012). Why Rumors Spread so Quickly in Social Networks. *Communications of the ACM*, *55*(6), 70–75. doi:10.1145/2184319.2184338

Doherty, N. F., & Ellis-Chadwick, F. (2010). Internet retailing: The past, the present and the future. *International Journal of Retail & Distribution Management*, *38*(11/12), 943–965. doi:10.1108/09590551011086000

Doherty, N. F., & Tajuddin, S. T. (2018). Towards a user-centric theory of value-driven information security compliance. *Information Technology & People*, *31*(2), 348–367. doi:10.1108/ITP-08-2016-0194

Dolnicar, S., & Grün, B. (2007). Cross-cultural differences in survey response patterns. *International Marketing Review*, *24*(2), 127–143. doi:10.1108/02651330710741785

Domazet, I. (2018). Digital Transformation of Business Portfolio through DCRM. In M. Radović (Ed.), *Digital Transformation - New Challenges and Business Opportunities* (pp. 214–235). London, UK: Silver and Smith Publishers.

Domazet, I., Lazić, M., & Zubović, J. (2018). Driving Factors of Serbian Competitiveness: Digital Economy and ICT. *Strategic Management: International Journal of Strategic Management and Decision Support Systems in Strategic Management*, *23*(1), 20–28. doi:10.5937/StraMan1801020D

Domazet, I., & Neogradi, S. (2018). Digital Marketing and Service Industry: Digital Marketing in Banking Industry. In N. Ray (Ed.), *Managing Diversity, Innovation, and Infrastructure in Digital Business* (pp. 20–41). Hershey, PA: Information Science Publishing.

Domínguez, L., & Brown, F. (2004). Measuring technological capabilities in Mexican. *CEPAL Review*, *83*(83), 129–144. doi:10.18356/872c3189-en

Donahue, J. D., & Zeckhauser, R. J. (2011). *Collaborative governance: Private sector roles for public goals in turbulent times*. Princeton, NJ: Princeton University Press. doi:10.1515/9781400838103

Donaldson, T. (1996). Values in tension: Ethics away from home. *Harvard Business Review*. Retrieved March 12, 2019, from https://hbr.org/1996/09/values-in-tension-ethics-away-from-home

Dor, D., & Elovici, Y. (2016). A Model of the Information Security Investment DecisionMaking Process. *Computers & Security*, *63*, 1–13. doi:10.1016/j.cose.2016.09.006

Dority, G. K. (2016). *Rethinking Information Work: a Career Guide for Liberian and other Information Professionals* (2nd ed.). Santa Barbara, CA: ABC-CLIO, LLC.

Dornberger, R. (Ed.). (2018). *Business Information Systems and Technology 4 0: New Trends in the Age of Digital Change* (Vol. 141). Cham, Switzerland: Springer. doi:10.1007/978-3-319-74322-6

Doty, D. H., & Glick, W. H. (1994). Typologies as a Unique Form of Theory Building: Toward Improved Understanding and Modeling. *Academy of Management Review*, *19*(2), 230–251. doi:10.5465/amr.1994.9410210748

Doug, J. G. (2018). Blockchain for Social Impact: Moving Beyond the Hype. *Technical Report*. Stanford Graduate School of Business.

Doyle, J. R. (2013). Survey of time preference, delay discounting models. *Judgment and Decision Making*, *8*(2), 116–135.

Dragoni, N., Giallorenzo, S., Lafuente, A., Mazzara, M., Montesi, F., Mustafin, R., & Safina, L. (2017). Microservices: yesterday, today, and tomorrow. In M. Mazzara & B. Meyer (Eds.), *Present and Ulterior Software Engineering* (pp. 195–216). Cham, Switzerland: Springer. doi:10.1007/978-3-319-67425-4_12

Drahota, A., & Dewey, A. (2008). The Sociogram: A Useful Tool in the Analysis of Focus Groups. *Nurs. Re.*, *57*(4), 293–297. doi:10.1097/01.NNR.0000313489.49165.97 PMID:18641498

Draško, T., & Božica, P. (2014). Control and optimization of complex biological systems. In *37th International Convention on Information and Communication Technology, Electronics and Microelectronics* (pp. 222-227). Opatija: IEEE.

Drucker, P. F. (1993). *The Post Capitalist Society*. London: Butterworth-Heinemann.

Dubin, R. (1978). *Theory Building* (Revised ed.). New York: The Free Press.

Duffy, B., Smith, K., Terhanian, G., & Bremer, J. (2005). Comparing data from online and face-to-face surveys. *International Journal of Market Research*, *47*(6), 615–639. doi:10.1177/147078530504700602

Duflo, E., Banerjee, A., Glennerster, R., & Kothari, D. (2010). Improving immunization coverage in rural India: A clustered randomized controlled evaluation of immunization campaigns with and without incentives. *British Medical Journal*, *340*(1), 2220. doi:10.1136/bmj.c2220

Duflo, E., Kremer, M., & Robinson, J. (2008). How high are rates of return to fertilizer? Evidence from field experiments in Kenya. *The American Economic Review*, *98*(2), 482–488. doi:10.1257/aer.98.2.482

Dunbar, R. I. M. (2012). Social cognition on the Internet: Testing constraints on social network size. *Philosophical Transactions of the Royal Society of London. Series B, Biological Sciences*, *367*(1599), 2192–2201. doi:10.1098/rstb.2012.0121 PMID:22734062

Durndell, A., Haag, Z., & Laithwaite, H. (2000). Computer self-efficacy and gender: A cross cultural study of Scotland and Romania. *Personality and Individual Differences*, *28*(6), 1037–1044. doi:10.1016/S0191-8869(99)00155-5

Durst, S., & Edvardsson, I. R. (2012). Knowledge management in SMEs: A literature review. *Journal of Knowledge Management, 16*(6), 879–903. doi:10.1108/13673271211276173

Durugbo, C. (2016). Collaborative networks: A systematic review and multi-level framework. *International Journal of Production Research, 54*(12), 3749–3776. doi:10.1080/00207543.2015.1122249

Dwight, S. A., & Feigelson, M. E. (2000). A quantitative review of the effect of computerized testing on the measurement of social desirability. *Educational and Psychological Measurement, 60*(3), 340–360. doi:10.1177/00131640021970583

Dwivedi, A. (2012). A higher-order model of consumer brand engagement and its impact on loyalty intentions. *Journal of Retailing and Consumer Services, 24*, 100–109. doi:10.1016/j.jretconser.2015.02.007

Earl, M. (2001). Knowledge Management Strategies: Toward a Taxonomy. *Journal of Management Information Systems, 18*(1), 215–233. doi:10.1080/07421222.2001.11045670

Easter, M. M., Davis, A. M., & Henderson, G. E. (2004). Confidentiality: More than a linkage file and a locked drawer. *IRB, 26*(2), 13–1. doi:10.2307/3564233 PMID:15069972

Ebert, J. E., & Prelec, D. (2007). The fragility of time: Time-insensitivity and valuation of the near and far future. *Management Science, 53*(9), 1423–1438. doi:10.1287/mnsc.1060.0671

Ebrahimifard, A., Amiri, M., Arani, M., & Parsa, S. (2016). Mapping BPMN 2.0 Choreography to WS-CDL: A Systematic Method. *Journal of E-Technology, 7*, 1–23.

Eccles, J. S., Roeser, R., Wigfield, A., & Freedman-Doan, C. (2006). Academic and motivational pathways through middle childhood. In L. Balter & C. S. Tamis-LeMonda (Eds.), *Child psychology: a handbook of contemporary issues* (pp. 325–356). New York, NY: Psychology Press.

Edgeworth, F. Y. (1881). *Mathematical physics: An essay on the application of mathematics to the moral sciences.* London: Kegan. Retrieved from https://archive.org/details/mathematicalpsy01goog

Edgeworth, F. Y. (1881). *Mathematical Physics: An Essay on the Application of Mathematics to the Moral Sciences.* Retrieved from https://archive.org/details/mathematicalpsy01goog/page/n6

Edison Research. (2018). Facebook declines for the first time in infinite dial history. *Blog – Latest news.* Retrieved February 15, 2019, from https://www.edisonresearch.com/facebook-declines-first-time-infinite-dial-history/

Edwards, R., & Fenwick, T. (2015). Critique and politics: A sociomaterialist intervention. *Educational Philosophy and Theory, 47*(13-14), 1385–1404. doi:10.1080/00131857.2014.930681

Edwards, W. (1954). The theory of decision making. *Psychological Bulletin, 51*(4), 380–417. doi:10.1037/h0053870 PMID:13177802

Edwards, W. (1961). Behavioral decision theory. *Annual Review of Psychology, 12*(1), 473–498. doi:10.1146/annurev.ps.12.020161.002353 PMID:13725822

Egbu, C. O. (2001). Knowledge management in small and medium enterprises in the construction industry: challenges and opportunities. *Managing Knowledge: conversation and Critiques. Proceedings of an international conference.*

Egbu, C. O., Hari, S., & Renukappa, S. H. (2005). Knowledge Management for Sustainable Competitiveness in Small and Medium Surveying Practices. *Structural Survey, 23*(1), 7–21. doi:10.1108/02630800510586871

Ehimagunmwende, C. (2016). *Challenges Facing SMEs Financing in Nigeria.* Available: https://www.linkedin.com/pulse/challenges-facing-smes-financing-nigeria-clifford-nosa/

Eid, M. I. (2011). Determinants of e-commerce customer satisfaction, trust, and loyalty in Saudi Arabia. *Journal of Electronic Commerce Research*, *12*(1), 78.

Eisenhardt, K. M. (1989). Agency Theory: An Assessment and Review. *Academy of Management Review*, *14*(1), 57–74. doi:10.5465/amr.1989.4279003

Eisenhardt, K. M. (1989). Building Theories from Case Study Research. *Academy of Management Review*, *14*(4), 532–550. doi:10.5465/amr.1989.4308385

Elbeltagi, I., & Agag, G. (2016). E-retailing ethics and its impact on customer satisfaction and repurchase intention: A cultural and commitment-trust theory perspective. *Internet Research*, *26*(1), 288–310. doi:10.1108/IntR-10-2014-0244

Ellis, K. (2004). Managing the Acquisition Process: Do Differences Actually Exist across Integration Approaches. In A. L. Pablo & M. Javidan (Eds.), *Mergers and Acquisitions: Creating Integrative Knowledge*. John Wiley & Sons.

Elshwimy, F., Algergawy, A., Sarhan, A., & Sallam, E. (2014). Aggregation of similarity measures in schema matching based on generalized mean. *Proceedings of the IEEE International Conference on Data Engineering Workshops* (pp. 74-79). Piscataway, NJ: IEEE Computer Society Press. 10.1109/ICDEW.2014.6818306

Engelsman, W. (2007). *Information Assets and their Value*. Academic Press.

Eniola, A. A., & Entebang, H. (2015). SME firm performance-financial innovation and challenges. *Procedia: Social and Behavioral Sciences*, *195*, 334–342. doi:10.1016/j.sbspro.2015.06.361

Epper, T., Fehr-Duda, H., & Bruhin, A. (2011). Viewing the future through a warped lens: Why uncertainty generates hyperbolic discounting. *Journal of Risk and Uncertainty*, *43*(3), 169–203. doi:10.100711166-011-9129-x

Erez, M., & Early, P. (1993). *Culture, self-identify, and work*. Oxford, UK: Oxford University Press. doi:10.1093/acprof:oso/9780195075809.001.0001

Eric, P. (2016). *Blockchain: Democratizes Trust Distributed Ledgers and the Future of Value*. Technical Report. Deloitte.

Erl, T., Merson, P., & Stoffers, R. (2017). *Service-oriented Architecture: Analysis and Design for Services and Microservices*. Upper Saddle River, NJ: Prentice Hall PTR.

Ernst, S. A., Brand, T., Lhachimi, S. K., & Zeeb, H. (2018). Combining Internet-Based and Postal Survey Methods in a Survey among Gynecologists: Results of a Randomized Trial. *Health Services Research*, *53*(2), 879–895. doi:10.1111/1475-6773.12664 PMID:28217941

Eshach, H. (2006). Bridging In-school and Out-of-school Learning: Formal, Non-Formal, and Informal Education. *Journal of Science Education and Technology*, *16*(2), 171–190. doi:10.100710956-006-9027-1

Esposito, E., & Evangelista, P. (2014). Investigating virtual enterprise models: Literature review and empirical findings. *International Journal of Production Economics*, *148*, 145–157. doi:10.1016/j.ijpe.2013.10.003

Estle, S. J., Green, L., Myerson, J., & Holt, D. D. (2007). Discounting of money and directly consumable rewards. *Psychological Science*, *18*(1), 58–63. doi:10.1111/j.1467-9280.2007.01849.x PMID:17362379

Estruch, A., & Álvaro, J. A. H. (2012). Event-driven manufacturing process management approach. In *10th Int. Conf. on Business Process Managament*, (pp. 120–133). Berlin: Springer.

Etzioni, A. (2012). The privacy merchants: What is to be done? *The Journal of Constitutional Law*, *14*(4), 929–951.

EU GDPR. (2018). The EU General Data Protection Regulation (GDPR) is the most important change in data privacy regulation in 20 years. *EU GDPR.ORG*. Retrieved June 1, 2018, from https://www.eugdpr.org/

Eucken, W. (1983). El orden de la competencia y su realización. In *La economía social de mercado: un proyecto económico alternativo* (pp. 21–40). Buenos Aires, Argentina: Centro Interdisciplinario de Estudios para el Desarrollo Latinoamericano. (Original work published 1956)

European Commission. (2005). The New SME Definition. User Guide and Model Declaration. European Commission.

Evans, Y., He, I. Y., & H. J. (2018). Analysis of published public sector information security incidents and breaches to establish the proportions of human error. *Proceedings of the Twelfth International Symposium on Human Aspects of Information Security Assurance (HAISA) 2018, 12*, 191–202.

Evans, A. M., & Krueger, J. I. (2009). The psychology and economics of trust. *Social and Personality Psychology Compass*, *3*(6), 1003–1017. doi:10.1111/j.1751-9004.2009.00232.x

Evans, M. (2007). Analysing Google rankings through search engine optimization data. *Internet Research*, *17*(1), 21–37. doi:10.1108/10662240710730470

Everitt, B. S., & Skrondal, A. (2010). *The Cambridge Dictionary of Statistics*. Cambridge, UK: Cambridge University Press. doi:10.1017/CBO9780511779633

Falcon, A. (2017). *10 Crowdfunding Sites To Fuel Your Dream Project*. HongKiat. Available: https://www.hongkiat.com/blog/crowdfunding-sites/

Fang, W. (2007). Using Google Analytics for improving library website content and design: a case study. *Library Philosophy and Practice*, 1-17.

Fang, Y., Qureshi, I., Sun, H., McCole, P., Ramsey, E., & Lim, K. H. (2014). Trust, satisfaction, and online repurchase intention: The moderating role of perceived effectiveness of e-commerce institutional mechanisms. *Management Information Systems Quarterly*, *38*(2), 407–427. doi:10.25300/MISQ/2014/38.2.04

Fan, W., & Yan, Z. (2010). Factrors affecting response rates of the web surveys: A systematic review. *Computers in Human Behavior*, *26*(2), 132–138. doi:10.1016/j.chb.2009.10.015

Faraj, S., & Azad, B. (2012). The materiality of technology: An affordance perspective. In P. Leonardi, B. Nardi, & J. Kallinikos (Eds.), *Materiality and Organizing: Social interaction in a technological world*. Oxford University Press. doi:10.1093/acprof:oso/9780199664054.003.0012

Farid, A. (2017). Measures of reconfigurability and its key characteristics in intelligent manufacturing systems. *Journal of Intelligent Manufacturing*, *28*(2), 353–369. doi:10.100710845-014-0983-7

Faulkner, D., Teerikangas, S., & Joseph, R. J. (2012). The handbook of mergers and acquisitions. Oxford, UK: Academic Press. doi:10.1093/acprof:oso/9780199601462.001.0001

Fawcett, J., Ayers, D., & Quin, L. (2012). *Beginning XML*. Indianapolis, IN: John Wiley & Sons.

Fehler, M. (2005). Techniques for Analysis and Calibration of Multi-Agent Simulations. Lecture Notes Computer Science, 3451, 305-321. doi:10.1007/11423355_22

Feldstein, M. S. (1965). The derivation of social time preference rates. *Kyklos*, *18*(2), 277–287. doi:10.1111/j.1467-6435.1965.tb02482.x

Felluga, D. F. (2015). *Critical theory. The key concepts*. New York: Routledge. doi:10.4324/9781315718873

Feng, L., Zhang, X., & Zhou, K. (2018). Current problems in China's manufacturing and countermeasures for industry 4.0. *EURASIP Journal on Wireless Communications and Networking*, *2018*(1), 90. doi:10.118613638-018-1113-6

Fenwick, T. (2010). (Un)doing standards in education with actor-network theory. *Journal of Education Policy, 25*(2), 117–133. doi:10.1080/02680930903314277

Fenwick, T. (2011). Reading educational reform with actor network theory: Fluid spaces, otherings, and ambivalences. *Educational Philosophy and Theory, 43*(S1), 114–134. doi:10.1111/j.1469-5812.2009.00609.x

Fenwick, T., & Edwards, R. (2010). *Actor-network theory and education.* London: Routledge. doi:10.4324/9780203849088

Fenwick, T., & Edwards, R. (2011). Introduction: Reclaiming and renewing actor network theory for educational research. *Educational Philosophy and Theory, 43*(S1), 1–14. doi:10.1111/j.1469-5812.2010.00667.x

Fenwick, T., Edwards, R., & Sawchuk, P. (2011). *Emerging approaches to educational research: Tracing the sociomaterial.* London: Routledge.

Fenwick, T., & Landri, P. (2012). Materialities, textures and pedagogies: Socio-material assemblages in education. *Pedagogy, Culture & Society, 20*(1), 1–7. doi:10.1080/14681366.2012.649421

Ferdous, F., Chowdhury, M. M., & Bhuiyan, F. (2015). Barriers to the Implementation of Human Resource Information Systems. *Asian Journal of Management Sciences and Education, 4*(1), 33–43.

Ferrari, A. (2012). *Digital Competence in Practice: An Analysis of Frameworks.* Retrieved from Fillis, I., & Wagner, B. (2005). E-business development: An exploratory investigation of the small firm. *International Small Business Journal, 23*(6), 604–634.

Fielding, R., Taylor, R., Erenkrantz, J., Gorlick, M., Whitehead, J., Khare, R., & Oreizy, P. (2017). Reflections on the REST architectural style and principled design of the modern web architecture. In *Proceedings of the 2017 11th Joint Meeting on Foundations of Software Engineering* (pp. 4-14). New York, NY: ACM Press. 10.1145/3106237.3121282

Financial Conduct Authority. (2015). *A review of the regulatory regime for crowdfunding and the promotion of non-readily realisable securities by other media.* Available at: www.fca.org.uk/static/documents/crowdfunding-review.pdf

Fine, B. (2005). From actor-network theory to political economy. *Capitalism, Nature, Socialism, 16*(4), 91–108. doi:10.1080/10455750500376057

Finkl, K., & Ploder, C. (2009). Knowledge Management Toolkit for SMEs. *International Journal of Knowledge Management, 5*(1), 46–60. doi:10.4018/jkm.2009010104

Finne, T. (1998). Special Feature: A Conceptual Framework for Information Security Management. *Computers & Security, 17*(4), 303–307. doi:10.1016/S0167-4048(98)80010-2

Fischer, E., & Reuber, R. (2003). *Competitiveness Strategy in Developing Countries: A Manuel for Policy Analysis* (G. Wignaraja, Ed.). London: Routledge.

Fishburn, P. (1978). *Theory of utility for decision-making.* Moscow: Science.

Fishburn, P. C. (1966). Stationary value mechanisms and expected utility theory. *Journal of Mathematical Psychology, 3*(2), 434–457. doi:10.1016/0022-2496(66)90023-X

Fishburn, P. C. (1968). Utility theory. *Management Science, 14*(5), 335–378. doi:10.1287/mnsc.14.5.335

Fisher, R. J. (1993). Social desirability bias and the validity of indirect questioning. *The Journal of Consumer Research, 20*(2), 303–315. doi:10.1086/209351

Fitzgerald, J. L., & Hamilton, M. (1997). Confidentiality, disseminated regulation and ethico-legal liabilities in research with hidden populations of illicit drug users. *Addiction (Abingdon, England)*, *92*(9), 1099–1107. doi:10.1111/j.1360-0443.1997. tb03667.x PMID:9374006

Fitzgerald, T. (2007). Building Management Commitment through Security Councils, or Security Council Critical Success Factors. In H. F. Tipton (Ed.), *Information Security Management Handbook* (pp. 105–121). Hoboken, NJ: Auerbach Publications.

Flaherty, D. (1989). *Protecting privacy in surveillance societies: The federal republic of Germany, Sweden, France, Canada, and the United States*. Chapel Hill, NC: The University of North Carolina Press.

Fleck, L. (1981). Genesis and development of a scientific fact. Chicago, IL: UP. doi:10.7208/chicago/9780226190341.001.0001

Flint & David. (2005). *The User's View of Why IT Projects Fail*. Gartner Report.

Fondevila Gascón, J. F., Rom Rodríguez, J., Mata Monforte, J., Santana López, E., & Masip Masip, P. (2015). Crowdfunding as a formula for the financing of projects: an empirical analysis. *Hermes Scientific Journal*. Available at: http://www.redalyc.org/articulo.oa?id=477647161003

Forbes, H., & Schaefer, D. (2017). Guidelines for successful crowdfunding. *Procedia CIRP*, *60*, 398–403. doi:10.1016/j.procir.2017.02.021

Forrester Research. (2017). *The digital transformation race has begun*. Retrieved March 5, 2019, from http://www.virtusadigital.com/wp-content/themes/the-box/images/digital-transformation/The%20Digital%20Transformation%20Race%20Has%20Begun.pdf

Forsyth, T. (2004). *Critical political ecology. The politics environmental science*. London, New York: Routledge. doi:10.4324/9780203017562

Fouad, N. A., & Santana, M. C. (2017). SCCT and Underrepresented Populations in STEM Fields: Moving the Needle. *Journal of Career Assessment*, *25*(1), 24–39. doi:10.1177/1069072716658324

Foucault, M. (1979). *Discipline and punish: The birth of the prison*. Harmondsworth, UK: Penguin.

Fouladi, R. T., Mccarthy, C. J., & Moller, N. P. (2002). Paper-and-pencil or online? Evaluating mode effects on measures of emotional functioning and attachment. *Assessment*, *9*(2), 204–215. doi:10.1177/1073191102009002011 PMID:12066835

Fountain, R. M. (1999). Socio-scientific issues via actor network theory. *Journal of Curriculum Studies*, *31*(3), 339–358. doi:10.1080/002202799183160

Fowler, F. J. (2002). Survey research methods (3rd ed.). Thousand Oaks, CA: Sage.

Fowler, R., Hodge, B., Kress, G., & Trew, T. (1979). *Language and control*. London: Routledge.

Fraillon, J., Ainley, J., Schulz, W., Friedman, T., & Gebhardt, E. (2014). *Preparing for Life in a Digital Age – The IEA International Computer and Information Literacy Study. International Report*. Amsterdam: IEA.

Francis, J. J., Johnston, M., Robertson, C., Glidewall, L., Entwistle, V., Eccles, M. P., & Grimshaw, J. M. (2010). What is an adequate sample size? Operationalizing Data Saturation for Theory-based Interview Studies. *Psychology & Health*, *25*(10), 1229–1245. doi:10.1080/08870440903194015 PMID:20204937

Frankham, J. (2006). Network utopias and alternative entanglements for educational research and practice. *Journal of Education Policy*, *21*(6), 661–677. doi:10.1080/02680930600969191

Frederick, S., Loewenstein, G., & O'Donoghue, T. (2002). Time discounting and time preference: A critical review. *Journal of Economic Literature, 40*(2), 351–401. doi:10.1257/jel.40.2.351

Frey, R. S. (2001). Knowledge Management, Proposal Development, and Small Businesses. *Journal of Management Development, 20*(1), 38–54. doi:10.1108/02621710110365041

Friend, C. (2019). Social contract theory. *Internet Encyclopedia of Philosophy*. Retrieved February 4, 2019, from https://www.iep.utm.edu/soc-cont/

Furner, C. P., Racherla, P., & Zhu, Z. (2014). A multinational study of espoused national cultural and review characteristics in the formation of trust in online product reviews. *International Journal of Services Technology and Management, 20*(1-3), 14-30.

Furner, C. P. (2013). Cultural determinants of information processing shortcuts in computer supported groups: A review, research agenda and instrument validation. *International Journal of Information Systems and Social Change, 4*(3), 17–32. doi:10.4018/jissc.2013070102

Furner, C. P., & George, J. F. (2009). Making it hard to lie: Cultural determinants of media choice for deception. *Proceedings of the 42nd Hawaii International Conference on System Sciences*.

Furner, C. P., & George, J. F. (2012). Cultural determinants of media choice for deception. *Computers in Human Behavior, 28*(4), 1427–1438. doi:10.1016/j.chb.2012.03.005

Furner, C. P., & Goh, S. H. (2013). Cultural Determinants of Socially Desirable Distortion in Computer Based Data Collection: A Multicultural Investigation. *International Journal of Social and Organizational Dynamics in IT, 3*(3), 51–67. doi:10.4018/ijsodit.2013070104

Furner, C. P., Mason, R. M., Mehta, N., Munyon, T. P., & Zinko, R. A. (2009). Cultural determinants of learning effectivness from knowledge management systems: A multinational investigation. *Journal of Global Information Technology Management, 12*(1), 30–51. doi:10.1080/1097198X.2009.10856484

Furner, C. P., & Zinko, R. A. (2017). The influence of information overload on the development of trust and purchase intention based on online product reviews in a mobile vs. web environment: An empirical investigation. *Electronic Markets, 27*(3), 211–224. doi:10.100712525-016-0233-2

Fyfe, T., & Crookall, P. (2010). *Social Media and Public Sector Policy Dilemmas*. Academic Press.

Galiani, S., Gertler, P., & Bando, R. (2016). Non-Contributory Pensions. *Labour Economics, 38*, 47–58. doi:10.1016/j.labeco.2015.11.003

Galpin, V. C. (2002). Women in Computing Around the World. *ACM SIGCSE Bulletin, 34*(2), 94–100. doi:10.1145/543812.543839

Gambardella, T. (2018). Gearing up to meet GDPR compliance requirements. *TechTarget*. Retrieved February 15, 2019, from https://searchcompliance.techtarget.com/video/Gearing-up-to-meet-GDPR-compliance-requirements

Ganguly, B., Dash, S. B., Cyr, D., & Head, M. (2010). The effects of website design on purchase intention in online shopping: The mediating role of trust and the moderating role of culture. *International Journal of Electronic Business, 8*(4-5), 302–330. doi:10.1504/IJEB.2010.035289

Gantz, J., Boyd, A., & Dowling, S. (2009). *Cutting the clutter: tackling information overload at the source*. IDC. Retrieved March 2, 2019, from https://www.xerox.com/assets/motion/corporate/pages/programs/information-overload/pdf/Xerox-white-paper-3-25.pdf

García del Junco, J., & García, R. (1995). Análisis de las principales capacidades de la gestión empresarial. *Dirección y Organización*, (13), 32-44.

Garcia, M. (2015). A process for developing efficient agent-based simulators. *Engineering Applications of Artificial Intelligence*, *46*, 104–112. doi:10.1016/j.engappai.2015.09.003

Garcia, M. (2016a). A hybrid approach with agent-based simulation and clustering for sociograms. *Inf. Sci.*, *345*, 81–95. doi:10.1016/j.ins.2016.01.063

Garcia, M. (2016b). A technique for automatically training agent-based simulators. *Simulation Modelling Practice and Theory*, *66*, 174–192. doi:10.1016/j.simpat.2016.04.003

Garcia, M. (2017). A technique for developing agent-based simulation apps and online tools with nondeterministic decisions. *Simulation Modelling Practice and Theory*, *77*, 84–107. doi:10.1016/j.simpat.2017.05.006

Gareau, B. J. (2005). We have never been human: Agential nature, ANT, and marxist political economy. *Capitalism, Nature, Socialism*, *16*(4), 127–140. doi:10.1080/10455750500376081

Gartner Report. (2017). *Gartner says worldwide public cloud services market to grow 18 percent in 2017*. Retrieved March 2, 2019, from https://www.gartner.com/newsroom/id/3616417

Gately, C. G., & Cunningham, J. A. (2014). Building Intellectual Capital in Incubated Technology Firms. *Journal of Intellectual Capital*, *15*(4), 516–536. doi:10.1108/JIC-07-2014-0087

Gaudeul, A., & Giannetti, C. (2017). The effect of privacy concerns and social network formation. *Journal of Economic Behavior & Organization*, *141*, 233–253. doi:10.1016/j.jebo.2017.07.007

Gbandi, E. C., & Amissah, G. (2014). Financing options for small and medium enterprises (SMEs) in Nigeria. *European Scientific Journal*, *10*(1), 327–340.

Gębczyńska, A. (2016). Strategy implementation efficiency on the process level. *Business Process Management Journal*, *22*(6), 1079–1098. doi:10.1108/BPMJ-01-2016-0004

Geetika, R., & Singh, P. (2014). Dynamic coupling metrics for object oriented software systems: A survey. *Software Engineering Notes*, *39*(2), 1–8. doi:10.1145/2579281.2579296

GEM Bogota. (2018). *GEM report Bogotá*. Secretaria Distrital de Desarrollo Economico de Bogota in alliance with EAN University.

Geng, R., Afshin Mansouri, S., & Aktas, E. (2017). The relationship between green supply chain management and performance: A meta-analysis of empirical evidences in Asian emerging economies. *International Journal of Production Economics*, *183*, 245–258. doi:10.1016/j.ijpe.2016.10.008

Gentner, D. (2002). The psychology of mental models. In N. J. Smelser & P. B. Bates (Eds.), *International encyclopedia of the social and behavioral sciences* (pp. 9683–9687). Amsterdam: Elsevier.

George, A. L., & Bennett, A. (2005). *Case Studies and Theory Development in Social Sciences*. Cambridge, MA: MIT Press.

Gerlmaier, A. (2011). Stress and burnout among IT professionals – searching for causes. In Burnout in der IT-Branche (pp. 53-89). Kröning: Asanger.

Ghauri, P., Hadjikhani, A., & Elg, U. (2012). The three pillars: Business, state and society: MNCs in emerging markets. In Business, Society and Politics (pp. 3-16). Emerald Group Publishing Limited.

Ghauri, P. N., & Grønhaug, K. (2005). *Research methods in business studies: A practical guide.* Pearson Education.

Ghobakhloo, M., & Azar, A. (2018). Business excellence via advanced manufacturing technology and lean-agile manufacturing. *Journal of Manufacturing Technology Management, 29*(1), 2–24. doi:10.1108/JMTM-03-2017-0049

Ghobakhloo, M., Azar, A., & Fathi, M. (2018). Lean-green manufacturing: The enabling role of information technology resource. *Kybernetes, 47*(9), 1752–1777. doi:10.1108/K-09-2017-0343

Ghobakhloo, M., Tang, S., Sabouri, M., & Zulkifli, N. (2014). The impact of information system-enabled supply chain process integration on business performance: A resource-based analysis. *International Journal of Information Technology & Decision Making, 13*(05), 1075–1113. doi:10.1142/S0219622014500163

Giachi, S. (2014). Dimensiones sociales del fraude fiscal: Confianza y moral fiscal en la España contemporánca. *Revista Espanola de Investigaciones Sociologicas, 145*, 73–98.

Giacomazzi, F., Panella, C., Pernici, B., & Sansoni, M. (1997). Information systems integration in mergers and acquisitions. A normative model. *Information & Management, 32*(6), 289–302. doi:10.1016/S0378-7206(97)00031-1

Gibson, J. (1986). *The ecological approach to visual perception.* Hillsdale, NJ: Lawrence Erlbaum.

Gigerenzer, G. (2014). *Risk savvy: How to make good decisions.* New York, NY: Viking.

Gigerenzer, G. (2016). Towards a rational theory of heuristics. In R. Frantz & L. Marsh (Eds.), *Minds, models and milieux: Commemorating the centennial of the birth of Herbert Simon.* Basingstoke, UK: Palgrave Macmillan. doi:10.1057/9781137442505_3

Giovanis, A. N., & Athanasopoulou, P. (2014). Gaining customer loyalty in the e-tailing marketplace: the role of e-service quality, e-satisfaction and e-trust. *International Journal of Technology Marketing, 9*(3), 288-304.

Gleasure, R., & Feller, J. (2016). A rift in the ground: Theorizing the evolution of anchor values in crowdfunding communities through the oculus rift case study. *Journal of the Association for Information Systems, 17*(10), 708–736. doi:10.17705/1jais.00439

Gliem, J. A., & Gliem, R. R. (2003). Calculating, Interpreting, and Reporting Cronbach's Alpha Reliability Coefficient for Likert-Type Scales. Academic Press.

Globalwebindex. (2018). Social: Flagship Report 2018. *Globalwebindex.* Retrieved March 4, 2019, from https://www.globalwebindex.com/hubfs/Downloads/Social-H2-2018-report.pdf

Gomart, E., & Hennion, A. (1999). A sociology of attachment: Music amateurs, drug users. In J. Law & J. Hassard (Eds.), *Actor network theory and after* (pp. 220–247). Oxford: Blackwell. doi:10.1111/j.1467-954X.1999.tb03490.x

Gómez-Plana, A. G., & Arzoz, P. P. (2011). Fraude Fiscal e IVA en España: Incidencia en un modelo de equilibrio general. *Hacienda Pública Española, 199*(4), 9–52.

Gong, W., Stump, R. L., & Maddox, L. M. (2013). Factors influencing consumers' online shopping in China. *Journal of Asia Business Studies, 7*(3), 214–230. doi:10.1108/JABS-02-2013-0006

González, J. (2009). *Teoría del desarrollo económico neoinstitucional. Una alternativa a la pobreza en el siglo XXI.* Porrua.

Goodman, S. E., & Ramer, R. (2007). Global Sourcing of IT Services and Information Security: Prudence before Playing. *Communications of the Association for Information Systems, 20*(1), 812–823.

Gosling, S. D., Vazire, S., Srivastava, S., & John, O. P. (2004). Should we trust Web-based studies? A comparative analysis of six preconceptions about Internet questionnaires. *The American Psychologist*, *59*(2), 93–104. doi:10.1037/0003-066X.59.2.93 PMID:14992636

Graebner, M. E., Heimeriks, K. H., Huy, Q. N., & Vaara, E. (2017). The process of postmerger integration: A review and agenda for future research. *The Academy of Management Annals*, *11*(1), 1–32. doi:10.5465/annals.2014.0078

Graydon, P., Habli, I., Hawkins, R., Kelly, T., & Knight, J. (2012). Arguing Conformance. *IEEE Software*, *29*(3), 50–57. doi:10.1109/MS.2012.26

Grebe, A., Spöhrer, M., & Stock, R. (2018). Popular narratives of the cochlear implant. In A. Görgen, G. Alfonso Nunez, & H. Fangerau (Eds.), *Handbook of popular culture and biomedicine. Knowledge in the life sciences as cultural artefact* (pp. 229–243). Cham: Springer.

Greenberg, A., & Collins, S. (1966). Paired comparison taste tests: Some food for thought. *JMR, Journal of Marketing Research*, *3*(1), 76–80. doi:10.1177/002224376600300109

Greenfield, P. M. (2016). Social Change, Cultural Evolution, and Human Development. *Current Opinion in Psychological*, *8*, 84–92. doi:10.1016/j.copsyc.2015.10.012 PMID:29506809

Green, L., Fry, A. F., & Myerson, J. (1994). Discounting of delayed rewards: A life-span comparison. *Psychological Science*, *5*(1), 33–36. doi:10.1111/j.1467-9280.1994.tb00610.x

Green, L., & Myerson, J. (2004). A discounting framework for choice with delayed and probabilistic rewards. *Psychological Bulletin*, *130*(5), 769–792. doi:10.1037/0033-2909.130.5.769 PMID:15367080

Gregor, S. (2006). The Nature of Theory in Information Systems. *Management Information Systems Quarterly*, *30*(3), 611–642. doi:10.2307/25148742

Greiner, M. E., Hmann, T. B., & Krcmar, H. (2007). A strategy for knowledge management. *Journal of Knowledge Management*, *11*(6), 3–15. doi:10.1108/13673270710832127

Grewal, D., Levy, M., & Kumar, V. (2009). Customer experience management in retailing: An organizing framework. *Journal of Retailing*, *85*(1), 1–14. doi:10.1016/j.jretai.2009.01.001

Griffith, T. L. (1999). Technology Features as Triggers for Sensemaking. *Academy of Management Review*, *24*(3), 472–488. doi:10.5465/amr.1999.2202132

Grimm, C., & Smith, K. (1997). *Strategy as action: Industry rivalry and coordination*. Cincinnati, OH: South-Western College Publishing.

Grint, K. (2004). Actor network theory. In G. Goethals, G. Sorensen, & J. MacGregor (Eds.), Encyclopaedia of leadership (pp. 5-8). Burns: Sage. doi:10.4135/9781412952392.n3

Grullon, G., Kanatas, G., & Weston, J. (2009). *Religion and Corporate (Mis)Behavior*. doi:10.2139srn.1472118

Grzeda, M. (1999). Career development and emerging managerial career patterns. *Journal of Career Development*, *25*(4), 233–247. doi:10.1177/089484539902500401

Guay, F., Marsh, H. W., & Boivin, M. (2003). Academic self-concept and academic achievement: Developmental perspectives on their causal ordering. *Journal of Educational Psychology*, *95*(1), 124–136. doi:10.1037/0022-0663.95.1.124

Gulaid, L. A., & Kiragu, K. (2012). Lessons learnt from promising practices in community engagement for the elimination of new HIV infections in children by 2015 and keeping their mothers alive: summary of a desk review. *Journal of the International AIDS Society, 15*.

Gunter, U., & Önder, I. (2016). Forecasting city arrivals with Google Analytics. *Annals of Tourism Research, 61*, 199–212. doi:10.1016/j.annals.2016.10.007

Gupta, B. (2013). Human Resource Information System (HRIS): Important Element of Current Scenario. *IOSR Journal of Business and Management, 13*(6), 41–46. doi:10.9790/487X-1364146

Haak-Saheem, W., & Darwish, K. T. (2014). The role of knowledge management in creating a culture of learning. Management Decision, 52(9), 1611–1629.

Haas, M. R., Criscuolo, P., & George, G. (2015). Which problems to solve? Online knowledge sharing and attention allocation in organizations. Academy of Management Journal, 58, 680–711. doi:10.5465/amj.2013.0263

Habeeb, S., & Sudhakar, K. F. (2019). Analyzing Causality Among the Service Quality, Customer Satisfaction and Behavioral Intention Variables with Respect to E-Shopping: An Empirical Take. *International Journal of Online Marketing, 9*(1), 38–59. doi:10.4018/IJOM.2019010103

Hacisalihzade, S., & Mansour, M. (1985). Solution of the multiple dosing problem using linear programming. *International Journal of Bio-Medical Computing, 17*(1), 57–67. doi:10.1016/0020-7101(85)90073-X PMID:3840459

Hackett, G., & Betz, N. E. (1989). An exploration of the mathematics self-efficacy/mathematics performance correspondence. *Journal for Research in Mathematics Education, 20*(3), 261–273. doi:10.2307/749515

Hackett, G., Esposito, D., & O'Halloran, M. S. (1989). The relationship of role model influences to the career salience and educational and career plans of college women. *Journal of Vocational Behavior, 35*(2), 164–180. doi:10.1016/0001-8791(89)90038-9

Hadjikhani, A., Lee, J. W., & Ghauri, P. N. (2008). Network view of MNCs' sociopolitical behavior. *Journal of Business Research, 61*(9), 912–924. doi:10.1016/j.jbusres.2007.10.001

Hadjikhani, A., Lee, J. W., & Park, S. (2016). Corporate social responsibility as a marketing strategy in foreign markets: The case of Korean MNCs in the Chinese electronics market. *International Marketing Review, 33*(4), 530–554. doi:10.1108/IMR-03-2014-0104

Hadjikhani, A., Leite, E., & Pahlberg, C. (2019). Business and Socio-Political Interaction in International Service Projects: The Case of Brazil. *Management International Review, 59*(1), 171–200. doi:10.100711575-018-0368-9

Hadjikhani, A., & Thilenius, P. (2005). 'The impact of horizontal and vertical connections on relationships' commitment and trust'. *Journal of Business and Industrial Marketing, 20*(3), 136–147. doi:10.1108/08858620510592759

Haferkamp, N., & Krämer, N. C. (2011). Social comparison 2.0: Examining the effects of online profiles on social-networking sites. *Cyberpsychology, Behavior, and Social Networking, 14*(5), 309–314. doi:10.1089/cyber.2010.0120 PMID:21117976

Ha, H. Y., Janda, S., & Muthaly, S. K. (2010). A new understanding of satisfaction model in e-re-purchase situation. *European Journal of Marketing, 44*(7/8), 997–1016. doi:10.1108/03090561011047490

Ha, H. Y., Muthaly, S. K., & Akamavi, R. K. (2010). Alternative explanations of online repurchasing behavioral intentions: A comparison study of Korean and UK young customers. *European Journal of Marketing, 44*(6), 874–904. doi:10.1108/03090561011032757

Haines, V. Y., & Petit, A. (1997). Conditions for Successful Human Resource Information System. *Human Resource Management, 36*(2), 261–275. doi:10.1002/(SICI)1099-050X(199722)36:2<261::AID-HRM7>3.0.CO;2-V

Hair, J. F., Anderson, R. E., Tatham, R. L., & Black, W. C. (1998). *Multivariate data analysis* (5th ed.). Upper Saddle River, NJ: Prentice Hall.

Hair, J. H., Babin, B. J., Anderson, R. E., & Tatham, R. L. (2006). *Multivariate Data Analysis.* Pearson Prentice Hall.

Håkansson, H., & Snehota, I. (1995). *Developing relationships in business networks.* Academic Press.

Håkansson, H., & Snehota, I. (2006). "No business is an island" 17 years later. *Scandinavian Journal of Management, 22*(3), 271–274. doi:10.1016/j.scaman.2006.08.001

Hallikainen, H., & Laukkanen, T. (2018). National culture and consumer trust in e-commerce. *International Journal of Information Management, 38*(1), 97–106. doi:10.1016/j.ijinfomgt.2017.07.002

Hamburg, I. (2019). Implementation of a digital workplace strategy to drive behavior change and improve competencies. In *Strategy and Behaviors in the Digital Economy.* IntechOpen. Retrieved May 16, 2019 from https://www.researchgate. net/publication/332494626_Implementation_of_a_Digital_ orkplace_Strategy_to_Drive_Behavior_Change_and_Improve_Competencies

Hammer, M., & Champy, J. (1993). *Reengineering the Corporation: A Manifesto for Business Revolution.* New York: HarperCollins.

Hansen, A. (2006). Do declining discount rates lead to time inconsistent economic advice? *Ecological Economics, 60*(1), 138–144. doi:10.1016/j.ecolecon.2006.03.007

Harbaugh, E. R. (2010). The effect of personality styles (level of introversion-extroversion) on social media use. *The Elon Journal of Undergraduate Research in Communications, 1*(2), 70–86.

Harison, E., & Boonstra, A. (2009). Essential competencies for technochange management: Towards an assessment model. *International Journal of Information Management, 29*(4), 283–294. doi:10.1016/j.ijinfomgt.2008.11.003

Harris, J. (2018). Ethical issues in social networking. *Cariblogger.* Retrieved April 7, 2018, from https://cariblogger. com/ethical-issues-in-social-networking/

Harris, S., & Spencer, E. (2015). *2015-2016 HR Systems Survey* (18th ed.). Academic Press.

Harrison, A., Wheeler, P., & Whitehead, C. (2004). *The Distributed Workplace: Sustainable Work Environments.* London: Spon Press.

Harrison, G. W., Lau, M. I., & Williams, M. B. (2002). Estimating individual discount rates in Denmark: A field experiment. *The American Economic Review, 92*(5), 1606–1617. doi:10.1257/000282802762024674

Hartford Business. (2014). *Millennials to take over by 2025.* Retrieved March 4, 2019. From http://www.hartfordbusiness.com/article/20140818/PRINTEDITION/140819969/millennials-to-take-over-by-2025

Harton, H., Green, L., Jackson, C., & Latane, B. (1998). Demonstrating Dynamic Social Impact: Consolidation, Clustering, Correlation, and (Sometimes) the Correct Answer. *Teaching of Psychology, 25*(1), 31–35. doi:10.120715328023top2501_9

Hartwick, E. R. (2000). Towards a geographical politics of consumption. *Environment & Planning A, 32*(7), 1177–1192. doi:10.1068/a3256

Ha, S., & Stoel, L. (2012). Online apparel retailing: Roles of e-shopping quality and experiential e-shopping motives. *Journal of Service Management, 23*(2), 197–215. doi:10.1108/09564231211226114

Haskins, B., & Nilssen, A. (2015). The collaborative enterprise: how enterprises are adapting to support the modern meeting. *Wainhouse Research*. Retrieved March 2, 2019, from https://www.logitech.com/assets/65076/wainhouse-wp-the-collaborative-enterprise.pdf

Haspeslagh, P. C., & Jemison, D. B. (1991). *Managing Acquisitions: Creating Value through Corporate Renewal*. Free Press.

Hassan, S. (2011). Friendship dynamics: Modeling social relationships through a fuzzy agent-based simulation. *Discrete Dynamics in Nature and Society, 2*, 118–124.

Hatlevik, O. E., Throndsen, I., Loi, M., & Gudmundsdottir, G. B. (2018). Students' ICT self-efficacy and computer and information literacy: Determinants and relationships. *Computers & Education, 118*, 107–119. doi:10.1016/j.compedu.2017.11.011

Hawk, S. T., van den Eijnden, R. J., van Lissa, C. J., & ter Bogt, T. F. M. (2019). Narcissistic adolescents' attention-seeking following social rejection: Links with social media disclosure, problematic social media use, and smartphone stress. *Computers in Human Behavior, 92*, 65–75. doi:10.1016/j.chb.2018.10.032

Hedger, M. M., Mitchell, T., Leavy, J., Greeley, M., & Downie, A. (2008). *Desk review: evaluation of adaptation to climate change from a development perspective*. Available: http://citeseerx.ist.psu.edu/viewdoc/download?doi=10.1.1.575.1027&rep=rep1&type=pdf

Hedges, L. V., & Olkin, I. (1985). *Statistical methods for meta-analysis*. Orlando, FL: Academic Press.

He, J., & Freeman, L. A. (2010). Are men more technology-oriented than women? The role of gender on the development of general computer self-efficacy of college students. *Journal of Information Systems Education, 21*, 203–212.

Helliwell, J. F., & Putnam, R. D. (2004). *The social context of well- being*. Philos. doi:10.1098/rstb.2004.1522

Helokunnas, T., & Kuusisto, R. (2003). Information Security Culture in a Value Net. *Engineering Management Conference, 2003. IEMC'03. Managing Technologically Driven Organizations: The Human Side of Innovation and Change*. 10.1109/IEMC.2003.1252258

Henderson, C., Evans-Lacko, S., Flach, C., & Thornicroft, G. (2012). Responses to mental health stigma questions: The importance of social desirability and collection method. *Canadian Journal of Psychiatry, 57*(3), 152–160. doi:10.1177/070674371205700304 PMID:22398001

Henderson, N., & Bateman, I. (1995). Empirical and public choice evidence for hyperbolic social discounting rates and the implications for intergenerational discounting. *Environmental and Resource Economics, 5*(4), 413–423. doi:10.1007/BF00691577

Henningsson, S., Yetton, P. W., & Wynne, P. J. (2018). A review of information system integration in mergers and acquisitions. *Journal of Information Technology*, 1–49.

Hennion, A., & Gomart, É. (1999). A sociology of attachment: Music lovers, drug addicts. In J. Law & J. Hassard (Eds.), *Actor-network-theory and after* (pp. 220–247). Oxford, UK: Blackwell.

Herath, T., & Rao, H. R. (2009a). Encouraging information security behaviors in organizations: Role of penalties, pressures and perceived effectiveness. *Decision Support Systems, 47*(2), 154–165. doi:10.1016/j.dss.2009.02.005

Herath, T., & Rao, H. R. (2009b). Protection motivation and deterrence: A framework for security policy compliance in organisations. *European Journal of Information Systems, 18*(2), 106–125. doi:10.1057/ejis.2009.6

Hermann-Röttgen, M. (2010). *Cochlea-Implantat: Ein Ratgeber für Betroffene und Therapeuten*. Trias.

Hernandez, A., & Resnick, M. (2013). Placement of Call to Action Buttons for Higher Website Conversion and Acquisition. *Proceedings of the Human Factors and Ergonomics Society Annual Meeting, 57*(1), 1042–1046. doi:10.1177/1541931213571232

Hernaus, T., Vukšić, V. B., & Štemberger, M. I. (2016). How to go from strategy to results? Institutionalising BPM governance within organisations. *Business Process Management Journal, 22*(1), 173–195. doi:10.1108/BPMJ-03-2015-0031

Herrmann & Jahnke. (2007). Work Process Oriented Introduction of Knowledge Management: Reconsidering the Guidelines for SME. In *I-KNOW '07. 7th International Conference on Knowledge Management*. Graz, Austria: Know-Center.

Hertwig, R., & Gigerenzer, G. (2011). Behavioral inconsistencies do not imply inconsistent strategies. *Frontiers in Psychology, 2*(292), 1–3. PMID:22110447

Hetherington, K., & Law, J. (2000). After networks. *Environment and Planning D. Space and Society, 18*, 127–132.

He, W., & Da Xu, L. (2014). Integration of distributed enterprise applications: A survey. *IEEE Transactions on Industrial Informatics, 10*(1), 35–42. doi:10.1109/TII.2012.2189221

Heyman, G. M. (1996). Resolving the contradictions of addiction. *Behavioral and Brain Sciences, 19*(4), 591–610. doi:10.1017/S0140525X00042990

Hickson, D. J., Hinings, C. R., McMillan, C. J., & Schwitter, J. P. (1974). The culture free context of organization structure: A trinational comparison. *Sociology, 8*(1), 59–80. doi:10.1177/003803857400800104

Higgins, G. E., Wilson, A. L., & Fell, B. D. (2005). An application of deterrence theory to software piracy. *The Journal of Criminal Justice and Popular Culture, 12*(3), 166–184.

Higgins, R. C. (2012). *Analysis for financial management* (10th ed.). Irwin, NY: McGraw-Hill.

Hinings, B., Gegenhuber, T., & Greenwood, R. (2018). Digital innovation and transformation: An institutional perspective. *Information and Organization, 28*(1), 52–61. doi:10.1016/j.infoandorg.2018.02.004

Hirschheim, R., & Klein, H. K. (1989). Four Paradigms of Information Systems Development. *Association for Computing Machinery. Communications of the ACM, 32*(10), 1199–1216. doi:10.1145/67933.67937

Hirschhorn, L. (2002). Campaigning for Change. *Harvard Business Review, 80*(7), 98–104. PMID:12140858

Hitt, M. A., Harrison, J. S., & Ireland, R. D. (2001). *Mergers & acquisitions: A guide to creating value for stakeholders.* Oxford University Press.

Hoch, St., & Loewenstein, G. (1991). Time-inconsistent preferences and consumer self-control. *The Journal of Consumer Research, 17*(4), 492–507. doi:10.1086/208573

Hodges, A., Balkany, T. J., & Butts, S. L. (2001). Cochlear implants in congenitally deaf children. In M. L. Pensak (Ed.), *Controversies in otolaryngology* (pp. 417–433). New York, NY: Thieme.

Hofstede, G. (2001). *Culture's Consequences: comparing values, behaviors, institutions, and organizations across nations* (2nd ed.). Thousand Oaks, CA: Sage.

Hofstede, G., Neuijen, B., Ohayv, D., & Sanders, G. (1990). Measuring organizational cultures: A qualitative and quantitative study across twenty cases. *Administrative Science Quarterly, 35*(2), 286–316. doi:10.2307/2393392

Hogg & Tindale. (n.d.). *Blackwell Handbook of Social Psychology: Group Processes.* John Wiley.

Holifeld, R. (2009). Actor-network theory as a critical approach in environmental justice: A case against synthesis with urban political ecology. *Antipode, 41*(4), 637–658. doi:10.1111/j.1467-8330.2009.00692.x

Holland, J. L. (1959). A theory of vocational choice. *Journal of Counseling Psychology, 6*(1), 35–45. doi:10.1037/h0040767

Holt-Lunstad, J., Smith, T. B., & Layton, J. B. (2010). Social relationships and mortality risk: A meta-analytic review. *PLoS Medicine, 7*(7), e1000316. doi:10.1371/journal.pmed.1000316 PMID:20668659

Hong, K. S., Chi, Y. P., Chao, L. R., & Tang, J. H. (2006). An empirical study of information security policy on information security elevation in Taiwan. *Information Management & Computer Security, 14*(2), 104–115. doi:10.1108/09685220610655861

Hoof, F., Jung, E.-M., & Salascheck, U. (2011). *Jenseits des Labors: Transformationen von Wissen zwischen Entstehungs- und Anwendungskontext.* Bielefeld: Transcript. doi:10.14361/transcript.9783839416037

Horberg, E. J., Oveis, C., & Keltner, D. (2011). Emotions as moral amplifiers: An appraisal tendency approach to the influences of distinct emotions upon moral judgments. *Emotion Review, 3*(3), 237–244. doi:10.1177/1754073911402384

Hörl, E. (2017). *General ecology: The new ecological paradigm.* London: Bloomsbury.

Hornsby, J. (2007). *An empirical investigation of the effects of discounting on privacy related decisions* (Dissertation). Nova Southeastern University.

Horowitz, J. K., & Carson, R. T. (1990). Discounting statistical lives. *Journal of Risk and Uncertainty, 3*(4), 403–413. doi:10.1007/BF00353349

Hosnavi, R., & Ramezan, M. (2010). Measuring the effectiveness of Human Resource Information System in National Iranian Oil Company. *Education, Business and Society, 3*(1), 28–39. doi:10.1108/17537981011022797

House, R., Javidan, M., Hanges, P., & Dorfman, P. W. (2002). Understanding cultures and implicit leadership theories across the globe: An introduction to the GLOBE project. *Journal of World Business, 30*(1), 3–10. doi:10.1016/S1090-9516(01)00069-4

Hoyos, T. A. (2014). Innovación y cambio tecnológico en la sociedad del conocimiento (2nd ed.). Ediciones ECOE, Universidad de la Sabana.

HRIS Technology Trends and Next-Generation Needs. (2015). Retrieved from https://www.comparehris.com/hris-technology-trends-and-next-generation-needs/

HRIS Trends for 2017. (2017). Retrieved from https://www.peoplematters.in/article/hcm-hrms-hris/hris-trends-for-2017-15025

Hsi, S. (2007). Conceptualizing learning from the everyday activities of digital kids. *International Journal of Science Education, 29*(12), 1509–1529. doi:10.1080/09500690701494076

Hsu, C. L., Wu, C. C., & Chen, M. C. (2013). An empirical analysis of the antecedents of e-satisfaction and e-loyalty: Focusing on the role of flow and its antecedents. *Information Systems and e-Business Management, 11*(2), 287–311. doi:10.100710257-012-0194-8

Huang, Y.-H., & Gramopadhye, A. K. (2016). Recommendations for health information technology implementation in rural hospitals. *International Journal of Health Care Quality Assurance, 29*(4), 454–474. doi:10.1108/IJHCQA-09-2015-0115 PMID:27142953

Hug, F. A., Choudhary, I. N., & Klassen, R. D. (2016). Social management capabilities of multinational buying firms and their emerging market suppliers: An exploratory study of the clothing Industry. *Journal of Operations Management, 46*(1), 19–37. doi:10.1016/j.jom.2016.07.005

Hui, J. S., Gerber, E. M., & Gergle, D. (2014). Understanding and leveraging social networks for crowdfunding: opportunities and challenges. In *Proceedings of the 2014 conference on Designing interactive systems* (pp. 677-680). Academic Press. Available: https://collablab.northwestern.edu/pubs/DIS2014_HuiGerberGergle.pdf

Hui, J. S., Greenberg, M. D., & Gerber, E. M. (2014). Understanding the Role of Community in Crowdfunding Work. In *Proceedings of the 17th ACM conference on Computer supported cooperative work & social computing* (pp. 62-74). Available: https://dl.acm.org/citation.cfm?id=2531715

Hu, L.-T., & Bentler, P. M. (1999). Cutoff criteria for fit indexes in covariance structure analysis: Conventional criteria versus new alternatives. *Structural Equation Modeling*, *6*(1), 1–55. doi:10.1080/10705519909540118

Hulme, A. (2014, June). Consumer credit roundup. *Credit Management*, 32–33.

Hüls, R. (1999). *Geschichte der Hörakustik: 2000 Jahre Hören und Hörhilfe*. Heidelberg, Germany: Median.

Hultin, L., & Mähring, M. (2014). Visualizing institutional logics in sociomaterial practices. *Information and Organization*, *24*(3), 129–155. doi:10.1016/j.infoandorg.2014.05.002

Iandoli, L., & Zollo, G. (2007). *Organizational Cognition and Learning. Building Systems for the Learning Organization*. New York: Information Science Publishing. doi:10.4018/978-1-59904-313-5

IBGE. (2016). *Aguas de Sao Pedro*. Retrieved May 8, 2019, from https://cidades.ibge.gov.br/brasil/sp/aguas-de-sao-pedro/panorama

IBM. (2019). Where does big data come from. *Big Data & Analytics Hub*. Retrieved January 21, 2019, from https://www.ibmbigdatahub.com/infographic/where-does-big-data-come

Ifinedo, P. (2012). Understanding information systems security policy compliance: An integration of the theory of planned behavior and the protection motivation theory. *Computers & Security*, *31*(1), 83–95. doi:10.1016/j.cose.2011.10.007

Ifinedo, P. (2014). Information systems security policy compliance: An empirical study of the effects of socialisation, influence, and cognition. *Information & Management*, *51*(1), 69–79. doi:10.1016/j.im.2013.10.001

Igloo. (2019). 2019 State of the digital workplace report. Retrieved June 18, 2019, from http://igloosoftware.lookbookhq.com/c/report-igloo-digital?x=QOKHau&_ga=2.218919897.1310781544.1560897722-686124159.1560897722

Igloo. (2017). Ro-Why: The business value of a digital workplace. Retrieved March 6, 2019, from https://www-cmswire.simplermedia.com/rs/706-YIA-261/images/RO_Why.pdf

Ignite, M. (2017). *Spark the Future*. Retrieved March 6, 2019, from https://slideplayer.com/slide/4875602/

Imache, R., Izza, S., & Ahmed-Nacer, M. (2012). An enterprise information system agility assessment model. *Computer Science and Information Systems*, *9*(1), 107–133. doi:10.2298/CSIS101110041I

Indrawati & Mas-Marhaeni. (2015). Predicting Instant Message Application Adoption using a Unified Theory of Acceptance & Use of Technology. *Proceedings of 5th International Conference on Computing and Informatics*.

Infocom. (2018). *Meetings in America: A study of trends, costs, and attitudes toward business travel and teleconferencing, and their impact on productivity*. A Verizon Conferencing White paper. Retrieved March 6, 2019, from https://e-meetings.verizonbusiness.com/global/en/meetingsinamerica/uswhitepaper.php#INTRODUCTION

International ICT Literacy Panel. (2007). *Digital Transformation. A Framework for ICT Literacy*. Author.

Invoice. (2019). *Best Crowdfunding Sites To Fund Your Business Ideas In Nigeria*. Available: https://invoice.ng/blog/best-crowdfunding-sites-in-nigeria/

ISACA. (2009). An Introduction to the Business Model for Information Security. *ISACA Journal*, 1–28.

Işik, Ö., Mertens, W., & Van den Bergh, J. (2013). Practices of knowledge intensive process management: Quantitative insights. *Business Process Management Journal*, *19*(3), 515–534. doi:10.1108/14637151311319932

ISO. (2006). *Enterprise integration -- Framework for enterprise modelling. ISO/CEN Standard 19439:2006*. Geneva, Switzerland: International Organization for Standardization.

ISO. (2010). *Systems and software engineering – Vocabulary. ISO/IEC/IEEE 24765:2010(E) International Standard*. Geneva, Switzerland: International Organization for Standardization.

Issa, T., Isaias, P., & Kommers, P. (2016). *Social Networking and Education: Global Perspectives*. Cham, Switzerland: Springer International Publishing. doi:10.1007/978-3-319-17716-8

ITU. (2017). *Global Cybersecurity Index (GCI) 2017*. ITU Report. doi:10.1111/j.1745-4514.2008.00161.x

Ivakhnenko, A., & Stepashko, V. (1985). *Noise-immunity modeling*. Kiev: Naukova dumka.

Iwe, C., & Bendict, H. (2013). Economic recession and investment on Human Resource Information Systems (HRIS). Perspectives on some South African firms. *Journal of Management Development*, *32*(4), 404–418. doi:10.1108/02621711311326383

Iyengar, S., & Brooks, R. (Eds.). (2016). *Distributed sensor networks: sensor networking and applications*. Boca Raton, FL: CRC Press.

Iyengar, S., & Kinder, D. R. (1987). *News that matter*. London: University of Chicago Press.

Iyer, A. (2018). Moving from Industry 2.0 to Industry 4.0: A case study from India on leapfrogging in smart manufacturing. *Procedia Manufacturing*, *21*, 663–670. doi:10.1016/j.promfg.2018.02.169

Jaafar, N. I., & Ajis, A. (2013). Organizational Climate and Individual Factors Effects on Information Security Faculty of Business and Accountancy *International Journal of Business and Social Science*, *4*(10), 118–131.

Jahan, S. (2014). Human Resources Information System (HRIS): A Theoretical Perspective. *Journal of Human Resource and Sustainability Studies*, *2*(02), 33–39. doi:10.4236/jhrss.2014.22004

Jain, S., Shao, G., & Shin, S. J. (2017). Manufacturing data analytics using a virtual factory representation. *International Journal of Production Research*, *55*(18), 5450–5464. doi:10.1080/00207543.2017.1321799 PMID:28924330

Jakob, W., & Blume, C. (2014). Pareto Optimization or Cascaded Weighted Sum: A Comparison of Concepts. *Algorithms*, *7*(1), 166–185. doi:10.3390/a7010166

Janeš, A. (2014). Empirical verification of the balanced scorecard. *Industrial Management & Data Systems*, *114*(2), 203–219. doi:10.1108/IMDS-04-2013-0195

Janeš, A., Biloslavo, R., & Faganel, A. (2017). Sustainable business model: A case study of Fonda.si. *Annales Series Historia et Sociologia*, *27*(1), 175–190.

Janiesch, C., Matzner, M., & Müller, O. (2012). Beyond process monitoring: A proof-of-concept of event-driven business activity management. *Business Process Management Journal*, *18*(4), 625–643. doi:10.1108/14637151211253765

Jankowski, J. (2013). Increasing Website Conversions Using Content Repetitions with Different Levels of Persuasion. *Intelligent Information and Database Systems*, 439-448. doi:10.1007/978-3-642-36543-0_45

Jeffery, M., & Leliveld, I. (2004). Best practices in IT portfolio management. *MIT Sloan Management Review*, *45*(3), 41–49.

Jegelevičiūtė, S., & Valančienė, L. (2015). Comparative analysis of the ways crowdfunding is promoted. *Procedia: Social and Behavioral Sciences, 213,* 268–274. doi:10.1016/j.sbspro.2015.11.536

Jeston, J., & Nelis, J. (2007). *Business Process Management. Practical Guidelines to Successful Implementations.* Amsterdam: Butterworth–Heinemann.

Jie, X. (2014). Research on the Realization of Human Resource Management System. *Advanced Materials Research, 926-930,* 3930–3933. doi:10.4028/www.scientific.net/AMR.926-930.3930

Jin, D., Chai, K.-H., & Tan, K.-C. (2014). New service development maturity model, *Managing Service Quality. International Journal (Toronto, Ont.), 24*(1), 86–116.

Jin, F. (2013). Epidemiological Modeling of News and Rumors on twitter. In *Proc. 7th workshop on Social Network Mining and Analysis.* ACM. 10.1145/2501025.2501027

Jitpaiboon, T., Dobrzykowski, D. D., Ragu-Nathan, T., & Vonderembse, M. A. (2013). Unpacking IT use and integration for mass customisation: A service-dominant logic view. *International Journal of Production Research, 51*(8), 2527–2547. doi:10.1080/00207543.2012.720727

Johnson, K. (July 9, 2018). What is consumer privacy and where is it headed? *Forbes.* Retrieved March 4, 2019, from https://www.forbes.com/sites/forbestechcouncil/2018/07/09/what-is-consumer-data-privacy-and-where-is-it-headed/#4f7fab731bc1

Johnson, D. (2009). *Ethical theory and business.* Upper Saddle River, NJ: Pearson Prentice Hall.

Johnson, R. D., Lukaszewski, K. M., & Stone, D. L. (2016). The Evolution of the Field of Human Resource Information Systems: Co-Evolution of Technology and HR Processes. *Communications of the Association for Information Systems, 38*(28), 533–553. doi:10.17705/1CAIS.03828

Johnston & Warkentin. (2017). Fear Appeals and Information Security Behaviors: An Empirical Study. *MIS Quarterly, 34*(3), 549. doi:10.2307/25750691

Joinson, A. (1999). Social desirability, anonymity, and Internet-based questionnaires. *Behavior Research Methods, Instruments, & Computers, 31*(3), 433–438. doi:10.3758/BF03200723 PMID:10502866

Jones-Evans, D. (1996). Technical entrepreneurship, strategy and experience. *International Small Business Journal, 14*(3), 15–39.

Jošanov, Pucihar, & Vrgović. (2016). Opinions and behavior of students about abuse of internet in social involvements: Gender analysis. *Business School.*

Joseph, L. (2018). Blockchain for Global Development. *Innovations, 12*(1/2), 10-17.

Jovane, F., Seliger, G., & Stock, T. (2017). Competitive Sustainable Globalization General Considerations and Perspectives. *Procedia Manufacturing, 8,* 1–19. doi:10.1016/j.promfg.2017.02.001

Jung, J., Ernstmann, N., Nitzsche, A., Driller, E., Kowalski, C., Lehner, B., ... Pfaff, H. (2012). Exploring the association between social capital and depressive symptoms: Results of a survey in German information and communication technology companies. *Journal of Occupational and Environmental Medicine, 54*(1), 23–30. doi:10.1097/JOM.0b013e318237a1b6 PMID:22157802

Juric, M., & Weerasiri, D. (2014). *WS-BPEL 2.0 beginner's guide.* Birmingham, UK: Packt Publishing Ltd.

Kahneman, D. (2011). *Thinking, fast and slow.* New York: Farrar, Straus and Giroux.

Kahneman, D., Slovic, P., & Tversky, A. (1982). *Judgment under uncertainty: Heuristic and biases.* New York: Cambridge University Press. doi:10.1017/CBO9780511809477

Kahneman, D., & Thaler, R. (1991). Economic analysis and the psychology of utility: Applications to compensation policy. *The American Economic Review, 81,* 341–346.

Kahneman, D., & Tversky, A. (1979). Prospect theory: An analysis of decision under risk. *Econometrica, 47*(2), 263–291. doi:10.2307/1914185

Kahneman, D., & Tversky, A. (2000). *Choices, values, and frames.* Cambridge, MA: Cambridge University Press. doi:10.1017/CBO9780511803475

Kahre, C., Hoffmann, D., & Ahlemann, F. (2017). Beyond business-IT alignment-Digital business strategies as a paradigmatic shift: A review and research agenda. In *Proceedings of the 50th Hawaii International Conference on System Sciences* (pp. 4706–4715). Academic Press. 10.24251/HICSS.2017.574

Kamp, A. (2018). Assembling the actors: Exploring the challenges of 'system leadership' in education through actor-network theory. *Journal of Education Policy, 33*(6), 778–792.

Kananu, K. M., & Nyakego, M. O. (2016). Challenges and Strategies in the Implementation of Human Resource Information Systems in Kenyan Universities. *Research on Humanities and Social Sciences, 6*(18), 148–161.

Kantis, H., Postigo, S., Federico, J., & Tamborini, F. (2002a). El surgimiento de emprendedores de base universitaria: en qué se diferencian? Evidencias empíricas para el caso de Argentina. Presentado en: RENT XVI Conference, Barcelona, Spain.

Kantis, H., Angelelli, P., & Moori, V. (2004). *Desarrollo emprendedor: América Latina y la experiencia internacional.* BID-FUNDES Internacional.

Kantis, H., Ishida, M., & Komori, M. (2002b). *Empresarialidad en economías emergentes: Creación y desarrollo de nuevas empresas en América Latina y el Este de Asia (No. 56558).* Washington, DC: Inter-American Development Bank.

Karau, S., & Williams, K. (1995). Social Loafing: Research Findings, Implications, and Future Directions. *Current Directions in Psychological Science, 4*(5), 135. doi:10.1111/1467-8721.ep10772570

Kariuki, M. M. (2015). Human Resource Information System and Competitive Advantage of Companies Listed in Nairobi Security Exchange in Kenya. *European Journal of Business and Management, 7*(21), 198–206.

Kasemsap, K. (2016). Multifaceted Applications of Data Mining, Business Intelligence, and Knowledge Management. *International Journal of Social and Organizational Dynamics in IT, 5*(1), 57–69. doi:10.4018/IJSODIT.2016010104

Kassim, N. M., Ramayah, T., & Kurnia, S. (2012). Antecedents and Outcomes of HRIS use. *International Journal of Productivity and Performance Management, 61*(6), 603–623. doi:10.1108/17410401211249184

Katrak, H., & Strange, R. (2002). Introduction and Overview. In H. Katrak & R. Strange (Eds.), *Small Scale Enterprises in Developing and Transition Economies.* Basingstoke, UK: Palgrave.

Katz, J. (1986). Desarrollo y crisis de la capacidad tecnológica Latinoamericana, el caso de la industria metalmecánica. Estudios sobre desarrollo tecnológico por BID/CEPAL/CIID/PNUD.

Katz, J. (2007). Cambios estructurales y desarrollo económico. Ciclos e creación y destrucción de capacidad productiva y tecnológica en América Latina. Revista de Economía Política de Buenos Aires, 1, 71-92.

Katz, J. (2000). Cambios estructurales y productividad en la Industria Latinoamericana, 1970-1996. *Revista de la CEPAL, 71,* 65–84.

Kautz, K., & Jensen, T. B. (2013). Sociomateriality at the royal court of IS: A jester's monologue. *Information and Organization*, 23(1), 15–27. doi:10.1016/j.infoandorg.2013.01.001

Kavanagh, M.J., Thite, M., & Johnson, R.D. (2009). The Future of HRIS. *Emerging Trends in HRM and IT*. Retrieved from file:///C:/Users/Matilda/Desktop/HRIS/Chapter17The%20future%20of%20HRIS.pdf

Kavanagh, M. J., Thite, M., & Johnson, R. D. (2015). *Human Resource Information Systems*. Sage Publications.

Kaygusuz, I., Akgemci, T., & Yilmaz, A. (2016). The impact of HRIS usage on Organizational Efficiency and Employee Performance: A Research in Industrial and Banking Sector in Ankara and Istanbul cities. *International Journal of Business and Management*, 4(4), 14–52.

Kay, R. H. (1990). The relation between computer literacy and locus of control. *Journal of Research on Computing in Education*, 22(4), 464–474. doi:10.1080/08886504.1990.10781935

Kazadi, K., Lievens, A., & Mahr, D. (2016). Stakeholder co-creation during the innovation process: Identifying capabilities for knowledge creation among multiple stakeholders. *Journal of Business Research*, 69(2), 525–540. doi:10.1016/j.jbusres.2015.05.009

Keeler, E. G., & Cretin, S. (1983). Discounting of life-saving and other non-monetary effects. *Management Science*, 29(3), 300–306. doi:10.1287/mnsc.29.3.300

Kehoe, C. M., & Pitkow, J. E. (1996). Surveying the territory: GVU's five www user surveys. *The World Wide Web Journal*, 1(3), 77–84.

Keith, M. J., Babb, J., Furner, C., Abdullat, A., & Lowry, P. B. (2016). Limited Information and Quick Decisions: Consumer Privacy Calculus for Mobile Applications. *AIS Transactions on Human-Computer Interaction*, 8(3), 88–130. doi:10.17705/1thci.00081

Keith, M., Babb, J., Furner, C. P., & Abdullat, A. (2015). The role of mobile-computing self-efficacy in consumer information disclosure. *Information Systems Journal*, 25(6), 637–667. doi:10.1111/isj.12082

Keller, L.R. & Strazzera, E. (2002). Examining predictive accuracy among discounting models. *Journal of Risk and Uncertainty, 24*(2), 143-160.

Keller, A. C., Smith, K. T., & Smith, L. M. (2007). Do gender, educational level, religiosity, and work experience affect the ethical decision-making of U.S. accountants? *Critical Perspectives on Accounting*, 18(3), 299–314. doi:10.1016/j.cpa.2006.01.006

Kelliher, F., Harrington, D., & Galavan, R. (2010). Spreading leader knowledge: Investigating a participatory mode of knowledge dissemination among management undergraduates. *Irish Journal of Management*, 29(2), 170–125.

Kelman, S. (2005). *Unleashing Change: A Study of Organizational Renewal in Government*. The Brookings Institute.

Kerin, R. A., Cron, W. L., & Peterson, R. A. (1977). Personalization, respondent anonymity, and response distortion in mail surveys. *The Journal of Applied Psychology*, 62(1), 86–89. doi:10.1037/0021-9010.62.1.86

Khalfallah, M., Figay, N., Barhamgi, M., & Ghodous, P. (2014). Model driven conformance testing for standardized services. In *IEEE International Conference on Services Computing* (pp. 400–407). Piscataway, NJ: IEEE Computer Society Press. 10.1109/SCC.2014.60

Khan, M. M., & Fasih, M. (2014). Impact of service quality on customer satisfaction and customer loyalty: Evidence from banking sector. *Pakistan Journal of Commerce and Social Sciences*, 8(2), 331–354.

Khan, M., Wu, X., Xu, X., & Dou, W. 2017. Big data challenges and opportunities in thehype of Industry 4.0. *2017 IEEE International Conference on Communications(ICC)*, 1–6.

Khan, S. A. R., & Qianli, D. (2017). Does national scale economic and environmental indicators spur logistics performance? Evidence from UK. *Environmental Science and Pollution Research International*, 24(34), 26692–26705. doi:10.100711356-017-0222-9 PMID:28956233

Khan, S. A. R., Qianli, D., SongBo, W., Zaman, K., & Zhang, Y. (2017). Environmental logistics performance indicators affecting per capita income and Sectoral growth: Evidence from a panel of selected global ranked logistics countries. *Environmental Science and Pollution Research International*, 24(2), 1518–1531. doi:10.100711356-016-7916-2 PMID:27785719

Khan, S. A. R., Zhang, Yu., Anees, M., Golpîra, H., Lahmar, A., & Qianli, D. (2018). Green supply chain management, economic growth and environment: A GMM based evidence. *Journal of Cleaner Production*, 185, 588–599. doi:10.1016/j.jclepro.2018.02.226

Khashman, I. M. A., & Khashman, A. M. (2016). The Impact of Human Resource Information System (HRIS) Applications on Organizational Performance (Efficiency and Effectiveness) in Jordanian Private Hospitals. *Journal of Management Research*, 8(3), 31–44. doi:10.5296/jmr.v8i3.9419

Kickstarter. (2016). *Seven things to know about Kickstarter*. Retrieved from https://www.kickstarter.com/about

Kim, H. W., Xu, Y., & Gupta, S. (2012). Which is more important in Internet shopping, perceived price or trust? *Electronic Commerce Research and Applications*, 11(3), 241–252. doi:10.1016/j.elerap.2011.06.003

Kim, S. H., Jang, S. Y., & Yang, K. H. (2016). Analysis of the Determinants of Software-as-a-Service Adoption in Small Businesses: Risks, Benefits, and Organizational and Environmental Factors. *Journal of Small Business Management*.

Kim, S. S., & Malhotra, N. K. (2005). A Longitudinal Model of Continued Is Use: An Integrative View of Four Mechanisms Underlying Postadoption Phenomena. *Management Science*, 51(5), 741–755. doi:10.1287/mnsc.1040.0326

Kim, S. S., & Son, J.-Y. (2009). Out of dedication or Constraint? A Dual Model of Post-Adoption Phenomena and its Empirical Test in the Context of Online Services. *Management Information Systems Quarterly*, 33(1), 49–70. doi:10.2307/20650278

Kim, Y., & Peterson, R. A. (2017). A Meta-analysis of Online Trust Relationships in E-commerce. *Journal of Interactive Marketing*, 38, 44–54. doi:10.1016/j.intmar.2017.01.001

Kindhäuser, U. (2007). Presupuestos de la corrupción punible en el Estado, la economía y la sociedad. Los delitos de corrupción en el Código penal alemán. *Política Criminal*, 3(A1), 1–19.

King, J. H., & Richards, N. M. (March 28, 2014). What's up with Big Data ethics? *Forbes*. Retrieved February 27, 2018, from https://www.forbes.com/sites/oreillymedia/2014/03/28/whats-up-with-big-data-ethics/#a344d0035913

Kingston, J. (2012). Choosing a knowledge dissemination approach. *Knowledge and Process Management*, 19(3), 160–170. doi:10.1002/kpm.1391

Kiparissides, A., Koutinas, M., Kontoravdi, C., Mantalaris, A., & Pistikopoulos, E. (2011). 'Closing the loop' in biological systems modeling—From the in silico to the in vitro. *Automatica*, 47(6), 1147–1155. doi:10.1016/j.automatica.2011.01.013

Kirby, K. N. (1997). Bidding on the future: Evidence against normative discounting of delayed rewards. *Journal of Experimental Psychology. General*, 126(1), 54–70. doi:10.1037/0096-3445.126.1.54

Kirby, K. N., & Herrnstein, R. J. (1995). Preference reversals due to myopic discounting of delayed reward. *Psychological Science*, *6*(2), 83–89. doi:10.1111/j.1467-9280.1995.tb00311.x

Kirby, K. N., & Marakovic, N. N. (1995). Modeling myopic decisions: Evidence for hyperbolic delay-discounting within subjects and amounts. *Organizational Behavior and Human Decision Processes*, *64*(1), 22–30. doi:10.1006/obhd.1995.1086

Kissmer, T., Stieglitz, S., Knoll, J., & Gross, R. (2018). *Knowledge workers' expectations towards a digital workplace. Americas Conference on Information Systems*. Retrieved May 16, 2019. From https://www.researchgate.net/publication/325809547_Knowledge_Workers%27_Expectations Towards_a_Digital_Workplace

Klassen, R. D., & Vereecke, A. (2012). Social issues in supply chains: Capabilities link responsibility, risk (opportunity) and performance. *International Journal of Production Economics*, *140*(1), 103–115. doi:10.1016/j.ijpe.2012.01.021

Klein, B., & Meckling, W. (1958). Application of operations research to development decisions. *Operations Research*, *6*(3), 352–363. doi:10.1287/opre.6.3.352

Klick, M. T. (2016). The Effect of State-Local Complementarity and Local Governance on Development: A Comparative Analysis from Post-War Guatemala. *World Development*, *82*, 1–13. doi:10.1016/j.worlddev.2016.01.005

Klyushin, D., & Petunin, Y. U. (2019). *Evidence-based medicine. The use of statistical methods*. Dialektika-Vil'yams. (in Russian)

Kneer, G. (2009). Akteur-netzwerk-theorie. In G. Kneer & M. Schroer (Eds.), *Handbuch Soziologische Theorien* (pp. 19–38). Wiesbaden, Germany: VS. doi:10.1007/978-3-531-91600-2_2

Knoke, B., Missikoff, M., & Thoben, K. D. (2017). Collaborative open innovation management in virtual manufacturing enterprises. *International Journal of Computer Integrated Manufacturing*, *30*(1), 158–166.

Knorr-Cetina, K. (1999). 'Viskurse' der Phyisk: Wie visuelle Darstellungen ein Wissenschaftsgebiet ordnen. In J. Huber & M. Heller (Eds.), *Konstruktionen Sichtbarkeiten* (pp. 245–263). Wien, Germany: Springer.

Knorr-Cetina, K. (1999). *Epistemic Cultures: How the Sciences Make Knowledge*. Harvard University Press.

Koeffer, S. (2015). Designing the digital workplace of the future -what scholars recommend to PR actioners. *International Conference on Information Systems*, Fort Worth, TX.

Kohlbacher, M., & Gruenwald, S. (2011). Process orientation: Conceptualization and measurement. *Business Process Management Journal*, *17*(2), 267–283. doi:10.1108/14637151111122347

Kohlborn, T., Mueller, O., Poeppelbuss, J., & Roeglinger, M. (2014). Interview with Michael Rosemann on ambidextrous business process management. *Business Process Management Journal*, *20*(4), 634–638. doi:10.1108/BPMJ-02-2014-0012

Koho, M., Torvinen, S., & Romiguer, A. T. (2011). Objectives, enablers and challenges of sustainable development and sustainable manufacturing: Views and opinions of Spanish companies. In *International Symposium on Assembly and Manufacturing (ISAM)*. IEEE. 10.1109/ISAM.2011.5942343

Koh, S. C. L., & Tan, K. H. (2006). Operational intelligence discovery and knowledge mapping approach in a supply network with uncertainty. *Journal of Manufacturing Technology Management*, *17*(6), 687–699. doi:10.1108/17410380610678747

Kondratova, I., & Goldfarb, I. (2004). Knowledge portal as a new paradigm for scientific publishing and collaboration. *Journal of Information Technology in Construction*, *9*, 161–174.

Koopmans, T. C. (1960). Stationary ordinary utility and impatience. *Econometrica*, *28*(2), 287–309. doi:10.2307/1907722

Koopmans, T. C. (1964). On flexibility of future preferences. In M. W. Shelly & G. L. Bryan (Eds.), *Human Judgments and Optimality*. New York: Wiley.

Koopmans, T. C., Diamonds, P. A., & Williamson, R. E. (1964). Stationary utility and time perspective. *Econometrica*, *32*(1/2), 82–100. doi:10.2307/1913736

Kopcso, D., & Pachamanova, D. (2017). *Case Article—Business Value in Integrating Predictive and Prescriptive Analytics Models*. INFORMS Transactions on Education.

Kosinski, M., Bachrach, Y., Stillwell, D. J., Kohli, P., & Graepel, T. (in press). Manifestations of user personality in website choice and behavior on online social networks. *Machine Learning*.

Kosinski, M., Stillwell, D., & Graepel, T. (2013). Private traits and attributes are predicable from digital records of human behavior. *Proceedings of the National Academy of Sciences of the United States of America*, *110*(15), 5802–5805. doi:10.1073/pnas.1218772110 PMID:23479631

Kostoska, M., Gusev, M., & Ristov, S. (2016). An overview of cloud interoperability. In *Federated Conference on Computer Science and Information Systems* (pp. 873-876). Piscataway, NJ: IEEE Computer Society Press. 10.15439/2016F463

Kotey, B., & Folker, C. (2007). Employee training in SMEs: Effect of size and firm type—Family and nonfamily. *Journal of Small Business Management*, *45*(2), 214–238. doi:10.1111/j.1540-627X.2007.00210.x

Kothari, C. R. (2004). *Research Methodology: Methods and Techniques*. New Age International.

Kotter John, P. (1998). Winning at Change. *Leader to Leader*, *10*(10), 27–33. doi:10.1002/ltl.40619981009

Kovach, K. A., & Cathcart, C. E. Jr. (1999). Human Resource Information System (HRIS): Providing Business with Rapid Data Access, Information Exchange and Strategic Advantage. *Public Personnel Management*, *28*(2), 275–283. doi:10.1177/009102609902800208

Kovács, G., & Kot, S. (2017). Economic and social effects of novel supply chain concepts and virtual enterprises. *Journal of International Studies*, *10*(1), 237–254. doi:10.14254/2071-8330.2017/10-1/17

Kowalska-Styczen, A., Malarz, K., & Paradowski, K. (2018). Model of knowledge transfer within an organisation. *Journal of Artificial Societies and Social Simulation*, *21*(2), 3. doi:10.18564/jasss.3659

Krumpal, I. (2011). Determinants of Social Desirability Bias in Sensitive Surveys: A Literature Review. *Quality & Quantity*, *47*(4), 2025–2047. doi:10.100711135-011-9640-9

Kulatunga, A., Jayawickrama, M., & Jayatilaka, P. R. (2013). Drivers and barriers to implement sustainable manufacturing concepts in sri lankan manufacturing sector. *Proceedings of the 11th Global Conference on Sustainable Manufacturing - Innovative Solution*, 172-177.

Kumar, R., Shaikh, B. T., Ahmed, J., Khan, Z., Mursalin, S., Memon, M. I., & Zareen, S. (2013). The Human Resource Information System: A rapid appraisal of Pakistan's capacity to employ the tool. *BMC Medical Informatics and Decision Making*, *13*(1), 104. doi:10.1186/1472-6947-13-104 PMID:24016066

Kuppuswamy, V., & Bayus, B. L. (2014). *Crowdfunding Creative Ideas: The Dynamics of Project Backers in Kickstarter*. UNC Kenan-Flagler Research Paper:2013-15.

Kuzmich, I., & Todurov, B. (2015). Dynamics of Secondary Pulmonary Hypertension after Cardiac Surgical Procedures in Patients with Low Left Ventricular. *Clinical Anesthesiology & Intensive Care*, *2*(6), 82–90.

Kwahk, G. (2012). Social impact theory: An examination of how immediacy operates as an influence upon social media interaction in Facebook fan pages. *The Marketing Review*.

Kyobe, M., Namirembe, E., & Shongwe, M. (2015). The Alignment of Information Technology Applications with Non-Technological Competencies of SMEs in Africa. *The Electronic Journal on Information Systems in Developing Countries, 67*(1), 1–22. doi:10.1002/j.1681-4835.2015.tb00483.x

Lafrenière, D., Menuz, V., Hurlimann, T., & Godard, B. (2013). Knowledge dissemination interventions: A literature review. *SAGE Open*, 1–14. doi:10.1177/2158244013498242

Laibson, D. (1997). Golden eggs and hyperbolic discounting. *The Quarterly Journal of Economics, 11*(2), 443–477. doi:10.1162/003355397555253

Laibson, D., Repetto, A., & Tobacman, J. (2003). A debt puzzle. In P. Aghion, R. Frydman, J. Stiglitz, & M. Woodford (Eds.), *Knowledge, information, and expectations in modern economics: In honor of Edmund S. Phelps* (pp. 228–266). Princeton, NJ: Princeton University Press.

Lamb, R., & Kling, R. (2003). Reconceptualizing users as social actors in information systems research. *Management Information Systems Quarterly, 27*(2), 197–235. doi:10.2307/30036529

Lapointe, C., & Fishbane, L. (2015). *The Blockchain Ethical Design Framework*. Georgetown.

Larichev, O. I. (1979). *Science and the art of decision making*. Moscow: Science.

Larsson, R., & Finkelstein, S. (1999). Integrating Strategic, Organizational, and Human Resource Perspectives on Mergers and Acquisitions: A Case Survey of Synergy Realization. *Organization Science, 10*(1), 1–26. doi:10.1287/orsc.10.1.1

Latour, B. (2005). Reassembling the social: An in-troduction to actor-network-theory. Oxford, UK: UP.

Latour, B. (1987). *Science in action: How to follow scientists and engineers through society*. Cambridge, MA: Harvard University Press.

Latour, B. (1992). Where are the missing masses the sociology of a few mundane artifacts. In W. Bijker & J. Law (Eds.), *Shaping technology/building society: Studies in socio-technical change* (pp. 225–264). London: MIT Press.

Latour, B. (1995). The "pedofil" of Boa Vista: A photo-philosophical montage. *Common Knowledge, 4*, 144–187.

Latour, B. (1996). On interobjectivity. *Mind, Culture, and Activity, 3*(4), 228–245. doi:10.120715327884mca0304_2

Latour, B. (1997). The trouble with actor-network theory. *Soziale Welt, 47*, 369–381.

Latour, B. (1999). *Pandora's hope: Essays on the real-ity of science studies*. Cambridge, MA: Harvard UP.

Latour, B. (1999a). On recalling ANT. In J. Law & J. Hassard (Eds.), *Actor network theory and after* (pp. 15–25). Oxford, UK: Blackwell.

Latour, B. (1999b). *Pandora's hope*. Cambridge, MA: Harvard University Press.

Latour, B. (2004). Why has critique run out of steam? From matters of fact to matters of concern. *Critical Inquiry, 30*(2), 225–248. doi:10.1086/421123

Latour, B. (2005). *Reassembling the social: An introduction to actor-network theory*. Oxford, UK: Oxford University Press.

Latour, J., & Crawford, T. (1993). An interview with Latour. *Configurations, 2*(2), 247–269. doi:10.1353/con.1993.0012

Laux, F. L., & Peck, R. M. (2007). *Economic perspectives on addiction: Hyperbolic discounting and internalities*. Social Science Research Network working paper. Retrieved November 3, 2015 at http://papers.ssrn.com/sol3/papers.cfm?abstract_id=1077613

Lavrakas, P. J. (2008). *Encyclopedia of survey research methods*. Thousand Oaks, CA: Sage Publications, Inc. doi:10.4135/9781412963947

Law, J. (1997). *Heterogeneities*. Paper presented at the 'Uncertainty, Knowledge and Skill Conference', Limburg University.

Law, J. (2007a). *Actor network theory and material semiotics, version of 25th April 2007*. Retrieved from: http://www.heterogeneities.net/publications/Law2007AntandMaterialSemiotics.pdf

Law, J. (1991). Introduction. In J. Law (Ed.), *A sociology of monsters: Essays on power, technology and domination*. London: Routledge.

Law, J. (1992). *Notes on the theory of the actor network: Ordering, strategy and heterogeneity*. Lancaster, UK: Centre for Science Studies, Lancaster University. Retrieved from http://www.comp.lancs.ac.uk/sociology/papers/Law-Notes-on-Ant.pdf

Law, J. (1996). Ontology and the mode of accounting. In J. Mouritsen & R. Munro (Eds.), *Accountability, power and ethos*. London: Chapman Hall.

Law, J. (1999). After ANT: Complexity, naming and topology. In J. Law & J. Hassard (Eds.), *Actor network theory and after* (pp. 1–14). Oxford, UK: Blackwell.

Law, J. (2003). *Traduction/Trahison: Notes on ANT*. Lancaster, UK: Centre for Science Studies, Lancaster University. Retrieved from http://www.comp.lancs.ac.uk/sociology/papers/Law-Notes-on-Ant.pdf

Law, J. (2004a). And if the global were small and noncoherent? Method, complexity, and the baroque. *Environment and Planning D. Space and Society*, *22*(1), 13–26.

Law, J. (2004b). *After method: Mess in social science research*. London: Routledge.

Law, J. (2007b). Making a mess with method. In W. Outhwaite & S. P. Turner (Eds.), *The Sage handbook of social science methodology* (pp. 595–606). London: Sage. doi:10.4135/9781848607958.n33

Law, J., & Hassard, J. (Eds.). (1999). *Actor network theory and after*. Oxford, UK: Blackwell Publishing/The Sociological Review.

Law, J., & Urry, J. (2003). *Enacting the social*. Lancaster, UK: Centre for Science Studies, Lancaster University. Retrieved from http://www.comp.lancs.ac.uk/sociology/papers/Law-Notes-on-Ant.pdf

Lawson, E., & Price, C. (2003). The Psychology of Change Management. *The McKinsey Quarterly*.

Le Ber, M. J., & Branzei, O. (2010). Value frame fusion in cross sector interactions. *Journal of Business Ethics*, *94*(S1), 163–195. doi:10.100710551-011-0785-1

Leander, K. M., & Lovvorn, J. F. (2006). Literacy networks: Following the circulation of texts, bodies, and objects in the schooling and online gaming of one youth. *Cognition and Instruction*, *24*(3), 291–340. doi:10.12071532690xci2403_1

Lee, A. S., & Baskerville, R. L. (2003). Generalizing Generalizability in Information Systems Research. *Information Systems Research*, *14*(3), 221–243. doi:10.1287/isre.14.3.221.16560

Lee, C., Lee, C. C., & Kim, S. (2016). Understanding information security stress: Focusing on the type of information security compliance activity. *Computers & Security*, *59*, 60–70. doi:10.1016/j.cose.2016.02.004

Lee, E. J., Kim, H. S., & Kim, H. Y. (2014). Relationships between core factors of knowledge management in hospital nursing organisations and outcomes of nursing performance. *Journal of Clinical Nursing*, *23*(23–24), 3513–3524. doi:10.1111/jocn.12603

Lee, N., & Brown, S. (1994). Otherness and the actor-network: The undiscovered continent. *The American Behavioral Scientist, 37*(6), 772–790. doi:10.1177/0002764294037006005

Lee, N., & Hassard, J. (1999). Organization unbound: Actor-network theory, research strategy and institutional flexibility. *Organization, 6*(3), 391–404. doi:10.1177/135050849963002

Lee, N., & Stenner, P. (1999). Who pays? Can we pay them back? In J. Law & J. Hassard (Eds.), *Actor network theory and after* (pp. 90–112). Oxford, UK: Blackwell. doi:10.1111/j.1467-954X.1999.tb03484.x

Lehner, B. S., Jung, J., Stieler-Lorenz, B., Nitzsche, A., Driller, E., Wasem, J., & Pfaff, H. (2013). Psychosocial factors in the information and communication technology sector. *Management Decision, 51*(9), 1878–1892. doi:10.1108/MD-12-2012-0876

Lehner, F. (2018). ICT Skills and Competencies for SMEs: Results from a Structured Literature Analysis on the Individual Level. In *The Impact of Digitalization in the Workplace* (pp. 55–69). Springer. doi:10.1007/978-3-319-63257-5_5

Lehnert, M., Linhart, A., & Roeglinger, M. (2017). Exploring the intersection of business process improvement and BPM capability development: A research agenda. *Business Process Management Journal, 23*(2), 275–292. doi:10.1108/BPMJ-05-2016-0095

Leite, E., & Bengtson, A. (2018). A business network view on value creation and capture in public-private cooperation. *Industrial Marketing Management, 73*, 181–192. doi:10.1016/j.indmarman.2018.02.010

Leonard-Barton, D. (1990). A Dual Methodology for Case Studies: Synergistic Use of a Longitudinal Single Site with Replicated Multiple Sites. *Organization Science, 1*(3), 248–266. doi:10.1287/orsc.1.3.248

Leonardi, P. M. (2013). Theoretical foundations for the study of sociomateriality. *Information and Organization, 23*(2), 59–76. doi:10.1016/j.infoandorg.2013.02.002

Leonardi, P. M. (2017). Methodological Guidelines for the Study of Materiality and Affordances. In M. Raza & S. Jain (Eds.), *Routledge Companion to Qualitative Research in Organization Studies*. New York: Routledge. doi:10.4324/9781315686103-18

Lepak, D. P., & Snell, S. A. (1999). The Human Resource Architecture: Toward a Theory of Human Capital Allocation and Development. *Academy of Management Review, 24*(1), 31–48. doi:10.5465/amr.1999.1580439

Lerner, J. S., Small, D. A., & Loewenstein, G. (2004). Heart strings and purse strings: Carryover effects of emotions on economic transactions. *Psychological Science, 15*(5), 337–341. doi:10.1111/j.0956-7976.2004.00679.x PMID:15102144

Lessig, L. (2006). *Code: Version 2.0*. New York, NY: Basic.

Levina, N., & Vaast, E. (2005). The Emergence of Boundary Spanning Competence in Practice: Implications for Implementation and Use of Information Systems. *Management Information Systems Quarterly, 29*(2), 335–363. doi:10.2307/25148682

Li, A., & Reb, J. (2009). A cross-nations, cross-cultures, and cross-conditions analysis on the equivalence of the alanced nventory of desirable responding. *Journal of Cross-Cultural Psychology, 40*(2), 214–233. doi:10.1177/0022022108328819

Liao, Y., Deschamps, F., Loures, E., & Ramos, L. (2017). Past, present and future of Industry 4.0 - a systematic literature review and research agenda proposal. *International Journal of Production Research, 55*(12), 3609–3629. doi:10.1080/00207543.2017.1308576

Li, G., & Wei, M. (2014). Everything-as-a-service platform for on-demand virtual enterprises. *Information Systems Frontiers, 16*(3), 435–452. doi:10.100710796-012-9351-3

Li, J., Zhang, Y., Man, J., Zhou, Y., & Wu, X. (2017). SISL and SIRL: Two knowledge dissemination models with leader nodes on cooperative learning networks. *Physica A*, *468*, 740–749. doi:10.1016/j.physa.2016.11.126

Lim, J. S., Chang, S., Maynard, S., & Ahmad, A. (2009). Exploring the Relationship between Organizational Cultural and Information Security Culture. *7th Australian Information Management Conference*.

Lim, K. K., Ong, Y.-S., Lim, M. H., Chen, X., & Agarwal, A. (2008). Hybrid ant colony algorithm for path planning in sparse graphs. *Soft Computing*, *12*(10), 981–994. doi:10.100700500-007-0264-x

Lin, C., & Lekhawipat, W. (2014). Factors affecting online repurchase intention. *Industrial Management & Data Systems*, *114*(4), 597–611. doi:10.1108/IMDS-10-2013-0432

Lin, J. W., & Lai, Y. C. (2013). Online formative assessments with social network awareness. *Comput. Educ.*, *66*, 40–53. doi:10.1016/j.compedu.2013.02.008

Linn, M. C. (1985). Gender equity in computer learning environments. *Computers and the Social Sciences*, *1*(1), 19–27. doi:10.1177/089443938500100103

Lin, S., & Kernighan, B. W. (1973). An Effective Heuristic Algorithm for the Traveling Salesman Problem. *Operations Research*, *21*(2), 498–516. doi:10.1287/opre.21.2.498

Lin, X., Featherman, M., Brooks, S. L., & Hajli, N. (2018). Exploring gender differences in online consumer purchase decision making: An online product presentation perspective. *Information Systems Frontiers*, 1–15.

Lin, Y., Luo, J., Cai, S., Ma, S., & Rong, K. (2016). Exploring the service quality in the e-commerce context: A triadic view. *Industrial Management & Data Systems*, *116*(3), 388–415. doi:10.1108/IMDS-04-2015-0116

Liska, R. (2018). Management Challenges in the Digital Era. In R. Brunet-Thornton & F. Martinez (Eds.), *Analyzing the Impacts of Industry 4.0 in Modern Business Environments* (pp. 82–99). Hershey, PA: IGI Global. doi:10.4018/978-1-5225-3468-6.ch005

Litt, E. (2013). Measuring users' internet skills: A review of past assessments and a look toward the future. *New Media & Society*, *15*(4), 612–630. doi:10.1177/1461444813475424

Liu, D. Q., Wu, Z. Q., Wang, Y. X., Guo, Q., & Liu, J. G. (2017). Optimal teaching strategy in periodic impulsive knowledge dissemination system. *PLoS One*, *12*(6), e0178024. doi:10.1371/journal.pone.0178024 PMID:28665961

Locher, C. (2005). Methodologies for Evaluating Information Security Investments - What Basel II Can Change in the Financial Industry. *Proceedings of the 13th European Conference on Information Systems*, 1–12.

Loewenstein, G. (1992). The fall and rise of psychological explanations in the economics of intertemporal choice. In G. Loewenstein & J. Elster (Eds.), *Choice over time* (pp. 3–34). New York: Sage.

Loewenstein, G., & Prelec, D. (1993). Preferences for sequences of outcomes. *Psychological Review*, *100*(1), 91–108. doi:10.1037/0033-295X.100.1.91

Lombardi, R. (2019). Knowledge transfer and organizational performance and business process: Past, present and future researches. *Business Process Management Journal*, *25*(1), 2–9. doi:10.1108/BPMJ-02-2019-368

London, M. (1993). Relationships between career motivation, empowerment and support for career development. *Journal of Occupational and Organizational Psychology*, *66*(1), 55–69. doi:10.1111/j.2044-8325.1993.tb00516.x

London, M., & Noe, R. A. (1997). London's career motivation theory: An update on measurement and research. *Journal of Career Assessment*, *5*(1), 61–80. doi:10.1177/106907279700500105

Lopes, T. P. (2006). Career development in foreign-born workers: Where is the career motivation research? *Human Resource Development Review, 5*(4), 478–493. doi:10.1177/1534484306293925

Lösch, A., Spreen, D., Schrage, D., & Stauff, M. (2001). Technologien als Diskurse – Einleitung. In *Technologien als Diskurse: Konstruktionen von Wissen, Medien und Körpern* (pp. 7–20). Heidelberg, Germany: Synchron.

Luce, R. D., & Suppes, P. (1965). Preference, utility, and subjective probability. In R.D. Luce, R.R., Bush, & E. Galanter (Eds.), Handbook of mathematical psychology, (pp. 103-189). New York: Wiley.

Luce, R. D., & Raiffa, H. (1957). *Games and decisions: Introduction and critical survey.* New York: Dover.

Luck, B. (2007). *Cyberbullying: an emerging issue bernadette luck, record of the communications policy & research forum.* Retrieved from https://apo.org.au/sites/default/files/resource-files/2007/10/apo-nid69033-1106296.pdf

Lu, J., Yu, C., Liu, C., & Wei, J. (2017). Comparison of mobile shopping continuance intention between China and USA from an espoused cultural perspective. *Computers in Human Behavior, 75*(3), 130–146. doi:10.1016/j.chb.2017.05.002

Luo, X., Warkentin, M., Johnston, A. C., & Luo, X. (2009). The Impact of National Culture on Workplace Privacy Expectations in the Context of Information Security Assurance. *Proceedings of the Fifteenth Americas Conference on Information Systems*, 1–6.

Luthra, S., Kumar, V., Kumar, S., & Haleem, A. (2011). Barriers to implement green supply chain management in auto industries using Interpretes structural modeling technique-an Indian perspective. *JIEM, 4*(2), 231–257. doi:10.3926/jiem.2011.v4n2.p231-257

MacKinnon, D., Cumbers, A., & Chapman, K. (2002). Learning, innovation and regional development: A critical appraisal of recent debates. *Progress in Human Geography, 26*(3), 293–311. doi:10.1191/0309132502ph371ra

Madala, H., & Ivakhnenko, A. (1994). *Inductive learning algorithms for complex systems modeling.* Boca Raton, FL: CRC Press.

Madden, G. L., Bickel, W. K., & Jacobs, E. A. (1999). Discounting of delayed rewards in opioid-dependent outpatients: Exponential or hyperbolic discounting functions? *Experimental and Clinical Psychopharmacology, 7*(3), 284–293. doi:10.1037/1064-1297.7.3.284 PMID:10472517

Madsbjerg, S. (2017). *It's Time to Tax Companies for Using Our Personal Data.* Retrieved from https://www.nytimes.com/2017/11/14/business/dealbook/taxing-companies-for-using-our-personal-data.html?rref=collection%2Fsectioncollection%2Fbusiness&action=click&contentCollection=business&region=stream&module=stream_unit&version=latest&contentPlacement=8&pgtype=sectionfront

Maheshwari, S. (December 24, 2018). Sharing Data for Deals? More Like Watching It Go With A Sigh. *The New York Times.* Retrieved March 5, 2019, from https://www.nytimes.com/2018/12/24/business/media/data-sharing-deals-privacy.html

Mahmood, S. (2008). *Corporate Governance and Business Ethics for SMEs in Developing Countries: Challenges and Way Forward.* Academic Press.

Mahoney, J. T., McGahan, A. M., & Pitelis, C. (2009). Perspective-the interdependence of private and public interests. *Organization Science, 20*(6), 1034–1052. doi:10.1287/orsc.1090.0472

Majumdar, T. (1958). *The measurement of utility.* London: Macmillan.

Makadok, R. (2001). Toward a synthesis of the resource-based and dynamic-capability views of rent creation. *Strategic Management Journal, 22*(5), 387–401. doi:10.1002mj.158

Malcolm, J., Hodkinson, P., & Colley, H. (2003). The interrelationships between informal and formal learning. *Journal of Workplace Learning*, *15*(7/8), 313–318. doi:10.1108/13665620310504783

Manago, A. M. (2012). The New Emerging Adult in Chiapas, Mexico: Perceptions of Traditional Values and Value Change among First-Generation Maya University Students. *Journal of Adolescent Research*, *27*(6), 663–713. doi:10.1177/0743558411417863

Mandal, P., & Bagchi, K. (2016). Strategic role of information, knowledge and technology in manufacturing industry performance. *Industrial Management & Data Systems*, *116*(6), 1259–1278. doi:10.1108/IMDS-07-2015-0297

Mandal, P., & Gunasekaran, A. (2003). Issues in implementing ERP: A case study. *European Journal of Operational Research*, *146*(2), 274–283. doi:10.1016/S0377-2217(02)00549-0

Marcella, A. (2015). *Blockchain Technology and Decentralized Governance: Is the State Still Necessary?* Academic Press.

Marcolin, B. L., Compeau, D. R., Munro, M. C., & Huff, S. L. (2000). Assessing User Competence: Conceptualization and Measurement. *Information Systems Research*, *11*(1), 37–60. doi:10.1287/isre.11.1.37.11782

Marek, E. (2017). *Redefining change management in the digital age*. Retrieved March 6, 2019, from https://www.itchronicles.com/itsm/redefining-change-management/

Marglin, S. A. (1963). The social rate of discount and the optimal rate of investment. *The Quarterly Journal of Economics*, *77*(1), 95–111. doi:10.2307/1879374

Markovic, M. R. (2008). Managing the organizational change and culture in the age of globalization. January 8. *Journal of Business Economics and Management*, *9*(1), 3–11. doi:10.3846/1611-1699.2008.9.3-11

Marks, M. L., & Mirvis, P. H. (2001). Making Mergers and Acquisitions Work: Strategic and Psychological Preparation. *The Academy of Management Executive*, *15*(2), 80-94.

Markus, M. L., & Benjamin, R. I. (1996). Change Agentry - the Next IS Frontier. *Management Information Systems Quarterly*, *20*(4), 385–407. doi:10.2307/249561

Markus, M. L., & Robey, D. (1988). Information Technology and Organizational Change: Causal Structure in Theory and Research. *Management Science*, *34*(5), 583–598. doi:10.1287/mnsc.34.5.583

Marquardt, R., Makens, J., & Larzelere, H. (1965). Measuring the utility added by branding and grading. *JMR, Journal of Marketing Research*, *2*(1), 45–50. doi:10.1177/002224376500200106

Marschak, J. (1950). Rational behavior, uncertain prospects, and measurable utility. *Econometrica*, *18*(2), 111–141. doi:10.2307/1907264

Marsden, P. (2010). *Social Commerce: Monetizing Social media*. London: GRIN Verlag.

Marsh, E. (2018). Understanding the Effect of Digital Literacy on Employees' Digital Workplace Continuance Intentions and Individual Performance. *International Journal of Digital Literacy and Digital Competence*, *9*(2), 15–33. doi:10.4018/IJDLDC.2018040102

Marsh, H. W., & Hocevar, D. (1985). Application of confirmatory factor analysis to the study of self-concept: First- and higher order factor models and their invariance across groups. *Psychological Bulletin*, *97*(3), 562–582. doi:10.1037/0033-2909.97.3.562

Martin, A., & Eloff, J. (2003). Information Security Culture. *Proc. of IFIP TC11 17th International Conference on Information Security*.

Martin, C. L., & Nago, D. H. (1989). Some effects of computerized interviewing on job applicant responses. *The Journal of Applied Psychology, 74*(1), 72–80. doi:10.1037/0021-9010.74.1.72

Marx, K. (1995). *Capital: A critique of political economy*. Moscow: Progress. (Original work published 1867)

Masalskyte, R., Andelin, M., Sarasoja, A.-L., & Ventovuori, T. (2014). Modelling sustainability maturity in corporate real estate management. *Journal of Corporate Real Estate, 16*(2), 126–139. doi:10.1108/JCRE-09-2013-0023

Mas-Colell, A., Whinston, M. D., & Green, J. R. (1995). *Microeconomic theory*. New York: Oxford University Press.

Mason, R. O. (1986). Four ethical issues of the information age. *Management Information Systems Quarterly, 10*(1), 4–12. doi:10.2307/248873

Mastrobuoni, G., & Weinberg, M. (2009). Heterogeneity in intra-monthly consumption patterns, self-control, and savings at retirement. *American Economic Journal. Economic Policy, 1*(2), 163–189. doi:10.1257/pol.1.2.163

Matentzoglu, N., Parsia, B., & Sattler, U. (2017). OWL Reasoning: Subsumption Test Hardness and Modularity. *Journal of Automated Reasoning*, 1–35. PMID:30069069

Matute, J., Polo-Redondo, Y., & Utrillas, A. (2016). The influence of EWOM characteristics on online repurchase intention: Mediating roles of trust and perceived usefulness. *Online Information Review, 40*(7), 1090–1110. doi:10.1108/OIR-11-2015-0373

Mauss, M. (2005). Techniques of the body. In M. Fraser (Ed.), The body: A reader (pp. 73–77). London, UK: Routledge.

Mazmanian, M., Orlikowski, W. J., & Yates, J. (2013). The autonomy paradox: the implications of mobile email devices for knowledge professionals.' Organization Science, 24, 1337–1357.

Mazur, J. E. (1987). An adjusting procedure for studying delayed reinforcement. In M. M. Commons, J. A. Nevvin, & H. Rachlin (Eds.), *Quantitative analyses of behavior*. Hillsdale, NJ: Lawrence Erlbaum.

Mbow, C., Skole, D., Dieng, M., Justice, C., Kwesha, D., Mane, L., & Virji, H. (2012). *Challenges and prospects for REDD+ in Africa: desk review of REDD+ implementation in Africa. Global Land Project Reports, 5. World Agroforestry Centre*. Nairobi, Kenya: ICRAF.

McAdam, R., & Reid, R. (2001). SMEs and Large Organisation Perceptions of Knowledge Management: Comparisons and Contrasts. *Journal of Knowledge Management, 5*(3), 231–241. doi:10.1108/13673270110400870

McAfee, A., Brynjolfsson, E., Davenport, T. H., Patil, D. J., & Barton, D. (2012). Big data: The management revolution. *Harvard Business Review, 90*(10), 60–68. PMID:23074865

McAsey, M., Mou, L., & Han, W. (2012). Convergence of the forward-backward sweep method in optimal control. *Computational Optimization and Applications, 53*(1), 207–226. doi:10.100710589-011-9454-7

McCleary, K., Asubonteng, P., & Munchus, G. (1995). The effects of advanced information technology on organizational design. *Health Manpower Management, 21*(2), 20–23. doi:10.1108/09552069510085870 PMID:10143260

McClure, S., Ericson, K., Laibson, D., Loewenstein, G., & Cohen, J. (2007). Time discounting for primary rewards. *The Journal of Neuroscience, 27*(21), 5796–5804. doi:10.1523/JNEUROSCI.4246-06.2007 PMID:17522323

McCormack, K. (2001). Business process orientation: Do you have it? *Quality Progress, 34*(1), 51–58.

McCormack, K. (2007). *Business Process Maturity. Theory and Application*. BookSurge Publishing.

McCormack, K., & Johnson, W. C. (2001). *Business process orientation: gaining the e-business competitive advantage*. Boca Raton, FL: St. Lucie Press. doi:10.1201/9781420025569

McCormack, K., Willems, J., van den Bergh, J., Deschoolmeester, D., Willaert, P., Indihar Štemberger, M., ... Vlahović, N. (2009). A global investigation of key turning points in business process maturity. *Business Process Management Journal*, *15*(5), 792–815. doi:10.1108/14637150910987946

McCrae, R. R., & Costa, P. T. (1982). Self-concept and the stability of personality: Cross-sectional comparisons of self-reports and ratings. *Journal of Personality and Social Psychology*, *43*(6), 1282–129. doi:10.1037/0022-3514.43.6.1282

McCrae, R. R., & Costa, P. T. Jr. (1983). Social desirability scales: More substance than style. *Journal of Consulting and Clinical Psychology*, *51*(6), 882–888. doi:10.1037/0022-006X.51.6.882

McDonald, H., & Adam, S. (2003). A comparison of online and postal data collection methods in marketing research. *Marketing Intelligence & Planning*, *21*(2), 85–95. doi:10.1108/02634500310465399

McDowell, W., Wilson, R., & Kile, C. Jr. (2016). An examination of retail website design and conversion rate. *Journal of Business Research*, *69*(11), 4837–4842. doi:10.1016/j.jbusres.2016.04.040

McKibben, W. B., & Silvia, P. J. (2017). Evaluating the distorting effects of inattentive responding and social desirability on self-report scales in creativity and the arts. *The Journal of Creative Behavior*, *51*(1), 57–69. doi:10.1002/jocb.86

McLaren, P. L., & Giarelli, J. M. (Eds.). (1995). *Critical theory and educational research*. Albany, NY: State University of New York Press.

McLay, A. (2014). Re-reengineering the dream: Agility as competitive adaptability. *International Journal of Agile Systems and Management*, *7*(2), 101–115. doi:10.1504/IJASM.2014.061430

Mclean. (2017). Melbourne's RMIT to Explore the Social Sciences of Blockchain. *ZDNet*. Retrieved from http://www.zdnet.com/article/melbournes-rmit-to-explore-the-social-science-of-blockchain/

McLean, C., & Hassard, J. (2004). Symmetrical absence/Symmetrical absurdity: Critical notes on the production of actor-network accounts. *Journal of Management Studies*, *41*(3), 493–519. doi:10.1111/j.1467-6486.2004.00442.x

Meehl, P. E., & Hathaway, S. R. (1946). The K factor as a suppressor variable in the MMPI. *The Journal of Applied Psychology*, *30*, 525–564. doi:10.1037/h0053634 PMID:20282179

Meier, S., & Sprenger, C. (2010). *Stability of time preferences*. IZA Discussion Paper 4756, Institute for the Study of Labor.

Melville, N., Kraemer, J., & Gurbaxani, V. (2004). Information technology and organizational performance: An integrative model of IT business value. *Management Information Systems Quarterly*, *28*(2), 283–322. doi:10.2307/25148636

Mengoni, M., Perna, A., Bevilacqua, M., & Giraldi, L. (2017). The role of business relationships in new product development. The case of Antrox-Nel Design. *Procedia Manufacturing*, *11*, 1351–1357. doi:10.1016/j.promfg.2017.07.264

Menkhoff, T., Wah, C. Y., & Loh, B. (2002). Towards Strategic Knowledge Management in Singapore's Small Business Sector. Presented at the *International Conference on Globalization, Innovation and Human Resource Development for Competitive Advantage*, Bangkok, Thailand.

Mentzer, J. T., DeWitt, W., Keebler, J. S., Min, S., Nix, N. W., Smith, C. D., & Zacharia, Z. G. (2001). Defining supply chain management. *Journal of Business Logistics*, *22*(2), 1–25. doi:10.1002/j.2158-1592.2001.tb00001.x

Merriam-Webster. (2018). Retrieved from http://www.merriam-webster.com/

Meshi, Tamir, & Heekeren. (2015). The Emerging Neuroscience, Trends in Cognitive Science. *Trends in Cognitive Sciences*, *19*(12), 771–782.

Meyer, A. G. (2009). *Estimating individual level discount factors and testing competing discounting hypotheses* (Dissertation). University of Colorado.

Meyer, A. G. (2013). Estimating discount factors for public and private goods and testing competing discounting hypotheses. *Journal of Risk and Uncertainty*, *46*(2), 133–173. doi:10.100711166-013-9163-y

Mezgár, I., & Rauschecker, U. (2014). The challenge of networked enterprises for cloud computing interoperability. *Computers in Industry*, *65*(4), 657–674. doi:10.1016/j.compind.2014.01.017

Michelmore, K., & Sassler, S. (2016). Explaining the gender earnings gap in STEM: Does field group size matter? *The Russell Sage Foundation Journal of the Social Sciences*, *2*(4), 194–215. doi:10.7758/rsf.2016.2.4.07

Microsoft Ignite. (2017). Spark the Future. Retrieved March 6, 2019, from https://slideplayer.com/slide/4875602/

Microsoft. (n.d.). *What is Blockchain?* Author.

Mifsud, D. (2014). Actor-Network Theory: An assemblage of perceptions, understandings, and critiques of this 'sensibility' and how its relatively under-utilized conceptual framework in education studies can aid researchers in the exploration of networks and power relations. *International Journal of Actor-Network Theory and Technological Innovation*, *6*(1), 1–16. doi:10.4018/ijantti.2014010101

Miliszewska, I., & Horwood, J. (2000). Women in Computer Science. In E. Balka & R. Smith (Eds.), *Women, Work and Computerization – Charting a Course to the Future* (pp. 50–57). Boston, MA: Kluwer. doi:10.1007/978-0-387-35509-2_7

Milkman, K. L., Rogers, T., & Bazerman, M. H. (2008). Harnessing our inner angels and demons: What we have learned about want/should conflicts and how that knowledge can help us reduce short-sighted decision making. *Perspectives on Psychological Science*, *3*(4), 324–338. doi:10.1111/j.1745-6924.2008.00083.x PMID:26158952

Milkman, K. L., Rogers, T., & Bazerman, M. H. (2009). Highbrow films gather dust: Time- inconsistent preferences and online DVD rentals. *Management Science*, *55*(6), 1047–1059. doi:10.1287/mnsc.1080.0994

Miller, P. (2012). Digital workplace business case: What is the financial value of investing in digital working? *Digital Workplace Group*. Retrieved March 6, 2019, from http://www.digitalworkplacegroup.com/wp-content/downloads/dwg-free/DWG-Digital-Workplace-Business-Case-Free-Report.pdf#page=1&zoom=auto,-274,848

Miller, R. (2017). *The Promise of Managing Identity on the Blockchain*. Academic Press.

Miller, Z. (2018). *The Entrepreneur's Guide to the Fees on Crowdfunding Platforms*. Available: https://www.thebalancesmb.com/entrepreneurs-guide-to-fees-on-crowdfunding-platforms-985187

Miller, A. (1971). *The assult on privacy: Computers, data banks and dossiers*. Ann Arbor, MI: University of Michigan Press.

Miller, C., & Bartlett, J. (2012). 'Digital fluency': Towards young people's critical use of the internet. *Journal of Information Literacy*, *6*(2), 35–55. doi:10.11645/6.2.1714

Miller, D., & Shamsie, J. (1996). The Resource-Based View of the Firm in Two Environments: The Hollywood Film Studios from 1936 to 1965. *Academy of Management Journal*, *39*(3), 19–543.

Miller, G. A. (1987). Meta-analysis and the culture-free hypothesis. *Organization Studies*, *8*(4), 309–326. doi:10.1177/017084068700800402

Miller, P. (2012). *The Digital Workplace: How Technology is Liberating Work*. TECL Publishing.

Miller, P., & March, A. (2016). *The Digital Renaissance of Work: Delivering digital workplaces fit for the future*. Routledge.

Mills, M. (2011b). Do signals have politics? Inscribing abilities in cochlear implants. In The Oxford handbook of sound studies (pp. 320-346). Oxford UP. doi:10.1093/oxfordhb/9780195388947.013.0077

Mills, M. (2011a). Hearing aids and the history of electronics miniaturization. *IEEE Annals of the History of Computing*, *33*(2), 24–45. doi:10.1109/MAHC.2011.43

Miltgen, C. L. (2009). Online consumer privacy concern and willingness to provide personal data on the internet. *International Journal of Networking and Virtual Organizations*, *6*(6), 574–603. doi:10.1504/IJNVO.2009.027790

Milton, N. (2010). *The Lessons Learned Handbook: Practical Approaches to Learning from Experience*. Witney, UK: Chandos Publishing. doi:10.1533/9781780631929

Minbaeva, D. B. (2013). Strategic HRM in building micro-foundations of organizational knowledge-based performance. *Human Resource Management Review*, *23*(4), 378–390. doi:10.1016/j.hrmr.2012.10.001

Ministry of Infrastructure. (2015). *Report on the Energy Sector in Slovenia in 2014*. Retrieved February 7, 2019, from http://www.energetika-portal.si/dokumenti/poslovna-porocila/porocilo-o-stanju-na-podrocju-energetike/

Ministry of Infrastructure. (2017). *Report on the Energy Sector in Slovenia in 2017*. Retrieved March 5, 2019, from http://www.energetika-portal.si/fileadmin/dokumenti/publikacije/agen_e/porae_2017.pdf

Minsky, H. P. (1977). Banking and a fragile financial environment. *Journal of Portfolio Management*, *3*(4), 16–22. doi:10.3905/jpm.1977.408609

Mitchell, M. S., Cropanzano, R. S., & Quisenberry, D. M. (2012). Social exchange theory, exchange resources, and interpersonal relationships: A modest resolution of theoretical difficulties. In *Handbook of social resource theory* (pp. 99–118). New York, NY: Springer. doi:10.1007/978-1-4614-4175-5_6

Mitta, V.K., Egede, P., Herrmann, C., & Sangwan, K.S. (2013). Comparison of Drivers and Barriers to Green Manufacturing: A Case of India and Germany. *Procedia CIRP*, 723-728.

Mittal, V. K., & Sangwan, K. S. (2014a). Prioritizing Barriers to Green Manufacturing: Environmental, Social and Economic Perspective. *Procedia CIRP*, *17*, 559–564. doi:10.1016/j.procir.2014.01.075

Mittal, V. K., & Sangwan, K. S. (2014b). Prioritizing Drivers for Green Manufacturing: Environmental, Social and Economic Perspectives. *Procedia CIRP*, *15*, 135–140. doi:10.1016/j.procir.2014.06.038

Modigliani, A. (1968). Embarrassment and embarrassability. *Sociometry*, *31*(3), 313–326. doi:10.2307/2786616 PMID:5681346

Mol, A. (1999). Ontological politics. A word and some questions. In J. Law & J. Hassard (Eds.), *Actor network theory and after* (pp. 74–89). Oxford, UK: Blackwell. doi:10.1111/j.1467-954X.1999.tb03483.x

Mol, A. (2002). *The body multiple: Ontology in medical practice*. Durham, NC: Duke University Press. doi:10.1215/9780822384151

Mol, A. (2010). Actor-network theory: Sensitive terms and enduring tensions. *Kölner Zeitschrift für Soziologie und Sozialpsychologie*, *50*(1), 253–269.

Mol, A., & Law, J. (1994). Regions, networks and fluids: Anaemia and social topology. *Social Studies of Science*, *24*(4), 641–671. doi:10.1177/030631279402400402 PMID:11639423

Moldavska, A., & Welo, T. (2017). The concept of sustainable manufacturing and its definitions: A content-analysis based literature review. *Journal of Cleaner Production*, *166*, 744–755. doi:10.1016/j.jclepro.2017.08.006

Molinillo, S., & Japutra, A. (2017). Organizational adoption of digital information and technology: A theoretical review. *The Bottom Line (New York, N.Y.)*, *30*(01), 33–46. doi:10.1108/BL-01-2017-0002

Mollick, E. (2014). The Dynamics of Crowdfunding: An Exploratory Study. *Journal of Business Venturing, 29*(1), 1-16.

Molloy, J. C., & Barney, J. B. (2015). Who Captures the Value Created with Human Capital? A Market-based View. *The Academy of Management Perspectives, 29*(3), 309–325. doi:10.5465/amp.2014.0152

Moreira, F., Ferreira, M., & Seruca, I. (2018). Enterprise 4.0–the emerging digital transformed enterprise? *Procedia Computer Science, 138*, 525–532. doi:10.1016/j.procs.2018.10.072

Morgan, J. (2013). *Five trends shaping the future of work*. Retrieved March 6, 2019, from https://www.forbes.com/sites/jacobmorgan/2013/06/20/five-trends-shaping-the-future-of-work/#777c696aece0

Moscovici, S. (1988). Notes towards a description of social representations. *Journal of European Social Psychology*, *18*(3), 211–250. doi:10.1002/ejsp.2420180303

Moser, I. (2005). On becoming disabled and articulating alternatives. The multiple ordering of disability and their interferences. *Cultural Studies, 19*(6), 667–700. doi:10.1080/09502380500365648

Moser, I. (2008). Making Alzheimer's disease matter: Enacting, interfering and doing politics of nature. *Geoforum, 39*(1), 98–110. doi:10.1016/j.geoforum.2006.12.007

Motsenigos & Young. (2002). KM in the U.S. government sector. *KM World, 11*.

Mourtzis, D., Vlachou, E., & Milas, N. (2016). Industrial Big Data as a result of IoT adoption in manufacturing. *Procedia CIRP, 55*, 290–295. doi:10.1016/j.procir.2016.07.038

Mujeeb, L. M. (2013). Importance of best human resource management practices and the need for human resource information system (HRIS) for the public health sector in Sri Lanka. *Sri Lanka Journal of Bio-Medical Informatics, 3*(2), 55–62. doi:10.4038ljbmi.v3i2.2449

Müller, J. M., Buliga, O., & Voigt, K. I. (2018). Fortune favors the prepared: How SMEs approach business model innovations in Industry 4.0. *Technological Forecasting and Social Change, 132*, 2–17. doi:10.1016/j.techfore.2017.12.019

Müller, J. M., Kiel, D., & Voigt, K. I. (2018). What Drives the Implementation of Industry 4.0? The Role of Opportunities and Challenges in the Context of Sustainability. *Sustainability, 10*(1), 247. doi:10.3390u10010247

Müller, S., & Zaracko, A. (2010). Haben gehörlose Kleinkinder ein Recht auf ein Cochleaimplantat? *Nervenheilkunde: Zeitschrift für Interdisziplinaere Fortbildung, 29*(04), 244–248. doi:10.1055-0038-1628755

Mulligan, T. (2016). Ethical Consequentialism. *Oxford Bibliographies*. Retrieved March 23, 2019, from http://www.oxfordbibliographies.com/view/document/obo-9780195396577/obo-9780195396577-0026.xml

Mummalaneni, V., & Meng, J. (2009). An exploratory study of young Chinese customers' online shopping behaviors and service quality perceptions. *Young Consumers, 10*(2), 157–169. doi:10.1108/17473610910964732

Munro, R. (1997). Proceedings of the 5th interdisciplinary Perspectives on Accounting Conference. *Power, Conduct and Accountability: Re-Distributing Discretion and the Technologies of Managing*.

Murdoch, J. (1998). The spaces of actor-network theory. *Geoforum, 29*(4), 357–374. doi:10.1016/S0016-7185(98)00011-6

Murphy, J. G., Vuchinich, R. E., & Simpson, C. A. (2001). Delayed reward and cost discounting. *The Psychological Record, 51*, 571–588.

Mutch, A. (2013). Sociomateriality - Taking the wrong turining? *Information and Organization, 23*(1), 28–40. doi:10.1016/j.infoandorg.2013.02.001

Mutingi, M., Musiyarira, H., Mbohwa, C., & Kommula, V. P. (2017). *An Analysis of Enablers and Barriers of Sustainable Manufacturing in Southern Africa* (Vol. 2). WCECS.

Myers, M. D. (2013). *Qualitative Research in Business and Management*. Sage Publications Inc.

Myers, M. D., & Newman, M. (2007). The qualitative interview in IS research: Examining the craft. *Information and Organization, 17*(1), 2–26. doi:10.1016/j.infoandorg.2006.11.001

Myerson, J., & Green, L. (1995). Discounting of delayed rewards: Models of individual choice. *Journal of the Experimental Analysis of Behavior, 64*(3), 263–276. doi:10.1901/jeab.1995.64-263 PMID:16812772

Nadarajah, D., & Kadir, S. L. S. A. (2016). Measuring Business Process Managementusing business process orientation and process improvement initiatives. *Business Process Management Journal, 22*(6), 1069–1078. doi:10.1108/BPMJ-01-2014-0001

Nagendra, A., & Deshpande, M. (2014). Human Resource Information Systems (HRIS) in HR planning and development in mid to large sized organizations. *Procedia: Social and Behavioral Sciences, 133*, 61–67. doi:10.1016/j.sbspro.2014.04.169

Nason, R. S., & Wiklund, J. (2015). An Assessment of Resource-Based Theorizing on Firm Growth and Suggestions for the Future. *Journal of Management*, 1–29.

National Manufacturing Competitiveness Council. (2006). *The National Strategy for Manufacturing*. Available from: http://nmcc.nic.in/pdf/strategy_paper_0306.pdf

National Post. (2019). *Millennials will overtake baby boomers as the largest U.S. population group in 2019*. Retrieved March 6, 2019, from https://nationalpost.com/news/world/millennials-will-overtake-baby-boomers-as-the-largest-u-s-population group in 2019

National Science Foundation. (2011). *Women, Minorities, and Persons with Disabilities in Science and Engineering*. Author.

National Science Foundation. (2014). *Integrated postsecondary education data system, 2013, completions survey*. National Center for Science and Engineering Statistics: Integrated Science and Engineering Resources Data System (WebCASPAR). Retrieved from https://webcaspar.nsf.gov

Nauta, M. M., Epperson, D. L., & Kahn, J. H. (1998). A multiple-groups analysis of predictors of higher level career aspirations among women in mathematics, science, and engineering majors. *Journal of Counseling Psychology, 45*(4), 483–496. doi:10.1037/0022-0167.45.4.483

Nawawi, A., & Salin, A. S. A. P. (2019). Capital statement analysis as a tool to detect tax evasion. *International Journal of Law and Management, 60*(5), 1097–1110. doi:10.1108/IJLMA-03-2017-0024

Ndii, M. Z., Carnia, E., & Supriatna, A. K. (2018). Mathematical models for the spread of rumors: a review. In F. L. Gaol, F. Hutagalung, & C. F. Peng (Eds.), *Issues and Trends in Interdisciplinary Behavior and Social Science, 8*. London: CRC Press; doi:10.1201/9781315148700-8

Nederhof, A. J. (1985). Methods of coping with social desirability bias: A review. *European Journal of Social Psychology, 15*(3), 263–280. doi:10.1002/ejsp.2420150303

Nehme, M. (2018). Regulating crowd equity funding–the why and the how. *Journal of Law and Society, 45*(1), 116–135. doi:10.1111/jols.12082

Nelson, L. J., & Cooper, J. (1997). Gender Differences in Children's Reactions to Success and Failure with Computers. *Computers in Human Behavior*, *13*(2), 247–267. doi:10.1016/S0747-5632(97)00008-3

Nespor, J. (2002). Networks and contexts of reform. *Journal of Educational Change*, *3*(3/4), 365–382. doi:10.1023/A:1021281913741

Neubauer, T. (2009). An empirical study about the status of business process management. *Business Process Management Journal*, *15*(2), 166–183. doi:10.1108/14637150910949434

Neuman, W., Russel, M. R. J., & Crigler, A. N. (1992). *Common knowledge*. Chicago: Chicago University Press. doi:10.7208/chicago/9780226161174.001.0001

New Generation Applications. (2018). 21 Big Data Statistics & Predictions on the Future of Big Data. *Blog*. Retrieved March 5, 2019, from https://www.newgenapps.com/blog/big-data-statistics-predictions-on-the-future-of-big-data

Ng, B. Y., Kankanhalli, A., & Xu, Y. (2009). Studying users' computer security behavior: A health belief perspective. *Decision Support Systems*, *46*(4), 815–825. doi:10.1016/j.dss.2008.11.010

Nguyen, D. H., de Leeuw, S., & Dullaert, W. E. (2018). Consumer behaviour and order fulfilment in online retailing: A systematic review. *International Journal of Management Reviews*, *20*(2), 255–276. doi:10.1111/ijmr.12129

Nguyen, T. H., Mewby, M., & Macaulay, M. L. (2015). Information Technology Adoption in Small Business: Confirmation of a Proposed Framework. *Journal of Small Business Management*, *53*(1), 207–227. doi:10.1111/jsbm.12058

Nicholson, J. D., & Stepina, L. P. (1998). Cultural values: A cross-national study. *Cross Cultural Management*, *5*(1), 34–49.

Niels, A., & Janneck, M. (2017). Understanding the Relations Between Self-concept and Causal Attributions Regarding Computer Use. In Harris, D. (Ed.), *Engineering Psychology and Cognitive Ergonomics: Performance, Emotion and Situation Awareness: 14th International Conference, EPCE 2017* (pp. 180-199). Springer International Publishing. 10.1007/978-3-319-58472-0_15

Niels, A., Guczka, S., & Janneck, M. (2016). The Impact of Causal Attributions on System Evaluations in Usability Tests. In *Proceedings of the 2016 CHI Conference on Human Factors in Computing Systems* (pp. 3115-3125). ACM. 10.1145/2858036.2858471

Niels, A., & Janneck, M. (2015). Computer-Related Attribution Styles: Typology and Data Collection Methods. In *INTERACT 2015, Part II, LNCS 9297* (pp. 274–291). Springer International Publishing. doi:10.1007/978-3-319-22668-2_22

Niels, A., Jent, S., Janneck, M., & Zagel, C. (2019). Correlations Between Computer-Related Causal Attributions and User Persistence. In T. Z. Ahram (Ed.), *Advances in Artificial Intelligence, Software and Systems Engineering* (pp. 242–251). Cham: Springer. doi:10.1007/978-3-319-94229-2_23

Noejovich, H. (2011). Ordoliberalismo ¿alternativa al "neoliberalismo"? *Economía*, *67*, 203–211.

Nolan Norton Institute. (1998). *Putting the Knowing Organization to Value*. White Paper. Author.

Nonaka, I. (1994). A Dynamic Theory of Organizational Knowledge Creation. *Organization Science*, *5*(1), 14–37. doi:10.1287/orsc.5.1.14

Nonaka, I., & Takeuchi, H. (1995). *The Knowledge-creating Company*. New York: Oxford University Press.

Norris, P., & Sanders, D. (2003). Message or medium? Campaign learning during the 2001 British General Election. *Political Communication*, *20*(3), 233–262. doi:10.1080/10584600390218878

North, A. S., & Noyes, J. M. (2002). Gender influences on children's computer attitudes and cognitions. *Computers in Human Behavior, 18*(2), 135–150. doi:10.1016/S0747-5632(01)00043-7

North, D. C. (1990). *Institutions, Institutional Change, and Economic Performance.* Cambridge University Press. doi:10.1017/CBO9780511808678

Noutsa, F. A., Kamdjoug, J. R. K., & Wamba, S. F. (2017). *Acceptance and Use of HRIS and Influence on Organizational Performance of SMEs in a Developing Economy: The Case of Cameroon.* Presented at World Conference on Information System and Technologies.

Novak, R., & Janeš, A. (2018). Business process orientation in the Slovenian power supply. *Business Process Management Journal.* doi:10.1108/BPMJ-05-2017-0130

Noyes, K. (2014). Why Investors Are Pouring Millions into Crowdfunding. *Fortune Magazine.* Available: http://fortune.com/2014/04/17/why-investors-arepouring-millions-into-crowdfunding/

Noys, B. (2010). *The persistence of the negative: A critique of contemporary continental thought.* Edinburgh, UK: Edinburgh University Press. doi:10.3366/edinburgh/9780748638635.001.0001

Nulty, D. D. (2008). The adequacy of response rates to online and paper surveys: What can be done? *Assessment & Evaluation in Higher Education, 33*(3), 301–314. doi:10.1080/02602930701293231

Nunes, M. B., Annansingh, F., & Eaglestone, B. (2006). Knowledge management issues in knowledge-intensive SMEs. *The Journal of Documentation, 62*(1), 101–119. doi:10.1108/00220410610642075

Nunnally, J. C. (1978). *Psychometric Theory.* New York, NY: McGraw-Hill.

O'Rourke, C., Fishman, N., & Selkow, W. (2003). *Enterprise architecture using the Zachman framework.* Boston, MA: Course Technology.

Ochsner, B. (2013). Teilhabeprozesse oder: Das Versprechen des Cochlea-Implantats. Augenblick. *Konstanzer Hefte zur Medienwissenschaft, 58,* 112–123.

Ochsner, B., & Stock, R. (2014). Das Hören des Cochlea Implantats. *Historische Anthropologie, 22*(3), 408–425. doi:10.7788/ha-2014-0308

Oguz, F., & Sengün, A. (2011). Mystery of the unknown: Revisiting tacit knowledge in the organizational literature. *Journal of Knowledge Management, 15*(3), 445–461. doi:10.1108/13673271111137420

Ojo, O., & Nwaokike. (2018). Disruptive Technology and the Fintech Industry in Nigeria: Imperatives for Legal and Policy Responses. *Gravitas Review of Business and Property Law, 9*(3). Available: SSRN: https://ssrn.com/abstract=3306164

Okada, E. M., & Hoch, S. J. (2004). Spending time versus spending money. *The Journal of Consumer Research, 31*(2), 313–323. doi:10.1086/422110

Olawumi, S. O., Lateef, L. A., & Oladeji, E. O. (2017). Financial Deepening and Bank Performance: A Case Study of Selected Commercial Banks in Nigeria. *Journal of Mathematical Finance, 7*(03), 519–535. doi:10.4236/jmf.2017.73028

Oliveira, T., Alhinho, M., Rita, P., & Dhillon, G. (2017). Modelling and testing consumer trust dimensions in e-commerce. *Computers in Human Behavior, 71,* 153–164. doi:10.1016/j.chb.2017.01.050

Oliver, D. G., Serovich, J. M., & Mason, T. L. (1995). Constraints and Opportunities with Interview Transcription: Towards Reflection in Qualitative Research. *Social Forces, 84*(2), 1273–1289. doi:10.1353of.2006.0023 PMID:16534533

Oliver, R. T. (1971). *Communication and culture in ancient India and China.* Syracuse, NY: Syracuse University Press.

Olken, B. A. (2009). Do television and radio destroy social capital? Evidence from Indonesian villages. *American Economic Journal. Applied Economics, 1*(4), 1–33. doi:10.1257/app.1.4.1

Olowe, F. T., Moradeyo, O. A., & Babalola, O. A. (2013). Empirical study of the impact of microfinance bank on small and medium growth in Nigeria. *International Journal of Academic Research in Economics and Management Sciences, 2*(6), 116–124.

Olson, C. B., Stander, V. A., & Merrill, L. L. (2004). The influence of survey confidentiality and construct measurement in estimating rates of childhood victimization among navy recruits. *Military Psychology, 16*(1), 53–69. doi:10.120715327876mp1601_4

Omega Management Group Corp. and Coveo. (2011). *The knowledge-driven support organization and its impact on the customer experience.* Retrieved March 6, 2019, from http://www.omegascoreboard.com/pdf/finalresults.pdf

Omerzel, D. G., & Antoncic, B. (2008). Critical Entrepreneur Knowledge Dimensions for the SME Performance. *Industrial Management & Data Systems, 108*(9), 1182–1199. doi:10.1108/02635570810914883

Onakoya, A., Fasanya, I., & Abdulrahman, H. (2013). Small and Medium Scale Enterprises Financing and Economic Growth in Nigeria-. *European Journal of Business and Management, 5*(4), 2222–2839.

Oost, D., & Chew, E. (2007). *Investigating the Concept of Information Security Culture: UTS.* Hoboken, NJ: Auerbach Publications School of Management Working Paper: No. 2007/6.

Organization for Economic Co-operation and Development (OECD). (2000). Small and Medium-sized Enterprises: local Strength, global reach. *OECD Policy Review,* 1-8.

Orlikowski, W. (2000). Using Technology and Constituting Structures: A Practice Lens for Studying Technology in Organizations. *Organization Science, 11*(4), 404–421. doi:10.1287/orsc.11.4.404.14600

Orlikowski, W. J. (2007). Sociomaterial Practices: Exploring Technology at Work. *Organization Studies, 28*(9), 1435–1448. doi:10.1177/0170840607081138

Orlikowski, W. J., & Scott, S. V. (2008). Sociomateriality: Challenging the Separation of Technology, Work and Organization. *The Academy of Management Annals, 2*(1), 433–474. doi:10.1080/19416520802211644

Orwell, G. (1949). 1984. New York: Harcourt Brace.

Osatuyi, B., & Passerini, K. (n.d.). Twittermania: Understanding how social media technologies impact engagement and academic performance of a new generation of learners, *Communications of the AIS.*

Oster, S.M. & Scott-Morton, F.M.S. (2005). Behavioral biases meet the market: The case of magazine subscription prices. *Advances in Economic Analysis & Policy, 5*(1), 1-32.

Ostroff, F. (2006, May). Change Management in Government. *Harvard Business Review.* PMID:16649704

Oulasvirta, A., Suomalainen, T., Hamari, J., Lampinen, A., & Karvonen, K. (2014). Transparency of intentions decreases privacy concerns in ubiquitous surveillance. *Cyberpsychology, Behavior, and Social Networking, 17*(10), 633–638. doi:10.1089/cyber.2013.0585 PMID:25226054

Ozga, J. (2009). Governing education through data in England: From regulation to self-evaluation. *Journal of Education Policy, 24*(2), 149–162. doi:10.1080/02680930902733121

Pablo, A. L. (1994). Determinants of Acquisition Integration Level: A Decision-Making Perspective. *Academy of Management Journal, 37*(4), 803–836.

Paine, L. S. (1994). Managing for organizational integrity. *Harvard Business Review*. Retrieved October 10, 2018, from https://hbr.org/1994/03/managing-for-organizational-integrity

Palacios-Marqués, D., Soto-Acosta, P., & Merigó, J. M. (2015). Analyzing the effects of technological, organizational and competition factors on Web knowledge exchange in SMEs. *Telematics and Informatics*, *32*(1), 23–32. doi:10.1016/j.tele.2014.08.003

Paluck, E. L. (2009). What's in a norm? Sources and processes of norm change. *Journal of Personality and Social Psychology*, *96*(3), 594–600. doi:10.1037/a0014688 PMID:19254106

Pandya, D. C., & Patel, D. N. J. (2017). Study and analysis of E-Governance Information Security (InfoSec) in Indian Context. *IOSR Journal of Computer Engineering, 19*(1), 4–7. doi:10.9790/0661-1901040407

Panetto, H., & Whitman, L. (2016). Knowledge engineering for enterprise integration, interoperability and networking: Theory and applications. *Data & Knowledge Engineering*, *105*, 1–4. doi:10.1016/j.datak.2016.05.001

Paoloni, P., Cesaroni, F. M., & Demartini, P. (2019). Relational capital and knowledge transfer in universities. *Business Process Management Journal*, *25*(1), 185–201. doi:10.1108/BPMJ-06-2017-0155

Pareto, V. (2014). *Manual of political economy*. Oxford, UK: Oxford University Press. (Original work published 1906)

Park, C., Vertinsky, I., & Becerra, M. (2013). Transfers of explicit vs. tacit knowledge and performance in international joint ventures: The impact of age. *International Business Review*, *24*(1), 89–101. doi:10.1016/j.ibusrev.2014.06.004

Parker, E. (2017). An actor-network theory reading of change for children in public care. *British Educational Research Journal*, *43*(1), 151–167. doi:10.1002/berj.3257

Parra, Argote, & Farro. (2018). Emprendimiento universitario: análisis de contraste entre la Universidad EAN Colombia y la Universidad Continental Perú. *Universidad EAN, 2018*, 7–38.

Parra, L., & Argote, M. (2013). La gestión en el proceso de creación empresarial: el caso de IN3 de la Universidad EAN de Colombia. In *Emprendimiento: diferentes aproximaciones*. Cuaderno de investigación. Editorial Universidad EAN.

Parra, L., & Argote, M. (2016a). Marco Conceptual para el Análisis de Brechas tecnológicas en el Sector Metalmecánico. Análisis de brechas tecnológicas en el sector.

Parra, L., & Argote, M. (2017). Data Analytics to Characterize UniversityBased Companies for Decision Making in Business Development Programs. In E. Rodriguez (Ed.), *Data Analytics Applications in Latin America and Emerging Economies*. CRC Press, Taylor and Francis.

Patrick, K., & Dotsika, F. (2007). Knowledge sharing: Developing from within. *The Learning Organization*, *5*(14), 395–406. doi:10.1108/09696470710762628

Patrignani, N., & Kavathatzopoulos, I. (2016). Cloud computing: The ultimate step towards the virtual enterprise? *ACM SIGCAS Computers and Society*, *45*(3), 68–72. doi:10.1145/2874239.2874249

Patriotta, G. (2003). *Organizational Knowledge in the Making - How Firms Create, Use, and Institutionalise Knowledge*. Oxford, UK: Oxford University Press.

Paulhus, D. L. (1991). *Measurement and control of response bias* (Vol. 1). New York: Academic Press.

Paul, P., & Saraswathi, R. (2017). The Internet of Things – A comprehensive survey. In *Proceedings of the International Conference on Computation of Power, Energy Information and Communication* (pp. 421-426). Piscataway, NJ: IEEE Computer Society Press. 10.1109/ICCPEIC.2017.8290405

Pautasso, C. (2014). RESTful web services: principles, patterns, emerging technologies. In A. Bouguettaya, Q. Sheng, & F. Daniel (Eds.), Web Services Foundations (pp. 31-51). New York, NY: Springer. doi:10.1007/978-1-4614-7518-7_2

Pavic, S., Koh, S. C. L., Simpson, M., & Padmore, J. (2007). Could e-business create a competitive advantage in UK SMEs? *Benchmarking: An International Journal, 14*(3), 320–351. doi:10.1108/14635770710753112

Pavlou, P. A., & El Sawy, O. A. (2006). From IT Leveraging Competence to Competitive Advantage in Turbulent Environments: The Case of New Product Development. *Information Systems Research, 17*(3), 198–227. doi:10.1287/isre.1060.0094

Pavlov, A. (2010). Modified algorithm with combinatorial selection and variables orthogonalization and its analysis. In Inductive modeling of complex systems (pp. 130-139). Academic Press.

Pedersen, M. R., Nalpantidis, L., Andersen, R. S., Schou, C., Bøgh, S., Krüger, V., & Madsen, O. (2016). Robot skills for manufacturing: From concept to industrial deployment. *Robotics and Computer-integrated Manufacturing, 37*, 282–291. doi:10.1016/j.rcim.2015.04.002

Pels, D. (1996). The politics of symmetry. *Social Studies of Science, 26*(2), 277–304. doi:10.1177/030631296026002004

Peltier, D. B., & Walsh, J. A. (1990). An investigation of response bias in the Chapman Scales. *Educational and Psychological Measurement, 50*(4), 803–815. doi:10.1177/0013164490504008

Peltier, J. W., Zhao, Y., & Schibrowsky, J. A. (2012). Technology adoption by small businesses: An exploratory study of the interrelationships of owner and environmental factors. *International Small Business Journal, 30*(4), 406–431. doi:10.1177/0266242610365512

Perangkaan, J., & Menteri, J. P. (2015). *Brunei Darussalam Statistical Yearbook 2015*. Academic Press.

Peregudov, F.I., & Tarasenko, F.P. (1989). *Introduction to system analysis*. Moscow: Radio and Communication.

Perez, J. R., & de Pablos, P. O. (2003). Knowledge management and organizational competitiveness: A framework for human capital analysis. *Journal of Knowledge Management, 7*(3), 82–91. doi:10.1108/13673270310485640

Pérez-López, S., & Alegre, J. (2012). Information technology competency, knowledge processes and firm performance. *Industrial Management & Data Systems, 112*(4), 644–662. doi:10.1108/02635571211225521

Perks, M. (2015). *Everything you need to know but were afraid to ask: the Digital Workplace*. Retrieved October 6, 2018, from https://www.unily.com/media/23747/the-digital-workplace-guide-whitepaper.pdf

Perlow, L. A. (2012). *Sleeping with your Smartphone: How to Break the 24/7 Habit and Change the Way You Work*. Boston, MA: Harvard Business School Press.

Peršič, A., Markič, M., & Peršič, M. (2016). The impact of socially responsible management standards on the business success of an organisation. *Total Quality Management & Business Excellence*. doi:10.1080/14783363.2016.1174059

Peslak, A. R. (2012). An analysis of critical information technology issues facing organizations. *Industrial Management & Data Systems, 112*(5), 808–827. doi:10.1108/02635571211232389

Peterson, R. A., & Kerin, R. A. (1981). *The quality of self-report data: Review and synthesis*. Chicago: American Marketing Association.

Petry, N. M., & Casarella, T. (1999). Excessive discounting of delayed rewards in substance abusers with gambling problems. *Drug and Alcohol Dependence, 56*(1), 25–32. doi:10.1016/S0376-8716(99)00010-1 PMID:10462089

Pettigrew, A. (1997). What is Processual Analysis? *Scandinavian Journal of Management, 13*(4), 337–348. doi:10.1016/S0956-5221(97)00020-1

Pew Research Center. (2015). *From Telephone to the Web: The challenge of mode of interview effects in public opinion polls.* Author.

Pew Research Center. (2018a). Social Media Use in 2018. *Pew Research Center: Internet & Technology.* Retrieved March 4, 2019, from http://www.pewinternet.org/2018/03/01/social-media-use-in-2018/

Pew Research Center. (2018b). American's complicated feelings about social media in an era of privacy concerns. *Pew Research Center: FACTTANK.* Retrieved March 4, 2019, from http://www.pewresearch.org/fact-tank/2018/03/27/americans-complicated-feelings-about-social-media-in-an-era-of-privacy-concerns/

Peyton Young, H. (2005). Social Dynamics: Theory and Applications. *Computational Economics,* 1–45.

Pham, T. S. H., & Ahammad, M. F. (2017). Antecedents and consequences of online customer satisfaction: A holistic process perspective. *Technological Forecasting and Social Change, 124,* 332–342. doi:10.1016/j.techfore.2017.04.003

Philip, B. (2017). How Blockchain Technology Could Change Our Lives. *European Union,* 1–24.

Pillania, R. K. (2006). Leveraging Knowledge for Sustainable Competitiveness in SMEs. *International Journal of Globalisation and Small Business, 1*(4), 393–406. doi:10.1504/IJGSB.2006.012187

Pillania, R. K. (2006c). Current status of storage and access of knowledge in Indian industry. *Journal of Information and Knowledge Management, 5*(1), 37–46. doi:10.1142/S0219649206001347

Pillania, R. K. (2008). Strategic Issues in Knowledge Management in Small and Medium Enterprises. *Knowledge Management Research and Practice, 6*(4), 334–338. doi:10.1057/kmrp.2008.21

Pillania, R. K. (2008b). Information technology strategy for knowledge management in SMEs. *Knowledge and Process Management, 15*(3), 41–49. doi:10.1002/kpm.311

Pink, B. (n.d.). *Australian Social Trends.* Australian Bureau of Statistics Catalogue no. 4102.

Pisa & Juden. (2017). *Blockchain and Economic Development: Hype vs. Reality. Technical Report.* Center for Global Development.

Plachkinova, M., & Maurer, C. (2018). Teaching case security breach at target. *Journal of Information Systems Education, 29*(1), 11–20. Retrieved from http://jise.org/Volume29/n1/JISEv29n1p11.html

Plaza, B. (2011). Google Analytics for measuring website performance. *Tourism Management, 32*(3), 477–481. doi:10.1016/j.tourman.2010.03.015

Ployhart, R. E., & Moliterno, T. P. (2011a). Emergence of the Human Capital Resource: A Mulitlevel Model. *Academy of Management Review, 36*(1), 127–150. doi:10.5465/amr.2009.0318

Ployhart, R. E., Nyberg, A. J., Reilly, G., & Maltarich, M. A. (2014). Human Capital Is Dead; Long Live Human Capital Resources! *Journal of Management, 40*(2), 371–398. doi:10.1177/0149206313512152

Poland, B. D. (1995). Transcription Quality as an Aspect of Rigor in Qualitative Research. *Qualitative Inquiry, 1*(3), 290–310. doi:10.1177/107780049500100302

Polanyi, M. (1962). *Personal Knowledge: Toward a Post- Critical Philosophy.* New York: Harper Torchbooks.

Polanyi, M. (1967). *The Tacit Dimension.* London: Routledge and Keoan Paul.

Pontryagin, L. S., Boltyanskii, V. G., Gamkrelidze, R. V., & Mishchenko, E. F. (1962). *The Mathematical Theory of Optimal Processes (English translation).* Geneva: Interscience.

Poole, M. S., & Van De Ven, A. H. (2004). *Handbook of Organizational Change and Innovation.* Oxford University Press.

Pope, D. G., & Sydnor, J. R. (2011). What's in a picture? Evidence of discrimination from Prosper.com. *The Journal of Human Resources, 46*(1), 53–92. doi:10.3368/jhr.46.1.53

Pöppelbuß, J., & Röglinger, M. (2011). What makes a useful maturity model? A framework of general design principles for maturity models and its demonstration in business process management. In *Proceedings of the 19th European Conference on Information Systems.* Helsinki, Finland: ECIS.

Popplewell, K. (2014). Enterprise interoperability science base structure. In K. Mertins, F. Bénaben, R. Poler, & J. Bourrières (Eds.), *Enterprise Interoperability VI: Interoperability for Agility, Resilience and Plasticity of Collaborations* (pp. 417–427). Cham, Switzerland: Springer International Publishing. doi:10.1007/978-3-319-04948-9_35

Porter, M. E., & Stern, S. (2002). National Innovative capacity. Academic Press.

Posner, R. A. (1981). The economic of privacy. *The American Economic Review, 71*(2), 405–409.

Posner, R. A. (2000). *Law and social norms.* Cambridge, MA: Harvard University Press.

Prat, A., & Strömberg, D. (2005). *Commercial television and voter information.* CEPR Discussion Paper 4989.

Prat, A., & Strömberg, D. (2013). *The political economy of mass media.* New York: Columbia University Working Paper. Retrievable at http://www.columbia.edu/~ap3116/papers/mediasurvey11.pdf

Prat, A. (2005). The wrong kind of transparency. *The American Economic Review, 95*(3), 862–877. doi:10.1257/0002828054201297

Prat, A. (2017). *Lecture notes 'Industrial Organization.* New York: Columbia University.

Preidel, C., & Borrmann, A. (2016). Towards code compliance checking on the basis of a visual programming language. *Journal of Information Technology in Construction, 21*(25), 402–421.

Pressman, S. (2011). La clase media en países latinoamericanos. *Revista Problemas del Desarrollo, 164*(42), 127–152.

PricewaterhouseCoopers. (2011). *Millennials at work: reshaping the workplace.* Retrieved March 6, 2019, from https://www.pwc.com/co/es/publicaciones/assets/millennials-at-work.pdf

Przybylski, A. K., & Weinstein, N. (2013). Can you connect with me now? How the presence of mobile communication technology influences face-to-face communication quality. *Journal of Social and Personal Relationships, 30*, 237 –246.

Puaschunder, J. M. (2016). Trust and reciprocity drive common goods allocation norms. In *Proceedings of the Cambridge Business & Economics Conference.* Cambridge, UK: Cambridge University. 10.5465/ambpp.2016.17526abstract

Puaschunder, J. M. (in progress). *On the collective soul of booms and busts.* Retrievable at https://papers.ssrn.com/sol3/papers.cfm?abstract_id=2799646

Puaschunder, J. M., & Schwarz, G. (2012). *The future is now: How joint decision making curbs hyperbolic discounting but blurs social responsibility in the intergenerational equity public policy domain.* Harvard University Situationist Law and Mind Sciences Working Paper.

Puaschunder, J. M. (2015). On the social representations of intergenerational equity. *Oxford Journal of Finance and Risk Perspectives, 4*(4), 78–99.

Puaschunder, J. M. (2017). Nudgital: Critique of Behavioral Political Economy. *Archives of Business Research*, *5*(9), 54–76. doi:10.14738/abr.59.3623

Putnam, H. (2002). On the rationality of preferences. In H. Putnam (Ed.), *The Collapse of the Fact-Value Dichotomy and Other Essays*. Cambridge, MA: Harvard University Press.

Putnam, R. D. (2000). *Bowling alone: The collapse and revival of American community*. New York: Simon & Schuster.

Quinn, M. J. (2017). *Ethics for the Information Age*. Hoboken, NJ: Pearson.

Qureshi, M. O., Kaur, M. K., & Sajjad, S. R. (2013). An empirical analysis of organizations using Human Resource Information System (HRIS) in India: An employee perspective. *International Journal of Economics and Management Sciences*, *2*(9), 54–63.

Racevskis, K. (1983). *Michel Foucault and the subversion of the intellect*. Ithaca, N.Y.: Cornell UP.

Racherla, P., & Furner, C. P. (2009). *Cultural determinants of consumers' evaluation of online product reviews: An uncertainty reduction perspective*. Paper presented at the International Conference on Information Systems - Cross Cultural Research on Information Systems SIG.

Rachlin, H., Raineri, A., & Cross, D. (1991). Subjective probability and delay. *Journal of the Experimental Analysis of Behavior*, *55*(2), 233–244. doi:10.1901/jeab.1991.55-233 PMID:2037827

Radovic, A., Gmelin, T., Stein, B.D., & Miller, E. J. (2017). *Depressed adolescents' positive and negative use of social media*. Academic Press.

Rahim Mosahab, P. C. (2010). *Service Quality, Customer Satisfaction and Loyalty: A Test of Mediation*. Academic Press.

Rahman, M.A., Qi, X., Jinnah, M.S. (2016). Factors affecting the adoption of HRIS by the Bangladeshi banking and financial sector. *Cogent Business and Management*, *3*, 1–10.

Rahman, M. A., Islam, M. D., & Qi, X. (2017). Barriers in Adopting Human Resource Information System (HRIS): An Empirical Study on Selected Bangladeshi Garments Factories. *International Business Research*, *10*(6), 98–105. doi:10.5539/ibr.v10n6p98

Rahman, Z. A., & Shah, I. M. (2015). Measuring Islamic Spiritual Intelligence. *Procedia Economics and Finance*, *31*(15), 134–139. doi:10.1016/S2212-5671(15)01140-5

Ramachandra, G., Iftikhar, M., & Khan, F. A. (2017). A Comprehensive Survey on Security in Cloud Computing. *Procedia Computer Science*, *110*, 465–472. doi:10.1016/j.procs.2017.06.124

Ramdani, B., Kawalek, P., & Lorenzo, O. (2009). Predicting SMEs' adoption of enterprise systems. *Journal of Enterprise Information Management*, *22*(1/2), 10–24. doi:10.1108/17410390910922796

Ramsey, F. P. (1928). A mathematical theory of savings. *Economic Journal (London)*, *38*(152), 543–559. doi:10.2307/2224098

Ranft, A. L., & Lord, M. D. (2002). Acquiring New Technologies and Capabilities: A Grounded Model of Acquisition Implementation. *Organization Science*, *13*(4), 420–441. doi:10.1287/orsc.13.4.420.2952

Ranga, M., Temel, S., Ar, I. M., Yesilay, R. B., & Sukan, F. V. (2016). Building Technology Transfer Capacity in Turkish Universities: A critical analysis. *European Journal of Education*, *51*(1), 90–106. doi:10.1111/ejed.12164

Rangriz, H., Mehrabi, J., & Azadegan, A. (2011). The Impact of Human Resource Information System in Strategic Decisions in Iran. *Computer and Information Science*, *4*(2), 81–88. doi:10.5539/cis.v4n2p81

Ranjbarian, B., Fathi, S., & Jooneghani, R. B. N. (2012). The Effect of Brand Extension Strategies upon Brand Image in the Sport Apparel Market. *International Journal of Academic Research in Business and Social Sciences, 2*(10), 48.

Ravasan, A. Z., Rouhani, S., & Asgary, S. (2013). A Review for the Online Social Networks Literature (2005-2011). *European Journal of Business and Management, 6*(4).

Ravesteyn, P., & Batenburg, R. (2010). Surveying the critical success factors of BPM-systems implementation. *Business Process Management Journal, 16*(3), 492–507. doi:10.1108/14637151011049467

Read, D. (2001). Is time-discounting hyperbolic or subadditive? *Journal of Risk and Uncertainty, 23*(1), 1, 5–32. doi:10.1023/A:1011198414683

Read, D. R. (1964). A quantitative approach to the comparative assessment of taste quality in the confectionery industry. *Biometrics, 20*(1), 143–155. doi:10.2307/2527623

Read, D. R., & van Leeuwen, B. (1998). Predicting hunger: The effects of appetite and delay on choice. *Organizational Behavior and Human Decision Processes, 76*(2), 189–205. doi:10.1006/obhd.1998.2803 PMID:9831521

Read, D., Frederick, S., & Airoldi, M. (2012). Four days later in Cincinnati: Longitudinal tests of intertemporal preference reversals due to hyperbolic discounting. *Acta Psychologica, 140*(2), 177–185. doi:10.1016/j.actpsy.2012.02.010 PMID:22634266

Read, D., Loewenstein, G., & Kalyanaraman, S. (1999). Mixing virtue and vice: The combined effects of hyperbolic discounting and diversification. *Journal of Behavioral Decision Making, 12*, 257–273. doi:10.1002/(SICI)1099-0771(199912)12:4<257::AID-BDM327>3.0.CO;2-6

Reed, D. D., & Martens, B. K. (2011). Temporal discounting predicts student responsiveness to exchange delays in a classroom token system. *Journal of Applied Behavior Analysis, 44*(1), 1–18. doi:10.1901/jaba.2011.44-1 PMID:21541113

Reed, M. I. (1997). In praise of duality and dualism: Rethinking agency and structure in organizational analysis. *Organization Studies, 18*(1), 21–42. doi:10.1177/017084069701800103

Reijers, H. A. (2006). Implementing BPM systems: The role of process orientation. *Business Process Management Journal, 12*(4), 389–409. doi:10.1108/14637150610678041

Rettinger, D. A., & Jordan, A. E. (2005). The relations among religion, motivation, and college cheating: A natural experiment. *Ethics & Behavior, 15*(2), 107–129. doi:10.120715327019eb1502_2

Reuben, E., Sapienza, P., & Zingales, L. (2010). Time-discounting for primary and monetary rewards. *Economics Letters, 106*(2), 125–127. doi:10.1016/j.econlet.2009.10.020

Reus, T. H., Lamont, B. T., & Ellis, K. M. (2016). A darker side of knowledge transfer following international acquisitions. *Strategic Management Journal, 37*(5), 932–944. doi:10.1002mj.2373

Reyt, J., & Wiesenfeld, B. M. (2015). Seeing the forest for the trees: exploratory learning, mobile technology, and knowledge workers' role integration behaviors. Academy of Management Journal, 58, 739–762.

Rezaei, R., Chiew, T., & Lee, S. (2014). A review on E-business interoperability frameworks. *Journal of Systems and Software, 93*, 199–216. doi:10.1016/j.jss.2014.02.004

Rheinberger, H.-J. (1997). *Toward a history of epistemic things: Synthesizing proteins in the test tube*. Stanford, CA: Stanford UP.

Richard, M. O., Chebat, J. C., Yang, Z., & Putrevu, S. (2010). A proposed model of online consumer behavior: Assessing the role of gender. *Journal of Business Research, 63*(9-10), 926–934. doi:10.1016/j.jbusres.2009.02.027

Richardson, H. S. (2018). Moral Reasoning. *Stanford Encyclopedia of Moral Reasoning*. Retrieved March 1, 2019, from https://plato.stanford.edu/entries/reasoning-moral/

Richman, W. L., Kiesler, S., Weisband, S., & Drasgow, F. (1999). A meta-analytic study of social desirability distortion in computer-administered questionnaires, traditional questionnaires and interviews. *The Journal of Applied Psychology*, *84*(5), 754–775. doi:10.1037/0021-9010.84.5.754

Ridgeway, C. L. (2001). Gender, Status, and Leadership. *The Journal of Social Issues*, *57*(4), 637–655. doi:10.1111/0022-4537.00233

RightScale. (2017). *State of the Cloud Report*. Retrieved March 6, 2019, from https://www.rightscale.com/blog/cloud-industry-insights/cloud-computing-trends-2017-state-cloud-survey#cloud-workloads

Riles, A. (2000). *The network inside out*. Ann Arbor, MI: University of Michigan Press. doi:10.3998/mpub.15517

Ritter, D., May, N., & Rinderle-Ma, S. (2017). Patterns for emerging application integration scenarios: A survey. *Information Systems*, *67*, 36–57. doi:10.1016/j.is.2017.03.003

Ritvala, T., Salmi, A., & Andersson, P. (2014). MNCs and local cross-sector partnerships: The case of a smarter Baltic Sea. *International Business Review*, *23*(5), 942–951. doi:10.1016/j.ibusrev.2014.02.006

Rivard, S. (2014). Editor's Comments: The Ions of Construction. *Management Information Systems Quarterly*, *38*(2), iii–xiii.

Roberts, A. S. (2010). *The logic of discipline: Global capitalism and the architecture of government*. New York: Oxford University Press. doi:10.1093/acprof:oso/9780195374988.001.0001

Robey, D. (1980). Computers and management structure: some empirical findings re-examined. In D. Katz, R. L. Kahn, & J. S. Adams (Eds.), *The Study of Organizations* (pp. 33–42). San Francisco, CA: Jossey-Bass.

Roblek, V., Meško, M., Dimovski, V., & Peterlin, J. (2019). Smart technologies as social innovation and complex social issues of the Z generation. *Kybernetes*, *48*(1), 91–107. doi:10.1108/K-09-2017-0356

Rodriguez, E. (Ed.). (2017). *Data Analytics applications in Latin America and emerging economies* (1st ed.). New York: Taylor and Francis. doi:10.4324/9781315164113

Roeser, T., & Kern, E. M. (2015). Surveys in business process management–a literature review. *Business Process Management Journal*, *21*(3), 692–718. doi:10.1108/BPMJ-07-2014-0065

Rokhman, W. (2010). The Effect of Islamic Work Ethics on Work Outcomes. *Electronic Journal of Business Ethics and Organization Studies*, *15*(1), 21–27. doi:10.4103/1817-7417.104699

Romi, S., & Schmida, M. (2009). Non-formal education: A major educational force in the postmodern era. *Cambridge Journal of Education*, *39*(2), 257–273. doi:10.1080/03057640902904472

Rose, N. (1996). *Inventing ourselves: Psychology, power and personhood*. Cambridge, UK: Cambridge University Press. doi:10.1017/CBO9780511752179

Rosenberg, M. J., & Hovland, C. I. (1960). Cognitive, Affective, and Behavioral Components of Attitudes. In Attitude organization and change: An analysis of consistency among attitude components (pp. 1-14). New Haven, CT: Yale University Press.

Rosen, I., Lane, R., Morrill, S., & Belli, J. (1991). Treatment plan optimization using linear programming. *Medical Physics*, *18*(2), 141–152. doi:10.1118/1.596700 PMID:2046598

Rosenthal, S. B. (2019). Situation Ethics. *Encyclopedia Britannica*. Retrieved March 12, 2019, from https://www.britannica.com/topic/situation-ethics

Ross, S. (2011). ROSI Scanarios. *Information Systems Control Journal, 3*. Available: https://www.isaca.org/Journal/archives/2011/Volume-2/Pages/What-is-the-value-of-security.aspx

Roth, A. V., Tsay, A. A., Pullman, M. E., & Gray, J. V. (2008). Unraveling the food supply chain: Strategic insights from China and the 2007 recalls. Journal Supply chain Management. *Global Rev. Purch. Supply, 44*(1), 22–39.

Roth, A., Singhal, J., Singhal, K., & Tang, C. S. (2016). Knowledge creation and dissemination in operations and supply chain management. *Production and Operations Management, 25*(9), 1473–1488. doi:10.1111/poms.12590

Rothaermel, F. T., Agung, S. D., & Jiang, L. (2007). University entrepreneurship: A taxonomy of the literature. *Industrial and Corporate Change, 16*(4), 691–791. doi:10.1093/icc/dtm023

Rothenberg, J. (1961). *The measurement of social welfare*. Englewood Cliffs, NJ: Prentice Hall.

Roxas, B., Battisti, M., & Deakins, D. (2014). Learning, innovation and firm performance: Knowledge management in small firms. *Knowledge Management Research and Practice, 12*(4), 443–453. doi:10.1057/kmrp.2012.66

Rudy, A. P. (2005). On ANT and relational materialism. *Capitalism, Nature, Socialism, 16*(4), 109–125. doi:10.1080/10455750500376065

Ruostela, J., & Lönnqvis, A. (2013). Exploring more productive way of working. World Academy of Science, Engineering and Technology, 73, 711-719.

Sadiq, U., Khan, A. F., & Ikhlaq, K. (2012). The Impact of Information Systems on the Performance of Human Resource Department. *Journal of Business Studies Quarterly, 3*(4), 77–91.

Sa, F., Rocha, A., & Cora, M. P. (2016). Potential Dimensions for a Local e-Government Services Quality Model. *Telematics and Informatics, 33*(2), 370–376. doi:10.1016/j.tele.2015.08.005

SagePeople. (2017). *Becoming a People Company-the Way to unlock fast track growth*. Retrieved from file:///C:/Users/Matilda/Downloads/Sage_People_Research_Report.pdf

Said, A. A. S. (2015). Positioning organisational culture in knowledge management research. *Journal of Knowledge Management, 19*(2), 164–189. doi:10.1108/JKM-07-2014-0287

Salanié, F., & Treich, N. (2005). Over-savings and hyperbolic discounting. *European Economic Review, 50*(6), 1557–1570. doi:10.1016/j.euroecorev.2005.05.003

Salmi, A., & Heikkilä, K. (2015). Managing relationships with public officials—A case of foreign MNCs in Russia. *Industrial Marketing Management, 49*, 22–31. doi:10.1016/j.indmarman.2015.05.026

Saloja, S., Furu, P., & Sveiby, K. (2005). Knowledge management and growth in Finnish SMEs. *Journal of Knowledge Management, 9*(2), 103–122. doi:10.1108/13673270510590254

Samdantsoodol, A., Cang, S., Yu, H., Eardley, A., & Buyantsogt, A. (2017). Predicting the relationships between virtual enterprises and agility in supply chains. *Expert Systems with Applications, 84*, 58–73. doi:10.1016/j.eswa.2017.04.037

Samuelson, P. A. (1937). A note on measurement of utility. *The Review of Economic Studies, 4*(2), 155–161. doi:10.2307/2967612

Santos, K., Loures, E., Piechnicki, F., & Canciglieri, O. (2017). Opportunities assessment of product development process in industry 4.0. *Procedia Manufacturing, 11*, 1358–1365. doi:10.1016/j.promfg.2017.07.265

Santos, S. J. D. (2015). Association Between Physical Activity, Participation in Physical Education Classes, and Social Isolation in Adolescents. *The Journal of Pediatrics*, *91*(6), 543–550. doi:10.1016/j.jped.2015.01.008 PMID:26113429

Saragiotis, P. (2019). Business process management in the port sector: A literature review. *Maritime Business Review*, *4*(1), 49–70. doi:10.1108/MABR-10-2018-0042

Sarkar, K. R. (2010). Assessing insider threats to information security using technical, behavioural and organisational measures. *Information Security Technical Report*, *15*(3), 112–133. doi:10.1016/j.istr.2010.11.002

Sarkis, J., Helms, M. M., & Hervani, A. A. (2010). Reverse logistics and social sustainability. *Corporate Social Responsibility and Environmental Management*, *17*(6), 337–354. doi:10.1002/csr.220

Sarrazin, H., & West, A. (2011). Underestanding the Strategic Value of IT in M&A. *The McKinsey Quarterly*, *1*, 1–6.

SAS. (2019). Big Data: What it is and why it matters. *Big Data Insights*. Retrieved February 2, 2019, from https://www.sas.com/en_us/insights/big-data/what io big data.html

Sassler, S., Glass, J., Levitte, Y., & Michelmore, K. (2016). The missing women in STEM? Assessing gender differentials in the factors associated with transition to first jobs. *Social Science Research*, *63*, 192–208. doi:10.1016/j.ssresearch.2016.09.014 PMID:28202143

Savin-Baden, M. (2015). *Rethinking Learning in an Age of Digital Fluency: Is being digitally tethered a new learning nexus?* Routledge.

Sax, L. J., Lehman, K. J., Jacobs, J. A., Kanny, M. A., Lim, G., Monje-Paulson, L., & Zimmerman, H. B. (2016). Anatomy of an Enduring Gender Gap: The Evolution of Women's Participation in Computer Science. *The Journal of Higher Education*, *88*(2), 258–293. doi:10.1080/00221546.2016.1257306

Sayes, E. (2014). Actor-network theory and methodology: Just what does it mean to say that nonhumans have agency? *Social Studies of Science*, *44*(1), 134–149. doi:10.1177/0306312713511867 PMID:28078973

Sayes, E. (2017). Marx and the critique of actor-network theory: Mediation, translation, and explanation. *Distinktion: Journal of Social Theory*, *18*(3), 294–313. doi:10.1080/1600910X.2017.1390481

Schillerwein, S. (n.d.). *The Digital Workplace: Redefining productivity in the Information Age.* Infocentric Research AG. Retrieved March 6, 2019, from file:///C:/Users/Admin/Downloads/The_Digital_Workplace_-_Whitepaper_-_Infocentric_Research.pdf

Schillmeier, M. (2007). Dis/abling practices: Rethinking disability. *Human Affairs*, *17*(2), 195–208. doi:10.2478/v10023-007-0017-6

Schimmel, N. (2007). Indigenous Education and Human Rights. *International Journal on Minority and Group Rights*, *14*(4), 425–453. doi:10.1163/138548707X247419

Schlenker-Schulte, C., & Weber, A. (2009). Teilhabe durch barrierefreie Kommunikation für Menschen mit Hörbehinderung. In Rhetorik: Ein internationales Jahrbuch. Band 28. Rhetorik und Verständlichkeit (pp.92-102). Tübingen: Max Niemeyer Verlag. doi:10.1515/9783484605817.92

Schmidt, F. (2011). A theory of sex differences in technical aptitude and some supporting evidence. *Perspectives on Psychological Science*, *6*(6), 560–573. doi:10.1177/1745691611419670 PMID:26168377

Schönborn, G., Cecilia Berlin, C., Pinzone, M., Hanisch, C., Georgoulias, K., & Lanz, M. (2019). Why social sustainability counts: The impact of corporate social sustainability culture on financial success. *Sustainable Production and Consumption*, *17*, 1–10. doi:10.1016/j.spc.2018.08.008

Schröder, C. (2011). Regional and enterprise-specific factors of growths dynamics in German ICT companies. In P. J. J. Welfens (Ed.), *Cluster- und Innovationsdynamik in Europa: Neue Perspektiven der Automobil- und ITK-Wirtschaft* (pp. 237–308). Stuttgart: Lucius & Lucius.

Schubmehl, D. (2014). Unlocking the hidden value of information. *IDC*. Retrieved March 6, 2019, from https://idc-community.com/groups/it_agenda/bigdataanalytics/unlocking_the_hidden_value_of_information

Schulz-Schäffer, I. (2000). *Sozialtheorie der Technik*. Frankfurt, Germany: Campus.

Schumpeter, J. A. (1949). *Economic theory and entrepreneurial history*. Cambridge, MA: Harvard University Press.

Schüttpelz, E. (2008). Der Punkt des Archimedes. Einige Schwierigkeiten des Denkens in Operationsketten. In G. Kneer, M. Schroer, Markus, & E. Schüttpelz (Eds.), Bruno Latours Kollektive. Kontroversen zur Entgrenzung des Sozialen (pp. 234-258). Frankfurt a. M., Germany: Suhrkamp.

Schweizer, L. (2005). Organizational Integration of Acquired Biotechnology Companies into Pharmaceutical Companies: The Need for a Hybrid Approach. *Academy of Management Journal*, 48(6), 1051–1074. doi:10.5465/amj.2005.19573109

Schwienbacher, A., & Larralde, B. (2010). Crowdfunding of small entrepreneurial ventures. In D. J. Cumming (Ed.), *The Oxford Handbook of Entrepreneurial Finance*. Oxford, UK: Oxford University Press.

Scott, S. V., & Orlikowski, W. J. (2013). Sociomateriality—Taking the wrong turning? A response to Mutch. *Information and Organization*, 23(2), 77–80. doi:10.1016/j.infoandorg.2013.02.003

Segoro, W. (2013). The influence of perceived service quality, mooring factor, and relationship quality on customer satisfaction and loyalty. *Procedia: Social and Behavioral Sciences*, 81, 306–310. doi:10.1016/j.sbspro.2013.06.433

Selznick, P. (1957). *Leadership in Administration: A Sociological Interpretation*. Evanston, IL: Row, Peterson & Co.

Sen, A. K. (1971). Choice functions and revealed preference. *The Review of Economic Studies*, 38(3), 307–317. doi:10.2307/2296384

Sen, A. K. (1977). Rational fools: A critique of the behavioral foundations of economic theory. *Philosophy & Public Affairs*, 6(4), 317–344.

Sen, A. K. (1993). Internal consistency of choice. *Econometrica*, 61(3), 495–521. doi:10.2307/2951715

Sen, A. K. (1995). Rationality and social choice. *The American Economic Review*, 85(1), 1–24.

Sen, A. K. (1997). Maximization and the act of choice. *Econometrica*, 65(4), 745–780. doi:10.2307/2171939

Sen, A. K. (2002a). Consistency of choice. In A. Sen (Ed.), *Rationality and freedom*. Cambridge, MA: Harvard University Press.

Sen, A. K. (2002b). Goals, commitment, and identity. In A. Sen (Ed.), *Rationality and freedom*. Cambridge, MA: Harvard University Press.

Senf, D. (2004). *Cochlea-Implantat: Mit dem CI leben, hören und sprechen: Ein Ratgeber für Eltern*. Idstein: Schulz-Kirchner.

Seppanen, V. (2002). Evolution of competence in software contracting projects. *International Journal of Project Management*, 20(2), 155–164. doi:10.1016/S0263-7863(00)00043-0

Serres, M. (1982). *The parasite*. Baltimore, MD: Johns Hopkins UP.

Seuring, S., & Miller, M. (2008). From literature review to a conceptual framework for sustainable Supply Chain Management. *Journal of Cleaner Production*, *16*(15), 1699–1710. doi:10.1016/j.jclepro.2008.04.020

Seven Reasons HR Technology Is So Hot Today. (2013, May). Retrieved from https://www.forbes.com/sites/joshbersin/2013/05/31/7-reasons-hr-technology-is-so-hot-today/#7dc154176fdc

Seyal, A. H. (2003). *An Investigation of E-Commerce Adoption in Micro Business Enterprise: Bruneian Evidence*. In 4th We-B conference, Perth, Australia.

Seyal, A. H. (2019). Evaluating Strategic Information Technology Planning Process: Lesson Learnt from Bruneian Small Businesses. In Strategy and Behavior in the Digital Economy. IntechOpen.UK.

Seyal, A. H., & Rahman, M. N. (2003). A Preliminary Investigation of E-Commerce Adoption in Small and Medium Enterprises in Brunei. *Journal of Global Information Technology Management*, *6*(2), 6–26. doi:10.1080/1097198X.2003.10856347

Seyal, A. H., Rahman, M. N., Sy, M. Y., & Siau, N. Z. (2017). Examining m-Learning in Higher Education: An Application of Theory of Planned Behavior. In A. H. Seyal & M. N. Rahman (Eds.), *Theory of Planned Behaviour: New Research*. Nova Publisher.

Shabir, Hameed, Safdar, & Gilani. (2014). The impact of social media on Youth: A case study of Bahawalpur City. *Asian Journal of Social Sciences & Humanities*, *3*(4).

Shackle, G. L. S. (1955). *Uncertainty in economics and other reflections*. Cambridge, UK: Cambridge University Press.

Shah, A. K., & Oppenheimer, D. (2008). Heuristics made easy: An effort-reduction framework. *Psychological Bulletin*, *134*(2), 207–222. doi:10.1037/0033-2909.134.2.207 PMID:18298269

Shaikh, A. (2016). *Capitalism: Competition, conflict, crises*. Oxford, UK: Oxford University Press. doi:10.1093/acprof:oso/9780199390632.001.0001

Shani, A., & Tesone, D. V. (2010). Have human resource information system evolved into internal e-commerce? *Worldwide Hospitality and Tourism Themes*, *2*(1), 30–48. doi:10.1108/17554211011012586

Shannon, C. E. (1948). A mathematical theory of communication. *The Bell System Technical Journal*, *27*(3), 379–423. doi:10.1002/j.1538-7305.1948.tb01338.x

Shashaani, L., & Khalili, A. (2001). Gender and computers: Similarities and differences in Iranian college students' attitudes towards computers. *Computer Education*, *37*(3-4), 363–375. doi:10.1016/S0360-1315(01)00059-8

Shavelson, R. J., Hubner, J. J., & Stanton, G. C. (1976). Self-Concept: Validation of Construct Interpretations. *Review of Educational Research*, *46*(3), 407–441. doi:10.3102/00346543046003407

Shehu, E., Papies, D., & Neslin, S. (2016). *Free Shipping and Product Returns*. Tuck School of Business Working Paper, (2864019).

Shibly, H. A. (2011). Human Resource Information Systems Success Assessment: An Integrative Model. *Australian Journal of Basic and Applied Sciences*, *5*(5), 157–169.

Shih, B., Chen, C., & Chen, Z. (2012). Retracted: An Empirical Study of an Internet Marketing Strategy for Search Engine Optimization. *Human Factors and Ergonomics in Manufacturing & Service Industries*, *23*(6), 528–540. doi:10.1002/hfm.20348

Shiri, S. (2012). Effectiveness of Human Resource Information System on HR Functions of the Organization- A Cross Sectional Study. *US-China Education Review*, *9*, 830–839.

Shui, H., & Ausubel, L. M. (2004). *Time inconsistency in the credit card market.* Social Science Research Network working paper. Retrieved October 25, 2015 at http://ssrn.com/abstract=586622

Siann, G., Macleod, H., Glissov, P., & Drundell, A. (1990). The effects of computer use on gender differences in attitudes to computers. *Computers & Education, 14*(2), 183–191. doi:10.1016/0360-1315(90)90058-F

Sia, S. K., & Soh, C. (2007). An Assessment of Package-Organisation Misalignment: Institutional and Ontological Structures. *European Journal of Information Systems, 16*(5), 568–583. doi:10.1057/palgrave.ejis.3000700

Siddiqui, S., & Singh, T. (2016). Social Media its Impact with Positive and Negative Aspects. *International Journal of Computer Applications Technology and Research, 5*(2), 71 - 75. Retrieved from http://www.ijcat.com/archives/volume5/issue2/ijcatr05021006.pdf

Siemens, G. (2013). Learning Analytics. *The American Behavioral Scientist, 57*(10), 1380–1400. doi:10.1177/0002764213498851

Sieverding, M., & Koch, S. C. (2009). (Self-) Evaluation of computer competence: How gender matters. *Computers & Education, 52*(3), 696–701. doi:10.1016/j.compedu.2008.11.016

Sikdar, A., & Payyazhi, J. (2014). A process model of managing organizational change during business process redesign. *Business Process Management Journal, 20*(6), 971–998. doi:10.1108/BPMJ-02-2013-0020

Silberberg, S. (2000). *The structure of economics: A mathematical analysis.* Boston: McGraw-Hill.

Sills, S. J., & Song, C. (2002). Innovations in survey research: An application of Web-based surveys. *Social Science Computer Review, 20*(1), 22–30. doi:10.1177/089443930202000103

Silverthorn, D. U. (2007). *Physiologie.* München, Germany: Pearsons.

Simon, H. A. (1957). *Models of man: Social and rational.* New York: Wiley.

Simon, H. A. (1959). Theories of decision making in economics and behavioral science. *The American Economic Review, 49*, 253–283.

Simon, H. A. (1979). Rational decision making in business organizations. *The American Economic Review, 69*(4), 493–513.

Simon, H. A., & Bartel, R. D. (1986). The failure of armchair economics. *The Challenge (Karachi), 29*(5), 18–25. doi:10.1080/05775132.1986.11471113

Simovic, V., & Radovic-Markovic, M. (2018). Modern business environment and entrepreneurship education. In M. Radović (Ed.), *Digital Transformation - New Challenges and Business Opportunities* (pp. 148–169). London, UK: Silver and Smith Publishers.

Şimşit, Z., Günay, S., & Vayvay, Ö. (2014). Theory of Constraints: A Literature Review. *Procedia: Social and Behavioral Sciences, 150*, 930–936. doi:10.1016/j.sbspro.2014.09.104

Singer, E., Van Hoewyk, J., & Neugebauer, R. (2003). Attitudes and Behavior: The Impact of Privacy and Confidentiality Concerns on Participation in the 2000 Census. *Public Opinion Quarterly, 65*(3), 368–384. doi:10.1086/377465

Sinha, J., & Kim, J. (2012). Factors affecting Indian consumers' online buying behavior. *Innovative Marketing, 8*(2), 46–57.

Siponen, M. (2005). Analysis of Modern Is Security Development Approaches: Towards the Next Generation of Social and Adaptable ISS Methods. *Information and Organization, 15*(4), 339-375.

Siponen, M., Pahnila, S., & Mahmood, M. A. (2010). Compliance with information security policies: An empirical investigation. *Computer, 43*(2), 64–71. doi:10.1109/MC.2010.35

Sirmon, D. G., Hitt, M. A., Ireland, R. D., & Gilbert, B. A. (2011). Resource Orchestration to Create Competitive Advantage: Breadth, Depth, and Life Cycle Effects. *Journal of Management, 37*(5), 1390–1412. doi:10.1177/0149206310385695

Sivakumar, K., & Nakata, C. (2001). The stampede toward Hofstede's framework: Avoiding the sample design pit in cross-cultural research. *Journal of International Business Studies, 32*(3), 555–574. doi:10.1057/palgrave.jibs.8490984

Škrinjar, R. (2010). *Increasing the process orientation maturity with the renovation and computerization of operations* (Unpublished doctoral dissertation). University of Ljubljana, Ljubljana, Slovenia.

Škrinjar, R., Bosilj-Vukšić, V., & Indihar-Štemberger, M. (2008). The impact of business process orientation on financial and non-financial performance. *Business Process Management Journal, 14*(5), 738–754. doi:10.1108/14637150810903084

Škrinjar, R., & Trkman, P. (2013). Increasing process orientation with business process management: Critical practices. *International Journal of Information Management, 33*(1), 48–60. doi:10.1016/j.ijinfomgt.2012.05.011

Slonim, R., Carlson, J., & Bettinger, E. (2007). Possession and discounting behavior. *Economics Letters, 97*(3), 215–221. doi:10.1016/j.econlet.2007.03.018

Smith, A., & Anderson, M. (2018). Social Media Use in 2018. *Pew Research Center: Internet & Technology.* Retrieved March 25, 2019, from https://www.pewinternet.org/2018/03/01/social-media-use-in-2018/

Smith, D. (2016). *Cloud computing deployments should begin with service definition.* Gartner Report. Retrieved March 6, 2019, from https://www.gartner.com/doc/reprints?id=1-G2H8FE&ct=160826&st=sb

Snyder, J. M. Jr, & Strömberg, D. (2010). Press coverage and political accountability. *Journal of Political Economy, 118*(2), 355–408. doi:10.1086/652903

Sobihah, M., Mohamad, M., Ali, N. A. M., & Ismail, W. Z. W. (2015). E-commerce service quality on customer satisfaction, belief and loyalty: A proposal. *Mediterranean Journal of Social Sciences, 6*(2), 260.

Soderberg, J., & Netzen, A. (2010). When all that is theory melts into (hot) air: Contrasts and parallels between actor network theory, autonomist Marxism, and open Marxism. *Ephemera, 10*(2), 95–118.

Sodhi, M. S., & Tang, C. S. (2011). Social enterprises as supply chain enablers for the poor. *Social-Economical Planning Science., 45*(4), 146–153. doi:10.1016/j.seps.2011.04.001

Sohrabi, S. N., Maple, C., Watson, T., & Solms, R. (2017). *Motivation and opportunity based model to reduce information security insider threats in organisations.* doi:10.1016/j.jisa.2017.11.001

Sohrabi, S. N., Von Solms, R., & Furnell, S. (2016). Information security policy compliance model in organizations. *Computers & Security, 56*, 1–13. doi:10.1016/j.cose.2015.10.006

Solis, B., & Littleton, A. (2017). *The 2017 state of digital transformation. altimeter.* Retrieved March 6, 2019, from file:///C:/Users/Mohsen/AppData/Local/Temp/Altimeter%20_%202017%20State%20of%20DT.pdf

Soloman, A., Breunlin, D., Panattoni, K., Gustafson, M., Ransburg, D., Ryan, C., ... Terrian, J. (2011). "Don't Lock Me Out": Life-Story Interviews of Family Business Owners Facing Succession. *Family Process, 50*(2), 149–166. doi:10.1111/j.1545-5300.2011.01352.x PMID:21564058

Solove, D. J. (2008). *Understanding privacy.* Cambridge, MA: Harvard University Press.

Sølvberg, A. M. (2002). Gender differences in computer-related control beliefs and home computer use. *Scandinavian Journal of Educational Research, 46*(4), 409–426. doi:10.1080/0031383022000024589

Sorensen, E. (2009). *The materiality of learning: Technology and knowledge in educational practice.* Cambridge, UK: Cambridge University Press. doi:10.1017/CBO9780511576362

Soros, G. (2018). *Remarks delivered at the World Economic Forum in Davos.* Retrieved at https://www.georgesoros.com/2018/01/25/remarks-delivered-at-the-world-economic-forum/

Soto-Acosta, P., Popa, S., & Martinez-Conesa, I. (2018). Information technology, knowledge management and environmental dynamism as drivers of innovation ambidexterity: A study in SMEs. *Journal of Knowledge Management, 22*(4), 824–849. doi:10.1108/JKM-10-2017-0448

Sowden, S., Lymberopoulos, E., Militaru, E., & Catmur, C. (2018). *Quantifying compliance and acceptance through public and private social conformity.* doi:10.1016/j.concog.2018.08.009

Sparrow, J. (2001). Knowledge Management in Small Firms. *Knowledge and Process Management, 8*(1), 3–16. doi:10.1002/kpm.92

Spender, J. C. (2002). Knowledge Management, Uncertainty, and an Emergent Theory of the Firm. In C. W. Choo & N. Bontis (Eds.), *The Strategic Management of Intellectual Capital and Organizational Knowledge* (pp. 149–162). Oxford, UK: Oxford University Press.

Spöhrer, M. (2013). Bilder der gelungenen Kommunikation. Das Cochlea Implantat in sozialen und medizinischen Denkkollektiven. *Das Zeichen*, 382-389.

Spöhrer, M. (2016a). *Film als epistemisches Ding.* Marburg: Schüren.

Spöhrer, M. (2016b). Vom Eigen- und Stellenwert der geisteswissenschaftlichen Wissensproduktion: Schreiben als Experimentalsystem. In A. Bartl & M. Famula (Eds.), *Vom Eigenwert der Literatur* (pp. 195–212). Würzburg: Königshausen & Neumann.

Spöhrer, M. (2017a). A cyborg perspective: The cochlear implant and actor-networking perception. In M. Spöhrer & B. Ochsner (Eds.), *Applying the Actor-Network Theory in Media Studies* (pp. 80–95). Hershey, PA: IGI Global. doi:10.4018/978-1-5225-0616-4.ch006

Spöhrer, M. (2017b). Applying actor-network theory in Production Studies: The formation of the film production network of Paul Lazarus' Barbarosa (1982). In M. Spöhrer & B. Ochsner (Eds.), *Applying the actor-network theory in media studies* (pp. 114–141). Hershey, PA: IGI Global. doi:10.4018/978-1-5225-0616-4.ch008

Spöhrer, M. (2018). Applying Actor-Network theory in media Studies: Theoretical (im)possibilities. In M. Spöhrer (Ed.), *Analytical frameworks, applications, and impacts of Actor-Network theory* (pp. 1–27). Hershey, PA: IGI Global.

Spychinger, M. B. (2010). Fehler als Erfahrung: Zur Rolle von Koordination und Diskoordination in bewussten Prozessen. In Was aus Fehlern zu lernen ist in Alltag, Wissenschaft und Kunst (pp. 31-54). Berlin, Germany: Lit.

Srite, M., & Karahanna, E. (2006). The role of espoused national culture values in technology acceptance. *Management Information Systems Quarterly, 30*(3), 679–704. doi:10.2307/25148745

Srivastava, M., & Rai, A. K. (2013). Investigating the Mediating Effect of Customer Satisfaction in the Service Quality-Customer Loyalty Relationship. *Journal of Consumer Satisfaction, Dissatisfaction & Complaining Behavior*, 26.

St. Jevons, W. (1871). *The theory of political economy.* London: Macmillan. Retrieved from http://www.econlib.org/library/YPDBooks/Jevons/jvnPECover.html

Stafford, J. E. (1966). Effects of group influences on consumer brand preferences. *JMR, Journal of Marketing Research, 3*(1), 68–75. doi:10.1177/002224376600300108

Stäheli, U. (2011). Das Soziale als Liste. Zur Epistemologie der ANT. In F. Balke, M. Muhle, & A. von Schöning (Eds.), *Die Wiederkehr der Dinge* (pp. 83–102). Berlin: Kadmos.

Stalder, F. (1997). *Actor-network theory and communication networks: Toward convergence.* Toronto: Faculty of Information Studies, University of Toronto. Retrieved from http://felix.openflows.com/html/Network_Theory.html

Stan, S. (2007). Beyond Information Security Awareness Training: It Is Time to Change the Culture. In H. F. Tipton (Ed.), Information Security Management Handbook (pp. 555–565). Academic Press.

Stanford University. (2019). Virtue ethics. *Stanford Encyclopedia of Philosophy.* Retrieved February 3, 2019, from https://plato.stanford.edu/entries/ethics-virtue/

Stanton, J. M. (1998). An empirical assessment of data collection using the Internet. *Personnel Psychology, 51.*

Stanton, J. M., Stam, K. R., Mastrangelo, P., & Jolton, J. (2005). Analysis of end user security behaviors. *Computers & Security, 24*(2), 124–133. doi:10.1016/j.cose.2004.07.001

Star, S. L. (1991). Power, technologies and the phenomenology of conventions: On being allergic to onions. In J. Law (Ed.), *A sociology of monsters: Essays on power, technology and domination.* London: Routledge.

Star, S. L. (1995). The politics of formal representations: Wizards, gurus, and organisational complexity. In S. L. Star (Ed.), *Ecologies of knowledge: Work, and politics in science and technology* (pp. 89–118). New York: State University of New York Press.

Statista. (2019). *Crowdfunding Worldwide.* Available: https://www.statista.com/outlook/335/100/crowdfunding/worldwide

Statistica. (2019). Number of social media users worldwide from 2010 to 2021 (in billions). *Statistica: The Statistics Portal.* Retrieved March 8, 2019, from https://www.statista.com/statistics/278414/number-of-worldwide-social-network-users/

Sterner, T. (1994). Discounting in a world of limited growth. *Environmental and Resource Economics, 4*(5), 527–534. doi:10.1007/BF00691927

Stewart, R., Bey, N., & Boks, C. (2016). Exploration of the barriers to implementing different types of sustainability approaches. *Procedia CIRP, 48,* 22–27. doi:10.1016/j.procir.2016.04.063

Stillson, P. (1954). A method for defect evaluation. *Industrial Quality Control, 11,* 9–12.

Strathern, M. (1996). Cutting the network. *Journal of the Royal Anthropological Institute, 2*(3), 517–535. doi:10.2307/3034901

Strohmeier, S. (2006). Research in e-HRM: Review and Implications. *Human Resource Management Review, 17*(1), 19–37. doi:10.1016/j.hrmr.2006.11.002

Strotz, R. H. (1957). Myopia and inconsistency in dynamic utility maximization. *The Review of Economic Studies, 23*(3), 165–180. doi:10.2307/2295722

Subramanian, N., Gunasekaran, A., Yu, J., Cheng, J., & Ning, K. (2014). Customer satisfaction and competitiveness in the Chinese E-retailing: Structural equation modeling (SEM) approach to identify the role of quality factors. *Expert Systems with Applications, 41*(1), 69–80. doi:10.1016/j.eswa.2013.07.012

Suchman, L., & Jordan, B. (1990). Interactional Troubles in Face-to-Face Survey Interviews. *Journal of the American Statistical Association, 85*(409), 232–241. doi:10.1080/01621459.1990.10475331

Su, D., & Huang, X. (2011). Research on online shopping intention of undergraduate consumer in China-based on the theory of planned behavior. *International Business Research, 4*(1), 86.

Sudman, S., & Bradburn, N. M. (1974). *Response effects in surveys: A review and synthesis.* Chicago: Aldine Publishing Co.

Sue, V. M., & Ritter, L. A. (2011). *Conducting online surveys.* Thousand Oaks, CA: Sage.

Su, J., Yang, Y., & Duan, R. (2018). A CA-based heterogeneous model for knowledge dissemination inside knowledge-based organizations. *Journal of Intelligent & Fuzzy Systems, 34*(4), 2087–2097. doi:10.3233/JIFS-162116

Sullivan, Y. W., & Kim, D. J. (2018). Assessing the effects of consumers' product evaluations and trust on repurchase intention in e-commerce environments. *International Journal of Information Management, 39*, 199–219. doi:10.1016/j.ijinfomgt.2017.12.008

Super, D. E. (1953). A theory of vocational development. *The American Psychologist, 8*(5), 185–190. doi:10.1037/h0056046

Super, D. E., Starishevsky, R., Matlin, N., & Jordaan, J. P. (1963). *Career development: Self-concept theory.* New York, NY: College Entrance Examination Board.

Suppes, P. (1961). Behavioristic foundations of utility. *Econometrica, 29*(2), 186–202. doi:10.2307/1909288

Sutherland, J.W., Richter, J.S., Hutchins, M.J., Dornfeld, D., Dzombak, R., Mangold, J., … Friemann, F. (2016). The role of manufacturing in affecting the social dimension of sustainability. *CIRP Annals - Manufacturing Technology, 65*, 689–712.

Su, X. (2006). *An Overview of Economic Approaches to Information Security Management.* Centre for Telematics and Information Technology, University of Twente.

Suzuki, G. (1957). Procurement and allocation of naval electronic equipments. *Naval Research Logistics Quarterly, 4*(1), 1–7. doi:10.1002/nav.3800040103

Sveiby, K. (1997). *The New Organizational Wealth: Managing and Measuring Knowledge-Based Assets.* San Francisco: Berret Koehler.

Sweet, T. M., & Zheng, Q. (2017). A mixed membership model-based measure for subgroup integration in social networks. *Social Networking, 48*, 169–180. doi:10.1016/j.socnet.2016.08.001

Sykes, E. R. (2011). Interruptions in the workplace: A case study to reduce their effects. *International Journal of Information Management, 31*, 38–394.

Symonds, J. (2000). Why IT Doesn't Appeal to Young Women. In E. Balka & R. Smith (Eds.), *Women, Work and Computerization – Charting a Course to the Future* (pp. 70–77). Boston, MA: Kluwer. doi:10.1007/978-0-387-35509-2_9

Tabak, D., & Kuo, B. (1971). *Optimal control by mathematical programming.* Englewood Cliffs, NJ: Prentice-Hall.

Taborga, C. P., Lusa, A., & Coves, A. M. (2018). A proposal for a green supply chain strategy. *Journal of Industrial Engineering and Management, 11*(3), 445–465. doi:10.3926/jiem.2518

Tajuddin, S. T. (2016). *The Role of "perceptions of information value" in information security compliance behaviour: a study in Brunei Darussalam's public organisations.* Loughborough University. Retrieved from https://dspace.lboro.ac.uk/2134/23261

Tamir, D. I., & Ward, A. F. (2015). Old desires, new media. In The Psychology of Desire (pp. 432–455). Guilford Press.

Tan, F. T. C., Tan, B., Wang, W., & Sedera, D. (2017). IT-enabled operational agility: An interdependencies perspective. *Information & Management, 54*(3), 292–303. doi:10.1016/j.im.2016.08.001

Tanriverdi, S., & Uysal, V. (2011). Cross-Business Information Technology Integration and Acquirer Value Creation in Corporate Mergers and Acquisitions. *Information Systems Research, 22*(4), 703–720. doi:10.1287/isre.1090.0250

Tarhan, A., Turetken, O., & Reijers, H. A. (2016). Business process maturity models: A systematic literature review. *Information and Software Technology, 75*, 122–134. doi:10.1016/j.infsof.2016.01.010

Teece, D. J. (2000). Strategies for Managing Knowledge Assets: The Role of Firm Structure and Industrial Context. *Long Range Planning, 33*(1), 35–54. doi:10.1016/S0024-6301(99)00117-X

Terstriep, J., & Lüthje, C. (2018). Innovation, knowledge, and relations–on the role of clusters for firms' innovativeness. *European Planning Studies, 26*(11), 2167–2199. doi:10.1080/09654313.2018.1530152

Terungwa, A. (2011). An empirical evaluation of small and medium enterprises equity investment scheme in Nigeria. *Journal of Accounting and Taxation, 3*(3), 79-90.

Thacher, J. B., Srite, M., Stepina, L. P., & Liu, Y. (2003). Culture, overload and personal innovativeness with information technolgoy: Extending the nomological net. *Journal of Computer Information Systems, 44*(1), 74–81.

Thaler, R. H. (1981). Some empirical evidence on dynamic inconsistency. *Economics Letters, 8*(3), 201–207. doi:10.1016/0165-1765(81)90067-7

Thaler, R. H., & Shefrin, H. M. (1981). An economic theory of self-control. *Journal of Political Economy, 89*(2), 392–406. doi:10.1086/260971

Thaler, R. H., & Sunstein, C. R. (2008). *Nudge. Improving decisions about health, wealth, and happiness.* New Haven, CT: Yale University Press.

Thatcher, J., Pu, W., & Pienta, D. (2018). IS Information Systems a (Social) Science? *Communications of the Association for Information Systems, 43*(1), 11.

The Economist. (2017). *Do Social Media Threaten Democracy?* Retrieved from https://www.economist.com/news/leaders/21730871-facebook-google-and-twitter-were-supposed-save-politics-good-information-drove-out

The Future of Accounting is Female: Women in Accounting are on the Rise - CPA Exam Hub. (2019). Retrieved from https://cpaexamhub.com/blog/future-accounting-female-women-accounting-rise/

The Punch Newspaper. (2018). *Crowdfunding: How to raise money from strangers.* Available: https://punchng.com/crowdfunding-how-to-raise-money-from-strangers/

Thiele, J. C., & Grimm, V. (2010). NetLogo meets R: Linking agent-based models with a toolbox for their analysis. *Environmental Modelling & Software, 25*(8), 972–974. doi:10.1016/j.envsoft.2010.02.008

Thite, M., Kavanagh, M. J., & Johnson, R. D. (2009). *Evolution of Human Resource Management and Human Resource Information Systems.* Retrieved from https://s3.amazonaws.com/academia.edu.documents/38322126/EVOLUTION.pdf?AWSAccess KeyId=AKIAIWOWYYGZ2Y53UL3A&Expires=1509386148&Signature=Ru%2BRbIY6CJD8 p%2FK2PXUN57lA5x8%3D&response-content- disposition=inline%3B%20filename%3DEvolution_of_Human_RE-souRcE_managEmEnt_a.pdf

Thompson Reuters. (2017). *Mergers and Acquisitions Review, Full Year 2017.* Retrieved from http://dmi.thomsonreuters.com/Content/Files/MALegalAdvisoryReview.pdf

Thomson, K. L., & Von Solms, R. (2005). Information security obedience: A definition. *Computers & Security, 24*(1), 69–75. doi:10.1016/j.cose.2004.10.005

Thorpe, R., Holt, R., Macpherson, A., & Pittaway, L. (2005). Using Knowledge within Small and Medium-Sized Firms: A systematic Review of the Evidence. *International Journal of Management Reviews, 7*(4), 257–281. doi:10.1111/j.1468-2370.2005.00116.x

Tisdell, C. (2017). Information technology's impacts on productivity and welfare: A review. *International Journal of Social Economics, 44*(3), 400–413. doi:10.1108/IJSE-06-2015-0151

Tomic, D., Muftic, O., & Baksa, S. (2005). *Computer 3D Spectral Analysis of Human Movements*. In Conference on Computer-Aided Ergonomics, Kosice, Slovakia. Retrieved from https://bib.irb.hr/prikazi-rad?rad=212840

Tomic, D. (2002). Spectral performance evaluation of parallel processing systems. *Chaos, Solitons, and Fractals, 13*(1), 25–38. doi:10.1016/S0960-0779(00)00223-X

Tommy, K., & Erik, P. (2018). What Blockchain Alternative Do You Need? In *Workshop on Cryptocurrencies and Blockchain Technology (LNCS), 11025*. Springer.

Tømte, C., & Hatlevik, O. E. (2011). Gender-Differences In Self-Efficacy Ict Related To Various Ict-User Profiles In Finland And Norway. How Do Self-Efficacy, Gender And Ict-User Profiles Relate To Findings From Pisa 2006. *Computers & Education, 21*, 393–402.

Tontini, G., da Silva, J. C., Beduschi, E. F. S., Zanin, E. R. M., & Marcon, M. D. F. (2015). Nonlinear impact of online retail characteristics on customer satisfaction and loyalty. *International Journal of Quality and Service Sciences, 7*(2/3), 152–169. doi:10.1108/IJQSS-02-2015-0021

Tran, H., Zdun, U., Oberortner, E., Mulo, E., & Dustdar, S. (2012). Compliance in service-oriented architectures: A model-driven and view-based approach. *Information and Software Technology, 54*(6), 531–552. doi:10.1016/j.infsof.2012.01.001

Tran, K., Morra, D., Lo, V., Quan, S. D., Abrams, H., & Wu, R. C. (2014). Medical students and personal smartphones in the clinical environment: The impact on confidentiality of personal health information and professionalism. *Journal of Medical Internet Research, 16*(5), 1–8. doi:10.2196/jmir.3138 PMID:24855046

Transparency International. (2019). *Corruption Perceptions Index 2018*. Berlin: Author.

Triandis, H. (1995). *Individualism and collectivism*. Boulder, CO: Westview.

Triola, M. (2009). *Elementary Statistics* (11th ed.). Boston, MA: Addison Wesley.

Trope, Y., & Fishbach, A. (2000). Counteractive self-control in overcoming temptation. *Journal of Personality and Social Psychology, 79*(4), 493–506. doi:10.1037/0022-3514.79.4.493 PMID:11045735

Troshani, I., Jerram, C., & Gerrard, M. (2010). Exploring the Organizational Adoption of Human Resource Information Systems (HRIS) in the Australian public sector. *21st Australian Conference on Information Systems*.

Truell, A. (2003). Use of the Internet tools for survey research. *Information Technology, Learning and Performance Journal, 21*(1), 31–37.

Turkle, S. (2015). *Reclaiming Conversation: The Power of Talk in a Digital Age*. New York, NY: Penguin Press.

Turner, J. R. (2014). Grounded Theory Building for the Workplace. *Performance Improvement, 53*(3), 31–39. doi:10.1002/pfi.21401

Tvenge, N., & Martinsen, K. (2018). Integration of digital learning in industry 4.0. *Procedia Manufacturing, 23*, 261–266. doi:10.1016/j.promfg.2018.04.027

Tzitzikas, Y., Manolis, N., & Papadakos, P. (2017). Faceted exploration of RDF/S datasets: A survey. *Journal of Intelligent Information Systems, 48*(2), 329–364. doi:10.100710844-016-0413-8

U.S. Department of Commerce. (2010). *How does commerce define sustainable manufacturing?* Retrieved from .http://www.trade.gov/competitiveness/sustainablemanufacturing/how_doc_defines_SM.asp

Uhl, A., & Gollenia, L. (2016). *Digital enterprise transformation: A business-driven approach to leveraging innovative IT*. New York, NY: Routledge. doi:10.4324/9781315577166

UNCTAD. (2014). *Findings on Services, Development and Trade*. Retrieved March, 29, from http://unctad.org/en/pages /PublicationWebflyer.aspx?publicationid=549

UNESCO. (2008). *Teacher Training Curricula for Media and Information Literacy*. Report of the International Expert Group Meeting. Paris: International UNESCO.

Uzun, H., & Poturak, M. (2014). Factors Affecting Online Shopping Behavior of Consumers. *European Journal of Social and Human Sciences*, (3), 163-170.

Vaara, E. (2002). On the Discursive Construction of Success/Failure in Narratives of Post-Merger Integration. *Organization Studies*, *23*(2), 211–248. doi:10.1177/0170840602232003

Vaara, E., & Monin, P. (2010). A Recursive Perspective on Discursive Legitimation and Organizational Action in Mergers and Acquisitions. *Organization Science*, *21*(1), 3–22. doi:10.1287/orsc.1080.0394

Valkokari, K., & Helander, N. (2007). Knowledge Management in Different Types of Strategic SME Networks. *Management Research News*, *30*(8), 597–608. doi:10.1108/01409170710773724

Vallhagen, J., Almgren, T., & Thörnblad, K. (2017). Advanced use of Data as an Enabler for Adaptive Production Control using Mathematical Optimization–An Application of Industry 4.0 Principles. *Procedia Manufacturing*, *11*, 663–670. doi:10.1016/j.promfg.2017.07.165

van der Aalst, W. M., Dumas, M., & ter Hofstede, A. H. (2003). Web service composition languages: old wine in new bottles? In *Proceedings of the 29th Conference on EUROMICRO*. Washington, DC: IEEE. 10.1109/EURMIC.2003.1231605

van der Pol, M., & Cairns, J. (2001). Estimating time preferences for health using discrete choice experiments. *Social Science & Medicine*, *52*(9), 1459–1470. doi:10.1016/S0277-9536(00)00256-2 PMID:11286369

van Laar, E., van Deursen, A. J., van Dijk, J. A., & de Haan, J. (2017). The relation between 21st-century skills and digital skills: A systematic literature review. *Computers in Human Behavior*, *72*, 577–588. doi:10.1016/j.chb.2017.03.010

van Laar, E., van Deursen, A. J., van Dijk, J. A., & de Haan, J. (2018). 21st-century digital skills instrument aimed at working professionals: Conceptual development and empirical validation. *Telematics and Informatics*, *35*(8), 2184–2200. doi:10.1016/j.tele.2018.08.006

Van Looy, A., De Backer, M., Poels, G., & Snoeck, M. (2013). Choosing the right business process maturity model. *Information & Management*, *50*, 466-488. doi: .06.002 doi:10.1016/j.im.2013

Van Looy, A., De Backer, M., & Poels, G. (2011). Defining business process maturity: A journey towards excellence. *Total Quality Management & Business Excellence*, *22*(11), 1119–1137. doi:10.1080/14783363.2011.624779

Van Schaik, C. P. (1983). Why are diurnal primates living in groups? *Behaviour*, *87*(1-2), 120–144. doi:10.1163/156853983X00147

Van Slyke, R. (1968). *Mathematical programming and optimal control theory*. Berkeley, CA: University of California.

Vanin, V., & Pavlov, A. (2004). Development and application of self-organization algorithms for modeling of complex processes and objects which are represented by the point former. In *Proceedings of Tavria State agrotechnical academy* (pp. 51–56). Melitopol.

Vargas, J. E. G. (2014). Universal Broadband Access in Developing Countries-The Case of Bolivia. *Proceedings of the 4th IEEE Global Humanitarian Technology Conference*, 597-602. 10.1109/GHTC.2014.6970344

Varma, R. (2011). Indian women and mathematics for Computer Science. *IEEE Technology and Society Magazine, 30*(1), 39–46. doi:10.1109/MTS.2011.940294

Vartabedian, M., Wells, G., & O'Reilly, L. (2018), Businesses Blast California's New Data-Privacy Law. *The Wall Street Journal*. Retrieved August 2, 2018, from https://www.wsj.com/articles/businesses-blast-californias-new-data-privacy-law-1530442800

Vartiainen, M. (2009). Working in multi-locational office – how do collaborative working environments support human centered design? *HCI, 10*, 1090–1098.

Vartiainen, M., Hakonen, M., Koivisto, S., Mannonen, P., Nieminen, M. P., Ruohomäki, V., & Vartola, A. (2007). *Distributed and Mobile Work – Places, People and Technology*. Helsinki: University Press Finland.

Vásquez, W. F., & Espaillat, R. (2016). Willingness to Pay for Reliable Supplies of Safe Drinking Water in Guatemala: A Referendum Contingent Valuation Study. *Urban Water Journal, 13*(3), 284–292. doi:10.1080/1573062X.2014.991741

Vázquez-Barquero, A. (2007). Desarrollo endógeno. Teorías y políticas de desarrollo territorial. *Investigaciones Regionales, 11*, 183–210.

Verbaan, M., & Silvius, A. (2014). The Impact of IT Management Processes on Enterprise Agility. *Communications of the IIMA, 12*(1), 7.

Verbano, C., & Crema, M. (2016). Linking technology innovation strategy, intellectual capital and technology innovation performance in manufacturing SMEs. *Technology Analysis and Strategic Management, 28*(5), 524–540. doi:10.1080/09537325.2015.1117066

Verborgh, R., Harth, A., Maleshkova, M., Stadtmüller, S., Steiner, T., Taheriyan, M., & Van de Walle, R. (2014). Survey of semantic description of REST APIs. In C. Pautasso, E. Wilde, & R. Alarcon (Eds.), *REST: Advanced Research Topics and Practical Applications* (pp. 69–89). New York, NY: Springer. doi:10.1007/978-1-4614-9299-3_5

Verschoor, C. V. (2013). Ethical Behavior Differs Among Generations. *Strategic Finance*. Retrieved January 5, 2019, from https://sfmagazine.com/wp-content/uploads/sfarchive/2013/08/ETHICS-Ethical-Behavior-Differs-Among-Generations.pdf

Vicente, M., Gama, N., & da Silva, M. (2014). A Business Motivation Model for IT Service Management. *International Journal of Information System Modeling and Design, 5*(1), 83–107. doi:10.4018/ijismd.2014010104

Vieru, D., & Rivard, S. (2014). Organizational Identity Challenges in a Post-Merger Context: A Case Study of an Information System Implementation Project. *International Journal of Information Management, 34*(3), 381–386. doi:10.1016/j.ijinfomgt.2014.02.001

Vieru, D., & Rivard, S. (2015). Knowledge Sharing Challenges during Post-Merger Integration: The Role of Boundary Spanners and of Organizational Identity. *International Journal of Business and Management, 10*(11), 1–12. doi:10.5539/ijbm.v10n11p1

Vinerean, S., Cetina, I., Dumitrescu, L., & Opreana, A. (2013). Modeling Trust To Study Consumers Acceptance Of Online Shopping. *Revista Economica, 65*(2), 72–90.

Vitalik, B. (2016). *Privacy on the Blockchain*. Ethereum Blog.

Von Krogh, G. (1998). Care in Knowledge Creation. *California Management Review, 40*(3), 133–154. doi:10.2307/41165947

von Neumann, J., & Morgenstern, O. (1953). *Theory of games and economic behavior*. Princeton, NJ: Princeton University Press.

Von Solms, B. (2000). Information Security -- the Third Wave? *Computers & Security, 19*(7), 615–620. doi:10.1016/S0167-4048(00)07021-8

Von Solms, R., & Van Niekerk, J. (2013). From information security to cyber security. *Computers & Security, 38*, 97–102. doi:10.1016/j.cose.2013.04.004

Voronin. (2017). *Multi-Criteria Decision Making for the Management of Complex Systems.* IGI Global; doi:10.4018/978-1-5225-2509-7

Voronin, A. N., Ziatdinov, Yu. K., & Kuklinsky, M. V. (2010). *Multi-criteria solutions: Models and methods.* Kiev: NAU.

Vroom, C., & von Solms, R. (2004). Towards information security behavioural compliance. *Computers & Security, 23*(3), 191–198. doi:10.1016/j.cose.2004.01.012

Wacjcman, J. (2000). Reflections on gender and technology studies: In what state is the art? *Social Studies of Science, 30*(3), 447–464. doi:10.1177/030631200030003005

Wade, M., & Hulland, J. (2004). Review: the resource-based view and information systems research: review, extension, and suggestions for future research. *Management Information Systems Quarterly, 28*(1), 107–142. doi:10.2307/25148626

Wagner, D., Vollmar, G., & Wagner, H.-T. (2014). The impact of information technology on knowledge creation: An affordance approach to social media. *Journal of Enterprise Information Management, 27*(1), 31–44. doi:10.1108/JEIM-09-2012-0063

Wagner, E. L., Moll, J., & Newell, S. (2011). Accounting logics, reconfiguration of ERP systems and the emergence of new accounting practices: A sociomaterial perspective. *Management Accounting Research, 22*(3), 181–197. doi:10.1016/j.mar.2011.03.001

Wagner, E., Newell, S., & Piccoli, G. (2010). Understanding Project Survival in an ES Environment: A Sociomaterial Practice Perspective. *Journal of the Association for Information Systems, 11*(5), 276–297. doi:10.17705/1jais.00227

Wagner, W., Lorenzi-Cioldi, F., Mankova, I., & Rose, D. (1999). Theory and method of social representations. *Asian Journal of Social Psychology, 2*(1), 95–125. doi:10.1111/1467-839X.00028

Wahab, M. A., Quazi, A., & Blackman, D. (2016). Measuring and validating Islamic work value constructs: An empirical exploration using Malaysian samples. *Journal of Business Research, 69*(10), 4194–4204. doi:10.1016/j.jbusres.2016.03.005

Walid, A., & Nicolas, S. (2017). Blockchain technology for social impact: opportunities and challenges ahead. *Journal of Cyber Policy*, 1-17.

Walter, F. E., Battiston, S., & Schweitzer, F. (2008). A Model of Trust Based Recommendation System on Social Network. *Autonomous Agents and Multi-Agent Systems, 16*(1), 57–74. doi:10.100710458-007-9021-x

Waltz, S. B. (2006). Nonhumans unbound: Actor-network theory and the reconsideration of "things" in educational foundations. *Journal of Educational Foundations, 20*(3/4), 51–68.

Wang, E., Myers, M. D., & Sundaram, D. (2012). *Digital Natives and Digital Immigrants: towards a Model of Digital fluency.* Paper presented at the ECIS.

Wang, C. H., Lu, I. Y., & Chen, C. B. (2008). Evaluating firm technological innovation capability under uncertainty. *Technovation, 28*(6), 349–363. doi:10.1016/j.technovation.2007.10.007

Wang, H., Gibbins, N., Payne, T., Patelli, A., & Wang, Y. (2015). A survey of semantic web services formalisms. *Concurrency and Computation, 27*(15), 4053–4072. doi:10.1002/cpe.3481

Wang, H., & Greiner, M. E. (2011). Prosper—The eBay for money in lending 2.0. *Communications of the Association for Information Systems, 29,* 243–258. doi:10.17705/1CAIS.02913

Wang, J.-P., Guo, Q., Yang, G.-Y., & Liu, J.-G. (2015). Improved knowledge diffusion model based on the collaboration hypernetwork. *Physica A, 428,* 250–256. doi:10.1016/j.physa.2015.01.062

Wang, R., Wiesemes, R., & Gibbons, C. (2012). Developing digital fluency through ubiquitous mobile devices: Findings from a small-scale study. *Computers & Education, 58*(1), 570–578. doi:10.1016/j.compedu.2011.04.013

Ward, M. L. (2003). *Understanding the role of entertainment media in the sexual socialization of American youth: A review of empirical research.* Academic Press.

Warner, J. T., & Pleeter, S. (2007). The personal discount rate: Evidence from military downsizing programs. *The American Economic Review, 91*(1), 33–53. doi:10.1257/aer.91.1.33

Warren, S., & Brandeis, L. (1890). The right to privacy. *Harvard Law Review, 4*(5), 193–220. doi:10.2307/1321160

Wayland, J., & Kuniholm, M. (2015). Legacies of Conflict and Natural Resource Resistance in Guatemala. *The Extractive Industries and Society, 3*(2), 395–403. doi:10.1016/j.exis.2016.03.001

Webster, J., Brown, G., Zweig, D., Connelly, C. E., Brodt, S., & Sitkin, S. (2008). Beyond knowledge sharing: knowledge withholding at work. In Research in Personnel and Human Resources Management. Bradford: Emerald Group Publishing. doi:10.1016/S0742-7301(08)27001-5

Weeger, A., Wang, X., & Gewald, H. (2016). IT consumerization: BYOD-program acceptance and its impact on employer attractiveness. *Journal of Computer Information Systems, 56*(1), 1–10. doi:10.1080/08874417.2015.11645795

Weeks, K. O. (2013). An Analysis of Human Resource Information Systems impact on Employees. *Journal of Management Policy and Practice, 14*(3), 35–49.

Weigold, A., Weigold, I. K., & Ressel, E. J. (2013). Examination of the equivalence of self-report survey-based paper-and–pencil and internet data collection methods. *Psychological Methods, 18*(1), 53–70. doi:10.1037/a0031607 PMID:23477606

Welch, C., & Wilkinson, I. (2004). The political embeddedness of international business networks. *International Marketing Review, 21*(2), 216–231. doi:10.1108/02651330410531411

Wendland, J., Lerch Lunardi, G. & Bittencourt Dolci, D. (2019). Adoption of health information technology in the mobile emergency care service. *RAUSP Management Journal.* Retrieved January 9, 2019, from . doi:10.1108/RAUSP-07-2018-0058

Wertenbroch, K. (1998). Consumption self-control by rationing purchase quantities of virtue and vice. *Marketing Science, 17*(4), 317–337. doi:10.1287/mksc.17.4.317

Westin, A. F. (1976). *Privacy and freedom.* New York: Atheneum.

Wetzel, I. (2002). Teaching Computer Skills: A Gendered Approach. In C. Floyd, G. Kelkar, S. Klein-Franke, C. Kramarae, & C. Limpangog (Eds.), Feminist Challenges in the Information Age (pp. 223-239). Opladen: Leske + Budrich. doi:10.1007/978-3-322-94954-7_17

White, M. (2012). Digital workplaces: vision and reality. *Business Information Review, 29*(4), 205-214.

Whitley, B. E. Jr. (1997). Gender Differences in Computer-Related Attitudes and Behavior: A Meta-Analysis. *Computers in Human Behavior, 13*(1), 1–22. doi:10.1016/S0747-5632(96)00026-X

Whittle, A., & Spicer, A. (2008). Is actor network theory critique? *Organization Studies, 29*(4), 611–625. doi:10.1177/0170840607082223

Wiig, K. (1993). *Knowledge Management Foundations*. Schema Press.

Wijnhoven, F. S., Stegwee, T. R., & Fa, R. T. A. (2006). Post-merger IT Integration Strategies: An IT Alignment Perspective. *The Journal of Strategic Information Systems, 15*(1), 5–28. doi:10.1016/j.jsis.2005.07.002

Wilke, A., Bollmann, U., Cazzaniga, S., Hübner, A., John, S. M., Karadzinska-Bislimovska, J., & Wulfhorst, B. (2017). The implementation of knowledge dissemination in the prevention of occupational skin diseases. *Journal of the European Academy of Dermatology and Venereology, 32*(3), 449–458. doi:10.1111/jdv.14653 PMID:29055149

Wilkins, A. L., & Ouchi, W. G. (1983). Efficient cultures: Exploring the relationship between culture and organizational performance. *Administrative Science Quarterly, 28*(3), 468–481. doi:10.2307/2392253

Williams, S., & Schubert, P. (2018). Designs for the digital workplace. *Procedia Computer Science, 13*, 478-485. Retrieved May 16, 2019 from https://www.researchgate.net/ publication/328472149_Designs_for_the_Digital_Workplace

Williams, C. C., & Franic, J. (2016). Beyond a Deterrence Approach Towards the Undeclared Economy: Some Lessons from Bulgaria. *Journal of Balkan & Near Eastern Studies, 18*(1), 90-106. doi:10.1080/19448953.2015.1094269

Williamson, D. (2010). Social Network Demographics and Usage. *eMarketer*.

Wilson, F. (2015). The Quality Maturity Model: Your roadmap to a culture of quality. *Library Management, 36*(3), 258–267. doi:10.1108/LM-09-2014-0102

Wimpenny, P., & Gass, J. (2000). Interviewing in Phenomenology and Grounded Theory: Is there a difference? *Journal of Advanced Nursing, 31*(6), 1485–1492. doi:10.1046/j.1365-2648.2000.01431.x PMID:10849162

Winner, L. (1980). Do artifacts have politics? In The social shaping of technology (pp. 26-38). Buckingham, YJ: Open UP.

Winner, L. (1993). Upon opening the black box and finding it empty: Social constructivism and the philosophy of technology. *Science, Technology & Human Values, 18*(3), 362–378. doi:10.1177/016224399301800306

Witzany, G. (2012). *Biocommunication of fungi*. Dordrecht: Springer. doi:10.1007/978-94-007-4264-2

Wold, H., Shackle, G. L. S., & Savage, L. J. (1952). Ordinal preferences or cardinal utility? *Econometrica, 20*(4), 661–664. doi:10.2307/1907647

Wolffram, A., Derboven, W., & Winker, G. (2009). Women withdrawers in engineering studies: Identity formation and learning culture as gendered barriers for persistence? *Equal Opportunities International, 28*(1), 36–49. doi:10.1108/02610150910933622

Wollschlaeger, M., Sauter, T., & Jasperneite, J. (2017). The future of industrial communication: Automation networks in the era of the internet of things and industry 4.0. *IEEE Industrial Electronics Magazine, 11*(1), 17–27. doi:10.1109/MIE.2017.2649104

Wong, K. Y. (2005). Critical Success Factors for Implementing Knowledge Management in Small and Medium Enterprises. *Industrial Management & Data Systems, 105*(3), 261–279. doi:10.1108/02635570510590101

Wong, K. Y., & Aspinwall, E. (2005). An Empirical Study of the Important Factors for Knowledge-Management Adoption in the SME Sector. *Journal of Knowledge Management, 9*(3), 64–82. doi:10.1108/13673270510602773

Woodbury, M. (2002). Women in Computing. In C. Floyd, G. Kelkar, S. Klein-Franke, C. Kramarae, & C. Limpangog (Eds.), Feminist Challenges in the Information Age (pp. 107-117). Opladen: Leske + Budrich. doi:10.1007/978-3-322-94954-7_9

Woods, K. M., & McNamara, J. R. (1980). Confidentiality: Its effects on interviewee behavior. *Professional Psychology, Research and Practice, 11*(5), 714–721. doi:10.1037/0735-7028.11.5.714 PMID:11650636

World Bank. (2017). *Global Outlook – A fragile recovery.* Retrieved March 8, 2019, from http://pubdocs.worldbank.org/en/216941493655495719/Global-Economic-Prospects-June-2017-Global-Outlook.pdf

Wouter, D., & Prat, A. (forthcoming). Attention in organizations. In Y. Bramoulle, A. Galeotti, & B. Rogers (Eds.), *The Oxford handbook of network economics.* Oxford, UK: Oxford University Press.

Wright, B. E. (2004). The Role of Work Context in Work Motivation: A Public Sector Application of Goal and Social Cognitive Theories. *Journal of Public Administration: Research and Theory, 14*(1), 59–78. doi:10.1093/jopart/muh004

Wright, P. M., Gardner, T. M., & Moynihan, L. M. (2003). The impact of HR practices on the performance of business units. *Human Resource Management Journal, 13*(3), 21–36. doi:10.1111/j.1748-8583.2003.tb00096.x

Wüst, K., & Gervais, A. (2018). Do you need a Blockchain? *Conference on Blockchain Technology.*

Wynne, B. (1996). SSK's identity parade: Signing-up, off-and-on. *Social Studies of Science, 26*(2), 357–391. doi:10.1177/030631296026002007

Xiaofen, T. (2013). Investigation on quality management maturity of Shanghai enterprises. *The TQM Journal, 25*(4), 417–430. doi:10.1108/17542731311314890

Xiaosong Peng, D., Liu, G. J., & Heim, G. R. (2011). Impacts of information technology on mass customization capability of manufacturing plants. *International Journal of Operations & Production Management, 31*(10), 1022–1047. doi:10.1108/01443571111182173

Xu, L., Xu, E., & Li, L. (2018). Industry 4.0: State of the art and future trends. *International Journal of Production Research, 56*(8), 2941–2962. doi:10.1080/00207543.2018.1444806

Xu, Q., Su, Z., Zhang, K., Ren, P., & Shen, X. S. (2015). Epidemic information dissemination in mobile social networks with opportunistic links. *IEEE Transactions on Emerging Topics in Computing, 3*(3), 399–409. doi:10.1109/TETC.2015.2414792

Xu, Y. J. (2017). Attrition of Women in STEM: Examining Job/Major Congruence in the Career Choices of College Graduates. *Journal of Career Development, 44*(1), 3–19. doi:10.1177/0894845316633787

Yang, H., Ma, K., Deng, C., Liao, H., Yan, J., & Zhang, J. (2013). Towards conformance testing of choreography based on scenario. In *Proceedings of the International Symposium on Theoretical Aspects of Software Engineering* (pp. 59-62). Piscataway, NJ: IEEE Computer Society Press. 10.1109/TASE.2013.23

Yazdanmehr, A., & Wang, J. (2016). Employees' information security policy compliance : A norm activation perspective. *Decision Support Systems, 92*, 36–46. doi:10.1016/j.dss.2016.09.009

Yetton, P., Henningsson, S., & Bjørn-Andersen, N. (2013). Ready to Acquire: The IT Resources Required for a Growth-by-Acquisition Business Strategy. *MIS Quarterly Executive, 12*(1), 19–35.

Yin, R. K. (2013). *Case Study Research: Design and Methods.* Thousand Oaks, CA: SAGE Publication.

Yin, R. K. (2015). *Qualitative research from start to finish.* Guilford Publications.

Yin, R. K. (2017). *Case study research and applications: Design and methods.* Sage Publications.

Yoo, Y., Lyytinen, K., & Heo, D. (2007). Closing the gap: Towards a process model of post-merger knowledge sharing. *Information Systems Journal, 17*(4), 321–347. doi:10.1111/j.1365-2575.2007.00248.x

Young, M., Young, R., & Zapata, J. R. (2014). Project, programme and portfolio maturity: A case study of Australian Federal Government. *International Journal of Managing Projects in Business, 7*(2), 215–230. doi:10.1108/IJMPB-08-2013-0034

Yousef, D. A. (1999). Commitment and Job Satisfaction in a. *Personnel,* (1958).

Yousef, D. A. (2000). *Organizational commitment as a mediator of the relationship between Islamic work ethic and attitudes toward organizational change.* doi:10.1177/0018726700534003

Yu, J., & Zhang, R. (2008). A dynamic analysis upon the knowledge dissemination within an organization. *2008 4th International Conference on Wireless Communications, Networking and Mobile Computing.* doi: 10.1109/WiCom.2008.2613

Yuan, F., & Woodman, R. W. (2010). Innovative behavior in the workplace: The role of performance and image outcome expectations. *Academy of Management Journal, 53*(2), 323–342. doi:10.5465/amj.2010.49388995

Yung, C. (2009). Entrepreneurial financing and costly due diligence. *Financial Review, 44*(1), 137–149. doi:10.1111/j.1540-6288.2008.00213.x

Zack, M. (1998). What Knowledge-Problems Can Information Technology Help to Solve. *Proceedings of the Fourth Americas Conference on Information Systems,* 644-646.

Zaib, T. (2017). Evaluating Narcissisim, Intention and Selfie Posting Behaviour among Housewives in Australia: An Extended TPB. In A. H. Seyal & M. N. Rahman (Eds.), *Theory of Planned Behaviour: New Research.* Nova Publisher.

Zanella, A., Bui, N., Castellani, A., Vangelista, L., & Zorzi, M. (2014). Internet of things for smart cities. *Internet of Things Journal, IEEE, 1*(1), 22–32. doi:10.1109/JIOT.2014.2306328

Zanero, S. (2017). Cyber-physical systems. *IEEE Computer, 50*(4), 14–16. doi:10.1109/MC.2017.105

Zanjani, S., Mehdi, S. M., & Mandana, M. (2008). Organizational Dimensions as Determinant Factors of KM Approaches in SMEs. *Proceedings of World Academy of Science, Engineering and Technology, 35.*

Zauberman, G., Kim, B. K., Malkoc, S. A., & Bettman, J. R. (2009). Discounting time and time discounting: Subjective time perception and intertemporal preferences. *JMR, Journal of Marketing Research, 46*(8), 543–556. doi:10.1509/jmkr.46.4.543

Zeng, F.-G. (2004). Compression and Cochlear Im-plants. In Compression: From cochlea to cochlear implants (pp. 184-220). New York, NY: Springer.

Zgurovsky, M., & Pavlov, A. (2019). The Four-Level Model of Planning and Decision Making. In *Combinatorial Optimization Problems in Planning and Decision Making: Theory and Applications* (pp. 347–406). Cham: Springer. doi:10.1007/978-3-319-98977-8_8

Zhang, Yu, Hêriş, G., & Khan, S. A. R. (2018). The relationship between green supply chain performance, energy demand, economic growth and environmental sustainability: An Empirical evidence from developed countries. *The Central European Journal of Social Science and Humanities, 14*(4), 479-494.

Zhang, Y., Fang, Y., Wei, K. K., Ramsey, E., McCole, P., & Chen, H. (2011). Repurchase Intention in B2C e-commerce - A relationship quality Perspective. *Information & Management, 48*(6), 192–200. doi:10.1016/j.im.2011.05.003

Zhao, L. J., Wang, J. J., Chen, Y. C., Wang, Q., Cheng, J. J., & Cui, H. (2012). SIHR rumor spreading model in social networks. *Physica A, 39*(7), 2444–2453. doi:10.1016/j.physa.2011.12.008

Zheng, H., Li, D., Wu, J., & Xu, Y. (2014). The Role of Multidimensional Social Capital in Crowdfunding: A Comparative Study in China and Us. *Information & Management, 51*(4), 488-496.

Zheng, X., Lee, M., & Cheung, C. M. (2017). Examining e-loyalty towards online shopping platforms: The role of coupon proneness and value consciousness. *Internet Research*, 27(3), 709–726. doi:10.1108/IntR-01-2016-0002

Zhu, Y., Li, Y., Wang, W., & Chen, J. (2010). What leads to post-implementation success of ERP? An empirical study of the chinese retail industry. *International Journal of Information Management*, 30(3), 265–276. doi:10.1016/j.ijinfomgt.2009.09.007

Zimmermann, O., Tomlinson, M., & Peuser, S. (2012). *Perspectives on Web Services: Applying SOAP, WSDL and UDDI to Real-World Projects*. New York, NY: Springer Science & Business Media.

Zinko, R., Furner, C. P., Royal, M. T., & Hall, A. (2010). Self-perceptions of our personal reputations: The mediating role of image in the development of organizational citizenship behaviors. *Journal of International Management Studies*, 5(1), 1–9.

Zinko, R., Furner, Z. Z., Hunt, J., & Dalton, A. (2017). Establishing a Reputation. *Journal of Employment Counseling*, 54(2), 87–96. doi:10.1002/joec.12056

Zinko, R., Tuchtan, C., Hunt, J., Meurs, J., Furner, C., & Prati, L. M. (2017). Gossip: A channel for the development of personal reputation. *The International Journal of Organizational Analysis*, 25(3), 516–535. doi:10.1108/IJOA-07-2016-1041

Zollo, M., & Reuer, J. J. (2010). Experience spillovers across corporate development activities. *Organization Science*, 21(6), 1195–1212. doi:10.1287/orsc.1090.0474

Zollo, M., & Singh, H. (2004). Deliberate learning in corporate acquisitions: Post-acquisition strategies and integration capability in U.S. bank mergers. *Strategic Management Journal*, 25(13), 1233–1256. doi:10.1002mj.426

Zoltan, A. (2016). Public policy to promote entrepreneurship: A call to arms. *Small Business Economics*, 47(1), 35–51. doi:10.100711187-016-9712-2

Zulhuda, S. (2010). *Proceeding 3rd International Coriference on ICT4M 2010 Information Security in the Islamic Perspective: The Principles and Practices*. Academic Press.

Zweben, S. (2011). Undergraduate CS Degree Production Rises; Doctoral Production Steady. 2009-2010 Taulbee Survey. *Computing Research News*, 23(3).

About the Contributors

Efosa C. Idemudia, an internationally known scholar, is an Associate Professor of Business Data Analytics program at Arkansas Tech University. Dr. Idemudia holds degrees from universities located on three different continents: a PhD in Management Information Systems from Texas Tech University, a Master's in Computer Information Systems from the University of Texas at El Paso, and an MBA in International Business from the Helsinki School of Economics and Business Administration; he completed his Fulbright at the Lagos Business School and Carnegie Fellow at Covenant University. He participated as a member of the University System of Georgia's Academic Advisory Committee for Computer Disciplines for five years and is a member of Strathmore Who's Who of Professionals. Dr. Idemudia taught both graduate and undergraduate students as a visiting scholar in the Computer Information Systems (CIS) Department at Georgia State University, which the U.S. News & World Report ranked within the top ten CIS departments in the United States. Currently, Dr. Idemudia is a member of the editorial boards for the International Journal of Technology Diffusion (IJTD); the Journal of Information Technology Management (JITM); Electronic Commerce Research and Applications; International Journal of Risk and Contingency Management (IJRCM); the International Journal of Management Science of AASCIT; the Engineering and Technology of AASCIT; American Journal of Science and Technology of AASCIT; the Journal of the Southern Association for Information Systems; the International Journal of Economic and Business Management; Control, Systems Engineering and The Africa Journal of Information Systems

* * *

M. Afshar Alam, PhD, is Professor, Dean and Head of Department in Department of Computer Science and Engineering, Jamia Hamdard, New Delhi, India. He has also served as Dean of the Faculty, Dean Student Welfare, Foreign Students Advisor in the university. He has teaching experience of more than 24 years. He has authored 9 books and guided PhD research works. He has more than 130 publications in international journal and conference proceedings. He has delivered special lectures as a various academic institutions and resource person at conferences He is a member of expert committees of UGC, AICTE and other national and international bodies. His research areas include software re-engineering, data mining, bioinformatics and fuzzy databases, sustainable development. He has recently co-authored book on "Green Computing approach towards Sustainable Development".

Mohsen Attaran is the 2004-05 Millie Ablin Outstanding Professor of Management at California State University, Bakersfield. He is the recipient of numerous awards for outstanding performance in teaching, research and community services. He is the author/co-author of three books, four book chapters, over one hundred articles, and ten commercial software packages. His research has been widely published in the major professional journals in his field. Professor Attaran has been a consultant for public and private organizations and has conducted numerous in-house workshops and seminars for Fortune 500 companies He is founder and president of Interactive Educational Services, Inc. with the aim of providing web portals and Mobile solutions to K-12 educational institutions. He has founded and managed several businesses in his career in a variety of technological fields including a Telehealth Doctor Visits, a subscription based virtual business, and a few non-profit organizations.

Sharmin Attaran is an Associate Professor of Marketing at Bryant University. She obtained her PhD in Marketing and Entrepreneurship from the University of Illinois at Chicago, her MBA from California State University Bakersfield, and her BA in Economics from UCLA. Dr. Attaran is an expert in the field of Digital Marketing and enjoys researching how technology aids marketing communication and marketing education. She also runs a successful digital marketing consulting business aiming at refining marketing strategies for businesses.

Toni Bakhtiar obtained a Sarjana Sains degree in mathematics in 1996 from Bogor Agricultural University, Indonesia, an M.Sc. degree in technical mathematics in 2000 from Delft University of Technology, the Netherlands, and a Ph.D. degree in information physics and computing in 2006 from the University of Tokyo, Japan. Dr. Bakhtiar is currently a professor of applied mathematics at Department of Mathematics, IPB University (a.k.a. Bogor Agricultural University), Indonesia, and a research fellow at International Center for Applied Finance and Economics (InterCAFE). His research interests lie primarily in the area of operation research, optimal control, mathematical modeling and computational aspect in economics. Dr. Bakhtiar is a member of Indonesian Mathematical Society (IndoMS), Indonesian Operations Research Association (IORA), and The Institute for Operations Research and the Management Sciences (INFORMS).

Umesh Banodha, Associate Professor in computer science & Information Technology at Samrat Ashok Technological Institute, Vidisha (M.P.), an Autonomous Institute, affiliated to Rajiv Gandhi Technical University, Bhopal. I did M.Tech. (Honors) and Ph.D. My Area of interest Software Engineering / Architecture, Databases, UML, object oriented, Programming Languages etc. I am member of various international / National journals. I published more than 15 research papers in various conferences and journals (National / International).

Neeta Baporikar is currently Director/Professor (Business Management) at Harold Pupkewitz Graduate School of Business (HP-GSB), Namibia University of Science and Technology, Namibia. Prior to this she was Head-Scientific Research, with Ministry of Higher Education CAS-Salalah, Sultanate of Oman, Professor (Strategy & Entrepreneurship) at IIIT Pune and BITS India. With more than a decade of experience in industry, consultancy and training, she made a lateral switch to research and academics in 1995. Dr. Baporikar holds D.Sc. (Management Studies) USA, PhD in Management, University of Pune INDIA with MBA (Distinction) and Law (Hons.) degrees. Apart from this she is Senate Member, Namibia University of Science and Technology, Namibia, External Reviewer, Oman Academic Accreditation Authority (OAAA), Accredited Management Teacher from All India Management Association (AIMA), Qualified Trainer form Indian Society for Training & Development (ISTD), International PhD Examiner, Doctoral Guide and Board Member of Academics and Advisory Committee in accredited B-Schools. Reviewer for international journals, she has to her credit several conferred doctorates, several refereed research papers, and authored books in the area of Entrepreneurship, Strategy, Management and Higher Education.

Leon Dario Parra Bernal, Ph.D.(c) in Economics (UNAM, México), is professor of the Institute of Sustanaible Entrepreneurship at EAN University, Colombia. Ms Development Studies (FLACSO), Mexico. More than fifteen years of teaching experience in Data Analytics, Labor Economics, Development Studies, Project Management, Entrepreneurship, Economic Geography, Public and Demography Policy in public and private universities in Colombia, Mexico and Bolivia (graduate and undergraduate). Academic Coordinator of the Master of Comparative Public Policy from FLACSO, Mexico in 2005 and 2006. Associate researcher of several projects of Public Impact Policy Evaluation and Latin American labor market Analysis. Adviser of the Ministry of Health in Mexico and UNAIDS to prepare the report MEGAS 2007 – 2008. Consultant of Population Fund UNFPA of the United Nations in Bolivia for poverty and labor markets studies in 2009 and 2010. Consultant of UNDP in Colombia in programs to support and strengthen entrepreneurship. Research Fellow in Scholl of Development Sciences (CIDES) of UMSA in La Paz - Bolivia between 2008 and 2010, sponsored by the government of Mexico and Santander Universities Program. Research Fellow of Brown International Advanced Research Institute (BIARI) of Brown University in 2011. Technical adviser of the Global Entrepreneurship Monitor Big DATA world project (2017-2018). Currently, he is working in several projects of Big Data and Data Analytics for Public, Private and International Organizations at Global Level.

Roshee Lamichhane Bhusal, M. Phil, is currently working as Lecturer and Placement In-charge, Kathmandu University School of Management, Kathmandu. Earlier she was Head of Academics for the BBA/MBA Programs at CG Institute of Management. Before joining academics, she has corporate exposure in different verticals of Chaudhary Group (CG) conglomerate as Manager (Business Development), Kathmandu, Nepal.

Simon Bourdeau is an associate professor at the School of Management of the University of Québec in Montreal (ESG-UQAM) since 2012. He is a researcher affiliated with several research groups and centers, including CEFRIO, CIRANO and GReSI (HEC Montréal). He holds a Ph.D. in information technology from HEC Montréal. His research interests include: IS project management, project teams' dynamics, operational risks, IT strategic planning and innovation. Since 2013 he is a certified LEGO© Facilitator© Serious Play ™ and uses this methodology in teaching and research and organizes workshops in private and public organizations.

Guillermo Calleja-Leal is Ph.D. in Geography and History, Complutense University of Madrid (Spain), and Ph.D. in Contemporary History, Phoenix International University (UK). Diploma from the European Technical Security Center (Belgium). International M.A. in Operational Safety on Extreme Risks (Spain). Member of the Royal Academy of History (Spain) and the Royal Academy of the Valencian Culture (Spain). Author of books on Military History, Security and Defense, Politics, and Anthropology. Dr. Calleja-Leal is a distinguished member of official organizations related to the military defense in Spain, and he is a USNA (United States Naval Academy) reference author.

Milenka Linneth Argote Cusi is co-founder of BI&DE SAS, bidem.com.co. Speaker. Member of the Data Science Specialization from Johns Hopkins University. Master in Statistical Demography at the Latinamerican Social Science Faculty, México. Systems Engineer, Escuela Militar de Ingeniería de Bolivia. Consultant & Researcher of EAN University, Colombia. Member of the Entrepreneurship Group of COLCIENCIAS in the highest category A1. She has more than fifteen years of experience as Data Scientist and in Development IA algorithms to support decision making in academic and productive sectors in many countries of Latin America. She has also participatedd in projects as: Big Data for Global Entrepreneurship Monitor (2018), Strengthening Data Analytics Capabilities in companies of Bogota (2017), Technological gaps Analysis in productive sectors in Colombia (2016) and Business census to students in EAN University (2013). Since 2012 she has experience in developing and implementing Data Analytics solutions in public and private sectors. She is active in developing algorithms of fuzzy time series using population data of Mexico and entreprenurship data of GEM, with the objective of forecasting data.

Oleksandr Davydko was graduated of Igor Sikorsky Kyiv Polytechnic Institute. In 2018 obtained Master degree qualification in Computer sciences program subject area. Fields of scientific interest: mathematical programming, operation research, bioinformatics.

José C. Delgado is an Associate Professor at the Computer Science and Engineering Department of the Instituto Superior Técnico (University of Lisbon), in Lisbon, Portugal, where he earned the Ph.D. degree in 1988. He lectures courses in the areas of Computer Architecture, Information Technology and Service Engineering. He has performed several management roles in his faculty, namely Director of the Taguspark campus, near Lisbon, and Coordinator of the B.Sc. and M.Sc. in Computer Science and Engineering at that campus. He has been the coordinator of and researcher in several international research projects. As an author, his publications include one book, 25 book chapters and more than 60 papers in international refereed conferences and journals.

Ivana Domazet is a Senior Researcher at the Institute of Economic Sciences and Associate Professor at the Faculty for Banking, Insurance and Finance, Union University, Belgrade. From 2010 she teaches courses on Marketing Management, Market Research and Competitiveness Enhancement (postgraduate studies). Her scientific interest refers to: Integrated Marketing Communications, Marketing Research and Strategy, CRM and Digital Marketing. She published a numerous papers related to foregoing topics. She is President of Scientific Council at the Institute of Economic Sciences, Vice-president of Board member of the Institute of Economics Sciences, Board member of the Institute of Social Science, member of Serbian Scientific Association of Economists and Serbian Marketing Association.

Jasmin Ehrhardt studied Psychology at the University of Hamburg. In her Bachelor thesis she developed a first version of the Computer-Related Self Concept (CSC) Questionnaire.

Pantry Elastic is currently a master student in applied mathematics at Department of Mathematics, Faculty of Mathematics and Natural Sciences, IPB University (a.k.a. Bogor Agricultural University), Indonesia. She received a Sarjana Sains degree in mathematics from Universitas Haluoleo, Indonesia, in 2016. Her research interests include the modeling in life sciences and economics.

Richard Herschel is a Professor in the Department of Decision & System Sciences Department at Saint Joseph's University. This department offers programs in Business Intelligence & Analytics at both the undergraduate and graduate levels. Before becoming an educator, Dr. Herschel worked at Maryland National Bank, Schering-Plough Corporation, Johnson & Johnson, and Columbia Pictures as a systems analyst. Dr. Herschel has researched and written extensively about knowledge management and business intelligence. He is the founding Editor of the International Journal of Business Intelligence Research and he served as the Educational Channel Expert for b-eye-network.com.

Sapna Jain, PhD, is working as an Assistant Professor in Department of Computer Science and Engineering, Jamia Hamdard University, New Delhi, India. Her research areas include data mining, sustainable development, green computing. She has recently co-authored book on "Green Computing approach towards Sustainable Development".

Jaharuddin is an associate professor at Department of Mathematics, IPB University, Indonesia. He obtained a Doktorandus, a Magister Sains, and a Ph.D. degrees in mathematics, all from Institute of Technology Bandung, Indonesia, in 1990, 1992, and 2004, respectively. Much of his research interests concern solution method in mathematical modeling. Dr. Jaharuddin is a member of Indonesian Mathematical Society (IndoMS).

Aleksander Janeš, PhD, is an Associate Professor and chair of the Department of Management, in the Faculty of Management at University of Primorska, Slovenia. His practice and research work is focused on business process management. The Faculty of Management offers undergraduate and postgraduate study programs in the area of management for profit and non-profit organizations. Before becoming an educator, Dr. Janeš worked at Poslovni sistem Mercator, d. d. (Business System Mercator, PLC) where he received company's award.

Monique Janneck is a professor for Human-Computer Interaction in the Department of Electrical Engineering and Computer Science at Luebeck University of Applied Sciences, Germany. She graduated in Psychology and earned a doctorate in Informatics with a thesis on the design of cooperative systems from a communication psychology perspective. Her research focus is on the interplay between human behavior, social structures and technological development: She is interested in the way humans interact with technology, the way theories and findings on human behavior can inform the design of information technology, and the way technology impacts individual, organizational, and social behavior and structures.

Nilofer A. Kazmi completed her PhD from CCS University, Meerut. She started her career as a lecturer at St. Xavier's College, Mumbai and then joined the University Grants Commission as Education Officer. She was promoted to the positions of Deputy Secretary, Joint Secretary, Additional Secretary and then served as Secretary, University Grants Commission, India. She has been a member of important committees in universities and Inter University Centres and other national and international Committees in the Government of India. She was awarded the Queen Elizabeth House Visiting Fellowship, Oxford University, U.K. to do a research study of the academic quality audit procedures followed in the U.K. Dr. Kazmi was nominated by the UNFPA to study the Population Education programmes in Indonesia, Thailand and the Philippines. She was invited as a team member by the governments of the Republic of Korea and Thailand to work out modalities for student and faculty exchange between India and these countries. She served on a high level committee of Government of India to study the community college system of the USA. She was awarded Doctor of Science (Honoris Causa) by Tumkur University in recognition of her contribution in the field of Adult Education and Population Education. Her area of interest is educational administration and sustainable education.

Diane Kirkland has an MBA from the Marshall School of Business at the University of Southern California with emphases in Marketing and Entrepreneurship, and a BA from the University of Southern California with emphases in Communications. She is a doctoral student at the Mitchell College of Business at the University of South Alabama. For the past four years, Diane has been a Lecturer at School of BPA, CSU-Bakersfield teaching Introduction to Marketing and Diversity in Business Organizations. Prior to lecturing at CSUB, Diane was the owner/operator of DMK-Designs, a high-end collection of Men's Furnishings sold at the TJX/Marshall's department stores. From 1995 through 2012, Diane worked as an international manufacturing consultant, matching the manufacturing needs of US-based electronics companies with synergistic China-based ISO9001 manufacturers.

Ravinder Kumar is an Associate Professor at Amity University, Noida, India. He holds a bachelor's degree in Mechanical Engineering with Honors. He did his Master's and Ph.D. from Delhi College of Engineering, University of Delhi, India. He has published about 50 research papers in reputed international journals and Conferences. His areas of interest include supply chain management and quality management in SMEs. He has published papers in journals such as Competitiveness Review: An International Journal, Global Journal of Flexible Systems and Management, IIMB Management Review, Benchmarking: an International Journal, International Journal of Pharmaceutical and Healthcare Marketing, International Journal of Business Information Systems, International Journal of Manufacturing Research, etc.

Emilene Leite, Ph.D., is an Assistant Professor at Örebro University School of Business, Sweden and also a researcher affiliated to Uppsala University. She graduated from Uppsala University, Sweden, holding a doctoral degree in Marketing. She has some years of experience in the financial industry and an executive MBA in Corporate Finance from FGV, Brazil. She also holds a master degree in Economics from Stockholm University and an MBA in Marketing Management from Gävle University in Sweden. Her research investigates the impact of relationships between business and socio-political actors on the strategy of multinationals companies operating in emerging markets. She teaches courses in marketing and international business.

Norfarrah Binti Muhammad Masdi is in their final year of their Masters coursework for Information Systems at SCI, Universiti Teknologi Brunei.

Denise Mifsud is the Gozo College Principal, besides being an independent education researcher and consultant, and a Fellow Associate of the Euro-Mediterranean Centre of Educational Research. She previously held a full-time lecturing post at the University of the West of Scotland as well as being a part-time lecturer at the University of Malta. She was awarded her PhD by the University of Stirling in 2015. Research areas of interest include educational policy analysis, generation, reception and enactment; leadership theories, with a particular interest in educational leadership, especially distributed forms; school networks and educational reform; power relations; Foucauldian theory; Actor-Network theory, as well as qualitative research methods, with a particular focus on narrative, as well as creative and unconventional modes of data representation. Of late, she has also been researching initial teacher education, with a particular focus on the construction and performance of professional identities in pre-service teachers. She has presented her research at various international conferences, besides winning the following academic awards: the 2014 American Education Research Association (AERA) Emerging Scholar Award; SAGE 2014 Early Research Bursary for EERA Annual International Conference 2014; and the SERA 2015 Estelle Brisard Memorial Prize.

Virginia Miori, Ph.D., is Professor and Chair of the Decision & Systems Sciences Department at Saint Joseph's University in Philadelphia, Pennsylvania. She is a graduate of the LeBow College of Business at Drexel University, holding a doctoral degree in Operations Research. She also holds an MS in Operations Research from Case Western Reserve University and an MS in Transportation from the University of Pennsylvania. She has 18 years of teaching experience and over 12 years of industry experience in developing and implementing statistical and operations research models in the area of supply chain/logistics. She is active in research in the areas of data ethics, healthcare efficiency and supply chain, manufacturing and transportation supply chain, scheduling and predictive analytics, and has received several research awards.

Ievgen Nastenko is a Head in department of biomedical cybernetics of National Technical University of Ukraine "Igor Sikorsky Kyiv Polytechnic Institute". Also from 1989 is a Head in department of Information Technologies and Mathematical Modeling of Physiological Processes of Amosov National Institute of Cardiovascular Surgery. He received Master degree of engineering in Kiev Civil Engineering Institute in 197. In 1989 he became a Ph.D. of biomedical cybernetics, in 2008 - Dr.Sc. of biophysics. Published 340 papers, including: 16 patents; 136 articles (30 – in foreign journals); 2 chapters in 2 books, 186 abstracts on topic of development and use the statistical and deterministic models in technique, biology and medicine.

Olena Nosovets received her MS in Computer Science from the National Technical University of Ukraine Igor Sikorsky Kyiv Polytechnic Institute in 2009. She became the Candidate of Technical Sciences in 2015. Defended the candidate dissertation in the specialty "Models and methods of cardiovascular system condition control in various human body's operating modes". Currently an assistant professor of biomedical cybernetics department of the Igor Sikorsky Kyiv Polytechnic Institute, Ukraine. She writes and presents widely on issues of inductive modeling, predicting modeling and causal analysis.

Rajko Novak, MSc, is a senior consultant and lecturer in the field of quality, business process management, strategic leadership and excellence. In these areas, he collaborates with several organizations including power supply industry. His practice and research work is focused on business process management.

Pavlov Oleksander was qualified as an engineer at the Kyiv Polytechnic Institute (KPI), specializing in Intelligent Decision-Making Systems (2002). In 2007 he got PhD with a thesis on self-organizing algorithms in the tasks of the increasing information value for geometrical models. Currently is an senior lecturer of computer science at department of descriptive geometry, engineering and computer graphics, National Technical University of Ukraine «Igor Sikorsky Kyiv Polytechnic Institute», the physics and mathematics faculty. His research interests are in the field of complex system modelling and pattern recognition.

Volodymyr Pavlov was qualified as an engineer at the Kyiv Polytechnic Institute (KPI), specializing in Automated Control Systems (1977). Defended the candidate dissertation in the specialty "Automatic control and regulation, technological processes control in the metallurgical industry". He Became the Candidate of Technical Sciences in 1981, worked as a junior researcher, senior researcher at the Kyiv Institute of Automation. Currently an assistant professor of biomedical cybernetics department of the National Technical University of Ukraine «Igor Sikorsky Kyiv Polytechnic Institute». His research interests and publications are in the field of inductive modeling, pattern recognition, causal analysis.

Julia Margarete Puaschunder holds Bachelor's degrees and Master's degrees in Philosophy/Psychology, Business, Public Administration and Doctorates in Social and Economic Sciences and Natural Sciences. Trained as a behavioral economist with Doctorates in Social and Economic Sciences as well as Natural Sciences and Masters in Arts, Business, Public Administration and Philosophy/Psychology, she has over 15 years of experience in applied social sciences empirical research in the international arena. After a line of research on Corporate and Financial Social Responsibility as well as Intergenerational Equity, her research focuses on Artificial Intelligence Ethics. Julia is included in the '2018 Marquis Who's Who in America and in the World' among the top 3% professionals around the globe. She was awarded the 2018 Albert Nelson Marquis Lifetime Achievement Award.

Lukman Raimi is an Assistant Professor of Entrepreneurship at the American University of Nigeria, Yola. He holds a PhD in Entrepreneurship & CSR from the Leicester Business School, De Montfort University Leicester, United Kingdom. Besides, he has two Master's degrees in Economics and Human Resources Management from University of Lagos. Previously, he was a Principal Lecturer and Coordinator of Training at the Centre for Entrepreneurship Development (CED), Yaba College of Technology Nigeria. He is a trained facilitator of Entrepreneurship at the Entrepreneurship Development Institute (EDI), Ahmedabad, India. He had undergone special training in Enterprise Education for Employability at the Pan African University Nigeria under the British Council's sponsorship. He had coordinated several Business Plan Competitions in Nigeria including serving as Mentor in the 2014 Business Plan Competition of Islamic Development Bank held in Morocco. He is an alumnus of Cumberland Lodge, Windsor, United Kingdom.

Jose Manuel Saiz-Alvarez is Ph.D. (Hons.) in Economics & Business Administration, Autonomous University of Madrid (Spain). Ph.D. (Hons.) in Sociology, Pontifical University of Salamanca (Spain). He is a member of the National System of Researchers of the National Council for Science and Technology (CONACYT) in Mexico and a regular member of the Mexican Academy of Sciences. Research Professor, EGADE Business School-Tecnologico de Monterrey (Mexico), and visiting professor, the Catholic University of Santiago de Guayaquil (Ecuador) and Autonomous University of Manizales (Colombia). Honorary Professor, Autonomous University of Madrid (Spain). Certificate of Recognition, Capitol House of Representatives of Puerto Rico. Diploma of Honor, Valahia University of Targoviste (Romania). He has given more than one hundred conferences in Europe and America and is the author of more than three hundred publications in his specialty. To date, he has supervised 74 doctoral theses and is a member of Editorial Boards and referee of numerous national and international journals. He is in the Who's Who in the World, from the 2011 Edition.

Kanak Saxena, Ph.D. in computer Science from the Devi Ahilya University, Indore, India. She is professor in the computer science & Information Technology Department at the Samrat Ashok Technological Institute affiliated to Rajiv Gandhi Technical University, Bhopal. Her Current research focuses on Database Systems, Parallel computing, Data Uncertainty and design and other interests include Network security and performance and Software Engineering. She is the member of editorial board of various international journals. She is the member of the international committee of the International Conference on Computer Science and Its Applications. She Published more than 80 research Papers in Various Conferences and Journals National / International).

Afzaal H. Seyal, Ph.D., is Assistant Professor Computing & Information Systems program area at School of Computing & Informatics, Universiti Teknologi Brunei, where he has been working since 1990. He obtained his first degree from Roosevelt University Chicago in Computer Science and subsequent PhD from LaSalle University in Management. He has an extensive research experience and produced over 90 papers in conferences and leading information systems journals such as Journal of Global IT Management (JGITM), Computer and Education, Behavior and Information Technology, Information Management, Business Process Management Journal (BPMJ) and Electronic Markets. His Google Scholar H-index=19 with 1410 citations. He served as editorial board member of JGITM and BPMJ. He has contributed six book chapters and chief editor of book Theory of Planned Behavior: New Research, published by Nova Publishers New York.

Nor Zainah Siau, Ph.D., is Senior Lecturer and Program Leader of Computing & Information Systems program at SCI. She received her M.Sc. in Computer Science from Coventry University and PhD in Computer Science from Loughborough University. She has twenty years of teaching experience and also has supervised the students' final year projects and has presented papers in the several international conferences.

Vladimir Simovic is a Research Fellow at the Institute of Economic Sciences and Associate Professor at the Faculty for Banking, Insurance and Finance, Union University, Belgrade. Ever since 2012 he teaches courses Information systems and Management information systems to undergraduate students and Contemporary information technology to PhD students. The areas of his professional interests are in e-Business in general and more specifically in business information systems, IT entrepreneurship, Internet marketing and e-Learning. He is a member of a Scientific Council at the Institute of Economic Sciences.

Markus Spöhrer is a Postdoc research associate in the Project „Techno-sensory processes of participation. App-practices and Dis/Ability". (Media and Participation, University of Konstanz). He studied American Studies, German and English literature (University of Tübingen, Germany) and Media Studies (University of Miami). He his doctorate in Media Studies at the University of Konstanz, Germany. His research and teaching focus on theories and methods of digital gaming, medial aspects of hearing, Actor-Network-Theory, techno-sensoria of Audio Games and stereoscopic media.

K. Francis Sudhakar is an Assistant Professor at department of School of Management, NIT Warangal in the area of Marketing. His interests are in Services Marketing and Consumer Behavior. He has teaching experience of 20 years in various subjects of Management.

Alamuri Suryanarayana is Professor and Dean (Academics) at Mantra School of Business Management, Hyderabad, India, and superannuated from Osmania University (OU) as the Dean, Faculty of Management in 2016. Earlier, he held the post of Chairperson, Board of Studies, Department of Business Management, OU, for two years during 2005-07 and served OU for more than 35 years. He is a Fellow Member of World Business Institute, Australia, and also a Fellow Member of International Society of Management. He is the recipient of Best Professor in HRM from World Education Congress in 2012. He has Four International Book Chapters (Three USA and One Germany) and several publications in Conference Proceedings, Journals, and Edited Books and over 100 paper presentations in both National and International conferences.

Habeeb Syed is currently a research scholar at National Institute of Technology Warangal in School of Management department in the area of Marketing. His interests are in Consumer Behavior and Services Marketing. He has a teaching experience of three years in various subjects of Management.

Sharul Tajuddin, Ph.D., is Assistant Professor in Networking and Security area, School of Computing & Informatics (SCI), Universiti Teknologi Brunei. He obtained his PhD from Loughborough University U.K. in Information Security area; Dr. Sharul has twenty-year of teaching experience in Computer Networking, Multimedia and Information Security. Dr Sharul work in information Security has been published in conference proceedings and leading journals including People and Information Technology.

Dragos Vieru is a full professor at TELUQ University of Quebec. He holds a Ph.D. degree in information technology from HEC Montreal and a M.Sc. degree in management of information systems from John Molson School of Business, Montréal, Canada. His research interests are in the areas of IT-enabled organizational change, knowledge sharing, IT sourcing, and IT governance. Dragos Vieru has published articles in several academic journals, notably in the Journal of Knowledge Management, the International Journal of Information Management, and the Journal of Information Technology Teaching Cases. He has over 15 years of professional experience in IT project management in the healthcare sector.

Sylvie Vincent-Höper is a research associate at the Department of Industrial and Organizational Psychology at the University of Hamburg. She worked as researcher at Stanford University (USA) and Stellenbosch University (South Africa) and held a temporary professorship at the Department of Work and Organizational Psychology at the University of Hamburg. Her research focus is investigating the underlying mechanisms of leaders' impact on employees' well-being, innovativeness, and success with a special consideration of gender-relevant implications.

Albert N. Voronin is a Doctor of Sciences (Eng.) and is a professor in the Department of Computer Information Technologies at the National Aviation University of Ukraine. Dr. Voronin is also a member of the American Mathematical Society.

Tom Yoon is an associate professor in the Department of Management Information Systems at Western Connecticut State University. He earned his Ph.D. in MIS from Florida State University. Prior to joining WCSU, he taught at Florida State University, Cleveland State University, and Metro State University of Denver. Before his academic career, he worked several years as an IT manager and software engineer. His current research interests include the adoption and diffusion of IT innovations, enterprise resource planning (ERP), business intelligence, mobile commerce, and service oriented architecture (SOA), His research publications appear in the IS journals, conference proceedings, and encyclopedias.

Robert Zinko is a visiting professor at Texas A&M University – Central Texas. He holds PhDs in both Marketing and Management, with research areas in personal and online reputation. His work has appeared in such journals as The Leadership Quarterly and Electronic Markets.

Index

A

acquisition channels 483, 486-488, 491-495, 498
Actor-Network Theory 135-136, 150, 212
agency 4-5, 138-139, 141-144, 147-148, 150, 205, 296, 361, 365, 380, 476
Agent Based Modeling 427, 434
agility 47, 85-88, 93-94, 97, 99, 114, 327, 333, 335, 343, 386, 390
ALPF2 304
anonymity 25-26, 34, 42, 169, 428
Ant Colony Optimization 425, 427-428, 439, 441
application 25, 50, 84, 86-88, 95-96, 98-101, 103, 105-108, 114, 120, 126, 161, 183, 230, 242, 252-253, 278, 281-282, 286, 293, 300, 306-307, 318-320, 329-330, 333, 348, 358, 365, 369, 439, 461, 466, 471-472, 474-475, 528-529, 531, 533, 538, 543
assemblage 5, 8, 21, 140, 143-144, 147, 210, 380
average session duration 483, 491-495
average user profile 483, 495

B

barriers 118, 123, 204, 218, 221, 225-226, 251-256, 258, 260, 330, 386-387, 392, 448, 543
behavioral economics 157-159, 161, 165-169, 171, 183-185, 187
behavioral intentions 558-559
blockchain 425, 427-442
Bogotá 525, 529, 535
bounce rate 483, 491, 493, 498
brain science 377, 551
Brunei Darussalam 499-500, 504-505, 508, 510-511, 515-517
Bruno Latour 206-207
business process management (BPM) 324-325, 343
business process orientation (BPO) 324-325, 327, 343

Business Process Orientation Maturity Model (BPOMM) 332, 343

C

career development 65-67, 69-70, 76-77
career motivation 65-66, 69-70, 72, 74-77
career success 66, 69-70
challenges 3, 43-44, 47-48, 50, 86, 123, 218-220, 227, 230, 235-237, 239-242, 246, 253, 295-296, 324-325, 334, 358-359, 390, 397-398, 402-403, 425, 427-428, 441-442, 446-449, 451-452, 455, 462-463, 484-485, 496, 502-503, 542, 555, 560, 564
change agent 43, 46-47, 50-51
clinical trials 308, 320
cochlear implant 201-203, 206, 209-212
collaboration 9, 49, 54, 57-58, 86-87, 96, 127, 244, 296-298, 300, 362, 386, 388, 390-397, 399, 403, 441, 447, 463, 542
collective behavior 244, 425-427, 429-437, 439, 441
Compartmental Models 478
competence 44, 46-47, 50, 53-54, 58-59, 119, 558
competitive advantage 46, 116-118, 122, 128, 174, 235-237, 239-240, 244, 246, 327, 500, 525, 559, 561, 563
competitiveness 54, 57, 117-118, 121, 245, 250, 254, 304, 386, 451, 556
compliance 84, 86, 88, 103, 105-107, 114, 158, 161, 171, 295, 317, 380, 390, 412, 427, 501, 504-506, 508-509
computer-related self-efficacy 68, 75, 77
confidentiality concerns 22-26, 28, 30-35, 42
conformance 84, 86, 88, 105-107, 114
consequentialism 409, 414, 420-421
consumer 107, 114, 161, 163, 177, 180-182, 186, 239, 326, 346, 386, 409-411, 427, 429, 550-561, 564-565
contextual analysis 115, 147, 257

control actions 305-307, 309, 312, 320

conversion rate 483, 487-495, 498

corruption 292, 295-296, 299, 301-302

coupling 27, 84, 86-88, 96, 99, 101-103, 105, 107, 114

crowdfunding 218-227, 229-230

culture 2, 22-23, 26-27, 30, 32, 34-35, 117, 121-123, 125, 127, 229, 253-254, 299-301, 325-326, 329, 331-332, 334, 336, 358, 367, 381, 389, 412, 432, 506, 508-509, 517, 527, 529

customer loyalty 556-557, 560-564

customer satisfaction 550, 554-558, 560-564

customer trust 555, 560-564

Cyberaddiction 364, 374

Cyberbullying 364, 373, 377

Cybersickness 363-364, 373, 377

D

DA capabilities 525, 528, 531, 534, 542-543

Data Analytics 178, 485, 525-526, 528, 531, 533, 539, 542-543

decision making 122, 158-162, 165-166, 169, 178, 183-184, 252, 279, 287, 290, 305-306, 327, 335, 388-389, 396, 421, 509, 525, 528-531, 533-534, 539, 543

democratisation of information 158-159

digital economy 44-46, 50, 52, 58, 525

digital fluency 43-50, 53, 57-58

digitalization 296, 304, 325, 336, 447, 451

Digital Laws 377

digital literacy 46, 299, 304

digital workplace 383-393, 395-396, 398-403

digital workplace solutions (DWS) 386

disability 201, 204-205, 211, 300

Dispersion of Responsibility 377, 379

disseminant 464, 466, 469, 472, 475-476

E

e-commerce 56-57, 184, 485, 550-555, 557-561, 564-565

education research 135, 140, 143, 145-146, 150

E-Government 241, 243, 295-296, 298-301, 304, 511

enterprise systems 3, 5, 15, 20

enthusiast 464, 469, 475

entrepreneurs 92, 127-128, 218-221, 224-226, 229-230, 530, 542

epistemic things 201-202, 205-207

espoused collectivism 27, 31-32, 42

espoused masculinity 27, 31-32, 42

espoused power distance 22, 27, 31-32, 42

espoused uncertainty avoidance 27, 31-32, 42

ethics 162, 184, 297, 409, 411-415, 420-421, 509, 558

exchange value 175-177, 179, 182

experimental systems 205-207, 209

external criterion 309, 312, 322

extrovert 409, 418

F

Facebook 169, 178, 181-182, 225-226, 345-349, 351-353, 355-356, 360-361, 364-365, 370, 410-411, 417, 420

financing 218-222, 224-227, 229-230, 300, 529-530, 542

fiscal policy 292-293, 298, 301-302, 304

G

gender differences 65-69, 73-76, 559

Generalized Variable 322

generic model 250-251, 258, 261

Google Analytics 483-487, 489-491, 495

governance 7, 86-87, 147, 158-159, 161, 165, 171, 175-179, 182-183, 185-187, 509

Grounded Theory 255-257

Group Method of Data Handling (GMDH) 309, 318, 322-323

H

heuristic information 439, 441

I

ignorant 412, 464, 469, 475

India 121, 126-127, 335, 348, 447, 550-555, 559-562, 564

Inefficiencies X 296, 304

Informal Learning 498

informal organization 352-353, 378

Information Communication Technology (ICT) 48, 120, 126-127, 236, 241, 246, 297, 300, 326, 328, 333, 335, 343, 359, 500

Information Perception Value 499-500, 504

information security 499-509, 515, 517

Information Work 384

innovation 57, 94, 116, 119, 122, 128, 178, 223, 236, 239-240, 245, 298, 326, 345, 351, 354, 363, 390-391, 402, 526, 529-530, 551

interoperability 84, 86-88, 96, 98-99, 101, 103-107, 114, 428

inter-organizational cooperation 235
introvert 409, 418
ISO 9001 325, 332-333, 343
IT infrastructure 48, 56, 259, 343, 394, 396
IT Knowledge 56, 343
IT operations 343

J

job 2, 26, 54, 66, 72, 121, 252, 298-299, 358, 386, 395, 403, 439, 506, 509, 517, 552
justice 296, 298, 301, 413

K

Kantianism 412-415, 420
knowledge dissemination 124, 461-465, 468, 475
knowledge management 115-120, 124, 126, 128, 461, 463
knowledge management system 461
knowledge transfer 57, 202, 461, 463

L

Latin America 242, 297, 300, 526, 529, 551
Learning sample 309, 313-316, 322
LinkedIn 298, 347, 350-352, 361, 417

M

maturity 88, 140, 324-325, 327-336, 343, 463, 529
maturity model 88, 329, 332, 334, 343
Media Skill 358, 373, 378
MNEs (multinational enterprise) 237
Model of the Optimal Structure 322
moderator 169, 173, 185-187, 555-556
monitoring 181, 236, 238, 242, 306, 308, 312, 402, 411-412, 538
morality 295, 414, 516
Moral Tax 299, 304
multicriteria 276, 278-285, 288-290

N

networks 48-49, 86, 95-96, 107, 125, 135-141, 143-144, 146-150, 178, 184, 186, 202-203, 206, 209-212, 227, 239, 244, 246, 298, 345-347, 360, 366, 370, 403, 410, 439, 463-464, 528, 538, 554, 558
Nigeria 218-223, 226-227, 229-230
non-formal education 483-485, 488, 494-495
Non-Formal Leaning 498
non-linear scheme of compromises 276, 289-290

normality 204-205, 210, 330

O

online surveys 24, 33
ontology 103, 137, 140, 142, 145, 147-148, 150, 255
optimal control model 461, 464, 466, 475, 479
Optimal Structure 309, 322
optimization 85, 94, 162, 236, 276-278, 280-285, 287, 290, 292, 296, 298, 302, 305-320, 328, 332, 425-428, 439, 441, 470, 486, 498, 528
Ordoliberalism 297, 304
organizational structure 2, 326-329, 331-332, 334

P

performativity 5, 7, 13-14, 20, 136
Pontryagin minimum principle 461, 464, 470, 472, 475, 480
post-merger integration 1-3, 9-10, 15, 20
power relations 135-136, 142, 148-150
practices 1-15, 20-21, 44, 47, 49, 54, 58-59, 116, 119-120, 122-125, 127, 136, 138, 140-141, 143, 145-146, 181, 201-202, 204-206, 208, 211, 219-223, 229, 292-293, 301, 306, 325, 328, 334, 345, 353, 360-362, 367, 383, 385, 412, 447, 449, 451, 508-509, 565
preferences 158-160, 162-167, 169-174, 178, 180, 182, 187, 283, 285-290, 353, 384, 401, 411, 418, 515
privacy 25, 157-158, 160-162, 167-171, 173-174, 177-187, 253, 259, 409, 411-414, 418-421, 428, 503-504, 555-556, 558
process theory 14-15, 21
provider 107, 114, 174-177, 187, 364, 557

Q

qualitative research 52, 219, 255, 500

R

reclaiming the common good of knowledge 158-159
Reconfigurations 5, 14, 16
repurchase intentions 550, 552, 554-555, 557, 559-564
resources 2, 44, 51, 58, 94-95, 107, 115-119, 122, 124-125, 127-128, 144, 182, 220-222, 225, 227, 236-242, 244, 246, 252-254, 292-293, 299-301, 325-327, 335, 343, 358-359, 367, 383, 439, 447, 449, 463, 484, 501-502, 517, 526-527, 529-530, 542-543

S

scalar convolution 279-285, 287-290
scarcity 335, 428
search engine optimization 486, 498
service 43, 56-57, 86, 88, 95-97, 101, 107, 114, 177,
    180, 186, 239-240, 242, 244, 253, 295, 326,
    330, 335, 343, 364, 386, 389, 396, 399, 403,
    410, 414, 427, 439, 447, 451, 498, 500, 503,
    536, 552, 554-564
service quality 552, 554-564
skills 43-51, 53-56, 58-59, 66-67, 69-70, 77, 117-
    118, 128, 227, 358, 360, 366, 439, 449, 543
Slovenian power supply business 324-325, 328, 333
smart city 235-237, 239-244, 428
Social Contract Theory 412-415, 420
Social Desirability Distortion 24-25, 42
Social Impact Theory 366-367, 369, 374, 379-381
socially desirable reporting 22-23, 30-32, 34
social media tolerance 416-418
social media usage 410, 417-418
social network 174, 184, 225, 229, 344-346, 348-
    349, 351, 353, 355-358, 361, 372-373, 410
socio-economic 168, 218-219, 221, 324, 326, 336,
    359
sociomaterial assemblage 5, 8, 21
sociomaterialism 135
sociomateriality 5, 21, 145
socio-political actors 235-240, 244, 246
soft factors 324, 326, 328-329, 332, 334-335
solitariant 464, 466, 472, 475
strategy 1, 7, 15, 53, 56, 86, 91-92, 115-118, 120,
    125, 143, 173, 182, 240, 246, 253, 293, 300,
    305, 307-308, 312, 317-320, 326, 328-329,
    332, 335, 357, 359, 388, 393, 395-399, 402,
    412, 462, 464, 469, 472, 475, 502, 504, 508,
    531, 533, 542-543, 552-553, 560
supply chain management 446-448, 451, 455, 462
sustainability 115, 235-236, 238, 242, 299, 327,
    446-452, 455, 530
SWOT 293, 298
symmetry 99, 135-136, 138-139, 141, 145-146, 149-
    150, 205

T

Tanzi-Oliveira Effect 301, 304
tax 158, 161, 171, 176, 178, 187, 277, 292-296, 298-
    301, 304
technical things 201-202, 205-209, 212
technological 43-48, 50-51, 53-59, 75, 85, 87, 94,
    115, 117, 119, 121, 125, 146, 168, 174, 176,
    181, 204, 206-207, 211-212, 236-237, 239-241,
    243, 246, 251, 254, 258-259, 299, 334, 403,
    428, 450, 496, 516, 525-531, 533, 538, 542-543
technological capabilities 121, 526, 530-531, 543
Testing Sample 323
thought collectives 206, 208-210
Training Sample 323
translation 30, 135-136, 138-140, 142-143, 146-148,
    150, 203, 205, 207-208, 210, 528
Twitter 169, 225, 346, 348-352, 361, 364-365, 370,
    410, 420
typology 43, 46, 50-53, 58, 68, 140, 150, 223

U

URL 487, 498
Utilitarianism 412-415, 420
utility function 281, 284, 288-290

V

virtual enterprise 84, 86, 96-97, 99, 106, 114
Virtue Ethics 412-415, 420
viscourse 208

W

Web Analytics 485, 498
website design 485, 555, 558-559
welfare 165, 292-293, 299, 302, 304, 326
women in STEM 65-66

Y

Youth 140, 344-345, 347, 353-355, 361, 374

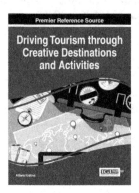

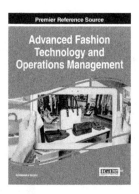

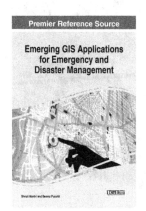
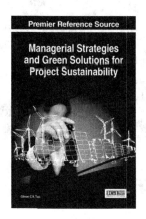

The Premier Reference for Information Science & Information Technology

100% Original Content
Contains 705 new, peer-reviewed articles with color figures covering over 80 categories in 11 subject areas

Diverse Contributions
More than 1,100 experts from 74 unique countries contributed their specialized knowledge

Easy Navigation
Includes two tables of content and a comprehensive index in each volume for the user's convenience

Highly-Cited
Embraces a complete list of references and additional reading sections to allow for further research

Included in:

InfoSci®-Books

Encyclopedia of Information Science and Technology Fourth Edition
A Comprehensive 10-Volume Set

Mehdi Khosrow-Pour, D.B.A. (Information Resources Management Association, USA)
ISBN: 978-1-5225-2255-3; © 2018; Pg: 8,104; Release Date: July 2017

For a limited time, receive the complimentary e-books for the First, Second, and Third editions with the purchase of the *Encyclopedia of Information Science and Technology, Fourth Edition* e-book.*

The **Encyclopedia of Information Science and Technology, Fourth Edition** is a 10-volume set which includes 705 original and previously unpublished research articles covering a full range of perspectives, applications, and techniques contributed by thousands of experts and researchers from around the globe. This authoritative encyclopedia is an all-encompassing, well-established reference source that is ideally designed to disseminate the most forward-thinking and diverse research findings. With critical perspectives on the impact of information science management and new technologies in modern settings, including but not limited to computer science, education, healthcare, government, engineering, business, and natural and physical sciences, it is a pivotal and relevant source of knowledge that will benefit every professional within the field of information science and technology and is an invaluable addition to every academic and corporate library.

Scan for Online Bookstore

Pricing Information

Hardcover: **$5,695**   E-Book: **$5,695**   Hardcover + E-Book: **$6,895**

Both E-Book Prices Include:
- *Encyclopedia of Information Science and Technology, First Edition E-Book*
- *Encyclopedia of Information Science and Technology, Second Edition E-Book*
- *Encyclopedia of Information Science and Technology, Third Edition E-Book*

*Purchase the Encyclopedia of Information Science and Technology, Fourth Edition e-book and receive the first, second, and third e-book editions for free. Offer is only valid with purchase of the fourth edition's e-book through the IGI Global Online Bookstore.

Recommend this Title to Your Institution's Library: www.igi-global.com/books

Printed in the United States
By Bookmasters